Encyclopedia of Catholic Social Thought, Social Science, and Social Policy

Volume 3: Supplement

Edited by
Michael L. Coulter
Richard S. Myers
Joseph A. Varacalli

THE SCARECROW PRESS, INC.
Lanham • Toronto • Plymouth, UK
2012

Published by Scarecrow Press, Inc.
A wholly owned subsidiary of The Rowman & Littlefield Publishing Group, Inc.
4501 Forbes Boulevard, Suite 200, Lanham, Maryland 20706
www.rowman.com

10 Thornbury Road, Plymouth PL6 7PP, United Kingdom

British Library Cataloguing in Publication Information Available

Library of Congress Cataloging-in-Publication Data

The earlier edition (volumes 1 & 2) of this book was previously cataloged by the Library of Congress as follows:

Encyclopedia of Catholic social thought, social science, and social policy / edited by Michael L. Coulter . . . [et al.].
p. cm.
Includes bibliographical references and index.
ISBN-13: 978-0-8108-5906-7 (hardcover : alk. paper)
ISBN-10: 0-8108-5906-8 (hardcover : alk. paper)
1. Christian sociology—Catholic Church—Encyclopedias. I. Coulter, Michael L., 1969–
BX1753.E595 2007
261.8088'282—dc22   2006038367

Volume 3: Supplement (2012) ISBN: 978-0-8108-8266-9

Printed in the United States of America

Contents

Abbreviations

AAS	*Acta Apostolicae Sedis*
ACHR	American Convention on Human Rights
ACS	American College of Surgeons
ANH	Assisted nutrition and hydration
AP	*Aeterni Patris* (Pope Leo XIII)
ASE	Association for Social Economics
BWL	*Jesus Christ, the Bearer of the Water of Life: A Christian Reflection on the "New Age"* (Pontifical Council for Culture)
CA	*Centesimus Annus* (Pope John Paul II)
CARA	Center for Applied Research in the Apostolate
CC	*Casti Connubii* (Pope Pius XI)
CCC	*Catechism of the Catholic Church*
CDF	Congregation for the Doctrine of the Faith
CEA	Catholic Economic Association
CFR	Community of the Franciscan Friars of the Renewal (Franciscan Capuchins)
CHA	Catholic Health Association
CIC	*Codex Iuris Canonici* (*Code of Canon Law*)
CRC	Convention on the Rights of the Child
CSDC	*Compendium of the Social Doctrine of the Church* (PCJP)
CSP	Congregation of St. Paul (Paulist Order)
CV	*Caritas in Veritate* (Pope Benedict XVI)
DA	*Doctoris Angelicis* (Pope Pius X)
Denz-Hün	Denzinger, Heinrich, and Peter Hünermann, *Enchiridion Symbolorum Definitionum et Declarationum de Rebus Fidei et Morum*, 40th ed.
DF	*Dei Filius* (First Vatican Council)
DH	*Dignitatis Humanae* (Second Vatican Council)
DI	*Dominus Iesus* (CDF)
DP	*Dignitas Personae* (CDF)
DVb	*Dei Verbum* (Second Vatican Council)
DVi	*Donum Vitae* (CDF)
EAPC	European Association for Palliative Care
ECE	*Ex Corde Ecclesiae* (Pope John Paul II)
EOC	Economy of Communion
ERD	*Ethical and Religious Directives for Catholic Health Care Services* (CHA)
EV	*Evangelium Vitae* (Pope John Paul II)
EWTN	Eternal Word Television Network
FC	*Familiaris Consortio* (Pope John Paul II)

FR	*Fides et Ratio* (Pope John Paul II)
GE	*Gravissimum Educationis* (Second Vatican Council)
GS	*Gaudium et Spes* (Second Vatican Council)
HET	Heterologous embryo transfer
HLA	Human Life Amendment
HPC	Pontifical Council for Health Pastoral Care
HV	*Humanae Vitae* (Pope Paul VI)
ICCPR	International Covenant on Civil and Political Rights
ID	*Immortale Dei* (Pope Leo XIII)
IDC	*Inscrutabili Dei Consilio* (Pope Leo XIII)
IM	*Inter Mirifica* (Second Vatican Council)
ITC	International Theological Commission
IVF	In vitro fertilization
LC	Legion of Christ
LG	*Lumen Gentium* (Second Vatican Council)
LLDP	*Marriage: Love and Life in the Divine Plan* (USCCB)
MDG	Millennium Development Goals
MV	*Mirari Vos* (Pope Gregory XVI)
NCCB	National Conference of Catholic Bishops
NGO	Nongovernmental organization
NHPCO	National Hospice and Palliative Care Organization
NL	*The Search for Universal Ethics: A New Look at the Natural Law* (ITC)
NRLC	National Right to Life Committee
OFM	Order of Friars Minor (Franciscan Order)
OP	*Ordo Praedicatorum* (Order of Preachers; Dominican Order)
OSB	Order of St. Benedict (Benedictine Order)
OSF	Order of St. Francis (Franciscan Sisters)
OSU	Order of St. Ursula (Ursuline Order)
OT	*Optatam Totius* (Second Vatican Council)
PCJP	Pontifical Council for Justice and Peace
PDG	*Pascendi Dominici Gregis* (Pope Pius X)
PPACA	Patient Protection and Affordable Care Act
PS	Palliative sedation
PSSC	Pontifical Council for Social Communications
PT	*Pacem in Terris* (Pope John XXIII)
PVS	Persistent vegetative state
QA	*Quadrigesimo Anno* (Pope Pius XI)
RH	*Redemptor Hominis* (Pope John Paul II)
R.Miss.	*Redemptoris Missio* (Pope John Paul II)
RN	*Rerum Novarum* (Pope Leo XIII)
RSM	Sisters of Mercy
SJ	Society of Jesus (Jesuit Order)
SM	Society of Mary (Marianist Order)
SRS	*Sollicitudo Rei Socialis* (Pope John Paul II)
SS	*Spe Salvi* (Pope Benedict XVI)
STh	*Summa Theologica* (St. Thomas Aquinas)
UDHR	Universal Declaration of Human Rights
UFL	University Faculty for Life
UN	United Nations
UNESCO	United Nations Educational, Scientific and Cultural Organization

UR	*Unitatis Redintegratio* (Second Vatican Council)
USCC	United States Catholic Conference
USCCB	United States Conference of Catholic Bishops
VS	*Veritatis Splendor* (Pope John Paul II)

Introduction to Volume 3

The original two volumes of the *Encyclopedia of Catholic Social Thought, Social Science, and Social Policy* were published in 2007. Those two volumes include 848 entries from more than three hundred contributors. The original volumes include a range of entries on the three areas noted in the title. First, the *Encyclopedia* includes entries on the foundational documents of Catholic social thought (e.g., *Rerum Novarum, Centesimus Annus*). Second, we incorporated entries reflecting the learning of various social sciences and other humanistic disciplines as this learning relates to Catholic social thought (e.g., alcoholism and drug abuse, and forgiveness and mercy). Third, the *Encyclopedia* contains entries that examine specific social policy questions (e.g., abortion, organ transplants).

Our effort to link Catholic social thought at a broad theoretical level to social science research and then to how the theory and social science research relate to specific policy questions is one of the defining features of the original volumes. Because we tried to explore the relevance of the Catholic intellectual tradition to diverse areas of concrete human and social problems, the *Encyclopedia* is less abstract than other efforts that explicate Catholic social thought. The distinctiveness of the original volumes is in their particularity; in them, we have explored a broad range of key documents and persons who developed Catholic social thought and also detailed the work of organizations that put that teaching into practice. A fuller explanation of the *Encyclopedia*'s approach is set forth in the original introduction, which is reproduced immediately following the introduction to this third, supplemental volume of the *Encyclopedia*.

This third volume continues the basic approach of the original volumes. The volume contains 202 entirely new entries from more than a hundred contributors. The original volumes included the work of outstanding scholars, and many of those scholars have also contrib-

uted to this volume. We are also pleased that we have been able to add to our list of contributors many other distinguished scholars.

There are several reasons for publishing this third, supplemental volume only five years after the original effort. First, Catholic social thought is a continuing reflection on the dignity of the human person and on the nature of the good society, and so there will continue to be a need for new volumes of the *Encyclopedia* to take account of recent historical developments. This volume fills that need.

These developments, of course, will continue in all three areas of the title. So, the third volume includes entries on new Church documents that set forth authoritative statements of Catholic social thought. Examples include entries on Pope Benedict XVI's important recent encyclicals (*Spe Salvi* and *Caritas in Veritate*) and on the Congregation for the Doctrine of the Faith's statement on the ethical implications of current issues of biomedical research (*Dignitas Personae*). This volume includes entries that discuss recent social science research that bears on issues important to Catholic social thought. An example of this type of entry is the entry on the social costs of pornography, which describes recent research on the topic. Further, this volume includes entries discussing social policy—e.g., embryo adoption and/or rescue—that have come to the fore in recent years.

Another reason for publishing a supplemental volume is to fill gaps in the original volumes. The scope of Catholic social thought is so wide that the number of topics that ought to be addressed to achieve a full understanding of the Catholic Church's teaching, and the implications thereof, is nearly infinite. Catholicism has something of importance to say on nearly every aspect of human and social existence. Although the effort that produced the original volumes was a lengthy, multiyear project, there were a variety of topics that, for one reason or another, were omitted. Accordingly, in this supplemental volume we have included entries on topics that we were not able to fit into the original volumes. We have, in particular, expanded our treatment of specific moral questions (e.g., infanticide, the treatment of ectopic pregnancies). We have, moreover, made a concerted effort to provide treatments, from a Catholic perspective, of a broader range of significant thinkers (e.g., John Stuart Mill and Leo Tolstoy) and ideas (e.g., multiculturalism, nominalism, and social Darwinism) in an effort to engage the cultural realities outside a narrow conception of what is of concern to the Catholic Church as an institution.

In an effort to emphasize the connections to the original volumes, we have in this third volume provided a list of all the entries in the three volumes. This comprehensive list is located at the end of this volume. This list will enable readers to see the richness of the three volumes and also make it easier for readers to explore interrelationships. Through the use of cross-referencing and an index, we have made an effort to direct the reader to related entries. We have also included bibliographies to identify fruitful sources of additional reading.

Our guiding principle throughout has been to reflect the full range of views within the broad umbrella of Catholic orthodoxy. Many issues relevant to Catholic social thought admit of differing prudential judgments. We have continued to attempt to reflect the legitimate

diversity of thought that does exist with the Catholic Church on contested issues and thinkers. We hope to illustrate the great diversity and pluralism that exist within the teaching of the Church. There are, of course, limits on the theories and prudential judgments that can properly be described as authentically Catholic. We believe that the rich teaching that has been set forth during the recent pontificates of Blessed Pope John Paul II and Pope Benedict XVI clearly articulates the bounds of Catholic orthodoxy, and we have endeavored to keep within those boundaries.

We understand that there is a continuing need for Catholic social thought to engage the pluralism and diversity of a complex global civilization. We hope that this volume will contribute to the never-ending process of bringing the Gospel message to bear on the realities of social life.

We would like to again thank our home institutions (Grove City College, Ave Maria School of Law, Nassau Community College–State University of New York and its Center for Catholic Studies). We also again express our profound gratitude to our families for their unwavering support during this project.

Michael L. Coulter
Richard S. Myers
Joseph A. Varacalli

Introduction to Volumes 1 and 2 (2007)

The Encyclopedia of Catholic Social Thought, Social Science, and Social Policy represents an attempt at a comprehensive and broad-ranging analysis of how the Catholic religious, moral, and intellectual tradition can and should shape society and social life. As the *Compendium of the Social Doctrine of the Church* states, Catholic social doctrine is designed to contribute to a proper understanding of *"man's place in nature and in human society"* (# 14). In its essence, Catholic social doctrine is "the accurate formulation of the results of a careful reflection on the complex realities of human existence, in society and in the international order, in the light of faith and of the Church's tradition. Its main aim is to interpret these realities, determining their conformity with or divergence from the lines of the Gospel teaching on man and his vocation, a vocation which is at once earthly and transcendent; its aim is thus to guide Christian behavior" (*SRS* # 41). As Pope John Paul II stated in *Veritatis Splendor*, an encyclical on moral theology, "In the face of serious forms of social and economic injustice and political corruption affecting entire peoples and nations, there is a growing reaction of indignation on the part of very many people whose fundamental human rights have been trampled upon and held in contempt, as well as an ever more widespread and acute sense of the need for a radical personal and social renewal capable of ensuring justice, solidarity, honesty and openness" (# 98).

This renewal can be based on the Church's social doctrine, which promotes a true humanism. Therefore, it is vitally important that this body of thought be better known—both to promote proper social development and to promote the saving message of the Gospel. As Pope John Paul II stated, "The teaching and spreading of her social doctrine are part of the Church's evangelizing mission" (*SRS* # 41).

The volume encompasses and combines three interdependent areas of scholarly inquiry. The first area

is Catholic social thought, traditionally understood as consisting of papal encyclicals, other Church statements and analyses that deal not only with the "social question" but also with other social institutions such as the family and education, and the writings, on the state of civilization, of both classical and contemporary Catholic intellectuals and scholars. The second area integrated into the volume consists of Catholic informed social scientific perspectives (methodologically analogous to, for instance, a feminist sociology, capitalist economics, Marxist history, and Freudian psychology) applied to concrete social issues and social problems. Finally, social policy analyses, statements, and proposals shaped by a Catholic worldview regarding government, civil, and other private sphere social institutions have been incorporated into this endeavor. In some cases, these three independent yet related levels of analysis have been incorporated into a single entry; in other cases, the multilayered nature of this intellectual endeavor is approached through the appropriate cross-referencing of entries.

The coeditors hope that readers will concur with the understanding that this encyclopedia represents much more than just a Catholic social thought encyclopedia per se—as important as that enterprise is. The attempt in this volume is much broader, trying as it does to apply a Catholic sensibility and critique to a wide variety of aspects of social existence, from intellectual and scholarly disciplines, to cultural and institutional structures, to the strategies and possibilities of government intervention in the lives of the citizenry.

As a perusal of the table of contents and list of contributors will attest, this encyclopedia consists of over eight hundred entries written by over three hundred authors. As large scale as this project is, no claim could possibly be made that it is completely comprehensive and exhaustive. It does hope, however, to establish a logic and a set of Catholic principles that point out to its users how omitted topics would, in theory, be treated and approached, thus setting the stage for future work in the field.

Some of the entries are thematic, analytical, and substantive; others short and primarily descriptive, with many intermediate. Moreover, many, but not all, of the contributing scholars are members of the Society of Catholic Social Scientists, the Fellowship of Catholic Scholars, and other groups that are supportive of the constitutive role that magisterial thought plays in authentic Catholic scholarship.

The guiding principle of Catholic orthodoxy, however, leaves plenty of room for prudential disagreements and scholarly debates over the interpretation of many issues. Examples of such legitimately debated issues would be the proper understanding of natural law, the suitable role of market-oriented solutions to social problems, the plausibility of a modern society based on distributist principles, the proper understanding of democracy as a political structure, the morality of the death penalty, and the proper application of the principle of subsidiarity. At the same time, it must be stressed that the pluralism in this volume is contained within the parameters of Catholic teaching. To do otherwise—to incorporate scholarly perspectives that cannot plausibly and honestly be said to emanate from an authentic Catholic framework—would be to severely compromise the utility, integrity, and purpose of this particular enterprise. It is one thing to acknowledge the utility of non-Catholic perspectives as useful counterpoints to a Catholic view, it is another to call an essentially non-Catholic analysis a Catholic one. It simply and needlessly confuses the needed and required intellectual and moral debate and comparison.

The scholarly field of vision of this volume is truly interdisciplinary and international in scope. Its organization breaks down conventionally understood disciplinary boundaries, exposes and explicates inevitable—if hitherto unrecognized—disciplinary connections, and combines expertise from such seemingly diverse areas such as theology, philosophy, history, sociology, political science, economics, psychology, social services, medicine, and law. Although anchored with a certain emphasis on the modern American context, cross-cultural and trans-historical analyses of Catholic social thought, social science, and social policy in this volume are very well represented, including contributions on the present and historical situation in Europe, Asia, Africa, and South America. The coeditors understand that American civilization and the Catholic Church in the United States with their respective visions and problems—as important as they are in history and in the contemporary situation—do not represent either the global community or the Church Universal.

The coeditors have attempted—and succeeded in most cases—to make sure that the encyclopedia entries were written in clear and lucid prose, eliminating unnecessary jargon. In some cases, the use of a complicated and complex language in an entry is an inevitable function of the topic or the intellectual discipline. The volume is envisioned to appeal to the well-educated layperson, whether Catholic or not, who wants a clear and accurate introduction to Catholic social thought and a Catholic-informed social science and social policy. Additionally, the coeditors envision that this encyclopedia could be used as an academic text or resource in a wide range of college and seminary courses, in America and worldwide.

The coeditors believe that this finished product represents a distinctive contribution to academic scholarship in at least two ways. First of all, it clearly presents a Catholic alternative in intellectual and moral public discourse at a time when the processes of secularization are eroding the likelihood of wide-ranging and necessary debates on a host of crucial intellectual and moral issues pertinent to the future of not only the American Republic but also the international world order. Second, the "three-layered" approach of the volume—again, enhanced through the use of cross-referencing—sets this encyclopedia apart from those Catholic social thought volumes that deal almost exclusively at the level of abstract philosophical and theological discourse. One certainly need not be a devotee and advocate for Catholic social thinking to find this encyclopedia of good use as a handy reference tool.

Michael L. Coulter
Stephen M. Krason
Richard S. Myers
Joseph A. Varacalli

· A ·

AETERNI PATRIS *Aeterni Patris* ("Of the Eternal Father") is an encyclical of Pope Leo XIII promulgated in 1879. In this encyclical, Leo sought to restore a central role for philosophy in Christian life. In particular, the encyclical promoted the scholastic method of St. Thomas Aquinas. The publication of *Aeterni Patris* spurred both a revival of Thomism in the Catholic Church and a century of papal pronouncements on Christianity and philosophy, culminating in the encyclical *Fides et Ratio* by Pope John Paul II.

The origins of *Aeterni Patris* lie with what was perceived by the Holy See as the philosophical crisis of modern times, both inside and outside the Church. The medieval synthesis of philosophy and theology was neglected and modern thought tended to set reason against faith, weakening both. In its dogmatic constitution on the Catholic faith, *Dei Filius* (1870), the First Vatican Council maintained the compatibility of revelation and human knowledge, declaring that "not only can faith and reason never be at odds with one another but they mutually support each other" (*DF* # 4: 10). As bishop of Perugia for 32 years, Cardinal Joachim Pecci, the future Pope Leo XIII, advocated the teaching of the Dominican Doctor Thomas Aquinas as an antidote to false conclusions of modern thought. Leo's first encyclical after becoming pope in 1878, *Inscrutabili Dei Consilio*, singled out Augustine and Thomas as exemplars of Christian philosophy (*IDC* # 13).

Leo promulgated *Aeterni Patris* on August 4, 1879, the second year of his papacy. It received the subtitle *On the Restoration of Christian Philosophy in Catholic Schools in the Spirit of the Angelic Doctor, St. Thomas Aquinas.* Leo was well known for his literary and scholarly merits, and the encyclical is written in elegant, classical Latin, often panegyric in praise of Thomas. It is divided into 34 numbered paragraphs.

In the first sections of *Aeterni Patris*, Leo outlines the role of philosophy in fortifying Christianity. Philosophy is both the handmaiden of faith and an intellectual discipline in its own right, necessary for the progress of human sciences. Since faith can be corrupted by "philosophy and vain deceit" (Colossians 2: 8), the magisterium is, however, compelled to oversee the right use of philosophy (*AP* # 1). Leo commends the early apologists and fathers of the church who employed philosophical methods to defend and advance Christianity in a pagan world, including Quadratus, Aristides, Hermias, Athenagoras, Lactantius, Victorius, Optatus, Hilary, Arnobius, Justin Martyr, Irenaeus, Clement of Alexandria, Origen, Tertullian, Jerome, Basil the Great, Gregory of Nazianzus, Gregory of Nyssa, Cyprian, Athanasius, and John Chrysostom (*AP* # 4, 11, 12). He especially praises Augustine as the greatest genius of the fathers, who combined the most refined secular learning with the loftiest faith, harmonizing natural philosophy and Christian revelation. Boethius and Anselm in the West and John Damascene in the East added to the patrimony of philosophy (*AP* # 13).

Christian philosophy reached its apex in medieval scholasticism. The scholastics systematized the early fathers, arranging their insights with diligence and skill and achieving an exemplary unity of human science and theological reflection. Leo quotes Pope Sixtus V on the glories of the two leading doctors of the Middle Ages, St. Thomas and St. Bonaventure, who enriched scholastic theology with order, beauty, and genius (*AP* # 14).

Aeterni Patris reaches its climax when Leo focuses on St. Thomas Aquinas, the Angelic Doctor, as the greatest of the scholastics and a perennial fountain of wisdom for Catholics. Thomas constitutes "the special bulwark and glory of the Catholic faith" because he "gathered together, encompassed and surpassed the teaching of all the other doctors." Leo quotes Cajetan, saying that because Thomas is "most venerated the ancient doctors of the Church [he] in a certain way seems to have inherited the intellect of all" (*AP* # 17). Thomas reached the heights of scholastic philosophy and theology because he was humble and lucid, had an encyclopedic knowledge and memory, lived a virtuous and unblemished life, was devoted to prayer, and was a lover of truth. He improved all aspects of philosophy and was a master of reasoning, although he always subjected the natural to the supernatural order and to sacred scripture. His scholastic method was rigorous, balanced, orderly, and fruitful. His thought embraced both human and sensible objects and the loftiest of divine and ethereal essences. At all times, he searched for the reasons and causes of things, discovering their underlying principles and laying the groundwork for later insights (*AP* # 18).

As a result, the perennial wisdom of Thomas Aquinas was recognized by the great religious orders, medieval schools and universities, and the ecumenical councils of Lyons, Vienna, and Florence, and the First Vatican Council (*AP* # 19–20, 22). Great praise was accorded to Thomas in papal bulls and briefs by Popes Clement VI, Nicholas V, Benedict XIII, Pius V, Clement XII, Urban V, Innocent XII, Benedict XIV, and Innocent VI (*AP* # 21). Unfortunately, the 16th century witnessed a plethora of new and tenuous philosophies that disdained the accomplishments of the scholastics and made an exaggerated recourse to human reasoning (*AP* # 24).

Leo concludes *Aeterni Patris* by describing the great advantages that would accrue from reviving the teaching of Thomas Aquinas: to Catholic youth, Catholic schools, the disciplines of theology and philosophy, the peace of society, and the arts and sciences (*AP* # 27–29).

Aeterni Patris constituted the first papal document entirely devoted to philosophy and the most elevated status accorded to Thomas in a magisterial document. For Leo, the impartial and wide-ranging perspective of Thomas represented the Catholic middle ground between two extremes that plagued the 18th and 19th centuries: rationalism, which discarded faith; and fideism, which disparaged reason. Leo was a remarkably farsighted pope, and his exhortation to revive Thomas was forward, not backward, looking. Whereas previous papal documents had been content to condemn false propositions of philosophy, *Aeterni Patris* was essentially positive, focusing on the merits of Thomas and the scholastic method.

For Leo, the rigor that Thomas brought to philosophy was necessary to make it a systematic discipline and hence capable of sustaining a scientific approach to theology (*AP* # 24). Thomas was the most modern of philosophers because his method was rooted in realism. Thomas and other scholastics such as Albert the Great reasoned to the supernatural from sensible and material things, an approach not at odds with the empirical method (*AP* # 30). Leo rejected any notion of antiquarianism, approving of new discoveries in philosophy (*AP* # 24) and excluding from his exhortation any theses from the scholastics that time has shown to be improbable, obscure, or obsolete. In like manner, he urged a return to the original writings of Thomas, wary of strange or stale derivations thereof (*AP* # 31). Although Leo gave priority to Thomas, his emphasis on Thomas's methodology, and his praise of other scholastics, implied an acceptance of the plurality of approaches that characterize Catholic theology and philosophy.

Leo took immediate steps to implement *Aeterni Patris*. On October 15, 1879, he established the Pontifical Academy of St. Thomas Aquinas, with the mission to foster research into the work of St. Thomas, to explain and defend his doctrine, and to disseminate his teaching. (Popes Pius XI and Paul VI would earn their doctorates in Thomistic philosophy from the Pontifical Academy.) Leo ordered a new, critical edition of Thomas's work, the Leonine edition. He mandated that the philosophy

of Thomas be taught in Catholic education and declared Thomas the patron saint of Catholic schools. He also recommended the study of Thomas to the other orders, in particular to the Jesuits in 1892 and the Franciscans in 1898.

With Leo's support, the turn of the 20th century saw a flowering of Thomism. By 1902, there were centers of neoscholastic studies in 14 countries, with about 206 new periodicals and about a thousand articles published annually. A new crop of Thomistic scholars emerged, including Etienne Gilson, who was profoundly moved by *Aeterni Patris*; Joseph Pieper; Joseph Marechal; and Jacques Maritain. Subsequent popes confirmed *Aeterni Patris*. In his *motu propio Doctoris Angelicis* (1914), Pius X renewed all of Leo's enactments promoting Thomas, requiring that the *Summa Theologica* be the fundamental text in institutions of apostolic right (*DA* # 11). The 1917 *Code of Canon Law* mandated that seminarians be instructed "according to the method, doctrines and principles of the Angelic Doctor" (Canon 1366). In the encyclical *Fausto Appetente Die* (1921), Pope Benedict XV congratulated the Dominican Order that "the Church declared the teaching of Thomas to be her own and that Doctor, honored with the special praises of the Pontiffs, the master and patron of Catholic schools" (# 7). Pius XI's 1923 encyclical *Studiorum Ducem (On St. Thomas Aquinas)* was devoted entirely to fostering Thomas's method; in it, Pius XI wrote that *Aeterni Patris* would alone be sufficient to render Leo's papacy glorious (# 11). In the celebrated encyclical *Humani Generis*, Pius XII confirmed that "the method of Aquinas is singularly preeminent both for teaching students and for bringing truth to light" (# 31). Paul VI's apostolic letter *Lumen Ecclesiae* (1974), commemorating the seventh centenary of the death of Thomas, described his synthesis of theology and philosophy as a safe hinge for the progress of Christian teaching.

Given Pope John Paul II's predilection for philosophy, he can be considered *Aeterni Patris*'s most direct heir. In his address to the Eighth International Thomistic Congress on September 13, 1980, at the close of its centennial celebration of *Aeterni Patris*, John Paul looked to understand the Thomistic renewal in light of the Second Vatican Council, as was his practice. According to John Paul, "the directives of *Aeterni Patris* of Leo XIII" prepared the way for the Council to seek "unity and continuity between authentic humanism and authentic Christianity, between reason and faith" (# 2). John Paul wrote one of his most significant encyclicals, *Fides et Ratio* (1995), to take up the question of faith and philosophy in the spirit of *Aeterni Patris* (*FR* # 100). In

Fides et Ratio, he elaborated on the incomparable value of Thomas's teachings and method—realistic, faithful, objective, transcendent (*FR # 43–44, 57–58*)—while confirming that the Church has no particular philosophy or exclusive method of her own (*FR # 49*).

Aeterni Patris must be considered one of the most significant of papal encyclicals. It is widely regarded that Pope Leo's encyclical *Rerum Novarum* (1891) launched the social teaching of the papacy, which with great insight addressed economic and social conditions over the course of the 20th century. Perhaps in the same way, Leo should be considered with *Aeterni Patris* to have launched a sustained meditation by the papacy on the relation of faith and reason, and philosophy and theology, culminating in *Fides et Ratio*. John Paul in his March 24, 1993, general audience spoke of the ordinary papal magisterium, which, even without making any *ex cathedra* definitions, can shed profound light on the human condition. There is perhaps no better illustration of this charism than the revival of Thomism and sound philosophical methods urged by *Aeterni Patris*.—Howard Bromberg

BIBLIOGRAPHY AND FURTHER READING: Brezik, Victor, ed. *One Hundred Years of Thomism: "Aeterni Patris" and Afterwards, a Symposium.* Houston: Center for Thomistic Studies, 1981; Bruni, Gerardo, and John S. Zybura. *Progressive Scholasticism: A Contribution to the Commemoration of the Fiftieth Anniversary of the Encyclical "Aeterni Patris."* St. Louis: B. Herder Book Co., 1929; Hill, Harvey. "Leo XIII, Loisy, and the 'Broad School': An Early Round of the Modernist Crisis." *Catholic Historical Review* 89, no. 1 (2003): 39–59; John Paul II. *Inter Munera Academiarum* [apostolic letter], January 28, 1998; John Paul II. Address to Participants at the Eighth International Thomistic Congress, September 13, 1980; Pereira, Jose. "Thomism and the Magisterium: From *Aeterni Patris* to *Veritatis Splendor*." *Logos* 5, no. 3 (2002): 147–83. *See also* AQUINAS, ST. THOMAS; FIDEISM; *FIDES ET RATIO*; POPE LEO XIII; RATIONALISM; THOMISM/NEO-THOMISM

AMERICA   *America* is a weekly journal of opinion published and edited by Jesuits from the United States. In continuous publication since April 17, 1909, it aims to provide critical but balanced analysis of current events and trends within the Catholic Church, this country, and the world at large. In recent decades, its orientation has generally been aligned with progressive tendencies within American Catholicism.

The founding editor, Rev. John J. Wynne, SJ (1859–1948), served for only two years but set a basic formula for each issue to which the magazine still adheres: an editorial, letters to the editor, a number of short articles, and various reviews of books, art, and culture. One of the founding editors of *The Catholic Encyclopedia*, Father Wynne also served from 1892 as the editor of *The Messenger of the Sacred Heart*, which had been founded in 1865 by Rev. Benedict Sestini, SJ, to be the chief publication of the Apostleship of Prayer for promoting the morning offering and the practice of consecration to the Sacred Heart of Jesus.

Convinced, however, of the need for a publication that would be broader in scope than this largely devotional magazine, he began a new venture called *The Messenger* in 1902. By 1909, he had renamed it *America* and envisioned it as an American counterpart to *The Tablet* of London. Its subtitle, *Catholic Review of the Week*, served to specify even further the distinctive perspective he intended. As conceived by its often combative founder, the magazine was to provide a record of Catholic achievements and a vehicle for the defense of Catholic doctrines. The very name *America* involved a bold but risky strategy, for the magazine needed to address issues pertinent to the Church in America and to gain Catholic influence on American culture without running afoul of ecclesiastical authorities concerned with the problems of modernism and Americanism.

By 1910, the Jesuit provincials of the United States were troubled by the financial affairs of the new magazine as well as by the polemical style of the editor. They appointed as his replacement Rev. Thomas J. Campbell, SJ, a former provincial, who served as editor until 1914. During his tenure and that of his successor, Rev. Richard H. Tierney, SJ (1914–1925), the journal developed extensive (if somewhat eclectic) coverage of foreign affairs through a network of Jesuit correspondents around the world. Besides its reports on World War I and on the persecution of Catholics by the Mexican government during the 1920s, the journal's main concerns were such domestic issues as the labor movement and economic conditions, poverty and child welfare, rising divorce rates and the need for social reform, and the need for ending discrimination against Negroes (then the preferred term), both within Catholic institutions and in the country at large. The editorials regularly exhibited support for such papal initiatives as Benedict XV's peace proposals and the nascent efforts at the development of modern Catholic social teaching, especially in the light of Leo XIII's extensive series of encyclicals on its various political, economic, and cultural aspects.

In the period between the world wars, the concerns of *America* under the editorial leadership of Rev. Wilfrid Parsons, SJ (1925–1936), and Rev. Francis X. Talbot, SJ (1936–1944), were dominated by economics, the Spanish Civil War, the rise of Adolf Hitler, and the looming threat of another war. The journal was clearly sympathetic to Spanish Catholics and supported at least certain aspects of Francisco Franco's party precisely because he was a Catholic. On the domestic front, the editorials became increasingly critical of Herbert Hoover's handling of the Depression, despite a respect for his accomplishments in postwar European reconstruction. The magazine praised Franklin Delano Roosevelt's introduction of unemployment insurance, the National Labor Relations Act, and increasing federal regulation of utilities. But articles through 1941 and the outbreak of World War II noted that Roosevelt's policies had still not brought the unemployment rate below a staggering 15%. Although the magazine remained consistently critical of the anti-Semitism of Father Charles Coughlin, even in the face of overwhelming support for Coughlin in letters from the readership, the editors loudly objected to governmental shutdown of Coughlin's radio broadcasts on free speech grounds.

With the coming of World War II, the editors modified the previously antiwar tone of the journal. Rev. John LaFarge, SJ, for instance, argued that war against totalitarianism was justifiable. Even after stepping down as editor in 1948, LaFarge indefatigably used his association with *America* to promote a conciliatory approach to ecumenism as well as to the struggle for interracial justice. Under the editorship of Rev. Robert Hartnett, SJ (1948–1955), editorials regularly criticized Sen. Joseph McCarthy, whom some Catholics of the period lionized for his vigorous anticommunism. Harnett also used the pages of *America* to counter the anti-Catholic polemics of Paul Blanshard and to defend the place of a Catholic voice in American public life. During the watch of Rev. Thurston Davis, SJ (1955–1968), the presidential candidacy of John F. Kennedy gave occasion for *America* to examine the question of Catholic officeholders and the persistence of prejudice against Catholics in the United States.

America vigorously supported the Second Vatican Council, not only in the frequent articles devoted to the analysis of conciliar debates and documents but through the swift publication of the first English edition of the documents by America Press. With its editorial of August 17, 1968, the journal took the controversial step of dissenting against Pope Paul VI's determination that all forms of birth control are inherently evil in *Humanae Vitae*.

During the terms of Rev. Donald R. Campion, SJ (1968–1975), and Rev. Joseph A. O'Hare, SJ (1975–1984), the editors of *America* labored to generate informed analysis and commentary on the main issues of the day, from the Vietnam War and the sexual revolution to the implementation of the liturgical changes after the Second Vatican Council and the departures of vast numbers of clergy and religious, with the inevitable effects on Catholic education, social service, and health care systems. During this period, *America* was resilient in supporting the difficult but steady progress of racial integration and social change in the United States.

In the most recent period, under the editorial leadership of Rev. George W. Hunt, SJ (1984–1998), Rev. Thomas J. Reese, SJ (1998–2005), who was reportedly forced to resign under pressure from the Vatican, and Rev. Drew Christiansen, SJ (since 2005), *America* has often been a venue (sometimes quite controversially) for debates on such topics as the Vatican's struggle with liberation theology, the proper liturgical role of the laity in light of the clergy shortage, the Catholicity of Catholic institutions of higher education, the morality of abortion, homosexuality, physician-assisted suicide, and the reform of health care.—Joseph W. Koterski, SJ

See also CATHOLIC PRESS, THE; SOCIETY OF JESUS

AMERIO, ROMANO (1905–1997) Romano Amerio, an Italo-Swiss philosopher, was born in 1905 in Lugano, Switzerland, where he died in 1997. His father was originally from Asti, Italy, while his mother came from a prominent family based in Lugano. His brother, Franco, became a Salesian. Having completed his studies, first of philosophy at the Catholic University of the Sacred Heart in Milan and then of classical philology in Munich, Romano Amerio taught for 40 years at the *lycée* in Lugano and for two years (from 1952 to 1954) at the Catholic University of Milan. Despite the repeated invitation by Father Agostino Gemelli to teach at the Catholic University of Milan during the Fascist years, Amerio refused to do so because he did not want to become a member of the Fascist Party, thus being infected, as he used to explain to his friends, by liberalism.

Amerio was one of the most refined and learned humanists of the 20th century; he edited the 34 volumes of the complete works of Tommaso Campanella, translated Augustine's *City of God*, and was a renowned expert on Dante, Manzoni, Leopardi, Sarpi, Epicurus, and other authors. He is, however, mainly remembered for having identified the two aspects, one metaphysical and the other theological, of the contemporary crisis of the Catholic Church and Western civilization. Amerio's theological reflection was so appreciated by his contemporaries that the bishop of Lugano, Angelo Jelmini, wanted Amerio to accompany him to the Second Vatican Council as a *peritus*.

Don Divo Barsotti has remarked that "talking about Romano Amerio is talking of an order of truth and charity, where the first is linked to the second one but precedes it. Essentially, according to Amerio, the worst evils in the Western thought of the 20th century, including Catholic thought, have mainly been due to a general disorder of the mind, whereby *caritas* [charity] is placed before *veritas* [truth], without realizing that this disorder upsets also the right understanding that we should have of the Most Holy Trinity. Before the time when Descartes's thought took hold of its heart, Christianity had always placed *veritas* before *caritas*, in the same way in which we know that it is the mouth of Christ-*Veritas* that breathes the Holy Spirit-*Caritas*, and not the other way round." After Descartes, it was the opposite. Amerio calls this metaphysical disorder, in *Iota Unum*, "dislocation of the divine Monotriad," liberalism being enthroned instead of the truth. Already in 1937, in a short essay on Descartes, Amerio had articulated his point that the *Logos*, namely the *idea* of love (as well as of will and freedom) precedes love (as well as will and freedom). In other words, love cannot be raised to the level of an absolute principle instead of the natural absolute principle, which is, in the reality of God as of all things, the Logos, the idea of everything. Subverting this order is, according to Amerio, the gravest subversion of the nature of Being, which first of all is, then thinks, and only lastly, after having thought, loves, wants, and freely chooses.

In *Zibaldone*, Amerio shows that liberalism derives from this "dislocation of the divine Monotriad," as the origin of the slow but encompassing subversion aimed at rendering civilization independent of God: yesterday, this subversion was violently accomplished by the Nazi-fascist and socialist-communist ideologies, while today it is cunningly accomplished by the ideology of capitalism, and also in its Catholic variants such as in some strains of personalism. Subverting the order of the Trinitarian essence, liberalism is, according to Amerio, intrinsically irreconcilable with Christianity, because it is irreconcilable with human nature: in itself, it is against nature. In *Iota Unum* and *Zibaldone*, Amerio adds that some segments in the Church, too, have recently bowed down to liberalism. On this, the Italian philosopher Augusto Del Noce wrote to Amerio that, to him too,

Catholic restoration, which the world badly needs, has in the "order of the essence" its ultimate philosophical problem.

Finally, according to Amerio, exclusive reliance on the pastoral over the dogmatic is a concession to liberalism. The answer to this state of affairs is the law of the historical conservation of the Church: the Church is lost if it loses the truth, but, as it is metaphysically impossible for the Church to lose the truth (discontinuity with tradition being metaphysically impossible, despite any effort in that direction), the solution, in Amerio's judgment, is rediscovering the dogmatic *munus* in its fullness, which allows the Church to assess every doctrine in light of her supernatural charism, and to defeat all attempts at discontinuity with the truth.—Enrico Maria Radaelli

BIBLIOGRAPHY AND FURTHER READING: Amerio, Romano. *Iota Unum: Studio delle variazioni della Chiesa cattolica nel secolo XX.* Edited by E. M. Radelli. Turin: Landau, 2009; Amerio, Romano. *Stat veritas: Seguito a "Iota unum."* Edited by E. M. Radelli. Turin: Landau, 2009; Amerio, Romano. *Zibaldone.* Edited by E. M. Radelli. Turin: Landau, 2010; Radaelli, Enrico Maria. *Romano Amerio: Della verità e dell'amore.* Lungro di Cosenza: Marco Editore, 2005; *Romano Amerio, il Vaticano II e le variazioni nella Chiesa cattolica del XX secolo.* Verona: Fede & Cultura, 2008. *See also CARITAS IN VERITATE*; LIBERALISM; SECULARIZATION

ANSCOMBE, G. E. M. (1919–2001) Gertrude Elizabeth Margaret Anscombe (commonly known as Elizabeth Anscombe) was born on March 18, 1919, the third child of an atheist father and nominally Anglican mother, who were schoolteachers. She became convinced of the truth of the Catholic faith on the basis of reading she did between the ages of 12 and 15. G. K. Chesterton was influential at that stage in her life. Her philosophical interests were already aroused. Reading a book on natural theology by a 19th-century Jesuit, she came across a "proof" of a "principle of causality" that she saw proceeded "from a barely concealed assumption of its own conclusion." Over a period of three years, before embarking on the study of philosophy at university, she made five attempts to produce an improved version, in each case coming to judge that it was vitiated by the same fault, though more cleverly disguised, as the one that had provoked her efforts.

Anscombe went to Sydenham High School for Girls and then, in 1937, to St. Hugh's College, Oxford. Her parents had been hostile to her efforts to become a Catholic, so it was only when she went to the university that she was in a position to receive instruction in the

Faith. This she had from Rev. Richard Kehoe, OP, at Blackfriars, Oxford, being received into the Church on April 27, 1938, at the age of 19. Unbeknownst to her, another undergraduate, Peter Geach (1916–), had been receiving instruction in his final year from the same Dominican priest and was received into the Church the following month. They were to meet shortly afterward and became engaged later that year. Geach had obtained a first in Greats that year; Anscombe was to obtain a first in 1941. They were married on December 26, 1941. Their marriage was to bear fruit in the lives of seven children as well as in intensely productive philosophical exchanges; Peter Geach was also to have a distinguished career as a philosopher and logician.

While still an undergraduate, Anscombe wrote the first part, "The War and the Moral Law," of a pamphlet that she coauthored with fellow undergraduate Norman Daniel, *The Justice of the Present War Considered* (1939). She judged the war unjust both because of the unlimited aims with which it was undertaken and, more particularly, because she identified a conditional intention on the part of the government to kill civilians. So, at the age of 20, she had firmly in place the basis for her subsequent opposition to nuclear deterrence policy and her opposition to the conferral of an honorary doctorate by Oxford University on former President Harry Truman.

In 1941, Anscombe went as a postgraduate student to Newnham College, Cambridge, and while there became a student and friend of Ludwig Wittgenstein (1889–1951) who then held the Chair of Philosophy at Cambridge University. She always engaged critically with his thought and had little time for his reflections on religion, but his influence on her was powerful, perhaps most of all through the example he gave of unrelenting intensity in addressing philosophical problems and his aversion to shallowness and pretension. Wittgenstein's substantial work in undermining the Cartesian assumptions behind the tradition of modern philosophy was also of great importance to her. A fair amount of her subsequent work can be seen as a reappropriation of much in Aristotle, Anselm, and Aquinas through dismantling the Cartesian obstacles to a just estimation of their writings. Wittgenstein appointed her one of his three literary executors, and she played a major role in editing and translating his unpublished works, besides lecturing on his work.

In 1946, she was appointed to a research fellowship at Somerville College, Oxford; in 1951 to a lectureship; and in 1964 to a tutorial fellowship. This was a period of intense work—of tutoring, lecturing, writing, translating, and editing—combined with bringing up a young family. Anscombe's own contributions to philosophy cover most areas of the subject, contributions distinguished by the acute manner in which she uncovered and challenged unquestioned assumptions. Most, though not all, of her teaching and writing was addressed to students of philosophy in whom she could not assume her own Catholic beliefs.

In 1956, Anscombe unsuccessfully opposed a proposal that Oxford University confer an honorary doctorate on ex-President Truman. She opposed it because "choosing to kill the innocent as a means to your ends is always murder," and Truman had ordered murder on a massive scale by signing the order to drop the atomic bombs on Hiroshima and Nagasaki. Some of the overwhelming majority who endorsed conferral of Truman's degree rationalized their position by saying one shouldn't make him responsible for the mass murder just because he signed his name at the foot of the order. Anscombe explained her opposition in a pamphlet, *Mr. Truman's Degree* (1956). She went on, however, to confront the roots of the specious exoneration of Truman in a series of lectures on intention, which were published the following year: *Intention* (1957).

Intentional actions, she wrote, are ones that an agent knows he is performing (without having to rely on observation) and to which he would have to allow the question "Why are you doing X?" to apply, and where the answer to the why question is a *reason* that either is backward looking (e.g., revenge) or constitutes a further intention, in particular the immediate and further objectives one is seeking to achieve. A range of actions are therefore identifiable under descriptions that specify the means chosen and ends aimed at. (So, for example, it is clear enough what Truman was aiming at in signing the order—the destruction of Japanese civilian populations—even if that was not his ultimate aim, and therefore the action-description "ordering mass murder" applies to what he did.) The work is dense and short (94 pages) and has been seminal—a book that restored philosophical interest in action theory. When the second edition (1963) was reprinted in 2000, Donald Davidson described it as "the most important treatment of action since Aristotle."

Anscombe's work made it clear that though an agent's own statements of his intentions have a certain authority, there are constraints on the intelligibility of those statements. They cannot, for example, suppress mention of his evidently chosen means to his chosen ends. Nor can an agent "redescribe" his ends when the facts of the case and the context make clear what he is aiming at. Intellectual maneuvers of this kind have not been uncommon in the history of Catholic moral theology, particularly in the application of the principle of double effect, with attempts to redescribe as side effects what are manifestly chosen effects. "The denial of [the principle of double effect] has been the corruption of non-Catholic thought, and its abuse the corruption of Catholic thought," Anscombe observed.

In Oxford in the 1950s, she confronted what she saw as and named the prevailing consequentialism of conventional morality and its academic defense. *Consequentialism*, as she defined it, consisted in the denial of a morally significant distinction between the intended and foreseen effects of one's choices; one was held to be equally responsible for both. In such a view, there cannot be absolute moral norms against, for example, killing the innocent, adultery, idolatry, or vicarious punishment. If my refusal to kill one innocent person whose death would save the lives of 19 others makes me just as much responsible for their deaths as I would have been had I intentionally killed them, then the absolute prohibition on intentionally killing the innocent must seem to collapse. Since unintended evils will result from many of our chosen actions and omissions, the belief that one is just as responsible for them as if one had aimed to bring them about will lead one to ground choices in attempted calculations about which outcome of different options will be the lesser evil. Such a conception of rational moral choice has entered Catholic moral theology under the name *proportionalism*, subverting the Church's teaching on absolute moral norms.

The diagnosis of consequentialism as a prevalent feature of modern moral philosophy appeared in a famous paper Anscombe published in 1958: "Modern Moral Philosophy." That paper also identified the moderns' distinctive use of the notions of moral duty, moral obligation, and the "moral ought," which Anscombe diagnosed as deracinated derivatives of a divine law conception of morality. In the absence of belief in a divine lawgiver, she recommended that secular moralists cease ungrounded invocations of "*moral* obligation" and return to an Aristotelian understanding of the virtues as what are required for human well-being. The article has been widely credited with initiating the revival of interest in virtue ethics.

Answerability for intentional actions does not exhaust what human beings are answerable for. One is answerable for foreseeable harmful side effects of one's choices, though one does not incur guilt if one's chosen course of action was required for sufficiently grave reasons. One is also answerable for omissions when one *could* and *should* have acted. And one may be guilty

of failure to act even when one is not aware that one *should* act, when ignorance of obligation is itself culpable ignorance, as in one who does not take the trouble to find out what he should take the trouble to find out.

Both before and after the publication of *Humanae Vitae*, Anscombe defended the Church's teaching on contraception, arguing that a woman who used the anovulent pill to render intercourse sterile, while clearly not engaging in the nongenerative-type behavior that the Church had always condemned, deliberately produced circumstances that rendered chosen acts of intercourse nongenerative as *intentional acts*. Such a choice was to be distinguished from having intercourse in circumstances in which the woman happened to be naturally infertile: generative-type behavior was not vitiated by any intentional bringing about of sterility. Anscombe argued that defense of the Church's teaching on contraception was essential to the intelligibility of the Church's teaching on chastity. Those who initially claimed to be making a case for the use of the pill only within marriage would soon be allowing other kinds of nonmarital, nongenerative acts.

In 1970, Anscombe moved from Oxford to the Chair of Philosophy at Cambridge, the chair once occupied by her teacher Wittgenstein. One of the subjects of her seminars in her first years there was "on killing human beings." Human beings are to be distinguished from the other animals in being spirit as well as flesh. The spirituality of human bodily life is exhibited in a number of ways: in the fact that a thought can be identified only by saying what is being thought and not by material happenings or any physical process; in the fact that human beings "move in the categories of innocence and answerability and desert"; in our requiring *justification* for certain courses of action. So, human beings possess a great dignity. It is radically contrary to recognition of that dignity to kill a human being for reasons of convenience or because one judges that he or she lacks a worthwhile life. Duly constituted civil authority may kill in defense of the common good, but since the foundation of its right to do so is the human need of protection from *unjust* attack, civil authority may never engage in or authorize the killing of the innocent. Our most basic right is our right not to be murdered.

Anscombe had always been clear in her opposition to abortion and euthanasia, regarding each nation that has "liberal" abortion laws as having become "a nation of murderers." Though her reading of the embryological evidence left her unconvinced that there was an individualized human form at the very earliest stages of development, she held that abortion at these stages was, if not the killing of an individual human being, at least the killing of "a living individual whole whose life is—all going well—to be the life of one or lives of more than one human being," which it would be pedantic not to call murder.

Anscombe's opposition to abortion was not merely intellectual. She joined two of her children in actions outside abortion clinics; there is a press photograph of her being dragged away by police on one occasion from the front of a clinic. The press reports, however, carefully avoided saying who the elderly protestor was.

Respect for human dignity, as Anscombe understood it, means not merely basic respect for human existence but also respect for the kind of life proper to the nature of human beings. And so, failure to see that human beings should be brought into existence only through natural procreation in the bond of marriage leads to a loss of recognition of human dignity. This is manifest in the status accorded to the human embryo in in vitro fertilization programs.

Anscombe used to wonder at times in the 1960s whether the Church's teaching on contraception would suffer the same neglect as its teaching on usury, usury being the demanding of interest on the mere strength of a loan. In a posthumously published paper (written in 1975), she presented the thesis that "the automatic right of money to bear interest is something that essentially goes with a stock market; and further is something that must go against prosperity unless trade and productivity are continually expanding. For if interest is paid, then either there must be a real increase of productivity, or there must be a flow of the country's money into the hands of the people who already have money (to them that have shall be given) or there must be inflation." Anscombe thought it highly regrettable that the Church should have fallen silent about usury since Benedict XIV's condemnation of it "in unretractable terms" in his encyclical letter *Vix Pervenit* of 1745. On so many moral issues, Anscombe was opposed to the conventional tenets and spirit of the age.

She retired from the Chair of Philosophy at Cambridge in 1986. She had been made a Fellow of the British Academy in 1967, and over the course of her career, she had been a regular visiting professor in a number of universities in the United States and on occasions in Germany, Spain, and South America. Many students testified to her outstanding abilities as a teacher. Concluding an obituary notice, her sometime colleague, Prof. Philippa Foot, wrote: "She was a very important philosopher and a great teacher. Many say 'I owe everything to her' and I say it too on my own account."

Large and important areas of Anscombe's work in philosophy have been left untouched in this account. There can be no substitute for reading Anscombe's own writings.—Luke Gormally

BIBLIOGRAPHY AND FURTHER READING: Anscombe, G. E. M. *Intention.* Oxford: Blackwell, 1957 (2nd ed., Cambridge, MA: Harvard University Press, 2000); Anscombe, G. E. M. *Collected Philosophical Papers.* Vol. 2, *Metaphysics and the Philosophy of Mind.* Oxford: Blackwell, 1981; Anscombe, G. E. M. *Collected Philosophical Papers.* Vol. 3, *Ethics, Religion and Politics.* Oxford: Blackwell, 1981; Foot, Philippa, "Obituary: Elizabeth Anscombe (1919–2001)." *Somerville College Record* (2001): 119–20; Geach, Mary, and Luke Gormally, eds. *Human Life, Action and Ethics: Essays by G E M Anscombe.* Exeter, England: Imprint Academic, 2005; Geach, Mary, and Luke Gormally, eds. *Faith in a Hard Ground: Essays on Religion, Philosophy and Ethics by G E M Anscombe.* Exeter, England: Imprint Academic, 2008. *See also* CONSEQUENTIALISM; DOUBLE EFFECT, PRINCIPLE OF; MORAL THEOLOGY: A SURVEY; PROPORTIONALISM

ANSELM, ST. (c. 1033–1109)

St. Anselm was born in Aosta, in northern Italy, around 1033. He was a natural born scholar, and throughout most of his youth he dedicated himself to the assiduous pursuit of knowledge. In 1060, when he was 26 years old, he entered the Benedictine monastery of Bec in northwestern France. This was a new foundation, having been established by Abbot Herluin in 1034. It was quickly to become the site of one of the most illustrious monastic schools in all of Europe. The founder of the school was Lanfranc of Pavia, who was prior at Bec when St. Anselm joined the community there. When Lanfranc was appointed the archbishop of Canterbury in 1063, St. Anselm succeeded him as prior and head of the monastic school. When Abbot Herluin died in 1078, St. Anselm was elected to take his place. Subsequently, just as he had succeeded him as prior, St. Anselm was to succeed Lanfranc as the archbishop of Canterbury, a position to which he was appointed in 1093.

St. Anselm's tenure as archbishop of Canterbury was not a particularly pacific one, for he was engaged in almost continuous conflict with the Crown, first with King William Rufus, and then with his successor and brother, King Henry I. What principally put archbishop and king at odds with one another was St. Anselm's opposition to the Crown's attempt to usurp powers and privileges that properly belong to the Church. The conflict grew so heated that St. Anselm had to endure two lengthy periods of exile, the first under William, from 1097 to 1100, the second under Henry, from 1103 to 1107. He was to live only two years after returning to his see at the end of the second period of exile, dying at Canterbury in 1109. He was canonized a saint in 1163 and declared a Doctor of the Church in 1720.

St. Anselm bears several notable titles. He has been called the Father of Scholasticism, the Last of the Fathers, and, because he was so devoted a student and disciple of St. Augustine, Augustinus Redivivus ("Augustine reborn"). It is common to identify him, along with St. Augustine, as a Christian Platonist. St. Anselm's motto, which perfectly captures the guiding spirit of this great theologian, was *Fides Quaerens Intellectum* ("Faith Seeking Understanding"). The order of the two terms in that motto was of critical importance: first there must be faith, and then understanding. He lived according to the principle that he had learned from St. Augustine, expressed in the statement "*Credo ut intelligam*" ("I believe in order that I may understand"). We must always begin with belief, the unquestioning acceptance of divine revelation, but then—and this is the most characteristic feature of his whole attitude—we must commit ourselves to the most vigorous exercise of our reason in order to broaden and deepen our comprehension of what we believe. Reason is the God-given means by which we expose to full view the intrinsic intelligibility of the truths of faith.

St. Anselm was convinced that the truths of faith could be proved by reason alone, even great mysteries such as the Trinity, the Incarnation, and the Redemption. In this, he doubtless was asking of human reason more than it is capable of delivering, but even though he fell short in his attempts to demonstrate the truth of the mysteries, those attempts nonetheless stand as noble and edifying monuments of theological discourse, and there is something lastingly admirable in his unswerving dedication to the proposition that faith and reason are completely compatible. The eminent medievalist Gerald B. Phelan paid St. Anselm the highest kind of compliment when he wrote of him: "No more vigorous defender of human reason ever lived than St. Anselm of Canterbury."

It is always a delight to read St. Anselm, for the clarity and cogency of his prose and for the impressive logic with which he weaves together his arguments. He addresses himself to believers, but to believers who assent to what they believe as rational creatures, and as such, he wants to show them that their belief is immeasurably enriched when they come to see that it is thoroughly reasonable. The corpus of St. Anselm's writings, as compared to that of St. Augustine or St. Thomas Aquinas, is relatively slight, but whatever it lacks in quantity is more than made up by its quality. Among his works are to be counted *On Truth, On Free Will, On the Fall of the Devil, On the Virginal Conception and Original Sin*, and *On the Procession of the Holy Spirit*. Most scholars agree that his three most important works are the *Monologion, Cur Deus Homo*, and the *Proslogion*.

In the *Monologion*, which owes not a little to St. Augustine's *De Trinitate*, he builds an imposing structure of intricately interrelated arguments whose purpose is to provide a rational basis for the doctrine of the Trinity. *Cur Deus Homo* ("Why God Became Man") takes the same approach toward the Incarnation and the Redemption. Here St. Anselm seeks to demonstrate that there is an irrefutable logic behind these mysteries that, once grasped, will make them all the more luminous.

The *Proslogion* ("A Discourse") is probably the most well known of St. Anselm's works, because it contains the famous "ontological argument." This has proven to be one of the most controversial arguments in the history of Western philosophy. It was taken exception to shortly after St. Anselm first published it, by a fellow monk, Gaunilo of Marmoutiers, and to this day, one can find philosophers and theologians who will energetically praise it or disparage it. The disparagers claim that the argument simply does not succeed in what it was attempting to do. But just what was it attempting to do? It is precisely over that question that the jury is split.

Those who defend the ontological argument assert that those who disparage it are simply missing St. Anselm's point, for those people say that he fails to demonstrate the existence of God, but they are wrong in that opinion because that is not at all what St. Anselm was attempting to do. In the argument, its defenders contend, St. Anselm begins with belief—specifically, with the belief that God does in fact exist. The purpose of the argument, then, is not to prove that God exists, but simply to show the reasonableness of believing that God exists. The defenders' is a thoughtful point of view, but unfortunately it finds no corroboration in the argument itself, which is clearly addressed to the fool, that is, to one who says in his heart that there is no God. Moreover, in his response to the monk Gaunilo, St. Anselm makes it quite clear that the purpose of his argument was to prove, to one who does not believe, the existence of God.

The gist of the ontological argument can be stated as follows: It is based upon an idea—the idea of God as a being a greater than which cannot be conceived. Now, anyone, even an atheist, can understand that idea;

he has it in his mind. But if he truly understands it, then he must see that it would be contradictory to suppose that it could exist *only* as an idea in his mind, for then it would not be a being a greater than which cannot be conceived, for to exist actually is greater than to exist only mentally. Therefore, God exists.

As the history of the controversy that has swirled around it clearly attests, the argument elicits an enduring fascination, but while respecting it for its many admirable qualities, in the end we have to agree with St. Thomas Aquinas that, insofar as the argument is to be accepted as an attempt at demonstration—and, again, this is how St. Anselm intended it be accepted—then it does not measure up to the task. The problem lies with the argument's starting point, an *idea* of God. As St. Thomas gently points out, mental existence—that is, an idea, even though it be the most sublime of ideas—is an insufficient basis for proving extramental existence.

Does this mean then that the argument, and the *Proslogion* as a whole, should be dismissed as not worthy of our serious attention and study? By no means. If this powerful little work does not demonstrate, in the strict sense, the existence of God, it offers us a veritable feast of profound theological reasoning as pertaining to the divine nature. In this, as in all of St. Anselm's works, we find brilliant example after brilliant example of a vibrant faith ever in search for deeper understanding.—D. Q. McInerny

BIBLIOGRAPHY AND FURTHER READING: Clayton, Joseph. *Saint Anselm*. Milwaukee: Bruce, 1933; Deane, Sidney Norton. *St. Anselm*. Chicago: Open Court, 1903; Hopkins, Jaspers. *A Companion to the Study of St. Anselm*. Minneapolis: University of Minnesota Press, 1972; Phelan, G. B. *The Wisdom of Saint Anselm*. Latrobe, PA: Archabbey Press, 1960; Rule, Martin. *The Life and Times of St. Anselm*. 2 vols. London: Kegan Paul, Trench, 1883. *See also* AUGUSTINE, ST.; REASON

ARENDT, HANNAH (1906–1975)

Hannah Arendt was one of the leading political philosophers of the 20th century. Born in Germany to a Jewish family, she left Germany in 1933 to escape the Nazis and lived in France for the next eight years, working for a number of Jewish refugee organizations. She came to the United States in 1941 and held a number of academic positions at various American universities. Her best known works are *The Origins of Totalitarianism* (1951), *The Human Condition* (1958), and *Eichmann in Jerusalem* (1963). At the time of her death, she had completed two out of three volumes of her last major philosophical work, *The Life of the Mind*.

Arendt was born on October 14, 1906, in Konigsberg, which then was the capital of Eastern Prussia. She grew up in a strictly regimented, but happy, family. In 1924, after the completion of her secondary education, she entered Marburg University, where she met Martin Heidegger, with whom she had a brief, but intense, romantic involvement. After a year of study at Marburg, she transferred to Freiburg University, where she attended lectures given by Edmund Husserl. In the spring of 1926, she began her doctoral studies at Heidelberg University under the direction of Karl Jaspers. Arendt completed her dissertation in 1929, which was titled *On Love and St. Augustine* (*Der Liebesbegriff bei Augustin*).

She fled Germany in 1933 to escape the growing threat posed by the Nazis. Arendt lived in Paris for six years (1933–1939), where she worked for a number of Jewish refugee organizations. In 1941, she fled France and moved to New York City, where she met influential writers and intellectuals who were associated with the journal *Partisan Review*. During the postwar period, she lectured at a number of American universities, including the University of Chicago.

Arendt wrote two of the most important works of her career shortly after coming to the United States. One of her most well-known books, *The Origins of Totalitarianism*, published in 1951, is a study of how the totalitarian regimes of Nazi Germany and Soviet Stalinism came about. In 1958, she published *The Human Condition*, her most important work in philosophy.

An important year for Arendt was 1963. First, she published *Eichmann in Jerusalem*, based on a series of articles she wrote for the *New Yorker*, which had sent her to cover the trial of Adolf Eichmann. The book, which described Eichmann as a petty bureaucrat and not a moral monster, caused deep controversy in Jewish circles. Also published that year was *On Revolution*, a comparative analysis of the American and French revolutions. In addition, she published three collections of essays that are of particular importance: *Between Past and Future*, *Men in Dark Times*, and *Crises of the Republic*.

At the time of her death in 1975, Arendt had completed the first two volumes, *Thinking* and *Willing*, of her last major philosophical work, *The Life of the Mind*, which was published posthumously in 1978. The third volume, *Judging*, was left unfinished, but some background material and lecture notes were published in 1982 under the title *Lectures on Kant's Political Philosophy*.

Arendt's political philosophy developed out of her contact with phenomenology. A characteristic attitude of phenomenologists was the questioning of foundational assumptions. For Husserl, her mentor, exposing and questioning presumptions was essential to his conception of philosophy—an idea that he developed in confronting the scientism that he believed had overtaken European philosophy. Arendt expressed this basic attitude in one of her most well-known phrases, "the banality of evil." This was her diagnosis of Eichmann. He was not a "moral monster" but a thoughtless bureaucrat who sputtered banal slogans: he had lost the ability to question his foundational assumptions.

Arendt's conception of politics was also influenced by her work on St. Augustine. From him, she came to view politics as occurring in the everyday acts of ordinary people rather than in grand gestures of the state. Her conception of politics is based instead on the implicit value and importance of civic engagement and collective deliberation about all matters affecting the political community. According to this perspective, politics finds its authentic expression whenever citizens gather together in a public space to deliberate about matters of collective concern. Political activity is valued not because it may lead to agreement or to a shared conception of the good, but because it enables each citizen to exercise his or her powers of agency, to develop the capacities for judgment, and to attain by concerted action some measure of political efficacy.

Nonetheless, Arendt was not an antiliberal thinker. She was a defender of constitutionalism and the rule of law, an advocate of fundamental human rights, and a critic of all forms of political community based on traditional ties and customs, as well as those based on religious, ethnic, or racial identity. Arendt's political thought cannot, in this sense, be identified with either the liberal tradition or the claims advanced by a number of its conservative critics.

The Life of the Mind developed out of her Gifford Lectures at the University of Aberdeen in Scotland. Through this work, she continued to develop her thought on the faculties of thinking and willing. In her discussion of thinking, she focuses mainly on Socrates and his notion of thinking as a solitary dialogue between me and myself. This appropriation of Socrates leads her to introduce novel concepts of conscience and morality. Arendt relied heavily on her reading of St. Augustine's notion of the will. She describes the will as an absolutely free mental faculty that makes new beginnings possible.

Catholics have had mixed responses to Arendt's thought. Her connections with Heideggerian thought have made her controversial among Catholic thinkers. Some view her restless methodological questioning to suggest a rejection of the philosophy of Being. But, her strong defense of those who bring questions of meaning, identity, value, and transcendence to public life has clear sympathies with 20th-century Catholic political thought. For example, her essay *On Revolution* contains a nuanced position that is critical of the thoughtlessness of the rights talk that characterized the French Revolution, but places the critique in the context of her defense of human dignity.—Kevin P. Lee

BIBLIOGRAPHY AND FURTHER READING: Arendt, Hannah. *Eichmann in Jerusalem*. New York: Penguin, 2006; Arendt, Hannah. *The Human Condition*. Chicago: University of Chicago Press, 1958; Arendt, Hannah. *On Love and St. Augustine*. Chicago: University of Chicago Press, 1998; Arendt, Hannah. *On Revolution*. New York: Penguin, 2006; Arendt, Hannah. *The Origins of Totalitarianism*. New York: Harcourt, Brace, Jovanovich, 1973; Your-Breuhl, Elizabeth. *For the Love of the World*. New Haven, CT: Yale University Press, 2004; Your-Breuhl, Elizabeth. *Why Arendt Matters*. New Haven, CT: Yale University Press, 2006. *See also* AUGUSTINE, ST.; HEIDEGGER, MARTIN; NAZISM; PHENOMENOLOGY; TOTALITARIANISM

ARON, RAYMOND (1905–1983) French sociologist, writer, and thinker Raymond Aron was renowned and very influential over some 50 years in the mid-20th century in a number of fields besides sociology, including political science and political commentary, history, philosophy, and strategic thinking. Aron was especially noted for his skepticism about and opposition to such ideologies as Nazism, fascism, and communism as well as variants of contemporary leftist ideologies that tended, as he saw it, to become secular religions.

Although often attacked as a man of the right, Aron was not a typical conservative but rather a "classical" secular liberal who habitually adopted realistic positions that much later in the United States would be styled "neoconservative." In his *Memoirs*, he described himself as "an analyst in the service of freedom."

Aron was a 1930 graduate in philosophy from France's elitist École Normale Supérieure, where he was a fellow student, roommate, and close friend of the later world-famous French existentialist philosopher Jean-Paul Sartre—who became a notable public rival of Aron's in France for a period extending over nearly a half century. Aron also pursued an academic career as a professor throughout most of his professional life. Among his academic appointments were his professorships at the Sorbonne from 1955 to 1968 and at the Collège de France from 1970 on. He guest-lectured frequently, particularly at universities in Germany and in the English-speaking world.

But Aron was best known as a journalist and commentator, his journalistic career dating from his editorship of *La France Libre* in London during World War II. Over some 30 years until 1977, he was a columnist for the widely read and quoted Parisian daily *Le Figaro*, and after that up until his death he contributed a weekly column to *L'Express*, a journal on the democratic left.

He was a prolific author of both scholarly and popular books, publishing more than 30 volumes, many of which were translated. His first important scholarly work, which grew out of his graduate work in Germany during the 1930s where he witnessed firsthand the rise of Nazism, was his *Introduction to the Philosophy of History: An Essay on the Limits of Historical Objectivity* (1938; Eng. trans., 1961).

Typical of his critiques of ideological extremism was his 1955 book *The Opium of the Intellectuals* (Eng. trans., 1957), a devastating polemic against, among others, his old school friend, Sartre, the latter by then a prominent Communist fellow traveler. Aron's battle against leftist forces and supposed "revolutionary" solutions extended up to his dissection of the 1968 student and worker uprisings in France in his *The Elusive Revolution: Anatomy of a Student Revolt* (Eng. trans., 1969).

As a major thinker on the subject of war and peace in what had become the nuclear age, Aron published, among other studies, his 1951 *Century of Total War* (Eng. trans., 1954) and especially his 1961 *Peace and War: A Theory of International Relations* (Eng. trans., 1966 and 1973). (Of possible interest to Catholic readers and students is the fact that Aron, himself a major contemporary moralist, almost never refers to or even indicates that he knows very much about the traditional Catholic "just war" teaching.)

Aron's more substantial scholarly studies include *The Industrial Society* (1966; Eng. trans., 1967) and, more importantly, his magisterial two-volume 1967 work *Main Currents in Sociological Thought* (Eng. trans., 1967), in which he analyzes the work and influence of the great pioneers on the European continent of the study of human society, namely, Montesquieu, Comte, Tocqueville, Marx, Durkheim, Pareto, and Weber.

In addition to his journalistic and scholarly work, Aron enjoyed a wide range of high-level personal contacts. He was a personal friend of U.S. Secretary of State Henry Kissinger, and he conferred regularly with those in power while keeping his distance and maintaining his independence. Though he worked for the Free French in World War II and knew Gen. Charles De Gaulle personally—and recognized the degree to which the latter was twice a modern "savior" of France—he was never formally a Gaullist and at times greatly displeased the French general and president. It almost goes without saying, given his opposition to colonialism, that Aron opposed the Algerian War, as he brought out in his 1957 *La Tragédie Algérienne* and his 1958 *L'Algérie et la République*.

As a political commentator, Aron was a strong supporter of the North Atlantic Treaty Organization and the Western Alliance, and he often found himself in sharp public opposition to the fashionable leftist French anti-Americanism of the day. Although not uncritical of some American policies and actions, he tried to be scrupulously fair—yet was generally regarded as "pro-American." His major work on this subject was his 1973 book *The Imperial Republic: The United States and the World, 1945–1973* (Eng. trans., 1974).

According to his personal testimonials, Raymond Aron proudly identified himself as a Jew, although the "pride" in question was mostly expressed in solidarity with his fellow Jews and against anti-Semitism. As far as religious Judaism was concerned, he described himself as a nonbelieving and nonpracticing Jew. He declared himself to be simply "incompetent" in religious matters. He did, however, respect religious belief and commitment, including by Catholics, and in his 1957 volume *Espoir et Peur du Siècle* (translated as *On War: Atomic Weapons and Global Diplomacy*, 1968), he included an epigraph quoting Pope Pius XII on "the flagrant contradiction of 20th-century man" between "confidence in modern man" as a result of the modern "technical revolution" and the "bitter reality" of endless modern wars and ruins. Aron was a major 20th-century thinker and commentator whose influence extended far beyond his native France.—Kenneth D. Whitehead

BIBLIOGRAPHY AND FURTHER READING: Aron, Raymond. *Main Currents in Sociological Thought*. With an Introduction by Daniel J. Mahoney and Brian C. Anderson. Foreword by Pierre Manent. New Brunswick, NJ: Transaction, 1998; Aron, Raymond. *Memoirs: Fifty Years of Political Reflection*. Translated by George Holoch. Foreword by Henry Kissinger. New York: Holmes & Meier, 1990; Aron, Raymond. *Peace and War: A Theory of International Relations*, Garden City, NY: Doubleday, 1973; Aron, Raymond. *Politics and History: Selected Essays by Raymond Aron*. Collected, translated, and edited by Miriam Bernheim Conant. New York: Free Press, 1978. *See also* SARTRE, JEAN-PAUL; SHILS, EDWARD A.; SOCIOLOGY: A CATHOLIC CRITIQUE

ASHLEY, BENEDICT M., OP (1915–) Father Benedict Ashley is an American Roman Catholic theologian and philosopher who was born Winston Norman Ashley in Neodesha, Nebraska, on May 5, 1915, to nonpracticing Protestant parents. By the time of his birth, World War I had been in progress for less than a year. Gifted with a powerful memory, Ashley remembers the homecoming parade for the returning U.S. troops in 1918. Already as a child, Ashley was curious about philosophical matters, noting in his memoirs an early love of Plato's works.

In 1933, during the Great Depression, Ashley went off to the University of Chicago on a competitive scholarship. While at the university, Ashley was influenced by its president, Robert Maynard Hutchins (1899–1977), and the philosopher Mortimer Adler (1902–2001) in their attempt to reform education by means of a "Great Books" curriculum. Their emphasis on Aristotelianism and Thomism providing guiding principles for education would leave a lasting impression on the young undergraduate.

After receiving his bachelor's and master's degrees in comparative literature in late 1937, Ashley looked forward to teaching English. At this time, Ashley was working on a novel and writing poetry. Novelists Norman Maclean and Thornton Wilder and writer/poet Gertrude Stein encouraged his early literary efforts. Although Ashley would also take courses from the process philosopher Charles Hartshorne and the logical positivist philosopher Rudolf Carnap, it was a course with Herbert Schwartz (a Jewish convert to Catholicism) on Thomistic philosophy (using Joseph Gredt's *Elementa philosophiae Aristotelico-Thomisticae*) that was especially important to his intellectual development.

Just prior to World War II, while still at the university, Ashley became a committed Marxist, indeed a card-carrying member of the Trotskyite Socialist Workers Party. Providentially, during this time of active Communist involvement, Ashley was also reading St. Thomas Aquinas. This reading of Aquinas, coupled with the influence of the Dominican chaplains at the university and two friends—Schwartz and Leo Shields—would spark his conversion to Catholicism.

After his baptism in 1938, Ashley was expelled from the Socialist Workers Party on account of his conversion. During this time, Ashley began doctoral studies in political science (rather than literature) at the University of Notre Dame—jumping at the chance to study at a Catholic university under a Catholic director. There, he wrote a thesis titled "Natural Slavery According to Aristotle and St. Thomas" (1941)—about the two philosophers he most admired—under the direction of Waldemar Gurian (1902–1954), an expert on Marxism and an émigré from Hitler's Europe.

More influential still than Gurian, however, was the French Catholic philosopher Yves Simon (1903–1961). From Simon, Ashley learned that Thomism was a philosophy that could be used to not only respond to the errors of modern thought but also offer its own answers to contemporary problems. In St. Thomas, Ashley found the kind of answers to his questions that Marx could not provide.

While still at the University of Chicago, Ashley felt called to the Dominican Order, having been exposed to their way of life by such Dominican chaplains as Father Timothy Sparks. Ashley described this call some years ago, saying that he had given himself to God in baptism and now he thought that he should "'go all the way' in following Christ and give myself to him in religious vows."

Once his doctorate was finished, Ashley applied and was admitted into the Chicago Province of the Dominican Order in the summer of 1941. His novitiate was made in River Forest, Illinois, at a time when the Midwest Province was thriving. After his novitiate, he was required to take the same course of study as the other students at the Aquinas Institute. This academic program consisted of three years in philosophy (then solemn profession in 1945) and three years in theology before ordination (in 1948), and a fourth year of theology after ordination. Post ordination, Father Ashley wrote a 290-page lectorate dissertation in theology, "Contemplation and Society" (1949).

As a young priest, Ashley would be deeply influenced by William H. Kane, OP (1901–1970), one of his former professors who held the view that the metaphysics of St. Thomas must be grounded in a sound philosophy of nature; without this grounding, it lacks foundation. This view would influence Ashley's way of conceiving the relationship between science and theology—one he argued was Aquinas's own position.

To put these views into practice, Kane, along with Ashley and classmate Raymond Nogar, OP (1916–1967), founded the Albertus Magnus Lyceum in 1951 in River Forest, for the purpose of fostering collaboration between Thomists and scientists. Although neither Ashley nor Nogar had formal training as a scientist, they were both well read in the philosophy and history of science. The Lyceum, which Ashley directed from 1958 to 1963, would have a limited impact on the Catholic philosophical world, but its research and publications would influence and inspire several young Dominicans in their later work, for example, William A. Wallace (1918–) and other "River Forest School Thomists."

Also in 1951, Ashley wrote his second doctoral dissertation in the Pontifical Faculty of Philosophy

(River Forest, Illinois) on the subject, "Aristotle's Special Physical Sciences: Physics and Chemistry," the essential part of which was published in two parts in the journal *New Scholasticism* in 1958. Ashley would then teach the history of philosophy in River Forest for almost 20 years, until 1969.

During the 1950s, Father Ashley (as the principal consultant) and his fellow River Forest Dominicans were engaged in the St. Xavier Plan of Liberal Education at the request of the Mercy Sisters at St. Xavier College (Chicago). The Dominicans were asked to provide them with theological assistance in revising the curriculum for their college and related high school and grade school. This project would enable the Dominican Fathers to implement their ideas about the relation of the modern and classical disciplines, centering on the issue of the role of natural science. It would also put into practice, as Ashley has noted, the educational ideals of Hutchins and Adler, with the focus not on the study of classical texts but on the classical disciplines revised to assimilate modern knowledge to the Aristotelian methodology. A work giving practical form to Ashley's educational philosophy was his *The Arts of Learning and Communication: A Handbook of the Liberal Arts* (1958).

Ashley would also take on various administrative positions during this period, beginning with his appointment in 1962 as regent of studies for the Chicago Province and also serving as chairman of the Midwest Association of Theological Schools and as a consultant for the U.S. Bishops Committee on Priestly Formation in 1965–1968.

This time of work in theological education coincided with the advent of the Second Vatican Council. Ashley had greeted the council with enthusiasm and joy. He was much encouraged by the council's efforts in such areas as ecumenism, evangelization, and openness to engaging the problems of the modern world in a fresh way. He also saw in its call for renewal the possibility of overcoming what he has referred to as the "narrowness" and "formalism" of the Dominican way of life at the time.

Ashley found the postconciliar period very disconcerting, however, as he dealt with the unintended results of the council. For example, as required by the council, the constitutions of the whole Dominican Order were totally revised for the first time in their seven-hundred-year history. While Ashley saw the revision as mostly successful, in actual practice many Dominicans not only abandoned authentic aspects of Dominican life but also left the order, and some even left the Church. Nonetheless, Ashley was able to get through this ex-

tremely difficult period of his life since his hope in the council's vision of reform was a source of strength.

What would open a new chapter in Ashley's life was his acceptance of Dominican Albert Moraczewski's (1920–2008) invitation in 1969 to become a faculty member at the Institute of Religion and Human Development at the Texas Medical Center in Houston. During his three years there, Ashley began to see medical ethics/bioethics as an important field where science and theology might meet, in addition to learning much about modern medicine and psychotherapy. Some of this learning would bear fruit in *Health Care Ethics*, a text he coauthored with Kevin O'Rourke, OP, and now in its fifth edition (2006). He would also begin at the Medical Center his major project, *Theologies of the Body: Humanist and Christian*, first published in 1985—a sweeping work of interdisciplinary scholarship tracing the anthropologies of the two "religions" in the book's subtitle, as well as showing the need for theology to integrate modern science.

In 1972, Ashley was called back to Dubuque, Iowa (where the theology faculty of the Chicago Province's Aquinas Institute—which has been called the Aquinas Institute of Theology since 1962—had been moved in 1950) to be regent of studies for Dominican students and to teach moral theology, rather than philosophy, as he had previously done. By this time, the students there seemed poorly trained in Thomism and more concerned with modern psychology and certain theological fads, as Ashley recalls.

In 1979, Ashley, along with former Lyceum colleague James A. Weisheipl, OP (1923–1984), received the Dominican Order's prestigious master of sacred theology (STM), a postdoctoral degree traditionally given to Dominicans who have taught and written with distinction. Other honors and awards would follow over the next 30 years.

Throughout the 1980s and 1990s, Father Ashley taught moral theology at Aquinas Institute of Theology (now in St. Louis, Missouri, and where Ashley is emeritus professor of moral theology), St. Louis University, and Kenrick-Glennon Seminary, among other places. From 1988 to 1992, Ashley taught as senior professor in the fledgling John Paul II Institute for Studies on Marriage and Family in Washington, D.C. There he would deliver in 1992 the annual McGivney Lectures, *Justice in the Church*, eventually published in 1996.

Since the mid-1990s, Ashley has continued to teach at various institutions, lecture throughout the world, and publish widely. His most recent book, *The Way toward Wisdom* (2006) sums up one of the central theses of his River Forest School of Thomism: natural science or natural philosophy is the starting point sine qua non for the study of metaphysics.

As for his moral theology, Ashley's book *Living the Truth in Love* (1996) shows how Christ is the fulfillment of the natural moral law; and if men are to imitate his life, they must have the infused theological virtues as well as acquire the cardinal virtues—both of which Ashley coordinates in a scripturally based moral theology. These are but two of the central ideas that Ashley has argued for over the course of his long and distinguished Dominican priesthood.—Mark S. Latkovic

BIBLIOGRAPHY AND FURTHER READING: Ashley, Benedict M., OP. *The Ashley Reader: Redeeming Reason.* Naples, FL: Sapientia Press, 2006; Ashley, Benedict M., OP. *Choosing a Worldview and Value System: An Ecumenical Apologetics.* Staten Island, NY: Alba House, 2000; Ashley, Benedict M., OP. *The Dominicans.* Collegeville, MN: Liturgical Press/Michael Glazier, 1990; Ashley, Benedict M., OP. *Justice in the Church: Gender and Participation.* Washington, DC: Catholic University of America Press, 1996; Ashley, Benedict M., OP. *Living the Truth in Love: A Biblical Introduction to Moral Theology.* Staten Island, NY: Alba House, 1996; Ashley, Benedict M., OP. *Theologies of the Body: Humanist and Christian.* St. Louis: Pope John Center, 1985 (2nd ed. with new preface, 1995); Ashley, Benedict M., OP. *The Way toward Wisdom: An Interdisciplinary and Contextual Introduction to Metaphysics.* Notre Dame, IN: University of Notre Dame Press, 2006; Ashley, Benedict M., OP, Jean deBlois, and Kevin O'Rourke, OP. *Health Care Ethics: A Catholic Theological Analysis,* 5th ed. Washington, DC: Georgetown University Press, 2006; Latkovic, Mark S. *The Fundamental Moral Theology of Benedict M. Ashley, O.P.: A Critical Study: Toward a Response to the Second Vatican Council's Call for Renewal in Moral Theology.* STD dissertation, Pontifical John Paul II Institute for Studies on Marriage and Family, Washington, DC, 1998. *See also* MORAL THEOLOGY: A SURVEY; PHILOSOPHY, DISCIPLINE OF; SIMON, YVES R.; THOMISM/NEO-THOMISM

ATHEISM The essence of atheism is simply the denial of the existence of God. It is an intellectual position that would seem to be as old at the human race itself, although its long history has been an erratic one. The seeds of atheism in Western society were planted in ancient Greece, initially by the pre-Socratic philosopher Democritus, who died around 370 BC. Democritus was the first philosophical materialist, the inventor of the atomic theory, and a determinist, after his own fashion. For him, the natural world, that is, the physical world, was the *only* world. In the following century, the philosopher Epicurus picked up the ideas generated by Democritus, embellished them, and gave them further development, and thus Epicureanism was born. In the century before the birth of Christ, the Roman poet Lucretius (d. 52 BC) gave powerful expression to the atheistic ideas propounded by Democritus and Epicurus in his poem *De Rerum Natura.* The Stoic philosophers, whose ideas deeply influenced Roman culture, gave much emphasis to Nature, which they effectively deified. Thus they were pantheists—which is to say atheists, for pantheism is but a polite form of atheism.

With the advent of Christianity, what appeared at the time to be an advancing tide of atheism was abruptly curbed, and for the first 12 centuries of the Christian era, atheism was a negligible factor in Western society. The focus of this entry is on atheism as manifested in the West, but it would be wrong to think that it is not to be found in Eastern society as well. Apart from the situation that obtains in some Eastern countries today, where atheism is a Western import, Eastern thought produced its own indigenous brands of atheism, most notably in the form of orthodox Buddhism.

In the 14th century, with the ascendency and eventual dominating presence of nominalism, we see the initial stage of what was in time to develop into modern atheism, and it should be emphasized that atheism, as a prominent feature of Western society, is very much a modern phenomenon. Nominalism, whose principal perpetrator was the English Franciscan William of Ockham, took the position that knowledge of God was to be had by faith alone, a position that came to be known as fideism. Nominalism succeeded in driving a wedge between faith and reason, declaring the latter to be impotent with respect to knowledge of all things divine. Because nominalism and the fideism it spawned asserted that human reason was incapable of proving the existence of God, it effectively rendered null and void the venerable discipline of natural theology.

Both the Renaissance and the Reformation made contributions to the growth of atheism in Western society, albeit indirectly. The Renaissance did this by its uncritical advocacy of the kind of humanism that was developed in classical Greece and Rome—a humanism that, for all its positive features, was fundamentally flawed because of its distorted understanding of the transcendent. The Reformation made its indirect contribution to modern atheism through the favoritism it showed toward fideism. One of the hallmarks of Protestantism, which sets it apart pronouncedly from Catholic

Christianity, is its abiding suspicion of human reason. But to be suspicious of human reason, and to fail to make proper use of it, is to neutralize one of the most formidable defenses against atheism.

Modern atheism, apropos of the time when it came fully into its own, can be regarded as coterminous with modern philosophy, which saw its birth in the 17th century and whose father is universally acknowledged to be the Frenchman René Descartes. Descartes himself was not an atheist—far from it—but the philosophy he developed can contribute in no small way to atheism. It is a philosophy that marks the triumph of idealism in Western thought, and the link between idealism and atheism is rather direct. This is because philosophical idealism represents a stance that puts more stock in the internal world of ideas than in the external world of things, giving precedence to the subjective over the objective. That way of thinking opens the path to atheism because it distances us from the objective order of things, where, exercising our reason, we come to know of God and things divine. We do not do this by simply exploring the inner sanctums of the mind. Philosophical idealism is virtually inseparable from what is called immanentism, a way of looking at the world that is antipathetic to everything having to do with the transcendent. The immanentist point of view is thoroughly naturalistic; it closes itself off from the supernatural. In his monumental study of modern atheism, *God in Exile*, Father Cornelio Fabro argues compellingly that immanentism is one and the same with atheism.

Besides Descartes, there have been, among the philosophers, several other major contributors to modern atheism, among them the Dutch philosopher Baruch Spinoza (1632–1677). For Spinoza, *Nature* and *God* were two words for the same thing, clearly showing that his atheism took the form of pantheism. The 18th century contributed substantially to modern atheism, through the work of the French philosophes, for example, especially Denis Diderot. It was in the 18th century that deism came into prominence, a movement which, though not explicitly atheistic, aided and abetted atheism because of its strong leanings toward immanentism.

The 19th was a banner century for the number of philosophers it produced who contributed to the growth of atheism. First and foremost among them was Georg Hegel, the colossus of German idealism. It has been rightly argued by more than one scholar that Hegel contributed more to modern atheism than did any other single philosopher. But there were three other philosophers, also German, whose contributions to atheism were not insignificant. Ludwig Feuerbach,

author of *The Essence of Christianity*, was the first to give full development to the notion that God is but a projection of man's deepest desires: God did not create man, but man created God, out of need. Karl Marx, who was much influenced by both Hegel and Feuerbach, was the father of collective atheism, in the form of dialectical materialism. Marx spurned religion, dubbing it famously the "opium of the people," but ironically gave birth to a movement that was to turn out to be nothing else than an elaborate ersatz religion. If Marx was the father of collective atheism, Friedrich Nietzsche was the father of individualistic atheism. Nietzsche's Zarathustra proclaimed the death of God, but this announcement, for Nietzsche, was not cause for rejoicing, for now man was absolutely alone. Nietzsche's atheistic philosophy, not surprisingly, eventually leads to nihilism.

It is indicative just to what extent atheism has taken hold in modern Western society that two of the major atheistic philosophers of the 20th century, Jean-Paul Sartre and Albert Camus, both won the Nobel Prize for literature. Sartre was a disciple of the German philosopher Martin Heidegger, another principal figure in modern atheism. The kind of atheistic existentialism propounded by Sartre and Camus was of the individualistic variety; all in all, it offers us a decidedly gloomy picture of the human condition. Sartre tried valiantly to convince the world that his existentialism was not really nihilistic, but his efforts were in vain. Finally, mention should be made of the psychologist Sigmund Freud, a committed atheist who saw much to admire in the evolutionism of Charles Darwin and whose role in the promulgation of atheism has been considerable, especially among the intelligentsia.

Atheism, in whatever age or culture it manifests itself, can take a number of different forms. It is customary to distinguish between absolute atheism and practical atheism. An *absolute atheist* is someone who deliberately denies the existence of God. A *practical atheist* claims to believe in God, but lives his life as if God did not exist. Jacques Maritain distinguished between the negative and the positive atheist. The *negative atheist* discards the idea of God out of pure indifference; the God question simply does not interest him. The *positive atheist* is, as it were, a true disbeliever, in a constant state of open warfare with theism.

It would be difficult to exaggerate the impact atheism has had on modern society. One has only to think of the collective atheism represented by Communism and consider the immense damage it has wrought in those countries where it managed to gain the ascendancy. Though more subtle, the influence of atheistic existentialism and of Freudianism has also been significant, especially in the realms of literature, the arts, and the mass media. The steady and energetic movement to bring about the total secularization of society, which we bear witness to today, must be considered, especially given its often decidedly antireligious attitude, to be an aspect of modern atheism.

One of the distinguishing features of contemporary atheism is its bold, swashbuckling militancy. It gives the impression of being a movement on the march, out to conquer the world for the cause of godlessness. This is suggested by a spate of books, recently published, written by atheists such as Sam Harris, Daniel Dennet, Richard Dawkins, and Christopher Hitchens, who show themselves to be fully prepared to take the offensive, and they are unsparing in their sword-wielding attacks on the enemy—theism in general and Christianity in particular. Their books contain nothing remarkably new in terms of the traditional atheistic ideas and arguments, but there is novelty in the acrimonious tone that is often to be found in them. These are zealous atheists, and they have a way with rhetoric, but there is something about their intense earnestness that makes a reader wonder if they do not "protest too much."

The sources of atheism are doubtless many, but two of the principal ones, as cited by Étienne Borne, are (1) the presence of evil in the world and (2) man's reckless confidence in his own intellectual prowess and what it has achieved. Since time immemorial there have been people who have denied the existence of God because they could not reconcile the existence of an all-good, all-powerful being with the presence of evil in the world, both physical and moral. This is probably the most common source of atheism. The other principal source, which has gained in strength in recent centuries, has to do with man's increasing mastery over nature, especially with the advent of modern science and technology, dissipating what were once thought to be impenetrable mysteries and giving man more control over his environment. This has led some people pridefully to decide that the "God hypothesis" is simply no longer necessary. For them, modern man has finally come of age; he is the new Prometheus, and no longer has any need of God.

Serious, committed atheists, especially if they are numbered among the intelligentsia, have a habit of insisting that atheism bears the clear mark of rationality, whereas to be a believer is to succumb to the irrational. This is, of course, to have things just upside down. Atheism represents the most flagrant way we can abuse our God-given reason, by exercising it in the futile attempt to deny the existence of the source of all being. A critical test of the inherent worth of any philosophy is found in the fruits it is capable of producing. In this respect, the philosophy of atheism has proven to be utterly barren. It rests on negation of the most radical kind, denying the source of all being. But to do that is, willy nilly, to commit oneself to non-being, and that is why atheism, in spite of itself, inevitably ends in nihilism.—D. Q. McInerny

BIBLIOGRAPHY AND FURTHER READING: Borne, Étienne. *Atheism.* New York: Hawthorne Books, 1961; Fabro, Cornelio. *God in Exile: Modern Atheism.* Westminster, MD: Newman Press, 1968; Maritain, Jacques. "The Meaning of Contemporary Atheism." In *The Range of Reason*, ch. 8. New York: Charles Scribner's Sons, 1953; Miceli, Vincent, SJ. *The Gods of Atheism.* Harrison, NY: Roman Catholic Books, 1971. *See also* AGNOSTICISM AND ATHEISM; HUMANISM; NIHILISM; PHILOSOPHY, DISCIPLINE OF; SECULARIZATION

AUGUSTINIANISM AND MEDIEVAL RELIGIOUS LIFE

While scholars debate not only what should be considered part of Augustinianism but even whether the term itself is misleading, some basics may be safely given. The term *Augustinianism* is used by scholars in medieval studies to describe religious orders (monks and nuns, often in cloistered communities) that have both taken their name from and based their collective "identities" in the person of St. Augustine. Prominent among these orders have been the Augustinian "Canons Regular" and the Augustinian "Hermits." These orders impacted medieval history strongly as part of what has been called the Augustinian Reform—a movement of religious/spiritual reform within those orders in the Middle Ages. (The term *Observant*, when thus capitalized, at least within medieval studies, usually refers to the phenomenon of such reformist religious orders.)

As distinct from the impact of St. Augustine's own religio-political thinking on Catholic social thought (for example, in his work *The City of God*), Augustinianism impacts that larger social arena through the basing of communal (and thus societal) identities in the *personage and life* of a saint, rather than strictly in their thought. The tension that arose from the rivalries among these orders contributed greatly to sociological thinking on the whole because religious communities in general were such an integral part of medieval society, not only religiously but also politically and economically. This tension stemmed from each order viewing itself as the most authentic representative of the way of life envisioned and lived by St. Augustine. The fact that the very survival of the orders often was dependent on a continuing intake of members made rivalry and debate all the more intense.

Several works of St. Augustine functioned as particularly normative for these orders. Much controversy currently surrounds the issue of whether one of these, the work known as the "Rule of St. Augustine" (or any of the works of which it is made up), was actually written by the saint himself, but there is little doubt that these orders took it as normative for their life on both the communal and the individual levels. The second work is the *Confessions* of St. Augustine. Since the primary emphasis for these orders was on a way of life, it is natural that this autobiography of sorts took pride of place for them.

These orders did not, however, *primarily* produce logical treatises drawing or arguing for conclusions from the *Confessions*. Rather, they built and defended their claims for their own superior authenticity in carrying on the work of the saint by writing (or commissioning) "Lives" of St. Augustine. In these, they arranged events and material from the *Confessions* in such a way as to portray the saint in a manner matching their own recognizable identity or the emphases of their order. (The practice of writing "lives" of saints is the subject of a distinct branch of inquiry within medieval studies known as hagiography.) In addition to these written works, these orders might occasionally employ religious art to portray the saint in their own way, such as the commissioning of a public statue of St. Augustine in the distinct robes of an Augustinian Hermit, rather than in the garb recognizably peculiar to the Canons Regular.

The rivalry between the Hermits and the Canons Regular in particular had some distinct impact on major European (and thus American) history and society. Martin Luther, the first prominent figure of the Protestant Reformation, was an Augustinian Hermit before his breach with Rome. Early in Luther's progression toward that breach, Pope Leo X became aware of his ideas and teachings. Leo famously dismissed the issue as just another "monks' quarrel." One scholar (Alison Frazier) has conjectured that the backdrop to Leo's statement is this often very heated rivalry and debate between the Hermits and the Canons Regular. Rome would have had had many reports of the rivalry (and decisions to make to keep peace between the two orders), and the writings of a Hermit (Luther) might have seemed to the pope to be simply another in a long list of outbursts, and his dismissal of the issue would understandably

have furthered tensions motivating Luther's departure. Thus, Augustinianism played at least some role in the Protestant Reformation, which so heavily impacted the shape of Europe at the end of the Middle Ages in innumerable ways. One can see a certain logic in the fact that the first major figure of the Protestant Reformation began as a member of a religious order so involved in the Augustinian Reform within the medieval church.

Finally, it is also pertinent to sociology (and related fields) that some scholars in medieval studies have devoted much research (and are continuing to do so) to the interplay between men's and women's religious communities within the realm of medieval Augustinianism. A prominent avenue of inquiry in this arena is the research of distinct practices among female communities (in things such as liturgical texts) that might yield communal identities distinct to those Augustinian religious women (distinct, that is, from their male counterparts, even though governed by the men's communities, and most often peacefully)—an issue of interest to those working in gender studies and related sociological fields.—M. Brett Kendall

BIBLIOGRAPHY AND FURTHER READING: Bynum, Carolyn. "The Spirituality of Regular Canons in the Twelfth Century: A New Approach." *Medievalia et Humanistica* 4 (1973): 3–24; Fassler, Margot. "The Augustinians of Paris and the Politics of Reform." In *Gothic Song: Victorine Sequences and Augustinian Reform in Twelfth-Century Paris*. New York: Cambridge University Press, 1993; Frazier, Alison. "A Layman's Life of St. Augustine in Late Medieval Italy: Patronage and Polemic," *Traditio* 65 (2010): 231–286; Frazier, Alison. *Possible Lives: Authors and Saints in Renaissance Italy*. New York: Columbia University Press, 2005. *See also* AUGUSTINE, ST.; AUGUSTINIANISM; MEDIEVAL MONASTICISM AND WESTERN CULTURE

· B ·

BARONI, GENO (1930–1984) Italian American priest Geno Baroni helped shape the social revolution in the 1960s and 1970s by influencing American thinking on civil rights, ethnic pluralism, neighborhood revitalization, coalition building, and urban affairs. He applied Catholic social doctrine in ministering to the poor. Father Baroni maintained links to the civil rights movement while contributing to President Lyndon B. Johnson's Great Society. He was the Catholic Church's coordinator of Dr. Martin Luther King Jr.'s March on Washington in 1963, participated in Freedom Summer in Mississippi in 1964, and joined the Selma March in 1965. Baroni was also instrumental in establishing the Head Start program. As a coalition builder, he opposed the growing polarization among white and nonwhite groups.

Baroni was born October 24, 1930, in Acosta, Pennsylvania, the son of Italian immigrants Guido and Josephine (Tranquillini). His father worked in a coal mine and was an organizer for labor leader John L. Lewis. Baroni himself was fired from a factory for organizing factory workers in Jamestown, New York.

He graduated from St. Mary's College in Emmitsburg, Maryland, in 1952 and entered the seminary there, becoming a priest in 1958. He then served at St. Columba's Church in Jamestown and St. Leo's in Altoona, Pennsylvania. Baroni taught high school, became active in community affairs, and set up credit unions for the needy. He was next assigned from 1960 to 1965 to the Washington, D.C., Parish of SS. Paul and Augustine, a merger of black and white parishes, later renamed St. Augustine in the 1980s. In working with the poor in neglected neighborhoods, he drew strength from the teachings of Popes Leo XIII, John XXIII, and Paul VI. He inspired social worker Mary Houston, who managed the V Street Center, a rundown convent that had been restored by the Church. Baroni inspired other young idealistic individuals to enter public service, including Sen. Barbara Mikulski of Maryland, Rep. Mary Kaptur of Ohio, and Dean Arthur Naparstek of Western Reserve University.

Working under the U.S. Catholic Conference as executive director of the Office of Urban Affairs (1965–1967) and director of the Urban Poverty Task Force (1967–1970), he supervised many antipoverty programs. The urban task force concept had emerged from the Catholic Conference's statements on race relations that produced the Campaign for Human Development, which, in turn, was the response to the 1967–1968 urban riots and the Kerner Report. The Kerner Report stated that the nation was moving toward two societies, one black and one white, separate and unequal.

Baroni's work propelled him to national attention. In 1974, *Time* named him one of 200 rising leaders. Robert F. Kennedy noticed this young priest working to overcome institutional racism and unequal opportunity and appointed him treasurer of the first Head Start program in Washington, D.C. At the time, Baroni was on the City's Human Relations Council and the Mayor's Commission on Economic Development.

At a time of national upheaval, Baroni became ever more conscious of his Italian ethnicity. He was founder and first president of the National Italian American Foundation, a vital organization based in Washington, D.C., whose goal was to protect Italian American interests. He believed that the foundation was an affirmation of ethnic pluralism in American life. With funding from the Ford Foundation, Baroni founded the National Center for Urban Ethnic Affairs, an organization that gathered data and promoted the interests of ethnic people, especially European Americans, in attempting to rebuild decaying ethnic neighborhoods. He also received grants from the Rockefeller Foundation.

President Jimmy Carter appointed this activist priest assistant secretary for neighborhood development, consumer affairs, and regulatory functions in the Department of Housing and Urban Development (HUD). Baroni was the first priest to hold such high public office. HUD Secretary Patricia Roberts Harris delegated to him the responsibility of working with inner city urban groups. He accelerated the fight to stimulate housing development for the disadvantaged and minorities. He helped push through the 1977 Community Reinvestment Act, which appropriated $5 billion for propping up the revitalization and self-help process in 21 cities.

In addition to his social activism, Baroni wrote numerous articles and lectured extensively. He edited *Pieces of a Dream* and wrote *Who's Left in the Neighborhoods*. He was a Fellow at the Kennedy School of Government at Harvard University. He served as a trustee on the Robert Kennedy Memorial Foundation, actively participated in the Miners Legal Defense Fund, and was honored by the American Italian Historical Association at its 16th Annual Conference in Albany, New York, 1983.

Geno Baroni died on August 27, 1984, in Washington, D.C., after a long battle with cancer. Soon after his death, his colleagues formed the Geno Charles Baroni Society of Empowerment, Change, and Social Invention to serve as a forum to combine policy with action to help people in need. His legacy also was enhanced in 1987 with the construction and dedication of the Geno Baroni Apartments at 1414 V Street, NW, in Washington, D.C., across from St. Augustine Parish where he served as assistant pastor in the 1960s. One-third of the 32 apartments were reserved for low-income tenants.

This son of humble Italian immigrant parents from a coal mining region of Pennsylvania was in the forefront of social change, fighting to revive the old neighborhoods, support urban blue-collar working families, and establish a network of church, civil rights, community, and political organizations to help the disadvantaged. Inspired by the teachings of the Catholic Church, he raised the consciousness of American Catholics to achieve equal justice for all.—Frank J. Cavaioli

BIBLIOGRAPHY AND FURTHER READING: Cavaioli, Frank J. "Geno Baroni, Italian American Civil Rights Priest." In *Shades of Black and White: Conflict and Collaboration between Two Communities,* edited by Dan Ashyk, Fred L. Gardaphe, and Anthony Julian Tamburri, 45–55. Staten Island, NY: American Italian Historical Association, 1999; O'Rourke, Lawrence M. *Geno: The Life and Mission of Geno Baroni.* Mahwah, NJ: Paulist Press, 1991. *See also* CIVIL RIGHTS MOVEMENT, THE; NEIGHBORHOOD; NEIGHBORHOOD AND THE ITALIAN AMERICAN CATHOLIC; SOCIAL CHARITY; SOCIAL JUSTICE

BASIL THE GREAT, ST. (330–379)

St. Basil the Great was a bishop, theologian, and reformer. As both churchman and theologian, he played a crucial role in the Church's resolution of the Arian crisis. As bishop, he established a modus vivendi for the Church in its dealings with secular authorities. As an ascetic, he composed a set of rules that continue to govern monasteries today. As an administrator, he founded institutional charities that set the model for the Church's future philanthropic work. He was also a liturgical reformer and served as patron and collaborator to many, including St. Gregory of Nazianzus, St. Gregory of Nyssa, St. Athanasius of Alexandria, and St. Ephrem of Syria. He is a Doctor of the Church, and in the East he is honored, with St. Gregory of Nazianzus and St. John Chrysostom, as one of the Three Holy Hierarchs.

Basil was one of nine children born to a well-to-do Cappadocian family that had been Christian for several generations. His parents, Basil and Emmelia, are also venerated as saints, as are two of Basil's siblings, Gregory (of Nyssa) and Macrina (the Younger). His ancestors included martyrs and confessors.

Basil's father was a teacher of rhetoric who tutored his children at home. He died when Basil was a teenager, however, and young Basil continued his academic studies at prestigious schools, first in his native Cappadocia, then for a year in the imperial capital Constantinople, and finally for six years at Athens. He studied under Libanius, the most renowned rhetorician of his time and an ardent proponent of the old ("pagan") religion; Basil sustained a warm relationship with Libanius throughout his life. At Athens, Basil made the acquaintance of a future emperor, Julian, the lapsed Christian who would, during his brief reign (360–363), initiate a drive to repaganize the empire. Also at Athens, Basil shared with his countryman and classmate

Gregory of Nazianzus a common life of philosophical study, prayer, and asceticism. He returned to Cappadocia to teach in 355.

At this time, Basil had a spiritual awakening that led him to seek baptism (it was customary, at that time, to defer baptism until adulthood). Having decided to devote his life to God, he embarked on a tour of places renowned for their asceticism—Palestine, Egypt, Syria, and Mesopotamia. He met with many solitaries and observed their life, but finally returned to Cappadocia to establish a religious community on a remote property in Pontus owned by his family. His mother and sister joined him there and drew a number of devout women. It was there that he composed his monastic "Rule," which he would continue to adapt and edit throughout his life. Through Basil's influence, contemplatives in the Church began increasingly to favor disciplined community life over the solitary life of the desert hermits (who could be wild and anarchic). Basil referred to the life he chose, life in community, as "the way that is in accordance with Christ's polity" (*Letters*, 150).

The fruit of his contemplation poured forth in his writing. His theological works and his letters drew attention for their erudition and their style. His old classmate Julian, now emperor, tried to entice Basil to life at court, but Basil refused.

He was ordained a priest by the bishop of Caesarea, Eusebius, around 362, and made an auxiliary bishop shortly afterward. It was a time of doctrinal crisis in the Church. Though Arian doctrine had been condemned by the Council of Nicaea in 325, it continued to mutate like a virus and spread through the world. In Basil's lifetime, most of the emperors in the East were Arian, and Arianism was effectively the state religion. Basil's bishop, Eusebius, was an ardent advocate of Nicene orthodoxy, but was not intellectually equipped for the subtleties of theological disputation; he was utterly dependent on Basil.

In addition to the Arian crisis, there came a social crisis in 368, when a series of natural calamities—including hailstorms, floods, and earthquakes—brought famine to the lands of Cappadocia. Basil was appalled when some merchants seized the opportunity to grow rich from the scarcity of food, leaving the poor to starve. Basil's preaching shamed the wealthy and led them to share what they had. He led by example as well, selling his inheritance and giving the proceeds over to relief efforts.

It was Basil's management of these dual crises that established his reputation with the Christian people. Upon the death of Eusebius in 370, Basil was made bishop of Caesarea. He served in that capacity, championing the Nicene faith, until his death in 379.

In the struggle against Arianism, Basil continued the work begun by Athanasius. Basil's articulation of the Nicene faith was profoundly influential in the proceedings of the First Council of Constantinople (380), which met the year after Basil's death and was led by his fellow Cappadocians, his brother Gregory of Nyssa and his friend Gregory of Nazianzus.

Historians say that Basil was the first to produce a sustained theological reflection on the Church's social concerns. It is a recurring theme in his homilies and letters, most of them addressed to groups of ascetics. The ideal monk is one whose prayer is augmented by work, he wrote, but whose work is done so "that they may have something to distribute to those in need" (*Letters*, 207).

Basil's doctrine was concretized in the construction of the campus known as the Basileidas. It was a vast complex of facilities built to serve a variety of needs—so vast that the locals referred to it as the "New City" and Gregory of Nazianzus compared it to the Seven Wonders of the ancient world. Basil's Catholic charities included a soup kitchen, poorhouses, a trade school, a hostel for needy travelers, personal care for the elderly, and a hospice for the dying. The staff of male and female ascetics dispensed food and medical care to all who approached, regardless of their religious affiliation. This was not something added to their devotions; it was integral to their religious life. This mixed life of prayer and action was Basil's ideal. But the duty to serve the poor applied to all Christians. In appealing to the rich, Basil often emphasized that it was in their own best interest to succor the poor, as they would be judged worthy of heaven based on the charity they demonstrated on earth.

In his eulogy for Basil, Gregory of Nazianzus described such pious charitable work as "the short road to salvation, the easiest ascent to heaven" (Oration 43.63). As such, it was, according to Basil, not merely the work of monks and nuns, but of all Christians.

As a respected and articulate spokesman for Nicene orthodoxy, Basil was a constant source of irritation to the Arian emperor Valens and the Cappadocian prefect Modestus. They sought to win Basil through threats and bribes, and they failed consistently. In his resistance, Basil demonstrated the value of detachment gained through a life vowed to poverty and celibacy. He had no fear of confiscation because he owned nothing.

When Modestus threatened him with exile, Basil replied: "I belong to no place. This earth in which I live is not mine. I should be in my own place in whatever country to which I was sent. I know that the whole earth is God's; and wherever I may be I consider myself a stranger and a pilgrim." Infuriated, Modestus said, "Never have I been spoken to with so much liberty," to which Basil replied: "That is perhaps because you have never yet met a bishop" (recounted in Gregory of Nazianzus, *Funeral Orations*, 43).

That was not the only time Basil had to defend the Church against encroachments by the state. Indeed, he had at least one close encounter with Valens himself, when the emperor appeared unannounced at a liturgy—and was given a place among the common people in the congregation. In his constant vigilance for the Church's freedom, Basil would serve as a model for bishops in all ages.

Basil recognized the Church as a universal society, inclusive of angels and saints, on earth and in heaven. He promoted unity—or, more precisely, communion—between his diocese and other sees throughout the world. He took an active interest in the difficulties of other bishops and congregations, attempting, for example, to mediate the long-running dispute over the episcopacy in Antioch and appealing repeatedly to Pope Damasus I to intervene in affairs in the East. Though Basil was repeatedly frustrated in his appeals to Rome, his efforts demonstrate his sense of the authority of the papacy and its role in promoting unity.

For Basil, the Church was one not only in space, but also in time. He placed a premium on sacred tradition, whose authority he placed alongside Scripture. He saw the liturgy as the ordinary conduit of tradition. It was there that apostolic doctrine was communicated "in a mystery" (*On the Holy Spirit*, 66). He strove to be faithful always to the doctrine he had received from "the Fathers" (e.g., *Letters*, 204.2, 28.1).

His efforts at liturgical reform were for the sake of the Church's overall vitality and fidelity to tradition. Historians sometimes call Basil's program a "monasticizing" of the city. He wanted the charitable work of the laity to flow from a sustained and disciplined life of prayer in community.

Basil's theological reflection produced insights that would be crucial to the development of a distinctive Christian social ethic. He affirmed in clear terms, for example, the universal equality of all men before God: "To every man belongs by nature equality of like honor with all men, and . . . superiorities in us are not according to family, nor according to excess of wealth, nor according to the body's constitution, but according to the superiority of our fear of God" (*Letters*, 262.1). Nor can one tribe or nation claim superiority to another: "The saints do not all belong to one country. Each is venerated in a different place. So what does that imply? Should we call them city-less, or citizens of the whole world? Just as at a common meal those things laid before the group by each are regarded as available to all who meet together, so among the saints, the homeland of each is common to all, and they give to each other everywhere whatever they have to hand" (Homily 338.2).—Mike Aquilina

BIBLIOGRAPHY AND FURTHER READING: Basil the Great. *On the Holy Spirit*. Translated by Stephen M. Hildebrand. Crestwood, NY: St. Vladimir Seminary Press, 2011; Basil the Great. *Letters*. Fathers of the Church, vols. 13 and 28; translated by Sr. Agnes Clare Way, CDP. Washington, DC: Catholic University of America Press, 1969; Basil the Great. *Against Eunomius*. Fathers of the Church, vol. 122; translated by Mark DelCogliano and Andrew Radde-Gallwitz. Washington, DC: Catholic University of America Press, 2011; Gregory of Nazianzus. *Funeral Orations*. Fathers of the Church, vol. 22. Washington, DC: Catholic University of America Press, 1953; Meredith, Anthony. *The Cappadocians*. Crestwood, NY: St. Vladimir Seminary Press, 1995; Quasten, Johannes. *Patrology*. Vol. 3, pp. 203–236. Allen, TX: Christian Classics, n.d.; Rousseau, Philip. *Basil of Caesarea*. Berkeley: University of California Press, 1994. *See also* CHURCH FATHERS, EARLY; GREGORY OF NYSSA, ST.; JULIAN THE APOSTATE; ORTHODOX CHURCHES, SOCIAL TEACHINGS OF

BAUDOUIN, KING (1930–1993) Born on September 7, 1930, Baudouin Albert Charles de Belgique became King of the Belgians in 1951, following the abdication of his father Leopold III. A popular monarch, he maintained public neutrality on national controversies, especially the incessant quarrel between the Dutch-speaking north (Flanders) and the French-speaking south (Wallonia). A devout Catholic, the king participated in the charismatic movement and founded the King Baudouin Foundation, a center for the promotion of economic development projects.

In 1990, King Baudouin abandoned his political neutrality in a dispute over abortion. On March 9, the Belgian parliament approved the legalization of abortion by a concurrent majority. Although a personal opponent of the law, Prime Minister Wilfried Maertens urged the king to sign the law. The royal signature to laws duly approved by the parliament, an act required for the law to be promulgated, had long been treated as a simple formality. Politicians warned Baudouin that

refusal to sign the law could result in political moves to force his abdication or even to abolish the monarchy.

On March 31, Baudouin sent Prime Minister Maertens a letter in which he announced his refusal to sign the iniquitous law. He asked the prime minister to release the letter to the parliament and to the nation at large. In it, the king unveiled the reasons for his opposition to the law. "This bill poses a grave problem of conscience for me. I fear that in effect it will be understood by a large part of the population as an authorization to practice abortion during the first 12 weeks after conception. I also have serious concerns about the clause permitting abortion to be practiced beyond 12 weeks if the child to be born is afflicted with 'a particularly grave anomaly recognized as incurable at the moment of diagnosis.'. . . I fear that the law will contribute to a palpable diminution of respect for the lives of the weakest around us."

The king's decision to refuse to sign the bill stunned the parliament and the nation. With a concurrent parliamentary majority supporting the bill and a monarch refusing to sign and thus promulgate it, Belgian society teetered on a constitutional precipice. In an astute political maneuver, Prime Minister Maertens resolved the crisis. Article 12 of the Belgian constitution stipulates that when the monarch is incapable of governing, any bills passed by parliament simply require approval by the Council of Ministers (the Belgian cabinet) in order to be promulgated. On April 4, a joint session of parliament declared that the throne was vacant, given the king's problem of conscience. The Council of Ministers promptly ratified and promulgated the controversial abortion law. The next day, the parliament declared that the throne was once again occupied, since the king's incapacity due to conscientious objection had been resolved, and Baudouin once again assumed his constitutional powers.

In his public remarks during the abortion controversy, the king limited himself to secular arguments appealing to rights, especially to the rights of the disabled. His posthumously published diary revealed the religious motivation that guided him during his resistance to legalized abortion: "The vise closes in on me over the problem of abortion. My God, all of this forces me to rely on You alone. . . . I have set sail alone with my conscience and my God. . . . If I hadn't done this [refused to sign the abortion law], I would have been sick my entire life for having betrayed the Lord." Long revered in the Belgian Catholic community, Baudouin's resistance to abortion had made him a virtual confessor of the faith on human life issues.

King Baudouin died of a heart attack on July 31, 1993. At the funeral Mass for the monarch, Gottfried Cardinal Daneels, the primate of Belgium, praised the conscientious resistance shown by the king during the parliamentary crisis over abortion: "For him [Baudouin] the conscience was absolute. It was the voice of the deepest part of the human person and the voice of God. He always followed it, even at the risk of his personal interest, even at the risk of putting the monarchy itself into question. He knew that human life was worth such a price."

The tomb of King Baudouin in the royal chapel at Laeken has subsequently become a site of pilgrimage for European pro-life activists. Many Belgian Catholics have signed petitions to open a canonical investigation that could eventually lead to the canonization of Baudouin as a saint of the Catholic Church.—John J. Conley, SJ

BIBLIOGRAPHY AND FURTHER READING: Conley, John J. "Remembering King Baudouin, Witness to Life." In *Life and Learning* 14 (2004): 113–119; Fralon, Alain José. *Baudouin: L'Homme qui ne voulait pas être roi.* Paris: Fayard, 2001; Suenens, Léon Josef Cardinal. *Le Roi Baudouin: Une Vie qui nous parle.* Oppem-Meise: Éditions Fiat, 1995. *See also* ABORTION; CONSCIENTIOUS OBJECTION: LIFE AND HEALTH CARE ISSUES

BELTRAME QUATTROCCHI, LUIGI (1880–1951) AND MARIA (1884–1965) The Church has known, throughout its history, saintly married couples, from Aquila and Priscilla to Basil the Elder and Emmelia (parents of St. Basil the Great and St. Gregory of Nyssa), to the Franciscan tertiaries Elzear and Delphina in medieval times, to married couples of Korean martyrs in modern times. As Blessed John Paul II remarked in his December 22, 2001, address to the Roman Curia, however, the Italians Luigi and Maria Beltrame Quattrocchi (both Franciscan tertiaries) were the first to be beatified "together as a couple, an eloquent testimony to holiness in marriage." Their beatification took place on October 21, 2001, 20 years after the apostolic exhortation *Familiaris Consortio*, seven years after the opening of their cause of beatification, and seven years before the beatification of the parents of St. Theresa of Lisieux (the day of whose death, on September 30, 1897, was also the day of Maria Beltrame Quattrocchi's first communion). The Beltrame Quattrocchis' liturgical memory is on November 25, their wedding anniversary. Their relics are at the Roman Shrine of Divine Love.

Luigi Beltrame Quattrocchi, a government attorney who declined promotions to safeguard his in-dependent judgment, was actively involved in Catholic lay apostolate throughout his life, together with his wife, Maria Corsini Beltrame Quattrocchi. She was also a spiritual author. Her most significant writings are *Lux vera* on the three spiritual breads (the bread of the word of God, the bread of life, and the bread of our own will), *Warp and Weft* (already in its title a program for every marriage, and a moving reflection on her own marriage written shortly after her husband's death), and *Let Us Uphold Life!* (her last writing and an invitation to put to good use the talents each one of us has received from God). Luigi and Maria were married at the Basilica of St. Mary Major in Rome on November 25, 1905, a few months after their engagement. They had four children (three of whom were present at their beatification ceremony): Filippo (then Don Tarcisio, a diocesan priest), Cesare (then Father Paolino, a Trappist monk), Stefania (then Mother Cecilia, a Benedictine cloistered nun), and Enrichetta (a consecrated laywoman who remained with her parents throughout their lives). From 1926 on, when more in love than ever, Luigi and Maria decided to live in chastity as brother and sister, a decision shared by such other Catholic couples as Jacques and Raissa Maritain.

Since their very beginning, the Beltrame Quattrocchis' marriage and family life were based on intense sacramental life and devotional practices: daily Mass in the morning, prayer over meals, recitation of the rosary in the evening, consecration to the Sacred Heart of Jesus. Their devotion was contagious: when confined to a shelter from the bombings in World War II, others would naturally join them in praying the rosary. This piety inspired their works of mercy toward their neighbors, from giving refuge to Jewish families in their apartment during the war to contributing to the preparation for marriage of young couples. They gave three religious vocations to the Church (those of three of their children), but also received much from the many priests and religious men (among whom was the great Dominican scholar Reginald Garrigou-Lagrange) who were close to their family. In this, too, they were an example of how religious and marital vocations strengthen each other.

While their married and family life was the result of the daily exercise of natural virtue and response to supernatural grace, it was also built on their morally upright and God-loving reaction to dramatic circumstances. During her fourth pregnancy, Maria developed a placenta disease that led her gynecologist to suggest abortion as the only way out of the almost sure death of mother and child. Despite the shock and sorrow, and over the contrary advice received from the gynecologist, Luigi and Maria fixed their gaze on the Crucifix and pronounced a firm no to abortion. The child, Enrichetta, was born healthy and would remain with Luigi and Maria until their deaths. In a way, this dramatic but highly edifying episode confirms Blessed John Paul II's remark that the Beltrame Quattrocchis are an "exemplary expression of the Italian people" (Homily of John Paul II, October 21, 2001). In Italy, acceptance of divorce in the 1970s led in a few years to acceptance of abortion. Against this escalation of immorality, the Beltrame Quattrocchis show to Italy and the whole world how the health of marriage and family life is inextricably intertwined with the acceptance of human life, no matter how worrisome the surrounding circumstances may be or wrongly be thought to be.—Maurizio Ragazzi

BIBLIOGRAPHY AND FURTHER READING: Beltrame Quattrocchi, Luigi and Maria. *Dal campo base alla vetta: Lettere d'amore.* Rome: Città Nuova, 2001; Beltrame Quattrocchi, Luigi and Maria. *Dialogando con i figli: Lettere d'amore.* Rome: Città Nuova, 2001; Beltrame Quattrocchi, Maria. *La trama e l'ordito: Radiografia di un matrimonio,* 5th ed. Rome: Fondazione Luigi e Maria Beltrame Quattrocchi, 2001; Beltrame Quattrocchi, Maria. *Lux vera: I tre pani,* 3rd ed. Sorrento: Monastero di S. Paolo, 1969; Beltrame Quattrocchi, Maria. *Rivalutiamo la vita!* Rome: La Famiglia Italiana, 1955; Beltrame Quattrocchi, Tarcisio. *Lui, lei, noi, loro: I beati Luigi e Maria Beltrame Quattrocchi. Testimonianze dirette.* Siena: Cantagalli, 2002. *See also* ABORTION; CHASTITY; CULTURE OF LIFE; DIVORCE; *FAMILIARIS CONSORTIO*; FAMILY; FATHERHOOD; ITALY; LAY APOSTOLATE; MARRIAGE; MOTHERHOOD

BENEDICT OF NURSIA, ST. (480–547) St. Benedict is the father of Western monasticism. Through Western monasticism, St. Benedict preserved much of what was valuable in the classical world. He also helped create a new civilization, Western Christendom, by synthesizing this classical inheritance with Catholicism and Germanic culture. St. Benedict's influence continues today most directly through the Benedictine Order, which is grounded in his famous *Regula Sancti Benedicti,* or Rule of St. Benedict.

Most of what we know about St. Benedict's life comes through Pope St. Gregory the Great's biography of St. Benedict, contained in his *Dialogues* (593). St. Benedict was born into a noble Roman family at Nursia, a village in the mountains north of Rome, in

480. St. Benedict lived during the time of the disintegration of the West. Toward the end of the fourth century, the Constantinian revival of the empire had begun to give way and the Germanic tribes again invaded: in 380, the Western Goths (Visigoths) attacked Constantinople; in 382, the Eastern Goths (Ostrogoths) invaded Asia Minor; in 396, the Western Goths overran Italy and in 410 sacked Rome; in 420, the Western Goths settled in Spain and established their own kingdom; in 429, the Vandals overran Roman North Africa and established a kingdom; in 450, the Angles and Saxons overran Britain; and four years prior to St. Benedict's birth, Odoacer deposed the last emperor of the West.

In his youth, St. Benedict went to Rome to study. However, when he was approximately 20 years old, he left Rome to escape the licentious world that had surrounded him. As Pope St. Gregory the Great wrote: "But for as much as he saw many by reason of such learning fall to dissolute and lewd life, he drew back his foot, which he had as it were not set forth in the world, lest, entering too far in acquaintance therewith, he likewise might have fallen into that dangerous and godless gulf."

St. Benedict settled in a town called Enfide (likely modern Affile) about 40 miles from Rome. After performing many miracles, becoming a hermit for three years, and establishing a number of monasteries, St. Benedict founded the famous monastery at Monte Cassino around 520. While there, St. Benedict wrote his Rule to govern the life of his monks.

The Rule represented a break with the preceding forms of monasticism in two ways: first, it established a communal, rather than solitary, monastic life; and second, it prescribed moderation, not austerity, in living. The Rule is divided into 73 chapters governing life in a Benedictine monastery. For example, chapters 39 and 40 regulate food and provide for two meals a day, including wine, and state that the abbot has the discretion to add to the fare. Emphasizing community life, the monks dined together.

Over the centuries, the Benedictine Order has contributed much to the Church and Western civilization. Numerous popes, missionaries, scholars, historians, and religious leaders came from the order. For example, Benedictines served as the primary missionaries to the Germanic peoples who settled in Europe.

In establishing Monte Cassino and writing his Rule, St. Benedict created Western monasticism. Men and women of faith entered monasteries to worship God, live in an intimate community with other Christians, and leave a declining world behind. The

Benedictine Rule of monastic life and the communal practice developed at Monte Cassino ordered the lives of most Western monks for the next six hundred years. During this time, monks preserved much of the culture, learning, texts, and practices of the ancient world that was falling away. The monastic communities preserved the corpus of the ancient world until the High Middle Ages when the new peoples of Europe were able to reclaim what was lost and begin to build a new, different, Christian civilization.

During their golden age, the monasteries of western Europe, modeled on St. Benedict's example, were centers of spiritual, intellectual, cultural, and economic life. As historian Christopher Dawson noted: "It was the monasteries that were the saviors of Christian culture and of the Christian way of life. The abbey was a microcosm of Christian culture, an island which preserved the tradition of Christian culture." The monks dutifully employed themselves in manual arts such as farming, liberal arts such as teaching, and speculative activities such as theology. St. Benedict was, therefore, instrumental in creating the means—the form of community—that preserved much of what was good from the classical world.

But that is not the end of the story. Western monasticism also played a crucial role in synthesizing a new, Christian civilization out of the remnants of the classical Roman and Greek civilization and the new Germanic cultures that had overtaken western Europe. Unlike their Eastern counterparts, who were retreating into the deserts, Western monasticism engaged with and created Western culture. Western monasticism, following St. Augustine and St. Basil, centered monastic life around the community. This corresponded with the West's philosophical commitment to man as a social being and its theological commitment to individual Christians being part of Christ's Mystical Body. Western monasticism's greater openness found its way into St. Benedict's Rule.

While the first step in achieving this synthesis was the preservation of classical thought and culture, the second step was bringing the Germanic conquerors of Europe to Christianity. The monks were instrumental in converting the tribes to Christianity. For example, in 596, Pope St. Gregory sent the Benedictine monk St. Augustine of Canterbury on a mission to England after Roman civilization had been eliminated by the tribal migrations. St. Augustine's mission brought with it St. Benedict's Rule and established the great monasteries at Hexham, Jarrow, and Wearmouth. The monks drawn to these monasteries came from both Roman and German stock. Besides Britain, monks following the Rule of St.

Benedict evangelized the tribes in northern and central Europe such as the Saxons, Danes, Swedes, Norwegians, Slavs, and Hungarians.

The monasteries served as centers for education of the new elites in western Europe along with the men (and women) of lower classes who became monks (and nuns) or who received their education as part of the monastery's charitable work. The monks inculcated their pupils with a common culture derived from antiquity and Catholicism.

The monasteries also assimilated positive aspects of the barbarian culture with the classical Christian tradition. For instance, Christian poetry used traditional Germanic metaphors. And the monks created Christian historiography whose subject was the new peoples of Europe, such as the Venerable Bede's *Ecclesiastical History of England* (731).

In this way, monasteries became the great cultural centers of Europe. During the missionary activity of the late eighth and early ninth centuries, which was carried out primarily by monks, the monasteries founded were not simple affairs. These monasteries were meant to serve as the religious, cultural, and economic centers of their areas. They included the trades and crafts necessary to create a thriving community.

Perhaps the most important practical aspect of the rise of Western monasticism along the lines created by St. Benedict was the economic success of the monasteries. The monks ventured into parts of the vast areas of Europe that had been left a wilderness through depopulation (caused by the barbarian invasions) and brought them into cultivation. When one monastery became overcrowded, the abbot would send a group of monks to establish a daughter house where the monks would repeat what had been done so often already: cutting down the forests and draining the swamps, building a monastery, cultivating the land, providing religious services to neighbors, educating, and performing charitable works.

Slowly, through the centuries, a new Christian society was created. This new entity, known as Christendom, was the product of—in no small measure—St. Benedict's monastic vision and his Rule.

This vision of a Europe united by a common faith, made possible by St. Benedict, continues to animate today. For example, Pope Paul VI declared St. Benedict the patron of Europe in 1964. More recently, Pope Benedict XVI has repeatedly urged Europe to find its identity in St. Benedict's example.

Beyond St. Benedict's role in the formation of Western civilization, he continues to influence through the Benedictine Order's ministries. Benedictines, living in prayerful community, operate many different types of ministries, including education, health care, and evangelization. Though united by St. Benedict's Rule, Benedictine monasteries around the world enjoy a significant degree of autonomy within their congregations, which are loose confederations of monasteries. This permits the monasteries to vary their ministries according to local circumstances.—Lee J. Strang

BIBLIOGRAPHY AND FURTHER READING: Butler, Cuthbert. *Benedictine Monachism: Studies in Benedictine Life and Rule.* London: Longmans, Green, 1924 (2nd ed., New York: Barnes & Noble, 1961). Gregory the Great. *Dialogues.* London: Philip Lee Warner, 1911. Knowles, David. *Christian Monasticism.* New York: McGraw-Hill, 1969. Strang, Lee J. "The Role of the Christian Legal Scholar: The Call for a Modern St. Benedict." *Notre Dame Journal of Legal Ethics and Public Policy* 20 (2006): 59–87. *See also* CHURCH FATHERS, EARLY; MEDIEVAL MONASTICISM AND WESTERN CULTURE

BERNANOS, GEORGES (1888–1948)

Georges Bernanos was one of the great Catholic novelists of the 20th century. Also, as a journalist and polemicist, he upheld and represented with integrity the best of the French spirit and tradition. This was at a time when, because of France's defeat and occupation in World War II, French morale and belief in France's civilizing mission had dropped to a historic low.

Born in Paris on February 20, 1888, Bernanos spent his formative years at a family home in the Pas-de-Calais region of northern France, a rather somber and windblown area where the action of most of his novels takes place. His family background was unquestioningly Catholic and conservative, and he even spent a couple of years in a minor seminary in the course of his education. The priesthood, though, was apparently never a question for him personally, although he retained many personal friendships with priests. Moreover, the profound and memorable portraits of a number and variety of the priests in his fiction rank among the best in all of Catholic literature.

But Bernanos was himself a layman who married and fathered six children, and, after he became established as a writer, he subjected his large family to a rather nomadic existence, moving restlessly from place to place within France and even abroad. His wife was Jeanne Talbert d'Arc, a direct descendent of one of the brothers of St. Joan of Arc—the latter being one of the author's constant heroines, whom he celebrated

throughout his life, including in the 1929 book *Jeanne, relapse et sainte* (*Joan, Relapsed and Saint*).

Coming out of such a traditional Catholic milieu, Bernanos early and quite consciously identified himself as a royalist, strongly opposed to the secularizing and anticlerical parties and governments of the day. He even took part in some of the demonstrations and scuffles of the activist Camelots du Roi. As early as 1908, he joined the major French right-wing (and anti-Semitic) party of the day, the Action Française. His break with the Action Française later became something of a cause célèbre, and he came to be considered a "traitor" to the cause by some of the French right—some of whom themselves went on to become Nazi collaborationists after the fall of France.

Prior to the outbreak of World War I, Bernanos had commenced a modest journalistic career as the editor of a small right-wing newspaper in Normandy. He began writing fiction stories around the same time, but they mostly saw publication only in later years. When the war which decimated his whole generation came, however, he volunteered and actively served in combat in the trenches. This was an experience that indelibly marked him for life and was reflected in his writing in various subtle ways (although none of his novels was ever *about* the war).

After the war, he followed political and public affairs and wrote about them in periodicals. Eventually, however, his disillusionment and even disgust with the postwar French parties and governments—leading up to what he considered to be the grave dishonor of the Munich agreements caving in to Hitler and later to the capitulation of the nation itself to the Nazis and the collaboration of the French Vichy government with them—motivated Bernanos to abandon his homeland in the late 1930s and move his family to Brazil, where he spent the war years. While there, he wrote some magnificent polemics favoring the Free French cause; they were published in such books as his 1942 *Lettre aux Anglais* (*Letter to the English*) and his *Le Chemin de la Crois-des-Âmes* (*The Way of the Cross of Souls*), published in 1948.

Bernanos began seriously to write fiction after being discharged following the 1918 armistice, and meanwhile he worked for several years as a traveling insurance salesman to support his family—an experience reflected in some of his vivid descriptions of small-town and rural France. It was several years, however, before he succeeded in getting a novel published. Then, in 1926, he dazzled France and even the world beyond with the publication of his novel *Sous le soleil de Satan* (*Under the Sun of Satan*), a brooding, mysterious tale about an unworldly and saintly priest, the Abbé Donissan, loosely modeled on the career of St. John Vianney, the famous curé of Ars and confessor; the novel also described at the same time a seemingly doomed young woman, Mouchette, who murders her lover, and whom the saintly priest strives to save. The priest's dialogues with Satan embodied as a woodsman in this novel created a sensation that went beyond the merely literary.

This first novel of Bernanos signaled the major themes that would characterize his fiction generally and that the author would expound and plumb even more acutely and profoundly in subsequent novels: heroic sanctity, the salvation of souls, the innocence of childhood, the workings of grace in human life, the mystery of iniquity in that same human life, the facing of painful death, and the lacerations of the human heart generally, which the prophet Jeremiah had considered "more tortuous than all else . . . beyond remedy" (Jeremiah 17). This is how the human heart is often depicted by Bernanos!

Comparisons of the work of the French novelist with that of the Russian novelist Fyodor Dostoevsky began with this first novel and continued to be made with some of his later novels. These later books treated these and similar themes with a literary talent and style that rarely fails to grip the reader, even though Bernanos is sometimes quite obscure—perhaps owing to the difficulty, sometimes even the impossibility, of expressing what the author somehow does grasp, if only obscurely, and is determined to try to express.

His next novel, *L'imposture* (*The Imposture*), was published in 1927 and is about a prominent French priest-intellectual, a member of the French Academy, the Abbé Cénabre, who has completely lost his faith, yet goes on publicly exploiting both his faith and his priesthood for reasons of worldly prestige. The novel also presents another simple, down-to-earth—and, again, saintly—priest, the Abbé Chevance, who tries to bring the "imposter" priest-intellectual back to the faith and help him save his soul.

The same Abbé Chevance appears in the next Bernanos novel, *La joie* (*Joy*), published in 1928. He appears there as the spiritual director, soon to pass away, of a young woman of an aristocratic but decadent family, Chantal de Clergerie, herself a saint and one of the most memorable of all of the characters of Bernanos. Chantal is eventually murdered by an anarchist Russian exile, Fyodor, working as a chauffeur for Chantal's family; he murders her essentially *because* she is a saint and he finds that intolerable.

Bernanos's next novel, *Un crime* (*A Crime*), published in 1935, represented an attempt to please the author's publisher with a "detective story" that would sell. Although the book contains unmistakable Bernanosian themes and treatments, it is not one of the author's best or most characteristic novels.

The book considered to be the author's masterpiece, *Journal d'un curé de campagne* (*The Diary of a Country Priest*), came out in 1936. It is the one book of Bernanos that is well known and read and has generally remained in print in English translation. It is an account written in the first person by a young curé of the country parish of Ambricourt; the priest's name is never given, and as the reader gradually learns in the course of reading the book, he is already afflicted with terminal stomach cancer—the same disease that took Bernanos's own life a dozen years later—but the country priest's observations and reflections on the Christian life, faith, and, especially, death in the faith of the Lord Jesus Christ place this book far above any mere sentimental or "pious" fiction. The book includes a lengthy and amazing dialogue in which the country priest reconciles the local countess, who had been consciously cursing God every day for 11 years because God had permitted the death of her young son. The conclusion of the book comes with the realization of the dying curé that "*tout est grace*"—"all is grace"! In 1950, Robert Bresson directed a classic French film based on this novel.

The remaining important literary works of Georges Bernanos include his 1937 *Nouvelle histoire de Mouchette* (*Story of a "New" Mouchette*), reprising the topic of a doomed young woman that so fascinated Bernanos; and his 1943 *Monsieur Ouine* (*Mr. "Oui"* or *Mr. "Non"*—it really makes no difference; it is all the same!), about a modern "hollow man" who has consciously succumbed to evil, though once again the book includes another of Bernanos's priests haranguing his wayward parishioners in their "dead parish." The book that followed was *Un mauvais rêve* (*An Evil Dream*), published in 1950 after the author's death; it focused on the theme of the "female sinner." Bernanos also wrote a number of short stories and novellas that figure among his published work.

Finally, in the last year of his life, Bernanos wrote the stark drama *Dialogues des Carmélites* (*Dialogues of the Carmelites*), published in 1949, recounting the story of a convent of nuns who were guillotined during the French Revolution. In this drama, the author proved that his insight into the Catholic religious life was equal to his understanding of the Catholic priesthood. French composer Francis Poulenc turned this Bernanos script into an outstanding opera in 1956.

Bernanos was primarily a novelist, but it should not be forgotten that he was also a lifelong, passionate, and prominent journalist and outspoken public advocate of justice who was listened to, sometimes with awe, in his day. Among his "polemical" works, besides those noted above, that must also be mentioned here is his 1938 *Les grands cimetières sous la lune* (*The Great Cemeteries beneath the Moon*). Like the leftist George Orwell—who in his book *Homage to Catalonia* ended up denouncing the left and all its works in the Spanish Civil War, after Orwell had found out at first hand in Spain what the left was actually doing there—so Bernanos, a rightist living in Majorca when the Spanish Civil War broke out, was so appalled by the violence and wrong of what "his side" also proved capable of doing that he accordingly denounced the right in what has been described as one of the greatest political polemics ever written.

Bernanos penned a half dozen or more other political polemics, and it should be remembered that, in addition to being a great Catholic novelist, he was very much a man of his own times—and one who did honor to the Catholic Church and the Catholic faith by the way in which he bore witness. His post–World War II nonfiction books included the 1944 *La France contre les robots* (*France against the Robots*) and his posthumous 1953 *La liberté, pourquoi faire?* (*Why Liberty, What's the Point?*).

Many of the novels of Bernanos have been translated into English at one time or other, mostly by university or other specialized presses, and, except for *The Diary of a Country Priest*, these books have not generally remained in print, although used copies of them in English can still sometimes be acquired on the Internet today. Few of the polemical works of Bernanos have been translated, however, and this is a pity, since they are often classic, even titanic, works of their type.

Georges Bernanos sincerely believed throughout his life in what he called "*la chevalerie Chrétien française*" (French Christian chivalry). It is hardly progress, nor does it speak well for our era, that few or none today believe in any such thing. After an unsuccessful operation at the American hospital in Neuilly, Bernanos died on July 5, 1948.—Kenneth D. Whitehead

BIBLIOGRAPHY AND FURTHER READING: Balthasar, Hans Urs von. *Bernanos: An Ecclesial Existence*. San Francisco: Ignatius Press, 1996; Bernanos, Georges. *Journal d'un curé de campagne*. Paris, Librairie Plon, 1936; Bernanos, Georges. *The Diary of a Country Priest*. Translated by Pamela Morris. London: Borisword, 1937; Speaght, Robert. *Georges Bernanos: A Study of the Man and the Writer*. New York: Liveright, 1974. *See also AC-TION FRANCAISE*; DOSTOEVSKY, FYODOR MIKHAILOVICH; PERCY, WALKER; TOLKIEN, J. R. R.

BERTONE, CARDINAL TARCISIO (1934–)

Addressing Cardinal Bertone on his 75th birthday and explaining why he had appointed him secretary of state (an unusual selection, as Cardinal Bertone is a religious, not a secular, priest and had no previous experience in diplomacy), Pope Benedict XVI wrote: "I have always admired your *sensus fidei*, your doctrinal and canonical training and your *humanitas*, which was of great help to us in creating, in the Congregation for the Doctrine of the Faith (CDF), an authentic family atmosphere, combined with a steady and firm working discipline."

Born to a pious family in Romano Canavese, Piedmont, Italy, in 1934, Tarcisio Bertone had been attracted to the Salesians of Don Bosco since his early youth and made his religious profession in 1950. Ordained in 1960, and having completed his studies in theology and canon law, he taught both disciplines at the Pontifical Salesian University in Rome. He became the dean of the canon law faculty in 1976 and was the rector of the university from 1989 to 1991. Since 1978, he had also been invited to teach at the Institute *utriusque iuris* of Lateran University. A consultor to several dicasteries of the Roman Curia since the 1980s, Bertone directed the working group within the Italian Bishops' Conference that translated into Italian the 1983 *Code of Canon Law*.

Made a bishop in 1989, two years later Bertone became the archbishop of Vercelli (the oldest diocese in Piedmont) and, as such, a successor to St. Eusebius, a faithful companion of St. Athanasius in the fight against Arianism. In 1995, Pope John Paul II called him back to Rome as the secretary of the CDF, headed by then Cardinal Joseph Ratzinger. Appointed in 2002 to head the archdiocese of Genoa and elevated to cardinal by Pope John Paul II in 2003, the current pope chose him as secretary of state in 2006 and camerlengo of the Holy Roman Church (an office of the papal household) in 2007.

As Cardinal Bertone himself remarked remembering one of his mentors, the great scholar and Austrian Salesian Cardinal Alfons Maria Stickler, three devotions have a typically Salesian flavor: those to the Eucharist, to the Virgin Mary, and to the pope. Cardinal Bertone's devotion to the Eucharist is in a way prefigured in his own name, Tarcisio being the teenage protomartyr of the Eucharist who gave his life to defend the Holy Species he was bringing to incarcerated Christians. The cardinal's devotion to the Virgin Mary was further nurtured by the role Pope John Paul II entrusted to him in the publication of the third part of the secret of Fatima, a task that brought him into contact with Sister Lucia, over whose funeral he presided in 2005. (He also represented the pope in 2007 at the celebrations of the 450th anniversary of the apparition of Our Lady of Montallegro near Genoa.) Finally, his devotion to the pope was shown on the many occasions on which both the current pontiff and his predecessor gave him delicate assignments, from participating in the drafting of the declaration *Dominus Iesus* to being part of the attempts of reconciliation with Archbishop Marcel Lefebvre, to handling the cases of Fathers Anthony De Mello and Tissa Balasuriya and the former archbishop Emmanuel Milingo.

In 2001, when he was the secretary of the CDF, his signature was appended after that of Cardinal Ratzinger under the note on the doctrinal decrees regarding the thought and writings of Antonio Rosmini-Serbati. During Cardinal Bertone's tenure as secretary of state, the Holy See ratified such multilateral treaties as the Convention on Cluster Munitions and signed bilateral agreements, including those with Andorra, Brazil, and Montenegro. Both in his official speeches and private interviews, Cardinal Bertone, in unison with Pope Benedict XVI and reaffirming Church teaching, has defended human life, from conception to natural death, and family life based on marriage between one man and one woman, against the many attacks and moral evils to which they are subject.—Maurizio Ragazzi

BIBLIOGRAPHY AND FURTHER READING: Bertone, Tarcisio. *The Last Secret of Fatima: My Conversations with Sister Lucia.* New York: Doubleday, 2008; Viani, Bruno. *Tarcisio Bertone: The Smiling Cardinal*, 3rd ed. (in Italian). Genoa: De Ferrari, 2006. *See also* CONCORDATS; EUROPE; FAMILY; HUMAN LIFE (DIGNITY AND SANCTITY OF); POPE BENEDICT XVI; POPE JOHN PAUL II; ROSMINI-SERBATI, ANTONIO; TREATIES IN CATHOLIC SOCIAL TEACHING

BIBLICAL NATURAL LAW Addressing the Romans, St. Paul reminds them of something they had been taught by the ancient Greeks, their own moral philosophers such as Cicero, and their consciences, namely, that there is a "law" they know and "do by nature," because it is "written on their hearts" (Romans 2: 14–15). The evangelist thus points to the Torah, or the Law of Moses, as being first a law that was given by God and known through the things he made, including all of creation, the entire physical universe, and, most impor-

tantly, the human being. This law was codified at Sinai as the Ten Commandments and later in the Word made Flesh who revealed the fullness of the New Covenant Law of Love.

It is important to note that the greatest of pagan philosophers had themselves rationally deduced many of the natural law principles revealed in Scripture, including the prohibitions against murder, adultery, robbery and theft, false witness, shamefulness, spite, and envy. Aristotle, for instance, had identified the like as intrinsic evils, and such evils were almost universally condemned in the ancient pagan codes of law. Paul's claim, then, was recognizable in its own time as a reasonable one.

The Bible is rich in its exposition of the natural law. The book of Genesis establishes that all creation takes its existence from God and that it is naturally good. The human person's existence within the created world is not just good, but "very good" (Genesis 1: 31). The human person is revealed as having been made in the divine image and likeness, with a mind to know both God and the good, a heart to love God and the good, and a free will capable of choosing for God and to do good. But the freedom of the will and man's desire for freedom can be abused, as it is in sin, which disorders the ability to accurately know and perceive the good, to properly love God and neighbor, and to impeccably choose the good for oneself and others. Genesis 2 then reflects on the natural inclination to marriage and the family, the fruitful love of men and women, and the procreation of new life in the context of a stable union producing a new social image of God in the family. In *The Theology of the Body*, Pope John Paul II offered the world a rich appreciation of the natural law contained in the opening chapters of Genesis, which reveal human beings as having natural inclinations to life, love and friendship, truth, goodness, freedom, happiness, monogamous family life, productive work, and community.

But as Genesis 3–4 shows, man's awareness of the natural law can be corrupted and diminished owing to the effects of sin. Therefore, they must be reminded that murder is evil, that polygamy introduces jealousy and disorder into marriage and family life, and that broken promises leave a train of wounded, grieving, and angry hearts. Thus is the intellect gradually darkened in its capacity to seek and know the truth and the good, thus is the will weakened in its capacity to choose the good, and thus is the heart disordered in its loves, often looking for God's love and others' love in "all the wrong places."

In Exodus, the great Covenant at Sinai reveals in stone what should be known in the heart, namely, that every human being has a deeply imbedded need for and desire to love and be loved by God and by other human beings, especially close family members, and that this love of God and of one's family and eventually others cannot tolerate murder, adultery, stealing, lying, and coveting. To be free, a person must free himself from slavery to the passions and appetites that incline him to sin, and this begins foremost in acknowledging that his creator and his ultimate destiny, God, cannot be ignored. When men ignore the God of truth and love, they enter the land of idolatry and pride, and there swiftly follows every woe known to human experience, thus preventing the human person from achieving the happiness they most ardently desire but too often misconstrue.

Throughout the Hebrew Scriptures, from the Torah to the historical books, the prophets and the wisdom literature, this basic cosmological and anthropological perspective is constantly reiterated. If man would only open his mind and heart to the gifts of the Holy Spirit, he might glimpse again through the haze his divine image and likeness and his divine origin and destiny. But too often foolish pride and selfish ego intrude, and so the invitation to love is not perceived and thus is too often rejected as darkness gathers, evils perpetuate, hearts are wounded, lives are ruined, and communities are destroyed, while hatred, sadness, and despair banish all thought of happiness.

The Christian New Testament furnishes a new appreciation of the natural law in light of a world marred by so much sin and error. The heart of the New Covenant fulfilled in Christ is summarized in the Sermon on the Mount (Matthew 5–7). Here the "law written on the heart" is revealed as a series of interior spiritual states of the soul rooted in virtues essential to the attainment of human health and happiness. The road to happiness or beatitude runs through the human heart, recognizing its need for holiness and wholeness. In the sermon, poverty of spirit (or humility) and meekness are identified as the first steps on the road to happiness. Humility properly recognizes and understands who we are as finite beings and who God is as Infinite Being and the author of all being.

Every human heart contains a desire for home, beauty, and the good, which are ultimately fulfilled only in unity with God the Father, who is the author of the life and love for which humans yearn. Pride rejects or ignores God, but humility is the first step on the road to godliness and prepares the soul to use its every gift and talent for the advancement of the good in complete faith and trust. A humble, trusting heart is able then to attain a proper understanding of mourning losses in a condition of well-ordered love, namely, love of God, who is the author of love and love itself, and then the love of neighbor as self. This well-ordered love then recognizes the value of family, friends, and wider society, allowing the soul to perceive the good and the just.

Justice is a natural inclination of the soul, but it is fulfilled only in a proper "love of neighbor as of self." Moreover, genuine love looks beyond justice to mercy and forgiveness. The heart that forgives injury is a healthy heart, one capable of recognizing its own and others needs for mutual reconciliation. A merciful heart is capable of purity that seeks every virtue and good and avoids vice and evil. Cleansed of vice, a heart finally achieves peace and is capable of peacemaking, which is so vital to the attainment of human happiness. Finally, the soul that has attained peace is able, even in the midst of persecution, to offer a blessing rather than a curse to the persecutor, thus forgiving evil rather than perpetuating it.

This life of holiness is not possible on human terms alone, but, as revealed in the New Testament, it is possible through grace. With the gifts of the Holy Spirit, revealed in Isaiah, the human intellect grows in knowledge, wisdom, and understanding and is thus capable of right judgment. But the heart needs courage, too, a gift of God's grace. Humble admission of the source of our capacity for knowing is itself possible only with the gifts of wonder and awe and pious love of God. A heart watered with the theological gifts of faith, hope, and love is thus able to enjoy the fruits of the Holy Spirit for which all human beings long and that can be realized only in a life of holiness. St. Paul identifies several of the fruits, including love, joy, peace, patience, kindness, generosity, faithfulness, gentleness, and self-control. Against such, he notes, there is no law. They embody the law and life of the spirit, which in itself provides a foundation of justice and the common good.

First principles of the natural law include a natural liberty of conscience and worship of God, the right to life and preciousness of life from the moment the gift is given by God to the moment it is taken by him, the right to the love and protection of a family, the rights of a man and woman to enter into a fruitful bond of lifelong and faithful conjugal love, the right to basic respect and dignity of persons and their freedom to develop and use individual talents and gifts, to seek and know the truth, and to choose the good. Added to these are the right and duty to seek and enjoy dignified work for the advancement of oneself, one's family, and the wider community and the right to seek happiness in light of justice and the common good in the full tranquility of order and peace. From these rights can be deduced other goods consistent with the natural law such as the natural right and even duties of self-defense, of protecting the innocent from harm, and of property necessary for a dignified life. The forms in which these rights are imbedded in human law will vary from place to place, but so long as human law respects underlying natural law principles, justice will be served along with social order and the common good.—Robert F. Gorman

BIBLIOGRAPHY AND FURTHER READING: John Paul II. *The Theology of the Body: Human Love in the Divine Plan.* Boston: Pauline Books & Media, 1997; Levering, Matthew. *Biblical Natural Law.* Oxford: Oxford University Press, 2008; Pinkaers, Servais, OP. *The Sources of Christian Ethics.* Washington, DC: Catholic University of America Press, 1995. *See also* COMMON GOOD; FAMILY; GOSPEL FOUNDATIONS; HUMAN LIFE; HUMAN RIGHTS; JUSTICE; SUBSIDIARITY; THEOLOGY OF THE BODY; VIRTUE-ETHICS

BIFFI, CARDINAL GIACOMO (1928–)

"We are not aware of any other episcopal Magisterium, at least in Italy, that so effectively combines the light of theological wisdom and the rigor of sacred science with convincing judgments and practical applications." These are the words with which Italian theologian Inos Biffi (no relation) described Cardinal Biffi's ministry.

Born in Milan in 1928, Giacomo Biffi entered the seminary of the Archdiocese of Milan, in Venegono Inferiore, in 1942. He was ordained in 1950 by (the now Blessed) Cardinal Schuster. In the 34 intervening years, until his appointment as archbishop of Bologna, Biffi served the Archdiocese of Milan—as a teacher (mainly of dogmatic theology) from 1950 to 1960, as a pastor (first in Legnano, a historical city outside of Milan, and then at St. Andrea in Milan) from 1960 to 1974, and finally as episcopal vicar for culture and auxiliary bishop to the archbishop of Milan from 1975 to 1984. In 1984, Biffi became the archbishop of Bologna (a role he would maintain for the subsequent 20 years), and he was made a cardinal a year later. He had the unique privilege of preaching the traditional spiritual exercises to the Roman Curia twice, first in 1989 on the invitation of (the now Blessed) Pope John Paul II, and then in 2007 on the invitation of Pope Benedict XVI.

Cardinal Biffi's coat of arms captures the three key features of his pastoral ministry: it has spokes representing his Christ-centric identity (the spoke being the Christ who links God and humanity); it reproduces a motto of St. Ambrose, the father and Doctor of the Church whom Biffi regards as his father and teacher; and the motto in question (*Ubi Fides Ibi Libertas*, "Where There Is Faith There Is Freedom") signals the impact of faith on the practical life of man.

That a Catholic priest, bishop, and cardinal should be Christ-centered in his approach might seem a platitude. But Biffi's way of reaching the man of today is to emphasize the importance of seeking the face of Christ, true God and true man. He also reads the products of human genius with the eyes of faith, such as unfolding the Pinocchio story in its archetypal meaning for the history of salvation.

Similarly, Biffi's attraction to St. Ambrose is not the result of mere erudite research. To the contrary, St. Ambrose represents the courageous witness who presents the fullness of faith in Christ to the decadent society of the fourth century, which has so many elements of similarity with the current time. Within the context of the initiatives that marked the 16th century of Ambrose's episcopal ordination, Biffi supervised the monumental work of the critical edition of all of Ambrose's writings and the preparation of the new liturgical books for the Ambrosian Rite. These are works of culture in the most noble sense of the word, as embraced by Biffi, namely, the cultivation of man through all that is good, right, and beautiful, as a reflection of the "cultivation" (or vine growing) of the Lord Jesus by God the Father (John 15: 1).

St. Ambrose's motto—that where there is faith, there is freedom—underlines that, in its proper and authentically human sense, freedom is based on truth and enlightened by faith. From this concept, Biffi draws crucial consequences for the social life and does not mince words in defense of the defenseless. Calling by name what is under everybody's eyes and avoiding any softening of language that would sound complacent, Biffi has written that "amidst the most infamous events of history and the many genocides, the greatest shame of the twentieth century remains the legalization and public financing of abortion," and that the "most cruel form of maltreatment, accepted as normal and civilized, is the destruction of the family."

Cardinal Biffi's memoirs, now in their second edition, show their author's wit and humility. (We are only who we are in God's eyes, as the curé of Ars used to say.) They constitute a clear reflection on the problems of the contemporary Church and society, accompanied by the serenity of the man of faith who knows that, at the end, truth prevails because Christ the Truth has saved the world.—Maurizio Ragazzi

BIBLIOGRAPHY AND FURTHER READING: Biffi, Giacomo. *Ambrogio Vescovo: Attualità di un maestro*. Cinisello Balsamo: Edizioni San Paolo, 1997; Biffi, Giacomo. *Approccio al Cristocentrismo: Note storiche per un tema eterno*. Milan: Jaca Book, 1993; Biffi, Giacomo. *The Man Christ Jesus: How the Lord Looked, Acted, Prayed, and Loved*. Translated by Charlotte J. Fasi. Manchester, NH: Sophia Institute Press, 2008; Biffi, Giacomo. *Memorie e digressioni di un italiano cardinal*, 2nd ed. Siena: Cantagalli, 2010; Biffi, Giacomo. *Pinocchio, Peppone, l'Anticristo e altre divagazioni*. Siena: Cantagalli, 2005; Biffi, Giacomo. *Ragione e vita: A che punto è la notte?* Siena: Cantagalli, 2004. *See also* ABORTION; FAMILY; FREEDOM; JESUS CHRIST; POPE BENEDICT XVI; POPE JOHN PAUL II

BIOTECHNOLOGY The predominance of science and technology is almost a defining feature of the modern age. Their success has led to the view that scientific knowledge supplants all other forms of knowledge and using technology uniquely expresses human creativity. More precisely, it is *biotechnology* that is now prevalent; ours is the biotech age. Biotechnology offers the possibility of engineering and manipulating the very biological basis of all life, including human life, and this is now a central concern in ethics, politics, economics, commerce, and health care.

Etymologically, *technology* implies not objects, but knowledge of *techne*, or craft skill. For Aristotle, *techne*, understood as "bringing forth," was conceived in terms of the different forms of causality in human action and was believed to be a specific intellectual virtue. In modern technology, the emphasis falls heavily on efficient cause and what is instrumentally useful to achieve an effect. For modernity, technology is allied to the construction of artifacts, tools, and machines. The prefix *bio-* indicates the specific focus of biotechnology: life itself. And since human life and life events are now so completely under the purview of medicine (a form of what some call "medicalization"), *biomedical* technology is the form in which most of us encounter biotechnology.

As with technology in general, biotechnology has invited a variety of critical philosophical, sociological, ethical, and theological responses, as well as both serious and popular debate in the media, which inevitably dwells on *utopian* and *dystopian* futures. The recognition of the embeddedness of biotechnology in systems of values and in wider political and cultural ideologies and aspirations has yielded a rich vein of critical literature, which itself has raised fundamental questions about anthropology and what it means to be a human be-

ing. The new discipline of *bioethics* seeks the values and moral norms to apply to the many possible applications of biotechnology. Some critics argue, however, that bioethics has become little more than the public relations department of many in the new biotechnology industries.

Biotechnology's roots in the commercial-industrial complex of modern bureaucratic society have given rise to critical analyses of the potential abuse of power and the danger of injustice, alienation, and marginalization of the vulnerable. Thoreau remarked that "men have become the tools of their tools," and the tendency of biotechnology to instrumentalize human beings has indeed become a central concern in bioethics.

Modern science challenged the Greek worldview of changeless forms, but its own mechanistic worldview was in turn transformed by an emerging perception of process, development, and change in nature. This helped to legitimize the idea that since human beings are living, changing organisms subject to the randomness of genetic inheritance, technology now enables us to manage, direct, and "enhance" ourselves and our future, realizing the desire to replace chance with man-made purpose. Still, current technology reveals the shaping ideology of Francis Bacon (1561–1626), who viewed the natural environment as a resource at the disposal of human beings and who believed that science could relieve fallen man's estate. From nature as a reserve to be plundered, it has been a short step to the view that human nature or, more precisely, living human bodies are also a resource to be exploited for a variety of purposes, many of which employ a medical rationale. Man is thus not only *homo faber* but has himself become the raw material for his constructive projects. And such self-exploitation shapes humanity's self-understanding. Critics such as Heidegger, Ellul, and Habermas have dwelt on the menacing and rapacious nature of much technology, a theme continued in the writings on biotechnology of Hans Jonas, Leon Kass, and Francis Fukuyama.

According to Robert Budd, the term *biotechnology* was coined around 1917 by Hungarian agricultural engineer and minister of nutrition Karl Ereky. Its original meaning was related to food production and agriculture. Ereky's *biotechnologie* was essentially a scientific program of pig fattening to achieve greater yield. Significantly, he coined the term *biotechnologische Arbeitsmaschine*, reflecting his understanding of the pig as a machine for food production. Budd compares this idea with the more comprehensive contemporary definition by the Organization for Economic Cooperation and Development: "Biotechnology is the application of scientific and engineering principles to the processing of materials by biological agents to provide goods and materials."

The immediate scientific roots of biotechnology included *zymotechnology*, industrial fermentation, including brewing and baking, which was greeted with enthusiasm for its economic potential. By the late 1920s, the term *biotechnologie* appeared in a standard German dictionary and meant the manipulation of microorganisms in production. Budd notes that the lines between animate and inanimate were becoming uncertain and also observes how the quest for contraceptive methods was a recurring element in modern biotechnology.

As scientific, ideological, and political interest in evolution and heredity grew, biotechnology became part of a wider social movement not only to understand human origins and growth, but to manipulate them. In 1936, Julian Huxley argued that biotechnology would become more important than mechanical and chemical engineering. Certain neologisms signaled a paradigm shift: *biosciences* indicated a new set of disciplines, *bioinformation* a new form of knowledge, *bioresources* the range of material available for research and utilization, *biopower* the nature of its potential impact on social relationships within civic society, *bioethics* the need for moral awareness of the problems raised by the new developments, and *bioeconomics* the relation of the new technology to commercial benefit in public and private spheres.

It was the prefix *bio-* that signaled the specificity of the new technology and that extended and sharpened the critical analysis that had been offered of technology in general. In 1962, Elmer Gaden wrote: "Biotechnology embraces all aspects of the *exploitation* and *control* of biological systems and their activities." Biotechnology in the medical context covers a wide range of interventions relating to human life, embracing reproductive medicine, clinical genetics, molecular biology, pharmacology, and neuroscience. Biomedical technology aims at diagnostic, therapeutic, or corrective interventions and increasingly at the enhancement of human capacities.

In the 1970s, prenatal genetic screening technology began to offer what would become a barrage of invasive and noninvasive techniques to detect structural and functional anomalies in the unborn child. This raised many ethical concerns, at the center of which was the question of a "new eugenics." With the fusion of industrial microbiology and genetics in the 1970s, recombinant DNA technology became the most dramatic technological tool in the "growing biotechnological arsenal," so that "for the first time in history we become

the engineers of life itself." Thus, genetics became the prism through which biotechnology was perceived and genetic engineering became the basis of the new biotechnology.

The medical and commercial potential in such technology was quickly exploited. Later, the Human Genome Project was developed to map and sequence the entire genetic constitution of the human being. Whatever therapeutic aspirations surrounded the initiative, its most immediate and enduring effect was to extend the scope of prenatal diagnosis, which in the absence of effective treatments for many genetic diseases increased the "diagnostic/therapeutic gap" and the medical elimination of "defective lives." Used in conjunction with in vitro fertilization, which reached its triumph with the first so-called test-tube baby in 1978 in the United Kingdom, techniques of genetic screening became central to the new reproductive technologies.

Biotechnology now manipulates human life and mechanisms of genetic inheritance through cloning, gene therapy, and cell nuclear transfer; animal-human hybrids and chimeras are further potential variations on artificial reproduction. Ian Wilmut claimed that cloning Dolly the Sheep has "taken us into the age of biological control." But by 2009, he thought adult stem cell research might be a more significant development for medicine, and many would agree.

As biotechnology meets neuroscience, greater manipulation of the brain offers new clinical possibilities. Developments in genetics, robotics, information, and nanoprocesses reflect a revolution in our understanding of genetic causality and the etiology of disease, opening the way to more extensive bioengineering with potential to cure illness, enhance human capacities, and extend our life span. What is called *nanotechnology* involves "manipulating the unimaginably small" (a nanometer is one-billionth of a meter) while preserving the functional possibilities of the larger entity. Some hope that nanotechnology will bridge the gap between mechanical and molecular capabilities and extend diagnostic and therapeutic applications by enhancing pharmacological therapies and surgical possibilities for the repair of brain and other tissue. Already, transcutaneous electrical and magnetic stimulation is being used in an exploratory way to treat brain-related illness, and the possibility arises of a brain prosthesis such as an artificial hippocampus to treat memory impairment caused by neural degeneration. Nanotechnology focusing on brain–computer interface—silicon chips interacting with neurons—is being explored by military scientists, but also by medical researchers seeking clinical applications to prevent or ameliorate cognitive decline in the aging brain.

Nikolas Rose claims that "these are not merely medical technologies or technologies of health, they are technologies of life" that change what it is to be a living biological organism. Does this refiguring of life's vital processes redefine human nature, its proper functioning, its beginning and end, and even what it means to be *living* at all? Rather than being a given, is the biological becoming wholly contingent? Certainly, such alteration of human beings and human society is reshaping procreation, parenthood, and family life, requiring us to navigate between the technologically possible and the morally permissible.

Serious moral evaluation of biotechnology requires the guidance available from forms of knowledge such as the wisdom arising from the poetic imagination, mythical narrative, and above all mystical spirituality. Catholic analyses of biotechnology, as found in *Donum Vitae, Evangelium Vitae*, and other magisterial documents affirm the need to subject all technology to ethical scrutiny. Catholic teaching proclaims the sanctity of human life and the dignity of the human person who, in his bodily-spiritual unity, is made in the image and likeness of God, redeemed by Christ, and called to eternal life with the Blessed Trinity. This teaching articulates the proper goals of medicine and what constitutes the good of human health; it also advocates the just allocation of resources and affirms the centrality of ethical and spiritual values in health care. Since biotechnology has contributed to a fundamental shift in our experience of the body, this critique, rooted in biblical revelation and shaped by philosophical and theological anthropology, exposes the tendency to instrumentalize, depersonalize, and alienate both technology's masters and its alleged beneficiaries. It also opposes naturalism and materialism and the tendency of the "technological imperative" to devalue the role of moral education and virtuous living in pursuing human fulfillment.

Theology challenges a restricted focus on biological manipulation, which distorts the deeply human activities of receiving and nurturing life (procreation rather than reproduction); it insists on humane care of our bodily lives and humble ways of approaching dying and death that transcend merely instrumental calculation. Theology questions any biotechnology that seeks to engineer human perfection or manufacture "immortality," proclaiming rather the gift of divine grace, spiritual transformation, and moral striving within community as our unique way of flourishing and salva-

tion. The very nature of the *human* is at issue in debates about the biotechnology with which medicine is now reshaping human life. There seems little evidence that humanity is yet anywhere near acquiring the wisdom and moral insight necessary to resolve many of the questions raised by such biotechnology in a way that protects and enhances, rather than diminishes, human beings.—John C. Berry

BIBLIOGRAPHY AND FURTHER READING: Brock, Brian. *Christian Ethics in a Technological Age.* Grand Rapids, MI: Eerdmans, 2010; Fukuyama, Francis. *Our Postmodern Future: Consequences of the Biotechnology Revolution.* New York: Farrar, Straus & Giroux, 2002; Shelley, Toby. *Nanotechnology: New Promises, New Dangers.* New York: Zed Books, 2006; Stehr, Nico, ed. *Biotechnology: Between Commerce and Civil Society.* New Brunswick, NJ: Transaction, 2004. *See also CARITAS IN VERITATE; DIGNITAS PERSONAE; DONUM VITAE;* EUGENICS; *EVANGELIUM VITAE;* TRANSHUMANISM

BODIN, JEAN (1529/30–1596) Jean Bodin was born in Angers, France. The son of a wealthy tailor, he was sent to Paris to study at the Collège des Trois Langues (now known as Collège de France), a newly established humanist school that focused on languages rather than on theology. Bodin's university training was at Toulouse (beginning in 1550), where he studied jurisprudence and subsequently lectured on Roman law before moving to Paris to take up legal and political duties.

At that time, a significant scholarly concern was to codify and universalize French law. While the professors at Toulouse by and large followed the traditional, scholastic method for applying the Code of Justinian and *Gloss* (the standard legal texts of the time) to contemporary situations, the influence of the Italian humanists, who emphasized historical context, was being felt. Bodin's first major work, *Methodus ad facilem historiarum cognitionem* (1566; *Method for the Easy Comprehension of History*), reflects this training and intellectual climate. In it, he sought to integrate his humanism, theology, and legal training in a universal philosophy of history. While the work is not of central contemporary importance, Bodin's acumen and scholarly knowledge are impressive as he attempts to provide a method for establishing a world history from which the student could draw lessons both moral and political. Further, in this work one finds the nucleus of Bodin's later theories. Two years later, he published *Response aux paradoxes de M. de Malestroit* (1566; *Response to the Paradoxes of Monsieur de Malestroit*), which contains his insights into economics.

By far Bodin's most lasting contribution is in political philosophy, specifically as laid out in *Les six livres de la République* (1576; *The Six Books of the Commonwealth*), which was written as a defense of monarchical authority in response to Huguenot constitutionalism. Given this work's importance, it is worth outlining its main points.

In book 1 of *Les six livres*, Bodin begins by defining the commonwealth as "the rightly ordered government of a number of families, and of those things which are their common concern, by a sovereign power." This right order distinguishes a legitimate political body from "a band of thieves or pirates" owing to its fidelity to the laws of nature. Contrasting his account with that of Plato, Bodin states that his aim is to discuss not a theoretical commonwealth, but one that could obtain in practice. While the family is the origin of the commonwealth, the source of its unity is the sovereign who binds its members together. And while consent is an important political concept for Bodin, more important is the naturalness of a hierarchical system as ordained by God for the purpose of pursuing the human good. In good Platonic or even Aristotelian fashion, Bodin affirms that being a citizen is not so much a matter of securing one's rights as of pursuing the common good. Thus, while the sovereign is answerable to God should he act viciously, his power is absolute and not to be questioned; his legitimacy is not the result of the people's consent but of his ordination by God.

Book 2 addresses the various types of regimes and begins with the traditional distinction between monarchy, democracy, and aristocracy. Yet, Bodin deviates from the classical framework by rejecting the essential distinction between good and bad regimes, as well as the possibility of a mixed regime. While Bodin lists further distinctions (e.g., between royal, despotic, and tyrannical monarchy), it would seem that, practically speaking, the concept of sovereignty overshadows the issue of the best type of regime: A clear preference for royal monarchy is present, yet any regime in which there is an indivisible sovereign will suffice for political life.

The third book turns to subordinate authorities in the commonwealth such as councilors, officers, magistrates, guilds, and estates. All must obey the sovereign and act as intermediaries between the people and sovereign. At the same time, Bodin reaffirms that such bonds are not servile or compulsory but are grounded in the mutual affection that begins in the family. Ultimately, subordinate authorities and even the sovereign himself exist to ensure that these natural relationships between members of families are just. It is friendship, and not fear, that binds the commonwealth together.

Book 4 begins with the admission that all commonwealths eventually submit to decay. This book examines the various causes of revolution and offers practical advice for preventing the dissolution of the commonwealth. Bodin asserts that cruelty is better than licentiousness, that a large commonwealth tends to be more stable than a small one, and that commonwealths must have one religion. Concerning the last point, while Bodin does not recognize what we would call religious liberty, he does state that it is generally best not to coerce people into observing the religion of the commonwealth, since this tends to drive people to atheism and immorality once they have lost the fear of God.

Book 5 addresses the types of regime best suited for various types of people. People are divided along climatic and latitudinal lines as Southerners, Northerners, and temperate-zoned peoples. Southerners are ruled by religion and given to contemplation. Northerners, by contrast, are given to the manual arts. Those in between are prudent and best suited for political affairs.

In the sixth and final book of *Les six livres*, Bodin turns to concerns about the maintenance of commonwealths. He begins by discussing the importance of a regular census for assessing conditions and knowing the people in the commonwealth. He then moves on to revisit the advantages and disadvantages of the types of regimes and reasserts that the best form of government is a monarchy that rules in accordance with what he calls "harmonic justice," that is, "distribution based on principle of equality as well as similarity."

Les six livres is often seen as setting forth the first theory of indivisible, absolute sovereignty. Whereas in *Methodus* Bodin had argued for a limited sovereignty, in that community consent and law are seen as having binding power on the king, *Les six livres* removes these limitations. This stronger notion of sovereignty was of incalculable influence on later political developments, given its centrality to subsequent theory and practice. In particular, he is sometimes seen as an early source for the modern liberal tradition, both in his understanding of sovereignty and in his focus on practice over theory (i.e., on a commonwealth that *could* exist over one that *ought to* exist). That being said, the many ways in which Bodin remains rooted within a classical framework mark him as an important figure who straddles both the medieval and modern worlds. Consider the following two examples.

The first difference between Bodin and the early modern thinkers who took up his notion of sovereignty is that Bodin retains the traditional view of humans as social and political animals. His definition of a commonwealth as a grouping of families rather than of individuals distinguishes him from his modern political heirs. Thus, even if we could call Bodin an absolutist, it is of a mitigated variety in that he does not attempt to reduce the commonwealth to isolated individuals ruled by an unlimited sovereign.

Second, despite the practical orientation of his political thought, Bodin unqualifiedly affirms the telos of human nature to be contemplation rather than action. Bodin's theory of the soul follows the traditional distinction between speculative and practical reason, giving the highest place in the commonwealth to those who live in terms of the speculative part of the soul— priests and philosophers. This is a marked contrast with much of modern political theory, which tends to denigrate contemplation as being useless. Thus, Bodin is wedded to a vision of human life and purpose that is fully in keeping with the Catholic intellectual tradition.

Toward the end of Bodin's life, he wrote a short work entitled *De la démonomanie des sorciers* (1580; *On the Demon-mania of Witches*) and two major volumes, *Colloquium heptaplomeres de rerum sublimium arcanis abditis* (1588, first published in 1857; *Colloquium of the Seven about Secrets of the Sublime*) and *Universae naturae theatrum* (1596). *Colloquium* is of interest both as a contemporary response to the Wars of Religion and as an early argument for toleration of various religions in one political regime. It could be said, then, to extend and modify his views of religions and politics as outlined in *Les six livres*. *Theatrum* deals with natural philosophy.

Concerning Bodin's own religious convictions, while some argue that he was more humanist than Catholic, more political theorist concerned with political stability than pious believer interested in the salvation of people's souls, or even a naturalist in matters of religion, there is no doubt that he operated within the Catholic milieu. Thus, Bodin should be seen as a Catholic political theorist whose response to the challenges of his day helped to shape subsequent social and political developments. Bodin died in 1596 and was given a Catholic burial (per his request) at the Church of the Franciscans at Laon.

What is lasting in Bodin's theory? Why would one turn to him to address contemporary themes in social and political theory? Given his influence on modern liberalism, studying Bodin can help us to understand the history behind the shaping forces of modernity. In doing so, one is able to discern more clearly the Catholic contributions to the development of political realities as well as the problematic deviations that must be rejected.

Focusing in particular on the notion of sovereignty, Jacques Maritain and others may be right to reject the theory of indivisible sovereignty modern liberalism inherited from Bodin. Yet, if Julian H. Franklin is correct, this doctrine is an accretion as a result of political circumstances (viz., the St. Bartholomew Massacre of 1572) that does not shape Bodin's general theory. The problem is not the doctrine of sovereignty as such, but that of *indivisible* sovereignty: Catholic theorists, even if not using the term, regularly spoke of sovereignty within the secular and sacred realms that mutually limited each other's jurisdiction, and the constitutionalist tradition spoke of mixed regimes in which sovereignty was shared.

Despite faults one might find within Bodin's system, it is important to recognize him as a transitional figure who retained a vision of human life as rooted in the organic development of politics out of family life and as ordered toward the contemplation of Truth as its ultimate perfection. And while he may be guilty of too closely associating church and state (not to mention giving the primacy to the state), nonetheless he maintains an orientation of earthly life toward the Heavenly Jerusalem that many of his modern liberal disciples abandoned. This traditional anthropology was subsequently replaced by an individualistic one that both failed to recognize man's social nature and often dogmatically denied any final purpose to human life. In short, Bodin shows us that many of the supposedly secular and modern contributions to social and political life are rooted in the Catholic tradition and can be embraced by being reconnected to their source of vitality, the Church.—Michael P. Krom

Bibliography and Further Reading: Bodin, Jean. *Six Books of the Commonwealth*. Translated by M. J. Tooley. Oxford, England: Blackwell, 1955; Franklin, Julian H. *Jean Bodin and the Rise of Absolutist Theory*. New York: Cambridge University Press, 1973; King, Preston T. *The Ideology of Order: A Comparative Analysis of Jean Bodin and Thomas Hobbes*. Portland, OR: Frank Cass, 1999. *See also* ARISTOTLE; AUTHORITY; MARITAIN, JACQUES; PLATO; SEPARATION OF CHURCH AND STATE; SOVEREIGNTY

BOSCO, ST. JOHN (1815–1888) St. John Bosco is the founder of the family of religious men (priests and brothers) and women (sisters) who are known as the Salesians. He was born in Becchi, Italy, on August 16, 1815. Bosco grew up not just poor but without a father, the man who gave life to him having died when his son was barely two years old. These two factors—poverty and fatherlessness—were to figure prominently in the life work of this saint.

While still a young man, Bosco came under the influence of St. Joseph Cafasso (1811–1860), the apostle to prisoners. With Cafasso's encouragement, Don Bosco, as he was later known, entered the diocesan seminary in Turin in 1835. Ordination came in 1841. Within his first year of priestly ministry, Don Bosco met a poor orphan, Bartolomeo Garelli, and decided to give instruction in advance of the boy's reception of First Holy Communion. Not much after that, Don Bosco began meeting regularly with a group of male youths to teach them the catechism.

Once again, Cafasso's assistance proved decisive for Don Bosco. This time, Cafasso introduced Bosco to the Marchesa di Barola, who owned and operated a boarding school for girls where Bosco, in time, became its chaplain. What the Marchesa di Barola did for disadvantaged girls, Don Bosco was intent on doing for boys. In Turin, he opened his own boarding school, placing his mother in charge of housekeeping there. The school later became known as the Oratory of St. Francis de Sales in honor of the 17th-century bishop of Geneva and Doctor of the Church.

Don Bosco's work caught the attention of powerful patrons who gave him access to material resources he could never have had on his own. Among the donations he received was a printing press, which he used for the dissemination of catechetical and devotional tracts. What the priest really needed, though, was other priests to help him carry out his apostolate with boys whom today we would call "at risk." So, in 1850, Don Bosco started training his own cadre of priests. In 1854, the priests recruited by Don Bosco formed an association under the patronage of St. Francis de Sales. This in turn led to the establishment of a religious congregation of priests in 1859. A brief time afterward, a lay member by the name of Joseph Rossi was accepted as the first Salesian brother. Papal approval for the congregation was conferred in 1868.

After gaining papal approval for the Salesian priests and brothers, Don Bosco founded with Maria Mazzarello the Institute of the Daughters of Mary Help of Christians in 1871. The members of this institute are better known today as the Salesian sisters. In 1874, Don Bosco created the Salesian Cooperators, a network of mostly laypeople who are not canonical members of the Salesians but support the apostolic endeavors of those in vowed life according to the charism of St. John Bosco. In 1875, the Salesians launched a mission in Argentina, their first outside Italy. Later that same year, a mission was sent to the United States.

Given Don Bosco's long history of training boys in the Catholic faith and equipping them with skills for gainful employment in a society that was changing from agrarian to industrial, a clear method is discernible in his work. The approach is known as the "preventative system" of education. It derives its name from the effort on the part of caring adults to remove youngsters from any occasions to sin. This could be done, Don Bosco believed, by a frequent recourse to sacramental confession and sacramental communion. Efficacious as the sacraments of Penance and the Eucharist are, Don Bosco also believed that education cannot be restricted only to the mind. It must be attentive also to the affective dimension of human development, with youngsters knowing that they are loved all the while they advance cognitively. The strategy favored by Don Bosco accented the critical influences exercised by religion, reason, and kindness. In his philosophy of education, Don Bosco found no place for corporal punishment. Instead, he held firmly that fatherly guidance can overcome many of the infirmities of spirit likely to affect adolescent boys.

In the 19th century as economic and social changes swept across Europe, there were fears in some quarters that the working classes would be lost to the Church. The Church, trying to position itself as the defender of the working classes, was fortunate indeed to have a figure like St. John Bosco. He and his confreres did not abandon the masses but remained close to them, just as the ideas of Karl Marx (1818–1883) were gaining momentum and his writings such as *The Communist Manifesto* (1848) and *Das Kapital* (1867) were becoming more popular. While many parts of Europe came to be dominated by socialist ideology and were openly hostile to religion, St. John Bosco and the Salesian charism represented another way of wrestling with the social question. It is the way of faith in action, working to transform the social order and rendering it more just. It succeeded, too, giving the Church's social teaching an early and prescient embodiment in the person of Don Bosco.

St. John Bosco was reputed to have worked miracles during his earthly life, and only slightly less so did he miraculously inspire others through his preaching. He died in Turin on January 31, 1888, was beatified in 1929, and was canonized in 1934. At his canonization, the saint was given the title of Father and Teacher of Youth by Pope Pius XI. He is venerated as the patron saint of Catholic publishers and young apprentices. Today, there are approximately 40,000 Salesian priests, brothers and sisters all over the world, active in about

120 countries. This makes the Salesians the third largest religious order of men in the Church after the Jesuits and the Franciscans. The Salesian sisters hold the distinction of being the largest order of consecrated women in the Church.—Robert J. Batule

BIBLIOGRAPHY AND FURTHER READING: Bosco, John. *The Spiritual Writings of Saint John Bosco.* Edited by Joseph Aubry and translated by Joseph Caselli. New Rochelle, NY: Salesians of Don Bosco, 1984; Stella, Pietro. *Don Bosco: Life and Works.* Translated by John Drury. New Rochelle, NY: Salesians of Don Bosco, 2005. *See also* EDUCATION, CATHOLIC: ELEMENTARY AND SECONDARY IN THE UNITED STATES

BURKE, CARDINAL RAYMOND LEO (1948–)

Raymond Leo Cardinal Burke was born on June 30, 1948, in Richland Center, Wisconsin, the youngest of six children. The parents of the future cardinal, Thomas F. and Marie B. Burke, operated a dairy farm. He attended Catholic parochial schools, first at St. Mary School in Richland Center from 1954 to 1959 and subsequently at St. Joseph School in Stratford, Wisconsin, from 1959 to 1962. Prayerfully discerning that he had a vocation to serve as a Catholic priest, the young Burke entered Holy Cross Seminary in La Crosse, Wisconsin, which he attended from 1962 until 1968, completing high school and several years of college study and formation.

As a seminary student, Burke excelled both in his academic and spiritual formation. Consequently, he was chosen to continue his philosophical studies at the Catholic University of America as a Basselin Scholar from 1968 to 1971, from which university he received his BA and MA in philosophy with highest honors. In 1971, Burke entered the Pontifical North American College in Rome and attended the Jesuits' Pontifical Gregorian University, where he completed his theological studies, again with the highest honors. His seminary classmates describe Burke as a holy, prayerful, intelligent, humble human being who desired nothing more than to serve God's people as a priest. Father Raymond L. Burke was ordained to the priesthood by Pope Paul VI in St. Peter's Basilica on July 29, 1975, on the Solemnity of SS. Peter and Paul.

Father Burke's first priestly assignment was as an associate at the Cathedral Parish of St. Joseph the Worker in La Crosse. During this time, he also taught at Aquinas High School in La Crosse. In obedience to his diocesan bishop, Burke returned to Rome from 1980 until 1983 to study canon law at the Pontifical Gregorian University, receiving his license and doctorate, summa cum laude. During his time as a doctoral student, the 1983 *Code of Canon Law* was promulgated, and Burke collaborated on a Latin–English dictionary of canonical terms in the new code—a dictionary that continues to be a reliable reference work. His 1984 Gregorian doctoral dissertation, *Lack of Discretion of Judgment Because of Schizophrenia: Doctrine and Recent Rotal Jurisprudence,* gained almost immediate recognition as an original contribution and definitive study of the subject. This work is notable not only for its significant substantive content but also for the careful and balanced canonical methodology employed throughout the study. Upon completion of his doctorate, Father Burke was named moderator of the Curia and vice chancellor of the Diocese of La Crosse. This period of his administrative service in the diocese was also rich in pastoral ministry, especially to farming families and to Hmong immigrants.

Burke again responded to the call of priestly obedience when, in 1989, Blessed Pope John Paul II named him the first American to hold the position of defender of the bond at the Apostolic Signatura. In Rome, Burke also served as member of the esteemed canon law faculty at the Gregorian University, where he taught in the jurisprudence program and directed doctoral dissertations. Additionally, he penned numerous scholarly articles on canonical and theological topics. After five years in this dual capacity as an official of the Roman Curia and a university professor, Monsignor Burke was named bishop of La Crosse on December 10, 1994. On the Solemnity of the Epiphany, January 6, 1995, Pope John Paul II ordained Bishop Burke in St. Peter's Basilica. With the grace of enlightenment, Bishop Burke inserted into his episcopal coat of arms the Latin words *Secundum Cor Tuum* ("According to Your Heart").

From the start of his episcopal ministry, Bishop Burke cultivated devotion to the Most Sacred Heart of Jesus. He continuously invited his flock to participate in the purifying and burning love of the Sacred Heart. During the Great Jubilee and Holy Year 2000, Bishop Burke enthroned the Sacred Heart in the Cathedral of St. Joseph the Worker. To encourage vocations to the priesthood, Burke reopened the high school seminary program. Keenly appreciative of the role of woman religious in the life of the Church, he nourished vocations to religious life. He tirelessly traveled his large rural diocese, frequenting parishes and schools, conferring the sacrament of Confirmation, defending the rights of family farmers, visiting the infirm and elderly, and showing great pastoral solicitude for his priests. Inspired by his great devotion to Our Lady, Bishop Burke founded the Shrine of Our Lady of Guadalupe, which he dedicated on July 31, 2008, and which quickly became a source of spiritual renewal for pilgrims from within and outside the diocese.

On December 2, 2003, Pope John Paul II appointed Burke as the archbishop of St. Louis. In the archdiocese, Archbishop Burke continued the indefatigable episcopal service that had characterized his earlier years in La Crosse. Continuing to promote devotion to the Most Sacred Heart, he enthroned the Sacred Heart in the Cathedral Basilica, where he created a Sacred Heart Altar consistent with the magnificent architectural structure of the edifice. At the heart of his plentiful ministry, Archbishop Burke contributed ample time and energy to the renewal of the Kenrick Glennon Seminary. Throughout his episcopal ministry, he continued to consult and write about various topics in canon law, theology, and the spiritual life. In 2007, he published an article, "Canon 915: The Discipline Regarding the Denial of Holy Communion to Those Obstinately Persisting in Manifest Grave Sin" (*Periodica* 96, 3–58). The scholarly article represents the mastery of the canonical sources and their integration with the theology of the Second Vatican Council. Archbishop Burke also supported the extraordinary form Mass and Rituals with all of their traditional beauty, reverence, and transcendence in the worship of God.

At the summit of his service as archbishop, his priestly obedience would be perfected when Pope Benedict XVI appointed him as prefect of the Supreme Tribunal of the Apostolic Signatura. In response to the Holy Father's need for his integration of holiness and intelligence, Archbishop Burke serenely accepted this new position and, without hesitation, left behind country, archdiocese, family, and many friends. On November 20, 2010, Pope Benedict created Archbishop Burke a cardinal, conferring the red hat upon him and entrusting him with all the profound responsibility of a member of the College of Cardinals of the Holy Roman Catholic Church.

Cardinal Burke has continued to be a forceful advocate for the culture of life. In so doing, he has encouraged Catholics to exercise their responsibilities in public life in a manner consistent with Catholic social teaching. He has also strongly urged Catholic institutions to maintain a strong Catholic identity.—John J. Coughlin, OFM

See also BERNARDIN, CARDINAL JOSEPH; CANON LAW; CHAPUT, CHARLES; O'CONNOR, JOHN CARDINAL

· C ·

CAMUS, ALBERT (1913–1960) Albert Camus was born into a working-class family in Mondovi, Algeria, on November 7, 1913. Though baptized a Catholic and raised in the faith by his mother (his father was killed in World War I when Albert was a child), he abandoned his religion while still a young man. At the age of 17, he contracted pulmonary tuberculosis, from which he nearly died, and for the rest of his days he had to deal with periodic flare-ups of that disease, a remarkable fact when one considers the high energy level at which he consistently lived his life.

From 1932 to 1936, Camus was a student of philosophy at the University of Algiers, working his way through that institution by holding down a variety of jobs. The thesis he wrote for his degree was on St. Augustine and Plotinus. In 1935, he founded a theater company, which he managed for the next four years, in the course of which, besides taking care of the business side of the enterprise, he wrote adaptations of plays, directed them, and acted in them as well. And thus began for him a lifelong and avid interest in the theater. It was during this period that he joined the Communist Party, but in relatively short order disenchantment on his part caused him to sever ties with that organization. As the years wore on, his negative attitude toward Communism became increasingly more pronounced. In 1938, he began his career as a journalist, writing for the *Alger Républicain*.

At the outbreak of World War II, unqualified for military service because of his tuberculosis, Camus moved to Paris and immediately became active in the French Resistance. He was eventually to become editor of *Combat*, a major underground newspaper, a position he continued to hold for a time after the war ended and the newspaper became a legal publication. Not long after his becoming established in Paris, he met and befriended Jean-Paul Sartre; however, the friendship was to be dissolved in 1951, rather tempestuously, because of sharp ideological differences between the two men. Camus's argument with Sartre had mainly to do with the latter's existentialist philosophy and with what Camus regarded as Sartre's unreasoning commitment to Communism. But both during and after their friendship, Camus and Sartre were numbered among France's most famous and influential intellectuals.

Camus's opinion that there was not a sharp distinction between literature and philosophy is tellingly exemplified in his own writings. He was a novelist of distinction, and three of his works, *The Stranger* (1942),

The Plague (1947), and *The Fall* (1956) continue to command devoted readers, especially in America, where Camus gained a popularity that seems never to have lagged. Camus was an accomplished playwright, and among his most well-known dramatic productions are *The Misunderstanding* (1944); *Caligula* (1945), which explored themes related to his notion of the absurd; and *The Just Ones* (1949). The two works by Camus that are principally philosophical in tone are *The Myth of Sisyphus* (1943) and *The Rebel* (1951). Camus was awarded the Nobel Prize for literature in 1957. His career as a writer, which showed every sign of having a number of promising developments yet to come, was brought to an abrupt halt on January 4, 1960, when he was killed in an auto crash. He was 47 years old.

Camus's philosophical thought, which is to be found as much in his novels and plays as in the two works named above, centered around the notion of rebellion in face of the absurd. He provides us with the most thorough explication of what he means by "the absurd" in *The Myth of Sisyphus*, a work that begins with the arresting assertion: "There is but one truly philosophical problem, and that is suicide." Why should that be so? Because man is an alienated creature, finding himself in an irrational universe that is completely antithetical to his deepest yearnings. And his life, besides being fraught with difficulties that he can neither surmount nor understand, culminates in the ultimate insult of death, which Camus describes as "the only reality." In view of this rather dire state of affairs, one might then suppose that suicide would be the logical choice for the absurd man, but in fact Camus rejects suicide as unacceptable, for that would represent undignified escapism. Nonetheless, it would be an equally escapist option on the part of the absurd man were he to succumb to hope. He must live a life where, as Camus puts it, there is no appeal. It is the fate of the absurd man to make the best he can of a hopeless situation. Like Sisyphus of ancient Greek myth, his role is relentlessly to exert himself in a task that, though meaningless—and indeed *because* of its very meaninglessness—becomes an act of uncompromising defiance, by which he discovers his dignity as a human being. It is through his unyielding revolt that the absurd man asserts his freedom.

The heart of the absurd man's painful condition, as Camus puts it in one place, is "the divorce between the mind that desires and the world that disappoints." What the human mind desires, and what the world cannot offer, is satisfaction for "that nostalgia for unity, that appetite for the absolute." For all the painful estrangement he feels because of the unfriendly cosmic setting

in which he finds himself, the absurd man has a burning love of life, taken in the sheer quantity of its varied experiences. And it is just his love of life that makes death so onerous a reality. He accepts his situation, but very much on his own terms—which is to say, rebelliously—and that means that he spurns any attitude that would smack of reconciliation or resignation. His lack of hope is not to be equated with despair, however; he is not a nihilist. He has sympathy for his fellow human beings, especially the poor, and he does what he can on their behalf, even though he realizes that in the end all his efforts are futile, for he is involved in a war where defeat is inevitable. The one glimmer of light in the otherwise oppressively dark world in which the absurd man finds himself has its source in his capacity to create. Creative activity can bring joy to the life of the absurd man, and although it cannot remove the darkness, it can at least lessen it somewhat.

The Rebel is an analytical, historical survey of what Camus regarded as the outstanding rebellious personages and movements, artistic and political, of modern times, beginning with the 18th century. The book develops many of the themes that were introduced in *The Myth of Sisyphus*, but now the emphasis is more on the social setting than on the individual. Rebellion is founded on individualism, but the individual is not alone. The rebellion we find advocated here has lost much of its forbidding starkness. The rebel is less repressed in spirit because he feels that somehow he is right, that his activity has value, that he might even manage to achieve, or at least make some progress toward, that order about which he had always dreamed. In contrast to existentialist thought, the rebel is willing to entertain the possibility that human beings share a common nature.

The book gives clear emphasis to Camus's disagreements with existentialism—which he regards as philosophical suicide because it essentially rests on negation—and to his vigorous opposition to Communism. The damning flaw of Communism is its mindless commitment to historical determinism, which gives it warrant to indulge liberally in mass murder, all for the sake of its purely theoretical constructs such as a purely utopian future. Unlike an absurdist view of the world, Communism is nihilistic; though claiming to be humanistic, it is in fact antihuman. Camus's rejection of Communism did not mean that he abandoned his deeply entrenched leftist and godless loyalties. The rebellious project he promoted was thoroughly secular in nature. His rebel turns his back on the whole supernatural order, and he does so with a kind of Luciferian adamancy.

Camus's philosophy of the absurd was doubtlessly sincerely held, but that does not save it from its essential superficiality. It was a point of view he had formulated as a very young man, and while he was to continue to develop it throughout the rest of his life, he never completely succeeded in ridding it of a certain adolescent quality, despite the powerful language in which it was consistently expressed. Though a formidable artist, Camus was not enough the philosopher to provide his rebel with that capacity for self-analysis that would have allowed him to liberate himself from a stance that—Camus's claim to the contrary notwithstanding—is unavoidably nihilistic. To turn one's back on the All, as the rebel does, is necessarily to settle for nothing. Camus's rebel finds himself at odds with the universe because he sees that universe as incapable of satisfying his nostalgia for unity, his aspiration for order, his appetite for the absolute. In light of that circumstance, there was a critically important question he failed to ask himself: Whence comes that nostalgia, that aspiration, that appetite? Successfully pursued, that question would have led him to the point where he ceased to be a stranger unto himself, for he would then have seen that he was himself integral to that unity for which he had always longed.—D. Q. McInerny

BIBLIOGRAPHY AND FURTHER READING: Aronson, Ronald. *Camus and Sartre*. Chicago: University of Chicago Press, 2004; Brée, Germaine. *Camus*. New Brunswick, NJ: Rutgers University Press, 1964; Champigny, Robert. *A Pagan Hero*. Philadelphia: University of Pennsylvania Press, 1969; Cruickshank, John. *Albert Camus and the Literature of Revolt*. London: Oxford University Press, 1959; Denton, David E. *The Philosophy of Albert Camus*. Boston: Prime, 1967; Hanna, Thomas. *The Thought and Art of Albert Camus*. Chicago: H. Regnery, 1958. *See also* NIHILISM; PHILOSOPHY, DISCIPLINE OF; SARTRE, JEAN-PAUL; SECULARIZATION

CARITAS IN VERITATE Pope Benedict XVI contributed to Catholic social teaching in his third encyclical, *Caritas in Veritate* (*Love in Truth*), dated June 29, 2009, and released in Rome a week later, on July 7, 2009. In so doing, Benedict took his place alongside other modern popes in addressing the issues of social welfare and social justice in the modern age.

The encyclical was drafted during a crisis in the world's economic system that erupted during the fall of 2008. It was, in part, a response to that crisis. At the time, some feared that a global economic "meltdown" might occur, bringing with it great human suffering and the end of an era of expanding world trade. These fears were so real that the promulgation of the text of the pope's encyclical, originally intended to commemorate the 40th anniversary of Pope Paul VI's *Populorum Progressio* was held back for nearly two years, in part to allow the extent and gravity of the economic crisis to be better seen and understood.

This caution of the Church's teaching authority in speaking about economic matters allows us to glimpse an important truth about all Catholic social teaching: social doctrine concerns essentially temporal, contingent matters. Precisely for this reason, social doctrine does not lend itself to dogmatic definition the way teaching on the Trinity or the Eucharist, for example, does. Social teaching, as Benedict teaches in *Caritas in Veritate*, must extrapolate from first principles of justice and right conduct to propose wise and just actions to individuals and governments to help build God's kingdom. But this does not make social doctrine unimportant or unnecessary, or the action of Christians in living according to that teaching less of an integral part of their moral duty as Christian believers. As Benedict writes, "Man's earthly activity, when inspired and sustained by charity, contributes to the building of the universal *city of God*, which is the goal of the history of the human family. In an increasingly globalized society, the common good and the effort to obtain it cannot fail to assume the dimensions of the whole human family . . . in such a way as to shape the *earthly city* in unity and peace, rendering it to some degree an anticipation and a prefiguration of the undivided *city of God*" (CV # 7).

Thus, the central concern of this encyclical is not to promulgate doctrinally binding dogmatic definitions with regard to human social and economic systems like capitalism, socialism, corporatism, or communism, but to shed light on a possible path toward greater justice and peace in human affairs, through actions of "love in truth," in order to build up the anticipated "undivided *city of God*."

On July 8, 2009, the day after the text of the encyclical was released in Rome, Benedict, at his Wednesday general audience, gave his own personal "analysis" of his just-published encyclical. *Caritas in Veritate* was inspired, Benedict said, by a passage in St. Paul's Letter to the Ephesians where "the Apostle speaks of acting according to the truth in love: 'Rather, living the truth in love, we should grow in every way into him who is the head, Christ.'"

Paul's teaching was that the guiding principle for all the actions of Christians should be "to live the truth in love." Benedict teaches that this is, in fact, the essence of *all* Catholic social doctrine. "The entire social doctrine of the Church," Benedict said, "revolves around the principle *caritas in veritate.*"

The opposite of *veritas* (truth), however, is falsehood, and the object of Benedict's encyclical is not only to set forth the truth but also to expose dangerous lies at the center of modern economic life, especially the lie that self-love or selfishness, not love for one's neighbor, is "good," and that a just and humane economic order can be built on the basis of selfishness.

In the West, it has become common to argue that selfishness, or self-interest, can be a basis for a dynamic economy and society because it so strongly motivates initiative. It is thus often considered "good" to be selfish, because this selfishness eventually brings about prosperity and happiness. But Benedict says this is a lie: "When those at the helm are motivated by purely selfish ends, instruments that are good in themselves can be transformed into harmful ones," he wrote. "It is man's darkened reason that produces these consequences" (*CV* # 36).

An age suffering from a "darkened reason" that proclaims the goodness of what is evil, needs to be converted. This is the central message of Pope Benedict in *Caritas in Veritate*. Mankind longs for, and deserves, an age not of "darkened reason," but of humble wisdom, an age of patient commitment to social and economic justice. In his encyclical, Benedict writes that a society that embraces the seductive but false idea that selfish passion is a solid basis for the organizing of human affairs is doomed to the frustration of its deepest hopes and longings. "In a climate of mutual trust, the market is the economic institution that permits encounter between persons," Benedict writes. "*Without internal forms of solidarity and mutual trust, the market cannot completely fulfill its proper economic function.* And today it is this trust which has ceased to exist, and the loss of trust is a grave loss" (*CV* # 35).

Benedict sets forth in his encyclical a vision for a human society that can provide the opportunity for rich and fulfilling human lives, with the joy of family life, with productive work, and without excessive anxiety over material needs, so that the world may become more nearly a place where men and women can become what St. Irenaeus says they are when they are truly alive: God's glory ("The glory of God is man alive"; St. Irenaeus of Lyons, *Against Heresies*, book 4, chapter 20, 7). Benedict's vision is a generous, expansive, confident Christian humanism that he offers to a world buffeted by economic crises and persuaded that competition and selfishness are the overarching motive forces

of human activity, not acts of "love in truth." The pope writes in his encyclical: "The Church has always held that economic action is not to be regarded as something opposed to society. In and of itself, the market is not, and must not become, the place where the strong subdue the weak" (*CV* # 36).

The roots of Benedict's beliefs in this regard go far back. The finance minister of Italy, Giulio Tremonti, said on November 20, 2008, that Benedict was the first to predict the crisis in the global financial system, referring to a "prophecy" in a paper Benedict wrote when he was a cardinal. As Cardinal Joseph Ratzinger in 1985, Benedict presented a paper entitled "Market Economy and Ethics" at a Rome event dedicated to the Church and the economy. He said a decline in ethics "can actually cause the laws of the market to collapse." And in an October 7, 2008, speech, Benedict, reflecting on crashing markets, concluded that "money vanishes, it is nothing" and warned that "the only solid reality is the word of God."

Thus, Benedict has long felt that virtue, trust, fair dealing, and a concern for the common good—and ethics of human solidarity, and ethics of "charity in truth"—would pay economic dividends, while selfishness, deception, greed, and vice would lead to a loss of trust and to eventual collapse in the financial markets.

In *Caritas in Veritate*, Pope Benedict tells us that the Church's social teaching has developed considerably in the 118 years between Leo XIII's *Rerum Novarum* in 1891 and 2009. The teaching developed, he tells us, in order to reflect changing economic, technological, and social situations. And Benedict uses one word to summarize the chief "novelty" the Church finds at the outset of the 21st century: globalization. "The principal new feature has been the explosion of worldwide interdependence, commonly known as globalization," Benedict writes. "Paul VI had partially foreseen it, but the ferocious pace at which it has evolved could not have been anticipated. Originating within economically developed countries, this process by its nature has spread to include all economies" (*CV* # 33).

One of Benedict's essential purposes in this encyclical, then, is to assess this "new thing" he calls "globalization." He seeks to explain how this unexpected, even unforeseeable, reality, brought about by new technologies—from global air travel to instantaneous global communication via computers, with accompanying rapid movements of capital worldwide—affects what the Church teaches about social justice and the common good. The chief proposal that the pope gives in response to this new globalization is that this globalization process requires some type of wise, equally global, authority to guide and control it for the common good.

Some worried readers of Benedict's encyclical saw in this papal proposal something to be feared, an embryonic "one-world government" inimical to the best interests of mankind, and so they criticized this aspect of the pope's teaching. But others noted that the pope was calling not for a "world government" but for a morally upright world "authority" to restrain excesses of a de facto "world order" that already exists and exercises great power, but does not do so in the interest of the poor and the weak. In this regard, the pope wrote: "To manage the global economy; to revive economies hit by the crisis; to avoid any deterioration of the present crisis and the greater imbalances that would result; to bring about integral and timely disarmament, food security and peace; to guarantee the protection of the environment and to regulate migration: for all this, there is urgent need of a true world political authority, as my predecessor Blessed John XXIII indicated some years ago. Such an authority would need to be regulated by law, to observe consistently the principles of subsidiarity and solidarity, to seek to establish the common good, and to make a commitment to securing authentic integral human development inspired by the values of charity in truth" (*CV* # 67).

The pope wrote this encyclical because he felt the sorrow of impoverished men and women who have little hope. "It is undeniable that the liberal model of the market economy, especially as moderated and corrected under the influence of Christian social ideas, has in some parts of the world led to great success," Benedict said when, as Cardinal Ratzinger, he spoke in Benevento, Italy ("Eucharist, Communion and Solidarity," June 2, 2002). "All the sadder are the results, especially in places like Africa, where clashing power blocs and economic interests have been at work. Behind the apparent beneficial models of development there has all too often been hidden the desire to expand the reach of particular powers and ideologies in order to dominate the market. In this situation, ancient social structures and spiritual and moral forces have been destroyed, with consequences that echo in our ears like a single great cry of sorrow."

The encyclical is a call for justice in economic dealings—for an end to the oppression of the weak by the strong due to economic policies marked by recklessness and deception, enriching a few and impoverishing many.

The use of technology is another key theme in the encyclical. At the official July 7 press conference that unveiled *Caritas in Veritate*, Cardinal Renato Martino,

president of the Pontifical Council for Justice and Peace (PCJP), along with the council's secretary, Archbishop Giampaolo Crepaldi, pointed to technology as a new "sign of the times." Cardinal Martino said that Cold War ideologies "have been replaced by the new ideology of technology" and that the "arbitrary nature of technology is one of the greatest problems of today's world." Archbishop Crepaldi explained that *Caritas in Veritate* is "the first time an encyclical deals with this theme [of technology] so fully."

The last chapter of the encyclical is devoted entirely to "the development of peoples and technology." Summarizing the previous five chapters, Pope Benedict writes that the "supremacy of technology tends to prevent people from recognizing anything that cannot be explained in terms of matter alone" (*CV* # 77) and advises that "development must include not just material growth but also spiritual growth" (*CV* # 76). In one of the most powerful passages in the encyclical, Benedict warns of the dangers an amoral technology poses to humanity. It could even create a type of mental and spiritual prison for most human beings, cutting them off from the transcendent, that is, ultimately, from God. "Technological development can give rise to the idea that technology is self-sufficient when too much attention is given to the 'how' questions, and not enough to the many 'why' questions underlying human activity," Benedict writes (*CV* # 70).

He continues: "The process of globalization could replace ideologies with technology, allowing the latter to become an ideological power that threatens to confine us within an *a priori* that holds us back from encountering being and truth. Were that to happen, we would all know, evaluate and make decisions about our life situations from within a technocratic cultural perspective to which we would belong structurally, without ever being able to discover a meaning that is not of our own making. The 'technical' worldview that follows from this vision is now so dominant that truth has come to be seen as coinciding with the possible. But when the sole criterion of truth is efficiency and utility, development is automatically denied. True development does not consist primarily in 'doing.' . . . Even when we work through satellites or through remote electronic impulses, our actions always remain human, an expression of our responsible freedom . . . . Moving beyond the fascination that technology exerts, we must reappropriate the true meaning of freedom, which is not an intoxication with total autonomy, but a response to the call of being, beginning with our own personal being" (*CV* # 70).

The encyclical contains an introduction, six chapters, and a conclusion. In the introduction, the pope recalls how "charity is at the heart of the Church's social doctrine" (*CV* # 2) and makes it clear that authentic human development has need of truth. In this context, he dwells on two "criteria that govern moral action" (*CV* # 6): justice and the common good.

Chapter 1 focuses on the message of Paul VI's *Populorum Progressio*, which "underlined the indispensable importance of the Gospel for building a society according to freedom and justice" (*CV* # 13).

Chapter 2 is entitled "Human Development in Our Time." Here, the pope discusses the global economic system and its bases. If profit, the pope writes, "becomes the exclusive goal, if it is produced by improper means and without the common good as its ultimate end, it risks destroying wealth and creating poverty" (*CV* # 21). He also dwells on the question of respect for life, affirming that "when a society moves towards the denial or suppression of life, it ends up no longer finding the necessary motivation and energy to strive for man's true good" (*CV* # 28).

Chapter 3, "Fraternity, Economic Development and Civil Society," opens with a passage praising the "experience of gift," often insufficiently recognized "because of a purely consumerist and utilitarian view of life" (*CV* # 34). Referring to *Centesimus Annus*, he highlights the "need for a system with three subjects: the market, the State and civil society" (*CV* # 38) and highlights the importance of "economic forms based on solidarity" (*CV* # 39). The chapter closes with a fresh evaluation of the phenomenon of globalization.

In chapter 4, "The Development of People: Rights and Duties; The Environment," he also dedicates attention to "the problems associated with population growth" and the family. States, he says, "are called to enact policies promoting the centrality and the integrity of the family" (*CV* # 44).

Chapter 5 is devoted to the "cooperation of the human family." Here, Pope Benedict highlights how "the development of peoples depends, above all, on the recognition that the human race is a single family" (*CV* # 53). Hence Christianity and other religions "can offer their contribution to development only if God has a place in the public realm" (*CV* # 56). The pope also makes reference to the principle of subsidiarity, which, he explains, "is the most effective antidote against any form of all-encompassing welfare state" (*CV* # 57). He dedicates the final paragraph of this chapter to the "urgent need" for "a true world political authority" with "effective power" (*CV* # 67).

Chapter 6 is entitled "The Development of Peoples and Technology." In it, the Holy Father warns against the "Promethean presumption" of humanity thinking "it can re-create itself through the 'wonders' of technology," adding: "A particularly crucial battleground in today's cultural struggle between the supremacy of technology and human moral responsibility is the field of bioethics" (*CV* # 74). The pope also expresses his concern over a possible "systematic eugenic programming of births" (*CV* # 75).

Finally, in the conclusion, Benedict XVI highlights how "development needs Christians with their arms raised towards God in prayer" just as it needs "love and forgiveness, self-denial, acceptance of others, justice and peace" (*CV* # 79).

The reception of the encyclical was varied. The secular press tended to criticize the pope's "conservative" stance on marriage and family issues. Among Catholics, there was a spectrum of opinion: some praised it; others found reason for complaint. And one prominent writer developed a theory of the text's history that prompted controversy and outrage. Catholic writer Donald Goodman of the *Distributist Review* said he found *Caritas in Veritate* "a mixed blessing" because, although it "contains numerous reaffirmations of the perennial social teaching of the Catholic Church, blazes new ground in some areas, and makes explicit what was only implicit in some earlier writings," it "leaves off a good deal of what was great and powerful in past statements of the Church's social teaching—most especially, it is completely devoid of any acknowledgment of Christ the King. . . . This is troubling."

Thomas Woods, author of *The Church and the Market: A Catholic Defense of the Free Economy*, was even harsher. The encyclical, he said, is a relatively unremarkable restatement of familiar themes from previous social encyclicals, containing policy recommendations that will attract no one to the Church and so represents a "gigantic missed opportunity," forgoing legitimate concerns and criticisms regarding the structure of the world's monetary systems for "platitudinous warnings about materialism and greed."

Many said they found clear signs that the encyclical was the work of several hands, and minds, and that this was a reason for the perplexity many felt in reading the document. The introduction and conclusion do seem clearly to be the product of Benedict himself, marked by his own personal theological emphasis and use of language and imagery. In the encyclical's six chapters, however, many passages and ideas seem just as clearly to be drawn from helpers and advisors who assisted the pope in preparing this text.

One of the pope's advisors on the upcoming encyclical was Father Mario Toso, a professor of social philosophy at the Pontifical Salesian University and from 2003 to 2007 the rector magnificus of the university. Toso is one of the leading social philosophers in Italy and a Salesian. As a consultor of the PCJP, he has taken part in studies on nonviolence and problems of land distribution.

The most radical presentation of the position that the encyclical seemed to have been stitched together from various sources came from George Weigel, who argued that the encyclical could be divided up into "red" and "gold" passages, the "red" passages written by officials of the PCJP, the "gold" sections written by Benedict himself. Weigel made the argument that "in the often unpredictable world of the Vatican," the PCJP had a different "agenda" for this encyclical than Benedict himself.

Weigel, noting that the PCJP sees itself as "the curial keeper of the flame of authentic Catholic social teaching," said the council prepared drafts of the encyclical that did not meet Benedict's approval. "It is one of the worst-kept secrets in Rome that at least two drafts of such an encyclical, and perhaps three, were rejected by Pope Benedict XVI," Weigel said. He continued: "Benedict XVI's long-awaited and much-delayed social encyclical seems to be a hybrid, blending the Pope's own insightful thinking on the social order with elements of the Justice and Peace approach to Catholic social doctrine."

Weigel said that the "clearly Benedictine" passages in the encyclical are the strong emphasis on the life issues (abortion, euthanasia, embryo-destructive stem-cell research) as social justice issues and the sections on the inherent linkage between charity and truth. And he concluded: "Those with eyes to see and ears to hear will concentrate their attention, in reading *Caritas in Veritate*, on those parts of the encyclical that are clearly Benedictine."

Weigel's analysis sparked outrage in some quarters. "The hubris of George Weigel knows no bounds," wrote Michael Sean Winters in *America*. "In his denunciations of the passages he dislikes, Weigel is not simply ideologically skewed but downright insulting to Pope Benedict. Weigel is wrong."

But Weigel was not alone in seeing something odd in the construction of this encyclical. Peter Steinfels of the *New York Times* wondered, "Why is *Caritas in Veritate* so poorly written?" and added: "That is meant as a serious, honest question. . . . The matter is all the more confounding since Benedict has often shown himself a graceful writer, and one who has insisted on the importance of beauty in communicating his Church's message."

The essential message of Benedict's encyclical remains the essential message of all Catholic social teaching: that we must combat the social injustice of our time by a return to Christian life and institutions, and by fixing men's eyes not on the passing things of this earth, but on the things that are above. It is a teaching that echoes the words of Pope Pius XI in his powerful 1931 encyclical, *Quadragesimo Anno*, written in the depths of the Great Depression. "It is obvious that not only is wealth concentrated in our times," Pius wrote, "but an immense power and despotic economic dictatorship is consolidated in the hands of a few" (*QA* # 105). "Economic dictatorship has supplanted the free market; unbridled ambition for power has likewise succeeded greed for gain; all economic life has become tragically hard, inexorable, and cruel (*QA* # 109). "'Wherefore,' to use the words of Our Predecessor, 'if human society is to be healed, only a return to Christian life and institutions will heal it.' For this alone can provide effective remedy for that excessive care for passing things that is the origin of all vices; and this alone can draw away men's eyes, fascinated by and wholly fixed on the changing things of the world, and raise them toward Heaven. Who would deny that human society is in most urgent need of this cure now?" (*QA* # 129).—Robert Moynihan

See also BIOETHICS; *DEUS CARITAS EST*; GLOBALIZATION; POPE BENEDICT XVI; SOLIDARITY; *SPE SALVI*; SUBSIDIARITY; TECHNOLOGY; WEIGEL, GEORGE

CASAROLI, CARDINAL AGOSTINO (1914– 1998) "You have always sought to love and serve men—all men of any peoples—accepting everyone in the light of God's providential design. . . . Your appreciation of the value of human intelligence, enlightened and fortified by Christian faith, and of the connatural fragility of man led you to that typical 'historical realism,' which accompanied you in your daily work and remains for us too a useful lesson for our lives" ("Pope John Paul II's Letter to Cardinal Agostino Casaroli on the Occasion of His XXV Year of Episcopal Ordination," *Osservatore Romano*, July 3, 1992).

Born in Castel San Giovanni near Piacenza, Italy, in 1914, Agostino Casaroli, having completed his early formation at the seminary in Bedonia and the Alberoni College in Piacenza, studied canon law at the Lateran University and diplomacy at the Pontifical Ecclesiastical Academy. Ordained in 1937, he joined the Secretariat of State three years later. Already entrusted with delicate assignments by Pope John XXIII, he was elevated to the episcopate by Pope Paul VI in 1967 and named secretary of the Congregation for Extraordinary Ecclesiastical Affairs. Then, in 1979, Pope John Paul II made him a cardinal at his first consistory. From that year until 1990, he was secretary of state and prefect of the Council for the Public Affairs of the Church. John Paul II also made him president of the Commission for the Vatican City State and, in 1984, charged him with representing the pontiff before the civil government of the Vatican City State. He died of cardio-respiratory complications in Rome in 1998 and is buried in the Roman Basilica of the Twelve Holy Apostles.

Agostino Casaroli's name is associated with the opening up of the Vatican relations with the former Soviet Bloc, a policy improperly known as *Ostpolitik* by a somewhat misleading analogy with the parallel developments of German policy toward Eastern Europe. Casaroli was first sent to several Eastern European countries by Pope John XXIII in 1963. Then, under Pope Paul VI, he was entrusted with negotiations with Hungary and the then Czechoslovakia and Yugoslavia. He was the special delegate of the Holy See to the Conference on European Security and Cooperation in Helsinki, Finland, in 1975, at which the Holy See was a discreet but forceful proponent of human rights and religious freedom.

Under John Paul II, in 1988, Cardinal Casaroli led the Holy See delegation to celebrate the millennium of Russian Christianity and met the newly elected secretary of the Communist Party, Mikhail Gorbachev, who would be received at the Vatican a year later. Assessing Vatican Ostpolitik is not an easy task, even if one only considers the plurality of popes and secretaries of state involved and the significant differences among Eastern European countries. In any event, Casaroli, who regarded himself as a man of dialogue and above all a faithful servant of all the popes he served, was the first to acknowledge the opportunities of this policy but also its shortcomings, flowing from the very nature and contradictions of the Communist system.

Restricting Casaroli's significance to the role he played in the policy toward Eastern Europe, though, would be a disservice to history and his own biography. In 1961 and 1963, he led the Holy See delegations to the Vienna Conferences on diplomatic and consular re-

lations; in 1964, he represented it at the exchange of the instruments of ratification of the modus vivendi with Tunisia; in 1971, he delivered the Vatican's instrument of adhesion to the nuclear nonproliferation treaty; in 1984, he signed the revised Concordat between the Holy See and Italy; a year later, he presided over the signing of the peace treaty between Argentina and Chile that was the result of the successful papal mediation between the two countries regarding the Beagle Channel dispute; and finally, in 1990, after signing in New York the Convention on the Rights of the Child, he represented the Holy See in Paris at the summit of heads of states that led to the adoption of the charter for a new Europe. To the end of his life, he was committed to his priestly ministry and to assisting young detainees (as he had done since the 1940s) in the jail for minors at Casal del Marmo, Rome.—Maurizio Ragazzi

BIBLIOGRAPHY AND FURTHER READING: Barberini, Giovanni, ed. *La politica del dialogo: Le carte Casaroli sull'Ostpolitik vaticana.* Bologna: Società editrice Il Mulino, 2008; Casaroli, Agostino. *The Martyrdom of Patience: The Holy See and the Communist Countries (1963–1989).* Translated by Marco Bagnarol. Toronto: Ave Maria Centre of Peace, 2007; Casaroli, Agostino. *Nella Chiesa per il mondo: Omelie e discorsi.* Milan: Rusconi, 1987; Comolli, Gian Maria, and Giacomo Sala Danna. *Agostino Casaroli per la fede e la giustizia.* Piacenza: Editrice Berti, 2004; Silvestrini, Achille, ed. *L'Ostpolitik di Agostino Casaroli, 1963–1989.* Bologna: Edizioni Dehoniane, 2009. *See also* COMMUNISM; CONCORDATS; HOLY SEE (INTERNATIONAL STATUS AND ROLE); INTERNATIONAL LAW; INTERNATIONAL RELATIONS: CATHOLIC PERSPECTIVE ON; POPE BLESSED JOHN XXIII; POPE JOHN PAUL II; POPE PAUL VI; TREATIES IN CATHOLIC SOCIAL TEACHING

CATHOLIC HEALTH ASSOCIATION OF THE UNITED STATES (CHA)

The Catholic Health Association of the United States (CHA) is the national membership organization of the Catholic health care ministry in the United States. "The Love of Christ Urges Us" (2 Corinthians 5:14) is its motto. Founded as the Catholic Hospital Association of the United States and Canada in 1915, a separate association was founded in Canada in 1954. In 1979, CHA adopted its present name.

According to the American Hospital Association's 2009 survey, there were 636 U.S. Catholic hospitals with 121,821 beds, representing 12.7% of hospitals and 15.1% of hospital beds in the nation. About one in six of all persons admitted to a hospital receives care in a Catholic facility. In addition to hospital facilities, CHA membership includes home health, hospice, and long-term care and assisted living facilities.

The roots of CHA are found in the development of the modern hospital. In the late 19th century, the American hospital was evolving from a place of welcome for the poor to a site for surgical interventions, made possible by advances in analgesia and antisepsis. Prior to the surgical advances, many middle-class persons could receive almost all available health care needs in their homes. In the mid-19th century, only approximately 16% of physicians ever made calls to local hospitals. Catholic, Protestant, and other not-for-profit hospitals in the United States were well positioned to become the sites of new medical treatment.

By the dawn of the 20th century, rapid and ongoing scientific advances and tremendous energy were present in the medical and hospital sectors of the nation. New associations of professionals, such as the American College of Surgeons, brought the spirit of reform to the variation of quality in the nation's hospitals. The College looked to rate hospitals based on their educational and quality standards. The "standardization" movement also sought to link hospitals to improved and accredited medical education.

An observer of these trends was Rev. Charles B. Moulinier, SJ, who was regent (the Jesuit superior's representative) at the medical school of Marquette University in Milwaukee. Father Moulinier supported standardization and held the perspective of medical education. As a result of a retreat he preached to hospital sisters, his conversation and concern about Catholic hospitals developed. In a conference planned with leaders of hospital sisters in 1914, he proposed an association of Catholic hospitals to facilitate the transition of the facilities through the challenges presented by standardization. The following year, CHA was established near Marquette University with Father Moulinier as president until 1928.

Standardization was an external challenge to Catholic hospitals that presented the need for an internal response if they were to survive. The two elements of response to external challenges and demands and internal development seem to characterize CHA in the decades since.

As noted, standardization represented an external review that eventually led to accreditation processes. Early voices within the new CHA structure expressed concern that the integrity of Catholic hospitals and the Catholic medical ethics tradition could be governed by external and secular accrediting authorities. Therefore, Father Moulinier had two major objectives: first, to provide educational resources for Catholic hospitals to meet the reasonable and scientific expectations of the new century, and second, to preserve the ministerial and moral ethos of the facilities. With respect to the moral concerns, Father Moulinier accepted the surgical ethics code of the College of Surgeons but also published a Catholic ethics code in the first issue of CHA's journal *Hospital Progress* (now *Health Progress*). The code of ethics published by CHA is the antecedent for the *Ethical and Religious Directives for Catholic Health Care Services (ERD)*.

The early decades of the 20th century saw the Church in the United States transition from the status of mission territory. During World War I, the National Catholic War Council was established as an organization of the nation's bishops. In 1919, the bishops created the National Catholic Welfare Council (which later became the National Catholic Welfare Conference). The council granted recognition to CHA that same year.

CHA became a gathering place for Catholic hospitals and the hierarchy during a turbulent period in the national health care sector. CHA suggested the development of diocesan health care liaisons of the Ordinary to Catholic hospitals of the diocese and to CHA itself. The significance of CHA for conversation *within* the Catholic health care ministry perhaps has less visibility but is of great significance for the history of the Church in the nation. It lies in the American experience of the movements of European immigration and the religious institutes of women and men who established hospitals, often at first for discrete ethnic populations. CHA provided a place for vowed religious and their unique and distinct charisms to meet each other and build a common and ongoing understanding of Catholic health care ministry.

Communities of vowed religious women are the primary sponsors of American Catholic hospitals, and sister leadership has been present in CHA from its founding. The constitutions of religious institutes of women did not, however, permit their leadership in national organizations at the early stages of CHA's history. As these constitutions were modified, vowed women religious assumed a range of leadership roles in CHA.

In recent decades, CHA continued its response to external political issues perceived as a threat to the ministry. If standardization presented a first risk, the profound economic disruption of the Great Depression brought a next and profound risk. Another challenge was presented by national developments in nursing education in the 1930s, which were seen as a risk to hospital-based nursing education. There were proponents of both college- and hospital-based nursing education in CHA.

Following World War II, CHA and the voluntary hospital sector opposed national health insurance initiatives introduced in Congress due to fear that nonprofit hospitals would be excluded from the national program. Reimbursement issues continue to be pressing issues for the health care sector, including the transitions to the Medicare and Medicaid programs in the 1960s. In the 1970s, CHA took an advocacy stance it still maintains based on human dignity and the moral right of basic health care access for all persons. This position was reflected in the Affordable Care Act of 2010. CHA found a major challenge to integrity in the years following *Roe v. Wade* (1973) when the threat of mandatory participation in procured abortion was a pronounced one, until the Church Amendment provided protection.

Pope John Paul II addressed CHA membership at a special assembly during the pope's 1987 pastoral visit. His speech remains the most significant charter statement for the health care ministry in the United States.

CHA has developed an increasing emphasis on the internal service dimensions of its work since the 1970s. The internal technical and scientific educational activities of CHA are no longer necessary. A more recent focus has been CHA's work in providing standards for "community benefit" programs so that Catholic hospitals can preserve their nonprofit status. Catholic health care ethics discussion has been a hallmark concern of CHA from the earliest summer educational sessions and the important presence of Rev. Gerald Kelly, SJ, who later figured in the development of *ERD*.

In recent decades, health care organizations have grown more complex while the number of professed religious in the ministry has continued to decline. In 1965, 97% of Catholic hospitals in the United States had administrators who were vowed religious. By 1985, the number of vowed religious had declined to about 30%. In the mid-1990s, CHA began an initiative for formation of laypersons for leadership in the Catholic health care ministry, which has its imperative in the Gospel mandate of compassion and service. The need for this type of lay formation is increasingly apparent; by 2010, less than 1% of administrators were vowed religious.

In "Catholic Health Ministry 2020: Steeped in Tradition, Focused on the Future," CHA has identified five goals for the ministry in its response to the Gospel and Catholic teaching and values: "Continue to champion the sanctity of life from conception to natural death," "Lead the development of sustainable, person-centered models of care across the continuum," "Meet the current and emerging needs of vulnerable persons," "Engage all who are called to serve through a ministry-wide commitment to formation," and "Broaden and deepen our relationships with the community of the Church."—Joseph J. Piccione

BIBLIOGRAPHY AND FURTHER READING: Catholic Health Association of the United States. "Our Vision for the Next Decade." St. Louis: CHA, 2010; Kauffman, Christopher J. "Church and Society: Developments during the Schwitalla Years, 1928–1947." *Health Progress*, May 1990, 29–37; Kauffman, Christopher J. "Development of a Service Organization: CHA from Post–World War II through Vatican II." *Health Progress*, June 1990, 29–37; Kauffman, Christopher J. "The Leadership of Father Moulinier: The Catholic Hospital Association Comes of Age, 1921–1928." *Health Progress*, March 1990, 41–48; Kauffman, Christopher J. *Ministry and Meaning: A Religious History of Catholic Health Care in the United States.* New York: Crossroad, 1995; Kauffman, Christopher J. "The Modern Association: Preserving a Catholic Presence in the U.S. Healthcare System." *Health Progress*, July–August 1990, 35–46; Kauffman, Christopher J. "The Push for Standardization: The Origins of the Catholic Hospital Asociation, 1914–1920." *Health Progress*, January–February 1990, 57–65; Kauffman, Christopher J. "Years of Transition: Internal Developments under Fr. Schwitalla, 1928–1947." *Health Progress*, April 1990, 33–41; Pentland, Sharon. "What's Past Is Prologue." *Health Progress*, January–February 1995, 55–71. *See also* ETHICAL AND RELIGIOUS DIRECTIVES FOR CATHOLIC HEALTH CARE SERVICES; WOMEN'S RELIGIOUS ORDERS AND THE SOCIAL APOSTOLATE

CENTER FOR APPLIED RESEARCH IN THE APOSTOLATE (CARA)

The Center for Applied Research in the Apostolate (CARA) is a Washington, D.C.-based nonprofit organization devoted to applied social scientific research that supports and advances the mission of the Catholic Church. CARA principally administers and analyzes surveys for Catholic parishes, dioceses, and other Church agencies. Its main ongoing programs include customized parish surveys, an annual (or more frequent) national telephone poll of American Catholics, a database of U.S. Catholic parishes, an annual census of Catholic seminaries, and the publication of *The CARA Report*, a quarterly digest of institutionally Catholic-oriented research. CARA also maintains nationally aggregated databases of information on the U.S. Church, including parishes, clergy, seminarian enrollments, vowed religious, and Catholic school enrollments, as well as American Catholic laity; conducts yearly data gathering for the annual reports and decision making of a number of Catholic organizations; and engages in contract research and consulting with and for a wide variety of national Catholic apostolates and groups, providing a full range of services for gathering and interpreting data, including focus groups, content analysis, and demographic mapping.

CARA's work is characterized by high standards of professional objectivity and the use of precise statistical methods and data validation. Its senior research associates all have graduate degrees in their academic fields and hold faculty positions at Georgetown University.

Conceived by Richard Cardinal Cushing, CARA was founded in 1964 after consultation among more than a dozen national apostolates, including several associations of religious orders, Serra International, and the Knights of Columbus. Its formation reflected the intersection of several forces: the growing confidence in scientific research to contribute to the solution of social issues, the emphasis of the Second Vatican Council on accurate sociocultural knowledge—discerning the signs of the times—for Church mission, and the ongoing national consolidation of Catholic institutional structures in America. In the background was the emergence of Catholic sociology from a separate emphasis on Catholic thought to the adoption of methods and ideas of the American academic mainstream. By the middle of the 20th century, the establishment of research and planning efforts to address social issues was well advanced in most sectors of American society. At about the same time began the formation of diocesan offices of research and/or pastoral planning, which exist today in about half of U.S. dioceses.

CARA was initially envisioned as an agent of universalism to help the American Church move into an era of global society. In his 1964 address inaugurating the Center, Archbishop (later Cardinal) Cody of New Orleans likened it, in purpose, to the recently formed World Bank or the U.S. Agency for International Development. CARA's role was to help move the U.S. Church from a parochial to a more universalist vision by the use of modern methods "so that American Catholics [can] function effectively in the universal apostolate of the Church." In the early 1980s, CARA was instrumental in founding, and was the administering agency in the Americas, of the World Values Survey, a widely used panel study of trends in social values.

Initially, CARA was expected not to do its own research primarily, but to enable scholarly reflection and collective social action by the wider Church. With the participation of a council of scholars, CARA was, according to Archbishop Cody, expected to "draw on the vast resources of the Church in the United States for the latest findings in sociology, Scripture, theology, psychology, missiology, area studies, anthropology, economics, catechetics, liturgy, agronomy, and any other relevant science [that will contribute to the success of the Church's spiritual and social mission]. It will promote such research by Catholic universities and professional groups"; only "some specialized research [would] be carried out by the center itself." It was purposely located in the national capital of Washington, D.C., to better "serve as a focal point for the continuing reexamination and rethinking of apostolic methods."

These lofty prophetic aims have diminished since the 1960s. With the growing emphasis on data-based management techniques, CARA developed in-house applied research expertise, which became increasingly valued on the micro rather than the macro level. Today CARA is primarily a center doing in-house applied studies for clients, employing contract researchers to augment the work of its full-time staff. Practically speaking, the need to market its services widely to American Catholics effectively limits controversial departures from mainstream American Catholic thought, either to the left or to the right, in CARA's work. The chair of CARA's board, moreover, has always been a cardinal or a bishop.

As an independent center governed by its own board of directors, CARA does not function with catechetical authority and must continually seek independent funding for its work. CARA addresses this reality by keeping its research descriptive, atheoretical, and detail oriented, leaving the decision making to the client Church agency and further reflection on its research to other Catholic university scholars. This strategy is reflected in CARA's stated policy "to let research findings stand on their own and never take an advocacy position or go into areas outside its social science competence." Today CARA's mission states three main goals: "to increase the Church's self-understanding; to serve the applied research needs of Church decision-makers; and to advance scholarly research on religion, particularly Catholicism."—D. Paul Sullins

BIBLIOGRAPHY AND FURTHER READING: Cody, John P. "His Excellency Announces the Center for Applied Research in the Apostolate." Washington, DC: CARA, 1964; Gannon, Francis X. "Bridging the Research Gap:

CARA, Response to Vatican II." *Review of Religious Research* 9, no. 1 (1967): 3–11; McCarthy, Richard D. "CARA Offers a Unique Service to Church in the United States," *Congressional Record* 116: 183, November 17, 1970.

CHAPUT, CHARLES (1944–) Charles Chaput is the archbishop of Philadelphia. Born in Concordia, Kansas, Chaput entered the Franciscan Capuchins in 1965 in Pittsburgh, Pennsylvania. Having obtained a bachelor's degree in philosophy from St. Fidelis College in 1967, Chaput then solemnly professed his vows as a friar in 1968. In 1970, he was awarded a master's degree in religious education from the Capuchin College in Washington, D.C., and was ordained a priest on August 29 that same year. In 1971, he earned a master's degree in theology from the University of San Francisco.

Between 1971 and 1974, then Father Chaput taught theology and gave spiritual direction at St. Fidelis, his alma mater in Herman, Pennsylvania. Continuing a service to his own order, he worked as executive secretary and director of communications for three years from 1974 to 1977. In 1977, he was named the pastor of Holy Cross Parish in Thornton, Colorado. That same year, he was also elected to the position of vicar provincial for the Capuchins of Mid-America. Three years later, Father Chaput took on the responsibilities of secretary and treasurer for this same province. In 1983, he became its chief executive and provincial minister.

In his 18th year of priestly ministry, Pope John Paul II chose him to be the bishop of Rapid City, South Dakota. Chaput's episcopal ordination took place in the diocesan cathedral there on July 26, 1988. Nine years later, Chaput was selected by the pontiff to be the fourth archbishop of Denver, succeeding James F. Stafford who went to serve in the Roman Curia as president of the Pontifical Council on the Laity. In 2011, Chaput was transferred by Pope Benedict XVI to the metropolitan see of Philadelphia, replacing Justin Cardinal Regali.

Archbishop Chaput is the author of two books. The first, *Living the Catholic Faith: Rediscovering the Basics*, grew out of a popular series of lectures he delivered in the Jubilee Year of 2000. The second is titled *Render unto Caesar: Serving the Nation by Living Our Catholic Beliefs in Political Life*. It calls upon Catholics not to retreat from the public square because of the unpopularity of Catholic teaching on controversial topics like abortion and the death penalty. Chaput presents a case in this volume for a more vigorous participation on the part of Catholics in the great moral questions of the day. This,

he contends, can only help the United States be true to the principles upon which it was founded.

Many of the themes taken up by Chaput in his second book are found in his columns in the *Denver Catholic Register*, the archdiocesan newspaper, and in addresses he has given before audiences around the United States. What Chaput eagerly wants for American Catholics is a profoundly serious engagement with the truth. He points out in *Render unto Caesar* that "the Gospel says that we will know the truth, and the truth will make us free (John 8: 32)—not comfortable; not respected; but free in the real sense of the word: able to see and do what's right." Doing what is right has a cost, however. "We can't follow Jesus Christ without sharing in his cross," the archbishop writes. Suffering on account of the truth is an inexorable part of the Catholic witness. Its purpose, according to Archbishop Chaput, is "to change the world, for the sake of the world, in the name of Jesus Christ." But changing the world cannot be accomplished, he explains, "without engaging in a hands-on way the laws, the structures, the public policies, the habits of mind, and the root causes that sustain injustice in our country."

Unfortunately, not much is going to be achieved in this realm, Chaput notes, until there is a revised and more accurate understanding of certain cultural shibboleths or catchwords. Take, for example, pluralism. Because Catholics live in a pluralistic society, some say, they ought not to act upon their ideas concerning what values should hold sway in the public square. Chaput cautions that "Catholics who use 'pluralism' as an alibi for their public inaction suffer from what the early church described as *dypsychia*. In other words, they're ruled by two conflicting spirits. They may speak like disciples, but their unwillingness to act paralyzes their words."

Another of these unassailable shibboleths is tolerance. Men and women of faith must be tolerant, they are told, lest their latent rigidity and inflexibility be obstacles to getting along with others. Chaput holds that "Catholics have the duty not to 'tolerate' other people but to love them, which is a much more demanding task. Justice, charity, mercy, courage, wisdom—these are Christian virtues; but not tolerance. . . . Real Christian virtues flow from an understanding of truth, unchanging and rooted in God, that exists and obligates us whether we like it or not. The pragmatic social truce we call 'tolerance' has no such grounding."

And then, of course, there is conscience. Conscience, when it is invoked, does lead people to opposite judgments and decisions. Further, conscience cannot be violated without doing serious harm to personal dignity. Thus, it is not possible to compel even Catholics to accept Church teaching. This is all true. What is often forgotten, though, is the importance of humility, what Archbishop Chaput calls the "willingness to put the matter to real prayer and the seriousness of [the] effort to accept the wisdom of the church and follow her guidance." This humility, if it were practiced, would preclude persons from organizing "dissent in the name of 'conscience,' especially in a media age that celebrates almost anyone who challenges authority." The effect of the misguided effort to mobilize dissent via the media is "[the tribalization of] Catholic life by turning the Church into a battleground for interest groups and personal ego."

In the intersection of faith and culture, where pluralism, tolerance, and conscience are found, there also are the issues that have so roiled a nation like the United States. How are issues like poverty, the death penalty, abortion, international debt, and others properly evaluated? Are they all the same? Archbishop Chaput assesses the issues this way: "Understanding the moral differences among social issues is critical. . . . Not all issues have the same gravity." He argues that some issues are "foundational," by which he means there are issues which in their nature ineluctably have to do with the most elementary of rights and duties. Abortion is a foundational issue. So are euthanasia and embryonic stem cell research. As issues, they pertain inescapably to the fundamental right to life. They also impose the duty of protecting innocent life. "Deliberately killing innocent human life, or standing by and allowing it, dwarfs all other social issues," the archbishop maintains.

Issues like housing, unemployment, and the environment do not disappear. However, neither are they foundational. When the right to life is secured first, then there is a foundation—a very broad one at that—for addressing other violations of justice.

The consistent ethic of life is not in disharmony with this understanding. The consistent ethic of life proposes a connection or correspondence between and among the various issues. It does not propose that all the issues are equally important. Were that so, there would not be a scale then for discerning the most urgent from the least urgent. Medical triage is a good illustration of this principle at work. Emergency room personnel treat life and death cases way ahead of those cases involving skin abrasions and sprained ankles. Decisions are made based on the gravity of the threat at hand. The consistency of the consistent ethic of life is in the bearing the issues have on the inherent dignity of the person. All the

threats to that inherent dignity are not judged to be of the same order and magnitude. Some are more immediate than others. Attacks against life itself are always more foundational than attacks against the quality of life.

A careful and accurate analysis of the social issues, leading to the considered judgment that the life issues are preeminent over other ones, signals something very important about citizenship. Archbishop Chaput comments: "If we really love this country, and if we really treasure our faith, living our Catholic beliefs without excuses or apologies, and advancing them in the public square, are the best expressions of patriotism we can give to the nation. American Catholics need to be *more* Catholic, not less; and not simply 'more Catholic,' but more *authentically and unselfishly Catholic.*" Living the Catholic faith now with integrity is the best way to anticipate the citizenship of heaven. (cf. Philippians 3: 20)—Robert J. Batule

Bibliography and Further Reading: Chaput, Charles. *Living the Catholic Faith: Rediscovering the Basics.* Ann Arbor, MI: Servant, 2001; Chaput, Charles. *Render unto Caesar: Serving the Nation by Living Our Catholic Beliefs in Political Life.* New York: Doubleday, 2008.

CHRYSOSTOM, ST. JOHN (c. 349–407) Patriarch of Constantinople (398–407) and renowned preacher, theologian, and Doctor of the Church, St. John was accorded the appellation Chrysostom ("Golden Mouth") because of the richness, vividness, and eloquence of his preaching. Considered one of the four great doctors of the Eastern Church—the others being SS. Athanasius, Basil, and Gregory of Nazianzus—he was a native of Antioch in Syria who as a young man became a monk and even lived as a hermit until bad health forced him to leave his cave and return to the city.

Ordained a deacon in 381, he busied himself with caring for the poor and the sick and also worked zealously as a catechist. After ordination as a priest in 386, he was given charge of the city's principal church, where over a dozen years his preaching made him famous in the East. In particular, a series of his sermons "On the Statues" helped reconcile the Antiochans who had rebelled against the Roman Empire over the imposition of new taxes and, during riots, had broken statues of the imperial family.

When the archbishopric of Constantinople became vacant in 397, St. John, on account of his fame, was chosen by the Byzantine emperor Arcadius to be the new patriarch. It was customary at that time for the emperor to choose the new patriarch as part of the tight control the Byzantine rulers continued to exercise over the Church. St. John tried to decline the appointment but was brought to Constantinople by a ruse that was practically an abduction and installed as archbishop.

But St. John Chrysostom did not prove to be exactly the "emperor's man." He was a genuine Catholic bishop and a serious reformer. He disciplined and removed clergy for laxity, and even sometimes for crimes, and prohibited live-in housekeepers in their residences. St. John deposed bishops guilty of simony (and thereby incurred the charge of exceeding his authority and jurisdiction in at least one notable case), ordered monks back to their monasteries and insisted on a regular religious life, and opened hospitals and tried to alleviate the condition of the poor. He reduced the Church's expenses and regularly inveighed against luxury and extravagant living in his sermons. He himself lived simply.

As patriarch of the principal imperial city, however, St. John could not avoid the politics and intrigue that went on, and he inevitably made enemies, if only when rendering necessary judgments. Among these enemies was Empress Eudoxia, who was persuaded to believe that he had targeted her as "Jezebel" in one of his sermons.

A formidable enemy turned out to be the patriarch of Alexandria, Egypt, Theophilus, who had resented St. John's installation at Constantinople over an Egyptian candidate he had favored. Theophilus was summoned to Constantinople by the emperor in 401 in the case of some Egyptian monks whom he had excommunicated but who had then appealed to the emperor in yet another ecclesiastical case being judged by the secular arm. Theophilus at first refused to respond to the imperial summons, but then as part of his defense strategy he decided to launch counteraccusations against St. John Chrysostom. In 403, he arrived in Constantinople with more than 20 of his Egyptian suffragan bishops in tow, along with a considerable amount of Alexandrian gold for bribes in his planned campaign against the patriarch of Constantinople.

In the capital, the Alexandrian patriarch first recruited to his cause a number of other disaffected bishops and then proceeded to convene these and his Egyptian bishops in what was called the Synod of the Oak across the Bosporus in Chalcedon. This false synod considered a number of trumped-up charges against St. John Chrysostom and then declared him deposed. St. John refused to appear or even recognize the charges against him—they *were* false—but the Emperor Arcadius

nevertheless ended up ratifying them and exiling the saintly patriarch.

Riots and disturbances broke out in the city when the populace learned that their beloved patriarch had been exiled, and the emperor was obliged to bring him back for what proved to be a temporary restoration. Later, after a statue of Empress Eudoxia was erected in front of the cathedral and became a scene of excesses, the patriarch did not hesitate to preach against those excesses, this time comparing the empress to Herodias, who had demanded the head of John the Baptist. The empress duly demanded the head of St. John Chrysostom, and, this time, he was exiled permanently to Armenia by the enraged Emperor Arcadius.

Because his residence in Armenia quickly became a place of pilgrimage for many of the Eastern Christian faithful, however, St. John was ordered to be exiled even farther away at a place some 600 miles from Constantinople across the Black Sea. Forced to march in sun and rain, heat and wind, across several rugged mountain ranges by his merciless guards, St. John Chrysostom, exhausted and at the end of his tether, died at Comara in Pontus on September 14, 407, uttering as his last words, "Glory to God in all things."

St. John had appealed his deposition to Pope Innocent I in Rome, who declined to recognize its validity and called for the convening of a council of bishops from both East and West to judge the case. The pope's judgment was ignored, however, and no such council was ever convened.

The saint was famed for his preaching, and many of the sermons are included in the *Patrologia Graeca* on a wide variety of themes, including especially expositions of Sacred Scripture. A number of his treatises are similarly extant on such subjects as the priesthood and the divinity of Christ. His letters, too, movingly throw light on his life and times. He preached especially eloquently on the Eucharist and has been called (unofficially) the Doctor of the Eucharist—about which he preached: "He who did this at the Supper is the same who now performs the act. We rank as ministers. It is He who consecrates and transmutes" (*Hom. 82 In Matt.*). St. John Chrysostom is commemorated on the Roman calendar on September 13.—Kenneth D. Whitehead

BIBLIOGRAPHY AND FURTHER READING: Bauer, C., *John Chrysostom and His Times*. Translated by M. Gonzaga; 2 vols. Westminster, MD: Newman Press, 1960–1961. Kelly, J. N. D., *The Story of John Chrysostom: Ascetic, Preacher, Bishop*. Ithaca, NY: Cornell University Press, 1995. See also BASIL THE GREAT, ST.

CICERO, MARCUS TULLIUS (106–43 BC) Marcus Tullius Cicero, lawyer, politician, orator, and philosopher, was one of the leading figures in the events of the Roman Revolution that ultimately ended in the Republic's dissolution. An outsider to the Roman aristocracy, Cicero's intellectual prowess, oratorical skills, and tenacious ambition earned him an influential position in the Senate and in Rome's political machine until he was murdered in an act of political vengeance in 43 BC. During his intermittent withdrawals from public life, Cicero wrote many political and philosophical treatises that still remain influential in both Catholic and secular circles.

Cicero was born on January 3, 106 BC, in Arpinum, a small town southeast of Rome. Son of a wealthy equestrian family, he showed exceptional academic talent at a young age. His father moved his family to Rome to provide young Cicero with the best possible education. Like other wealthy Roman boys, Cicero studied logic, literature, and philosophy in both Rome and Athens, but he concentrated especially on rhetoric, honing his abilities to compose and deliver speeches. After studying law and joining the Roman bar, Cicero's tremendous oratorical talent helped him rise from obscurity.

Cicero first came to prominence as a defense attorney in 80 BC. He then spent two years studying in Greece. Upon his return, he married Terentia, whose patrician blood added to his political stature. In 76 BC, Terentia bore him his first of two children, his beloved daughter Tullia, who was a great source of joy for him until her death in 45 BC. He began his ascent of the *cursus honorum*, the ladder of Roman public offices, when he was elected quaestor in 75 BC at the youngest possible age. He served his term in Sicily, where he impressed inhabitants with the honest and just administration of his duties.

Service in Sicily provided the groundwork for Cicero's political breakthrough: his prosecution of Verres, the corrupt former governor of Sicily, in 70 BC. Against overwhelming odds, Cicero defeated Hortensius, Rome's leading lawyer at the time, and forced Verres into exile. His victory established him as head of the Roman bar and made him famous throughout the Republic. This latter fact was critical in providing a base for Cicero's run for higher office, as he lacked the three main components of a winning campaign: a patrician family name, enormous wealth, and military glory.

Cicero reached the pinnacle of Roman offices when he was elected praetor for 66 BC and consul for 63 BC, both at the youngest possible age. He thus became the first *novus homo*, a "new man" who was the first in his family to hold the highest office, since Gaius Marius in 107 BC. As consul, he successfully uncovered and prosecuted a planned coup d'état led by Lucius Sergius Catilina in 63 BC. This was the greatest achievement of his political career, earning him a thanksgiving festival and the bestowed title of Pater Patriae, Father of his Country.

After his consulship, Julius Caesar joined with Pompey the Great and Marcus Crassus to form what historians call the First Triumvirate. This surreptitious political alliance pushed Cicero, who refused the invitation to join them because he knew their subversive intentions, to the margins of political life. After enduring a year of forced exile and the futility of politics under the triumvirs, Cicero retired to private life, where in 56–55 BC he wrote philosophical treatises on the ideal form of government and on rhetoric, the most famous being the *De Legibus*, *De Re Publica*, and *De Oratore*.

In the late 50s BC, Cicero returned to public life. He was elected augur in 53 BC and then served in 51 BC as proconsular governor of Cilicia in Asia Minor, where he again won praise from residents on account of his just ruling. When he returned to Rome the following year, Caesar and Pompey were on the brink of civil war. Cicero, who had begrudgingly supported Pompey in earlier years, joined the Senate in backing him against Caesar, whom he deemed a greater threat to the constitution. Caesar defeated Pompey in 48 BC, and then implemented a program of clemency for his former enemies, including Cicero, who was able to return to Rome in 47 BC after Caesar personally pardoned him.

With Caesar possessing unprecedented and unbridled power in Rome, Cicero mourned the Republic and its vanquished freedom. At the same time, he suffered two personal setbacks: he divorced Terentia after 30 years of marriage in 46 BC, and he lost his daughter Tullia a year later. The latter event sent him into depression and another retirement to private life. Again for solace he turned to writing, producing more works on oratory and philosophy, including the *Brutus*, *Tusculanae Disputationes*, *De Amicitia*, and *De Officiis*.

Cicero was not part of the conspiracy against Caesar in 44 BC, but he was overjoyed at the event. At age 62, he returned to the political arena as the senior leader of the constitutional faction in their rivalry with the Caesarians, led by the now sole consul Marc Antony. Deeming Antony as great a threat to the Republic as Caesar, Cicero delivered a series of fiery speeches, the *Philippics*, denouncing Antony and his ambitions. Cicero also supported the 18-year-old Octavian, Caesar's adopted heir, and advocated for giving the boy exceptional authority in hope of playing him against Antony. A strict constitutionalist throughout his career, Cicero's bending of the laws to grant official power to Octavian had an ironic effect: the boy eventually joined forces with Antony, and then 13 years later he personally brought the Republic and her constitution to their final end.

After Antony and Octavian aligned in 43 BC, they proscribed their political enemies, with Antony placing Cicero at the top of his list. Cicero aborted an attempt to escape, and he met his death on a deserted road at the hands of Antony's men on December 7, 43 BC. By the order of Antony, Cicero's head was cut off, and his right hand and tongue, the instruments with which he wrote and delivered the *Philippics*, were nailed to the rostra in the Roman Forum.

The elegant prose and philosophical depth of Cicero's writings made him the most widely read and revered Latin author in the West for centuries. During the Renaissance, the recovery of over 800 of his private letters, written between 68 and 44 BC and originally published by his personal secretary Tiro, revealed the complexity of Cicero's personality. He was exceptionally vain and excessively liable to flattery. Throughout his life, he remained proud of his accomplishments as a *novus homo*, yet he also resented what he perceived as the aristocracy's sustained hostility toward him. He often waffled when faced with difficult decisions, and although he was a man of principle and a deep believer in the constitution, he occasionally compromised his convictions for the sake of political expediency.

Cicero's writings on law, government, and philosophy contributed to the development of Catholic thinking in these areas. Influenced both by Stoicism and Platonic philosophy, Cicero composed the earliest complete account in Latin of natural law reasoning, a tradition he learned from the Stoics. In a famous passage in book 3 of *De Re Publica*, he wrote, "The true law is right reason in accord with nature, known widely by all, constant and ever lasting, which by its commands bids man to duty, and by its prohibitions deters him from wrong." Cicero expressed this understanding of the natural law as early as 20 years of age in the work *De Inventione Rhetorica*, writing in book 2 that "the law of nature is not what is born in opinion, rather it is a certain force implanted in nature, like religion, loyalty, gratitude, revenge, obedience, and truth."

According to Richard A. Horsley, Cicero departed from his Stoic predecessors by distinguishing God from the law, a mark of the Platonic influence in his thought. This distinction is evident both in *De Legibus* and in *De Re Publica*. In the latter work he calls God, the creator and ruler of all, the founder and judge of the law of nature. This distinction is also presupposed in the Catholic understanding of creation and of the natural law.

St. Thomas Aquinas cited Cicero twice in his treatise on law in the *Prima Secundae* of his *Summa Theologiae*, and both references are to the same passage in book 2 of the *De Inventione Rhetorica*. St. Thomas employed this passage (cited in q. 91, Article 3, and q. 95, Article 2) to demonstrate how human laws are reasoned from the precepts of natural law: "Justice came forth from nature; then certain practices became customs from reasonableness of advantage. Afterwards fear of the laws and religion confirmed what came from nature and was approved by custom." St. Thomas cited Cicero on a number of other occasions throughout the *Summa Theologiae*, especially on the virtues and vices.—David G. Bonagura Jr.

Bibliography and Further Reading: Everitt, Anthony. *Cicero: The Life and Times of Rome's Greatest Politician*. New York: Random House, 2003; Horsley, Richard A. "The Law of Nature in Philo and Cicero." *Harvard Theological Review* 71 (1978): 35–59; Mitchell, Thomas N. *Cicero: The Ascending Years*. New Haven, CT: Yale University Press, 1979; Mitchell, Thomas N. *Cicero: The Senior Statesman*. New Haven, CT: Yale University Press, 1991. *See also* AQUINAS, ST. THOMAS; *FIDES ET RATIO*; NATURAL LAW; VICES; VIRTUES

COLLECTIVE CONSCIENCE The word *conscience* has traditionally referred only to individual conscience, but modern analyses of social phenomena have led some philosophers and social scientists to use the term *collective conscience* and similar terms such as *social conscience, public conscience*, the *conscience of peoples*, and the *conscience of society*. Moreover, the term *conscience* bears a certain ambiguity, referring sometimes to the mental state called "consciousness" and at other times to the act of moral judgment. In the former sense, *collective conscience* refers to a certain awareness shared among the members of a group or of an entire society; in the latter sense, it refers to shared moral judgment. The concept of collective conscience with its moral connotations entered Catholic social thought in the early 20th century and has slowly increased in use to the present time. Both magisterial and scholarly documents have used the term, though without in-depth analysis of its relation to Catholic social thought.

In the Catholic tradition, the collective conscience of any group depends upon the consciences of its individual members. Just as the members of a social institution, and not the institution itself, really perform institutional actions, so the members of that institution make moral judgments about institutional actions. A society or social institution is said to have a collective conscience by an analogy to individual persons having a conscience. Individual conscience is a personal act of moral judgment, and collective conscience is an act of moral judgment shared among persons related to each other in a society or social institution.

The collective conscience of a social institution deserves respect because of the respect due to the individuals organized to act on its behalf. The collective conscience of a society is manifest, for example, in its civil laws and its culture. The collective conscience of an institution is manifest in its policies and its culture. Just as individual persons are bound to seek and preserve true moral judgments, they are sometimes bound to share those moral judgments in society and its institutions, for example, regarding conscientious objection. From the perspective of Catholic tradition, collective conscience derives its dignity from the same foundation as individual conscience: natural and divine law.

A collective conscience may also be mistaken. Because a collective conscience includes the consciences of at least two, and often many, people, a collective conscience differs significantly from an individual conscience. Thus it does not bind in the same way, for a person is ultimately bound to follow one's own conscience. Moreover, "conflicts of conscience" among a group are conflicts among persons, whereas an individual's doubtful conscience represents a conflict within that person's moral reasoning.

The concept of a collective conscience originated not in Catholic social thought but in the secular science of sociology. Pioneer of sociology Emile Durkheim (1858–1917) first offered a scientific definition of the term *conscience collective* ("collective" or "common" consciousness) in his book *De la division du travail social* (1893; *The Division of Labor in Society*). At the beginning of the industrial revolution in the late 19th century, Durkheim attempted to describe the forces unifying industrial society. He argued that social life is unified by a similarity of consciousness among the members of a society and by the social division of labor. Those who work together come to share a similarity of consciousness—a collective conscience. In a later work, *Les formes élémentaires de la vie religieuse* (1912; *The Elementary Forms of Religious Life*), Durkheim argued that the foundational categories of thought are of religious origin and that societies form around religious ideals. When a set of religious ideals gains intensity in the consciousness of many people, they form a society in order to live out those ideals. The collective consciousness arises from this shared world of sentiments, ideas, practices, and images and synthesizes them so that they preserve a certain rationality. Thus, according to Durkheim, collective or common consciousness signifies the whole complex of beliefs, sentiments, and mores common to the members of the same society.

The term *conscientiae collectivae* ("collective conscience") first appears in papal documents in *Pascendi Dominici Gregis* (1907; *On the Doctrines of the Modernists*) of Pope Pius X (1835–1914). The pope used the term to describe a modernist view—to be rejected—that the Catholic Church should be understood as "the product of the collective conscience" (*PDG* # 23) of God's people. According to such a view, the collective conscience originates in the individual person's need to communicate one's faith to others and becomes collective as individuals form themselves into societies to preserve and communicate their faith. In the modernist theory, the Church in the spiritual order would be similar to a democratic political state in the temporal order. Pius X criticizes the proposition that Church doctrine evolves through the encounter between the magisterium and the Church's "collective conscience," which in practice would be formed by leading individuals who advance progressive judgments against traditional ones.

Despite the negative judgment of Pope Pius X regarding the modernist use of the term, *collective conscience* in Catholic social thought has developed as a neutral term used to describe a social phenomenon. Pope John Paul II used the term in the encyclical *Evangelium Vitae* (1995) when discussing the vulnerability of democratic processes to institutionalize values that do not respect the dignity of the human person. Here the usage of "collective conscience" changes from a notion posited in an ideology criticized by the magisterium—that is, modernism—to a social reality presumed to exist. In this encyclical, a collective conscience is not identical with public opinion and still less with the majority opinion. It is the interrelationship of moral judgments among all the members of a political society, such as a nation-state. It is the fallible and fragile moral basis for political judgment in a democratic society. Inasmuch as the collective conscience recognizes the objective grounds of morality in the natural law, democratic processes establish laws that respect the dignity of the human person and that are capable of maintaining peace.

By contrast, inasmuch as the collective conscience opposes this law, democratic processes tend to establish unjust law and to look merely toward empirical means, such as public opinion and majority vote, to regulate opposing interests.

In his social encyclical *Caritas in Veritate* (2009), Pope Benedict XVI continues developing the concept of collective conscience in Catholic social thought as he discusses the need for progress in ethical analyses to match the advances in technological possibilities. This moral progress in society emerges from an "ethical interaction" and "reciprocity" of consciences that is based upon moral truths in the natural and divine law and leads to true moral judgments about social practices. A well-formed collective conscience witnesses especially to the universal moral laws of human thriving and peace, and Catholic social thought has called attention to universal declarations of human rights as an expression of collective conscience. In particular, *Caritas in Veritate* recalls the need to cultivate a public conscience that recognizes a universal right to food and access to water. The encyclical also reminds us that a lack of respect for fundamental rights corrupts a society's conscience and well-being, for instance, when the lack of respect for life in some reproductive technologies and the use of embryos promote ways of moral reasoning incapable of maintaining justice and social peace.

Two other Catholic documents speak of the need for the collective conscience of some societies to examine the moral meaning of historical events. In preparation for the Jubilee Year 2000, the International Theological Commission published "Memory and Reconciliation: The Church and the Faults of the Past" (1999), which reflected upon how "purification of memory" is possible through the recognition of the faults of the past. This document suggests that the members of a society are at times called to cooperate in an act of judgment upon their common memory and responsibility for past actions. This social judgment is the work of both personal and collective consciences that arrive at a shared moral judgment about historical events that affects present social relationships and promotes reconciliation. The formation of conscience leading to collective judgment is ultimately perfected in Christ's liturgy, though prepared for in studies such as those undertaken by the International Theological Commission. The need for such discernment before Christ is expressed by the Pontifical Council for Promoting Christian Unity in cooperation with the Commission on Faith and Order of the World Council of Churches. Publishing jointly "Resources for the Week of Prayer for Promoting Christian Unity and throughout the Year 2005," these two representative councils urged different Christian communities to examine their collective consciences before Christ, the foundation of the one church.

Magisterial documents of the 20th century take collective conscience to be a human social reality ultimately ordered to God through Christ. Scholarly analyses of the Church's social doctrine also use the term, but without systematic analysis of its meaning within that body of thought. Collective conscience is a shared judgment about social activities that promotes social justice and peace inasmuch as it witnesses to the natural and divine law. This collective conscience has authority and indeed forms individual consciences for social action without removing individual responsibility.—Grattan T. Brown

BIBLIOGRAPHY AND FURTHER READING: Durkheim, Emile. *The Elementary Forms of the Religious Life.* Translated by Joseph Ward Swain. Mineola, NY: Dover, 2008; John Paul II. *Evangelium Vitae: Encyclical Letter on the Value and Inviolability of Human Life.* Boston: Pauline Books & Media, 1995. *See also CARITAS IN VERITATE*; CONSCIENCE; *EVANGELIUM VITAE*

CONDOMS AND AIDS　The Catholic Church is opposed to the use of condoms to stop the spread of acquired immune deficiency syndrome (AIDS). It holds that this objective can only be achieved by the practice of chastity and the reservation of sexual intercourse to marriage. Even if, in individual cases of intercourse, a condom can retard the transmission of the human immunodeficiency virus (HIV), programs based on the dissemination of condoms are counterproductive because they promote promiscuity and infidelity.

Assuming that condoms can, to some degree, prevent the transmission of HIV during particular acts of sexual intercourse, the question arises as to whether, in light of the grave consequences of contracting AIDS, it might be permitted for married couples to use condoms during sexual intercourse when one of the spouses is infected. This question might be rephrased as: Is the use of a condom in this particular case condemned by the Church's teaching on the illicit character of contraception in general?

The answer to this question depends on addressing two more specific questions: First, is the use of a condom in such cases a choice to sterilize marital intercourse? Second, is the use of a condom in such cases the corruption of a true act of marital intercourse? Both these questions are disputed even among those moralists who agree with the Church's teaching on contraception as it is found in the encyclical *Humanae Vitae*.

The answer given to the first question—whether in this case there is a contraceptive choice—depends on the weight given to the intention of the spouses and the intrinsic nature of the act itself. The principle of double effect is not applicable here. This is because the principle of double effect requires that we already know how to categorize the act and whether this act is good or at least indifferent, in light of which an evil side effect might be tolerated. What is at stake here is an accurate description of the object of choice in the first place.

Those moralists who make intention the decisive factor in describing the object of human action claim that, in the case at hand, spouses are not choosing to sterilize their sexual intercourse. Rather, they are choosing to stop infection and the consequent sterility is a by-product. Sterilization is outside of the scope of their choice: it is *praeter intentionem*. The choice involved is not a contraceptive choice and, accordingly, does not fall within the condemnation of contraception found in *Humanae Vitae*. Therefore, according to these moralists, were the Church to permit the use of condoms in these cases, it would not be changing its teaching on contraception at all.

Other moralists who give more weight to the nature of any given human action disagree. They claim that certain acts have an imbedded meaning that cannot be shed whatever the intention of the agent might be. For example, one cannot give a baby shampoo to drink and claim to intend to be rehydrating him. The nature of the act cannot embody such an intention. Therefore, these moralists claim that, despite the intention of the spouses, any couple employing a condom necessarily chooses a kind of action that renders the marital intercourse sterile, and this is decisive for categorizing the action: it is an act of contraception.

It is certain that factors other than the intention of the person acting can be significant in describing the object of an action. In such cases, the circumstance of the action (including the consequences) can become what is called the "principal condition" of the object of choice. For example, a person might choose to play a song on his guitar for the edification of his friends. However, if a circumstance of this action is that he does it loudly, at 3 a.m., and under the bedroom window of the neighbor's house, this action would be called "disturbing the peace." The circumstances of where and when are principal conditions of the object that change the object of choice. Applying this to the case at hand, some moralists claim that while the spouses directly

chose marital intercourse, the circumstance of sterilization (how the act is done) is a principal condition of the object; accordingly, it changes the act into an act of contraception.

Yet, sometimes a circumstance that otherwise would change the object of choice, does not. This happens when there is a good reason to tolerate an otherwise vitiating circumstance. For example, a surgeon should always ask consent of a patient before operating. Lack of consent would be a circumstance that makes an otherwise good action bad. This circumstance would become the principal condition of the object, even though it is not directly chosen: the surgeon directly intends to operate, and the lack of consent is a circumstance since it describes the way he acts, not what he chooses. Yet, in an *emergency*, the surgeon may proceed without consent, and this otherwise bad circumstance is now not morally significant. In this way, some moralists claim that the circumstance of sterilization can be tolerated given the gravity of becoming infected by HIV. In this case, the use of a condom would not change the object of the action.

In *Veritatis Splendor*, John Paul II emphasized the importance of concentrating on the object of human action in order to forestall an approach to morality where the end justifies the means (cf. *VS* # 76–78). Yet the Church has not indicated precisely how to weigh the contribution of intention of the agent and the intrinsic nature of an action in determining the object of a human act. This means that neither side of the debate can, at present, be certain that it is correct.

In conclusion, there is no unanimity among orthodox moralists as to whether the choice involved is a choice for contraception, and few would claim with certainty that it is definitely so. This being the case, the debate has moved toward addressing the second question: Is the use of a condom in such cases the corruption of a true act of marital intercourse?

This debate depends on the premise that there is an archetype act of marital intercourse and that all those acts of marital sex that fall short of this are perverted and hence wrong. It is proposed that the archetype act is that act of intercourse that would consummate a marriage.

According to canon law, a marriage is consummated when the spouses "have performed between themselves in a human manner the conjugal act which is per se suitable for the generation of children, to which marriage is ordered by its very nature and by which the spouses become one flesh" (*CIC* 1061 §1). The traditional interpretation of this is that, for consummation, the husband must penetrate his wife and deposit semen (though not necessarily sperm) in her vagina. Since this is precluded by the use of a condom—though not by a contraceptive pill—sexual intercourse with a condom is not the kind of act by which a marriage can be consummated. Therefore, condomized sexual intercourse, even in the case at hand, appears to be a perversion of marital intercourse and, accordingly, illicit.

This conclusion is apparently strengthened by the observation that a man without semen cannot consummate a marriage. It is not enough to *intend* to inseminate, the husband really must do so. Moreover, when a condom is used to prevent HIV infection, there is an intention to prevent ejaculation into the vagina, even if there is no intention to sterilize the intercourse.

A possible weakness with the consummation argument is that canon law is potentially reformable. It is risky to build an argument on the law alone; ultimately, it must be founded on the theological reasons *behind* the law. Furthermore, some moralists question why the canonists demand vaginal ejaculation. The law says the consummating act must be "per se suitable for the generation," and this might suggest that what precludes consummation is an intention to sterilize the act of intercourse. In that case, those moralists who claim there is no such intention in the case of condoms and HIV will reject the canon law consummation argument.

It seems significant, though, that canon 1061 §1 also speaks of the act of consummation as being that which effects a "one flesh union." It might be argued that condoms preclude such a union, whereas the pill does not, since in the latter case the bodies of the spouses are in a more profound contact and the husband does truly leave something of himself in his wife. Condoms would pervert the marital act by undermining its unitive dimension.

If the use of a condom even in the case of HIV infection is intrinsically evil, two more positions would need to be rejected: appeal to the principle of "the end justifies the means" or to the principle of "the lesser of two evils." In both cases, there would be a direct choice to do what is evil, and this is never morally upright.

In *Light of the World*, Pope Benedict XVI stated that an HIV-infected prostitute who uses a condom to prevent infection has taken "a first step in a movement toward a different way, a more human way, of living sexuality." This cannot be taken to mean the use of condoms is tolerated, let alone promoted. It is equivalent to noting that a mugger who leaves his victim with a few dollars to get a bus home shows an inkling of decency

that might, one day, lead him to stop mugging people altogether.—William Newton

BIBLIOGRAPHY AND FURTHER READING: Fisher, Anthony. "HIV and Condoms within Marriage." *Communio* 36, no. 2 (2009): 329–359; Long, Steven. "The False Theory Undergirding Condomistic Exceptionalism." *National Catholic Bioethics Quarterly* (2008): 709–731. Rhonheimer, Martin. "On the Use of Condoms to Prevent Acquired Immune Deficiency Syndrome." *National Catholic Bioethics Quarterly* 5, no. 1 (2005): 37–48; Smith, Janet. "The Morality of Condom Use by HIV-Infected Spouses." *Thomist* 70 (2006): 28–69. *See also* AIDS; CONDOMS; CONTRACEPTIVE MENTALITY; *HUMANAE VITAE*; MORAL THEOLOGY: A SURVEY

COPE, BLESSED MOTHER MARIANNE (1838–1918)

Barbara Koob was born on January 23, 1838, and baptized the following day in what is now the west-central part of Germany. Her family emigrated to Utica, New York, in 1839 and joined St. Joseph Parish, where she received her First Holy Communion and Confirmation. In the 1850s, she became a naturalized U.S. citizen with her father and siblings. Although she felt an early calling to the religious life, family obligations interfered with her wishes. She left school after completing an eighth-grade education and for nine years worked in the Utica Steam Woolen Mills to support her ailing father and her siblings. The month after her father's death, confident that her siblings could support themselves, she began her religious life. On November 19, 1862, at the Church of the Assumption in Syracuse, New York, she took the name Sister Marianne and was invested in the Sisters of St. Francis. In 1863, she was professed as a sister and began her work teaching in the new schools that the order founded and staffed.

Several administrative appointments on a number of governing boards of her religious community dramatically changed her vocation from educator to nurse-administrator. In the 1860s, she played a major role in the creation and organization of two of the first hospitals in the central New York area: St. Elizabeth's in Utica (1866) and St. Joseph's in Syracuse (1869), both staffed by the Franciscan sisters. The hospitals reflected the charism of the order and had unique charters that stated that the hospitals would provide for the sick without regard to ethnicity, religion, or color. Among the first 60 registered American hospitals, they were unique in their antidiscrimination policy. Mother Marianne also initiated distinctive and innovative medical and sanitary practices, such as the daily antiseptic cleansing of halls and rooms and the cleansing of hands before ministering to the patients. Other innovative practices included the acceptance of medical students from the College of Physicians and Surgeons to do clinical work in her hospital; the formation of patients' rights, which allowed patients to decide if they wished to be seen by medical students; and the acceptance and care of alcoholic patients who were refused at other hospitals. While criticized for some of these policies, she was a woman ahead of her times. Her hospital experience was invaluable to the next chapter of her life.

As superior general of her order, Mother Marianne was the only one to respond favorably for a call to open a hospital for lepers (the Hansen Disease Community) in the Sandwich Islands in 1883. She personally accompanied six of the 35 sister volunteers who responded to her new mission in Honolulu. Her accomplishments included the creation of Malulani Hospital, the first general hospital on the island of Maui; her criticism of the abuse of leprosy patients at the Branch Hospital at Kakaako, which resulted in transferring the overcrowded hospital to her order; and the opening of Kapiolani Home for the homeless female children of leprosy patients. This whirlwind of activities delayed and eventually canceled her expected return to Syracuse, because her leadership was declared by government and church authority to be essential to the success of the mission.

As a result of her work, two years later she was decorated by King Kalakaua of Hawai'i with the medal of the Royal Order of Kapiolani. Because of their reputation for unselfish and courageous treatment of the outcasts of Hawai'i, Mother Marianne and her sisters were requested to open a new home for leprous women and girls at the Kalaupapa settlement on Molokai. This brought her into direct contact with the "Apostle of the Lepers," Father Damien de Veuster, during the last months of his life. She and her sisters physically cared for him, but also comforted him by assuring him that the patients at the Boys' Home at Kalawao on the opposite end of the settlement would be taken care of after his death. This promise taxed her administrative qualities, for not only did she care for these young male patients but she also supervised the building of a new structure, found a benefactor for this enterprise, and then successfully transferred the home into the capable hands of Father Damien's assistant and an order of brothers. Her sisters then returned to the home she had opened to care for the girls and women inflicted with Hansen's disease.

In addition to the physical care of these patients, Mother Marianne was aware of the psychological needs of these women. She organized music, art, and sewing classes and encouraged the women to wear vibrant clothing and to plant colorful plants around their homes and hospitals. She also encouraged the local pastor to give religious training to her patients, both Catholic and non-Catholic. Mother Marianne died on August 9, 1918, after a courageous lifetime devoted to Christian action. Her canonization process is in its final stages, as a second miracle has been approved by the Vatican Medical Board. Her legacy continues in Hawaii and Syracuse, where the Sisters of St. Francis of the Neumann Communities have an enduring presence in the fields of education and health care.—Marynita Anderson

BIBLIOGRAPHY AND FURTHER READING: Durkin, Mary Cabrini, OSU, with Mary Laurence Hanley, OSF. *Mother Marianne of Molokai: Valiant Woman of Hawaii;* Strasbourg, France: Éditions du Signe, 1999; Hanley, Mary Laurence, OSF, and O. A. Bushnell. *Pilgrimage and Exile.* Honolulu: Mutual, 2009. *See also* HOSPITAL; WOMEN'S RELIGIOUS ORDERS AND THE SOCIAL APOSTOLATE

· D ·

DAMIEN OF MOLOKAI, ST. (1840–1889) Joseph de Veuster, later known as Damien of Molokai, was the seventh of eight children and was born on January 3, 1840, in Tremelo, Flemish Brabant (now known as Belgium). The son of a farmer-merchant, he was expected to take over the family business and studied at Braine-le-Compte for a professional business degree. Instead, however, he followed his two older sisters and an older brother into the religious life.

At 18, de Veuster rebelled against his parents' wishes and joined his brother Auguste (Father Pamphile) as a novice brother in the Congregation of the Sacred Hearts of Jesus and Mary and the Perpetual Devotion to the Blessed Sacrament at Louvain. He adopted the religious name of Damien, made his first vows on February 2, 1859, took his final vows on October 7, 1860, and received his minor orders in 1863. Yearning to be a missionary, the next year, he voluntarily took his ill brother's place on a foreign mission. After a difficult and harrowing five-month voyage, he arrived in Honolulu, the Kingdom of Hawai'i. His new bishop encouraged him to further his studies, and in 1864 he was ordained to the priesthood. From 1864 until 1873, he worked as a parish priest in the rugged regions of northern Oahu and personally built several chapels. He embraced the local traditions and enhanced the religious ceremonies with the colorful Hawaiian culture.

In 1865, the government of Hawai'i recognized the public health problem caused by leprosy among its native people and implemented the Act to Prevent the Spread of Leprosy by forcing lepers to leave their families and live in two leper colonies, Kalaupapa and Kalawao, which were isolated at the east end of the Kalaupapa Peninsula on Molokai. The government expected the settlers to carve out their own existence and to farm their own food. No medical care was provided, and the people were too weak to fend for themselves.

Realizing the lepers' needs but also the danger of this new assignment, the local bishop asked for priest-volunteers to provide spiritual care for the 816 lepers. Father Damien was the first to volunteer, decided to stay permanently in the colonies without reinforcements, and single-handedly transformed the two colonies into more comfortable environments. In 1873, after first building the parish church of St. Philomena, he erected the first houses for the lepers. He then personally took care of their immediate needs: treating ulcers, building coffins, digging graves, and providing proper burials without regard for their religion. Damien provided a wholesome safe existence for them by enforcing laws; organizing farms; erecting hospitals, schools, and orphanages; building a water system, roads, and wharves; and teaching them to play musical instruments and sing in the church choirs.

Despite his long hours toiling for the lepers, Damien's life was grounded in spirituality, which he shared with his lepers. His life and example fostered daily prayer, the rosary, adoration to the Blessed Sacrament, daily Mass, and the Divine Office. He learned their languages and showed his lack of fear of their disease by sharing their food. For the first time, these lepers were treated with compassion, dignity, and respect. He became their advocate to the local and royal governments, often traveling to plead for and demand better services, which outraged government officials and other local leaders. His efforts brought little assistance to the lepers, but resulted in a personal attack against his good name and reputation. In a point-by-point open letter rebuttal in the *Pacific Commercial Advertiser*, Robert Louis Stevenson vindicated this false attack on Father Damien and not only restored his good name but also predicted his rise to sainthood for his heroic virtue.

In 1884, when Father Damien scalded his foot and felt no pain, he realized he had contracted leprosy. He received care from Dr. Masanao Goto, a leprosy special-ist who used holistic methods in his treatment of the disease, but Damien was well familiar with the futility of a cure for this disease. He spent his last five years in a frenzy completing his building projects and implementing his goals for his leper friends. In these last years, he sought assistance to continue the care for his people. Damien found solace when his assistant and Civil War veteran Joseph Dutton; Father Conrardy, a Belgian priest; Mother Marianne Cope, a nurse, administrator, educator, and Sister of St. Francis from Syracuse, New York; and James Sinnett, a nurse from Chicago, promised to continue his compassionate care for his people. Four people with different skills took the solitary place of the "Apostle to the Lepers."

After 15 years serving the leper colonies, Father Damien was forced to retire to his bed on March 23, 1889, after renewing his vows and was given last rites. He died at age 49 on April 15, 1889. His canonization process was initiated in 1977 by Pope Paul VI and completed on October 11, 2009, by Pope Benedict XVI. The symbols of this Apostle of the Lepers are the dove and the tree. He is honored in both the Roman Catholic (feast day: May 10) and U.S. Episcopal churches (joint feast day with Mother Marianne Cope: April 15). In addition, Damien of Molokai has been immortalized in sculpture, literature, and film.—Marynita Anderson

BIBLIOGRAPHY AND FURTHER READING: Barry, Michaels. *St. Damien de Veuster, Missionary of Moloka'i*. Boston: Pauline Books & Media, 2009; Bunson, Margaret, and Matthew Bunson. *Apostle of the Exiled: St. Damien of Molokai*. Huntington, IN: Our Sunday Visitor, 2009; Stewart, Richard. *Leper Priest of Moloka'i*. Honolulu: University of Hawai'i, 2000; Tayman, John. *The Colony: The Harrowing True Stories of the Exiles of Molokai*. New York: Simon & Schuster, 2007. *See also* COPE, BLESSED MOTHER MARIANNE; HEALTH CARE POLICY; SAINTS AND SOCIAL ACTION

DANTE ALIGHIERI (1265–1321)   Dante Alighieri ranks among the very best of poets of Western civilization. His *Commedia*, which was subsequently titled *The Divine Comedy*, is an unparalleled literary achievement that has been studied for almost seven centuries. Other works of Dante include the *Convivio*, *Monarchia*, *La vita nuova*, and *De vulgari eloquentia*.

Dante was born in Florence about May 1265 of Alighiero di Ballincione and Bella degli Abati. The Alighieris were well respected and claimed descent from an ancient Roman family. His education would have been that of the Trivium—grammar, logic, and rhetoric—and Quadrivium—arithmetic, geometry, astronomy, and music.

Dante married Gemma Donati to whom he had been betrothed at the age of 12, and they had four children: Pietro, Jacopo, Antonia, and Beatrice. However, when he was nine years old, he had met a young girl, Beatrice Portinari, with whom he fell in love. It was a distant, very reserved love, and Beatrice was probably unaware of the depth of his affection for her. Her death in 1290 deeply affected him, and he immortalized Beatrice by including her as a figure in *The Divine Comedy*.

In his younger years, Dante wrote romantic poetry and formed a close friendship with a fellow poet, Guido Cavalcanti. His later works were more philosophical and show the influence of Thomistic philosophy.

Dante lived during a time of violent political conflict between Italian city-states and the Guelph and Ghibelline political factions. The Alighieri family was associated with the Guelphs, who supported the pope, against the Ghibellines, who supported the emperor. Victory of one faction often meant loss of property, death, or exile to the members of the other faction. Dante himself participated in the Battle of Compaldino in 1289, which ended in a Guelph victory for Florence. With the Guelphs in control, Dante entered political life in 1295. In 1300, the Guelphs themselves divided into two factions: the White Guelphs and the Black Guelphs. With the intrigue of Pope Boniface VIII, the Black Guelphs took control of Florence, and the White Guelphs, including Dante, were sent into exile in 1301.

Dante was forced to leave his family, and he never again set foot in his beloved Florence. He found support and shelter in sympathetic families outside of Florence and in 1306 began his great work, *The Divine Comedy*, which he continued to write until his death in 1321 from malaria contracted from traveling. He is buried in Ravenna.

Among the most notable achievements of Dante was his contribution to the Italian language. Prior to Dante, serious literary work was composed in Latin. *The Divine Comedy* and some of Dante's other works, however, were written in his Tuscan dialect. So great was the poetic power that Dante drew from his dialect that it became the standard form of a unified Italian language. Indeed, modern Italian owes as much to Dante as English owes to Shakespeare.

Dante studies fell into decline until the mid-19th century when serious studies of *The Divine Comedy* were renewed. *The Divine Comedy* is now one of the most heavily annotated literary works in the West.

In Dante's work, we find the interplay of two great themes: justice and love, at both the natural and supernatural levels. Plato also dealt with these themes in, for example, *Republic, Symposium*, and other Socratic dialogues. But Dante's approach is thoroughly Christian, which presumes the need for salvation. It is easy to understand Dante's concern with justice. He had seen and personally experienced the effects of injustice, which tore apart the social fabric of Italy with constant warring, intrigue, betrayals, and vengeance. Justice is the moral glue that holds society together. It governs the social relationships between individuals and between men and the state. Without justice, said St. Augustine, what are kingdoms but gangs of robbers? There is no commonwealth without it. In his *Monarchia*, Dante considered the world to be in an ideal state under the rule of a benevolent monarch. In *The Divine Comedy*, however, we see that justice cannot be obtained without supernatural grace.

The Divine Comedy begins: "Midway upon the journey of our life. . . ." Although Dante is both the author and protagonist wayfarer of the story, traveling through hell, purgatory, and heaven, he represents all of us. This is our life, our spiritual journey, not just his.

The Divine Comedy is divided into three parts: *Inferno, Purgatorio*, and *Paradiso*. Dante the wayfarer begins the journey by awakening in a dark wood, the forest of sin and error. He cannot escape by himself. His way is blocked by three beasts, representing lust, ambition, and greed. The soul of the Roman poet Virgil, representing the good of the intellect, comes to lead Dante out of the dark wood. Virgil is sent by Beatrice (divine wisdom), St. Lucy, and the Blessed Virgin (divine grace). The lesson here is that the intellect is fructified by grace. Without it, the intellect cannot be instrumental in one's salvation. Nor can we save ourselves. We need the prayers of others.

Virgil first leads Dante into hell to see the effects of sin upon the souls of the damned. The inscription over the gates of hell states that justice moved God—Divine Power, Wisdom, and Love—from all eternity to create it. We, as readers, travel along with Dante the wayfarer as he engages in dialogues with the damned, some of whom are very engaging in their discourse. They cleverly make excuses for their sins and draw sympathy from those with whom they converse. The readers are drawn into the same temptations as Dante to feel sorry for the damned. But it must be remembered that the damned are in hell not because they committed sins—all of us, even the saints, have sinned to some degree or another—but because they refused to repent.

Our time of earthly life is a time of grace. But at death, the will becomes fixed. The punishment of the damned is that they can no longer repent. Their suffering is to eternally experience the fullness of their sins. Not only have the damned lost the good of the intellect, but they have also lost the good of community. So inwardly turned to their own egos are these souls that they hardly recognize the existence of their neighbors, much less develop a relationship or communication with them.

Hell has a spiritually meaningful topography. It consists of a series of circles arranged in a funnel-shaped structure, with the widest circles at the top where those guilty of the sins of incontinence are punished. At the lower levels, we find those guilty of the more serious sins of malice, fraud, betrayal, and hate. At the very bottom is Satan seen crushing the archtraitors Judas, betrayer of Christ, and Brutus and Cassius, betrayers of Caesar, in three enormous mouths. The topography of hell warns us of the structure of sin. Little sins draw us into bigger sins. Sins of incontinence lead to more serious sins of fraud and violence. Were it not for God's grace, the world would fall into a moral abyss from which recovery would be impossible.

In purgatory, Dante meets the souls of other sinners. But these are the repentant sinners. They are saved, but they need to be purged of their sins. Unlike the souls of the damned, these souls form a true community. Like the communion of the faithful on earth, they help each other to progress spiritually. They suffer for their sins, but it is fruitful, redemptive suffering, not the spiritually useless suffering of the damned.

In purgatory, the defects of love are cured. At the bottom level, the most serious sins—pride, envy, anger—involve perverted love for things that ought not to be loved. At the next level is sloth, which is inadequate love. And finally at the upper part of purgatory, the sins of excessive love—avarice, gluttony, and lust—are purged. These defects in love are cured not only by punishments but also by instruction from examples of the lives of the saints and the Blessed Virgin.

Finally, Dante is brought into heaven, where he is taught by the saints. Eventually, he is granted a vision of God Himself, "the Love that moves the sun and the other stars."

The Divine Comedy was intended to be a practical work. The reader is meant to be drawn into the same journey and same vision as Dante's, to let this experience be transformative of one's own life, and to become a channel of God's grace, without which there is neither justice nor community in this life or the next. The poem itself is a channel of God's grace. Perhaps this is why *The Divine Comedy* has earned the honor of a papal encyclical devoted to its merits: *In Praeclara Summorum* of Pope Benedict XV, promulgated on April 30, 1921.—Adrian T. Calderone

BIBLIOGRAPHY AND FURTHER READING: Calderone, A. "*The Divine Comedy* as a Part of Catholic Education." *Homiletic and Pastoral Review* (1996): 47–52; Cassell, A. K. *Dante's Fearful Art of Justice.* Toronto: University of Toronto Press, 1984; Gilson, E. *Dante and Philosophy.* New York: Sheed & Ward, 1949; Toynbee, P. *Dante Alighieri: His Life and Work*, Mineola, NY: Dover, 2005. *See also* GRACE; JUSTICE; LITERATURE; SALVATION; SHAKESPEARE, WILLIAM

DAWKINS, CLINTON RICHARD (1941–)   Clinton Richard Dawkins, commonly known as Richard Dawkins, is a prominent evolutionary biologist and perhaps the world's best known proponent of atheism. Born to British parents on March 26, 1941, in Nairobi, Kenya, he studied zoology at Balliol College, Oxford, where he earned a DPhil degree in 1966. Dawkins has taught at the University of California at Berkeley and at the University of Oxford, where he was appointed Simonyi Professor for the Public Understanding of Science in 1995. He has been a fellow of New College, Oxford, since 1970 and has received numerous honorary doctorates. Dawkins has delivered many lectures and served on the editorial boards of several journals such as *Skeptic*.

Chief among Dawkins's contributions to evolutionary biology is the central role played by the gene. In *The Origin of Species* (1859), Charles Darwin had laid out the theory of evolution by natural selection, offering an explanation for Earth's vast diversity of living organisms. Darwin's theory did not, however, definitively state what it was that is favored by natural selection—whether the individual, the population group, the species, or something else entirely. Lacking knowledge of contemporary genetics, Darwin himself was in a poor position to answer this question.

Some biologists, attending to the phenomenon of altruistic and self-sacrificial behavior, believed that natural selection acted upon whole groups or species. Dawkins took issue with this view in his first book, *The Selfish Gene* (1976). In this work, Dawkins defended the idea that the gene is the principal object of natural selection, although it is also true that individual organisms are selected for survival insofar as they are the "survival machines" by which genes survive and replicate. Dawkins applied this reasoning to a variety of biological phenomena; in particular, he argued that it explains phenomena that at first sight seem to go against the idea of natural selection, such as the behavior of organisms that engage in altruism or that limit the number of their offspring. *The Selfish Gene* remains among the most famous and widely read of Dawkins's books.

Dawkins is also known for his coinage and popularization of the word *meme*, meaning a unit of cultural transmission that corresponds to the gene as a unit of biological transmission. Memes are any products of human culture that propagate from mind to mind; they range from recipes to phrases to styles of footwear. Dawkins argued that memes evolve as independent entities in the "meme pool," just as do genes in the gene pool. Consequently, he criticized some of his colleagues for assuming that even cultural phenomena such as religion must originally have arisen because they served a biological advantage for the groups in which they developed. Dawkins argued instead that memes prosper by replicating themselves, not by replicating their hosts. As an example, he pointed out that the custom of clerical celibacy cannot offer its practitioners a biological advantage; a gene for celibacy must inevitably die out. A *meme* for celibacy, however, may serve its own advantage: a celibate cleric may wield more influence over his followers and hence be more successful in persuading some of them to imitate his own lifestyle.

Dawkins is well known for his vocal defense of atheism and criticism of religious belief. In *The God Delusion* (2006), Dawkins undertook the ambitious task of not only refuting traditional arguments for the existence of God but also producing a positive argument to the contrary, and further showing that the whole edifice of religion is not only wrong but a threat to society as well. Dawkins's treatment of the traditional arguments is not extensive; he attempted to refute St. Thomas Aquinas's famous "five ways" in the space of approximately three pages, and his generally superficial presentation of these and other theistic beliefs has led to criticism that Dawkins does not grasp Christian theology well enough to criticize it in a serious fashion. Theologian Alister McGrath, in *Dawkins' God: Genes, Memes, and the Meaning of Life* (2007), called Dawkins's understandings of religious belief, such as that faith means believing in something without any evidence, "an embarrassment to anyone concerned with scholarly accuracy" (102). Dawkins's notion of faith is rejected by the Catholic Church, which holds that the existence of God can be known by the natural power of reason and that God has given external signs of credibility to his revelation precisely because the act of faith must be in accord with reason (*DF* # 2.1, 3.4).

Dawkins's principal argument against the "God Hypothesis" centers on the idea of complexity and statistical improbability. Dawkins argues that, although the fundamental reason for positing the existence of God is to explain the complexity and appearance of design in the universe, "a God capable of designing a universe, or anything else, would have to be complex and statistically improbable" (*The God Delusion*, 153). The more complex a system is, the more improbable it is, unless its complexity can be explained through prior causes, which presumably is not the case where God is concerned. From these premises, Dawkins concludes that to posit God as the first cause is to assume a more complex, and hence less probable, first principle of things.

Dawkins further argues that religious belief is a positive harm to society, leading to fundamentalist rejection of science, religious wars, and ruthlessly intolerant and immoral cultural norms. In contrast, he states, atheism as such has not produced such evils. Although atheists such as Joseph Stalin have done evil things, they have not done them in the name of atheism. Notably, Dawkins compares the religious upbringing of children to child abuse, even suggesting that sexual abuse of children is a lesser evil than religious indoctrination, and that the Roman Catholic Church has been "unfairly demonized" over the former issue, the latter being ultimately a more destructive activity.

Dawkins is an avid promoter of rationalism and skeptical inquiry. In 2006, he founded the Richard Dawkins Foundation for Reason and Science, a nonprofit organization aimed at promoting a rationalist scientific worldview and combating religious fundamentalism and superstition. The foundation also contributes to the support of secular humanitarian charities such as the International Red Cross.—Michael J. Bolin

BIBLIOGRAPHY AND FURTHER READING: Dawkins, Richard. *The Blind Watchmaker.* New York: W. W. Norton, 1996; Dawkins, Richard. *The God Delusion.* Boston: Houghton Mifflin, 2006; Dawkins, Richard. *The Selfish Gene.* New York: Oxford University Press, 1989; McGrath, Alister. *Dawkins' God: Genes, Memes, and the Meaning of Life.* Malden, MA: Blackwell, 2007. *See also* AGNOSTICISM AND ATHEISM; DARWIN, CHARLES; EVOLUTION

DEISM The word *deism* is derived from the Latin *Deus*, which means God, so we have in that etymological information a clear enough indication that, whatever else deism might be said to have been, it was not a form of atheism. Like Christianity, then, it was theistic;

however, in sharp contrast to Christianity, it was in fact a form of theistic minimalism.

With respect to just about every key doctrine, deism was directly, and even belligerently, antithetical to Christianity. It was prepared to acknowledge, along with Christianity, the existence of God and that he is the originating source of the universe in which we live. But even here, on this most fundamental of points, there was not to be found perfect agreement. Some deists, like Christians, recognized God as the Creator, in the strict sense of the term; that is, they subscribed to the notion that there was nothing antecedent to God's creative act (*creatio ex nihilo*). Other deists saw God as simply the Divine Architect—one who gave shape and order to the present universe, but in doing so worked with preexisting matter which was in a chaotic state; he thus acted much in the same way as did the demiurge in Plato's *Timaeus*.

The God of deism was a remote and impersonal being (in this respect, he would seem not to be radically dissimilar to Aristotle's Prime Mover) who, once he had constituted the universe in its present form, withdrew from the scene, as it were, because the autonomy of operation he had given to his workmanship required no need of continual supervision on his part. The natural laws that God had established as an integral part of the universe were sufficient for its smooth and perpetual functioning. This was, according to the deists' way of thinking, precisely as it should be, for the architect of the universe, being himself perfect, could only bring about a perfect universe, that is, one which could function flawlessly on its own. It would be somehow unbecoming for God to intervene in the workings of the universe once he had formed it and set it in motion.

The God of deism was preeminently a rational God, and the most explicit manifestation of the divine reason was to be found in the laws of nature, which should serve, for man, as the most effective means by which he, using his own reasoning powers, comes to a knowledge of God. The laws established by God governed the physical universe, to be sure, but they also had important application to the moral universe of man. For deism, the only true religion was a rational religion, which is to say, a religion whose tenets, in order to be acceptable, had to pass the tests set up by human reason. In other words, human reason was elevated, by deism, to function as the final arbiter in deciding what was, and what was not, true religion.

As it turned out, human reason, as exercised by the deists, found all the major doctrines of Christianity to be severely wanting and brushed them aside with care-less ease. Deism rejected the doctrine of the Trinity, for example, and with that move there was no question of acknowledging the divinity of Christ. It also rejected divine revelation, miracles (these would represent an improper intervention in human affairs on God's part), the priesthood ("priestcraft" became one of deism's favorite pejoratives), the sacraments, and the efficacy of prayer.

Deists were ambivalent regarding the subject of divine providence. Some accepted what was more or less the Christian understanding of the doctrine, but the majority opinion drew a distinction between general providence and particular providence, accepting the former, dismissing the latter. Their notion of general providence had it that God was attentive to the universe taken as a whole, but in the manner of an absentee landlord. The particular providence that was rejected by the deists was the idea that God was at all concerned with individual human beings. This went hand in hand with the denial of the efficacy of prayer. The most extreme deists also rejected the idea that there was a future life and adopted a worldview that was really not much different from outright materialism.

Deism is commonly associated with the 18th century, the so-called Age of Reason, but it saw its origins in the previous century. Among the causes of deism, the Reformation and the scientific revolution can be cited as chief. The Reformation, ignoring tradition and the magisterium, settled upon Sacred Scripture as the sole source of Christian truth, with the individual effectively then becoming the authoritative interpreter of Scripture. This had two effects. First, it made for the inevitable proliferation of Protestant sects. Second, it served to undermine the intrinsic authority of Scripture as authentic divine revelation, and this was something that deism took great pains to exploit. The deists came to regard the Bible as an entirely human product, to be approached with the same critical attitude as any other classic text of world literature. Deism interpreted the scientific revolution, with its stunning successes in various fields, as definitive proof of the incomparable prowess of human reason, which was to be taken as the supreme standard by which all things, including religion, were to be judged.

As to its genesis, deism was very much an English phenomenon, and the Englishman Lord Herbert of Cherbury (1583–1648) is often identified as the Father of Deism. He published a series of books—*De veritate* (*On Truth*) in 1624, *De religione laici* (*On the Religion of the Layman*) in 1645, and *De religione gentilium* (*On the Religion of the Pagans*) in 1663—that spelled out many of the ideas that were to become the commonplaces of deist thought. Other English contributors to that thought were John Toland, who published *Christianity Is Not Mysterious* (1696); Anthony Collins, who produced an influential text entitled *Discourse of Free-Thinking* (1713); and Matthew Tindal, the author of *Christianity as Old as the Creation* (1730).

The most prominent proponent of deist thinking in France was Voltaire—he has been described by one historian as "the achetypal deist"—but mention should also be made of Jean-Jacques Rousseau. Voltaire was a lifelong Anglophile, and he can be given most of the credit for importing the English movement into his native country. There were two salient features of French deism: it was militantly anticlerical, which, given the setting, was one and the same as being anti-Catholic (Voltaire was tolerant toward religion so long as the religion in question wasn't Catholicism); and it was adamantly opposed to monarchical government, and in that respect deism could be cited as one of the contributors to the French Revolution. The chief figures of deism as it manifested itself in Germany were philosopher Moses Mendelssohn and philosopher and playwright Gotthold Lessing.

Given that it sprang up in England, it is not surprising that deism would eventually take root in the English colonies in America. The two major deist works that find a place in early American literature are *Reason, the Only Oracle of Man* by Ethan Allen, published in 1784, and *The Age of Reason* by Thomas Paine, published 10 years later in 1794. The latter work was not given a welcome reception by the American public; in fact, it had the effect of transforming Paine's status as a hero of the Revolution to that of a persona non grata. From the opinions they expressed here and there in their writings, it is evident that both Benjamin Franklin and Thomas Jefferson also had definite leanings toward deism.

Perhaps deism is most accurately described as a "secular religion." It was a religion in the sense that it gave at least token acknowledgment to the possibility that there was a supernatural realm to be taken into account. It was secular in the sense that, for all practical purposes, it gave prominence of place to the natural realm. God may be in his heaven, but neither the place nor its divine resident need be of much concern to earth-dwelling man.

Never a popular movement, deism was the brainchild and the preoccupation of the intelligentsia, and its proponents assumed an elitist attitude. Voltaire, for example, thought that the masses were not sufficiently rational to be able to appreciate and benefit by a religion based on reason alone, and he believed that they should be encouraged to continue to believe in "myths" such as hell, with its threat of eternal punishment, for that would ensure their living orderly, nondisruptive lives. Though it saw its heyday in the 18th century, not a few of the ideas fostered by deism are alive and well today—within Freemasonry, for example. Also, it seems that some deist ideas find currency within certain circles of liberal Protestantism.—D. Q. McInerny

BIBLIOGRAPHY AND FURTHER READING: Byrne, Peter. *Natural Religion and the Nature of Religion: The Legacy of Deism.* London: Routledge, 1989; Champion, Justin A. I. "Deism." In *Columbia History of Western Philosophy,* 437–445. New York: MJF Books, 1999; Lauer, Rosemary Z. *Mind of Voltaire: A Study in "Constructive Deism."* Westminster, MD: Newman Press, 1961; Morais, Herbert Montfort. *Deism in Eighteenth-Century America.* New York: Russell & Russell, 1960. *See also* ARISTOTLE; REASON; SCIENCE; VOLTAIRE

DE KONINCK, CHARLES (1906–1965)

Though Charles De Koninck is not as well known, among English-speaking readers, as Jacques Maritain and Étienne Gilson, he deserves to be considered with them as one of the major figures of the Thomistic revival that was inaugurated by Pope Leo XIII's 1879 encyclical, *Aeterni Patris.* He certainly ranked among the most illustrious Thomist philosophers at work on the North American continent during the middle decades of the 20th century, and his influence, though limited to date, has been considerable.

Charles De Koninck was born in Torhout, Belgium, a small town near Bruges, on July 29, 1906. When he was eight years old, his family emigrated to the United States, settling in Detroit, but three years later his father decided to send his then 11-year-old son back to Belgium to be educated there, beginning at the College at Ostend. The young boy had a natural bent for mathematics and science, and his original intent was to pursue his studies in those fields. However, his tutor persuaded him that he would be better advised to follow the classics course. This he did, and with great success, becoming highly proficient in Greek and Latin. This was not done at the expense of the sciences, however, and he pursued studies in physics and chemistry at the École Normale at Torhout.

Under the direction of the Belgian Dominicans, De Koninck engaged in an intensive study of the works of St. Thomas Aquinas from 1925 to 1928, which proved to be a telling chapter in his life, for henceforth he was to be a totally dedicated student of the thought of Aquinas. In 1934, De Koninck received his doctorate in philosophy, summa cum laude, from Louvain University. His dissertation, "The Philosophy of Sir Arthur Eddington," was written under the direction of Prof. Fernand Renoirte.

No sooner had he finished his graduate studies at Louvain than he was invited to join the faculty of the Higher Institute of Philosophy at Laval University in Quebec City, Canada. He was to spend his entire academic career at Laval. In 1933, the year prior to receiving his doctorate and moving to Canada, De Koninck married Zöe Decruydt, and together they were to have 12 children, every one of whom came to share their father's passion for learning, several of them ending up with doctoral degrees.

Given his interests and educational background, De Koninck's appointment at Laval was specifically for the field of the philosophy of nature, and most of the courses he taught there over the years were in that discipline and those related to it. He also taught courses that concentrated exclusively on the works of Aquinas. De Koninck was the dean of the Faculty of Philosophy at Laval from 1939 to 1956 and was reappointed to that post in 1964, a year before his death. Besides being an energetic and captivating lecturer, he was an assiduous writer, and he published numerous philosophical works on a wide variety of subjects, most of them in the form of articles, written in French.

Along with A.-M. Parent, De Koninck founded the journal *Laval theologique et philosophique*, in which many of his own articles appeared. Besides a doctorate in philosophy, De Koninck also held a doctorate in theology (from Laval), and in his capacity as a theologian, he was often consulted by churchmen in Quebec on a variety of matters. Over the years, he held positions as visiting professor at the University of Mexico, McMaster University, Purdue University, and the University of Notre Dame, and he lectured at any number of other universities throughout North and South America. De Koninck was a member of the Royal Society of Canada and the Roman Academy of St. Thomas. He further served as *theologus* (official theologian) of Cardinal Maurice Roy during the Second Vatican Council, the only layman to hold such a position. He was in Rome in this capacity when he died of a sudden heart attack on February 15, 1965, at the age of 58.

It was during De Koninck's 30-year tenure at Laval, and chiefly because of the dynamic influence he exerted there, that the institution became what was arguably the principal center for Thomistic studies on the North American continent. He was the mentor to scores of graduate students, many of them from the United States, who went to Laval with the express purpose of studying under him. Then, armed with Laval licentiates or doctorates and deeply imbued with a love for the thought of St. Thomas, they took positions in colleges and universities across the United States and Canada and carried on the scholastic tradition to which they had been given a matchless introduction.

De Koninck was a Thomist after the mind of St. Thomas himself, which is to say that he saw the principal object to be truth, not who stated the truth. Although he had an astonishingly deep and comprehensive knowledge of the works of St. Thomas, he never regarded his role to be that of a mere parrot of the thought of the Common Doctor. To be a Thomist, for him, was not to be antiquarian, for the thought of St. Thomas, in all its essentials, was a source of immeasurable philosophical and theological riches, timeless in quality, and it was the task of the modern Thomist to apply St. Thomas's thought to present-day issues and problems. And this he did with remarkable success. Like Maritain, De Koninck saw St. Thomas's thought as singularly exemplary of the perennial philosophy, freighted with that wisdom of which the modern world had so desperate a need.

Though De Koninck's interests as a philosopher were quite diverse, as evidenced by the variety of subjects on which he wrote, his principal contributions were in the fields of the philosophy of nature, represented by works such as *Cosmos* (1934) and *The Hollow Universe* (1960), and in social or political philosophy, represented by works such as *The Primacy of the Common Good* (1943) and *In Defence of St. Thomas* (1945). De Koninck had a thoroughgoing knowledge of modern science, and he harbored a warm respect for its accomplishments. But he was concerned that the empirical sciences, because of the narrow approach each of them necessarily takes toward the study of nature, were giving us a simplistic notion of physical reality, a notion that had little, if any, connection with the view of that reality we have through our common experience. De Koninck saw no conflict between science and religion; his understanding of the physical universe was fully accepting of everything that science had beneficially to say about its nature, but he felt that the scientific view, because of its limitations, had to be lodged within a larger, all-encompassing theological view. The universe was best seen as a grand work of art, and the Artist was God.

The Primacy of the Common Good and *In Defence of St. Thomas* are worthy to be regarded as two of the most trenchant works on the common good written in the 20th century. De Koninck develops his notion of the common good, based on principles laid down by St. Thomas, in opposition to a position he identifies as "personalism," which is a form of individualism that is injurious to any community because it gives distorted emphasis to the person at the expense of the common good. There is no denying the unique dignity of the human person, given that his final end is God, but for De Koninck the person is able to flourish, as a person, only when properly subordinate to the common good, be that of the family, of the political community, or ultimately and most importantly, of the analogous common good who is God Himself. De Koninck saw the kinds of totalitarian regimes established by Fascism and Communism as totally antipathetic to the common good, however they might tout the term, for in these regimes the person, as person, is effectively obliterated under the crushing weight of an ideologically driven juggernaut, the antithesis to a genuine community.

De Koninck's theological writings constitute a category unto themselves and are eminently worthy of serious study, particularly those having to do with the field of Mariology. He had an ardent devotion to the Blessed Virgin Mary, and it has been conjectured that works like his *Ego Sapientia: The Wisdom That Is Mary* (1943) were contributing factors toward the proclamation of the dogma of the Assumption by Pope Pius XII in 1950.

The circumstance that the works of Charles De Koninck are not as well known as they ought to be among English-language readers will happily soon be remedied, thanks to the initiative of philosopher Ralph McInerny—a student of De Koninck who wrote his doctoral dissertation under his direction—who established a project that will culminate in the publication in English, by the University of Notre Dame Press, of all of the major works of his much-admired mentor. With the completion of this project, many more people will have access to the works of one of the most distinguished Thomistic philosophers of recent times.—D. Q. McInerny

BIBLIOGRAPHY AND FURTHER READING: Armour, Leslie. "The Philosophy of Charles De Koninck." In *The Writings of Charles De Koninck*, edited by Ralph McInerny, vol. 1. Notre Dame, IN: University of Notre Dame Press, 2008; George, Richard J. "Teacher-Scholar: The Traditional Wisdom of Charles De Koninck." *American Benedictine Review* (1965): 586–597; McInerny, Ralph. "Charles De Koninck: A Philosopher of Order." *New Scholasticism* 39, no. 4 (1965): 491–516; McInerny, Ralph, ed. and trans. *The Writings of Charles De Koninck.* 2 vols. Notre Dame, IN: University of Notre Dame Press, 2008–2009. *See also* GILSON, ÉTIENNE HENRY; MARITAIN, JACQUES; McINERNY, RALPH; THOMISM/NEO-THOMISM

DEMOCRATIC THEORY Democratic theory is a field of study that examines the theory and practice of democracy. It consists of a broad range of approaches by which scholars attempt to define the term, evaluate its necessary principles, and determine the conditions under which it is established and sustained. It utilizes normative, philosophical, and empirical analysis and is closely associated with the subdiscipline of comparative politics within the general subject of political science.

Research in this area focuses on democracy's origins, beginning with the Athenian model of democracy and reviewing how it has evolved over time into contemporary democratic political regimes. It explores the works of political theorists whose ideas help to explain its foundations and functions. Among democracy's earliest writers are Plato and Aristotle. During the Enlightenment, numerous philosophers, including Jean-Jacques Rousseau, John Locke, Baron de Montesquieu, and James Madison, made notable contributions. Modern thinkers include the likes of John Rawls and Hannah Arendt. Their works investigate human nature, social contracts, political stability, and revolution.

As an area of study, democratic theory is relatively new in political science. It began with the publication of Robert Dahl's *A Preface to Democratic Theory* in 1956. In this book, Dahl discusses two competing theories of democracy—Madisonian and populist theory—and comes to the conclusion that they do not adequately explain how modern democracies work. He constructs a new model, which he calls "polyarchy," to solve the problems he finds in the classical approaches to understanding democracy.

Dahl's *Preface* and his subsequent works, including *Pluralist Democracy in the United States* (1967), *Polyarchy* (1971), *Dilemmas of Pluralist Democracy* (1983), and *Democracy and Its Critics* (1989), have led other scholars to contribute to the development of this new field. Seymour Martin Lipset in his seminal work *Economic Development and Political Legitimacy* (1959) investigates the conditions that create democracies, such as wealth, education, and industrialization. Arend Lijphart focuses on the internal workings of the democratic political system, its institutions, electoral systems, and political parties. Juan Linz and Alfred Stepan write about the decline of democracies in *The Breakdown of Democratic Regimes* (1978). And Samuel Huntington considers the waves of democratization in *The Third Wave* (1991) in reaction to the significant number of countries that were transitioning to democracy in the post–Cold War era.

Because of its diverse nature, democratic theory is a difficult field to study and describe. While there is a general consensus that its essential conditions include participation, competition, and civil and political liberties, there is little agreement on what democracy means and how to institute it. Scholars struggle whether to separate or combine its social, economic, and political components. There are numerous conceptions of it in the literature—direct democracy, aggregative democracy, polyarchy, radical democracy. Several typologies have been proposed to classify the different democratic systems based upon political and economic criteria. Political theorists have produced competing theories to describe, explain, and predict it depending on their differing views on human nature, the state of nature, political institutions, and the existence of natural rights. Given this high degree of diversity within the field and the challenges it poses, scholars continue to value and study the concept of democracy.

Traditionally, the Catholic Church does not offer a particular political and economic model by which individuals should live. The Church believes that societies must make these decisions based upon their own historical circumstances. Its duty is to provide social teaching to orient society's members toward the common good. This is done by informing each individual's conscience to assure that it is properly formed. It is also achieved by articulating the moral principles upon which a society should be built and ought to function, which is ultimately the protection and promotion of the dignity of the human person.

When it comes to democracy, the Church's views are guarded. While it values the participation and choice provided by such a system, it also recognizes the associated vulnerability and abuses.

Historically, there has been an attitude of distrust toward democracy by the Church. This was based on several factors. First, revolutionary democracy in Europe was often founded upon the philosophies of religious indifference and subjective moral autonomy, which led to the destruction of tradition. New democratic leaders often accused the Church of supporting the old regimes and the privileges it had secured under them. Second, the new freedoms unleashed by democracy witnessed the arrival of a dangerous secular ideal and the demise of Christian virtue. Third, these democratic experiences spilled over into a demand for the democratization of the Catholic Church, calling for the elections of Church leaders, including the pope. Finally, democracy's ties to capitalism and nationalism also raised a series of issues for the Church.

Some of these criticisms of democracy have carried over into the modern day. In his encyclical letter *Evangelium Vitae*, Pope John Paul II discusses how ethical relativism has been used within the context of a democracy to legitimize grave crimes and the denial of freedom. There is a serious temptation to substitute democracy for morality, whereby majority rule becomes the source of "truth." Democracy should be properly viewed as a means to an end, not an end in itself. Its morality is not automatic—it is only moral insofar as it conforms to objective moral law. Without this foundation, a democracy becomes vulnerable to the interests of those in power who are in a position to manipulate the system.

In spite of these potential shortcomings, the Catholic Church recognizes that democracy possesses certain positive characteristics, particularly when compared to other forms of governance. Pope John Paul II in *Centesimus Annus* makes the case that democracy best guarantees the participation of the citizens to elect and hold accountable those who govern them, to secure the peaceful transition of power, and to ensure respect for human rights. It is a type of political system that is based on the rule of law and, when authentically practiced, is one that is grounded in natural law. It is supported by a values system that respects human rights and is committed to the common good. Without these, a democracy becomes vulnerable to regime change.

The Catholic Church also prefers that political power be divided among several sources within a society, rather than being concentrated in the hands of one or a few individuals and institutions. This division of power increases the probability of a balanced order where checks can be applied to help maintain political power within its proper boundaries. The end result is a reduction in abusive government. Democracy promotes a general sense of shared responsibility between elected officials and their constituents. Citizens are in a position to hold their political leaders accountable. The civil and political liberties associated with democracy offer its citizens several avenues to check authority: elections, the ability to run for office, referenda, and the right to petition. Citizens are also capable of receiving greater amounts of information through a free media about the activities of their elected officials and the workings of government, thus resulting in a higher degree of equality.

Likewise, the rule of law protects the government from the arbitrary rule of the masses. Structures and procedures are put into place to moderate an impassioned, hostile public, who could potentially make demands that threaten the system. Elected officials operating within these bounds are free to contribute to the common good, acting according to the principle of service rather than personal gain.

While democracies experience to one degree or another the practical problems of corruption and excessive bureaucratization, the rule of law, participation, and accountability provide solutions not available in other types of government. If authentically practiced, a democracy affords its citizens the rights and freedoms to live the way they ought to live as they proceed on their pilgrimage to unity with God in the kingdom of heaven.—Andrew M. Essig

BIBLIOGRAPHY AND FURTHER READING: Dahl, Robert A. *A Preface to Democratic Theory.* Chicago: University of Chicago Press, 1956; John Paul II. *Centesimus Annus.* 1991; Hyland, James L. *Democratic Theory: The Philosophical Foundations.* Oxford, England: Manchester University Press, 1995; Rommen, Heinrich A. *The State in Catholic Thought: A Treatise in Political Philosophy.* St. Louis: B. Herder, 1955. *See also* DEMOCRACY; EVANGELIUM VITAE; NATURAL LAW

DENNETT, DANIEL (1942–) Daniel Dennett is a philosopher of science with interests in biology, cognitive science, and the mind. Recently, he has gained notoriety for his critique of religion as nothing more than an evolutionary adaptation. Dennett's strong attacks on religion, especially Christianity, have placed him among the pantheon of new atheists that includes Richard Dawkins, Sam Harris, and Christopher Hitchens.

Dennett was a student of W. V. Quine as an undergraduate at Harvard University before attending Oxford University for his doctorate. Dennett is currently the Austin B. Fletcher Professor of Philosophy and the codirector of the Center for Cognitive Sciences at Tufts University. He has also been the recipient of numerous distinctions, including a Fulbright Fellowship and two Guggenheim fellowships; he was named Humanist of the Year in 2004 by the American Humanist Association.

At the core of Dennett's work are his cognitive theories examining both the content and consciousness of the mind. In his book *Brainstorms* (1978), Dennett's view of free will has two stages. When a choice is posed to us, there is a "consideration generator" in our mind that in a somewhat undetermined process suggests possible considerations. The mind then selects relevant considerations for a rational selection process. The choice of considerations is predictive of the agent's

choice. For Dennett, his approach allows an agent of decision making to engage in a process that has an element of randomness at the stage of posing relevant considerations, but also permits conscious deliberation in the narrowing of possible considerations and a final decision. This deliberation is guided by the desires and beliefs of the decision maker.

Continuing his exploration of cognitive processes, Dennett in *The Intentional Stance* (1987) recognizes three levels of explaining the action of an object. We can view an object as a physical phenomenon that is merely the result of physics and chemistry or as the result of design or a form of engineering. A third possibility is the intentional stance that describes human actions as forms of belief, thinking, and intent. Dennett favors employing the intentional stance in explaining phenomena without any commitment to any deeper reality guiding the process. He concludes that what the self believes and thinks is an operationally valid concept that can provide us with some capacity to predict behavior.

These decision processes are part of the broader human phenomenon known as consciousness. In *Consciousness Explained* (1991), Dennett explores through a theory of "neural Darwinism" how evolution explains some of the content-producing features of consciousness. As part of his discussion of neural Darwinism, he introduces heterophenomenology, a view that assumes that people do subjectively experience in consciousness certain feelings. The subjective experiences of anger, love, and so forth are accurate expressions of our feelings, but are not necessarily accurate representations of what is actually occurring. The objective reality of consciousness results from the mind employing a "multiple draft" process that recognizes that phenomena present many forms or drafts of an experience in many parts of the brain that are eventually reconciled.

Ever the empiricist, Dennett contends that there is no aspect of mind beyond the objective aspect of reality. Hence, he rejects the notion of "qualia." Some cognitive theorists use the term *qualia* to describe the aspects of an entity that remain when you remove all of its objective aspects. For example, the experience of the redness of a ripe tomato is more than the sum of its chemistry and physics. For Dennett, the perspective of an intentional stance includes no such mysterious entities, because nothing is outside a causal system of material events, including qualia.

Darwin's Dangerous Idea (1996) is Dennett's explicit exploration of evolutionary theory. Dennett portrays evolution as an algorithmic process, a "set of rules for calculation or problem solving." This algorithmic process requires "substrate neutrality"; that is, it must be simple, be applicable in all conditions, and produce the same results every time. This process can be discovered through reverse-engineering of biological species. Dennett starts from an existing species and works from the present back to its adaptations in the past revealing its algorithmic processes. The resulting algorithms are not necessarily absolute truths, but probable truths that utilize intuition and inference.

Since the algorithmic process of evolution is self-contained, it does not require a designer, intelligent or otherwise. This simple mechanism is the adaptation of species through natural selection. With this advance in the natural sciences, there is no need for a deus ex machina in biology, a God who acts like a "skyhook," lifting species upward into more complex forms like a crane—the cranes raise one another without anybody at the controls. This "dangerous" idea eliminates the need for God in the evolution of species.

So what happens to human development? It takes an interesting turn with the advent of cultural evolution through memes. A *meme* is a replicable form or idea of a human person or society that is adapted over time by a culture. This new form of cultural evolution through memes places Dennett at odds with the more narrow genetic determinism of sociobiology.

In the realm of morality, Dennett claims that there are no absolute truths or even certain ethical rules as the result of evolutionary biology. We must make choices without any certainty as to the correctness of our actions. If there is moral uncertainty in his evolutionary vision, Dennett offers some compensation with claims for the spectacular beauty and diversity of the world created by evolution.

Dennett's book is posing ideas dangerous not only for religion but also for some Darwinian theorists. He took aim, for example, at Stephen Jay Gould, who was not enamored of what he considered to be Dennett's naïve adaptation position. Gould had argued in a famous paper, "The Spandrels of San Marco," that many structures in the animal world are not adapted for any advantage. Dennett countered in *Darwin's Dangerous Idea* that Gould is trying to opt out of the mandates of the algorithm of evolution.

In his book *Breaking the Spell: Religion as a Natural Phenomenon* (2006), Dennett explores the evolutionary causes of religion. Taking on the issue of whether it is possible to scientifically analyze religion, he writes that religion evolved from the need to avoid harm and find the useful in our environments. This skill, in the form of a "hyperactive agent-detecting device," allowed us

to realize that we lived in a world with other minds. The ability of the device went too far, however, and attributed beliefs and desires to inanimate objects. This animism eventually resulted in more complex forms of deities who have special knowledge. Classes of priests arose to broker this special knowledge through increasingly sophisticated ritual processes. These specialized forms of knowledge were given special protection through the ideal of belief in belief that allowed this special knowledge to become even more arcane and inaccessible.

The critique of this book by Christians has been lively, with a number of complaints lodged against Dennett. One is that Dennett poses a closed system often based on unproven assumptions and sheer speculation. For example, the notion that religious forms are the result of adaptive cultural memes seems to be contradicted by the rich experiential dimension of faith traditions that employ personal experiential discoveries and reason that are arguably not just mimetic repetitions of preconscious and invisible forms replicating themselves in our cultural forms and common life.

The attacks on *Breaking the Spell* have come not just from orthodox Christians. Leon Wieseltier notes in the *New York Times Book Review* that the empirically oriented Dennett paradoxically engages in a highly speculative analysis. He even cites Dennett for the admission that science has not proven his claims. Moreover, Wieseltier claims that Dennett, at a minimum, is overreaching in claiming a biological advantage and adaptation for common human activities and feelings. For example, can we force all of art and literature into the ambit of this claim? One final argument against Dennett is that if the reason he employs is a biological artifact of evolution, then why is it not merely an adaptation and no longer an independent form of objectivity that justifies Dennett's analysis of religion?

Dennett's analysis of religion has led to a number of debates, including a famous one with Cambridge professor of historical theology Alister McGrath that resulted in a book, *The Future of Atheism* (2008). In the debate and book, Dennett posits his naturalistic view of species development through evolutionary adaption that excludes a supernatural cause. Religions are culturally replicable memes that evolve in and through human societies. Religions are like viruses; they are parasites out "for themselves." They survive by occupying space in minds and being passed on to new generations. In response, McGrath notes that Dennett advocates an unsupported and unobserved hypothetical entity, the meme. Moreover, isn't atheism also a meme? If the answer is yes, then what is the basis for determining mimetic orthodoxy between religion and atheism? Finally, McGrath wonders why there is no scientific evidence supporting Dennett's position.—Phillip M. Thompson

BIBLIOGRAPHY AND FURTHER READING: Dennett, Daniel. *Breaking the Spell: Religion as a Natural Phenomenon.* New York: Viking, 2006; Dennett, Daniel. *Consciousness Explained.* Boston: Little, Brown, 2006; McGrath, Alister. *The Future of Atheism.* Minneapolis: Fortress Press, 2008. *See also* ATHEISM; DAWKINS, CLINTON RICHARD; PINKER, STEPHEN

DIGNITAS PERSONAE   *Dignitas Personae* is an instruction by the Congregation for the Doctrine of the Faith, dated September 8, 2008, and expressly approved by Pope Benedict XVI, that offers responses to various bioethical questions beyond what was provided in *Donum Vitae* (1987). *Dignitas Personae* seeks to encourage biomedical researchers to be respectful of the dignity of every human being and to contribute to the formation of conscience in regard to various questions about procreation and scientific research.

Like the encyclicals *Evangelium Vitae* and *Veritatis Splendor*, *Dignitas Personae* draws upon the light of both faith and reason to set forth an integrated vision of human life and is intended to provide moral guidance not just for Catholics but for "all who seek the truth" (*DP* # 3). As an ecclesial document, it falls within the ordinary magisterium (*Donum Veritatis* # 18) and should be received by Catholics "with the religious assent of their spirit" (*DP* # 37).

The first of the instruction's three parts reviews the anthropological, theological, and ethical principles that ought to govern the moral analysis of the specific problems regarding procreation considered in the second part and of the issues relevant to recently developed procedures for manipulating human embryos and the human genome raised in the third part.

At the core of the document are carefully worded statements of two fundamental theses about human life. The first is about the inviolable right of any innocent person to life: "The human being is to be respected and treated as a person from the moment of conception; and therefore from that same moment his rights as a person must be recognized, among which in the first place is the inviolable right of every innocent human being to life" (*DP* # 4). The second is about marriage as the proper context of procreation: "The origin of human life has its authentic context in marriage and in the family, where it is generated through an act which expresses the reciprocal love between a man and a woman. Procreation which is truly responsible vis-à-vis the child to be born must be the fruit of marriage" (*DP* # 6).

Like *Donum Vitae* and *Evangelium Vitae*, *Dignitas Personae* avoids committing itself to any particular theory of animation or ensoulment, but it does assert that the embryo has "the dignity proper to a person" (*DP* # 5). The reasoning that *Dignitas Personae* employs for defending the view that personal rights must be granted from the moment of conception is based on solid scientific evidence regarding the continuity of any individual's development from the moment a zygote has formed and on philosophically precise distinctions: "The reality of the human being for the entire span of life, both before and after birth, does not allow us to posit either a change in nature or a gradation in moral value" (*DP* # 5). But the document also clearly admits that there are theological reasons for holding the above-mentioned positions on human personhood and on marriage: the facts that every human being is made in the image of God (*DP* # 8) and that the acts that make procreation possible need to reflect God's own trinitarian love (*DP* # 9).

To forestall the objection that the Church has no business passing judgment on medical research, the document distinguishes between the *technical* evaluation of scientific claims, which is indeed restricted to those with professional competence, and the *moral* evaluation of any action in any field, for unconditional respect is due always and everywhere to every human being. For the Church to remind scientists that the end of a research program does not ethically justify using any and every means is not to compromise the legitimate autonomy of the sciences but only to be faithful to her own mission of forming consciences (*DP* # 10).

The second section of the document assesses the range of techniques that have been devised for assisting fertility. They are judged morally permissible so long as they respect (1) every human being's right to life and to physical integrity; (2) the unity of marriage, understood as requiring "reciprocal respect for the right within marriage to become a father or mother only together with the other spouse" (*DP* # 12); and (3) the distinctively human values of sexuality, which are taken to require that procreation take place only as a result of the marital communion between a husband and wife.

In light of the normative status of these principles, the document encourages the practice of adoption, so that children who lack parents may receive a home, and it praises research directed at the prevention or correction of sterility. It finds morally licit the use of medical techniques that facilitate conjugal acts of sexual intercourse and that assist them to achieve fertilization by removing obstacles. In continuity with *Donum Vitae*, however, *Dignitas Personae* expressly forbids all artificial insemination, including intracytoplasmic sperm injection, a procedure in which germ cells taken from the man are injected directly into a woman's oocyte in a test tube (*DP* # 17). Because of the inevitability in these techniques that procreation will be separated from the conjugal act of the spouses, the document thus forbids not only the use of surrogate mothers and sperm banks but also techniques in which it is the gametes of spouses joined in marriage that are being used to try to obtain conception.

Unsurprisingly, the document also criticizes all techniques of in vitro fertilization for accepting the sacrifice of numerous embryos (*DP* # 15)—both those embryos that are deliberately destroyed by being directly discarded as likely to be suffering some genetic defect (*DP* # 22) and the vast numbers that are not transferred into the uterus but frozen (*DP* # 18). The Church, the document reminds us, must defend the sacred and inviolable character of every human life from conception until natural death precisely because God's love does not differentiate between newly conceived infants, children, adults, and the elderly. God sees in each of them "an impression of his own image and likeness" (*DP* # 16).

On the question of what to do with the vast number of embryos that have already been frozen, the document finds there to be unresolvable problems of injustice to the individuals so conceived, for none of the solutions proposed (e.g., using the embryos experimentally for research or therapeutically for treating diseases, thawing them without reactivating them and then treating them as if normal cadavers, offering them to infertile couples, or permitting them to be prenatally adopted) is without problems. Hence, *Dignitas Personae* echoes Pope John Paul II's appeal to halt the production of human embryos so as to respect their basic human rights (*DP* # 19).

Part of the second section is given to the consideration of procedures that are actually abortive, despite the use of other terminology. In commenting, for instance, on one of the practices currently in clinical use after the transfer of multiple embryos into the mother's womb, the document condemns "embryo reduction" (the procedure in which some of the embryos or fetuses in the womb are directly exterminated) as the intentional abortion of innocent human beings (*DP* # 21). Likewise, the document condemns devices such as the

intrauterine device (IUD) that interfere with embryos before their implantation, "morning-after pills," and pharmaceuticals like RU-486. Even though the use of such devices and drugs may not actually cause an abortion on every use (for conception does not occur after every act of sexual intercourse), the person who seeks to prevent an embryo's implantation or to dislodge it "generally intends abortion" (*DP* # 23).

The third section of *Dignitas Personae* reviews newly devised treatments that involve the manipulation of the embryo or the human genome. The document makes a careful distinction between somatic cell gene therapy, which seeks to reduce or eliminate genetic defects in the cells of a particular patient, and germ line cell therapy, which aims at correcting genetic defects in an individual's offspring. Somatic cell gene therapy can be morally licit if one can establish that those being treated will not be exposed to excessive risks to their health or physical integrity and if they or their legitimate representatives give informed consent (*DP* # 26). But germ line cell therapy, the document concludes, is not morally permissible in the present state of research, for the considerable risks connected to any genetic manipulation are not fully controllable and one may not morally undertake action that could possibly cause grave harm to these individuals. In particular, the "eugenic mentality" and the inclination to "take the place of our Creator" that are expressed or latent in the use of genetic engineering to strengthen the gene pool must be renounced (*DP* # 27).

In regard to human cloning, the document rejects the notion that there is any moral difference between "reproductive cloning" (done in order to obtain the birth of a baby) and "therapeutic cloning" (done for the sake of medical therapy or research). Human cloning is "intrinsically illicit in that . . . it seeks to give rise to a new human being without a connection to the act of reciprocal self-giving between the spouses and, more radically, without any link to sexuality" (*DP* # 28). In its determination that both reproductive and therapeutic cloning involve a serious offense to the dignity of the person, the document makes clear that even an otherwise beneficent intention cannot correct for a practice that is intrinsically wrong.

As part of its review of the therapeutic use of stem cells, *Dignitas Personae* insists that researchers must consider how the stem cells are obtained. Techniques of animal-human hybridization and those that involve taking them from a living human embryo in a way that invariably causes the death of the embryo must be regarded as gravely wrong, but methods that do not cause serious harm to the subject from whom the stem cells are taken are generally licit (e.g., when taken from an adult, or from the blood of the umbilical cord at the time of birth, or from those individuals who have died of natural causes during the fetal stage of their development) (*DP* # 32). The document expresses serious doubts but stops short of passing a definitive judgment about the techniques such as altered nuclear transfer (ANT) or oocyte assisted reprogramming (OAR) for obtaining stem cells with a pluripotency like that of embryonic stem cells without actually being embryos (*DP* # 30).

Finally, the document notes the grave moral disorder involved in experimenting on human embryos, for they have a right to the same respect owed to a child once born and to every person (*DP* # 34). It concludes with reminders about the problem of moral complicity involved in the research use of "biological material" illicitly obtained by individuals other than the researcher (*DP* # 35). Here the document invokes the standard distinction between material and formal cooperation with evil and warns of fallacious reasoning even in regard to material cooperation, as well as the complete impermissibility of formal cooperation, with evil.

The judgments and the reasoning present in *Dignitas Personae* do not replace or alter those of *Donum Vitae*. Rather, the 2008 document confirms the 1987 document, especially in regard to the debates that arose because of the earlier document's criticisms of such techniques as in vitro fertilization. Like its predecessor, *Dignitas Personae* exhibits the Church's concern to protect the dignity of nascent human life and conjugal love and to provide guidance for the proper formation of consciences on such matters as preimplantation genetic diagnosis, gene therapy, and "emergency contraception."

It is significant that the document does not yet definitively resolve all current questions. For instance, the document apparently tends in the direction of regarding embryo-rescue as illicit, but it stops short of saying so unambiguously (*DP* # 19). While a couple attempting an embryo transfer simply to resolve their infertility would clearly be acting illicitly by violating the goods of marriage, the document does not comment on the morality of an embryo adoption undertaken merely with the intention of rescuing unwanted embryos. Likewise, the instruction does not treat the morality of other assisted reproductive technologies such as gamete intra-fallopian transfer (GIFT) and intrauterine insemination (IUI).—Joseph W. Koterski, SJ

BIBLIOGRAPHY AND FURTHER READING: Brugger, E. Christian, ed. "Symposium on *Dignitas Personae*," *National Catholic Bioethics Quarterly* 9, no. 3 (2009); Grabowski, John S., and Christopher Gross, "*Dignitas Personae* and the Adoption of Frozen Embryos: A New Chill Factor?" *National Catholic Bioethics Quarterly* 10, no. 2 (2010): 307–328; Hilliard, Marie T. "*Dignitas Personae* and Emergency Contraception." *Ethics & Medics* 34, no. 2 (2009): 3–4; Latkovic, Mark S. "The Dignity of the Person: An Overview and Commentary on *Dignitas Personae*." *National Catholic Bioethics Quarterly* 10, no. 2 (2010): 283–305. *See also DONUM VERITATIS; DONUM VITAE;* EMBRYO ADOPTION AND/OR RESCUE; EUGENICS

"DOCTRINAL NOTE ON SOME QUESTIONS REGARDING THE PARTICIPATION OF CATHOLICS IN POLITICAL LIFE"

The "Doctrinal Note on Some Questions Regarding the Participation of Catholics in Political Life" was issued by the Congregation for the Doctrine of the Faith (CDF) in January 2003 (although dated 2002). In issuing the document, the CDF made clear that it was addressing the role of Catholics "in today's democratic societies," where, "in a climate of true freedom, everyone is made a participant in directing the body politic" (# 1). For Catholics, the document makes clear, the political freedom and power attendant to citizenship in a democratic polity carry with them certain responsibilities, beginning with the duty *to* participate, then involving questions of *how* we participate, and *to what purpose.*

Citing the *Catechism of the Catholic Church,* the CDF notes that Christians from the days of the early Church have been called to "play their full role as citizens" (# 1). "It is a mistake," the document stresses, "to think that, because we have here no lasting city, but seek the city which is to come, we are entitled to shirk our earthly responsibilities; this is to forget that by our faith we are bound all the more to fulfill these responsibilities according to the vocation of each" (# 9). As such "the lay faithful are never to relinquish their participation" in *all* those areas of public life—"economic, social, legislative, administrative and cultural"—that affect "the common good" (# 1). We are reminded of the instruction of the Second Vatican Council that to the Catholic laity falls the duty "to impress the divine law on the affairs of the earthly city" (*GS* # 43).

The CDF then focuses specifically on how Catholics are called to contribute through the political process: "by voting," of course, but "in other ways as well" (# 1). In a democracy, we have the opportunity for greater participation: actively supporting or opposing particular candidates, contacting our elected officials to urge support or opposition for various legislative and policy initiatives, even seeking and holding office ourselves.

There is a temptation, though, to separate Catholic social thought from the political realm. This has been particularly prevalent in the United States in recent decades. In 1960, then presidential candidate John F. Kennedy, seeking to mollify Protestant concerns about his Catholicism, assured members of the Greater Houston Ministerial Association, a Protestant group, of his commitment to an "absolute . . . separation of church and state" and proclaimed that a President's "religious views" should be no more than "his own private affair." Since that time, many American Catholics have taken guidance from Kennedy's formulation.

This view has been vigorously opposed, notably in a March 1, 2010, address, also in Houston, "The Vocation of Christians in American Public Life," by Archbishop Charles Chaput. Kennedy's speech, the archbishop said, has had the effect of "walling religion away from the process of government in a new and aggressive way" and "divid[ing] a person's private beliefs from his or her public duties."

That is manifestly *not* the Church's teaching on the role of religion in public life. As the CDF makes clear, it is "the lay Catholic's duty to be morally coherent. . . . There cannot be two parallel lives in their existence: on the one hand, the so-called 'spiritual life,' with its values and demands; and on the other, the so-called 'secular' life, that is, life in a family, at work, in social responsibilities, in the responsibilities of public life and in culture" (# 6). Catholics fulfill our civic responsibilities precisely when we allow our consciences to guide us in "infusing the temporal order with Christian values" (# 1). Our involvement in political life should be as Catholics—directed not toward self-interest but toward the common good, and seeking not to impose our views but to contribute the insights of Catholic moral and social teaching to public policy deliberations.

To be sure, the doctrinal note emphasizes the need to distinguish "between the domains proper to religion and to political society," lest sectarian religious laws be imposed through civil law in ways that violate religious freedom and even threaten other human rights (# 6). There is a critical difference, however, between such "confessional values" and broader ethical and moral considerations that affect the common good. These "do not require from those who defend them the profession of the Christian faith, although the Church's teaching confirms and defends them" (# 5). And such moral and ethical truths are no less legitimate in a "pluralistic society" because they happen to accord with Catholic teaching; nor should the voices of certain adherents be excluded from the public square because their Christian faith may have helped them in recognizing these truths (# 6).

Within the guiding principles of the Church's moral and social teaching, the CDF stresses "the legitimate freedom of Catholic citizens to choose among the various political opinions that are compatible with faith and the natural moral law, and to select, according to their own criteria, what best corresponds to the needs of the common good" (# 3). "It is not the Church's task to set forth specific political solutions—and even less to propose a single solution as the acceptable one—to temporal questions that God has left to the free and responsible judgment of each person," the doctrinal note explains. "It is, however, the Church's right and duty to provide a moral judgment on temporal matters when this is required by faith or the moral law" (# 3).

In short, the legitimate prudential judgments of Catholic citizens as to which public policies best serve the common good must be informed by and consistent with the Church's moral and social teachings—teachings that are based on "moral law rooted in the nature of the human person, which must govern our understanding of man, the common good and the state" (# 2).

It should be emphasized here that this concept of a natural law, inscribed by God on every human heart and discernible through the gift of reason, while much denigrated in modern society, is hardly inconsistent with American democracy. It is, in fact, the very basis of the Declaration of Independence.

There are times, the doctrinal note observes, when "political activity comes up against moral principles that do not admit of exception." The CDF cites as examples attacks on the sanctity of human life, such as abortion and euthanasia; threats to the integrity of the family; modern forms of slavery; and violations of religious freedom (# 4).

Even on such fundamental principles, for example, the sacredness of life and opposition to abortion, the doctrinal note makes clear that a public official or citizen may—as long as their commitment to the moral principle is clear and unambiguous—support imperfect laws or policies designed to limit the harm caused by an unjust law, if it is not possible to immediately overturn the law completely. On other issues—for example, complex questions of war and peace or "development of an economy that is at the service of the human person and of the common good"—there can be varying prudential judgments as to the "practical implementation" of the principles of Catholic social teaching (# 4). "Very often," the Second Vatican Council's Pastoral Constitution on the Church in the Modern World (*Gaudium et Spes*) explains, a layperson's "Christian vision will suggest a certain solution in some given situation. Yet it happens rather frequently, and legitimately so, that some of the faithful, with no less sincerity, will see the problem quite differently." In such cases, "no one is permitted to identify the authority of the Church exclusively with his own opinion. Let them, then, try to guide each other by sincere dialogue in a spirit of mutual charity and with anxious interest above all in the common good" (GS # 43).

At the same time, the CDF's doctrinal note deplores cases in recent years "within some organizations founded on Catholic principles, in which support has been given to political forces or movements with positions contrary to the moral and social teaching of the Church on fundamental ethical questions" (# 7). We might cite as a recent example the 2009 effort of the group Catholics United to support the nomination of Catholic Kansas governor Kathleen Sebelius to be U.S. Secretary of Health and Human Services, minimizing her long and consistent record of support for virtually unrestricted abortion—including late-term, partial birth abortion—as being balanced by her support for other issues on Catholic United's agenda. The group went so far as to attack Kansas City archbishop Joseph Naumann for criticizing the governor's pro-abortion record.

"No Catholic can appeal to the principle of pluralism or to the autonomy of lay involvement in political life to support policies affecting the common good which compromise or undermine fundamental ethical requirements," the CDF makes clear (# 5). It is absolutely true, as the doctrinal note says, that "the Christian faith is an integral unity, and thus it is incoherent to isolate some particular element to the detriment of the whole of Catholic doctrine. A political commitment to a single isolated aspect of the Church's social doctrine does not exhaust one's responsibility towards the common good" (# 4).

Some accuse pro-life Catholics of just such an "isolation" of a single issue, and it is true that simply opposing abortion does not fulfill our broader obligation to work toward the common good of all. At the same time, as the doctrinal note stresses, the sanctity of human life is a fundamental moral principle that cannot be compromised, and "those who are directly involved in lawmaking bodies have a *grave and clear obligation to oppose* any law that attacks human life" (# 4). Moreover, the abortion mentality that drives the mass destruction

of preborn human life is demonstrably more than a "single issue," affecting as it does society's attitudes toward *all* vulnerable populations: the poor, the disabled, the elderly, and the terminally ill, for example. Even the late Cardinal Joseph Bernardin, foremost voice for the "seamless garment" approach to life issues, emphasized that "a society which destroys human life by abortion under mantle of law unavoidably undermines respect for life in all other contexts."

And so, while Catholics should not support candidates or parties solely because they oppose abortion—without regard to their positions on other fundamental moral principles—the CDF seems clearly to recognize that the larger problem today is among Catholics who would disregard a candidate's active *support* for abortion because they embrace other aspects of the candidate's agenda—even though these may in many cases involve policy positions that are legitimately subject to differing prudential judgments.

Finally, the CDF stresses the obligation of Catholics to defend our own right to be heard in the public square—not out of self-interest, but as essential to the promotion of the common good. The document warns against an "intolerant secularism" that would disqualify Christians from a voice in the public square because their views are informed by their faith. Such "marginalization" of the Christian voice would undermine the goal of "true consensus" in a pluralistic society; open the road to "moral anarchy" in which the weak would be even more vulnerable to the strong; and "threaten the very spiritual and cultural foundations of civilization" (# 6). We might in this context recall the words of one of America's Founding Fathers, John Adams: "Our Constitution is designed only for a moral and religious people. It is wholly inadequate for any other."

The seriousness of this responsibility—to defend and use our right to be heard in the public square—was underscored by the U.S. Catholic bishops in their 1998 document "Living the Gospel of Life: A Challenge to American Catholics." Catholics in America "have been changed by our culture too much," the bishops wrote, "and we have changed it not enough" (# 25). As the Congregation for the Doctrine of the Faith made clear, that must change if we are to serve the common good in the way that Catholics are uniquely situated to do: bringing the Gospel to bear on the "earthly city" by contributing the Church's moral and social teachings to our pluralistic society's public policy deliberations.—Richard Hinshaw

BIBLIOGRAPHY AND FURTHER READING: Bernardin, Joseph. "A Consistent Ethic for Church and Society."

Address to the annual meeting of Diocesan Pro-Life Directors, Denver, Colorado, August 8, 1988; Congregation for the Doctrine of the Faith. "Doctrinal Note on Some Questions Regarding the Participation of Catholics in Political Life." 2002. Available at http://www.vatican.va/roman_curia/congregations/cfaith/documents/rc_con_cfaith_doc_20021124_politica_en.html; U.S. Conference of Catholic Bishops. "Living the Gospel of Life: A Challenge to American Catholics." Washington, DC: U.S. Catholic Conference, 1998. *See also* CHAPUT, CHARLES; CONSISTENT ETHIC OF LIFE (SEAMLESS GARMENT); FAITHFUL CITIZENSHIP; KENNEDY, JOHN F.

DOMINUS IESUS   On August 6, 2000, the Congregation for the Doctrine of the Faith (CDF) issued a declaration entitled *Dominus Iesus: On the Unicity and Salvific Universality of Jesus Christ and the Church*. The document was signed by Cardinal Joseph Ratzinger, then prefect of the CDF (later Pope Benedict XVI), and Archbishop Tarcisio Bertone, the secretary of the CDF (later the Vatican secretary of state). Pope John Paul II ratified, confirmed, and ordered the declaration to be published on June 16, 2000.

Dominus Iesus ("Lord Jesus") is generally understood as a response to certain misunderstandings and misapplications of the Second Vatican Council on ecumenism and interreligious dialogue. Some believe a more proximate reason for the document was concern about the Catholic Church in Asia, especially India, where bishops were trying to evaluate certain new theological ideas of religious pluralism and various experiments in Catholic practice (e.g., the use of Hindu symbols and scriptures in Catholic settings). The document itself notes that its purpose is not to answer "questions that are matters of free theological debate, but rather to set forth again the doctrine of the Catholic faith in these areas, pointing out some fundamental questions that remain open to further development, and refuting specific positions that are erroneous or ambiguous" (# 3).

The document is divided into an introduction (# 1–4) followed by six thematic topics and a conclusion. The six themes are: I. The Fullness and Definitiveness of the Revelation of Jesus (# 5–8); II. The Incarnate Logos and the Holy Spirit in the Work of Salvation (# 9–12); III. Unicity and Universality of the Salvific Mystery of Jesus Christ (# 13–15); IV. Unicity and Unity of the Church (# 16–17); V. The Church: Kingdom of God and Kingdom of Christ (# 18–19); and VI. The Church and Other Religions in Relation to Salvation (# 20–22).

The introduction acknowledges a tension between the Church's mandate to proclaim Jesus Christ as "the way, the truth and the life" (John 14: 6) and the awareness that other religions "often reflect a ray of that truth which enlightens all men" (*DI* # 2; see also *Nostra Aetate*, # 2). But this tension is not the problem. Instead, the problem is that the Church's "constant missionary proclamation is endangered today by relativistic theories that seek to justify pluralism, not only *de facto* but also *de iure* (or *in principle*). As a consequence, it is held that certain truths have been superseded" (*DI* # 4). Among these allegedly superseded truths are: "the definitive and complete character of the revelation of Jesus Christ, the nature of the Christian faith as compared with the belief in other religions, the inspired nature of the books of Sacred Scripture, the personal unity between the Eternal Word and Jesus of Nazareth, . . . the unicity and salvific universality of the mystery of Jesus Christ, the universal salvific mediation of the Church, . . . and the subsistence of one Church of Christ in the Catholic Church."

Earlier popes (e.g., Leo XII, Gregory XVI, and Pius IX) had condemned religious indifferentism. *Dominus Iesus*, though, is focused on more recent expressions of religious relativism since the Second Vatican Council. These can be traced to various philosophical and theological presuppositions such as the "elusiveness and inexpressibility of divine truth," "relativistic attitudes about truth itself," and "the radical opposition posited between the logical mentality of the West and the symbolic mentality of the East" (*DI* # 4). No names are mentioned in the text of *Dominus Iesus*, but one footnote refers to the 1985 Notification of the CDF concerning the book *Church, Charism and Power* by Rev. Leonardo Boff, OFM. The document might also have other theologians in mind, such as John Hick, Hans Küng, Anthony De Mello, Paul Knitter, Tissa Balasuriya, and Jacques Dupuis.

In exploring theme I, numerous scriptures are given that testify to Jesus Christ as "the definitive self-revelation of God" and the Christian dispensation as "the new and definitive covenant" (*DI* # 5). To claim, therefore, that the Christian revelation is imperfect or incomplete or merely "complementary" to revelations given in other religions is "contrary to the Church's faith" (*DI* # 6).

The definitive revelation of Christ demands "the obedience of faith" (*DI* # 7; cf. Romans 1: 5 and 16: 26 and 2 Corinthians 10: 5–6). Faith is not simply "a personal adherence of man to God" but also "a free assent to the whole truth that God has revealed" (*DI* # 7).

Faith requires adherence both to God who reveals and to the truth that he reveals. Theological faith is a supernatural virtue that cannot be compared to belief in other religions. The distinction between "theological faith and belief in the other religions" must be *firmly held*" (*DI* # 7). Although the sacred writings of other religions might contain some elements that can nourish a relationship with God, they cannot be compared to the inspired texts of the Old and New Testaments (*DI* # 8).

In theme II (the Incarnate Logos and the Holy Spirit in the work of salvation), the CDF makes it clear that Jesus of Nazareth cannot be considered a "finite, historical figure" who reveals the divine "in a way complementary with other revelatory and salvific figures" (*DI* # 9). Any separation of the economy of the eternal Word from the economy of the Incarnate Word, Jesus Christ, must be rejected. Also to be rejected is attributing to the divine Logos "a salvific activity . . . exercised 'in addition to' or 'beyond' the humanity of Christ" (*DI* # 10).

Dominus Iesus repudiates the notion that the Holy Spirit has a salvific mission apart from the Christian economy of salvation. Instead, "there is only one salvific economy of the One and Triune God, realized in the mystery of the incarnation, death and resurrection of the Son of God, actualized with the cooperation of the Holy Spirit, and extended in its salvific value to all humanity and to the entire universe" (*DI* # 12).

Theme III (unicity and universality of the salvific mystery of Jesus Christ) presents another truth that must be "*firmly believed*": that the history of salvation has been brought to its fulfillment in "the incarnation, death and resurrection" of Jesus Christ, who is the "Son of God, Lord and only Savior" (*DI* # 13). This is supported by multiple New Testament passages (e.g. 1 John 4: 14 and 1: 29; Acts 4: 12, 10: 36, and 10: 42–43). As a truth of the Catholic, it must also be firmly believed "that the universal salvific will of the One and Triune God is offered and accomplished once for all in the mystery of the incarnation, death and resurrection of the Son of God" (*DI* # 14).

Dominus Iesus encourages the work of theologians who are seeking to explore how "the historical figures and positive elements" of other religions "may fall within the divine plan of salvation" (*DI* # 14). These "participated forms of mediation," however, can "acquire meaning and value *only* from Christ's own mediation, and they cannot be understood as a parallel or complementary to his" (*DI* # 14).

Theme IV explains the unicity and unity of the Church founded by Jesus Christ. Along these lines, "the

Catholic faithful *are required to profess* that there is a historical continuity—rooted in the apostolic succession—between the Church founded by Christ and the Catholic Church" (*DI* # 16). *Dominus Iesus*, section 16, repeats the important passage of *Lumen Gentium*, namely, that the Church of Christ "subsists in [*subsistit in*] the Catholic Church, governed by the Successor of Peter and by the bishops in communion with him" (*DI* # 16; cf. *LG* # 8). The CDF explains that the Second Vatican Council used the expression *subsistit in* "to harmonize two doctrinal statements: on the one hand that the Church of Christ, despite the divisions which exist among Christians, continues to exist fully only in the Catholic Church, and on the other hand, that 'outside her structure, many elements can be found of sanctification and truth'" (*DI* # 16; cf. John Paul II, *Ut unum sint*, # 13; *LG* # 15; and *UR* # 3). It is essential to realize that these elements of sanctification and truth "derive their efficacy from the very fullness of grace and truth entrusted to the Catholic Church" (*DI* # 16; cf. *UR* # 3).

Footnote 56 makes it clear that outside of the Church's visible structure, "there exist only *elementa Ecclesiae*—which being elements of that same Church—tend and lead toward the Catholic Church." In fact, "there exists a single Church of Christ, which subsists in the Catholic Church governed by the Successor of Peter and by the bishops in communion with him" (*DI* # 17). Separated churches that have retained apostolic succession and a valid Eucharist are "true particular Churches," but ecclesial communities that have not preserved apostolic succession and a valid Eucharist "are not Churches in the proper sense" (*DI* # 17; cf. CDF, "Note on the Expression 'Sister Churches,'" June 30, 2000). Nevertheless, many members of ecclesial communities are "by Baptism incorporated into Christ and thus are in a certain communion, albeit imperfect, with the Church" (*DI* # 18; cf. *UR* # 3). Catholics, though, cannot "imagine that the Church of Christ is nothing more than a collection—divided, yet in some way one—of Churches and ecclesial communities; nor are they free to hold that today the Church of Christ nowhere really exists and must be considered only as a goal which all Churches and ecclesial communities must strive to reach" (*DI* # 17).

Theme V (The Church: Kingdom of God and Kingdom of Christ) strives to overcome any separation between the Kingdom of God and the Church. Some theologians, minimizing the centrality of Christ, hope for a kingdom that is more theocentric than Christocentric (or ecclesiocentric). According to the CDF, "such theses are contrary to Catholic faith because they deny the unicity of the relationship which Christ and the Church have with the kingdom of God" (*DI* # 19).

In theme VI (The Church and the other religions in relation to salvation), there is a reaffirmation of the Second Vatican Council's teaching that "the Church, a pilgrim now on earth, is necessary for salvation" (*DI* # 20; cf. *LG* # 14). This is a truth that must be firmly believed (*DI* # 20), but it should not be set against "the universal salvific will of God" (cf. 1 Timothy 2: 4) and the recognition that, for those "who are not formally and visibly members of the Church," salvation "is accessible by virtue of a grace which, while having a mysterious relationship to the Church, does not make them formally part of the Church, but enlightens them in a way which is accommodated to their spiritual and material situation" (*DI* # 20). This grace is given "in ways known to God himself" (*DI* # 21). Nevertheless, such grace comes from Christ and is communicated by the Holy Spirit. Although non-Christians can be saved, Christ remains the only Savior, and the Church must never be considered as merely *one way* of salvation alongside other religions that are "seen as complementary to the Church or substantially equivalent to her" (*DI* # 21).

Dominus Iesus goes so far as to acknowledge that other religious traditions "contain and offer religious elements that come from God"; moreover, some of their prayers and rituals "may assume a role of preparation for the Gospel" (*DI* # 21). Nevertheless, these prayers and rituals cannot be put on the same level as the Christian sacraments, and it must not be overlooked that these other religions "insofar as they depend on superstitions and other errors (cf. 1 Corinthians 10: 20–21) constitute an obstacle to salvation" (*DI* # 21). Members of other religions can receive divine grace, but "*objectively speaking* they are in a gravely deficient situation [*in statu gravis penuriae obiective*] in comparison with those who, in the Church, have the fullness of the means of salvation" (*DI* # 22). This rules out all forms of religious indifferentism and relativism, characterized by the belief that "one religion is as good as another" (*DI* # 22). The Church, faithful to her missionary call, must strive to bring the truth of Christ to all people. Certainly, there is an equality of dignity with respect to those who participate in interreligious dialogue, but this does not translate into an equality of doctrine, especially with regard to Jesus Christ. When proclaiming the Gospel to all people, the Church must always be "guided by charity and respect for freedom" (*DI* # 22).

After the appearance of *Dominus Iesus*, many Catholic leaders, including Francis Cardinal George of Chicago, praised it for its much-needed opposition to religious relativism. Others, though, were concerned that the document's tone might come across as overly severe in some ecumenical settings. Nevertheless, many evangelical Christians were very pleased with the document's clear affirmation of Christ as the only Savior (even if they were less enthusiastic about the centrality given to the Catholic Church). Some Jewish leaders criticized the document for its affirmation of Christ as the only way of salvation, but others were aware that the Church must be true to her own principles. The most unfortunate reactions came from some secular journals, which falsely claimed that *Dominus Iesus* taught that only Catholics could be saved. Anyone reading the document, however, would realize that this is not at all what the document teaches (cf. # 20–22). Cardinal Ratzinger, in an interview published in *L'Osservatore Romano* on November 22, 2000, expressed his "sadness and disappointment at the fact that the public reaction, with a few praiseworthy exceptions, had completely disregarded the Declaration's true theme" (English ed., 10).

Several subsequent documents of the CDF have expanded upon or commented on the topics addressed by *Dominus Iesus*, most significantly the "Responses to Some Questions Regarding Certain Aspects of the Doctrine on the Church" (2007) and "Doctrinal Note on Some Aspects of Evangelization" (2007). As with *Dominus Iesus* itself, these documents provide numerous citations from the Second Vatican Council showing that the council has not been properly studied and comprehended in certain Catholic circles (especially on the question of *subsistit in* of *LG* # 8). Unfortunately, various forms of relativism, pluralism, and indifferentism remain problems for the Church today. Catholics, though, should be grateful for documents like *Dominus Iesus* that clearly and calmly proclaim the truth about Jesus Christ and the one, holy, catholic, and apostolic Church.—Robert L. Fastiggi

BIBLIOGRAPHY AND FURTHER READING: Becker, Karl, SJ. "An Examination of *Subsistit In*." *L'Osservatore Romano*, English ed. December 14, 2005, p. 11; Denzinger, Heinrich, and Peter Hünermann. *Enchiridion symbolorum definitionum et declarationum de rebus fidei et morum*, 40th ed. Freiburg: Herder, 2005; George, Francis, and Bernard Law. "What *Dominus Iesus* Reaffirms." *Origins* 30, no. 15 (September 21, 2000): 228–231; Imbelli, Robert, Philip Kennedy, and Marty E. Marty. "Rome and Relativism: *Dominus Iesus* and the CDF." *Commonweal* 27 (October 20, 2000): 12–13; John Paul II. "The Purpose of *Dominus Iesus*." *Origins* 30, no. 19 (October 19, 2000): 299; Pope, Stephen J., and Charles Hefling, eds. *Sic et No: Encountering "Dominus Iesus."* Maryknoll, NY: Orbis, 2002; Ratzinger, Joseph. "Answer to Main Objections against *Dominus Iesus.*" *L'Osservatore Romano*, English ed. November 22, 2000, p. 10; Ratzinger, Joseph. *Truth and Tolerance: Christian Belief and World Religions.* Translated by Henry Taylor. San Francisco: Ignatius Press, 2004; Sullivan, Francis A., SJ. "The Impact of *Dominus Iesus* on Ecumenism." *America.* October 20, 2000, pp. 10–11; Sullivan, Francis A., SJ. "*Quaestio Disputata*: Response to Karl Becker, S.J. on the Meaning of *Subsistit In.*" *Theological Studies* 67, no. 2 (2006): 395–409; Weakland, R. "On the Document's Ecumenical Impact." *Origins* 30, no. 17 (October 5, 2000): 267.

See also CHURCH, THE (NATURE, ORIGIN, AND STRUCTURE OF); ECUMENISM; EVANGELIZATION; *LUMEN GENTIUM*; MORAL RELATIVISM; RELIGIOUS PLURALISM, THE POLITICAL PROBLEM OF; RELIGIOUS RELATIVISM/INDIFFERENTISM; SALVATION; THEOLOGY

DOSTOEVSKY, FYODOR MIKHAILOVICH (1821–1881)

A Russian writer of the 19th century, Fyodor M. Dostoevsky inspired thinkers and artists of highly disparate convictions: from Christian apologists like Nikolai Berdyaev to secular existentialists like Albert Camus. His immense impact on contemporary culture comprises, among other influences, an extension of anti-utopian discourse by his effective critique of socialism and communism on the grounds of their threat to human dignity and freedom; an inspiration to the existentialist vein of thought; and a thorough renovation of the novel as a genre. This stimulating author is best known as a novelist, yet he also produced marvelous short stories, journalistic writings, critical essays, and speeches.

Born in a modest apartment inside St. Mary's hospital for the Moscow poor, where his father worked as a state surgeon, Dostoevsky derived from his early impressions of life's hardships a profound sense of responsibility for and spontaneous responsiveness to human suffering. The future writer's gentle and pious mother was in charge of her children's early education and instilled in them an undying love of literature and religious devotion. After the death of his mother in 1837, Fyodor was sent to study free of charge at the Military Engineering Academy in St. Petersburg. This strikingly modern and Westernized capital of the tsarist Russian Empire figures prominently in almost all of Dostoevsky's works, forming an apt stage for the country's torturous political, social, and spiritual tensions between its Slavic past and its West-bound future.

In 1844, the aspiring author's literary interests led him to neglect his professional duties, which in turn forced him to retire from the military after just one year of service. Having abandoned a career as an officer, Dostoevsky devoted himself fully to studying and translating from a wide range of European authors. He also wrote his first novel, *Poor Folk* (1846), which the majority of literary critics met with overwhelming enthusiasm.

Dostoevsky was originally heralded in the 1840s literary milieu as a new genius of the then popular Natural School, which prioritized mimetic depiction of social injustice. Despite this warm welcome, Dostoevsky quickly detached himself from the circle of critical realists on both aesthetic and religious grounds, and his next work, *The Double* (1846), received a harsh critical response as too mystical and obscure. In 1847, driven by despair and self-doubt, Dostoevsky joined a clandestine philosophical society whose members discussed political issues in the light of utopian social teachings (mainly by the French communist Charles Fourier). Although Dostoevsky did not share the predominantly atheist views of this conspiracy, he nonetheless became infatuated with Christian Socialism, the main articulations of which he imbibed from the banned pamphlet *Words of a Believer* (1834), written by the Catholic priest Hugues-Félicité Robert de Lamennais.

In 1849, Dostoevsky was arrested for his alleged anti-tsarist activities and, after months of interrogations, received a death sentence. Only at the last moment of his torturous mock execution did he learn of the tsar's clemency; he then spent four hellish years at hard labor and six more years of exile in Siberia. Under the reign of a more liberal Tsar Alexander II, Dostoevsky returned to St. Petersburg, where together with his brother Mikhail he began publishing a politically moderate literary journal, *Time*. Here, Dostoevsky printed his *The House of the Dead* (1862), a fictional memoir of a convict. This expressive, compassionate, and psychologically profound account of extreme suffering remained one of the most popular books during the writer's life. Hence, Dostoevsky's spiritual journey took him from his youthful enthusiasm for utopianism to a mature appreciation of human nature and divine grace. In Siberia, Dostoevsky claimed to have undergone a radical conversion into Orthodox Christian faith, which he brilliantly and emotively vindicated in all of his post-Siberian works. Better than any other writer of the time, Dostoevsky successfully placed Christianity at the center of the broadest ideological debate in order to engage his contemporaries in the process of rediscovery rather than rejection of its timeless ideal.

As Dostoevsky's writing matured and acquired its characteristic features in *Notes from Underground* (1864), he launched his masterful attack on discourses of Russia's increasing modernization and secularization. With its elusive and exhibitionistic tone, this first-person narrative also initiated Dostoevsky's provocative inquiry into the unseemly underside of the human psyche. Here, the so-called underground man articulates Dostoevsky's complex reaction to modernity heralded in Russia by general infatuation with positivist rationality, utility, and progress. By his impassioned assertion of human freedom and dignity even at the expense of utter absurdity and irrationality, the underground man heroically resists materialism, empiricism, utopianism, and idolatrous faith in science. Despite the allure of this articulate protestation, the protagonist fails to engage lovingly with other human beings and thus falls into a parasitic and miserable existence as a lonely hoarder of regrets and grudges. Thanks to its uncompromising defense of individual freedom, this text gained the acclamation of Friedrich Nietzsche, Lev Shestov, Albert Camus, Andre Gidé, Franz Kafka, and countless other writers who explored human alienation and individual isolation.

Already in *The Notes*, Dostoevsky attempted to supplement his antihero's derisive negation of conventions with a tentative statement of hope in the possible transformation of human personality through spiritual illumination; however, he succeeded at the challenging task only in his first great novel, *Crime and Punishment* (1866). Influenced by the fashionable teachings of voluntarism and amorality, this novel's hero, Rodion Raskolnikov, murders a greedy pawnbroker to assert his individual right. Despite his grand ambition, Rodion fails to use the spoils of his daring deed to benefit either humanity or his own family and eventually confesses his crime to the authorities. Torn between his coldly calculating mind and passionately caring heart, Raskolnikov discovers the need to repent through Sonya Marmeladova, a meek and saintly young woman who sacrificed herself in order to save her family from destitution. As the murderer is sent to Siberia, Sonya follows him to nurse his tragically split psyche back to spiritual health.

In *The Possessed* (1872), Dostoevsky's most polemic novel, the writer represented terrorism as a major ailment of modernity. Having identified nihilism as the main ideological force behind this violent political practice, Dostoevsky asserts that such violent and uncompromising denial of all values stems logically from atheism. In this bitterly sarcastic novel, the author also revealed the horrifically destructive potential of socialism as a totalizing ideology, which consumes and annuls the complex humanity of its carriers. Here as elsewhere, Dostoevsky presented Westernization of Russia as a ruinous path of development because the Western ideal of individualism fractured human community and threatened to disintegrate all social, moral, and spiritual ties between people.

The Brothers Karamazov (1880), the last and best known novel by Dostoevsky, contains the widest range of characters embodying complex ideas. With its pivotal murder of a profligate father and the diverging plot lines of his three sons' real or potential regeneration, the tragic story of the Karamazov family symbolizes the universal situation of humanity devastated by violence and seeking transcendence. This novel is a culminating articulation of Dostoevsky's lifelong engagement with such contrasting worldviews as human solidarity (which recognizes universal responsibility for evil in the world) and extreme individualism (which asserts personal autonomy). Through his character of the holy monk Zosima, Dostoevsky shows how all are guilty for every evil in the interconnected human reality of sin and suffering, and how each person can participate in the redemptive transformation of the whole of being through his or her unique practice of active love. The regenerative trajectories of the Karamazov brothers seem to prove that grace continuously engenders new goodness, beauty, and truth despite degradation or destruction of individual lives.

Because of his intense inquiry into moral and religious problems of modernity, Dostoevsky continues to be a timely and highly relevant author who can be viewed as a strong ally in the world's current battle with terror as sophisticated annihilation of human dignity and life. Moreover, Dostoevsky's influence penetrates all levels of Western culture. Dostoevsky's contemporaries already began to comprehend questions of Russia's place in the world through his Slavophile ideas; however, it was the next generation, especially the first wave of immigrants from postrevolutionary Russia, who began interpreting and participating in their cataclysmic existence directly through Dostoevskian concepts of Christian personalism, philanthropy, authenticity, and positive freedom. Where Dostoevsky's contemporaries saw merely a compelling writer with a peculiarly uneven style, 20th-century readers discovered a colossal figure of a metahistorical visionary and a spiritual genius, as well as a highly innovative artist. In contrast to another Russian literary giant, Leo Tolstoy, whose realistic prose glorifies matter and flesh, Dostoevsky is recognized as a supreme master of largely symbolic and pneumatological writing.

The Christological focus of Dostoevsky's writings "damaged" his intellectual reputation in Russia both during his life and after his death. The liberal press of the 19th century regarded him as a reactionary who defended outlived ideals of Orthodoxy and autocracy, while the Soviet regime either banned or neglected his works due to their emphatic religiosity. Despite these hurdles, Dostoevsky's art continues to inseminate new spiritual discoveries, as evidenced by the extensive engagement with his works by such theologians as Pope Benedict XVI, Henri de Lubac, Stewart Sutherland, and Peter Kreeft, to name just a few.—Svetlana Corwin

BIBLIOGRAPHY AND FURTHER READING: Frank, Joseph. *Dostoevsky: The Mantle of the Prophet, 1871–1881.* Princeton: Princeton University Press; London: Robson, 2002; Gibson, A. Boyce. *The Religion of Dostoevsky.* Philadelphia: Westminster Press, 1973; Girard, R. *Resurrection from the Underground.* New York: Crossroad, 1997; Leatherbarrow, W. J. *A Devil's Vaudeville: The Demonic in Dostoevsky's Major Fiction.* Evanston, IL: Northwestern University Press, 2005; Pattison, George, and Diane Oenning Thompson, eds. *Dostoevsky and the Christian Tradition.* Cambridge: Cambridge University Press, 2001. *See also* LAMENNAIS, HUGUES-FÉLICITÉ ROBERT DE

DOUGLAS, MARY (1921–2007) Mary Douglas was one of the most widely respected British social anthropologists of her generation. Her work elaborated and expanded on a fundamental principle of the sociologist Emile Durkheim: that how we organize our communities determines the shape of our cultural institutions like religion. Her complex methodology sought to objectively analyze individual and collective experience on their own merits rather than force the facts into a predetermined theoretical framework. Douglas's approach used multiple disciplines and time frames to allow meaningful comparisons across a diverse body of human experience. Although her work assumes that social conditions and relations determine the form and structure of belief systems and cultural ideals, Douglas was not a hard-core social determinist. But her approach did counter what she perceived as an excessive Western focus on the individual and the drive to maximize self-interest.

The preference for a communal understanding of society was developed early. After the death of her mother at age 12, Mary Douglas was raised by her maternal grandparents and attended school at the Roman Catholic Sacred Heart Convent in Roehampton, England. There, she learned the value of a hierarchical order for structuring and providing a deep sense of solidarity. At the convent, she was also exposed to the influence of Catholic social encyclicals like *Rerum Novarum* and *Quadragesimo Anno* that favored communal obligations over individual rights.

After attending Oxford University, where she studied politics, philosophy, and economics, Douglas worked in the British Colonial Office from 1943 to 1947. She then began her research for her DPhil at the Oxford Institute of Social Anthropology. The leading British African anthropologist, fellow Catholic E. E. Evans-Pritchard, headed the institute. Evans-Pritchard became her teacher, mentor, and model. He taught the young Douglas the value of deriving one's conclusions from observations and not from excessive theorizing or fashionable generalizations.

The fieldwork for her doctorate was on the Lele, a matrilinear society living in the remote highlands of the southern Belgian Congo. This research led to the publication of *The Lele of Kasai* in 1963, which described their gerontocracy, complex marriage arrangements, and cults. She would return briefly to this region in 1983 and be alarmed by the environmental devastation and the role of the indigenous Catholic Church in promoting witch hunting.

Douglas's most famous and influential work was *Purity and Danger: An Analysis of the Concepts of Pollution and Taboo* (1966), which explored the relationships between dirt, holiness, impurity, and hygiene. This book has gone through numerous editions and was published in 15 languages. *Purity and Danger* assumes that context and social history are the essential elements that can clarify the differences between the sacred or clean and the unclean or impure.

Purity and Danger demonstrated how rituals and rules are not merely superstitions but mirror social institutions. For example, Douglas proposed that the kosher laws of the Hebrew people were not primitive health regulations or randomly chosen tests of a people's commitment to their God; instead, the laws were about symbolic boundary maintenance. Prohibited foods were those that did not fit neatly into any category. Classifications produced anomalies that could be categorized as matter out of place, a form of dirt or pollution. Douglas had a subtle position, however, and she recognized that there were times when breaches of a routine classification had the capacity to renew the world symbolically.

In *Natural Symbols: Explorations in Cosmology* (1970), Douglas continued her groundbreaking work by proposing a group-and-grid system to place an individual in a society. A "group" posits an individual within or without a bounded social entity and was divided into the categories of hierarchical, sectarian, competitive individual, and isolates. The "grid" defines an individual's social role within networks of social privileges, claims, and obligations. The group-and-grid analysis suggests the forms of social structures, including patterns of beliefs and morality. Working-class families often demonstrate a group and grid with a more restrictive code of personal action, where hierarchy and position are more commanding, than is the case in more prosperous families, where a more elaborate code of conduct stresses the competing of many different interests.

Natural Symbols also took exception to some trends of the 1960s, including the liturgical reforms of the Second Vatican Council and student protests. Douglas questioned the doctrinal latitude and the dissolving of categories and important administrative and intellectual distinctions. The postconciliar Church seemed confused about what makes ritual and symbols meaningful. More specifically, she questioned the changes in the Mass, the wearing of habits by nuns, and the requirement of abstinence. On the issue of abstinence, for example, the changing of a communal rule against eating of meat on Friday to an individual decision made the following of the rule less likely as it lost its role as a shared symbol. Through its reforms, the Church made such self-denying acts less rather than more intelligible.

The Second Vatican Council reforms in the Church seemed to undermine differentiated and bounded systems of hierarchy that were essential to maintaining complex social structures. In their wake, these reforms left chaos, not renewal. Douglas advocated a "benign" hierarchy that did not exercise arbitrary power but was inclusive, had full communication in all directions, and had natural balancing corrections. A balancing correction for strict rules, for example, was the granting of a loving privilege. The benign hierarchy model had advantages in providing clearly stratified and specialized roles for each person that made such a structure capable of being resilient and tenacious when confronting adversity because it could organize effectively.

As for student protesters and their mass demonstrations, Douglas argued that the demands for complete freedom were not, as was often assumed at the time, a cry for compensation from deprivation. Rather, the students were following historical precedents in lacking clearly articulated roles or group allegiances. As a result, their youthful lives were focused on ego-centered competitions and fleeting social relations.

After *Natural Symbols*, Douglas went in a variety of new directions. She explored how contemporary societies assessed environmental risks, the means by which consumers communicate social concerns, the relationship between rituals and jokes, the rational basis of witchcraft accusations, and the etiquette of eating and drinking. In these forays, Douglas demonstrated considerable dexterity in exploring across cultures and disciplines to mine insights.

In examining the role of community, her work exceeded the normal scope of social anthropology and has been influential in fields like psychology, politics, economics, risk analysis, and biblical criticism. In the last couple of decades of her life, Douglas learned Hebrew and worked with Jewish scholars to produce books on the books of Numbers and Leviticus and the writers of and forms utilized in the Pentateuch. These works were extensive meditations on the literary construction and social context of these sacred texts.

Never far from her reflections, the Catholicism of Mary Douglas provoked one critic, eminent Cambridge anthropologist Edmund Leach, to accuse her of employing her anthropological studies as a means for Catholic "propaganda." Douglas's relationship to Catholicism, grounded initially in her family's deep faith and her experience at a convent school, was complex. A devout Catholic, she appreciated the value of hierarchical Church structures—when benign—to provide structure, meaning, tradition, charity, and a thick form of community. The Church also nurtured the virtues of stability, loyalty, and completion. She was not against change, however, in the post–Vatican II Church, but thought reforms should seek to develop appropriate rituals for flexible institutional forms instead of adopting a 1960s attitude of antiritualism. As for the role of women, she did not seek to eliminate the hierarchy or an all-male celibate priesthood. Instead, she advocated for a Catholic Commission of Women to be a counterpoint to the male hierarchy and provide the hierarchy with advice on issues such as contraception, abortion, biogenetics, and euthanasia.

Critics of Douglas's body of work have accused her of a lack of rigor and attention to detail. She was also criticized as being too theoretical. Her group-and-grid analysis, for example, was accused of providing uncertain criteria or being overly deterministic. In her defense, Douglas eventually admitted to some errors in her works, including problems with group-and-grid theory and her early claims about Hebrew dietary laws.

Despite such criticisms, the works of Mary Douglas remain highly influential and have provided the essential foundations for cultural theory, which focuses on institutions, the discourses they initiate, and the discourses that support them. The honors accorded Douglas also suggest the importance of her writings. She was elected a member of the British Academy and presented the Gifford Lectures in 1989. She was named a Commander of the British Empire in 1992 and Dame Commander of the British Empire in 2006. A *Sunday Times* survey of "Makers of the Twentieth Century" listed *Purity and Danger* among the 100 most influential works since 1945.—Phillip M. Thompson

BIBLIOGRAPHY AND FURTHER READING: Douglas, Mary. *Natural Symbols: Explorations in Cosmology*, 2nd ed. New York: Routledge, 1996; Douglas, Mary. *Purity and Danger: An Analysis of the Concepts of Pollution and Taboo*. New York: Routledge, 1966. Fardon, Richard. *Mary Douglas: An Intellectual Biography*. New York: Routledge, 1999. *See also* ANTHROPOLOGY; DURKHEIM, EMILE

DOWN SYNDROME Down syndrome is a chromosomal condition typically causing relatively mild to moderate cognitive impairment. It is often associated with physical features such as almond-shaped eyes slanting upwards (often with beautiful white specks in the iris, called Brushfield's spots), slightly flattened facial features, and a short stature. Down syndrome is named after English doctor John Langdon Down (1828–1896), who classified people with the physical characteristics of Down syndrome into a particular category that he referred to as a "Mongolian" type. As a result of this incorrect theory, Down syndrome was commonly referred to as Mongoloidism, and people with Down syndrome as Mongoloids; this language is now considered offensive. The possessive nomenclature of "Down's syndrome" is also disfavored in the United States, but is still commonly used in the United Kingdom.

In 1958, French geneticist and first president of the Pontifical Academy for Life, Dr. Jerome Lejeune (1926–1994), identified the presence of the extra 21st chromosome as the most common cause of the condition, leading some to refer to Down syndrome generally as Trisomy 21. Dr. Lejeune has been declared a Servant of God by the Vatican, an early step in the process of canonization.

Down syndrome is a common genetic disorder, occurring in people across the globe, in all races. Estimates of its incidence vary, but the consensus seems to settle near the National Down Syndrome Society's figure of one in every 733 babies born. Down syndrome always involves a disorder in the 21st chromosome of the human genome. Chromosomes are tiny rod-shaped structures in the nucleus of every cell that carry a person's genes. Typically, each parent provides 23 chromosomes—23 in the egg and 23 in the sperm—creating a cell with 46 chromosomes at conception. Each of these 23 different chromosomes inherited from one parent has a counterpart that can be matched with the 23 chromosomes of the other parent. Most people with Down syndrome (approximately 95%), however, have 47 chromosomes instead of the usual 46; they have three of the 21st chromosome in every single cell of their bodies. The extra chromosome typically comes from the egg, but can also come from the sperm or even take place in the first cell division after conception. About 3–4% of cases of Down syndrome are caused by "translocation," in which the extra 21st chromosome is attached to a different chromosome, leaving the person with 46 total chromosomes. The rarest form of Down syndrome, called "mosaicism," is thought to be caused by an error in the first few cell divisions that causes only some cells in the body to have 47 chromosomes; the rest have the typical 46.

People with Down syndrome almost always have some form of cognitive impairment, typically in the mild to moderate range. People with Down syndrome can also have other cognitive disabilities, such as autism spectrum disorder or attention deficit disorder. An increased risk for some physical conditions is associated with Down syndrome. The Down Syndrome Medical Interest Group publishes the comprehensive *Health Care Guidelines for Individuals with Down Syndrome*, explaining these conditions and outlining recommendations for monitoring and treatment. Virtually all people with Down syndrome have hypotonia, or a reduced muscle tone. Approximately half of all babies with Down syndrome are born with various heart defects; a much smaller percentage are born with various gastrointestinal abnormalities. Children with Down syndrome are at increased risk for developing leukemia and related blood disorders, hypothyroidism, and ear, sinus, and upper respiratory tract infections. Alzheimer's disease is more common and can appear at an earlier age in people with Down syndrome than in the general population.

On the other hand, people with Down syndrome appear to be at less risk than the general population for coronary atherosclerosis, stroke, high blood pressure, breast cancer, lung cancer, mouth cancer, and other common solid tumors. As people with Down syndrome receive more informed medical care, their life expectancy has risen dramatically—from an average of 25 years in 1983 to 60 today. Significant research on Down syndrome is being conducted to explore, among other things, the cognitive issues caused by Down syndrome (including its connection with Alzheimer's disease); the links between Down syndrome and lower risks of certain cancers and heart diseases; and the reasons for substantially higher survival rates and lower relapse rates for children with Down syndrome who get acute myeloid leukemia. This research is important for its potential benefit for the general population as well as for people with Down syndrome.

While the precise identification of the genetic causes of Down syndrome gives sharp focus to much of this research, it also makes prenatal identification of the condition relatively easy, raising significant moral issues. There are two general categories of prenatal tests for Down syndrome. One category is screening tests, which estimate the statistical risks that the baby a woman is carrying might have Down syndrome. These tests are routinely offered to pregnant women during prenatal care, in the form of various combinations of blood tests and urine tests. Based on analysis of substances in the mother's blood and urine and the baby's gestational age, these tests provide statistical probabilities that the baby will have Down syndrome. These tests are sometimes combined with extremely detailed ultrasound examinations that look for additional markings that might indicate Down syndrome. While this type of testing is noninvasive and presents no risk to the health of the baby, it also provides only statistical probabilities that the baby will have Down syndrome.

The second category of tests, diagnostic tests, involves invasive tests examining the chromosomes of the baby. Small samples of tissue from the placenta (in chorionic villus sampling, or CVS) or amniotic fluid (in amniocentesis) are extracted, and the chromosomes of the baby are examined. These tests provide definitive prenatal diagnoses of Down syndrome, but they also slightly increase the risk of miscarriage. New tests are being developed that will likely allow a definitive diagnosis of Down syndrome through noninvasive testing in the first trimester of pregnancy.

The increasing prevalence of prenatal testing for Down syndrome presents difficult moral issues. There is currently no prenatal therapy that addresses any of the cognitive or health issues raised by Down syndrome. Thus, parents who receive prenatal diagnosis of Down syndrome can only use the information to either help prepare for the additional complications that might accompany the birth of their child or to decide to abort their child. *Evangelium Vitae* acknowledges both these possibilities, warning: "Special attention must be given to evaluating the morality of *prenatal diagnostic techniques*

which enable the early detection of possible anomalies in the unborn child. . . . When they do not involve disproportionate risks for the child and the mother, and are meant to make possible early therapy or even to favor a serene and informed acceptance of a child not yet born, these techniques are morally licit. But since the possibilities of prenatal therapy are today still limited, it not infrequently happens that these techniques are used with a eugenic intention which accepts selective abortion in order to prevent the birth of children affected by various types of anomalies. Such an attitude is shameful and utterly reprehensible, since it presumes to measure the value of a human life only within the parameters of 'normality' and physical well-being, thus opening the way to legitimizing infanticide and euthanasia as well" (*EV* # 63).

Growing public concern for the potentially eugenic implications of prenatal testing has led to enactment of laws such as the Prenatally and Postnatally Diagnosed Conditions Awareness Act of 2009, also known as the Kennedy-Brownback Act, which encourages providing accurate, up-to-date information and support for parents who receive a diagnosis of Down syndrome or other disabilities either prenatally or up to a year after the birth of their child. Similar concerns prompted enactment of the Genetic Information Nondiscrimination Act of 2008, which prohibits employers or health insurers from discriminating in any way based on genetic information obtained through any sort of testing.

Nevertheless, most parents who receive a prenatal diagnosis of Down syndrome abort their babies. A 1999 meta-analysis of data from studies worldwide concluded that about 92% of women who receive a definitive diagnosis of Down syndrome choose to abort their children. There is no way of knowing how many women abort babies who do *not* have Down syndrome based solely on the statistical probabilities of the screening tests. It is clear, however, that the absolute number of babies born with Down syndrome in the world is decreasing as testing becomes more widespread, even though women are tending to have children at older ages and the risk of having a child with Down syndrome increases as women age. Studies conducted in 2004 and 2005 in the United States show that 15% fewer babies with Down syndrome were born in 2005 compared to 1989, though analysis of maternal age trends indicates there should have been a 34% increase.

The tragic irony of this trend is that increased social acceptance of people with disabilities in the mainstream of life and advances in medical care continue to improve the quality of the lives of people with Down syndrome and their families. Today, children with Down syndrome are routinely educated with their nondisabled peers in school and participate in extracurricular activities and sports leagues. Adults with Down syndrome attend college, hold jobs, and get married. They write books, achieve popular celebrity as stars on hit television shows like *Life Goes On* and *Glee*, and pursue their vocations in contemplative religious communities, such as the Little Sisters Disciples of the Lamb in Le Blanc, France.

Research supports what families of children with Down syndrome often experience firsthand—the unexpected ways in which their lives are enriched, rather than tragically burdened, by the experience of intimately living with and loving a person with a disability. Studies show that families with children with disabilities have about the same positive outcomes, in terms of parent stress, family functioning, and marital satisfaction, as families without. Families with disabled children tend *not* to seek prenatal screening tests for subsequent children, based on their firsthand experience of how the burdens of caring for such a child can be outweighed by surprising benefits. Even more compelling than these scientific conclusions, though, is the growing library of books written by parents of children with disabilities, in which they describe the many unexpected joys and rewards of raising such a child, including the beautiful and dramatic way that loving such a child helps us to understand that *all* of our children are gifts, and all are equally loved into being by God.—Elizabeth R. Schiltz

BIBLIOGRAPHY AND FURTHER READING: Groneberg, Jennifer. *Roadmap to Holland*. New York: New American Library, 2008; Pueschel, Siegfried M. *A Parent's Guide to Down Syndrome: Toward a Brighter Future*. Rev ed. Baltimore: Paul H. Brookes, 2000; Schiltz, Elizabeth. "Living in the Shadow of Mönchberg." In *The Cost of Choice: Women Evaluate the Impact of Abortion*, edited by Erika Bachiochi, 42–49. San Francisco: Encounter Books, 2004; Skotko, Brian G. "Mothers of Children with Down Syndrome Reflect on Their Postnatal Support." *Pediatrics* 115, no. 1 (January 2005): 64–77; Skotko, Brian G. "Prenatally Diagnosed Down Syndrome: Mothers Who Continued their Pregnancies Evaluate Their Health Care Providers." *American Journal of Obstetrics and Gynecology* 192 (2005): 670–677; Soper, Kathryn L., ed. *Gifts: Mothers Reflect on How Children with Down Syndrome Enrich Their Lives*. Bethesda, MD: Woodbine House, 2007; Soper, Kathryn L., ed. *Gifts 2: How People with Down Syndrome Enrich the World*. Bethesda, MD: Woodbine House, 2009; Vredevelt, Pam. *Angel behind the Rocking Chair: Stories of Hope in Unexpected Places*.

Sisters, OR: Multnomah, 1997. *See also* ABORTION; CONSISTENT ETHIC OF LIFE (SEAMLESS GARMENT); DISABILITIES (PERSONS WITH); *EVANGELIUM VITAE*; HUMAN DIGNITY

DUHEM, PIERRE (1861–1916) Pierre Duhem was a French physicist, mathematician, and historian and philosopher of science. He was the oldest child of a large family, and his parents tried to provide as fine an education for him as possible. After the death of his parents, however, Duhem had to discontinue his studies with the Jesuits in order to provide for the family. Eventually, he made his way back to his studies, enrolling at the noted École Normale Supérieure, where he was a high-achieving student all of his years. Duhem married in 1890, but tragedy soon struck in his life, for his wife was to die during childbirth, along with his newborn child. He never remarried after that.

After completing his studies, Duhem became a physicist, and he posited the notion that generalized thermodynamics was a foundation for physical theory. He thought that physics, chemistry, mechanics, and so on should be derivable from the first principles of thermodynamics. In the philosophy of science, he is known for his work on theory and experiment. In the history of science, a particular concern here, he declared that the history of science that had been written by the philosophes of the Enlightenment was distorted and inaccurate.

Duhem was not a theologian, but he was a noticeably "believing physicist" who was firmly convinced that the Enlightenment and emergent Protestantism had portrayed the Catholic Church as hostile to science (and progress) and indeed an oppressor of science. Duhem's massive, 10-volume *Le système du monde: Histoire des doctrines cosmologiques de Platon à Copernic* (1913) explicated an alternative perspective on the history of science, one that placed the Church in a central role in the origins and development of science. Instead of a view of the Middle Ages as a dark age in the history of science, he posited that Catholics such as St. Albert the Great, Roger Bacon, Jean Buridan, Robert Grosseteste, and a host of others created an intellectual climate that included scientific imagination and experimentation that paved the way for the development of later modern science. For Duhem—and later for Rev. Stanley L. Jaki, OSB, a disciple of Duhem who promoted Duhem's contributions in his many works—the true history of science had never seen the light of day.

After his massive exposition of the critical role of the Church in the development of science, Duhem was tireless in his objections to the views of the predominantly liberal, anticlerical disciples of the legacy of the French Enlightenment philosophes of an earlier period. For this, he paid a heavy price. Marcelin Berthelot, an important figure in the French scientific establishment of that time, declared that Duhem would never be able to teach in Paris. This turned out to be true, for Duhem ended up teaching in provincial universities far from Paris for the remainder of his life. This is only one example of the treatment he received for opposing the prevailing ideas of his era.

Duhem published more than 40 books and about three hundred articles, essays, and reports. He wrote important works in theoretical mechanics, the philosophy of physics, and the history of science (especially on the medieval origins of science). Duhem put together an impressive scholarly career in a relatively short life span, passing away at 56 years of age in 1916. Perhaps his most lasting contribution was his new view of the history of science, a view that encompasses the Christian and religious origins of science. Duhem's perspective attempts to correct the inaccurate, egregious, and unjust distortions of the role of the church and science in the past. Pierre Duhem never received the attention he deserved in his lifetime, but as the years pass, it appears that he is finally receiving the acclaim due him.—Thomas D. Watts

BIBLIOGRAPHY AND FURTHER READING: Ariew, Roger. "Pierre Duhem." In *The Stanford Encyclopedia of Philosophy*, Fall 2011 ed., edited by Edward N. Zalta, http://plato.stanford.edu/archives/fall2011/entries/duhem/; Duhem, Pierre. *Le systéme du monde: Histoire des doctrines cosmologiques de Platon à Copernic.* Paris: A. Hermann, 1913; Jaki, Stanley L., *Scientist and Catholic: An Essay on Pierre Duhem.* Front Royal, VA: Christendom Press, 1991; Jaki, Stanley L. *Uneasy Genius: The Life and Work of Pierre Duhem.* The Hague: Nydoff, 1984. *See also* ENLIGHTENMENT, AGE OF THE; JAKI, STANLEY L., OSB; POSITIVISM; SCIENCE

· E ·

ECONOMY OF COMMUNION (EOC) In his 2009 social encyclical *Caritas in Veritate*, Pope Benedict XVI notes one recent sign of economic hope—the development of a "broad intermediate area" of "traditional companies which nonetheless subscribe to social aid agreements in support of underdeveloped countries . . . and the diversified world of the so-called 'civil economy' and the 'economy of communion'" (*CV* # 46).

Several commentators connected the pope's description of businesses that consider profit as "a means for achieving human and social ends" (*CV* # 46) and the Focolare Movement's global Economy of Communion (EOC) network. For example, George Weigel acknowledges the influence that the Focolare's EOC academics had in drafting the document, noting that this school of thought merits further discussion. One of the pope's economic advisors, Stefano Zamagni, also has noted that the EOC project and Communion and Liberation's Company of Works have long demonstrated how the social vision of solidarity and fraternity can fully "enter" into economic life.

Since the origins of the Focolare Movement in war-torn Trent, inspired by the example of the first Christian community (Acts 2: 44–45), Focolare communities have practiced a "communion of goods" aimed at meeting the basic needs of all participants. Such needs, however, often outstripped resources.

During a visit to Brazil in 1991, Chiara Lubich was moved by the circumstances of the people, including Focolare members, living in the *favelas* that surround São Paolo. In light of Pope John Paul II's then recent *Centesimus Annus*, she and the local communities reflected on how to respond to these needs. From their deliberations emerged the idea of launching a new economic model, which they called the Economy of Communion. EOC businesses would generate jobs and commit to a three-part division of their profits: (1) direct aid to people in need; (2) educational projects to help foster a "culture of giving"; and (3) the continued growth and development of the business. Initial businesses began with the active participation of hundreds of people who pooled their resources, often even selling chickens or other livestock to purchase "shares" for the initial capital.

There are now more than 700 EOC businesses throughout the world, most small and medium size; only a few have more than 100 employees. In the United States, EOC businesses include an environmental engineering firm, a violin atelier, a language school, a tutoring service, a law office, an organic farm, and various consulting businesses. North American EOC firms sustain their vision through contact with local Focolare communities and their business-to-business network with other EOC firms throughout the continent and the world. Quarterly conference calls, an annual national convention, and occasional international meetings provide opportunities to sustain their commitment to the project and refine their ideas.

For example, Clare Marie DuMontier's Visitation Law Office in Appleton, Wisconsin, provides guardianship services for the elderly. DuMontier had considered leaving the profession because of the conflict that permeated the legal environments in which she had worked. But in an interview in *Our Sunday Visitor*, she describes the simple yet essential benefit of her connection with the EOC that attracted her: "What I love about working in an Economy of Communion business is that my entire life in Christ is united—my work, as well as my family life and community life."

The businesses commit themselves to infusing all their relationships—with employees, customers, suppliers, regulatory agencies, the general public, and the environment around them—with values of love and respect. One such business is Consort International, a manufacturer of high-quality string instruments. John Welch, Consort's CEO, knew a dealer who was having serious financial trouble and had a large outstanding balance with Consort, so from time to time, Welch would call to see how he was doing.

How do EOC businesses function in a competitive environment? John Mundell is the founder and CEO of Mundell & Associates, an environmental reclamation consulting firm in Indianapolis. "It's a twist on the American way, but in an EOC business, we try to see competitors not as the ones to beat, but as people with whom we can build relationships. Since we started, we have tried to follow the principle of never speaking ill of a competitor. It's tempting when someone calls seeking negative information, but we refrain. We compete only by the quality of our product and our service. We have even helped people in our area to establish similar companies, sharing with them how we started, how to avoid the mistakes that we made, and sending along résumés of good people when they don't serve our own employment needs. Also, when asked to testify in court, it is tempting to go on about a competitor's mistakes. But I try to make it a point to also say what they did right."

Mundell continued: "We saw one result of building these kinds of relationships when we were involved in a fairly large bid for a sophisticated project in another state. When the attorney for the city stood up to say how our references checked out, he confessed that he had spoken not only with our client referrals, but also with our competitors. 'I tried to get the dirt on this company, to find out what they do not do well, and I have never heard such glowing remarks from competitors. I have no reservations about hiring these people.'"

EOC businesses also consider how to foster reciprocal relationships in their local environments. For example, because he wanted to spur economic develop-ment in a distressed part of the city, Mundell decided to relocate the company's offices there. "We decided to hire local people to fix the roof and do the landscaping. We have developed close relationships with the coffee shops and restaurants in the neighborhood and have offered our employees gift certificates to be used at these businesses. The local Catholic school was not able to support much curricular enrichment, so we sponsored a workshop for them on protecting wildlife and hired another business that was also going through a hard time to develop it. Our employees also volunteer at the food pantry in the nearby Disciples of Christ church. As a service to the community, some of our employees and their spouses helped to fix up a run-down house in a poorer part of our neighborhood. It just so happened that a television crew came by that day, and seeing what we were doing, they featured us on the evening news. Because of that coverage, three years later we obtained a $50,000 contract."

Those helped by EOC businesses are active participants in the project—part of the same community, committed to living the culture of giving. This culture assumes that everyone, of any economic status, has something to give—understanding, attention, forgiveness, a smile, time, talents, ideas, or help. Sharing one's needs, with dignity and sincerity, is an essential contribution to the life of communion.

The poor also share their experience of how God's love reaches them through the help they receive. As a woman from Uruguay who received EOC aid wrote: "I have experienced the love of our heavenly Father on many occasions, but I never thought he would even help me with my teeth. Through the help I received I was able to take care of an infection I had. I felt extremely happy, as if I were the Father's favorite child."

Direct aid from the EOC has been used primarily to provide temporary assistance for the unemployed, for students who cannot afford schooling, and for those facing unexpected illness or personal calamity. Many who are receiving help relinquish it as soon as they establish minimal economic independence. A young man from Nigeria who used EOC aid to finish high school and find a better job wrote: "Now it is time for me to help someone else whom I do not know but who needs my small contribution, as I was helped. I ask God that he may always give me a heart as big as his, in order to see others' needs."

The EOC has also established credit and micro-credit programs. For example, a Serbian mushroom farm used an EOC loan to install a heating, ventilation, and irrigation system and to purchase a delivery van.

A small Indonesian supermarket received seed funds to subsidize prices so that those without means could buy necessities at a discount; the store in turn was able to employ 14 additional people. A Brazilian bakery purchased equipment and now employs four full-time and two part-time workers. A loan helped a Bulgarian family farm survive a drought; within the year, they repaid a large part of the loan. EOC funds helped a Croatian stocking factory purchase a fabric machine, creating new jobs.

For those who participate in the Economy of Communion, sharing profits with those in need is a logical expression of their identity as members of the universal human family and an expression of their connection to this family. Similarly, the protagonist in the work of the community to improve economic and social structures is not an individual being generous or being ingenious in solving problems. Rather, when the community builds relationships of mutual love through which they discover how they can be "gifts" for each other, the protagonist is the presence of Christ among them.—Amy Uelmen and Thomas Masters

BIBLIOGRAPHY AND FURTHER READING: Bruni, Luigino, ed. *The Economy of Communion: Toward a Multi-Dimensional Economic Culture*. Hyde Park, NY: New City Press, 2002; Economy of Communion website, http://edc-online.org; Gold, Lorna. *New Financial Horizons: The Emergence of an Economy of Communion*. Hyde Park, NY: New City Press, 2010; Lubich, Chiara. "The Charism of Unity and Economy." In *Essential Writings: Spirituality, Dialogue, Culture*, 269–289. Hyde Park, NY: New City Press, 2007; Norris, Thomas J. "The New Sociality: An Economy of Communion." In *The Trinity: Life of God, Hope for Humanity*, 113–130. Hyde Park, NY: New City Press, 2009; Uelmen, Amelia J. "*Caritas in Veritate* and Chiara Lubich: Human Development from the Vantage Point of Unity." *Theological Studies* 71 (2010/2011): 26–45. *See also* CARITAS IN VERITATE; LUBICH, CHIARA, AND THE FOCOLARE MOVEMENT

ECTOPIC PREGNANCY An ectopic (or extrauterine) pregnancy occurs when a fertilized egg implants in some part of the mother's body other than the uterus. In the vast majority of cases, the fertilized egg implants in one of the fallopian tubes. In rare cases, the implantation may take place in the ovaries, the abdomen, or the cervix. An ectopic pregnancy in a fallopian tube may tear or rupture the fallopian tube. This can lead to severe internal bleeding, which is life-threatening to the mother. Ectopic pregnancies are the

leading cause of maternal death in the first trimester in the United States. Approximately 40–50 women die each year in the United States as a result of ectopic pregnancies. The incidence of ectopic pregnancies has increased in recent decades. This increase is due to increases in pelvic inflammatory disease, sexually transmitted diseases, failed tubal sterilizations, and the use of fertility treatments.

There are various ways to treat ectopic pregnancies, and these various options raise significant moral questions. (In some cases, the embryo or fetus has died and these moral difficulties are no longer present; however, here we are concerned with cases in which the embryo or fetus is still alive. The moral issue does not change whether the unborn child is an embryo or a fetus. The developing human organism from fertilization until the end of the eighth week of gestation is typically referred to as an *embryo* and thereafter as a *fetus*.)

In its *Ethical and Religious Directives*, the U.S. Conference of Catholic Bishops states that "in the case of extrauterine pregnancy, no intervention is morally licit which constitutes direct abortion" (*ERD* # 48). In *Evangelium Vitae*, Pope John Paul II defines *abortion* as the "deliberate and intentional killing, by whatever means it is carried out, of a human being in the initial phases of his or her existence, extending from conception to birth" (*EV* # 58). The *Ethical and Religious Directives* continues: "Abortion (that is, the directly intended termination of pregnancy before viability or the directly intended destruction of a viable fetus) is never permitted. Every procedure whose sole immediate effect is the termination of pregnancy before viability is an abortion, which, in its moral context, includes the interval between conception and implantation of the embryo" (*ERD* # 45). However, "operations, treatments, and medications that have as their direct purpose the cure of a proportionately serious pathological condition of a pregnant woman are permitted when they cannot be safely postponed until the unborn child is viable, even if they will result in the death of the unborn child" (*ERD* # 47).

There are four options to treat ectopic pregnancies that are discussed in the literature: expectant management, salpingectomy, salpingostomy, and the administration of methotrexate. In *expectant management*, the mother is carefully monitored and there is no surgical or chemical intervention. In 40–64% of cases, the threat to the mother is resolved by a spontaneous abortion. This treatment option is universally regarded as morally permissible when medically indicated. But if the human embryo continues to develop, other treatment options may be appropriate.

Salpingectomy involves the removal of the fallopian tube along with the embryo. There are total salpingectomies (which involve the removal of the entire fallopian tube) and partial salpingectomies (which involve the removal of only a portion of the fallopian tube). Partial salpingectomies are preferable to total salpingectomies because they can preserve the functioning of the affected fallopian tube; the basic moral issue, however, is the same. Salpingectomies are regarded as morally permissible even though the removal of the tube involves the death of the embryo. This treatment is considered to satisfy the principle of double effect, although the removal of the tube reduces and may eliminate the woman's potential fertility.

The standard account of double-effect reasoning is that it is permissible for an actor to act to secure a good effect bound up with evil if (1) the act considered independently of the evil is good or indifferent, (2) the actor intends the good and foresees but does not intend the evil either as a means or an end, (3) the good does not follow as an effect from the evil, and (4) one's obligations to achieve the good counterbalance those to avoid the evil. A salpingectomy is thought to satisfy the principle of double effect in the same way that a hysterectomy to remove a cancerous uterus has been justified even when the woman is pregnant and the hysterectomy results in the death of the unborn child. The removal of the tube is good because (1) the tube presents a danger to the mother, (2) the surgeon intends the good (to eliminate the threat to the mother posed by the affected tube) and does not intend, although he foresees, the evil (the death of the embryo) as a means or as an end, (3) the good (saving the life of the mother) does not follow as an effect from the evil (i.e., if it were possible to save the embryo by implanting it in the uterus, that would not frustrate the aim of the salpingectomy, to eliminate the affected tube's threat to the mother), and the good—saving the mother's life—would not be outweighed by the evil, the death of the embryo.

Salpingostomy involves the removal of the embryo while leaving the fallopian tube intact. This method is preferable from the standpoint of the woman's potential fertility, since the fallopian tube remains intact. A number of moral theologians, however, condemn the morality of salpingostomy on the theory that it involves a direct abortion. According to this view, the operation is performed on the embryo for the benefit of the mother; the death of the embryo (which generally occurs when it is removed from the tube) is the means of saving the life of the mother and preserving her fertility. But the good motives for the salpingostomy do not justify performing an intrinsically evil act (a direct abortion). (Again, if it were possible to remove the embryo and implant it in the uterus, then the "removal" would not inevitably lead to the death of the embryo. There is some medical literature that states that this transfer has been done, but there is no regular practice of this type of transfer.)

The *use of methotrexate* is another treatment option that preserves the woman's potential fertility. The use of methotrexate ends the pregnancy by halting cell growth. Methotrexate interferes with implantation and placenta formation and thus effectively aborts the embryo. A number of moral theologians also condemn the morality of the use of methotrexate to treat an ectopic pregnancy on the same grounds that they condemn salpingostomy—that methotrexate involves a direct abortion.

A number of moral theologians have defended the morality of salpingostomy and methotrexate. Such defenses have come from those who subscribe to consequentialism. These defenses involve weighing the good and bad consequences likely to flow from these treatments and conclude that the benefits to the mother (protecting her life, health, and potential fertility) outweigh the harms (primarily the death of the embryo). But such defenses have also come from those who defend an orthodox view of moral reasoning and who subscribe to the teaching of *Veritatis Splendor* and *Evangelium Vitae.*

The defenses of salpingostomy and methotrexate are based on the idea that these treatments do *not* involve a direct abortion. Rather, these theories contend, these treatments are morally permissible because they do not involve the intentional killing of an unborn child. These moral theologians contend that salpingostomy and the use of methotrexate are ways to treat the pathological condition presented by the tubal pregnancy. These methods then are analogous to a salpingectomy—treating a pathological condition with the unintended but foreseen death of the embryo.

Thus, there is considerable disagreement about the morality of salpingostomy and the use of methotrexate to treat ectopic pregnancies. This debate involves highly contested issues such as how to understand the scope of intention in moral reasoning and the nature of double effect reasoning. The magisterium has not yet taken a definitive position on these contested treatment options.—Richard S. Myers

BIBLIOGRAPHY AND FURTHER READING: Bowring, Kelly. "The Moral Dilemma of Management Procedures for Ectopic Pregnancy." In *Life and Learning*

XII: Proceedings of the Twelfth University Faculty for Life Conference, edited by Joseph W. Koterski, SJ, 97–126. Washington, DC: University Faculty for Life, 2003; Guevin, Benedict M., OSB. "The Use of Methotrexate or Salpingostomy in the Treatment of Tubal Ectopic Pregnancies." *National Catholic Bioethics Quarterly* 7 (2007): 249–256; Kaczor, Christopher. "The Ethics of Ectopic Pregnancy: A Critical Reconsideration of Salpingostomy and Methotrexate." *Linacre Quarterly* 76 (2009): 265–282; Rhonheimer, Martin. *Vital Conflicts in Medical Ethics: A Virtue Approach to Craniotomy and Tubal Pregnancies*. Edited by William F. Murphy Jr. Washington, DC: Catholic University of America Press, 2009. *See also* CONSEQUENTIALISM; DOUBLE EFFECT, PRINCIPLE OF; ETHICAL AND RELIGIOUS DIRECTIVES FOR CATHOLIC HEALTH CARE SERVICES; *EVANGELIUM VITAE*

EDUCATION, CATHOLIC: ELEMENTARY AND SECONDARY IN THE UNITED STATES

The first school within the territorial expanse of what is now the United States was a Catholic school, established by the Franciscans in Florida in 1606. The opening of schools in all the Spanish territories was a pattern followed in California and New Mexico as the Franciscans sought to educate the children of both the colonists and the Native Americans.

The French exploration of the New World led to the opening of the first school for boys in New Orleans in 1722 by a Capuchin friar; the Ursuline nuns began a girls' school in that city five years later. These schools became prototypes of those to spring up along the St. Lawrence River and in St. Louis, Kaskaskia, Mackinaw, Detroit, Vincennes, and Maine (where a Catholic school existed as early as 1640).

In the British colonies, Catholics experienced relative freedom only in Maryland (as long as Catholics ruled) and in Pennsylvania; it was in places such as these that Catholic education began its development into the system it is today. The groundwork laid during the colonial period served as the foundation for the massive Catholic educational effort that would flourish within 50 years of the ratification of the Constitution.

The First Provincial Council of Baltimore in 1829 asserted: "We judge it absolutely necessary that schools be established in which the young may be taught the principles of faith and morality, while being instructed in letters." The bishops of the nation made that judgment a matter of law in 1884 at the Third Plenary Council of Baltimore.

Much of what parochial schools became and still are came about through a series of events played out in New York City. The chief protagonist was Archbishop John Hughes, who, from 1840 to 1842, was embroiled in a heated controversy over Catholic children and their education. His first complaint centered on the overt anti-Catholicism in the public schools. When assurances were given that the most offensive aspects of this bigotry would be stopped, he next attacked Bible reading in the schools as a sectarian religious exercise unacceptable to the Catholic community. He was joined in this battle by Unitarians, Jews, other religious minorities, and atheists.

Archbishop Hughes's most notable achievement was gaining for immigrants the right to operate and control their own schools. He was unsuccessful in obtaining public funds for the schools, though, and began to rely on religious orders to provide low-cost, quality education, moving away from the lay teachers who actually predominated in the Catholic schools before that time. His decision to abandon the battle with secular authorities served as further impetus for the establishment of a separate school system for U.S. Catholics. He believed strongly and sincerely that "the days have come, and the place, in which the school is more necessary than the church."

Not all American bishops agreed with Hughes on either the necessity of Catholic schools or the desirability of state aid. Archbishop John Ireland of St. Paul, Minnesota, expressed a cautious but clear desire to utilize the public schools. Ireland's suggestions along these lines were vehemently attacked by many of his brother bishops, most notably by John Lancaster Spalding, Bishop of Peoria. He contended, like Hughes, that "without parish schools, there is no hope that the Church will be able to maintain itself in America." Unlike Hughes, though, Spalding recoiled from the thought of any kind of governmental assistance for parochial schools, for fear of governmental interference.

While the first Catholic school operated on this continent as early as 1606, it took more than two centuries for these institutions to be organized into anything resembling a system. A German-born Redemptorist and naturalized U.S. citizen named John Neumann accomplished that feat. As the fourth bishop of Philadelphia, Neumann established a diocesan board of education with clerical and lay representatives from every parish in the diocese. Through this body of advisors and due to his own personal drive, parochial education prospered in Philadelphia and became a unified, coherent system, making Philadelphia a model for the nation and Neumann "the father of parochial schools in America."

By 1892, Philadelphia's Archbishop Patrick John Ryan had appointed a priest to full-time work as diocesan superintendent of schools. The commitment to Catholic education continued to grow, and under Cardinal Dennis Dougherty, a unique system of free Catholic high schools flourished. What was a priority for the ordinary was expected to be a priority for his clergy, as pastors unwilling to open parish schools were threatened with removal.

Some U.S. bishops opted for an "assimilationist" form of Catholicism (condemned in 1899 by Pope Leo XIII as "Americanism" in *Testem Benevolentiae*), which maintained that Catholic doctrine should be presented in a way that would cause as little difference to surface with Protestants as possible. The Americanists were opposed to parochial schools. When the *Code of Canon Law* was enacted in 1917, however, they had to face this strong statement: "Catholic children are not to attend non-Catholic, neutral or mixed schools." Where no other alternative was available, the bishop himself had to determine what dangers to the Faith existed and then judge if a dispensation from the law would be tolerable.

The rationale behind this stringent injunction was explained clearly by Pope Pius XI in *Divini Illius Magistri* (1929): "The so-called 'neutral' school from which religion is excluded, is contrary to the fundamental principles of education. Such a school moreover cannot exist in practice; it is bound to become irreligious" (# 79). While this kind of thinking has been characterized by some as a "fortress" or "siege" mentality, few observers can doubt that the American public school is a potent example of a "neutral" school system becoming irreligious de facto and, some would add, de jure.

The Fathers of the Second Vatican Council considered Catholic education extensively as they followed the trajectory of Church teaching to that point and contributed to its development as well. Several comments bear notice from *Gravissimum Educationis* (1965): "The Church's involvement in the field of education is demonstrated especially by the Catholic school. . . . Therefore, since it can contribute so substantially to fulfilling the mission of God's people, and can further the dialogue between the Church and the family of man, to their mutual benefit, the Catholic school retains its immense importance in the circumstances of our times too. . . . As for Catholic parents, the Council calls to mind their duty to entrust their children to Catholic schools" (# 8).

In 1971, the American bishops issued a pastoral letter on Catholic education, *To Teach as Jesus Did*. It became the standard by which to judge all Catholic schools, outlining as it did the goals and objectives for all Catholic institutions of learning. Included is the following statement: "[Catholic schools] are the most effective means available to the Church for the education of children and young people." Some commentators have noted the irony that in that very same year, bishops were closing schools at the rate of one a day.

Pope Paul VI's bicentennial message to the Church in the United States contained praise for the American Catholic school system and an encouragement to continue the tradition: "The strength of the Church in America [is] in the Catholic schools." Nor was it sheer coincidence that the two U.S. citizens Paul VI canonized in observance of our bicentennial, Bishop John Neumann of Philadelphia and Mother Elizabeth Ann Seton of New York, were prime movers in the parochial school effort.

The first thorough analysis of Catholic education in modern times was offered by the Vatican Congregation for Catholic Education in 1977. *The Catholic School* probed every aspect of the educational process and also recognized the fact that some people had suggested phasing out Catholic schools. Its conclusion was that "to give in to them would be suicidal."

Pope John Paul II's esteem for the American Catholic school system was evident in his 1979 videotaped message to the National Catholic Educational Association gathered in Philadelphia that year for its annual convention, in which he said that he hoped to give "a new impulse to Catholic education throughout the vast area of the United States of America." He went on to say: "Yes, the Catholic school must remain a privileged means of Catholic education in America . . . worthy of the greatest sacrifices." He likewise referred to the Catholic school as the "heart of the Church." Pope Benedict XVI has followed the same pattern, devoting an entire address to Catholic education during his 2008 pastoral visit to the United States.

At its peak, Catholic schooling in the United States reached more than half the target population—an achievement unique in Church history. The post–Vatican II confusion had a most deleterious effect on the schools, though, especially in the mass exodus of thousands of clergy and religious, which, in turn, raised doubts about the future of these schools. In addition, a mode of thinking that had taken root in many sectors of the Catholic community questioned the very desirability and existence of a separate Catholic school system. Further, Catholic movement from cities to suburbs found many dioceses unprepared or unwilling to provide the Catholic schools needed to accommodate the population shift. The end result was a halving of the Catholic school population in a 40-year period.

Challenges facing Catholic schools include escalating costs, a small but persistent Catholic homeschooling movement, and failure to reach the children of new immigrants. With heavy reliance on lay teachers and other costs due to increasing commitment to professionalism, tuition has skyrocketed in recent years, thus putting Catholic education out of reach for many parents. Perhaps the hardest hit have been those of the middle-income bracket, who often do not qualify for tuition assistance programs because of the appearance of financial ability. Creative means are being sought in many dioceses to address this problem.

A perennial goal of the Catholic Church in the United States has been to obtain justice for parents of children in religiously oriented schools through government assistance in the form of tax credits or vouchers. Where even some limited such assistance has been forthcoming, enrollment hemorrhaging has stabilized in many instances. The *Compendium of the Social Doctrine of the Church* (2004) takes aim at governments that make genuine freedom of choice in education burdensome: "Public authorities must see to it that 'public subsidies are so allocated that parents are truly free to exercise this right without incurring unjust burdens. Parents should not have to sustain, directly or indirectly, extra charges which would deny or unjustly limit the exercise of this freedom'" (*CSDC* # 241).

Homeschooling had not been common among Catholics until recent years, but has been increasing. This phenomenon has its origins in two realities. First, many Catholics have been heavily influenced by Fundamentalist and Evangelical Christians, who turned to homeschooling in large numbers as a result of the strong pattern of secularization that infected the government schools, on which they had hitherto relied. Second, in places where Catholic schools were losing their unique Catholic identity, parents often determined to take matters into their own hands by providing what they believed would be a more authentic Catholic education than seemingly was being offered by Catholic schools of their experience. Inasmuch as these parents are usually rather orthodox in their theology and practice and likewise have larger families, their absence from the Catholic schools has had a negative impact on the schools in certain places. Such parents assert that their

practice is in keeping with Church teaching, especially as that relates to their being the "primary educators" of their children. The *Compendium of the Social Doctrine of the Church*, however, also teaches that "parents are the first educators, not the only educators, of their children. It belongs to them, therefore, to exercise with responsibility their educational activity in close and vigilant cooperation with civil and ecclesial agencies" (*CSDC* # 240).

Historically, the Church in the United States, especially during the major waves of immigration of the late 19th and early 20th centuries, considered the Catholic education of the immigrants' children to be a top priority, thus ensuring at one and the same time the lifelong identification of children with the Catholic Church, along with their concomitant entrance into the mainstream of American social and political life. For at least two generations, that policy has been noted in the breach more than in the observance, particularly with regard to Hispanic Catholics, so that fewer than 4% of their children attend Catholic schools. Cognizance of this pastoral lacuna has finally been acknowledged in *To Nurture the Soul of a Nation: Latino Families, Catholic Schools, and Educational Opportunity* (2009), which sets a goal of 1 million Hispanic children in Catholic schools by 2020.

With the passage of time, and much wiser for the experience, the Catholic community in the United States has demonstrated a renewed interest in Catholic education, as enrollments have stabilized and even increased in many dioceses, especially in high-growth areas. Schools are on the rebound, in terms of reclaiming a truly Catholic identity, highlighted in surveys done by various sociologists that show that graduates of postconciliar Catholic schools continue to be markedly different from their public school counterparts, especially in regard to Sunday Mass attendance, attitudes on abortion, willingness to consider a priestly or religious vocation, and generosity to the local parish (both in service and donations).

At yet another level, the success story of Catholic schools in the United States occurs with regularity in the academic realm. John Coleman of the University of Chicago documents an impressive performance record for Catholic high school students, which indicates that they outperform not only public school students but also—and amazingly so—students from secular private schools. The reason for the success, according to Coleman, is religious and moral values and the coordination between home and school. These two aspects take on the greatest significance when considering the incredible achievements of youngsters in inner-city Catholic schools. As new challenges and new opportunities emerge, it is safe to say that new forms of governance and financing will be needed to ensure that Catholic schools remain a vital part of American Catholic life.—Peter M. J. Stravinskas

BIBLIOGRAPHY AND FURTHER READING: Bryk, Anthony S., Valerie E. Lee, and Peter B. Holland. *Catholic Schools and the Common Good*. Cambridge, MA: Harvard University Press, 1993; Buetow, Harold A. *The Catholic School*. New York: Crossroad, 1988; Burns, James, et al. *A History of Catholic Education in the United States*. New York: Benziger, 1937; Hancock, Curtis L. *Recovering a Catholic Philosophy of Elementary Education*. Mount Pocono, PA: Newman House Press, 2005; O'Brien, J. Stephen. *Mixed Messages: What Bishops and Priests Say about Catholic Schools*. Washington, DC: National Catholic Educational Association, 1987; Stravinskas, Peter M. J. *Constitutional Rights and Religious Prejudice: Catholic Education as the Battleground*. Pine Beach, NJ: Newman House Press, 2009. *See also DIVINI ILLIUS MAGISTRI*; EDUCATION, CATHOLIC: ELEMENTARY AND SECONDARY IN CANADA; EDUCATION, CATHOLIC: HIGHER EDUCATION IN CANADA; EDUCATION, CATHOLIC: HIGHER EDUCATION IN THE UNITED STATES; EDUCATION, PUBLIC: HIGHER EDUCATION IN THE UNITED STATES; *GRAVISSIMUM EDUCATIONIS*; HOME SCHOOLING

EMBRYO ADOPTION AND/OR RESCUE   Because babies conceived in vitro frequently fail to implant in a woman's womb, fertility clinics routinely retrieve and fertilize several ova. One or several may be implanted immediately, others cryopreserved by being put into a reservoir of liquid nitrogen. Many embryos thus frozen will be orphaned. Thousands of embryonic human persons are now so imprisoned. What morally licit act or acts, if any, can be done on behalf of these tiny human persons? The central question is this: Is it morally permissible for a woman to have a biologically unrelated, abandoned, and frozen human embryo transferred from the freezer to her womb—a process known as Heterologous Embryo Transfer (HET)—and then nurture it until birth as a means of protecting its life?

Three different answers to the question are given by Catholic scholars loyal to magisterial teaching: (1) HET is *intrinsically evil*; (2) HET is morally permissible for a *married* woman who with her husband could "adopt" such babies prenatally, nurturing them first in the "home" provided by the wife's womb and then, after birth, in the home provided by husband and wife together; (3) HET is morally permissible not only for a *married* woman who with her husband adopts the child prenatally and who will care for the child after birth but also for a *single* woman who can "rescue" such children by having a cryopreserved or "frozen" embryo transferred from its reservoir to her womb, there to nurture it until birth and then give it up for adoption to a married couple.

Some scholars such as Msgr. William B. Smith think that certain passages in *Donum Vitae* support the first answer. One is the text stating that the "spare" embryos produced by in vitro fertilization (IVF) and not transferred to the body of their mother suffer an "absurd fate" with no possibility of *morally licit means* of survival. Others such as Mary Geach find support for this answer in this *Donum Vitae* passage: "The procreation of a new person . . . must be the fruit and the sign of the mutual self-giving of the spouses. . . . The fidelity of the spouses in the unity of marriage involves reciprocal respect of their right to become a father and a mother only through each other." Catherine Althaus defends this view in light of Blessed John Paul II's "theology of the body."

Luke Gormally and others claim that two sentences in *Dignitas Personae* reject embryo adoption: "It has also been proposed, solely in order to allow human beings to be born who are otherwise condemned to destruction, that there could be a form of 'prenatal adoption.' This proposal . . . presents various problems not dissimilar to those mentioned above [the problems mentioned above were medical, legal, and psychological]. . . . It needs to be recognized that the thousands of abandoned embryos represent a *situation of injustice which in fact cannot be resolved*" (*DP* # 19).

Other scholars such as Germain Grisez, Geoffrey Surtees, William E. May, Peter Ryan, SJ, and E. Christian Brugger seek to refute these claims. Of greater importance, Archbishop Rino Fisichella, president of the Pontifical Academy of Life when *Dignitas Personae* was published, and the United States Conference of Catholic Bishops have both explicitly said that the question of HET is still open.

St. Thomas Aquinas and Pope John Paul II teach that human acts are *morally* specified by the "object" rationally chosen by the moral agent and that one can grasp this object only from the perspective of the acting person (*STh* I–II, q. 18; *VS* # 78). John Paul and St. Thomas insist that this object freely chosen is also the *proximate* or *immediate end* of the action, chosen as the means to attain a *further* or *remote end*. Both the means chosen (the moral "object") and further end for whose sake it is chosen must be good if the act is to be good. There is, moreover, a crucial difference between the "natural species" of an act (e.g., sexual intercourse) and its "moral species" (marital intercourse, fornication, adultery, incest). Properly identifying HET's specifying moral object is, therefore, crucial.

The basic argument that HET is intrinsically immoral condemns the procedure because it violates the good of marriage and is an unchaste kind of act. Defenders of this position—among them Nicanor Pier Giorgio Austriaco, OP, Mary Geach, Nicholas Tonti-Filippini, Tadeus Pacholzyck, Christopher Oleson, and William Stempsey, SJ—maintain that the conjugal act is inwardly oriented not only to the bodily union of the spouses (its unitive aspect) but also toward the procreation of new human life (its procreative aspect) in such a way that pregnancy is not merely the fruit of the act but is caused by it. Thus, any woman, married or single, seeking pregnancy outside the conjugal act is engaging in an act that is intrinsically evil because it is a grave violation of marital fidelity.

Many other scholars—including Germain Grisez, E. Christian Brugger, William E. May, Peter Ryan, SJ, Christopher Tollefsen, Thomas V. Williams, LC, John Berkman, and the "early" Helen Watt—judge the above argument erroneous. Grisez, Brugger, May, Ryan, and Tollefsen rebut this argument with the counterargument that pregnancy is *not* a part of the genital act, even when the genital act (its "natural" species) is a "marital act" (its "moral" species), and that the woman is made pregnant *not* by the inseminating male or the genital act but by the child conceived as a result of the genital act. Thus, when a woman accepts an embryo into her womb via embryo transfer, she does not imitate the marriage act. The object specifying the woman's act is not to violate her marriage (a morally bad object) but to transfer an abandoned frozen child from its canister to her womb and to nurture it until birth (a morally good object).

Some authors such as Berkman, the early Watt, and Kristen Carey affirm that HET is morally permissible for a married woman "preadopting" a frozen embryo but not for an unmarried woman "rescuing" the embryo and giving it up for adoption after birth. In their judgment, the adopting woman's specifying moral object is to have a frozen embryo transferred from the canister to the wife's womb as the means of preadopting the child into a home where, after birth, both wife and husband can care for it. This moral object is good and does not violate any human good nor is it a violation

of marriage. However, they reject the claim that a single woman can licitly choose to have the abandoned embryo transferred to her womb to nurture it until birth and then give it up for adoption.

Watt later changed her view on this and took the position that HET is immoral with one exception: if the cryopreserved embryo is removed from its canister and transferred into the womb of its genetic mother, who will then also be its gestational and sociological mother—that is, only with a prior material relationship that will continue—then HET is permissible.

The third position contends that HET is morally permissible for an unmarried woman seeking to rescue a frozen embryo, nurture it in her womb, and then give it up for adoption. Williams distinguishes between "becoming a mother" (through the marital act, nonmarital genital sex, or IVF) and "being a mother." Because today there is a separation of motherhood into distinct stages caused by new reproductive methods, "being a mother" can be divided into genetic, gestational, social, and other stages. Williams then argues that recent developments in Catholic theology (in particular, those initiated by the work of Pope Pius XII and above all by John Paul II) have provided solid grounds for defending this view. He thus proposes that the adopting or rescuing of frozen embryos violates no basic human goods and can be considered a "sometimes heroic act of kindness toward extremely needy members of the human community."

Grisez, May, Brugger, Ryan, and Tollefsen argue that if, like John Paul II and Aquinas, we properly identify the object morally specifying human acts and, as John Paul insists, put ourselves into the position of the acting person, we will see that it is morally right for a married woman with her husband to adopt an abandoned and frozen embryo prenatally whom they will educate and care for as their child after birth. And we will also see that it can be morally good for a single woman to rescue such an abandoned and frozen embryo, nurture him or her in her womb until birth, and then give the baby up to a married couple for adoption.

In the case of the married woman, the object morally specifying her act is definitely not to violate her marriage but rather "to transfer this unborn human baby from the freezer to her womb and to nurture it there until birth." This is the *means* the woman chooses to save the child's life, and the saving of its life is the *further* or *remote end* of her act. This freely chosen object includes her being pregnant, insofar as pregnancy is required in order to nurture the child in her womb. This object is not opposed to any good of human persons, but itself protects the great good of life in the abandoned and frozen embryo.

The argument of Berkman, Carey, and initially Watt is that the single woman is acting as a "surrogate" mother and thus violating the teaching of *Donum Vitae*. These authors, replying to this objection, emphasize that the woman is not choosing to bear the child for the benefit of other persons, as does a surrogate mother as defined by *Donum Vitae*, but only for the benefit of the child. Nor is she cooperating in the evil of those who arranged and/or managed the IVF. The nurture she proposes to give does not involve her in the wrongs already done to the baby, and it will be given for the baby's good and not the good of other persons. In giving the child up for adoption after birth, she is not abandoning responsibilities she assumed in having the baby. Nor is she cooperating in any evil project undertaken by the technicians whose aid is needed in transferring the baby from the freezer to her womb. On the contrary, while they usually cooperate in immoral activities, on this occasion these technicians are cooperating with the woman in treating the baby as a person whose life is intrinsically good and worthy of protection.—William E. May

BIBLIOGRAPHY AND FURTHER READING: Althaus, Catherine. "Can One 'Rescue' a Human Embryo? The Moral Object of the Acting Woman." *National Catholic Bioethics Quarterly* 5, no. 1 (Spring 2005): 113–141; Althaus, Catherine. "Human Embryo Transfer and the Theology of the Body." In *The Ethics of Embryo Adoption and the Catholic Tradition*, edited by Sarah-Vaughan Brakman and Darlene Fozard Weaver, 43–68. New York: Springer, 2007; Berg, Thomas V., and Edward J. Furton, eds. *Human Embryo Adoption: Biotechnology, Marriage, and the Right to Life*. Philadelphia: National Catholic Bioethics Center, and Thornwood, NY: Westchester Institute for Ethics & the Human Person, 2006; Brakman, Sarah-Vaughan. "*Real* Mothers and Good Stewards: The Ethics of Embryo Adoption." In *The Ethics of Embryo Adoption and the Catholic Tradition*, edited by Sarah-Vaughan Brakman and Darlene Fozard Weaver, 119–138. New York: Springer, 2007; Brown, Brandon P., and Jason T. Elbert. "Ethical Considerations in Defense of Embryo Adoption." In *The Ethics of Embryo Adoption and the Catholic Tradition*, edited by Sarah-Vaughan Brakman and Darlene Fozard Weaver, 103–108. New York: Springer, 2007; Brugger, E. Christian. "In Defense of Transferring Heterologous Embryos," *National Catholic Bioethics Quarterly* 5, no. 1 (Spring 2005): 96–112; Brugger, E. Christian, ed. "Symposium on *Dignitas Personae*." *National Catholic Bioethics Quarterly* 9, no. 3 (Autumn 2009): 461–484; Carey, Kristen Ann. "Ethical and Religious Directives for a Catholic Embryo Adoption Agency: A Thought Experiment." In *The Ethics of Embryo Adoption and the Catholic Tradition*, edited by Sarah-Vaughan Brakman and Darlene Fozard Weaver, 251–274. New York: Springer, 2007; Geach, Mary. "Are There Any Circumstances in Which It Would Be Morally Admirable for a Woman to Seek to Have an Orphan Embryo Implanted in Her Womb?" In *Issues for a Catholic Bioethic*, edited by Luke Gormally, 341–346. London: Linacre Centre, 1999; Geach, Mary. "Rescuing Frozen Embryos." In *What Is Man, O Lord? The Human Person in a Biotech Age; Proceedings of the Eighteenth Bishops' Workshop*, edited by Edward J. Furton, 217–230. Boston: National Catholic Bioethics Center, 2002; Grisez, Germain. *The Way of the Lord Jesus*. Vol. 3, *Difficult Moral Questions*. Quincy, IL: Franciscan Press, 1997; Haas, John M. "*Dignitas Personae* and the Question of 'Embryo Adoption.'" National Catholic Bioethics Center, 2008, http://www.ncbcenter.org/page.aspx?pid=1010; Kaczor, Christopher. "Artificial Wombs and Embryo Adoption." In *The Ethics of Embryo Adoption and the Catholic Tradition*, edited by Sarah-Vaughan Brakman and Darlene Fozard Weaver, 307–322. New York: Springer, 2007; May, William E. *Catholic Bioethics and the Gift of Human Life*, 2nd ed. Huntington, IN: Our Sunday Visitor, 2008; May, William E. "The Morality of 'Rescuing' Frozen Embryos." In *What Is Man, O Lord? The Human Person in a Biotech Age; Proceedings of the Eighteenth Bishops' Workshop*, edited by Edward J. Furton, 201–215. Boston: National Catholic Bioethics Center, 2002; Napier, Steven. "*Dignitas Personae* and the Question of 'Embryo Adoption.'" National Catholic Bioethics Center, 2008, http://www.ncbcenter.org/page.aspx?pid=1010; Napier, Steven. "Frozen Embryo Adoptions Are Morally Objectionable." In *The Catholic as Citizen: Debating the Issues of Justice; Proceedings from the 26th Annual Conference of Catholic Scholars*, edited by Kenneth Whitehead, 84–101. South Bend, IN: St. Augustine's Press, 2004; Smith, William B. "Rescue the Frozen?" *Homiletic and Pastoral Review* 96, no. 1 (October 1995): 72–74; Stempsey, William E., SJ. "Heterologous Embryo Transfer: Metaphor and Morality." In *The Ethics of Embryo Adoption and the Catholic Tradition*, edited by Sarah-Vaughan Brakman and Darlene Fozard Weaver, 25–42. New York: Springer, 2007; Surtees, Geoffrey. "Adoption of a Frozen Embryo." *Homiletic and Pastoral Review* 96, no. 4 (August–September 1996): 8–9; Tollefsen, Christopher. "Could Human Embryo Transfer Be Intrinsically Immoral?" In *The Ethics of Embryo Adoption and the Catholic Tradition*, edited by Sarah-Vaughan Brakman and Darlene Fozard Weaver, 85–102.

New York: Springer, 2007; Watt, Helen. "Are There Any Circumstances in Which It Would Be Admirable for a Woman to Seek to Have an Abandoned Embryo Transferred into Her Womb?" In *Issues for a Catholic Bioethic*, edited by Luke Gormally, 347–352. London: Linacre Centre, 1999; Weaver, Darlene Fozard. "Embryo Adoption Theologically Considered: Bodies, Adoption, and the Common Good." In *The Ethics of Embryo Adoption and the Catholic Tradition*, edited by Sarah-Vaughan Brakman and Darlene Fozard Weaver, 151–160. New York: Springer, 2007. *See also* BIOETHICS; *DIGNITAS PERSONAE*; *DONUM VITAE*; HUMAN EMBRYO; MORAL THEOLOGY: A SURVEY

EMOTIVISM   Emotivism is the name given by philosopher Alasdair MacIntyre to a peculiar attitude toward moral reasoning whose central tenet is the rejection of the idea that there is an objective moral order, embodying principles and standards according to which the ethical value of human actions is to be determined. Emotivism is in essence moral subjectivism, which is to say, it represents a position that maintains that the only proper and legitimate source for the determination of moral right and wrong is the individual person. In traditional moral theory, the role of the individual is, to be sure, of central importance, for it is up to him to determine what is right or wrong in particular cases. But the individual does this by referring to objective principles and standards. From the point of view of moral subjectivism, on the other hand, the individual not only judges but also establishes the standards according to which he judges. He thus becomes, in moral matters, both judge and legislator.

In traditional ethical moral philosophies, such as that developed by Aristotle and later refined and enriched by St. Thomas Aquinas, it was taken as axiomatic that there was an objective moral order. Just as there are objective laws that govern the physical universe (the laws of nature), so there are objective laws that govern the moral universe (the natural law). Accepting this state of affairs, it is the duty of the individual, as a moral agent, to foster a lively awareness of the basic principles and standards of the natural law, so that, through the exercise of the virtue of prudence, he can reason rightly from those general criteria to particular cases. The individual is thus always operating within an established moral structure that was not of his own devising.

Emotivism rejects the traditional way of viewing man's situation as a moral agent. To the extent that it recognizes a moral order at all, that order is seen as something that has its origin in the individual and hence is necessarily private and, for all practical purposes, exclusive. Determining right and wrong is the sole prerogative of the individual, and that action is reducible to the personal preference of the individual. In the final analysis, it is the emotions, or feelings, that are to be regarded as decisive in moral matters.

The moral subjectivism to which emotivism directly translates leads inevitably to moral relativism. The logic here is clear enough. If my individual preference is the foundation for my moral choices, the same holds true for every other individual, and that being the case, the chance of there ever being any common principles and standards in which all can share is rendered quite remote, if not entirely impossible. With no acknowledged objective principles or standards, there is no logical basis upon which any one individual preference can claim to be superior to any other. Moral relativism thus reigns supreme.

Instances of emotivism have manifested themselves at various times over the course of the history of Western philosophy, but it is only in modern times that emotivism has become a pervasive phenomenon. It would require but a brief glance at the state of contemporary culture to recognize the commanding role emotivism plays therein. Today many people are content to feel, rather than to think, their way to moral resolutions. As for the specific philosophical sources for the prevalence of emotivism in our day, one influential work that deserves special mention is *Principia Ethica* (1903) by British philosopher G. E. Moore.

MacIntyre calls attention to a rather devious aspect of the methodology of emotivism: the fact that its promoters tend to advance its cause through what have all the appearances of rational arguments founded upon principles but which are really elaborate disguises that serve to mask the fundamental premise of emotivism—that moral choice is reducible to personal preference. In fact, emotivism takes the position that there are not, and cannot be, any rational justification for our moral choices.

One of the more revealing features of MacIntyre's thoroughgoing critique of emotivism is his pointed claim that its methodology, besides being pseudorational, is also manipulative. The emotivist will argue that it is simply personal preference that decides moral issues, but in this he is being not a little deceptive, for what he is really attempting to do—and here is where the manipulation comes in—is to persuade you that it is *his* personal preferences that are to be preferred. What tends to happen, therefore, in any community, is that its governing moral criteria turn out to be the personal preferences of its most powerful persuaders.

Because of the subjectivism and relativism that emotivism necessarily entails, whenever it gains the ascendency, any genuinely rational discourse regarding moral matters quickly evaporates. By either ignoring or openly repudiating the natural law, emotivism removes those foundational principles and standards necessary to resolve critical moral issues. Faced with a situation of this sort, the only recourse for the dedicated emotivist is lamely to recommend the continuance of the conversation—an altogether futile gesture, for the conversation in question has neither direction nor finality.

MacIntyre developed a moral thesis that is directly opposed to emotivism, and he provides three reasons for considering emotivism a failed mode of moral philosophy. First, it rests upon circular reasoning: Moral judgments are said to express feeling of approval, but that approval is then identified as moral approval. Second, though emotivism attempts to persuade us otherwise, the two claims "Act *X* is good," and "I prefer *X*" are simply not equivalent. Third, any reliable moral theory should endeavor to explain the *meaning* of the language used in moral discourse, but emotivism limits itself to explaining the *use* of that language. It seems reasonable to conclude that emotivism is another form of utilitarianism.—D. Q. McInerny

BIBLIOGRAPHY AND FURTHER READING: MacIntyre, Alasdair. *After Virtue: A Study in Moral Theory.* Notre Dame, IN: University of Notre Dame Press, 1981; Moore, G. E. *Principia Ethica.* Cambridge: Cambridge University Press, 1903. *See also* MacINTYRE, ALASDAIR C.; MORAL RELATIVISM; SUBJECTIVISM

ENTREPRENEUR An entrepreneur is a businessperson who perceives what people want or need, envisions how to make it available, and, taking the risks, brings together the people, resources, and institutions to produce it. This is not simply a business owner or manager. It refers to the essential combination of skills: of sensing what is wanted given changing conditions or even perceiving what might be wanted in the future, being alert to information and opportunities, and having the ability to make it happen. In economics and business, the entrepreneur is critically important to respond to changing market, technological, and social conditions, linking up what people want with the capacity to provide it.

In Catholic thought, particularly in the latter 20th century, the entrepreneur has been recognized as witnessing to the superiority of the human dimension of the economy (*CA* # 32), as well as for creating places in which people can work their vocations, produce output that truly benefits and is appreciated by others, and grow in community with others.

An entrepreneur requires several vital skills. The most important of these may be alertness to new information regarding opportunities and perception of what people want or might want. This involves an unusual awareness of others, both of what they want or need now and of how that may change with rapidly varying production and demand conditions. On the demand side, people want goods or services in light of their needs and interests, but also given their income and in relation to other goods and services. As these change, demand for what the entrepreneur sells will fluctuate enormously. Production conditions vary rapidly as well. New technologies arise that alter what is possible or efficient.

An entrepreneur also needs prudence, optimism, drive, courage, perseverance, and a capacity to work with and coordinate others. Producing a successful good or service doesn't simply happen on its own. First, it is not certain one will succeed, and thus entrepreneurship clearly requires a willingness to take risks and optimism that it will work out. But this must be tempered with prudence about what is truly feasible. This is not simply reckless risk-taking, but practical, prudent action, in the real-life context of uncertainty in rapidly changing conditions.

Furthermore, it doesn't happen instantly. After one has an idea about how to provide something old in a new way, or something totally new, comes the hard work of careful analysis, planning, and proving the idea to others—partners, financiers, and customers themselves. And it doesn't happen alone. In most cases, entrepreneurs must bring together and draw from the gifts, talents, and hard work of others: collaborators, workers in the firm, networks of others outside it for support, advice, sales, and so on. As Pope John Paul II wrote, this requires important virtues: "diligence, industriousness, prudence in undertaking reasonable risks, reliability and fidelity in interpersonal relationships, as well as courage" (*CA* # 32). Moreover, recognizing that the success of the free market economy rests on the entrepreneur points to people as the most important resource (*CA* # 31).

Understanding about the role of the entrepreneur developed slowly over the past few centuries, but took off rapidly in economic and business writings and Church teaching in the late 20th century. Among the earliest substantial reflections was that developed in the mid-1700s by Richard Cantillon. A merchant himself, he was familiar with the constant fluctuations of production and demand conditions and the risks involved in trying to bring goods and services to the market. Not surprisingly, his work recognized the frequent changes to which producers had to respond. These ideas were developed more fully by French political economist Jean-Baptiste Say in the early 1800s, who also coined the term *entrepreneur* ("one who undertakes"). In order to succeed, Say noted that the entrepreneur needed to have judgment, perseverance, and knowledge and be willing to take risks in the face of possible failure, dealing with constantly changing conditions on both production and demand sides.

Unfortunately, these insights did not deeply impact the economics profession until later in the century. Adam Smith, who wrote *Wealth of Nations* in 1776, had a description of market functioning that was too automatic, with too little sense of the importance of the entrepreneur, and this vision dominated the field until the 1870s.

Picking up from Say, Carl Menger and his followers in the Austrian school (beginning in the late 1800s) emphasized how quickly circumstances changed and how, as a result, market prices depend upon rapidly varying subjective values. Rejecting a more mechanistic system moving inexorably toward equilibrium balance, the Austrians recognized both that only through entrepreneurs could the market adjust toward any equilibrium and that in many cases the entrepreneur's actions (developing new products or ways of doing things) in fact *disrupted* equilibrium. This was developed more completely in the work of Ludwig von Mises and Friedrich Hayek, who rejected socialist central planning as impossible because the state could never adapt (or create) as quickly as a free market system. Not only would incentives for providing what people want be weak, but there could be no prices to capture the information about relative valuations that people have and that entrepreneurs use.

In the early to mid-20th century, renowned economic historian Joseph Schumpeter (himself within the Austrian school) likely deserves the most credit for popularizing the role of the entrepreneur within the mainstream economics profession. This included pointing out how the profession had overemphasized the division of labor following Smith, and illuminating the creative destruction and human initiative and creativity that more accurately characterize capitalism. Others extended these insights. Israel Kirzner emphasized the critical role of the discovery process and alertness to information and opportunity, while George Gilder drew attention to creative private initiative serving what others want.

By the 1970s, these insights were increasingly verified by the massive failures of the centrally planned economies: their inefficiency, their dreary and oppressive work conditions and apathetic workers, their poor quality output, their chronic shortages, and their products little tailored to what people wanted. Technological progress, large-scale production, education, and the division of labor weren't enough. Without incentives that arise from private property (one gets the returns from one's property, including one's business), from prices and profits, and most especially from individuals free to pursue businesses to produce what people want, the scarce resources of society will not be well organized to meet those demands. Most importantly, *someone* has to have the awareness, sense the changes, take the risks, persevere with their ideas, and assemble and motivate others. Centrally planned economies raised up these tasks too high organizationally (placing decision makers far from those interested in the output), strangled them too much with bureaucratic and political entanglements, and eliminated the incentives.

By the 1980s, these insights were recognized more broadly within the economics and business fields. In economics, this was also associated with a general move away from Keynesian top-down steering of the economy (not outright ownership) in macroeconomic policy and away from excessive regulation on the microeconomic side, both toward freeing individual entrepreneurs.

Development of Church teaching on the entrepreneur had to unite several strands: not only these recognitions of greater efficiency within the secular literature but also in the context of the overall system: what constitutes the true good, work, vocation, and true human development—that is, growth in love of God, virtue, and community.

Historically, the earliest related statements in Scripture or tradition concern simply work or money or business, as one would expect of an era in which goods and services changed little over the decades. In the Middle Ages, the scholastic theologians developed ever more sophisticated reasoning regarding how markets functioned. Those in the Spanish school at Salamanca, in particular, appear to have recognized how market prices balanced interests of buyer and seller.

But the analysis developed rapidly with the social encyclicals. Across the last century, this involved developments in understanding the system, as well as creativity, subsidiarity, human work and vocation, and the community of persons. In *Rerum Novarum*, Leo XIII rejected socialism and class warfare and stressed the importance of private property and private initiative. While recognizing problems within capitalism in the midst of the Great Depression, Pius XI (in *Quadragesimo Anno*) added to this emphasis on the role of private initiative and developed the principle of subsidiarity. Socialism violated subsidiarity by placing the decisions too high, leaving people with too little responsibility. The Second Vatican Council furthered this progression by recognizing both the critical role of the laity to transform the world in their individual positions as well as the vocation of individuals and the importance of personal development with growth in virtue as one works and fulfills that vocation. John Paul II completed this with his analysis of work in *Laborem Exercens*, which provided substantial exploration of the objective (technical) dimension and subjective dimension (what the work means for the worker) of work. The subjective dimension highlighted growth in virtue and ability as people worked, and personal vocation to transform the world, as well as to grow in relationship with others—something businesses did in creating a community of persons producing for others.

These themes were united with the role of the entrepreneur in *Centesimus Annus*. After the collapse of Communism, it became apparent that without incentives to make what people want, the system failed to provide effectively or efficiently. But this didn't just matter for efficiency. State producers had little incentive to consider what people wanted and were slow to change. The system did not solve alienation and help people sense that their work mattered and was a source of development. Instead, workers felt that they were mere cogs in a giant machine with little authority or freedom and little incentive to work well, given guaranteed employment and low pay unrelated to productivity and the high probability that the poor work of others in the chain would undermine one's efforts for ultimate users of the output. Naturally, this weakened the idea that work was good and the attraction of vocation.

The entrepreneur is thus critical for work and vocation. It takes a person to properly read the circumstances and adjust production accordingly. In the free market, the entrepreneur has the incentives, drive, and creativity to predict what people want and to try to bring it to market. Thus, by living out his vocation, the entrepreneur critically not only creates the conditions in which others have work (which Communism also provided) but also raises the chances that the work one does will be valued by others and can be one's gift to others. This is a challenge for any economy, but it becomes imperative when conditions are changing rapidly.

Following the creator, people are called to their vocation, to develop themselves via their work, and to bring their gifts and talents in service to others to transform the world. The entrepreneur's work helps to insure that people sense work as important in benefiting others, that they are creative, and that they have a vocation. In addition, as in the Trinity, we are called to be in communion. More than ever in history, we have to work with others in producing output. In creating productive businesses, the entrepreneur creates possibilities for us to develop in relation with others as well. As Anthony Percy argues, properly understood and carried out with God's will, the entrepreneur's vocation both provides for the common good and more effectively enables others to live out their vocations.—John D. Larrivee

BIBLIOGRAPHY AND FURTHER READING: Chafuen, Alejandro. *Faith and Liberty: The Economic Thought of the Late Scholastics*. Lanham, MD: Lexington Books, 2003; Gilder, George. *The Spirit of Enterprise*. New York: Simon & Schuster, 1984; Kirzner, Israel. *Discovery and the Capitalist Process*. Chicago: University of Chicago, 1985; Percy, Anthony. *Entrepreneurship in the Catholic Tradition*. Lanham, MD: Lexington Books, 2010; Skousen, Mark. *The Making of Modern Economics: The Lives and Ideas of the Great Thinkers*, 2nd ed. Armonk, NY: M. E. Sharpe, 2009. *See also* AUSTRIAN SCHOOL OF ECONOMICS; *CENTESIMUS ANNUS*; SUBSIDIARITY; SUPPLY-SIDE ECONOMICS

ESCHATOLOGY IN ANCIENT, MEDIEVAL, AND MODERN THOUGHT   Eschatology is the study of "last things" (*eschatos*, in Greek, means "last" or "final"). In Catholic theology, eschatology means death, final judgment, purgatory, and heaven and hell—most specifically heaven and hell, which most properly belong to "eternity" (discussed below), following final judgment.

Catholic eschatology begins with the two religiophilosophical strands that melded in the inception of Christianity in the New Testament: Jewish apocalypticism and Greco-Roman thought. The former arose in the Second Temple period (between the building of the Second Temple after the return from the Babylonian exile—which began with the destruction of the First Temple in 586/7 BC—and the final destruction of that Second Temple by the Romans in AD 70), in the works known as Jewish Apocalypses: 1 Enoch, 2 Baruch, and 4 Ezra. The book of Daniel is also apocalyptic in nature, but in the Hebrew canon of the Old Testament it falls within the latest section, "Writings"; the first two, "Law" and "Prophets," are not *properly* eschatological, but rather, in the Prophets, *proto-eschatological* (this clarification applies specifically to the literal sense of the Prophets at the time of original composition; for Catholic theology, all Scripture is eschatological in its fulfillment in Christ, its "spiritual sense").

For the Israelite/Jewish religion, the Jerusalem temple was the *true* completion of creation, as the center of the land promised by God (Genesis 12–22). The destruction of that temple made it difficult to envision fulfillment of that promise in the present world and age, and thus belief arose in a next, final world/age in which the promise would be fulfilled. At the center of this system were the figure of the Messiah (a final Davidic king) and the Temple Mount (Zion), both functioning as distinctly part of this world/age, but as the *final* stage, the "Messianic age," a bridge to the next. Some scholars surmise that, in the absence of the temple, the mount would operate as the land fulfillment: the land was promised in this world/age and the promise needed to be *at least partially* fulfilled *literally* in this world/age, a role that the mount would fulfill in the Messianic age as the location of the Messiah's work. The next world/age would *immediately* follow the Messianic age (just before formation of the modern state of Israel in 1948, several major strands of Judaism opposed its formation on the grounds that the land promise cannot be fulfilled politically without the final Messiah). Predictions of the number of years of the Messianic age in the New Testament book of Revelation (with Jesus as the true Messiah and the true fulfillment of the temple) are thought to be modeled on similar numerological predictions in the Jewish Apocalypses.

Greek philosophy brought new concepts into interaction with Second Temple Judaism. For Judaism, the Messianic age was historical (of this world) in nature. The next world/age, while believed firmly, was largely unknown regarding its nature (except, for example in 2 Baruch, the element of the true temple that transcends, but bases, the earthly historical copies); concepts were not yet readily available with which to think about that world. Now philosophers such as Plato spoke of things outside of time and historical, material particulars— universal "forms." These are now part of the base for the Christian concept of eternity, that which is beyond the particulars of the time and the history of this world.

In Christian history, concepts of a clearly delineated (in a set number of years) Messianic age persisted. In the Middle Ages, "millenarianism" drew on the 1,000-year reign described in the book of Revelation.

This construct of prediction continues today in the form of "millennialism," the belief that the Second Coming of Christ will happen in relation to a 1,000-year period of tribulation (among these beliefs, there is variance as to whether the true Second Coming will happen before or after this period).

Current Catholic theology does not concern itself with a historical 1,000-year period leading up to the transition to eternity. Rather it resembles Greek philosophy's emphasis on the relation of the universal (Christianity's "eternity") to the present historical age. According to some scholars, Plato did not see such a sharp divide (a dualism) between these realms as he was previously thought to propound, but rather some form of participation by the lower, historical realm in the higher, "eternal" realm. Catholic theology views the Messianic age as one in which, since the time of Christ (through the Incarnation, the entering of the second person of the eternal Trinity into historical space and time in a concrete, historical person), history participates in and is defined by eternity in a radically new and mystical way.

The standard term for the Second Coming, *Parousia*, receives a unique interpretation in Catholic theology. Literally (from its Greek roots), the term means "being (*ousia*) alongside (*para*)." Mystical Catholic theology takes this term as intricately tied to the "Real Presence" of Christ in the Eucharist/Blessed Sacrament (the historical *re*-Presentation of the Calvary sacrifice through the ongoing sacrifice of the Mass). This teaching sees the Messianic age as that between the historical first coming of Christ and the final Second Coming, an age in this world in which the Eucharistic presence grounds the new participation of this world in the next, while maintaining the Second Coming as a unique future event leading into the *full* eschaton (the age of the "Church Triumphant"). No specific time frame is given for how long this present age (the Messianic age of the "Church Militant") will last.

Present societal systems are defined by the eternal "society" of heaven. Magisterial Church teaching guards against the conflation of the eschatological (eternal) and the purely temporal. For instance, complete justice cannot be realized until its eschatological fulfillment in heaven (cf. *CCC* # 676). Rather, true justice functions as a goal to be striven for in this age, in hopes of true fulfillment in heaven. While the Church as the "mystical body of Christ" is a model of the true, final society, it is just that and is not meant to function as a legal ruling body in present *political* society.

Systems such as Marxism have been described as eschatological because they do posit a final event that will end the present order (for Marxism, definitively ending class oppression and struggle). This is, however, a modified sense of the term functioning simply on the concept of finality. Its "next world" will still be part of the present order of history—it will not have even the limitedly defined "beyond" of the Jewish apocalyptic next world/age. The magisterial teaching of the Church rejects Marxism and other systems that deny a distinct "eternal" world. Briefly put, for Marxism the historical defines the eschatological, rather than, as in magisterial Catholic theology, the eschatological/eternal defining and radically transforming the historical. The influence of Marxism on liberation theology varies among individual theologians within that movement.—M. Brett Kendall

BIBLIOGRAPHY AND FURTHER READING: Collins, John J. *The Apocalyptic Imagination: An Introduction to the Jewish Matrix of Christianity.* New York: Crossroad, 1984; Durrwell, Francois-Xavier. "Eucharist and Parousia." Translated by Peter Jones. *Lumen Vitae* 26 (1970): 273–315. Wainright, Geoffrey. *Eucharist and Eschatology.* London: Epworth, 1978; *See also* ESCHATOLOGY; LIBERATION THEOLOGY; MARXISM; MILLENARIANISM

ETHICAL AND RELIGIOUS DIRECTIVES FOR CATHOLIC HEALTH CARE SERVICES

Ethical and Religious Directives for Catholic Health Care Services is an ecclesial document for Catholic health care institutions in the United States and for the individuals working within them. Catholic health care is a long-standing sponsored ministry of the Church. In the United States, the first Catholic hospital was founded in the 18th century. Perhaps the most widely recognized ecclesial document in Catholic health care ministry in the United States, it is often identified as the *Directives* or simply *ERD*. Periodic revision of *ERD* is currently developed through a consultation process by the Committee on Doctrine of the U.S. Conference of Catholic Bishops (USCCB). Revisions are submitted to the Congregation for the Doctrine of the Faith (CDF) for review and then presented to the USCCB at its annual meeting for approval. Approval by the USCCB constitutes a recommendation to the local ordinary for promulgation in a particular diocese.

ERD addresses the foundations of the Church's health care ministry and a range of issues within it. The stated purpose of the document (expressed in the preamble to the 2009 edition) is twofold: to "reaffirm the ethical standards of behavior in health care that flow from the Church's teaching about the dignity of the human person" and "to provide authoritative guidance on certain moral issues that face Catholic health care today." *ERD* is addressed to all persons involved in this Church-sponsored ministry, from sponsors and administrators to individual professionals as well as patients. The preamble states that "the moral teachings that we profess here flow principally from the natural law, understood in light of the revelation Christ has entrusted to his Church."

ERD is well recognized and used in Catholic health care because, upon promulgation by the local ordinary, the document is required for incorporation into the policy of all the health care ministries in the particular diocese. "Catholic health care services must adopt these Directives as policy, require adherence to them within the institution as a condition for medical privileges and employment, and provide appropriate instruction regarding the Directives for administration, medical and nursing staff, and other personnel" (*ERD* # 5). *ERD* is policy and has normative quality for the facility. It contains a mandate for its instruction to a spectrum of health care personnel.

ERD has gone through three stages (or generations) of development. The first generation involved the development of Catholic hospital ethics codes. Since the 1970s, *ERD* has been identified with the hierarchy of the United States. The genealogy of *ERD* can, however, be traced to the foundation in 1915 of the Catholic Health Association (CHA), which was originally known as the Catholic Hospital Association of the United States and Canada.

The early decades of the 20th century were significant as the era of standardization in American hospitals. This movement led to new standards of professionalism for hospitals, as well as new standards for medical and nursing education. Ethics codes were a manifestation of this spirit of improvement. Rev. Charles B. Moulinier, SJ (the first president of CHA) was very supportive of standardization and was eager that Catholic hospitals advance into the new expectations. Father Moulinier encouraged CHA to accept the invitation of the American College of Surgeons (ACS), founded in the standardization spirit in 1913, to accept its "Minimum Standard" for hospitals. This prompted opposition from some CHA member institutions, which objected that a secular standard would be normative in Catholic hospitals. Nevertheless, with the support of Cardinal Gibbons and Archbishop Messmer of Milwaukee (where the CHA offices were then located), CHA accepted the ACS standards at its 1918 convention.

Although it continued to accept the ACS code, the 1921 CHA convention adopted a code of ethics developed by Father Michael Bourke. This code was published in the first issue of the CHA journal *Hospital Progress* (now *Health Progress*). The "Bourke Code" listed immoral surgical procedures and practices. Often printed on a single sheet and posted in surgery suites, it was found useful by many Catholic hospitals but was not seen as an official statement of Catholic moral norms. The 1921 CHA convention also formed a permanent committee headed by Father Bourke with the goal of developing an ethics code. But none was forthcoming, and CHA did not return to the ethics code question until 1946. In the interim, a number of dioceses, including Hartford, Toledo, Grand Rapids, and Los Angeles, developed their own codes.

In 1946, the CHA Executive and Administrative Boards established a committee on medical ethics. Because the initial CHA executive directors were Jesuits, several Jesuit moral theologians, including Rev. John Clifford, SJ, and Rev. T. L. Buscaren, SJ, were invited to collaborate with diocesan directors of hospitals (who represented bishops in a liaison role to hospitals) on a code.

A year later, Rev. Gerald Kelly, SJ, was charged with the task of developing a code of ethics. He also took on responsibility for medical-moral articles in *Hospital Progress* and was to have a position of prominence in Catholic health care ethics in the United States until his death two decades later. Father Kelly's code was published by CHA in 1949 with the title *Ethical and Religious Directives for Catholic Health Care Services* and bore the approval of the archbishop of St. Louis. From the outset, this code was recognized to have authoritative status only where adopted by a local ordinary. By 1954, a second edition had 60 specific directives with sequential numbering in its several sections, like the *Code of Canon Law*. At the 36th annual meeting of the bishops of the United States, these directives received the approval of the body. Recognition was given to their wide spread and that almost 48,000 copies were in print. By 1955, 107 dioceses had adopted the code.

A second generation of *ERD* may be identified with the 1969 initiative taken by the administrative board of the United States Catholic Conference (USCC) to revise the 1954 directives. Behind the initiative was what Msgr. Harrold Murray, director of the USCC Department of Health Affairs, called "rumblings of concern" at a time of cultural and theological questioning. Monsignor Murray was approached by CHA executive director Rev. Thomas Casey, SJ, in the

mid-1960s on a range of issues, including increasing application of the principles of cooperation in tubal ligation procedures. Local demand for this procedure was particularly vocal when the Catholic hospital was the sole facility in a community.

Rev. Richard McCormick, SJ, Rev. John Connery, SJ, and Rev. Paul McKeever were the three theologians named by the USCC to submit a revision of *ERD* to the USCC Committee on Health Affairs, and their task was completed in October 1970. Their draft did not, however, address cooperation issues in the body of the text, but rather in the preamble, and it was written in such a manner that USCC reviewers saw judgment of cooperation questions was placed in the hospital administrator rather than in the local bishop. Accordingly, Archbishop John F. Whealon, chairman of the Committee on Doctrine, wrote a new preamble that reserved judgment to the ordinary on whether a particular situation was a legitimate application of the principles of cooperation. The assembled bishops accepted the revision in 1971.

In 1975, a revision of the 1971 *ERD* incorporated the first reference to the principles of cooperation. A new concluding sentence was added to Directive 12: "Catholic hospitals are not to provide abortion services based upon the principle of material cooperation." This had the effect of preventing application of the principle of material cooperation (a proposed relationship more remote than formal cooperation) to institutional participation in abortion. It was an important statement in the tumultuous wake of *Roe v. Wade* in 1973.

The third generation of *ERD* may be identified with the 1994 edition, a significant editing and reformatting of the text with significant expansion of the historical and theological content. *ERD* now spoke more directly to the phenomenon and shape of Catholic health care, a revision of critical importance as the number of vowed religious continued to decline and lay leadership has become more widespread. In addition to an expanded introduction section, each of the six parts of *ERD* now had its own introduction, followed by the numbered individual directives. These introductions allowed the reader to better understand Catholic teaching and set the context for the content of the specific directives.

A preamble and general introduction provide a scriptural, ecclesial, and theological orientation within *ERD*. Both the Gospel imperative and charisms of the religious institutes that founded Catholic health care in the nation are evoked by the primacy of the virtue of charity. It states: "The mystery of Christ casts light on every facet of Catholic health care: to see Christian love as the animating principle of health care."

Parts 1 through 3 of *ERD* can be seen as foundational. Part 1, "The Social Responsibility of Catholic Health Care Services," identifies the ecclesial nature of this traditional apostolate in the Church and states that facilities "must adopt these Directives as policy." It utilizes principles of Catholic social teaching to relate that concern for the poor and the marginalized must be expressed "in concrete action at all levels of Catholic health care." Part 2, "The Pastoral and Spiritual Responsibility of Catholic Health Care," contains many statements on spiritual care similar to the 1975 *ERD*. Since the 1994 edition, the section on pastoral care, placed at the conclusion of the 1975 edition, is now in a more prominent location. Part 3, "The Professional–Patient Relationship," seems at the heart of *ERD*. It expresses the dignity of the human person and the prudential decision making required for particular treatment situations. An emphasis on trust and personal relationship in the caregiving context suggests the historic charism of vowed religious and their dedication to their patients. In addition, the new emphasis on these themes is evidence of the influence of the personalist philosophy of Pope John Paul II on a generation of Catholic teaching.

The remaining three parts are more topical. Part 4, "Issues in Care for the Beginning of Life," addresses norms for acceptable reproductive technologies to assist married couples, defines abortion, and prohibits material cooperation with abortion, as well as warning of "the danger of scandal in any association with abortion providers."

Part 5, "Issues in Care for the Dying," affirms the obligation for truthful clinical information to persons that they may have "appropriate opportunities to prepare for death." The 2009 revision (fifth edition) of *ERD* addresses the question of assisted nutrition and hydration (ANH). The 2001 edition had recognized that this question had not been resolved; a 2004 allocution of Pope John Paul II and a 2007 response and application of CDF were reflected in the 2009 edition. ANH is now identified as having the goal of care, not treatment, and should "in principle" be provided to all patients unless excessively burdensome to the patient or for a patient who "draws close to inevitable death." Other aspects of this part include support for the burden–benefit standard in medical decision making, and the high moral warrant for effective pain management to benefit dying persons. Death is addressed as a "reality" in this state of life and in light of the witness to the Church's belief "that God has created each person for eternal life."

Part 6, "Forming New Partnerships with Health Care Organizations and Providers," was new to the 1994 edition. It addresses the ongoing reconfiguration of health care in the nation and recognizes that there are opportunities for Catholic health care to help "realign the local delivery system" as well as "serious challenges" presented to Catholic identity and integrity in some partnership proposals. The traditional principles of cooperation are presented, and judgment on moral analysis and any scandal issues is reserved to the bishop. Part 6 of the 1994 edition had the most edits in the 2001 *ERD*. It clarifies impermissible cooperation in sterilization from the 1994 edition's description of the 1975 CDF document *Quaecumque Sterilizatio*. Based on the confusion it caused, the appendix on cooperation analysis was removed for the 2001 edition.

True to the spirit of the third-generation *ERD*, since 1994 a conclusion section ends on a theological note. Sickness is seen as a sign of our human frailty, and compassion is identified as a sign of the discipleship of the Church and sign of "the final healing that will one day bring about the new creation and that is the ultimate fruit of Jesus' ministry and God's love for us."—Joseph J. Piccione

BIBLIOGRAPHY AND FURTHER READING: Griese, Orville N. *Catholic Identity in Health Care: Principles and Practice.* Braintree, MA: Pope John Center, 1987; Kauffmann, Christopher J. *Ministry and Meaning: A Religious History of Catholic Health Care in the United States.* New York: Crossroad, 1995; O'Rourke, Kevin, OP, Thomas Kopfensteiner, and Ron Hamel. "A Brief History: A Summary of the Development of the *Ethical and Religious Directives for Catholic Health Care Services.*" *Health Progress,* November–December 2001, 18–21; Smith, Russell E. "The Principles of Cooperation and Their Application to the Present State of Health Care Evolution." In *The Splendor of Truth and Health Care: Proceedings of the Fourteenth Workshop for Bishops,* 217–231. Braintree, MA: Pope John Center, 1995.

EUGENICS According to Luigi Cavalli-Sforza and Walter Bodmer, "the aim of eugenics is the improvement of the human species by decreasing the propagation of the physically and mentally handicapped, i.e., *negative* eugenics, and by increasing that of the 'more desirable types,' i.e., *positive* eugenics." The term *eugenics* was coined by Francis Galton in 1883, though the idea can be found in Plato.

For Galton, eugenics was "the study of agencies under social control that may improve or impair the racial qualities of future generations either physically or mentally." He also described it as the "science of improving stock . . . to give the more suitable races . . . a better chance of prevailing speedily over the less suitable." Galton regarded eugenics as a "scientific religion and a guide to morality" and spoke of the "religious significance of the doctrine of evolution," which imposed "a new moral duty . . . to further evolution." In 1908, he said that eugenics "must be introduced into the national consciousness as a new religion." This reshaping of social policy and the ethics of procreation according to eugenic principles would require radical intervention into human reproduction, so that "what nature does blindly, slowly, and ruthlessly, man may do providently, quickly, and kindly." Eugenics sought to use knowledge of heredity to control the quality of human beings to prevent the perceived degeneration of the "gene pool" and of civilization itself. It belongs within the intellectual tradition of the Darwinian theory of evolution, the Malthusian "struggle for existence," and Herbert Spencer's "survival of the fittest."

The Eugenics Education Society, established in England in 1907, aimed to "promote eugenic teaching, to spread a knowledge of the laws of heredity . . . to effect improvement of race," and to "further eugenic teaching at home, in the schools, and elsewhere." It drew support from across the political spectrum and from medical professionals, medical scientists, educationalists, academics, social planners, and social scientists, who remained its major advocates. Galton sought the support of those who were in positions to shape public opinion and public policy. Lyndsay Farrell notes that supporters viewed eugenics as a "scientifically based ideal which could be used to guide policy and practice over a wide range of problems in health and welfare." Eugenics also appealed to literary elites, idealists, and early feminists. Some ministers of religion were also enthusiastic in preaching eugenics.

Although there were moderates as well as extremists among their ranks, early eugenicists were invariably concerned about the propagation of those variously described as the "feeble-minded," the "unfit," the "residuum," or the "social problem group"—elastic categories that included the urban poor, the illiterate, immigrants, the mentally disabled, criminals, alcoholics, and other groups perceived as morally degenerate or deviant. The initial desire for segregation and prohibition of marriage soon led to more vigorous proposals for sterilization. The Mental Deficiency Act in England in 1913 and the ruling in the *Buck v. Bell* case in 1927 in the United States (which rejected a constitutional challenge to compulsory sterilization laws) were perceived

as successes for the eugenics movement. The birth control movement, itself rooted in neo-Malthusianism and pioneered by eugenicists such as Marie Stopes in the United Kingdom and Margaret Sanger in the United States, gradually appealed to eugenicists in general as a means to control the undesirable.

Eugenicists constructed a rhetoric of revulsion and rejection against those thought to be a threat to class stability, racial purity, and the health of society, understood as an organic corporate entity that could be afflicted with sickness or disease. Here can also be traced the influence of Nietzsche's malign ideology of anticompassion. Eugenics, as "social hygiene" and "race betterment," appealed to many in the United Kingdom and the United States and also found support in Latin America, Scandinavia, France, Eastern and Central Europe, Russia, Australia, Canada, and more recently Singapore and China. Nazi eugenic policies attracted wide interest; American scientist Harry T. Laughlin framed a model eugenic sterilization law that the Nazis adopted and which fellow scientist Frederick Osborn judged "the most exciting experiment that had ever been tried."

Eugenics can also be understood as a protean term whose various meanings can be discerned only by cross-cultural historical research. Such research has increasingly revealed many variations on the idea of controlling heredity. Eugenics has survived and flourished partly because of the adoption by its proponents of rhetorical camouflage or what Mark Adams calls "protective coloration." In this sense, eugenics may be considered a parasitic idea that, as well as possessing intrinsic appeal, has fed off other ideals, aspirations, and anxieties found within social, medical, and political thought.

Daniel Kevles spoke of the "history of a dirty word," one prominent part of which was the association with Nazism, and suspicion and opposition has invariably accompanied the progress of eugenics. That association often clouds contemporary debate, giving rise to the need for a more careful analysis to identify continuities and discontinuities between the old and new eugenics. It is no longer possible to accept the once widely held view that eugenics disappeared in disgrace following the Nazi experiment in race hygiene culminating in mass murder by the state. Instead, eugenics in Germany emerged within a specific medical ideology supported by medical professionals, scientific researchers, health care economists, and state bureaucrats prior to the emergence of the Third Reich. Moreover, eugenics both predated Nazism and continued its progress in the postwar period.

Since eugenics came to be associated with class prejudice and racism in the United Kingdom, racial segregation and anti-immigration in the United States, and genocide in Nazi Germany, some later advocates preferred to avoid the term altogether or qualify it with adjectives such as *reform* eugenics or *medical* eugenics, or to focus on the social implications of genetics, or to pursue eugenic goals through less obvious means.

C. P. Blacker, a major strategist of the British Eugenics Society, sought to embed eugenics in medical philosophy as part of the ambition to achieve greater scientific and technological control of human reproduction to achieve improvement in the quality of human beings. He advocated what he called "crypto-eugenics," exploring the eugenic aspects of contemporary social problems and especially reproductive health. In 1960, the Society's council proposed that "the Society's activities in crypto-eugenics should be pursued vigorously, and specifically that the Society should increase its monetary support for the FPA [Family Planning Association] and the IPPF [International Planned Parenthood Federation]." These two bodies appeared in the membership lists of the Eugenics Society into the 1970s. Thus was ensured the enduring influence of eugenics on key pressure groups in the late 20th century, particularly those advocating birth control, abortion law reform, population control, and eventually screening technologies in medical genetics. Some eugenicists also supported the legalization of euthanasia.

The Eugenics Society changed its name to the Galton Institute in 1988. Its conferences continued to attract leading geneticists and professionals in the fields of health and social policy. In the United States, eugenics also had its leading advocates in the same fields. Associated above all with Cold Spring Harbor, eugenics developed its own scientific rationale, and when the so-called new genetics emerged and drove the Human Genome Project, the international discussion of its social and ethical implications invariably featured eugenics at its very center. Popular support had made possible the legalization of coercive sterilization, which persisted for decades in many states. In both the United States and the United Kingdom, this popular support was apparent in the growth of the population control movement, whose eugenic dimension was never far from the surface.

The obsession of the early eugenicists with the "social problem group" was expressed in the late 20th-century eugenic demographic agenda, which perceived the Third World as a global social problem. But the initial crude population control agenda, centered on the danger of a "population explosion," was gradually transformed into a program of "reproductive health" and "reproductive rights" for the less developed nations, a shift engineered by the skilled marketing strategists in various antinatalist international nongovernmental agencies and United Nations bodies. The crucial role of eugenicists in creating and entrenching both the birth control and population control movements has been firmly established. For the eugenics movement, quality control through medical genetics would also become a necessary corollary of quantity control through contraception.

Kevles claimed that "the spectre of eugenics hovers over virtually all contemporary developments in human genetics." David Braine argues that since 1948 there has been a revival of eugenics aimed at a healthy and vigorous, physically and intellectually able population and that the new eugenics can now draw upon a more sophisticated expertise. Certainly, biomedical technology offers eugenic possibilities of which Galton and his early followers could only dream.

Some who defend this new orientation in eugenics apply qualifying adjectives to distinguish it from coercive state-imposed versions. They speak of *ethical* eugenics, *utopian* eugenics (Kitcher), or *liberal* eugenics (Agar) and emphasize the role of parental choice in eugenic abortion, cloning, and genetic engineering to enhance the characteristics of offspring. Such eugenics is widely defended if decisions are left to parents as part of an ideology of "personal choice" and "reproductive rights." But many question such a distinction in view of the various forms of coercive pressure in health education and counseling services, inadequate funding and poor resource allocation for the care of disabled children, the persistence of social stigma, and the risk of creating a genetic "underclass," often implicating the insurance industry and the vigorous promotion of certain screening procedures by health care systems. Some believe that such social pressure offers a "backdoor to eugenics." The early Eugenics Society envisaged precisely the cumulative eugenic effect of individual parental choices, informed by societal pressure. Some bioethicists argue for the desirability of imposing a eugenic duty requiring parents to use the whole range of interventions now available to achieve eugenic outcomes for the good of society.

Eugenics, as the "quality control of human beings by the quality control of human reproduction," has featured prominently in public policy discussion of genetics in recent decades, especially relating to the extension of prenatal screening and selective abortion, the new reproductive technologies, and human genetic enhancement, as well as in the contentious field of sociobiology. Many recent genetic research projects seem to represent a "new eugenics."

More radically, some entertain grandiose eugenic aspirations, seeking to replace the so-called genetic lottery by greater human control and purposive intervention to direct the course of evolution. In proposing a new eugenics, Richard Lynn advocates the extensive use of biotechnology and mechanisms of social engineering to control the quantity and quality of human populations to realize each society's aspiration to compete in the global conflict for the flourishing of the fittest. The aim is to reverse the global dysgenic forces at work in modern societies. Similarly, David Galton proclaims that "the new eugenic technology may become a vital weapon to prevent future genetic deterioration of our species." In such schemes, the role envisaged for the medical profession is that of distinguishing the fit from the unfit—worthwhile lives from meaningless lives—and the clinical elimination of the latter. From sterilization, prenatal destruction of human life, and pediatric euthanasia to the removal of the elderly infirm, such eliminative medicine, with its claimed economic benefits, implements a modern form of eugenics characteristic of what Pope John Paul II in *Evangelium Vitae* (1995) called the "culture of death."

Kevles noted that the Catholic Church has long been a "staunch opponent of eugenics." Early Catholic responses engaged seriously and critically with eugenics. Some opposed its flawed reasoning and scientific pretensions as well as its quasi-religious claims. Others conceded in principle the need for eugenic improvement and espoused general eugenic *ideals* while opposing as immoral most of the *methods* advocated, judging them an assault on natural rights and justice. Still others proposed a form of "Catholic eugenics" centered not on medical intervention but on moral and spiritual improvement through adherence to Christian faith and the practice of virtue and prayer. Catholic commentators challenged the inhumane nature of the "Galton school of eugenics," as some called it, and sought to rescue the unfit from stigma and rejection. This was heartfelt, since Catholics, with many of their numbers among the Irish and other immigrant groups in the lower social strata in both the United Kingdom and the United States, were routinely castigated as a dysgenic presence in society. Catholics often found themselves the target of the eugenic rhetoric of revulsion, even from eugenic enthusiasts in other churches. Another line of argument, which G. K. Chesterton developed, saw eugenic

advocates as proto-fascists, guilty of "Prussianism," the preparedness to use brutal state bureaucracy to achieve their utopian goals.

Catholic moral theology was more nuanced, avoiding the simple assertion that eugenics was invariably undesirable or unethical. The description of an aspiration or procedure as "eugenic" was not thought to settle the question of its moral propriety. The Church's own canonical rules on consanguinity had in part a eugenic rationale. Insofar as eugenic programs aimed to reduce the incidence of genetic illness among the population, they could be seen as a form of preventive medicine and thus morally defensible. The question remained: What were the ethical parameters within which eugenic aims could be pursued?

A distinction between eugenic aims and methods became central in Catholic thinking. Pope Pius XI's encyclical *Casti Connubii* in 1930 stated: "What is asserted in favor of the social and eugenic 'indication' may and must be accepted, provided lawful and upright methods are employed within the proper limits; but to wish to put forward reasons based upon them for the killing of the innocent is unthinkable." He spoke of the "very grave crime" of "taking the life of the offspring hidden in the mother's womb . . . for medical, social, or eugenic 'indication.'" He also affirmed that whatever its validity, eugenics must not be the supreme norm of human action.

In recent decades, the Catholic Church's critique has been directed at racist eugenics in population policies and eugenic practices in biomedicine. In *Sollicitudo Rei Socialis* in 1987, John Paul II expressed alarm at governments in many countries launching systematic campaigns against birth, which are often financed from abroad in the form of tied aid. These constitute a "form of oppression" of the poorest populations and sometimes lead to racism, or "the promotion of certain equally racist forms of eugenics."

As for medical eugenics, *Humanae Vitae* (1968) acknowledged that "serious reasons" could exist for limiting births, which could be understood to allow for eugenic considerations, though it rejected illicit methods such as contraception, sterilization, and abortion. Some Catholic medical ethicists incorporate a eugenic element in the concept of "responsible parenthood," while making clear that this is not the rejection of a disabled child as such, but rather a realistic evaluation on the part of parents of their ability to meet the particular demands of caring for such a child. The Holy See's document for the International Year of Disabled Persons in 1981 affirmed: "Medicine loses its title of nobility when instead of attacking disease, it attacks life.... Prevention should be against the illness, not against life."

Donum Vitae (1987) observed that some embryos in in vitro fertilization procedures are "sacrificed for various eugenic, economic or psychological reasons." This "dynamic of violence and domination" is morally objectionable, belonging as it does to "the abortion mentality." It involves domination over the life and death of one's fellow human beings, which can lead to "a system of radical eugenics." In *Evangelium Vitae*, John Paul II rejected "eugenic abortion, justified in public opinion on the basis of a mentality ... which accepts life only under certain conditions and rejects it when it is affected by any limitation, handicap or illness." Though prenatal diagnostic techniques were deemed acceptable for valid reasons, "it not infrequently happens that these techniques are used with a eugenic intention which accepts selective abortion in order to prevent the birth of children affected by various types of anomalies. Such an attitude is shameful and utterly reprehensible, since it presumes to measure the value of a human life only within the parameters of 'normality' and physical well-being, thus opening the way to legitimizing infanticide and euthanasia as well." *Reflections on Human Cloning* (1997) by the Pontifical Academy for Life argued that cloning belonged to "the eugenics project" (a modern form of "positive eugenics") and so was subject to all the ethical and juridical judgments that have condemned that project.

Eugenics has often sanctioned unjust discrimination against "inferior" human beings and subjugated individuals and families to the perceived needs of the collective. Such discrimination against the weakest members of society violates justice, without which the moral fabric of society begins to unravel. It threatens civilization itself, the survival of which depends on how we treat the weakest and most vulnerable. When health policy aims directly at reducing the numbers of the "genetically defective" by the eugenic tools of prenatal screening and abortion, society adopts a strategy of weeding out its weakest members with a search-and-destroy strategy. There is a chilling parallel between the concept of "meaningless lives" in modern bioethics and the idea of *lebens lebensunwerten* (lives unworthy of life) coined in Germany in 1920. The eugenic culling of the unfit, the weak, and the unwanted was first practiced systematically as part of animal husbandry. The danger is that as human society increasingly adopts similar eugenic strategies, we, too, practice the morality of the farmyard. Since the Catholic Church rejects any ideology that undermines justice and the common good, it remains opposed to any resurgent eugenics that threatens the sanctity of human life and the dignity of persons and that marginalizes vulnerable and suffering members of the human family.—John C. Berry

BIBLIOGRAPHY AND FURTHER READING: Black, Edwin. *War against the Weak: Eugenics, and America's Campaign to Create a Master Race*. New York: Four Walls, 2003; Blacker, C. P. *Eugenics: Galton and After*. London: Duckworth, 1952; Burleigh, Michael. *Earthly Powers: The Clash of Religion and Politics in Europe from the French Revolution to the Great War*. London, HarperCollins, 2005; Cavalli-Sforza, Luigi L., and Walter F. Bodmer. *The Genetics of Human Populations*. San Francisco: W. H. Freeman, 1971; Farmer, Ann. *By Their Fruits: Eugenics, Population Control, and the Abortion Campaign*. Washington, DC: Catholic University of America Press, 2008; Farrell, Lyndsay. "The History of Eugenics: A Bibliographical Review." *Annals of Science* 36 (1979): 112; Galton, Francis. *Essays in Eugenics*. London: Eugenics Education Society, 1909; Galton, Francis. "Eugenics: Its Definition, Scope and Aims." *Nature* 70 (1904): 82, 112–113; Galton, Francis. Foreword. *Eugenics Review* 1 (April 1909); Galton, Francis. *Inquiries into Human Faculty and Its Development*. London: Macmillan, 1883; Galton, Francis. *Memories of My Life*. London: Methuen, 1908; Kemp, N. D. A. *"Merciful Release": The History of the British Euthanasia Movement*. Manchester, England: Manchester University Press, 2002; Paul, Diane B. *Controlling Human Heredity: 1865 to the Present*. New York: Humanity Books, 1995; Paul, Diane B. *The Politics of Heredity: Essays on Eugenics, Biomedicine, and the Nature-Nurture Debate*. Albany: State University of New York Press, 1998; Schenk, F., and A. S. Parkes. "The Activities of the Eugenics Society." *Eugenics Review*, 1968, 142–175; Searle, G. R. *Eugenics and Politics in Britain, 1900–1914*. Leyden, The Netherlands: Noordhoff International, 1976; Weindling, Paul. *Health, Race, and German Politics between National Unification and Nazism, 1870–1945*. Cambridge: Cambridge University Press, 1989. *See also* CULTURE OF DEATH; CULTURE OF LIFE; *EVANGELIUM VITAE*; SANGER, MARGARET; SOCIAL DARWINISM

EVIL IN CHRISTIAN LITERATURE   Literature affords us a window into the human heart, explaining to us through fiction suffering and salvation, which in the words of Miguel de Unamuno is the "tragic sense of life." The greater the writer, the easier it is to identify with the created characters. This entry focuses on writers who were believing Christians and whose fictional characters recognize evil and through this experience triumph over it.

C. S. Lewis, often associated with England and Oxford, was born in Belfast, and always considered Ireland his home. Clive Staples Lewis was born on November 29, 1898, the second son of Albert and Flora Lewis. He experienced early parental loss when, at the age of nine, his mother died. After witnessing fierce conditions fighting in France during in World War I, Lewis turned to atheism, but subsequently converted to Christianity at the age of 29.

All of Lewis's writings reflect his sincerely held beliefs in the Anglican communion. He has come to be known as one of the greatest of Christian apologists. In July 1940, during a prayer service, an idea for a book suddenly struck Lewis. He decided to write a book that would consist of letters from an elderly devil to a young devil who had just begun to work on his first "patient." The purpose was to expose the devil's use of psychology to undermine the faith of a young man and to give a scenario of temptation from the diabolic point of view.

The Screwtape Letters consists of 31 letters from Screwtape, an older and experienced devil, to his young, novice nephew, Wormwood. The events in the life of the patient are ordinary daily occurrences, but they are meant to show how choices have eternal consequences. The advice that Uncle Screwtape gives is that the patient should consider feelings to be more important than knowledge. Petty annoyances with his mother and others are to be exaggerated. It is best to keep the patient believing that devils are comic figures, not really something that sophisticated people would believe in. Pleasures are to be shown as being something to be pursued at all costs because they are healthy and satisfying. The patient is to be attracted by friends who are modern thinkers. Even innocent pleasures could be used as a distraction. He is to be kept away from the real purpose of worship by "church shopping." Screwtape becomes enraged because the patient has fallen in love with a sincere Christian girl. Because it is wartime, Screwtape warns Wormwood not to have the patient die in a bombing raid. To have him die so quickly would prevent further seduction. However, this is the death he does experience, and Screwtape tells his nephew: "You have let a soul slip through your fingers."

A close friend of Lewis's was J. R. R. Tolkien, born John Ronald Reuel Tolkien in the Orange Free State, South Africa, on January 3, 1892. Tolkien returned to England with his family when he was three years old. There, his mother, with her two sons, converted to Roman Catholicism, suffering the enmity of her family. Tolkien was educated at the Birmingham Oratory, begun by Blessed John Henry Newman in 1849, and lived on the grounds of the oratory until his mother's untimely death at the age of 34. Tolkien became a professor of Anglo-Saxon at Oxford University, where he remained until his retirement.

Tolkien's best known work is *The Lord of the Rings*. It is a three-volume series, comprising *The Fellowship of the Ring*, *The Two Towers*, and *The Return of the King*. In *The Fellowship of the Ring*, the ring represents the power to rule others. It is a special ring that was forged by a dark lord and has been stolen. Eventually it comes to be in the possession of Bilbo Baggins. It is the one ring that is missing from the complete set of rings, but it is the most important one, for it has the power to grant complete dominion. Bilbo disappears, but he has bequeathed the ring to Frodo, his nephew, who now must roam Middle-earth to destroy the ring and its fiercesome powers. Problems arise among the fellowship of Frodo's supporters. There are many crises, but Frodo grows in charity during his journey. The choices are real choices between good and evil. The enemy is very wise, but not wise enough to conquer goodness. Frodo must take the ring back to where it was forged to break its evil power. Even after he is wounded, he continues on his quest because of the responsibility that was placed on him.

Georges Bernanos was one of a group of writers in France around the time of World War I who became known as the French Catholic Literary Revival. Bernanos was born in Paris on February 20, 1888, to Catholic parents. Educated at the Sorbonne in the arts and law, he became a playwright, essayist, and novelist. His novels are set in the mostly Catholic Artois region of northern France, as he spent most of his youth in Fressin (Pas de Calais). Fressin was then the center where clerical meetings were held, bringing Bernanos into contact with many priests.

Bernanos's most famous novel, *The Diary of a Country Priest*, was written in the late 1930s and won the Grand Prix of the Académie Francaise. The book purports to be a diary, written in the first person, of a young priest on a mission to his first assigned parish. The curé encounters all the problems of life as seen through the microcosm of a small European village. His parishioners are a mixture of upper class, bourgeois, and peasants. He sets goals for himself that are almost impossible to keep, intending to visit every parishioner in his district. In so doing, he encounters their conversations, troubles, anger at God, and gossip. Intertwined with this duty are his usual priestly obligations, like teaching catechism classes and visiting the sick. The curé himself is from a poor family, thus adding to the scorn some feel toward him and bringing to light the injustices of small bourgeois thinking. The harder the curé works, the more he feels he is being unsuccessful. His health deteriorates, and he is diagnosed with stomach cancer. One of the parishioners delights in spreading rumors about him implying that he is an alcoholic. Although he suffers all these injustices, the curé continually feels his inadequacy both as a person and as a priest. However, in the end on his deathbed, he utters his final redemption: "Does it matter? Grace is everywhere."

Norway has given the world one of the most important Catholic novelists in the person of Sigrid Undset. Undset was born in Denmark on May 20, 1882, to a Norwegian archeologist father and a Danish mother. The family moved permanently to Norway when Sigrid was two years old. She was a gifted artist, but eventually channeled her creative talent into writing. After some success in writing novels, she moved to Rome, married the Norwegian painter Anders Svarstad, and raised five children and stepchildren. In 1919, she ended her seven-year marriage to Svarstad. Again living in Norway, she then began her great historical epic trilogy, *Kristin Lavransdatter*. Undset converted to the Catholic Church in 1925 and was awarded the Nobel Prize for literature in 1928. The Nazi occupation of her country in 1940 forced her to leave Norway. Undset lived in Brooklyn, New York, until 1945, when she was able to return to her beloved Lillehammer, where she died in June 1949.

Kristin Lavransdatter is a trilogy composed of *The Bridal Wreath*, *The Mistress of Husaby*, and *The Cross*. It is a story set in early 14th-century Norway full of historical facts and descriptive landscapes. It is not about people important to the story of Norway, but just the everyday people in a remote part of Norway who undergo the ordinary and extraordinary vicissitudes of living under harsh and stark conditions in a Catholic environment. It is the fictional life story of Kristin, a beautiful and self-willed young girl who marries, has a family, and eventually meets her death during the Black Plague. *The Bridal Wreath* begins when Kristin is a young child strongly devoted to her father. Not having any brothers, she becomes close to a neighbor's son, who falls in love with her. However, her father has her betrothed to another young man, Simon, who is considered a good match. Kristin meets Erlend Nikulausson, a handsome and dashing young man who is somewhat of a scoundrel. Kristin falls deeply in love with him and decides that he is the one with whom she wants to be married.

They meet several times surreptiously and eventually become intimate. There are complications to their marriage in that Erlend has a paramour who has borne him two children. Kristin's betrothal must be broken, and Erlend has to settle his problems before the marriage can take place. They eventually marry, but Kristin must bear the burden of her sin for the remainder of her life with the romantic but unpredictable Erlend. In the following two books, Kristin becomes a mature woman and grows in her married life through the many sorrows she experiences in raising the seven sons she bore Erlend. Catholic ritual plays a large part in the lives of the characters, especially of Kristin's father, a devoted and religious man. It is the story of joy and sorrow, sin and forgiveness, and suffering and redemption.

Flannery O'Connor is one of the writers in the American Southern Gothic tradition—writers who focus very often on the grotesque in human nature. She was born in Savannah, Georgia, in 1925, the only child of devoutly Roman Catholic parents. She was educated in Southern schools in what is known as the "Bible Belt," a region that undoubtedly influenced her writing. Her work consists mainly of short stories and two novels that reflect her deeply held Christian faith. The amount of writing O'Connor has left behind was not prolific because of her death at the age of 39 from a rare form of lupus. In 1972, she posthumously received the National Book Award for the book *Flannery O'Connor: The Complete Stories*.

O'Connor's short story collection *A Good Man Is Hard to Find, and Other Stories* is considered by some to be her best. The story that gives the title to the collection is about a family—a grandmother, her son and daughter-in-law, and their three children—going on a car trip. The grandmother tells most of the story, which is really all about her. As they pass a cemetery, she calls attention to the Sunday-best clothing she is wearing because, should she meet a tragic end, the world would know that she is "a lady." There is foreboding in this scene—one already suspects that something tragic is going to happen. The family picks up a hitchhiker known as the Misfit, who it turns out is the escaped prisoner that the grandmother has been speculating about all along. He murders the entire family. However, before she is shot three times, Grandmother ultimately talks to the murderer about Jesus. He is obviously bitter and would like to believe in redemption, but is not certain. It is at the moment of her death that the grandmother has an epiphany—she stops thinking about herself. The Misfit through his evil acts and depth of feeling has saved the grandmother's soul by a moment of grace.

There is a salient feature in all of these Christian writers: The evil their protagonists endure is part of the tragic aspect of life, but in the end they are redeemed by faith.—Clara Sarrocco

BIBLIOGRAPHY AND FURTHER READING: Bernanos, Georges. *The Diary of a Country Priest.* New York: Macmillan, 1937; Lewis, C. S. *The Screwtape Letters and Screwtape Proposes a Toast.* New York: Macmillan, 1967; O'Connor, Flannery. *A Good Man Is Hard to Find, and Other Stories.* Orlando, FL: Harcourt, 1977; Tolkien, J. R. R. *The Lord of the Rings.* New York: Ballantine Books, 1965; Undset, Sigrid. *Kristin Lavransdatter.* Translated by Charles Archer. New York: Knopf, 1946. *See also* BERNANOS, GEORGES; EVIL; LEWIS, C. S.; LITERATURE; O'CONNOR, FLANNERY; TOLKIEN, J. R. R.

· F ·

FAITHFUL CITIZENSHIP Faithful Citizenship is an initiative established by the U.S. Conference of Catholic Bishops (USCCB) to educate Catholics on their civic responsibilities. It is based upon the Catholic Church's position that individuals have a moral responsibility and obligation to participate in the political process. The *Catechism of the Catholic Church* states that it is the duty of citizens to contribute, along with the civil authorities, to the good of society in the spirit of truth, justice, solidarity, and freedom (# 2239). The Church's *Code of Canon Law* also emphasizes that the Christian faithful are "bound by a particular duty to imbue and perfect the order of temporal affairs with the spirit of the gospel and thus to give witness to Christ, especially in carrying out these same affairs and in exercising secular functions" (*CIC* # 225§2). The source of this civic responsibility cited in these two important texts of the Catholic Church originates in the sacrament of baptism, whereby all men and women are called to a vocation of holiness as sons and daughters of God and to fulfill Jesus' calling to be "perfect, as your heavenly Father is perfect" (Matthew 5: 48).

Faithful citizenship as a concept addresses the relationship between religion and the state. The Church acknowledges the distinction between the political community and the Church, but these two realms are not mutually exclusive. Morality overlaps both. Religion provides the foundation from which moral judgments can be made, and these judgments should be applied to the exercise of political power. According to Catholic social teaching, the primary goal of state power guided by morality is the promotion of the inherent dignity of the human person and the common good. The exercise of political power inevitably raises questions about the nature of right and wrong and what constitutes the common good. When faced with such important issues, citizens rely upon their religious beliefs to guide them to potential solutions. Given the serious nature of politics and what is at stake, Catholics must consider how to act in the public square.

There are serious challenges that Catholics are confronted with when discerning their relationship to the state. An overwhelming temptation exists to detach morality from the political process in the name of separation of church and state, thereby relegating religion to the private space and barring it from the public square. Scandal and confusion are the by-products of this temptation. There are Catholic politicians who reject their faith for political expediency, which adds a degree of legitimacy to the notion that religion should be reserved to an individual's private conscience. In some instances, bishops, priests, and religious have not stepped forward in defense of the Church, or when they have participated in the political process, they have not done so in manner that is consistent with the official teachings of the Catholic Church. And the Catholic laity may avoid their civic duty or act contrary to the Church's teachings.

Recognizing the gravity of this situation, the USCCB has published numerous documents since 1976, culminating in the Faithful Citizenship initiative in 2007, to help guide Catholics in fulfilling their civic responsibilities. One of the more influential guides for Catholics is "Living the Gospel of Life: A Challenge to American Catholics." Released by the USCCB in 1998, this substantial document focuses primarily on the dignity of the human person. It recognizes the challenges that Catholics face as they enter the political process, in particular the problems of false pluralism and moral relativism. The document calls for the development of virtue, conviction, and a sense of duty and obligation to serve the common good.

A year later, the U.S. bishops followed up with another document, "Faithful Citizenship: Civic Responsibility for a New Millennium," which outlined the issues facing Catholics on the 2,000th anniversary of the birth of Jesus Christ. This statement begins with the evidence that numerous problems do exist in society and asks the questions that individuals need to consider in the face of these challenges. It continues with the call to faithful citizenship, highlights the assets that Catholics possess in the public square, and relates the numerous themes of Catholic social teaching.

On the eve of the 2004 presidential election, the USCCB issued another statement, entitled "Faithful Citizenship: A Catholic Call to Political Responsibility." This work touches upon many of the common themes associated with faithful citizenship—duty, obligation, responsibility, the role of the Church, and the importance of a properly formed conscience. It provides a detailed application of Catholic social teaching and the moral priorities—protecting human life, promoting family life, and pursuing social justice.

Between 2003 and 2007, the U.S. bishops also published abbreviated statements to remind Catholics of their civic duty and the Church's official teachings. These include "On Our Civic Responsibility for the Common Good" (2004), "Catholics in Political Life" (2004), "Task Force on Catholic Bishops and Catholic Politicians" (2004), and "Statement on Responsibilities of Catholics in Public Life" (2006). The Congregation for the Doctrine of the Faith also presented its views on faithful citizenship in its "Doctrinal Note on Some Questions Regarding the Participation of Catholics in Political Life" (2002). This document clarifies the special responsibility that Catholics have in bringing society to a deeper understanding of human life.

The central concern of all of these documents is protecting and promoting the inherent dignity of the human person. They also convey the message that not every issue has an equal moral claim. Particular actions—abortion, euthanasia, embryonic stem cell experimentation, human cloning, same-sex marriage—are intrinsically evil and can never be justified. These issues are referred to as non-negotiable because they are always morally wrong and do not advance the common good. The documents also articulate the Church's social teaching on other issues that Catholics need to consider when participating in the public space—poverty, economic development, discrimination, immigration, the death penalty, among others. All of these issues, both non-negotiable and important, create an integral unity that cannot be isolated from one another, although some distinctions do exist, of which all Catholics must be mindful.

In 2007, the USCCB issued "Forming Consciences for Faithful Citizenship: A Call to Political Responsibility from the Catholic Bishops of the United States." This work builds upon much of the material already published by the USCCB and has become the centerpiece of the Faithful Citizenship initiative. It provides guidelines on the political responsibilities of Catholics by helping them in forming their consciences in accordance with the teachings of the Catholic Church, as well as developing a sense of duty to participate in the political process well beyond simply voting. It recognizes that faithful citizenship involves more than an obligation and duty to participate in public life. It also emphasizes the critical element of a properly formed conscience. This provides an individual with the ability to make moral judgments of right and wrong, and, when properly formed, conscience bears witness to the authority of truth in reference to the supreme good to which all persons are drawn. An official USCCB website has been set up—www.faithfulcitizenship.org—that highlights this document and provides numerous sources of additional information for parish and school leaders, diocesan and community leaders, Catholic youths, and the media. It offers videos and podcasts in addition to general prayer and reflection resources.

This USCCB initiative—together with the numerous USCCB documents, the *Code of Canon Law*, the *Catechism of the Catholic Church*, and the *Compendium of the Social Doctrine of the Church*, among other sources—creates a full body of literature that directly addresses a Catholic's responsibility in the public square. Faithful Citizenship is a call to all Catholics to fulfill their civic and moral duty and obligation to participate in the political process with a properly formed conscience, with a particular emphasis on the dignity of the human person and the common good.—Andrew M. Essig

BIBLIOGRAPHY AND FURTHER READING: Chaput, Charles J. *Render unto Caesar: Serving the Nation by Living Our Catholic Beliefs in Political Life*. New York: Doubleday, 2008; United States Conference of Catholic Bishops. "Forming Consciences for Faithful Citizenship: A Call to Political Responsibility from the Catholic Bishops of the United States." Washington, DC: U.S. Catholic Conference, 2007; United States Conference of Catholic Bishops, "Living the Gospel of Life: A Challenge to American Catholics." Washington, DC: U.S. Catholic Conference, 1998. *See also* COMMON GOOD; CONSCIENCE; HUMAN DIGNITY; STATE, CATHOLIC THOUGHT ON

FARLEY, MARGARET, RSM (c. 1936–) Margaret Farley, a prominent ethicist, graduated from Cathedral High School in St. Cloud, Minnesota, in 1953, received her BA in English literature from the University of Detroit in 1957 and her MA in philosophy from the same university in 1960. From 1962 to 1967, she taught philosophy at Mercy College in Detroit and was a visiting lecturer of philosophy at the University of Detroit in 1966–1967. In 1970, she earned her MPhil in religious studies with a concentration in ethics from

Yale University and in 1973 her PhD in religious studies, again with a concentration in ethics, from the same university. Farley has taught at Yale since 1971. She became a full professor there in 1984 and was later named the Gilbert L. Stark Professor of Christian Ethics in the Department of Religious Studies and the Yale Divinity School. She is now a professor emerita.

Farley has received many honors, among them 11 or more honorary degrees, the John Courtney Murray Award for Excellence in Theology from the Catholic Theological Society of America, and the Luce Fellowship in Theology for 1996–1997 for her essay "The Act of Freedom: Key to the Relational Self." She has served as president of the Catholic Theological Society of America and the Society of Christian Ethics.

The author, coauthor, or editor of six books and scores of essays and monographs, Farley is recognized as one of the leading feminist authors of our day. She is an ardent advocate of the ordination of women, gay rights, abortion, contraception, and masturbation and a severe critic of papal teachings. She was a cosigner of the advertisement published in the October 7, 1984, issue of the *New York Times* by Catholics for Free Choice declaring that "a diversity of opinions regarding abortion exists among committed Catholics."

Farley maintains that only a feminist consciousness can adequately address the situation of women. This consciousness, she holds, shows the need for a radical reexamination of our concepts of the human and how urgent it is to incorporate the experience of all persons and groups, in particular the experience of women. She is convinced that acknowledging women's experience will revolutionize theological ethics and transform the moral imagination, as the "old order" (of women's unquestioned inferiority to men) gives way to new possibilities for recognizing the potential of women and indeed of all human beings. She argues for a feminist-inspired "common morality" whose basic premise is that human experience, especially contemporary feminist experience, reveals the divine. According to her—and this is of capital importance—contemporary feminist experience has an authority that surpasses other sources of moral guidance. Farley regards Scripture and tradition as unreliable because they are "confusing" and self-contradictory. She regards modern scientific sources as helpful, in that they reflect lived "reality," but regards them as clearly subordinate to feminist experience.

With other feminists, Farley rejects interpretations of sexual difference that claim that such differences are "complementary," which she understands to mean "that we are 'halves' of persons who will be 'whole' only when we find our gendered complement." She therefore proposes that we speak of "mutuality," recognizing that persons of the same sex can find themselves "mutually" attracted. She criticizes narrow understandings of the ends of sexual expression that ignore or trivialize the potential for union, intimacy, pleasure, and mutuality. In her opinion, the virtue of justice—understood in light of women's experience—must determine the morality of sexual relationships, including not only such sexual acts as heterosexual genital sex, homosexual acts, masturbation, and so forth but also such social institutions as marriage and the family within which sexual relationships are set.

Moreover, Farley contends, justice understood in this way shows the grave injustice of "traditional" Catholic teaching (in particular, that proposed by the ecclesial magisterium) of the nature of commitment, bioethics, marriage and divorce, and same-sex relations. Farley considers *pleasure*—sexual pleasure in particular—as a basic human good; in truth, pleasure is *not* a basic good but rather an emotional experience whose goodness depends on the kind of activity eliciting it.

Farley several times affirms that "my body" is "me" and cannot be separated from "my mind." It might then appear that she rejects contemporary dualism, which separates the "person" from his or her body. This, however, is not the case. Despite seemingly identifying the body with the self, Farley is a dualist. Thus, she declares that when transsexuals have "their bodily identity" altered by surgery, they affirm more deeply their "personal identity," and she definitely denies that unborn human beings are "persons."

Farley affirms that the two basic features of human personhood are autonomy and relationality. These, she maintains, "are 'obligating features' because they *ground* an obligation to respect persons as *ends in themselves.* . . . Persons are autonomous in the sense that they have a capacity for *free choice . . . self-determination*," that is, she continues, "the capacity to set our own agenda."

Farley contends that the recognition of autonomy and relationality as basic to personhood is most important because it helps to show the inadequacy of interpretations of moral obligation that propose moral norms without adequately taking into account "pastoral" consideration of individual capacities and vulnerabilities. In one of her more recent works, *Personal Commitments*, Farley claims that recognizing this, along with the many human limitations, leads to a reappraisal of past magisterial teachings—for example, on same-sex relations—that derive ethical norms from biological "givens" in isolation from a consideration of the potentialities of human persons adequately and integrally considered. Awareness of our historicity and therefore the partiality of our knowledge reinforce this.

According to Maura Ryan, one of her supporters, Farley recognizes that all human choices involve reasons and emotions, and both our reasons and our emotions are subject to evaluation. The problem for our moral lives (and our moral theories) is precisely how, in light of what norms, we are to evaluate love or judge the appropriateness of our care. Ryan declares: "Farley's proposal is deceptively simple: love (or care, or compassion) is just when it takes account of the concrete reality of the beloved, when it is 'formed by respect for what God has made—for human freedom, relationality, embodiment, historical and cultural formation, uniqueness, and the potentiality of fullness of life in an unlimited future.'" She then appeals to Farley's *Compassionate Respect* to illustrate concretely what this means. In that work, Farley excoriates those who oppose helping the poor women of Africa from the danger of being infected by the AIDS virus, in particular the ecclesial magisterium, of grave injustice. Farley ignores totally that AIDS infection is lowest in those countries where the government, respecting the traditions of the African people, supports programs of abstinence before marriage and fidelity in marriage as the only way to practice "safe sex."

It is especially noteworthy that nowhere in her writings does Farley consider love as the selfless giving of oneself, a giving whose archetypal example is Jesus' selfless gift of himself to us on the cross. This kind of love is precisely what he commands us to give in his "new commandment": "A new commandment I give to you, that you love one another: just as I have loved you, you also are to love one another" (John 13: 34). This is the kind of love at the heart of Blessed John Paul II's understanding of love. It is the kind of love a man and a woman promise to each other when, through "irrevocable" consent, they choose each other as spouses and in so doing not only point to but inwardly participate in the love-giving, life-giving, grace-giving bridal union of Christ as head of his bride and body, the Church. Moreover, this kind of love is at the heart of marriage and is the reason why, "for the good of the spouses and their offspring as well as of society, the existence of the sacred bond [of marriage] (*sacrum vinculum*) no longer depends on human decisions" (*GS* # 48). In other words, the marriage of Christians is indissoluble, and divorce does not in fact "dissolve" the marital union or bond, which is rooted in the very being of the spouses as part of the identity they gave to each other and to themselves when they gave their irrevocable consent

to marriage. Farley completely ignores this truth in her advocacy of divorce and remarriage. This is a major inadequacy of her understanding of love.

In conclusion, Farley's theological Christian ethics reject the God-given authority of the magisterium, vested in the pope and bishops in union with him, to teach authoritatively in Christ's name, and for it substitutes the authority of contemporary feminist experience.—William E. May

BIBLIOGRAPHY AND FURTHER READING: Curran, Charles E., Margaret Farley, and Richard A. McCormick, SJ, eds. *Feminist Ethics and the Catholic Moral Tradition.* Paramus, NJ: Paulist Press, 1996; Farley, Margaret. *Compassionate Respect: A Feminist Approach to Medical Ethics and Other Questions.* Paramus, NJ: Paulist Press, 2000; Farley, Margaret. *Just Love: Framework for a Christian Sexual Ethics.* New York: Continuum, 2006; Farley, Margaret. *Personal Commitments: Beginning, Keeping, Changing.* New York: Harper & Row, 1986; McGlynn, J. V., and Margaret Farley. *A Metaphysics of Being and God.* Englewood Cliffs, NJ: Prentice-Hall, 1966; Ryan, Maura, and Brian Linnane, SJ, eds. *A Just and True Love: Feminism at the Frontiers of Theological Ethics: Essays in Honor of Margaret A. Farley.* Notre Dame, IN: University of Notre Dame Press, 2007. *See also* DISSENT; FEMINISM; JOHNSON, ELIZABETH; MAGISTERIUM

FEUERBACH, LUDWIG ANDREAS (1804–1872) Ludwig Feuerbach was born in Landshut, Bavaria. After studying theology at the University of Heidelberg, he transferred to the University of Berlin, where he concentrated on philosophy and was a student of G. W. F. Hegel. In short order, he became a dedicated Hegelian. In 1830, Feuerbach published his first book, *Thoughts on Death and Immortality,* in which he denied the immortality of the soul. This led to his dismissal from the position he had secured at the University of Erlangen and thus ended his brief academic career.

Before the end of the decade, Feuerbach had become disenchanted with Hegelianism, chiefly on account of its idealism, and in 1839 he published *Towards a Critique of Hegel's Philosophy.* This had the effect of establishing him as a notable dissenter from the reigning Hegelianism, and he became the titular head of a group known as the Young Hegelians. By this time, Feuerbach had, in his own philosophy, developed an entirely naturalistic view of the world, which not only set him against orthodox Hegelian doctrine but also, more significantly, turned him into a militant crusader against religion in general and Christianity in particular. This state of affairs saw its culmination in the publication, in 1841, of *The Essence of Christianity*. The book had a pronounced impact in Germany and, after 1853, in the English-speaking world as well, thanks to a translation of the work done by novelist George Eliot (Mary Ann Evans).

In 1844, Feuerbach published *On the Essence of Faith in Luther's Sense*, in which he argued that the proper understanding of religion, that is, as something entirely human, was to be found in implicit form in Protestant theology. This reflected his larger thesis that all Christian theology is at bottom anthropology, for it is essentially about man. Following his repudiation of Hegelianism, Feuerbach began to formulate schemes for an entirely new direction to be taken by philosophy, and he wrote two books, *Provisional Theses for the Reformation of Philosophy* and *Principles of the Philosophy of the Future*, both published in 1843, which reflected his thinking along those lines.

Unquestionably the most well known and influential of Feuerbach's works is *The Essence of Christianity*. It became something of a general source book for dedicated atheists in the years following its publication, and among those who were profoundly influenced by the book were Karl Marx and Friedrich Engels. In the preface to its second edition, published in 1843, Feuerbach, clearly on the defensive, writes that in the book he has only presented a "faithful, correct translation of the Christian religion." The "translation" in question, presumably, was primarily intended for Christians themselves, so that they might be made aware of the fact, which they should accept as salutary, that the object of their belief is not what they think it is. The central thesis of the book can be stated as follows: God, as understood by Christianity—that is, as a distinct being, separate from nature—does not exist. Such a being is a pure illusion. What Christianity, and religion in general, chooses to call "God" is no more than a projection of a multiplicity of variegated human feelings. "The essence of religion," Feuerbach explains, "is the immediate, involuntary, unconscious contemplation of human nature as another, a distinct nature." God as God "is only an object of thought," and what religion identifies as the attributes of the divine nature are no more than the attributes of human nature, writ large as it were, and assigned transcendental status.

In the first part of the book, entitled "The True or Anthropological Essence of Christianity," Feuerbach sets about to "deconstruct" various tenets of the Christian religion, giving special attention to the mysteries. For example, the Trinity, according to his analysis, is nothing else than "man's consciousness of himself in his

totality"; the omnipotence of God is nothing else than "subjectivity exempting itself from all objective conditions and limitations, and consecrating this exemption as the highest power and reality"; and prayer is nothing else than "the wish of the heart expressed with confidence in its fulfillment," that is, merely the relation of the human heart to itself.

The Essence of Christianity, though burdensomely repetitious, is nonetheless a rather ingenious book, for it is so wrought as to give an undiscerning reader the impression that it is a work that reflects the highest scientific standards. It is, in fact, anything but that. Beneath its showy surface, what we discover are congeries of arguments that, though proposed with impressive rhetorical force, are singularly uncompelling. The method Feuerbach employs bears a semblance to genuine argumentation, but only that, and therein lies the deception. His method is simple and straightforward. He begins by laying down a proposition, and then proceeds to cite numerous scriptural and theological texts, many of the latter culled from the writings of Martin Luther, which purportedly support that proposition. But the problem here is that just about every one of the propositions he lays down is simply a bare assertion on his part. They are anything but manifestly true and indeed are, to put it mildly, highly questionable. So, for example, Feuerbach makes assertions such as "Man is the God of man," "God is the self-consciousness of man," and "God is man's *alter ego*," and we are apparently to accept them as true simply because Ludwig Feuerbach says they are true. The propositions he proposes should be, rightly, the conclusions of arguments, but they are not such because there are no premises that precede them. The abundance of textual material he provides, which supposedly stands as evidence in support of the propositions, in fact serves only as interesting but inapplicable addenda. The truth of the propositions themselves is simply assumed; it is by no means demonstrated.

Apart from that not insignificant problem, the book is also beset by any number of problems relating to logic, psychology, metaphysics, and epistemology, and these have a deleterious effect on the philosophical soundness of the work as a whole. Apropos of logic, Feuerbach takes the altogether remarkable position that, in any proposition, subject and predicate are identical. If this were to be taken seriously, propositional logic would be rendered meaningless. Feuerbach's psychology is not a little shaky, as is evidenced, for example, by his claim that the object of feeling is feeling. If this were true, sense knowledge would not, as it emphatically does, put us in contact with the external world. Feuerbach's metaphysics would have it that "every being is and by itself infinite." This could only be said by someone who has rejected the infinite God and is therefore led, following a line of reasoning that is consistent with his theory, to make man, the source of the supposedly illusory God, an infinite being. The man-made God is infinite because man, the maker, is infinite. Feuerbach's epistemology tells him that human understanding is "neutral, impassible, not to be bribed, not subject to illusions—the pure, passionless light of intelligence." It is only when man is not under the dictatorial influence of his feelings, and makes full use of his intelligence, that he is able to free himself from the kinds of illusions to which religion has become enslaved.

Feuerbach turned his back on Hegelianism because he took exception to its idealism. In his own mind, he considered himself to be, as a philosopher, a staunch realist, boasting that he did not "generate the object from the thought, but the thought from the object." Feuerbach may have put Hegelianism behind him, but the same cannot be said of idealism. He was in fact an idealist through and through, and there is ample evidence for this in *The Essence of Christianity*. There we are constantly coming across statements such as "the object of the intellect is intellect objective to itself," "Consciousness of the objective is the self-consciousness of man," and "The understanding is to itself the criterion of all reality." What is the import of Feuerbach's idealism, apropos of the central thesis propounded in *The Essence of Christianity*, that God and everything pertaining to God is but a projection of human feelings? He would have us believe that, having subjected Christianity to a thorough scientific examination, he discovered, as an objective matter of fact, that it was all no more than an elaborate instance of wish fulfillment. But that is not what happened. Feuerbach did not investigate Christianity, or religion in general, as objective reality. What he did was, first, to formulate in his own mind a complex of theses as to what the "essence" of Christianity was, whose connection with the objective reality displayed the highest kind of tenuousness, and then he projected those theses onto the objective reality. In sum, Feuerbach succumbed to just the kind of illusory thinking that, quite falsely, he had accused Christians of employing.—D. Q. McInerny

BIBLIOGRAPHY AND FURTHER READING: Chamberlain, William B. *Heaven Wasn't His Destination: The Philosophy of Ludwig Feuerbach*. London: George Allen, 1941; Kamenka, E. *The Philosophy of Ludwig Feuerbach*. London: Routledge & Kegan Paul, 1970; Wartofsky, M. *Feuerbach*. Cambridge: Cambridge University Press, 1977. *See also* AGNOSTICISM AND ATHEISM; HEGEL, GEORG WILHELM FRIEDRICH; HUMANISM; MARX, KARL; MARXISM

FIDEISM Fideism, as the name indicates, has to do with matters pertaining to faith, and it is adhered to by people who are themselves believers. It is not so much a systematic body of thought as it is a general point of view, the principal feature of which is an erroneous notion regarding the relation between faith and reason. Fideism effectively attempts to drive a wedge between faith and reason, under the supposition that they should operate in two quite different and separate realms. The basic claim of fideism is that faith is the only source of true, completely reliable, knowledge of God and things divine.

In its most extreme form, fideism would tend to regard human reason, as applied to matters of faith, as positively dangerous. The argument would go somewhat as follows: If we attempt to apply human reason to our knowledge of God and things divine—knowledge that can come to us only through revelation—then that knowledge will inevitably suffer distortion. Moreover, by applying our reason to matters of faith, we are effectively insulting God, by failing to put full confidence in his revelation. As fideism sees things, our duty as believers is simply to believe, blindly as it were, not attempting to understand the truths that have been revealed to us. The most extravagant form of fideism would be expressed by the Latin phrase *Credo quia absurdum*, "I believe because it is absurd."

Apart from the fact that fideism is an erroneous doctrine, because it actually undermines the faith whose purity and integrity it is purportedly defending, there is the additional and not insignificant problem that it proposes a program that is, from a psychological point of view, quite impossible to implement with any kind of consistency. We are rational creatures, and, as such, there is nothing to which we can give serious and meaningful volitional commitment—as we do in a very special way in the commitment of faith—that is not directly affected by the operations of our rational faculty. Fideism mistakenly supposes that the act of faith can consist of an isolated, raw act of the will; this cannot be the case for the simple reason that a voluntary act of that sort is not possible, for we can only will what we know. An act of the will is always a response to knowledge that is provided to the will by the intellect.

Throughout Christian history there have been, from time to time, certain believers who have taken a decidedly negative attitude toward reason as it relates to faith. Not uncommonly, this was a response to the ways in which reason can sometimes be perversely employed to distort the truths of faith, and to that extent such an attitude was understandable. However, there is no logical justification for rejecting something that is intrinsically good—that is, human reason—because it is capable of being abused. The Protestant Reformation ushered in an appreciable increase of fideism in Christian thought, which is not surprising, for a deep-set suspicion of human reasoning (Martin Luther set the tone here) is one of the defining marks of Protestantism. The 19th century saw another pronounced upsurge in fideism; this came as a reaction to the excessive rationalism that was the hallmark of the 18th century, the self-styled Age of Reason.

If there is anything that prominently distinguishes Catholic Christianity, it is its total and unvarying commitment, from the earliest days of the Church, to the proposition that not only is there no conflict between faith and reason but the two are completely and harmoniously compatible. St. Augustine's dictum that he "believed in order to understand," and the motto by which St. Anselm guided his theological studies, "Faith Seeking Understanding," perfectly reflect the Catholic position. Faith and reason are in fact inseparable. To make the initial act of faith, we need to have at least a rudimentary understanding of that to which we are giving our assent. Then, once we have accepted the gift of faith, in all its unfathomable riches, the mind employs itself in an endless exploration of those riches.

Modern philosophy, especially in the person of Immanuel Kant (1724–1804), has contributed substantially to the growth of fideism, which is a prominent feature of contemporary thought. Kant, in repudiating traditional metaphysics, and the natural theology that accompanies it, contended that any attempt to prove the existence of God through natural reason was futile. He staunchly maintained that we cannot conclude the reality of God through rational processes. To be sure, we acknowledge God's existence, but we do this simply by laying it down as a postulate, much as we would lay down a postulate in mathematics. Kant offered a set of arguments that proved, to his satisfaction, that the existence of God cannot be proved. As a matter of fact, those proofs fail, but so commanding was Kant's influence that many philosophers have been persuaded by them, firmly believing Kant had dealt the death blow to natural theology.

The denial that the existence of God can be proved by natural reason is one of the central tenets of fideism, a tenet that Catholics confidently reject for two reasons.

First, from the point of view of philosophy, it is simply a matter of fact that God's existence can be demonstrated, as has been done in an especially impressive manner by St. Thomas Aquinas. There is no more conclusive proof that something can be done than the fact that it actually has been done. Second, from the point of view of religious belief, the First Vatican Council formally defined it as an article of faith that the existence of God, and certain of his attributes, can be demonstrated by natural reason. To be sure, faith tells us that God exists, but so does reason.—D. Q. McInerny

BIBLIOGRAPHY AND FURTHER READING: First Vatican Council, *Constitutio Dogmatica de Fide Catholica* ("Dogmatic Constitution on the Catholic Faith"), chapters 3 and 4; Knox, R. A. *Enthusiasm: A Chapter in the History of Religion*. New York: Oxford University Press, 1950. *See also* AQUINAS, ST. THOMAS; *FIDES ET RATIO*

FILM AND CATHOLIC SOCIAL THOUGHT

The place of cinema in the media of social communications is unique. Like the printed word, it is mass produced, and like radio, it reaches large audiences at once and is not limited to the literate. Yet as a visual medium, film is more easily accessible and universal than either. Television has become more culturally pervasive, and the Internet and the advent of social media continue to revolutionize social communications. Yet as a vehicle of man's artistic aspirations, the enduring achievements of cinema have yet to be rivaled by newer media.

Cinema has been both a topic of Catholic social thought and action—ecclesial and lay—and a venue in which Catholic social thought has been variously represented by Catholic filmmakers, filmmakers influenced by Catholicism, and filmmakers depicting Catholic characters or communities shaped by Catholic principles. Accordingly, this entry treats first film as a subject of Catholic social thought and then Catholic social thought as a principle within the cinema world.

From an early date, the power of film to reach all ages and classes of society was of interest and concern to Catholics. In the United States, this concern became national in scope in connection with a number of World War I–era films created by social hygiene advocates, notably the government-sponsored films *Fit to Fight* (1918) and *End of the Road* (1919), which were opposed by the National Catholic War Council, the forerunner to the U.S. Conference of Catholic Bishops. Aimed at combating venereal disease, these films ostensibly promoted chastity, but cast sexuality more as a matter of health than morality; *Fit to Fight* also touted the military's prophylaxis program as a second line of defense.

The first mention of cinema in a papal document came in Pius XI's *Divini Illius Magistri* in 1929. Addressing Christian education, Pius XI noted that the cinema, along with radio and books, "can be of great utility for instruction and education when directed by sound principles," though these media are "only too often used as an incentive to evil passions and greed for gain." Groups that highlight the dangers of immoral books and films or that promote wholesome theatrical and cinematic venues for the young were praised by the pope.

In that same year, a far-reaching effort to work out those "sound principles" both in theory and in application was carried out in the United States: the Motion Picture Production Code, the road map for Golden Age Hollywood morality. Instigated by Cardinal George Mundelein of Chicago and created by Rev. Daniel Lord, SJ, and Martin Quigley, a lay Catholic and editor of the *Motion Picture Herald*, the Production Code sought to apply Catholic natural law theory to articulate universal principles governing the use of art and entertainment generally, and cinema in particular. Both entertainment and art, the Code held, are universally recognized as important elements in the lives of societies and human beings and have the potential either to "improve the race, or at least to re-create and rebuild human beings exhausted with the realities of life," or else to "degrade human beings."

Among its guiding principles, the Code proposed that "the sympathy of the audience should never be thrown to the side of crime, wrong-doing, evil or sin." This was distinguished from sympathy for sinners or criminals themselves. Law, "natural or human, shall not be ridiculed, nor shall sympathy be created for its violation." As part of human experience, sin and evil are valid dramatic material, but they must be presented in their proper moral light, in ways not apt to incite lower passions or inspire imitation. Topics addressed included depictions of violence, theft, sex, and religion. Motion pictures must uphold "the sanctity of marriage and the home." Acts of revenge might be positively depicted in period pieces, but in modern times they should never be justified. Patriotism was to be honored; the flag and the heritages of other nations were to be respectfully and fairly treated.

Although the motion picture studios officially adopted the Code in 1930, effective enforcement came only under boycott pressure from the Catholic Legion of Decency, formed in 1933 and in 1934 renamed the National Legion of Decency. Catholic layman Joseph I. Breen oversaw the Production Code Administration from 1934 to 1954.

Both the Production Code and the Legion of Decency were praised by Pius XI in the first papal encyclical devoted to the subject of cinema, *Vigilanti Cura* (1936), which called for and led to the formation of similar national film offices in countries around the world. *Vigilanti Cura* emphasized the social dimension of film, which addresses not individuals but gatherings of men congregating in their communities. Social action regarding immoral films had not only more closely united laity and bishops than almost any other recent issue, the pope noted, but had also brought together Protestants, Jews, and others. Misused, Pius XI said, the power of cinema can foster prejudice and bigotry directed toward social classes, nations, and peoples. Properly used, it can instill appreciation of the glories of one's own and of other nations, foster understanding and goodwill among classes, and "lend useful aid to a new and more equitable ordering and government of human society."

In 1948, Pius XII established the office that would become the Pontifical Commission of Social Communications. This office helped prepare Pius XII's important documents dealing with film: a pair of 1955 apostolic exhortations to Italian film industry representatives on the "ideal film," and the encyclical *Miranda Prorsus* (1957), which addressed cinema, radio, and television.

The apostolic exhortations to the film industry consider the world of cinema with respect to economic as well as artistic and technical considerations. Given the economic interests created by the cinema, along with its influence on social life particularly among youth and the poor, the medium's use cannot be left to purely economic drivers, the pope stated. The "civil and moral heritage" of peoples and families must be defended, and public and ecclesiastical authorities can and should establish mechanisms for evaluating films, offering appropriate information to the public and, if necessary, censuring or even banning films.

In *Miranda Prorsus*, while reaffirming the role of national film offices, Pius XII discussed the need for forming audiences to evaluate media presentations appropriately. He also addressed the responsibilities of critics, exhibitors, distributors, and filmmakers. *Miranda Prorsus* laid the groundwork for the Second Vatican Council decree *Inter Mirifica* (1963), which set forth an integrated Catholic doctrine of communications media, including the press.

Inter Mirifica laid new stress on the significance of the media with respect to "cultural and artistic" worth, as well as religious and moral values. At the same time, the Second Vatican Council's decree affirmed "the absolute primacy of the objective moral order," which "alone is superior to and is capable of harmonizing all forms of human activity, not excepting art, no matter how noble in themselves." While reaffirming the responsibilities of filmmakers, critics, and the state, *Inter Mirifica* developed the obligations of audiences to become discriminating, well-informed users of the media.

Going further, the 1971 pastoral instruction *Communio et Progressio* developed a true philosophy of communications media rooted in man's social nature and in soteriology. Social communication is ordered toward "the unity and advancement of men living in society," the instruction stated, and the increasing centrality of communication in modern society "exactly coincides with the Christian conception of how men should live together." Christ reconciled us to God, but also "laid the foundations of unity among men." By divine providence, the communications media exist to help men "fashion a new language" to promote understanding, charity, and communion.

John Paul II had a lifelong affinity for the dramatic arts and gave more than a dozen addresses significantly or entirely relating to film. In 1995, speaking to the Pontifical Commission for Social Communications, he highlighted the universality of film and its ability to influence public opinion and culture, the "indivisibility" of freedom which excludes moral evil, and the proper orientation of art to truth, goodness, and beauty.

While having less to say about the cinema in particular, Benedict XVI has repeatedly addressed the communications media generally. In *Caritas in Veritate* (2009), noting how integral a part of "the life of the human family" the media have become, Pope Benedict critiqued approaches to the media based on economic-driven efforts to dominate the market, arguing that "the meaning and purpose of the media must be sought within an anthropological perspective," that is, "a vision of the person and the common good that reflects truly universal values."

From the early days of silent film, social topics were a major concern in American cinema, but in general Hollywood reflected a solidly Protestant milieu until the Golden Age, when Catholic images and themes became increasingly popular. In Europe, Catholic filmmakers, subjects, and concepts played various roles in the developing cinema of 1930s France, the neorealist movement of postwar Italy, the French New Wave, the Polish Film School and later "cinema of moral anxiety," and other movements, many of which cross-pollinated one another both stylistically and thematically. Beyond Europe, Catholic social thought can be found touching films from Asia, Africa, and elsewhere.

Key social themes in cinema include the dignity of the human person, the dignity of labor, social and economic inequalities, just and unjust uses of capital, an option for the poor, and the right to associate. Other important themes include marriage and the family, private property and the universal destination of goods, subsidiarity, life issues, discrimination and human solidarity, civil rights, just and unjust wars, education, natural law and human justice, and the role of the Church in society.

The U.S. film industry developed in an age of widespread reform movements, and the "social problem" film was a popular genre in the 1910s and 1920s. Reflecting the prevailing Protestant culture, the urban immigrant poor, often Catholics, were often depicted as victims of their own moral weakness regarding drink, crime, and sexual immorality. A partial counterexample, Catholic director Raoul Walsh's *Regeneration* (1915), adapted from Catholic writer Owen Kildare's memoir, emphasized the role of environment in the protagonist's checkered history. Silent films in other genres, from the Douglas Fairbanks Sr. swashbuckler *The Mark of Zorro* (Fred Niblo, 1920) to the comedy *Modern Times* (Charlie Chaplin, 1936), presented socially significant themes (solidarity with the oppressed poor, the effects of industrialization) in ways influenced by Catholic sensibilities.

In the 1930s, as American Catholicism became an increasingly assertive element within the cultural mainstream, Catholic subjects and themes in Hollywood films grew more common. Such filmmakers as John Ford, Frank Capra, and Leo McCarey brought Catholic sensibilities to their work; other factors included the relevance of Catholic social thought and action in relation to the Great Depression and the New Deal, as well as the influence of the Production Code Administration and the Legion of Decency.

Ford's *How Green Was My Valley* (1937) and *The Grapes of Wrath* (1940) each dramatized the plight of a family from a rural labor community dependent on wealthy capital interests who make economic decisions abstracted from human consequences, devastating the communities. Labor unions played a role in both films, while family ties remained central to the films' concerns. Capra's populist comedies frequently featured predatory tycoons, but he also celebrated heroes who made socially responsible use of capital for the common good in *American Madness* (1932), *Mr. Deeds Goes to Town* (1936), and *It's a Wonderful Life* (1946).

Not infrequently, the standard of Catholic social thought has been carried in cinema by clerical and religious characters both historical and fictional. *Boys Town* (1938) celebrated the work of Father Edward Flanagan on behalf of disadvantaged and often delinquent boys. Other Depression-era films, including *San Francisco* (1936) and *Angels with Dirty Faces* (1938), depicted fictional counterparts to Father Flanagan, socially conscious reformer priests engaging social inequities and acting as moral guide and advocate for the marginalized and at-risk, especially youth.

In Europe, a popular Church-sponsored French film, Léon Poirier's *L'Appel du silence* (*The Call*, 1936), dramatized Brother Charles de Foucauld's military career and religious vocation in North Africa. More ambiguously, Robert Bresson's debut film *Les Anges du Péché* (*Angel of the Streets*, 1943) highlighted the work of the Sisters of Bethany, an order that works with—and accepts as postulants—women with criminal backgrounds. Maurice Cloche's *Monsieur Vincent* (1947) celebrated the social work of St. Vincent de Paul, whose dramatic contributions to Western social awareness included founding the first permanent institutions for charitable assistance to the poor.

Inspired in part by the gritty "poetic realist" films of 1930s French cinema—which highlighted the urban poor in Parisian slums as victims of bourgeois apathy, ruthless bankers, and a corrupt system—the neorealist cinema of postwar Italy emphasized the desperate economic and moral condition of the poor and working class, particularly in the war-shattered cities. Among the best known examples is *Ladri di biciclette* (*Bicycle Thieves*, Vittorio De Sica, 1948) which depicted the moral and domestic toll suffered by impoverished individuals and families in postwar Rome; Church efforts to alleviate those consequences were also briefly seen.

While the French realist films almost never proposed revolutionary action, Italian neorealism more readily embraced Socialist doctrine, though not without convergences with Catholic social thought. This convergence was best dramatized by Roberto Rossellini's pioneering *Roma, città aperta* (*Rome, Open City*, 1945), which depicted solidarity between Catholics and Communists against the Nazi regime, personified in the partisan priest Dom Pietro and the Communist leader Manfredi. Rossellini's *Francesco, giullare di Dio* (*The Flowers of St. Francis*, 1950), a playful adaptation of the *Little Flowers* focusing on Brother Juniper, was among the films of its milieu that most clearly refused to reduce man to an economic or political being.

While Leo McCarey's hugely popular *Going My Way* (1944) and *The Bells of St. Mary's* (1945), starring Bing Crosby as Father Chuck O'Malley, contributed significantly to the mainstreaming of American Catholicism, they also subverted both the social message and the spirituality of the Hollywood priest, emphasizing attractiveness and cultural hipness over substance. The clerical activist returned in Golden Age Hollywood's strongest expression of Catholic social thought, *On the Waterfront* (Elia Kazan, 1954). Based on the real-life crusade of a pair of Jesuit "waterfront priests" to unite oppressed Hoboken stevedores against the corrupt bosses of their own labor union, the film depicted an initially nonactivist priest undergoing a social awakening and taking a Christologically inflected message of solidarity and justice to the dockworkers. The right of workers to organize was both subverted and affirmed; the role of the state in securing workers' rights and enforcing justice was acknowledged in connection with Marlon Brando's testimony against the union bosses.

A strain of Catholic thought ran through the French New Wave of the late 1950s and early 1960s. Most of the filmmakers were Catholic or from Catholic backgrounds (the Protestant Jean-Luc Godard being a notable exception) and had worked as critics for the influential journal *Cahiers du Cinéma*, cofounded by the renowned Catholic critic André Bazin.

Éric Rohmer, a devout Catholic, explored the moral dimensions of love, commitment, and fidelity in such works as *Six Moral Tales*. In a medium that has often emphasized male perspectives, Rohmer gave thoughtful treatment to female characters. Several of François Truffaut's films could be considered a *via negativa* through similar territory ("Monogamy is impossible, but anything else is worse," he once quipped). One of Truffaut's most intriguing explorations of man as a social being was *L'Enfant sauvage* (*The Wild Child*, 1970), a fact-based account of the attempted socialization of a feral child discovered in an Aveyron forest.

The neorealist-influenced *L'Albero degli zoccoli* (*The Tree of Wooden Clogs*, Ermanno Olmi, 1978) offered a documentary-like ethnographic portrait of an Italian peasant community that remains among the richest cinematic expressions of Catholic social principles on a virtual compendium of themes. Ample attention is given to the rhythms of peasant life and labor with its hardships and joys, the centrality of family, marriage, and procreation, the duty of parents to educate their children, and the role of religion. The holiness of marriage and of the marital embrace is touchingly portrayed in an unusual wedding night in a convent. Economic inequalities and the unjust use of wealth trumping the universal destination of goods are dramatized to devastating effect in the climactic crisis.

Activist priests exhibiting solidarity with the needy have seldom been depicted enjoying the support of the hierarchy; at times, they have been opposed by it. The Jesuit missionaries in Latin America in the British film *The Mission* (Roland Joffé, 1986) not only opposed the slave trade but strove to advance the autonomy, self-sufficiency, and economic well-being of the natives through cooperative farming techniques and education; however, their efforts were undone by politics with Church complicity. The Belgian film *Daens* (Stijn Coninx, 1992) depicted a 19th-century priest crusading against child labor and unhealthy working conditions, inspiring a public outcry that was quelled by the ruling classes with the support of the hierarchy.

Romero (John Duigan, 1989), starring Raúl Juliá as Archbishop Óscar Romero, primate of El Salvador, offered a rare depiction of a high-ranking member of the episcopate crusading against political corruption and repression, though opposed by other members of El Salvador's hierarchy. Like the Jesuits in *The Mission*, Romero preached a "theology of liberation" while rejecting reductive forms of liberation theology, including lawless Marxist resistance.

Other films meriting attention include: *Norma Rae* (1979), a fact-based film about a textile factory worker who inspires her coworkers to unionize; *Dekalog* (*The Decalogue*, Krzysztof Kieślowski, 1988), a Polish series of 10 one-hour films set in modern Warsaw exploring moral issues; *Dead Man Walking* (Tim Robbins, 1995), a fictionalized account of Sister Helen Prejean's death-row efforts on behalf of a condemned convict; *Central do Brasil* (*Central Station*, Walter Salles, 1998), a Brazilian drama about a misanthropic middle-aged woman who reluctantly assumes an ambiguous responsibility for a half-orphaned boy; the films of American Catholic John Sayles, such as *Men with Guns* (1998), a drama about military repression in Latin America; the films of the Belgian brothers Jean-Pierre and Luc Dardenne, for example, *Le fils* (*The Son*, 2002), a drama about a carpenter who teaches at a juvenile rehabilitation center and takes an unusual personal interest in one troubled youth; *Shooting Dogs* (*Beyond the Gates*, Michael Caton-Jones, 2005), a fictionalized account of a martyred priest's efforts to prevent bloodshed during the 1994 Rwandan genocide; *Tsotsi* (Gavin Hood, 2005), a South African film about a young thug who discovers a baby in the back seat of a stolen car; *Longford* (Tom Hooper, 2006), a biographical film about Frank Pakeham, Earl of Long-

ford, a social reformer and Catholic convert; and *Des hommes et des dieux* (*Of Gods and Men*, Xavier Beauvois, 2010), a fact-based drama about French Trappist monks in Algeria peaceably coexisting with Muslim neighbors until being kidnapped by Muslim terrorists and murdered.—Steven D. Greydanus

BIBLIOGRAPHY AND FURTHER READING: Blake, Richard A. *AfterImage: The Indelible Catholic Imagination of Six American Filmmakers*. Chicago: Loyola Press, 2000; Doherty, Thomas. *Hollywood's Censor: Joseph I. Breen and the Production Code Administration*. New York: Columbia University Press, 2007; Malone, Peter. *Through a Catholic Lens: Religious Perspectives of Nineteen Film Directors from Around the World*. Plymouth, England: Rowman & Littlefield, 2007; McDannell, Colleen. *Catholics in the Movies*. Oxford: Oxford University Press, 2008; Smith, Anthony Burke. *The Look of Catholics: Portrayals in Popular Culture from the Great Depression to the Cold War*. Lawrence: University of Kansas Press, 2010. *See also CARITAS IN VERITATE; DIVINI ILLIUS MAGISTRI; MEDIA INFLUENCES; SOCIAL COMMUNICATIONS*

FISHER, ST. JOHN (1469–1535) St. John Fisher, Bishop of Rochester, died as a martyr under King Henry VIII of England on June 22, 1535. His severed head was impaled on London Bridge and, as it did not corrupt after many days and was becoming a pilgrimage destination, was thrown into the Thames just in time to free the pike for the display of the head of St. Thomas More, Fisher's friend and better known companion in martyrdom.

Fisher's reputation as a conscientious pastor, capable administrator, and compassionate example to his flock was, in his day, conjoined with his reputation as a forceful intellect and assiduous scholar who possessed perhaps the finest library in Europe. A number of scholars have noted Fisher's posthumous influence at the Council of Trent. Fisher was the first Lady Margaret's Professor of Divinity at Cambridge University, having convinced Lady Margaret Beaufort, mother of Henry VII, to create that post, along with two colleges (Christ's and St. John's). Fisher brought the famed Desiderius Erasmus to Cambridge in 1511 to teach Greek.

Though More's Catholic humanism is more celebrated today, it is quite likely, as Richard Rex has argued, that Fisher's was the model synthesis of Renaissance and medieval Christian elements. Fisher had ample opportunity to display his brilliance, for he became embroiled in two of the most important controversies to affect 16th-century England: the issue of the radical theology of Martin Luther and the "King's Great Matter," that is, Henry VIII's desire for an annulment of his marriage to Catherine of Aragon.

Long before Henry VIII felt compelled to execute his grandmother's spiritual director, he leaned heavily upon him, as upon More, to counteract the influence of Luther. In his early reign, the king was no friend of heresy. His *Defense of the Seven Sacraments* (1521) was a statement about sound doctrine and enduring public order. For it, he was styled "Defender of the Faith." Fisher defended his king's book against Luther's rejoinder (*Contra Henricum regem Angliae*, 1522) in an important text known as the *Defense of the Royal Assertion* (1525).

Luther's early theological commitments had ultimately led him to attack the doctrinal authority of the papacy in favor of *sola scriptura*, that is, the sole sufficiency of scripture in matters of doctrine. Fisher's *Confutation of Luther's Assertion* (1523) provides a thoroughgoing defense of the papal authority, essentially what is known as "papal monarchy." This concept was knit up into the positions of both Fisher and Henry as they inveighed against the ideas of Luther; therefore, it is ironic that Fisher and the king would later part company on just this concept when it came to the king's "divorce." Herein is the key to understanding Fisher's life and death. It is Fisher's constancy and Henry's fecklessness that strikes the inquirer. Though Fisher's fortunes were reversed, his mind was not. *He* was the true defender of the faith, who was destined to seal that defense with his life.

The story of the King's Great Matter is famous but widely misunderstood. Catherine of Aragon had been married for a short time to Henry's older brother, Arthur, until his death in 1502. It was agreed that Catherine should pass to Henry when he was of a marriageable age. The marriage was solemnized in 1509 and lasted until its "annulment" by Thomas Cranmer in 1533. Scruples concerning the marriage with Catherine developed in the king's mind probably due to the coincidence of two forces: first, the failure to have obtained a male heir to the throne and, second, his passion for Anne Boleyn. Henry's passion for Anne fit into a larger pattern of affairs and mistresses.

Henry's scruples were aided by his reading of Leviticus 20: 21, which forbids marriage to the wife of one's brother. Medieval scholastics had long debated the meaning of the passage, though a plurality had regarded the prohibition as unsuited to a Christian context. First, unlike the Jews, Christians did not allow divorce, so it was technically impossible to marry the wife of one's brother, unless she was a widow. Furthermore, a countervailing passage from the Old Testament, Deuteronomy 25: 5, suggested that Levirate marriage (from the Latin *levir*, a husband's brother) was laudable, even necessary, in the case of one's brother's widow. Most Christians know of this tradition from the dilemma posed to Jesus by the Pharisees regarding marriage in heaven (Matthew 22: 24 et al.). Finally, if there were doubts about such a Levirate arrangement, the pope could dispense all parties from such a prohibition, since it was not of the Lord, due to his plenary powers of judgment.

Pope Julius II had in fact done this in 1503. The royal handlers of the youthful Catherine and Henry assumed that such a dispensation was necessary and had secured it for the couple before their marriage in 1509. In his battle for an annulment, Henry attacked the validity of this dispensation, first by declaring that it was secured by political intrigue and fraud, a claim that was utterly refuted by an archive of papal correspondence. Later, and more radically, Henry attacked the ability of the pope to dispense from a biblical commandment and, at the same time, declared that the pope's "dispensing power" was no greater than that of any bishop. Of course, in this argumentation, Henry was attributing an absolute character to the Leviticus passage (which was doubtful) and was operating with an eye toward procuring the annulment of his marriage from his own archbishop of Canterbury, without the concurrence of the pope. A great irony in Henry's new position on authority is how it mirrors that of Martin Luther.

Henry's way to an annulment was somewhat hampered by the fact that the marriage of Catherine and Arthur was never consummated. This meant that a dispensation from an impediment ("affinity") was technically never needed, and that Catherine had always been free to join Henry in holy matrimony. In a famous courtroom scene, Catherine opposed Henry to his face, declaring that she had married him as a virgin and that he knew it! The king offered no rebuttal.

From all that has been said, it is clear that Henry had no case for the annulment of his marriage. St. John Fisher had powerfully argued all the relevant positions in favor of the liceity of the marriage in treatises of 1529 and 1530. Henry regarded this as unforgiveable and relied instead on the legion of theologians and bishops who were eager to put themselves in the king's good graces by taking his side in the matter. It was a shameful display of sycophancy, sometimes undergirded in secret (for Henry was a practical religious conservative) by a commitment to reformed thought from the

Continent. This was certainly true in the case of Henry's Archbishop of Canterbury, Thomas Cranmer, who proclaimed an annulment of the royal marriage in 1533. Pope Clement VII responded with excommunications for both Henry and Cranmer.

Fisher was sent to the Tower of London in April 1534 for his refusal to take the oath of supremacy, part of the Act of Succession of March 30, which declared Henry the supreme head of the Church in England. On May 20, 1535, shortly before his execution, Fisher was made a cardinal by Pope Paul III. For his part, the king intimated that he would send Fisher's head to Rome to receive the red hat.

Fisher's life and death played out against the backdrop of Catholic bishops in a Catholic country under a Catholic monarch. His story cannot be anachronistically transformed into an object lesson on the errors of Anglicanism, for no such thing existed in Henry's time. Sadly, the situation demonstrates the cowardice and defection from Catholic faith and order of the majority of the English bishops of the time.

The history of Fisher's time introduces us to a political revolution, a stage in the genesis of the omnicompetent or Leviathan state, with its secular theory of self-contained sovereignty and centralized power. Henry began by wishing for an annulment and ended by asserting his power over every facet of church and society. Nor is the prominent role of Parliament in Henry's time a contradiction of this revolution. Henry manufactured a compliant Parliament, manipulating it toward his own ends. Its rise to unprecedented importance came at the expense of the real mediating structures of culture and civil society: Catholic nobility, significant families, the independent episcopacy, the parish, and the papacy. Later, during the time of King Charles I, Parliament would play a role analogous to that of Henry, only this time dispatching a king and the remnants of sacral authority in an established church, providing a further act in the drama of absolutism.

Fisher sacrificed himself on behalf of the God-given role of the pope as the center of authority in the Church and on behalf of the freedom of the Church (*libertas ecclesiae*) to mold culture according to the Gospel. There is, of course, also a particular emphasis on the sanctity of the marriage bond.

In the terms of Catholic social teaching, Fisher saw that only a sovereignty that the state shares with the Church could contribute to actual subsidiarity and to a solidarity that is more than merely political. St. John Fisher was canonized in 1935, along with St. Thomas

More, by Pope Pius XI. Fisher and More share the feast day of June 22.—Ronald B. Thomas Jr.

BIBLIOGRAPHY AND FURTHER READING: Rex, Richard. *Henry VIII and the English Reformation.* New York: Palgrave MacMillan, 2006; Rex, Richard. *The Theology of John Fisher.* Cambridge: Cambridge University Press, 1991; Surtz, Edward, SJ. *The Works and Days of John Fisher.* Cambridge, MA: Harvard University Press, 1967. *See also* MORE, ST. THOMAS; SEPARATION OF CHURCH AND STATE

FOX-GENOVESE, ELIZABETH (1941–2007)

Elizabeth Fox-Genovese, an adult convert to the Catholic faith, was a scholar as notable for her bravery as for her brilliance. Her father, Edward Whiting Fox, was a professor of modern history at Cornell University. Although he was not a believer, he admired the intellectual and cultural achievements of Christianity and imparted this admiration to his daughter. Elizabeth earned her BA at Bryn Mawr College and her MA and PhD from Harvard University. She taught at the State University of New York at Binghamton and at the University of Rochester, then for more than 20 years at Emory University, where she was Eleonore Raoul Professor of the Humanities and the founding director of the Institute for Women's Studies.

After what Fox-Genovese described as her "long apprenticeship" in the world of secular liberal intellectuals, it was careful reflection on the central moral questions of our time that led her first to doubt and then to abandon both liberalism and secularism. Needless to say, this did not endear her to her former allies.

At the heart of her doubts about secular liberalism (and what she described as "radical, upscale feminism") was its embrace of abortion and its (continuing) dalliance with euthanasia. At first, she went along with abortion, albeit reluctantly, believing that women's rights to develop their talents and control their destinies required its legal permission availability. But Fox-Genovese was not one who could avert her eyes from inconvenient facts. For her, euphemisms such as "products of conception," "termination of pregnancy," "privacy," and "choice" ultimately could not hide the fact that abortion is the deliberate killing of a developing child in the womb. She came to see that to countenance abortion is not to respect women's privacy or liberty but to suppose that some people have the right to decide whether others will live or die. In a statement that she knew would enflame many on the left and even cost her valued friendships, she declared that "no amount of past oppression can justify women's oppression of the most vulnerable among us."

Fox-Genovese knew that public pro-life advocacy would be regarded by many in the intellectual establishment as intolerable apostasy—especially from one of the founding mothers of women's studies. She could have been forgiven for keeping mum on the issue and carrying on with her professional work on the history of the American South. But keeping quiet about fundamental matters of right and wrong was not in her character. And though she valued her standing in the intellectual world, she cared for truth and justice more. So she spoke out ever more passionately in defense of the unborn.

The more she thought and wrote about abortion and other life issues, the more persuaded she became that the entire secular liberal project was misguided. Secular liberals were not *deviating* from their principles in endorsing killing whether by abortion or euthanasia in the name of individual choice; they were *following* them to their logical conclusions. But this revealed a profound contradiction at the heart of secular liberal ideology, for the right of some individuals to kill others undermines any ground of principle on which an idea of individual rights or dignity could be founded.

Even in her "long apprenticeship," she was never among those who disdained religious believers or held them in contempt. As a historian and social critic, she admired the cultural and moral achievements of Judaism and Christianity. As her doubts about secularism grew, she began to consider seriously whether religious claims might actually be true. Reason led her to the door of faith, and prayer enabled her to walk through it. As she herself described her conversion from secularism to Catholicism, it had a large intellectual component; yet it was, in the end, less her choice than God's grace.

Fox-Genovese continued her scholarly labors, especially in collaboration with her husband Eugene Genovese, an eminent historian of American slavery. Cambridge University Press published their masterwork, *The Mind of the Master Class.* Soon after Fox-Genovese's own religious conversion, her husband (who had long been an avowed Marxist, but who had gradually moved in the direction of cultural and political conservatism) returned to the Catholic faith of his boyhood under the influence of his beloved wife.

As if she had not already antagonized the intellectual establishment enough, Fox-Genovese soon began speaking out in defense of marriage and sexual morality. Her root-and-branch rejection of the ideology of

the sexual revolution—an ideology that now enjoys the status of infallible dogma among many secular liberal intellectuals—was based on a profound appreciation of the centrality of marriage to the fulfillment of men and women as sexually complementary spouses; to the well-being of children, for whom the love of mother and father for each other and for them is literally indispensable; and to the health of society as a whole, which depends on the marriage-based family for the rearing of responsible and upright citizens. If her pro-life advocacy angered many liberal intellectuals, her outspoken defense of marriage and traditional norms of sexual morality made them apoplectic.

Elizabeth's marriage to Eugene was a great love story. They were two very different personalities, perfectly united. He was the head of the family; she was in charge of everything. Their affection for each other created a kind of force field into which friends were drawn in love for both of them. Although unable to have children of their own, they lavished parental care and concern on their students and younger colleagues, who in turn worshipped them.

Fox-Genovese left a double legacy: many fine students who themselves went on to distinguished careers as scholars, and a raft of superb works of historical scholarship and social criticism—works admired by honest scholars across the political spectrum. Even more importantly, her life provides an unsurpassed example of intellectual integrity and moral courage. Her fervent witness to the sanctity of human life and the dignity of marriage and the family will continue to inspire.—Robert P. George

BIBLIOGRAPHY AND FURTHER READING: Fox-Genovese, Elizabeth. *Feminism Is Not the Story of My Life.* New York: Knopf Doubleday, 1996; Fox-Genovese, Elizabeth. *Feminism without Illusions: A Critique of Individualism.* Chapel Hill: University of North Carolina Press, 1991. *See also* ABORTION; FEMINISM; FEMINISM IN THE CHURCH; GENOVESE, EUGENE D.

· G ·

GARRIGOU-LAGRANGE, RÉGINALD, OP (1877–1964) Réginald Garrigou-Lagrange, the preeminent Catholic theologian before the Second Vatican Council, was a faithful Thomist in the classic tradition of the great Dominican commentators, from Cajetan and Francesco Silvestri to John of St. Thomas and Billuart. His scholarship encompassed philosophy, theology, and spirituality, giving rise to a forceful unity of vision that constitutes a treasure of knowledge and inspiration for Catholics of all times.

Born Gontran-Marie in Auch, near Toulouse in France, in 1877, Garrigou-Lagrange had what he called his conversion while studying medicine in Bordeaux: reading Ernest Hello's *Life, Science and Art,* he instantly realized that Church doctrine is the absolute truth on God and man. This led him to abandon his medical studies and, in 1897, to become a Dominican novice in Amiens, taking the name of Réginald after the early Dominican Blessed Réginald of Orleans.

Garrigou-Lagrange studied theology at the Saulchoir under the Dominican Father Ambroise Gardeil, who would have a lasting impact on the direction of his intellectual endeavors. He also studied philosophy at the Sorbonne, where he attended the classes of Henri Bergson and met Jacques Maritain. In the meantime, he received priestly ordination in 1902. In 1909, shortly after Garrigou-Lagrange had started teaching at the Saulchoir and published his first writing on the philosophy of being, the master general of the Dominicans, Blessed Hyacinthe-Marie Cormier, called him to Rome to teach dogmatic theology at the recently established Angelicum. This was the beginning of a formidable intellectual adventure that would last for more than half a century: from 1918 to 1959, he commented on all the main treatises of the *Summa Theologica*; in 1915, he started teaching Aristotle's *Metaphysics*; and in 1917, encouraged by Pope Benedict XV, he founded the first chair of spiritual theology, which he taught until 1960 and whose classes were attended not only by university students but also by prelates and major superiors.

His intense teaching and scholarly production (his bibliography comprises more than 700 writings, mainly in Latin and French) were accompanied by an equally intense commitment as a spiritual director. From 1922 to 1937, Garrigou-Lagrange preached in Meudon, outside of Paris, at almost all the annual retreats of the Thomist Study Circles, which he had cofounded with the Maritains. His advice was eagerly sought by all the pontiffs from Benedict XV to John XXIII (and the young Karol Wojtyla had been his student in the 1940s). In 1955, Pope Pius XII named him a consultor to the then Holy Office, with whose secretary (Cardinal Ottaviani) he had a mutual relationship of great esteem. John XXIII appointed him to the central preparatory commission for the Second Vatican Council, but his health, which started deteriorating in 1960, did not allow Garrigou-Lagrange to carry out this work. He died in Rome in 1964, after receiving the last sacraments,

and was lauded by Pope Paul VI as a faithful servant of the Church and the Holy See.

In reaffirming the validity of the philosophy of being, in the Aristotelian-Thomistic tradition, Garrigou-Lagrange was not proposing ideas of a distant past but was faithful to the perennial concept of truth against all modernist and neo-modernist pretensions. Contrary to their attempt to replace the philosophy of being with the philosophy of action, Garrigou-Lagrange went right to the core of the matter, holding that truth is, in its classic definition, the alignment of the intellect and its object (*adaequatio rei et intellectus*), not the alignment of the understanding with life (*adaequatio realis mentis et vitae*). This philosophical premise was vital because, as he used to say in the footsteps of St. Thomas Aquinas, a small error in the principles becomes a big error in the conclusions (*parvus error in principio magnus est in fine*). From these philosophical premises, Garrigou-Lagrange regarded theology not as a systematic exposition of some vague religious experience, but as sacred doctrine, true science of God. Likewise, the main traits of his spiritual theology (a field he had embraced under the early inspiration of the Spanish Dominican Juan González Arintero) reflect Thomistic teaching.

Endowed with a unique capacity of drawing summary and effective conclusions from his vast analytical investigation, Garrigou-Lagrange was able to bring into a composite and internally consistent whole the three aspects of wisdom: philosophy (rooted in natural reason), theology (rooted in supernatural faith), and spiritual theology (rooted in the gifts of the Holy Ghost), in a spirit that always sought faithfulness to the truth and Church tradition, not distracting novelty for the sake of sounding original.

Garrigou-Lagrange's life was as exemplary as his scholarship. He lived with rigorous discipline 64 years as a Dominican friar (daily Mass, silent meditation, communal exercises, recitation of the rosary), he was austere in everything (including the simplicity of his cell and his reserved attitude toward food and drink), and his ability to concentrate and make the most of his time was outstanding. His acceptance of sickness and death was likewise worthy of such a remarkable figure. As the great Italian painter Piero della Francesca had been hit in the sense from which his art flowed, namely, his sight, the great thinker Garrigou-Lagrange was hit in his reasoning abilities, affected by Alzheimer's disease during his last years. In his moments of lucidity, he would thank God for this trial and turn to the recitation of the rosary as the only meaningful response to his condition.—Maurizio Ragazzi

BIBLIOGRAPHY AND FURTHER READING: Garrigou-Lagrange, Réginald. *God, His Existence and His Nature: A Thomistic Solution of Certain Agnostic Antinomies.* St. Louis, MO: B. Herder, 1934; Garrigou-Lagrange, Réginald. *Reality: A Synthesis of Thomistic Thought.* Translated by Patrick Cummins. St. Louis, MO: B. Herder, 1950; Garrigou-Lagrange, Réginald. *The Three Ages of the Interior Life, Prelude of Eternal Life.* Translated by Timothea Doyle. St. Louis, MO: B. Herder, 1947–1948; Nichols, Aidan. *Reason with Piety: Garrigou-Lagrange in the Service of Catholic Thought.* Naples, FL: Sapientia Press, 2008; Peddicord, Richard. *The Sacred Monster of Thomism: An Introduction to the Life and Legacy of Réginald Garrigou-Lagrange, O.P.* South Bend, IN: St. Augustine's Press, 2005; "Reginaldi Garrigou-Lagrange: In Memoriam," *Angelicum* 42 (1965): 3–272. *See also* AQUINAS, ST. THOMAS; ARISTOTLE; DOMINIC, ST., AND THE DOMINICAN TRADITION; MARITAIN, JACQUES; MODERNISM AND NEO-MODERNISM; OTTAVIANI, CARDINAL ALFREDO; POPE BENEDICT XV; POPE BLESSED JOHN XXIII; POPE JOHN PAUL II; POPE PAUL VI; POPE PIUS XII; THOMISM/NEO-THOMISM

GAY/LESBIAN THEORY The gay/lesbian liberation movement is a powerful, highly organized, and very widespread international effort meant to establish homosexual activity as part of the normal, socially accepted range of human sexual behavior; encourage individuals starting at a young age to explore having a possible gay or lesbian identity through sexual experimentation; and transform all social institutions—education, law, family, media, art, religion—to embrace and support these changes. Its members hold somewhat diverse views on the nature of sexuality and advocate different social change strategies, but overall they share certain core theories and visions of the person and society, many of which emerged out of feminism—especially lesbian and radical feminism—a generation earlier. These core theories and visions can be discerned in different contexts of movement action: political activism, the production of art and literature, popular media, the substance of educational curricula from grade school through college, and the articulation of religious beliefs. They are typically completely at odds with an authentically Catholic worldview: in fact, it is common for gay/lesbian thinkers to identify much of organized Christianity, and especially "patriarchal" Catholicism, as a main enemy in their culture war because of its very long-standing, explicit teaching that homosexual behavior is intrinsically immoral. Thus, activists and theorists especially relish their all-too-many allies within the Christian camp.

The Church and gay/lesbian theory articulate completely opposing sociologies of sex and gender. In social science, the term *sex* refers to one's biological, physical nature, while *gender* refers to the social expectations attached to that underlying bio-identity in a particular society. Catholic teaching begins with the notion, articulated from Genesis forward, that individuals are born male or female biologically and that this biological reality strongly shapes a set of complementary gender roles men and women live throughout life. Anthropologically, there are cultural differences in how societies define male and female gender roles: who is expected to do what work and rituals, has what type of authority, or wears what sort of clothing and adornment. There have been some cultures past and present where occasional homosexual activity has been considered normal. But the Church holds that beneath such surface differences in customs is a divinely designed, universal, heterosexual dynamic that prescribes opposite-sex attraction and marriage, and raising children to understand that males and females have unique but balancing strengths and weaknesses.

Thus, for the Church, sex and gender are very closely intertwined: heterosexuality is the foundation for rightly ordered personal and social life. Varying this basic template profoundly risks not only the moral lives of individuals but also the long-term viability of their society, by disrupting the pattern of natural human reproduction and corrupting the God-given cultural system built around it. The Church also teaches that as moral and political ideas evolve toward greater justice, a society should challenge painfully sexist norms and seek to improve them—for example, by fostering greater access for women to educational attainment or certain occupations, or encouraging more men to participate actively in child care and stop using physical power as a weapon in relationships. But in so doing, society must not deviate from its heterosexual basis as a divinely ordained social architecture.

Exceptions occur—for example, with physically ambiguous hermaphrodites; the transgendered, who experience a haunting disjuncture between their physical sex and their felt sexual self; or bisexuals and homosexuals. Catholicism treats these cases as wounded minds and souls endangered by sin and thus in need of healing and spiritual guidance. Their personal degree of sinfulness depends on how intentionally and deliberately they are challenging God's order. So the Church has taught and teaches today, incorporating as it goes valid findings from the social sciences about human nature, human experience, and cultural variations in gender customs.

Gay/lesbian theory fundamentally upends this entire structure of truth, arguing that sex and gender can be stretched apart. Differences within gay/lesbian theory are often about how wide a split between them there can or should be. But one widely shared position is *social constructionism*: the notion that sexual identity is not fixed and binary but, rather, open-ended, plastic, and primarily a result of social learning. Cultures select which sexualities to normalize, validate, and socialize children into out of all the possible ones that could exist. Constructionism finds its roots in Freud's claim of human polymorphous sexuality, Kinsey's later pseudoscientific but enormously influential studies of human sexual variability, the tradition of philosophical relativism, and more recently feminism's effort to destroy the "hegemony" of traditional male and female roles.

Constructionism's main challenge to opponents is circular: You *mistakenly* believe your heterosexual gender scripts are "natural" and inevitable because of ethnocentrism—that is, thinking that your particular ways of life are somehow best and true, the only possible ways—but instead they, too, are just social constructions. From these positions follows the often vehement hostility to Catholicism for its assertion that sexual identity *is* biologically grounded and its affirmation of a natural law foundation for nurturing heterosexual gender roles.

Gay/lesbian theorists argue that the "heteronormative" social universe should be deconstructed and rebuilt to align social norms and institutions with the authentic sexual diversity they believe we are capable of. But how much diversity is there, and why? In answering these questions, gay/lesbian social constructionism can take "weak" or "strong," liberal or radical forms. The issue here is how deep the role constructing goes, how radical the gender indeterminacy is, and thus how far social change needs to be taken.

In the weak form, often called *essentialism*, some biological or other "inner" factors that *seem like* biology still play a primary role in shaping gender behavior. Theorists emphasize that sex is still a powerful determinant of gender roles; it is just that our previous binary vision of the bio-sexual infrastructure is wrong. Bisexuality, transsexuality, or homosexuality (indeed some essentialists believe there are biological bases for pedophilia, hebephelia, and other sexual proclivities) is said to originate with genes, hormonal intrauterine environments, brain architecture, and so forth that cause later behavior. There exists a whole research tradition in homosexual studies seeking to identify first causes

of this type, in humans and also other kinds of animals. But since these inner forces and factors have turned out not to be readily identifiable scientifically, theorists often rely on individuals' reported experience of "feeling determined by something way inside from very early on" as an evidentiary claim. Sex and gender are still connected, but since there are more bio-sexes, there are more possible socially expressed genders.

In the strong form, often known as *queer theory*, more radical constructionists challenge the essentialist, bio-deterministic model of where gender roles come from. Here, the construction of who we are "goes all the way down" to the level of biology itself, the study of which is seen as essentially a political activity that either favorably supports polymorphous sexuality or not. Queer researchers seek to cut the causal tie linking sex and gender altogether, thereby *deprivileging* the concept of gender as a meaningful framework for human classification. In sociological terms, they seek to *destroy gender as a master status*. Once "compulsory heterosexuality" is thus undermined, a path is opened to champion a kind of triumph of the will as the key factor in shaping one's sexual "preferences." Biology may or may not be involved in such preferences, but that is less salient than choice.

Versions of queer theory have been around as long as feminism, but now it is much more mainstream: for example, the term often appears in descriptions of interdisciplinary college women's studies programs, where it is posed as an especially daring, deep form of "critical thinking" capable of cutting to the core of our society's heterosexist norms and values. There is also some evidence that gay men are more likely to espouse the rather deterministic essentialist position than are lesbians, many of whom come to homosexual relations later in life and emphasize them as an intentional, often political response to earlier destructive heterosexual experiences.

These strands of constructionism have powerful implications for the gay/lesbian movement, because they come tightly packaged with three other theoretical emphases: (1) experiential, expressive individualism; (2) a power-based theory of social order; and (3) the claiming of homosexual or other gender identities as an ascribed social status like race or age.

Gay/lesbian theory first asserts that the highest social good is an individualistic personal freedom to choose to live one's sexual life as one feels necessary. Society must be aligned with that expressive individualism to allow and encourage it. Thus, for example, the family is voluntaristically defined as whomever one decides to include, and marriage is simply a socially formalized relationship between any group of people who declare their mutual commitment. Religion is often brought to bear to justify these ideas: there are growing strains of pro-gay/lesbian theology in many Christian denominations, including the Episcopal Church, the United Church of Christ, and other liberal groups. Catholics, too, have their version, in such pseudo-Catholic groups as DignityUSA and its allies in dissidence. When religion is not invoked as a justification, gay/lesbian theory invokes secular humanistic principles of fairness and authenticity upon which to build its moral rationales. Queer theorists take this a step further, saying we should make up our own justifications for our individual liberty and never rely on any contaminated institutions to do so.

Drawing heavily from Marxism and feminism, the power-based theory of social order asserts that traditional genders only *seem* natural because society's heterosexual power elites, seeking to retain their advantaged position, impose and repeatedly reaffirm them in clever, deceptive ways, making their actual relativity hard to detect. This occurs through early childhood socialization, later schooling, the media, law, and religion; it involves both suppressing the alternate visions of masculinity and femininity that homosexuality offers, such as pliant and receptive manliness or aggressive or assertive femaleness, and strongly condemning same-sex attractions as deviant.

The third leg of the theoretical stool involves the relationship between homosexuality and efforts to achieve social change. Both types of gay/lesbian constructionists claim that homosexuality is an *ascribed status*: that is, a life-determining social position based on a powerful social label. But they articulate this for slightly different reasons. From an essentialist perspective, homosexuality is analogous to race or age: it is an accident of birth and human biology, or may as well be, because of how culture treats it. As an ascribed status resulting from biological or other causes, homosexuality should therefore have no moral significance at all, because morality requires some realm of choice. Homosexuals are thus unfairly judged as willfully sinful and deviant, when homosexuality is simply another gender added to the two more common ones. Homosexuals deserve the same social equality as heterosexual women or brown people or the elderly have aspired to, for the same reasons. This is why so much of advocates' energy goes into searching for the precultural causes, say, in the biology of brain physiognomy or hormonal balances, for why people "are" nonheterosexual.

Unfortunately for this stance, early scientific claims touted by the movement for this are not holding up: even quite pro-gay professional groups like the American Psychological Association are now admitting that there is no substantial, replicable research at this time to support the position that homosexuality is strongly genetic or neurological. Despite this, activists still often claim that in their *personal* experience, being gay or lesbian *feels* as if it is determined from deep inside, so it may as well be considered in the same way. The political upshot of this perspective is to pursue the role of minority in society and claim the need for social *reform*, as other minority groups have done to make room in the existing system for those previously excluded and oppressed. This more mainstream version of gay/lesbian theory frames its politics as a very familiar battle for civil rights, a rejection of prejudice and discrimination based on status ascription, and the pursuit of an expanded liberal democracy. First there was black liberation, then women's liberation, now gay/lesbian liberation. First there was racism, then sexism, now heterosexism.

On the other hand, more radical or queer theorists strongly dispute the essentialist claim of a third (or maybe even fourth or fifth) gender and its reformist implications. Since gender is not at all stable as far as we know and is subject to perpetual revision by people in the flux of their lives, a society must be created that does not think in terms of categories at all—beyond statuses of any sort, ascribed *or* achieved. It may be true that for now, in the current liberal democracy, those stigmatized as minorities should struggle for more liberty and rights. But the main goal is to overturn all social structures that require sexuality to be stable enough to be classified. Queer politics are thus revolutionary, seeking to transcend democratic pluralism. The point is to be free to fluidly construct and reconstruct one's own sexual identity and social roles; even if biology is shaping that process, it should not matter at the personal or social level. Politics is meant to eliminate the entire oppressive system of social categorization based on identities and statuses altogether, not simply to toy with how many tolerated categories there are.

Putting all these theoretical pieces together, gay/lesbian theory forms the basis for advocating a package of particular social changes, whether the goal is liberal reforms or longer-term revolution. First, social space has to be created for individuals to discover that homosexuality is what they enjoy and can be pursued legitimately. The movement thus organizes strongly around helping people, especially young people, "question" their gender socialization before it can warp their authentic selves, using tools like support groups, community organizations, and interest groups within occupational settings. Even the Republican Party has its pro-gay Log Cabin national organization. The movement thus acquires recruits.

Further, details of surrounding culture must be revised. For example, the highly voluntaristic terms *sexual orientation* and *sexual preference* are used propagandistically to signal that one's sexuality is a result of personal awareness and choice, not slavish adherence to traditional sexual scripts. Heterosexuals aligning with gay/lesbian ideology also use this terminology for themselves, to signal that they do not assign greater ontological reality to their historically more acceptable sexual identities either. "Coming out" is also ritualized as an act of courageously facing social opprobrium and joining others in a process of personal and social liberation. Law, family structure, and the workplace must be transformed to align with the new cultural norms, to enable these freed individuals to live out their homosexuality and relationships without stigma, following their own cultural standards.

Lastly, public impressions created by the raw sexuality inherent in the movement's nature—which after all is about having sex with who you want when you want and being quite open about it—are carefully managed to advance the sexual revolution without stimulating a backlash from moderates and liberals whose sympathies and alliances are needed and who tolerate some sexual change but don't really condone, and may even be repulsed by, the more dramatic forms of sexual expression that the movement draws out. Even in its moderate forms, gay/lesbian theory is a profoundly challenging theory of libidinous social sexuality and sexual sociality, in the tradition, for example, of the earlier bohemian free love movement and the social radicalisms of Wilhelm Reich and Herbert Marcuse. Achieving this sexual revolution involves a balance.

When the organized gay/lesbian movement acts out and up in public in order to attract recruits, demonstrate political clout, and assert homosexual identity as legitimate—for example, in gay pride events and Internet portal networks—the movement must handle quite carefully the huge diversity of sometimes orgiastic or highly deviant sexual activity that activism makes visible. This has been true since the earliest "homophile" demonstrations some decades ago, whose leaders consciously put forth a middle-class, folks-next-door image of gays and lesbians and told more visibly deviant groups to stay home. Today, queer theory's movement influence becomes especially problematic, for it takes the position

that any and all claims of a firm objective standpoint from which to judge morality are mere phallocentrism. Phallocentrism, that is, asserting the primacy of the heterosexual male and his way of thinking, is said to permeate all fields of human endeavor from art to zoology. The only way to overcome phallocentrism is to let all other previously closeted centrisms loose, giving equal legitimacy to any and all standpoints and sexual experiences: all sexual activity short of killing can be legitimized. This can make for a very provocative pride event.

Consider, for example, the avowedly queer group Sisters of Perpetual Indulgence. At pride events, its members mockingly don a religious habit, and their political theater often includes explicit desecrations and sexual acting-out in or around Catholic venues like churches. Or consider leather fetishists, who might be engaged in sexual activities and flaunting their way of dressing on a parade float. Seeing these, what will the larger public start to think about gay/lesbian activism and activists? And can movement leaders again tell them to stay home this time around?

In short, the homosexual movement presses for huge social changes in our culture and institutions, but must tread carefully so that homosexuality retains an aura of broad acceptability and regularity. Sociologically speaking, it must normalize its deviance cautiously. Thus, a strong tension persists now within the gay/lesbian movement, which is also reflected in its theorizing, between weak and strong constructionists, between liberal and radical approaches to social change in movement public presentation, materials, and events.

Church teachings defining all homosexuality as immoral will not change. But, as the ideas and theories driving the gay/lesbian movement acquire ever greater acceptance and social approval, its social teaching may have to become both more nuanced and more forthright. Reliable studies indicate that while perhaps 10% of all people in our culture experience some sort of same-sex episode at one time or another in their lives for various reasons, most often during youth, 2% or less of people claim an actual deep-seated gay or lesbian identity. An even tinier sliver adopt the more radical postidentity stance espoused by queer theory. Yet that group seems much larger because of its enormous, highly leveraged impact on our world today, locally, nationally, and internationally. The Church must work harder to affirm its life-giving theories of the person, sexuality, and social life in terms that more people can access and more clearly oppose the social changes in law and custom demanded by gay/lesbian theory.—Stephen R. Sharkey

BIBLIOGRAPHY AND FURTHER READING: Brink-mann, Susan. *The Kinsey Corruption: An Exposé on the Most Influential "Scientist" of Our Time.* West Chester, PA: Ascension Press, 2004; Butler, Judith. *Gender Trouble: Feminism and the Subversion of Identity.* New York: Rout-ledge, 1990; Eisenbach, David. *Gay Power: An American Revolution.* New York: Carroll & Graf, 2006; Fuss, Di-ana. *Inside/Out: Lesbian Theories, Gay Theories.* New York: Routledge, 1991; O'Leary, Dale. *One Man, One Woman: A Catholic's Guide to Defending Marriage.* Manchester, NH: Sophia Press, 2007; Sterling, Anne Fausto. *Sexing the Body: Gender Politics and the Construction of Sexuality.* New York: Basic Books, 2000; Summers, Claude, ed. *glbtq: An Encyclopedia of Gay, Lesbian, Bisexual, Trans-gender, and Queer Culture.* Chicago: glbtq, 2005; Wolfe, Christopher, ed. *Homosexuality and American Life.* Dallas: Spence, 1999. *See also* CULTURAL RELATIVISM; FEMINISM; HOMOPHOBIA; HOMOSEXUALITY; MARRIAGE AND DOMESTIC PARTNERSHIP LAW; POSTMODERNISM; SAME-SEX UNIONS; SEXISM; SEXUALITY (HUMAN); SOCIAL CON-STRUCTIONISM; THEOLOGY OF THE BODY

GENOVESE, EUGENE D. (1930–) Eugene D. Genovese is one of the most important and con-troversial American historians of his generation. His work—both what he has written alone and what he has coauthored with his wife, historian Elizabeth Fox-Genovese—is seminal for the understanding of slavery, the relationship of slaves and masters, and the relation-ship of the Southern United States to the North and the rest of the world. Genovese also has played a critical role in several professional and cultural debates from the 1960s through the 2000s.

Genovese was born in Brooklyn to an Italian American, Catholic, working-class family in 1930. At the age of 15, he left the Church and became a member of the Communist Party. Although the formal affiliation with the party did not last long, Genovese's sympathy for Karl Marx and use of Marx's critique of capitalist society has remained a lodestar throughout his career. Even as Genovese moved from the political left to the right later in his career—he returned to the Catholic Church in 1996—Genovese remains indebted to Marx and especially Marx's class analysis.

Genovese earned his undergraduate degree at Brooklyn College and then his doctorate at Columbia University in 1960. He taught at the Polytechnic In-stitute of Brooklyn and then Rutgers University. His Rutgers career ended with a maelstrom after a newly tenured Genovese announced at a teach-in, "I do not fear or regret the impending Viet Cong victory in Vietnam. I welcome it." The announcement of sympa-thy for insurgents in Vietnam by a Marxist member of the faculty at a state school led to turmoil on campus and beyond. New Jersey Republican gubernatorial candidate Wayne Dumont made firing Genovese a centerpiece of his ultimately unsuccessful campaign in 1965. Although Rutgers did not fire Genovese, he left Rutgers at the end of the 1966–1967 academic year. In 1969, he was hired at the University of Rochester, where he remained until 1986, when Elizabeth Fox-Genovese accepted an appointment at Emory Univer-sity. Genovese himself taught at various schools after he left Rochester, including a joint appointment at Emory, the Georgia Institute of Technology, Georgia State, and the University of Georgia. He retired from teaching in 1996.

Always a provocateur, Genovese found himself at the eye of many of the era's most contentious debates. In 1968, he vigorously defended novelist William Styron, whose Pulitzer Prize–winning *The Confes-sions of Nat Turner* (1968) came under attack by black nationalists. Although he was against the Vietnam War, he opposed efforts by members of the American Historical Association to pass a resolution against the Vietnam War in 1969; he believed that the organi-zation should be open to and represent historians who dissent from the dominant political view of the profession. Many saw Genovese's election in 1978 to the presidency of the Organization of American His-torians at the age of 48 as a symbol of the profession's openness to those on the left, but such gestures did not reassure Genovese. He remained concerned that the profession had marginalized many, including both political conservatives and practitioners of traditional historical approaches. These concerns led Genovese, his wife, and other historians to establish the Histori-cal Society in 1998; Genovese served as the society's first president until 2000.

Genovese's early work—notably his books *The Political Economy of Slavery* (1965) and *The World the Slaveholders Made* (1969)—introduced a new and sophis-ticated Marxist analysis to American historiography. Be-cause the South was a slave society—one where slavery dominated as the mode of production—Genovese saw it as fundamentally different from the capitalistic North. The antagonisms between the North and the South were based upon the different modes of production, and Genovese's work helped revitalize a new version of Wil-liam Seward's view of the Civil War as an "irrepressible conflict." More than that, Genovese's efforts—especially when considered along with the works of such European historians as E. P. Thompson and Eric Hobsbawm—freed Marxist historiography from the shackles of Marxist teleology. These historians jettisoned Marx's economic determinism, instead putting Marx's understanding of class formation and struggle at the heart of their histories. As a result, they wrote Marxist history that respected the contingency of history, which allowed them to influence other historians in ways that earlier Marxist historians did not. Genovese's work also showed sensitivity to ideas and culture, something that had often been lacking in earlier Marxist historians.

Reflecting on the arc of his career at the end of the millennium, Genovese observed that he had needed to take a "detour" from his study of slaveholders. To understand the slaveholders, he needed to understand the slaves, and so he undertook a study of American slaves. Published in 1974, *Roll, Jordan, Roll* won the Bancroft Prize and remains Genovese's most influential book.

Genovese's interpretation of slavery relied upon two important ideas: hegemony and paternalism. Drawing upon the work of Italian Marxist Antonio Gramsci, who emphasized the importance of culture, Genovese described the South as a place where slaves and slaveholders alike generally accepted the contours of a slave society. Instead of fighting a class war that focused on preserving or destroying slave society, masters and slaves focused their battles on more limited goals. Masters tried to get slaves to acknowledge their authority, while slaves worked to create customary rights that protected them and their communities in a world where slaves were legally another form of property. Genovese argued that both sides accepted that there existed an organic relationship between the slaves and slaveholders, which Genovese called "paternalism." For the masters, paternalism validated their authority and undermined attempts to create solidarity among slaves. For the slaves, paternalism meant that their owners recognized their humanity and gave them a basis for claiming customary rights. Accepting paternalism, slaves created a way to resist the dehumanizing implications of slavery without launching a frontal assault on the Southern slave regime. Although the slaves did not attack the slave society in which they lived, slaves did develop a culture in which they could express their humanity even as they accepted to some extent their position as slaves. Genovese found the fullest expression of African American culture in the black church.

Following *Roll, Jordan, Roll* and *From Rebellion to Revolution* (1979), a short book that argued that the French Revolution led slaves to oppose slavery itself rather than their own personal enslavement, Genovese returned to the study of slaveholders. In *The Fruits of Merchant Capital* (1983), Genovese and Fox-Genovese refined his conceptualization of the relationship of the slaveholding South to the expansion of capitalism in the North and throughout the Western world. According to the Genoveses, the Southern slaveholding system was a product of the modern capitalistic world and participated in the capitalist world markets, but the class of Southern slaveholders ultimately opposed the expansion of capitalistic ideas of property in the South. In *The Mind of the Master Class* (2005), the Genoveses reviewed the slaveholders' understanding of religion and history, and in *Slavery in White and Black* (2008), they examined the slaveholders understanding of slavery, especially "slavery in the abstract," by which they mean slavery understood without reference to racial or other accidental factors. In both books, they describe in incredible detail the impressive yet ultimately unsuccessful effort of Southerners to produce an ideology that could withstand the relentless expansion of a capitalist worldview.

The return of Genovese to the Catholic Church in 1996—which followed shortly after Fox-Genovese's conversion to Catholicism in 1995—marked a remarkable shift in a person who had been a self-identified Stalinist for half a century. Although Genovese decided that he could no longer defend his atheism intellectually, he did not disavow his earlier historical work when he returned to the Church. In fact, if one focuses on social thought alone, Genovese's return to the Church may be seen as a new attempt to solve what Genovese has always seen as the central social and political problem facing people in the modern world: laissez-faire capitalism creates enormous amounts of wealth, but it sunders the traditional relationships within society. In particular, it frees the elites from traditional responsibilities that they would otherwise have for the lower class.

Genovese studies the slaveholders so intensely because they tried to create an alternative path to modernity in which the elites accept their responsibilities to the members of the lower class. The slaveholders' attempt to create a just society failed, much as the efforts to create a sustainable modern Marxist state failed, but they were both—to Genovese's mind—doing the right thing by trying to stand up to unfettered individualism. Understood this way, it is not surprising that Genovese has found a home in the Catholic Church, which clearly rejects the idea that individuals are autonomous and one's responsibility for another is limited to those things that one has agreed to do.—Patrick H. Breen

BIBLIOGRAPHY AND FURTHER READING: Genovese, Eugene D. *In Red and Black: Marxian Explorations in*

Southern and Afro-American History. New York: Pantheon, 1971; Genovese, Eugene D. *Roll, Jordan, Roll: The World the Slaves Made.* New York: Pantheon, 1974; Kolchin, Peter. "Eugene D. Genovese: Historian of Slavery." *Radical History Review* 88 (2004): 52–67; Novick, Peter. *That Noble Dream: The "Objectivity Question" and the American Historical Profession.* New York: Cambridge University Press, 1988; Paquette, Robert Louis, and Louis A. Ferlegar, eds. *Slavery, Secession, and Southern History.* Charlottesville: University Press of Virginia, 2000. *See also* FOX-GENOVESE, ELIZABETH; MARXISM; SLAVERY

GROESCHEL, BENEDICT F., CFR (1933–)

Born on July 23, 1933, and raised in Jersey City, New Jersey, Rev. Benedict F. Groeschel, CFR, knew at an early age that he was called to religious life. Upon graduating from high school in 1951, he entered the Franciscan Capuchins and was solemnly professed in 1952. His ordination to the priesthood came on June 30, 1959.

At the beginning of his priestly ministry, Father Groeschel was intent on emphasizing the corporal works of mercy. In 1960, he was a chaplain to Children's Village, a facility for emotionally disturbed youngsters in Dobbs Ferry, New York. In 1967, Groeschel founded the St. Francis Home, a safe haven for young men, in the Greenpoint section of Brooklyn, New York. The priest cofounded with Christopher Bell in 1985 Good Counsel Homes, residences for pregnant women who might otherwise abort their unborn children.

Twelve years into his priestly ministry, in 1971, Columbia University in New York awarded Father Groeschel a doctorate in psychology. Ever since then, he has used his expertise as a psychologist to assess candidates for religious life and the diocesan priesthood, conducting interviews with them and administering testing to ascertain psychological soundness and then sharing his findings with bishops, vocation directors, and religious superiors. As a psychologist, Groeschel has also worked with priests and consecrated men and women who have experienced difficulties in the course of their ministries and apostolates. He has held a membership in the American Psychological Association since 1971.

Along the way, Groeschel developed a national and international reputation for giving spiritual direction and retreat conferences. Under Terence Cardinal Cooke in New York, he was made the archdiocesan director of the Office of Spiritual Development. John Cardinal O'Connor, Cooke's successor, confirmed Father Groeschel in this position and made the priest the promoter of the cause of Cardinal Cooke's canonization. The founder of the Trinity Retreat House in Larchmont, New York, Groeschel remains on its staff and is still in demand as a retreat master and keynote speaker at various conferences in the United States and abroad. The widespread acclaim for Groeschel as a spiritual director and retreat master is traceable in no small measure to the friar's gift for storytelling and his keen sense of finding the lighter side of things amid the seriousness of life.

A key moment of vocational discernment for the Capuchin friar came in 1987. Along with eight other confreres in the Capuchin Order, Groeschel cofounded the Community of Franciscan Friars of the Renewal (CFR) under the patronage of the cardinal-archbishop of New York, John O'Connor. In the early days of the order, Father Groeschel was the superior and a Council member. Since its inception, the order has experienced remarkable growth, and there is now a combined total of nearly 150 friars and sisters. Not surprisingly, they observe the Capuchin tradition, dedicating themselves to preaching reform and caring for the homeless in such places as New York City; Newark, New Jersey; Fort Worth, Texas; and Albuquerque, New Mexico. Outside the United States, the Community of Franciscan Friars of the Renewal has a presence in Ireland, England, Honduras, and Nicaragua.

In a career that has been at least partly academic, Groeschel has taught at Fordham University and Iona College, both New York institutions. Similarly, he has had an association with the Immaculate Conception Seminary in Lloyd Harbor, New York. He has also been a longtime faculty member at St. Joseph's Seminary in Yonkers, New York, and his most recent affiliation has been with the Institute for Psychological Sciences in Arlington, Virginia.

Groeschel's writing and publishing have been voluminous. He has authored more than 45 books, some of which have been translated into other languages. Many of his book titles are devotional in character, but not all reflect this orientation. There is *Spiritual Passages* (1984), a work that examines the rich interplay between psychological makeup and spiritual development, and *Courage to Be Chaste* (1985), a volume that takes a look at the virtue required to achieve mastery over sexual temptations and urges. In *Reform of the Renewal* (1990), Groeschel considers how calls for renewal in the Church devolve into meaningless rhetoric unless they are accompanied by personal conversion. Over and above the books, Groeschel's wisdom and wit continue to be available every month in a column he writes for *The Priest*, a magazine published by Our Sunday Visitor.

The influence of the New Jersey–born friar is seen also in his appearances on the Eternal Word Television Network and his work as a consultant to worthy Catholic organizations such as the Cardinal Newman Society. Groeschel serves as an advisor to this Virginia-based association, which has as its purpose enhancing the Catholicity of the Church's universities and colleges in the United States. The Cardinal Newman Society turns to Groeschel because his is a respected voice on Catholic issues with many people today. Groeschel's love for the Church is unassailable, and he is admired for many things, not least being his unwillingness to compromise on the hard truths of the Gospel.

In 2004, Groeschel suffered a near-fatal accident as a pedestrian when an automobile struck him in Florida. After a long, arduous convalescence, he was able to resume his work of preaching, writing, and counseling. Since his accident, Father Groeschel has published more than 10 books, including what might be his most impressive work of all, *I Am with You Always* (2010).—Robert J. Batule

BIBLIOGRAPHY AND FURTHER READING: Groeschel, Benedict F. *Courage to Be Chaste*. Mahwah, NJ: Paulist Press, 1985; Groeschel, Benedict F. *The Reform of Renewal*. San Francisco: Ignatius Press, 1990; Groeschel, Benedict F. *Spiritual Passages*. New York: Crossroad, 1984. *See also* CARDINAL NEWMAN SOCIETY; FRANCISCAN TRADITION, THE; O'CONNOR, JOHN CARDINAL; PSYCHOLOGY (DISCIPLINE OF)

GUARDINI, ROMANO (1885–1968) Romano Guardini is perhaps best known in the United States as a theologian, a "precursor of Vatican II" whose visions of the Church and the liturgy influenced both Popes John Paul II and Benedict XVI in spiritual and intellectual ways. Some may also know him as a writer of beautiful, profound devotional works such as *The Lord* or *The Art of Praying*. More specialized students of ecclesiology may know him as a major figure in the European liturgical reform movement that expanded out from Benedictine monasteries and shaped liturgical debate for the entire 20th century.

In Europe, Guardini is acknowledged as an intellectual giant whose works spanned theology, philosophy, art and literature, pedagogy, social criticism, and spiritual formation—for which he received prestigious awards also given to the likes of Albert Schweitzer, Ernst Bloch, and Martin Buber. Especially in Germany and Italy, his homelands, he is studied widely, and his collected works, running to many volumes, are eagerly gathered and published. The Bavarian Catholic Academy offers a Romano Guardini Prize.

By contrast, in North America, with the exception of occasional reprints of a smattering of his devotional and liturgical writings and a brief flurry of publications marking the centennial of his birth in the 1980s, most of Guardini's opus and influence has remained largely in the shadows. Yet things are beginning to turn. English-speaking scholars and the public, hungry to understand the intellectual and theological roots of Benedict XVI, are realizing that Guardini was one of his major inspirations. Their personal paths crossed several times, especially in Berlin and Munich after World War II. In 1965, Father Joseph Ratzinger dedicated his now famous work *What It Means to Be a Christian* to Guardini "with gratitude and admiration." Cardinal Ratzinger's 1999 work *Introduction to the Spirit of the Liturgy* takes direct inspiration from Guardini's 1918 book *The Spirit of the Liturgy*, which helped make Guardini influential. And today Pope Benedict often refers to Guardini in presentations and books.

Additionally, Guardini's influence on such major American Catholic figures as Dorothy Day, Thomas Merton, and Flannery O'Connor is becoming more well known. With the recent American republication of his seminal works *The End of the Modern World* and its more informal and lyrical precursor *Letters from Lake Como*, as well as out-of-print analyses of his work, such as Hans Urs Van Balthasar's *Romano Guardini: Reform at the Source*, audiences are (re)discovering an incisive and original thinker who largely anticipated the critique of modernism in contemporary social thought, developed a clear vision of the struggles of postmodernism, and formulated a methodology for analyzing culture and social institutions employing what he termed the Catholic weltanschauung.

Guardini was born in Verona, Italy, in 1885, but grew up with his family in Mainz, Germany. For the rest of his life, Italy and Germany were his homes, but he tended to see himself as transnational. Initially very uncertain about his future direction at university (writing later that this period of his life was a "sad comedy"), he lost his faith altogether. But then he recovered it and eventually pursued priestly ordination—over his father's objections and despite a discouraging seminary experience at Mainz, which was then rigidly authoritarian and whose faculty often viewed his questioning as insubordinate. He was ordained in 1910.

Guardini's early parish pastoral assignments taught him two important lessons. First, he was better suited for a university career that could include pastoral work as well. But second, while it was critical to reach youths and thus pursue pedagogy as a key to Church vitality, typical youth groups he encountered badly needed reform. They were more about socializing and attending meetings out of customary obligation; prayer was formulaic, and doctrines were discussed as rules to follow. This was all useless, Guardini concluded: without freedom and intellectual substance, the Church would die. He carried this lesson with him later as both a professor to his students and mentor to a Catholic youth group, Quickborn, whose mandate and focus he helped morph from concern mostly with the problems of personal maturity—moral conduct, chaste living, friendship—into a broader, national vehicle for cultural and political study and action for younger Catholics, deeper relations with the Church itself, and an organ for the advancement of democratic thought in the Weimar period. He also directed a related journal. These activities suffered under the Nazis after 1933.

During World War I, Guardini earned his theology degree at the University of Freiburg and afterwards his habilitation at Bonn, with work on St. Bonaventure. In the process, he began the shift in his own intellectual and spiritual wellspring away from the prevalent neoscholasticism toward the Platonic-Augustinian tradition—with its focus on the existential freedom embedded in authentic obedience—that ran through the rest of his later work.

In 1923, though a very new teacher, Guardini found himself appointed to a newly created Chair of the Philosophy of Religion and the Catholic Worldview (Weltanschauung) at the University of Berlin. This chair was meant to open some space in the overwhelmingly Protestant, secularizing, anti-Catholic academic culture of Germany for discussion of the newly invigorated Catholic thought emerging in the aftermath of World War I. For months, he suffered great isolation as a faculty member, but over time he began to attract increasing numbers of students, colleagues, and even townspeople to his lectures interested in the Catholic "return from exile." Guardini held this chair at Berlin until 1939, when the Nazis terminated it.

During World War II, Guardini was under a sort of house arrest at the home of an old friend and spent his time writing. From 1945 to 1948, he held a similarly named chair at the University of Tübingen, then the same chair at Munich until he retired from teaching in 1962. In 1961, he was called to consult with the liturgical preparatory commission for the Second Vatican Council but could not participate for reasons of health. He died in 1968.

Two key aspects of Guardini's critical social vision may be highlighted here. The first is his definition and application of the concept of a Catholic worldview or weltanschauung. Guardini stood against the relativizing historicism and sociologism of Weber, Dilthey, Troeltsch, and Jaspers. He defined his task not as comparatively studying the social conditions shaping the Catholic worldview, but rather as *encountering* man and society employing an ever more developed Catholic sensibility: to offer interpretations of concrete, living ideas, people, cultural products, events, and social trends with a Catholic gaze grounded in revelation and Catholic doctrine, seen as sources of freedom and truth. He used his academic position to unpack for audiences what it means to think like a Catholic about aspects of the world, giving them the intellectual and spiritual tools to better encounter the world themselves. Thus, for example, over his lifetime he taught about and produced detailed studies of poets and writers seen as living companions along life's path, such as Dostoevsky, Rilke, and Dante; of philosophers and theologians like Pascal, Kierkegaard, St. Augustine, and Plato; of the fundamentals of Christian life, including the Bible, Jesus, the nature of faith and grace, the liturgy, prayer, and saints; and about social order and change—the collapse of medieval society and the rise of modernism, the charm of ancient cathedrals and places, the role of technology in human consciousness, the tragic consequences of atheism, the loneliness of man in a disenchanted world, and the relationship among faith, the Church, and society.

Methodologically, Guardini's encounter with the world works by creating an open space to allow for an object of study to be perceived in its totality, in its inner workings. Guardini's gaze is not that of a Cartesian or Kantian abstract mind, imposing categories on the world and seeking general theories or models, but rather of one experiencing the constant tension between the inner nature of an object and the tendency of the observer to overpower it by imposing an understanding. The Catholic weltanschauung seeks to draw out the concrete, living reality of what is studied, in a manner analogous to seeking the ultimate truth of Christianity in Christ Himself, the full person, not by formulating a set of abstract ethical principles. Its rigor is similar to that demanded by Buber's I-Thou dyad or Scheler's phenomenology: If one can restrain one's egoistic impulses, a door is opened to perceive reality deeply.

The second aspect of Guardini's vision is his analysis of man's autonomy, the collapse of modernism, and the emergence of a new postmodern way of life in which a radical choice for God combats the relativism and meaninglessness of the dominant culture. He carried this out in ways that subverted routine categories. Guardini once quipped, "I am a conservative with my gaze turned forward." In this, he was rejecting the common accusation that Catholicism had to mean nostalgia for throne-and-miter Christendom or loyalty to reactionary political causes. He also bent standard liberalism, writing, "Personally I believe myself to be a democrat—and immediately add: a Catholic democrat who recognizes absolute values and objective authorities as givens."

Guardini took a dim view of much sociology of his day, insofar as it tended toward determinism and downplayed the autonomous consciousness of individuals (not to mention the role of Providence) in social organization. He wrote frequently about all sorts of sociopolitical issues, framing them as questions of value systems and ethics: the culture of Nazism, the Jewish question, Gandhi's movement, patriotism, abortion, revolutions, democracy, pluralism and freedom, the nature of power, and the death penalty—just to give a few examples. All these topics were broached under a canopy of awareness that man's relationship to nature and himself was changing. Whereas once nature was a given—a fact of life, evidence of God's work—in the industrial era, nature had become an object of manipulation, and reason's goal was less to seek God than to increase scientific, rational control over as much of nature—both in the world and within man himself—as possible. This encouraged man to see himself as the author of his own experience, needing God less and less as reason and faith are split apart and the latter's value questioned. Twentieth-century totalitarianisms are testimonies to the end points of such a development.

But also, more personally, man's autonomy is ever more radically threatened by systems of control and a loss of an existential sense of "place" in the cosmos. Though we by nature seek to locate ourselves that way, we are more and more placeless in a world that is just so much data. This situation generates tremendous anxiety: the times are inherently tragic and sad, Guardini thought. The truly human, faith-inspired response to it all is a kind of radical search for God once again: to seek our real place in the created cosmos, but on terms that respect our new knowledge of that cosmos.

As modernism's failures—such as Nazism, the collapse of delusional visions of progress, the rape of the world—become more evident, economic and cultural systems in the uncertain postmodern world mass-produce ever more powerful illusions of personal control and uniqueness. (Think of our McDonaldized social systems, objects, and environments, sold as giving us each what we want, our way.) In this situation, we face a test: What is a genuine person? Where is God? What is the true nature of freedom? Facing the test can result in what Guardini did not live to see: the leap of faith in hope, the call to be not afraid, the resurgence of personalism, and the radical choice to be Catholic brought forth by John Paul II and now Benedict XVI.

Guardini can be an intriguing role model for Catholic social thinkers today. He struggled his entire life with a society increasingly indifferent to God, drowning in a dangerously distracted popular culture, and beset by totalitarian impulses. In response, he sought to create conditions for reflectivity and authentic piety by offering revelation, the Mass, and reason. His effort to renew the liturgy by integrating ancient beauty and meaning with contemporary relevance and language strikes a remarkably current chord, since he neither romanticized the hierarchical clericalist church in which he was formed nor advocated the often heterodox reforms that banalized collective prayer.

Throughout his life, Guardini maintained a just balance between the horizontal and vertical, the earthly and sacred dimensions of life—something the contemporary Catholic renewal is working to repair. Further, for much of his career, he struggled with German academia: initially because of its Protestant-inspired, overtly anti-Catholic secularization and positivism, and later because his Catholicism threatened the Nazi regime. And because his scholarship was essentially interdisciplinary, Guardini fit only awkwardly into the highly specialized departmental culture whose walls secured academic identities and bases of power. Today's Catholic social scientists, facing not so dissimilar conditions on their campuses, could have much to learn from Guardini's at times melancholy, but glorious, witness.—Stephen R. Sharkey

BIBLIOGRAPHY AND FURTHER READING: Guardini, Romano. *The End of the Modern World and Power and Responsibility.* Wilmington, DE: ISI Books, 1998 (originally published in German in 1951); Guardini, Romano. *Letters from Lake Como: Explorations in Technology and the Human Race.* Grand Rapids, MI: Eerdmans, 1994 (originally published in German in 1923); Guardini, Romano. *Opera Omnia VI: Scritti Politici.* Brescia: Morcelliana, 2005; Krieg, Robert, CSC. *Romano Guardini: A Precursor of Vatican II.* Notre Dame, IN: University of Notre Dame Press, 1997; Krieg, Robert, CSC (ed.). *Romano Guardini: Proclaiming the Sacred in a Modern World.* Chicago: Archdiocese of Chicago Liturgy Training Publications, 1995; Reber, Joachim. *Incontro con Romano Guardini*. Lugano: EUPress, 2001; von Balthasar, Hans Urs. *Romano Guardini: Reform from the Source*. San Francisco: Ignatius Press, 2010 (originally published in German in 1970, revised in 1995). *See also* MODERNISM AND NEO-MODERNISM; POPE BENEDICT XVI; POPE JOHN PAUL II; POSITIVISM; SECULARIZATION; SOCIOLOGY OF KNOWLEDGE: A CATHOLIC CRITIQUE

· H ·

HEGEL, GEORG WILHELM FRIEDRICH (1770–1831)   Georg Hegel was born in Stuttgart on August 27, 1770, the eldest of three children; his father was a financial officer in the government of the state of Würtemberg. After graduating from the Stuttgart Latin School at age 18, Hegel enrolled in the University of Tübingen, where Friedrich Schelling and Johann Schiller were among his fellow students. There he studied theology, classical languages, and literature, graduating in 1793. It was while Hegel was at Tübingen that he developed an abiding love for the culture and literature of ancient Greece and imbibed the ideas and ideals of the Romanticism that was then dominating the intellectual climate of opinion. It was his infatuation with Romanticism that helps explain the enthusiasm he showed for the French Revolution. Hegel's theological studies at Tübingen had the ironic effect of leading him away from orthodox Christian belief, as he appropriated the views associated with the Higher Criticism movement, signing on to the distorted interpretations it gave to Sacred Scripture and to Christianity in general. At this time, he wrote a life of Jesus (later destroyed by him), which supported the specious distinction between the historical Jesus and the Jesus of faith, according to which the historical Jesus, as presented in the Gospels, was to be regarded in the main as a mythical fabrication.

After graduating from Tübingen, Hegel for a time acted as a tutor in that city, and later in Bern and Frankfurt, and then, in 1805, he became a professor at the University of Jena. It was while at Jena that he wrote his first major work, *The Phenomenology of Spirit*, completing it, so the story goes, on October 13, 1807, the day Napoleon's troops captured the city. Having fled from Jena, Hegel was for a short time a newspaper editor in Bamberg. From 1808 to 1816, he was headmaster of the gymnasium in Nuremberg. It was during his time at Nuremberg that Hegel, now age 41, married the 20-year-old Maria von Tucher.

During this period, Hegel wrote the two-volume *Science of Logic*, which he considered to be his most important work and which earned him an appointment to the chair of philosophy at the University of Heidelberg in 1816. The title of this work is somewhat deceptive, for it is not, as one might expect, a disquisition on formal logic; rather, it is an exposition of the fundamental tenets of his general philosophy. In 1817, at the University of Heidelberg, he published his *Encyclopedia of Philosophy*. Because of that work, he was offered in 1818 the prestigious position of the chair of philosophy at the University of Berlin, where he would become the most famous philosopher in Germany; as one historian has put it, "From that time [i.e., his appointment at Berlin] to the end of his life he ruled the philosophical world."

It was during his tenure at Berlin that Hegel published *The Philosophy of Right* (1821), a work in which he propounds his social and political thought and, specifically, holds up the Prussian monarchy as a model for government, thus indicating how far he had departed from the liberal ideas he had entertained as a youth at Tübingen. Hegel's political thought has been misconstrued by not a few of his commentators, and it certainly would not be right, as philosopher Karl Popper has done, to see him as the precursor of the modern totalitarian state. Hegel died in Berlin on November 14, 1831, a victim of a cholera epidemic that was then plaguing the city. The last of his major works, *The Philosophy of History*, a collection of lectures he gave in Berlin, was published posthumously.

Hegel was the principal figure in a philosophical movement known as German Idealism, which had its originating source in the thought of Immanuel Kant (1724–1804) and among whose other major figures were Johann Fichte (1762–1814) and Friedrich Schelling (1775–1854). It is difficult to give a reliable summary account of Hegel's philosophy, the principal reason for this being the obscure, sometimes positively opaque, quality of his writing style. Hegelian scholar Gustav Mueller has called Hegel the "world's worst stylist," and because of the difficulties posed by his highly problematic texts, Hegel has generated, as another scholar has aptly noted, much controversy over both the meaning of his thought and its philosophic import. Hegel would have benefited from a good editor. Despite the difficulties provided by his texts, which are not to be minimized, it is possible to lay out a reasonably accurate account of the main contours of his thought.

The first thing to be recognized about that thought is its sweeping comprehensiveness. Hegel was an ambitious, magnanimously inclusive thinker, who endeavored to incorporate the whole of reality. Philosophy, for him, was all-encompassing in its scope, not only in terms of what it sought to examine and understand as relating to present-day thought but also in terms of the sympathetic attitude it took toward the entire past history of philosophy. Hegel's philosophical outlook has a pronounced historical aspect to it; in fact, history plays a central role in his thought. Past philosophies are not falsified and discarded but, as amended, are gathered up by and integrated into the grand, ascending progress of human cogitation.

A key notion in Hegel's philosophy is *dialectic,* a term that has its origin in the Greek and whose basic meaning is a discussion. It takes at least two to discuss, and what is often revealed in discussion is a conflict of opinion, a conflict grounded in contradiction. It is the task of the philosopher to engage in an ongoing, laborious dialogue with Being, in all its myriad manifestations, in order to discover its essential dialectical—which is to say, its two-sided—quality. He comes to see that every idea has its contradictory, but neither of the terms of the contradiction cancels out its opposite; the two somehow coexist, in something like a perpetual and seemingly productive tension. "All Being," Hegel writes, "is a dialectical unity of opposites." By the untiring exercise of his freedom, by which he is uniquely identified, the philosopher learns to rise above mere reason, which is not dialectical, and to adopt a comprehensive view of things, which allows him to embrace contradictories, and by doing so to arrive at a kind of philosophic resolution. Hegel is rightly identified as an idealist philosopher, for ideas—his ideas—serve as the controlling engine of his system. To be sure, the philosopher engages dialectically with the objective order of things, but he always does so on his own terms, which means that, in the final analysis, it is the mind of the philosopher that sets the parameters by which reality is to be properly identified and assessed.

Hegel has been, and remains, one of the most influential philosophers of modern times, and his influence has been, for the most part, predominantly detrimental. One has only to recall the impact his thought had on Karl Marx and Ludwig Feuerbach. This is not to say, however, that there are not to be found in his philosophy some good, even brilliant, ideas. But taking his philosophy as a whole, as a system, it cannot be regarded as a reliable road to truth.

Hegel is sometimes identified as a pantheist, which, given the common understanding of pantheism, does not seem to be defensible. In any event, in the *Encyclopedia of Philosophy,* he explicitly states that his philosophy is *not* pantheistic. He also explicitly states that neither is his philosophy theistic; he rejects theism because it "personifies the Absolute, instead of thinking of it as ground of the absolute value of the person." One must be very cautious of Hegel's language. He uses the term *God* throughout his works, but the referent is always, as Blaise Pascal would have been very quick to notice, the "God of the philosophers," never the God of Abraham, Isaac, and Jacob. For Hegel, God is "the pure dialectical essence of all Being which objectifies itself in its own otherness . . . [and] maintains its identity in and through its non-absolute and finite self-manifestations." In another place, he writes: "From the concrete actuality of the finite ethical sphere emerges the idea of God or the Absolute." God—the *idea* of God—is the product of human societal circumstances. Hegel regards Christianity as the "absolute religion," but the Christianity he proposes for this signal honor is his own brainchild and has nothing at all to do with Christianity itself.—D. Q. McInerny

BIBLIOGRAPHY AND FURTHER READING: Desmond, William. *Art and the Absolute: A Study of Hegel's Aesthetics.* Albany: State University of New York Press, 1986; Gadamer, Hans-Georg. *Hegel's Dialectic.* New Haven, CT: Yale University Press, 1976; Kaufmann, Walter Arnold. *Hegel: A Reinterpretation.* New York: Doubleday, 1966; Miklowitz, Paul S. *Metaphysics to Metafictions: Hegel, Nietzsche and the End of Philosophy.* Albany: State University of New York Press, 1998; Mueller, Gustav Emil. "Georg Wilhelm Friedrich Hegel." In Georg Wilhelm Friedrich Hegel, *Encyclopedia of Philosophy,* translated by Gustav Emil Mueller, 8–53. New York: Philosophical Library, 1959; Norman, Richard. *Hegel's Phenomenology: A Philosophical Introduction.* London: Ashgate, 1991; Solomon, Robert. *In the Spirit of Hegel.* New York: Oxford University Press, 1985; Taylor, Charles. *Hegel.* Cambridge: Cambridge University Press, 1979. *See also* FEUERBACH, LUDWIG ANDREAS; MARXISM; PHILOSOPHY, DISCIPLINE OF

HEIDEGGER, MARTIN (1889–1976) Martin Heidegger was one of the most influential philosophers of the 20th century; his thought contributed to the development of existentialism, hermeneutics, phenomenology, political theory, psychology, and theology. He is known particularly for *Being and Time,* in which he developed his critique of traditional metaphysics that was influential for postmodern theorists (especially Jacques Derrida, Michael Foucault, and Jean-François Lyotard). He is viewed as a controversial figure due to his involvement with the Nazi Party and his affair with his student, political philosopher Hannah Arendt.

Heidegger's thought centered on ontology in *Being and Time*. He attempted to investigate being (*Sein*) by developing a phenomenological analysis of human existence (*Dasein*). He was critical of the entire tradition of Western philosophy (including Thomism) because he believed that philosophers continually subvert the question of being and that this has resulted in nihilism in modern thought. In *Being and Time*, he sought to rethink, or think for the first time (at least since the Pre-Socratics), the splendor of the appearance of beings.

Heidegger was born to a devout Catholic family in Messkirch, a small city in southern Germany, on September 26, 1889. His father, Friedrich, was a sexton in the Church of St. Martin, after which he named his son. The parish no doubt was central to his family life. The family home is described as "a small but impeccably neat masonry house not more than thirty yards across the courtyard" from the church. As a young adult, Heidegger studied at a Jesuit gymnasium in Freiburg. At 17, he was introduced to Pope Leo XIII's 1879 encyclical *Aeterni Patris* and to scholastic philosophy. An important text for him during this period was Franz Brentano's book on being in Aristotle's thought, *On the Manifold Meaning of Being According to Aristotle*, written in 1862 when Brentano was 22 years old, living in a Dominican house, and contemplating seminary. The book had the effect of drawing Heidegger to Aristotelian philosophy and to the phenomenology that developed out of Brentano's thought, particularly that of Edmund Husserl. This early exposure to Aristotelian metaphysics and phenomenology would shape his adult life.

Heidegger became a Jesuit novice for a brief period, but was discharged for "health reasons." He left the seminary in 1911 to study theology at Freiburg University, where he read broadly in philosophy, paying particular attention to neoscholasticism, neo-Kantianism, and phenomenology. In 1913, he completed his dissertation, *Doctrine of Judgment in Psychologism*, which drew from Husserl's *Logical Investigations* and was written under the direction of a neo-Kantian philosopher, Heinrich Rickert. Psychologism was the belief associated with neo-Kantianism that held that all philosophical inquiry could be reduced to empirical psychology. Husserl's work rejected psychologism, arguing that it conflated logical necessity and psychological contingency.

Heidegger's habilitation thesis, which he completed in 1915, was titled *Duns Scotus's Doctrine of Categories and Meaning*. It illustrates that during this period he sought to "think" the questions of medieval philosophy—to develop an authentic philosophical critique of the history of philosophical problems that was autonomous of tradition and questioning of its foundational assumptions (he would call this attitude the *problemsgeschite*). The origins of the attitude can be found in Husserl's approach to philosophy, which he described as early as 1911 in his essay, "Philosophy as a Strict Science," and many years later in his last book, *The Crisis of the European Sciences*. Heidegger would cite Husserl with approval when he concluded that "the stimulus for investigation must start, not with the philosophies, but with issue and problems." (This is an idea that was influential at the time, perhaps through the work of Carl Braig, a philosopher who influenced Husserl's conception of philosophy.) What concerned Heidegger in this work were problems of logic and language and their relationship to reality. His approach was to question the foundational assumptions of Scotus's thought as it approached these issues. Of significance is his awareness of the interrelationship among philosophical problems and the presumptions of the philosophical systems that inform them—that any particular philosophical problem belongs to a horizon of presumptions and questions. He would later call this the "hermeneutic situation." His task was to understand the difference between the modern and medieval hermeneutic situations.

In 1916, Heidegger joined the Freiburg faculty and thereby became a colleague of Husserl. He married Thea Elfride Petri the following year. In 1918, he was called to military service, serving for only 10 months. When he returned to Freiburg in January 1919, he announced his rejection of the "system of Catholicism." Soon afterward, he was appointed as Husserl's assistant and began lecturing on phenomenology and Aristotle. Although he continued to highly regard Husserl's *Logical Investigations*, Heidegger did not accept Husserl's turn to transcendental phenomenology. He soon began a radical reinterpretation of Husserl's phenomenology that would eventually lead to his original work in *Being and Time*.

The most fruitful period of his career was in the 1920s, while he was a professor at Marburg University. In 1927, he published *Being and Time*, which earned Heidegger a full professorship at Marburg. A year later, Heidegger was awarded the chairmanship of the Department of Philosophy at Freiburg University. During the next few years, he published *What Is Metaphysics?* and *Kant and the Problem of Metaphysics*. These works illustrate that Heidegger had moved from the Husserlian method to his own original approach to phenomenological ontology.

Following his time at Marburg, Heidegger's life became controversial. He became a rector of the University of Freiburg while the position was politically sensitive and under Nazi scrutiny. And while he held this post, he produced a number of addresses that were supportive of the Nazi cause. His work on the poetry of Hördering is often cited as indicative of his support for the Nazi view of Germany. His thought is also said to have become less systematic. In the years between the end of the war and his death in the 1970s, he became more reclusive, although he still continued to publish a number of works, including his lecture "What Is Philosophy?" He also is said to have become romantically involved with his student, Arendt, who would become a distinguished political philosopher. Heidegger was subject to "de-nazification" during the postwar period. Eventually he was allowed to resume teaching at Freiburg. He died on May 26, 1976, and is buried in Messkirch.

At the core of Heidegger's thought is his conception of the distinction between beings and Being. The distinction itself is one that would have been familiar to Catholic philosophers of his time. As Etienne Gilson argued, it is a distinction with which St. Thomas Aquinas was well acquainted. It is fundamental to a proper understanding of the belief that God created all things to believe that the act of existing is necessarily mysterious since it is divine and prior to the perception of beings. Gilson believed that the whole history of philosophy could be read as a series of attempts to substitute something other than the mystery of Being for Being itself.

Heidegger agreed with this analysis of philosophy to the extent that he argued that the "thought of Being" is constantly falling into neglect or oblivion (*Seinsvergessenheit*), which is to say that the question of Being gets reduced to a horizon of questions about a region or area of beings. Questioning Being, as such, is avoided. Heidegger's critique encompasses Gilson's, however, because he includes Thomistic metaphysics, whether "existentialist" or "essentialist," within the scope of the oblivion of Being. The problem with Thomism for Heidegger is in its analysis of beings: Thomism begins with presumptions about the actuality of things described within the Christian narrative of Creation (this is "onto-theology"). Heidegger believed that genuine philosophy exposes such presumptions and seeks to ask the underlying questions anew, without knowingly assuming metaphysical conclusions.

Being and Time is Heidegger's attempt to work out a phenomenological analysis of the experience of Be-

ing that is free of the metaphysical presumptions of the Christian understanding of Creation. He wants to ask anew the question of the appearance of beings, apart from metaphysical presumptions. To do this, he turns to the phenomenological method that looks to lived-experience. In Heidegger's analysis, what is distinct about the experience of Being is that the experiencer "comports toward" it. He means that persons have a self-conscious awareness of Being about which they must take responsibility. He uses the term *Dasein* to refer to the agent that comports toward Being, and he notes that fundamental to this comporting agent is temporality—it comports toward Being in time.

The reception of Heidegger's thought among Catholics has been mixed. He is rejected by neo-Thomistic philosophers, who tend to view his work as deepening the idealism that is characteristic of modern philosophy since Descartes. It has been more influential with Catholic thinkers who are influenced by recent French philosophy. For example, in *God without Being*, Jean-Luc Marion accepts aspects of Heidegger's critique of being and argues for exploring alternate approaches for theology.

In his 1998 encyclical *Fides et Ratio*, Pope John Paul II called on philosophers "to move from phenomenon to foundation," through a movement from immanent to transcendent (*FR # 82*), teaching that philosophy must be of a "genuinely metaphysical range" (*FR # 83*). This would seem to be contrary to Heidegger's assertion that philosophers cannot avoid the subversion of Being.—Kevin P. Lee

BIBLIOGRAPHY AND FURTHER READING: Caputo, John D. *Heidegger and Aquinas.* New York: Fordham University Press, 1982; Heidegger, Martin. *Being and Time.* Translated by John Macquarrie and Edward Robinson. New York: Harper & Row, 1962; Heidegger, Martin. *Introduction to Philosophy.* New Haven, CT: Yale University Press, 2000; Heidegger, Martin. *The Phenomenological Interpretation of Kant's Critique of Pure Reason.* Bloomington: University of Indiana Press, 1997; Heidegger, Martin. *What Is Called Thinking?* New York: HarperCollins, 1976; Kerr, Fergus. *After Aquinas.* Oxford, England: Blackwell, 2002; Safranski, Rudiger. *Martin Heidegger: Between Good and Evil.* Translated by Ewald Osers. Cambridge, MA: Harvard University Press, 1999; Yöur-Breuhl, Elizabeth. *For the Love of the World.* New Haven, CT: Yale University Press, 2004. *See also* ARENDT, HANNAH; ARISTOTLE; GILSON, ÉTIENNE HENRY; PHENOMENOLOGY; POSTMODERNISM; THOMISM/NEO-THOMISM

HIPPOCRATIC OATH Medicine is perhaps the most respected of professions. Not only are knowledge and competence required, as they are of other professions, but something more is demanded of a physician. It is embodied in an ethical imperative usually expressed in an oath taken upon entry (usually at graduation) into the field of medicine. The oath, the prototype being the Hippocratic Oath, is a covenant between the physician and the patient, as well as society, to treat the sick in a competent and ethical manner.

Greek medicine was a combination of science and art. It was *techne*, or knowledge, realized when put into practice. But this techne had to be combined with *phronesis*, or practical wisdom, which was learned over time by being an apprentice to an experienced physician. Another element required by the Greeks was virtue, or probity of life. The Hippocratic Oath sums up the essentials of what the Greeks thought should be reflected by a good physician and also what should be good medicine.

While the Oath invokes pagan gods of healing (it was composed 400 years before Christ), it is essentially Christian in its philosophy and ethics. It is a virtue-based, deontological moral code in conformity with Aristotelian and Thomistic natural law.

There are various translations of the Oath. A classical version reads as follows: "I swear . . . [to Greek gods] that I will fulfill according to my ability and judgment this oath and this covenant: To hold him who has taught me this art as equal to my parents and to live my life in partnership with him . . . ; to give a share of precepts and oral instruction and all the other learning to my sons and to the sons of him who has instructed me to pupils who have signed the covenant and have taken an oath according to the medical law, but no one else. I will apply dietetic measures for the benefit of the sick according to my ability and judgment; I will keep them from harm and injustice. I will neither give a deadly drug to anybody who asked for it, nor will I make a suggestion to this effect. Similarly I will not give to a woman an abortive remedy. In purity and holiness I will guard my life and my art. I will not use the knife . . . but will withdraw in favor of such men as are engaged in this work. . . . I will come for the benefit of the sick, remaining free of all intentional injustice, of all mischief and in particular of sexual relations with both female and male persons, be they free or slave. What I may see or hear in the course of the treatment or even outside of the treatment in regard to the life of men, which on no account one must spread abroad, I will keep to myself,

holding such things shameful to be spoken about. If I fulfill this oath . . . , may it be granted to me to enjoy life and art, being honored with fame among all men for all time to come; if I transgress it and swear falsely, may the opposite of all this be my lot."

The Oath reflects covenants of the physician with the gods, his teacher, his students, and his patients. The first section is the covenant between the doctor and the transcendent powers that govern human destiny. The second relates to teachers and to the importance of passing this tradition to future generations of physicians. Sections 3, 4, and 5 discuss medical treatments. The Greeks believed that bodily homeostatic balance was essential to health and that herbal and dietetic regimes were means to attain this equilibrium. These paragraphs proscribed abortion and euthanasia. Sections 6 and 7 address physician probity; they require confidentiality and abstaining from sexual relations with patients' families. The final section mentions the rewards and/ or sanctions for fulfilling or failing to honor this oath.

The genius of the Oath is widely acknowledged. Its insistence, and the profession's acknowledgment, that the physician be competent and virtuous is perhaps the single most important reason that medicine has consistently been the highly regarded profession that it is. But the Oath has been criticized by Steven Miles, among others, for being paternalistic, sexist, and essentially a set of rules of etiquette maintained by a privileged club. It also lacks an articulated imperative for compassion.

This is somewhat surprising, because it was the Greek thinkers, particularly Aristotle, who discussed the meaning of love. Natural love is directed to the acquisition of a good object as perceived by the intellect. Aristotle emphasized two goods and therefore two forms of love: *eros*, or desire for a physical good, and *philia*, or desire for the good of human friendship. Christianity, citing Christ's sacrificial death, elevated a third form of love, *agape*, or altruistic self-giving to another, to a higher level. Agape gained its special significance in the New Testament. Compassion is an aspect of agape and is the emotional response that results in a desire to help a fellow human being who is suffering from an illness or disease.

Greek medicine, as reflected in the Hippocratic Oath, emphasized clinical competence combined with an intellectual ethical imperative of not harming. Margaret Mead has noted that a distinctive feature of the Oath was that it required the separation between curing and killing, and that this prohibition on killing is "a priceless possession." As presented by M. B. Etziony,

Greco-Roman, Chinese, and Hindu medical writers hinted at the concept of compassion, but it was not expressly promoted. Christian medical practitioners, taking their cue directly from Christ, were not only directed to cure but also encouraged to emphasize the humaneness of the doctor–patient relationship. This elevated love to a higher level: agape. More recently, bioethics, with its academic obsession with analytic principles, has discounted Christian medical compassion. It is not surprising, then, that the Oath has often been modified in recent years to eliminate the portions that are inconsistent with cultural realities; it is most common, for instance, for recent medical school graduates to take a version of the Oath that omits the prohibitions on euthanasia and abortion.

From the beginning of recorded history, medicine has been considered the most respected of human professions, the clergy perhaps excepted. This is not surprising given that health is probably our most cherished possession. It should also be noted that all major human cultures have medical oaths and there are remarkable similarities between them.

There are, however, distinct differences between Greek and Roman attitudes about the dignity of the human person compared to those of the Christian. In the mind of the Greek or Roman, the dignity of the person flowed from their Greek or Roman citizenship. If you were a citizen of the state, you had full civil rights; the foreigner and slave had none. For the Christian, one's dignity is a right emanating from his being made in the image and likeness of God. Christ required his disciples to love one another. The Hippocratic Oath required technical competence and adherence to the natural law, but not necessarily charity or compassion.

Christianity has added the dimension of compassion to the physician's ethic. It was not emphasized by the Greeks. But Christ, "having compassion on them" (Matthew 20: 34), was considered a "healer" who admonished his disciples to care for the sick. It would be unfortunate if our technology and bureaucracy were to mitigate the spirit and ethos of the Hippocratic Oath and the Christian component of compassion.—Patrick Guinan

Bibliography and Further Reading: Etziony, M. B. *The Physician's Creed.* Springfield, IL: Charles C Thomas, 1973; Miles, Steven. *The Hippocratic Oath and the Ethics of Medicine.* New York: Oxford University Press, 2004. *See also* BIOETHICS; *DEUS CARITAS EST*; HUMAN DIGNITY

HOBBES, THOMAS (1588–1679) Thomas Hobbes, born in 1588, earned his bachelor's degree at Oxford University. He engaged in careful study of Greek and Latin authors, served as a tutor, and engaged in scholarly pursuits. Although he worked in various fields—philosophy, physics, history, and mathematics—he is best known as a political philosopher, as demonstrated in *De Cive* (1642) and *Leviathan* (1651). Hobbes died in 1679 and was interred at St. John the Baptist Church in Derbyshire, England.

Thomas Hobbes's thought was at the foundation of a revolutionary 17th-century understanding of human nature, the human good, and politics. That thought was revolutionary philosophically, morally, socially, and politically and (of particular interest to Catholics) with regard to the place of the Church in relation to the political order. The new thought soon came to be called "modern," to contrast it both from the medieval Christian understanding and from classical pagan political philosophy (Plato and Aristotle).

Hobbes's revolution took its philosophic bearings from his diagnosis of the harmfulness of earlier moral and political thought. The "Greek and Latin authors" influenced men to favor "tumults" "with the effusion of so much blood . . . that there was never anything so dearly bought, as these western parts have bought the learning of the Greek and Latin tongues."

So Hobbes took his political bearings from understanding the political problem as tumults (wars, especially civil wars) and efforts by the governed to control their rulers (i.e., more wars). While he was thinking in particular of the English Civil War, that particular war revealed to him the political problem everywhere and always. To remedy the political problem so understood, Hobbes's explicit aim was first that his own moral and political teachings should replace the older ones in the universities, which "are the fountains of civil, and moral doctrine." But ultimately he aimed to replace the older ideas in the minds of rulers and subjects as well.

To achieve civil peace, Hobbes reconceived the status of the individual and his relation to the state. Civil peace required each individual's consent both to the existence of society and to obeying the political "sovereign" (Hobbes's term for a ruler who should have all legal power in a state). That required giving every individual a compelling and reliable reason to obey, a reason understandable even to those of limited understanding. Hobbes found that reason in the fear of death and the consequent desire for self-preservation. That desire he considered the strongest passion in most men most of the time and hence the most reliable basis for securing their obedience. If one obeyed, one's life (and the means to life) would be secured by the political sovereign; otherwise, it would not.

Paradoxically, Hobbes acknowledges that this solution to the political problem requires the sovereign to have absolute power over all aspects of individual and social life, but only for the sake of preserving the lives of individuals. In this sense, Hobbes teaches the necessity of "unlimited government." The idea that political power has no other purpose than to secure each individual's life makes Hobbes the founder of modern individualism. Of particular interest to Catholics, Hobbes's state is forbidden to have a concern either for the souls of its citizens or for their virtue beyond what is required for civil peace. In this sense, Hobbes teaches the necessity of "limited government." The result is a paradox and perhaps a contradiction: legally unlimited government for the sake of government limited in its purpose.

So, to the extent that the modern political world supposes the individual, his rights, and his consent to be the origin and foundation of society, justice, and political life, and that securing those rights by securing civil peace is the sole purpose of government, Hobbes is modernity's founding political philosopher. This modernity deemphasizes (compared to both classical and Christian antecedents) bringing political life into line with justice understood as transcending the boundaries of the political order. Appeals to *that* kind of justice only cause more tumults. The truncated remains of justice, for Hobbes, are only the "command of the sovereign." And "law" is only the command of the sovereign ("legal positivism"). Hobbes does not regard as law what Catholics call "divine law" (or "natural law," understood as rational creatures' participation in the divine law).

Hobbes's political and moral teaching goes together with his philosophical "materialism." Materialism is that way of thinking in which everything in the universe (i.e., everything that exists) consists in the purposeless motion of matter. So, there is no such thing as Christians would call "spirit" nor a transcendent or eternal goal of human life; there is not even what Aristotle would call "happiness," but only "a perpetual and restless desire of Power after power, that ceaseth only in Death." If the modern world understands man and his life in terms of the purposeless motion of matter, then Hobbes founded the modern way of understanding the world. And to the extent that the modern world finds no purpose to human life beyond its comfortable self-preservation, Hobbes is the founding father of the modern world.

Hobbes's materialism rejects Aristotelian/Thomistic teleology, the idea that all natural beings have natural purposes that determine what is good for those beings. For human beings, that natural purpose was thought to be "happiness," that condition of self-sufficiency in which one has all that one needs and hence desires nothing more. By denying the existence of happiness, no natural purpose remains for human life. There does remain the natural and ceaseless desire for ever more power, but that is not for Hobbes a "purpose" but only a "means to some future apparent good." Although Hobbesian man desires peace for the sake of self-preservation, Hobbes is explicit that there can be no limit to how much power one must have in order to secure peace, because one cannot be certain how much power those who threaten peace and self-preservation might have. Hobbes's thought shows that the price of making political peace the goal of human life is to consume human life in the unlimited pursuit of power for the sake of self-preservation. Whenever one thinks about human life as merely about pursuing power (intellectual, political, economic, or whatever) and mere self-preservation, without reference to the natural end of happiness or of the supernatural end of eternal life, one is thinking within Hobbes's framework.

Both classical and Christian political philosophers taught that human beings are designed to live together (whether the designer was nature, as with Aristotle, or God, as with St. Augustine and St. Thomas Aquinas). In contrast, Hobbes denied this and asserted that men are natural enemies, and hence that competition, rather than mutual dependence or regard, characterizes man's original (i.e., natural) condition. Hobbes calls this natural condition the "state of war." In that state, man's life is "solitary, poor, nasty, brutish and short" because there is no natural authority to protect us from each other. But Hobbes aims to show us how to overcome this awful condition. We can do so, not because God has providentially given us a natural social order and government (he hasn't), but because human reason can show us how to create these by our own effort (consent). Man can remedy what God's providence failed to provide. Hobbes's book *Leviathan* explains what is required to do that. To the extent that modern society, including the family and parental authority, is thought to be merely a human construct, rather than natural, Hobbes's book is the bible of the modern world.

Whether Hobbes's teaching is in any way Christian is disputed. He spends fully half of *Leviathan* "reinterpreting" biblical revelation to try to convince believers that it is compatible with his materialism. It is doubtful, on Hobbes's basis, that there can be a state of being such as Christians have called "heaven." Everything in Hobbes's universe is material, and whatever is not material is not part of the universe. So "god," "spirit," and the human soul are material, not immaterial. And, since everything material is perpetually in the process of coming into being and passing away, these also constantly change. In particular, there is no final resting place or condition, no heaven or hell as Christians have understood those things, but rather dissolution into nothingness. The practical meaning of Hobbes's teaching, therefore, while perhaps not a strict theoretical atheism, implies a practical atheism. His thought neither requires nor implies the existence of a god, of providence, or an eternal and unchanging purpose of human life. It implicitly denies the existence of the biblical God as Catholics (and other Christian traditions) understand him.

Notwithstanding what a Catholic would call Hobbes's atheism, Hobbes is very concerned with religion. Wars involving religion had torn Europe apart in the 16th and 17th centuries. Hobbes's political teaching aims to remedy the problem of civil war, and his remedy crucially involves religion. For the sake of civil peace, he denies that any state can have more than one sovereign, that is, one legal ruler. And there should be no legal limits on the power of that ruler. Hence the notion that the power of government can be limited (by a constitution for example) is rejected by Hobbes.

Of relevance for Catholics, Hobbes denies that the Church can have any sphere of authority that is independent of the state. Since the Roman emperors had recognized the Church as of divine origin (no later than the sixth century), the state had recognized a separation between the Church's sphere of authority and that of political rulers. The Church ruled over its clergy and over spiritual aspects of the laity's lives (e.g., such matters as marriage and family). But Hobbes thought "two sovereigns" over the same territory had been the occasion of tumults, notably the 16th- and 17th-century Wars of Religion. The problem was neither the "Protestant Revolt" against the Church nor political rulers' use of religious division to aggrandize their own power, but rather the Church's independence of political rule. Accordingly, he taught, there can be only one sovereign in every country, and the Church must be absolutely subordinate to that sovereign. Henceforth, the state would acknowledge the Church not as divinely ordained but as existing by the will of the sovereign.

The standard secular histories of political philosophy attribute the idea that human beings have "natural rights" to early modern thought (Hobbes and John Locke [1632–1704]). Though less well remembered, there was a pre-Hobbesian natural rights teaching de-veloped, especially in the 16th century by neoscholastic thinkers such as Bellarmine, Vitoria, and Suarez. But Hobbesian natural rights differ decisively from the Catholic understanding. The latter is an inference from Jesus' teaching that we are to "love our neighbor as ourselves." This means that our duties to others do not stop at the boundaries of our family, tribe, nation, or country. In this context, to say that we have duties to those very different from us can be stated from the point of view that those others have claims that we are obligated to respect. Those claims can be, and were, called natural rights.

Hobbes's very different understanding is that natural rights are based on human psychology. They are desires that are so strong that it is unreasonable to ask anyone to give them up. The foundational natural right is to life. It is a "right," first, because most men most of the time desire to preserve themselves and, second, since there is no gain to any individual in giving up his life, it is unreasonable to expect him to do so. Hobbes's natural rights are constructed from loving our *own* life above all else, combined with the prudential calculation that we have to recognize others as having the same natural right to life so they will live with us in peace.

All other Hobbesian natural rights are derived from the fundamental natural right to life. Our right to property is derived from our need for property in order to preserve ourselves. Similarly, our natural right to liberty exists because we need it to be free from the threat of death from others or the sovereign. So, Hobbes's natural rights are fundamentally self-regarding, in contrast to Christian natural rights, which are fundamentally other-regarding.

The difference in how the two understandings work out in practice can be illustrated as follows. For Hobbes, there is a natural punishment for failure to respect others' natural rights: These others will resist such oppression and try to kill you. This argument works for those capable of making trouble for you, but it does not work for those who cannot harm you (e.g., the unborn, the aged, etc.). Hobbes's reason for these latter having natural rights thus lacks a sanction. Hence, Hobbes's teaching opens the door to abortion and the culture of death generally, even within a political order apparently based on natural rights (as in the Declaration of Independence). In contrast, the Catholic understanding is that our duty to love others extends even to those who cannot harm us if we fail to recognize their rights. It therefore closes the door to abortion and the culture of death.—Gary D. Glenn

BIBLIOGRAPHY AND FURTHER READING: Holloway, Carson. *The Way of Life: John Paul II and the Challenge of Liberal Modernity.* Waco, TX: Baylor University Press, 2008; Mintz, Samuel I. *The Hunting of Leviathan.* Cambridge: Cambridge University Press, 1969; Oakeshott, Michael, ed. *Leviathan, or The Matter, Forme and Power of a Commonwealth Ecclesiastical and Civil.* Oxford, England: Blackwell, 1946; Sabine, George. *A History of Political Theory.* New York: Holt, Rinehart & Winston, 1966; Strauss, Leo. "Thomas Hobbes." In *Natural Right and History*, 166–201. Chicago: University of Chicago Press, 1953. *See also* LOCKE, JOHN; POLITICAL PHILOSOPHY

HOMICIDE   Homicide represents the "extreme form of violence." There is a lack of consensus as to the nature of homicide. Popularly, it refers to the killing of one person by another. Traditionally, criminal law divides homicide into two crimes: *murder* (the unlawful killing of another human being with malice aforethought) and *manslaughter* (the unlawful killing of another human being *without* malice aforethought). The Model Penal Code adds a category of *negligent homicide*. At the same time, some acts of homicide may be justifiable (e.g., self-defense) or excused (e.g., insanity). Some forms of killing, such as abortion or assisted suicide, are treated in varying ways, depending in large part on the degree of social disapproval of such behavior.

Explanations of violence share a common characteristic, according to criminologist Richard Rosenfeld: They "are based less on the inherent qualities of the behavior than on the social and moral status of victim and perpetrator." For example, the behavior of criminals is more likely explained as the acts of those who have moral or social defects. In contrast, violence by persons considered "morally upright," such as law enforcement agents, medical doctors, or soldiers, are more readily explained in terms of a legal and moral obligation. Furthermore, discussions of abortion and euthanasia similarly can reflect more about the status of the unborn or those disabled or in extreme pain than on the behavior itself. Such explanations also suggest differences regarding the redeemability of persons.

Homicide is pervasive. According to a report of the World Health Organization in 2002 entitled *Violence and Health*, homicide presents a serious health problem: "Each year, more than 1 million people lose their lives as a result of self-inflicted, inter-personal, or collective violence." Additionally, the United States, in spite of a significant declining rate of violent crime since the mid-1990s, maintains a high rate of gun-related lethal violence and also leads the world in homicides committed without guns. Finally, racial oppression and eco-

nomic inequality typically are identified as contributing causes to lethal violence.

Homicide affects the human community, but is not distributed equally among all social groups. Several demographic identifiers—age, gender, race, social class, and neighborhood environment—are especially significant. According to data compiled by the U.S. Department of Justice and annual National Crime Victimization Surveys, homicide rates for both offenders and victims are higher for young adults than for any other age group. While males are at higher risk than females, younger women, especially racial and ethnic minorities, are more likely to be killed or assaulted by an intimate other in their lives than are men. Also, women who are young, poor, and foreign born are more likely to be victims of femicide (murder of women). Likewise, African Americans and Hispanics with lower social and economic status are significantly overrepresented as both offenders and victims of homicide in comparison to non-Hispanic whites. Finally, according to ecology-based research, the cohesiveness of a neighborhood community, based on mutual trust and responsibility, contributes to less violence. In summary, homicide especially targets those persons and groups who are deprived of adequate social, economic, and political resources or whose rights as persons are not clearly defined.

Catholic social teaching develops themes that provide a deeper understanding of homicide as the extreme form of violence. The principle of human life and dignity conveys that every person, as a child of God, has inherent worth that is not earned by material achievement. In *Evangelium Vitae*, Pope John Paul II emphasizes that all persons possess dignity "without any distinction of race, nationality, religion, political opinion or social class" (# 18). As a result, there is no person or group who is or should be socially classified as "unredeemable." In this context, the Church does not support capital punishment because it diminishes respect for life and deprives a person of the opportunity to reform himself or herself.

In *Evangelium Vitae*, John Paul describes the "equal personal dignity" of every human person and notes that we all have responsibility for others. We are indeed our brothers' and sisters' keepers (# 8)! Catholic social teaching, therefore, emphasizes the social nature of the human person. In this regard, Pope Benedict XVI, in *Caritas in Veritate*, describes charity grounded in truth as the "principal driving force" that underlies personal development and collective unity (# 1).

The absence of respect for one another contributes to a "lack of solidarity" with society's weakest or more vulnerable members and to violence in its extreme form. For example, genocide and femicide especially victimize those who are socially, economically, and politically most vulnerable.

The principle of respect for dignity and life also extends to controversy over embryonic stem cell research. Catholic moral teaching rejects research that involves the killing of human persons in the embryonic stage. Euthanasia, too, is condemned as a grave violation of the natural law, "since it is the deliberate and morally unacceptable killing of a human person" (*EV* # 65). Furthermore, in its 2000 report *Respect for the Dignity of the Dying*, the Pontifical Academy of Life emphasizes that the autonomy of every person obligates one to respect and be responsible for the gift of life both in self and others. Therefore, the act of willful self-destruction contradicts the responsibility to preserve one's own life.

While not all forms of killing are socially disapproved, the *Catechism of the Catholic Church* states: "The legitimate defense of persons and societies is not an exception to the prohibition against the murder of the innocent that constitutes intentional killing" (# 2263). St. Thomas Aquinas in his *Summa Theologica* states that in legitimate defenses, the act of self-defense is intended to preserve the life of self or another, while the killing of the aggressor or perpetrator is not intended directly (II–II, 64, 7).

Catholic social teaching related to homicide presents an apparent paradox. In a position statement on the American criminal justice system entitled *Responsibility, Rehabilitation, and Restoration*, the U.S. Conference of Catholic Bishops (USCCB) echoes policy trends and scholarship in society that emphasizes the significance of the protection of society and offender accountability as goals of criminal sentencing. The USCCB, however, also maintains that all persons, offender and victim alike, are redeemable based on the inherent worth of the gift of God-given life. Within this context, John Paul II, at a papal Mass in 1999, referring to *Evangelium Vitae* # 27, urged all followers of Christ to respect the dignity of human life "even in the case of someone who has done great evil." Also, *Gaudium et Spes* states that behavior related to "any type of murder, genocide, euthanasia, or willful self-destruction" opposes life and human dignity (# 27). But although this seems paradoxical, those who do such acts do not relinquish their dignity as persons (*GS* # 28).

Homicide is more meaningfully understood within the context of Catholic social teaching. In this vein, the effectiveness of public social policy should be evaluated based on its ability to foster the protection of the poor and vulnerable in society and to respect the redeemability of all persons.—Alfred R. D'Anca

BIBLIOGRAPHY AND FURTHER READING: Rosenfeld, Richard. "Homicide and Serious Assaults." In *The Oxford Handbook of Crime and Public Policy*, edited by Michael Tonry, 25–50. New York: Oxford University Press, 2009; Sampson, Robert J., and Stephen W. Raudenbush. "Neighborhoods and Violent Crime: A Multilevel Study of Collective Efficacy." *Science* 277 (1997): 918–924. *See also* ABORTION; DEATH PENALTY; EUTHANASIA; HUMAN LIFE (DIGNITY AND SANCTITY OF); POPE JOHN PAUL II; *REDEMPTOR HOMINIS*

HOSPITAL   The hospital, as we know it, is a Catholic idea and institution. A hospital can be defined as a facility where inpatient medical and nursing care is delivered. It was not present in the Hippocratic and Galenic medical cultures. Its precise beginning can be traced to AD 550 and the Samson Xenon (Greek for hospital) in Byzantium. The motivating spirit for the hospital's origin came from Christ himself. The unique aspect of the hospital was the concept of Christian compassion, not previously seen in health care.

Sickness was particularly difficult for patients in the ancient world. Because of ignorance of the pathophysiology of disease, therapy focused on the balancing of the four humors (choleric, melancholic, phlegmatic, and sanguine) by means of dietetics, herbs, purging, and bloodletting. Physicians made house calls, and patients were cared for at home. The majority of patients, the poor and slaves, were nursed by their families, if at all.

The ethos of Christianity was profoundly different from those of other prevailing Mediterranean cultures. Christ performed miracles to manifest his divinity. Thirty-four of Christ's 44 miracles were of a healing nature. The Gospels repeatedly refer to Christ as being compassionate ("He had compassion on them," Matthew 20: 30). Indeed, compassion is a recurring characteristic attributed to Christ. Concern for the poor and the ill was passed on by Christ's mandate to his disciples. In the early Church, the deacons were specifically tasked to care for the sick in the Christian community.

As the Church emerged from persecution, religious houses and monasteries were founded, and part of their mission was to care for travelers, the poor, and the sick. Compared to the chaotic and barbaric West, the Eastern Roman Empire in Byzantium was administratively supportive of monastic activities. In 550, the Samson Xenon was founded to provide both inpatient medical care as well as food and nursing. This was the first formal hospital. The concept spread, eventually to the Moslem world, as well as to the more pacified areas of western Europe.

Throughout the Middle Ages and early Renaissance, hospitals were Church-run by males, especially the military hospital orders emanating from the Crusades. As the Italian city-states gained wealth and power, hospital management was assumed by wealthy donors and the city-states. The Protestant Reformation was a major disruption in the care of the sick. The monasteries were confiscated for their wealth, leaving no agency to care for the poor, the orphaned, and the sick. In England alone, five hundred hospitals were closed during the Reformation. On the other hand, the Church continued to promote good nursing and hospital care. St. Vincent de Paul and St. Louise de Marillac were reforming nursing and health care in 1633, two centuries before Florence Nightingale.

The critical difference was the shift from a Church-based mandate of compassion in addition to medical and nursing care to state-sponsored welfare. For the former, the patient's soul as well as his body was important. This concept of compassion was the principal goal in Church-sponsored hospitals but not in municipal or Crown-run institutions. These became the "poorhouses" where the orphans, poor, and sick were warehoused.

The first hospital in the New World was established by Hernán Cortés in Mexico City in 1524. The first Catholic hospital was Charity Hospital, opened in French New Orleans in 1782, and the first in the United States was Mother Elizabeth Seton's Baltimore Infirmary, opened in 1823. The 300 years between 1524 and 1823 saw little medical progress because of the unchanged Galenic therapeutics and the lack of compassion in nursing care. This gradually advanced in the United States with the influx of the various orders of religious sisters, mostly from Europe, often at the behest of the local American bishop. Between 1850 and 1950, 560 Catholic hospitals were opened by orders of female religious.

These sisters were religious first and their years of spiritual formation emphasized Christ's love for the poor and the sick, which they carried over into their nursing care. Many of these women came to the United States to specifically care for impoverished and persecuted immigrant poor, orphans, and the sick. The difference between the civic "almshouse" mentality of institutionalizing the poor and sick and the compassionate Christian care of the sisters was stark and, to this day, little appreciated.

In 1915, the Catholic Hospital Association of the United States and Canada (CHA) was formed. The CHA was initially overwhelmingly composed of hospitals run by religious sisters guided by the Catholic values of compassion and love for the sick patients. Circumstances have changed, however, especially in the past 50 years since the Second Vatican Council. There has been a shift in the focus of the ministering sisters from living in community and wearing distinctive religious garb to living a lay life and conforming to the spirit of the world. The ministering esprit de corps has diminished. Lay administrators are now assuming control of Catholic hospitals. By 1981, a majority of Catholic hospital chief executive officers were lay. These administrators, usually men, never received the formation in self-sacrifice that the nuns did.

Medicine has changed, as well, with government and third-party involvement. Combinations of hospitals, now called "systems," have come together to enhance efficiency and income. Unfortunately, there has been a simultaneous diminution of the pastoral aspects of Catholic health care, which has eroded traditional Christian compassion and charity. Efforts should be made to revitalize the evangelizing and compassionate original mission of Catholic hospitals.—Patrick Guinan

BIBLIOGRAPHY AND FURTHER READING: Guinan, Patrick. "Christ the Physician." *Linacre Quarterly* 68 (2001): 315–318; Miller, Timothy. *The Birth of the Hospital in the Byzantine Empire.* Baltimore: Johns Hopkins University Press, 1985. *See also* PALLIATIVE CARE; SETON, ST. ELIZABETH ANN BAYLEY; VINCENT DE PAUL, ST.

HUME, DAVID (1711–1776) Regarded by many scholars as the most important philosopher to have written in the English language, David Hume was also an influential historian, economist, and essayist. Often presented as a radical skeptic whose chief importance was his influence on Immanuel Kant, Hume was also a moral conservative and political Tory. While primarily known today as the author of *A Treatise of Human Nature: Being an Attempt to Introduce the Experimental Method of Reasoning into Moral Subjects* (1739–1740), Hume was better known to his contemporaries as an essayist and historian. His writings on economics were an important influence on the work of Adam Smith, and his political works exerted wide influence on the American founding, through such statesmen as Alexander Hamilton and James Wilson.

Hume was born in Edinburgh, Scotland, on May 7, 1711. His father Joseph, who held a modest estate and practiced law, died shortly after Hume's second birthday, leaving his mother Katherine to raise David and his older siblings, John and Katherine. In 1723, at the age of 12, Hume attended Edinburgh University along with his brother. Hume spent nearly three years at the university, reading widely in both ancient and modern philosophy, history, literature, mathematics, and science. Since Hume's patrimony was inadequate to provide for his support, his family encouraged him to study law, but Hume found the pursuit contrary to his temperament. After a brief, unsuccessful attempt at a life of business in Bristol, Hume moved to France in 1734, eventually settling in the small town of La Flèche in Anjou, home to the Jesuit college that had educated René Descartes. Between 1734 and 1737, Hume wrote much of his first great work, *A Treatise of Human Nature*, which he published in three volumes upon his return to England.

Hume's *Treatise* has the avowed intention of extending to moral subjects the method of experimental reasoning applied by Isaac Newton to natural philosophy. Largely on account of this work, Hume is frequently presented as the culmination of the tradition of British empiricism inaugurated by Francis Bacon, as well as the greatest philosopher in a triumvirate that includes John Locke and George Berkeley. In this common account, British empiricism, which attempts to explain all human knowledge in terms of sensory experience, is contrasted with "Continental rationalism," which claims that at least some of the content of our knowledge is derived from the principles of reasoning themselves. Whatever their disagreements, both of these modern philosophic schools are united in their opposition to the classical rationalism of Aristotle and the scholasticism of St. Thomas Aquinas.

Nevertheless, Hume's later works offer a response to the corrosive doubt introduced to moral philosophy by Descartes. They also attempt to ameliorate the political danger posed by the abstract theories espoused by social contract theorists such as Locke. Much of the current academic interest in Hume centers on his *Treatise*, however, in part because its extended theory of ideas suits our contemporary preoccupation with epistemological questions. In his later work, Hume took some care to distance himself from the *Treatise*. His reasons for doing so are a matter of debate, but a careful consideration of his mature work is essential to any understanding of Hume.

Hume was very disappointed by the reception of his *Treatise*, later remarking that it "fell *dead-born from the press*," without stirring the least public interest. Hume seems to have attributed the public failure of the *Treatise*

more to its form than its content. In 1740, in an attempt to generate interest, he published an anonymous pamphlet entitled *Abstract of a Book Lately Published: Entitled, A Treatise of Human Nature, etc., Wherein the Chief Argument of That Book Is Farther Illustrated and Explained* (1740), in which he represented his pivotal account of cause and effect.

Hume seems to have anticipated the possibility that the *Treatise* would prove controversial, though; he published it anonymously after having removed several provocative sections, including a chapter discussing miracles. If his intention was to avoid a reputation for skepticism and atheism, however, his efforts were unsuccessful; contemporaries such as William Warburton and Samuel Johnson decried Hume as both skeptic and atheist, and this ill reputation forever impeded Hume's ability to secure an academic post. While Hume eventually achieved financial security, his varied career included service as a tutor to the Marquess of Annandale, secretary to Lt. Gen. James St. Clair, librarian to the Edinburgh Faculty of Advocates, and chargé d'affaires of the British Embassy in Paris.

While Hume objected that his *Treatise* had been misunderstood, he never repudiated its substance. Hume eventually recast it in the form of two shorter, more carefully written works. *An Enquiry Concerning Human Understanding* (as revised in 1758) presents the chief arguments of book 1 of the *Treatise*, "Of the Understanding," while restoring the controversial section that denies that miracles can be supported by evidence. *An Enquiry Concerning the Principles of Morals* (1751), which Hume judged to be his finest work, refines the arguments he first presented in books 2 and 3 of the *Treatise* ("Of the Passions," and "Of Morals," respectively). Taken together, however, the *Enquiries* present a more moderate Hume.

Throughout his work, Hume distinguishes what he calls "demonstrative reasoning" from "moral reasoning." Demonstrative reasoning concerns the relation among the ideas men form out of data they receive through their senses. According to Hume, propositions relating ideas are intuitively or demonstratively certain when they can be shown to be without contradiction. Such propositions are discoverable by the operation of human thought, but they do not depend on external reality. Propositions involving facts, on the other hand, cannot be demonstrated, because no matter of fact permits logical contradiction. The contrary of any matter of fact would itself be a fact. For Hume, we gain our knowledge of external reality through the testimony of our senses and our memory.

According to Hume, reasoning about facts rests on an elusive relationship we call "cause and effect." In his account, human beings commonly infer causal relationships between events. The physical workings of the natural world, however—for example, the interaction of forces behind a collision of billiard balls—are always remote from what we happen to identify as factual events. Hume concludes that we never actually experience cause and effect. Consequently, we cannot know with any certainty how (or even whether) facts relate to one another; neither, as we have seen, can we know this through demonstrative reasoning. Hume nevertheless acknowledges that people *believe in* cause and effect and that they are reasonable to do so. Hume traces this belief to a natural principle of the human mind called "custom." The mind effortlessly infers a connection between events when it experiences their constant conjunction. Hume makes no claim to having reached the ultimate cause of this human propensity; he merely denies that men obtain certainty when drawing conclusions from experience.

In what way, then, might Hume be considered a moderate? First, Hume denies that causality is a mere fiction of the human mind. The intention of his skeptical analysis is to demonstrate that there are degrees and kinds of certainty, despite the claim of philosophers such as Descartes that genuine knowledge must rest on clear and certain premises. Hume demonstrates that probable knowledge is sufficiently sound for most of our purposes.

Second, Hume's probabilistic account of knowledge has analogous implications for moral and political life. In addition to his *Enquiries*, Hume published several collections of essays, including *Essays, Moral and Political* (1741–1742) and *Political Discourses* (1752). Unlike the *Treatise*, Hume's essays found considerable success, eventually earning him fame on the Continent as well as in England. In his moral and political works, Hume argues that reason alone cannot serve as the foundation for morality. While reason may play some role in articulating moral positions, only the sentiments give rise to the praise and blame necessary to sustain moral life. According to Hume, an action or quality is regarded as virtuous or vicious insofar as it brings pleasure or pain to an observer. Even though such responses arise within the individual, Hume denies that they are primarily self-centered. Men naturally approve of qualities or actions that they recognize as agreeable or useful, whether or not they themselves are immediate beneficiaries. Hume argues that human beings naturally possess sympathy for one another.

This sympathy is a rather weak sentiment and does not amount to natural benevolence; yet it is sufficient for human beings to be aware of the moral experiences and affections of others. Unlike many social contract theorists, Hume denies that man is naturally asocial. It is natural for human beings to live in community and consequently to make moral judgments.

For Hume, however, knowledge of right and wrong is not a matter of demonstrable certainty. In this, he stands apart from pure conventionalists who equate morality with whatever the law requires. Nor does Hume agree with the Catholic natural law tradition insofar as it identifies clear and unvarying precepts. Nevertheless, Hume does not consider himself a moral relativist. For him, judgments about right and wrong come about through custom in a way analogous to the inference of cause and effect. Moral norms arise in response to the particular needs of social life, what Hume terms "utility." Since the moral customs of a culture develop over a long period of time, they represent the accumulated experience of society. While customs may vary between cultures because of differences in circumstance and experience, such variance is neither infinite nor arbitrary. Just as Hume believes that cause and effect is real, so too he suggests that there is a consistent human nature that influences the shape of moral customs. Identifying the causes of particular moral judgments is more a matter of experience than demonstration for Hume, and he compares good judgment to the acquisition of taste. This opinion helps account for Hume's interest in historical studies, where he sought to uncover empirical evidence of man's moral nature. Hume's six-volume *The History of England from the Invasion of Julius Caesar to the Accession of Henry VII* (1754–1762) provides an example of such an inquiry.

Hume spent his final years in Edinburgh revising his works and socializing with friends. He died August 25, 1776.—Travis Cook

BIBLIOGRAPHY AND FURTHER READING: Capaldi, Nicholas. *Hume's Place in Moral Philosophy*. New York: P. Lang, 1989; Copleston, Frederick Charles. *A History of Philosophy, Volume V, Part 1*. Garden City, NY: Image Books, 1964; Danford, John W. *David Hume and the Problem of Reason: Recovering the Human Sciences*. New Haven, CT: Yale University Press, 1990; Livingston, Donald W. *Hume's Philosophy of Common Life*. Chicago: University of Chicago Press, 1984; Mossner, Ernest Campbell. *The Life of David Hume*, 2nd ed. Austin: University of Texas Press, 1980. *See also* ENLIGHTENMENT, AGE OF THE; SCOTTISH ENLIGHTENMENT THOUGHT

· I ·

IGNATIUS OF LOYOLA, ST. (c. 1491–1556) The centenary book commemorating the founding of the Society of Jesus (Jesuits) closes with an elegy on the death of St. Ignatius of Loyola bearing the epitaph *Non coerceri maximo, contineri tamen a minimo, divinum est—* "Not to be encompassed by the greatest, yet all the while to be contained by the littlest, that is divine." Perhaps no other saint has achieved this more radically and more enduringly than Ignatius, tirelessly stressing how the ordinary circumstances of everyday life speak to the faithful about God. Ignatius insisted that if Christians only reflected deeply on their experiences and the consequent movements of their hearts, they would come to meet the Triune God in the deepest desires of their souls. Contrary to many practices of the 16th century, Ignatius thus counseled against extreme mortifications and against relegating God to the overtly religious and encouraged Christians to see how the mundane gifts of one's daily life were in fact God's invitations to greater union.

Iñigo López de Loyola was born into a noble family, the youngest of 13 children in or around the year 1491. The family castle of Loyola lay just south of the Pyrenees in the Basque region of today's northeast Spain. He was brought to court early, spending his youth in the household of Juan Velázquez de Cuéllar, treasurer to King Ferdinand of Aragon. From there, he signed on for service in the household of the Duke of Nájera and viceroy of Navarre. In 1515, when cited for brawling in a hostelry in Loyola, Iñigo could claim that he had received the tonsure (not an unusual custom of his day) so as to be treated with the more lenient benefits afforded those with clerical status, the Church being to him then nothing more than a juridical convenience.

In 1521, when the King of France contested Charles of Habsburg, the newly elected Holy Roman emperor (who was also the king of Spain), the armies of Spain and France met along the Pyrenees at a siege at Pamplona. Here a cannonball ripped through Iñigo's right leg, and he was duly carried back to the family castle. While in Loyola, he asked his sister-in-law to retrieve for him some tales of chivalry, but she instead brought him Ludolf of Saxony's *Vita Christi* as well as the *Flos Sanctorum*, the Spanish translation of Jacob de Voragine's anthology of saints' lives, *The Golden Legend.* Iñigo noticed that when his mind turned to tales of chivalry and conquest, his zeal would sensibly soar, but only for a brief moment; on the other hand, when he read the trials and feats of St. Francis of Assisi and St.

Dominic, he was initially unresponsive, but the more he thought of the saints' courage and daring, the more ablaze his soul burned. Iñigo could not help but wonder what he, too, might be able to accomplish for an immortal sovereign, Jesus Christ. Here is the beginning of Ignatian contemplation: praying with oneself in the scene and from there drawing how one feels and senses in response to God's promptings.

From Loyola, Iñigo set out to live the simple life of a penitent beggar in the hope of finding God's will for his life. The first stop on this journey was the Benedictine Abbey of Montserrat where, in great symbolism, he laid his sword at the altar of the renowned Black Madonna. He next came to the little town of Manresa and spent a year (1522–1523) there in prayer and deep contemplation. Here he composed the kernel of his *Spiritual Exercises* (on which he continued to work for many years), a guidebook for Christians desirous of growing in deeper conversion and love of Christ and his Church. Fervent with the life of Jesus, he traveled to Jerusalem to live where Jesus lived. Given the hostilities between Muslims and Christians at this time, he was forced to cut short his stay in the Holy Land. Yet sensing his need for both community and education, Iñigo spent the next 11 years (1524–1535) studying humanities and theology (at Barcelona, 1524–1526; Alcalá, 1526–1527; Salamanca, 1527; and Paris, 1528–1535), emerging from the University of Paris as Ignatius, *magister artium.*

In 1534, Ignatius and six others (most notably, St. Francis Xavier and Blessed Peter Favre) vowed lives of chastity and poverty so as to serve Christ, in the Holy Land if possible. As these early companions met in Venice in the hope of traveling to Jerusalem, however, battles between the Turkish and Venetian fleets made Mediterranean voyages impossible. Ordained a priest in Venice in 1537, Ignatius left for Rome, while the others promised to meet him there at the end of April 1538. On the way into the Eternal City, Ignatius experienced a mystical vision at La Storta, a pivotal moment in his life. In this tiny village just 10 miles northwest of Rome, Jesus Christ appeared to him and promised "to be propitious at Rome," which only strengthened Ignatius to endure the upcoming deliberations with Vatican officials about the founding of a new and distinct type of religious order. In fact, Ignatius proved a visionary with his request for a type of men's religious life not yet experienced in the Church, but he also proved to be a formidable opponent when challenged. Against many Roman cardinals' opposition and much to their dismay, Pope Paul III granted oral approval to the first *Formula of the Jesuit Institute* (September 3, 1539) and then confirmed the Society of Jesus a year later with his papal bull *Regimini Militantis Ecclesiae* (September 27, 1540).

With this approbation, Paul III also granted Ignatius and his companions the numerous privileges many curial officials had been so actively resisting. As such, Ignatius was the first to abandon many of the customary practices of religious life: a distinctive habit, the tonsure, and most noticeably, praying the Divine Office in choir and in common. While these were certainly innovative, Ignatius's vision of the vowed life was the most revolutionary. He extended the canonical 12-month novitiate to two years and then introduced the profession of dispensable, simple vows. Unlike the perpetual vows of monastic and mendicant orders hitherto, Ignatius desired that his men profess simple vows, undergo a decade-plus regime of intellectual and character formation before priestly ordination, and only then a third year of probation (the Tertianship), which would finally incorporate a Jesuit fully into the order with solemn vows. In this way, Ignatius could "release" any man (and one woman, Isabel Roser) under vows who proved unsuitable for mission. In return for this lengthy process, the fully formed members of the Society of Jesus would be the first religious to profess a special "fourth vow" to the Holy Father to go wherever in the world the pope saw the Church's greatest need.

Despite his pilgrim soul, Ignatius would never again travel far from Rome. Elected superior general, Ignatius served the ever-growing society from his room near today's Gesù Church in Rome. Here Ignatius displayed a unique combination of pragmatism and mysticism. He loved his late-night gazing upon the stars from his balcony in the (then) dark and quiet Roman streets; he was given to long moments of prayerful contemplation and often wept copiously during the celebration of Mass. As quickly as he could be lifted to heaven, however, he could be just as swiftly put back on earth, having fostered an unmatchable growth and success in the Church's history of religious life. From 1540 until his death on July 31, 1556, the Society of Jesus grew to well over a thousand members (only about 40 of whom were fully professed), with more than a hundred houses dispersed among 12 governing provinces—from India to Portugal, from Upper Germany down through Sicily—and with 33 colleges (with six more approved for the fall before Ignatius's death).

The *Spiritual Exercises* end with Ignatius's "Contemplation to Attain Divine Love," where we learn that "love ought to find its expression in deeds more than in words" (§230). The whole of Ignatius's spirituality sought to express itself in the service of others. While there are no developed principles of the social apostolate in the writings of Ignatius, the practical implications of how he envisioned bringing the Gospel to the marginalized abound. The one indispensable doctrine was his insight that, in order to effect enduring social amelioration, permanent structures would first have to be established. Ignatius therefore sought to found organized, thoroughly financed, and legally recognized structures that could carry out its intended works well beyond the life of any one of its members. He was simply brilliant in securing the right associations (socially, legally, and financially) to make such institutions flourish: for example, he invited members of the pope's family to help him set up his house for reformed prostitutes (Casa Marta), while also establishing a safe place for the unfortunate young daughters of prostitutes (La Casa dell'Vergine Miserabile), as well as countless lay confraternities filled with members who were quite capable in helping to underwrite such works as Ignatius envisioned.

From Ignatius's own hand, we have nearly seven thousand letters (an overwhelmingly majority after 1547), the most of any 16th-century writer; we also possess his *Spiritual Diary*, which includes his attached *Deliberation on Poverty* (1544); the Jesuit *Constitutions* (1546); and his *Autobiography*, dictated to Gonçalves da Câmara in 1553. Still, Ignatius will forever be known as the author of the *Spiritual Exercises* (begun in 1522), which are not so much to be read as to be experienced, and the Church around the world continues to ponder these meditations and draw from them everlasting fruit.

Ignatius of Loyola still stands as a great religious visionary, surely a mystic, and no doubt a fruitful priest and pastor of souls. He cherished those around him and brought a Basque's love of this life and the earth's bounty to a soul also intent on heaven. He worshipped the Trinity, followed Jesus, adored the Eucharist, and displayed a knight's love for his lady, Mary. Above all, however, he was a man of prayer so deep and intimate that it could not help but lead to action. He was canonized in 1622.—David Vincent Meconi, SJ

BIBLIOGRAPHY AND FURTHER READING: Idigoras, J. Ignacio Tellechea. *Ignatius of Loyola: The Pilgrim Saint.* Chicago: Loyola Press, 1994; Lacouture, Jean. *Jesuits: A Multibiography.* Washington, DC: Counterpoint, 1997; O'Malley, John W. *The First Jesuits.* Cambridge, MA: Harvard University Press, 1995; *St. Ignatius of Loyola: Personal Writings.* Edited by Philip Endean and Joseph Munitiz. New York: Penguin Classics, 1997. *See also* SAINTS AND SOCIAL ACTION; SOCIETY OF JESUS; XAVIER, ST. FRANCIS

INFALLIBILITY   Infallibility is preservation from the possibility of error. It is an attribute of the nature of God, who is omniscient and omnipotent. According to the Catholic faith, God bestows infallibility on his Church, which is manifested most clearly in its teaching magisterium—the episcopal college with its head, the pope. The Church's charism of infallibility is evident from Sacred Scripture, theological necessity, and Church history. It extends to the entire deposit of revelation, that is, the totality of the Church's teaching on faith and morals. The doctrine of papal infallibility was solemnly defined in the First Vatican Council and explained in the broader context of episcopal authority in the Second Vatican Council.

Among the religious groups and figures of the world, the Catholic Church is not alone in claiming infallibility, although its claim has been expounded with the greatest theological emphasis and elaboration. Infallibility is participation in the prophetic office of Jesus Christ and is a gift of the Holy Spirit. As such, it is an essential charism of the Church. As the Church is the universal instrument of salvation, God guarantees that the Catholic faith will be preserved and preached without error until the end of time. The infallibility of the Church is thus closely linked to its indefectibility.

Infallibility is manifested in the Church in various modes. By a supernatural sense of the faith, the entire People of God cannot err in belief when, "from the bishops to the last of the faithful," they manifest a universal consent in matters of faith and morals (*LG* # 12; *DVb* # 10). As a teaching Church, infallibility is located explicitly in the college of bishops, successor to the apostolic college. When Jesus Christ founded the church on Peter, he assured him that "the Gates of Hell will not prevail against it" (Matthew 16: 18). At the Last Supper, Jesus promised the apostles that "the Holy Spirit will teach you all truth" (John 16: 13). In the Great Commission, Jesus commanded the apostles to teach all nations, promising to stay with them until the end of time (Matthew 28: 18–20). St. Paul calls the Church "the pillar and ground of the truth" (1 Timothy 3: 15). Paul told the Thessalonians to receive the apostles' teaching "not as human words but, as it truly is, the Word of God" (1 Thessalonians 2: 13). The apostles attributed the decrees of the Council of Jerusalem to the Holy Spirit (Acts 15: 28). It is a traditional belief that the apostles received the gift of personal infallibility at Pentecost. Infallibility was exhibited by the early Church in its confessions of faith, its writing and canonization of Scripture, and the unanimous teaching of the fathers. Although the early Church was dogged by controversy, the creeds of the ecumenical councils were accepted as without error, and their canons as inviolable.

The infallibility of the Church extends to the fullness of the deposit of revelation. This deposit extends to all dogmas that are directly propounded to the faithful; it can also extend to secondary truths that are necessary "to guard fully, explain properly and define efficaciously the very deposit of faith," as Bishop Vincent Gasser related to the bishops of the First Vatican Council. Theologians have sought to understand the boundaries of infallibility in such questions as discernment of the natural law, approval of religious orders, and canonization of saints.

Although the bishops do not possess infallibility individually, the college of bishops can exhibit infallible teaching in two ways. The first is through their ordinary and universal magisterium. When the bishops, although dispersed throughout the world, in the course of their daily ongoing mission teach authoritatively and uniformly in communion with the pope that a matter of faith and morals is to be definitively held by the faithful, their teaching is infallible. Second, the bishops also teach infallibly in extraordinary circumstances, such as when in valid ecumenical councils they proclaim a truth of the Catholic faith. In the Church's 21 ecumenical councils, the bishops defined without error the major Trinitarian, Christological, and ecclesiastical dogmas.

The pope exercises infallibility in his capacity as successor to St. Peter when he teaches *ex cathedra*, that is, when as supreme teacher of the faith he solemnly defines a doctrine of faith or morals. The scope of papal infallibility is coextensive with that of the Church. The pope derives infallibility from the charism of his office and not from his own character or the consent of the Church.

Papal infallibility is one of the more distinctive and, to the larger world, contested of Catholic doctrines. Nevertheless, it is evident that the infallibility of the Roman See and more specifically of the Roman pontiff was believed from the beginning of the Church, even though not articulated with the precision of the First Vatican Council. When Christ gave the primacy to Peter (Matthew 16: 18; Luke 22: 31–32; John 21: 15–17), he granted him infallibility in the solemn exercise of this authority. In the second century, St. Irenaeus wrote that because of its greater authority, "all Christians must agree with the Church of Rome," which has "kept the apostolic tradition" (*Against Heresies*, book 3, chapter 3). In 252, St. Cyprian of Carthage wrote of the "seat of Peter whence apostolic faith is derived and whither no errors can come" (*Epistulae* 59: 14).

The Synod of Milan in 389 stated that the creed of the apostles "the Roman Church has always kept and preserved undefiled" (*Ambrose Letters*, 42). In 420, Bachiarius of Spain wrote that "none of the heresies could gain hold of or move the Chair of Peter, that is the See of faith" (*Professio Fidei* 2). In 450, Blessed Theodoret of Syria wrote of the faith of the Holy See as "free from heretical taint," which has "preserved the Apostolic Grace unsullied" (Epistle 116 to Renatus). The Formula of Hormisdas, which was signed by the Eastern bishops in 519 and ended the Acacian schism, stated that "in the Apostolic See, the Catholic religion has always been preserved immaculately." The Formula of Hormisdas was professed at the eighth ecumenical Council of Constantinople (869–870) and at the reunion Council of Florence (1431–1435). It was also cited in the First Vatican Council (1869–1870), which formally defined the doctrine of papal infallibility in the dogmatic constitution, *Pastor Aeternus*.

Papal infallibility can be both underestimated and exaggerated. Critics such as Hans Küng, August Bernhard Hasler, Peter Chirico, and Brian Tierney have unconvincingly challenged its historical support. Of the most commonly alleged claims of papal error—those of Popes Virgilius, Liberius, and Honorius—Msgr. Ronald Knox wrote: "Here have these popes been, fulminating anathema after anathema for centuries—certain in all human probability to contradict themselves or one another over again. Instead of which you get this measly crop of two or three alleged failures!"

The scope of papal infallibility may be exaggerated as well. In theological terms, infallibility must be distinguished from *revelation*, in which God makes known new supernatural truth. The infallible magisterium arrives at a sure and fuller understanding of the faith, but proposes no new dogmas. Infallibility is not *inspiration*, by which God influences the language of humans such that God can be called the principal author of the utterance. Papal infallibility does not equate with *impeccability*, which constitutes sinlessness. The pope and bishops are not oracles. In expounding the faith, they must "by fitting means diligently strive to inquire properly into that revelation and to give apt expression to its contents" (*LG* # 25).

Likewise, papal infallibility is misperceived if it is aggrandized as the sole criteria of faith. There is a modern tendency to demand that all Catholic teaching be proclaimed by the papacy to be received as definitive. Although the Immaculate Conception of Mary (*Ineffabilis Deus*, 1854) and her Assumption (*Munificentissimus Deus*, 1950) were infallibly defined by the pope, most

Catholic teaching partakes of the ordinary and universal magisterium. For this reason, recent popes have decided against resolving controversies through the extraordinary papal magisterium. Rather, they have chosen to attest to teachings rendered infallible by the ordinary and universal teaching of the Church. Examples include the reservation of the priesthood to men (*Ordinatio Sacerdotalis*) and the moral teachings regarding the taking of innocent human life, abortion, and euthanasia (*Evangelium Vitae*). Infallibility is best understood as ultimately the charism of the Church. For example, it is the Church's constant and ordinary teaching that demonstrates the certainty of the prohibition against artificial contraception. Thus Pope Paul VI in his encyclical *Humanae Vitae* (1968) serenely explained and ratified the Church's constant and infallible teaching as to the regulation of births, without resorting to extraordinary proclamations.

The doctrine of infallibility gives certitude to Church teaching unrivaled in any other dimension of human life. The pope is enabled by the Holy Spirit to teach with infallibility so that "the whole church is preserved in unity, and, resting on its foundation, can stand firm against the gates of hell" (*Pastor Aeternus* 4: 7). The charism of infallibility allows the Church to proclaim its mission authoritatively and with clarity. The luminous defining of Christian mysteries achieved at great cost in the first councils cannot be retracted, and the multifarious heresies cannot be reasserted.

Although the doctrine of papal infallibility has been called an obstacle to ecumenism, in fact the charism does not permit the untrammeled or even whimsical authority of the pope, as each infallible proclamation adds an unchangeable rock to the edifice of the faith. Infallibility is necessary for the exercise of papal authority, because it is essential for the unity of the Christian faith. While the Supreme Pontiff is able to exercise his jurisdiction freely and without restraint, his teaching is shaped and even constrained by the Church's body of infallible teachings, which, having been proclaimed as without error in the past, guides the magisterium in the future.—Howard Bromberg

BIBLIOGRAPHY AND FURTHER READING: Dulles, Avery. "Newman on Infallibility." *Theological Studies* 51 (1990): 434–449; Gasser, Vincent. *The Gift of Infallibility*, 2nd ed. Edited by Rev. James O'Connor. San Francisco: Ignatius Press, 2008; Küng, Hans. *Infallible? An Inquiry*. Garden City, NY: Doubleday, 1971. *See also* AUTHORITY; DISSENT; MAGISTERIUM; TRADITION: ITS MEANING AND PURPOSE;

VATICAN COUNCIL, FIRST; VATICAN COUNCIL, SECOND

INFANTICIDE Infanticide can be defined as the intentional killing, as a means or as an end, of a human newborn. The Second Vatican Council condemns infanticide in unequivocal terms: "For God, the Lord of life, has conferred on men the surpassing ministry of safeguarding life in a manner which is worthy of man. Therefore from the moment of its conception life must be guarded with the greatest care while abortion and infanticide are unspeakable crimes" (*GS* # 54). This denunciation rearticulates unbroken Christian teaching from *Didache* of the first century, which stated, "You shall not procure an abortion, nor practice infanticide." Infanticide was widely practiced in the ancient world, but Christian practice and teaching from the very beginning understood intentionally killing infants as incompatible with love of one's neighbor.

In recent years, the practice of infanticide has—along with abortion—become more widely practiced. In particular, female infanticide and sex-selection abortion in China and India have resulted in gross imbalances in the gender ratios of these countries, leading to other social ills. Infanticide has also found contemporary defenders who, usually in attempts to justify abortion, extend what they call "reproductive rights" to the time after birth.

Most modern defenders of infanticide, including Peter Singer, Michael Tooley, Jeff McMahan, and others, defend it on the same basis that many people defend abortion. The human being shortly after birth, they say, is biologically human but is not a "person," that is, a member of the moral community with dignity and rights. Since newborns are not persons, they do not have rights such as the right to life, and so it is morally permissible to kill them.

What then is a "person" on the view of those who defend infanticide? Retrieving a definition of *person* suggested by John Locke, defenders of infanticide often define a person as a being with self-awareness, self-consciousness, and desires for the future. A human infant is not aware of his or her existence and cannot plan for the future, and so is not a person. Since the human infant is not a person, it does not violate the baby's rights to be intentionally killed.

And why is self-awareness so important? Without self-awareness over time, the defender of infanticide reasons, a being cannot have an interest in continuing to live. If a being does not have an interest in what happens to it, if it does not matter to the being one way or the other, then that being cannot have rights—which are there to protect interests. A rock has no self-awareness and so does not care whether someone destroys it or uses it as a tool. By contrast, human beings with self-awareness do (characteristically) care about being destroyed or used as tools. However, if a human being has no self-awareness, then this human being cannot care about being destroyed or used for the good of others. So, human beings without self-awareness cannot have interests, and since rights are conceived of as protecting interests, such human beings without self-awareness also do not have rights.

There are intellectual, logical, and moral problems with these justifications of infanticide. First, there is no reason to adopt this understanding of "person," resting as it does on a misunderstanding of Locke. There is no evidence whatsoever that Locke advocated infanticide. Locke was writing about personhood as an account of human *responsibility*, not personal *moral worth*. As Patrick Kain points out with respect to Immanuel Kant, and the same holds true for Locke, "personhood and responsibility does not entail that each person acts or has acted, or that each is always able to act; it only entails that *when* or *if* a person does act, she may be held responsible for her actions" (66).

Second, if *current* self-awareness is necessary for personhood, then our right to live is endangered every time we lose consciousness, such as during surgery. Indeed, we lose our fundamental rights and dignity and then gain them back many times over the course of our lives. This is absurd. We should therefore reject the proposition that self-awareness is necessary for having rights.

Of course, someone in surgery has the *capacity* for consciousness that is not able to be actualized until the anesthetic wears off. If current self-awareness is not necessary, but rather the capacity for consciousness, then the human infant should count as a person since the human infant has the root capacity for consciousness that is not yet able to be actualized or may not ever be able to be actualized due to illness or handicap.

A third reason to reject infanticide is that defenders of the practice misconstrue the relationship of interests and rights. "Interests" can used in two different senses: a subjective sense of what a being happens to desire at the moment, and an objective sense of what would be good for a being to have regardless of what the being desires. Certain rights are inalienable—such as the right to life and the right to liberty—which means that these rights do not depend upon the desires or subjective interests of those who have these rights. Even if someone is not "interested" in being a free person, his right to liberty remains. People have a duty not to enslave a woman, even if she (perhaps because of brainwashing) wishes to be another person's slave. Similarly, even if a depressed person expresses no interest in living, it is wrong to intentionally kill such a person. The right to live does not depend upon whether a human being is interested in living in a subjective sense. To live and to be free are goods for human beings in an objective sense. In other words, the right to life and the right to liberty are objectively in the interest of all human beings, regardless of the shifting states of an individual human being's self-awareness or desires. In the objective sense of interests, rights protect the interests or fundamental goods of human beings.

Another way to critique infanticide is to note that innocent adult human beings have the right to live, and the right not to be intentionally killed, and that there is no morally significant difference between human infants and human adults such that infants merit lesser protection. If anything, infants merit *greater* protection, since adults might be unlawful aggressors who may legitimately be killed in self-defense, but such a situation could never happen with infants, who are always innocent and never unlawful aggressors. Of course, many differences exist between human infants and human adults, among them size, level of dependency, use of language, bodily strength, and many other aspects of maturity and physiological development. But none of these characteristics is relevant to whether or not a being has a right to live. So, since innocent human adults have a right to live and there is no morally significant difference determining basic moral worth between innocent adults and innocent infants, human babies also have a right to live.

A final way to defend infanticide is by restricting its use to only very sick infants whose lives will be painful. If we assume that human infants are persons, such killings are simply cases of direct euthanasia, intentionally killing (by act or omission) in order to destroy a human being judged not worthy of living. Such killing, like all other violations of the right to live of the innocent, is intrinsically evil. All disabled and gravely sick human beings, including all newborns, merit respect and care.

However, although life is a good for every human being, it does not follow that every treatment is worthwhile and should be administered. With adults as with newborns, the burdens and benefits of treatment must be carefully considered in decisions to begin, continue, or discontinue treatment. In some cases of disabled newborns, a treatment will be rightly judged more burdensome than beneficial, and such treatments may be discontinued or not begun, even if, as a side effect, the baby's life is not extended. Such cases are not infanticide, since the death of the newborn is not chosen as a means or as an end, but rather death is accepted as a side effect of refraining from burdensome treatment.—Christopher Kaczor

BIBLIOGRAPHY AND FURTHER READING: Hassoun, Nicole, and Uriah Kriegel. "Consciousness and the Moral Permissibility of Infanticide." *Journal of Applied Philosophy* 25, no. 1 (2008): 45–55; Kaczor, Christopher. *The Ethics of Abortion.* New York: Routledge, 2010; Kain, Patrick. "Kant's Defense of Human Moral Status." *Journal of the History of Philosophy* 47, no. 1 (2009): 59–102; Lindemann, Hilde, and Marian Verkerk. "Ending the Life of a Newborn: The Groningen Protocol." *Hastings Center Report* 38, no. 1 (2008): 42–51; McMahan, Jeff. "Infanticide." *Utilitas* 19, no. 2 (2007): 1–29. *See also* ABORTION; EUTHANASIA; PARTIAL BIRTH ABORTION

INTEGRATION OF PSYCHOLOGY AND PHILOSOPHY As the word *integrate* means "to unify," the "integration of psychology and philosophy" refers to the project of bringing psychology and philosophy into a closer relationship with each other. In a Catholic setting, this integration would generally occur through philosophy serving as some kind of foundation of or context for psychology.

There are three main motives for such integration. First, it is felt that psychology, as a specialized branch of knowledge, relies on philosophical presuppositions as much as any other specialized branch: the integration of psychology and philosophy, then, will make these presuppositions explicit and evaluate them, so that the most suitable ones may be used. Second, it may be argued, from the very nature of a university, that psychology as much as any other discipline needs to be brought in relation to the rest of knowledge, and that only the disciplines of philosophy and theology, with their general scope and import, can play this integrative role: on this view, then, the integration of all of knowledge implies the integration of each special discipline with philosophy.

These first two motives do not depend on the distinctive object of study of psychology. The third motive, however, does: Psychology as a theoretical discipline seems to deal with realities that arguably are greatly illuminated by philosophical inquiry, such as reason, the will, the emotions (or "passions"), interpersonal relations, and love. (Indeed, *psychology* means literally "study of the soul," which philosophy classically regarded as its own task.)

Similarly, psychology as a practical and clinical discipline inevitably examines philosophical questions, such as how mental illness and health are to be defined, whether some treatments should be ruled out on ethical grounds, and the manner and extent to which responsibility may be compromised by mental pathology. In general, psychology seems to presuppose some view of human nature and the purpose of human life, but these are appropriately studied by philosophy.

It is clear that the integration of psychology and philosophy (henceforth "integration") can look like an important project only to those who regard these disciplines as distinct and yet close enough for the union or harmonizing of the two to be fruitful or even necessary. That is why integration began to seem important only in the 20th century and typically among Catholic psychologists and philosophers.

Psychology, for most of its history, was not regarded as distinct from philosophy, just as indeed most scientific disciplines were regarded as areas within "natural philosophy." The first works in psychology, Plato's *Phaedo*, *Republic*, and *Timaeus* and Aristotle's *De Anima*, were investigations carried out by philosophers with deeper metaphysical and theological motivations; "faculty" psychology, begun by Aristotle, was developed by medieval philosophers; and antecedents of associationist psychology were set down by the philosophers John Locke and David Hume. Psychology broke away from philosophy and established itself as a separate discipline only at the end of the 19th century.

In Europe, this separation was an instance of the scientific community's aversion in general to the then dominant philosophical school of Georg Hegel. In the United States, philosophy had become so "psychologized"—so assimilated to psychology in its interests and methods—that it was philosophy that had to break away from psychology: so, for instance, when philosophers at the time wanted to organize themselves into a professional association, they called it the American Psychological Association (founded in 1892), in reaction to which the American Philosophical Association was later formed (in 1900).

Philosophy could mark itself out as a separate discipline, of course, only if it could claim either some special area of expertise or a method of arriving at knowledge distinct from the methods of natural science. Indeed, philosophers were highly receptive to the development, at the turn of the 20th century, of new logical techniques by Gottlob Frege and Bertrand Russell and the new phenomenology of Edmund Husserl precisely because these methods held forth the promise of a distinctively "logical" and not "psychological" method in philosophy. But the upshot was that philosophy, so marked out, could not possibly be brought in relation to psychology, as the *a priori* is entirely distinct from the *a posteriori*, and as conceptual analysis is distinct from empirical investigation; nor would such philosophers have wanted to do so and risk subverting philosophy. At most, one might engage in philosophy *of* psychology, or the conceptual analysis of psychological concepts ("philosophical psychology"), understood as a contribution to ethics or action theory, not psychology.

At the same time, psychology once separated from philosophy, and wishing to model itself on the physical sciences, was especially prone to embrace, either deliberately or implicitly, various forms of determinism, materialism, and positivism that would seem to be both philosophical positions and prejudicial to a sound psychology.

Protestant clinicians sought a remedy and corrective in the integration of *theology* with psychology, especially as advocated by the Christian Association for Psychological Studies (founded 1956) and followed later by the American Association of Christian Counselors (founded 1986, with its academic division, the Society for Christian Psychology). Fuller Theological Seminary and later the Rosemead School of Psychology at Biola University became the leading academic centers of this movement, which now includes dozens of programs and several journals (such as the *Journal of Theology and Psychology* and *Edification*). Protestant clinicians generally relied on theology, not philosophy, as a standard and judge of psychological science, from a conviction that Scripture plays that role as regards all human endeavors, and presumably as a result, too, of the underdevelopment of philosophical anthropology in Protestant thought.

The Catholic response has been mixed. In the first two decades of the 20th century, the Catholic clinical community took the lead incorporating findings of the psychological sciences into its therapeutic and pastoral ministries and in amplifying therapy with a spiritual dimension. But the Catholic contribution to the integration of philosophy and psychology has been limited, centered mainly in the work of the Institute for the Psychological Sciences (IPS) in Arlington, Virginia, founded in 1999, and its scholars (notably Father Benedict Ashley, Christian Brugger, Paul Vitz, and Daniel Robinson) and clinicians (especially Gladys Sweeney and William Nordling). This group has now developed a systematic interpretation of integration known as the IPS Model, which includes major theological, philosophical, and psychological components.

The fact that Catholics' initiative of integration has arisen so late relative to their Protestant colleagues may be explained by the importance of Thomism as an intellectual framework for Catholics before the 1960s, since clinicians educated up to that time would typically have received so thorough an education in Thomist philosophy as to find any materialistic and deterministic aspects of psychological theories implausible. On the other hand, the limited extent of the Catholic response in recent years is to be explained largely by the secularization of Catholic universities and the subsequent imperfect implementation of *Ex Corde Ecclesiae*, which charges Catholic universities, including presumably their psychology departments, with a task that would include integration: "The distinctive and primary responsibility of a Catholic university is 'to join together existentially, precisely by one's intellectual effort, two orders of realities which one is very often inclined to set in opposition, as if they were at odds: the progressive search for the truth, and the certitude of already knowing the font of truth'" (*ECE # 1*). At the same time, the tradition of Aristotelian Thomism, the more recent flourishing of realist phenomenology among Catholic thinkers, and the Catholic personalist movement (led by Gabriel Marcel and Emmanuel Mounier) supply tremendous resources for integration.

The tasks of integration may be categorized as positive, negative, and "bridge." The positive task is to build up a satisfactory general account of human nature from a philosophical point of view, giving due place to human freedom, rationality, relationship, and embodiedness, and then from this basis to offer specific philosophical treatments of phenomena important to psychology, which can serve as the framework for psychological inquiry. A good example of the execution of this positive task would be *Love and Responsibility* of Karol Wojtyla, which sets down a personalist anthropology and then, on that basis, offers accounts of romantic love and marriage that have exceptional psychological insight. Again, the philosophical framework of the virtues, developed by Aristotle and St. Thomas, provides the best foundation for the recent school of "positive psychology."

The negative task is to reveal and then refute erroneous philosophical commitments of psychological theories or research, such as determinism and materialism, and substance dualism. Perhaps the most important such task is to reveal the pervasive influence on mainline psychology of substance dualism and of a corresponding Baconian approach to the natural world.

The bridge task is to develop philosophical accounts that point to, or look to be complemented by, theological accounts—in other words, to deal with psychology in such a way that it is more easily illuminated by theological considerations. A good example of this last task would be how Wojtyla's use of the "personalist principle" in *Love and Responsibility* ("Love others as beings who have ends, not as mere means") is illuminated in turn by the "logic of the gift" presented in Christian revelation. That is, *Love and Responsibility* stands to the theology of the body in the way that, in the Catholic intellectual tradition, the integration of philosophy and psychology stands to the integration of theology and psychology.—Michael Pakaluk

BIBLIOGRAPHY AND FURTHER READING: Brugger, Christian, ed. "Catholic Psychology." *Edification* 3, no. 1 (2009): 1–86; John Paul II. Address to Members of the American Psychiatric Association and the World Psychiatric Association, January 4, 1993; Stevenson, Daryl H., Brian E. Eck, and Peter C. Hill, eds. *Psychology and Christian Integration: Seminal Works That Shaped the Movement*. Batavia, IL: Christian Association for Psychological Studies, 1997; Vitz, Paul C. *Psychology as Religion: The Cult of Self-Worship*, 2nd ed. Grand Rapids, MI: Eerdmans, 1994. *See also* AMERICAN CATHOLIC PSYCHOLOGICAL ASSOCIATION; PHILOSOPHY, DISCIPLINE OF; PSYCHOLOGY (DISCIPLINE OF); VITZ, PAUL C.

INTERNATIONAL LAW AND THE RIGHT TO LIFE   The right to life is, as a general matter, recognized in international law. The 1948 Universal Declaration of Human Rights (UDHR), a nonbinding statement of principle that is the wellspring of modern international human rights law discourse, declares: "Everyone has the right to life." The 1966 International Covenant on Civil and Political Rights (ICCPR), codifying portions of the UDHR in binding form, amplifies: "Every human being has the inherent right to life. This right shall be protected by law. No one shall be arbitrarily deprived of his life."

The scope of such a right is contested, however, and disagreement exists on whether the unborn child is included within its ambit; abortion proponents assert that a right to abortion can be grounded in international law. As traditionally understood, there are two principal sources of "hard" obligation in international law: treaties and customary international law. In addition, some authority exists for including "general principles common to the major legal systems of the world," but this is generally regarded as a "supplementary" secondary source that can be referenced in "special circumstances."

Obligations set forth in treaties are considered binding upon sovereign nations that have negotiated, signed, and ratified them. Means by which nations ratify treaties vary, but in the United States, the Constitution requires the "advice and consent" of two-thirds of the Senate.

One regional treaty, the 1968 American Convention on Human Rights (ACHR), explicitly protects unborn life: "Every person has the right to have his life respected. This right shall be protected by law, and, in general, from the moment of conception." Another regional treaty, the African Charter on Human and People's Rights on the Rights of Women in Africa, also known as the Maputo Protocol, permits abortion in certain circumstances.

Beyond regional conventions, no global treaty references abortion, and thus nations that protected the unborn in their laws and constitutions at the time such treaties were negotiated evidently intended to leave such laws untouched. No global treaty explicitly protects unborn life with language as expansive as that contained in the ACHR; proposals by Chile and Lebanon at the time of the drafting of the UDHR to include such a reference were dropped due to the opposition of the Soviet Union, which had legalized abortion.

The right to life of the unborn may nevertheless be inferred from the text of certain global treaties, namely, the ICCPR and the 1978 Convention on the Rights of the Child (CRC). Under general interpretive principles contained in the Vienna Convention on the Law of Treaties, any such inferences must be made "in good faith in accordance with the ordinary meaning to be given to the terms of the treaty in their context."

The ICCPR provides that "Sentence of death shall not be imposed for crimes committed by persons below 18 years of age and shall not be carried out on pregnant women." As nonminor women convicted of crimes "most serious" may otherwise be put to death, the independent life interest protected by the ICCPR is that of the unborn child.

The preamble to the CRC states that the child "needs special safeguards and care, including appropriate legal protection, before as well as after birth." While preambles are not binding, they provide an interpretive "context," per the Vienna Convention. Moreover, the CRC defines a "child" as "every human being below the age of 18 years," thereby setting a ceiling, but no floor, as to which persons are covered.

Customary international law is defined as "a general and consistent practice of states followed by them from a sense of legal obligation," also known as *opinio juris*. The process by which norms become customary over time is imprecise, but evolves and requires nearly universal consent. The U.S. Supreme Court, in *Sosa v. Alvarez-Machain*, has identified disregard of "safe conducts," infringements of the rights of ambassadors, and piracy on the high seas as violating customary norms. In addition, consensus holds that the international slave trade is proscribed by custom as well as treaty.

No "general and consistent" practice of states followed by them from a "sense of legal obligation" with regard to abortion is discernable. Even if one were to survey domestic laws throughout the world and attempt to discern "custom" from that—though that is not what customary *international* law is—such domestic laws range from those extremely protective of unborn life (e.g., the constitutions of Ireland, Chile, the Philippines, and Madagascar) to the permissive, such as in Canada and the United States.

No right to abortion can therefore be derived from "hard" law obligations. Since the mid-1990s, however, abortion proponents have sought to elevate nonbinding jurisprudence into "soft" norms, which they claim require nations to liberalize laws on abortion.

One source of such soft norms are recommendations and interpretations issued by treaty compliance committees directing countries to liberalize laws to comply with abortion norms they read into the text of treaties. Such committees are empowered only to receive reports from nations on progress toward implementing them, however, and cannot act as unelected and unaccountable supralegislatures rewriting the domestic laws and constitutions of signatory states.

A right to abortion is also claimed to be consistent with nonbinding outcome documents issued at global conferences on population (Cairo, 1994) and women (Beijing, 1995). Neither document contains such a right, however, and both affirm that "Any measures or changes related to abortion within the health system can only be determined at the national or local level according to the national legislative process."

Abortion proponents have brought litigation in national courts asserting the existence of abortion rights in international law. In 2006, the activist Constitutional Tribunal of Colombia struck down Colombia's penal protections of unborn life based in part on soft-law jurisprudence created by treaty compliance committees and what it discerned as "evolving" human rights norms. Subsequently, the Supreme Court of Mexico rejected such arguments in upholding a liberalized law in Mexico City, and the Supreme Court of Chile interpreted right-to-life provisions found in the ICCPR, UDHR, and ACHR as buttressing its constitution's protection of unborn life.

With respect to Catholic social thought, international law was once considered a subset of natural law, and its early development was influenced in large part by Catholic jurists such as Francisco Suarez and Francisco de Vittoria. Such roots can also be discerned in the UDHR, whose iteration of "universal" principles was heavily influenced by natural-law thinkers such as the Thomist Jacques Maritain and the Maronite Catholic Charles Malik of Lebanon. Modern international law theory is dominated by legal positivism, however, leaving open the question of what ultimately grounds fundamental human rights, including the right to life. Modern theorists sympathetic to natural law, such as Nicholas Wolterstorff, have questioned whether the modern human rights project commenced in 1948 is sustainable without restoring an understanding of human dignity predicated upon an objective, theistic basis.—Piero A. Tozzi

BIBLIOGRAPHY AND FURTHER READING: Glendon, Mary Ann. *A World Made New: Eleanor Roosevelt and the Universal Declaration of Human Rights.* New York: Random House, 2002; Scott, James Brown. *The Catholic Conception of International Law* (1934). Clark, NJ: Lawbook Exchange, 2008; Sylva, Douglas, and Susan Yoshihara. "Rights by Stealth: The Role of UN Human Rights Treaty Bodies in the Campaign for an International Right to Abortion." *National Catholic Bioethics Quarterly* 7 (2007): 97ff.; Tozzi, Piero A. "International Law and the Right to Abortion." New York: Catholic Family and Human Rights Institute, 2010; Wolterstorff, Nicholas. *Justice: Rights and Wrongs.* Princeton, NJ: Princeton University Press, 2008; Zampas, Christina, and Jamie M. Gher. "Abortion as a Human Right: International and Regional Standards." *Human Rights Law Review* 8, no. 2 (2008): 249–294. *See also* UNESCO; UNITED NATIONS

· J ·

JAKI, STANLEY L., OSB (1924–2009) Rev. Stanley Ladislas Jaki, OSB, contributed significantly to our understanding of cosmology, the history and philosophy of science, theology, philosophy, and more. Jaki was born in Györ, Hungary, in 1924. He received his early education from the historic abbey school at the famed Hungarian Archabbey of Pannonhalma (founded in 996 by Prince Géza, the second largest abbey by area in the world, exceeded in size only by Monte Cassino). His intelligence and broad learning were in evidence even at an early age, and he eventually obtained his doctorate in theology from the Pontifical Institute of San Anselmo in Rome in 1950.

Jaki joined the Benedictines in 1942, professed his solemn vows in 1944, and was ordained a priest in 1948. He then arrived in the United States, where unfortunate complications from a tonsillectomy resulted in his inability to effectively use his voice for several years. Jaki then enrolled in a doctoral program in physics at Fordham University (studying under the Nobel laureate and discoverer of cosmic rays Prof. Victor F. Hess), receiving his degree in 1957. Remarkably, at the age of 33, he possessed two doctorates (theology and physics) and had also completed extensive studies in philosophy, mathematics, foreign languages, and other subjects. He joined the faculty at Seton Hall University in 1965 and became a Distinguished University Professor there in 1978. His noted scientific work *The Relevance of Physics* (1966) was followed by many other works, including his autobiography, *A Mind's Matter: An Intellectual Autobiography* (2002).

Jaki employed his vast erudition in his earnest, diligent, and lifelong quest for the truth. He set out on a quest to uncover and explicate the real story of religion and science in the Middle Ages (and throughout history) and became enamored of the work of Pierre Duhem (1861–1916), a noted French physicist, philosopher of science, mathematician, and historian of science. Duhem was a firm Catholic, a "believing physicist," who thought that the Enlightenment and Protestantism had influenced the manner in which historians portrayed the Catholic Church as an enemy of science and of progress. In *Uneasy Genius: The Life and Work of Pierre Duhem*, Jaki explicates how much Duhem paid for his beliefs throughout his life, alternately vilified or ignored by fellow scientists and historians of science.

Duhem published a 10-volume work in 1913 that notably impacted Jaki, *Le systéme du monde: Histoire des doctrines cosmologiques de Platon a Copernic.* For Duhem, as for Jaki, the real history of science had never been told, a history that would portray the Church as a central figure in the development of science. In *The Savior of Science* (2000), Jaki noted that science had undergone a series of "stillbirths," failed attempts at a sustained science on the part of a number of historic cultures. Christian monotheism alone, Jaki stated, provided sufficient underpinnings for scientific advancements. In his book *Christ and Science* (2000), Jaki discussed four reasons for the unique, distinctive birth of science in Christian western Europe. First, the Christian belief in the Creator provided a foundation stone for thinking about nature; indeed, only a truly transcendental Creator could be powerful enough to create a nature that included autonomous laws without the Creator's power over nature being diminished in any way. Second, it put all material beings on the same level. Unlike the Greek cosmos, in the Christian cosmos there could be no divine bodies. Third, humankind was created in the image of the Creator, God, with a rationality that somehow shared in God's own rationality. Fourth, humankind, created by God, cannot dictate to nature what it should be. The noted scientific experimental method owes much to this Christian matrix. Great Christian scientists arose out of this encouraging and stimulating environment.

For Jaki, several biases have impacted the development of science over the centuries: empiricism, idealism, and anticlericalism. A number of events impinged at the same time to contribute to a hostile atmosphere with respect to the Church and science. The combined hostility of the "encyclopedists" of the Enlightenment, the rise of Protestantism, and other factors created an environment in which the Church was almost automatically assumed to be antiscience, hostile to progress, and so forth. The Church was therefore unfairly and inaccurately portrayed by historians, scientists, and others, and this pervaded the intellectual currents of the day, down to the present. Thus, it is not surprising that British philosopher Bertrand Russell stated that traditional religion had been engaged in a prolonged conflict with scientific knowledge. Yet, in this respect, it would come as a surprise to many people to learn that many craters on the moon are named after Jesuit scientists. Other distinguished Catholics were influential scientists. Other examples include the Dominican St. Albert the Great, a renowned naturalist, and the Augustinian Gregor Mendel, the father of modern genetics.

Jaki saw himself as an engaged participant in the "culture wars," and he found it difficult to comprehend how someone could *not* be an active participant. He certainly experienced anti-Catholicism in his life, and he agreed with Duhem that the Enlightenment and the rise of Protestantism (both conservative and liberal) both contributed to an animus and to a diminution of the Church's many contributions to science and civilization. He was pained to see the Church he loved so much besieged by various modern intellectual and cultural currents. He used the term "Aquikantists" to refer to an attempted "miscegenation" between St. Thomas Aquinas and Immanuel Kant. This is often referred to as "transcendental Thomism," and Jaki had little use for it. His interest in G. K. Chesterton, John Henry Newman, and apologetics was an attempt to combat the numerous fallacies and errors of the day. As for atheism, Jaki affirmed that one must surely say "Creator" in order to say "Cosmos." This is a central tenet of his cosmology.

He was certain of his beliefs, which were firmly anchored in God. No one will accuse Jaki of pantheism, for he clearly separated the Creator from creation. His theology was clearly stated and earnestly believed. As for evolution, Jaki takes a balanced approach, parallel in some respects to that of Christoph Cardinal Schönborn, OP, in his book *Chance or Purpose? Creation, Evolution and a Rational Faith* (2007) and of Raymond Nogar, OP, another priest-scientist, in *The Wisdom of Evolution* (1963). Science and a rationally anchored faith in God, he believed, do not involve a necessary tension or antagonism. Jaki was not a "creationist" per se, nor did he advocate evolutionism, an ideology that reduces all of reality to seemingly meaningless, mindless processes. Jaki believed in the original creation of the entire universe by God. Humankind was also created by God, in God's wondrous image. If there is some kind of evolutionary process at work, then for Jaki it is certainly "baptized," for it is unmistakably under God's everlasting control.

In future years, Jaki's many contributions should achieve increasing recognition—recognition that he richly deserved but did not always achieve in his lifetime. Still, he did receive several coveted awards and honors, including the Lecomte du Nouy Prize from Rockefeller University in 1970, the noted Templeton Prize in 1987, Gifford Lectureships at the University of Edinburgh, lectureships at Oxford, and a number of other honors in various countries.

Already there are signs of increasing recognition of Jaki's accomplishments. An international conference was held in Rome on April 13, 2010, to commemorate the first anniversary of his death. During the conference, the Stanley Jaki Foundation was initiated. The first president of the foundation is Father Paul Haffner, who did so much to bring Jaki's noted work to a wider audience through the publication of his 1991 and 2009 books on Jaki's contributions. Antonio Columbo, the secretary of the foundation, has stated that more of Jaki's manuscripts will be published in the years ahead.

Jaki was a noble, brilliant, forthright monk, scientist, historian of science, cosmologist, apologist, fierce combatant in the "culture war," and much more. His memory will long endure.—Thomas D. Watts

BIBLIOGRAPHY AND FURTHER READING: Haffner, Paul. *Creation and Scientific Creativity: A Study in the Thought of S. L. Jaki*. Front Royal, VA: Christendom Press, 1991; Jaki, Stanley L. *Christ and Science*. Royal Oak, MI: Real View Books, 2000; Jaki, Stanley L. *A Mind's Matter: An Intellectual Autobiography*. Grand Rapids, MI: Eerdmans, 2002; Jaki, Stanley L. *The Savior of Science*. Grand Rapids, MI: Eerdmans, 2000. *See also* DUHEM, PIERRE; ENLIGHTENMENT, AGE OF THE; SCIENCE

JOACHIM OF FIORE (c. 1135–1202) Joachim of Fiore (also known as Joachim de Fiore or de Flora) was a south Italian abbot and monastic founder. He is most famous for his writings on the theology of history, which in certain respects approached millenarianism. His followers often regarded him as a prophet, and although he disclaimed prophetic gifts himself, he wrote of certain spiritual experiences in which God gave him to understand the historical patterns in Sacred Scripture and, indeed, the meaning all of human history. After his death, his more radical followers exaggerated certain of his ideas into a clearly heterodox current of thought often called "Joachimitism" and differentiated by many scholars from "Joachimism," which expounded his thought more soberly and closer to his own mind. Because of the complex, symbolic, and allusive nature of his writing and due to lingering questions about authorship of certain controverted works, his exact relationship with his more extreme enthusiasts is hard to entirely resolve.

Joachim was born a Calabrian, son of a notary who was well placed in the court of the Norman kings of Sicily. As a young man, Joachim underwent a religious conversion in conjunction with a pilgrimage to Jerusalem and resolved to give up a worldly life. After some time as a hermit, he showed great talent as a preacher of moral reform and was ordained a priest. Convinced by a monk that his abilities would be wasted in the secular clergy, he next turned to monastic life and was elected abbot of a small Benedictine house (Corazzo) then loosely connected with the Cistercian order.

Although he is sometimes listed as a Cistercian, Joachim's relations with the Cistercians were complicated. They were initially strong supporters of his efforts as a monastic reformer and theological writer, and eventually he won incorporation of his house into the order. The affiliation, however, did not last long (1188–1192), as Joachim by then had a renown of his own, and his accustomed independence made submission to the requirements of the Cistercian general chapter difficult.

Since his relations with the papacy were good, Joachim was able to gain independence from the monks of Citeaux and to found his own Florensian order, which at its height was to reach around 40 monasteries, centered on his own new house of Fiore. Although the customs of the Florensians remained for the most part quite close to Cistercian observance, his relationship with his former order remained difficult for the rest of his life.

Joachim's theologizing reflects the strong Augustinian, mystical, and scriptural currents in 12th-century thought, but is at odds with the newly emerging scholastic method; indeed, he sharply attacked the orthodoxy of Peter Lombard, whose *Sentences* was already becoming a benchmark for this approach. Above all, Joachim's work is characterized by strong originality, especially in its very prominent eschatology. Before his time, most medievals interpreted the apocalyptic elements in the Scripture, most notably the book of Revelation, in spiritualizing terms that focused on their significance for the journey of the individual soul to God and his judgment. Joachim, however, reinaugurated a kind of interpretation that was not shy about identifying given institutions and persons with apocalyptic figures in Scripture. This undeniably struck a chord in his contemporaries, who were living through (to their consciousness) great changes in Church, society, and politics associated with the High Middle Ages, as well as the fears and expectations occasioned by such occurrences as the appearance of new monastic movements and heresies and the fall of Jerusalem to Saladin (1187). All this seemed in need of special explanation, which helps to account for the not inconsiderable popularity of Joachim's writings in his own lifetime, as well as the support he received from prominent figures in the Church and state, including Popes Lucius III, Urban III, Clement III, and Celestine III. Although he was moderately papalist in his politics, interpreting the eschatological Babylon as the Holy Roman Empire of his day, it is notable that he nonetheless managed to gain the esteem and admiration of members of the imperial family. Yet, his works also occasioned considerable opposition and disbelief from the outset of his career as a theological writer.

At the core of Joachim's method of exegesis was a complex, interrelated, and overlapping set of extended correspondences (*concordia*) between the events of the Old and New Testaments and, more broadly, their respective eras of salvation history. These correspondences were structured on certain key theological numbers, especially two, three, and seven. Some characteristic examples will illustrate: Just as the Israelite people gave rise to the great hermits and spiritual leaders Elijah and Elisha but eventually split away from the Jewish people (represented by Jerusalem) and came to grief, so the Greek Church gave rise to great monks and theologians but eventually split schismatically from the people of God. Likewise, just as there were seven great persecutions of the Israelites of old, so there would be seven great persecutions of the Church, whose leaders correspond to the seven-headed beast of the Apocalypse (Revelation 13), most of whom Joachim thought he could recognize: the sixth head was Saladin and his successors, and the last, the Antichrist proper, was soon to come. Between this immanent persecution perpetrated by the last head and final persecution of the Church in the time of Gog and Magog (comprising the tail of the beast), there would be the primary manifestation of the "thousand-year" reign of God and his saints, promised in Revelation 20. This would be a time of peace and intense spiritual development of a new, perfected monasticism.

Joachim was careful not to set a specific date for the beginning of this new state of the world, and he cautioned against interpreting apocalyptic time spans in Scripture (including the thousand years of the millennium itself) too literally. Yet all the same, he thought that he might see the Antichrist in his own lifetime and that he was specially charged by God to forewarn believers of the coming tribulation. He also thought he could at least determine the number of human generations into which history could be divided, as well as each of its major ages.

The most characteristic and controversial of his manifold schemes of history was his famous threefold division of world history into three overlapping ages (*status*) based on the predominance of a different person of the Holy Trinity. The age of the Father began with Adam, reached maturity with the giving of the law under Moses, and ended with Christ. The age of the Son began with King Josiah, matured with the Incarnation and the preaching of the Gospel, and was to end soon after Joachim's time. The last age, that of the Holy Spirit, began with St. Benedict and his establishment of the monastic life and would soon come to maturity in the new pure and reformed monasticism he thought would soon emerge and which would herald the millennium. It would end at the Last Judgment. Each age had its own spiritual and social character: In the age of the Father, the married state had predominated in the people of God, and it was the age of the rigorous old Law; in the age of the Son, the secular clergy were predominant, and it was the time of the preaching of the Gospel and the greater freedom of the New Law of Christ. In the final age, it would be the monastic order that would spiritually lead the people of God in a time of peace and deepened spiritual freedom and contemplative understanding. In this time, as God promised, his Spirit would be poured out on all mankind. All, even laypeople, would hold goods in common on the pattern of monks. The Jews would be peacefully converted, and all the world would recognize the authority of the pope, who could then devote himself to contemplation, rather than laborious struggle for the faith. Joachim never sought to deny the traditional twofold division of salvation history or the validity and finality of the New Testament, but his new threefold division would be his main focus, and some of his followers would come to be fixated on it, almost to the exclusion of others.

The posthumous fate of Joachim's work and reputation was complicated. Upon his death, he commended his works to the pope for correction. His own Florensian order was allowed to venerate his sanctity liturgically. Nonetheless, Pope Innocent III and the Fourth Lateran Council formally condemned as erroneous his heresy accusation against Peter Lombard's Trinitarian doctrine. At the same time, both Innocent III and his successor, Honorius III, were at pains to stress Joachim's own piety and basic orthodoxy.

By the middle of the 13th century, opinions about the Calabrian abbot became more sharply polarized. More extreme Joachimists emerged—many associated with the emerging Spiritual wing of the Franciscan order in its struggle with the mainstream over apostolic poverty—and their views occasioned major controversies. They identified the mendicants, especially the Franciscan order itself, as the new spiritual monasticism that would lead Christian society and set the date for the beginning of the new age in 1260, proclaiming Emperor Frederick II the Antichrist. One of the most extreme, Gerardo of Borgo San Donnino, claimed the writings of Joachim himself were to replace the New Testament itself in the dawning Age of the Spirit. Pope Alexander IV condemned Gerardo's version of the three stages of salvation history in 1255, and although Joachim was not explicitly included in the condemnation, some regard it as falling on his version of the idea as well. A local Church synod in Arles, France, condemned Joachim by name in 1260. St. Thomas Aquinas regarded him as ignorant in theology and argued against many of his distinctive positions, whereas St. Bonaventure mostly rejected the problematic three ages with their potential to derogate from the primacy of Christ in history, while finding more use for some of Joachim's secondary interpretations of the course of time in his own theology of history.

Although Joachim continued to have strong proponents in the 13th and 14th centuries, among them the radical Franciscan Peter Olivi and Dante Aligheri, his own order declined and was eventually reabsorbed by the Cistercians. The failure of the third age of the Spirit to materialize, as well as the failure of others of his followers' prophecies, led to further diminution of his stature, although occasional revivals of some of his ideas can be found in later history, as among some of the Anabaptist radicals of the 16th century or the eccentric sometime Jesuit Guillaume Postel. Some historians have seen in Joachim a forerunner of modern utopian ideologies, and indeed some of the 18th- and 19th-century utopians (e.g., Lessing, Comte, and the followers of Saint-Simon) admitted a fascination with the Calabrian abbot. Their concerns, though, are largely remote from his, and he is probably best interpreted as one of the periodic Catholic theologians whose originality helps shape the theological discourse of a period of Church history but proves marginal in the longer run.   Paul J. Radzilowski

BIBLIOGRAPHY AND FURTHER READING: Emmerson, Richard K., and Bernard McGinn, eds. *The Apocalypse in the Middle Ages.* Ithaca, NY: Cornell University Press, 1992; McGinn, Bernard, ed. *Apocalyptic Spirituality.* New York: Paulist Press, 1979; McGinn, Bernard. *The Calabrian Abbot: Joachim of Fiore in the History of Western Thought.* London: Macmillan, 1985; Ratzinger, Joseph. *The Theology of History in St. Bonaventure.* Chicago: Franciscan Herald Press, 1971; Reeves, Marjorie. *Joachim of Fiore and the Prophetic Future,* 2nd ed. Stroud, England: Sutton, 1999. *See also* AUGUSTINIANISM; FRANCISCAN TRADITION, THE

JOHNSON, ELIZABETH, CSJ (1941–)   Elizabeth A. Johnson, a Sister of St. Joseph, was born in 1941. She received her PhD at the Catholic University of America and is now a Distinguished Professor of Theology at Fordham University, New York. She has served on the board of directors of theological magazines and societies and has received 14 honorary doctorates, besides other academic awards. Widely known as a feminist theologian, her writings have been translated into several languages. These include *Consider Jesus* (1990); *She Who Is: The Mystery of God in Feminist Theological Discourse* (1992, 2002); *Women, Earth, and Creator Spirit* (1993); *Truly Our Sister* (2003); and *Quest for the Living God* (2007).

Johnson regards the Catholic Church as a social structure where women are unjustly deprived of equal access to power. She hopes to transform the institution from inside by making women's experience the chief measure of truth for Catholic doctrines and practices. This is the basis for her reinterpretation of Catholic doctrines in feminist terms, for since both Scripture and tradition are in her view distorted by patriarchy, they cannot be used for women's flourishing without first being subjected to feminist criticism. She uses the apophatic way and insists God is unnameable in order to free women from the allegedly oppressive names Father and Son, but she lays this strategy aside once she gives her deity the name Sophia.

As a feminist theologian, Johnson specifically condemns the sin of heterosexism and wants the flourishing of women of different sexual orientations. On this point, she cites lesbians Adrienne Rich and Audre Lorde, who were neither Catholics nor theologians. She deplores Blessed Pope John Paul II's idea of complementarity because it does not do justice to homosexuals, bisexuals, and the intersexed, whose diversity to her mind bespeaks the multidimensional character of humanity. One thing Johnson finds repugnant is the glorification of Mary as "asexual," since it disparages sexually active women. However, a feminist may redefine the Virgin Mary in a subversive way to make the events of her life serve the cause; for example, Mary's virginity need not mean an absence of sexual experience, since the virgin goddesses of antiquity took lovers, and the Magnificat could be reinterpreted as protesting the suppression of women's voices. Johnson is repelled, too, by the official portrait of Mary as humble and submissive to the divine will. She complains that when John Paul II, in *Redemptoris Mater*, listed the womanly virtues, he failed to promote the true dignity of women by leaving out such virtues as self-actualization and the overthrow of oppression. Johnson deplores the traditional idea of motherhood because it allows women no reproductive choice and relegates them to the private sphere where they engage in self-sacrifice.

Johnson objects to the dogma of the Trinity as a profoundly masculine image of God. It has a Father who generates a Son, and the two breathe forth a Spirit who is referred to as "he." She contends that the names Father, Son, and Spirit are only symbolic and that the Trinity is a theological construct that may be replaced with something more acceptable to feminists, namely, the triune mystery of Sophia, consisting of Sophia-Mother, Sophia-Jesus, and Sophia-Spirit. In discussing her new construct of the Trinity, Johnson refers more than once to the Kabbala. She warns us that we create an idol when we think of God literally as King, Lord, or Father and constantly use the pronoun *he*. The Fatherhood of God is not an intrinsic part of revelation, but a metaphor that, if taken in a naive way, becomes oppressive. Women can turn to other models of revelation, such as their own inner experience, to expand Scripture's images for God.

About Christology, Johnson says that it originally empowered women, but soon became the doctrine that most oppressed them. As the early Church developed, Christology was taught more and more from a male viewpoint, and Jesus was turned into the image of a male God whose representative at the altar had to be a male. By the end of the first century, men in authority were using their position as a model for the divine and erasing the original plurality in Jesus' speech about God. Liturgies and sermons were starting to use the patriarchal language that is still embedded in the Church's public prayers. Since then, the emphasis on Jesus' maleness has been the main reason why God is always referred to as "he." While she concedes that Jesus said, "He who sees me sees the Father" (John 14:9), Johnson argues that it is uncritical and naive to interpret the line literally and make the man Jesus into a revelation of the Father-God. She also laments that John's Gospel calls Jesus *Logos*, a name linked in ancient Greek philosophy to the male principle. Interpreting the fourth Gospel anew, she asserts that the prehistory of Jesus was instead the story of Wisdom (Sophia), though John disguised it as that of Logos.

Johnson repeats more than once that Jesus is the human being Sophia became. He spoke Sophia's words and did her deeds. Though Sophia may be only an allegory for divine wisdom found in the late books of the Old Testament, Johnson treats that image as the true and final revelation of God. Jesus as Sophia Incarnate was externally male, but he was a revelation of God as female—She Who Is. And besides, according to Johnson, Sophia was not only incarnate in Jesus as her prophet but also fully in control of him at all times—inspiring, sending, guiding, and resurrecting.

The Cross, for Johnson, was not the repayment to God of the debt due for sin. Rather, it symbolized the self-emptying of male domination. It was Sophia suffering the final pangs of pregnancy and struggling to bring her new creation to birth. As for the Resurrection, Johnson speaks of Jesus' disciples experiencing him as risen and expressing their feelings by calling him Christ. Afterward, they wrote community-building documents called Gospels in which they chose to retain some memories and abandon others. Paul was the first to interpret Jesus as Son of God, Mark followed him,

and by the end of the first century, Christians said that Jesus was the Son of God from conception, while John pushed this identity back before conception.

In addition to being a feminist theologian, Johnson is also an ecofeminist. In *Women, Earth, and Creator Spirit* (1993), she draws from the writings of Teilhard de Chardin and Thomas Berry to explain how human consciousness is only a more intense form of material energy. Without need for supernatural intervention, our intelligence arose from the universe itself, which is also intelligent and self-organizing. The Big Bang was already a Pentecost. She warns that human beings are damaging the planet by unbridled reproduction and that they need to extend moral standing to other species and ecological systems so as to live in divine solidarity with them. Johnson wonders why human beings think themselves more important than trees and why they value spirit more highly than matter. Moreover, she denies firmly that God is uncontaminated by matter and utterly transcendent. The solution to our ecological crisis, she proposes, is for us to shift our moral attention from human beings to the natural world as a sacrament of divine presence and to see its desecration as deeply sinful. The chief criterion of the morality of our actions should be whether they contribute to a sustainable life on earth.

Finally, Johnson is a strong advocate for women in the priesthood. She claims that, at first, every Christian was a priest without distinction and that Jesus never ordained his apostles or set up an all-male priesthood. She blames Luke for focusing exclusively on Peter and Paul in the book of Acts and suppressing the stories of women apostles who had preached, prophesied, and held leadership roles. Since sexist structures are embedded in the Bible, she urges the feminist theologian to use the hermeneutics of suspicion as well as the hermeneutics of reconstruction to discover the submerged histories of women in the early Church.

Johnson dismisses the Vatican pronouncement *Inter Insignores* (1976) against the ordination of women, calling it naive, simplistic, and theologically erroneous. If women cannot act *in persona Christi* at the Eucharist, she argues, it undercuts the meaning of baptism, by which women are made icons of Christ and thereby entitled to participate in the governance and ministry of the Church. In an article published in *Commonweal* on January 26, 1996, Johnson faults a just-released Vatican statement on women's ordination, *Ordinatio Sacerdotalis*, for its lack of persuasive reasoning, drawing her key response to it from the Second Vatican Council's *Declaration on Religious Freedom*, which states that truth cannot be imposed by force. She explains that the feminist theologian cannot in conscience accept the Church's teaching about the all-male priesthood, and so, the *Declaration* is her warrant for ongoing resistance. However, that resistance must not be construed as disloyalty or rebellion, but as loyalty and service. Johnson compares dissenting feminists like herself to St. Catherine of Siena and says she writes only out of concern for the truth. Though she dissents from the institutional authorities, she does so for the sake of the wider Church of the faithful.

In March 2011, the Committee on Doctrine of the U.S. Conference of Catholic Bishops issued a statement on Sister Johnson's book *Quest for the Living God*, concluding that the book "contains misrepresentations, ambiguities, and errors that bear upon the faith of the Catholic Church as found in Sacred Scripure, and as it is authentically taught by the Church's universal magisterium."—Anne Barbeau Gardiner

See also DISSENT; FARLEY, MARGARET, RSM; FEMINISM; FEMINISM IN THE CHURCH; MAGISTERIUM

JULIAN THE APOSTATE (331–363) Julian the Apostate was born into the imperial family of the Roman Empire in 331. Julian's father, Julius Constantius, was a stepbrother of Constantine the Great, who had legalized Christianity in the Edict of Milan. When Constantine died in 337, his three sons, fearing that Julius Constantius was a threat to their reign, conspired to kill his family; Julian and his brother Gallus, however, were saved due to their young age.

Julian was raised by Eusebius of Nicomedia, an Arian bishop. In addition to studying Scripture under Eusebius's tutelage, Julian became versed in Homer, Hesiod, Plato, Aristotle, and the Hellenistic tradition. Julian studied under some of the most influential thinkers of his time, including the sophist Libanius. In 355, the Roman emperor Constantius II appointed Julian the Caesar of Gaul, where he proved to be one of the greatest military commanders of the fourth century. His most important military engagement was at Strasburg, where he successfully defeated the Alamanni, a barbarian clan that had invaded Roman Gaul.

At the height of his military success, Julian's army declared him coemperor of the Roman Empire. Constantius II, the existing emperor, prepared to wage war against Julian, but died before a civil war could take place. Once Julian was decreed the sole emperor of the Roman Empire, he abandoned the Christian faith and openly made sacrifices to the Roman gods. Ju-

lian believed that the legalization of Christianity had weakened the mores of the empire. In order to appease the gods, Julian reopened all the pagan temples that had been closed by his last two Christian predecessors, Constantine and Constantius II. Julian also declared religious toleration throughout the Roman Empire with the hope that religious liberty would intensify the theological differences among the Christian sects and thus weaken Christianity.

The ultimate goal of Julian's reign was to repaganize and de-Christianize the Roman Empire. Julian removed the Christian clergy's tax exemption, taxed ecclesiastical profits, confiscated certain churches, exiled St. Athanasius, and forced all his soldiers to worship the Roman gods. He even attempted to rebuild the Jewish Temple of Jerusalem in an effort to weaken the faith of devout Christians. In response to these edicts, persecution of Christians grew. A "mob rule" of ordinary pagan citizens killed bishops, clergy, and laypeople throughout the Eastern Empire. Julian took no action in response to the persecution, indicating his subtle support of it.

Julian's most significant edict was his *Rescript on Christian Teaching*, an imperial order that banned Christians from teaching at secular universities. Decreed on June 17, 362, Julian wrote, "Since the gods have granted us liberty, it seems to me absurd that men should teach what they do not believe to be sound." Julian was very aware of the link between morality and education. Since Christians were atheists in the eyes of pagans, Julian deemed that Christians were not morally capable of teaching the pagan classics. Julian identified cultural Hellenism with theological paganism. St. Gregory of Nazianzus rebutted Julian in his *First and Second Invective against Julian* by arguing that Christians could benefit from pagan philosophy and literature, even if it was not divinely inspired.

Although Julian attempted to rid Christianity of its intellectual status, he was very aware of Christianity's achievements. Julian recognized that Christians committed many works of charity. In his letter to his friend Arsacius, the emperor wrote that Christians were making many converts through the exercise of *agape*, or love. Julian wanted pagan priests to mimic the charitable acts of the Christian clergy. To accomplish this formidable task, Julian demanded that pagan priests develop a more ascetic life, avoid jests and obscenities, ban erotic fiction, wear plain attire, and refrain from such luxuries as theater and chariot racing.

In addition to his edicts, Julian wrote many treatises, including *The Caesars*, *Misopogon* ("The Beard-Hater"), and *Against the Galileans*. In the latter treatise, Julian rehashed the arguments of Celsus and Porphyry in an attempt to debunk the legitimacy of Christianity. Julian dismissed Christianity as a cult, argued that pagan philosophy had produced more outstanding heroes than Christian theology, and concluded that Christians were nothing more than disobedient Jews. According to Julian, Christianity was a threat to the Roman Empire.

Julian's attempt to repaganize the empire failed for several reasons. For one thing, Julian reigned for only 18 months and his immediate successor, Jovian, was a Christian. Some historians also argue that Julian's project failed because of how well-grounded Christianity had become during the fourth century. According to this view, Julian's failure demonstrates the difficulty of imposing a political solution on a civilization with a deeply embedded and opposing religious and cultural view.

Beginning in the Renaissance, Julian was seen as a hero by many critics of the Church, including Edward Gibbon, Algernon Swinburne, Henrik Ibsen, and Gore Vidal, among others. In particular, Gibbon's thesis, which stated that Christianity hastened the fall of the Roman Empire, had many similarities with Julian's own arguments in *Against the Galileans*. Devout Catholics have also responded, in one way or another, to Julian's legacy. Julian is mentioned in several of Pope Benedict XVI's books and encyclicals. Cardinal John Henry Newman believed that Julian, despite his many faults, was a specimen of pagan virtue.

Julian died in a campaign against the Persian Empire while fighting in the front lines. By the end of the century, Christianity was the official religion of the Roman Empire. In the words of the 19th-century poet Algernon Swinburne, Julian was the "last pagan."—Thomas F. X. Varacalli

BIBLIOGRAPHY AND FURTHER READING: Ammianus Marcellinus. *Later Roman Empire (354–378)*. Translated by Walter Hamilton. New York: Penguin, 2004; Bowersock, G. W. *Julian the Apostate*. Cambridge, MA: Harvard University Press, 1978; Julian. *The Loeb Classical Library of the Collected Works of Julian*. Translated by Wilmer C. Wright. Cambridge, MA: Harvard University Press, 2006; Murdoch, Adrian. *The Last Pagan*. Rochester, VT: Inner Traditions, 2003. *See also* BASIL THE GREAT, ST.; CHURCH FATHERS, EARLY; *FIDES ET RATIO*; NATURAL LAW

· K ·

KENNEDY, JOHN F. (1917–1963)   John Fitzgerald Kennedy was the 35th President of the United States and the first Catholic to be elected to that office. Many viewed his election as a symbolic marker of the maturation and assimilation of the Catholic Church in the United States, although his personal ethics and view of the relationship between religion and politics raised questions concerning his fitness as the chief Catholic figure in American public life.

Kennedy was the second child of Joseph and Rose Kennedy, a wealthy and politically connected couple who came from prominent Irish Catholic Boston families. The Kennedys had eight other children. Robert F. Kennedy became attorney general of the United States under his brother and was assassinated during his campaign for the Democratic nomination for president in 1968. Edward Kennedy became a U.S. senator from Massachusetts, serving for almost five decades until his death in 2009. A sister, Eunice Kennedy Shriver, who also passed away in 2009, founded the Special Olympics in 1968.

The beneficiaries of Irish political power in Boston and entrepreneurial riches acquired through banking, real estate, and other ventures, Joseph and Rose were able to offer their children all the perks of American society. In 1938, Joseph was appointed U.S. ambassador to Great Britain. Meanwhile, John graduated from Choate boarding school and matriculated at Harvard University. After his graduation in 1940, he entered the Navy. He survived the destruction of the PT boat that he commanded and garnered accolades for his leadership in saving his crew.

On the strength of his war hero status, his father's fortune, and his own budding political skills, Kennedy was elected to the U.S. House of Representatives in 1946 as a Democrat. Six years later, he was elected to the Senate. During his period as a senator, he married Jacqueline Bouvier and published a Pulitzer Prize–winning book, *Profiles in Courage*. In 1960, he was nominated by the Democratic Party for president and narrowly defeated then vice president Richard Nixon in the general election. After serving fewer than three years as president, he was assassinated on November 22, 1963.

Some Protestant and secular polemicists raised the issue of Kennedy's religion in the course of the presidential election. Norman Vincent Peale, for example, headed a group of 150 Protestant ministers who publicly opposed Kennedy's election. Still, the intensity of anti-Catholicism in American politics—by no means insignificant in 1960—had declined since the first Catholic to run for president on a major party ticket, Al Smith, was defeated in 1928. Kennedy's adroit handling of the religious question also helped to disarm anti-

Catholic critics. That Catholics supported him disproportionately is certain: some 80% of his coreligionists cast their ballots for him.

Kennedy's policy positions were not unusual in the Democratic Party of the 1950s and 1960s, though some of them would be considered conservative today. For example, he proposed a series of income tax cuts, which were implemented after his death. At the same time, his New Frontier program envisioned federal funding for education, medical care for the elderly, and economic aid for rural regions. On race, he was progressive in the context of the time and became increasingly so over the course of his presidency, finally proposing civil rights legislation that would pass under his successor, Lyndon Johnson. In foreign affairs, scholars remain divided about whether Kennedy was a "Cold Warrior" taking a hard line against Communism, or a standard liberal adopting a more conciliatory stance. There is evidence to support both positions. For example, he escalated U.S. involvement in Vietnam, but also supported aid to Communist Yugoslavia (against the wishes of many Catholic bishops).

Although Catholics debated these issues, few argued that any of Kennedy's policies contradicted Catholic teaching. Catholic observers have found reason to praise a number of his policies, such as his concern for racial equality, his creation of the Peace Corps, and his opposition to worldwide Communism. An exception was Kennedy's education policy—support for federal funding of education yet opposition to parochial school aid—which put him at odds with the bishops' national organization, the National Catholic Welfare Conference. A case could be made that Kennedy's New Frontier program, insofar as it centralized funding and control of social programs in the federal government, was not in accord with the principle of subsidiarity, but opposition to these policies came from conservative circles and were not cast as specifically Catholic objections. Subsequent debate about Kennedy's meaning and legacy as a Catholic figure has focused less on his public policy and more on his personal practice of Catholicism and his statements on church and state.

Kennedy clearly identified himself as a Catholic and regularly attended church. He was a member of the Knights of Columbus and was on friendly terms with the archbishop of Boston, Cardinal Richard Cushing. (Cardinal Francis Spellman of New York, meanwhile, supported Nixon during the 1960 campaign.) Some believe that Pope John XXIII's intervention during the Cuban Missile Crisis influenced Kennedy's actions.

At the same time, Kennedy's moral code has been called into question. Claims that Kennedy engaged in numerous extramarital affairs both before and during his tenure as president were neither widely reported nor entirely suppressed at the time. Evidence uncovered by later investigators confirms a pattern of sexual promiscuity. Accusations of ties to organized crime and unethical political methods are similarly widespread, though not as indisputable; the most common is the charge that Kennedy benefited from the assistance of the Chicago mafia during the 1960 election.

Kennedy's views on church and state are more publicly accessible. To counter the anti-Catholic critics who surfaced during the 1960 campaign, the Catholic candidate fashioned a response meant to put to rest definitively any accusation of divided loyalty. He had first broached the subject in a widely noted 1959 interview published in *Look* magazine, where he stated, "Whatever one's religion in private life may be, for the office-holder, nothing takes precedence over his oath to uphold the Constitution and all its parts—including the First Amendment and the strict separation of church and state." He also announced that he had reversed his stands in favor of state aid to parochial schools and diplomatic recognition of the Vatican. The article elicited significant negative reaction from the Catholic press and many bishops.

The most famous expression of Kennedy's position was a speech he delivered to the Greater Houston Ministerial Association in September 1960. "I believe in an America where the separation of church and state is absolute," he declared. "I do not speak for my church on public matters; and the church does not speak for me." On policy matters, he insisted, he would make decisions "in accordance with what my conscience tells me to be in the national interest, and without regard to outside religious pressure or dictates."

Historians are still sorting out the provenance of the Kennedy speech. It has been suggested that speechwriter Theodore Sorensen asked for input from at least three prominent Catholic figures: Bishop John Wright of Pittsburgh, Jesuit theologian John Courtney Murray, and *Commonweal* editor John Cogley. The degree to which these advisors approved the final product remains a matter of debate. In a 1968 interview, Cogley confirmed his advisory role, but doubted that Wright or Murray had any significant input. Murray later admitted speaking briefly with Sorensen shortly before the speech, but implied that his influence was minimal if any. Without question, Murray generally kept his distance from Kennedy's campaign and church–state pronouncements. In 1967, Murray wrote in a personal letter that he believed Kennedy had been "far more of a separationist than I am."

While it is widely acknowledged that Kennedy's articulation of the relationship between religion and public office was politically successful, many Catholic commentators point to the Houston speech as the initiation of a harmful trend in Catholic political engagement: the justification of political positions contrary to Church teaching by characterizing them as private views that should not be imposed on public policy. In a March 2010 address, Archbishop Charles Chaput of Denver furnished an instance of this criticism of Kennedy's speech: "It began the project of walling religion away from the process of governance in a new and aggressive way. It also divided a person's private beliefs from his or her public duties."

The election of John F. Kennedy as president was a watershed yet ambivalent moment in the history of American Catholicism: A Catholic had been approved for the nation's highest office, but in the process had denounced religious influence on politics. Kennedy's impact on the implementation of Catholic social teaching in American politics is similarly complicated. While he understandably did not explicitly invoke Catholic principles, one might plausibly consider his policy record to be largely consistent with a genuinely Catholic approach to questions of public order. At the same time, his insistence on absolute separation of religious and political concerns, especially in retrospect, must be considered an inadequate characterization of the relationship between Catholic belief and public life.—Kevin E. Schmiesing

BIBLIOGRAPHY AND FURTHER READING: Campbell, Colleen Carroll. "The Enduring Costs of John F. Kennedy's Compromise." *Catholic World Report*, February 2007; Carty, Thomas J. *A Catholic in the White House? Religion, Politics, and John F. Kennedy's Presidential Campaign*. New York: Palgrave Macmillan, 2004; Casey, Shaun. *The Making of a Catholic President: Kennedy vs. Nixon, 1960*. New York: Oxford University Press, 2009; Collier, Peter, and David Horowitz. *The Kennedys*. New York: Summit, 1984; McAndrews, Lawrence J. "The Avoidable Conflict: Kennedy, the Bishops, and Federal Aid to Education." *Catholic Historical Review* 76 (April 1990): 278–294; Reeves, Thomas C. *A Question of Character: A Life of John F. Kennedy*. New York: Three Rivers Press, 1997.

KING, THOMAS M., SJ (1929–2009) Thomas King was the second of four children born to William H. and Catherine M. (Mulvihill) King of Pittsburgh,

Pennsylvania. He and his older brother William, who preceded him into the Jesuit order, had two younger sisters, Martha and Catherine Marie. Following his graduation from Central Catholic High School in Pittsburgh, Thomas earned a bachelor's degree in English at the University of Pittsburgh; a master's in education at Fordham University; a licentiate in sacred theology at Woodstock College, Maryland; and a doctorate in sacred theology at the University of Strasbourg, France. Father King taught theology at Georgetown University from 1968 until 2009. A distinguished scholar, Professor King's writings include books and articles on the Jesuit paleontologist and philosopher Pierre Teilhard de Chardin, Trappist monk/author Thomas Merton, and French philosopher Jean-Paul Sartre.

In response to what he considered an "invitation" from Jesus to become a priest, King entered the Society of Jesus in 1951 and was ordained in 1964. He chose the Jesuit order because the "process of learning and knowing" was important to him. After earning his doctorate in 1968, Father King began teaching theology at Georgetown. One of the first theology courses he taught was "The Problem of God," a course that became very popular with students and one he continued to teach regularly over the next four decades. This first year, he noted, was a year of turmoil for the nation. It was the year when Martin Luther King Jr. and Robert F. Kennedy were assassinated and when the United States' involvement in Vietnam was being strongly protested on American campuses. Consequently, in 1969, King moved from his residence with the Jesuit community into a freshman dorm in order to be more readily available to students. His discussions with them—both in and out of class—helped many discern their vocations.

During his second year at Georgetown, Father King began celebrating an 11:15 p.m. Mass six nights a week in Dahlgren Chapel. This Mass became a treasured memory for countless alumni over the next 40 years. Many recall the candlelit chapel, Father's deeply spiritual homilies, his great reverence for the Eucharist, and his practice of reading the first Gospel of St. John at the conclusion of each Mass. In addition, King offered an annual Mass on campus to celebrate the coming of Christmas, and, because the work of Teilhard de Chardin influenced him so profoundly, he would also celebrate the anniversary of his ordination to the priesthood by saying a Mass in the crypt underneath the chapel in Copley Hall.

At times of unrest—for example, when students were demonstrating against the U.S. presence in Vietnam, grieving the loss of life following the September

11, 2001, attack on the World Trade Center, or mourning the death of a student—he would offer special Masses. During his last few years, King went beyond the campus to offer Mass on Monday evenings for prisoners at the Arlington County jail. While students recall his scholarship and ability to clarify difficult concepts, they often remember even more vividly his laughter, keen sense of humor, and unfeigned interest in their lives, especially as they related to God. Indeed, in 1999, the university's student newspaper, the *Hoya*, named King "Georgetown's Man of the Century," noting that no one had had "a more significant presence on campus and effect on students than Father King."

As cofounder (1989) and first president of University Faculty for Life (UFL), a position he held for 15 years, King helped establish and implement the mission and goals of this pro-life organization. He believed that through research, dialogue, and publication, UFL could accomplish academically what no other organization in America could do. In particular, he encouraged holding annual conferences where pro-life scholars would have the opportunity to offer papers on issues related to abortion, infanticide, and euthanasia. Select papers from these conferences appear in UFL's peer-reviewed journals and are distributed to hundreds of university libraries. From its beginning, Father King coedited UFL's quarterly newsletter, *Pro Vita*, which provided a venue for members to discuss life issues and to learn of each other's achievements. Always interested in the upcoming generation, King served as faculty advisor for Students for Life at Georgetown University and helped host its annual Cardinal O'Connor Conferences. These conferences continue to draw together college and high school students from around the country on the day preceding the annual March for Life in Washington, D.C.

Additionally, King was an active member of the Knights of Columbus and Pax Christi. Although not a complete pacifist, he opposed many wars, particularly those he believed the country could not win, and emphasized the peaceful prevention of conflict whenever possible. Significantly, his cofounding of Cosmos and Creation (1982), an association that explores the relationship between science and theology, demonstrates Father King's extraordinary gift for bringing people together in their search for truth.—Jane H. Gilroy

BIBLIOGRAPHY AND FURTHER READING: King, Thomas M., SJ. "Abortion: Why This Issue." *Life and Learning XV: Proceedings of the Fifteenth University Faculty for Life Conference* 15 (2006): 113–119; King, Thomas M., SJ. *Teilhard's Mass: Approaches to "The Mass on the World."* Mahwah, NJ: Paulist Press, 2005; King, Thomas

M., SJ. "A Writer Loses Himself: A Study of Thomas Merton." *Chicago Studies* 24, no. 1 (1985): 69–86. *See also* ABORTION; RIGHT TO LIFE MOVEMENT; SOCIETY OF JESUS; UNIVERSITY FACULTY FOR LIFE

KÜNG, HANS (1928–)   Beginning around and at the Second Vatican Council in 1962–1965, Swiss theologian Hans Küng, although still only in his early 30s, was one of the most prominent and best known Catholic theologians in the world. He served as a *peritus*, or theological expert, at the council, and at the same time was publishing such best-selling books as *The Council, Reform, and Reunion* (1961), which helped bring to the council the worldwide attention it garnered at the time.

Within two years after the end of the council, however, other books by Küng came under critical examination by the Congregation for the Doctrine of the Faith (CDF) in Rome. These books included a major opus, his 1967 *Die Kirche* (*The Church*, 1968) and, especially, his 1970 study *Unfehlbar? Eine Anfrage* (*Infallible? An Inquiry*, 1971). The ultimate result of the examination by the CDF of these and some of his later books, along with the eventual outcome of extensive and prolonged exchanges of views between him, the CDF, and the German bishops' conference over nearly a decade, was the formal judgment issued by the CDF on December 18, 1979, that Küng could "no longer be considered a Catholic theologian or function as such in a teaching role."

In spite of this condemnation, Küng continued over the next three decades to be one of the most prolific and widely read theological authors in the world. He was widely featured as a speaker, journalist, and popular media gadfly and "star" on religious and theological subjects. Moreover, in spite of the negative Roman judgment against him, he went right on presenting himself as a "Catholic theologian," and he continued to be generally accepted as such by many, both Catholic and non-Catholic. In later years, he became recognized as an ecumenist and expert on world religions, as exemplified in such books of his as the 1986 book coauthored with three other experts, *Christianity and the World Religions: Paths of Dialogue with Islam, Hinduism, and Buddhism.*

Hans Küng was born on March 19, 1928, near Lucerne, Switzerland, and attended a coeducational German gymnasium there. Later, residing at the Collegium Germanicum in Rome, he studied for more than seven years in the Eternal City, including at the papal and Jesuit Gregorian University. He was ordained a diocesan priest in Switzerland. Later, in 1957, he took his doctorate in theology at the Institut Catholique in Paris, producing a highly praised dissertation on justification in the work of the distinguished Swiss Protestant theologian Karl Barth. He eventually became a professor of dogmatic and ecumenical theology and director of the Institute of Ecumenical Research at the University of Tübingen in Germany, which remained his permanent base, although he also taught frequently as a visiting professor at universities in Europe, Asia, and America—from which he received numerous honorary degrees. Küng's status at Tübingen had to be based on a special arrangement, since as a result of the 1979 Roman declaration that he was no longer a Catholic theologian, he could not be part of the Catholic theological faculty there, nor could he serve on the university's Protestant theological faculty.

For his part, Father Küng never accepted the Church's judgment that he was no longer a Catholic theologian. Yet he also publicly and sometimes sensationally refused to accept Church judgments and teachings on not a few other points. The 1979 CDF judgment against him, however, was based primarily on Küng's book *Infallible?* which examined the question of the Church's infallibility as that question had arisen with regard to the 1968 encyclical of Pope Paul VI, *Humanae Vitae*. This papal encyclical reiterating the Church's moral condemnation of the use of contraception was rejected by large numbers of Catholics when it was issued, and statistics today confirm that its teaching is still not accepted by most Catholic married couples. In 1968, hundreds of Catholic theologians, mostly in Europe and North America, publicly dissented from the teaching of the encyclical that "each and every marriage act must remain open to the transmission of life" (*HV* # 11). Generally speaking, these theological dissenters justified their dissent from the teaching of a papal encyclical by claiming that the teaching in question was not infallible. Hence, presumably, Catholic theologians *could* licitly dissent from a teaching that was possibly reformable. Such was the common argument, very widely accepted at the time (as it still is).

Küng's study of the infallibility question, however, had convinced him that the Catholic Church's traditional condemnation of the use of contraception had been consistently taught by the Church at all times and everywhere, and hence he believed that this teaching *was* infallible, according to the Church's established criteria concerning infallible teachings. However, it was also manifestly *wrong*. But if a Church could be mistaken about one of her "infallible" teachings, then what

followed logically was that the Church was *not* necessarily infallible. This was essentially Küng's argument.

In Küng's judgment, the Church was what he called "indefectible" in truth: The Church could not and would not depart from the basic truths of revelation concerning salvation in Jesus Christ, but at the same time the Church could not necessarily always be right in every detail. Indefectibility meant that the Church would persevere in truth despite being capable of error in some respects.

Such an open denial of the Church's infallibility, however, went against the plain and definite teaching of both the First and Second Vatican Councils that the Church *was* infallible in certain of her teachings on faith and morals universally proposed to the faithful to believe—not to speak of contradicting such acts of the teaching Church as Blessed Pope Pius IX's promulgation of the doctrine of the Immaculate Conception in 1854 and that of Pope Pius XII of the doctrine of the Assumption in 1951. Having examined Küng's analysis and arguments, the CDF ultimately had no choice but to condemn his position, since Küng quite aggressively refused to reconsider his position: *he*, not the Church, was in the right.

Father Küng's theological works exhibit over and over again this same pattern of asserting a position of his own against an established position of the Church. He believes and insists that Church teachings may be modified in the light of modern theological research and argument.

For example, in his *Theology for the Third Millennium: An Ecumenical View* (1988), Küng himself clearly recognized that binding Church teaching verified at the Councils of Lyons (1274), Florence (1439), and Trent (1547) has always held that "there were seven sacraments instituted by Christ"—a teaching that has been many times reaffirmed and that is, not incidentally, also firmly held by the Eastern Orthodox Church. Küng, however, while he agrees that the institution of the sacraments of baptism and the Eucharist can be verified in the New Testament, nevertheless holds that "the information given in the New Testament about the other sacraments speaks a different language, and the traditional proof texts cannot bear the weight of evidence and interpretation they are credited with"—as if the Church's traditional teaching on the seven sacraments reposed *only* on New Testament texts! For Küng, however, modern scholarly study of those texts outweighs the long teaching and practice of the Church and is decisive. Given this kind of approach and thinking, it cannot be surprising that the Catholic Church has formally judged Küng not to be a Catholic theologian in spite of his pretensions to the contrary.

It might be asked on what basis Küng considers that he *does* remain a Catholic theologian. In a 1980 essay entitled "Why I Remain a Catholic," he spoke of his love and admiration for the Swiss Catholic milieu and tradition in which he was raised and his view that Protestantism was too disjointed and splintered. All in all, the Catholic tradition was to be preferred. He claimed to represent what he called "an evangelical catholicity . . . concentrated and organized in the light of the Gospel. . . . Being Catholic means being ecumenical in the fullest sense." What must be noted, however, is that in spite of his insistence that he himself remains within the bounds of Catholicity, his judgment of "being Catholic" is quite clearly based not on what the Catholic Church itself defines as Catholicity, but upon what he himself decides—in other words, he employs Protestant "private judgment" to establish the particular Catholicity that he professes.

Although the Catholic Church's official judgment on Father Küng cannot be gainsaid—he is *not* a "Catholic theologian" in any true sense of the term— he nevertheless remains one of the major religious and theological figures of his own time. Those desiring to understand the post–Vatican II situation of the Catholic Church also need to understand what Küng represents if they are accurately to understand the turbulent years that followed the council. For the sake of this understanding—if not for the sake of any authentic truth of Christianity that it contains—probably the best of Küng's many books to consult is his *Christ Sein* (*On Being a Christian*, 1976).—Kenneth D. Whitehead

BIBLIOGRAPHY AND FURTHER READING: Küng, Hans. *On Being a Christian.* Translated by Edward Quinn. Garden City, NY: Doubleday, 1976; Küng, Hans. "Why I Remain a Catholic." In *Consensus in Theology? A Dialogue with Hans Küng and Edward Schillebeeckx,* edited by Leonard Swidler. Philadelphia: Westminster Press, 1980; Swidler, Leonard, ed. *Küng in Conflict.* Garden City, NY: Doubleday, 1981. *See also* CONGREGATION FOR THE DOCTRINE OF THE FAITH; CURRAN, CHARLES E.; DISSENT; McBRIEN, RICHARD P.

· L ·

LACORDAIRE, JEAN BAPTISTE-HENRI DOMINIQUE (1802–1861) Jean-Baptiste Henri-Dominique Lacordaire, who was reputed to be the greatest pulpit orator of the 19th century, was born on

May 13, 1802, and died November 21, 1861. When he was four years old, his father died. He was brought up a Catholic, and his mother provided that he receive legal training at Dijon. He then went to Paris and, even though he was underage, he was allowed to handle cases in court.

Lacordaire had lost his faith early in life, but then he had a conversion experience and regained it. He asked to be accepted as a seminarian in Paris and was ordained in 1827. He was then appointed a chaplain to a convent and at the College Henri IV. When Bishop John Dubois of New York visited Paris in search of priests for his diocese, he spoke to the young Lacordaire and told Lacordaire that he would make him his vicar general and rector of his seminary. Before Lacordaire could leave for New York, however, Hugues-Félicité Robert de Lamennais started a newspaper called *L'Avenir* and offered Lacordaire a job as a writer, which he accepted. Lacordaire and Comte Charles de Montalembert met at the office of the newspaper and were the principal contributors. On the one hand, the writing was strongly ultramontane; on the other hand, they strongly supported religious freedom and freedom of speech and the press.

Lancelot C. Sheppard's comment on the relationship between Lacordaire and Lamennais is that there was a contrast between the two. Sheppard writes that Lacordaire's close collaboration with Lamennais lasted for a little less than two years, but "their names were linked together in one way or another for many years to come, generally to Lacordaire's detriment." When their positions were criticized by Pope Gregory XVI, Lacordaire ended the close relationship.

In the late 18th and 19th centuries, the most important word in the political history of France was *liberalism.* Prior to the French Revolution of 1789, the dominant political theory was that of the Ancien Régime and the papal monarchy, and the bishops were mostly Gallicans. The government was a monarchy, at first an absolute monarchy; church and state were united, and the Church was supported by the monarchy. In 1789, the revolution began with a solemn Pontifical Mass and procession led by the archbishop of Paris. A meeting was called of the Estates General. The most radical proposals were made by the clergy, including some of the bishops, such as Talleyrand, who joined themselves to the Third Estate and ended up with the majority of votes. The "liberal" position demanded separation of church and state and the secularization of all the schools.

After the double fall of Napoleon I, the Bourbon dynasty was restored in the person of King Louis XVIII and then King Charles X. When the July Monarchy took power in 1830, Louis Philippe became King of the French. The July Monarchy was overthrown in 1848, and the Second Republic was established. Prince Louis Napoleon, nephew of Napoleon I, became president from 1848 to 1852.

In 1838, Lacordaire went to Rome, where he entered the Order of St. Dominic with the further intention of reestablishing the order in France. Lacordaire served twice as provincial of the French province, but his time as superior was a time of controversy in the order over the celebration of the liturgy of the hours.

Elections were held in April 1848. Fifteen priests were elected to the Constituent Assembly, of whom three were bishops. Lacordaire was elected deputy of Marseilles with two thousand votes. Lacordaire took his seat in the Assembly in his white Dominican habit and on the extreme left of the Assembly. He remained in the Assembly for only 11 days and spoke twice, without any great effect. He resigned on May 13, explaining that he felt he had to draw a line between the passions and parties and his impartiality as a religious.

In 1852, the Second Republic was overthrown, and the Second Empire was established (1852–1870). Louis Napoleon was then known as the Emperor Napoleon III. During this period, Catholic liberals like Lacordaire and Montalambert were ultramontane, that is, strong supporters of the papacy. At the same time, their Catholic liberalism was focused on freedom of education, freedom of the press, and election of representatives. They wanted to establish a constitutional government and the rule of law, parliamentary government, and the protection of private property. As Catholics, they looked for civil equality, political liberty, and freedom of conscience. After the defection of Lamennais, Lacordaire and his friend Montalambert became the principal Catholic liberals. John H. Hallowell, in his foreword to Father Finlay's book on Montalambert, has identified many of these political positions.

The liberal Catholic positions were all lost in the Third Republic (1870–1914), but many of them were eventually taken up again. Many of these positions were supported by Pope Leo XIII, especially through his great encyclical *Rerum Novarum*. The emphasis in Catholic social teaching was refocused away from the concern of parliamentary political organization to a concern for the poor, in the tradition of the German bishop of Mainz, William Emmanuel Baron von Kettler, and his concerns about labor reform.

Hallowell traces the development from hostility between the Church and Liberalism to the liberal political and social ideas of Pope John XXIII in his encyclicals *Pacem in Terris*, *Mater et Magistra*, and *Gaudium et Spes* and the Second Vatican Council's *Pastoral Constitution on the Church in the Modern World*. Toward the end of his life, Lacordaire was honored by being elected to the Academie Francaise.—George P. Graham

BIBLIOGRAPHY AND FURTHER READING: Finlay, James C., SJ. *The Liberal Who Failed: Montalembert, 1810–1870*. With a foreword by John H. Hallowell. Washington, DC: Corpus Books, 1968; Hales, E. E.Y. *Pio Nono*. New York: P. J. Kennedy & Sons, 1954; Hales, E. E.Y. *Revolution and the Papacy*. Notre Dame, IN: Notre Dame University Press, 1966; Shepherd, Lancelot. *Lacordaire: A Biographical Essay*. New York: Macmillan, 1964. *See also* LAMENNAIS, HUGUES-FÉLICITÉ ROBERT DE; *MIRARI VOS*; *PACEM IN TERRIS*; RELIGIOUS LIBERTY; ULTRAMONTANISM

LAMENNAIS, HUGUES-FÉLICITÉ ROBERT DE (1782–1854)

Hugues-Félicité Robert de Lamennais—a priest, writer, social and political critic, and theorist—was one of the most significant figures in Church and social history in the middle of the 19th century. He was born in St. Malo on the coast of Brittany in 1782, near the birthplace of writer, diplomat, and one of the founders of French romanticism and the neo-Catholic movement François-René de Chateaubriand (1768–1848). Few people played a more significant role in laying the foundations of the modern Catholic social tradition than Lamennais. Few would suffer a more wrenching fall from grace.

Paradox marked Lamennais's unusually eventful and active life. Extravagantly talented and hardworking, principled and courageous, a writer of great charm and force, Lamennais also could be stubborn, excruciatingly sensitive, and tragically intransigent when convinced of the rightness of his views. Moody, reclusive, and by his own description an "unusually ugly" man, he nonetheless drew an extraordinarily influential circle to himself. Pope Leo XII was said to have admired Lamennais so much that he kept a portrait of him in his private chambers in the Vatican and gave consideration to making him a cardinal. In contrast, Leo's successor, Pope Gregory XVI would condemn Lamennais's teachings—key aspects of which nevertheless eventually would find adoption in the documents of the Second Vatican Council.

After his mother's death when he was five years old, an uncle took charge of Lamennais's education. The uncle, a devoté of Jean-Jacques Rousseau's theories of education, locked the boy in his well-stocked library and let him read as he desired. This broad, if perhaps not fully balanced, education gave Lamennais an extensive exposure to contemporary philosophical and political thought.

Devout as a child, Lamennais fell away from his Catholic beliefs during his adolescence. Under the guidance of his brother Jean, a priest ordained in 1804, Lamennais returned to the faith and received his First Holy Communion that year, at age 22. For the next several years, Lamennais taught mathematics at a college recently founded by the Church, where his brother taught theology. There, under Jean's guidance, Lamennais engaged in an intense study of Scripture, the Church Fathers, the schoolmen, and the work of contemporary theologians. He received the tonsure and minor orders in 1809 and, after a period of tortured indecision, took holy orders in 1816. Lamennais never held a formal ecclesiastical position. Nevertheless, he was a devoted teacher and spiritual guide to many, including such notables as Victor Hugo, who, deeply impressed by Lamennais, made his first confession to him and remained his close friend for a number of years.

One might roughly divide Lamennais's work, at least until the mid-1830s, into five elements: theoretical and practical efforts to renew the Church and society in the wake of the French Revolution; an attempt to state an integrative philosophy of authority; the development of a powerful and politically liberal argument for papal authority and for the separation of church and state; the development of a liberal Catholicism, which situates the Church in the conditions of modernity; and most fundamentally of all, reconstituting the grounds for human solidarity and for relieving the conditions of the working poor.

Lamennais's first two works, which he wrote with his brother, set much of the foundation for his subsequent undertakings. The first, *Reflections on the State of the Church in France during the Eighteenth Century and Its Current State* (1809) was seized by the state. The work charged the philosophes with responsibility for the chaos and dissolution of society that flowed from the revolution and traced their errors to the reformers. It reflects his firmly held view that, without religion, society is impossible. The second work, *The Tradition of the Church on the Institution of Bishops* (1814), argued for the exclusive right of the pope to institute bishops.

Lamennais's 1817 work *Essay on Indifference in Matters of Religion* catapulted him to fame. Cartesian notions of rationalism that asserted individual reason as the ground of certainty and the ultimate arbiter of reality, the Reformation's bequest to the Enlightenment,

Lamennais argued, undermined the basis for religion and society alike. Whatever its shortcomings, Lamennais also built an argument for "absolute truth," through which the principle of unassailable authority could be established. This philosophical position, known as traditionalism, is one that Lamennais shared with the philosopher, statesman, and royalist Louis de Bonald (1754–1840). Truth, Lamennais argued, demonstrates itself through general reason (*sensus communis*), that is, in the understandings that have gained the universal assent of people through time. The way we know, Lamennais insists, reveals the innate social character of our humanity. Lamennais also emphasized the social nature of Catholicism and the way the faith united members of society in bonds of love. A huge success, the *Essay on Indifference* was quickly translated into several European languages and caught the attention of many, including Alexis de Tocqueville, who became well acquainted with Lamennais's work.

In 1825–1826, Lamennais published *Religion Considered in Its Relations with the Political and Civil Order*, in which he developed arguments for the separation of the Church from state authority. He also set forth his arguments for the primacy of papal authority in matters concerning the Church, a stance known as ultramontanism, referring to one who looks over the mountains toward Rome for authority. Lamennais's position put him in conflict with much of the French hierarchy, who adhered to Gallicanism, a set of propositions including the view that temporal authority limits papal authority and that a general council of the bishops is superior to the teaching authority of the pope.

Lamennais rested his ultramontanist arguments in part on a defense of the person from the exercise of the overweening power of the temporal state. For Lamennais, the pope acts as the "supreme defender of justice and of the rights of humanity," a role Gallicanism obstructs. State support of religion, he argued, also encourages people to consider religion from a political point of view, which eventually transforms religion into a subordinate institution, leading to "indifferentism": the idea that one may assume a stance of indifference to any of the truth claims religion makes.

Always one to put words into action, Lamennais grounded a new foundation for the training of priests, the Congregation of St. Peter, which was intended to replace the Jesuits. Their training put a premium on the ability to analyze and engage the culture. Firmly convinced that the laity would have a major role to play in the development and application of Catholic thought in modernity, the brothers Lamennais also opened a house of study for laymen, who were free to study what best suited their needs and talents in light of the goal of developing Catholic thought and applying it to the social fabric.

The high point of Lamennais's influence in the Church and the events that would lead to the tragic end of his priestly career came in 1830 with the founding of the journal *L'Avenir* (*The Future*), whose masthead carried the motto "God and Liberty." Lamennais summarized the "doctrines" of *L'Avenir* as consisting in six points: religious liberty, liberty of education (which he called the first liberty of the family), liberty of the press, universal suffrage, liberty of association, and the abolition of centralization. Lamennais's arguments concerning the role of association and the importance of decentralization of decision making played an important role in the development and articulation of two core principles in Catholic social thought, solidarity and subsidiarity. In a remarkable essay entitled "What Catholicism Will Be in the New Society," Lamennais appealed for the reunification of science and religion, which he said constitute two modes of knowing that are naturally inseparable. Among other things, he noted that freedom of association would promote religious toleration and social peace, and he forecast the role the Church and its clergy would be called on to play in confronting the social question and the issues surrounding work.

With a readership across Europe and even in the United States, *L'Avenir* became as controversial as it was widely read. Lamennais suspended its publication in 1831, after which he rather naïvely went to Rome to seek papal sanction of his liberal Catholicism. The result was the encyclical *Mirari Vos* (*On Liberalism and Religious Indifferentism*). The letter never mentions Lamennais by name, and it condemns a variety of teachings and positions having nothing to do with Lamennais. It did, however, also sternly denounce a number of the doctrines of *L'Avenir*. Deeply stung, Lamennais made a submission, and when reports called his intentions into question, an emotionally spent Lamennais made a second, unqualified submission. He also announced his resolve to refrain from further exercise of his priestly faculties.

Considering himself free to write on temporal and political issues, Lamennais published the pamphlet "Words of a Believer" in 1834. Apocalyptic in tone and imagery, the work decried political tyranny and the oppression and exploitation of the peasants and the working class. The book was a sensation, and translations of it appeared across Europe. Pope Gregory XVI condemned it ("perpetually") in the 1834 encyclical *Singulari Nos* (*On the Errors of Lamennais*). That encyclical ended Lamennais's remarkable role in the Church, but not his concern with the poor or his deep engagement with the social question. He continued to write and late in his life, along with Tocqueville, was elected to a committee to draft a new constitution for France in the wake of the Revolution of 1848. When his draft, which Tocqueville supported, was rejected, Lamennais resigned and could not be convinced to return.

Never excommunicated, and despite the entreaties of his brother Jean, Lamennais refused reconciliation with the Church. At his insistence, he was buried in a pauper's grave without any ritual. An admiring essay published in *Putnam's Monthly Magazine* shortly after his death described Lamennais as "saddened but not subdued by disappointment."—Thomas C. Kohler

BIBLIOGRAPHY AND FURTHER READING: Stearn, Peter N. *Priest and Revolutionary: Lamennais and the Dilemma of French Catholicism.* New York: Harper & Row, 1967; Vidler, Alexander R. *Prophecy and Papacy: A Study of Lamennais, the Church, and the Revolution.* New York: Charles Scribner's Sons, 1954. *See also* CATHOLIC SOCIAL THOUGHT; EUROPE; SEPARATION OF CHURCH AND STATE; SUBSIDIARITY; ULTRAMONTANISM

L'ARCHE AND JEAN VANIER (1928–) Canadian philosopher Jean Vanier has devoted his life to exposing the dignity and unique gifts of the vulnerable and marginalized, particularly people with intellectual disabilities. Vanier was a founder of the international ecumenical movement L'Arche, a federation of over 130 faith-centered communities in more than 30 countries. In these small residential communities, people with and without intellectual disabilities live together in familial communion, revealing and nurturing the particular gifts of people with intellectual disabilities. Vanier also cofounded Faith and Light, an international ecumenical association of predominantly parish-based groups supporting people with mental disabilities and their families in fostering relationships with their communities and churches, with an emphasis on participation in religious pilgrimages. Both of these movements, as well as the associated Faith and Sharing retreat movement, are concrete manifestations of the theological insights at the heart of much of Vanier's writing.

Vanier's written work and the international movements he inspired testify to the conviction expressed in the Charter of the Communities of L'Arche: that people with intellectual disabilities "are a living reminder to the wider world of the essential values of the heart without which knowledge, power and action lose their meaning and purpose. Weakness and vulnerability in a person, far from being an obstacle to union with God, can foster it. It is often through weakness, recognized and accepted, that the liberating love of God is revealed."

Vanier was born on September 10, 1928, in Geneva, Switzerland, where his father, Maj. Gen. Georges Vanier, was serving in the Canadian diplomatic corps. His father's diplomatic and military service kept the family in Europe for much of Vanier's childhood, first in England and then briefly in France until its invasion by Germany in 1940. In 1941, they returned to Canada, where Georges continued in his life of public service. Georges Vanier eventually became the first Roman Catholic governor general of Canada.

Jean Vanier's earliest years seemed to be setting him on a trajectory to follow his father's footsteps. In 1942, when he was only 13 years old, he decided to apply for admission to the Royal Naval College in Dartmouth, England. His father's reaction when confronted with this decision profoundly influenced the course of Vanier's life. Georges told him: "I trust you. If this is what you want to do, then you must do it." Vanier later explained that his father thus taught him at an early age that he could trust his intuitions, which would lead him down many unconventional paths. Vanier successfully completed his studies and joined the British Royal Navy just as World War II was ending. At age 20, he became an officer in the Canadian Navy, serving on Canada's only aircraft carrier, the *Magnificent*.

However, Vanier's parents modeled not only lives of public service but also lives of religious devotion. Both Georges and Vanier's mother, Pauline, have been nominated for beatification as exemplars of the vocation of marriage. Vanier found it increasingly difficult to ignore the pull toward the spiritual life modeled by his parents. Toward the end of his years as a naval officer, he was attending daily Mass, reading the Divine Office during his night watches, and spending much of his free time in service projects for the poor. In 1950, he resigned his commission in the navy to explore what he thought might be a vocation to the priesthood.

He began to study with the Dominican priest Père Thomas Philippe, who was directing a French community of priests and lay scholars called L'Eau Vive ("Living Water"). Within a year, Vanier became the director of L'Eau Vive, while also studying philosophy at the Institut Catholique de Paris. In 1956, he left L'Eau Vive, spending the next couple of years largely in seclusion as he continued his studies and struggling with the gradual realization that his vocation was not to the priesthood.

In 1962, he successfully defended his doctoral dissertation, later published as *Made for Happiness: Discovering the Meaning of Life with Aristotle* (2001). He returned to Canada in 1963 to teach ethics at St. Michael's College at the University of Toronto. Though he was an extremely popular teacher, Vanier's formal academic career did not last long.

Vanier had stayed in close contact with his spiritual mentor, Père Thomas, who had become the chaplain at Val Fleuri, a home and workshop for intellectually disabled men in the small village of Trosly-Breuil in northern France. With Thomas's encouragement, Vanier responded to the call to share his life with the people with mental disabilities living in the inhumane conditions then prevalent in the large asylums to which they were commonly abandoned. On August 4, 1964, Vanier moved into a modest house with no indoor toilets in Trosly-Breuil, along with two former inhabitants of such an asylum—Raphael Simi and Philippe Seux. Vanier called this new community "L'Arche," after Noah's Ark. He later explained that the name signified many things: the safety that Noah's Ark had provided to the vulnerable animals, God's first covenant between God and humanity, and Mary, who carried Jesus safely in her womb.

This small community rapidly attracted volunteers from around the world. Some of these helpers were inspired to form similar communities in their home countries. A L'Arche community named Daybreak opened near Toronto in 1969. The next year, the Asha Niketan in Bangalore, India, welcomed its first members. In 1975, the International Federation of L'Arche Communities was formed to provide an organizational framework for the rapidly expanding network that today consists of more than 130 communities on five continents.

The tensions that accompanied this growth and that continue to present challenges to L'Arche reflect the movement's complexity. Though inspired by the Roman Catholic faith of its founder, L'Arche International is an ecumenical and interfaith movement in which specific communities reflect and respect the varying faith traditions of their members. L'Arche communities also welcome people without any religious affiliation, though the centrality of prayer and trust in God are fundamental to L'Arche's identity. There can also be tension between the need for L'Arche communities to adhere to state-established standards of professional care for people with disabilities and the priority of friendship and hospitality in a communal life modeled after the family. Related to this is the possibility of tension between the disability rights movement's stress on the independence and self-determination of people with disabilities and L'Arche's reverence for weakness and vulnerability as the means through which God's love for his people is most powerfully revealed. The wide diversity of L'Arche communities throughout the world reflects different accommodations to these sorts of tensions.

All L'Arche communities are nevertheless united in their desire to create homes that welcome and reveal to the world the gifts of persons with mental disabilities, who are typically among the poorest and most marginalized members of society. L'Arche communities are intended to serve as prophetic, countercultural witnesses of the spirit of the Beatitudes. Central to the spirituality of L'Arche is the conviction that people with mental disabilities are powerful teachers of the wisdom of the heart that is so often neglected in our culture's definitions of success. In the words of St. Paul: "God has chosen the foolish and the weak in order to confound the wise and the strong" (1 Corinthians 1: 27). Reflecting this belief, the website of L'Arche International identifies Jean Vanier as its founder and his original housemates, Raphael Simi and Philippe Seux, as its cofounders.

People with mental disabilities living in L'Arche communities are referred to as the "core members." Some core members hold jobs in their local communities; others spend their time in the constant care of L'Arche "assistants"—the people without mental disabilities who choose to live with the core members. Some assistants commit themselves to a celibate, single life, while others are married. Some spend only a short time in L'Arche communities, while others dedicate their entire lives to L'Arche. In 1999, L'Arche introduced a program of formation for assistants known as the Ecole de Vie. This provides instruction in the philosophy and spirituality underlying L'Arche, as well as opportunities to reflect upon the often turbulent demands of daily life in L'Arche communities. At some of these retreats, assistants can publicly announce their assent to the invitation "to live a covenant in L'Arche with Jesus and with all your brothers and sisters, especially the poorest and the weakest." L'Arche's companion movements, the Faith and Light family and pilgrimage movement and the Faith and Sharing retreat movement, foster the spiritual lives of the core members, as well as people with mental disabilities who do not live in L'Arche communities, their families, and their friends.

Vanier's advocacy for people with intellectual disabilities, as well as other marginalized groups such as prisoners and the poor, has been honored by many awards, including the Companion of the Order of Canada, France's Legion of Honor, the Paul VI International Prize, the Community of Christ International Peace Award, the Rabbi Gunther Plaut Humanitarian Award, and the Gaudium et Spes Award. His literary legacy documents the spiritual insights underlying his life of service, most notably in such works as *Becoming Human* (1998), based on his extremely popular Massey Lectures broadcast by the Canadian Broadcasting Corporation, and *Community and Growth* (1979), his classic work on community life. In the words of Canadian academic and author Michael W. Higgins: "Vanier's contribution has been to call into question the very standard by which we judge 'success.' He is the consummate subversive of the value system that equates human dignity with utility."— Elizabeth R. Schiltz

BIBLIOGRAPHY AND FURTHER READING: Clarke, Bill. *Enough Room for Joy: Jean Vanier's L'Arche.* New York: Paulist Press, 1974; Downey, Michael. *A Blessed Weakness: The Spirit of Jean Vanier and L'Arche.* New York: Harper & Row, 1986; Nouwen, Henri J. M. *The Road to Daybreak: A Spiritual Journey.* New York: Doubleday, 1988; Spink, Kathryn. *The Miracle, the Message, the Story: Jean Vanier and L'Arche.* Mahwah, NJ: HiddenSpring, 2006; Vanier, Jean. *An Ark for the Poor: The Story of L'Arche.* Toronto: Novalis, 1995; Whitney-Brown, Carolyn, ed. *Jean Vanier: Essential Writings.* Maryknoll, NY: Orbis, 2008. See also DOWN SYNDROME; FAMILY; HUMAN DIGNITY; PREFERENTIAL OPTION FOR THE POOR

LA SALLE, ST. JOHN-BAPTIST DE (1651–1719)

John-Baptist de La Salle, canonized in 1900, was born in a mansion at Rheims, France, to a family of the lesser nobility. His father was a judge, and his mother (who was very pious) was of a noble family. During his early life, times were bad in France. In Paris, murders and crimes were frequent. The king was a mere child. But then things began to change, and the reign of Louis XIV began. De La Salle was acknowledged for his piety even from his earliest days, and he was noted for spiritual exercises, prayer, and pious reading. As a child, he learned to serve Mass and gave signs that he had a vocation to the priesthood.

After private tutors, de La Salle was sent to the College des Bons Enfants. The curriculum was classical. A thorough knowledge of Latin and Greek was required. At age 11, de La Salle received the tonsure, the first step toward the priesthood.

When de La Salle was 16, a wealthy relative of the family conferred on him the rich benefice of canon of the Cathedral Chapter of Rheims. It was taken for granted that those who became canons intended to become priests, and that the money they received would help pay the expenses of their education. In 1669, he qualified for the degree of master of arts.

De La Salle entered the Seminary of St. Sulpice in 1670. He remained there for 18 months, and it introduced him to the spirituality of the French School in the footsteps of Cardinal de Berulle (1575–1629). While at St. Sulpice, de La Salle took courses at the Sorbonne in theology, and he obtained a doctorate in theology in 1680 from the University of Rheims. While a seminarian, de La Salle spent Sundays and all feast days teaching catechism to poor children. Jansenism was rising in France, and de La Salle was armed against the insidious doctrines of that heresy at St. Sulpice.

When de La Salle had to return to Rheims in 1672 after the death of both his parents, he became friendly with Nicholas Roland, a fellow canon of the Cathedral of Rheims, who became his spiritual director. In the spring of 1679, Adrian Nyel arrived in Rheims with the idea of forming a school for poor boys. He came with several letters of introduction, including one to de La Salle. When de La Salle became aware of the project, he invited Nyel to stay at his house. This was the opening step in de La Salle's commitment to education.

Nyel's plan was simple: a school for poor boys. The problem was that he would start a school and then move on to start another school without properly completing its organization. It was difficult to get a supply of trained teachers. In 1681, de La Salle invited the teachers in schools for the poor into his own family home to share everything with himself and his family. De La Salle began to train them for their work, but his teachers began to find his restrictions irksome, and one by one they left. De La Salle was then faced with the problem of giving up his canonry and his family wealth. He began by resigning his canonry, and he used his family money to buy food for the poor.

De La Salle continued recruiting teachers and focused on the careful training of the masters, not only for their school work but also for their religious formation. Gradually, de La Salle began to realize that his work of training teachers and poor children required that the teachers be formed into a religious community, which he named the Brothers of the Christian Schools. He wanted them to take the usual vows, but did not want them to become priests. He felt that if they became priests, they would be distracted from their educational work by their ministerial duties.

De La Salle broke away from the attempt to educate children working with them one by one, which left most of the group to do whatever they wanted during the school period. De La Salle saw that they had to be taught in classes, where the teacher could work with the entire group at the same time. De La Salle was the first to set up training colleges as such (normal schools) and to inspire his teachers with a father's love for their pupils. He also focused on the mother tongue, French, rather than Latin.

De La Salle's establishment of the Christian Brothers led to their taking of vows. In 1684, about a dozen of his teachers took vows to dedicate their lives to teaching the children of the poor and to live in poverty and self-sacrifice, with de La Salle as their leader.

As Daniel-Rops has said, de La Salle was indeed an extraordinary man. He became a stern ascetic using the discipline, wearing a hair shirt, and sleeping on a plank. He fasted more than rules allowed. De La Salle was a mystic and a spiritual writer in the French School of Berulle.

The work of the Christian Brothers created controversy because they offered education without payment. Lawsuits were instituted against them, and justice was thwarted by lying witnesses. The great majority of the brothers remained loyal to de La Salle even when, almost outlawed, he was forced to leave Paris. A bishop tried to have him replaced as superior of the institute, but the directors of all of his houses wrote a letter together in 1714, commanding him in the name of the society to return and to place himself at their head. He died in 1719. When he died, the Brothers of the Christian Schools numbered 274 members. In 2009, after many religious communities had lost large numbers of members, the Christian Brothers still had more than five thousand members.—George P. Graham

BIBLIOGRAPHY AND FURTHER READING: Battersby, W. J. *De La Salle*. London: Longman's Green, 1950; Daniel-Rops, Henri. *The Church in the Seventeenth Century*. New York: Dutton, 1963. *See also* JANSENISM; SAINTS AND SOCIAL ACTION

LEJEUNE, JEROME (1926–1994) Jerome Lejeune was the second of three sons, born to a small business owner near Paris on April 3, 1926. His grandfather was a veterinarian who took him on rounds, possibly awakening his interest in medicine, since, as a young man, he had a desire to be a country doctor. In 1944, Lejeune began his medical studies at the Paris School of Medicine. He graduated in 1951 and became an assistant to Dr. Raymond Turpin. That same year, he married Birthe Bringsted in Denmark; the couple had two sons and three daughters while residing in Paris. Lejeune was a devoted family man, returning home for lunch with the family with whom he enjoyed Sundays in the country.

In 1958, in Turpin's lab, Lejeune discovered that individuals with Down syndrome have three copies of the 21st chromosome instead of two, a condition he named Trisomy 21. His discovery was published in January 1959 by the French Academy of Sciences and replicated by Brown and Jacobs in 1959. As a result, he was honored with the chair of fundamental genetics at the Paris School of Medicine. In 1963, President John F. Kennedy awarded him the Kennedy Prize, and in 1969 he received the highest award in genetics, the William Allan Memorial Award from the American Society of Human Genetics. Lejeune was an advisor to French president Georges Pompidou, appearing frequently on French TV as a scientific expert. He was also associated with the World Health Organization, the French Institute's Academy of Moral and Political Sciences, the French Academy of Medicine, the American Academy of Arts and Sciences, the Royal Swedish Academy, the National Academy of Medicine in Argentina, and the University of Santiago, Chile. He held four honorary doctorates.

Lejeune dedicated his life to research and caring for those with Trisomy 21, declaring, "Because every new human being belongs to our species from the moment of conception, each new human being is entitled to life, and, if she is sick, to our devotion." He believed that researchers should maintain a connection with clinical practice, and thus he treated more than nine thousand children in his medical practice at Necker Children's Hospital. "The parents," Lejeune said, "know their child's disease—it has been described to them as horrible, and they have been advised to abort—but they don't know their child." He spent many hours in his clinical practice teaching parents to see their child with Trisomy 21 as their son or daughter rather than as a diseased child. He would take calls at night when distraught parents had just received a diagnosis, feeling he had no right to make them wait one night in distress.

Lejeune's speeches and papers give bold witness that the unborn child's humanity is a scientific fact, not an opinion imposed on society by Christians. Over 30 years, he made 164 presentations worldwide, including testifying in 1981 in front of the U.S. Senate during an abortion debate. Lejeune described the fetus as Tom Thumb, a little man complete in every way, but no larger than a man's thumb. His publication "The Con-

centration Can" (1992) describes the fate of thousands of tiny human embryos held in suspended animation waiting to be used in in vitro fertilization procedures or destroyed at will.

In 1989, Lejeune was an expert witness in a divorce trial in Maryville, Tennessee, where a couple was fighting for possession of seven frozen embryos. The trial was a landmark case and was covered extensively on American television. The mother wanted to give the embryos up for adoption, while the father wanted the embryos destroyed. Lejeune considered it a revival of the trial of Solomon and testified so compellingly that human life begins at conception that Judge W. Dale Young awarded custody of the embryos to the mother. He was convinced that the embryos were not property to be divided but children to be awarded in custody. The decision was, however, reversed on appeal; the plight of frozen embryos, as Lejeune's testimony made clear, continues to be a matter of profound injustice.

Despite his reputation and discoveries regarding serious anomalies (he also identified the Cri du Chat syndrome and discovered the link between inadequate intake of folic acid by pregnant women and neural tube defects in their unborn children), Lejeune was never awarded the Nobel Prize. It may have been a reaction to his insistence that life begins at conception and on the right of disabled individuals to be born. This clashed with the social climate where activists were working for the legalization of abortion, beginning with the disabled. It was the discovery of Trisomy 21 that enabled researchers to develop amniocentesis, the most common method of prenatal diagnosis. The rate of abortion of unborn babies diagnosed with Trisomy 21 is 92%, inspiring Lejeune's lifelong quest to find a cure in order to save such children from what he termed "chromosomal racism." He felt it would take less intellectual effort to find a cure for Trisomy 21 than to send a man to the moon.

Lejeune's convictions left him few allies, and he had to search for funding for his research. Nevertheless, he was close friends with Pope John Paul II. The two met when Lejeune was giving a conference on the beginning of life at the Institute for the Family in Krakow, when Karol Wojtyla was still a cardinal. As pope, John Paul appointed Lejeune to the Pontifical Academy of Sciences. As he was dying of lung cancer in 1994, at the pontiff's request, Lejeune drafted the bylaws and Oath of the Servants of Life for the newly formed Pontifical Academy for Life. He served as president for only 33 days, dying on Easter Sunday 1994. He felt as though he was deserting his patients for whom he had promised to find a cure.

Lejeune was praised by Pope John Paul II as "a man for whom defending life had become an apostolate." The pope made a special visit to Lejeune's grave during his visit to Paris for World Youth Day. Servant of God Jerome Lejeune's cause for canonization was opened on June 28, 2007, by the archbishop of Paris. His family formed the Jerome Lejeune Foundation shortly after his death to continue his legacy by funding research into cure and treatment of Trisomy 21, advocacy, and medical care for thousands of patients with Trisomy 21 and other intellectual disabilities of genetic origin.—Leticia C. Velasquez

BIBLIOGRAPHY AND FURTHER READING: Jerome Lejeune Foundation website, http://www.jeromelejeune.org; Lejeune-Gaymard, Clara. *Life Is a Blessing*. Philadelphia: National Catholic Bioethics Center, 2011. *See also* ABORTION; BIOETHICS; DOWN SYNDROME; *EVANGELIUM VITAE*; HUMAN LIFE (DIGNITY AND SANCTITY OF); NATIONAL CATHOLIC BIOETHICS CENTER; PONTIFICAL ACADEMY FOR LIFE

LEWIS, C. S. (1898–1963) Author of more than 40 books, 200 essays and sermons, and 80 poems, Clive Staples Lewis was one the very greatest Christian apologists ever to have written in English; a formidable religious thinker, psychologist, and devotional writer; a philosopher and poet; a fiction writer who arguably produced benchmarks in religious allegory, the first-person novel, children's fantasy, and science fiction; and one of the foremost literary historians and critics of the 20th century. He really was, as he famously described himself in his inaugural lecture as the first professor of medieval and English literature at Cambridge University, an Old Western Man, and he consistently reminds us that "anything not eternal is eternally out of date."

Because he never wrote a book on, or described at length, any whole theory of social thought or policy, one must (with a few exceptions) look at individual essays to discern elements of Lewis's social philosophy. In "Willing Slaves of the Welfare State," for example, he makes clear the basis of his objection to all collectivist paradigms: "Our effective masters must be more than one and fewer than all. But the oligarchs begin to regard us in a new way.... All that can really happen is that some men will take charge of the destiny of the others.... Have we discovered some new reason why, this time, powers should not corrupt as it has done before?"

Alongside that distaste are a number of conservatively disposed beliefs. Lewis trusted the validity of reason, defended natural law, generally relied upon

tradition ("mere Christianity"), held to an objective view of creation (both natural and supernatural) and to the legitimacy of its claims upon us (our moral and aesthetic responses are trainable and ought to be ordinate), distrusted emotion as a guide to truth, and refused to equate progress with innovation or to see it as inevitable. Wounded in the trenches of World War I, his patriotism compelled him to proclaim the duty of men (not women) possibly to die for their country; but he steadfastly refused "to live for it."

As a social philosopher, Lewis is both a prophetic philosopher and a cultural critic. As a philosopher, he is broadly moral; keenly, even intuitively, attentive to culturally subterranean assumptions; intellectually fresh, penetrating, and analytical; anticipatory; and typically admonitory. The *loci classici* are the meditation *Abolition of Man* and the novel *That Hideous Strength*. In these, he offers dispositive statements on natural law and human nature, and on the working of these in the realm of practical events (ethics) and on aspects of the broader culture (education). Lewis anticipates (though not in detail, of course; prophetic philosophers leave matter, method, and dates to the pure prophet) cloning, legalized and epidemic abortion, legalized euthanasia, genetic engineering, and the rampant redefinition of fundamental, axiomatic premises (e.g., "family").

The cultural critic, less well known than the prophetic philosopher, is, on the other hand, a diagnostician, looking both around and back. This Lewis appears in such essays and sermons as "Is History Bunk?" "Modern Man and His Categories of Thought," and "Learning in Wartime," a sermon preached on December 22, 1939, in which Lewis stated: "The war creates no absolutely new situation: it simply aggravates the permanent human situation so that we can no longer ignore it. Human life has always been lived on the edge of a precipice." This insistence on a long and somewhat subversive—and often surprising—perspective is common in Lewis. Typical are "Democratic Education" and "Sex in Literature." In the latter, he writes, "When the prevalent morality of a nation comes to differ unduly from that presupposed in its laws, the laws must sooner or later change and conform to it. This is the case with 'obscene' literature."

The critic comes closest to a theory of social policy in two essays, "The Humanitarian Theory of Punishment" and "Equality." In them, we note Lewis's characteristic subversion of contemporary unexamined assumptions, cultivating instead Old Western assumptions respecting both human nature and the role of the state. His typically adversarial stance is evident in both.

On punishment, he writes: "The Humanitarian theory removes from Punishment the concept of Desert . . . the only connecting link between punishment and justice. . . . Thus when we cease to consider what the criminal deserves and consider only what will cure him or deter others . . . we now have a mere object, a patient, a 'case.'"

Lewis is at least as severe and unsentimental when discussing equality, a zeal for which he seems to regard as semi-superstitious: "I do not think that equality is one of those things . . . which are good simply in themselves and for their own sakes. . . . When equality is treated not as a medicine or a safety-gadget but as an ideal we begin to breed that stunted and envious sort of mind which hates all superiority."

Lewis's long perspective and intellectual severity, as well as his relentless uprooting of apparently axiomatic truths, are ubiquitous in his social and cultural criticism. He certainly distrusted the "science" in "social science," asserting that we cannot study men, "we can only get to know them." That is, he rejected any method that would massify people and study them as such.

His personal alms-giving was largely secret, often spontaneous, and (thanks to his lawyer, Owen Barfield, who established what came to be known as the Agape Fund) finally systematic: Lewis gave away roughly two-thirds of his income. Although beyond his own circle this giving was largely unknown during his lifetime, his historical perspicacity was very well known indeed. In a letter of November 5, 1933, Lewis wrote: "Did you see that [Hitler] said 'the Jews have made no contribution to human culture and in crushing them I am doing the will of the Lord.' Now as the whole idea of the 'Will of the Lord' is precisely what the world owes to the Jews, the blaspheming tyrant has just fixed his absurdity for all to see in a single sentence, and shown that he is as contemptible for his stupidity as he is detestable for his cruelty." And in "The Seeing Eye," he contemplates the possibility of humanity meeting an alien rational species: "I observe how the white man has hitherto treated the black, and how, even among civilized men, the stronger have treated the weaker. . . . I do not doubt that the same story will be repeated. . . . Nor was the failure [of English exploration] relieved by any high ideal motives. . . . The actual record of early Protestantism in this field seems to be 'blank as death.'"

In light of that judgment, one might inquire into what sort of Protestant Lewis was. In 1933, when he was 34 years old and not quite two years a Christian, C. S. Lewis published his first book that was not poetry, *The Pilgrim's Regress*, an allegorical Dream Vision. It took him all of two weeks to write. In this paradig-matic effulgence, Lewis did not trouble himself greatly over a conception of "church." And yet there she is, unostentatious, but no mere scenic touch, Mother Kirk rocking away at the very edge of the Canyon (at the depths of which lies baptism), dispensing her guidance. Though modest, she is dispositive—commanding, magisterial, utterly reliable. For example, she saves John by instructing him to take off his clothes, to dive deeply (explaining *how* one dives), and to find a narrow, frightening tunnel which, if negotiated, will bring him across the river. He obeys. The success of John the Pilgrim's journey has depended upon his meeting and heeding Mother Kirk. Furthermore, John will do himself no good by searching for another Mother Kirk; she is not one among several to be sampled.

But Lewis could not have become a Catholic (even though the suspicion was abroad that he might: at least one reviewer of *Pilgrim's Regress*, first published in America by Sheed and Ward, thought Lewis *was* a Catholic). For example, two weeks after Lewis's death, Father Guy Brinkworth discussed in the *Tablet* an exchange of letters with Lewis from the 1940s. "In the letters I received from him," wrote Brinkworth, "he time and time again asked specifically for prayers that God might give him 'the light and grace to make the final gesture.' He even went so far as to ask in a postscript to one of his letters for 'prayers that the prejudices instilled in me by an Ulster nurse might be overcome.'" Late in life, his dear brother Warren, while in Ireland, seriously considered taking instruction in Catholicism. Upon hearing of this, "Jack," as Lewis was known to his family, rushed to him to argue Warren out of his decision. There he entered into debate with a local priest and, according to George Sayer (Lewis's pupil, friend, and biographer, who heard the tale from Warren), got much the worse of it.

On the other hand were Lewis's many Catholic beliefs and practices: meatless Fridays; belief in the efficacy of, and regular practice of, auricular confession; belief in the Real Presence and the taking of Holy Communion frequently within the Anglican Church; belief in the Apostolic Succession and in the efficacy of prayers for the dead. He believed in the ordained priesthood of Canterbury, of Rome, and of the East and firmly opposed the ordination of women to the priesthood. More telling is his *publicly affirmed* belief in purgatory. We see this in *Letters to Malcolm*, of course, as "Lenten lands." But we see it, too, in *The Screwtape Letters* (letter 31): Not only is the Patient *not* finally saved by his baptism alone, but after his death (saved indeed, but by a close call—the patient was subject to temptation until the very end, when death, as is so often the case in Lewis, intervened), he is due a good "scrubbing."

In the essay "Christian Reunion" (unpublished during his lifetime), Lewis describes his reservation about Catholicism: the requirement that he "accept in advance any doctrine. . . . It is like being asked to agree not only to what a man has said but to what he's going to say." He continues: "To you the real vice of Protestantism is the formless drift which seems unable to retain the Catholic truths, which loses them one by one and . . . cannot be classified as Christian by any tolerable stretch of the word. To us the terrible thing about Rome is the recklessness (as we hold) with which she has added to the *depositum fidei*. . . . You see in Protestantism the Faith dying out in a desert: we see in Rome the Faith smothered in a jungle."

Kenneth Mason, in his pamphlet *Anglicanism: A Canterbury Essay*, writes: "If anyone asks, what is the final authority in matter of doctrine in Anglicanism? The reply must be, that there is no final authority." As for "differences of opinion . . . [the English temperament] would rather see the matter left unresolved, with dogmas held undogmatically." Perhaps that is why Lewis could say, and mean, "The great point is that in one sense there's no such thing as Anglicanism."

Withal, C. S. Lewis is difficult to categorize in terms common to the discourse of social thought and policy. His imaginative effusions are as radical as nature, his reason as conservative as the multiplication tables, and his spirit as liberated as the open arms of the Cross at which he worshipped.—James Como

BIBLIOGRAPHY AND FURTHER READING: Aeschliman, Michael D. *The Restitution of Man: C. S. Lewis and the Case against Scientism*. Grand Rapids, MI: Eerdmans, 1983; Holmer, Paul L. *C. S. Lewis: The Shape of His Faith and Thought*. New York: Harper & Row, 1976; Lewis, C. S. *God in the Dock: Essays on Theology and Ethics*. Edited by Walter Hooper. Grand Rapids, MI: Eerdmans, 1970; Lewis, C. S. *Present Concerns*. Edited by Walter Hooper. New York: Harcourt Brace Jovanovich, 1986; Meilander, Gilbert. *The Taste for the Other: The Social and Ethical Thought of C. S. Lewis*. Grand Rapids, MI: Eerdmans, 1978. *See also* CHESTERTON, GILBERT KEITH; LITERATURE; TOLKIEN, J. R. R.; PERCY, WALKER

LIFE-GIVING LOVE IN AN AGE OF TECHNOLOGY *Life-Giving Love in an Age of Technology* is the first pastoral letter of the U.S. Conference of Catholic Bishops (USCCB) dedicated to the topics of infertility and reproductive technologies. It was developed by the USCCB's Committee on Pro-Life Activities in collaboration with the Committee on Doctrine and the Committee on Laity, Marriage, Family Life, and Youth and approved by the full body of the USCCB in November 2009.

The text is a companion document to an educational resource on the topic of contraception approved by the U.S. bishops in November 2006 entitled *Married Love and the Gift of Life*. During that document's preparation, certain bishops questioned whether it should include a discussion of reproductive technologies in order to fill out the picture on the integral relationship between the unitive and procreative goods of marriage. The bishops decided to limit that text to the single issue of contraception. One year later at its November 2007 meeting, the assembly of bishops approved a formal request from the Committee on Pro-Life Activities to develop a new document offering pastoral guidance on the Church's teaching concerning reproductive technologies. The document is similar in length to its 2006 sister document and shares the common format of an introductory section followed by questions and answers. *Life-Giving Love* also complements the USCCB's statement on embryonic stem cell research released in June 2008 by providing a deeper consideration of the source of the problem of frozen embryos, proposed as subjects for experimentation, as a result of couples choosing in vitro fertilization (IVF).

Life-Giving Love was published one year after the release of the Vatican instruction *Dignitas Personae (On Certain Bioethical Questions*, 2008) by the Congregation for the Doctrine of the Faith (CDF). It derives its normative ethical principles from *Dignitas Personae*, as well as from the 1987 CDF instruction that stands as *Dignitas Personae*'s doctrinal predecessor, *Donum Vitae (On Respect for Human Life in Its Origin and On the Dignity of Procreation)*. Its framework for defending human life is also shaped by Pope John Paul II's encyclical *Evangelium Vitae* (1995).

Although *Live-Giving Love* includes an appendix with references to these documents for further reading, the text itself makes no explicit reference to them. This was intentional. The document is addressed specifically to Catholic couples suffering from infertility and aims both in idiom and format to be as accessible as possible to a popular audience. It eschews a technical and scholarly tone, aiming rather at a presentation that is positive, uplifting, and pastoral. To further this aim, it includes five sidebars with testimonials from Catholic spouses who have suffered from infertility, including those who have benefited from morally legitimate fertility treatments. It attempts to balance a sincere empathy for their painful experience with clear guidance on ethically legitimate alternatives. Acknowledging that some spouses experience a temptation to appeal to wrongful solutions to bring children into the world, the document responds by exhorting couples to hope in God and surrender to his design for family life.

Live-Giving Love begins by establishing marriage as the proper context for considering questions related to procreation. Its teaching on marriage is rooted in the theological anthropology found in Genesis 1 and 2. God creates man and women for a complementary one-flesh communion characterized by the dual goods of *procreation* (Genesis 1: 28) and *spousal unity* (Genesis 2: 24). Marriage therefore is a procreative and unitive type of relationship in which a man and woman, having consented to an exclusive lifelong partnership, consummate their union by becoming one flesh through sexual intercourse. At the foundation of this revealed teaching is the moral conclusion that marriage is the justifying basis for genital sexual expression and procreation.

The meaning of marital intercourse derives from the meaning of marriage. Taking its name from marriage itself (the marital act), intercourse is a unique procreative and unitive type of act. Disrespect for procreation or spousal unity is disrespect for the marriage. Two correlative moral conclusions follow: procreation should not be intentionally excluded from marital sexual intercourse (i.e., acts intentionally contracepted are intrinsically evil, as taught in *Humanae Vitae*), and procreation should not take place outside of sexual intercourse (i.e., babies should be the fruit of married love, as taught in *Dignitas Personae* and *Donum Vitae*). The bishops write: "The Church's teaching on sexual morality is a reflection on these two goods and on how, in the unfolding of God's plan for marriage, they should not be separated."

The same moral conclusion regarding procreation is reached by reflecting upon the duties we owe to human life in its origins. A child is a person possessing personal dignity and value. Children, therefore, should come into the world in a manner congruent with their natures, that is, they should be conceived in a personal way, respected as persons from their first moments of existence. Bringing children into the world through marital love is treating them in a way befitting of persons. Formulating this normative truth in terms of the rights of children, the bishops teach: "Children have a right to be conceived by the act that expresses and embodies their parents' self-giving love."

The bishops end their preliminary analysis by teaching that when spouses procreate, they cooperate with God in bringing new life into existence. This gift of sharing in God's creative act requires that spouses treat human life in its origins as God desires—in the words of the text, "in a uniquely personal way." And although the desire to bring children into the world "is positive and natural," not all means of doing so "respect this great gift."

The remainder of the document is dedicated to a moral assessment of forms of reproductive technology. It begins by discussing heterologous and homologous artificial insemination and surrogate motherhood. Applying the principle of Catholic moral reasoning which states that techniques that assist the marital act in achieving its proper reproductive end are in principle legitimate, and techniques that substitute for the marital act are not, the bishops show how each of these options violates this principle and in so doing deprives children of the fully personal context they deserve when coming into the world.

The text then turns to IVF. Applying the same principle, it teaches that because through IVF new life does not come into the world as fruit supervening upon a self-giving act of marital love, but rather as the object of an act of production, the technique is wrong. IVF depersonalizes a child at his most vulnerable stage of existence, which is not only an injustice against the child but also a violation of the good of marriage.

In examining human cloning, the document teaches that when we create a human being not for his or her own sake "but as a 'copy' of someone else, he or she is treated as a thing or even a commodity, not as a person. This is a gross violation of human dignity."

The bishops then address a question that may be on the minds of couples suffering from infertility: "Must we abandon hope of conceiving a child?" Without elaborating any specific possibility, the bishops mention options such as "hormonal treatment," "conventional or laser surgery to repair damaged or blocked fallopian tubes," and "means for alleviating male infertility factors" that do not replace the marital act. They specifically recommend the "techniques of natural family planning (NFP)," which can assist couples in maximizing their chances of conceiving.

The text reminds infertile married couples that their marriage is still meaningful and can still fulfill its "full Christian purpose." Although every couple is called to remain open to God's gift of new life, no one can assure the gift will be received. When it is not, the suffering can be intense. The whole Church therefore should receive such couples with "sympathy and support." Quoting a beautiful statement by Pope John Paul II to infertile couples, the text reads: "To couples who cannot have children of their own I say: you are no less loved by God; your love for each other is complete and fruitful when it is open to others, to the needs of the apostolate, to the needs of the poor, to the needs of orphans, to the needs of the world" (Homily at Mass for Families, Onitsha, Nigeria, February 13, 1982).

Finally, the document commends infant adoption to couples unable to conceive. When it turns to the question of so-called embryo adoption, it provides no clear moral guidance. Rather, like *Dignitas Personae* from which its statements are drawn, it offers ambiguous cautions against the practice.

The text concludes by returning to the dignity of children: "Children are not parents' possessions to manufacture, manipulate, or design; rather they are fellow persons with full human dignity, and parents are called to accept, care for, and raise them as new members of God's family and his Kingdom. Children deserve to be 'begotten, not made.'"—E. Christian Brugger

See also HUMAN EMBRYO; HUMAN LIFE (DIGNITY AND SANCTITY OF); NATURAL PROCREATIVE TECHNOLOGY

LOUIS OF GRANADA, VENERABLE (1504–1588)

Venerable Louis was born in Granada, Spain, in 1504, an era of conquest and expansion of the Spanish Empire. Just years before his birth, Christopher Columbus had discovered the Americas in the service of King Ferdinand and Queen Isabella; the colonization of the Western Hemisphere was under way. On the Iberian Peninsula, the Moors were defeated and the king desired to strengthen his reign over the former Moorish stronghold of Granada. Accordingly, he encouraged Spaniards to move to that city to counterbalance the Moors living there.

Louis's father, Francis Sarria, settled in Granada with Louis's mother. Sarria died when Louis was five years old, leaving his wife destitute. Without a man in the house, Louis's mother was subjected to vicious gossip and insults. Louis recollected getting into a fistfight with another boy one day. While Louis was begging alms in front of the Dominican monastery, the other boy shouted out for all to hear that Louis's mother was a whore. The mayor of Alhambra, Count de Tendilla, was passing by and admired Louis's courage in taking on a boy twice his size. From that day on, Louis was under the sponsorship of the count, who was responsible for

his education. In due time, Louis joined the Dominicans at the Convent of the Holy Cross and became a friar preacher on June 15, 1524.

Louis devoted himself to the pursuit of scholarship. Never in his entire life did he regret abandoning the world and all the things of the world: marriage, career, power, creature comforts. Louis was called out of the world to a life of prayer and study. He was an outstanding student who mastered the course of study, the *ratio studiorum*, which consisted of Latin, grammar, philosophy, and theology. In 1529, Louis was admitted to the College of St. Gregory in Valladolid. In gratitude for his education at the Convent of the Holy Cross, he changed his name from Louis de Sarria to Louis of Granada.

At the College of St. Gregory, Louis undertook a rigorous program of logic, philosophy, theology, and exegesis. All the time, he was preparing to become an inspiring preacher. However, he was also drawn to labor in the missionary fields and offered to become a missionary to Mexico. This offer was rejected by his superiors, which Louis stoically accepted as the will of God, then turned his attention to spiritual writing. In 1539, he wrote a treatise on prayer, which would evolve into the widely read *Book of Prayer and Meditation*. In 1544, the title of preacher general was granted to him by the Dominican order with permission to preach anywhere in Spain. At the age of 42, Louis was becoming famous as a preacher and writer; in 1552, he became confessor of Queen Catherine of Portugal.

A period of trial and frustration commenced in Louis's life. He had become a favorite at the royal court, and the nobles made excessive demands on his time, calling him to resolve trivial arguments. Louis could have lived at the palace, but chose instead to live in a cell at the Dominican monastery. His vocation was to preach and write, not to entertain royalty. Although he counseled the aristocrats, he had little stomach for the ways of the worldly. At the monastery, Louis would arise at 4 a.m. and spend two hours in prayer and contemplation. He especially delighted in reading the Bible and praying the rosary. At 6 a.m., Louis would celebrate Mass in a private chapel, then return to his cell to write on spiritual matters.

His writings were based on the Scriptures and the Fathers of the Church, especially St. Augustine and St. Thomas Aquinas. Louis endeavored to preach and write for the layman, not just the theologian. His goal was to inspire everyone to a life of holiness and charity. He averred that the most unlearned person can and should draw close to God through love and service to others.

In more than 35 years of writing, Louis composed 49 spiritual works. Two of his books, *Book of Prayer and Meditation* and *The Sinners Guide*, were translated into 25 different languages. Spanish missionaries disseminated the books of Louis all over the world, from native Indians in the Americas to the small Christian community in Japan. Missionaries returning to Spain brought back an amazing account. St. Rose of Lima wrote that her reading of the *Book of Prayer and Meditation* so infuriated the devil that he snatched the book from her hands and threw it into the garbage. St. Teresa was so enamored of *The Sinners Guide* that she credited it with converting a million souls.

Louis never boasted of the success of his preaching and writings, but gave all the credit to God. Louis's heartfelt desire was that people would turn away from sin and toward God through his spoken and written words. This was his mission and life's work. Louis's earthly journey came to an end on December 31, 1588. Having been in ill health for some time, he died in his cell with all the friars praying for him.

One of the seven precepts of the church is to participate in the Church's mission of evangelization of souls. Venerable Louis fulfilled this goal with estimable success through his preaching and spiritual writings. However, a few critics within the Dominican order were disdainful of him because Louis asserted that holiness can be attained by the laity, not just by the clergy and religious. Persons who practice the evangelical counsels of poverty, chastity, and obedience, he taught, are not necessarily more holy than persons who do not yet embrace the theological virtues of faith, hope, and charity. Venerable Louis's teachings were approved by the Council of Trent and Pope Paul IV. He also received a letter of commendation from Pope Gregory XIII, who lauded "the sublime doctrine and practical piety" of this learned and holy man. Venerable Louis of Granada was a theologian for the laity and would have applauded wholeheartedly the reforms of the Second Vatican Council.—Alexander LaPerchia

BIBLIOGRAPHY AND FURTHER READING: Dorcy, Mary Jean, OP. *Saint Dominic's Family*. Rockford, IL: Tan Books, 1983; Ghezzi, Bert. "Evangelization." Chapter 8 of *The Heart of a Saint: Ten Ways to Grow Closer to God*. Ijamsville, MD: Word Among Us Press, 2007; Louis of Granada, OP. *Pathways to Holiness*. Translated by Jordan Aumann, OP. Staten Island, NY: Alba House, 1998; Louis of Granada, OP. *The Sinners Guide*. Rockford, IL: Tan Books, 1985. *See also* DOMINIC, ST., AND THE DOMINICAN TRADITION; LAY APOSTOLATE

LUBICH, CHIARA (1920–2008), AND THE FOCOLARE MOVEMENT Chiara Lubich was the founder of the Focolare Movement. Born January 22, 1920, in Trent, Italy, Lubich was the second of four children. From her mother, a devout Roman Catholic, she absorbed a deep religious sensitivity. She described her father, a Socialist, as "large of heart" and broad of mind. In the late 1920s, he lost his job, and the family fell into poverty. She worked her way through school, eventually becoming an elementary school teacher.

Because of its location near a strategic pass through the Dolomite Alps, during World War II, the Allies bombed Trent heavily. As the violence demolished their possessions, relationships, and hopes, Lubich and other young women her age confronted an inescapable question: Is there an ideal worth living for that no bomb can destroy? The answer opened itself before them—this ideal was God, a God who is love, whose personal love enveloped every aspect of their lives.

In the bomb shelters, they read and reread the Gospels. Nearly 60 years later, the experience for Lubich was still vivid: "It was as if we had never read, 'Love your neighbor as yourself'—all of a sudden we understood, ah, it's that old lady who can't run to the shelter; it's the mother struggling with her five crying children—let's help them!" They read, "Ask and you shall receive" (Luke 11: 9). "We asked on behalf of the poor," Lubich recounts, "and each time we were filled with God's gifts: bread, powdered milk, jelly, wood, clothing . . . which we took to those who needed them." Filled with the freedom and joy of a life based on the Gospel, they shared their stories, and their group expanded.

In January 1944, a priest brought communion to the home of Doriana Zamboni, one of the young women with Lubich, who was too ill to leave her house. Afterward, the Capuchin asked Lubich when she thought that Jesus had suffered the most. She answered that it might have been in the Garden of Olives. He responded, "I believe, rather, it was what he felt on the cross when he cried out, 'My God, my God, why have you forsaken me?'" When the priest left, Lubich turned to her friend and said, "If Jesus' greatest pain was his abandonment by his Father, we will choose him as our Ideal, and that is the way we will follow him." Years later, Zamboni reflected, "From that day on, Chiara spoke to me often, in fact, constantly, of Jesus forsaken. He was *the* living personality in our lives."

The first Focolare house emerged as a spontaneous response to particular circumstances. On May 13, 1944, Lubich watched as air raids destroyed her family home. Afterward, her family proposed that they take refuge in the countryside. She, however, sensed that she had to remain in Trent with her friends to do something for those who most resembled Jesus forsaken.

Her family trudged toward the mountains, and she turned toward the city. Many years later, the scene remained vivid in her memory: "The destruction was total: trees had been uprooted, houses were in ruins, roads were covered with debris. Tears came to my eyes . . . and I let them flow." A frantic woman sprang out at a street corner, grabbed Lubich, and screamed, "Four of mine have died, do you understand?" She recalls, "As I consoled her I understood that I had to forget about my own grief in order to take on that of the others."

Among the ruins, she found all of her friends alive. Since their homes, too, had been destroyed and their families had fled, they began to live together in a small apartment that came to be known as the *focolare* (Italian for "hearth") because of its warm family atmosphere.

In the shelters, conscious that any moment could be their last, they searched for words that might express what Jesus expected of them. When they read, "This is my commandment, that you love one another as I have loved you" (John 15: 12), they recognized how he had loved—he gave his life. Lubich recalls gathering in a circle and making a pact: "I am ready to give my life for you; I for you, I for you; all for each one."

That pact generated new light and energy to understand what loving one another meant. "We are not always asked to die for one another, but we can share everything: our worries, our sorrows, our meager possessions, our spiritual riches." They also began to discern an almost tangible living presence of Christ in the community. "We saw our lives take a qualitative leap forward. Someone came into our group, silently, an invisible Friend, giving us security, a more experiential joy, a new peace, a fullness of life, an inextinguishable light. Jesus was fulfilling his promise to us: 'Where two or three are gathered in my name, I am there among them' (Matthew 18: 20)."

At another moment, they read Jesus' solemn prayer the night before he died: "That they may all be one. As you, Father, are in me and I am in you" (John 17: 21). Lubich describes that moment: "It was not an easy text to start with, but one by one those words seemed to come to life, giving us the conviction that we were born for that page of the gospel." She recalls, "One thing was clear in our hearts: what God wanted for us was unity. We live for the sole aim of being one with him, one with each other, and one with everyone. This marvelous vocation linked us to heaven and immersed us in the one human family. What purpose in life could be greater?"

Within five months after the war's end, a community of about 500—young men and women, married couples, children, the elderly, members of men's and women's religious orders, priests—had joined them in living this spirituality of unity.

In 1948, Lubich met Igino Giordani, who in the 1920s had headed the press office of the newly created Popular Party. During the 1930s, when he was director of *Fides*, the magazine of the Pontifical Society for the Propagation of the Faith, Giordani became known for his frank, combative style. In June 1946, he was elected to Parliament, where he helped lay the foundations of the postwar Italian republic. Lubich came to his office accompanied by three Franciscans—a Conventual, a Friar Minor, and a Capuchin—groups that had differed quite forcefully about how to live their founder's rule. For Giordani, seeing them together was "already a miracle." He noted in his memoir that when Lubich spoke, he heard the voice for which he had been waiting. "She put holiness within reach of everyone. She tore down the grille which separated the world of the laity from the mystical life. She put into the public square the treasures of a castle to which only a few had been admitted. She rendered God near, making people discover Him as father, brother, friend, present to humanity."

Giordani helped Lubich and the little group understand that they had a "charism," a gift from God to be shared not only with Catholics but with all of humanity—men and women; single and married; laypeople, clergy, and religious; adults and children. Giordani's desire to be an integral part of a Focolare household, even though he was a married man, led Lubich to understand that Focolare houses were not only to be constituted by single men or women but also to include married men and women who feel the same call to live for unity.

Each Focolare house generally includes at least four single women or men who live in community, as well as at least one, but usually many more, married women or men who remain with their families but partake fully in the life of the house. These houses serve as points of focus for wider communities of people who feel called to live out this charism of unity in their particular circumstances—laypeople from a broad spectrum of society ("adherents"), priests, religious men and women, young people ("gen"), men and women who feel called to bring the spirituality into their communities and workplaces ("volunteers of God"). In 2011, there were 742 of these Focolare houses in 83 nations.

Throughout the 1950s, many met this new spirituality through personal relationships and the ever larger summer gatherings in the Dolomites at the Mariapolis ("City of Mary"). In 1959, people from 26 countries gathered there. Giordani describes the scene: "All united they consecrated their own countries to God, in order to make of all peoples the one people of God, applying the instruction that Lubich had drawn from the gospel: 'Love the country of the other as you love your own.'"

By the late 1950s, the Focolare movement had spread throughout Italy, and by the early 1960s across Europe. On March 23, 1962, Pope John XXIII issued an official approval of the movement under the name Opera di Maria ("Work of Mary"), because its purpose, like Mary's, is to make Jesus present in the world.

In the early 1950s, Lubich had begun to hear from members of the underground Church behind the Iron Curtain about their dramatic situation. East Germany was willing to receive the help of medical professionals from other countries, so in 1961 and 1962 she sent 10 doctors and nurses who were members of the movement. At the annual Leipzig commercial fair, they could communicate with Focolare communities that had sprung up in Hungary, Czechoslovakia, Yugoslavia, Russia, Lithuania, and Poland.

The *focolarini* first visited Recife, Brazil, in 1958, where two priests who had attended the Mariapolis had brought a Focolare community to life. The movement spread quickly throughout Brazil, Argentina, and the rest of Latin America. Missionary priests and sisters helped to develop the movement in Asia, as well, beginning in Manila in 1966, then Korea, Japan, Hong Kong, Taiwan, and throughout Asia. The movement reached Australia in 1967, and subsequently New Zealand and Oceania.

Because Patriarch Athenagoras frequently invited Lubich to Istanbul, a Focolare house was opened there in 1967. From Turkey, the movement spread to Greece, Lebanon, Egypt, and eventually throughout the Middle East.

In the early 1960s, a bishop from Cameroon requested help on behalf of the Bangwa, a tribe in his diocese with a 93% infant mortality rate due to encephalitis. In 1965, Focolare members went to live in the Bangwa community, subsequently establishing a clinic and offering technical support to develop the economic infrastructure. The burgeoning population of Fontem, the village of the Bangwa, is now served by a highly regarded hospital and school, and its local industry has made it self-sufficient. From its beginnings in Fontem, the movement has spread throughout Africa.

In North America, the first Focolare house opened in Manhattan on September 14, 1961. Over the next 30 years, the movement spread throughout the United States and Canada. In 2011, there were Focolare houses in New York, Chicago, San Antonio, Houston, Dallas, Los Angeles, Washington, D.C., Columbus (Ohio), Atlanta, Toronto, Montreal, and Vancouver. North America has a "permanent Mariapolis," one of 33 such "little cities" of the Focolare around the world. Located in Hyde Park, New York, it provides a practical example of a community that lives by the law of the Gospel. It also serves as a gathering place for conferences, workshops, and retreats.

By the early 21st century, the Focolare movement had established itself in 182 countries with more than 140,000 core members and over 2 million affiliates, including 30,000 friends of non-Christian faith traditions. John Paul II's spontaneous remarks to a 1990 gathering of 10,000 young focolarini express the movement's ongoing aspiration: "The perspective of a united world is the great expectation of people today . . . toward a civilization that is truly expressed in the civilization of love."

On the Focolare's 60th anniversary in December 2003, John Paul II commended its members for their work as "*apostles of dialogue*, the privileged way to promote unity: dialogue within the Church, ecumenical and interreligious dialogue, dialogue with non-believers." The pope's statement explains how the Focolare's work has taken shape. While remaining faithful to their own spiritual roots, members open themselves, as Lubich has described it, "to the reality of being one human family in one Father: God." As the movement spread throughout the world, spontaneous contact among neighbors of differing Christian churches helped to sustain ecumenical dialogue. Open, trusting relationships with Buddhist, Hindu, Muslim, or Jewish friends paved the way for interfaith dialogue.

Lubich has received the Templeton Prize for Progress in Religion (1977), the UNESCO Prize for Peace Education (1996), and the Council of Europe's Human Rights Prize (1998); honorary citizenships in Rome and numerous other cities; and 16 honorary doctoral degrees in a variety of disciplines. The citation for the 2001 Defender of Peace Prize, presented by two Hindu-Gandhian institutions in India, acknowledged her use of "the most powerful human force of love and a strong faith in the unity of all humankind as espoused in the teachings of Jesus Christ," which has enabled her "to play a tireless role in sowing the seeds of peace and love among all peoples."

As the Focolare movement has spread and grown, structures have developed for outreach to families, professionals, youth, and parishes. Similarly, initiatives to serve local needs have developed into more than a thousand projects for social and economic development and improvement of health, education, and living conditions.

During natural disasters or other emergencies, the Focolare's global networks facilitate the communication of victims' immediate needs and channel resources directly to them. Because of the strong bonds of mutual love that permeate this global network, disaster relief can reinforce the personal relationships that already have been built, transcending the anonymous distribution of goods.

The Focolare takes a systematic approach to development funding through Action for a United World, a nongovernmental organization (NGO) known internationally by its Italian name, Azione per un Mondo Unito (AMU). It raises funds and awards grants for international development work conducted from the perspective of a spirituality of unity, promoting participation and shared responsibility, reciprocity, and respect for the dignity of local cultures and social structures. Another Focolare NGO, New Humanity, is now recognized by the UN Economic and Social Council as one of the 122 NGOs worldwide that hold general consultative status.

Even as Lubich's health began to decline, she updated the General Statutes, initially approved in 1990 by the Pontifical Council for the Laity. Just a few months before her death, the Pontifical Congregation for Catholic Education approved the Sophia University Institute. This university, an important element of Lubich's vision, offers interdisciplinary graduate degrees in "Foundations and Perspectives of a Culture of Unity."

Lubich died peacefully on March 14, 2008, at her home in Rocca di Papa, outside Rome. At her funeral, 30,000 gathered in and around the Roman Basilica of St. Paul outside the Walls. The gathering included representatives of the main Christian churches and all the major religions, acknowledging the global impact of her life and her spirituality.

In his eulogy, Vatican secretary of state Cardinal Tarcisio Bertone summed up the impact of her life: "She formed individuals who were love itself, who lived the charism of unity and communion with God and with their neighbor; people who spread 'love-unity' by making themselves, their homes and their work a 'focolare.' . . . This is a mission possible [for] everyone be-cause the Gospel is within everyone's reach: bishops and priests, children, young people and adults, consecrated and lay people, married couples, families and communities, all are called to live the ideal of unity."

In July 2008, 516 representatives from the world-wide Focolare communities gathered in Rome to elect new leadership. Above all else, they wished to remain faithful to Lubich's legacy, as expressed in the General Statutes: "Mutual and constant love, which makes unity possible and brings the presence of Jesus among all . . . is the norm of norms, the premise to every other rule." This helped them to open themselves to what the Holy Spirit was suggesting for the movement's future. After two rounds, their nearly unanimous choice as president was Maria Voce, a 72-year-old lawyer who had worked for many years with Lubich to draft the revised statutes.

In a message read at Lubich's funeral, Pope Benedict XVI gave thanks to God "for the gift given to the Church of this woman of intrepid faith, humble messenger of hope and peace, founder of a vast spiritual family that embraces many fields of evangelization." Lubich herself described the encounter with the Lord for which she hoped: "When I arrive to your door and you ask me my name, I will not say my name, I will say my name is 'thank you,' for everything and forever."—Amy Uelmen and Thomas Masters

BIBLIOGRAPHY AND FURTHER READING: Gallagher, Jim. *A Woman's Work: The Story of the Focolare Movement and Its Founder.* Hyde Park, NY: New City Press, 1998; Lubich, Chiara. *Essential Writings: Spirituality, Dialogue, Culture.* Hyde Park, NY: New City Press, 2007; Masters, Thomas, and Amy Uelmen. *Focolare: Living a Spirituality of Unity in the United States.* Hyde Park, NY: New City Press, 2011. *See also* CIVILIZATION OF LOVE; ECONOMY OF COMMUNION; ECUMENISM

· M ·

MAGUIRE, DANIEL C. (1931–)   For many years a professor of moral theological ethics at Marquette University in Milwaukee, Daniel C. Maguire is one of the foremost members of what in the postconciliar era of the Catholic Church must be considered a veritable "school" of Catholic moral theologians who dissent from Church teaching. This contrarian movement began with the issuance by Pope Paul VI of the encyclical *Humanae Vitae* in 1968, when hundreds of Catholic theologians publicly dissented from the encyclical's reaffirmation of the Church's traditional teaching that every use of marriage must remain open to the transmission of life (*HV* # 11). Since then, members of this nonconforming theological school have continued to espouse positions at variance with the teaching of the Church while claiming to remain Catholic theologians in good standing.

Since most of these same dissenting theologians have not generally been either corrected or otherwise disciplined by the Catholic bishops—except in such cases as those of Fathers Hans Küng and Charles E. Curran where the Congregation for the Doctrine of the Faith in Rome insisted upon formal and public disciplinary action—nor have they generally been dropped from the faculties where they have continued to teach, they have been able to continue to present themselves plausibly as Catholic religious and theological voices. Dr. Maguire, a former priest now twice married, has continued for more than 40 years to be a prominent member of this school of theologians.

On the evidence of his considerable publication record—over 150 articles and more than 10 books—Maguire is well trained and highly knowledgeable in the field of Catholic theology. He holds a doctorate of sacred theology (1969) from the Gregorian University in Rome, and before coming to Marquette, he taught moral theology at the Catholic University of America. In his works, Maguire demonstrates an extensive knowledge and sometimes even an impressive mastery of the subject matter of various aspects of both historical and contemporary moral theology. His departures from Catholic orthodoxy are thus neither trivial nor accidental, but rather are quite conscious and studied; he knows exactly what he is doing. Moreover, he does address and engage with real questions and dilemmas and generally provides reasoned arguments and citations in support of his positions—but quite regularly they are not the Church's positions.

Being knowledgeable in the field of Catholic theology is not the same as being a Catholic theologian. Maguire, for example, does not accept that the questions and dilemmas he deals with can ultimately and sometimes definitively be settled by the Catholic Church's magisterium. For him, as for the members of the dissenting school to which he belongs, he does not accept the teaching of the Second Vatican Council that "theological subjects should be taught in the light of faith under the guidance of the magisterium of the Church" (*OT* # 16); instead, he apparently believes theologians are able to function independently of Church authority on the basis of their acquired theological knowledge and expertise.

Beginning with writings of his published around the time of the issuance of *Humanae Vitae*, Maguire adopted, advocated, and defended positions that were intended to undermine the credibility of the encyclical. These positions included a denial that the Church's interpretation of the natural law was continuous with its power to expound divine revelation authentically and a similar denial that it could teach infallibly on moral questions. Such positions directly contradicted Pope Paul VI's teaching in *Humanae Vitae* (# 4)—based on citations from several of his predecessors—affirming the Church's competence to interpret the natural law. Moreover, the well-known First Vatican Council definition of the pope's infallibility expressly included the phrase "faith *and* morals" (emphasis added), indicating that the Church *can* teach infallibly on moral questions, and it has done so in the case of, for example, the Council of Trent's teaching on marriage. Maguire typically evades this latter question by saying that the term *morals* as it appears in the First Vatican Council conciliar definition is not itself defined.

More than merely dissenting from particular Church teachings, however, Maguire denies the nature of the Church's magisterium itself. For him, the magisterium does not reside in the teachings of the popes and the bishops in communion with him; rather, Maguire frequently speaks of the Church's "*hierarchical* magisterium," as if there were more than one kind of magisterium, or teaching authority, in the Church. In an influential article published in the journal *Cross Currents* (1968), Maguire wrote: "It would be better to speak of the *magisteria* of the Church. We would then consider not just the papal and episcopal magisteria but the *equally authentic* magisterium of the laity and the magisterium of the theologians" (emphasis added). This assertion is plainly incompatible with the Second Vatican Council's teaching that "the task of giving an authentic interpretation of the Word of God, whether in its written form, or in the form of Tradition, has been entrusted to the living teaching office of the Church *alone*" (*DV* # 19; emphasis added).

Thus, although Maguire—like the members of his dissenting theological school generally—likes to invoke the Second Vatican Council as the basis of his ability to hold positions at variance with the Church's teaching, he does not scruple in the slightest to dissent from the council's plain teachings whenever it suits his purpose. Such dissent from a conciliar teaching ratified by the pope, as from a papal encyclical, already constitutes a violation of the Second Vatican Council's *Lumen Gentium* (# 25), which strictly requires "loyal submission of the will and intellect . . . to the authentic teaching authority of the Roman Pontiff, even when he does not speak *ex cathedra*."

If this were not so, the faithful would not be able to rely on what the Second Vatican Council calls the "sacred and certain teaching of the Church," as again the council requires them to do in forming their consciences (*DH # 14*). The dissenting theologians simply do not see that the Church could no longer really teach at all if their understanding of the Church's teaching authority represented the correct view.

Yet Maguire consistently holds to these—and other—erroneous views in his writings. Precisely because they dissent from what the authentic magisterium proposes, his branch of theologians is obliged to rely on their acquired knowledge and theological expertise. Maguire even appears to consider the theological opinions arising thereby to be superior to magisterial teaching—precisely *because* they are putatively based on research or "science." The result of this approach is a supposed pluralism in Catholic teaching that he insistently trumpets. It is not just that he disagrees with Church teaching; he believes his theological opinions are equal to or superior to Church teachings and represent alternative "Catholic" teachings that are valid.

In a particularly notorious case, Maguire drafted (along with his then wife Marjorie Maguire and Frances Kissling) a paper entitled "A Catholic Statement on Pluralism and Abortion," which appeared as a paid advertisement in the October 7, 1984, edition of the *New York Times*. This ad claimed that a "diversity of opinions" existed in the Catholic Church on the subject of abortion. The statement was signed by 97 Catholics, including four male and 22 female religious, bringing about a major national scandal that lasted for years before Church authorities finally succeeded in obtaining retractions from most of the signatories involved. Maguire's position as a tenured Catholic moral theologian was apparently never affected by this travesty.

Again, in 2007, Maguire wrote and had the temerity to send out to all of the American Catholic bishops two pamphlets entitled *Moderate Roman Catholic Position on Contraception and Abortion* and *A Catholic Defense of Same-Sex Marriage*. Responding to this challenge, the Committee on Doctrine of the U.S. Conference of Catholic Bishops issued a "public correction" of Maguire's views, although this was surely a mild rebuke considering the provocation. Responding to the bishops, the Marquette University theologian reiterated his claim that there are multiple magisteria in the Catholic Church and declared that it was "arrogant" on the part of the Catholic bishops to claim what he called "a monopoly on insight in the Catholic community."

Maguire's published scholarly works reflect his consistent stance that the Catholic Church is *not* the "teacher of truth" that the Second Vatican Council said it was (*DH # 14*) and that theologians enjoy a status independent of Church authority based on their acquired theological expertise. The pamphlets he sent out to the bishops, for example, certainly reflected the views he had set out at greater length in such books as his *Sacred Choices: The Right to Contraception and Abortion in Ten World Religions* (2001) and *Sacred Rights: The Case for Contraception and Abortion in World Religions* (2003). It is notable that these evils are characterized by him both as "sacred" and as "rights."

Daniel Maguire's basic positions are laid out in his 2008 book *Whose Church? A Concise Guide to Progressive Catholicism*, which aims to show, inter alia, how "Vatican stances on contraception, abortion, gay marriage, and stem cell research violate not only common sense and ethical values but also the teaching of the gospel and its demands for justice and love." Considering his positions and his penchant for provocative public challenges, it is not surprising that in March 2010, Dr. Maguire publicly called on Pope Benedict XVI to resign the papacy for having failed, in Maguire's view, to act properly in the course of the Church's clerical sex-abuse crisis.—Kenneth D. Whitehead

BIBLIOGRAPHY AND FURTHER READING: Maguire, Daniel C. "Moral Inquiry and Religious Assent." In *Contraception: Authority and Dissent*, edited by Charles E. Curran. New York: Herder & Herder, 1969; Maguire, Daniel C. "Morality and Magisterium." *Cross Currents* 18 (1968). Reprinted in Charles E. Curran and Richard A. McCormick, SJ, eds., *The Magisterium and Morality*. New York: Paulist Press, 1982; Maguire, Daniel C. *Whose Church? A Concise Guide to Progressive Catholicism*. New York: New Press, 2008. *See also* DIGNITATIS HUMANAE; DISSENT; *HUMANAE VITAE*; INFALLIBILITY; KÜNG, HANS; MAGISTERIUM; MORAL THEOLOGY: A SURVEY; NATURAL LAW

MANHATTAN DECLARATION The Manhattan Declaration, "A Call of Christian Conscience," is a historic statement by Catholic, Protestant, and Orthodox religious leaders calling on Christians to protect the sanctity of life, the institution of marriage, and religious liberty. Although there are many issues of importance in the public square, the Manhattan Declaration urges Christians of every denomination to work to protect these three basic goods, all of which, the document argues, are under peculiar and sustained attack in recent times.

Although consistent with Catholic social teachings, the declaration is broadly ecumenical in language and appeal. The three primary drafters of the declaration were Catholic scholar Dr. Robert P. George, evangelical leader Charles Colson of Prison Fellowship, and Dr. Timothy George, professor at the Beeson Divinity School at Samford University. It was issued on November 20, 2009, in Washington, D.C. At the release, Pentecostal leader Harry Jackson, Tony Perkins of the Family Research Council, Ron Sider of the Palmer Theological Seminary, and Jim Daly of Focus on the Family joined Cardinal Justin Rigali of Philadelphia, Archbishop Donald W. Wuerl of Washington, and Archbishop Charles J. Chaput of Denver. Other prominent signers included Metropolitan Jonah Paffhausen, primate of the Orthodox Church in America; Archpriest Chad Hatfield of St. Vladimir's Orthodox Theological Seminary; Rev. William Owens, president of the Coalition of African-American Pastors; Robert Duncan, primate of the Anglican Church in North America; and Peter J. Akinola, primate of the Anglican Church in Nigeria.

The preamble of the Manhattan Declaration invokes the Christian heritage of resistance to infanticide, the slave trade, the claims of divine rights of kings, and racially discriminatory laws. It also notes the Christian work of caring for the sick and dying, helping the poor and destitute, and reaching out in humanitarian service to suffering individuals around the world. Invoking "the light of the truth that is grounded in Holy Scripture, in natural human reason (which is itself, in our view, the gift of beneficent God), and in the very nature of the human person," it calls on "all people of goodwill, believers and non-believers alike, to consider carefully and reflect critically on the issues we here address as we, with St. Paul, commend this appeal to everyone's conscience in the sight of God."

The document states: "In this declaration we affirm: 1) the profound, inherent, and equal dignity of every human being as a creature fashioned in the very image of God, possessing inherent rights of equal dignity and life; 2) marriage as a conjugal union of man and woman, ordained by God from the creation, and historically understood by believers and non-believers alike, to be the most basic institution in society and; 3) religious liberty, which is grounded in the character of God, the example of Christ, and the inherent freedom and dignity of human beings created in the divine image." The signatories "pledge to each other, and to our

fellow believers, that no power on earth, be it cultural or political, will intimidate us into silence or acquiescence."

In regard to the sanctity of life, the Manhattan Declaration calls on "all officials in our country, elected and appointed, to protect and serve every member of our society, including the most marginalized, voiceless, and vulnerable among us." The declaration specifically notes threats to life from abortion, "embryo-destructive research," and the movements to promote assisted suicide and euthanasia. It admonishes: "We must be willing to defend, even at risk and cost to ourselves and our institutions, the lives of our brothers and sisters at every stage of development and in every condition."

As threats to the marriage culture, the declaration singles out the "culture of divorce," glamorization of promiscuity and infidelity, "unilateral divorce," and the proposed redefinition of marriage to include "same-sex and multiple partner relationships." It notes "genuine social harms" that would follow marriage redefinition: "the religious liberty of those for whom this is a matter of conscience is jeopardized," "the rights of parents are abused as family life and sex education programs in schools are used to teach children that an enlightened understanding recognizes as 'marriages' sexual partnerships that many parents believe are intrinsically non-marital and immoral," and "the common good of civil society is damaged when the law itself, in its critical pedagogical function, becomes a tool for eroding a sound understanding of marriage on which the flourishing of the marriage culture in any society vitally depends." Signers pledge "to labor ceaselessly to preserve the legal definition of marriage as the union of one man and one woman and to rebuild the marriage culture."

Threats to religious liberty noted include efforts "to weaken or eliminate conscience clauses" protecting health care providers, "the use of anti-discrimination statutes to force religious institutions, businesses, and service providers" to "comply with activities they judge to be deeply immoral or go out of business," and the prosecution of Christian clergy "for preaching Biblical norms against the practice of homosexuality."

The declaration ends with a powerful statement: "We will not comply with any edict that purports to compel our institutions to participate in abortions, embryo-destructive research, assisted suicide and euthanasia, or any other anti-life act; nor will we bend to any rule purporting to force us to bless immoral sexual partnerships, treat them as marriages or the equivalent, or refrain from proclaiming the truth, as we know it, about morality and immorality and marriage and the family. We will fully and ungrudgingly render to Caesar what is Caesar's. But under no circumstances will we render to Caesar what is God's."

Archbishop John C. Nienstedt of St. Paul and Minneapolis described the document as an attempt to "light a fire" that he hoped "will catch on and touch the troops in the rank and file." After the declaration was issued, Cardinal Rigali, Archbishop Wuerl, Archbishop Timothy Dolan of New York, and Archbishop Joseph E. Kurtz of Louisville asked all Catholic bishops in the United States to introduce the document to their dioceses and encourage clergy and members to add their names as signatories.—Maggie Gallagher and William C. Duncan

See also FAMILY; MARRIAGE; NATURAL LAW

MARGARET OF CASTELLO (1278–1320)

Margaret of Castello was born a blind, lame dwarf in the town of Metola within the papal state of Massa Trabaria during the Middle Ages. Her aristocratic parents, Parisio and Emilia, told everyone that their daughter died shortly after birth. Parisio, a powerful political official, did not want his enemies to be glad of his misfortune in having such a creature for a child, so he sequestered little Margaret in a room in the castle and expunged all records of her name. Besides her nurse, the only person who knew Margaret was alive was the village priest, Padre Cappellano, who had baptized her upon her birth. This pious priest visited Margaret regularly, teaching her academic subjects and social skills. Margaret was blessed with superior intelligence and a great desire to learn. Cappellano grounded Margaret in the basics of the Catholic faith.

When Margaret was six years old, she was almost discovered by guests of her parents, whereupon her father had her locked up in a cell near a remote church outside her hometown of Metola. Margaret remained in the cell until she was 20 years old. At this time, some German pilgrims arrived in Metola with some exciting news. They reported that miraculous cures were taking place at the shrine of a recently deceased Franciscan, Fra Giacomo of Castello. This man was reported to have performed many miracles when alive.

Although Parisio was initially incredulous, he was in a heady state over some military success and perceived the hand of God in his personal affairs. He came to believe that God was backing him in all his undertakings and would grant him yet another great triumph. If God was working miracles among the rabble flocking to the tomb of Fra Giacomo, then certainly he would vouchsafe a mighty miracle for

the illustrious Parisio of Massa Trabaria. Thus, after 13 years of incarceration, Margaret was released to make a pilgrimage to the shrine of Fra Giacomo of Castello. After an arduous journey to Città di Castello through mountain trails, Margaret's parents deposited her at the tomb of the holy friar at the Church of San Francesco. Parisio ordered his daughter to beseech God to cure her lameness and give her sight. But when no miracle occurred, the parents abandoned Margaret, never to see her again.

Although sightless in a strange city, Margaret was free at last. Her cheerful, friendly nature soon won a circle of friends among the poor, including beggars, with whom she lived for several years. Gradually, a few wealthy families heard about Margaret and invited her to live with them. She repaid their hospitality by cooking and cleaning for them, as well as looking after their children, despite her blindness. A kindhearted noblewoman, Lady Gregoria Venturino, eventually welcomed Margaret into her home as a permanent guest. Now Margaret could spend her time visiting the sick at the city hospital and inmates at the city prison. Her great love of God impelled her to help those who were in need. People came to admire Margaret, who was loving and caring even though she could have become hateful and bitter over her parents' rejection and her physical deformities.

It was at this time during her life that Margaret became a lay sister in the Dominican order, donning the black-and-white habit of the *mantellate* ("veiled ones"). God granted special gifts to Margaret to help others, and she could foretell future events. She counseled those who were troubled and effected spiritual and physical healing of people. Like her role model, Jesus, Margaret wore herself out helping others; like him, she died at the age of 33. Margaret expired in the town of Castello on April 13, 1320, after a brief illness.

A well-known miracle recorded by the medieval biographers occurred right after Margaret's death—in fact, at her funeral. At the Mass for the deceased Margaret, the parents of a mute girl who was unable to walk carried her to Margaret's coffin and prayed to Margaret to intercede for their daughter at the throne of God. Soon all the people in the church were calling on Margaret to secure a miracle from God, and their petitions were heeded. The little girl on the ground next to Margaret's body rose to her feet without any help. She had never been able to walk, yet now she glided with ease around the coffin. She had never been able to talk, but now she exclaimed joyfully to the crowd: "I have been cured through Margaret's prayers." Margaret's passion to help others had not been halted with her death. The little girl's parents and all present rejoiced in an outburst of thanksgiving to God. This posthumous miracle was witnessed by hundreds of people who believed they were in the presence of a saint.

The story of Margaret's life and miracles spread rapidly throughout Massa Trabaria and the neighboring republics. On October 19, 1609, Pope Paul V beatified Margaret of Castello. As a sign of her sanctity, God has permitted Margaret's body to remain incorrupt through the centuries. Her body has not decomposed and is enshrined in a glass coffin at the School for the Blind, Città di Castello, Italy. The greater miracle is that Blessed Margaret triumphed over all obstacles in her quest to love. Blessed Margaret's generous spirit posits that our disabilities or personal misfortunes do not diminish our capacity to love and do good. Her life trumpets the dignity and worth of every person.—Alexander LaPerchia

BIBLIOGRAPHY AND FURTHER READING: Bonniwell, William R., OP. *The Life of Blessed Margaret of Castello*. Rockford, IL: Tan Books, 1983; Delaney, John J. *Dictionary of Saints*. Garden City, NY: Doubleday, 1980; Koenig-Bricken, Woodeene. *365 Saints*. New York: HarperCollins, 1995. *See also* PERSONHOOD, HUMAN

MARRIAGE: LOVE AND LIFE IN THE DIVINE PLAN

Marriage: Love and Life in the Divine Plan is a pastoral letter of the U.S. Conference of Catholic Bishops (USCCB). The letter, issued in November 2009, summarizes Church teaching on marriage and family life in light of the Second Vatican Council and the writings of Popes Paul VI, Blessed John Paul II, and Benedict XVI. In particular, it draws on the thought of John Paul II, especially as found in his "theology of the body."

The introduction to the pastoral letter recalls God's gift of marriage to man and woman at creation and how original sin ruptured the spousal communion willed by God, who still blessed marriage and whose Son-Made-Man redeemed marriage, elevating the marriage of Christians to the dignity of a sacrament of grace. It teaches that marriage is natural for all men and women as God's gift and ends by noting difficulties in understanding marriage today.

Part 1 of *Marriage: Love and Life in the Divine Plan* considers the natural institution of marriage. It defines marriage and discusses its essential purposes and then discusses some of the most pressing challenges currently facing marriage. Marriage is a lifelong partnership, exclusive and faithful, established by the free marital consent of a man and a woman and ordered toward the good of the spouses and the procreation of children. God, its author, has endowed it with its essential attributes. Once marriage has been validly entered and consummated, the bond uniting husband and wife cannot be dissolved by their will. It lasts until death and is the foundation of the family, the basic cell of society.

Key ideas of John Paul II's theology of the body are central here. Marriage is based on the fact that man and woman are different as male and female but the same as persons uniquely suited to be helpmates for each other. Their differences are complementary, distinct bodily ways of being open to God and one another, of answering the vocation to love. While spouses are more than their bodies and their union includes personal and spiritual levels, their bodily differences relate them to each other and, in their bodily union in the conjugal act, enable them to cooperate with God in bringing new persons made in his image into existence. The resulting family is a new kind of communion of persons that is the origin and foundation of society. The two ends or purposes of marriage are the "good of the spouses" and "procreation of offspring." After naming the good of spouses, the pastoral letter says immediately: "Thus, the Church teaches that marriage is both unitive and procreative . . . inseparably both" (*LLDP*, 11).

John Paul II's theology of the body affirms that the human body has a spousal significance. "The human body by its very nature signifies that we humans are directed to relationship . . . for it is only in relationship that we achieve a true wholeness as a communion of persons" (*LLDP*, 12). In explaining the *unitive* meaning of the conjugal act, the pastoral letter uses passages from the Song of Songs (2: 16, 4: 9–10) and Tobit (8: 5–7) that John Paul employed in his catechesis on the spousal meaning of the body.

Love is expansive and life giving. Marriage, as ordered to the procreation of human life, is not only love giving but life giving, and children are the "supreme gift of marriage" (*GS* # 50). Spouses are called to cooperate with the love of the Creator and the Savior in enriching his family with children. But many spouses who ardently desire to share life and love with children cannot do so because of infertility. This is a tragedy, but the marital union is a distinctive communion of persons and an infertile couple manifests this.

Spouses, after child-rearing years have passed, must stay involved with their children and especially with their grandchildren. They can also "nurture the needy, the disabled, and the abandoned with works of justice and charity" (*LLDP*, 15).

The two ends of marriage are inseparably related through "conjugal love," which expresses the unitive dimension of marriage "in such a way as to show how this meaning is ordered toward the equally obvious procreative meaning" (*LLDP*, 15). Conjugal love is by nature faithful, exclusive, and meant to be fecund. Procreation is a participation in God's own ongoing creativity. The transmission of life is a concrete realization of the man and woman's gift of themselves to one another. The unitive and procreative meanings of marriage are joined as two aspects of the same self-giving.

The bishops identify four fundamental challenges to marriage: contraception, same-sex marriage, divorce, and cohabitation.

Regarding contraception, the pastoral letter reaffirms the "inseparable connection willed by God and unlawful for man to break on his own initiative" (*HV # 12*). It rejects the claim that as long as the marriage as a whole is open to children, each individual act of intercourse need not be: "A marriage is only as open to procreation as each act of intercourse is, because the whole meaning of marriage is present and signified in each marital act. Each marital act signifies, embodies, and renews the original and enduring marital covenant between husband and wife" (*LLDP*, 18). When the spouses engage in the conjugal act, they speak what John Paul II called the "language of the body," one of personal communion in complete and mutual self-donation. Contraception changes the language of the body. It no longer speaks the language of selfless giving of one's whole person to the other but gives a contradictory meaning—the refusal to give oneself entirely, for one deliberately withholds his or her fertility from the other spouse.

The claim that persons of the same sex can marry is one of the most troubling contemporary developments. This attempt to redefine marriage ignores that male–female complementarity is essential to marriage, for this is what enables spouses to give and receive one another in the only bodily kind of act through which new human life can be given. This way of describing marriage regards male–female complementarity as irrelevant. But "the true nature of marriage . . . is a witness to the precious gift of the child and to the unique roles of a mother and father. Same-sex unions are incapable of such a witness. Consequently, making them equivalent to marriage disregards the very nature of marriage" (*LLDP*, 22). This claim also ignores the truth that children need both a father and a mother in order to flourish.

The charge that opposition to same-sex unions as marital is a form of unjust discrimination is erroneous. It is not unjust to oppose such unions, but rather just to defend the reality that marriage is based on the sexual complementarity of men and women whose intimate bodily union is the kind of union through which new human persons come to be. The Church condemns homosexual acts but does not condemn homosexuals and in fact loves them and helps them to practice the virtue of chastity and to have close intimate friends who are loved chastely.

Marriage is meant to be a lifelong covenantal union, and spouses promise each other fidelity until death. Divorce claims to dissolve this union, but it cannot. Jesus teaches that divorce cannot be reconciled with the binding nature of marriage as intended by the Creator (Matthew 19: 3–9). Quarrels and misunderstandings can be found in all marriages, reflecting the consequences of original sin. But God's plan for marriage persists, and he continues to offer mercy and healing grace.

In some cases, though, divorce may be the only solution to a morally unacceptable situation, for instance, when the safety of a spouse or children is at risk. No one in a marriage is obliged to maintain common living with an abusing spouse.

The pastoral letter urges validly married Catholics who have suffered the pain of divorce to make frequent use of the sacraments, especially the sacraments of Holy Eucharist and Reconciliation. Although the Church cannot recognize the validity of civil unions, it encourages those who have divorced and remarried civilly to participate in parish life and attend the Sunday Eucharist, even without receiving the sacrament.

Divorced persons who wish to marry in the Catholic Church should seek counsel about ways to remedy their situation, including the suitability of a declaration of nullity when there is no longer any hope of reconciliation. Such a declaration does not dissolve a marriage, but rather is a declaration that no valid marriage existed from the beginning because the requirements for valid consent were not met at the time of the wedding. If a declaration of nullity is granted and there are no other restrictions, both parties are free to marry in the Catholic Church.

Today, many unmarried couples cohabit in a sexual relationship. Sexual intercourse outside of marriage is gravely immoral, because such intercourse is meant to express conjugal love, a selfless giving of oneself to the other, and unmarried persons have failed to commit themselves to each other. Although some couples think that premarital cohabitation can help them find out whether they are compatible, social science research shows that cohabitation can harm a couple's chances for a stable marriage. More importantly, cohabiting couples commit the serious sin of fornication. This does not conform to God's plan for marriage and is always wrong and objectively sinful.

Nothing can take the place of the binding lifelong commitment of marriage. A refusal to make a public lifelong commitment is at the heart of cohabitation. Cohabitation also deprives children of their right to a stable home headed by a man and a woman who have committed themselves to each other in a lifelong marital union and are prepared to care for their children and to educate them. Here, too, the findings of the social sciences confirm that the best environment for raising children is a stable home provided by the marriage of their parents. "The family is the *original cell of social life* . . . the natural society in which husband and wife are called to give themselves in love and in the gift of life. Authority, stability, and a life of relationships within the family constitute the foundations for freedom, security, and fraternity within society" (*CCC* # 2207).

The second part of the pastoral letter considers the sacrament of matrimony and the importance of marriage in the life of the Church. Although marriage remains the good gift that God created it to be, a blessing not lost because of the Fall, original sin has had bad consequences for married life. Because men and women became wounded by sin, their marriages have become distorted.

Baptism by the power of the Holy Spirit transforms men and women into a new creation, removing sin and elevating them to share in God's own divine life. Jesus has raised the marriage of Christians to the dignity of a sacrament and in so doing has restored marriage to its original meaning and beauty, what the Creator intended it to be "in the beginning." He made marriage the visible embodiment of his love for his bride, the Church, revealing his love as the purest and deepest love and by doing so revealing the deepest meaning of marital love as self-giving on the model of God's inner life and love. The marital union is an image of Christ's union with the Church, a participation in the covenant between Christ and the Church. "The natural meaning of marriage as an exchange of self-giving is not replaced, but fulfilled and raised to a higher level" (*LLDP*, 31).

Marriage: Love and Life in the Divine Plan emphasizes marriage as a sacrament. The *Catechism* states: "Christian marriage . . . becomes an efficacious sign, the sacrament of the covenant of Christ and the Church" (*CCC* # 1617). The pastoral letter continues: "An 'efficacious sign' is one that does not merely symbolize or signify something, but actually makes present what it signifies. Marriage signifies and makes present to baptized spouses the love of Christ by which he formed the Church as his spouse" (*LLDP*, 32). Christian married couples are called to a more-than-natural love; they are called to love each other with the supernatural love that Christ has for his Church. Their free gift of themselves to each other, given when they made their marriage vows of love and fidelity, participates in Christ's love of his bride the Church to the end.

The spouses are the ministers of this sacrament. For Catholics of the Latin Rite, a "canonical form" requires their consent to marriage to be received by an authorized bishop, priest, or deacon who is the Church's official witness. Eastern Catholic Churches require the assistance and blessing of an authorized bishop or priest.

The Holy Spirit empowers spouses to will to do the acts of courtesies and love owed each other. Formed by Christ's self-giving love for his bride the Church, they can perform acts of self-giving love to benefit themselves, their families, and the whole Church.

In Ephesians 5: 22, St. Paul instructed wives to be "subordinate to their husbands as to the Lord." His way of speaking was influenced by the customs of his day, but as John Paul II explained, this saying must "be understood and carried out in a new way," in light of what St. Paul said immediately before: "Be subordinate to one another out of reverence for Christ (Ephesians 5: 21)." John Paul emphasized that this is something new, an "innovation of the Gospel."

By espousing himself to the Church, Christ revealed the inner life of the Trinity, a communion of Persons: Father, Son, and Holy Spirit. The Church is itself a communion of persons sharing in God's Trinitarian life and love. Married love signifies and participates in the Trinitarian life of God. The revelation of God as a Trinity of Persons in intimate communion is the most profound and central mystery of faith. It gives us definitive knowledge of God, the source of all other divine mysteries, including both the mystery of our creation in the image and likeness of God and the mystery of marriage and the family. "The Trinity is a loving and life-giving communion of equal Persons. The one God is the loving inter-relationship of the Father, the Son, and the Holy Spirit. To be created in the image and likeness of God means . . . that human beings reflect . . . the communal life of the Trinity. Human beings were created not to live solitary lives, but to live in communion with

God and with one another, a communion that is both life-giving and loving" (*LLDP*, 36).

This Trinitarian image in marriage and family is shown first in the truth that marriage, like the Triune Persons, is a communion of love between coequal persons; it is shown in the life of the family, where "parents and children, brothers and sisters, grandparents and relatives are called to live in loving harmony" (*LLDP*, 37). It is manifested, secondly, in the life-giving nature of the Triune community of Persons and of the life-giving nature of the marital union, in which spouses cooperate with God by giving life to new persons.

The communion of persons formed by Christian spouses and their children is a kind of microcosm of the Church. Thus, the Fathers of the Church and Second Vatican Council used the term "domestic Church" to describe the nature of the Christian family. It "constitutes," as John Paul II said, "a specific revelation and realization of ecclesial communion, and for this reason . . . it can and should be called a domestic church" (*FC* # 21). All family members are called to practice the foundational Christian virtues, but parents have the grave responsibility to foster these virtues. They are also called to have their children baptized and to be their first evangelizers and teachers of the faith, encouraging them to love and receive the sacraments of Reconciliation, Confirmation, and the Eucharist. Because Christ's presence in the family makes it a domestic church, the family's participation in the Eucharist, especially the Sunday Eucharist, is most important.

In addition to our common Christian vocation to marriage, marriage itself is a specific kind of vocation. It is a vocation to love one's spouse with the same love that Christ has for his Church and to bear children, if this is God's will, and educate them in this kind of love. Spouses must help each other become saints. Young men and women have the obligation to discern whether God is calling them to the married life or to the priestly or religious life or to a single life in the world. Those called to marriage must prepare themselves for marriage. In childhood, they received remote preparation for marriage in their own homes, primarily from their parents; they received proximate preparation at puberty, which meant education in the meaning and nature of marriage, parenthood, and human sexuality. Their immediate preparation, which takes place during the weeks and months prior to their wedding, should be a journey in the faith. Christian married couples are to "become what they are" (*FC* # 17), that is, living members of a communion of persons defined by the

unbreakable spousal love of Christ for the Church. This requires constant effort.

The vocation to marriage is a vocation to holiness; marriage is for spouses the way they are to sanctify each other and thus reach the heavenly kingdom. Catholic spouses must live the theological virtues of faith, hope, and charity, the virtues infused into them by the Holy Spirit when they were baptized. Charity or love is the form or soul of all the virtues, and the spouses must acquire, with the never-failing help of God's grace, the human virtues of prudence, justice, temperance, and fortitude.

Two key virtues for Catholic spouses are chastity—a manifestation of the virtue of temperance—and gratitude. They must be grateful to God for his great gift of marriage, to one another for their selfless gift of themselves to one another, to the family that God gives to them, to the Church of which they are living members, and to the world in which they live their daily lives and in which they are to sanctify themselves, their children, and all with whom they are meant to live in fellowship and harmony. This gratitude fosters a spirit of hospitality, especially to the poor, in whom Catholic spouses are to see Christ himself and to serve him.

Through baptism, Catholic spouses, like all the baptized, have received a new identity: that of children of God, adopted brothers and sisters of Jesus Christ, sharing his divinity as he shares their humanity. Despite their human weaknesses and sins, they are empowered by Christ's redemptive love not only to signify but also to share his everlasting spousal love for the Church. The love given them by Christ is powerful enough to transform them more and more into his likeness and to transform their love for each other to participate ever more deeply in his spousal love for the Church.

Catholic spouses encounter in the Eucharist the source of their marriage, Jesus Christ. This encounter helps them realize that their marriage and the family resulting from it are to embrace the Church of which they are a living part and the world in which they live their daily lives. The Eucharist, which means "thanksgiving," is where the spouses can fully express their gratitude, their thanksgiving, to God the Father for his supreme gift, the gift of his risen Son, who, in turn, bestows most fully the divine life and love of the Holy Spirit. And the Eucharist commits the spouses to serve the poor and needy, and this hospitality in turn builds up the Church, making it an even stronger witness to Christ's love.

Christian marriage is a sign of the coming Kingdom, a sign of hope and loving witness to human dignity. Christ moves Catholic couples to ever greater heights of love. Christian married love prepares the spouses for eternal life, when the Church of which they are living members will be truly itself, and when the spouses with the whole communion of saints can celebrate the heavenly wedding banquet.

In conclusion, this pastoral letter of the USCCB is a sign of the conference's commitment, formally initiated in November 2004 when it issued a National Pastoral Initiative for Marriage, to communicate the riches of the Catholic faith on the meaning and gift of marriage. The USCCB prays that the pastoral letter's vision of marriage will be the foundation for many works of evangelization, catechesis, pastoral care, education, and so on in dioceses, parishes, schools, and elsewhere. *Marriage: Love and Life in the Divine Plan* is both a call for and an ongoing commitment to a comprehensive and collaborative ministry to marriage and married people.—William E. May

See also *FAMILIARIS CONSORTIO*; FAMILY; MARRIAGE; THEOLOGY OF THE BODY

MARY   All Catholic doctrines about Mary flow from what the Second Vatican Council describes as the "intimate and indissoluble bond" (*arcto et indissolubili vinculo*) that unites Mary to her divine Son (*LG #* 53). According to St. Thomas Aquinas, God, in his almighty power, could have chosen many different ways to redeem the human race (cf. *STh* III, q. 30, art. 2). It was his choice, though, to restore human nature by being "born of a woman" in the fullness of time (Galations 4: 4). All this points to the central role played by Mary in the history of salvation. While there are many Catholic teachings about Mary, four are considered infallible: her perpetual virginity; her dignity as the Mother of God; her preservation from original sin in the Immaculate Conception, and her bodily Assumption into the glory of heaven.

Although the Gospels refer to the brothers and sisters of Jesus, none of them are ever identified as the sons or daughters of his mother. The Church has always understood these "brothers and sisters" as "close relations of Jesus, according to an Old Testament expression" (*CCC #* 500). Moreover, Church Fathers, such as St. Gregory of Nyssa and St. John Chrysostom found indirect witness to Mary's perpetual virginity in passages such as Luke 1: 34 ("How shall this happen, since I do not know man?") and John 19: 26–27 (the entrustment of Mary to the Beloved Disciple). All the great Fathers and Doctors of the Church uphold Mary's perpetual virginity, and Mary is spoken of as "ever-virgin"

in the liturgical prayers of both East and West and in important councils of the Church, such as the Second Council of Constantinople (553), the Lateran Council under Pope Martin I (649), the Profession of Faith of the Council of Trent (1564), and the Second Vatican Council's *Lumen Gentium* (# 69, 1964). Although never formally defined as a dogma, the perpetual virginity is considered infallible by reason of the ordinary universal magisterium of the Church, according to the criteria expressed by the Second Vatican Council (*LG #* 25).

Mary's perpetual virginity confirms the miraculous character of the conception and birth of Jesus. Mary as ever virgin also provides a model of consecrated virginity that has proven spiritually fruitful over the centuries. Some Church Fathers, applying the prophecy of the closed gate of Ezekiel 44: 2 to Mary, believed her virginal womb was so sanctified by the presence of the Lord that it was only fitting for her to remain ever virgin.

The dogma of Mary as the Mother of God follows from the divinity of her Son, Jesus. Mary, of course, is not the mother of the Trinity or the divine nature of Jesus, but, because the child she conceived and bore in her womb is divine, she must be honored as the Mother of the Word Incarnate. The Council of Ephesus in 431 solemnly affirmed Mary as the *Theotokos*, the birth-giver of God or "God-bearer." Mary's dignity as the Mother of God is, therefore, a solemn dogma proclaimed by an ecumenical council.

Mary's Immaculate Conception was not dogmatically defined until 1854, but it enjoyed widespread support for centuries before then. The angel's greeting of Mary as "full of grace" (*kekaritoméne*) in Luke 1: 28 was seen as testimony to her status as she who has been and continues to be "graced" by God. Moreover, early Church Fathers such as St. Justin Martyr (d. 165) and St. Irenaeus (c. 125–202) identified Mary as the "New Eve," the associate of her divine Son, the "New Adam," in the work of redemption, undoing the bondage brought about by the disobedience of the original Eve and Adam. This Eve/Mary parallelism led subsequent Church Fathers such as St. Ephraem of Syria (c. 306–373) to exalt Mary as free from any "flaw" or any "stain" (*Hymn* 27, v. 8). Later, St. Germanus of Constantinople (c. 635–733) would refer to Mary as "wholly without stain" and St. John of Damascus (c. 690–749) would speak of the "all pure seed" of St. Joachim, giving rise to the most holy child in St. Ann's womb.

Medieval theologians such as Aquinas and St. Bernard of Clairvaux (1090–1153), however, stopped short of affirming Mary's Immaculate Conception because they believed it would take away from the dignity of Christ as the Savior of all if he were not also his mother's Savior. Aquinas, therefore, believed that Mary did indeed contract original sin, but she was purified from it before she was born (*STh* III, q. 27, art. 2, ad 2). This prompted Franciscan theologians such as William of Ware (d. c. 1305) and Blessed John Duns Scotus to develop the concept of "anticipatory redemption" or "pre-redemption" (*praeredemptio*) as a solution. The merits of Christ could be applied to Mary in anticipation of her future role as the Mother of the Word Incarnate. In this way, Christ *would be* her Savior not by *cleansing* her from original sin but by *preserving* her from it.

In 1477, Pope Sixtus IV, a Franciscan, approved a feast day in honor of Mary's Immaculate Conception, and in 1483, he forbade anyone from criticizing this feast. The Council of Trent, in its 1546 decree on original sin, stopped short of endorsing Mary's Immaculate Conception, but stated that it had no intention of including under original sin "the blessed and immaculate Virgin Mary, the Mother of God" (Denz-Hün, 1516).

By 1708, the Immaculate Conception was granted papal support as a universal feast for the Catholic Church, and by the early 1800s, numerous petitions were being sent to the pope to define the Immaculate Conception as a dogma. After receiving near unanimous support from the bishops of the Catholic world, Pope Pius IX, in 1854, defined the Immaculate Conception as a solemn and infallible doctrine of the Catholic faith.

The fourth infallible Marian dogma is her Assumption, body and soul, into the glory of heaven. Since Patristic times, the "woman clothed with the sun" of Revelation 12: 1 was identified with Mary reigning with her Son in heaven. Mary was also identified with the Ark of the Covenant in the heavenly temple (cf. Revelation 11: 19). As early as the fifth century, there was a feast day in honor of Mary's "falling asleep" (*koimesis* in Greek, *dormitio* in Latin); by the seventh century, this feast was called the Assumption. Church Fathers, such as St. Gregory of Tours (d. 593), St. Germanus of Constantinople, and St. John of Damascus all explicitly affirmed Mary's Assumption into heaven after her earthly life had ended.

Even though the Feast of Mary's Assumption was celebrated liturgically in both the Christian East and West, it had never been solemnly defined. After receiving numerous petitions for such a solemn definition and near unanimous support from his brother bishops, Pope Pius XII defined Mary's Assumption into heaven as a dogma in 1950. He left open, however, the question whether she died before her Assumption, by using the phrase "when the course of her earthly life was finished" (Denz-Hün, 3903).

In addition to the four infallible Marian dogmas, there are numerous other Catholic doctrines and devotions to Mary. She is extolled as a heavenly intercessor, the model of virtues, and teacher. Moreover, she is honored as the Queen of Heaven, and special devotion is given to her "Immaculate Heart." Some Catholics have petitioned the pope to proclaim solemnly Mary as "Advocate, Coredemptrix and Mediatrix of all graces." The Second Vatican Council did speak of Mary as Advocate and Mediatrix (*LG* # 62), but it chose not to use the term *coredemptrix*. The *Acts* of the council explain that the term *Coredemptrix*, although most true in itself, would be difficult for the "separated brethren" (i.e., the Protestants) to understand (*Acta Synodalia Concilii Oecumenici Vaticani Secundi*, vol. 1, part 4, 99).

Marian devotions, such as the Rosary, have received enthusiastic and consistent endorsement from popes since the 16th century. Recent popes have also recognized Mary's importance for Catholic social doctrine. In his 1987 encyclical *Sollicitudo Rei Socialis* (issued during the Marian year of 1987–1988), John Paul II recognized Mary as the one who appeals to her Son when "they have no more wine" (*SRS* # 49; cf. John 2: 3). Moreover, "she is the one who praises God, the Father because 'he has put down the mighty from their thrones and exalted those of low degree; he has filled the hungry with good things, and the rich he has sent away empty' (Luke 1: 52–53). Her maternal concern extends to the *personal* and *social* aspects of people's life on earth" (*SRS* # 49). In a similar vein, Pope Benedict XVI, in his 2007 encyclical *Spe Salvi*, points to Mary as a "star of hope" for those traveling the often "dark and stormy" voyage of life (*SS* # 49). The numerous apparitions of Mary, especially to St. Juan Diego in 1531, testify to her ongoing solidarity with the poor and the humble of the earth.—Robert L. Fastiggi

BIBLIOGRAPHY AND FURTHER READING: Anderson, Carl, and Chavez, Eduardo. *Our Lady of Guadalupe: Mother of the Civilization of Love*. New York: Doubleday, 2009; Denzinger, Heinrich, and Peter Hünermann. *Enchiridion symbolorum definitionum et declarationum de rebus fidei et morum*, 40th ed. Freiburg: Herder, 2005; Gambero, Luigi. *Mary and the Fathers of the Church*. Translated by Thomas Buffer. San Francisco: Ignatius Press, 1999; Haffner, Paul. *The Mystery of Mary*. Herefordshire, England: Gracewing, 2004; Miravalle, Mark, ed. *Mariology: A Guide for Priests, Deacons, Seminarians, and Consecrated Persons*. Goleta, CA: Queenship, 2007; Nolan, Mary Catherine, OP. *Mary's Song: Living Her Timeless Prayer*. Notre Dame, IN: Ave Maria Press, 2001; Trouve, Marianne Lorraine, FSP, ed. *Mother of Christ, Mother of the Church: Documents on the Blessed Virgin Mary*. Boston: Pauline Books & Media, 2001. *See also COLLABORATION OF MEN AND WOMEN IN THE CHURCH AND IN THE WORLD, ON THE*; FEMINISM; MOTHERHOOD; *MULIERIS DIGNITATEM*

MASS MEDIA AND CATHOLIC SOCIAL THOUGHT

The mission of the Church is to "go into the whole world and proclaim the gospel to every creature" (Mark 16: 15). The Church recognizes not only the advantage but also the necessity of using media—also commonly referred to in Church documents more broadly as "social communications"—in this mission. It uses the Internet, TV, film, radio, and print media to reach and influence not just the individuals but also the masses and even the whole of human society. The Church teaches that the true purpose of social communications is to cause a reflection of and participation in the Trinity, which comes to humanity in and through the Son, who is the Word made flesh. Through God's communication of himself and his salvation through the Word, Jesus Christ, man is called to share in the communion of Father, Son, and Holy Spirit.

As the methods and uses of mass media have rapidly expanded, the Church has issued a number of documents addressing the issues surrounding mass media. Many of the recent popes have spoken on the topic. The Second Vatican Council also turned its attention to communications media. Moreover, although not strictly speaking "magisterial," various helpful documents have also been released by different curial offices and episcopal bodies. For example, the Pontifical Council for Social Communications (PSSC)—originally created in 1948 as the Pontifical Commission for the Study and Ecclesiastical Evaluation of Films on Religious or Moral Subjects and transformed into its current office in 1989—has been responsible for a number of documents on mass media.

These documents generally seek to guide the faithful through an understanding of the purpose of mass media, as well as the potential benefits and harms of media for both creators and consumers. Used in accord with their correct purpose and with proper concern for the dignity of the human person, media can produce extraordinary benefits. Used for base and evil purposes without regard to human dignity, however, media have the power to accomplish immense harm.

As social communications become ever more globalized, so do the potential harms and benefits of their use.

The Church offers insight into the potential positive and negative impacts of media, giving special attention to five key forces of modern society: economic, political, cultural, educational, and religious. Because media have a powerful and often global impact, the moral responsibility of choosing to use media for a good end falls not only to those who receive them but especially to those who produce and control them. Their responsibility lies not only in transmitting content that promotes the welfare of the soul but also in employing the appropriate medium to do so, "for [a given medium's] influence can be so great that men, especially if they are unprepared, can scarcely become aware of it, govern its impact, or, if necessary, reject it" (*IM* # 4).

Social communications have become indispensable to the functioning of economic structures around the world. In many ways, media can and do accomplish real good for humankind in this aspect. Among other things, media facilitate communication that cultivates market competition and product improvement and enables consumers to make informed choices. Media also equip businesses with tools to grow, thus helping to provide greater employment and economic prosperity.

On the other hand, media can also be abused to serve the economic interests of only a few. Nations and peoples who lack the communications technology to keep pace with an international economy increasingly dependent on information become further marginalized and struggle all the more to develop. Communications technology has become a basic condition of survival, and communicators have a responsibility both to inform more prosperous nations of these injustices and to provide marginalized nations with the information and technology necessary to participate in the global economy.

Media can also have a positive impact on politics. Social communications have created platforms for building and sustaining political communities. Within these political communities, particularly within democratic ones, media give citizens a means to inform and to remain informed about current issues, policies, campaigns, politicians and candidates, and events. Media also encourage accountability of those in office by providing a means to reveal corruption and abuse and at the same time to praise competence and true devotion to the masses.

Media can serve to facilitate abuse and injustice in politics, as well. Politicians can use media to spread falsehoods and propaganda. Rather than encouraging informed participation by citizens, politicians might use media to manipulate the people with an aim to accomplish certain agendas. The effect becomes particularly damaging when these agendas support unjust policies, the violation of fundamental human rights, the exploitation of certain groups, or oppressive regimes. Political advertising and public relations are not the only danger here; entertainment media can also promote unethical agendas that influence the political participation of the citizens.

The cultural impact of social communications can benefit the human person in many ways. Media open the door for many people to encounter beauty and truth in art, music, literature, and drama. The communication of wisdom and knowledge through cultural artifacts serves the development of humankind. Entertainment media, too, can bring communities together, uplift weary spirits, and even inspire people to heroism. Cultural heritage and traditions can be both celebrated and passed on to younger generations through media.

Like economics and politics, culture can also be negatively impacted through the abuse of media. Advertising, journalism, and entertainment media each present their own dangers. While it is often argued that media simply reflect the popular culture of the times, media's ability to sway culture must not be overlooked. Advertising too often promotes cultural attitudes of materialism and consumerism and can even be used to sell products and services that demean the human person. The temptation for journalists is to report half-truths and oversimplifications that can result in cultural discrimination or misunderstandings of complex issues. Entertainment media are especially prone to grave moral dilemma when they treat in bad taste subjects that ought to be revered. Gratuitous sexual and violent content degrades the humanity of both the creators and the viewers. The pornography industry, tragically so prevalent in many cultures around the world, is one such example of the extreme degradation of humanity for the sake of entertainment.

The opportunities for education have only increased with the availability of media. The Internet has been especially instrumental in supplying a means of learning to remote regions of the world, the homebound, prisoners, and many others. Media tools are being used in education and learning for all ages, from the very young to the elderly. Educational and training videos in the workplace can make important information available to all employees in an efficient manner. The spread of educational materials and learning tools through media helps to promote literacy and intellectual pursuit.

Media that are not produced for educational purposes, however, can serve to distract people from intellectual pursuit. By their very nature, entertainment media often encourage slothful behavior; they seek to draw an audience in and keep their attention indefinitely. In addition, if the content is simple and panders to base desires in man, media might even be said to dull the mind. Media that are created for educational purposes can be abused, too. If media aim to indoctrinate rather than educate or to control knowledge rather than increase it in the general population, they become a distortion of authentic education and an offense to human freedom.

Finally, the religious impact of social communications has been beneficial to many. Mass media provide an extraordinary opportunity for evangelization and catechesis, especially to those who would not otherwise have access to the Gospel message. News and information about religious events and people can be transmitted to countless faithful. In some cases, media have even offered the homebound opportunities to participate in worship. Through media, millions around the world are able to experience World Youth Day and other pastoral visits by the Holy Father, even if they cannot attend the events in person.

The abuse of social communications can come from both those who disdain religion and those who seek to promote it. Secular media risk marginalizing or trivializing religion. Even if they are not altogether hostile toward religion, they might promote false religions and religions that conform to secularism and relativism rather than the tradition of the Church. Dangers exist for those on the other side, as well. Religiously zealous individuals might be tempted to view all media with skepticism and negative judgment, thus condemning even those media that are good and fruitful. Furthermore, religious media can become propaganda if they lose their sense of objectivity and fair treatment of other faiths. Like politics, religion can be advertised as a marketplace option, playing on the emotions of consumers rather than proposing truth to men and women of goodwill. These and other harms can result from the abuse of media for the sake of religion.

The PSSC presents some basic ethical principles to help guide media creators and consumers in their use of mass media. It addresses three areas to which these principles apply: the message, the process, and structural and systemic issues.

The primary ethical principle states, "The human person and the human community are the end and measure of the use of the media of social communication; communication should be by persons to persons for the integral development of persons" (*Ethics in Communications* # 21). Media should never violate the human dignity of the individual person by their content, their process of communication, or their internal structures and policies.

The second ethical principle suggested by the PSSC draws a connection between the good of the individual and the common good. Media should be vigilant that their content and process do not cause divisions and conflict between groups, for such tension is contrary to the common good. This principle also applies to systemic and structural issues in media, where communicators in prosperous regions of the world should recognize a responsibility to assist and share media resources with less developed nations.

A third ethical principle relates to the freedom of expression. While public policy should always strive to protect the freedom of expression, there are certain forms of communication that, by their nature, forfeit any right to be expressed: libel and slander, obscenity and pornography, content that advances hatred and discrimination against particular groups, and gratuitous depictions of violence. The PSSC suggests that professional communicators develop ethical codes for their content and process, and the public, including religious bodies, should be invited to participate in defining and enforcing these norms.

Consumers, too, have an ethical responsibility: namely, to be discerning of the content they choose to consume. The consumer should make a conscientious effort to educate himself regarding the morality of the content as well as the internal structures and policies of media companies who produce it. The Church views responsible media consumption as an important aspect of the formation of the conscience. It is especially imperative for parents to teach their children to be able to approach and evaluate media with a critical and informed conscience.

The Church also has certain responsibilities and obligations with regard to mass media. The first of these is to be a model of excellence in its standards of communication—in message, process, and structure. The Church has a duty to encourage the faithful to use media to communicate the Gospel message. Representatives of the Church have a responsibility for honesty and openness with journalists; it is only with such honesty that the Church can maintain its credibility in the public square. Finally, the Church has an obligation to train its members, especially clergy, seminarians, and laypeople who work for it, to communicate ethically and well.—Tara Stone, Michael Barber, Dominic Iocco, and Derry Connolly

BIBLIOGRAPHY AND FURTHER READING: PSSC. *Ethics in Advertising.* Vatican City: Libreria Editrice Vaticana, 1997; PSSC. *Ethics in Communications.* Vatican City: Libreria Editrice Vaticana, 2000; PSSC. *Ethics in Internet.* Vatican City: Libreria Editrice Vaticana, 2002. *See also* FILM AND CATHOLIC SOCIAL THOUGHT

MAY, WILLIAM E. (1928–) William E. May is an American moral theologian known for his many writings and contributions in fundamental moral theology, Thomistic natural law theory, sexual ethics, and bioethics, as well as his defense of magisterial teaching. He was born in St. Louis, Missouri, on May 27, 1928, to Robert May (a Presbyterian, but later a convert to Catholicism) and Mary Armstrong (a Catholic). Although May's childhood coincided with the Great Depression, he had a happy upbringing. His family included a younger and older sister. The love, faith, and devotion of his parents and the example set by many dedicated and pious priests and religious eventually inspired May to enter the high school seminary in St. Louis.

May's hope to become a priest was cut short several years later, however, when, while studying for the priesthood in college, he began to suffer from what was diagnosed as petit mal epilepsy—at that time an "irregularity" to Holy Orders. After teaching in an Archdiocese of St. Louis high school for two years as a seminarian, hoping his medical condition would resolve on its own, May discerned, when it did not, that he was not called to a priestly vocation. He would eventually marry Patricia Keck in October 1958 and with her would have seven children. After his marriage, he never again experienced petit mal symptoms.

May earned bachelor's and master's degrees from the Catholic University of America in Washington, D.C., in the early 1950s and ended up working as an editor for Newman Press in 1954 before landing a job with Bruce Publishing in Milwaukee (1955–1968). He then worked for Corpus Instrumentorum in Washington, D.C. (1969–1970). During the period of the 1960s, May began his lifelong personal and professional association with philosopher Germain Grisez, whose innovative "new natural law theory" May would disseminate and continue to defend up to this day. May edited two of Grisez's books: *Contraception and the Natural Law* (1964) and *Abortion: The Myths, the Realities, and the Arguments* (1970).

In 1968, May received his PhD in philosophy from Marquette University, writing a dissertation on the metaphysics of French philosopher Henri Bergson, specifically his understanding of the reality of matter. That same year, he signed a letter circulated by Father Charles Curran in July protesting Pope Paul VI's encyclical *Humanae Vitae*, which upheld Church teaching on contraception. May almost immediately repented of this act; when his wife learned he had signed the dissenting document, she just gave him a look of utter contempt, he recalls. But it was not until several years later that he publicly retracted his signing of the document. During the last 40 years, he has come to be one of the foremost defenders of the encyclical and the Church's teaching on the existence of absolute moral norms.

From 1971 until 1991, May taught moral theology at Catholic University—first in the Department of Religion (1971–1975), where he replaced the ex-priest and moral theologian Daniel Maguire, and then in the School of Theology and Religious Studies (1975–1991). From 1991 until his retirement in 2008, he taught at the recently founded John Paul II Institute for the Study of Marriage and the Family in Washington, D.C. He has lectured all over the world and taught as a visiting professor at several academic institutions. Over the course of his long career, he has published—not counting popular pieces and dozens of book reviews—well over 250 scholarly articles and directed more than 20 doctoral dissertations. Since his retirement, May has been a senior fellow at the Culture of Life Foundation, also in Washington, continuing to write and to speak at conferences, as well as remaining active in various professional societies such as the Fellowship of Catholic Scholars, of which he was an early founding member and its president from 1985 to 1987.

During his years at Catholic University, May wrote many well-received and widely used texts, including *Human Existence, Medicine, and Ethics* (1977), *Catholic Sexual Ethics* (1985), and *An Introduction to Moral Theology* (1991). The years spent at the John Paul II Institute produced similarly well-reviewed and often-used texts, such as *Catholic Bioethics and the Gift of Human Life* (2000) and *Marriage: The Rock on Which the Family Is Built* (1995). Those years spent teaching also saw May translate a number of works by such renowned theologians as Livio Melina and the late Ramón García de Haro, as well as editing many collections—notable among these, *Principles of Catholic Moral Life* (1981) was based on a conference at Catholic University that May helped organize and whose purpose was to counter the rampant propor-

tionalism and dissent in moral theology at the time. In 2006, he published a brief memoir, *Standing with Peter*. The third editions of *Catholic Sexual Ethics* and *Catholic Bioethics* are forthcoming.

In 1986, May and John Finnis were the first laymen to be appointed (by Pope John Paul II) to the International Theological Commission, where May sat for two terms until 1997. He has also been a member of many other commissions and councils. May has additionally been the recipient of numerous awards and honors, among them the Cardinal Wright Award (1979), the Pro Ecclesia et Pontifice medal (1991), and the Paul Ramsey Award in Bioethics (2007).

Central to the moral thought of May is his conviction that the human person is a *bodily* being—a "body-person," as he likes to say. He often contrasts the "holistic" anthropology of the Catholic Church with the "dualistic" anthropology of the secular culture. Dualism involves an existential separation of the person from his or her body, seeing the latter as a subpersonal reality and merely an "instrument" that the person uses to realize more "personal values." He will apply these contrasting anthropologies to issues in sexual ethics and bioethics, speaking of the "integralist" versus the "separatist" understanding of the human person. The former anthropology respects the bond established by God between the unitive and procreative meanings of sexuality, but the latter separates them in such actions as contraception and artificial reproductive techniques.

May is fond of speaking of a "threefold dignity" of the human person, linking this to free choice, conscience, character, and virtue. The first kind of dignity, which is inalienable, is the one that human beings are gifted with in their creation by God, in his "image and likeness," as the book of Genesis records it. The second, like the first, is also intrinsic, but is a "work" of the person—an achievement brought about by free human choices to perform virtuous action, thus establishing for oneself a morally good character. (But the opposite is also the case: by performing morally evil actions, the person gives himself or herself a morally bad character, thus taking away from his or her dignity.) The third, again intrinsic, is a work of God's grace elevating the baptized to the status of children of God.

As noted, May is a prominent proponent of the "Grisez school" of moral theology, collaborating with its members and helping to develop, but especially to defend, its natural law theory and apply it to specific moral issues. The key to understanding this approach to natural law is the idea of inviolable and incommensurable "basic human goods," of which proponents list eight.

Not being moral in nature, these "principles of practical reasoning" are in need of *normative* principles—what they call "modes of responsibility"—to indicate which choices violate "integral human fulfillment," or what amounts to the ideal perfection of every human person in every human good. A third level of natural law precepts is what this school identifies as "specific moral norms," which function to direct the free choices of human persons to choose in morally good ways. Some of these norms are absolute—for example, the one against killing innocent human life—but most are not. Its overarching "first principle of morality" holds that we are always to choose in such a way that every basic good is respected as a good and none treated as an evil—that is, damaged, destroyed, impeded, and so on through human choice and action.

May is also known as an ardent defender of the Church's teaching (including the teaching of the ordinary magisterium) and a vigorous but fair opponent of revisionist moral thought, in particular the moral methodology of proportionalism. Proportionalism became the dominant ethical system after the Second Vatican Council, with such figures as Josef Fuchs, SJ, Louis Janssens, and Richard McCormick, SJ, among its most articulate and influential theorists. May has shown that proportionalist assertions that their thought is not accurately described in the encyclical *Veritatis Splendor* (1993) could not in any way be supported. He has also written widely against their efforts to reject intrinsically evil acts and these acts' corresponding exceptionless moral norms. Some give May credit for actually coining the term *proportionalism*.

May has sought to respond to the Second Vatican Council's call for renewal in moral theology by being sensitive to its desire that moral theology be both more fully nourished by the Sacred Scriptures and more firmly centered on the person of Jesus Christ. His *Introduction to Moral Theology* shows a remarkable effort to root theological ethics in the Bible and to focus it on faith in Christ and the mysteries of his life, demonstrating, against contrary opinions, the *specificity* of the Christian moral life. One way that we remain faithful to Christ and grow in holiness, May argues, is by discerning, adopting, and living out our personal vocations in charity by keeping the Ten Commandments and living the Beatitudes of the Sermon on the Mount.

On specific moral issues, May has argued forcefully against the "culture of death," and in support of the "culture of life," by showing how contraception, fornication and adultery, homosexual acts, masturbation, artificial reproductive technologies, abortion, embry-

onic stem cell research, and euthanasia/assisted suicide all transgress moral absolutes and thus harm human goods and violate the dignity of the human person. On some of these issues, at least where the Church has not taught in a definitive way or at all, May has changed his mind (e.g., he is now in favor of the use of methotrexate and salpingostomy to treat ectopic pregnancy). May was also one of the first moral theologians to seriously question the equation of "brain death" with human death. He has, moreover, been a prominent defender of the practice of adopting/rescuing frozen embryos but a consistent critic of both the gamete intra-fallopian transfer (GIFT) procedure to achieve pregnancy and the use of condoms by married couples to prevent the transmission of HIV/AIDS.

May has shown himself to be a thinker open to a wide range of philosophical and theological influences throughout his career, including the late Protestant ethicist Paul Ramsey. Although he is associated with the Grisez school of moral thought, May has written of the appeal more traditional neo-Thomists such as the Dominicans Benedict Ashley, Romanus Cessario, and the late Servais Pinckaers have for him. He has also done much to make better known and understood John Paul II's theology of the body.

May's approach to moral theology is, if anything, through and through practical—one might even say, "pastoral"—in its concerns. That is, May's way of doing moral theology shows itself to be an effort to assist people to come to make "true moral judgments" and "good moral choices," as he often phrases it. Since human persons are not yet fully the "beings that God wants them to be," May believes that the effort to become those beings in a world wounded by sin (original, personal, and social) requires divine grace and the determined effort of human freedom to cooperate with this grace. Although hobbled in recent years with some health issues, May has continued to be a productive and influential writer.—Mark S. Latkovic

BIBLIOGRAPHY AND FURTHER READING: May, William E. *Catholic Bioethics and the Gift of Human Life*, 3rd ed. Huntington, IN: Our Sunday Visitor, 2011; May, William E. *An Introduction to Moral Theology*, 2nd ed. Huntington, IN: Our Sunday Visitor, 2003; May, William E. *Marriage: The Rock on Which the Family Is Built*, rev. and expanded ed. San Francisco: Ignatius Press, 2009; May, William E. *Moral Absolutes: Catholic Tradition, Current Trends, and the Truth*. Milwaukee: Marquette University Press, 1989; May, William E. *Standing with Peter: Reflections of a Lay Moral Theologian on God's Loving Providence* Bethune, SC: Requiem Press, 2006; May, William

E. (with John Ford, SJ, Germain Grisez, Joseph Boyle, and John Finnis). *The Teaching of "Humanae Vitae": A Defense.* San Francisco: Ignatius Press, 1988; May, William E. *Theology of the Body in Context: Genesis and Growth.* Boston: Pauline Books & Media, 2010; May, William E., Ronald Lawler, OFM Cap., and Joseph Boyle Jr. *Catholic Sexual Ethics: A Summary, Explanation and Defense*, 3rd ed. Huntington, IN: Our Sunday Visitor, 2011. *See also* BIOETHICS; DISSENT; FAMILY; GRISEZ, GERMAIN; MAGISTERIUM; MARRIAGE; MORAL THEOLOGY: A SURVEY; NATURAL LAW; THEOLOGY OF THE BODY

McBRIEN, RICHARD P. (1936–) Father Richard P. McBrien, a priest of the Archdiocese of Hartford, Connecticut, ordained in 1962, in the years following the Second Vatican Council (1962–1965) came to be one of the best known Catholic theologians and commentators on Catholic Church affairs in the United States. This prominence primarily was due to his many books, the academic positions he held, and the long-running syndicated column he wrote for Catholic newspapers. He became especially popular with the secular media, where he was frequently invited to serve as a "Catholic spokesman" on a wide variety of subjects that arose in the news.

Holding a doctorate in theology (1967) from the Jesuit and papal Gregorian University in Rome, Father McBrien taught theology at the Pope John XIII National Seminary in Weston, Massachusetts (1965–1970), and at Boston College (1970–1980). He was long a luminary of the Catholic Theological Society of America and served as its president in 1973–1974. In 1980, McBrien became a professor of theology at the University of Notre Dame, serving until 1991 as chairman of the Theology Department.

Primarily an ecclesiologist, McBrien has nevertheless ventured into a wide range of Catholic subjects, historical, theological, and even political. Many of his books, some of them veritable tomes, have been bestsellers; some of them have been considered the kind of seemingly authoritative works on the subjects they cover, regularly placed on the shelves of public libraries. His books include *Who Is a Catholic?* (1971), *Catholicism* (1980, 1994), *Caesar's Coin: Religion and Politics in America* (1987), *101 Questions and Answers on the Church* (1996), *Lives of the Saints* (2001), *Lives of the Popes* (2006), and *The Church: The Evolution of Catholicism* (2008). McBrien also served as the general editor of the 1,341-page *HarperCollins Encyclopedia of Catholicism* (1995), described as "the most comprehensive, easy-to-use one-volume guide to the world's largest religious tradition."

Credentials, accomplishments, and published writings such as these not surprisingly established McBrien as a major post–Vatican II Catholic voice widely considered to be authoritative on the subjects he covers. Although this may be the case at least in some respects, serious reservations must nevertheless be noted concerning the extent to which McBrien can be considered to be an authentic, authoritative Catholic spokesman. In the post–Vatican II era notable for widespread theological dissent from the official teachings of the magisterium of the Church, McBrien has rather conspicuously *not* distinguished himself in upholding and defending authentic magisterial teaching. Rather, a salient aspect of his work has not infrequently been to call into question the truth and validity of some Catholic teachings—a type of approach in which he joins some of his theological contemporaries in implying or claiming this to have been sanctioned by the Second Vatican Council. He has sometimes also articulated theological positions that he suggests can represent valid alternatives to Church teachings considered by liberal opinion to be outmoded or superseded. In the same way, he treats favorably or at least neutrally theologians and thinkers whose work undermines and sometimes even contradicts established Catholic teaching.

Father McBrien himself is generally factually correct in what he writes about Catholic teaching in the sense that, for the most part, he correctly states what the Catholic teaching is. Moreover, on the evidence of his books, his knowledge of a very wide range of Catholic teaching proves to be both extensive and impressive. But then he often features side by side with the authentic Catholic teaching the opinions of those who call that teaching into question—as if theological opinion and magisterial teaching were all on the same level.

This tendency of his to equate magisterial teaching with sometimes dissenting theological opinion can be seen, for example, in his choice of collaborators for his *HarperCollins Encyclopedia of Catholicism*, in which open dissenters from Catholic teaching can be found listed as contributors alongside others apparently loyal to the magisterium of the Church. Similarly, in his 2008 volume entitled *The Church*, McBrien lists as his authorities on the subject of the Church's magisterium the most prominent post–Vatican II American dissenter from that same magisterium, Father Charles E. Curran, and another author whose book on the magisterium is ambivalent on the extent to which magisterial teaching is binding on the faithful, Father Francis Sullivan.

Another method of McBrien's is to imply that a teaching might be changeable or reformable even when he does not register outright dissent against it. Thus, in *101 Questions and Answers on the Church*, he states—although both the First and Second Vatican Councils taught that the authority of the Church was *not* dependent upon the consent of the faithful—that nonreception of a teaching by the faithful might eventually invalidate it. "A modern example of nonreception, or at least partial non-reception," he writes, "is the widely negative response to *Humanae Vitae* by Catholic married couples of child-bearing age."

One more favorite method of his is to include in his treatment of a given subject a wide variety of opinions on the teaching in question, some of them dissenting opinions, while not himself explaining or differentiating between those opinions that are within the boundaries of what Catholic teaching allows and those that are not compatible with authentic Catholic teaching and perhaps even contradict it.

A notable case illustrating these shortcomings in McBrien's work is afforded by the attempt by the Committee on Doctrine of the U.S. Conference of Catholic Bishops (USCCB) to clarify or correct some of the positions in his best-selling book *Catholicism*. The committee was particularly concerned because of this book's popularity and because it was being widely used as an introductory text on Catholicism, especially by young people. The committee therefore in 1981 began what was described as a "constructive and fruitful dialogue" with the author to bring the book more into line with what its title already said it was, namely, an authentic account of Catholicism.

Initially, the author agreed to cooperate. He even seems to have made a number of corrections in a study edition of the book, but then, in 1985, the bishops' committee issued a statement in which it spoke about the "confused and ambiguous" treatment of a number of topics in the second edition of the book, including its presentation of the virginal conception of Jesus, the perpetual virginity of Mary, and the binding force of Marian dogmas and its lack of support for the Church's teaching on contraception and the ordination of women. The committee requested that these points be corrected in future editions, but when the third edition of the book came out in 1994, these points had still not been corrected.

Hence, in a November 1995 letter to Father McBrien from the chairman of the USCCB Committee on Doctrine, it was clearly stated that the committee's "expectation ha[d] not been fulfilled." A meeting with McBrien was requested at which it was suggested that these matters might be cleared up. Instead, this priest-author rather rudely rejected the bishops' suggestion for a meeting, and in a series of exchanges, went on to reject the notion that his book was in any way an "introductory text" that might mislead inquirers. McBrien demanded to know who his "accusers" were (as if there needed to be any accusers to establish that some of his treatment was at variance with the Church's understanding). All in all, McBrien's response to the request of the USCCB committee to meet and clear matters up amounted to a practical denial on his part that the bishops of the Church possessed any authority over the writings of a modern Catholic theologian. McBrien never met with the committee, and the text of *Catholicism* that had been criticized stands as written.

The response of the Committee on Doctrine was neither to discipline the defiant theologian himself nor to ask that his book *Catholicism* be withdrawn or banned, in spite of its manifold deficiencies as identified by the committee. Rather, the response of the USCCB committee was simply to issue, on April 9, 1996, a lengthy "review" of *Catholicism* prepared by the staff of the committee, setting forth the major errors and ambiguities of the work. This review concluded that *Catholicism* contained statements that were "inaccurate or at least misleading," that there was in the work "an overemphasis on the plurality of opinion within the Catholic theological traditions," and that the book overstated "the significance of recent developments within the Catholic tradition."

While the publication of this unfavorable review of *Catholicism* by the Committee on Doctrine scarcely enhanced the reputation of the author, neither could it be said that it represented any effective disciplining of a theological author determined to propagate questionable positions purporting to be Catholic doctrine. Meanwhile, as can be verified by the (partial) listing of his works above, most of McBrien's major works were published *after* his *Catholicism* was found to be deficient by the USCCB Committee on Doctrine, yet it does not appear that these later books have ever been questioned in official quarters. The result is that Father McBrien continues to be widely accepted as an authority on Catholic teaching and practice.—Kenneth D. Whitehead

BIBLIOGRAPHY AND FURTHER READING: McBrien, Richard P. *Catholicism*, rev. ed. San Francisco: Harper-

SanFrancisco, 1994; "Review of the Third Edition of Father Richard P. McBrien's *Catholicism*." *Origins* 25, no. 43 (April 18, 1996). *See also* DISSENT; GREELEY, ANDREW M.; KÜNG, HANS

MEDIEVAL MONASTICISM AND WESTERN CULTURE

The ascetic life (from Greek *askesis*, "athletic discipline") arose within ancient Christian society and deeply affected that society precisely by being set apart from it. When persecution of Christians in the Roman Empire ceased in the early fourth century, the martyr as "witness" to the more perfect practice of the faith was replaced by the witness of voluntary heroic asceticism. The first *monachoi* ("solitary ones," from the Greek *monos*, "alone") lived in deserted regions of Egypt, Palestine, and Syria, first as hermits (from the Greek *eremos*, "deserted place"), but soon together as cenobites (from the Greek *koinos bios*, "common life"), that is, in communities, composed either of men or women leading a celibate life (from the Latin *caelebs*, "unmarried"). This meant a Christian life lived in voluntary denial of comfort and wealth and to a degree of spiritual and moral excellence not considered possible in the normal situation of an individual or family living "in the world." But this kind of life is meant to be well publicized in Christian society: their "anchoretic" life (from the Greek *anachoreo*, "to withdraw") is not absolute—one would, after all, still live with others, and the Christian ideal is not only to be pursued for its own sake (attainment of individual salvation) but must be shared and communicated to bring others along and to bring the world closer to God through prayer and example. Not all persons are "called" to this: hermits and monastic communities follow Christ radically, supporting themselves by manual labor, interceding for the Church and world, and exerting themselves in love of neighbor and help for the needy.

The historical development of monasticism in society from about 300 to 1300 shows an epic struggle to realize these principles through various movements of reform. This history can be divided into four stages.

In the first stage of late antiquity (300–600), the movement of monasticism in both hermit and cenobite varieties originated with SS. Anthony, Paul the Hermit, and Pachomius by the start of the fourth century. This was spread to the Latin-speaking world by the mid- to late fourth century through the efforts of highly literate travelers such as SS. Athanasius, Jerome, Cassian, and Sulpicius Severus. A synthesis of episcopal and monastic leadership (in men so different as SS. Martin of Tours and Augustine) popularized the ideal in the Western Church and brought Christianity to rustic areas of Gaul and even outside the empire to the Celtic islands. In Ireland, monasticism soon absorbed the fifth-century diocesan structures of St. Patrick and, blending with tribal power, overflowed the island: by the late sixth and early seventh centuries, SS. Columba and Aidan had established monasteries (Iona and Lindisfarne) in northern Britain, and St. Columbanus had planted a series of monasteries in Gaul (e.g., Luxeuil) and northern Italy (Bobbio).

Meanwhile, as the western parts of the empire underwent political subdivision by the Vandals, Goths, Franks, and Lombards, hermits and monastic communities multiplied, among whom St. Benedict of Nursia (480–547) deserves the greatest attention. Starting out as a hermit (in youthful flight from a morally debased student climate at Rome), he finished as an abbot at Monte Cassino, south of Rome, where he composed his Rule. The Rule of St. Benedict, with its concision and wise balance of spirituality and practicality, is now recognized (by comparison with its predecessors) to have been a classic summation and reform of existing practices. But the monastery where it was composed was destroyed by the Lombards soon after Benedict's lifetime; the surviving monks fled to Rome, where Pope Gregory the Great (R. 590–610) would become the Rule's promoter, praising its "discretion and clarity" (*Dialogues* II, 36).

The second stage of development was in the early Middle Ages (600–c. 1050). The Benedictine Rule was not an instant success: for centuries, it was still "mixed" in the monasteries of Frankish Gaul with other rules, such as that of the Irishman Columbanus. It was probably fully adopted first by Anglo-Saxons, and in the seventh and eighth centuries English monk-missionaries like St. Boniface (and SS. Leoba and Walburga) established the Rule of St. Benedict on the Continent, while helping build the future Carolingian Church and empire. New diocesan structures came into being along with new monasteries (masculine, such as Fulda, Lorsch, and Reichenau, or feminine, such as Heidenheim), and bishops, abbots, and abbesses worked in close cooperation with the political lords. Charlemagne's great cultural standardization of liturgy, laws, and texts was completed by his successor, Louis the Pious, who, at the Aachen Councils of 816 and 817, and with the counsel of Abbot Benedict of Aniane (the "Second Benedict"), decreed the Rule of St. Benedict to be the universal standard of Latin Christendom.

A new wave of invasions halted the progress of monasticism and the spread of Benedict's Rule: Western Christendom would soon suffer the breakup of the Carolingian empire and the Viking, Magyar, and Saracen attacks of the ninth and 10th centuries. Monasteries were among the first targets of plunder and devastation both in the British Isles and on the Continent, and those that survived were widely subject to secularism and decline through feudal patronage and military domination. But the work of Benedict of Aniane was not in vain, as new or newly reformed monasteries in Burgundy (Cluny, 909), Lorraine (Gorze, 913), and England (Glastonbury, 940; Bath 959) looked back to the Carolingian ideal.

Cluny, in particular, whose uniqueness consisted in its commendation to the papacy at its founding by William of Aquitaine, was free to elect its own abbots. Under a series of excellent, long-lived abbots, Cluny grew into a huge network of priories and affiliated abbeys. By 1095, it had over a thousand dependencies, and Pope Urban II, a former Cluny monk, stopped there to consecrate the largest church in Christendom ("Cluny III") on his way to preach the First Crusade.

During the 10th and 11th centuries, Benedictine monasteries multiplied and flourished throughout Europe, most of them in close cooperation with the German emperor, the kings of France and England, and other magnates. Monks were the professional intercessors, securing salvation for society. But great changes were ahead.

The third stage of monastic development took place in the 11th and 12th centuries (1050–1200). There were internal and external issues: the interpretation of the Rule had shifted to an emphasis on liturgy, increased public prayer, and pageantry, and the monks did much less manual work, less spiritual reading, and less individual prayer than was prescribed in the Rule. At the same time, the typical Benedictine monastery had become a part of the manorial economy and was generally supported by the labor of tenants; the wealth and power of the Cluniac empire was, however, becoming a subject of criticism. While the transnational spiritual leadership of Cluny, and its high standards, had at first encouraged emperors and popes to work to eliminate simony and a married clergy, the progress of reform finally led to conflict, as the pope was declared supreme over the emperor in the matter of investiture of bishops. The abbot of Cluny acted as a negotiator. And there was a reaction *against* Cluny in the direction of a richer spiritual life: new varieties of monasticism flowered, especially the Augustinian canons, who lived in cities near the cathedrals and performed the works of Martha rather than Mary, using the Rule of St. Augustine as a more archaic ideal.

Then there were the new hermit-cenobitical orders of Italy (Vallombrosa, Camalduli) and the Carthusians in France, and finally, the Cistercians. The latter two types were based on a fresh, stricter interpretation of the Rule of St. Benedict, bringing a more personal spirituality to the monk and more remote locations for new, self-sufficient monasteries. At the same time, both types also introduced a new institution: lay brothers—quasi second-class monks—who worked in support of the choir-monks while belonging to monastery with their own, simpler routine of prayer. The Cistercians were a huge success and grew to over three hundred houses all over Europe by the middle of the 12th century. Unlike Cluny, each Cistercian monastery, though uniform, was autonomous with its own abbot, and all the abbots met every three years in a general chapter.

The fourth stage occurred from 1200 to 1400. By the beginning of the 13th century, a further stage of social development called forth a new spiritual response. The growing cities and towns of Italy, France, the Rhineland, and England were creating a new, urban mentality, and the new orders of friars (from the Latin *fratres*, "brothers") created by SS. Francis and Dominic responded with a community that lived without landed property, as mendicants (from *mendicare*, "to beg"). Francis's idea was to follow the person of Christ, as such, without the baggage of tradition; Dominic's was to dedicate oneself to the study of Christian learning in order to preach the faith and fight heresy. Both orders profited from the advances in organization made by the Cistercians, and both were closely allied with the papacy from their beginnings. Finally, both movements were involved with the new institution of the university, which had developed from the cathedral schools in the major cities of Paris, Bologna, and Oxford.

The achievements of the monastic tradition are impressive. Medieval monastic culture was nurse, pedagogue, and influential companion to early Europe. Beginning as a spontaneous movement on the eastern fringe of the Roman Empire, it spread to the Atlantic Ocean and converted northern Europe in the sunset of ancient Rome. In the form of Benedictinism, it grew strong in alliance with new Christian kings, and after weathering the post-Carolingian destruction, gradually recovered itself, turning increasingly to the pope in Rome for approval. In a second phase, the monastic tradition provided new inspiration and guidance to the evolving Christian society in new forms, like Cistercianism and the mendicant orders.

By their disciplined life of prayer, the monks and nuns sought salvation, but they did a lot of other things, too: in particular, they preserved the learning and texts of the ancient classics and the Fathers. Monastic theological culture, wrote Jean Leclercq, "was the necessary precondition for the Scholastic Golden Age" and the Renaissance. In painting, sculpture, and architecture, monks produced the Romanesque and prepared the way for the Gothic. Modern Western music was given its basic structure by the tradition of chant. Medieval monks and nuns excelled in farming techniques, financial management of properties, reclamation of wasteland, the development of the water-driven mill, and the practice of metalworking and other arts.

The growth of modern science and society has overshadowed all these achievements, and it may be tempting to conclude that monasticism and other forms of the religious life are a thing of the past. But curiously, periods of destruction of monasticism have regularly been followed by movements of the resurgence of the religious life, as seen by the Jesuits after the Protestant Reformation, and the 19th- and 20th-century proliferation of new religious congregations in France after the French Revolution. The 20th century has been challenged as never before by attacks on human dignity, and the Second Vatican Council has pointed to the laity as the new prime mover in evangelization. Those who are not monks or nuns are still called to study their achievements and admire their example, while staying in the secular world and sanctifying society from within.

One especially important task today is the cultivation of a Catholic liberal arts education, which in its roots is the legacy of the medieval monks and nuns. The University of Dallas, for example, has had on its faculty many Cistercian monks who came after seeking refuge from Communist oppression in Hungary in 1956; there is still a flourishing Cistercian monastery nearby the campus. Belmont Abbey College, in Belmont, North Carolina, had its origin in 1876 through the efforts of the Benedictine monk-missionaries Boniface Wimmer and Leo Haid. At that time, North Carolina had the fewest Catholics of any state. The abbot of Belmont Abbey long functioned as the bishop of the entire state of North Carolina. In 1976, a century after the founding of the monastery, a diocesan structure was established, and the small liberal arts college, formerly staffed largely by monks but now almost entirely by laypersons, is playing its part in a new resurgence of Catholic higher education, as the young and old monks of Belmont Abbey continue their daily round of prayers.—Gerald Malsbary

BIBLIOGRAPHY AND FURTHER READING: Brooke, Christopher. *The Age of the Cloister: The Story of Monastic Life in the Middle Ages.* Mahwah, NJ: Hidden Spring, 2003; Lawrence, C. H. *Medieval Monasticism: Forms of Religious Life in Western Europe in the Middle Ages*, 2nd ed. London: Longman, 1989; Leclercq, Jean. *The Love of Learning and the Desire for God: A Study of Monastic Culture.* Translated by Catherine Misrahi. New York: Fordham University Press, 1982; Schmitt, Miriam, and Linda Kulzer, eds. *Medieval Women Monastics: Wisdom's Wellsprings.* Collegeville, MN: Liturgical Press, 1996; Southern, Richard W. *Western Society and the Church in the Middle Ages.* Harmondsworth, England: Penguin, 1970. *See also* BENEDICT OF NURSIA, ST.; DOMINIC, ST. AND THE DOMINICAN TRADITION; FRANCISCAN TRADITION, THE

MENTAL RESERVATION "The eighth commandment forbids misrepresenting the truth in our relations with others. This moral prescription flows from the vocation of the holy people to bear witness to the God who is the truth and wills the truth" (*CCC* # 2464). The virtue of truthfulness "consists in showing oneself true in deeds and truthful in words, and in guarding against duplicity, dissimulation, and hypocrisy" (*CCC* # 2468). Truthfulness is essential to social harmony. As St. Thomas Aquinas stated, "Men could not live with one another if there were not mutual confidence that they were being truthful to one another."

The Church has condemned offenses against the truth in the strongest terms. "Lying is the most direct offense against the truth. To lie is to speak or act against the truth in order to lead someone into error. By injuring one's relation to truth and to his neighbor, a lie offends against the fundamental relation of man and his word to the Lord" (*CCC* # 2483). Lying is a profanation of speech and violates man's obligation to justice and charity. It harms the liar. In a lie, the speaker states outwardly something at variance with the speaker's mind. This division between the speaker's inner and outer selves violates a proper sense of self-integration and authenticity. Lying is particularly harmful in the social order. "Lying is destructive of society; it undermines trust among men and tears apart the fabric of social relationships" (*CCC* # 2486).

This simple, straightforward condemnation of lying masks a number of complexities. There is no obligation to reveal all the truth that one knows. Some have argued that lies may be permissible in certain situations—for instance, to save the life of another. A common example is the situation of Nazis coming to a house in search of a Jewish family that the homeowner has been hiding. If the Nazis ask whether the Jewish family is inside the house, some have argued that the homeowner is entitled to lie.

The clear weight of the Church's teaching is that one must not lie, even to save a life. This follows from the idea that lying is always wrong and that one may not do evil to achieve a good or to avoid harm.

Some contend that a lie can be avoided by invoking the idea of "mental reservation." This technique, the theory contends, is a way to answer without lying. The idea of mental reservation has been invoked frequently (with great controversy) in recent years in connection with the issue of clergy sexual abuse. The idea is also frequently invoked in the context of medical ethics and counseling.

"Mental reservation" is used in two senses. According to the idea of *strict mental reservation*, the speaker adds—in his mind—a qualification to the clear meaning of the words spoken, and the words and the mental reservation *together* state a truth. So, for example, if a married woman is asked whether she has committed adultery and she answers, "I have not committed adultery," and adds—in her mind—the qualification "on Tuesday," her statement is true, according to the idea of strict mental reservation, if she has committed adultery only on Wednesdays. Another common example occurs when a feverish patient asks his doctor about his temperature and the doctor says, "Your temperature is normal," while adding—in his mind—the qualification "for someone in your condition." Under this approach, the entire idea of lying would virtually be eliminated. Someone would need never commit the sin of lying, because he could avoid the sin by stating a falsehood in order to deceive by simply including an appropriate mental qualification or reservation.

The idea of strict mental reservation has been condemned by the Church. An assertion that states a "truth" only with a mental reservation is a lie—a statement against the truth with the intent to deceive—and "by its very nature, lying is to be condemned" (*CCC* # 2485). Pope Innocent XI condemned the idea of strict mental reservation in 1679. So, one would not be permitted to lie even to the Nazis.

The idea that the obligation to avoid lying extends only to those who have the *right to know* the truth is not included in the Catholic view of lying. That idea—that one must not lie only to one "who has the right to know the truth"—was indeed included in the 1994 edition of the *Catechism of the Catholic Church*, but the phrase was eliminated in the 1997 edition.

In *Aquinas: Moral, Political and Legal Theory*, John Finnis explains the problem with so-called necessary lies: "Those who lie to the Gestapo enter . . . into the Nazis' politics of manipulation." It is necessary not to lie to the Nazis. Avoiding a lie "affirm[s] the human dignity of everyone concerned. . . . The good consequences of such an affirmation (and of refusing to join and promote the culture of liars) cannot be estimated, but should not be overlooked when considering the bad consequences—equally incalculable though more palpable and affecting—risked in rejecting the option of lying."

According to the idea of *broad* or *wide mental reservation*, either the circumstances (of time, place, or person) are such that the words spoken or the presence of an equivocal word or phrase might be thought to imply a falsehood that the speaker allegedly avoids by a mental reservation. In this context, the mental reservation when combined with the circumstances of the statement or the ambiguous nature of the words spoken is thought to avoid a lie.

Only the first situation—when the circumstances of the speech avoid the lie—is clearly accepted. For example, assume that someone has confessed a sin to a priest. If the priest is asked whether the person is guilty of the sin confessed, the priest is permitted to answer "I don't know." That statement is false, but—because of the circumstances—it will be understood that the priest is saying, "I don't know (apart from the confessional)." Another common example is when a criminal defendant pleads not guilty even though he is actually guilty of the crime charged. The plea is false, but in this context the statement is a formula that simply means that this is how the defendant wants his case to proceed. The use of the expressions in these two examples does not fall within the definition of lying set forth above. As Germain Grisez asserts in *The Way of the Lord Jesus*, these "expressions can obscure the truth, even if no one is deceived, and so can be effective without expressing an assertion believed to be false. The use of such expressions is not lying." This use of mental reservation is viewed as not troublesome at all, and so it is not limited by a "good cause" qualification.

The use of a mental reservation with equivocal or ambiguous speech is more controversial. Two famous examples illustrate this use of mental reservation. St. Raymond of Penafort posed the example of the murderous pursuer. When the pursuer asks about his intended victim's whereabouts, a person who is hiding the potential victim says, "*Non est hic.*" That phrase is apparently ambiguous in Latin and could mean either "He is not here" or "He does not eat here." Another example of the use of ambiguity (with a mental reservation) is the story of Abraham in chapter 20 of Genesis. Abraham tells Abimelech that Sarah is his sister. The statement is literally true, because Sarah was in fact Abraham's half-sister. Abraham did not disclose that Sarah was also his wife, however, because he feared that he would be killed if Abimelech thought that Sarah and Abraham were married.

Many commentators assert that the two communications noted above are not lies. According to this approach, the person hiding the intended victim stated a truth (the intended victim does not eat there) and mentally restricted his meaning to that sense of the Latin phrase, while permitting (and in fact intending) the pursuer to take the false sense of the phrase (he is not there). Similarly, Abraham stated a truth (Sarah was indeed his sister) and mentally restricted his words to that meaning.

Yet, as Abraham later admitted, the statement was intended to mislead Abimelech. Abraham, to save his life, intended that his hearers believe a falsehood (that Sarah was not his wife). As a result, some commentators regard these statements as lies. Under this view, the person hiding the intended victim lied because he communicated something (that the intended victim *was not* there) and that communication was other than what the person believed (in fact, knew) to be the case (that the person *was* there). Abraham lied because what he communicated (that Sarah *was not* his wife) was something that was at variance with what he believed (knew) to be the case (that Sarah *was* his wife). According to Grisez, "Such a mental reservation depends for its success entirely upon the false sense of the expression, whose true sense remains irrelevant to the communication. Thus, it both expresses something at odds with what has in mind and carries out the intent to deceive, and so is a lie."

One sees here the risk of the use of broad mental reservation when employed by the use of equivocal or ambiguous words. The technique is frequently used to deceive, and that is why some commentators regard such use of mental reservation as sinful. The strength of the view that such communications are lies is perhaps revealed by the fact that commentators who approve of broad mental reservation note that it must be restricted to situations involving good cause. This limitation is thought necessary because a generous use of broad mental reservation could lead to a habit of deception,

and perhaps to lying, with the attendant risk to the mutual trust necessary in society.—Richard S. Myers

BIBLIOGRAPHY AND FURTHER READING: Boyle, Joseph. "The Absolute Prohibition of Lying and the Origins of the Casuistry of Mental Reservation: Augustinian Arguments and Thomistic Developments." *American Journal of Jurisprudence* 44 (1999): 43–65; Finnis, John. *Aquinas: Moral, Political and Legal Theory.* New York: Oxford University Press, 1998; Griffiths, Paul J. "The Gift and the Lie: Augustine on Lying." *Communio* 26 (1999): 3–30; Griffiths, Paul J. *Lying: An Augustinian Theology of Duplicity.* Grand Rapids, MI: Brazos Press, 2004; Grisez, Germain. *The Way of the Lord Jesus*, vol. 2. Quincy, IL: Franciscan Press, 1993. *See also* LYING; MORAL THEOLOGY: A SURVEY

MERRY DEL VAL, CARDINAL RAPHAEL (1865–1930)

"I have chosen him because he is an expert linguist. He was born in England and educated in Belgium; he is Spanish by nationality but he has lived in Italy. He is the son of a diplomat and is a diplomat himself; he is acquainted with the problems of every country. He is very modest; he is a very holy man. He comes here every morning and informs me about all the problems of the world. I never have to make a single observation. Moreover, he does not know the meaning of the word compromise." This is how St. Pius X, shortly after his elevation to the papacy in 1903, explained why he had selected Cardinal Raphael Merry del Val as his secretary of state.

The son of a diplomat and of Spanish, Irish, English, Scottish and Dutch ancestry, Raphael Merry del Val was born in London in 1865 and educated in England, Belgium, and Italy. Before completing his studies in philosophy, theology, and canon law, he had already become a privy chamberlain supernumerary and a member of papal delegations to London, Berlin, and Vienna (earning him the title of monsignor when he was only a subdeacon). Ordained in Rome in 1888, Merry del Val became a member of the pontifical family and, in 1896, the secretary of the Pontifical Commission to study the validity of the Anglican orders. Entrusted with a delicate mission to Canada in 1897–1898 (opening the way to new relations between Canada and the Holy See), in 1899 he became the president of the Pontifical Ecclesiastical Academy, where the diplomats of the Holy See are taught and where he had been a student more than 10 years earlier on the express insistence of Pope Leo XIII. This pope had immediately realized, at their first encounter, that the many talents of the young Merry del Val should be placed at the service of the Holy See.

Consecrated to the episcopate in 1900 by Cardinal Rampolla, at the time secretary of state and his immediate predecessor in this office, Merry del Val became the secretary of the 1903 conclave that would elect Pope Pius X; it was the sudden death of the then secretary of the consistorial congregation, and therefore the conclave, that led the College of Cardinals to select Merry del Val for this task. His appointment in 1903 as secretary of state (an office he held until Pius X's death) was surprising, on account of both his youth (Merry del Val was only 38) and the fact that, for the first time, the post went to a non-Italian. Made a cardinal by Pius X in 1903 and the Archpriest of the Vatican Basilica the year of that saintly pope's death, Merry del Val remained a distinguished member of the Roman Curia under both Popes Benedict XV and Pius XI.

Cardinal Merry del Val participated (and obtained a number of votes) in the conclaves of 1914 and 1922, was until his death the secretary of the Holy Office (at a time when the prefect of that supreme dicastery was still the pope), and was twice a papal legate to Assisi on the occasion of the centennial celebrations of the finding of the body and the death of St. Francis. While still active in the Roman Curia and in the many works of charity and spiritual direction that had marked all his life, Merry del Val died of an appendicitis on February 26, 1930. He was buried next to Pope Pius X in the grotto of the Vatican basilica. The process for his beatification was opened in 1953, in between Pius X's beatification (1951) and canonization (1954).

Under Pope Leo XIII, Merry del Val had played a key role in drafting *Apostolicae Curae* (1896), in which the pope declared, in conformity with earlier papal pronouncements, that all Anglican ordinations were "absolutely null and utterly void." As he was a faithful interpreter of the will of Leo XIII's successor, it is difficult to detect Merry del Val's personal contribution to the monumental reform and forceful defense of the Church under the intense papacy of Pius X. In the turbulent relations with France (which unilaterally denounced the concordat with the Holy See and adopted in 1905 a law of rigid separation between church and state that led to persecution against the Church), the secretary of state was as firm as the pope he served. The relations with Italy, on the other hand, improved while the Roman question was still open and benefited from the informal contacts between Merry del Val and the Italian minister of education at the centennial celebration in Assisi in 1926. In 1910, Cardinal Merry del Val refused (as a matter of diplomatic propriety) a request for an audience with the pope presented by Theodore Roosevelt (the former president of the United States) because, on his visit, the former president had meetings with the Methodists and Freemasons of Rome, both known for their harsh hostility to the pope. In 1914, it was Merry del Val who signed the concordat with Serbia.

The perfect harmony between the pope and his secretary of state emerged also in their fight against modernism, the synthesis of all heresies. The root of heresy is pride, and it is no wonder that the name of Merry del Val should remain linked to the litany of humility, which he composed in 1895 and recited after every Mass. Both Pius X and Cardinal Merry del Val, despite their different personality and upbringing, were first and foremost men of faith, convinced that, amidst the politics and compromise of diplomatic life, Church policy must be guided by adherence to the truth (hence Pius X's appeal of "always going by the right path") and the salvation of souls (hence St. John Bosco's motto on Merry del Val's sepulcher: "Give Me Souls and Take Away the Rest"). For this reason, the forceful action by the pope and his secretary of state, and their mutual relations, remain exemplary beyond their time and circumstances.—Maurizio Ragazzi

BIBLIOGRAPHY AND FURTHER READING: Buehrle, Marie Cecilia. *Rafael, Cardinal Merry del Val*. London: Sands & Co., 1957; Cenci, Pio. *Il Cardinale Raffaele Merry del Val* [in Italian]. Rome: LICE and Roberto Berruti & C., 1933; Dal-Gal, Jerome. *The Spiritual Life of Cardinal Merry del Val*. New York: Benzinger Brothers, 1959; Javierre, José Maria. *Merry del Val* [in Spanish], 2nd ed. Barcelona: J. Flors, 1965; Merry del Val, Raphael. *Memories of Pope Pius X*. Westminster, MD: Newman Press, 1951; Merry del Val, Raphael. *Spiritual Diary*. New York: Exposition Press, 1964; Merry del Val, Raphael. *Spiritual Directions*. London: Burns, Oates & Washbourne, 1937; Murphy, Harriet, ed. *The Spiritual Writings of Raphael Cardinal Merry del Val (1865–1930)*. Leominster, Herefordshire, England: Gracewing, 2009. *See also* EUROPE; MODERNISM AND NEO-MODERNISM; POPE BENEDICT XV; POPE LEO XIII; POPE PIUS X, ST.; POPE PIUS XI

MILL, JOHN STUART (1806–1873) John Stuart Mill was born in London on May 20, 1806, the eldest of nine children. He was the son of James Mill, a political thinker and activist who was for a time the assistant and collaborator of Jeremy Bentham, the originator of utilitarianism. The young Mill's education was conducted entirely under the tutelage of his strict and demanding father, and it was quite an extraordinary education. John began the study of Greek at age three, Latin at seven, logic at 12, and political philosophy at 13. When he was 14, he spent a year studying in France. By the time he had reached the age where he would have been going off to college, he had already acquired a remarkably thorough education. It was not without its disadvantages, however, and in 1826, when Mill was 20 years old, he underwent an emotional crisis that was in great part attributable to what he saw as an education that had been too one-sided—a heavy emphasis on intellectual analysis, while paying insufficient attention to the feelings. To extricate himself from the pit of dejection into which he had fallen, he cultivated a liking for music and poetry, developing a special fondness for the poetry of William Wordsworth.

In 1823, when Mill was 17, he was given a position in the British East India Company, where he worked for 35 years, until the company was dissolved in 1858. This proved to be a perfect employment, in that it provided him with ample free time to devote to his various intellectual pursuits and to the writing in which he soon became deeply engaged. Besides the several books he published over the course of his life, he was a regular contributor to a number of important literary periodicals of the day, most notably the *Westminster Review*, a journal for which he served as editor for a time. Over the course of his life, he corresponded with many of the major figures of the Victorian Era. In 1830, Mill traveled to France while the revolution was taking place there, during which time he met the Marquis de Lafayette. He had an abiding interest in French affairs and French thought and was considerably influenced in his own thought by the likes of Saint-Simon, Auguste Comte, and Alexis de Tocqueville. In 1849, Mill married Harriet Taylor, a woman to whom he was extravagantly devoted and whom he regarded as the guiding light of his life. Mill served as a member of Parliament, representing Westminster, from 1865 to 1868. He died in Avignon, France, on May 8, 1873.

Mill's first major book, *A System of Logic*, a distinguished work particularly noteworthy for its impressive comprehensiveness, was published in 1843. His other major works are *Principles of Political Economy* (1848), *On Liberty* (1859), *Considerations on Representative Government* (1861), *Utilitarianism* (1863), *The Subjection of Women* (1869), and *Autobiography* (1873). Over the years, Mill published four collections of his periodical pieces, which went under the title of *Dissertations and Discussions.*

Mill has been described by one historian as the greatest British philosopher of the 19th century. However that point might be argued, there is no denying the influence he has had, especially in moral philosophy, in the years since his death. Mill was totally committed to the utilitarianism that had been developed by Jeremy Bentham. He tells us in his *Autobiography* (which is principally an account of his intellectual development) that he was fairly swept off his feet when he first read Bentham. "The feeling rushed upon me that all previous moralists were superseded," he writes, "and that here indeed was the commencement of a new era in thought." The principles of utilitarianism were subsequently to guide every aspect of his thought, especially that having to do with political philosophy. Mill did not regard himself as a mere theoretician but as a social reformer, and he intended that his writings should have a practical impact upon the public to whom they were addressed. "I had what might be called an object in life," he explains in his *Autobiography*, "to be a reformer of the world."

The pivotal concept in Mill's political philosophy was the notion of individual liberty, to which he gave great emphasis and which was consonant with the antipathy he harbored toward a large and intrusive government with its meddling bureaucracies. He maintained that government should never play a dominant role in education. Mill shows a commendable sensitivity toward the importance of subsidiarity as applied to public affairs. Though he enthusiastically supported social equality—he was no fan of the British aristocracy—Mill confessed that he was worried that increased equality could result in a society where a bland uniformity of opinion and practice would eventually prevail. Toward the end of his life, doubtless because of the influence of the thought of Saint-Simon, he tended to show himself increasingly favorable toward socialism, but it had to be a socialism that was without intrusive government and that allowed for the maximum in individual liberty.

Mill thought that *On Liberty* was likely to survive longer than anything else that he had written, with the possible exception of *A System of Logic*. He was surely right about *On Liberty*. As for his logic book, that has not managed to elicit a continuing readership, which says nothing against the inherent merits of the book. To the sustained popularity of *On Liberty* must be added that of *Utilitarianism*. What has become today the governing maxim of morality in the minds of many people—that one may do whatever one pleases so long as it brings no harm to others—can be traced to the influence of John Stuart Mill. That principle, as just stated, may be a simplistic expression of the central thesis of *On Liberty*, but it is not a gross distortion of it.

Because the central purpose of *On Liberty* is to champion "individuality," it is seriously hampered by the fact that this term is never given precise definition. We are told that it is the same thing as "development," but that is not much help. Individuality is expressed by nonconformity, even eccentricity, for the "individual" is one who stands stalwartly opposed to the prevalent opinions of his day. An individual's "own mode of laying out his existence is the best," simply because "it is his own mode." Mill, who was genuinely altruistic in his thinking and who termed egotism a moral vice, tried valiantly to reconcile his commitment to what is in fact a radical individualism with his sensitivity to larger social goods—he tells us that social virtues come before self-regarding virtues—but in the end he is not successful in doing this, with the result that we are left with a moral point of view that is seriously lopsided.

The basic idea that Mill explicates in *Utilitarianism*, which can be read as a modified version of the system propounded by Bentham, is the principle of utility, or the Greatest Happiness Principle, which holds that any action is right to the extent that it promotes happiness (i.e., pleasure), and wrong to the extent that it promotes unhappiness (i.e., pain). In this pronouncedly defensive and sometimes testy work, Mill takes up arms to combat what he regards as a raft of misunderstandings regarding the principle of utility. Though his version of utilitarianism has not a few things to recommend it, in comparison to that offered by Bentham, it nonetheless falls considerably short of serving as a reliable moral philosophy. The principal reason for this is to be found in the fact that it represents a entirely naturalistic way of looking at man and his place in the great scheme of things. Mill had no practical understanding of the reality of the supernatural order, and without that, paradoxically, one's understanding of the natural order is then inevitably distorted. Another major problem with Mill's utilitarian morality is that it is essentially a form of consequentialism, which systematically either ignores or denies outright the fact that human acts can be intrinsically good or intrinsically evil, a position that Mill's system made it unavoidable that he should adopt, albeit implicitly. Whatever positive elements might be found in his moral philosophy, it is, taken as whole, irremediably flawed.

Though Mill's education was in many respects very impressive, he himself was aware of its deficiencies, but that awareness did not extend as far as it should have. Besides ignoring the arts and humanities, his education offered him nothing by way of a healthy knowledge of religion, which was not the result of careless oversight on the part of Mill's father. The younger Mill's ignorance of religion was to become a permanent, and debilitating, feature of his life and thought. By his own admission, he grew up with a negative attitude toward religion, and he informs us that he came to look upon modern religion "exactly as I did upon the ancient religion, as something which in no other way concerned me." His negative attitude toward religion seems to have intensified over the years, as is evident in his writings, especially in books like *On Liberty* and *Utilitarianism*, where we find a lively prejudice against Christianity, especially Catholicism. In the end, religion, like so much else in his thought, was viewed from a narrow utilitarian perspective.—D. Q. McInerny

BIBLIOGRAPHY AND FURTHER READING: Anschutz, R. P. *The Philosophy of J. S. Mill*. New York: Oxford University Press, 1953; Borchard, R. *John Stuart Mill: The Man*. London: C. A. Watts, 1957; Britton, Karl. *John Stuart Mill*. London: Penguin Books, 1953; Donner, Wendy. *The Liberal Self: John Stuart Mill's Moral and Political Philosophy*. Ithaca, NY: Cornell University Press, 1991; Ten, C. L. *Mill on Liberty*. Oxford: Oxford University Press, 1980. *See also* CONSEQUENTIALISM; LIBERALISM; POLITICAL PHILOSOPHY; SOCIALISM; UTILITARIANISM

MILLENNIUM DEVELOPMENT GOALS Extreme poverty afflicts more than one billion people who survive on less than one U.S. dollar a day. The Millennium Development Goals (MDG) promise to eradicate extreme poverty and hunger, cutting them in half by 2015. Christ said, however, that the poor will be with us always (Matthew 26: 11; cf. Mark 14: 7; John 12: 8). The *Compendium of the Social Doctrine of the Church* explains that Christ's admonishment is meant to warn us against a false messianism and those who promise utopia—a new heaven on earth—before his final return (*CSDC* # 183). On the other hand, the MDG may be a sign of God's kingdom "actively seeking a new social order in which adequate solutions to material poverty are offered" (*CSDC* # 325). The reality may lie somewhere in between.

The MDG aspire to address some of the most pressing problems facing developing countries and are laid out in eight goals, 20 targets, and 56 indicators. The eight goals are to eradicate extreme poverty and hunger; achieve universal primary education; promote gender equality and empower women; reduce child mortality; improve maternal health; combat HIV/AIDS, malaria, and other diseases; ensure environmental sustainability; and develop a global partnership for development.

Released in August 2001, the MDG were supposed to encapsulate the principles found in the Millennium Declaration signed previously by 147 heads of state at the Millennium Summit during the United Nations (UN) General Assembly on September 8, 2000. The working committee that drafted the MDG also drew upon a 1996 report by the Organization for Economic Cooperation and Development (OECD) entitled *Shaping the 21st Century: The Contribution of Development Cooperation* and a multiagency group report (by the UN, OECD, World Bank, and International Monetary Fund) released in 2000 called *A Better World for All*, commonly referred to as the "International Goals." Both of these sources included the target of "sexual and reproductive health." This target, understood by many to include a right to legal abortion, was too controversial to be included in the Millennium Declaration. Attempts to include it into the MDG stalled negotiations and threatened final consensus until it was dropped.

The first goal, eradicating extreme human poverty, has three targets: halving the proportion of people whose income is less than a dollar a day from 1990 levels by 2015; achieving full and productive employment and decent work for all; and halving from 1990 to 2015 the proportion of people who suffer from hunger. There are nine indicators that measure whether these targets have been met. The indicators to determine whether poverty has been cut in half consider the proportion of the population living on less than $1 a day, the poverty gap ratio (i.e., the incidence multiplied by the depth of poverty), and the share of the poorest quintile in national consumption. The second target, achieving full and productive employment and decent work, is measured by the following four indicators: the growth rate of the gross domestic product per person employed, the employment-to-population ratio, the proportion of employed people living below $1 per day, and the proportion of own-account and contributing family workers in total employment. To assess whether hunger has been halved, one must measure the prevalence of underweight children under five years of age and the proportion of the population below a minimum level of dietary energy consumption.

The Holy See has supported the MDG to the extent that they express a "preferential option for the poor." It has warned, however, that the MDG can be reached only if poor persons are placed at the center of development. The integral development of persons who are poor is the key to authentic development, not improvements in markets and infrastructure per se. That is why Pope Benedict XVI writes in *Caritas in Veritate* that the social virtue of solidarity is the ladder that lifts up the poor, and why he warned that we must find ways to "feed the world's population" because "on this earth there is room for everyone" (*CV* # 50) without resort to "practices of demographic control" (*CV* # 28).

The second goal is to achieve universal primary education. There is one target for this goal, namely, to ensure that by 2015 children everywhere, both boys and girls, will be able to complete a full course of primary schooling. There are three indicators to assess this outcome: the net enrollment ratio in primary education, the proportion of pupils starting grade 1 who reach grade 5, and the literacy rate of 15- to 24-year-olds.

Education is essential to integral social development. The UN Convention on the Rights of the Child (CRC) guarantees primary education as a basic human right and stipulates that signatories to the treaty shall "make primary education compulsory and available free to all." Unfortunately, as of 2007, more than 115 million children worldwide are denied the most basic education.

MDG promoter Jeffrey Sachs, in his best-selling book *The End of Poverty*, singled out religion and culture passed on by way of the family as an obstacle to development because he believes they tend to deny women a right to education, which delays or blocks altogether "demographic transition" (a process whereby increases in basic health and public welfare remove the physical and psychological need for large families in order to stave off abject poverty). Bringing children to school without affirmation of the rights of parents as the primary educators of their children (*Charter of the Rights of the Family, art. 5*) is suspect. As Marguerite Peeters warns in *Globalization of the Western Cultural Revolution*, UN agencies are using girls' education to radically transform culture. Girls' education is not just about bringing girls to school, she says, but about inculcating in them an awareness of their rights, their autonomy and control over their life, and other values of the "new postmodern ethic."

The third goal is to promote gender equality and empower women. The elimination of gender disparity in primary and secondary education in all levels of education by 2015 is the target of this goal. There are three indicators to assess this target: the ratio of girls to boys in primary, secondary, and tertiary education; the share of women in wage employment in the nonagricultural sector; and the proportion of seats held by women in national parliaments. In the developing world, about

94 girls per 100 boys went to primary school in 2006. Women's participation in the political process has increased since 1990.

One suspicious feature in this goal is that *gender* is not defined, although *MDG Report 2008* claimed gender is "a human right at the heart of achieving the Millennium Development Goals." Various UN agencies "in the spirit" of the Beijing Platform for Action, however, have interpreted *gender* to mean a changeable social construct.

The Church condemns "theories that consider gender identity as merely the cultural and social product of the interaction between the community and the individual, independent of personal sexual identity without any reference to the true meaning of sexuality" (*CSDC* # 224). The Holy See in its reservation on the 1995 Beijing Platform for Action said that gender must be read in context and noted that the document referred to "both genders," "male and female." Goal 3 seems innocuous; this is no guarantee, however, that gender, left undefined, will not be used by overreaching UN agencies as a catalyst for social change, including a push for broad homosexual rights.

The fourth goal, reducing child mortality, targets reducing by two-thirds from 1990 levels the under-five mortality rate by 2015. The three indicators by which this will be measured are the under-five mortality rate, the infant mortality rate, and the proportion of one-year-old children immunized against measles. The child mortality rate for children under five years of age had improved from one in five in 1960 to one in 10 in 1990. The *MDG Report 2008* states that rates of child mortality have continued to improve, but a child born in a developing country is still 13 times more likely to die before age five than one in a developed nation.

While international agencies recognize a link between maternal education and child mortality, they fail to note the link between strong families and child mortality. The Holy See reminded UN delegates that "to protect the family means to protect the children." Therefore, "efforts should be intensified to recognize the social role of the family which is irreplaceable for the common good."

Another concern is that goal 4 is ideologically underinclusive in its definition of *children*. The preamble of the CRC assures each child's integrity "before as well as after birth," which demonstrates that children in utero have the same right to freedom from violence as any other member of the human family. The Holy See encouraged UN delegates to "see to it that the welfare of children is always given priority during all the stages of their development, right

from the moment of conception when they become individual human beings. The international community should assure the well-being of children through political action at the highest level."

The fifth goal, improving maternal health in the developing world, will be reached if the maternal mortality ratio is reduced by three-fourths from 1990 to 2015. To determine if this target has been reached, two factors are to be considered: the maternal mortality ratio and the proportion of births attended by skilled health personnel. There are, the UN admits, methodological problems that make it difficult to accurately assess progress in this area. The *MDG Report 2006* acknowledges that the data for maternal deaths in the developing world are "unreliable" with "wide margins of uncertainty."

Besides the methodological problems associated with this goal, UN bureaucrats promote sexual and reproductive health, including "safe" abortion, as the primary way of improving maternal health. They rely on the misinterpretation of UN human rights treaties by treaty-monitoring bodies and UN agencies to force abortion into goal 5. On the other hand, the Holy See and the pro-life and family nongovernmental organization coalition promotes skilled care at delivery and access to emergency obstetric care as the keys to reducing maternal mortality, which follows more closely the admonition of the 1994 Cairo Program of Action: "Governments should take appropriate steps to help women avoid abortion, which in no case should be promoted as a method of family planning."

Another problematic feature with goal 5 is its silence on the dignity and worth of motherhood. Mary Ann Glendon, former U.S. ambassador to the Holy See, twice urged UN delegates at the "Beijing + 10" conference in 2005 to consider motherhood in a favorable light, as did the founders of the United Nations, who insisted with equal vigor on "women's equality" and "protection for the family, motherhood and childhood." The Holy See views women's health holistically, considering their overall and comprehensive health care needs so as to secure for women the right to the highest standard of health care during pregnancy and the right to deliver children in a clean, safe environment, with adequate professional help.

The sixth goal is to combat HIV/AIDS, malaria, and other diseases. There are three targets: first, halting and beginning to reverse the spread of HIV/AIDS; second, providing by 2010 universal access to treatment for HIV/AIDS for those in need; and third, halting and beginning to reverse the spread of malaria and other major diseases by 2015. There are 10 indicators that mark progress toward these targets.

According to the *MDG Report 2005*, more than 20 million people have died of AIDS since it first appeared, more than 15 million children have lost one parent to this disease, and in sub-Saharan Africa, malaria afflicts an estimated 350 million to 500 million people a year, killing 1 million annually. Tuberculosis kills 1.7 million people each year. In 2004, there were nearly 9 million new cases of tuberculosis, 741,000 of them among people living with HIV.

Behavior change is important in combating the spread of HIV/AIDS, as Ugandan president Yoweri Museveni's successful abstinence campaign proved—HIV incidence rate in Uganda has been declining since 1989. The *MDG Report 2006* confirmed that several countries report success in reducing HIV infection rates through interventions that promote behavior change. UN agencies, however, send a mixed message by recommending both behavior change (abstinence before and fidelity within marriage) and condom usage. The Catholic Church, the single largest contributor to the fight against HIV/AIDS (more than one-fourth of HIV and AIDS treatment centers worldwide are Catholic based), is critical of linking behavioral change with condom usage to achieve HIV/AIDS prevention.

Pope Benedict XVI, during his 2009 trip to Africa, said that continent's HIV/AIDS epidemic "can't be resolved with the distribution of condoms: on the contrary, there is a risk of increasing the problem. The solution can only be found in a double commitment: first, a humanization of sexuality, that is, a spiritual and human renewal that brings with it a new way of behaving with one another; and second, a true friendship, also and above all for those who suffer, the willingness—even with sacrifice and self-denial—to be with the suffering."

The seventh goal is to ensure environmental sustainability. This goal has four targets: integrate the principles of sustainable development into country policies and programs and reverse the loss of environmental resources; achieve a significant reduction in the rate of biodiversity loss by 2010; halve by 2015 the proportion of people without sustainable access to safe drinking water and sanitation; and achieve by 2020 a significant improvement in the lives of at least 100 million slum dwellers.

MDG Report 2005 states that almost one billion people live in slums "characterized by overcrowding, little employment or security of tenure, poor water, sanitation and health services, and widespread insecurity." Improvements in slum dwellers' lives occur when laws protect them from forced and unlawful eviction and when policy provides for their access to credit to invest in their home.

Unfortunately, the MDG reports tend to view the fertility of the poor as part of the problem of underdevelopment. The Holy See counters that "demographic growth is fully compatible with an integral and shared development" (*CSDC* # 483). Respect for nature reveals that nature has own innate "grammar" that sets limits on its wise use with respect to the poor, future generations, and humanity as a whole (*CV* # 51). The innate grammar of nature is also seen in human nature. Pope Benedict challenged us to respect "human ecology" so that each person's right to life and to a natural death are honored and the unnatural and inhumane practices of contraception, in vitro fertilization, and embryo-destructive research are shunned (*CV* # 51).

The eighth goal is to develop a global partnership for development. This goal has six targets: provide for rule-based trading and financial systems, including good governance, tariff and debt relief, the special needs of landlocked and small islands, long-term debt and credit reform, essential drugs, and new technologies. These six targets are assessed by 16 specific indicators and several unspecified ones. Selected indicators not related to specific goals include population, total fertility rate, life expectancy at birth, adult literacy rate, and gross national income per capita.

As of 2008, only five countries have met the MDG targets. For the poorest countries, official aid and charitable donations are the main source of foreign financing, whereas trade ranks first for the middle-income countries. Money sent home by migrants working in foreign countries accounted for $34 billion, which directly benefits recipient families.

Pope Benedict XVI has said that aid to poor countries must respect both subsidiarity and solidarity so as not to create dependency and should be distributed with the involvement of local churches. The principal form of assistance needed in developing countries is the gradual penetration of the products of poor countries into the international markets. Too often in the past, aid has served to create only fringe markets for the products of the rich donor countries (*CV* # 58).

Pope John Paul II taught that development must be marked by a "spirit of friendship" (*SRS* # 39) and recognition of the fact that the human race is a single family. The Holy See calls for a reform of the United Nations, economic institutions, and international finance "so that the concept of the family of nations can acquire real teeth" (*CV* # 67). To give voice to poorer nations, foster international cooperation, and manage the global economy, integral disarmament, food security, the environment, and migration, "there is urgent need of a true world political authority." This was envisaged by the Charter of the United Nations so as to secure "authentic integral human development inspired by the values of charity in truth" (*CV* # 67).

If the United Nations fails to promote a relational anthropology, it could menace the world with a new collectivism. Some social scientists fear this is happening today given the United Nations' ideological commitment to sexual and reproductive rights and gender mainstreaming, combined with its move to link up with Big Business and Big Government in global human rights and development projects.

In conclusion, the MDG promoters are convinced that the only way out for those living in extreme poverty is a "big push" of development aid from rich countries, administered through UN agencies. Although the Church imposes no single economic answer to the challenges posed by poverty and no single economic model contains a totally adequate response, Pope Benedict recommends an incremental approach to development as being more respectful of our relational human nature (see *CV* # 47). He cautioned against overreliance on technological solutions to development often predicated upon a fatalistic vision of the world governed by "impersonal forces or structures independent of the human will" (*CV* # 42). There is a "danger constituted by utopian and ideological visions," he warned, furthered by "technocratic ideology," that place the ethical and human dimensions of development in jeopardy (*CV* # 14). To undermine human ecology and respect for its natural law (*CV* # 59) of relationality is to reduce the human person to "a mere means for development," which is typical of "types of messianism which give promises but create illusions" (*CV* # 14).

Ultimately, for the MDG to succeed, they need not so much a messianistic "big push" from the United Nations, Big Business, and Big Government as a little help from God: "Without him, development is either denied, or entrusted exclusively to man, who falls into the trap of thinking he can bring about his own salvation, and ends up promoting a dehumanized form of development" (*CV* # 11).—D. Brian Scarnecchia

BIBLIOGRAPHY AND FURTHER READING: Peeters, Marguerite. *The Globalization of the Western Cultural Revolution*. Brussels, Belgium: Institute for Intercultural Dynamics, 2007; Scarnecchia, D. Brian, and Terrence McKeegan. *The Millennium Development Goals in the Light of Catholic Social Teaching*. New York: International Organizations Research Group, 2009. *See also* AIDS; *CARITAS IN VERITATE*; DEVELOPING WORLD AND FOREIGN AID; ECONOMIC DEVELOPMENT, CHURCH TEACHING ON; INTERNATIONAL LAW AND THE RIGHT TO LIFE; PREFERENTIAL OPTION FOR THE POOR; UNESCO; UNFPA; UNITED NATIONS

MINDSZENTY, JÓZSEF CARDINAL (1892–1975)

The Venerable József Cardinal Mindszenty was born József Pehm on March 29, 1892, in the village of Mindszent in western Hungary. His parents owned a farm, and his father had been village magistrate. During his school years, Mindszenty was active in the Catholic Youth Movement.

After graduation, Mindszenty entered the seminary. He was ordained a priest on June 12, 1915, and appointed as an assistant pastor. He taught Latin and religion in the state high school in Zalaegerszeg, a major city in western Hungary. In 1917, his book on spiritual problems, *The Mother*, was published.

In late 1918, as World War I came to an end and the Austro-Hungarian Empire collapsed, King Charles IV withdrew and Count Kàrolyi took command of the revolutionary government in Budapest. In 1919, as Kàrolyi's socialist government prepared for elections, Mindszenty assumed a leadership role in the newly founded Christian Party. He launched a campaign against the Socialists, and in response, on February 9, Kàrolyi had him arrested and interned in the episcopal palace.

On March 21, 1919, the Communists took over and proclaimed the dictatorship of the proletariat. Mindszenty was transferred to a real jail and was held there until late July, when the Communist regime fell. On October 1, he was assigned to the parish of Zalaegerszeg where he would remain for many years. In 1927, he was appointed administrator of the Zala region. Mindszenty was responsible for founding new places for priests, establishing schools, and furthering pastoral activity throughout the diocese.

In 1941, with his homeland threatened by Hitler's aggression, Mindszenty dropped his birth name and adopted the name by which he would become known, defiantly incorporating part of his home village's name. Pope Pius XII appointed him diocesan bishop of Veszpré. On March 19, 1944, the German military launched Operation Panzerfaust, invading Hungary on the pretext of safeguarding communications. Six days later,

Mindszenty was named the bishop of Esztergom, the seat of the Catholic Church in Hungary.

The Nazis installed a puppet government in Budapest and issued anti-Jewish decrees as soon as they took over. From almost the first day of German occupation, Nuncio Angelo Rotta and the Hungarian bishops, including Mindszenty, worked to help improve the treatment of the Jews. By midsummer, however, despite the Church's efforts, 437,000 Jews had been deported from Hungary. Pope Pius XII requested that Hungarian bishops "intercede publicly on behalf of Christian principles and to protect their fellow citizens, especially Christians, unjustly affected by racial regulations." Mindszenty was one of the first to do so.

Admiral Miklós Horthy, the regent of the Kingdom of Hungary, agreed to work against the deportations and even signed a peace agreement with the Soviet Union. German authorities, however, removed Horthy from power and put Hungary under the control of a group of Hungarian Nazis known as the Arrow Cross, and the deportations resumed. The pope and his representatives, including Mindszenty, made many more protests, issued a report documenting the Vatican's work with the Jews of Hungary, and encouraged Catholics to help the victims. Almost every Catholic Church in Hungary provided refuge to persecuted Jews during the autumn and winter of 1944.

Mindszenty joined the Independent Smallholders' Party, which stood in opposition to the Arrow Cross Party. On October 31, 1944, the Catholic bishops of western Hungary addressed a memorandum to Premier Ferenc Szálasi, pointing out the perils to Hungary's cultural sites and population if western Hungary were made a battleground where Hungarians would fight the Russians (as Hitler and the Arrow Cross were demanding). Mindszenty personally took the memorandum to Budapest. On November 27, he was arrested and later transferred to the Köhida jail. Due to his outspoken opposition to government policies, he was charged with treason and put in prison. He was not released until after the Soviets "liberated" Hungary the following year.

On September 15, 1945, Mindszenty was appointed primate of Hungary and archbishop of Esztergom. On February 18, 1946, he was elevated to cardinal by Pope Pius XII. His titular church in Rome was Santo Stefano Rotondo.

Unfortunately, the departure of the Nazis led to only a brief respite for the people of Hungary. Mindszenty was soon in conflict with the new Communist regime. He did not believe in a separation of church and state and fought fiercely against secularization of church-run primary and secondary schools. He also continued to use the feudal title of prince-primate (*hercegprímás*) even after the use of nobility, peerage, and royal titulature were outlawed by the 1946 parliament (under Soviet influence).

Matters came to a head in 1948 when the cardinal refused to let the government secularize the Catholic schools. The government had Mindszenty arrested during the 1948 Christmas season. Before being taken away, Mindszenty left a note explaining that he had not been part of any conspiracy against the government and if a "confession" were ever produced by the government, it would be the product of coercion. While incarcerated, the cardinal was relentlessly tortured in order to coerce a confession for "crimes against the state."

While he was imprisoned by the Communist government, he allegedly confessed to working with Americans against the state of Hungary. The government released a book called *Documents on the Mindszenty Case* containing evidence against Mindszenty, including his confession. Among other forced confessions, Mindszenty supposedly admitted that he had orchestrated the theft of Hungary's crown jewels (including the Crown of St. Stephen) with the explicit purpose of crowning Otto von Habsburg emperor of Eastern Europe. He also allegedly admitted that he had schemed to remove the Communist government; that he had planned a Third World War; and that, once this war was won by the Americans, he himself would assume political power in Hungary. Mindszenty later said he had been beaten with rubber truncheons until he agreed to these fabrications.

In January 1949, Mindszenty was put on trial as a Nazi war criminal. He was charged with treason, conspiracy, and offenses against the Communist government's laws. He was also labeled a spy and a terrorist. His trial began on February 3, but the result was never in question; Mindszenty would be convicted and imprisoned. The sham trial generated worldwide condemnation, including a UN resolution. Three days after it started, the handwriting experts who had fabricated the "evidence" used to frame Mindszenty—Hanna Sulner and her husband—escaped to Vienna, where they denounced the trial as a farce and displayed microfilms of the phony documents on which the trial had been based. In July 1950, Sulner again described the details of Mindszenty's framing in a series of articles published in the *New York Herald Tribune*.

During the Hungarian uprising of 1956, Mindszenty was released from prison and returned to Budapest. On November 2, he praised the insurgents. The following day, he made a radio broadcast in favor of the recent anti-Communist developments. Unfortunately, his freedom lasted only a short while. Soon the Communists regained control, and Mindszenty sought asylum in the U.S. Embassy in Budapest. He lived there for the next 15 years.

In the embassy, Mindszenty wrote his memoirs, in which he explained how he had been framed: "It seemed to me that anyone should at once have recognized this document [the 'final confession'] as a crude forgery, since it is the product of a bungling, uncultivated mind." He continued: "But when I subsequently went through foreign books, newspapers, and magazines that dealt with my case and commented on my 'confession,' I realized that the public must have concluded that the 'confession' had actually been composed by me, although in a semiconscious state and under the influence of brainwashing. This was the explanation offered for the many spelling errors and the confused language of the document. It was also assumed that the police had had handwriting experts retouch parts of the test; but that the police would have published a document they had themselves manufactured seemed altogether too brazen to be believed."

On September 23, 1971, under the Vatican's pressure, the Communist government of Hungary allowed Mindszenty to leave the country. In exchange, Pope Paul VI declared Mindszenty a victim of "history" (instead of Communism) and annulled the excommunication imposed on his political opponents.

Mindszenty moved to Vienna, but despite being out of the nation, he continued his primacy of the Hungarian Catholic Church. Finally, in December 1973, the Holy See allowed the 82-year-old primate to step down, but it did not put anyone else in his place until after Mindszenty died.

The cardinal died in Vienna in 1975. In 1991, as soon as Hungarian Communism collapsed, the democratically elected government in Budapest had his remains sent to Esztergom, where he had served as bishop. He was interred in the basilica, the tallest building in Hungary and one of the biggest churches in the world.

Mindszenty is remembered in many ways. His life and his battle against the Soviet secret police was the subject of the 1950 film *Guilty of Treason*. In 1955, Mindszenty's trial was the subject of another fact-based movie, *The Prisoner*, starring Alec Guinness. The Mindszenty Museum in Esztergom, which opened after Communism collapsed, is a monument to his life and to the Soviet framing of him. A commemorative statue of Mindszenty stands at St. Ladislaus Church in

New Brunswick, New Jersey. He is also remembered in Chile, with a memorial in the same park (Parque Bustamante) in which a monument to the martyrs of the 1956 Hungarian Revolution stands. The Cardinal Mindszenty Foundation is an international educational organization based in St. Louis, Missouri.—Ronald J. Rychlak

BIBLIOGRAPHY AND FURTHER READING: Mindszenty, József. *Memoirs.* New York: Macmillan, 1974; Shuster, George Nauman. *In Silence I Speak: The Story of Cardinal Mindszenty Today and of Hungary's "New Order."* London: Gollancz, 1956; Swift, Stephen K. *The Cardinal's Story: The Life and Work of Jozsef, Cardinal Mindszenty.* New York: Macmillan, 1950. *See also* COMMUNISM; POPE PIUS XII; POPE PIUS XII AND THE JEWS

MIRARI VOS Although Pope Leo XIII's *Rerum Novarum* of 1891 is considered the flagship encyclical of modern social teaching due to its width of scope and depth of analysis, the social encyclical tradition had its official inception before the French Revolution, in 1740 with Benedict XIV's *Ubi Primum*. Nevertheless, the publication of *Rerum Novarum* is the primary landmark, along with the French Revolution, by which any particular encyclical can be not only quantitatively located but also qualitatively categorized. The encyclical *Mirari Vos* was written by Pope Gregory XVI in 1832, two years after the republican revolutions in France, Belgium, Ireland, and the Papal States; 17 years after the Restoration period inaugurated by the Congress of Vienna; and more than three decades after the French Revolution. *Mirari Vos*, then, is postrevolutionary with regard to chronological location and pre-Leonine when it comes to strategic categorization.

While all the encyclicals of the Church authoritatively declare foundational principles of and errors against Catholic social teaching, due to differing social and historical contexts and exigencies, as well as the personalities of papal authors, encyclicals differ, sometimes dramatically, in the particular principles they declare, their method and scope, and the kind and level of practical direction offered. Sometimes these contexts and authors differ to such an extent that one finds it difficult to recognize sufficient continuity and harmony between certain encyclicals. Such is the case when comparing encyclicals written during the historical context of post–French Revolution Europe with those written with an eye to post-Communist Europe and North America; and when comparing the very different ecclesial personalities of Gregory XVI and Blessed John Paul II. Understanding this context is especially important for a fruitful contemporary engagement with both Leonine (1878–1958) and, *a fortiori*, pre-Leonine (1740–1878) social encyclicals, for there is considerable difference in both substantive content and rhetorical tone between these and the more recent encyclicals. Thus, before undertaking a section-by-section analysis of the contents of *Mirari Vos*, it is necessary to discuss its historical and strategic context.

The most relevant impetus for the writing of the encyclical was not an abstract idea but a concrete person: Abbé Hugues-Félicité Robert de Lamennais, a French priest of a bourgeois Breton family. His early writings were severely ultramontane and traditionalist, much akin to Gregory's position; however, upon seeing the effects of Gallicanism upon French Catholicism, with the "state" suffocating and neutering the French clergy and laity alike, and being positively influenced by the American experiment in religion-friendly separation of church and state and government neutrality, Lamennais began to advocate an entirely new form of ultramontanism: an alliance of the pope and the *people*, as opposed to the liberal, bourgeois, aristocratic elite. Church and democracy were now to be married; and throne and altar, now showing signs of a dysfunctional and abusive relationship, needed to be divorced. Lamennais, together with the Dominican priest Henri Lacordaire and layman Comte Charles de Montalembert, began the journal *L'Avenir* to promote the movement, which at the time was considered radical, liberal, and progressivist—that is, anti-Catholic—to traditionalist ultramontanes like Gregory XVI.

Lamennais was so sure of the goodness of the new democratic movement that he sought a personal audience with the pope to get his official approval. But the pope was of a firmly aristocratic and monarchical temper and had just put down serious civil rebellions in the Papal States; instead of granting Lamennais a private audience, he wrote *Mirari Vos*, which repudiated the movement in no uncertain terms. Gregory's next encyclical, *Singulari Nos*, written two years later, would condemn Lamennais by name and his booklet, *Parole d'un croyant*. The pope also wrote to Lamennais personally, demanding he reject the new democratic movement and accept legitimist absolutist monarchy and its traditional relations with the Church. Lamennais's reaction to Gregory's rejection of his views was a tragic one, as he eventually lost his faith in Rome and even in Christian revelation itself.

For Pope Gregory, Lamennais's teaching was revolutionary, pernicious, and ultimately anti-Catholic, though perhaps noble and Christian in intention. Its effect would be to pull the Church into an alliance with the anti-Catholic spirit of the Reformation, Enlightenment, and French Revolution, and the best practical strategy for the Church at the time was to uphold the alliance of throne and altar as a vital institutional and cultural bulwark against this diabolical spirit. One could say this in defense of Lamennais: If the main evil against which he fought was state encroachment upon the rights and freedoms of the Church in France, he had great intellectual and moral support in the writings and actions of the prerevolutionary popes and Gregory XVI himself, and as later history has shown, this encroachment was only to get worse under the so-called democratic republics of the late 19th and early 20th centuries. He was not wrong to criticize the legitimist states of his time, to advocate democratic forms of government as an alternative to the often ecclesially hostile Restoration monarchies, or to recognize the apparently good social and political fruits of self-professed heretical liberals. What the pope condemned, however, was the erroneous suggestion, more explicitly expressed in Lamennais's later writings, that the democratic revolution, as long as the Church supported it (and perhaps even if it did not), would be a sort of panacea, an infallible means by which Church and people could produce a utopian paradise where the Holy Spirit would reign uncluttered by outdated and suffocating worldly politics.

Pope Pius IX would affirm Gregory's condemnation of liberalism, separation of church and state, and the democratic ethos in toto in *Quanta Cura* and its attached *Syllabus of Errors* (1864). And in *Vehementor Nos* (1905), Pope St. Pius X would condemn the 1905 legal edict of separation of church and state in France, though he did accept it practically as a fait accompli. The Church would, however, eventually accept the practical irreversibility of the bourgeois, republican political and economic revolution, even to the point of defending freedoms and rights once condemned as liberal and revolutionary: freedom of religion, freedom of association, and freedom of education. This seeming reversal of the traditional stance toward "modern civilization," while more tentative and oblique in the writings of Pope Leo XIII, appears quite straightforward and comprehensive in *Gaudium et Spes* and *Dignitatis Humanae*. The question of precisely how to interpret this apparent discontinuity is still open, though recently Pope Benedict XVI has insisted on a "hermeneutic of continuity."

Having considered the historical and strategic context within which the encyclical was written, we can now examine its contents. Introducing the encyclical, Pope Gregory uses strong language to depict the Church as having recently been besieged by great evils on the part of "insolent and factious men": "You know what storms of evil and toil, at the beginning of Our pontificate, drove Us suddenly into the depths of the sea. If the right hand of God had not given Us strength, We would have drowned as the result of the terrible conspiracy of impious men" (*MV* # 1). This is in reference to the 1831 civil rebellion led by Giuseppe Mazzini's Giovine Italia in the Papal States.

A paragraph from the beginning of the encyclical captures the gravity and profundity of the pope's assessment of the Church's situation: "We speak of the things which you see with your own eyes, which We both bemoan. Depravity exults; science is impudent; liberty, dissolute. The holiness of the sacred is despised; the majesty of divine worship is not only disapproved by evil men, but defiled and held up to ridicule. Hence sound doctrine is perverted and errors of all kinds spread boldly. The laws of the sacred, the rights, institutions, and discipline—none are safe from the audacity of those speaking evil. Our Roman See is harassed violently and the bonds of unity are daily loosened and severed. The divine authority of the Church is opposed and her rights shorn off. She is subjected to human reason and with the greatest injustice exposed to the hatred of the people and reduced to vile servitude. The obedience due bishops is denied and their rights are trampled underfoot. Furthermore, academies and schools resound with new, monstrous opinions, which openly attack the Catholic faith; this horrible and nefarious war is openly and even publicly waged. Thus, by institutions and by the example of teachers, the minds of the youth are corrupted and a tremendous blow is dealt to religion and the perversion of morals is spread. So the restraints of religion are thrown off, by which alone kingdoms stand. We see the destruction of public order, the fall of principalities, and the overturning of all legitimate power approaching. Indeed this great mass of calamities had its inception in the heretical societies and sects in which all that is sacrilegious, infamous, and blasphemous has gathered as bilge water in a ship's hold, a congealed mass of all filth" (*MV* # 5).

Here, the pope issues a clarion call to the bishops as good shepherds to "never abandon the sheep" in the midst of "so-many ravenous wolves" and to "labor and diligently take care that the faith may be preserved amidst this great conspiracy of impious men who attempt to tear it down and destroy it" (*MV* # 6, # 8). The Church must remain unified in and under the authority of the Roman pontiff, who holds "the full

power of nourishing, ruling, and governing the universal Church" (*MV* # 8), to protect it from the secular powers that would dethrone and make it conform to their image by promoting the spurious need in the Church for "restoration and regeneration" (*MV* # 9).

The initial "conspiracy" examined in the encyclical is the liberal attack on clerical celibacy and the sacrament of marriage; the pope reminds the bishops that the Church has every right and duty to preserve these sacred practices and institutions intact, as they are under its full jurisdiction and no one else's. Next, the pope tackles "indifferentism," the opinion "spread on all sides by the fraud of the wicked who claim that it is possible to obtain the eternal salvation of the soul by the profession of any kind of religion, as long as morality is maintained" (*MV* # 13). The perennial Church teaching on salvation outside the Church is that it is possible, though only through the extrasacramental graces that God can bestow upon souls rightly disposed to them, especially those souls in invincible ignorance about the necessity of entering the Catholic Church for salvation. This may seem in tension with the statement in the Athanasian Creed cited by the pope: "Without a doubt, they will perish forever, unless they hold the Catholic faith whole and inviolate" (*MV* # 13). But the pope is directing his admonition to believing Catholics in danger of being seduced to leave the Church in the futile hope of finding salvation elsewhere—that is, those in danger of the sin of apostasy and heresy. For *them*, there *is* no salvation outside the Catholic Church.

For the pope, the political analogue of religious indifferentism is the legal protections for liberty of conscience and freedom of the press and the civil movement against censoring "bad books" (*MV* # 14–16). It is the pope's direct and explicit attack on liberty of conscience that appears to be in direct tension with, if not contradiction to, the teaching on religious liberty of the Second Vatican Council. Here the pope condemns "that absurd and erroneous proposition which claims the liberty of conscience must be maintained for everyone" (*MV* # 14). But what the pope is condemning, as is clear from the social and historical context and his descriptions that follow, is an *unrestrained license* of belief, as if one were not duty bound to search for the Truth, hold on to it when found, and obey it in one's conscience. It is analogous to Leo XIII's judgment that "the liberty of thinking and publishing whatsoever each one likes, without any hindrances, is not in itself an advantage over which society can wisely rejoice. On the contrary, it is the fountainhead and origin of many evils" (*ID* # 32).

Now, what *Dignitatis Humanae* upholds is the *civil* right not to be coerced into a certain belief, not the *moral* right of holding whatever belief one desires to hold simply because one desires it; it explicitly insists on every person's moral duty to the Truth. The distinction between civil and moral rights was not yet explicitly made by the popes, at least in the area of freedom of conscience, and here Gregory collapses moral error and sin with its legal and political embodiment and application in 1830s Italy and France. This was a reasonable strategic and rhetorical move on the part of the pope in light of the religiously indifferent and even anti-Catholic rhetoric with which the legal and political agenda of freedom of conscience was promoted.

The remainder of the encyclical examines the general attack on "the trust and submission due to princes" (*MV* # 17), which the pope equates with an attack on the authority of God himself. The pope also cites the separation of church and state as a great threat to the authority of the state, but a boon for the "shameless lovers of liberty." Since the state derives all of its authority from God, to remove the Church's official, formal sanction of and union with the state is to court political rebellion and revolution (*MV* # 20).

There is probably no single document of the Church, excepting Pius IX's *Syllabus of Errors*, that is more vehement and explicit in its condemnation of "modernity" than *Mirari Vos* of Pope Gregory XVI. When comparing it to the modernity-affirming *Gaudium et Spes* of the Second Vatican Council, which Cardinal Joseph Ratzinger called a "counter-syllabus," it is, it must be admitted, difficult to recognize the continuity. Yet, the Church, while adopting a more nuanced stance toward secular culture at the Second Vatican Council and even before, has never essentially rescinded this condemnation. When understood as a constellation of ideas and set of practices that have at their heart the rejection of the divine identity and authority of the Catholic Church, combined with the attempt to "free" man from the only institution that can truly liberate him, the Catholic Church is as antimodern as it ever was.—Thaddeus J. Kozinski

Bibliography and Further Reading: Holland, Joe. *Modern Catholic Social Teaching.* Mahwah, NJ: Paulist Press, 2003; Kozinski, Thaddeus J. *The Political Problem of Religious Pluralism: And Why Philosophers Can't Solve It.* Lanham, MD: Lexington Books, 2010; Rao, John. "Lamennais and the Abyss." *Letter from the Romans* no. 5 (September 2000): 1, 21–27; Schuck, Michael J. *That They Be One: The Social Teaching of the Papal Encyclicals, 1740–1989.* Washington, DC: Georgetown University Press, 1991; Storck, Thomas. "Liberalism's Three Assaults." *Homiletic & Pastoral Review* 100, no. 4 (2000): 8–16. *See also* CIVIL LIBERTIES; COMMON GOOD; *DIGNITATIS HUMANAE*; FREEDOM OF SPEECH; HUMAN RIGHTS; LAMENNAIS, HUGUES-FÉLICITÉ ROBERT DE; NATURAL LAW; RELIGIOUS LIBERTY; RELIGIOUS RELATIVISM/INDIFFERENTISM

MOLLA, ST. GIANNA BERETTA (1922–1962)

Gianna Beretta Molla was a 20th-century woman—a doctor, wife, and mother—whose loving act of martyrdom exemplifies unwavering trust in God and is a powerful inspiration to modern-day Catholics. She was born in Magenta, Italy, on October 4, 1922, to Alberto and Marie and was baptized seven days later in the Basilica of San Martino. The family relocated to Bergamo when she was three years old, and she spent a large part of her childhood there. The 10th of 13 children, Gianna grew up in a household dedicated to serving the Lord; the family attended daily Mass and frequently prayed together. Alberto and Marie, both Third Order Franciscans, were devoted to teaching their children, a duty they viewed as part of God's mission for them. As a result of this tutelage, Gianna was able to receive her First Communion on April 4, 1928, at the age of five, at the parish of Santa Grata in Bergamo.

Intelligent, though not exceptionally gifted in her schoolwork, Gianna earned a reputation as an extremely hard worker, and her diligence came to fruition in her teenage years as she began to receive grades that were much improved. Perhaps even more successful than her studies was her involvement in Azione Cattolica (Catholic Action), an apostolic group Gianna joined at the age of 12, along with others in her family. She contributed a great deal to the organization and acted as a leader both during her time studying medicine and after she graduated and began working as a doctor. She loved to work with and mentor the youngest members of the group and persisted with her responsibilities despite the difficulties and dangers posed by the war raging through Europe. Her service to Azione Cattolica clearly had as much of an impact on her as it did on those with whom she worked; the organization's motto, "Prayer, Action, Sacrifice," was one by which Gianna lived.

As a young woman, Gianna was certain of her calling in life; in her eyes, the medical profession was a divine mission. She wrote: "Jesus says, 'Whoever visits the sick is helping me.' This is a priestly mission. Just as the priests can touch Jesus, so we doctors touch Jesus in the bodies of our patients: in the poor, the young, the old, and children. Jesus makes himself seen in our midst." In 1949, she graduated with honors from the University of Pavia with degrees in medicine and surgery. A year later, Gianna opened a clinic near her hometown of Magenta and continued her studies at the University of Milan, earning a specialized degree in pediatrics in 1952. She had dreamed of joining her brother Enrico in Brazil to do missionary work, but many factors, including her own poor health, prevented her from doing so. Although it was painful for Gianna to give up this ambition, she showed great strength in understanding that God had other plans, saying, "All the Lord's ways are beautiful because their ends are one and the same: to save our own soul and to succeed in leading many other souls to heaven, to give glory to God." Gianna continued her medical practice, becoming known as a compassionate doctor who truly cared about her patients and often helped them pay for treatment in times of financial hardship. She also became greatly involved in service work, especially in Azione Cattolica.

Despite her demanding schedule, Gianna took the time to appreciate the beauty of God's creation by enjoying skiing and mountain climbing. She also loved the theater and the opera; Gianna found great joy in life. In 1954, while working in the clinic, she met Pietro Molla, an engineer. The couple was married on September 24, 1955, in the Basilica of San Martino in Magenta. Pietro expressed his desire to form a "truly Christian family" with his wife and asked their "heavenly mother" to bless them with children. Gianna shared his enthusiasm for starting a family, writing that they would "become collaborators with God in His creation and so we will be able to give him children that love him and serve him." Their prayers were answered in 1956, when Gianna gave birth to Pierluigi. Mariolina (also known as Maria Zita) was born in 1957, and Laura became a part of their family in 1959. During this time, Gianna managed to balance her work as a doctor with her responsibilities as a wife and mother. Although she suffered two miscarriages after Laura was born, she continued to raise her young children in a strongly Catholic environment just as Marie and Alberto had raised her, teaching them about Jesus and praying with them daily.

Gianna was in the second month of her pregnancy with a fourth child in 1961 when a fibroma developed in her uterus. She was presented with options: an abortion would be safest for her but would directly kill her unborn child; a hysterectomy, too, would end the baby's life but save her own; removal of the fibroma itself would preserve the life of the child but carried many potential risks. The teaching of the Church allowed Gianna the option of the hysterectomy, as the operation does not directly kill the child; the death would be an unintended consequence as opposed to the objective of the surgery. Her doctor recommended an abortion as the best way to save the mother's life. However, the choice was clear to Gianna. "With hope and faith I have entrusted myself to the Lord," she declared. "I trust in God, yes; but now it is up to me to fulfill my duty as a mother. I renew to the Lord the offer of my life. I am ready for everything, to save my baby."

Gianna left no doubt in anyone's mind as to her intentions. "If you must decide between me and the child, do not hesitate: choose the child—I insist on it. Save the baby." Gianna Emanuela was delivered by Caesarean section on April 21, 1962, and her mother died seven days later of septic peritonitis. She was buried in a cemetery near Magenta.

Gianna Beretta Molla was beautified 32 years after her death by Pope John Paul II in 1994, the International Year of the Family. The miracle that made her canonization possible was confirmed in 2003, when Elisabeth Comparini Arcolino, a mother expecting her fourth child, tore her placenta and lost amniotic fluid. Bishop Diogenes Silva Matthes of Brazil spoke to Arcolino and prayed for the intercession of Blessed Gianna to save the baby. On May 31, a healthy baby was delivered by Caesarean section. On May 16, 2004, Molla was officially declared a saint of the Catholic Church. Pietro, then 91 years old, and their three surviving children, along with the Arcolino family, attended the ceremony. The Holy Father described the new saint as a "holy mother" who "remained heroically faithful to the commitment she made on the day of her marriage."

Today, organizations such as the Society of St. Gianna, which is dedicated to promoting the family and respect for life, and the St. Gianna Physicians Guild, which urges doctors to make and encourage pro-life decisions, work to spread the witness of St. Gianna's heroic act. Her life and martyrdom inspire modern-day Catholics to respect life and, as John Paul II said, "liv[e] as a response to the divine call."—Clare E. Myers

BIBLIOGRAPHY AND FURTHER READING: Molla, Pietra. *Saint Gianna Molla: Wife, Mother, Doctor.* Ft. Collins, CO: Ignatius Press, 2004; Society of St. Gianna website, http://www.saintgianna.org. *See also* ABORTION; CATHOLIC ACTION

MOMIGLIANO, ARNALDO (1908–1987) Arnaldo Momigliano was an Italian Jewish historian who specialized above all in the historiography and cultural history of the Greek and Roman world and the place of Judaism and Christianity within it. His interests were wide, however, and extended in some degree to the whole history of Western erudition, especially about history and religion.

Momigliano was born into a pious and broadly educated orthodox rabbinical family from Piedmont, Italy, and remarked later in life that much of his scholarly activity was informed by his attempt to understand the Jewish, Christian, and Roman heritages that shaped the world of his youth, defined by the small town of Caraglio in which he grew up. He initially studied philosophy at the University of Turin, but eventually switched to classical studies. His academic career started brilliantly in his native Italy, and he published his first monograph, on the Maccabean tradition in history, at age 22, as well as two other works in the next four years on the Emperor Claudius as an author and Alexander the Great. Momigliano's early training and orientation in history largely followed the liberal Italian tradition of Benedetto Croce, and he regarded himself as an Italian patriot. He was willing to swear loyalty to the Fascist regime to retain his university position at Turin, but was ultimately required to give it up in 1938 as Mussolini's regime turned increasingly anti-Semitic.

He left for England and was able to continue his historical research at Oxford University and University College London. Although in an institutionally somewhat marginal position in England during World War II, Momigliano made fruitful contact with German émigré scholars as well as British classical studies circles. After the war, an academic position at the University of Turin was formally restored to him, but he continued to reside and teach mostly in England, holding a number of positions there, most significantly at University College London. Toward the end of his scholarly career, especially after retiring from University College in 1974, he spent considerable time in Pisa and as a visiting professor at the University of Chicago. These years lived mostly in exile from his native Italy saw Momigliano develop his favorite and most characteristic form of scholarly writing: the learned essay. All three of his most important later books devoted to single topics—*Alien Wisdom, The Development of Greek Biography,* and *The Classical Origins of Modern Historiography*—were in fact more specially constructed sequences of such pieces than conventional monographs.

Momigliano's vision of the Western tradition saw it as emerging from several dynamic streams of intercultural interaction and the mutual understandings (and misunderstandings) that unfolded between the peoples of the ancient Mediterranean. To him, the transforma-

tions in historical culture and sense of tradition were at the core of this process. He consequently researched such topics as the role the experience of Persian dominance had on the Greek and Jewish interpretation of the past, the intercultural politics of the Hellenistic age, the limitations of Greek knowledge of foreign languages, the successive stages and strategies of Romans in their accommodation to Greek culture, and the role and dilemmas of subject peoples like Greeks, Celts, and Jews in the Roman Empire.

Momigliano had also an important interest in the consequences of the triumph of Christianity and the Church in late antiquity, and indeed, he had a significant influence on the subsequent English-language historiography of this era, both directly and through his student Peter Brown. To Momigliano, the Western tradition of historiography was based mainly on Greek roots, in the form of both the writings of Greek historians on politics and public endeavor and those of Greek antiquarians and geographers who specialized in the history of artifacts, documents, inscriptions, and social practices and customs. This tradition was then enriched by a Roman sense for national history and the Judeo-Christian sense for universal history with a sacred meaning.

His general view of traditional Western religion is respectful, yet his strong devotion to modern critical methods means that its fundamental tone and approach is not especially pious. It should be noted that the breadth of Momigliano's learning makes his scholarly achievement hard to categorize simply. He was, for instance, also quite interested in the post-ancient fate of the Western tradition of historical inquiry, and he retained an openness to emerging interdisciplinary approaches, such as those stemming from cultural anthropology.

In his last years, Momigliano warned against the tendency of certain contemporaries to reduce history to rhetoric and ideological concerns, thereby slighting the importance of facts in history. On the one hand, he pointed out that radical skepticism about history was not new in the Western tradition, but at the same time, he worried about the increasing sophistication of such skeptics. To him, this was in part because in the West history was long focused on the mature adult reader and came late into the university curriculum, where it had to justify its presence. This led to the exaggerated claims for the discipline, which tried to derive too much of human morality and other values from human history. In an age in which traditional Western ethical beliefs and religion were under challenge, it also provided the temptation to make history the instrument of ideology, to which the postmodernists then abandoned themselves.

While not denying an incidental rhetorical aspect to historiography, Momigliano thought it essential to avoid all ideological and literary reductions of history. Thus, he urged historians to always remember the importance of evidence and traditional critical methods, while at the same time to practice intellectual humility by realizing that though history can provide much knowledge relevant to guiding human action in the present, the principles that make such knowledge actionable lie outside the range of the historical discipline per se.—Paul J. Radzilowski

BIBLIOGRAPHY AND FURTHER READING: Grafton, Anthony. "Arnaldo Momigliano: A Pupil's Notes." *American Scholar* 60, no. 2 (1991): 235–252; Momigliano, Arnaldo. *Alien Wisdom: The Limits of Hellenization.* Cambridge: Cambridge University Press, 1971; Momigliano, Arnaldo. *The Classical Foundations of Modern Historiography.* Berkeley: University of California Press, 1990; Momigliano, Arnaldo. "History in an Age of Ideologies." *American Scholar* 51, no. 4 (1982): 495–507; Momigliano, Arnaldo. *On Pagans, Jews, and Christians.* Hanover, NH: Wesleyan University Press, 1987; Steinberg, Michael P., ed. *The Presence of the Historian: Essays in Memory of Arnaldo Momigliano.* Special issue, *History and Theory* 30 (1991). *See also* HISTORY (ACADEMIC DISCIPLINE OF); SHILS, EDWARD A.

MONTFORT, ST. LOUIS-MARIE GRIGNION DE (1673–1716)

The founder of two religious orders and the author of numerous hymns, poetry, treatises, and books, most notably *True Devotion to the Blessed Virgin,* St. Louis Grignion de Montfort left a lasting impact on prerevolutionary France through his numerous missions among the poor, while he and his writings have had a particularly strong influence on popular piety and Marian devotion in contemporary times, particularly since the reign of Pope John Paul II (1978–2005). Montfort was beatified in 1888 and canonized in 1947.

Louis-Marie Grignion was born in the small village of Montfort in the region of Brittany, France, on January 31, 1673, the second of 18 children. He would later add "de Montfort" to his name to emphasize the place of his reception of baptism, a sacrament central to the understanding of his spirituality. The family soon moved to the nearby village of Iffendic, where he spent the first 11 years of his life under the watch of his devout parents.

Montfort enrolled in the Jesuit College of Thomas à Becket in the city of Rennes in 1684. He received an education that influenced his spiritual outlook, not only from his Jesuit teachers but also from an uncle who was a priest in Rennes and from friends he met, including Claude Poullart des Places, the founder of the Holy Ghost Fathers. At the end of his eight years there, Montfort decided he was being called to the priesthood, and through advice from his spiritual director, he decided to go to Paris.

Evidence that Montfort was committed to living out the Gospel can be seen within the context of his journey from Rennes to Paris. Giving away all his possessions to the poor he met at the gate of Rennes, he traveled as a pilgrim, relying completely on Divine Providence for his needs. Arriving in Paris in the clothing of a beggar, Montfort enrolled in the Seminaire St.-Sulpice, one of the great centers for priestly formation at the time. He immersed himself in his studies, particularly Holy Scripture, the Fathers of the Church, and St. Thomas Aquinas, as well as the beginnings of the "French School," a movement of spirituality within which Montfort himself would be classified. This school, founded by Cardinal Pierre de Berulle and continued by others such as Jean-Jacques Olier, founder of the Sulpicians, blended a strong devotional life with a focus on the person of Jesus Christ, encouraging the pursuit of sanctity through a personal experience of him. This approach would deeply affect Montfort, not only in the deeply personal relationship with Christ that he developed but also in his understanding of the key role the Virgin Mary plays in this experience. Montfort also saw the approach of the French School as a path that all—rich or poor, educated or uneducated, young or old—could live out, an understanding that would be key to Montfort's future apostolate.

Montfort was ordained a priest on June 5, 1700, but he was still unsure of how exactly God wanted him to live out his priestly vocation. He volunteered to assist in some local parish missions as well as working in the poorest areas of the city of Poitiers. At this time, he met Marie-Louise Trichet, with whom Montfort would eventually start the religious community known as the Daughters of Wisdom. But Montfort was struggling with questions of God's plan for himself, and he wondered if he possibly was called to go as a missionary to Canada or the Far East. Deciding to seek the counsel of the pope, Clement XI, he was told that there was a great need for him in France. Pope Clement granted Montfort the prized title of "missionary apostolic," being in a sense sent out by the pope.

With a renewed sense of purpose and complete trust in Providence, Montfort made his way through the countryside of France, focusing particularly on the peasantry of the Vendée region. Imitating the "poor Christ," he traveled from town to town like an 18th-century St. Francis of Assisi, carrying nothing but a simple knapsack over his shoulder with a few books and articles of clothing, carrying out parish missions on the theme of the great love of God and his Mother, erecting Calvary shrines throughout the Vendée, and urging a renewal of baptismal vows by all the people. Testaments exist to this day in many of these places about how Montfort's visit transformed the villages and restored a culture of faith.

Montfort drew much criticism from two camps, though. First, many of the clergy, including many bishops, believed Montfort's style lacked the dignity and decorum a priest was expected to exhibit. Some bishops saw Montfort as an eccentric, even a radical, and forbade him from working in their dioceses—orders he always obeyed. The other camp that opposed him was the growing followers of Jansenism. This form of Calvinism with Catholic externals despised Montfort's message of God's passionate love for each person, a personal relationship with the Crucified God, and a reliance on God's tender Mother. These teachings contradicted the Jansenist god of fiery justice and anger. Hostility against Montfort reached such a level that many assassination attempts were made on his life, the last of which, a poisoning, severely injured his health. Montfort continued to give missions, but gradually pleurisy began to overtake his already compromised body. After giving his last mission at St.-Laurent-sur-Sevre, he died on April 28, 1716.

Montfort had dreamed of forming a group of priests and brothers who would live like the Apostles, preaching missions throughout France. Though many attempts were made, and even a rule drawn up, the Company of Mary, as it would be known, did not form until just before his death and would not get formal papal approval until 1748, from Pope Benedict XIV. Montfort's work and devotion would be carried on by the Montfort Fathers throughout the Vendée. Many historians believe the work of Montfort and his disciples inspired the Vendée resistance to the anticlerical Revolution of 1792.

In our own times, Montfort's writings have grown in popularity. Since Blessed Pope Pius IX, papal praise has been showered on the writings of St. Louis de Montfort, particularly his *True Devotion to the Blessed Virgin*. This work calls for a renewal of one's baptismal vows, along with a consecration of oneself completely to Jesus Christ through Mary, placing all one's good works, merits, and prayers in the hands of Mary to be presented to Jesus. Through this offering, according to Montfort, one becomes an instrument of Mary to bring about the reign of Jesus Christ in the world. Along with later figures such as Blessed William Joseph Chaminade and St. Maximilian Kolbe, Montfort predicted an "age of Mary," when, through those consecrated to her, Mary would bring about the triumph of Christ and his Church over its enemies.

Following the Second Vatican Council, some believed that devotion to the Virgin Mary had become outmoded, a hindrance to ecumenical dialogue, and an obstacle to a direct relationship with Jesus Christ. With the election of Pope John Paul II, however, Marian devotion began to return to the Catholic Church. John Paul, who himself had said that Montfort's book "was a turning point" in his life, and in fact took the motto of Montfort's consecration, "Totus Tuus" ("I Am All Yours"), as his own episcopal motto, clearly pointed the Church toward the spirituality of Montfort, particularly in the encyclical *Redemptoris Mater*. In light of this growing devotion to the Virgin, *True Devotion* has gained many adherents, particularly those of the "JP II generation," who borrowed much of their own spirituality from that of John Paul II. Many other groups, such as the Legion of Mary, the Apostolate for Family Consecration, and the Blue Army, to name a few, have all been inspired by *True Devotion*. Montfort's other writings, including *The Secret of the Rosary*, *The Secret of Mary*, *Love of Eternal Wisdom*, and *Friends of the Cross*, continue to be published in numerous languages, read, and studied, and there has been discussion about Montfort being declared a Doctor of the Church.—James Krug

BIBLIOGRAPHY AND FURTHER READING: Davies, Michael. *For Altar and Throne: The Rising in the Vendée, 1793–1796*. St. Paul: Remnant Press, 1997; DeFiores, Stefano, ed. *Jesus Living in Mary: Handbook of the Spirituality of St. Louis-Marie de Montfort*. Bay Shore, NY: Montfort, 1994; Gendrot, Marcel, SMM, ed. *Make Way for Jesus Christ: The Message of St. Louis de Montfort*. Translated by John Molloy, SMM. Bay Shore, NY: Montfort, 1984; Montfort, Louis-Marie Grignion de. *The Collected Writings of St. Louis Mary de Montfort*. Bay Shore, NY: Montfort, 1987; Perouas, Louis, SMM. *A Way to Wisdom: Louis Marie Grignion de Montfort and His Beliefs*. Bay Shore, NY: Montfort, 1982; Vasey, Vincent R., SM. *Chaminade: Another Portrait*. Dayton, OH: Marianist Resources Commission, 1987; Weigel, George. *Witness to Hope: The Biography of Pope John Paul II*. New York: Cliff Street Books/HarperCollins, 1999. *See also* FRENCH REVOLUTION

MORE, ST. THOMAS (1478–1535)

MORE, ST. THOMAS (1478–1535) Thomas More was a lawyer, author of *Utopia* and other classic works, lord chancellor of England, Catholic martyr, and saint. He is the patron of statesmen and politicians.

More was born on February 7, 1478, in London, about 20 yards from the birthplace of St. Thomas à Becket, martyred three centuries earlier. John More, Thomas's father, was a respected London lawyer. He provided a thorough education for Thomas, his oldest son, at St. Anthony's school, focusing on Latin, Greek, rhetoric, logic, and oratory. Thomas showed such promise that in 1490 he was taken as a page in the household of John Cardinal Morton, archbishop of Canterbury and lord chancellor of England, and then sent by Morton to study at Canterbury College, Oxford. Subsequently, More studied law for seven years at the Inns of Court before being called to the bar in 1501. During this time, he began a practice of daily Mass, prayer, and mortification to which he would adhere his entire life.

In 1510, More was elected to Parliament and became an undersheriff of London. Already known as an outstanding lawyer and judge, More began to acquire a reputation as a writer and humanist scholar, based on his translations of Greek and Latin poetry, his history of Richard III, and his friendship with the leading humanists of Europe, in particular, the great Erasmus (1466–1536). In 1516, More completed and published *Utopia*, a classic of Western literature. Written in Latin, it is a fantastic tale in which the character Raphael Hythloday describes the imaginary island of Utopia (a Greek amalgam of "nowhere" and "good place"). The Utopians are a pre-Christian society organized along rational and egalitarian custom: property is held in common; the economy is efficient and without class distinction; war and capital punishment are scorned; and marriage is a practical affair with divorce as a remedy. Commentators have debated how much of *Utopia* can be attributed to More's beliefs (with Marxist Karl Kautsky even claiming More as the first communist). In fact, there is little in Utopian life that cannot be derived from the speculations of the classical philosophers or the example of the New Testament Christians. It is perhaps best to evaluate the society of *Utopia* not on its own terms but in ironic contrast to the corruptions of Christian Europe.

More's humanism also showed in the life of his family. After his first wife Jane died, leaving four children, More married Lady Alice Middleton. They presided over an extended household of children, adoptees, wards, tutors, servants, and friends, known for its generosity, warmth, and piety. More insisted on a broad-ranging and humanistic education for his entire household; his beloved daughter, Margaret, was widely reputed to be the most learned female in England.

In 1518, More's career entered a new stage. King Henry VIII and his powerful lord chancellor, Thomas Cardinal Wolsey, employed More as royal secretary, diplomat, and counselor. As a reward for his expert service, More was knighted in 1521. By 1523, as speaker of the House of Commons, he had become the most important and efficient administrator of Henry's court, after Wolsey. More's literary efforts entered a new stage as well, in response to Martin Luther's Protestant revolt. Discarding his critiques of lazy clerics and obscure scholastics, More devoted his writing to polemics against the Lutheran heresy that he saw threatening Christendom. More advised Henry in writing a defense of the Catholic seven sacraments, which earned the monarch the title "Defender of the Faith" from Pope Leo X. In 1528, More published the first of a series of polemical books against William Tyndale, the famous translator of the English Bible and writer of Protestant tracts.

On October 25, 1529, More reached the summit of his political career when he was appointed lord chancellor (Wolsey having been dismissed in disgrace), the first layman to occupy this office, the highest in England. With great energy and clarity, More presided over the Court of Chancery, the Star Chamber, and Parliament and conducted the sundry affairs of state. He oversaw legislation reforming clerical abuses, drafting the Statute of Uses, and relieving the king of certain debts; negotiated trade with Spain; and supervised measures—including prosecutions—against Lutheranism in England.

But there was one affair of state More could not master: the king's "Great Matter," Henry VIII's desire to annul his marriage to Queen Catherine. Henry had married the Spanish-born princess of Aragon in 1509 and, although for 20 years she had been a model queen and wife, their only living child was a daughter, Mary. Henry needed a male heir, and also desired Anne Boleyn, a winsome maid at court, who refused to submit to Henry's overtures without prospect of matrimony.

Already in 1527, Henry had advanced grounds for declaring his marriage null. As Catherine had first been married to Henry's deceased older brother, Prince Arthur, Pope Julius II had dispensed Henry and Catherine from the prohibitions of canonical consanguinity in 1504 so they could wed. But Henry now claimed that the papal dispensation was in violation of divine law and was therefore invalid. The king bent the entire political machinery of his realm—clergy, scholars, canonists, diplomats, courtiers—to persuade Pope Clement VII to agree. Cardinal Wolsey's failure to achieve this goal was the cause of his disgrace.

Chancellor More was content to leave the decision to the Holy See. He refrained from any public declaration on the matter (although he did privately inform Henry of his opinion), but dutifully presented Henry's cause to Parliament. However, as Henry began to dispute not only the pope's decision but also his authority, More, a convinced believer in the unity of Christendom under the papacy, could no longer serve. On May 16, 1532, the day after the English clergy submitted to the sole authority of the king, More resigned as chancellor.

More hoped to retire to a quiet family life of letters on his Chelsea estate, but Henry's crafty and ambitious secretary of state, Thomas Cromwell, compelled Parliament to pass an Act of Succession on March 23, 1534, declaring the progeny of Henry and Anne heirs to the throne. More was willing to accept the monarchical succession as determined by Parliament, but was not willing to swear an oath rejecting the jurisdiction of the pope. For this refusal, an act of attainder was passed against him, and on April 17 he was imprisoned in the Tower of London, along with Bishop John Fisher, who also refused. In prison, More devoted himself to prayer, penance, and profound meditations on the passion of Jesus Christ, which have been published (*A Dialogue of Comfort against Tribulation: The Sadness of Christ*) and are classics of Christian spirituality.

On November 17, 1534, Parliament passed the Supremacy Act, proclaiming "that the King, our sovereign lord, his heirs and successors, kings of this realm, shall be taken, accepted, and reputed the only supreme head in earth of the Church of England called *Anglicana Ecclesia*; and to enjoy . . . all honors, dignities, pre-eminences, jurisdictions, privileges, authorities, immunities, profits and commodities [so] appertaining."

Again, More refused to swear to the spiritual supremacy of the king. To More's precise legal mind, such refusal could not violate the Treason Act, which punished only "maliciously speaking" against the king's supremacy. Nevertheless, More was tried on July 1, 1535, in Westminster Hall before a special commission. Testimony was introduced, certainly perjured, that More had by word denied the king's supremacy. More was convicted of high treason and sentenced to death by hanging, drawing, and quartering, but only after he gave a stirring defense of the freedom of the church and the primacy of the pope. His sentence of death, commuted to beheading, was carried out on July 6.

Although a total repudiation of Rome would be accomplished within a century, paradoxically More's stature in English history would only be enhanced. As literary indications of this, the 1592 play *Sir Thomas Moore* favorably depicts his popularity and courage, most notably in the portion of the play scholars believe was written by William Shakespeare; in *Gulliver's Travels* (1726), Jonathan Swift includes More in a "sextumvirate" of great men of history—in firmness of mind, in benevolence, in true love of country—"to which all the ages of the world cannot add a seventh"; and Robert Bolt's preface to *A Man for All Seasons* quotes Samuel Johnson's description of More as "the person of the greatest virtue these islands ever produced."

With the restoration of a Catholic hierarchy in England in 1850, the cause for More's canonization was opened. On May 19, 1935, Thomas More and John Fisher were declared saints by Pope Pius XI. (In a fine example of ecumenism, the Anglican Church calendar commemorates More on July 6.) Bolt's stirring 1960 play *A Man for All Seasons* (a 1520 description of More's genius), subsequently made into an Academy Award–winning movie, brought an attractive—and accurate—depiction of More to the broader public. In 2000, Pope John Paul II declared More the patron saint of statesmen and politicians, citing More's "imperishable example of moral integrity," his "exercise of virtue," and his defense of the "primacy of conscience."

More's personal virtues and achievements remain attractive. He was a consummate lawyer, an accomplished and impeccably honest statesman, an influential scholar and humanist, a powerful satirist and polemicist, and a man devoted to his family and farsighted in education, at all times witty, loyal, tender, conscientious, and willing to make the ultimate sacrifice for his beliefs. All this is not denied (despite recent attempts to vilify More for his actions against heretics), but for many modern social writers and thinkers, More's personal qualities are irrelevant. As philosopher David Hume wrote in *The History of England* (1762) of More's martyrdom: "Nothing was wanting to the glory of this end, except a better cause." More is seen as the representative of the feudal, medieval England that had to be swept aside in favor of a dynamic, mercantilistic nation-state, free from ancient and foreign attachments. More's age had passed. As a modern biographer writes, "The initiative had passed to Cromwell who was indeed the man for a new age."

This is a shortsighted view. The "new age" of Cromwell may have been the 16th and 17th centuries, but More looks to our age and beyond. Modern times show how well More knew the heart of society and the heart of man. In his defense of the indissolubility of marriage—"I know well that ye seek my blood, for as that I would not condescend to the King's second marriage," he declared at his sentence—he stood against the modern threat to the family. In his defense of the human conscience, he foreshadowed resistance to the totalitarian state, which would leave men no recourse save the dictates of the tyrant. In his defense of papal primacy, he stood for freedom of religion in relation to the state and for the essential communion that constitutes the Catholic Church. "No temporal man may be the head of the spirituality," More stated at trial.

More's life was blessed with an abundance of temporal gifts few possess. But his death speaks of the preeminent gift that is owed to God. St. Thomas More is the patron of statesmen and politicians because while exercising the most exquisite talents in generous service to the king and showing "constant fidelity to legitimate authority and institutions," he served not power but God's justice (John Paul II). On the block, his last words were: "I die the King's good servant and God's first."—Howard Bromberg

BIBLIOGRAPHY AND FURTHER READING: Ackroyd, Peter. *The Life of Thomas More*. New York: Anchor Books, 1999; Bolt, Robert. *A Man for All Seasons: A Play in Two Acts*. New York: Random House, 1960; John Paul II. "Apostolic Letter Proclaiming Saint Thomas More Patron of Statesmen and Politicians." October 23, 2000; Kautsky, Karl. *Thomas More and His Utopia*. London: Lawrence & Wishart, 1979 (originally published in 1888); Marius, Richard. *Thomas More: A Biography*. New York: Knopf, 1984; Martz, Louis L. *Thomas More: Search for the Inner Man*. New Haven, CT: Yale University Press, 1990; Maynard, Theodore. *Humanist as Hero*. New York: Macmillan, 1947; More, Thomas. *The Complete Works of St. Thomas More*. 15 vols. New Haven, CT: Yale University Press, 1974–1997; Reynolds, E. E. *The Field Is Won: The Life and Death of Saint Thomas More*. Milwaukee: Bruce, 1969; Roper, William, and Nicholas Harpsfield. *Lives of Sir Thomas More*. New York: Everyman's Library, 1963; Stapleton, Thomas. *The Life and Illustrious Martyrdom of Sir Thomas More*. New York: Fordham University Press, 1984; Wegemer, Gerard B., and Stephen Smith, eds. *A Thomas More Source Book*. Washington, DC: Catholic University of America Press, 2004; Wegemer, Gerard B. *Thomas More on Statesmanship*. Washington, DC: Catholic University of America Press, 1996. *See also* ARISTOCRACY; FISHER, ST. JOHN; GNOSTICISM, POLITICAL; HUMANISM; LITERATURE; POLITICAL SCIENCE; SOCIETY IN CHRISTIAN FANTASY; UTOPIANISM

MULTICULTURALISM The term *multiculturalism* admits of more than a single meaning. It can be used in a purely descriptive way, referring to the obvious fact that there are to be found in the world a multitude of different cultures, coincident with the multitude of different peoples or nations. It is taken to be axiomatic that any particular nation, such as the United States, is identified by a distinct national culture that sets it apart from other nations. In the first half of the 20th century, there were established in universities throughout the country a number of American Studies departments or programs; the principal occupation of the new discipline to which this gave rise was the study of what was confidently identified as American culture.

A culture, generally understood, is a set of beliefs, attitudes, habits, and practices that is shared by a given people and that creates a social atmosphere within which they live and breathe and identify themselves as a distinct collective entity—a community, specifically by reason of what they have in common. To use a different image, a culture can be thought of as the glue that binds a particular society together and constitutes it as a society. One of the most important elements composing a culture is a shared belief in and deference toward a transcendent object of one sort or another. This could be religious in nature (gods, or God himself) or entirely secular (the "dictatorship of the proletariat"), and it determines the shape and direction a particular culture will take. A common language is often an important component of a culture.

There has been a tendency of late to give "culture" a more narrow application, and we hear references made to the culture of a particular corporation or profession, but this uses the term analogically. In the commonly accepted understanding of the term, a culture applies to a people or a nation.

In recent decades, particularly in the United States, the term *multiculturalism* has taken on a new and quite distinct set of meanings, and it now refers to a particular position, a worldview, that is heavily laden with ideology. In point of fact, multiculturalism has become something very much like a movement, for it has definite organization behind it, and it has developed a number of explicit programs, which it studiously endeavors to implement, often with energetic singleness of purpose. As a movement, most of the activities of multiculturalism are concentrated in the field of education, especially on the elementary and secondary levels within the public schools. But it makes its influence felt within the broader culture as well, such as in the mass media—though here in rather subtle ways—and in politics. As an indication of the place it has come to have in politics, it is interesting to note that in the Canadian province of Manitoba there is a government-appointed minister of multiculturalism.

There is not to be found in multiculturalism, regarded as an ideological movement, perfect uniformity of doctrine, but there is a common thread of agreement among many of its advocates in the decidedly negative attitude they take toward Western culture. A special target of pointed criticism is what is called "Eurocentricism," a presumably widespread attitude on the part of Europeans, and their descendants outside Europe, which assumes that Western culture is superior to all other cultures. One can be led to believe, listening to some of the more passionate denunciations of Western culture by multiculturalists, that it is to be regarded as the cause of most of the world's woes and that it is inferior to all the other cultures.

That last claim is inconsistent with the notion that all cultures are equal, one of the mainstays of multiculturalism. While at first blush an apparent expression of disinterested magnanimity, the claim that all cultures are equal in fact serves to support an important aspect of multiculturalism's ideological agenda, for it is but an indirect way of advocating the notion of cultural relativism and all that implies. Cultural relativism, like multiculturalism itself, represents a distinct ideological point of view, the central proposition of which is the denial of the existence of universal principles and standards, especially regarding the moral realm, that apply to the human family as a whole. What this comes down to is simply a denial of the natural law. Multiculturalism, then, is a movement that is inspired in great part by a dedication to moral relativism and militant secularism, both of which are powerful influences in the times in which we live.

Those who actively promote multiculturalism say that they do so because they desire to foster ethnic diversity within the society to which they belong. That is the positive aim of their efforts. Negatively, they seek to discourage, if not positively prevent, what they call collective integration or assimilation. The latter would result, they argue, only in a culturally homogeneous society, which they regard as a bad thing, whereas an ethnically diverse society, which they are striving to realize, would result in a society that would be composed of many cultures, all of which would be equal to one another and all of which would coexist in perfect harmony.

The notion that it would be possible to have a single, coherent society composed of many distinct cultures, all exercising the same level of pacific influence, which is central to the thinking of multiculturalism, is eminently contestable. Whatever one might want to say about the notion as pure theory, we have an abundance of history that shows that it is a theory that has never seen realization. Given the very nature of culture, and what could be described as its functional purpose for a society, it is, practically speaking, impossible to have a single, coherent society that is not marked by a single, dominant culture, for it is just that culture that enables a society to *be* a society—that is, a single, coherent unit. As a matter of practical fact, then, a multitude of distinctly different cultures can result in only one thing: a multitude of distinctly different societies.

Unlike what advocates of multiculturalism want to believe, a society with a dominant culture—and it must have a dominant culture, otherwise it would not be a society—does not imply a society that lacks diversity, for a dominant culture does not preclude, and may even actively foster, any number of vibrant subcultures within its all-embracing ambit. But it is the very nature of a subculture that it is subordinate to the dominant culture, and loyalty to a subculture therefore diminishes loyalty to the dominant culture, the culture shared by everyone in the society. The two—dominant culture and subculture—are not in conflict, but in fact complement one another.

The advocates of multiculturalism feel themselves under obligation actively to promote diversity, but this is a mistake. Diversity will take care of itself, for human beings have almost a natural propensity for diversification, which is healthy in itself but must be held in check. If it gets out of control, this urge to be different can lead, within any society, to the kind of divisive factionalism that so concerned the authors of *The Federalist Papers*. What needs to be worked at in any society, actively and continuously, is *unity*, not diversity; emphasis must be put on what human beings have in common, what makes them essentially the same, and not on what differentiates them.

It is safe to say that no civil society is ever going to see perfect unity and harmony among its members; even so, that nonetheless remains an ideal the striving for which no society, if it wants to sustain itself as a society, can ever afford to abandon. Apart from that, though, the supposition that any society can in fact sustain itself without a common culture—a culture that, by definition, is shared by all—lacks any logical support. It is simply an erroneous idea, an unworkable theory.

One of the most remarkable omissions to be found in the thinking behind multiculturalism is the absence of any balanced understanding of the common good and the vitally important role that must play in any society. A particular society may be characterized by a common culture, which performs its basic function of lending coherence and unity to the society, but that coherence and unity will be fragile and tenuous—and so then will be the society itself—if the common culture is not deeply imbued with and guided by the dictates of the common good. The common good—the *true* common good, not its cheap substitutes—is the good as affecting all human beings in terms of their essential nature, as creatures with an eternal destiny. Because, then, there is but a single common good for all men, which is ultimately God himself, there should ideally be a common culture for all men. It is the creation of that common culture—a human culture in the fullest and most meaningful sense—toward which we should be bending all our efforts.—D. Q. McInerny

BIBLIOGRAPHY AND FURTHER READING: Howard, Thomas. *Chance or the Dance: A Critique of Modern Secularism.* San Francisco: Ignatius Press, 1970; Pieper, Josef. *Leisure, the Basis of Culture.* New York: New American Library, 1963; Senior, John. *The Restoration of Christian Culture.* San Francisco: Ignatius Press, 1983; Verene, Donald Philip, ed. *Man and Culture: A Philosophical Anthology.* New York: Dell, 1970; Wallace, Anthony F. C. *Culture and Personality.* New York: Random House, 1961. *See also* CULTURAL RELATIVISM; CULTURE; PLURALISM

MUSSOLINI, BENITO (1883–1945)　Prime minister of Italy from October 1922 to July 1943 and founder of the Fascist political party, Benito Mussolini was born on July 29, 1883, in the village of Predappio in the province of Forli in the region of Emilia-Romagna, Italy. The village is midway between Ravenna and Florence near the east coast of Italy. His father, Alessandro, a blacksmith, part-time journalist, ardent socialist, and anticlerical, named his son for the Mexican revolutionary Benito Juarez. His mother, Rosa, was a churchgoing elementary school teacher who saw to it that Benito began his education at age 9 under the Salesian fathers at Faenza, 20 miles from his home. He lasted there only a year, however, and by 1894 was in secular schools, where he eventually earned a certification and began his career as an elementary school teacher at age 19. Mussolini became a member of the Socialist Party, emigrated to Switzerland, and became something of a Marxist agitator before being expelled by the Swiss back to Italy. He taught in various private and public schools in Forli and the Italian Riviera, anticlericalism

and advocacy of violence being his most consistent pedagogical values.

One of the most important years in Mussolini's career was 1909. The Socialist Party in Trent, impressed by his growing reputation as a rhetorically gifted radical, chose him as secretary of the local organization and gave him editorial duties on the weekly socialist supplement, *La Vita Trentino.* As part of these duties, Mussolini wrote a weekly serial that became quite popular and was eventually collected and published as a novel, *The Cardinal's Mistress.* Set in Trent between 1648 and 1658, the work displays Mussolini's sensitivity for the poor—poverty was something he had experienced in his early life—as well as his hatred of the Church hierarchy and the Austrians who had historically occupied parts of northern Italy. Frederick III, the Holy Roman emperor, and the pope are the villains of the piece who poison the cardinal's mistress. By 1912, at the age of 29, Mussolini was appointed editor of Italy's official Socialist newspaper, *Avanti.*

At first, following the standard Socialist line at the time, he opposed Italian participation in what was to become World War I, but as with most of the Socialist parties in Europe, he ultimately came out in favor of war and specifically in Italian intervention on the side of the Allies—if only because the hated Austrians were their enemies. For this betrayal, he was expelled from the party. He went to war, and by 1919 he had begun to create a right-wing, nationalistic, anticommunist ideology that was to become Fascism. By 1921, the ideology had become a formal political party, and on October 30 the following year, Mussolini became the youngest prime minister in Italy's history at the invitation of King Victor Emmanuel III. Like German president Paul von Hindenburg a decade later, the king and his advisors hoped that moving Mussolini from the opposition to the government would end both the growing Communist threat and the more immediate threat of several hundred thousand Black Shirts marching on Rome. This royal decision would lead eventually to the end of the monarchy in 1946.

Mussolini, as president of the Council of Ministers, faced three tasks in uniting the Italian people: the first was the problem of poverty, epitomized in the north–south dichotomy of industry and wealth and characterized by the mass exodus of southerners to the Americas; the second was the military, which alone could frustrate his totalitarian ambition to create new Italians in the Fascist image; and the third was the church–state problem, as intense in Italy as in the Third French Republic.

Besides his role as prime minister, Mussolini also appointed himself minister of foreign affairs and minister of the interior. This neutralized the military until he could find a war for them. His charisma and magnificent speeches succeeded in temporarily uniting the Italian people and persuading the parliament to grant him dictatorial powers.

With respect to the Church, Mussolini and Pope Pius XI agreed to end the 60-year standoff between the Italian government and the papacy occasioned by the unification of Italy and the 1870 confiscation of the Papal States, including the Vatican itself, by the troops of King Victor Emmanuel II. On February 11, 1929, the Lateran Pacts were signed, by which the Italian government recognized the sovereignty of the pope over the Vatican City as an independent state in international and domestic relations, Catholicism as the official and sole religion of Italy, and protection of the dignity of the pope by the same *lese majeste* laws that protected the Italian monarch. Also, a modest financial compensation was afforded the papacy for the seizure of its territories, and a concordat was produced that guaranteed the Church and its clergy various benefits (exemption from military service, the administration of several basilicas, civil recognition by the Italian state of church weddings, and religious instruction in public elementary and secondary schools by those approved by the Church). While the state agreed to recognize Church lay organizations, within two years conflict arose over the independence of Catholic youth groups and the pressure brought by Fascism to limit the political freedom of these groups.

Avenging an 1896 Italian defeat, Mussolini pleased Italian nationalists by his 1935 invasion of Ethiopia. The subsequent condemnation and sanctions by the League of Nations caused "Il Duce," as he was now known, to withdraw Italy from the League in 1937. In the next year, the Chamber of Deputies was persuaded to end its session, and Mussolini became dictator. At the height of his power, however, he made the fatal mistake of joining Nazi Germany in World War II.

On July 23, 1943, with the Americans and British landing in Sicily, the Fascist Grand Council, constitutionally the highest power in Italy, with the agreement of the king, removed the Duce from his position as head of government. Imprisoned by the new government and exiled to the mountains of Abruzzi, Mussolini was rescued by German airborne troops and established as the puppet ruler of the mini-republic of Salo on Lake Garda in Lombardy, a territory not too much larger than what had been left to the Vatican. As the German army in Italy disintegrated, the partisans closed in on Mussolini. The cardinal archbishop of Milan, Ildefonso Schuster, arranged a meeting between Mussolini and the partisans, but this came to nothing and the Communist partisans eventually captured him as he fled toward Lake Como and the Swiss border. Mussolini and his mistress were executed on April 28, 1945, and notoriously their bodies hung upside down from a lamppost in Milan. A million other Italians had lost their lives in the war.—William J. Parente

BIBLIOGRAPHY AND FURTHER READING: Bosworth, R. J. B. *Mussolini.* London: Oxford University Press, 1980; Kent, Peter C. *The Pope and the Duce.* New York: St. Martin's Press, 1981; Neville, Peter. *Mussolini.* London: Routledge, 2004. *See also* FASCISM; ITALY; PAPAL STATES; SOCIALISM

· N ·

NATIONAL CATHOLIC REGISTER The *National Catholic Register* is a national biweekly newspaper, owned and operated as of February 1, 2011, by the Eternal Word Television Network (EWTN). Its editorial and business offices are in Irondale, Alabama. It also hosts a Web log where writers post news items and commentary and readers respond with comments of their own. The circulation of the printed newspaper in 2009 was 35,000.

The *Register* carries international and national news, features, and commentary of interest to a Catholic readership. An official statement of purpose says in part: "By dynamically presenting Church teaching and tradition with the news, the paper gives readers a distinct advantage: they become informed participants in the realm of politics, media, business, the arts, education, bioethics, etc."

The *Register* traces its origins back to March 17, 1900, when the first issue of a newspaper called the *Denver Catholic* was published as the official publication of the Diocese (now Archdiocese) of Denver, Colorado. In 1913, at a time when the newspaper was failing, its direction was taken over by a priest named Matthew Smith. Under his leadership, the circulation grew, finances were stabilized, and modern printing presses were purchased.

In 1927, Monsignor Smith launched a new venture—a national edition of what was by then called the *Denver Catholic Register*. In a message to readers appearing in the inaugural issue, he wrote: "If you like a Catholic paper with snap, vigor, courage, here it is. If you like one that is easy to read, here it is. If you like one that will always be loyal to the Church and has no selfish axe to grind, here it is." Smith also founded the Register System of Newspapers, with the national edition as its centerpiece. Under this scheme, the editorial operation in Denver published editions tailored to the needs of individual dioceses and featuring local news supplied by them, with editorial material relating to the international and national scenes supplied by the national edition. At its peak in the 1950s, the Register System included some 35 diocesan newspapers with a combined circulation of 850,000, while the *National Catholic Register* had a circulation of nearly 1 million.

Another component of the Register System operations under Monsignor Smith was a journalism school where students were trained for work in the Catholic press. The *Register* under Smith campaigned for fair treatment of migrant workers, battled the Ku Klux Klan, promoted the rights of Mexicans, and supported the Christian unity movement. It also published many features in the areas of apologetics and catechesis.

Over time, however, technological advances enabled a growing number of dioceses to begin publishing newspapers of their own, and the Register System declined. Eventually the *National Catholic Register* was sold to a California Catholic businessman and entrepreneur named Patrick J. Frawley Jr., who had made a fortune in PaperMate pens, Technicolor, and Schick razors and was an active supporter of conservative causes.

In the 1970s, the *Register*, now published in Los Angeles, entered vigorously into the controversies of the immediate post–Vatican II period, becoming a prominent voice of traditional Catholicism in that troubled era. Reflecting ideological divisions that now took hold in the Catholic press as a whole, the newspaper was often contrasted with the "other" *NCR*—the *National Catholic Reporter*—which began publication in these years and rapidly became a champion of liberal views.

Ownership of the *Register* changed hands again in 1995, when the newspaper was purchased by the Legion of Christ, and Circle Media, Inc., was established to publish it and a companion periodical called *Catholic Twin Circle* (later, *Faith and Family* magazine). At that time, editorial headquarters were transferred to Connecticut. Rev. Owen Kearns, LC, was named publisher and editor in chief. The *Register* retained its unabashedly conservative Catholic orientation and continued to carry a mix of international and national news and commentary along with features covering a wide range of topics in the areas of religion, culture, politics, the arts, and entertainment.

The *Register*'s link to the Legionaries of Christ became a source of embarrassment to the newspaper when it was disclosed that Father Marcial Maciel, the founder of the religious group who died in 2008, had sexually abused seminarians, fathered illegitimate children, and misappropriated funds. The *Register*'s publisher then took the unusual step of apologizing to readers and critics of Father Maciel for having defended him in the belief that he was innocent of the charges against him.

In mid-January 2011, EWTN announced that it planned to acquire the *Register*. According to a statement from the network, "Recent trends in the publishing world, coupled with fallout within the Legion [of Christ] after disclosures that their founder . . . led a double life, made it impossible for the order to continue publishing the paper." The purchase took place on February 1. The *Register*'s editorial and business offices are now in Irondale, Alabama. EWTN plans to continue to develop the *Register*'s online presence and to integrate the *Register* with EWTN's global presence on the Internet.

Like other Catholic periodicals today, and the print media generally, the *National Catholic Register* currently faces serious challenges arising from technological changes and the changing demographics of audiences resulting in changing tastes.—Russell Shaw

BIBLIOGRAPHY AND FURTHER READING: Catholic Press Association. *2009 Catholic Press Directory*. Chicago: Catholic Press Association, 2009; Kelly, George A. *The Battle for the American Church*. Garden City, NY: Doubleday Image Books, 1981. *See also* CATHOLIC PRESS, THE; *NATIONAL CATHOLIC REPORTER*; OUR SUNDAY VISITOR; *WANDERER, THE*

NATIONAL CATHOLIC REPORTER The *National Catholic Reporter* is a national newspaper published two times a month in Kansas City, Missouri. Besides its print edition, it also publishes news and commentary on its Internet site. The circulation of the printed newspaper in 2010 was 44,000.

The *Reporter* carries news, features, and commentary about the Catholic Church as well as about other events and issues as viewed from the particular perspective it represents. In the years since the Second Vatican Council, it has been an important voice of "progressive" Catholicism in the United States. Unlike most, though not all, other American Catholic newspapers that are owned and published by dioceses or religious institutes, it celebrates its independent status.

The newspaper's mission statement emphasizes a link to the Second Vatican Council. It says in part: "Having developed through the inspiration of the Second Vatican Council, our spirit is independent, our management lay, our vision ecumenical. We attempt to contribute to the Catholic conversation by supporting freedom, honesty, openness and shared responsibility . . . and by promoting the vision of a pilgrim church intimately linked with humanity and its history." The *Reporter* is often contrasted with the "other" *NCR*—the *National Catholic Register*—a biweekly newspaper that pursues a generally conservative line.

The *National Catholic Reporter* was founded in 1964, with its first issue published on October 28 of that year. The founding editor was Robert G. Hoyt, a Catholic journalist who had worked at the *Denver Catholic Register* before coming in 1949 to Kansas City where, with the encouragement of Archbishop Edwin V. O'Hara, he and several colleagues launched a five-day-a-week newspaper called the *Catholic Sun-Herald*. The *Sun-Herald* survived for six months, then went out of business.

In 1957, Hoyt was named editor of the *Catholic Register*, the Kansas City diocese's edition of the Register chain of newspapers, and in 1964 he and others began the *National Catholic Reporter*. In the early days, Bishop Charles H. Helmsing of Kansas City allowed the national newspaper to share premises with the diocesan paper as a cost-saving measure.

The *National Catholic Reporter*'s circulation rose rapidly, beginning from an initial base of 11,000 and soon rising to 100,000. But in 1968 the circulation figure began to drop, eventually reaching 35,000. In 1971, Hoyt was fired after refusing a request from the board of directors to resign.

Meanwhile, the newspaper's relations with Bishop Helmsing deteriorated. In 1967, the *Reporter* attracted much attention by publishing leaked copies of documents from the Pontifical Commission on Population, Family, and Birth-Rate, popularly known as the Birth Control Commission. The commission had originally been established by Pope John XXIII and was expanded by Pope Paul VI to advise him. The leaked documents showed a majority of commission members to be in favor of change in the Church's teaching on contraception, something the *National Catholic Reporter* also supported; the following year, Pope Paul published the encyclical *Humanae Vitae* reaffirming that same teaching as the teaching of the Church. The publication of the leaked documents was among the reasons cited by Helmsing for issuing a condemnation of the newspaper and challenging its right to use "Catholic" in its name. Sixty-six Catholic journalists thereupon signed a statement taking issue with the condemnation over its understanding of the "legitimate boundaries" of religious journalism.

Besides the leaked documents of the Birth Control Commission, other major stories covered by the *National Catholic Reporter* over the years have included the Second Vatican Council and its postconciliar implementation; the Vietnam War, which it opposed; and the clergy sex abuse scandal. Starting in 1985, the *Reporter* was one of the first national publications in the United States to give continuing attention to the sex abuse problem. Among the columnists whose work has appeared regularly in the paper are Father Richard McBrien, Sister Joan Chittister, and Bishop Thomas Gumbleton. Its current editor is Tom Fox, who also served as editor from 1980 to 1998 and publisher from 1998 through 2003.

In establishing the *National Catholic Reporter*, Hoyt said he sought to promote in Catholic journalism the same standards of honesty and openness in reporting the news that existed in the secular press. Leaving aside the question of whether secular news media themselves consistently observe those standards, the *Reporter* is generally credited with having contributed to the realization of Hoyt's stated goal, and it has won many awards for excellence from the Catholic Press Association of the United States and Canada. But the paper also has been criticized for ideological bias and a tilt in favor of progressive Catholicism and dissent, not only in its editorial and opinion pages but in its news coverage as well, together with an excessive readiness to dispute and oppose statements and actions of the Holy See and the bishops. Like other periodicals, the newspaper now faces challenges to adapt to new technology and the changing tastes of audiences in the 21st century.—Russell Shaw

BIBLIOGRAPHY AND FURTHER READING: Catholic Press Association. *2010 Catholic Press Directory*. Chicago: Catholic Press Association, 2010; Kelly, George A. *The Battle for the American Church*. Garden City, NY: Doubleday Image Books, 1981. *See also* CATHOLIC PRESS, THE; *NATIONAL CATHOLIC REGISTER*; OUR SUNDAY VISITOR; *WANDERER, THE*

NATURAL LAW AND *THE SEARCH FOR UNIVERSAL ETHICS: A NEW LOOK AT THE NATURAL LAW* In December 2008, Pope Benedict XVI welcomed the International Theological Commission (ITC) at the conclusion of its work on a draft of *The Search for Universal Ethics: A New Look at the Natural Law*. Regarding this project, the Holy Father declared: "I repeat the necessity and the urgency, in today's context, to create in culture and in civil and political society the indispensable conditions of the natural moral law. Also thanks to the study that you have undertaken on this fundamental argument, it becomes clear that the natural law constitutes the true guarantee offered to each one to live in freedom and in the respect for his dignity as a person, and to feel protected from any ideological manipulation and from all abuse perpetrated based on the law of the strongest. We all know well that in a world formed by the natural sciences the metaphysical concept of the natural law is almost absent, incomprehensible. Moreover considering its fundamental importance for our societies, for human life, it is necessary that there be a new response and that in the context of our thought this concept is made comprehensible: being itself bears in itself a moral message and an indication for the paths of law." The ITC's work was completed shortly thereafter, and the Congregation for the Doctrine of the Faith approved the text after the conclusion of the ITC's final session on December 6, 2008. The text consists of an introduction, five substantive chapters, and a conclusion.

The introduction raises the vital question of the existence of objective moral values that have a universal bearing on uniting humanity and procuring peace and happiness in the world. These are issues that frequently find their way into jurisprudential discussions of civil law. For example, one should not forget the contributions that the natural law has made to developments in the law of authentic human rights. The introduction posits the objective notion that, in spite of differences among the members of the human family, there is a universal essence and nature of the person that guides him to fundamental truths applicable to all humans and the societies in which they exist. This notion is fundamental to the Catholic Church's long-standing teaching about the essential value of the common good that inextricably unites the interest of each person and all members of the human family. As the ITC notes, "The search for a common ethical language concerns all men" (*NL* # 3).

Another important point about the universal ethics sought through the right reason of the natural law is to provide a necessary counterpoint to the tendency in the world to manifest or interpret "the rights of man by separating them from the ethical and rational dimension that constitutes their foundation and their end, to the profit of a pure utilitarian legalism" (*NL* # 5). It is thought by some that in order to overcome the claim that there is a universal ethic and truth, relativism is essential to "safeguard the pluralism of values and democracy" (*NL* # 7). The difficulty with this positivist approach to the law is that it remains satisfied in declaring what is just by the subjective standards of those to whom the law-making and law-interpreting processes are entrusted. The alternative to this, advocated by the ITC, is "that persons and the human community are capable, by the light of reason, of knowing the fundamental guidelines for moral action in conformity with the very nature of the human subject, and of expressing them in a normative manner, in the form of precepts or commandments. Such fundamental precepts, objective and universal, are called to found and to inspire the ensemble of the moral, juridical, and political determinations that regulate the life of man and of society. They constitute its permanent critical instance and assure the dignity of the human person in the face of the fluctuations of ideology" (*NL* # 9).

The ITC then goes on to elaborate its argument for a universal ethic based on the natural law by developing its theses in five chapters. The first, "Convergences," draws attention to the common moral patrimony between the Catholic understanding of a universal ethic based on the natural moral law and certain parallels with the great religious and philosophical wisdoms expressed throughout human history that acknowledge the universal and objective moral order and eschew relativism and subjectivity. This chapter concludes by arguing that the natural law not only avoids the conformism often associated with the positivistic and totalitarian attitudes of the contemporary age but also reinforces authentic personal freedom by defending those marginalized and oppressed by those institutions forgetful of the common good.

The second chapter, "The Perception of Common Moral Values," considers how the human person can identify fundamental principles of moral experience and formulate or discover the precepts of the natural law that have universal appeal and can inspire the moral life of any person. However, in spite of these common moral values, it is evident that assaults on the dignity of the human person persist into the contemporary age. In this context, recognition of the constant and necessary interplay between rights and responsibilities is essential to the advancement of the universal moral values that underpin the common good. The recognition of the fundamental principle of seeking that which is good and avoiding that which is evil—drawing on the first principle of the law as argued by St. Thomas Aquinas—is at the core of the common moral values. Also vital to endeavors dealing with this first principle is the formation of the moral person, which prepares the way for identification of moral norms. This formation and identification are inextricably related.

The third chapter, "The Theoretical Foundations of the Natural Law," provides the transition from common experience to concepts in which the philosophical, metaphysical, and religious foundations of the natural law can be identified as moral norms take shape. It is through this transition that the moral subject is led to the judgments of conscience where the moral requirements that impose themselves in concrete situations can be acknowledged. This process leads the subject from oneself to the objective standards universal to the natural moral law. Here the subject encounters the truth of authentic freedom, that is, freedom *for*, rather than freedom *from*, the truth so essential to the natural law and the universal ethics for which it supplies an apt foundation.

The fourth chapter, "The Natural Law and the City," provides insight into the regulatory function of the natural law in public and political life that is common to all people and their societies. It is here that the person in the public square must take stock of the law produced by the society in which this person and others subsist. Here is where the universal natural law and the natural right of each person engage one another. This engagement necessitates recognition that the person is at the center of the political and social order, because each person is an end and not a means to an end. At the same time this response emerges, it must be acknowledged that the person is a social being by nature and essence; therefore, for each person to flourish, there must be a social network established with others and regulated by the civil law guided by the natural law.

As the ITC notes, the natural law is the normative background in which the political order is called to move so that society may fulfill correctly its own mission of serving the person, who is prior to society. In this fashion, the four pillars of social life long associated with the Catholic intellectual tradition in modern times—freedom, truth, justice, and love—are satisfied for one and for all. These four values correspond to the requirements of an ethical order in conformity with the natural law and the rights to which each subject is entitled in his or her society.

The repeated reference to the natural law in the life of this "city" impels ongoing reliance on the kind of reason that avoids a political order that is threatened with the arbitrary, of particular interests, of organized untruth, or of the manipulation of spirits. In essence, the natural law contains the idea that the law of the state must necessarily be established on the principle of subsidiarity, which respects persons and intermediate bodies and regulates their interactions.

The fifth and final chapter, "Jesus Christ, Fulfillment of the Natural Law," demonstrates that the Christian understanding of the regulatory function of the civil law acquires its maturity within salvation history as established by the Incarnation. The application of human reason aligned with the natural moral law will lead the Christian to recognize the proper destiny of the human person. As the ITC explains, "Through the natural light of reason, which is a participation in the divine light, men are able to examine the intelligible order of the universe in order to discover the expression of the wisdom, beauty and goodness of the Creator" (*NL* # 103). What interferes with this light and the wisdom that emerges from it is the application of the human will, which is inclined to sin rather than to the good. Nonetheless, the person inclined to the good that emerges from the application of right reason will identify and acknowledge the wisdom of the Golden Rule—Do unto others as you would have them do to you. This acknowledgment is perfected in the person of Christ, who is "the living law, the supreme norm for all Christian ethics" (*NL* # 109).

These five chapters bring the ITC to its conclusions regarding the universal ethics based on the natural law. In essence, the commission recognizes that the one human family should pursue the common enterprise of identifying and living by common norms that promote justice and peace vital to the world and its peoples. In this regard, the natural law is the foundation for the universal ethics that can best promote the common human nature shared by one and all. The certitude of this claim is that the natural moral law is "inscribed" on the hearts of everyone because this normative deposit is accessible through the reason of virtually every person.

The natural moral law is not itself a list of definitive and immutable precepts, but is the inspiration held in common that can enable everyone in the search for the objective foundation at the foundation of an ethics that is universal and accessible. While easily identifiable with the fundamental teachings of the Catholic Church, the natural moral law and the universal ethics it supports are widely held and can be confirmed by others in dialogue respectful of the religious convictions and traditions of those not a part of the Christian community.

International society, in particular, is a place well suited to carry on this dialogue, as it is there that people who are inspired for the search for the truth about the human person will from the Christian faith, other faiths, and no faith find and mutually acknowledge the existence and the roles of the just norms that promote peace and harmony among all societies and their members. From the Church's perspective, this dialogue and the discoveries made through it offer the best chance of securing the common good that protects the dignity of every human person by ensuring the dignity of all. Moreover, this dialogue will enable all to better understand and accept the source of personal and collective morality that is crucial to the entire human family and its individual members.—Robert John Araujo, SJ

See also AQUINAS, ST. THOMAS; *FIDES ET RATIO*; NATURAL LAW

NATURAL RIGHTS   Natural (or human) rights are rights that are inherent in human nature. A *right* is a moral capacity or faculty of a person to have something, to act in some way, or to have another not interfere with one's actions or possessions. This is in contradistinction to a mere physical power one may have over something. When one claims a "natural" right, on its face it may tell us very little about what the right is—what its content is or whether it even qualifies as one. To know what natural rights are, one must have knowledge of human nature. Indeed, the very claim of a right is a claim about an aspect of human nature.

Human beings do not create themselves, but find themselves having been created by a creator—God. They have been created in such a way, with a specific nature, that makes them the types of beings that they are. They are rational and social, possessing an intellect to know the good and a will to choose the good, intrinsically ordered to a life of virtue in communion with others and eternal life with God. As a result of this nature, we can recognize by the use of our reason that human persons have a certain value or dignity that is not possessed by any other creature. Additionally, by means of God's revelation, we know that we are made in God's image and that, due to Christ's incarnation, death, and resurrection, our nature is redeemed and called to share in the life of God. This reinforces and elevates our understanding of the dignity we have as human persons. It is this dignity that gives rise to the natural rights of the person that are universal, inviolable, and inalienable.

The specific rights that flow from our dignity as persons are intrinsically related to the person's end or ultimate good for which he was created. To achieve his end, the person participates in a number of goods that are fitting to and in accordance with the fulfillment of human nature. These different natural goods help determine the different natural rights claims. To make a true rights claim, these goods of man's nature, freedom, the

natural moral law, the social and political community, the common good, and even man's relationship to God must be properly understood.

A good example that demonstrates the connection between these accompanying truths is the right to religious freedom. This natural right—rooted in the dignity of the human person—is a right to civil freedom consisting in immunity from coercion in religious matters. It is a right of noninterference by another private person or governmental authority. Yet this is not a natural right to believe in *any* religion, but is rather a right connected to the end for which the right is given. As the Catholic Church teaches, it is not a moral license to adhere to error nor a right to err, but rather a right to be free from coercion while fulfilling one's duty to seek out and come to know the truth about God, as God reveals himself fully in the Catholic Church, and then to live by that truth (*CSDC* # 421; *CCC* # 2104).

Because the act of searching out and accepting the Faith can be accomplished only by a free exercise of intellect and will, it excludes coercion of someone who might be erroneous in his judgment about the truth of God. The right is the means to the end, and it is this end that sets the limits to the exercise of one's right to religious freedom, as it must always be subject to the higher common good with respect to public order and objective moral norms. An obvious example would be limiting the exercise of the right when, in the name of one's religion, one commits murder. Here, the right so contravenes its purpose and violates a fundamental truth of the moral law that the political community has an obligation to limit the right for the sake of the common good.

At play here is the principle that one does not have a moral right to commit a moral wrong. In other words, if one has a moral obligation not to act in a certain way, then it is contradictory to claim that one has a moral right to commit the morally evil action. A right is a claim of what is due to someone as a matter of justice, but it is never due a person, as a matter of justice, to commit a moral evil. One might, however, have a legal or civil right—not a moral or natural right—to commit evil in the sense mentioned above. There could be a law that prevents a private person or the government itself from interfering with or preventing one from committing an immoral action, but noninterference does not give one the moral right to commit the wrong. Thus, one might be allowed legally and de facto, but not morally, to commit evil. This is analogous to our relationship with God: He allows us the free choice to commit evil de facto, but we do not have a right to violate God's divine and natural law.

The determination of *which* moral wrongs persons will not have a *legal* right to engage in is a matter of prudential judgment based on the understanding of the natural moral law, fundamental natural rights of others, and the common good. It is to be noted, however, that although natural rights are intimately tied to the social and political community, it does not mean that the government creates or is the source of these rights. The source of any natural right is human nature, which has its source in God.

The explication of the right to religious freedom also demonstrates the intrinsic relation between natural rights and natural law: Rights are mostly understood in relation to the moral laws that rights-bearing persons have a duty to follow—in this case, the duty to seek the truth about God. I say "mostly" because some natural rights exist irrespective of any duties. For instance, the unborn person does not have any duties or responsibilities, or more precisely cannot exercise his duty to achieve the end for which he is created a temporal life of holiness and eternal life with God—yet he still has a right to life simply because of the inherent goodness of his life. The other sense in which the natural law is linked to natural rights concerns the duties of other persons: The natural law obliges one not to violate the rights of another. In these two ways, there is a complementarity with respect to moral duties and rights, both of which are rooted in the same human nature.

Natural rights have not been without some controversy, even among Catholics. Some argue that they do not exist at all. Others claim that they are merely a part of a cultural construct, not grounded in human nature. Others say that natural rights originated either with medieval theologian William of Ockham or with the modern liberal political philosophies of Thomas Hobbes, John Locke, and Jean-Jacques Rousseau—all of whom root them in the autonomous individual in order to secure self-preservation, thereby privileging self-interest to the point where rights are incompatible with the natural law, virtue, the common good, and the whole Christian order. The counterview to the origin of natural rights, for which there is ample historical evidence, is that before (and after) Hobbes and Locke, many Catholic jurists, canon lawyers, philosophers, and theologians did understand some natural rights as subjective moral powers or capacities inhering in the individual person. These rights were not, however, rooted in the autonomous individual, severed from the natural law or community, but rather were interwoven with the rational and social nature of the human person always understood in relation to the divine, natural, canon, and civil laws within the respective communities.

What is evident with respect to the Catholic perspective is that over the last 50 years, most notably beginning with Pope John XXIII's encyclical *Pacem in Terris*, the Catholic Church has been a strong proponent of natural rights. To some, this is surprising, because the Church had seemingly condemned the movement toward natural rights, especially as expressed in France's *Declaration on the Rights of Man*. Some believe that the Church has changed its position toward natural rights, now accepting and advocating what it once rejected, while others argue that these condemnations are historically contingent and are not teachings of the Church. Others insist that these positions would seem to put the teaching authority of the ordinary magisterium into question, and therefore, upon closer reading of the papal documents, one can discern that the Church is consistent in its condemnation of the rights of old because they were either put forth as rights ultimately not given by God, or even against God and the Church, or tied to a religious indifferentism, or severed from the teleological nature of the human person, that is, the goods for which the rights exist. Thus, it is argued that these condemned rights are the same ones that the Church condemns today, and, more importantly, the Church has put forth a proper understanding of these rights. This is clear in the way the Church specifies some rights: "the right to life . . . the right for a child to live in a united family and in a moral environment conducive to the growth of the child's personality; the right to develop one's intelligence and freedom in seeking and knowing the truth . . . the right to share in the work that makes use of the earth's material resources, and to derive from that work the means to support oneself and one's dependents . . . the right to have and to rear children through the responsible exercise of one's sexuality" (*CSDC* # 155).

There are some Catholics who lament the Church's use of rights language, claiming it leads, at worst, to the very individualism and selfishness the Church denounces. They point out that the current ubiquity of rights language in political discourse, court decisions, international documents, and popular culture creates ever expanding claims of rights and a focus on the autonomous individual, leading to an undermining of community and the emphasis on the right to be independent from others, law, custom, tradition, the moral law, and from God. In other words, it is a natural right to *choose*, irrespective of the content of the choice. It also is argued that the use of rights language makes it difficult to overcome the distinction between the Catholic Church's understanding of rights and the false understanding so prevalent today. At best, they claim that the use of rights language needs to be complemented much more by, and ultimately be subordinate to, talk of the priority of duties and obligations, gift, virtue, the common good, and God.

What should be clear from the Church's teaching is that whether or not one uses the term *rights*, the human person is due, out of justice, certain things, both material and spiritual, or is due noninterference by others. The term *natural rights* is used for the ontological reality of the person in relation to the goods he is due so that he might achieve his end of a life of virtue and holiness in this world and eternal life in the next. Although perhaps not emphasized as some would like, the Church does combine rights with other truths concerning the human good, the moral law, theology of communion, and God, as most recently evidenced in Pope Benedict XVI's encyclical *Caritas in Veritate* (# 43). The Church teaches these truths in hopes of countering both the false claims of rights not rooted in human nature and the neglect or violation of other basic rights that are inherent to man's nature.—Steven Brust

BIBLIOGRAPHY AND FURTHER READING: Brett, Annabel. *Liberty, Right and Nature: Individual Rights in Later Scholastic Thought*. Cambridge: Cambridge University Press, 1997; Fortin, Ernest. "On the Presumed Medieval Origin of Individual Rights." In *Classical Christianity and the Political Order: Reflections on the Theologico-Political Problem*, edited by Brian Benestead. Lanham, MD: Rowman & Littlefield, 1996; Helmholz, Richard. "Natural Human Rights: The Perspective of the *Ius Commune*." *Catholic University Law Review* 52 (2003): 301–325; Kraynak, Robert. *Christian Faith and Modern Democracy: God and Politics in the Fallen World*. Notre Dame, IN: University of Notre Dame Press, 2001; MacIntyre, Alasdair. *After Virtue*. Notre Dame, IN: University of Notre Dame Press, 1981; Oakley, Francis. *Natural Law, Laws of Nature, Natural Rights: Continuity and Discontinuity in the History of Ideas*. New York: Continuum International, 2005; Reid, Charles J., Jr. "The Canonistic Contribution to the Western Rights Tradition: An Historical Inquiry." *Boston College Law Review* 33 (1991): 37–92; Rowland, Tracey. *Culture and the Thomist Tradition after Vatican II*. London: Routledge, 2004; Strauss, Leo. *Natural Right and History*. Chicago: University of Chicago Press, 1950; Williams, Thomas. *Who Is My Neighbor? Personalism and the Foundations of Human Rights*. Washington, DC: Catholic University of America Press, 2005. *See also DIGNITATIS HUMANAE*; FREEDOM OF SPEECH; LOCKE, JOHN; *PACEM IN TERRIS*; RELIGIOUS LIBERTY

NEIGHBORHOOD AND THE ITALIAN AMERICAN CATHOLIC

If one takes the time to examine contemporary films or peruse modern books in which Italian Americans are depicted as central characters, positively or pejoratively, there are several constant themes one will almost surely encounter. The importance of family, the centrality of the family meal, and, unfortunately, the existence of organized crime are just some common issues with which Italian Americans are often associated. While we may very properly and validly dispute many of the stereotypes we find in these and similar modern media depictions, there is one common theme about which little is directly written and on which there has been little extensive research, certainly from a theological perspective. This is the centrality and sacredness of the "neighborhood," a term used with frequency and precision by many Italian Americans and a theme that permeates many Italian American stories, both real and fictional.

For Italian Americans, the reality of the neighborhood transcends the typical definition of a geographical area. For many of Italian descent in America, this term connotes something much deeper than what one may read on a map and means much more than a group of people who share a zip code. It connotes an intimate network of families and institutions that come together to form one larger community. More accurately, they form one larger family. The "space" in which the neighborhood resides, often transcending the official boundaries of areas as laid down by the local or state government, is seen as sacred, a form of communal family property. In most cases, this reality takes on a spiritual dimension and is an expression of the typically southern Italian notion that the sacred and the secular are neither easily separated nor should they be.

In fact, the Italian understanding of neighborhood is in many ways a theological expression that touches upon the Catholic understanding of God's working in the world, the centrality and sacredness of family, and various other Catholic theological concepts not often associated with a geographic area. While this may be dismissed as a mere cultural expression or a misguided expression of popular religious sentiment, in some sense, what is present here is a well-developed ecclesiology in which the understanding of the church and of the human family extends beyond the borders of a physical building. God, his powerful saints, and all of

God's providential workings extend into each and every aspect of human life and human endeavor. The faith—and more specifically God and, to a lesser extent, his saints—has direct involvement in the life of the people that cannot be confined to one physical building, however sacred and central that building might be to them.

In his foundational work on the issue of Italian Americans and their "religion of the streets," *The Madonna of 115th Street*, Robert Orsi refers frequently to what he terms the "Domus-Centered mentality of Italian-Americans," a worldview that animates much of their understanding of community, neighborhood, and reality as a whole. Such a mentality, imbued with strong Catholic notions of God and Providence, can be called the meta-narrative through which Italian Americans, traditionally, understand all that is. Defined succinctly, the *domus* refers to the immediate family, relatives of any kind and to any degree, as well as all of those who are not related by blood but are worthy of being part of the domus. Such persons are called *comari* and *compari*. In other words, union through blood is sacred, but so is union through locale, and once such a union has been established, it is for life, similar to actual family. The neighborhood, therefore, in the words of Salvatore Primeggia and Joseph Varacalli, is an "entity that is painstakingly maintained, much more than simply a place of residence" for the very reason that it is an extension of the domus; it is one rather large family dwelling.

In light of this, the traditional Italian propensity for very public and outdoor *festas*—in which the entire community joyously celebrates a given saint, especially the Virgin Mary—is much more than an ostentatious display of devotion or an excuse to eat popular delicacies. Rather, it is a distinct theological expression noting the sacredness of the streets, a means of literally blessing the area and processing through the Italian neighborhood, demonstrating that the entire world is God's place of worship and that all of the neighborhood really constitutes the local church.

Long before the Second Vatican Council, this Italian notion of neighborhood embraced a vision of Church as Communion, through which all persons are intimately united as one domus, one family. In this vision, the church building is a sacred and beloved place to gather, but the Church itself is the People of God, and the world itself is truly the space in which the Lord is worshipped and the Gospel is lived.—Philip A. Franco

BIBLIOGRAPHY AND FURTHER READING: Franco, Philip. "The Traditional Italian Festa: Toward a Theology of Communion and Catechesis." Doctoral dissertation, Fordham University, New York, 2005; Orsi, Robert. *The Madonna of 115th Street: Faith and Community in Italian Harlem, 1880–1950*. New Haven, CT: Yale University Press, 2002; Primeggia, Salvatore, and Varacalli, Joseph A. "The Sacred and the Profane among Italian American Catholics: The Giglio Feast." *International Journal of Politics, Culture and Society* 9 (1996): 423–449. *See also* COMMUNITY; FAMILY; NEIGHBORHOOD; PARISH AS AN AGENT OF EVANGELIZATION

NEUMANN, ST. JOHN (1811–1860) St. John Nepomucene Neumann, named after a 14th-century Bohemian martyr, was himself born in Bohemia (today the Czech Republic), where he studied for the priesthood, but then without being ordained emigrated to the United States, where he became a missionary priest and was later named the fourth bishop of Philadelphia. He became the first American bishop and the second U.S. citizen to be canonized.

John Neumann was born in Prachatitz, Bohemia, on March 28, 1811. He was educated in the Gymnasium of Pious Workers in Budweis, Bohemia, and then, in 1831, entered the diocesan seminary. Later he studied at the School of Theology at the Charles-Ferdinand University in Prague. He completed his studies in 1835, but was not immediately accepted for ordination to the priesthood because the Diocese of Budweis already had a surplus of priests.

Young Neumann had already decided, however, that he wanted to become a missionary in America, and so he set out almost immediately for New York. He arrived there with nothing more than the suit on his back and a dollar in his pocket. He was, however, soon accepted for ordination by Bishop John Dubois of New York and was ordained to the sacred priesthood on June 23, 1836.

At that time, there was a great need for German-speaking priests in western New York to minister to the rapidly growing numbers of immigrants from Germany, so Father Neumann was sent to the area around Buffalo and Niagara Falls to work with these communities. Actually, he was proficient in as many as six languages and was able to fill ministerial needs in a number of communities.

Throughout his priestly life, Neumann was a veritable workhorse and labored unstintingly. Four years of such labor in western New York in relative isolation, however, convinced him of his own need for religious community life and support. Accordingly, he sought to join the Redemptorist order (the Congregation of the

Most Holy Redeemer). He entered the order's novitiate in Pittsburgh and took his vows in Baltimore in 1842. Some six years later, he was named provincial supervisor of the order in the United States, and subsequently he was assigned to a parish in Baltimore. Then, in 1851, Neumann was appointed by Blessed Pope Pius IX to be the fourth bishop of Philadelphia, a diocese that earlier had declined to accept him for ordination.

Neumann was ordained to the episcopate in Baltimore on March 28, 1852, by Archbishop Patrick Kenrick. As a bishop, he took as his model the founder of the Redemptorist order, St. Alphonsus Liguori, making the care of the poor one of his first priorities. All the years of his episcopacy were intensely busy. More than 80 churches were constructed in the Philadelphia area during his tenure, and he began the construction of the Cathedral of St. Peter and St. Paul. All this activity reflected an outstanding record of achievement on the bishop's part in what would turn out to be an episcopacy that lasted less than a decade.

As a parish priest, Neumann had already been heavily involved in the development of the parochial school movement in the United States, and he organized the parochial school system in Philadelphia on a sound and solid basis. He was also necessarily involved with the growth of religious orders in the United States, including the Holy Cross Sisters, the Holy Cross Brothers, the Sisters of Notre Dame de Namur, the Immaculate Heart Sisters, and the Christian Brothers. He was the founder of the Sisters of the Third Order of St. Francis in Philadelphia, an order that observed the "active" Franciscan practice; these sisters both taught in his schools and staffed his orphanage. The expansion of parochial education during the episcopacy of Bishop Neumann was as remarkable as the increase in the number of parishes; the number of students in Catholic schools increased nearly 20-fold during those same years.

In addition to his work as a bishop and administrator, Neumann also found time to write many articles for Catholic newspapers and periodicals, many of which did not always appear under his byline. He had already produced in German the *Kleine Katechismus* (1846) and a more extensive *Katolischer Katechismus* (also in 1846), along with another book in German on the history of the Old and New Testaments for use in the Catholic schools. Among other things, as bishop, he established the Forty Hours Devotions on a diocesan basis.

Neumann was indefatigable and regularly bore heavy burdens, yet he did not even consider himself worthy or capable of being a bishop, seeing himself as a kind of "country boy" in the midst of smart Philadelphia society. He was a man small in stature, humble and retiring in manner—though obviously possessed of considerable talents considering his many accomplishments. Nevertheless, he actually tried to step down, and eventually he was given a coadjutor, Bishop James F. Wood. Neumann never failed to carry out his episcopal duties scrupulously, however, and he even made his *ad limina* visit to Rome in 1854, where he was present for the formal promulgation of the doctrine of the Immaculate Conception of the Blessed Virgin Mary. The American bishops in Baltimore had already selected Mary under this title to be the patroness of the United States.

The future saint died suddenly, falling on a street in Philadelphia on January 5, 1860. His saintliness had been recognized by some during his lifetime, and when extraordinary favors began occurring apparently obtained through his intercession, there began a much closer and thorough examination of his whole life and activities. His cause was formally introduced in 1897, and he was declared venerable by Pope Benedict XV in 1921, beatified by Pope Paul VI in 1963, and canonized by the latter in 1977. He is commemorated annually by the Church on January 5.—Kenneth D. Whitehead

BIBLIOGRAPHY AND FURTHER READING: Curley, Michael J., CSSR. *Bishop John Neumann, C.S.S.R., Fourth Bishop of Philadelphia: A Biography.* Philadelphia: Bishop Neumann Center, 1952; Langan, T. *John Neumann, Harvester of Souls.* Huntington, IN: Our Sunday Visitor, 1976. *See also* EDUCATION, CATHOLIC: ELEMENTARY AND SECONDARY IN THE UNITED STATES; SAINTS AND SOCIAL ACTION

NEW AGE MOVEMENT: *JESUS CHRIST, THE BEARER OF THE WATER OF LIFE: A CHRISTIAN REFLECTION ON THE "NEW AGE"*

There are a wide variety of philosophies and movements that come under the umbrella of the New Age movement with no specific head or main tenets. New Age beliefs are as widely varied as Wiccan and Hinduism; there are pantheistic, polytheistic, and theosophic creeds, as well as the more popular occult practices, including tarot readings, numerology, astrology, yoga, and spiritism.

These movements are dissimilar in practice and conviction, but all have roots in the belief that the Age of Aquarius is upon us and the Earth is moving out of the Age of Pisces. This new age will usher in a greater consciousness, and the enlightened will have, as a result, greater psychic abilities and be more in tune with the powers of the Earth. This will instill greater oneness among people and God. But who and what God *is* is open to different interpretations, with great emphasis on a person's individual experience of the spiritual world. Most New Agers believe in the universality of God; that is, everything that exists has a divine nature and shares in the divine nature of everything else that exists. This is called *pantheism,* the first of the New Age beliefs to be examined.

Pantheism—from the Greek *pan,* which means "everything," and *theos,* "god"—is the belief that everything is God or that God is in everything. This negates God as creator of the universe and serves to confuse by placing God in a chicken-and-egg type of problem: A created Creator exists in all that is created. This assumes a contradiction—that the Creator is a created creature. But God has no creator, because he is not in fact created or made. In a pantheistic view, God is best seen as a way of relating to the universe and is characterized by a belief in the sacredness of nature.

One of the modern fathers of pantheism was a Dominican friar named Giordano Bruno, who lived in 16th-century Italy. He was an accomplished astronomer and mathematician who antedated Copernicus in his belief that the sun is the center of our universe and the surrounding stars are similar in structure to the larger sun. Bruno also wrote and taught extensively his conclusion that God resided in all things: "Nature is none other than God in things. Whence all of God is in all things. Think thus, of the sun in the crocus, in the narcissus, in the heliotrope, in the rooster, in the lion."

Bruno was later burned as a heretic for his beliefs, but the pantheistic Pandora's box had been opened, and it became the religion of popular elitists in the 18th and 19th centuries. Prominent figures associated with pantheism include Samuel Coleridge, Ralph Waldo Emerson, Walt Whitman, and Henry David Thoreau; later ones include D. H. Lawrence, Albert Einstein, and Frank Lloyd Wright. The movement experienced a huge resurgence in the late 20th century and became the underpinnings to the renewed interest in paganism. It also supports various environmental movements, which often take the innocuousness of things like organic food and preserving open spaces around the country and turn them into an idolatry of Earth and a pursuit of utopianism.

"What has been successful is the generalization of ecology as a fascination and a resacralisation of the earth, Mother Earth or Gaia, with the missionary zeal characteristic of Green politics. . . . In such a vision of a closed universe that contains "God" and other spiritual beings along with ourselves, we recognize here an implicit pantheism" (*BWL* 2.3.1). This recognition of God in all things pervades New Age thinking, but is a fundamental departure from the Christian perspective. "As Christians, we believe on the contrary that 'man is essentially a creature and remains so for all eternity, so that an absorption of the human I in the divine I will never be possible'" (*BWL* 2.3.1).

From pantheism, a natural progression is to theosophy or, in the ancient form, the direct mystical knowledge of God, the world, and all human beings. Modern theosophy was founded in 1875 by Helena Blavatsky, a Russian medium, and Henry Olcott. The Theosophical Society of New York attempted to establish a universal brotherhood that would not make distinctions between race or creed. This brotherhood would recognize that there was some truth in all religions and encourage study of them in conjunction with philosophy and science in order that all humanity, through this study, could evolve to perfection and discover people's latent powers. In *Isis Unveiled* (1877), Blavatsky wrote: "Our examination of the multitudinous religious faiths that mankind, early and late, have professed, most assuredly indicates that they have all been derived from one primitive source. It would seem as if they were all but different modes of expressing the yearning of the imprisoned human soul for intercourse with supernal spheres. . . . Combined, their aggregate represents one eternal truth; separate, they are but shades of human error and the signs of imperfection."

Madame Blavatsky was exposed to be a fraudulent medium in the 1890s, but her occult teachings continued to thrive. Theosophy finds its roots in Hinduism and as such its spiritual home in India. It proposes that one can come to know God through the direct intuition of his essence. This is best accomplished when an individual is in tune with the Earth and its elements. Theosophists find that this essence gives them harmony with the universe and imparts to them some of the secret forces of nature. They can then impart these secrets to the world through revelation and tradition. Theosophists use the trappings of Christianity by implying there is revelation and tradition. But in the Christian tradition, knowing God comes from revelation inspired by the Holy Spirit, human reasoning, and sacred scripture, not by some inner communal process that somehow expands to include the Earth, sun, and stars.

Blavatsky was also passionately concerned with the women's liberation movement and wrote frequently that the Judeo-Christian and Islamic traditions held women accountable for the fall of man, through

Eve, and were therefore repressive. She spent the latter part of her life studying Hinduism, the forefather of theosophy. Blavatsky "urged people to return to the mother-goddess of Hinduism and to the practice of feminine virtues. This continued under the guidance of Annie Besant who was in the vanguard of the feminist movement. Wicca and women's spirituality carry on this struggle against patriarchal Christianity today" (*BWL* 2.3.2).

In her magnum opus, *The Secret Doctrine: The Synthesis of Science, Religion, and Philosophy*, Blavatsky rails against Christianity and makes the case for Lucifer being the savior of man. Her writings and feminist ideology have fostered the modern occult movement, which is female dominated and is often concerned with either the powers and worship of various pagan goddesses or actual communication with spirits and demonic beings. It is a short trip to Satanism.

This threat is real and dangerous to all those baptized Catholics who participate, even innocently, in behavior that opens the door to the occult. Occult practices and beliefs have certainly been an offshoot of New Ageism; they are more about gaining power and less about self-actualization or spiritual awareness. Horoscopes, psychic readings, tarot cards, and Ouija boards all open the door to evil precisely because they seek the power to be like God. "Let there not be found among you anyone who immolates his son or daughter in the fire, nor a fortune teller, soothsayer, charmer, diviner, or caster of spells, nor one who consults ghosts and spirits or seeks oracles from the dead. Anyone who does such things is an abomination to the Lord, and because of such abominations to the Lord, your God is driving these nations out of your way. You, however, must be altogether sincere toward the Lord, your God" (Deuteronomy 18: 10–13).

In 1 John 5: 18–21, John tells us that, while we are begotten by God who protects us and to whom we belong, the entire world is under the power of the Evil One. Satan is real and enters this world through these seemingly innocent practices. Opening these doors courts disaster with your soul. Baptized and confirmed Christians have renounced Satan and his dark and evil kingdom. We are called upon to keep our eyes fixed on the Resurrected Christ and thereby gain the kingdom of light. Anything else is false.

The New Age movement is a response to a deep spiritual search for answers to life's most important questions. But the answer that the movement provides comes from a turn inward, toward the sovereign self. Its solutions must, therefore, be rejected. New Age solutions ignore the transcendent God and authentic religious meaning. As the Pontifical Council for Culture notes in *Jesus Christ, the Bearer of the Water of Life: A Christian Reflection on the "New Age,"* the Church and its members must respond to this spiritual longing by reiterating the "call . . . to come closer to Jesus Christ and to be ready to follow Him, since He is the real way to happiness, the truth about God and the fullness of life for every man and woman who is prepared to respond to His love" (*BWL* 1.5).—Mary Ellen Barrett

BIBLIOGRAPHY AND FURTHER READING: Groothuis, Douglas. *Unmasking the New Age.* Nottingham, England: IVP Books, 1986; Lewis, C. S. "Christianity and 'Religion.'" Chapter 11 of *Miracles.* London: G. Bles, 1947; Pacwa, Mitch, SJ. *Catholics and the New Age.* Cincinnati, OH: Servant Books, 1992. *See also DOMINUS IESUS*; NEW AGE MOVEMENT; PAGAN SPIRITUALITY; PELAGIANISM; THEOSOPHY

NIETZSCHE, FRIEDRICH (1844–1900) Philosopher and self-proclaimed anti-Christian Friedrich Nietzsche is seen today as the principal thinker of moral relativism. Born in 1844 in Roecken in eastern Germany, Nietzsche's father died when he was only four years old. In his upbringing, Nietzsche felt the decline of Christian belief acutely; his forebears were Lutheran pastors back to the beginning of the 17th century, but his religious environment was much more one of social and cultural betterment than of serious beliefs and piety. Sent to an elite boarding school, the young Nietzsche excelled in classics but not in any other subject. Intensely interested in the doctrines of Christianity, he planned on studying theology, but by the end of his time there, he had ceased believing in the Christian teachings, which he saw as an obstacle to the striving for truth. Turning to philology, Nietzsche's work so impressed the foremost classicist at the University of Leipzig, Friedrich Ritschl (1806–1876), that he was awarded a doctorate without examination and appointed to a professorship at Basel University when he was only 24 years old, all on the basis of his mentor's recommendation. He taught there for 10 years, after which he retired due to poor health.

Nietzsche's restless intellect was unfit for a narrow career in philology, in any case. His first book was on the classical notion of tragedy, but it won him the scorn of his colleagues, who saw it as below the basic standards of their discipline. In *Die Geburt der Tragoedie aus dem Geiste der Musik* (1872; *The Birth of Tragedy*, 1909), Nietzsche held that there were two perspectives on the human condition taken by the Greeks: the Apollonian and the Dionysian. The former is that of dispassionate reason, the latter the joy of intoxicated frenzy. The greatness of Greek tragedy was its ability to merge these two principles and keep them in balance. As a result, Nietzsche looked with suspicion on the founder of Western philosophy, Socrates, as leading to an exaggeration in the Western tradition on Apollonian and its rational detachment, and a reevaluation of Socrates continued as a motif in Nietzsche's work.

During his years at Basel, Nietzsche became an acquaintance of composer Richard Wagner (1813–1883), and the close relationship that developed between them was very important to Nietzsche throughout his life. It was Wagner's personality that especially affected Nietzsche; the composer's intellectual impact on him was very small. Both men were influenced by the philosophy of Arthur Schopenhauer (1788–1860). Nietzsche also found in Schopenhauer the figure of a philosopher who could also write elegantly.

Nietzsche himself was the most gifted stylist in modern philosophy, which often makes it difficult to discover exactly what he intended to say. But his aphoristic style, which commenced in 1878 with the first book of *Menschliches, Allzumenschliches* (1886; *Human, All Too Human*, 1909), is also part of the message of his thought, which opposes philosophical system-building and looks to the prephilosophical experiences that are lost in the creation of a comprehensive system of thought. The fragmentary style enacts the truth that we cannot fully grasp the whole of being with our linguistic formulations, though nevertheless our lives are lived in tension with it. Nietzsche would rather be falsely seen as a materialist, for example, than as reifying the nonobjective horizon of existence.

Ultimately Nietzsche had to break with Wagner, who was arrogant and insulting toward him, but the impact of the man stayed with him, and he wrote about Wagner up until the end of his career. Nietzsche also fundamentally disagreed with Wagner over the role of myth. Rationality alone is insufficient for man's existence, and myth is also needed for life, Nietzsche believed. Reality in its fullness can never be grasped by finite minds, but man simply cannot live in the absence of all explanations for random events and therefore seeks an intention or meaning behind what appears as meaningless fate. In a society where bourgeois equality was spreading, the level of public life was being degraded and art privatized—a situation against which Wagner reacted by turning art into an overwhelming assault on the senses, fashioning himself and his art as a mythological experience and compelling the public to take notice. Nietzsche admired this to a degree, yet found Wagner's *Ring* cycle of operas nauseating, for example, and began writing *Human, All Too Human* as a result of his disappointment with it. For Nietzsche, instead of possessing religious authority, myth was a game played for the sake of life.

Nietzsche thus offers us a philosophy that wishes to affirm and foster life by critiquing the metaphysical foundations of modernity. His work *Jenseits von Gut und Boese* (1886; *Beyond Good and Evil*, 1906) attempted to destroy the modern prejudice that the will to truth is automatically life affirming. Untruth is in fact a condition of life. Here, Christian nobility is not necessarily opposed to Nietzsche's thought: The example Christ left us of love and service to those beneath one, a path in which one does not insist on one's own rights but rather is open to suffering, is an altogether different approach from the search for a comprehensible truth that would justify social divisions, for example. The idolization of success in the modern world means the social hierarchy is seen as an exact mirror of personal and moral worth, something that Nietzsche, whose career failed and who wrote while living on the margins of society, could never accept. At the same time, though, Nietzsche was gravely concerned to avoid *ressentiment*, envy coupled with impotence, the self-poisoning of the mind he clearly diagnosed in *Zur Genealogie der Moral* (1887; *On the Genealogy of Morals*, 1967), where it is described as being the origin of morality. Most morality is based on utility, that is, what is useful to the community. According to its etymological origins, the term *morality* means the customs of the community, and insofar as communities reflect not only man's nature but also his fallenness, Christianity does not object to Nietzsche here, either.

Because he does without the conceptual language of morality and metaphysics, Nietzsche's philosophy is difficult to label with traditional categories. Compounding this problem is the fact that Nietzsche's great work, *Also Sprach Zarathustra* (1892; *Thus Spoke Zarathustra*, 1896), is written in fictional form. Nietzsche sought a nobility that modernity impedes with its claim to universal knowledge, particularly about good and evil. The noble person who says yes to his life is beyond the slave-morality of utility and attempts at the same time to affirm both the whole and his limited part in it. This task was an existential one for Nietzsche. He knew not only failure and betrayal but physical suffering as well, as he had to deal with poor health throughout his life. Despite his illnesses, Nietzsche never settled down and planted roots anywhere, instead wandering around Germany, Switzerland, France, and Italy. He collapsed at the end of 1888 and spent his remaining years suffering from insanity. His breakdown was most likely not hereditary, but rather the effect of syphilis contracted in his youth.

Nietzsche's fundamental insight is the inability of morality to justify itself. Morality is too narrowly individualist and cannot be self-grounding; its source is the inarticulate experience of a greater whole that cannot be captured in formulas that would be intellectually grasped and then applied. Nietzsche realized he was closer to being a Christian theologian than a moralist. Even the title *Human, All Too Human* indicates how Nietzsche wanted to place himself outside of the human, into the presence of God. His fascination with Schopenhauer and Wagner, his break with each, and the scorn he then heaped on them represents more than anything else his sense of their betrayal of their own promise. And his relation with Christianity is the same: Simply put, Christianity has betrayed Christ.

It is also true, however, that Nietzsche saw traditional Christianity as the principal obstacle to the new way of life he wanted to promote. He preached the "death of God," first in 1882 in the first edition of *Die Froehliche Wissenschaft* (1887; *The Gay Science*, 1974), though this should not be identified as some final proposition of Nietzsche. Rather, in it Nietzsche continued to carry out the critique of morality to its end point; rather than a revolt against God, the pronouncement "God is dead" involved the will to become like God, which is logically implied in Christianity. The attempt to live without ressentiment can only be a search for God. Nietzsche's negative critique of the god of the philosophers does not actually oppose Christ as much as a Christianity that fails in its quest to stay true to its founder. In his last lucid year, he produced a work called *Der Antichrist* (1895). It has been translated into English as *The Antichrist* (1896), but could just as well be translated *The Anti-Christian*.—Philip J. Harold

BIBLIOGRAPHY AND FURTHER READING: Hollingdale, R. J. *Nietzsche: The Man and His Philosophy*, rev. ed. Cambridge: Cambridge University Press, 1999; Kirkland, Paul E. *Nietzsche's Noble Aims: Affirming Life, Contesting Modernity*. Lanham, MD: Lexington Books, 2009; Safranski, Ruediger. *Nietzsche: A Philosophical Biography*. Translated by Shelley Frisch. New York: Norton, 2002; Walsh, David. *The Modern Philosophical Revolution: The Luminosity of Existence*. Cambridge: Cambridge University Press, 2008. *See also* ATHEISM; MORAL RELATIVISM; NIHILISM; POSTMODERNISM; SECULARIZATION

NOMINALISM   Nominalism is a position in philosophy or theology that in one way or another denies the real, extra-mental existence of any referent for "universals," that is, for universal terms, like *man*, considered in general such as in the sentence "Man is a rational animal." Classically, to nominalists, universals exist only in the human mind, and all really existing things are inherently *individual*. Nominalism is logically opposed to realism, which in some sense asserts the extra-mental existence of a real referent for universals.

Nominalism most especially refers to the nominalistic tendency that existed in a variety of different forms throughout the history of speculative thought of medieval Western Christendom, starting from the positions of such early antirealists as Roscelin (d. c. 1125). It became in many ways the dominant form of scholastic thought about universals in the 14th, 15th, and (in some places) 16th centuries, in the wake of the success of William of Ockham (d. c. 1348) and his intellectual offspring in defining the terms of the debate.

It is from Ockham that the term *nominalism* has acquired a broader association with a set of metaphysical and ethical positions, including radical application of the principle of parsimony (Ockham's razor) even to the point of reducing Aristotle's 10 categories of *being* to only two (substance and accident), denial of absolute certainty to any proposition whose opposite cannot be shown to involve a contradiction, assertion that God can do anything that does not involve a *logical* contradiction insofar as he does not freely bind himself otherwise by his promises and ordinances, and a stress on the relative freedom and ethical primacy of the human will as opposed to intellect on the pattern of the divine freedom. The emphasis on divine freedom and God's absolute power in Ockham's thought tends to accentuate the contingency of the natural created order. When combined with his reservations about the epistemological prospects of our intellect in earthly life, it results in an air of uncertainty around metaphysical truths like the existence of God and the immortality of the human soul, as compared to earlier generations of scholastic thinkers. A corollary of this is that theology and philosophy, according to Ockham, lie relatively further from each other in method and conclusions than they do for, say, St. Thomas Aquinas.

Earlier scholars were prone to attribute to Ockham and late medieval nominalism a "linguistic turn" in logic, which shifted the primary focus away from the relation of thought with being, to questions about the signification of words. Although all nominalist thinkers reflected this linguistic interest in their logical writings, in truth the fashion for a language-centered logic grew out of the earlier, 13th-century work of the moderate realist Peter of Spain. His "terminism" so defined the logical interests of the Late Middle Ages that even figures like the Thomist St. Vincent Ferrer (d. 1419) expounded logic according to the basic pattern it established.

Before saying more about any of these matters, it should be noted that scholarship of recent generations has shown late medieval nominalism to be a diverse movement, begetting a variety of important thinkers who could and did differ, even on fundamental questions. Although it took its general inspiration from him, it was far from being simply a "School of Ockham." For example, John Buridan (d. c. 1361), one of the most important of the Paris nominalists of the 14th century, was critical of Ockham's logic and embraced a position on the relation of will and intellect that was arguably closer to Aquinas's intellectualism than Ockham's voluntarism. Meanwhile, Buridan attacked the much more radical nominalism of his Paris colleague Nicolas of Autrecourt (d. c. 1369), who was willing to take Ockham's premises to more far reaching (and skeptical) conclusions than Ockham himself ever did, denying, for instance, that one could ever be certain of causes from a study of effects, or even that one could ever infer with certainty the existence of a substance from the existence of an accident. Very much unlike Ockham, he seems to have wielded the "razor" in order to deny there was any need to posit human free will as a real causal factor! Autrecourt thus foreshadowed in significant degree the position of certain modern philosophers, such as David Hume, on these issues. Uniquely among the major nominalist scholastics, some of his positions were formally condemned by the pope during his own lifetime.

Divergences from Ockham (and each other) can likewise be found among the English nominalists of the 14th century, such as the Franciscan Adam of Wodeham (d. 1358) and the Dominican Robert Holcott (d. 1349), whereas the Italian-born Gregory of Rimini (d. 1358), Prior General of the Augustinian Hermits, synthesized both French and English strains of nominalism with a rigorous Augustinianism. Many nominalists of the period spanning the late 14th to mid-15th centuries, on the other hand, were eclectics like Marsilius of Inghen (d. 1396) or Jean Gerson (d. 1429). Characteristically, they blended (sometimes liberally) ideas of non-nominalist scholastic thinkers, like Aquinas, into their thought. Only late in the 15th century did nominalism begin to coalesce into a clear "school" in self-conscious opposition to other scholastic approaches, especially a resurgent Thomism. What follows about nominalist ethics and political theory, therefore, will be based mostly on positions of Ockham, but with reference to the thought of others, as expedient.

Ockham's ethics reflect his voluntarism in that he stresses the complete freedom of God in establishing whatever moral order he willed in creation. Ockham therefore insists that God could have conceivably created a world with a notably different moral order than he actually did. Indeed, notoriously, Ockham argues that God could have, in his absolute power, created a moral order in which it would be virtuous to hate him, as it were, for the sake of a more fundamental love of him! This position was controversial enough that not all nominalist thinkers saw fit to agree with him, even among some of his more faithful followers, as in the case of Gabriel Biel (d. 1495).

It needs to be noted, though, that in Ockham's account God is not, in actual fact, capriciously willful. He has bound himself by establishing a certain natural order, and in addition, he has freely bound himself in a yet deeper way by revelation. Indeed, natural law is central to Ockham's political philosophy. Yet, the natural and supernatural moral orders tend to pull apart radically on further analysis in Ockham's thought. Natural law, as something accessible to the reason of even pagan philosophers, capable of being cultivated by them in natural human freedom, belongs to the sphere of virtues but not to the sphere of supernatural merit. This merit operates fundamentally by God's absolute power and alone infuses the charity toward God that makes him recognize a soul as his own and worthy of eternal life. God, in fact, by his ordered power has deigned to link supernatural merit with the virtues cultivated by human free will and (in a different way) with the actions of the sacramental ministry of the Church, but it was not necessary that he do so. Moreover, the continuous operation of grace is not so much *through* them as *together with* them. Although grace is thus inextricably bound up with the assent of human free will, as well as to the sacraments, its operation is already in an ontological sense quite alien from both in Ockham's theology, albeit in a very different way than they would be for Martin Luther. Most later nominalist theologians followed Ockham on these issues, although a few demurred in important ways, notably Gregory of Rimini, who protested in the name of St. Augustine that he gave too much scope in salvation to human free will.

Ockham's political and ecclesiological writings are the product of his last years and cannot be easily extricated from the struggle over the meaning of "apostolic poverty" carried on between Pope John XXII and those Franciscans (himself included) who wished to interpret it as strictly excluding any true ownership. To this end, Ockham argues that, according to natural law, Adam and Eve had no property, but only a natural right of use, and that even after the Fall, private property is only *possible*, not necessary, under natural law. Yet Ockham went further than this, as he was convinced that John XXII was actually a heretic for denying what previous popes had asserted on these issues and therefore no true pope. Under the influence of his protector, Louis of Bavaria, whose imperial claim Pope John had rejected, Ockham created a new synthesis of scholastic thought, certain canon and civil law conventions of self-governance, and the earlier imperialist tradition of medieval political theory. By his account, assent of the governed, however customarily given, is necessary to establishment of legitimate authority in Church or state, even for offices like the papacy, whose actual power flows straight from God. Likewise, any Christian can dissent from papal authority in the name of the Catholic truth, and "the wise," those with other kinds of authority (such as the emperor), can in an emergency intervene to depose a heretical or unworthy pope. Although the point is debated, some scholars have seen the influence of Ockham's voluntarism and stress on the metaphysical importance of the individual in this lionizing of popular assent.

Although Ockham explicitly rejected the claim of his more radically imperialist contemporary Marsilius of Padua (d. c. 1342) that the papacy is merely a human institution, he did closely analogize the pope to the emperor in terms of the limits of his ordinary authority. Just as the emperor can interfere in the affairs of the papacy only in emergencies, so it is with the pope in the affairs of the empire. Ockham not only denied the plenitude of papal power in civil affairs, but he even tended to slight the doctrinal role of the papacy and to see it merely as the seat of highest ecclesiastical jurisdiction.

Although Ockham's political thought was widely viewed as heterodox by later generations, the use of civil law models in formulating ecclesiology proved to be the spirit of the age. The unprecedented crisis of the Great Schism (1378–1415) eventually gave rise to the conciliarist movement, which, besides ending the schism at the Council of Constance under the leadership of the great nominalist theologians Pierre Cardinal D'Ailly (d. 1420) and his student Gerson, also asserted the role of the Council in the Church to be like that of the emerging parliaments in many late medieval monarchies. It should be pointed out, though, that nominalists of the period actually had a great variety of positions on controversial issues in political theory. For instance, whereas Buridan was a proponent of absolute monarchy, his student Nicole Oresme (d. 1382) argued for the superiority of Aristotle's mixed constitution and interpreted later medieval estates monarchies with their parliamentary institutions in Aristotelian terms. He also condemned some fiscal and economic practices often associated with monarchs of the time, such as inflationary debasement of the currency, which he argued violated the common good.

The position of nominalism in the history of the Church and Western civilization is paradoxical. On the one hand, there is no doubt that nominalism was once the mainstream position among Catholic theologians in many places in Europe (especially northern Europe) and that nominalist theologians took the lead in defending orthodoxy against the radical, antitraditional realism of John Wycliff (d. 1384) and his followers, among them the Czech Hussites. It is also notable that nominalists like Johannes Eck (d. 1543) were prominent among Luther's most consistent opponents in Germany, as he veered ever more sharply away from Catholic positions during his dispute with Rome over indulgences and justification. It cannot be denied that many men of undoubted piety were nominalists in theology—St. John Cantius (d. 1473) and Gerson, for instance (earlier in their respective careers, at least). Furthermore, late medieval natural philosophers, among whom nominalists were prominent, provided the leaders of the scientific revolution of the 17th century with some crucial ideas, as Buridan's student Albert of Saxony (d. 1390) did for Galileo on problems of motion, impetus, and acceleration. Indeed, it can be maintained that the nominalist tendency to see creation as ordered but deeply contingent may have encouraged a turn away from a more necessitarian Aristotelianism to an attitude that recommended empirical study of nature to determine just what kind of world God actually *did* create. Some have even seen the nominalist stress on a self-contained sphere of human free will in the created order as a kind of scholastic equivalent to the attitudes of contemporaneous Renaissance humanism and its exultation of the natural capacities of man.

Yet, on the other hand, it must be admitted that nominalism helped pave the way for the often caustic skepticism of modern thought by its hesitations about the ability of reason to prove metaphysical propositions like the immortality of the soul or even the existence of God. Some have argued its stress on God's absolute freedom, especially with regard to natural and revealed moral law, offended the religious sensibilities of the popular piety (and perhaps was even *intended* to shake up complacent religious sentimentality!), thus alienating many from rational theology and encouraging a certain tendency to implicit fideism not uncommon in the late Middle Ages. Indeed, many have discerned a fideistic tendency at the heart of nominalism itself, in its relatively sharp circumscription of what we can know about God by natural reason as opposed to by faith, and the tendency found in some nominalist theologians (like D'Ailly and Gerson) to denigrate speculative knowledge of God in favor of direct, mystical knowledge of him. It cannot be doubted the increasingly abstruse side of nominalist logic helped condition an overreaction by some Renaissance humanists against scholastic education in general. Furthermore, the subjective coloring of nominalist anthropology likely helped shape the religious subjectivism of the young Martin Luther, while providing him with few clear, workable answers to his doubts about justification. It needs to be remembered, though, that few, if any, of these consequences were foreseen, much less intended, by the founding thinkers of late medieval nominalism.—Paul J. Radzilowski

BIBLIOGRAPHY AND FURTHER READING: Black, Antony. *Political Thought in Europe, 1250–1450.* Cambridge: Cambridge University Press, 1992; Boehner, Philotheus, and Stephen F. Brown, eds. *Ockham: Philosophical Writings,* rev. ed. Indianapolis: Hackett, 1990; Gilson, Etienne. *History of Christian Philosophy in the Middle Ages.* London: Random House, 1954; Oberman, Heiko A. *The Harvest of Medieval Theology: Gabriel Biel and Late Medieval Nominalism,* 3rd ed. Grand Rapids, MI: Baker Book House, 2000; Spade, Paul Vincent, ed. *The Cambridge Companion to Ockham.* Cambridge: Cambridge University Press, 1999; Swiezawski, Stefan. *Dzieje Filozofii Europejskiej XV Wieku* [*The History of European Philosophy in the Fifteenth Century*]. Vols. 1–5. Warsaw: Akademia Teologii Katolickiej, 1974–1980; Vignaux, Paul. *Nominalisme au XIVe Siècle.* Montreal: Institute d'Études Médiévales, 1948; Zupko, Jack. *John Buridan: Portrait of a Fourteenth-Century Arts Master.* Notre Dame, IN: University of Notre Dame Press, 2003. *See also FIDES ET RATIO;* OCKHAM, WILLIAM OF; REASON

· O ·

OAKESHOTT, MICHAEL (1901–1990) Michael Oakeshott was a British philosopher of the 20th century, whose contributions included significant writings in political thought, the philosophy of history, and epistemology. He is perhaps best known for his critique of the "rationalist" spirit, which he saw encroaching on or eliminating traditional and customary ways of living and attaining knowledge, and for an analysis of the relationship between human freedom and civil association. Born in Chelsfield, Kent, Oakeshott, with the exception of service in World War II, spent nearly his entire adult life in academia, first at Cambridge University, then a brief stint at Oxford University, and from 1951 until his retirement at the London School of Economics.

Oakeshott's first major work, published in 1933, was *Experience and Its Modes,* a work that set forth his basic metaphysical and epistemological understanding of reality. It is an understanding steeped in the idealist philosophy of G. W. F. Hegel and the British Idealists, in which all reality (and the experience of reality) is understood as a world entirely of thoughts or ideas. We comprehend this world of ideas through what Oakeshott refers to as the modes of experience, which are various ways of understanding experience from a distinctive and particular perspective. Among the most prominent modes in contemporary human conduct are history (experience viewed under the category of the past), science (under the category of quantity) and, above all, practice (under the category of willful change). The practical mode is the one in which we live most of our lives, involving everything from changing our diet to changing our political party; it is the continual effort to change a given unsatisfactory situation into an ought-to-be. No mode, however, no matter how prominently it factors in our lives, can render a completely coherent account of experience. All have inherent limitations.

This last proposition suggests the motive force behind Oakeshott's difficult and dense treatise. Beyond elucidating an idealist epistemology, *Experience and Its Modes* urges the different modes to refrain from encroaching upon each other and pretending to be what they are not. It may be obvious that morality has nothing to say about the accuracy of a scientific formula, but it is perhaps less obvious that the reverse is also largely true. Science can help fashion a new drug, but it has nothing to say about the morality of using that drug to perform assisted suicide or euthanasia. Oakeshott was clearly alarmed by what he saw as the arrogance of certain disciplines presuming to dictate conclusions to others, and above all by what has come to be known as scientism—the belief that all reality can be best understood through the premises and methods of science. From this perspective, *Experience and Its Modes* is Oakeshott's opening salvo in a lifelong battle against not only scientism but all forms of reductionism, which he saw as always corrupting and harmful.

In the later 1930s, Oakeshott's focus shifted noticeably. In *Experience and Its Modes*, political theory is little discussed, and amid citations of Hegel, Immanuel Kant, John Stuart Mill, and the various British Idealists, there is not one of Thomas Hobbes, the philosopher about whom Oakeshott would write most often. Yet only two years later, Oakeshott published his first essay on Hobbes, in 1946 his famous introduction to *Leviathan* appeared, and nearly 50 years later, Hobbes would figure significantly in Oakeshott's last major political writing, "The Rule of Law" (1983).

Scholars debate just why and how Oakeshott's turn to Hobbes arose, but it seems reasonable to speculate that the rise of the totalitarian movements and a world war were significant in chastening enthusiasm for the progressive and statist implications of Hegelian and idealist thought. In Hobbes, Oakeshott seems to have found a more sober and skeptical account of the state, shorn of any perfectionist temptations. Most strikingly, Oakeshott argues that Hobbes was a kind of proto-liberal, one who "is not an absolutist precisely because he is an authoritarian" (*Rationalism in Politics*, 282). Oakeshott meant in part that, for Hobbes, acknowledging the legitimacy of political authority did not require affirming the truth or rightness of any given laws it might make. One was free to retain one's convictions about a host of matters, while acknowledging the need for civil authority to preserve the peace. This insight into the dynamic between political authority and freedom would be a central concern of Oakeshott's ongoing philosophical reflections on politics.

In 1962, *Rationalism in Politics*, a collection of Oakeshott's essays, was published. It remains his best known work and is generally considered the best entrée into his thought. Underlying the disparate topics of *Rationalism in Politics* is a recurring theme, a kind of warning to humanity against those Oakeshott viewed as the dubious characters of our time: the Ideologue, the Collectivist, the Utopian, the Determinist, the Reductionist, and their ringleader, the Rationalist. For Oakeshott, all of these characters stand indicted for undermining life as an adventure—a unique, freely chosen, and unpredictable journey—and seeking to replace it with life as mechanism, complete with owner's manual. The Rationalist, for example—not to be confused with the man of reason, but a character who emerges from the post-Renaissance, post-Reformation crisis of faith—can abide neither the untidiness of the traditionalist, living life according to custom and habit, nor the idio-syncratic ways of the bohemian. Both stymie progress. For the Rationalist, endless progress is ours to achieve if we embrace life's difficulties as a series of scientific and technological problems to be solved—finding the "rational" solution to everything from a better garden to a better marriage.

Oakeshott's most sustained and systematic reflections on political thought occur in *On Human Conduct* (1975). Here Oakeshott demonstrates the essential character of free agency in the human individual, the theoretical character of political society best suited for such an individual (what Oakeshott calls simply "civil association"), and Europe's historical record in approximating such a civil association in practice. In the ideal civil association, government is the proverbial traffic officer, disinterested as to where any particular citizen is going, but wanting to ensure that all reach their destinations safely and with minimal interference to each other. It is the politics of free individuals pursuing their infinitely varied goals and interests in peace and order. By contrast, the rationalist ruler already knows what is best for his citizens, and therefore what their goals and interests *should* be, even if they in their ignorance disagree. All that remains for the state is to effectively harness citizen energies and resources to achieve such goals, whether in the hard collectivism of the totalitarian state or the soft collectivism of the welfare state. Oakeshott tended to downplay any moral to be drawn from his works, characterizing them usually as philosophical inquiries, and *On Human Conduct* is certainly that. But it is also clearly a broadside at the collectivist ideology that had been so dominant in the 20th century and that in 1975 showed no signs of receding anytime soon.

In 1983, Oakeshott published his last major work, *On History, and Other Essays*, and no treatment of Oakeshott would be complete without at least a brief mention of his understanding of history—the field to which, after political theory, he devoted his most intense reflection. Essentially, Oakeshott sought to both understand what makes the historical past different from other modes of the past and, as seen in *Experience and Its Modes*, to protect history from being overwhelmed by other modes and especially by the practical past. Where the practical mode seeks to use the past to justify and validate present concerns and beliefs, the distinct achievement of history is precisely to eschew such goals in favor of simply making the past more intelligible by showing how different events are contingent (touch upon each other) in time and place. Oakeshott profoundly admires the intellectual achievement of wresting the historical mode from other perspectives on the past (analogous, he notes, to astronomy evolving from astrology), and he is zealous to preserve it. Toward that end, he never says that the working historian must be utterly pure in remaining within the historical mode (a perspective that would disqualify most of the great works of history), but at the very least he should be cognizant of when he has slipped into the practical past. Analyzing the events that most coherently explain the Confederacy's defeat in the U.S. Civil War is, Oakeshott wants to insist, something quite different from describing the war as America's greatest tragedy.

Of the many aspects of Oakeshott's life and intellectual pursuits, one of the more difficult to discern is his relationship to Christianity, a matter that still awaits further biographical studies. In terms of his writings, a number of Oakeshott's earliest essays (written in the 1920s) deal with Christianity, but it must be said that when read chronologically they suggest a man gradually moving away from an orthodox understanding of the faith. The bulk of his mature writings has very little to say about religion. *On Human Conduct* contains a brief but eloquent affirmation of the role religious belief plays in dealing with the sufferings and trials of the human condition, but, if not denying, certainly gives no ringing affirmation of the truth of religious belief itself. While Oakeshott was far from indulging in the hostility toward Christianity found in so many contemporary intellectuals—he had sympathy for the moral contributions it has made, as well as for its appreciation of the mystery in human existence that yields to no ready calculus—he seemed to remain something of a sympathetic skeptic.

Catholic social thinkers will part ways with Oakeshott in his seeming unwillingness to acknowledge moral absolutes, or at least to acknowledge such traditional foundations for them as natural law and divine sanction. And in his concern for the individual, Oakeshott has been criticized for giving too little thought regarding the intermediate associations of society as well as for the demands of the common good. On the other hand, such thinkers will likely sympathize with Oakeshott's defense of human freedom, the uniqueness of the individual, and the value of tradition, as well as in his anti-utopianism, which owes more than a little to St. Augustine. In fact, Augustine is one of the thinkers Oakeshott came to admire most (even if he never got around to writing significantly about him), no doubt because few persons had better understood man's earthly limitations or reflected more soberly on their implications for politics. Oakeshott may not be as sure as Augustine about where man's ultimate goal lies, but he is quite sure it is not to be found lurking somewhere in the Houses of Parliament.—Paul T. Foster

BIBLIOGRAPHY AND FURTHER READING: Corey, Elizabeth Campbell. *Michael Oakeshott on Religion, Aesthetics, and Politics.* Columbia: University of Missouri Press, 2006; Franco, Paul. *The Political Philosophy of Michael Oakeshott.* New Haven, CT: Yale University Press, 1990; Fuller, Timothy. "The Work of Michael Oakeshott." *Political Theory* 19 (August 1991): 326–333; Gerencser, Steven Anthony. *The Skeptic's Oakeshott.* New York: St. Martin's Press, 2000; Grant, Robert. *Oakeshott.* London: Claridge Press, 1990. *See also* AUTHORITY; HEGEL, GEORG WILHELM FRIEDRICH; HOBBES, THOMAS; POLITICAL PHILOSOPHY; TRADITION

O'CONNOR, FLANNERY (1925–1964) Flannery O'Connor is a leading Catholic fiction writer of the 20th century. She was born Mary Flannery O'Connor in Savannah, Georgia, on March 25, 1925, the only child of Edward and Regina (Cline) O'Connor. Both of her parents came from long-standing Southern Catholic families. When she was 12, her family moved to the small town of Milledgeville, the former antebellum capital of Georgia, so that her father could take a job with the Federal Housing Administration. When she was 15, her father died of disseminated lupus erythematosus, a debilitating autoimmune disease. After attending mostly parochial schools, Flannery enrolled in the Georgia State College for Women, earning a social sciences degree in 1945.

Always a bookish person, Flannery discovered in college her talent for writing fiction. From 1945 to 1947, she studied at the famous Writer's Workshop at the University of Iowa, developing friendships with some of America's most noted writers, friendships she would cultivate her entire life. After earning her master of fine arts degree in 1947, she studied at Yaddo, the celebrated writer's colony in New York.

Her Northern idyll came to an abrupt end in 1951 when she was diagnosed with lupus, the incurable disease that killed her father. She returned to her 500-acre family dairy farm, Andalusia, located 12 miles outside of Milledgeville to live with her mother. For the remainder of her life, her daily routine consisted of taking care of the peafowl and other birds on the farm, suffering through cortisone treatments for lupus, practicing her Catholic faith, and writing.

From an early age, O'Connor took a rigorous, disciplined approach to the craft of writing. Her 32 published short stories are replete with trenchant prose, brilliant imagery, and dramatic effect. Her first novel, *Wise Blood* (1952), reveals that O'Connor had both assimilated the work of contemporary writers, most notably Nathanael West's *Miss Lonelyhearts*, and achieved an original style of her own. In her second and final novel, *The Violent Bear It Away* (1960), O'Connor powerfully combines Old and New Testament themes of prophecy, baptism, sin, and forgiveness.

All of O'Connor's fiction shows a startling maturity and consistency of style. Her stories are set in the Deep South, and her fiction incorporates the racial antagonisms of her region. Her characters are haunted by religious quests and confronted with stark epiphanies and searing moral choices. O'Connor's prose is spare and wry, her imagery pointed. Her stories consist mostly of dialogue, and with her great talent for irony and for dialect, the words of her characters reveal layers of unintended meaning, as well as unwitting humor and genuine comic effect.

Although O'Connor is often described as a writer of Southern gothic or grotesque fiction, she considered herself as foremost a Catholic writer. While there are occasional Catholic characters and explicit references to the Eucharist in her fiction—such as in "A Temple of the Holy Ghost"—O'Connor drew mostly on the Protestant landscape of rural Georgia. Paradoxically, she was best able to plumb Catholic themes by means of her often extravagantly Protestant and primitive characters, who seek to inflict Christ on a bland, secular world. Her stories bring to the surface an ironic humor that underlies even the most pained religious search. In *Wise Blood*, the protagonist Hazel Motes preaches "the Church of Christ without Christ." O'Connor neither condemns nor mocks her religious zealots; their absurdities point to a transcendent world, opposed to nihilistic visions of other modern authors. The highlight of her stories, she wrote, is the sudden opportunity for grace that overtakes her protagonist, which must be accepted or denied. In her story "The River," for example, she makes use of a Protestant ritual of a crude baptism in a local river to uncover themes of original sin, blasphemy, the Fall, cleansing, and accidental grace.

O'Connor's Catholic faith underlies her fiction, but in her essays and speeches her religious devotion is explicit. She wrote the essay "The Church and the Fiction Writer" for the March 30, 1957, issue of *America* and "The Catholic Novelist in the Protestant South" in 1963. Her marvelously phrased and wide-ranging letters disclose her profound Catholic belief, her prayer life, and her daily attendance at Mass. The suffering brought on by her disease deepened her faith; she accepted and did not protest her condition. O'Connor described the Eucharist as the "center" of her existence: "All the rest of life is expendable."

Since her premature death from lupus at the age of 39 on August 3, 1964, her reputation as a writer has magnified. Her literary work has been examined in numerous full-length studies and journal articles. *Wise Blood* has entered the canon of American classical literature, and her finest short stories such as "A Good Man Is Hard to Find," "The Artificial Nigger," "The Late Encounter with the Enemy," The Life You Save May Be Your Own," "Everything That Rises Must Converge," "Parker's Back," and "Judgment Day" are classics of the form. O'Connor's essays and lectures were collected and published in 1969 with the title *Mystery and Manners*. In 1971, her *Complete Stories* was published, winning the National Book Award. Her letters were published in 1979 with the title *The Habit of Being*. In 1988, the Library of America published her *Collected Works*; she was the first post–World War II writer to be included in this prestigious series. Her reputation as a great American author and one of the greatest of modern Catholic writers is secure.—Howard Bromberg

BIBLIOGRAPHY AND FURTHER READING: Gooch, Brad. *Flannery: A Life of Flannery O'Connor*. New York: Little, Brown, 2009; Gordon, Sarah. *Flannery O'Connor: The Obedient Imagination*. Athens: University of Georgia Press, 2003; Kilcourse, George, Jr. *Flannery O'Connor's Religious Imagination: A World with Everything Off Balance*. New York: Paulist Press, 2001; McMullen, Joanne, and Jon Peede, eds. *Inside the Church of Flannery O'Connor: Sacrament, Sacramental, and the Sacred in Her Fiction*. Macon, GA: Mercer University Press, 2007; Murray, Lorraine. *The Abbess of Andalusia: Flannery O'Connor's Spiritual Journey*. Charlotte, NC: St. Benedict Press, 2009; Wood, Ralph. *Flannery O'Connor and the Christ-Haunted South*. Grand Rapids, MI: Eerdmans, 2004. *See also* EVIL IN CHRISTIAN LITERATURE; LEWIS, C. S.; LITERATURE; PERCY, WALKER

O'CONNOR, JOHN CARDINAL (1920–2000)

John O'Connor, who was to become the archbishop of New York from 1984 to 2000, was born on January 20, 1920, the fourth of five children in what he called a blue-collar, "ordinary family" in southwest Philadelphia, a neighborhood of Irish-, Italian-, and Eastern European–descended families. Thomas and Dorothy O'Connor raised their children in an atmosphere of religious devotion that included appreciation of the human rights of working people. Thomas was a skilled interior painter, specializing in the installation of gold leaf on the ornamental ceilings of auditoriums and churches. O'Connor described his father as a "union man" with a concern for justice and the dignity of the individual person and with little sympathy for those he perceived to be "multimillionaire[s]" who "had made [their] money on the backs of the poor or [by] exploiting the coal miners or the railroad workers."

O'Connor attended public and Catholic schools before entering St. Charles Borromeo Seminary in Wynnewood, Pennsylvania. He was ordained in 1945. During his subsequent seven years of service as assistant pastor in a Philadelphia parish, he also taught in Catholic high schools, ministered in psychiatric wards, and established special programs for the instruction of mentally handicapped children, whose care remained one of his lifelong concerns.

During the Korean War, O'Connor became a Navy chaplain—a two-year stint that would become a 27-year career. In 1964, after assignments at sea and stateside, O'Connor joined the Third Marine Division and accompanied it on a combat tour in Vietnam. There, he celebrated Mass daily, sometimes under fire, tended the wounded, counseled traumatized soldiers, wrote letters to families of the dead, and ventured into combat zones where soldiers were otherwise without pastoral care. For his courage and dedication, he was awarded the Legion of Merit.

He continued his chaplaincy at the Marine Corps school in Quantico, where he implemented religious instruction specifically tailored to the base's mentally handicapped children, working actively to identify and draw out children whose existence had previously gone ignored and unspoken, a product of social stigma. Moreover, rather than living in the officers' quarters to which he was entitled, he lived off base so that service members could visit him in privacy. While at Quantico, O'Connor earned his PhD in political science at Georgetown University and attained the rank of rear admiral. After 27 years, he retired from uniformed service in 1979 when Pope John Paul II ordained him auxiliary bishop of the military vicariate, the diocese overseeing U.S. military chaplains across the world.

Although he wholeheartedly backed the United States' involvement in Vietnam at the time, O'Connor later tempered and reformulated his views. He stepped back from his stance that intervention was morally necessary to stop Communist expansion and liberate the South Vietnamese. In doing so, he noted his prior failure to take into account the war's enormous cost in resources and innocent lives, the brutal experiences of American forces on the ground, and the political motivations of many Washington decision makers. He

would later condemn American aid to counterrevolutionary guerrillas in Central America; question the development of ever more dangerous weapon systems; participate in a National Conference of Catholic Bishops (NCCB) committee that rejected the testing, development, and deployment of nuclear weapons and condoned their possession strictly for deterrent purposes; and criticize, according to just-war principles, the moral justification for the 1999 NATO bombardments in the former Yugoslavia.

While O'Connor served only eight months as bishop of Scranton, Pennsylvania, his time there affirmed his commitment to human dignity and workers' rights. Installed in June 1983, he made the welfare of teachers in the diocese's Catholic schools—whose attempts to organize for better wages had been rebuffed in the past by parish principals and pastors—a central priority. In his first letter to the diocesan priests, he insisted that a just wage for parish teachers was "absolutely essential" and made clear that every teacher had a right to form bargaining associations without fear of pressure, harassment, or other retaliation. (Conversely, he also asserted the right of any teacher freely *not* to associate.) O'Connor came through on this promise, setting in motion a substantial pay increase for teachers in the diocese's parochial schools.

He was also known for his mixture of compassion and ebullience—ministering to the handicapped, visiting the bedsides of the sick, marching in Labor Day festivals, conversing with students at the local university. Also during this time, he disseminated videos emphasizing the NCCB position against the testing, production, and deployment of new nuclear weapons systems and oversaw the appointment of Mary Ellen Keating as diocesan director of communications, the first laywoman to be named to such a high position in the Scranton diocese.

O'Connor was appointed the archbishop of New York in 1984 and was named a cardinal in 1985. During his tenure in New York, O'Connor never wavered from Vatican doctrine on issues such as abortion and homosexuality. Just before his installation at St. Patrick's Cathedral in March 1984, the soon-to-be archbishop appeared on a New York talk show and discussed his views on abortion, equating the practice with Nazi extermination policies. These comments provoked backlash from Jewish groups—the cardinal had stated, unartfully, "Now, Hitler tried to solve a problem, the Jewish question." Moreover, women's rights organizations were incensed that the painful choice to undergo an abortion should be equated with Nazi activity at Dachau. The cardinal was known as a vigorous proponent of pro-life views. Among other initiatives, he inspired the founding of the Sisters of Life, a new religious community whose members take a special vow to protect and enhance the sacredness of human life. As recognition of his role in defending life, there is an annual student conference (the Cardinal O'Connor Conference on Life) held at Georgetown University in conjunction with the March of Life.

The cardinal also strongly opposed the extension of equal employment rights to homosexuals, immediately taking over the archdiocese's ongoing legal challenge to a mayoral order prohibiting employment discrimination on the basis of sexual orientation among city contractors. He would later denounce a city council bill protecting homosexuals from discrimination as shielding sin and sponsor a subsequent referendum drive for its repeal. O'Connor's outspokenness on these matters prompted the *New York Times* to recommend he adopt a "change of tone" if he hoped to be effective as archbishop of New York. While never backing down from these principles, he did drop the abortion–Holocaust analogy and mended fences with Jewish leaders around the world, including participating in the 1993 peace talks between Israelis and Palestinians.

Moreover, despite his opposition to gay rights legislation, O'Connor was dedicated—even in the face of opposition—to caring for the victims of the AIDS epidemic. When Queens and Upper West Side residents protested vehemently against archdiocesan plans to house homeless AIDS patients in treatment centers there, he did not back down. The cardinal, working in conjunction with Mother Teresa, remained committed to the plan of providing archdiocesan facilities for their housing. In fact, the archdiocese had been operating a shelter for AIDS victims at a location kept undisclosed for the protection and privacy of its residents. The archdiocese had also established a hotline for victims to obtain referrals for screening and placement.

Cardinal O'Connor made the promotion of workers' rights a central component of his leadership as archbishop of New York. In 1984, health care workers reached an agreement with the League of Voluntary Hospitals and Homes—representing some 48 private hospitals and nursing homes in New York City: In return for a 5% raise, the workers agreed to end their 47-day strike. The league, however, never fulfilled its end of the bargain, an action upheld in 1985 by the National Labor Relations Board when challenged by Local 1199 of the Drug, Hospital and Health Care Employees Union, which represented health care workers on the lower ends of the pay spectrum such as technicians, nurses, nurses' aides, housekeepers, ward clerks, cooks, and social workers. Even though four archdiocesan hospitals were League members, O'Connor announced that he was prepared to honor the 1984 deal, instructing the head of the archdiocese's hospitals division to reach a just contract with the union without regard to potential conflicts with the league. The archdiocese followed through on its promise. In 1986, O'Connor announced that he had reached an agreement with the Local 1199 workers at the archdiocese's hospitals that reinstated the original agreement that the League had broken and applied the 5% raise retroactively from 1984.

O'Connor would continue to advocate on behalf of Local 1199, and his willingness to provide just wages to the archdiocese's hospital employees would have a resounding effect for employees in many nonarchdiocesan hospitals. In 1987, the cardinal and Jesse Jackson, along with Local 1199 president Georgiana Johnson, called on the city to increase wages and benefits for home health care workers, which were largely dictated by city, state, and federal subsidies to the agencies that employed them.

Perhaps his most significant work on behalf of Local 1199 occurred in conjunction with the efforts of Johnson's successor as president, Dennis Rivera. In 1989, the archdiocese agreed to annual pay increases of 8.5% per year and an array of benefit improvements such as child care, increased pension contributions, and voluntary training programs to give workers the ability to obtain more skilled positions. While the contract covered only 4,200 of the union's members, it put significant pressure on other institutions in the League of Voluntary Hospitals and Homes, who together employed some 50,000 Local 1199 workers, to agree to similarly favorable terms. In fact, several months later another league hospital agreed to a contract covering its own Local 1199 employees containing very similar provisions; in doing so, the hospital admitted that the archdiocese's agreement had materially advanced the union's bargaining position. In a matter of days, Rivera's coordinated efforts led to agreements covering all Local 1199 workers employed by league members that would produce salary increases of some 21% over the next three years. In 1992, O'Connor and Rivera again teamed up to organize a massive rally in opposition to Gov. Mario Cuomo's proposed Medicaid cuts that, the cardinal asserted, could "only make the poor poorer" and make the already inadequate health care system worse.

O'Connor also worked on behalf of labor associations in sectors other than health care. He negotiated on behalf of striking members of the Newspaper Guild of New York and, when Rupert Murdoch took over the *New York Post*, pleaded with Murdoch to treat fairly the guild members who had lost their jobs as a result of the strike by rehiring them rather than finding new employees. Behind the scenes, O'Connor spearheaded the drive to unionize thousands of limousine drivers in New York City, as well. He delivered testimony in Congress denouncing corporations' practice of simply firing and replacing those employees who organize and strike for better wages and treatment. Generally, the cardinal was recognized as playing an integral role in the resurgence of cooperation between clergy and workers for the promotion of workers' welfare.

In one of his last sermons before succumbing to complications from brain cancer, O'Connor reaffirmed his commitment to the labor cause. He reminded the audience of his father Thomas and his union roots, quipping to an assemblage of labor leaders, "I [insist] that my casket have a union label." He announced the formation, in partnership with the New York City Central Labor Council, of a Commission on the Dignity of Immigrants to aid them in employment grievances, as well as in areas such as discrimination and naturalization.

Cardinal O'Connor died on May 3, 2000. His death occasioned the issuance by Local 1199 of a tribute, calling him "the patron saint of working people" and quoting Rivera saying, "He was a very important figure in the lives of our organization and was a defender of the rights of working people." For his championing of labor rights, Congress posthumously awarded the cardinal the Congressional Gold Medal, the highest honor that Congress can bestow on a civilian.

This outpouring of respect can be summed up by O'Connor's response in a 1993 interview to a question regarding the disconnect between the pervasive lip service paid to religion in popular culture and politics and the actual practice of the Church's social teaching: "For too long a time there was a danger in our forgetting that the church is always countercultural. When the culture seems to be completely sympathetic with the church, there is always the danger of the church being lulled into the values of the culture [and forgetting the] sense of urgency about converting the culture. Nevertheless, I think this culture can be converted."—Daniella E. Keller and David L. Gregory

BIBLIOGRAPHY AND FURTHER READING: Hentoff, Nat. "Profiles: I'm Finally Going to Be a Pastor." *New Yorker*, March 23, 1987; O'Connor, John J. *A Chaplain Looks at Vietnam*. Cleveland: World, 1968; Pace, Eric. "Catholic Hospital Employees Will Receive 5 Percent Raise." *New York Times*, September 26, 1986; Pace, Eric. "Ruling Backs Hospital League." *New York Times*, September 8, 1985; Steinfels, Peter. "Death of a Cardinal; Cardinal O'Connor, 80, Dies; Forceful Voice for Vatican." *New York Times*, May 4, 2000. *See also* ABORTION; BURKE, CARDINAL RAYMOND LEO; "DOCTRINAL NOTE ON SOME QUESTIONS REGARDING THE PARTICIPATION OF CATHOLICS IN POLITICAL LIFE"; NUCLEAR WEAPONS; SISTERS OF LIFE; UNIONS

ORIGINAL SIN The dogma of original sin is essential for a proper understanding of Catholic social doctrine. The *Compendium of the Social Doctrine of the Church*, issued by the Pontifical Council for Justice and Peace in 2004, notes that the "marvelous vision of man's creation by God is inseparable from the tragic appearance of original sin" (# 115). A similar observation is made by Pope Benedict XVI in his 2009 encyclical *Caritas in Veritate*: "The Church's wisdom has always pointed to the presence of original sin in social conditions and in the structure of society" (# 34).

The *Catechism of the Catholic Church* describes original sin as "the deprivation of original justice and holiness" (# 405). Unlike personal sin, original sin involves a sin that is "contracted" and not "committed." This is why original sin can be called sin "only in an analogical sense," since it is "a state and not an act" (*CCC* # 404).

The dogma of original sin underscores the truth that moral evil does not come from God but from the choices of free and rational creatures. God created everything good (Genesis 1: 31), but angels and men have sinned, and because of this, "*moral evil*, incommensurably more harmful than physical evil, entered the world" (*CCC* # 311). Because the devil, represented by the serpent, induces man to sin (Genesis 3), the fall of the angels must have preceded the fall of man. The Catholic Church teaches that "the devil and the other demons were indeed created by God naturally good, but they became evil by their own doing. As for man, he sinned at the suggestion of the devil" ("Profession of Faith of the Fourth Lateran Council"; Denz-Hün, 800). The fall of the angels is not explicitly described in Scripture. Theologians have explained this fall in various ways down through the centuries, usually as a combination of pride and envy toward God. Some, like the Jesuit Francisco Suárez (1548–1617), have suggested that Lucifer rebelled when God revealed his plan to become man.

The introduction of moral evil into cosmic history by the fall of the angels is followed by the fall of man, which is described in the third chapter of Genesis using "figurative language" (*CCC* # 393). Even though the biblical description of the fall is figurative, it refers to a "primeval event, a deed that took place at the beginning of the history of man" (cf. *CCC* # 393; *GS* # 13). The consequences of the fall of Adam and Eve disclose the fundamental effects of original sin: namely, death and corruption (Genesis 3: 19), suffering and hardship (Genesis 3: 16–19), and the tendency to sin, which is shown by the murder of Cain (Genesis 4: 8) and the increase of human wickedness (Genesis 6: 5).

While the narrative of the Fall in Genesis 3 is foundational for the dogma of original sin, the Church believes that this dogma can only be grasped in light of Christ, the Redeemer (cf. *CCC* # 388–389). Thus, the New Testament is essential for knowing the deeper truth about original sin: that all human beings are implicated in Adam's sin just as Christ offered sacrifice for the sins of all men (cf. Romans 5: 12–21; *CCC* # 402–403). Although Genesis 3 describes Eve as sinning first, the Pauline doctrine of Christ as "the New Adam" points to original sin as the "sin of Adam" because Adam is "the type of the one who was to come" (Romans 5: 14).

Early Church Fathers such as St. Irenaeus (c. 130–202) describe Mary as "the New Eve" who parallels Christ, the New Adam. The doctrine of Mary as the new Eve and "Mother of the living" (cf. Genesis 3: 20) contains the seeds of the dogma of the Immaculate Conception solemnly defined by Pope Pius IX in 1854: Mary as the Mother of the New Adam was preserved free from all stain of original sin from the first instant of her conception. This was due to "the singular grace and privilege of Almighty God" and "in view of the merits of Jesus Christ, the Savior of the human race" (Denz-Hün, 2803). Moreover, because of her preservation from original sin, Mary never underwent bodily corruption when her earthly life was over. This is the dogma of the Assumption, solemnly defined by Pope Pius XII in 1950, who decided to leave open the question whether Mary died before being assumed, body and soul, into the glory of heaven. If she did die, however, it was not because of original sin. According to Suárez, Mary died not because of original sin, but because she wished to be in solidarity with her Son's death and resurrection.

The Church recognizes that the transmission of original sin "is a mystery that we cannot fully understand" (*CCC* # 404). Following the writings of St. Augustine, the Church rejected the teaching of Pelagius (c. 355–425), who believed the sin of Adam was one of bad example and that original sin harmed only Adam and Eve and not their descendents (cf. Denz-Hün, 222, 223, 239, 371, 372, 1510–1514). The Council of Trent, in 1546, repeated the earlier condemnations of Pelagianism and taught that original sin "is transmitted by propagation, not by imitation" (Denz-Hün, 1513) and "is in all men, proper to each" (*CCC* # 404; cf. Denz-Hün, 223, 231).

There have been debates about how original sin is transmitted. Some (e.g., Peter Lombard, 1100–1160) believed that original sin is contracted by the lust or concupiscence that accompanies every sexual act, even in marriage. This view, sometimes attributed (incorrectly) to St. Augustine is no longer held. Instead, the view of St. Thomas Aquinas expressed in *Summa Theologica* (I–II, q. 81, art. 1) is generally accepted. According to this view, original sin is transmitted by the human nature received in human propagation, a human nature that is linked, materially and morally, to the sin of Adam (cf. *CCC* # 404).

The theory of evolution does not challenge the transmission of original sin. In his 1950 encyclical *Humani Generis*, Pius XII taught that Catholics were free to pursue research into evolutionism insofar as it pertains to the outward bodily form, but not with respect to the immortal soul, which is immediately created by God (Denz-Hün, 3896). Pius XII, however, believed it important to uphold "monogenism" (the belief in a single human origin) over "polygenism" (the belief in multiple human origins) because "it is in no way apparent how such an opinion [polygenism] can be reconciled with what the sources of revealed truth and the documents of the Church's Magisterium propose with regard to original sin, which proceeds from a sin actually committed by an individual Adam and which, through generation, is passed on to all and is in everyone as his own" (cf. Denz-Hün, 3897; Romans 5: 12–19).

Following the teachings of Aquinas, many Catholic theologians distinguish between the "formal aspect" of original sin, which is the "deprivation of original holiness and justice," and the material effects, which are primarily bodily death, ignorance, suffering, and concupiscence, that is, the inclination to sin (cf. *CCC* # 405). Original sin, therefore, involves both the deprivation of holiness (sanctifying grace) and a wounded human nature. This deprivation of sanctifying grace is overcome by baptism, which, "by imparting the life of Christ's grace, erases original sin and turns a man back towards God" (*CCC* # 405). The material effects of original sin, however, persist in man after baptism and "summon him to spiritual battle" (*CCC* # 405; cf. *STh* I–II, q. 82, art. 3).

The Catholic Church's understanding of original sin differs somewhat from that of most Eastern Orthodox, who tend to understand original sin as primarily solidarity in death and human weakness. Father John Meyendorff, for example, believes that the consensus in the Orthodox tradition is to identify original sin as mortality and weakness rather than inherited guilt. He links the Latin understanding of original sin as "inherited guilt" to the Vulgate translation of Romans 5: 12: "Sin came into the world through one man and death through sin, and so death spread to all men as all sinned in him (*in quo omnes peccaverunt*)." According to Meyendorff, the Greek phrase "*eph ho pantes hemarton*" should be more accurately translated as "because all have sinned," not "as all sinned in him." Recent Catholic translations of the Bible agree with Meyendorff on the translation of Romans 5: 12, but the Vulgate notion of inherited guilt can still be found in Romans 5: 19 if not 5: 12.

The Catholic understanding of original sin also differs from that of classical Protestant theologians such as Martin Luther and John Calvin, who tended to understand human nature after the Fall as totally depraved and corrupt rather than wounded. Moreover, they tended to believe that concupiscence itself is sin and not simply the inclination toward sin. For Luther, this meant that we are justified solely by the imputation of Christ's justice (*simul justus et peccator*). We are *declared* just rather than *made* just. The Council of Trent in 1547 rejected this Protestant understanding of justification as well as the Lutheran-Calvinist denial of free will in fallen man (cf. Denz-Hün, 1529, 1554, 1555).

Liberal Protestantism tends to downplay classical Protestant themes such as human depravity, sin, and damnation. Instead, the emphasis is on ethics and the "social gospel." Jesus is seen more as a model of human righteousness in solidarity with the oppressed rather than the Redeemer of fallen man. This deemphasis on original sin has also influenced certain movements of contemporary Catholicism, especially "liberation theology." The deemphasis extends, at times, to the abandonment of the teaching that "baptism or the desire for it" is necessary for salvation (cf. the Council of Trent's Decree on Justification; Denz-Hün, 1524). Once original sin is obscured, then the need for faith in Christ, baptism,

and membership in the Church is also diminished. It is not surprising then that new forms of Pelagianism have emerged as well as various forms of religious relativism and indifferentism. If there really is no deprivation of grace due to original sin, then the need for Jesus as the Savior can be obscured or abandoned.

In contrast to these liberal notions, recent magisterial documents have reaffirmed the dogma of original sin. The Second Vatican Council observed that "from the very onset of his history man abused his liberty, at the urging of the Evil One. Man set himself against God and sought to attain his goal apart from God" (*GS* # 13). In his 1966 address to theologians at a symposium on original sin, Pope Paul VI criticized those authors who more or less deny "that the sin which has been such an abundant source of evils for mankind has consisted above all in the disobedience which Adam, the first man and figure of the future Adam, committed at the beginning of history" (*AAS* 58 [1966]: 654). In his 1968 "Credo of the People of God," Paul VI reaffirmed the dogma of original sin as taught by the Council of Trent. Pope John Paul II devoted his Wednesday general audiences of September 8–October 8, 1986, to the topic of original sin, noting that the dogma of original sin can help modern man cope with the more "mysterious and distressing aspects of evil" and prevent him from wavering between "a hasty and unjustified optimism and a radical pessimism bereft of hope." Pope Benedict XVI reflected on the all too obvious effects of original sin in his general audience of December 3, 2008, noting that "as a consequence of this evil power in our souls, a murky river developed . . . which poisons the geography of human history."

The dogma of original sin helps to explain the mystery of evil in human history. It also serves as an antidote to superficial optimism and despondent pessimism. From a Catholic perspective, original sin is a truth that moves us toward deeper faith and trust in Jesus Christ, the Savior of the human race.—Robert L. Fastiggi

BIBLIOGRAPHY AND FURTHER READING: Denzinger, Heinrich, and Peter Hünermann. *Enchiridion symbolorum definitionum et declarationum de rebus fidei et morum*, 40th ed. Freiburg: Herder, 2005; Haffner, Paul. *The Mystery of Creation*, rev. ed. Herefordshire, England: Gracewing, 2010; Meyendorff, John. *Byzantine Theology*. New York: Fordham University Press, 1974; Yarnold, Edward, SJ. *The Theology of Original Sin*. Notre Dame, IN: Fides, 1971. *See also* CATECHISM OF THE CATHOLIC CHURCH; EVIL; PELAGIANISM; SIN (PERSONAL AND SOCIAL)

OTTAVIANI, CARDINAL ALFREDO (1890–1979) *Semper Idem* ("Always the Same"): This was the episcopal motto of Cardinal Alfredo Ottaviani. As Christ is the same yesterday, today, and tomorrow, so is the deposit of the faith, of which Ottaviani was for years the chief defender as the pope's right hand in his role as head of what was then the Holy Office and is now the Congregation for the Doctrine of the Faith (CDF).

Born in the popular Roman district of Trastevere in 1890, Ottaviani was educated at the Pontifical Roman Seminary and the Athenaeum St. Apollinare (now the Lateran University), obtaining doctorates in philosophy, theology, canon law, and civil law. Ordained in 1916, Ottaviani was the personal secretary of Pope Pius XI, who nominated him, in 1928, to the Secretariat of State, where he spent seven years. He was then made an assessor of the Holy Office in 1935. Ottaviani's name would remain indissolubly linked to this dicastery until his death. He was its pro-secretary from 1953 (when Pope Pius XII made him a cardinal) to 1959, then its secretary until 1966, and until 1968 the first pro-prefect of what had become the CDF. Made an archbishop in 1962, Ottaviani was the cardinal protodeacon at the 1963 conclave and, in this capacity, announced the election of Pope Paul VI and crowned him with the *triregnum*. He died of bronchial pneumonia at the Vatican in 1979, and his remains are at St. Salvatore in Ossibus next to the premises of the CDF.

Ottaviani combined theological insight and erudition with a formidable legal mind. In his early years at the Roman Curia, he worked closely with the then secretary of state, Cardinal Gasparri, during the negotiations of the Lateran Pacts that would settle the "Roman Question" in 1929. Among his academic achievements, Ottaviani authored what would become the standard work on public ecclesiastical law before the Second Vatican Council, a treatise that reached several editions both in its expanded version for lawyers and its abridged compendium for theologians.

Though maliciously vilified by some for his firm conviction that doctrinal orthodoxy (*rectitudo fidei*) is the unavoidable premise of right action (*rectitudo morum*), his capacity to distinguish between denunciation of the error and love for the errant earned him the respect of his many enemies. At the Second Vatican Council, he was widely acknowledged as an evenhanded president of the Preparatory Theological Commission. Likewise, his unbending anticommunism, reflected in the 1949 decree expressly acknowledging as apostates and ipso facto excommunicating those Catholics who would profess and spread Communist doctrine, did not prevent him

from being on good personal terms with the then head of the Italian Communist Party, which was the largest one in Western Europe.

Ottaviani's philosophy of life was to fear nothing but sin and to serve the Church even when this entails a personal cost. This explains why he could publicly voice his concerns on the new Order of the Mass in his 1969 letter to Pope Paul VI, coauthored with Cardinal Bacci and known as the "Ottaviani intervention," while still remaining a faithful and appreciated servant of the Church. It was this fidelity that Pope John Paul II, in the homily at his funeral, identified as the constant feature of Ottaviani's life. He had a great heart (worthy, in biblical terms, of an outstanding priest and true man of God), which prompted him to give refuge to persecuted Jews and anti-Fascist militants during World War II and, among his many commitments, to continue ministering to the destitute young men of the Oratory of St. Peter and the needy girls of the Oasis of St. Rita in Frascati, for all of whom he was a fatherly figure.—Maurizio Ragazzi

BIBLIOGRAPHY AND FURTHER READING: Cavaterra, Emilio. *Il prefetto del Sant'Offizio: Le opere e i giorni del cardinale Ottaviani*. Milan: Mursia, 1990; Cekada, Anthony, ed. and trans. *The Ottaviani Intervention: Short Critical Study of the New Order of Mass*. West Chester, OH: Philothea Press, 2010; Leoni, Francesco. *Il cardinale Alfredo Ottaviani, carabiniere della Chiesa*. Rome: Editrice Apes, 2002; Lesourd, Paul, and Jean-Marie Ramiz. *Alfredo Cardinal Ottaviani*. Notre Dame, IN: University of Notre Dame Press, 1964. *See also* CHURCH, INDIRECT POWER OF (*POTESTAS INDIRECTA*); COMMUNISM; EXCOMMUNICATION; LITURGY AND SOCIAL ORDER; POPE JOHN PAUL II; POPE PAUL VI; POPE PIUS XI; POPE PIUS XII; VATICAN COUNCIL, SECOND

OUR SUNDAY VISITOR Our Sunday Visitor Publishing Company is located in northeastern Indiana in the town of Huntington. Today, it is the largest Catholic publishing house in the United States and publisher of a weekly Catholic newspaper bearing the name *Our Sunday Visitor*. It grew out of one priest's determination to counter anti-Catholicism in the early 20th century in the Hoosier State.

Father John Noll, a native of Fort Wayne, Indiana, one of 19 children, was a pastor in several parishes who demonstrated a strong interest in catechesis and communications. When a periodical called *The Menace* began to be distributed, he became concerned about its anti-Catholic content, so Noll decided to launch a national Catholic weekly to refute the propaganda directed against the Church in the pages of *The Menace*. The first issue of *Our Sunday Visitor* made its debut on May 5, 1912. The original press run was 35,000, and it sold for a penny.

Growth was extremely rapid at the beginning. By the end of its first year, the circulation had soared to 200,000. A year later, in 1913, circulation for the newspaper reached 400,000. The apex for readership came in the early 1960s, when it was estimated that 1 million Catholics were following the news through *Our Sunday Visitor*.

Fighting anti-Catholicism was but one part of Father Noll's vision. He was also concerned about giving Catholics solid content every week with news stories and editorials applying what the Catholic faith authentically teaches. This has been a hallmark of the newspaper through two world wars, the Cold War, the collapse of Communism, and the threats that now come from the various types of terrorism. The steadiness of *Our Sunday Visitor* has been manifested throughout the seasons of the Church's life, too. It supported the reforms of the Second Vatican Council, gave a favorable assessment to the encyclical *Humanae Vitae* when other publications showed hostility, and championed the call of Pope John Paul II for a new evangelization. This posture of being with the Church remains unchanged as the newspaper prepares to observe its centennial in 2012.

Archbishop Noll's guiding spirit from his 44-year role as editor is still in evidence at *Our Sunday Visitor*. Although the Catholic population in the United States has shifted dramatically since his death in 1956, the newspaper he founded continues to serve the Church by shoring up the Catholic identity of its readers. At the turn of the 20th century, immigration, with its inevitable social dislocation, challenged Catholic identity. In the 21st century, an even greater challenge to Catholicism comes from a pervasive and deep secularism. Additional challenges come from the contemporary privatization of religion and the disaffection of many people today from institutions like the Church that provide moral training and guidance. Still, with every issue, *Our Sunday Visitor* (current circulation 51,000) reminds American Catholics that they are to be salt and light (cf. Matthew 5: 13–14) in precisely those places where people are hungry for the Gospel and long to be set free by its truth.

The impact of Our Sunday Visitor Publishing today reaches well beyond the newspaper. For instance, the company publishes *The Priest* (circulation 5,000), a monthly magazine—started by Noll in 1925 under the title *The Acolyte*—filled with essays and articles appealing to the Catholic clergy. Other publications from Our Sunday Visitor are *The Catholic Answer* (circulation 39,000) and *My Daily Visitor* (circulation 26,000).

Besides these periodicals, the company also publishes a number of book titles every year. Those who have published books through Our Sunday Visitor include the outstanding moral theologian Dr. William May; Father Benedict Groeschel, a founder of the Franciscan Friars of the Renewal; the Norbertine Father Alfred McBride; and Father John Peter Cameron, a Dominican. Mention must also be made of the catechetical texts for children the company produces every year for Catholic parishes and schools. And it does not stop there. Our Sunday Visitor Publishing makes available catechetical pamphlets for home and classroom use under the title *What the Church Teaches*. It also prints offering envelopes for parishes that contract for this service. Our Sunday Visitor Institute, a nonprofit corporation, assists deserving Catholic organizations annually with grants to carry out their catechetical and educational work. Our Sunday Visitor Publishing Company is a member of the Catholic Press Association, with Gregory Erlandson as its current president and publisher.—Robert J. Batule

BIBLIOGRAPHY AND FURTHER READING: Ball, Ann. *Champion of the Church: The Extraordinary Life and Legacy of Archbishop Noll*. Huntington, IN: Our Sunday Visitor, 2006; Jacquet, Lou. "75 Years of the Church in America." *Our Sunday Visitor*, May 3, 1987; "OSV in Focus: Our Mission and Message." *Our Sunday Visitor*, November 9, 2003. *See also* CATHOLIC PRESS, THE; *HOMILETIC AND PASTORAL REVIEW*; *NATIONAL CATHOLIC REGISTER*; *NATIONAL CATHOLIC REPORTER*; *WANDERER, THE*

· P ·

PALLIATIVE SEDATION   Palliative sedation (PS) is a pharmacological intervention for patients in a dying state when no other methods to relieve their suffering have been successful. PS can have a sound clinical basis as a response to the needs of patients who have entrusted their care to health care professionals. Two concerns are present. First, PS sometimes lacks consistent definition within clinical practice. Second, a significant challenge to PS has been presented by advocates of assisted suicide and euthanasia, who advocate PS as a means to advance their agenda. Consequently, PS receives ongoing attention for both its clinical models and ethical rationale.

Loving and effective care of the sick is a moral imperative arising from the Gospel. The healing miracles of Jesus Christ are both signs of the kingdom of God present in the person of Jesus as well as concern for the specific needs of the person who seeks healing intervention. The identification of Jesus himself with the sick ("I was sick and you took care of me," Matthew 25: 36) and the teaching on the Good Samaritan (Luke 10: 25–37) are further impetus for Christian care of the sick. Over the course of centuries, care of the sick monk has been seen as care for Christ himself, as found in the rules of St. Basil the Great and St. Benedict in the Eastern and Latin monastic traditions. A proliferation of institutes of vowed religious women and men were established specifically to care for the sick. In the United States, 19th-century hospitals were often places of refuge for the poor; with the advent of modern antisepsis and analgesia, hospitals were positioned as sites for new surgical interventions and evolved into contemporary hospital centers.

Care of the dying is a recognizable dimension of Catholic health care. In classical accounts of the death of the saints, narrative is often given of the vigil kept with the dying. The death of St. Francis of Assisi (1226) is a paradigm case. The dying person witnessed to their hope and faith by their trust in the face of profound illness and death and by reception of the sacraments. Vigil with the dying entailed attentive presence as well as interventions to relieve pain. Catholic practice in recent centuries finds an example of solicitude for the dying in the death of St. Joseph, with many 19th-century hospital motherhouse chapels and churches (including St. Patrick's Cathedral in New York) bearing stained-glass windows of Joseph, on his deathbed, attended by Jesus and Mary. Catholic tradition, including magisterial teaching, encourages relief of pain in the dying, so that death can be as serene as possible, facilitating acceptance of death as a final act of faith. A concern that a person at risk of death in the midst of great pain could have their exercise of faith burdened supported a strong pastoral basis for effective pain management.

PS is utilized in contemporary hospice and palliative care. As the modern hospital became the locus for more intensive surgical interventions in the late 19th century, hospice and palliative care became responses to concerns about the overmedicalization in hospitals of human death and chronic and progressive disease. Hospice care specifically responds to persons who experience a progressive disease state and are terminally ill. In the United States, hospice is primarily provided in the homes of patients, but is also provided in long-term care centers, residential hospices, and hospitals. Palliative care addresses patients who are not necessarily dying but are seriously ill. Primarily a hospital service, palliative care is oriented to pain control, symptom management, and providing a disease trajectory overview so that the patient can make prudent treatment and care decisions.

Both hospice and palliative care are normally provided by interdisciplinary teams of physicians, nurses, pastoral care workers, and social workers. The team approach is intended to support a more integrated assessment and response to the patient so that pharmacologic interventions would be taken within a more comprehensive understanding of the patient as person. Accordingly, the most proficient teams have developed the foundational competency for a dynamic presence to and with the patient, to accompany the patient in decision making and to address pain and symptom management in the final months prior to death. This vision of integrated care can be undermined by a failure of team formation or excessive reliance on medical interventions as response to patient needs.

Sedation by medication is used in a range of clinical applications. Intensive Care Unit patients often receive a combination of pain and sedation medications, for example. Sedation can lightly or significantly reduce consciousness for a period of time. "Respite sedation" is used to determine whether a temporary period of sedation is sufficient to reduce the patient's burden of suffering. As consciousness is necessary for human personal and moral action, consciousness represents a human good. To deprive a person of consciousness can be an injustice. If consciousness is lost as a foreseeable side effect of pursuit of another good medical or care goal with the consent of the patient or the patient's representative, however, this sedation is prudent and just. The principle of double effect would be utilized within the prudential reasoning process. When sedation is indicated in the face of intolerable suffering in the face of imminent death, it should be provided after the patient has fulfilled his or her spiritual responsibilities.

PS can help address either intractable physical pain (found in a minority of cases) or for intolerable existential suffering and anguish. For patients experiencing refractory physical pain, PS is widely affirmed as clinically indicated. More controversial is use of PS for existential suffering. Based on the professional's fidelity to the patient, human suffering should first be eased by the caring and ongoing presence of persons who become companions with the one who suffers, learning the person's spiritual and existential needs. Physical massage therapy and human touch also are precursors to pharmacological interventions. When indicated, the lowest amount of medication to reduce consciousness can be pursued for the patient's good.

Of particular difficulty is the patient who may have no religious orientation, sense of existential acceptance, or meaning in life. In these cases, requests have been made for a deep, continuous sedation, even prior to the final disease state and without nutrition and hydration support. The intent of PS in these instances is not relief of suffering with the side effect of reduced or lost consciousness, but rather taking away consciousness, intending a hastened death. The intention is one of causing death—euthanasia. When deep, continuous sedation is used in a situation in which the patient is not imminently dying, the patient's death would not be caused by the sedative medication but by the absence of nutritive support. In use of sedation, ordinary care measures should not be interrupted. The range of care measures should be evaluated on a case-by-case basis; a person who is imminently dying would not necessarily benefit from placement of a new line to provide assisted nutrition and hydration.

The very troubling advocacy of misuse of PS to cause death has cast a pall of suspicion over PS in the minds of many people. In the face of the international phenomenon of euthanasia practiced under the cover of PS, many clinicians around the world support new guidelines for the use of PS and the preservation of its integrity. The International Association of Catholic Bioethicists held a working colloquium in July 2011 on the practical clinical and moral issues of PS, funded by the three U.S. associations of the Order of Malta and hosted by the National Catholic Bioethics Center.

In the United States, the National Hospice and Palliative Care Organization (NHPCO) issued a position statement and commentary on PS for imminently dying terminally ill patients in 2010. NHPCO stated: (1) PS should be available for the "small number of imminently dying patients whose suffering is intolerable and *refractory*"; (2) the goal of PS should be symptom relief and not unconsciousness itself; (3) PS should be considered on a case-by-case basis in an interdisciplinary team conference; (4) PS requires additional and specific professional education; (5) NHPCO could not take a position on existential suffering and encouraged more ethical exploration of the issue; and (6) PS "is categorically distinct from euthanasia and assisted suicide" when properly administered. Regarding assisted nutrition and hydration (ANH), NHPCO recognized that the lightly sedated patient would still be able to take nutrition by mouth. It noted the significance of providing ANH and other care measures, but stated that such

should be a distinct analysis from PS itself, based on the need of the imminently dying patient.

The European Association for Palliative Care (EAPC) in 2009 published a framework it recommends for the use of sedation in palliative care, which provides greater consideration of specific issues than the NHPCO statement. The most common symptoms for use of sedation are identified as "agitated delirium, dyspnoea [or dyspnea—shortness of breath or labored breathing], pain and convulsions." EAPC identifies a well-developed list of "problem practices" with respect to PS: (1) "abuse of sedation," when particular "clinicians sedate patients approaching the end of life with the primary goal of hastening the patient's death [which] has been called 'slow euthanasia'"; (2) "injudicious use of palliative sedation," when sedation is used as the first step in addressing the patient's situation, rather than within an integrated and careful response, or is used by overwhelmed health care professionals or in response to family, and not patient, need; (3) "injudicious withholding of PS" while pursuing therapeutic options that are not successful; and (4) "substandard clinical practice of PS," when there is an appropriate symptom but no proper assessment by the interdisciplinary team, no proper monitoring of distress, or "hasty dose escalation," among other things.

Care of the terminally ill is particularly important at a time of diminished religious faith in contemporary culture (*GS* # 18–22). It is an opportunity for solidarity with persons in their profound dependency and vulnerability, and it manifests Christian love of family members and professionals (*CCC* # 2279). "It is therefore through Christ, and in Christ, that light is thrown on the mystery of suffering and death which, apart from his Gospel, overwhelms us" (*GS* # 22).—Joseph J. Piccione

BIBLIOGRAPHY AND FURTHER READING: Cherny, Nathan I., Lukas Radbruch, and Board of the European Association for Palliative Care. "European Association for Palliative Care (EAPC) Recommended Framework for the Use of Sedation in Palliative Care." *Palliative Medicine* 23, no. 7 (2009): 581–593; Kirk, Timothy W., and Margaret M. Mahon. "National Hospice and Palliative Care Organization (NHPCO) Position Statement and Commentary on the Use of Palliative Sedation in Imminently Dying Terminally Ill Patients." *Journal of Pain and Symptom Management* 39, no. 5 (2010): 914–923; Perkins, Ignatius, OP. "A Christian Journey of Hope." *Ethics & Medics* 30, no. 8 (2005): 3–4; Pius XII. Speech on the religious and moral implications of analgesia, February 24, 1957. *See also* ARTIFICIAL/ASSISTED NUTRITION AND

HYDRATION; ASSISTED SUICIDE; EUTHANA-
SIA; PALLIATIVE CARE

PAPAL DOCUMENTS Papal documents are issued by the pope or by the Roman Curia under his
authority. They manifest his doctrinal, juridical, and pastoral authority over the universal Church. Promulgated
by the oldest continuous institution in the West, papal
documents have both religious and historic significance
and have helped give rise to their own field of study—
diplomatics. Legislative decisions of the pope, issued
in official letters known as *decretals*, were collected in
registers and were an important source of canon law.
By the Middle Ages, papal documents had become
highly formalized and were commonly known by their
method of authentication, as *bulls*. With the worldwide
teaching of the papacy in the last century, the *encyclical
letter* has become perhaps the most influential of papal
documents.

The range of papal documents reflects the complexities of administering a worldwide church. They
are variously classified according to their format, their
method of authentication, their juridical content, their
mode of promulgation, and other factors. The typology
of documents has varied over two millennia. Although
the classification of papal documents through history
is complex and often inconsistent, their variety demonstrates the breadth, range, and flexibility with which
the papal office is equipped to sustain the Church and
teach the world.

The varieties of papal documents can perhaps best
be understood as the following types: (1) *constitutions*,
which address important matters of Church polity or
Church doctrine; (2) *decretals*, which constitute papal
juridical decisions, either as *rescripts* (responses to questions posed to the pope) or as *motu propios* (answers proposed on his own initiative); and (3) *encyclicals*, pastoral
letters sent to the bishops of the church. Historically,
these documents were promulgated in the form of *bulls*
or *briefs*.

The Roman chancery is entrusted with drawing
up and promulgating papal documents. The innova-
tions and traditions of the chancery played a decisive
role in the development of letter writing and official
documentation in the West. Since 1865, papal documents have been promulgated in the official gazette of
the Holy See, the *Acta Sanctae Sedis* and since 1909 the
Acta Apostolicae Sedis. Most papal documents are issued
in Latin, often with official translations. Despite the
importance of the form and method of a document, in
the end significance must be accorded to the words and

intent of the Roman pontiff, such that it can be said,
"He who heareth you, heareth Me" (Luke 16: 10).

As is evident from the New Testament, the apostles
exercised their supervisory authority by writing letters
to the far-flung churches of Christendom. The first and
second letters of Peter manifest pastoral care for the
universal Church. The first popes continued to settle
doctrinal questions in ecclesiastical letters. In the first
century, Pope Clement wrote to the church in Corinth
restoring presbyters who had been deposed. In the second century, Pope Victor wrote to the bishops of Asia
to unify the date for celebrating Easter. With the rise of
Christianity as the religion of the Roman Empire, papal
documents took on an increasingly legal character, reflecting the heritage of imperial Rome. The pontificates
of Julius (R. 337–352) and Damasus (R. 366–384) contain the first mention of papal secretaries and notaries
to prepare, copy, send, and receive papal documents, as
well as papal registers and archives.

Most papal documents were classified as letters
(*episotolae* or *litterae*), although precise distinctions have
since been drawn among the various types. Legal mat-
ters were classified as *epistolae praecepta*, *decreta*, or *senten-
tiae*. An *epistola synodica* was written upon the advice of
a Roman synod of presbyters. *Tomes* addressed dogmatic
questions, such as the famous Tome of Pope St. Leo the
Great to St. Flavian in 449, which definitively formulated the dogma of the two natures in one person of
Christ and was proclaimed at the Council of Chalcedon
in 451. The formula of Pope St. Hormisdas achieved the
end of the Acacian schism in 519. It was signed by the
bishops of the East and was a *libellus*.

Both the terminology and typology of papal documents shifted with the advent of the medieval papacy.
By and large, papal letters were classified according to
their method of sealing and presentation. *Letters close*
were sealed for private use; *letters open* (*patent*) were delivered unsealed and were meant as public documents.
The majority of letters were also classified according to
their legislative authority—*constitution* (forerunner of
the apostolic constitutions), *decretalis*, *edictum*, or *statu-
tum*. Papal replies to an individual case were classified as
either *mandata*, *responsa*, or *rescripta*. *Privilegia* conveyed
papal grants of jurisdiction, property rights, and titles to
churches, religious houses, and clergy. A *chirograph* was a
papal letter addressed to the Roman Curia.

The sealing and authentication of papal documents were made elaborate to prevent forgeries, which
were common enough in any event. Documents became highly formalized, as is customary with legal and
diplomatic papers. They were distinguished in name,

type of parchment, folds, signature, papal seal, insignia, script employed, and salutation. The more solemn papal letters took the name "bull" from their method of authentication, which was a leaden ball. A bull was characterized by the initial *protocol* (invocation, names and titles of the pope and the addressee, and greeting), the *contextus* (preamble, narration, disposition, and sanctions), and the concluding *eschatocal* (the pope's signature, date, and location).

The modern registering of papal letters began with Pope Innocent III (*R.* 1198–1216). The first modern archival office was created in 1612 and is now referred to as the Vatican Secret Archives. Diplomatics, the study of ancient official documents, can be said to have begun with the Benedictine J. Mabillon (1632–1707), who wrote the first comprehensive study of papal documents. The Vatican Library estimates that more than 30 million papal documents have been issued. Taking the period 1909 to 1976 as an example, 1,681 documents were promulgated as apostolic constitutions, 2,067 as apostolic letters, and 78 as encyclicals. As noted by the Second Vatican Council, religious obedience to the papal magisterium takes into account the character of the papal documents, as well as the force and emphasis of the teaching contained therein (*LG #* 25).

Given modern means of communication, forgery of papal pronouncements is no longer possible and papal documents have been greatly simplified in form and type, with elaborate presentation now being purely ceremonial. As terminology has carried over from earlier periods, however, the nomenclature of papal documents bears reviewing. There are various categories of papal documents—decretals, bulls and briefs, apostolic constitutions, motu proprios, apostolic letters, and encyclicals—each of which will be treated below.

Historically, decretals were letters embodying a papal decision, usually on questions of discipline, faith, or morals. The first decretal letters are considered to be Pope Damasus's address to the bishops of Gaul around 365 and Pope Siricius's letter to a Spanish bishop, Himerius of Tarragona, in 385. Significantly, decretals from the outset exhibited a concern for the universal Church. In form, they reflected the influence of the imperial responses of the Roman Empire, which expressed juridical decisions in the form of letters. Decretals were collected in canonical collections and were the major source of the *Corpus Juris Canonici*, the legislative canons of the Church before the codification of 1917. Some of the more notable decretal collections include *Canones Urbicani* (fifth century), *Collectio Dionysiana* (525), *Decretals of Gratian* (c. 1150), *Decretals of Pope Gregory IX* (1234), *Constitutiones Clementinae* (1317), and the various collections known as *Extravagantes*. Recently popes have made use of decretal letters to proclaim canonizations.

Papal bulls were issued from the sixth century and became prevalent in the eighth century, when the pope became responsible for governing the Papal States. The papacy of Leo IX (*R.* 1049–1054) saw the regularization and expansion of the work of the chancery, and papal bulls took on a fixed form, seal, signature, and salutation. The intricately designed leaden seal that gave bulls their name showed the name and insignia of the pope on the obverse and depicted SS. Peter and Paul on the reverse; it was attached to the document by a hemp or silk cord for authentication. Papal bulls traditionally began with the pope's name, his title as "Bishop, servant of the servants of God" (*Episcopus, servus servorum dei*), and a clause of perpetuity (*in perpetuam memoriam*). The *incipit* is the first few words of the message, from which the title is derived. Bulls conclude with blessings or prohibitions.

Bulls were classified as cameral, consistorial, curial, half-bulls, secret bulls, or golden bulls. Most major papal pronouncements were promulgated as bulls, including documents establishing the College of Cardinals (1059), establishing the Dominican order (1216), convoking the Second Crusade (1145), defining papal primacy (1302), stating the necessity of the Church for salvation (1441), excommunicating Martin Luther (1521), promulgating the Tridentine rite (1570), establishing the Gregorian calendar (1582), condemning Jansenism (1713), and summoning the First (1868) and Second (1961) Vatican Councils.

A brief was a medieval modification of the bull. Briefs were employed for expedited decisions and less formal letters and were sealed with stamped wax. The oldest preserved papal brief is from Pope Boniface IX in 1390. Papal briefs were issued to dispense King Henry VIII from the prohibition against marrying his brother's widow, to suppress the Society of Jesus in 1773, and to restore the English Catholic hierarchy in 1850.

Apostolic constitutions represent the most solemn form of papal document and were usually issued in the format of a bull. Apostolic constitutions state important legislative, liturgical, and dogmatic pronouncements of the Church. The infallible papal definitions of the Immaculate Conception of Mary (*Ineffabilis Deus*, 1854) and of her Assumption (*Munificentissimus Deus*, 1950) were apostolic constitutions in the format of bulls. The most important documents of the two Vatican Councils were promulgated as dogmatic constitutions. The *Code of Canon Law* was promulgated in the apostolic constitution *Sacrae Discipli-nae Leges* (1983) and the *Catechism of the Catholic Church*, in *Fidei Depositum* (1992). A series of 20th-century apostolic constitutions revised the rules for electing the pope, culminating in *Universi Dominic Gregis* (1996).

A motu proprio (Latin for "of one's own will") is a signed document of the pope issued on his own initiative. In this manner, they differ from most decretals, which were answers to petitions or rescripta. Thus, *a motu proprio* does not depend on the truth of the case narrated in a rescript. The first motu proprio is usually attributed to Pope Innocent VIII in 1484. Decrees of Popes John Paul II and Benedict XVI permitting the Tridentine Mass were promulgated by motu proprio.

Papal letters remain an essential and increasingly flexible medium for the papal mission. Apostolic letters by Pope Pius IX (*Epistle to the Easterns*, 1848) and Leo XIII (*Praeclara Gratulationis Publicae*, 1894) urging reunion of the churches were rejected in encyclicals of the Eastern Orthodox patriarchs. Pope Paul VI's luminous *Credo of the People of God* (1968) was an apostolic letter in the motu proprio form. John Paul II reserved ordination to men in the apostolic letter *Ordinatio Sacerdotalis* (1994).

An *apostolic epistle* is a letter addressed to a specific group. An *apostolic exhortation* is a papal document encouraging a portion of the church to carry out an ecclesiastical activity or mission. A *consistorium* convokes a meeting of members of the hierarchy. Oral pronouncements of the pope can be issued as homilies or allocutions. John Paul II created a new format for papal documents in the collections of teachings he delivered in his pastoral visits to the countries of the world. Papal agreements, congratulatory messages, addresses, appointments, excommunications, dispensations, and the like are usually issued as letters. The Roman Curia issues documents of its own.

Modern encyclicals began in the 18th century as letters written by the pope to the Catholic bishops on a pastoral matter. In recent pontificates, they have often been addressed to all people of goodwill, and as John Paul II indicated in his general audience of March 10, 1993, have the "value of universal teaching." In *Humani Generis* (1950), Pope Pius XII wrote that encyclicals, even though not partaking necessarily of the pope's supreme teaching authority, can require assent from Catholics, as they "are taught by the ordinary magisterium." The encyclical *Aeterni Patris* (1879) called for a revival of Thomism, which helped spark a century of papal pronouncements on faith and reason, culminating in John Paul's encyclical *Fides et*

Ratio (1998). The encyclicals *Casti Connubii* (1930) and *Humanae Vitae* (1968) addressed questions of birth control and marital life. The social teaching of the papacy was launched with the encyclical *Rerum Novarum* (1891) and was elaborated in more than 10 encyclicals by subsequent popes, including *Quadragesimo Anno* (1931), *Mater et Magistra* (1961), *Populorum Progressio* (1967), *Laborem Exercens* (1981), and *Centesimus Annus* (1991). In earlier centuries, the most important papal documents were legislative and dogmatic. With the emergence of the modern papacy as a pastoral voice to much of the world, it can be surmised that the encyclical has become the most influential of papal documents.—Howard Bromberg

BIBLIOGRAPHY AND FURTHER READING: Carlen, Claudia, ed. *Papal Pronouncements: A Guide, 1740–1978.* 2 vol. Ypsilanti, MI: Pierian Press, 2010; Fenton, Joseph. "The Doctrinal Authority of Papal Encyclicals." *American Ecclesiastical Review* 121 (August 1949): 136–150; Grote, Heiner. "Rome's Official Statements: How and What? Towards a Typology of Documents." *Ecumenical Review*, January 1994; Levillain, Philippe, ed. *The Papacy: An Encyclopedia.* 3 vols. New York: Routledge, 2002; Morrisey, Francis, OMI. *Papal and Curial Pronouncements: Their Canonical Significance in Light of the 1983 Code of Canon Law*, 2nd ed. Ottawa: St. Paul University, 2001; Sayers, Jane. *Original Papal Documents in England and Wales from the Accession of Pope Innocent III to the Death of Pope Benedict (1198–1304).* New York: Oxford University Press, 1999; Sullivan, Francis, SJ. *Creative Fidelity: Weighing and Interpreting Documents of the Magisterium.* New York: Paulist Press, 1996. *See also* AUTHORITY; *CATECHISM OF THE CATHOLIC CHURCH*; CONCORDATS; ENCYCLICAL(S); INFALLIBILITY; MAGISTERIUM

PARISH AS AN AGENT OF EVANGELIZATION

There is much talk in contemporary theological discourse regarding the issue of evangelization, understood as the ongoing and active invitation offered to all people to come to know Christ and to deepen their relationship with Christ in and through the Catholic Church. This manner of offering the Gospel is distinct from proselytism, which carries with it a connotation of overly aggressive recruitment. Such efforts, when taken to their extreme, often disregard human freedom and personal conversion, seeking to make polemic, intellectual arguments that assist with bolstering the numbers of a specific group. Evangelization, understood properly, neither pokes nor prods, but offers, helps, and actively invites one to the Church. It is neither the passive welcoming of a person who happens to stumble into the church nor the brutish dragging of reluctant souls through the doors. True evangelization is much deeper than both of those approaches. More than arguments, written treatises, or smiling ministers of welcome, it is the multifaceted "proclamation of Christ and his Gospel [Greek: *evangelion*] by word and the testimony of life" (*CCC* # 905; cf. 861). Paraphrasing his predecessor, Blessed Pope John Paul II tells us, "Evangelization—which has the aim of bringing the Good News to the whole of humanity, so that all may live by it—is a rich, complex and dynamic reality, made up of elements, or one could say moments, that are essential and different from each other, and that must all be kept in view simultaneously" (*Catechesi Tradendae*, 18).

In the Catholic context, many in the Church today, in various capacities and at various levels within the Church's structure, are discussing what John Paul II termed the "new Evangelization." By this, the pope referred to both the new methods that we must use to offer the Gospel as well as the fact that, in the contemporary postmodern context, even those who are already baptized often need to be offered the Gospel. "In summary, the new Evangelization is primarily the 'clear and unequivocal proclamation of the person of Jesus Christ, that is, the preaching of his name, his teaching, his life, his promises and the Kingdom which he has gained for us by the paschal mystery'" (*National Directory for Catechesis*, 17).

For many Catholics, for better or worse, the local parish is the first and perhaps the sole personal connection the individual makes with the universal Catholic Church. In this local manifestation of Church, the person comes to know the faith, meet the faithful, and hopefully develop a faith-filled relationship with the Triune God. In short, the parish is, for many, *the* experience of the Church. The parish can be called the front line, then, in the work of evangelization. Eloquent talks given by popes and bishops, as well as wonderful programs that are developed to offer people the truth of the Faith, will not meet with success if they are not "filtered" down to the people on the local level and experienced directly and personally. It is therefore primarily here in the parish that the success of evangelization is measured and from here that the ongoing invitation to all is both made and received. Furthermore, extraparochial evangelization efforts must, by their very nature, lead people to the Eucharistic community that is the parish. It is possible, therefore, to have an effective and wider net of evangelization cast, only to have those who have been set ablaze with faith quite disappointed when they return to their local parish and find that, perhaps for

the larger community, the flames of evangelical fervor do not burn so brightly.

As we are reminded in the directory for catechesis—the Church's handbook of sorts for all things educational and formational—"The Christian community is the origin, locus, and goal of catechesis. Proclamation of the Gospel always begins with the Christian community and invites [people] to conversion and the following of Christ. It is the same community that welcomes those who wish to know the Lord better and permeate themselves with a new life. The Christian community accompanies catechumens and those being catechized, and with maternal solicitude makes them participate in her own experience of the faith and incorporates them into herself" (*General Directory for Catechesis*, 254). Thus, the community—specifically the local community—is an indispensible part of evangelization. Only when the community is consciously aware of this fact and acts upon it can evangelization truly bear fruit.

While a plethora of methods, programs, and theories of evangelization exist, comment on their specific content is beyond the scope of this discussion. What is essential is that successful evangelization by the parish community must necessarily transcend the walls of classrooms and even the walls of the church building. The parish must make a concerted effort to reach out to the local community, meet the people where they are, and make personal connections. This is the point of success, when the faith becomes not an intellectual endeavor but a deep personal encounter with Christ through his Church. The point of it all is not knowledge *about* Christ, but knowledge *of* Christ. When the person feels an intimate connection to the Church as manifested in the local community—when he feels his life story to be intimately woven and inextricably linked with the story of the local Church community—this is successful evangelization. It is at this "moment" within the endeavor of evangelization that the individual truly becomes a part of the parish community and will likely remain a committed contributor to the life of the local church.

Parishes can achieve these goals in myriad ways, depending on their individual, unique situations. One very effective tool is to demonstrate the connectedness of the aforementioned "stories" of the person and the parish through the telling and retelling of the lives of the saints, recognizing and celebrating ethnically significant traditions in doing so and thereby making an intimate connection between culture and faith. This is a prime example of the evangelical importance of what is termed "popular religion." Succinctly defined, popular religion is the intersection of the Catholic Faith as expressed in and through local culture. In many cases since the Second Vatican Council, a conscious or unconscious turn toward a more intellectual and "modern" approach to the Faith may have hindered local parochial evangelization. As theologian Elizabeth Johnson affirms: "There is . . . a growing scholarly interest in popular religion, long neglected because of rationalistic bias. . . . [Popular religion] helps communities to create meaningful lives in stressful circumstances" (*Friends of God and Prophets*, 11).

It is indeed a truism to say that all evangelization is local, for it is here in the parish that the Gospel is proclaimed and lived by, through, and for the local woman and man who encounters the Lord. Through the dialogue with popular local culture, the Gospel takes deep root and grows in the hearts of these people.—Philip A. Franco

BIBLIOGRAPHY AND FURTHER READING: Congregation for the Clergy. *General Directory for Catechesis*. Washington, DC: USCCB, 1997; John Paul II. *Catechesi Tradendae: On Catechesis in Our Time*. Boston: Pauline Books & Media, 1997; Johnson, Elizabeth. *Friends of God and Prophets: A Feminist Theological Reading of the Communion of Saints*. New York: Continuum Books, 1993; U.S. Conference of Catholic Bishops. *National Directory for Catechesis*. Washington, DC: USCCB, 2005.

PARTIAL BIRTH ABORTION   Late-term, partial birth abortion began to gain public attention in 1992, when Ohio abortionist Dr. Martin Haskell delivered a paper on the procedure—which he termed "intact dilation and extraction"—at a meeting of the National Abortion Federation. He described the process of guiding the preborn child feet first through the birth canal until just the head remained in the uterus, at which point he would pierce the skull and suction out the brain and spinal fluid, so that the collapsed skull could pass through the mother's partially dilated cervix. Haskell said the procedure, which to that point he had used more than 700 times, caused less bleeding and internal trauma to the mother than other late-term abortion methods.

While Dr. Haskell's description was cold and clinical, it did not differ in substance from the heart-rending eyewitness account of a partial birth abortion given by formerly "pro-choice" nurse Brenda Pratt Shafer in 1993: "The mother was six months pregnant. The baby's heartbeat was clearly visible on the ultrasound screen. The doctor went in with forceps and grabbed the baby's legs and pulled them down into the birth canal. Then he delivered the baby's body and arms—everything but the head. The doctor kept the baby's head just inside the

uterus. The baby's little fingers were clasping and unclasping, and his feet were kicking. Then the doctor stuck the scissors through the back of the head, and the baby's arms jerked out. The doctor opened the scissors, stuck a high-powered suction tube into the opening and sucked the baby's brains out. Now the baby was completely limp."

As the gruesome nature of the procedure became more widely known, public outcry grew. Even such staunch political supporters of legal abortion as Sen. Daniel Moynihan (who labeled the procedure "infanticide") and former New York City mayor Ed Koch called for it to be outlawed. Congress responded by passing such a ban in 1995, but it was vetoed by President Bill Clinton, citing concerns about women's health and fetal abnormalities should the procedure be outlawed.

The president's assertions were contradicted by numerous sources, however, including Dr. Warren Hern, author of what was at the time the leading textbook on abortion procedures, who stated that partial birth abortion was in fact "potentially dangerous" to the mother because turning the baby to the breach position risks "amniotic fluid embolism or placental abruption." Ultimately, the American Medical Association, a supporter of legal abortion, also publicly stated that there are no valid medical indications for partial birth abortion and joined the call to prohibit the procedure.

Over the next several years, a number of states passed their own bans on partial birth abortion, but this effort was seemingly derailed by the U.S. Supreme Court in 2000, when it held unconstitutional Nebraska's ban on partial birth abortion (*Stenberg v. Carhart*). Congress kept trying, however, and in November 2003, President George W. Bush signed into law a federal ban on partial birth abortion. That law, too, was challenged in the courts, with three federal courts of appeals invalidating the Act. On appeal, the Supreme Court in 2007 upheld the constitutionality of the federal ban on partial birth abortion in *Gonzales v. Carhart*.

For the pro-life movement, partial birth abortion presented both an opportunity and a challenge. "We saw that this could be used to educate people about how violent and abusive abortions are," said the National Right to Life Committee's Douglas Johnson. Describing the reality of partial birth abortion allowed pro-lifers to focus public attention on what is done to a child in an abortion, and "when the child is discussed, we win," said Patrick Mahoney of the Christian Defense Fund.

Even the court cases that ultimately struck down bans on partial birth abortion helped shine a light on the cruelty not only of that particular procedure but also of abortion in general. In the Nebraska case, for example, Supreme Court justices John Paul Stevens and Ruth Bader Ginsburg—both supporters of legal abortion—based their rejection of a partial birth abortion ban on their judgment that it was not appreciably different from other methods of abortion. "They agreed that the whole business, by whatever procedure, is brutal, gruesome and destructive of 'potential life,'" wrote *Chicago Tribune* columnist Steve Chapman. Yet, "they think it enjoys the full protection of the U.S. Constitution."

In a 2004 U.S. District Court case in New York challenging the 2003 federal ban, Judge Richard Casey focused his line of questioning on what is done to the baby in the procedure and brought out expert medical testimony that the child will experience "prolonged and excruciating pain." Supreme Court justice Anthony Kennedy, writing the majority opinion in 2007 upholding the federal ban, reiterated that various other abortion procedures were at least as barbaric as the partial birth method.

The challenge for the pro-life movement was to avoid being drawn into a singular focus—or, more likely, allowing politicians to singularly focus on—banning partial birth abortion, which accounted for less than 1% of abortions every year in America. For politicians—with polls consistently showing large majorities in favor of banning this particular procedure—this could be seen as a way of appeasing pro-life voters without having to tackle what many saw as the far less politically popular effort to prohibit *all* abortions. Pro-life activists had to avoid falling into the trap of trying to *separate* partial birth abortion from other types of legal abortion in a shortsighted effort to gain support for a ban from supporters of *Roe v. Wade*. Court rulings such as those cited above made clear that this horrific, late-term procedure was a *natural consequence* of *Roe v. Wade*, and it was incumbent upon the pro-life movement to make that case if partial birth abortion was to be an effective teaching instrument in dramatizing the injustice of virtually unrestricted abortion that had been ushered in by that 1973 Supreme Court ruling.

Ultimately, pro-lifers have used the partial birth abortion issue effectively: to focus attention on the life of the preborn child, and thereby on the cruelty and injustice of abortion; to highlight the extreme dimensions of *Roe v. Wade* and of a pro-choice lobby that would not even agree to restrictions on this gruesome, late-term procedure; to give hope and encouragement to the pro-life movement by "chang[ing] the momentum," in Mahoney's words, and by scoring a significant legisla-

tive and legal victory; and to attempt to save at least *some* lives by banning one abortion procedure, while the effort goes forward to restore legal protection for *all* children in the womb.—Richard Hinshaw

BIBLIOGRAPHY AND FURTHER READING: Ruse, Cathy Cleaver. "Partial-Birth Abortion on Trial." *Human Life Review* (Spring 2005); Shafer, Brenda Pratt. Statement before the Subcommittee on the Constitution, Committee on the Judiciary, U.S. House of Representatives Hearing on The Partial-Birth Abortion Ban Act (HR 1833), March 21, 1996. *See also* ABORTION; RIGHT TO LIFE MOVEMENT; *ROE v. WADE/ DOE v. BOLTON*

PATIENT PROTECTION AND AFFORDABLE HEALTH CARE ACT OF 2010

There should have been a Catholic victory celebration on March 23, 2010. Health care reform had finally passed Congress and was signed that day by President Barack Obama. The U.S. Conference of Catholic Bishops (USCCB), the Catholic Health Association (CHA), and most students of Catholic social teaching had long sought such legislation. Recrimination, however, was more prominent than celebration. How did this happen? What is the likely future of Catholic teaching and U.S. health care policy?

The reform legislation of 2010 contained provisions long sought by the principal Catholic groups: health insurance reform, near-universal coverage of all U.S. residents, quality-improvement measures, and initiatives toward cost control. Sharp disagreements, however, broke out between the USCCB (supported by many Catholics) and the CHA (supported by other Catholics) over the new law's abortion, conscience protection, and immigrant coverage provisions. These disagreements became the focus of anger, rupturing the formerly close relationship between the USCCB and CHA.

Following more than a year of intense debate in Congress and the public (and nearly 100 years of failure to enact reform proposals), Congress passed President Obama's highest legislative priority: the Patient Protection and Affordable Care Act (PPACA). The reforms are very complex (reflecting the complexity and size of the health care system itself) and are to unfold over a decade. In broad outline, this legislation aims to expand access to health insurance to 32 million uninsured persons (out of an estimated 46 million in 2010). It proposes to do this by (1) expanding eligibility for Medicaid among low-income, working-age adults who do not have the resources to purchase private insurance; (2) requiring that virtually all citizens and legal residents purchase health insurance, either through their employer or individually through state-created insurance "exchanges"; and (3) providing financial assistance to individuals and employers to make insurance affordable. In addition, PPACA has complex financial penalties for certain employers and individuals who disobey the mandate.

PPACA also reforms the health insurance market by requiring private insurance companies to eliminate denial of coverage for preexisting conditions, to cover young adults on their parents' plan under certain conditions, to eliminate annual and lifetime coverage limits, and to narrow the gap between highest and lowest charges for insurance. Exempt from coverage requirements and subsidies are all persons residing in the U.S. illegally and persons whose incomes are too high to qualify for Medicaid but too low to afford private insurance even with the subsidies available. This last point was a focus of dissatisfaction with PPACA by the USCCB, CHA, and other Catholic groups, who believe that *all* persons have the right to health care coverage.

The health care reform legislation further included changes in Medicare coverage and in payments to private insurance companies offering Medicare Advantage insurance policies. To improve the quality of care, PPACA included subsidies for hospitals and physicians to acquire electronic health information technology, as well as penalties for low-quality care such as hospital-acquired infections and preventable hospital readmissions. To reduce acceleration in health care spending, the law authorized experiments with new forms of delivery that require greater cooperation and continuity of care among hospitals, rehabilitation facilities, physicians, and others involved in patient care.

The principles of Catholic social thought most pertinent to PPACA are justice, common good, subsidiarity, and solidarity, as well as the prohibition against abortion and protections for the consciences of health care workers regarding illicit prescriptions and procedures. Although different Catholic groups and individuals initially favored a variety of approaches to achieving these principles, the major Catholic groups agreed that the approach embodied in PPACA reformed a dysfunctional health care system (with major access, quality, and spending inadequacies and injustices) toward a better system, particularly in its coverage and insurance reforms. These would move closer to justice (adequate coverage for all) and a more inclusive system for all (common good and solidarity). Many Catholic groups lobbied Congress for these principles in the legislation,

but the USCCB and CHA were particularly active and worked closely together until the very end of the process. A few bishops and some smaller groups, such as the Catholic Medical Association, did object to the national scope of the reform, arguing that subsidiarity required state-based and private market-based reforms.

All Catholic groups aggressively lobbied against health care reform providing coverage or federal payment for elective abortions and insisted that it should protect the conscientious refusal of Catholics and others to participate in abortions, sterilizations, abortifacient or contraceptive prescriptions, and other otherwise lawful medical procedures that violate their religious or moral consciences. They found support among congressional Republicans and, somewhat surprisingly, among numerous Democrats. At the outset of the process, and throughout the legislative debate, the White House and both parties agreed that any reform legislation should embody the principles of the decades-old Hyde Amendment, which prohibits federal payment for abortions using Department of Health and Human Services funds (except in cases of rape, incest, or danger to the life of the mother), and of long-standing legislative protection of provider conscience.

During negotiations on the major provisions of the reform bill during 2009, a small group of senators and representatives quietly negotiated abortion and conscience language. Because the Republicans were mostly pro-life, negotiations principally involved the House and Senate leadership, the White House, and key pro-life and pro-choice Democrats. The House side was led by Rep. Bart Stupak of Michigan and the Senate side by Sen. Robert Casey of Pennsylvania. Ultimately, the House passed the Stupak Amendment to implement the Hyde provisions in the new law. All major Catholic groups supported this language. This amendment specified that no funds authorized or appropriated under the reform law, including subsidies, may be used for elective abortions or for benefits packages that include such abortions.

Because the Senate legislation needed a 60% vote to avoid a filibuster, negotiations in that body had a different dynamic, and its abortion language became different from the House's. The unified Catholic position began to fray after Senate passage in December 2009, with some believing the Senate language to be inadequate and others judging it equivalent to Hyde and Stupak. The Senate language prohibits the secretary of health and human services from requiring the coverage of any abortions as part of the essential health benefits package and prohibits insurance companies from using federal funds, including subsidies, to pay for abortions except those allowable under the Hyde Amendment.

There was hope that a House–Senate conference committee would merge the bills and adopt the Stupak language. When the Senate partisan balance shifted in early 2010 following the Massachusetts special election to replace the late Sen. Edward Kennedy, there was no hope that a conference committee, followed by a new House and Senate vote, could produce legislation in 2010. Therefore, the White House and congressional Democrats adopted a strategy of passing the Senate legislation in the House, along with a budget reconciliation bill that would meld the fiscal, but not the legislative, language of the two versions. The decisive House vote had to be on the Senate language.

As the vote neared, Representative Stupak brokered an agreement that pro-life Democrats would vote for passage and that the president would issue an executive order to implement the bill consistent with the Stupak Amendment. This deal became the breaking point between Catholic groups. The USCCB strongly urged defeat of the Senate bill in the House because, not containing the Stupak Amendment, it was insufficiently pro-life. The bishops were joined by the Catholic Medical Association, the National Catholic Bioethics Center, and conservative Catholic activists (who objected not only to the abortion language but also to the expansion of federal power in health care). CHA, on the other hand, urged passage of the legislation because, in its judgment, the abortion provisions were strongly pro-life, containing the same protections as Stupak in different words. The CHA was joined by the Leadership Conference of Women Religious; Network, a progressive lobby group led by women religious; and liberal and progressive Catholic groups.

This split was particularly painful for the USCCB and CHA, which had worked closely for decades to obtain the expanded coverage and system delivery reform promised by PPACA. The bishops' conference also felt that, as moral teachers for the Catholic Church, groups such as CHA should have bowed to their judgment. Some in the USCCB and in Catholic circles argued that CHA had compromised principle by accepting federal payment for abortions in order to acquire broadened coverage. CHA, however, believes that PPACA's language does in fact preserve Hyde Amendment principles and does not entail federal funding of abortion. Moreover, it finds the legislation to be pro-life because it contains support for adoptions and special provisions for prenatal and other help for women to carry their children to term. The CHA does not, therefore, agree

that it made a moral compromise on abortion. The points of contention are as follows.

First, the USCCB and its allies argue that because PPACA requires at least one private plan on each state insurance exchange to *include* abortion coverage, federal subsidies will fund abortion for the first time. CHA and its allies, however, counter that the law's language explicitly prohibits use of federal funds for abortions *beyond those already allowed* by Hyde. Moreover, the states can forbid abortion coverage on the exchanges, and any plans that do cover abortion must strictly segregate federal subsidies from the added personal premiums that an enrollee must pay for that coverage.

Second, pro-life opponents of the law argue that its additional funding for community health centers will encourage or even require such centers to provide abortions. Supporters, however, argue that existing laws and regulations governing community health centers, as well as provisions of PPACA itself, prevent such result.

Third, opponents of PPACA argue that the executive order cannot be enforced against the flawed provisions of the underlying law and that, in any case, executive orders can be rescinded by the same or subsequent presidents. This objection also draws upon the basic suspicion of many bishops and other Catholics about the abortion intentions of the Democratic Party generally and of President Obama specifically. CHA and other supporters of the reform law contend that, although executive orders are weaker than legislative language, the provisions of the PPACA law itself, as described above, are strongly pro-life, and the executive order will govern implementation during the Obama administration.

Finally, Catholic opponents argued that the new law does not adequately protect conscience rights. Supporters counter that the law preserves existing federal laws protecting the rights of those who object to providing, paying for, or covering abortions.

Given these sharp divisions, what happens from mid-2010 into the future? Clearly, both the USCCB and CHA are disturbed by the division. They will engage in dialogue to resolve the differences, as well as cooperation to monitor federal and state regulations that implement PPACA over the next 10 years. The effort will be to ensure interpretations of the law consistent with expansion of insurance coverage and with prohibition of federal funding for abortion. There is strong goodwill on each side to come together again on health care reform.

At the level of Catholic social teaching itself, the critical question is this: Given that the bishops individually and collectively are the moral teachers of the faithful, to what extent does their teaching authority extend to the interpretation of legislative language? During and immediately after the debate on PPACA, the USCCB seemed to claim the authority to direct conscience in the interpretation of legislative language around abortion. If so, then in principle such should extend to obedience to the bishops' interpretation of *other* legislation and executive decisions, such as on Social Security, immigration, length of prison sentences, and war. Yet, traditionally, interpretation of particular legal and political actions has been left to the prudential judgment of the laity. The debate over Catholic social teaching and health care reform in 2010, then, may leave lasting questions for the evolution of Catholic social teaching itself.—Clarke E. Cochran

BIBLIOGRAPHY AND FURTHER READING: DiNardo, Daniel, William Murphy, and John Wester. "Setting the Record Straight." Press release, May 21, 2010, available at http://www.usccb.org/news/archived. cfm?releaseNumber=10-104; "Health Care." Special issue. *Journal of Catholic Social Thought* 7, no. 1 (Winter 2010); Jost, Timothy Stoltzfus. "Episcopal Oversight." *Commonweal*, June 4, 2010, pp. 8–9; Nairn, Thomas. "Catholics Understand Health Care as a Right." *Health Progress*, March–April, 2010, pp. 58–60; Staff of the *Washington Post. Landmark: The Inside Story of America's New Health-Care Law and What It Means for Us All.* New York: Public Affairs, 2010. *See also* ABORTION; COMMON GOOD; HEALTH CARE POLICY; JUSTICE; SOCIAL JUSTICE; SOLIDARITY; SUBSIDIARITY

PAULIST PRESS   Paulist Press is the publishing arm of the Missionary Congregation of St. Paul (Paulist Fathers). Based in Mahwah, New Jersey, it publishes a wide array of scholarly and popular works in fields relevant to Catholicism, including theology, history, liturgy, and spirituality.

The mission of Paulist Press is to bring the good news of the Gospel to Catholics and people of other religious traditions; support dialogue and welcome good scholarship and religious wisdom from all sources across denominational boundaries; and foster religious values and wholeness in society, especially through materials promoting healing, reconciliation, and personal growth.

Father Isaac Hecker, an American convert to Catholicism, founded the Paulist congregation in 1858. Hecker's ambitious vision was nothing less than the conversion of the United States to Catholicism, and this vision inspired the Paulists' focus on evangelism

through the spoken and written word. The Paulists' first publishing effort was a weekly magazine, *Catholic World*, which was printed from 1865 to 1995. It was revived in 2006 as an online journal.

In 1881, the Paulists founded the Columbus Press in New York City; it was renamed Paulist Press in 1913. In keeping with the society's mission, its initial focus was on apologetics, explaining the teachings of the Church in popular fashion through such brisk-selling works as *The Question Box* by Rev. Bertrand Conway, CSP.

Paulist Press capitalized on the increasing educational level and wealth of the U.S. Catholic community in the post–World War II era. By the late 1960s, it was the largest Catholic distributor and publisher in the world. One of the press's significant initiatives was Catholic Library Services (CLS), a program that developed into a separate company, the American Library and Educational Services Company (ALESCO).

With the splintering of American Catholicism that occurred following the Second Vatican Council, Paulist Press became associated with the "liberal" wing of the Church. The press tracked post–Vatican II theological developments in its major series, *Concilium: Theology in the Age of Renewal*. Dissenting theologians such as Father Charles Curran and Rev. Richard McCormick, SJ, have been mainstays of its publishing program. On Catholic social teaching, besides Curran and McCormick, the press publishes such authors as Rev. Kenneth Himes, OFM, and Mark and Louise Zwick. Although few authors associated with a more conservative reading of the Church's social tradition have appeared in Paulist's booklists, the press's offerings reflect a variety of views, many of which exhibit fidelity to the Church's magisterial teaching.

Paulist Press remains a major Catholic publisher of hardcover and paperback books, audio and video tapes, educational programs, and parish resources. Its *Classics of Western Spirituality* series has presented more than 90 volumes of the original writings of significant spiritual teachers—predominantly Christian but also Jewish, Islamic, and Native American. It has continued its tradition of popularly oriented catechetics in series such as *101 Questions* and *What Are They Saying About*. In recent years, Paulist Press has expanded into online ventures, including TheCatholicWorld.com and CathNews USA, a daily news service.—Kevin E. Schmiesing

BIBLIOGRAPHY AND FURTHER READING: Gillis, James. *The Paulists.* New York: Macmillan, 1932; O'Brien, David. *Isaac Hecker: An American Catholic.* Mahwah, NJ: Paulist Press, 1992. *See also* HECKER, ISAAC

PELLEGRINO, EDMUND D. (1920–) Edmund Daniel Pellegrino was born on June 22, 1920, in Newark, New Jersey, but spent his early years in Brooklyn, New York. Edmund was one of four sons born to Michael J. and Marie (Catone) Pellegrino, both of whom were first-generation Italian Americans. He credits his parents' teaching and examples with instilling in him the benefit of keeping faith central to his life. Pellegrino attended a Jesuit high school, which provided him with a rigorous education emphasizing classical studies. He earned his bachelor of science degree in 1941 from St. John's University, a Vincentian institution, where he majored in chemistry and philosophy, graduating summa cum laude with honors in chemistry.

Pellegrino's high school and college education convinced him that faith was not opposed to science. His interest in medical ethics and the philosophy of medicine, subjects he would write about prolifically in the future, was founded upon the philosophical and theological studies at these Catholic schools. He cites, for example, the writings and work of two 13th-century clerics, Roger Bacon, a Franciscan, and Albertus Magnus, a Dominican, which provided him with unambiguous examples of faith and science working together.

In 1944, Pellegrino married Clementine Coakley, and they would become the parents of seven children. That same year, he earned his medical degree from New York University College of Medicine. Dr. Pellegrino then interned at New York's Bellevue Hospital (1944–1945) and held residencies at the Goldwater Memorial Hospital, Columbia University (1945–1946), and at Bellevue Hospital (1948–1949). Between these two residencies, Pellegrino served as chief of medical service at the Army Air Force Regional Hospital, Maxwell Field, Montgomery, Alabama (1946–1948).

During a research fellowship in kidney physiology and kidney disease in the Department of Medicine at New York University (1949–1950), he contracted tuberculosis, which took three years to cure. He spent these years as a supervising physician at the Homer Folks Tuberculosis Hospital in Oneonta, New York (1950–1953). These experiences helped him appreciate even more the unique relationship between doctors and patients, which he refers to as a "covenant," that is, a solemn agreement, as opposed to a contractual business arrangement. He believes, and also taught his students, that when physicians take an oath, they pledge publicly to use their medical knowledge for the betterment of the patients entrusted to them.

Throughout his career, even while working as a practicing clinician, research scientist, and teacher,

Pellegrino readily accepted leadership positions. In 1952, he became the first chairman of the Department of Medicine of a new rural hospital, the Hunterdon Medical Center in Flemington, New Jersey. Although at the age of 32 he felt unprepared for this role, he did not hesitate to take on the additional responsibility, attributing his confident approach to his liberal high school education. Within a year, he became director of the hospital as well as chief of medical services (1953–1959), launching an experimental program that combined excellent health care, research, and teaching, which was uncharacteristic at that time for a rural hospital. Maintaining his interest both in clinical medicine and academics, Pellegrino continued to teach clinical medicine once a week at New York's Bellevue Hospital during this period.

Having established his reputation as director of what under his aegis had become an outstanding community hospital, Pellegrino was offered the opportunity to be an influential force in a second rural hospital, this time at the University of Kentucky's newly founded College of Medicine in Lexington. Here he served as professor, chairman of the Department of Medicine, director of medical service, and senior physician from 1959 to 1966. He also established an excellent continuing education program for practicing doctors, just as he had done at Hunterdon. In these capacities, Pellegrino met with patients and worked with academic administrators, as well as with members of the medical community. He and the hospital's founders shared the philosophy that the best clinical teaching environment was one that gives first place to patient care. Working with a team, he helped put into motion plans that reflected his educational and medical philosophy. As a result, the design of the physical plant situated the clinical and science departments in close proximity, thus encouraging daily consultations among their departmental members in a collegial environment.

While at the University of Kentucky, Pellegrino helped form a curriculum that combined courses from both the humanities and sciences, a newly emerging idea in the early 1960s but one that helped set a new and valuable trend in medical education. On a practical level, he implemented his humanistic ideals by eliminating the system whereby the poor would sit lined up on benches waiting for outpatient treatment. Instead, he saw to it that rich and poor alike met with their doctors in private offices by appointment. He developed his own keen understanding of the needs of the underprivileged by volunteering in area clinics. Significantly, his ready acceptance of lecture engagements, participation in academic programs, and teaching abilities earned him the respect of the academic community to such a degree that his colleagues elected him chairman of the university's Senate.

By 1966, after helping to establish strong foundations in Hunterdon and Lexington, Pellegrino moved on to the State University of New York at Stony Brook. During his seven years there (1966–1973), he held various teaching and administrative positions, becoming Stony Brook's first dean of the School of Medicine (1968–1972), as well as director and first vice president of its Health Sciences Center. In these capacities, he was able to apply the same philosophy he held in Kentucky—reverence for human life, allegiance to the Hippocratic Oath, and commitment to the patient–physician covenant—but at Stony Brook, this was exercised on a much larger scale than before. In addition to outlining the direction for the teaching, health, and research programs, Pellegrino helped design the physical facilities for the Center's library, medical school, and hospital, thus setting the course for this institution. During that same period, he founded and was the first editor of the *Journal of Medicine and Philosophy* (1968–), a scholarly publication that consistently explores ethical and philosophical questions arising from current advances in science and medicine. The journal and Pellegrino's accomplishments were instrumental in expanding the dialogue concerning the ethics of new biotechnological advances both in the United States and abroad.

After his tenure at Stony Brook, Pellegrino became a consultant, and later administrator, for the University of Tennessee (1973–1975), where he fostered the development of a statewide medical system incorporating satellite clinical campuses as part of the center. In addition to his administrative positions, Pellegrino taught medicine, continuing to integrate the study of the humanities into the medical program. While he was still at Tennessee, Yale University contacted him, asking for assistance in putting together a medical center in Hartford, Connecticut. He accepted, becoming president and chairman of the board of Yale's New Haven Medical Center (1975–1978).

By the time Pellegrino became president of the Catholic University of America in Washington, D.C., in 1978, medical students across the country were benefiting from the type of programs he had envisioned and supported throughout his career. In addition to their medical training, they were engaged in the study of the ethical and human dimensions of their profession. In

the following years, this movement grew, spreading to other parts of the world.

In 1982, Pellegrino moved across the city to Georgetown University. During his tenure as John Carroll Professor of Medicine and Medical Ethics at the Georgetown University Medical Center (1982–2000), he held several other noteworthy positions, as director of Georgetown's Kennedy Institute of Ethics (1983–1989), Center for the Advanced Study of Ethics (1989–1994), and Center for Clinical Bioethics (1991–1996). As John Carroll Professor Emeritus of Medicine and Medical Ethics at Georgetown (2000–), Pellegrino continues to influence ethical decision making in the field of medicine.

Pellegrino's writings cover a broad range of topics that include such controversial human life issues as abortion, cloning, and stem-cell research. He has authored or coauthored more than 20 books and over 630 published items. He argues the necessity of examining the philosophical and ethical aspects of contemporary medical issues before putting new procedures into practice. Such preliminary studies are essential in order to provide a framework for making virtue-based ethical decisions concerning the latest biotechnological discoveries. As chairman of the President's Council on Bioethics (2005–2009), Pellegrino oversaw the issuance of in-depth papers and reports regarding such challenges: *Human Dignity and Bioethics*, *The Changing Moral Focus of Newborn Screening*, and *Controversies in the Determination of Death*.

Because of his reputation as an expert in both medicine and morality, Pellegrino has been invited to serve on influential committees and boards that affect worldwide practices, including the Pontifical Academy for Life (1994–) and the Committee on Bioethics of UNESCO (2004–). As further testimony to his excellent reputation, Pellegrino has been named a fellow of the Hastings Center (2005-) and has been asked to serve on 26 editorial boards, including those of the *Encyclopedia of Bioethics* (1974), the *Journal of the American Medical Association* (1987–), and the Catholic Health Association of the United States (2000–). As of 2010, he had received more than 50 honorary degrees from colleges and universities in the United States and Canada and more than 40 outstanding awards. Pellegrino's remarkable foresight in introducing the study of the humanities into medical training and promoting the rational discussion of moral, medical, and scientific issues have merited him this well-deserved recognition.—Jane H. Gilroy

BIBLIOGRAPHY AND FURTHER READING: Kilner, John F. *Cutting-Edge Bioethics: A Christian Exploration of Technologies and Trends.* Grand Rapids, MI: Eerdmans, 2002; Mitchell, C. Ben. *Biotechnology and the Human Good.* Washington, DC: Georgetown University Press, 2007; Monagle, John F., and David C. Thomasma. *Health Care Ethics: Critical Issues for the Twenty-First Century.* Sudbury, MA: Jones & Bartlett, 2005; Pellegrino, Edmund D. *The Philosophy of Medicine Reborn: A Pellegrino Reader.* Edited by H. Tristram Engelhardt Jr. and Fabrice Jotterand. Notre Dame, IN: University of Notre Dame Press, 2008; Thomasma, David C., ed. *Festschrift: The Influence of Edmund D. Pellegrino's Philosophy of Medicine.* Dordrecht, The Netherlands: Kluwer Academic, 2010. *See also* ABORTION; BIOETHICS; CLONING; HIPPOCRATIC OATH; PONTIFICAL ACADEMY FOR LIFE; VIRTUE-ETHICS

PERSISTENT VEGETATIVE STATE, FEEDING AND HYDRATING PERSONS IN A

A "persistent vegetative state" (PVS) can be described as a condition marked by the following behaviors: a state of apparent vigilance, some alteration of sleep/wake cycles, and an absence of signs of awareness of self or environment and of response to environmental stimuli. The term does not correspond to a specific anatomical abnormality or injury, although patients who exhibit the behaviors suffer from severe brain injury.

It was long thought that PVS patients, notwithstanding their mysterious "waking cycles," are incapable of all conscious activity. But recent scientific evidence demonstrates that some PVS patients can respond consciously to stimuli in the environment, including painful stimuli.

When the U.S. bishops first began to teach on the care due to patients in a persistent vegetative state, they were divided on the matter. In 1990, the Texas bishops judged that someone in this condition suffered a "lethal pathology which, without artificial nutrition and hydration will lead to death" and that withholding or withdrawing assisted nutrition and hydration (ANH) from such persons simply acknowledges that "the person has come to the end of his or her pilgrimage and should not be impeded [by ANH] from taking the final step." Some individual bishops (e.g., Louis Gelineau of Providence, Rhode Island) issued similar statements.

In 1992, the Committee for Pro-Life Activities of the National Conference of Catholic Bishops published a document that considered current medical literature on the PVS condition and different positions taken by moral theologians on the question of morally requisite care. The committee stated that it did not find persuasive the argument that, since persons in the PVS condition can no longer consciously pursue spiritual goals, providing them ANH is futile and/or unduly burdensome. The committee concluded: "We hold for a presumption in favor of providing medically assisted nutrition and hydration to patients who need it, which presumption would yield in cases where such procedures have no medically reasonable hope of sustaining life or pose excessive risks or burdens."

In the same year, the Pennsylvania bishops issued a similar document, in which they declared: "As a general conclusion, in almost every instance there is an obligation to continue supplying nutrition and hydration to the unconscious patient. There are situations in which this is not the case [e.g., when a patient's body can no longer assimilate the food and so its provision is useless], but these are exceptions and should not be made into the rule." They judged that ANH is "clearly beneficial in terms of preservation of life," does not add a "serious burden" in the vast majority of cases, and consequently is in principle morally obligatory. Other individual bishops (e.g., James McHugh of Camden, New Jersey, and John Myers of Peoria, Illinois) and certain state bishops' conferences (e.g., the Missouri Conference of Catholic Bishops) issued statements reaching conclusions similar to the Pro-Life Committee and the Pennsylvania bishops.

Kevin O'Rourke, OP, is the best known advocate during this time of the view that ANH for persons in the vegetative state is *not* morally required. He claimed that his position was based on an address of Pope Pius XII to a congress of anesthesiologists in which the pope emphasized that "life, health, [and] all temporal activities are in fact subordinated to spiritual ends." He continued that "normally one is held to use only ordinary means" to prolong life, that is, "means that do not involve any grave burdens for oneself or another." The pope concluded, "A stricter obligation would be too burdensome for most men and would render the attainment of the higher, more important good too difficult." O'Rourke interpreted Pius as saying that a means is "extraordinary," and hence not obligatory, if it does not enable a person to strive for the spiritual purpose of life. This position was also taken by his colleague Benedict Ashley, OP, in their *Health Care Ethics* in editions published prior to 2004. O'Rourke and Ashley also claimed that persons in the vegetative state were suffering from a "fatal pathology" and that all ANH does is preserve "mere physiological functioning."

O'Rourke's interpretation of Pope Pius's address was criticized by others. Although a means of preserving life is "extraordinary" and not morally required if it *prevents* a person from pursuing the spiritual purpose of life, they argued, it is not extraordinary when "*ineffective . . . in helping a person strive for the spiritual purpose of life.*" Some mentally impaired infants, children, and senile elderly people are (and will remain) incapable of making judgments and choices and thus cannot pursue the "spiritual goal of life," but to deny them the food and water they need to survive would be gravely immoral. Such means, so long as they are adequate to sustain bodily life, are always "ordinary" or "proportionate."

Several ethical truths and principles are relevant to this matter: (1) human bodily life, however burdened, is still a good of the person, integral to his or her being; (2) it is always gravely immoral intentionally to kill an innocent human being, that is, to deprive him or her of the good of life itself; (3) means chosen to preserve human life are morally obligatory if they are morally (if not necessarily medically) ordinary or proportionate; (4) means chosen to preserve human life are not obligatory—and in fact their withholding or withdrawal may be morally indicated—if they are morally (again, not necessarily medically) extraordinary or disproportionate; and (5) means are extraordinary or disproportionate if the means chosen are either futile (useless) or burdensome. Treatments can be burdensome for different valid reasons such as extreme pain that is unable to be regulated, extreme cost, interference with activities in which one legitimately wishes to engage although suffering from a fatal pathology, or compelling a person to leave loved ones and families to move to another area (e.g., moving to Arizona from Washington, D.C.).

As John Finnis shows, one can make judgments about the burdensomeness of different medical treatments, because there are ways of objectively assessing the cost, pain, and grave impositions on one's lifestyle and so forth. But one can never measure the worth of a human life, because it is of incalculable worth and not capable of being measured. One cannot put a price on it because it is priceless.

On March 20, 2004, Pope John Paul II delivered an address on the subject of providing ANH to persons in a PVS, based on current medical and scientific findings relevant to the vegetative state. The pope included the following principal ideas: First, "*A man, even if seriously ill or disabled in the exercise of his highest functions, is and always will be a man,* and he will never become a 'vegetable' or an 'animal'" (# 3; emphasis in original). Second, sick persons, including those in a vegetative state, have a right to basic health care, which includes "nutrition, hydration, cleanliness, warmth, etc.," "appropriate rehabilitative care," and monitoring "for clinical signs of eventual recovery" (# 4). Third, ANH is "in principle" morally required for persons in a PVS. The Holy Father affirmed: "I should like to underline how the administration of food and water, even when provided by artificial means, always represents a *natural means* of preserving life, not a medical act. Its use, furthermore, should be considered, in principle, *ordinary and proportionate*, and as such morally obligatory, insofar as and until it is seen to have attained its proper finality, which in the present case consists in providing nourishment to the patient and alleviation of his suffering" (# 4; emphasis in original). Fourth, one must never make a person's life contingent on its quality. "It is not enough to reaffirm the general principle according to which the value of a man's life cannot be made subordinate to any judgment of its quality . . . ; it is necessary to promote the *taking of positive actions* as a stand against pressures to withdraw hydration and nutrition as a way to put an end to the lives of these patients" (# 6; emphasis in original). Fifth, "It is necessary, above all, *to support those families* who have had one of their loved ones struck down by this terrible clinical condition" (# 6; emphasis added).

After John Paul II's address, the U.S. bishops realized the need to revise the directive treating this issue in the *Ethical and Religious Directives for Catholic Health Care Services (ERD)*, a set of ethical norms governing the activities of Catholic health care facilities in the United States. In the fourth (2001) edition of the *ERD*, Directive 59, dealing with the administration of ANH, read as follows: "There should be a presumption in favor of providing nutrition and hydration to all patients, including patients who require medically assisted nutrition and hydration, as long as this is of sufficient benefit to outweigh the burdens involved to the patient."

The bishops knew that some Catholic health care providers and ethics committees were claiming that this directive allowed removing or withholding ANH from PVS patients. In order to bring the directive in line with the papal teaching and prevent this serious misinterpretation, the U.S. bishops at their fall 2009 plenary meeting reformulated the relevant directive, which now states: "In principle, there is an obligation to provide patients with food and water, including medically assisted nutrition and hydration for those who cannot take food orally. This obligation extends to patients in chronic and presumably irreversible conditions (e.g., the 'persistent vegetative state') who can reasonably be expected to live indefinitely if given such care. Medically assisted nutrition and hydration become morally optional when they cannot reasonably be expected to prolong life or when they would be 'excessively burdensome for the patient or [would] cause significant physical discomfort, for example resulting from complications in the use of the means employed.' For instance, as a patient draws close to inevitable death from an underlying progressive and fatal condition, certain measures to provide nutrition and hydration may become excessively burdensome and therefore not obligatory in light of their very limited ability to prolong life or provide comfort."

Like the 2004 papal address, this reformulation acknowledges that nutrition and hydration may be removed when no longer proportionate to their end (i.e., when they are no longer needed to sustain life) or when their administration is gravely burdensome to the patient. It is important to note that the directive does *not* say that ANH may be removed if a person judges that his *life* on a feeding tube is too burdensome. The burden referred to here arises from the administration of ANH itself. The intention in withdrawing the ANH is to free the patient from the burdens imposed by artificial feeding; the fact that the patient's death may be hastened by the act is accepted as a foreseen but unintended effect. But to remove ANH with the intention of ending the life of a patient because the judgment has been made that *life* in the PVS is too burdensome (i.e., performing an act *in order to* bring about death) is euthanasia. It follows that the directive should not be interpreted as permitting the removal of food and water from patients who are not dying. This is one of the misinterpretations the reformulation of the relevant ERD directive was intended to correct.

The major negative responses Pope John Paul II's address elicited held that it marked "a significant departure from the Roman Catholic bioethical tradition" and that it was not in conformity with the 1980 *Declaration on Euthanasia* from the Congregation for the Doctrine of the Faith (CDF) primarily because it imposes excessively severe burdens on the families of such persons. These objections are misplaced, however.

John Paul II's address is entirely compatible with "traditional Catholic teaching." In *Evangelium Vitae*, he explicitly appealed to the CDF's 1980 *Declaration on Euthanasia* to distinguish euthanasia "from the decision to forgo . . . medical procedures which no longer correspond to the real situation of the patient, either

because they are by now disproportionate to any expected results or because they impose an excessive burden on the patient and his family. . . . [Doing so] is not the equivalent of suicide or euthanasia; it rather expresses acceptance of the human condition in the face of death" (*EV* # 65). The pope obviously judged it appropriate to withhold or withdraw the provision of nutrition and hydration for legitimate reasons (e.g., futility or excessive burdensomeness).

Not long after his March 20 address, Pope John Paul II delivered another address, on November 12, 2004, in which he reaffirmed the Catholic tradition teaching that treatment that is "ineffective or obviously disproportionate to the aims of sustaining life or recovering health" may be withheld or withdrawn. This address is in conformity with, and in no way contrary to, his teaching in March on the obligation, in principle, to provide food and hydration to the permanently unconscious "insofar as and until it is seen to have attained its proper finality, which in the present case consists in providing nourishment to the patient and alleviation of his suffering" (March 2004 address, # 3).

Nor does the pope impose excessively grave burdens on families. In most cases, the burdens imposed by feeding and hydrating patients in a PVS are proportionate to feeding and hydrating those paralyzed from the neck down or suffering loss of all limbs. Admittedly, the total care of persons in each of these states can and does impose burdens—they must not only be fed and hydrated, but kept warm in the winter, cool in the summer, given shelter, and so forth. But these persons are not the only ones whose care causes burdens: staying up at night with an infant child, caring for an elderly parent, and tending to the needs of a gravely sick spouse or disabled child or sibling all impose burdens. But these types of care are morally required by the Golden Rule and are honored by any civilized society. Justice requires that others accept the duties associated with caring for disabled persons, and Christian charity deepens that duty. Moreover, withholding or withdrawing ANH would not eliminate the burden of caring for disabled persons until they die; their *death* ends the caregiver's burden. But to remove ANH *in order to* bring about death so that one may be free of the burden of caring for another is euthanasia.

In 2007, the CDF, in its "Responses to Certain Questions of the United States Conference of Catholic Bishops Concerning Artificial Nutrition and Hydration" and the accompanying commentary, vigorously defended Pope John Paul's 2004 address and showed why criticisms leveled against it are seriously in error. From this, it is clear that, with rare exceptions clearly indicated, ANH is morally required for persons in the persistent vegetative state.—William E. May and E. Christian Brugger

BIBLIOGRAPHY AND FURTHER READING: Ashley, Benedict M., OP, Jean deBlois, CSJ, and Kevin O'Rourke, OP. *Health Care Ethics: A Catholic Theological Analysis*, 5th ed. Washington, DC: Georgetown University Press, 2006; Ashley, Benedict, OP, and Kevin O'Rourke, OP. *Health Care Ethics: A Theological Analysis*, 4th ed. Washington, DC: Georgetown University Press, 1997; Brugger, E. Christian, and William E. May. "Are Food and Water Ordinary Measures?" *Zenit*, May 10, 2010; Cahill, Lisa Sowle. "Catholicism, Death and Modern Medicine," *America* 192, no. 14 (2005): 14–17; Committee for Pro-Life Activities, National Conference of Catholic Bishops. *Nutrition and Hydration: Moral and Pastoral Reflections.* Washington, DC: USCCB, 1992; Congregation for the Doctrine of the Faith, *Declaration on Euthanasia (Jura et Bona)*, May 5, 1980; Congregation for the Doctrine of the Faith, "Responses to Certain Questions of the United States Conference of Catholic Bishops Concerning Artificial Nutrition and Hydration"; Finnis, John. *Fundamentals of Ethics*. Washington, DC: Georgetown University Press, 1983; International Federation of Catholic Medical Associations and the Pontifical Academy for Life. "Life-Sustaining Treatments and Vegetative State: Scientific Advances and Ethical Dilemmas." International Congress, Rome, March 17–20, 2004; Jesuit Consortium of Bioethical Schools. "Undue Burden? The Vatican and Artificial Nutrition and Hydration." *Commonweal*, February 13, 2009; John Paul II. "Life-Sustaining Treatments and Vegetative State: Scientific Advances and Ethical Dilemmas." Address, March 20, 2004; May, William E. *Catholic Bioethics and the Gift of Human Life*, 2nd ed. Huntington, IN: Our Sunday Visitor, 2008; O'Rourke, Kevin, OP. "The A.M.A. Statement on Tube-Feeding: An Ethical Analysis." *America* 155 (1986): 321–333; Pius XII. "The Prolongation of Life: Allocution to the International Congress of Anesthesiologists" [November 24, 1957]. *Pope Speaks* 4 (1958): 396; Shannon, Thomas A., and James Walter. "Implications of the Papal Allocution on Feeding Tubes." *Hastings Center Report* 34, no. 4 (July–August 2004): 18–20. *See also* BIOETHICS; LIFE, ORDINARY AND EXTRAORDINARY MEANS OF SUSTAINING

PERSONA HUMANA   On December 29, 1975, the Congregation for the Doctrine of the Faith (CDF) promulgated "Declaration on Certain Questions Concerning Sexual Ethics," usually referred to as *Persona Humana* after the first two words of the Latin text. It was signed by the prefect of the CDF, Cardinal Franjo Šeper, and the secretary, Archbishop Jérôme Hamer. It had been approved for promulgation by Pope Paul VI on November 7 and was presented to the public on January 15, 1976.

Although in the days immediately following its presentation several supportive articles were published in the Holy See's official newspaper, *L'Osservatore Romano*, in general—especially in the English-speaking world—it was greeted with dissent and dismissal. The fundamental reason for this was that the document reiterated what the Holy See knew were three of the then most assailed teachings of Catholic (that is, natural law-based) sexual ethics: the immorality of premarital sex, homosexual acts, and masturbation. It also confronted issues of a more theoretical character, such as the thesis, rejected by the document, that a mortal sin is committed only when one makes an explicit "fundamental option" rejecting God and not, for instance, when one performs a single act of masturbation.

In 2006, the successor to Cardinal Šeper, Cardinal Joseph Ratzinger, explained that the literary form of the document as a "declaration" indicates that it "formalizes an already existing position of the Church, articulating in a more binding manner certain objective principles in the field of sexual morality." The future pope also noted that *Persona Humana* is a pastoral document and invited pastors of souls to apply its objective principles to individual cases with prudence and understanding.

A fairly brief document, *Persona Humana* is divided into 13 numbered sections. The first four depict the societal situation that obliged the CDF to speak out on these disputed issues. The first lines refer to the judgment of learned men of our day that sexuality so characterizes the individual person that upon it depends his or her progress toward psychological and spiritual maturity and insertion into society. The document acknowledges, therefore, the contribution of the social sciences, and yet it singles out certain educators, teachers, and moralists as promoting behaviors incompatible with Church teaching and the exigencies of human nature (# 1). The one idea explicitly criticized in these early sections is the idea that neither in human nature nor in revealed law can there be found any "absolute and immutable norm" regarding particular acts other than the general obligation of charity and respect for human dignity (# 4).

In the final sentence of section 5, the document states the fundamental principle of all sexual morality and so also the one that governs its own particular teaching: "The use of the sexual function has its true meaning and moral rectitude only in true marriage [*in matrimonio legitimo*]." In section 7, therefore, it opposes those who would say that sexual union before marriage by a couple with the firm intention of marrying is moral; it insists, on the contrary, that the constant teaching of the Church is that no genital action outside of publicly ratified marriage can be legitimate. In a note, it cites in support papal teachings from the 13th, 15th, 17th, and 20th centuries. In a way, this attention given to the sexual activity of engaged couples dates *Persona Humana*. Thirty-five years after its publication, the sexual activity of engaged couples is less of a pressing issue—but *only* because sexual activity between those with no such firm intention to marry is so prevalent even among those who call themselves Catholics.

Homosexual relations are treated in section 8. The document recognizes a distinction between homosexual tendencies that are transitory and curable and those that are due to "some kind of innate instinct or a pathological constitution," but it denies that, even in the latter case, sexual acts can be morally acceptable. It explicitly rejects the position of those who maintain that people of a permanent homosexual orientation might enter into unions similar to marriage (*communionem matrimonii consimilem*). Quoting in full Romans 1:24–27, the CDF asserts that homosexual acts lack the order proper to sexual acts considered as such. The section's last sentence reads: "This judgment of Scripture does not of course permit us to conclude that all those who suffer from this anomaly [*deformitate*] are personally responsible for it, but it does attest to the fact that homosexual acts are intrinsically disordered [*suapte intrinseca natura . . . inordinatos*]." In Cardinal Ratzinger's 2006 comments on *Persona Humana*, he notes that this remark was misinterpreted by some in such a way that the homosexual tendency itself (as distinct from homosexual acts) was portrayed as either indifferent or even good. This misinterpretation, he says, was dealt with by the CDF in the 1986 "Letter on the Pastoral Care of Homosexual Persons" (# 3). There, the homosexual tendency is described as "objectively disordered [*obiective inordinata*]." The same teaching is repeated in the *Catechism of the Catholic Church* (# 2358).

In section 9, *Persona Humana* says that, according to the constant tradition of the Church, masturbation is "an intrinsically and seriously disordered act." Again, it cites in support papal teachings, some of them of considerable antiquity. One such teaching of particular topical interest is an 11th-century letter from Pope Leo

IX to St. Peter Damien in which the pope commends the latter's letter 31 [*opusculum* 7], also known as *Liber Gomorrhianus*. In this work, the saint argues that priests who engage in unnatural vice in different degrees—solitary masturbation, masturbation with another, emission of semen "between the thighs," and anal intercourse—should be deposed from the priesthood. He speaks explicitly and harshly of priests who abuse boys and young men and of prelates who fail to discipline them. *Persona Humana*'s section 9, however, is concerned mostly with the arguments of those who would judge masturbation (in many instances) as normal behavior and therefore not a grave matter. The document acknowledges that, especially among adolescents, psychological imbalance or habit can diminish true deliberation to such an extent that "subjectively there may not always be serious fault"; it insists nonetheless that, since such acts contradict essentially the end of the sexual faculty, they are in themselves seriously disordered.

Since acts of masturbation appear to certain scholars to be of such slight significance morally, this discussion leads very naturally into a consideration of the nature of sin and the so-called fundamental option. The document, of course, acknowledges that there is such a thing as a "fundamental option towards God," but it insists, in opposition to some prominent moral theologians of the day, that this option can be altered radically by particular sexual acts, "especially when, as often happens, these have been prepared for by previous more superficial acts" (# 10).

As already mentioned, when it was first published, opposition to *Persona Humana* was widespread. This opposition is well documented in Richard McCormick's "Notes on Moral Theology: 1976." As was to be expected, it took various forms, only one of which—philosophically and theologically, the most important one—can be considered (very briefly) here.

Many of the critics of *Persona Humana* complain that its methodology is "deductive." Reading through it, though, one is hard-pressed to identify a syllogism (two premises and a conclusion). The objection of the critics seems, instead, to be not to the document's methodology but to its endorsement of the view that there are exceptionless moral precepts, which it applies to particular acts. The objection is, therefore, not to the methodology but to the teaching itself. The critics' own methodology tends to run together two essentially distinct spheres of analysis: the objective and the subjective. It is one thing to consider the intelligible character of an act (including its possible lack of intelligibility due to an absence of order to the proper end); it is quite another to ask whether the person performing the act is doing so voluntarily. The critics in question wish to import the latter subjective consideration into the sphere of objective analysis so as to render the latter—in itself—less demanding. But this confusion of distinct spheres only renders ethical analysis less precise and less accurate.—Kevin L. Flannery, SJ

BIBLIOGRAPHY AND FURTHER READING: Peter Damian. *Letters.* Translated by Owen J. Blum. Washington, DC: Catholic University of America Press, 1990; Congregation for the Doctrine of the Faith, Joseph Cardinal Ratzinger, et al. "Dichiarazione circa Alcune Questioni di Etica Sessuale: Considerazioni della Congregazione per la Dottrina della Fede." *Documenti e Studi*, 20. Rome: Libreria Editrice Vaticana, 2006; May, William E. *Catholic Sexual Ethics.* New Haven, CT: Catholic Information Service, 2001; McCormick, Richard A. "Notes on Moral Theology: 1976." *Theological Studies* 38 (1977): 57–114.

PIEPER, JOSEF (1904–1997) Josef Pieper was born in Elte, a small village in Westphalia, Germany, where his father was the schoolteacher. When he was eight years old, the family moved to Münster, where Pieper subsequently attended the 1,100-year-old Gymnasium Paulinum. It was while he was a student there, having outgrown a youthful fascination for the works of Søren Kierkegaard, that he was introduced to St. Thomas Aquinas, and thus began for him a lifelong dedication to the study and exposition of Thomistic thought. After studying at the University of Münster, Pieper then went on to the University of Berlin, where he earned his PhD in philosophy at the age of 24. His doctoral dissertation was entitled "The Ontic Foundation of Morality in Thomas Aquinas," and in it he contested the notion, which is regarded as virtually a truism in much contemporary ethical philosophy, that it is illegitimate to move from *is* to *ought* in moral reasoning. Pieper demonstrated that this is an entirely specious notion and that, as a matter of fact, every *ought* is grounded in the *is*, which is to say, all the moral tenets by which we govern our lives have their roots in actual reality, in the objective order of things. To suppose otherwise is to open the door to subjectivism and moral relativism.

After receiving his doctorate, Pieper was for several years an assistant at the Institute for Social Research at the University of Münster, where conducting seminars comprised part of his duties. It came as an appreciable shock to him when, in 1933, the Nazi Party took control of the German government, for, as he explains in his autobiography, *No One Could Have Known*, he and the people with whom he associated hardly gave a thought to politics. But those in politics had nonetheless given more than a thought to him; in short order, he was prohibited from giving public speeches, his first book was taken off the market and the firm that had published it shut down, and he was blocked from taking a position on a university faculty. Even so, given his background, he was able to secure a position during the war years in the testing service of the air force, and this allowed him to support his family. By a bit of ingenious maneuvering that prevented him from being bothered by the regime, and backed by a publisher not easily intimidated, he managed to publish a number of books during the war years that were intended to serve as a basic library for lay Christians and, he wrote later, "to provide a counterweight to the ever-increasing pressure of the Nazi world view."

When the war ended and a democratic government was restored in Germany, he received an appointment to the faculty at the University of Münster, where he remained for his entire academic career, continuing his teaching long after others would have retired and maintaining throughout his reputation as a captivating lecturer who always dealt with substantive issues. Over the years, he lectured at many universities in the United States, and in 1962 he made an extensive lecture tour of India. Pieper died in 1997.

It is difficult to give a precise characterization of Pieper as a philosopher. He certainly can be identified as a Thomist, and an exceptionally good one; indeed, he could be said to have been a Thomist in much the same way as was St. Thomas himself—which is to say that he was principally interested in the truth and therefore sought it out wherever it could be found. Pieper was as assiduous a student of Plato and Aristotle as he was of Aquinas, and he was ready to recognize sound and defensible ideas even when they came from a philosopher with whom he for the most part disagreed. In all, he can be most accurately identified as one who sought to put himself in the mainstream of what Pope Leo XIII identified in his encyclical *Aeterni Patris* as the "perennial philosophy."

Pieper was a popular philosopher, in the sense that his books appealed to a wide audience, but the basic explanation for his popularity is to be found in the succinct, carefully focused character of all of his books, and the fact they are written in a prose style that is remarkable for its clarity and cogency. One of Pieper's greatest strengths as a philosopher was his ability to communicate complex and even profound ideas to a general audience in a lucid and compelling manner.

This was the result of a very conscious effort on his part, in which he modeled himself on Aquinas. For Pieper, the principal purpose of philosophy was "to reflect on the totality of the real." But because the "real" concerns everyone, philosophers should attempt to address everyone in reporting the results of their reflections.

Pieper wrote on a wide variety of subjects, proving himself to be a philosopher whose interests were as catholic as they were Catholic. Because there is such a remarkable balance to be found among all of his books in terms of the quality of the contents of each, it is difficult to single out any one of them for special praise, and there is no one of his books that could be called his magnum opus. To mention just a few titles, by way of providing a sampler of his work: In *Leisure, the Basis of Culture*, Pieper takes up philosophic arms against a narrow and wrongheaded practicality that would reduce all life to profit-motivated work. The leisure he advocates here is not idleness, but contemplative rest, a state of quiet in which one can listen to the real. *The Four Cardinal Virtues*, besides giving an especially insightful overall analysis of the most important of the moral virtues, is particularly valuable for the way in which it restores a sound understanding of prudence, the chief of the moral virtues. *Living the Truth* provides convincing evidence of Pieper's prowess as a metaphysician. The subtitle of *In Defense of Philosophy* is *Classical Wisdom Stands Up to the Modern Challenge*, and the book meets the challenge with verve, making the strongest kind of case for the need to return to a right understanding of philosophy as the pursuit of wisdom. In *Tradition: Concept and Claim*, Pieper argues tellingly that it is of the very nature of tradition, correctly conceived, that it must be handed on just as it has been received, that is, unchanged. *In Search of the Sacred* provides a pointed analysis of the kind of errant theological thinking that led to the confusion in the Church following the Second Vatican Council, a confusion most evidently displayed in the liturgy. A secularized, desacralized society, he argues, can only eventuate, sooner or later, in a dehumanized society.

Philosopher Ralph McInerny has described Pieper's *Guide to Thomas Aquinas* as "one of the best introductions to the thought of St. Thomas by one of the leading figures in the Thomistic revival." In the preface to *Guide to Thomas Aquinas*, Pieper wrote that the purpose of the book was to present a portrait of Aquinas "as he truly concerns philosophical-minded persons today, not merely as a historical personage but as a thinker who has something to say to our own era." The statement perfectly reflects how Pieper himself responded to

Aquinas and his works. All of his writings on the saint have the effect of demonstrating that the thought of the Common Doctor, in all its essentials, is timeless and as such lends itself to universal application. The peculiar genius of Pieper, as a Thomist, was the constructive and illuminating way he applied the thought of St. Thomas to contemporary issues and problems. He productively developed that thought, going beyond Aquinas in dealing with a variety of subjects, but always in a way that was perfectly consonant with the spirit of Aquinas's thought.

Poet T. S. Eliot, who himself had studied philosophy up to the point of a doctorate, rightly saw that the poverty of so much modern philosophy lay in the fact that it was lacking in insight and wisdom, and he just as rightly saw that what set Josef Pieper apart as a philosopher was that these two precious possessions were his. Eliot went on to make an especially perspicacious observation about Pieper when, taking note of his originality, he identified it as "subdued and unostentatious." Pieper's originality was subdued because of the utter seriousness with which he took the enterprise to which he was totally dedicated. It was unostentatious because Pieper never called attention to himself. As a philosopher, he showed edifying consistency in keeping himself focused on the principal purpose of philosophy: the pursuit of truth. Pieper's insights were derived from his wisdom, and his wisdom was owed, fundamentally, to his realization that a philosophy not founded upon theology is barren.—D. Q. McInerny

BIBLIOGRAPHY AND FURTHER READING: Austenfeld, Thomas. "Josef Pieper's Contemplative Assent to the World." *Modern Age* 42, no. 4 (2000): 372–382; *Josef Pieper: An Anthology*. San Francisco: Ignatius Press, 1989. *See also* McINERNY, RALPH; PHILOSOPHY, DISCIPLINE OF; THOMISM/NEO-THOMISM

PINCKAERS, SERVAIS-THÉODORE, OP (1925–2008)
Servais Pinckaers was a Belgian Dominican moral theologian best known in the English-speaking world for his book *The Sources of Christian Ethics*—a groundbreaking work in fundamental moral theology attempting to respond to the Second Vatican Council's (1962–1965) call for renewal in the discipline and anticipating by almost two decades the scriptural and virtue-informed approach to moral theology of the *Catechism of the Catholic Church* (French, 1992; English, 1994; revised 1997) and the encyclical *Veritatis Splendor* (1993). The Holy See appointed Pinckaers to serve on the commission charged with preparing the *Catechism*—of which he is said to have helped draft its

moral section—as well as the commission charged with preparing *Veritatis Splendor*. It should be no surprise then to see reflected in these historic magisterial documents some of the moral vision of Father Pinckaers.

Pinckaers was born in Liège, Belgium, in the fall of 1925 and grew up in the village of Wonck in Belgium's Walloon region. Twenty years later, he entered the Dominican Order, studying theology at the Studium (study house) of the Belgian Dominicans at La Sarte, in the town of Huy. Here in 1952, the year after his priestly ordination, he received a license in sacred theology under the direction of the dogmatic theologian and future cardinal, Jérôme Hamer, OP, writing a licentiate thesis on another future cardinal's landmark book, Henri de Lubac, SJ's *Surnaturel: Études historiques* (1946).

De Lubac's work, like the *nouvelle théologie* movement in general that it was identified with, was controversial at the time for its understanding of the nature–grace relationship, but was one that Pinckaers largely approved, especially its emphasis on the notion of the "natural desire" to see God. Still, Pinckaers did not agree with everything in de Lubac's treatise. For example, as he expressed it in a later essay, he took issue with the Jesuit's characterization of St. Thomas Aquinas's understanding of human nature (under Aristotle's influence) as "self-sufficient." Rather, Pinckaers argued, human nature for the Common Doctor is "open to God and His grace."

Pinckaers saw the thesis of the *desiderium naturale visionis dei* as the position held by Aquinas himself. Pinckaers made clear, however, that this desire does not, for him or for St. Thomas, "impose any demands on God." As he saw the matter, already within the "natural desire" there is etched an unwillingness to violate the supernatural character of God's gifts (e.g., the Incarnation, his grace) to human beings.

Pinckaers's studies for the license were followed beginning in 1952 by work toward his doctorate at the Pontifical University of St. Thomas Aquinas in Rome, popularly known as the Angelicum. His dissertation, "La vertu d'espérance, de Pierre Lombard à St. Thomas d'Aquin" ("The Virtuous Nature of Hope, from Peter Lombard to St. Thomas Aquinas," 1954), was directed by Louis-Bertrand Gillon, OP, and examined the medieval theology of hope. Parts of it would be published as articles in the 1950s, and these in turn were incorporated into an early book of his, *Le renouveau de la morale* (1964).

In the course of his doctoral studies, Pinckaers also attended the classes of such notable theologians as Frenchman and future cardinal Paul-Pierre Philippe,

OP; Italian and future cardinal Mario Luigi Ciappi, OP; and the famous Thomist Reginald Garrigou-Lagrange, OP (1877–1964). By attending the latter's classes, Pinckaers was exposed to this formidable French Thomist who had directed Karol Wojtyla's doctoral thesis on faith in St. John of the Cross. He was well known for, among other things, his traditional scholasticism, writings on the spiritual life, and hostility to the historical method in theology—a method that Pinckaers much favored, as seen in his theological training at La Sarte and throughout his career, and very much on display in his most famous work, *The Sources of Christian Ethics*.

Pinckaers obtained his doctorate in sacred theology in 1954 and then taught moral theology at the Studium at La Sarte from 1954 to 1965. It was here, as most of the few (and brief) biographies of Pinckaers available note, that he would begin a project of the renewal of moral theology and, by doing so, anticipate the Second Vatican Council's own call for renewal of the discipline by several years. Most of these biographies also note his *Le renouveau de la morale* as evidence of his early efforts at renewal.

His time spent at La Sarte, both as student and as teacher, were apparently important for developing the key ideas of Pinckaers's moral theology. In an essay in the English-language edition of the theological journal *Communio*, Pinckaers identified the principal "sources" of his moral theology—which served, too, as key elements of his vision of a renewed moral theology—as: (1) the attraction to the Eucharist that he felt from infancy; (2) the primacy of the Word of God as the principal and preeminent source of theology, superior to any merely human word; (3) studying and teaching theology at the feet of St. Thomas Aquinas, using the texts of the *Summa Theologica*—a study that also included his awareness of the patristic component to Aquinas's thought, especially that of St. Augustine; and (4) the necessity of studying ancient and modern philosophers so as to be open to all that is human. Each of these elements, as well as an awareness of the importance of a proper method for moral theology and a correct understanding of the role of experience, is among his lampposts in *Sources*.

Finally, the biographies of Pinckaers note that after the study house at La Sarte was closed in 1965, he went to the Dominican priory at Liège and engaged in pastoral ministry for the next eight years—years that attuned Pinckaers to the pastoral dimension one sees in his work. It most assuredly helped form his ideas on the importance of moral theology being closely bonded to spirituality so as to better overcome the split between faith and culture/morality so characteristic of the modern world and so worrisome to the Fathers of the Second Vatican Council (cf. *GS # 43*). Popular works—and he wrote many of these, even late in life—such as *The Pursuit of Happiness*, acutely demonstrate this awareness by a focus on the centrality of the Beatitudes of the Sermon on the Mount for happiness.

In 1972–1973, Pinckaers spent a year at the University of Fribourg in Switzerland as an invited professor. He returned there in 1975, in the French-language chair in fundamental moral theology, and taught at the university for the next 25 years. During this time, Pinckaers also served on the papally appointed International Theological Commission (1992–1997), an advisory body to the Congregation for the Doctrine of the Faith, and in 1990, received the Dominican order's most prestigious honor, its master of sacred theology.

For the last decade of his life, Father Pinckaers remained in Fribourg as emeritus professor until his death on April 7, 2008, at the age of 82. In all, he had published some 25 books and over three hundred articles, both popular and scholarly. In the last years of his life, he spent time writing books on such favorite subjects of his as St. Augustine and virtue.

In some respects, Pinckaers might well be called the "moral theologian of the Beatitudes." Thus, Thomas O'Meara, OP, is correct to call him a "biblical Thomist." At the heart of his *Sources of Christian Ethics*—there is probably no better work to examine to survey the basic orientation and content of Pinckaers's moral theology—is the central importance of the Sermon on the Mount and the Beatitudes for Christian ethics.

Like Augustine before him, Pinckaers sees in the Lord's Sermon the "Magna Carta" or model of Christian ethics. He emphasizes and contrasts a moral theology built on the foundation of the Beatitudes with the 400-year tradition of the manuals of moral theology—running from the Council of Trent in the 16th century to Vatican II in the 20th and written in Latin by priests for the training of future priests—with their emphasis on duty and obligation stemming from nominalism. This would predispose the manuals not only to "legalism" but also to largely neglect such themes as beatitude, happiness, suffering, and love—the very sorts of themes that are predominant in the Bible—and overemphasize another biblical theme: sin.

According to Pinckaers, moral theology is the science of the meaning of life, and the Sermon on the Mount is Christ's answer to the question posed by the ancient pagan philosophers: How is man to attain happiness? Most importantly, Pinckaers sees the Beatitudes,

as did Augustine, as seven "stages" of the Christian life—moving from humility to purity of heart. Thus, for Pinckaers, the essential elements of Christian moral theology include grace, the Word of God, the sacraments, the Gifts of the Holy Spirit, the moral and theological virtues, and prayer (Pinckaers focuses on the Our Father and links its seven petitions to the Beatitudes, as did Augustine and Aquinas). These are some of the key features that give the Christian moral life its unquestioned uniqueness and essential dynamism.

Although Pinckaers robustly defends the existence of moral absolutes from such revisionist Catholic theologians as the proportionalists, he shies away from placing an emphasis on law, precepts, and commands as central to Christian ethics. We obey because we love, Pinckaers reminds us; we do not love because we obey. What gives the believer's moral life its specificity, then, is *faith in Christ* and the Christian virtues that flow from this life of faith. Hence, for Pinckaers, the Ten Commandments retain all of their validity, but at their core, he stresses, is the dual love commandment: the love of God and neighbor.

Pinckaers notes that for St. Paul, faith is the "source" of morality, giving rise to a "new being" and a transformation of the person in his totality, feelings included. With the Holy Spirit within the believer, transforming his very existence, it is now possible to "imitate" Christ. While rooted in faith, the Christian moral life centers on charity (*agape*), the Spirit's "greatest gift."

This, too, is the approach of Aquinas, as Pinckaers shows in a chapter of the *Sources* devoted to demonstrating the thoroughly Christian character of his moral teaching. At the heart of the "new law" (or "evangelical law"), for St. Thomas, is "chiefly the grace itself of the Holy Spirit, which is given to those who believe in Christ" (*STh* I–II, q. 106, art. 1). The Sermon functions as the "text" of this "interior law" of freedom. Therefore, Pinckaers emphasizes, unlike modern moral theories of obligation, Aquinas reconciles freedom and law in the grace and charity infused into us by the Holy Spirit.

Pinckaers's project in *Sources*, among other places, is also to show how far moral theology has strayed from this Augustinian and Thomistic vision of Christian ethics by tracing, beginning with William of Ockham's nominalism in the 14th century and continuing with the post-Tridentine manualists up to Vatican II, the path away from what he calls the "freedom for excellence" (i.e., the freedom to do the good, a virtuous freedom open to the spontaneity of the Holy Spirit) to the "freedom of indifference" (the dispassionate freedom to choose either good or evil without the spontaneous and natural attraction to the good).

In *The Dominicans*, Benedict M. Ashley, OP, expresses well this historical moral theology of Pinckaers when he notes that his fellow Dominican has "worked for a more thorough revision of moral theology based on a historical understanding of the effects of voluntarism in the late Middle Ages and on a return to a morality of character rather than of legality and casuistic decision. . . . This entails an opposition to the theory of Proportionalism advocated by some Jesuit theologians and others which seems to revive the least desirable aspects of Probabilism."

Despite Father Pinckaers's decided emphasis on the virtues (theological and moral) and the Scriptures, he does not ignore, by any means, the prominent role given to the natural moral law and its precepts in traditional Catholic theological ethics. In fact, he devotes a lengthy chapter of some 55 or so pages to natural law in *Sources*. But he stresses its roots in the natural inclinations of human nature—inclinations that are not just "biological" but "spiritual," because they are indeed at the source of voluntary free action and thus at the source of morality as the "seeds" of the virtues.

These inclinations both enliven and dynamically point us to various goods that fulfill us and lead to our flourishing: human life, sexual union, friendship, society, truth, and so on. Corresponding to each of them are precepts of the natural law and the virtues. Without at all downplaying the fact that natural law is a work of human reason, Pinckaers wants to recover the idea that the natural law, "imposed externally when taught, was in reality written in the human heart—in the very nature of our human faculties of reason and will, at the root of free action" (*Sources*, 405).

If one can find fault with Pinckaers's moral theology, at least as set forth in his classic work *The Sources of Christian Ethics*, it is in his seeming lack of interest in providing ordinary Christians with a practical method for going about making a concrete moral decision, such as we find in the moral thought of Germain Grisez. Of course, for Pinckaers, this might seem like the old casuistry, with its emphasis on cases of conscience. This, too, could largely explain Pinckaers's lack of attention to specific moral issues in his other writings, although he clearly recognizes the need for moral theology to give practical answers to today's moral problems, as the manualists did in their day.

Given both his high standard of Christian scholarship and large body of writings, with their scriptural, historical, and spiritual orientation, Father Pinckaers

should remain a theologian to be studied and discussed for years to come—hopefully not just in moral theology but in spiritual theology as well. I believe this to be true for, with St. Thomas, as Dominique Khoury-Hélou observes, Pinckaers has proposed for our day a moral theology of the good and the virtues based on the new law, while insisting on the supernatural end of the Christian life whose principal elements are faith, the Holy Spirit, and the grace that comes to us in the sacraments of the Church.—Mark S. Latkovic

BIBLIOGRAPHY AND FURTHER READING: Cessario, Romanus, OP. "Hommage au Père Servais-Théodore Pinckaers, O.P.: The Significance of His Work." *Nova et Vetera*, English ed., 5, no. 1 (2007): 1–16; Cessario, Romanus, OP. "On the Place of Servais Pinckaers (+ 7 April 2008) in the Renewal of Catholic Theology." *Thomist*, 73, no. 1 (2009): 1–27; Cessario, Romanus, OP. "Theology at Fribourg," *Thomist* 51, no. 2 (1987): 325–366; May, William E. "Recent Moral Theology: Servais Pinckaers and Benedict Ashley," *Thomist* 62, no. 1 (1998): 117–131; O'Meara, Thomas F., OP. "Interpreting Thomas Aquinas: Aspects of the Dominican School of Moral Theology in the Twentieth Century." In Stephen J. Pope, ed. *The Ethics of Aquinas*, 355–377. Washington, DC: Georgetown University Press, 2002; Pinckaers, Servais, OP. *Morality: The Catholic View*. South Bend, IN: St. Augustine's Press, 2001; Pinckaers, Servais, OP. *The Pinckaers Reader: Renewing Thomistic Moral Theology*. Edited by John Berkman and Craig Steven Titus. Washington, DC: Catholic University of America Press, 2005; Pinckaers, Servais, OP. *The Pursuit of Happiness—God's Way: Living the Beatitudes*. Staten Island, NY: Alba House, 1998; Pinckaers, Servais, OP. *The Sources of Christian Ethics*. Translated by Mary Thomas Noble, OP. Washington, DC: Catholic University of America Press, 1995 (original French ed., 1985); Sherwin, Michael S., OP. "Eulogy for Fr. Servais Theodore Pinckaers, O.P." *Nova et Vetera*, English ed., 7, no. 3 (2009): 549–553. *See also* BIBLICAL NATURAL LAW; GARRIGOU-LAGRANGE, REGINALD, OP; GRACE; GRISEZ, GERMAIN; NATURAL LAW; THOMISM/NEO-THOMISM; VIRTUES

PINKER, STEPHEN (1954–) Stephen Pinker is a Canadian American experimental psychologist, cognitive scientist, and author of popular scientific writings. His research has been in the areas of mental imagery, shape recognition, visual attention, children's language, and the neural basis of words and grammar. He is interested in many aspects of language and mind, but he is especially known for his work in cognitive processes, a computational theory of the mind, and evolutionary psychology. Most recently, Pinker has entered into debates on the merits of religions and religious perspectives as one of the "new" atheists.

Pinker was born of Jewish parents in Montreal and received his undergraduate degree in psychology from McGill University and his PhD in experimental psychology at Harvard University. He has taught at the Massachusetts Institute of Technology, Stanford University, and Harvard. Pinker's work has resulted in his receiving the Early Career Award (1984) and Boyd McCandless Award (1986) from the American Psychological Association, and the Troland Research Award (1993) from the National Academy of Sciences. He was twice a finalist for a Pulitzer Prize, in 1998 and 2003. *Time* named him one of the 100 most influential scientists and thinkers in the world in 2004.

Pinker's initial research was in the field of how the brain processes optical phenomena, specifically how three-dimensional space is represented as mental images and the range of attention that the eye holds beyond its focus. He also analyzed how we focus on charts and graphs. Pinker then turned to the area of the language development of children and wrote a book on how children acquire the words and grammatical structures of their native language. A subsequent text focused on the ability of children to correctly use different verb forms in sentences. These works launched a two-decade interest in the use of regular and irregular verbs and how the use of such verbs involved key processes in language development such as memory and syntax.

In 1994, Pinker published his first work for a general audience, *The Language Instinct*. In accessible prose, he introduced his claim that language is fundamentally a biological adaptation that is vibrant, flexible, and constantly evolving. He rejected a number of common assumptions, like the claims that the average person's grammar is poor, that the quality of language is declining, and that other primates can learn language. Language, he wrote, is an evolutionary adaptation, a developed instinct responding to the specific problem of communication among hunter-gatherers. *Instinct*, for Pinker, is a nonintentional but highly effective response to a problem; a *technology* would be an intentional response to a problem. This evolutionary schema became the foundation on which he developed his language theory. The book draws on the work of Noam Chomsky positing that language has a universal grammar for deciphering how any given language works. We do not reason to grammar structures in other languages, but already have the software for deciphering basic structures

of that language. This language processing has a specific location in the brain. Pinker deviated from Chomsky, however, in his claim that language is an inherited feature of humanity that was created and refined by natural selection.

Building on his work in *The Language Instinct*, Pinker offers an evolutionary explanation of our mental processes in *How the Mind Works*. Deploying his evolutionary and cognitive psychology, Pinker tackles a wide array of issues such as how we developed vision, reasoning, emotions, humor, feminism, emotion, art, and even the meaning of life. According to him, our mental processes developed from natural selection to respond to issues in our ancient past as hunter-gatherers. In this book, Pinker also develops in detail the idea that the brain is a computational entity. The mind applies the relevant algorithms in our brain organs or modules to process information. For example, our eyes turn data into meaningful chunks of information to be evaluated step by step according to the appropriate algorithm to get a specific output. This capacity has allowed our species to outsmart animals, plants, and even fellow human beings. Certain mental states, such as pain, may not be susceptible to such an algorithm, however; they are "qualia," or nonrepresentational mental states.

Pinker's foundational ideas of the evolutionary development of the brain, computational psychology, and his views on religion have solicited much criticism. Some language theorists have objected to his hard distinction between innate and learned knowledge. Geoffrey Sampson, in *Educating Eve: The Language Instinct Debates*, rejects the idea that we are genetically hardwired to learn language through fixed structures in our brains. Rather, he asserts that we are good at learning languages because human beings are good at learning "anything that life throws at us"; it is a general learning capacity and not a specific feature of the brain that is the key to our linguistic evolution.

Some feminists have decried Pinker's claim that certain female behaviors are hardwired into women. He responds by defending equity feminism but not relenting on gender feminism. For Pinker, differences between men and women are not entirely socially constructed.

Another prominent critic of Pinker has been evolutionary biologist Stephen J. Gould, who engaged in a series of heated exchanges with Pinker in the *New York Review of Books*. Gould claimed that Pinker engaged in narrow and barren "cocktail party" speculation in overemphasizing adaptation through natural selection as the primary mechanism for developing human language.

Gould concluded that biological evolution is partly the result of adaptation, but also the result of historical contingency, genetic drift, unselected neutrality, and many other factors.

Responding to Gould, Pinker offers the brain and the eyes as examples of finely tuned body systems that could not have arisen from genetic drift or any other nonadaptive mechanism. Moreover, Gould's nonadaptive "spandrels" often are co-opted into becoming adaptive advantages. As for the claim of brazen environmental speculations, Pinker notes the abundance of archeological and ethnographic evidence supporting his conclusions.

In addition to language theorists, feminists, and fellow evolutionists, Pinker has received criticism for his computational claims of the brain from humanists who detect a severe form of materialist reductionism. Ideas are created in a culture and are deposited in the mind. Moreover, Pinker's position may eliminate free will, deep meaning, and purpose. In regard to the latter, Pinker responded that there are two levels of analysis. Meaning and purpose can be a neuro-psychological phenomenon on one level, and yet we can also examine these issues at another level in terms of how we live our lives.

Another controversial area of recent interest for Pinker is the related issue of morality. He seems to lean both toward and against an evolutionary determinism. He favorably invokes what he perceives as a growing body of evidence that morality is more than internalized lessons. Some people seem to lack a moral sense almost in the same way that color-blind people lack the capacity to discern colors, and the absence of this moral faculty seems to be because they did not genetically receive this evolutionary adaptation. Pinker is no advocate for a punishment-free system, though, because the incentives of a criminal system may influence even those without the moral faculty. Moreover, the inheritance of a reduced moral faculty is not an excuse for all actions, because we have free will and a universal human nature that in general has the desire for life, liberty, and the pursuit of happiness.

It is the implication of Pinker's ideas (such as his views on evolutionary psychology) for religion that has aroused the most passionate response to his works. In addition, he has ignited much criticism for his probing of why religion can be both an irrational and yet robust system of beliefs. Pinker notes that religious practices and rules provide practical social benefits. Ancestor worship helps the elderly be taken care of, religious rites of passage provide guidance on delineating the age of responsibility, and costly initiations insure group loyalty. Hence, practical, if "baser," motives maintain religious beliefs and systems.

The criticisms from the religious community are diverse. Some, like novelist Tom Wolfe, worry that neuroscience has eliminated the idea of a soul and replaced it with an organ, the brain. He has also proposed at Harvard a course on "Reason and Faith," stating that faith is a belief in "something without a good reason to believe in it."

Such forays into public discussions of religion have prompted strong responses. Theologian Paul Griffiths, in the journal *First Things*, criticizes Pinker for his article in the *New Republic* attacking President George W. Bush's Bioethics Council's report *Human Dignity and Bioethics*. For Griffiths, Pinker errs in part in seeming to suggest that religious attachment to dignity makes it inherently problematic merely because of associations to institutions like the Catholic Church. Pinker also is incorrect in denouncing dignity because it has numerous definitions. This variability justifies Pinker in offering the concept of adopting autonomy as a more fixed and sure foundation for assessing bioethical issues. Griffiths counters this assumption by noting that autonomy is every bit as relative and fungible as human dignity. Finally, Griffiths chides Pinker for not realizing that autonomy and human dignity are both grounded in highly complex understandings of what it means to be human and that these understandings are what dispose us to certain public policy and ethical conclusions.

Pinker wants to avoid this debate by excluding the dignity perspective without probing the justifications and ultimate claims of autonomy. If Pinker did pursue this analysis, it would lead him to understand that such terms dispose us to think and advocate for specific claims based in our understanding of what it means to be human.—Phillip M. Thompson

BIBLIOGRAPHY AND FURTHER READING: Feser, Edward. *The Last Superstition: A Refutation of the New Atheists*. South Bend, IN: St. Mary's Press, 2008; Griffiths, Paul. "The Very Autonomous Steven Pinker." *First Things* (August–September 2008): 19–21; Pinker, Steven. *How the Brain Works*. New York: Norton, 1999; Pinker, Steven. *The Language Instinct*. New York: Perennial/HarperCollins, 1994; Sampson, Geoffrey. *Educating Eve: The Language Instinct Debates*, rev. ed. London: Continuum, 2005. *See also* ATHEISM; DAWKINS, CLINTON RICHARD; EVOLUTION

PONTIFICAL COUNCIL FOR HEALTH PASTORAL CARE   On February 11, 1985, Pope John

Paul II instituted the Pontifical Commission for the Pastoral Assistance to Health Care Workers, which in 1988 was reinstituted as the Pontifical Council for the Pastoral Assistance to Health Care Workers. In 1998, in keeping with its mission of supporting those who receive, as well as give, health care, the council was given a second name: the Pontifical Council for Health Pastoral Care (HPC), which is more commonly used.

HPC's mission is to coordinate the activities of different dicasteries of the Roman Curia as they relate to the practice and development of medical and mental health care and the specific problems encountered by those who both receive and provide such care. It is tasked to explain, defend, and spread Church teaching on health-related issues in the study and practice of professional and pastoral health care. HPC works to foster the work of diverse Catholic international organizations and offers various levels of guidance and support to diverse groups and associations of professional and pastoral caregivers, as well as lay receivers of such care. The dicastery also studies health care policy development and related programs and initiatives at both national and international levels, and it invites the collaboration of experts, especially through "ad hoc" task forces, in service of these efforts.

HPC maintains contact with local churches throughout the world, especially through meetings with various national and regional bishops' commissions charged with concerns for health pastoral care issues, and also through bishops' *ad limina* visits to Rome. Such meetings allow the dicastery both to learn directly about the various health care problems faced by local churches and to sensitize the churches to problems particularly relevant in their respective regions, if not worldwide.

Notable initiatives of HPC include the institution, in 1992 by John Paul II, of the World Day for the Sick, which is celebrated annually on February 11, the Feast of Our Lady of Lourdes. The pope commonly writes a message of encouragement to one or more groups, which is presented during the day's celebrations by a special envoy whom he appoints. Another initiative is an annual international conference held in the Vatican each November on topics concerning science and the practice of medicine.

Notable publications by the dicastery include *Charter for Health Care Workers* in 1995 and the pastoral handbook *Church: Drugs and Drug Addiction* in 2002. HPC also produces the quarterly magazine *Dolentium Hominum: Church and Health in the World*, which is published in Italian, Spanish, French, and English.—Philip M. Sutton

See also HEALTH CARE POLICY; HIPPOCRATIC OATH; HOSPITAL

PONTIFICAL COUNCIL FOR THE FAMILY

Pope Paul VI instituted the Committee for the Family in 1973. The 1980 Synod of Bishops was devoted to the Christian family, and the Synod Fathers called for the creation of centers to study and promote the Church's teaching on marriage and family life. In response, Pope John Paul II established the Pontifical Institute for Studies on Marriage and the Family—now the Pontifical John Paul II Institute for Studies on Marriage and Family—and the Pontifical Council for the Family (PCF). PCF was instituted in 1981 and elevated to a dicastery of the Roman Curia in 1983. The Pontifical John Paul II Institute and PCF complement one another. The institute has a more scholarly focus and is designed to deepen the understanding of the different aspects of human love, marriage, and the family from the theological, ethical, and anthropological point of view. PCF has a more pastoral approach.

PCF is responsible for promoting the apostolate of the family and pastoral ministry to individual and groups of families. This dicastery helps Christian families fulfill their educational and apostolic mission by offering them the teaching and guidance of the Church's magisterium, especially on the issues of responsible procreation and the defense of human life from conception to natural death. In caring for families and defending human life at all stages of development, PCF exercises particular competence in and responsibility for the theology and catechesis of the family; promoting conjugal and family spirituality; educating and protecting the rights of the family and the child; preparing couples for marriage; and forming and supporting the laity in providing pastoral care to their own and others' families.

This dicastery also examines a number of related issues that affect society as a whole, including families who practice a different or no faith. These issues include sex education, contraception, sterilization, abortion, population demographics, ethical and pastoral problems related to AIDS and other bioethical problems, and national and international legislation and policies regarding these issues, as well as marriage, the family, and the protection of human life. PCF is charged to respond assertively to educate and support those persons and organizations responsible for confronting directly any antifamily and anti-life legislation at the national and international level.

PCF fulfills its mission in part through interdicastery cooperation, especially with the Congregation for the Doctrine of the Faith, the Pontifical Council for Health Pastoral Care, and the Pontifical Academy for Life. Since 1994, at the request of various bishops' conferences, PCF has organized courses for bishops and pastoral workers to update them on recent developments concerning marriage, the family, human life, and related ethical issues from the perspective of the Church's magisterium. PCF also collaborates closely with pro-life and pro-family movements and associations.

In 1994, which the United Nations proclaimed the International Year of the Family, PCF assumed responsibility for organizing World Meetings (or Encounters) of Families. Such meetings have been held in Rome (1994 and again in 2000, which was part of the Vatican-declared Jubilee of Families); Rio de Janeiro (1997); Manila (2003); Valencia, Spain (2006); and Mexico City (2009). The next is scheduled for Milan, Italy, in 2012.

In 1996, PCF began publishing a quarterly review, *Familia et Vita*, which contains articles by scholars and pastors with expertise in family and human life topics. The articles appear in the original languages of the authors, with summaries in five languages, including English. The dicastery has also published a number of papers, monographs, and books regarding the family, human life, and related issues.

Notable PCF publications, reflecting the breadth of concerns it deals with, include: *Charter of the Rights of the Family* (1983), *From Despair to Hope: The Family and Drug Addiction* (1991), *Ethical and Pastoral Dimensions of Population Trends* (1994), *The Natural Methods for the Regulation of Fertility: The Authentic Alternative* (1994), *Humanae Vitae: Prophetic Service for Humanity* (1995), *The Truth and Meaning of Human Sexuality: Guidelines for Education within the Family* (1995), *Preparation for the Sacrament of Marriage* (1996), *Declaration on the Decrease of Fertility in the World* (1998), *The Family and Human Rights* (1999), *Family, Marriage and "de Facto" Unions* (2000), and *Family and Human Procreation* (2006). These and other publications are available in various languages, either at the Vatican website or for purchase from PCF.

It would only be fair to recognize the particular contributions of Alfonso Cardinal López Trujillo to the growth and activity of PCF. He served as its president from 1990 until his death in 2008, and many of his addresses may be found on the PCF Vatican website. PCF's current president is Ennio Cardinal Antonelli.—Philip M. Sutton

See also ALCOHOLISM AND DRUG ABUSE; *CHARTER OF THE RIGHTS OF THE FAMILY*; *FAMILY AND HUMAN PROCREATION*; *FAMILY AND HUMAN RIGHTS, THE*; TRUJILLO, ALFONSO LÓPEZ

PORNOGRAPHY, SOCIAL COSTS OF   In 2010, the Witherspoon Institute of Princeton, New Jersey, published *The Social Costs of Pornography: A Statement of Findings and Recommendations*, edited by Mary Eberstadt and Mary Anne Layden. The booklet was the fruit of a conference of 54 scholars held in Princeton in December 2008, sponsored by the Witherspoon Institute and cosponsored by the Institute for the Psychological Sciences. This conference, which sought to show the social costs of pornography, was the first multidisciplinary exploration of this issue in the Internet age by scholars and writers. Later that year, the institute published *The Social Costs of Pornography: A Collection of Papers*, edited by James R. Stoner Jr. and Donna M. Hughes.

There were eight key findings in the booklet coedited by Eberstadt and Layden: (1) pornography is now readily available and consumed widely in our society in large part because of the Internet; (2) contemporary pornography differs qualitatively from past pornography because it is found everywhere and is increasingly hardcore; (3) its consumption can harm women, (4) children, and (5) persons not immediately connected to its consumers, as well as (6) its consumers; (7) pornography consumption is morally and philosophically problematic; and (8) pornography ought to be regulated legally even though it does not harm everyone.

Although the 54 signatories were not unanimous in their recommendations, they regarded the following as "guidelines" for the kinds of initiatives needed to reduce the current harms caused by consumption of pornography, particularly via the Internet: (1) The therapeutic community, should "take the lead both in amassing new evidence and in disseminating that evidence at the highest levels of public opinion and governance." (2) Educators and other teachers should be attentive to ongoing research into the effects of pornography consumption and integrate its findings into curricula as appropriate. (3) Journalists, editors, bloggers, and others who influence public opinion should lead in investigating the effects of pornography. (4) Private industry can do a lot; for example, all corporations should make clear there is no tolerance for pornography in the workplace and help employees who have become addicted and dependent on pornography to break their habits, and the hospitality industry ought not provide television movies of pornographic material.

(5) Popular culture and celebrities should use their bully pulpit to discourage the popularization and acceptance of pornography and the banal justification that "everybody does it." (6) Government at various levels can do much; for example, the government should make it a condition for operating an Internet server that service not be offered to sites that propagate obscenity, and the government should require that all "adult" material (print and digital) carry a warning about the addictive potential of pornography and consequent possible psychological harm to the consumer.

The Social Costs of Pornography: A Collection of Papers has a foreword by Jean Bethke Elshtain and an introduction by coeditors Stoner and Hughes and is composed of three parts. Part 1 is called "Evidence of Harm" and includes five essays; Part 2, "Moral Perspective," has three essays; and Part 3, "Dilemmas of Law and Policy," also has three essays. It concludes with a note on contributors, an appendix of selected research findings, and an index.

In an essay in part 1, Pamela Paul, a well-informed journalist, asserts that our entire culture has become "pornified" and that the pornification of culture and the widespread use of pornography negatively affect millions of people. The other essays in part 1 are by recognized scholars and professionals who do research themselves or regularly consult scientific studies of pornography and its harms.

Norman Doidge, a psychiatrist, psychoanalyst, and expert in studies of the brain and its neurological "plasticity," says that the current pornography epidemic graphically shows that sexual tastes can be acquired. "Pornography delivered by high speed Internet connections satisfies the prerequisites for neoplastic change [of the brain]," he writes (29). Pornographers want us to believe that pornography is purely instinctive, but, Doidge argues, this is *not* true, because if it were, pornography would be unchanging. In reality, the *content* of pornography is dynamic, and changes in its content can lead to the development of acquired tastes. A generation ago, Doidge observes, "hard-core pornography" meant the presentation of sexual intercourse between two aroused partners, displaying their genitals, while "soft-core" meant pictures of women in various states of undress, baring their breasts. But hard-core has evolved. Today it is dominated by the "sadomasochistic themes of forced sex, ejaculations on women's faces, and angry anal sex, all involving scripts fusing sex with hatred and humiliation." Today the comparatively tame soft-core pictures that appeared in *Esquire* and similar magazines of bygone years now appear on mainstream media all

day long, "in the pornification of everything, including television, rock videos, soap operas, advertisements, and so on" (30).

During the mid- to late 1990s, Doidge treated or evaluated many men with basically the same story: all had acquired a taste for a kind of pornography that troubled or even disgusted them and had disturbing effects on their sexual excitement, their interpersonal relationships, and sexual potency. Although it is usually hard to get information about private sexual preferences, this is not the case with pornography today, because its use is increasingly public. "This shift," Doidge observes, "is illustrated by the change from calling it 'pornography' to the more casual term 'porn'" (31–32).

This has resulted in a cultural situation where, as Stoner and Hughes say in their summary of Doidge's essay in the introduction, "men find that pornographic attitudes have invaded their minds and relationships as well as their computers. . . . Clinical findings reveal that pornography use can become addictive, and users find it very hard to stop even when facing the loss of their relationships, families, and jobs" (xvii).

Layden, a psychotherapist and director of the University of Pennsylvania's Psychopathology Program in the Department of Psychiatry, offers scientific evidence of pornography's harms and emphasizes that pornography is a potent teacher of beliefs, behaviors, and attitudes toward women and children, interpersonal relationships, and the meaning of human sexuality. Contemporary pornography, especially that readily accessible to adolescents and adults (and even children) on the Internet, reinforces the "rape myth," which holds that women themselves are to blame for being raped because deep down they *want* to be raped and *ask* to be raped by dressing and acting provocatively. Research Layden cites offers evidence that "males shown imagery of a woman aroused by sexual violence and then shown pornography that involved rape were more likely than those who hadn't [been shown the pornography] to say that the rape victim suffered less, that she enjoyed it, and that women in general enjoy rape" (59–60). And this is precisely what pornographers want males to believe and act on.

A meta-analysis of 33 studies showed that exposure to either violent or nonviolent pornography increases acts of sexual violence. "Taken as a whole, they indicate that many kinds of pornography and frequent use of pornography are connected to both violent fantasies and actual violent sexual assaults, with violent pornography having the greatest negative effect" (64–65). Layden notes studies showing that the kinds of sexual violence perpetrated against women other than rape are negatively affected by pornography consumption. Many women will be sexually harassed on their jobs or elsewhere. According to Layden, battered women, including battered wives, experience significantly more sexual violence if the men battering them are frequent users of sexually explicit pornography (65).

Layden cites studies showing that male pornography users, especially those who consume it frequently, end up viewing women simply as objects for their gratification. They become emotionally detached and uninterested in any interpersonal relationship, concerned only to satisfy their lustful desires. As a result of this, the women whom they abuse, whether prostitutes or their wives, suffer severe depression, guilt feelings, and similar harms (67–68).

The essays by Roger Scruton, Hadley Arkes, and Hamza Yusuf in part 2 address pornography's moral harms to individuals and societies, and in particular to the family. Scruton begins by affirming that his argument is not that pornography is itself wrong or evil, but about the nature of the sexual act and the desire expressed in it. Examining five modern "myths" about sexual desire, he rejects them because they all regard the sexual act, whatever form it takes, as a means to something else—pleasure, sexual orgasm, relief from internal pressure, or what have you. They ignore the truth that this act, precisely because it is an act of a thinking and willing *person*, is intrinsically meaningful as an act of *giving and receiving a unique kind of love*. This is the only kind of love that can "make one" a being who is not a substitutable, replaceable, and disposable thing but rather a nonsubstitutable, irreplaceable, and nondisposable *person* of flesh and blood and mind (113–125). Scruton's argument is rooted in the truth that human acts not only get things done in the external world (i.e., have effects or consequences) but also get things *said*, for they reveal our being as moral beings to ourselves and to others. We are the kind of persons we are—loving or lustful; self-giving or self-centered and self-loving; adulterers, fornicators, masturbators, or loving spouses—because we are what we do so that one can say that our moral character is our integral existential identity as shaped by our free, self-determining choices.

Arkes takes what he calls a "natural-law approach" to show that pornography is wrong in principle and in itself. It is not only wrong for its harmful consequences but is intrinsically wrong or evil because it refuses to respect and honor the natural exclusivity and intimacy of sexual relations and their procreative potential and in fact violates these priceless goods. In addition, he argues

that what is wrong in principle cannot be ignored by law without teaching that wrong is right, or at least "all right" (127–142).

Yusuf's brilliant and thought-provoking essay, skillfully integrating gems from the Platonic Socrates, the Bible and the Koran, and medieval Muslim and Christian thinkers (Imam al-Ghazali and St. Thomas Aquinas), argues that "true love—not the bestial 'love' of lust—is the desire to give pleasure to the other as well as to receive it." Since love can be destroyed by acts of betrayal, a virtue is needed to protect love. That virtue is chastity, which "enables one to ethically commit to another without the destructive element of betrayal" (153). Indeed, "chastity has been a steadfast guardian of human well being and an effective restraint from falling into the potentially bottomless pit of lust and wantonness. . . . Chastity in the Islamic tradition is, as in the Hellenistic and Christian tradition, seen as one of the four cardinal virtues [associated with temperance], and one that protected the individual from his own destructive inclinations as well the community from moral disintegration caused by licentiousness" (154–155).

More could be said about this helpful essay, in particular the parallels Yusuf draws between the Catholic understanding of the seven capital sins and the Islamic understanding of degrees of progression in the spiritual life. Lustful desire, he argues, betrays love, whereas chastity protects and enables love to flourish.

Part 3 has two essays—Stoner's and Gerard V. Bradley's—that address dilemmas of law and policy from the perspective of professors very familiar with constitutional law, while a third—K. Doran's—documents the magnitude of the pornography industry and suggests ways of curbing its power by, for example, enforcing copyright laws. Stoner and coeditor Hughes summarize the thrust of his and Bradley's papers. Their contributions argue that the question is to find a way to confront pornography's serious harms in a context shaped by constitutional doctrines and powerful interests that are strongly opposed to any effort at regulation. Although, as Bradley points out, the value of public morality has been widely misunderstood, "the situation is not hopeless in the face of mounting evidence of unmistakable wrong and measurable harm." Contemporary constitutional law allows full regulation only of hard-core and child pornography. Nonetheless, "actual regulation in most jurisdictions and certainly on the internet does not, at present, approach what is constitutionally permitted." They concur that "in the end it is a matter of public opinion and political will" (xviii).

The two publications of the Witherspoon Institute on the social costs of pornography examined here are of great importance. Their findings ought to be widely disseminated so that public opinion can be alerted to the terrible harms pornography is causing and aroused to take effective political action to change current doctrines of constitutional law to help counter these harms.—William E. May

BIBLIOGRAPHY AND FURTHER READING: Eberstadt, Mary, and Mary Anne Layden, eds. *The Social Costs of Pornography: A Statement of Findings and Recommendations.* Princeton, NJ: Witherspoon Institute, 2010; Stoner, James R., Jr., and Donna M. Hughes. *The Social Costs of Pornography: A Collection of Papers.* Princeton, NJ: Witherspoon Institute, 2010. *See also* CHASTITY; CONTRACEPTIVE MENTALITY; FREEDOM OF SPEECH; *HUMANAE VITAE*; PORNOGRAPHY; SEXUALITY (HUMAN); SIN (PERSONAL AND SOCIAL)

PRICE CONTROLS Price controls are efforts by governments to legally require a price, typically different from the equilibrium that would have occurred in the market on its own. A *price ceiling* is when the state sets a price *below* the market price, while a *price floor* is when the state sets a price *above* the market price. While price controls are one means to achieve a just price or just wage (concepts reflected in Catholic social thought), they are only likely to work or be the best policy under certain circumstances, for example, when markets are incomplete or not competitive and governments cannot provide more targeted assistance. Consequently, just wages and prices are not synonymous with, nor do they require, price controls.

Under the right conditions, price controls may be the appropriate policy to meet the conditions of justice and to achieve a correspondence between the value customers place on goods with the costs of bringing it to market. Price ceilings are typically set on necessities like food, fuel, or shelter (e.g., rent control) with the intent to make goods or services available to people too poor to afford them. These may be appropriate if a small group of suppliers (a monopoly or oligopoly) has managed to control the sales in a market and keep the price artificially high. On the other hand, price floors are set to provide suppliers with a minimum price, the most common being minimum wages and agricultural price supports. Minimum wages may make sense if a small group of employers manages to pay wages that are below the amount an individual worker earns for the firm (the marginal revenue product). This is more likely in very rural markets with few employers, especially if

workers cannot travel easily. In these cases, price controls can help correct the concentration of power.

But price controls are unlikely to work when sufficient competition exists on both the demand and supply sides of the market. Market prices result from real underlying circumstances. Under competitive conditions (i.e., when there are enough buyers and sellers interacting with each other), market prices arise from the balancing of the interests of the buyers and sellers. Market demand reflects the cumulative valuations potential customers have for the good or service, in light of their needs and wants in the face of alternative options, as well as the resources they have. Supply incorporates the costs to society of bringing the good or service to market, given the technological and production conditions, as well as the opportunity costs of doing so (producing that good at the expense of other goods that could be made or other uses to which the producers could devote their time, money, risk, effort, etc.). Both are aggregate concepts, across multiple people, and change continually in light of varying demand, opportunities, substitution possibilities, needs, production conditions, and so on.

A basic relationship for demand is that marginal benefit declines as more units are consumed, either because some people have more additional units or because the sales are to people who do not value the good or service as much in the first place. On the other hand, the marginal cost tends to rise as more units of given goods are produced. This may be because the opportunity cost of taking the resources away from alternative uses rises or because, beyond some point, firms experience diminishing marginal productivity. The combination of these two simple forces results in a market price. Firms search for customers who will pay them to produce goods, that is, enough to cover the cost of producing those goods. But since the marginal benefit is declining, the additional sales they make are to people who are willing to pay only lower and lower prices. At some point, firms can no longer find customers who are willing to cover the cost of producing additional units. Conversely, customers can no longer find producers who can afford to produce the good for as little as they are willing to offer. That point is the equilibrium price and its resulting quantity.

It may be that some people cannot or do not want to pay that price, but that doesn't change the fundamental reality that producers must be able to meet their costs or they will not be able to stay in business. Similarly, some potential producers cannot or do not want to produce for a price that low, but that doesn't change the fundamental reality that some people do not value the output that much in the face of other needs they have to meet and the resources in their stewardship.

Attempts to set prices above or below the market equilibrium must confront these realities. Take rent control as an example. Governments that set price ceilings (below the market price) will find that many more people are now willing to rent an apartment at that lower price. On the other hand, since supply represents real costs suppliers face, many landlords will stop renting their apartments because those newer rents do not cover the costs of upkeep. The result is shortages. Over time, many producers who remain are likely to lower quality, be more selective in renting, move to other forms of real estate, or get out altogether. Black markets typically result, with smaller amounts of lower quality apartments renting at higher prices to small numbers of the well-off who can afford the high prices and the risks of buying illegally. Overall, these actions reduce the supply of housing in the short and long run, as well as its quality, making it harder for the least well-off to find housing—which is exactly the opposite of the policy's intent.

A similar dynamic applies to price floors. A higher minimum wage induces entry of many higher skill workers into the market, who then compete with the original low-skill/low-wage worker. On the other hand, firms will reduce the overall number of workers they want to hire due to the increased price, and they will tend to prefer the most skilled workers whose personal productivity is likely to exceed the minimum wage. In many cases, these jobs go to secondary workers in households headed by a person who is already earning a substantial income and/or to productive workers who find it worthwhile to work only when the price hits a high enough level. The combination of both factors provides an incentive to not hire low-skill workers. Again, the intended beneficiaries are those likely to be hardest hurt by the policies.

Rather than achieving justice, price controls often violate some conditions of justice (and efficiency) by being poorly targeted in costs and benefits. Many price ceilings may force poor producers to accept lower prices from customers who should pay more. For example, many sellers, for instance, elderly landlords, are little better off, or even poorer, than their tenants. Rent control forces them to accept lower rent from some renters who can and ought to be paying more. Similarly, many business owners (and their customers) may be poorer than the families of some of the workers, and a higher minimum wage forces them to pay more to those workers who need it less.

In these cases, the price controls actually transfer income from the poor to the better off: some costs are borne by some producers and consumers who cannot afford it, and some benefits go to individuals who do not need it. For the minimum wage, this is compounded by the fact that the minimum wage increases the chance that many low-skill workers will be priced out of employment altogether.

Both price ceilings and price floors have been tried for thousands of years, with consistent (and thus predictable) effects: shortages, surpluses, disinvestment or overinvestment in a sector, poor targeting, the poor being hurt by the policies the most, and so forth. For example, during the French Revolution, the authorities attempted to force a low price on food to make it more affordable in the cities. Despite a bountiful harvest, this artificially low price was below the cost of production and transportation, and thus many farmers withheld their crops from sale, resulting in shortages in the cities. Naturally, black markets developed, and the rich were the ones most likely to get the food.

In recent decades, alternative policies have been developed that achieve the goals of assisting the poor without these problems of price controls. For example, food or rent vouchers (replacing price ceilings), based upon income and paid for by the government, can insure that only poor individuals receive assistance with their necessities and do not penalize poor producers or cause other distortions. Wage subsidies can replace minimum wage price floors by offering to subsidize the wages of low-income individuals and can be based upon overall household income, thus targeting assistance directly to those most in need, while the cost is spread more generally across society. It should be added that, while more effective, these laws in no way remove the need for individual acts of charity as well.

Given their potential problems in markets that are adequately competitive and the possibility of far more effective assistance programs, it is clear that price controls cannot be synonymous with the concepts of "just prices" or "just wages." Critical to this distinction is recognizing the difference made by such factors as the completeness of markets, the degree of competition, availability of substitutes, the general increase in well-being of the population overall, and the feasibility of government action.

For most of human history, market exchange was not very developed. Producers rarely had consistent quality of goods; buyers bought few things and even then only occasionally. Thus it was easy to consider isolated exchanges, that is, at an individual level, to assess what would be a fair balance of the needs of the buyers and sellers, *for that individual transaction.* As more producers and consumers interacted, such an analysis became unrealistic: sales could have been made to other customers; customers could have gone to other sellers. Catholic theologians of the late Middle Ages thus recognized the mechanism by which the market price roughly balanced off the needs of the multiple customers and producers.

But not always. In cases in which market power allows some producers to gain at the expense of others, price controls make sense. The use of the term "just price" covers both circumstances, recognizing that market prices often are just, while in some cases they are not. This can be seen in *Centesimus Annus:* "A person who produces something other than for his own use generally does so in order that others may use it after they have paid a just price, mutually agreed upon through free bargaining" (# 32). Catholic teaching also recognizes that mere agreement to prices doesn't constitute justice or fulfill love, a point made by Leo XIII in *Rerum Novarum* (# 44): the fact that wages are freely agreed upon may not be sufficient given that work is necessary and personally important and that some may be effectively extorted into such agreements. Maintaining this distinction is important because it preserves the concept of just price, without erroneously limiting it or linking it to market prices or to policies that often may be neither just nor prudent.—John D. Larrivee and David McGinley

BIBLIOGRAPHY AND FURTHER READING: Chafuen, Alejandro. *Faith and Liberty: The Economic Thought of the Late Scholastics.* Lanham, MD: Lexington Books, 2003; Schuettinger, Robert L., and Eamonn F. Butler. *Forty Centuries of Wage and Price Controls: How Not to Fight Inflation.* Washington, DC: Heritage Foundation, 1979; Sowell, Thomas. *Basic Economics: A Common Sense Guide to the Economy,* 3rd ed. New York: Basic Books, 2004. *See also* CENTESIMUS ANNUS; JUST PRICE; JUST WAGE; *RERUM NOVARUM*

PRISONS Prisons were known in early Rome and in medieval Europe, where they served principally as places of confinement for those awaiting trial and sentence or for debtors. Inmates lived in extremely dire conditions. According to the *Oxford History of the Prison: The Practice of Punishment in Western Society*, in the Middle Ages, other forms of punishment, such as hanging, branding, and mutilation, were more popular. The penal system remained informal and disordered until reform movements in the early 19th century, especially evident in the United States, that were directed to the reform and individualized treatment of the prison inmate. With concern over apparent post–Revolutionary War crime increases and over the disintegration of the family, America embarked distinctively to establish the penitentiary, a correctional system that reflected the spirit of Quakers and Puritans and housed prisoners in isolation and solitude to permit them to contemplate their wrongdoing and reform themselves. By 1850, however, such a rehabilitative model was deemed a failure. Focus was placed more prominently on control of prisoners, reinforced by gothic architectural fortress structures and hard labor. The result was an experience of confinement that was monotonous in its isolation and routine. According to John Irwin in *The Warehouse Prison*, prisons were considered places for inmates to "do time."

The rehabilitative goal, however, was maintained during much of the 20th century, characterized by an indeterminate, offender-based sentencing system that incorporated such new legislation and practices as classification and treatment of prisoners to offset retribution-oriented penal sanctions. In the mid-1970s, in the context of a "tough on crime" attitude in America, as well as growing skepticism by academics and penal authorities, the rehabilitative goal was abandoned in favor of retributive punishment that spawned an escalation in the building of prisons and in the prison population. This resulted in a pattern of mass imprisonment in America that reflects an enormous and continuing increase in the number of inmates, growing racial-ethnic disparities in the prison population, and the use of prisons to house nonviolent drug offenders.

The nature of prison life also changed. For example, American prison reform in the 19th century, more humane than the brutal sanctions of past history, was founded not on inmates' deep-seated human dignity but rather on an attempt to regulate the disproportionate imposition of criminal sanctions. In this system, prisoners essentially were viewed as unredeemable individuals who needed to be controlled and disciplined. Both the Pennsylvania and Auburn penal models represented environments where prisoners lived together in isolation. In the 20th century, following World War II, a more rehabilitative approach emerged that sought to change the more austere and retribution-oriented emphasis of the past. Prisons became known as "correctional facilities," characterized by the classification of inmates, programs of treatment, and early parole release based on a demonstrated pattern of compliant behavior. The contemporary operation of prisons characterized by mass imprisonment in America has been described by scholars as fostering control and depersonalization of the inmate that, in turn, comprises the "warehousing of prisoners." As a result, the American prison system can create the experience of "men doing nothing."

Catholic social teaching provides a perspective to critically examine American prisons. It rejects the philosophy of retribution that governs criminal punishment and that views prisons as simply a means to administer punishment for crime. Catholic social teaching also questions the nature of the prison experience for inmates. Punishment that is based on strict retribution is more offense oriented than offender oriented and is inconsistent with the teachings of the Church. As expressed by Pope John XXIII in *Pacem in Terris*, belief in human dignity reflects the capacity of each person to reform himself or herself. Therefore, by acts of criminal behavior, offenders do not become less human. All persons are redeemable based on their divinely rooted human nature. Pope John Paul II, in his message for the Jubilee in Prisons in 2000, appealed to all governments "to make prison life more human" by establishing prisons not as places for prisoners to do time but rather as environments in which inmates have the opportunity for self-reform. He stated that "time belongs to God" and "those who are in detention must not live as if their time in prison had been taken from them completely: even time in prison is God's time." Therefore, John Paul's message affirmed, imprisonment that does not address the deep-seated needs of every person who is incarcerated and provide an opportunity for self-reform would be "an act of vengeance on the part of society."

The U.S. Conference of Catholic Bishops, in *Responsibility, Rehabilitation, and Restoration: A Catholic Perspective on Crime and Criminal Justice* (2000), reflected on high incarceration rates as having been accompanied by harsher punitive measures such as mandatory minimum sentences and escalating prison brutality. Furthermore, the principle of solidarity emphasizes that offenders as well as victims of crime are to be considered as more than social issues; rather, they possess deep-rooted dignity as members of one human family. Therefore, according to Catholic teaching, establishing a humane prison system necessitates public policy that addresses the needs of vulnerable groups in society and punishment that is defined by a rehabilitative purpose rather than more exclusively by inmate isolation and control. According to John Paul II, "prison should not be a corrupting influence, a place of idleness and even vice, but instead a place of redemption" (Message for the Jubilee in Prisons # 7).—Alfred R. D'Anca

BIBLIOGRAPHY AND FURTHER READING: D'Anca, Alfred R. "A Different Promise: Catholic Social Thought and Criminal Punishment in America." *Catholic Social Science Review* 14 (2009): 217–243; Foucault, Michel. *Discipline and Punish*. London: Allan Lane, 1977; Irwin, John. *The Warehouse Prison*. Los Angeles: Roxbury, 2005; McCormick, Patrick J. "Just Punishment and America's Prison Experiment." *Theological Studies* 61 (2000): 508–531; U.S. Conference of Catholic Bishops. *Responsibility, Rehabilitation, and Restoration: A Catholic Perspective on Crime and Criminal Justice*. Washington, DC: USCCB, 2000. *See also* CRIMINAL JUSTICE SYSTEM: A CATHOLIC CRITIQUE; CRIMINOLOGY

PROSTITUTION Prostitution, the act of exchanging sexual activity for money, usually between a man and a woman who are not married to each other, has been explicitly forbidden from the very beginning of the Judeo-Christian tradition. This prohibition is based on several principles: the dignity of the human person, the sanctity of marriage, the suitability of the family for raising children, and the dictates of natural law.

The dignity of humankind and the sanctity and purpose of marriage have been expounded in Scripture. In the first chapter of the first book of the Bible, in the first telling of the creation story, God confers dignity upon man and woman equally by creating them in his image and proclaiming that all his creation is good, implying that human sexuality is also good (Genesis 1: 26–27). Prostitution denies a person's dignity, reducing that person to a thing of sexual pleasure. It defiles both the prostitute and the client who are made in God's image. In Genesis 2, the retelling of the creation story, God establishes marriage as the venue in which sexuality should be expressed and children should be raised. Man and the suitable female partner God has created for him shall become "one flesh" (Genesis 2: 18, 26).

Throughout the ancient world, prostitution was accepted, even ritualized in pagan temples. Yet, when God led the Hebrew slaves out of bondage in Egypt and set them apart as his people, he gave them statutes by which they shall live and by which they shall be recognized, forbidding the practices they had witnessed while living in pagan society that assaulted their dignity and debased the marriage bond. Two of these commandments, the sixth and the ninth, explicitly delineate the boundaries of sexual conduct: "You shall not commit adultery" (Exodus 20: 14) and "You shall not covet your neighbor's wife" (Exodus 20: 17). Both of these commandments give explanation in Leviticus 18 and Deuteronomy 22 where instances of forbidden sexual intercourse are enumerated and their punishments mandated.

In the New Testament, Jesus repeats the fact that humans are valuable. "Are not five sparrows sold for two small coins? Yet not one of them has escaped the notice of God. . . . Do not be afraid; you are worth more than many sparrows" (Luke 12: 6–7). Jesus reinforced and expanded earlier teaching on the sacredness of matrimony, stressing the sinfulness of lustful thoughts and the indissolubility of the marriage bond (Matthew 4: 27–28, 31–32).

St. Paul emphasized the indwelling of the Holy Spirit as a reason for the dignity of humankind. He reminded his followers that they were valuable also because the Son of God died for their redemption. "Do you not know that your body is a temple of the Holy Spirit within you, which you have from God? You are not your own; you were purchased with a price" (1 Corinthians 6: 19–20). He also wrote of the sanctity of marriage: "Each of you know how to acquire a wife for himself in holiness and honor, not in lustful passion" (1 Thessalonians 4: 2–7).

Despite the teachings of the Church, prostitution was prevalent and not criminalized during Western history. Even St. Augustine and St. Thomas Aquinas, who clearly condemned prostitution, believed that the civil law ought not to outlaw the practice. Aquinas's view was that the civil law should not prohibit all sinful acts. Aquinas cited natural law in condemning prostitution, and in fact, he thought that prostitution was a mortal sin. Since natural law dictated that sexual intercourse was intended for procreation and that the family was the appropriate setting for the proper upbringing of children, engaging in prostitution perverted the marriage act, endangered family structure, and was therefore a violation of natural law.

The Church has never wavered in its teaching that the human being, made in God's image and redeemed by the sacrifice of the cross, deserves respect and honor. Indeed, the exhortation of the fifth-century pope St. Leo the Great that Christians should recognize their dignity is repeated today in the introduction to the *Catechism of the Catholic Church*. In 1227, Pope Gregory IX, recognizing that women were driven to prostitution by lack of economic opportunities, established a religious order for those wishing to reform their lives, the Order of St. Mary Magdalene. In 1582, prompted by the reformist attempts of Protestants to outlaw prostitution, Pope Sixtus V suggested the death penalty for prostitutes; this punishment was, however, not enforced.

In the 20th century, the Pastoral Constitution on the Church in the Modern World, *Gaudium et Spes*, proclaimed by Pope Paul VI on December 7, 1965, restated the principle of humankind being made in the image of God, and the sinfulness of objectifying them: "Whatever insults human dignity, such as . . . prostitution . . . where people are treated as mere instruments of gain . . . are infamies indeed. They poison society. . . . Moreover, they are a supreme dishonor to the Creator" (*GS* # 27).

In his first encyclical, *Redemptor Hominis*, Pope John Paul II repeated St. Paul's teaching concerning the sacrifice of the cross restoring human dignity (*RH* 10.1). John Paul II continually reaffirmed the Church's teaching on the purpose and indissolubility of marriage and also reaffirmed the Church's traditional teaching on matters of sexual morality, including reaffirming the prohibition on prostitution in his encyclicals *Veritatis Splendor* (1993) and *Evangelium Vitae* (1995).—Florence Maffoni Scarinci

BIBLIOGRAPHY AND FURTHER READING: Dever, Vincent M. "Aquinas on the Practice of Prostitution." *Essays in Medieval Studies* 13 (1996): 39–50; Ditmore, Melissa Hope. *Encyclopedia of Prostitution and Sex Work.* Santa Barbara, CA: Greenwood, 2006; Orme, Nicholas. "The Reformation and the Red Light." *History Today* 37, no. 3 (1987): 36–41.

PUBLIC GOODS A *public good* is a good or service with two properties: it is both *nonrival*, which means that one person's consumption has no effect on the benefit of the good for another person, and *nonexcludable*, which means that one cannot prevent people from consuming a good or receiving the benefits pertaining thereto. While the challenges of nonrivalry and nonexcludability were explored by David Hume and Adam Smith, the systematic modern treatment began with Nobel laureate Paul Samuelson's classic work on the topic.

The issue of public goods arises because they are a form of "market failure," that is, a circumstance in which free markets, left to their own, would be unlikely to provide an efficient amount of the good or service. In this case, it is because some people can free ride on the provision by others. As a result, some means other than direct payment will likely be necessary for them to be provided, for example, by government or some third party such as advertising. Since the term *public good* refers narrowly only to goods and services that meet these characteristics based upon a strict utilitarian framework, it is not synonymous with the concept of *common good* from Catholic social teaching, which refers to overall well-being of society.

Perhaps the most common example of public good is national defense. It is nonrival because a family in Kansas receives just as much benefit from defense against enemies as a family in Nebraska or Oklahoma, and it is nonexcludable because families in those other states cannot prevent that family in Kansas from benefiting from any defense they would provide. If not provided by some centralized authority capable of collecting payment for the service, people could free ride on the provision of defense by others. Other examples include ideas, radio broadcasts, roads, fireworks, and parks, though in these latter cases, crowding may become a problem and thus they are not perfectly rival. Nonetheless, the problem for all of them, even if in degree, still remains: how society obtains the efficient amount of them, by market or by government.

The issue of efficiency arises from the characteristics of the goods. Since private goods benefit only the purchaser, the efficient point will be when the marginal benefit of the next unit equals the marginal cost to provide that unit. The market equilibrium for private goods is likely to achieve this, because the person will stop when it is no longer worthwhile to himself, and this will have no effect on others since the good is rival.

On the other hand, in the case of public goods, because they are nonrival, multiple people can benefit from the same goods at the same time. Unlike private goods, in which a dollar spent by one person benefits only that person, a dollar spent on a fireworks display can benefit many watchers simultaneously, generating potentially more utility per dollar (at least initially).

Because multiple people are benefited simultaneously by the public good, the optimal amount of public good occurs when the marginal *social* benefit (the *sum* of the marginal benefits of all those affected) equals the marginal cost of provision. Markets are unlikely to provide this amount for public goods because multiple people can benefit from what is provided by others (nonrival), and those who provide any of the good/service have no way to recover their costs of providing it because they cannot prevent those who want to use it from doing so (nonexcludability). The result is that only those with the greatest benefit would provide the good or service and would do so only for their own enjoyment, though others would likely free ride. Those providing it would stop at the point efficient for them alone, where their own marginal cost balances their own marginal benefit. But this is too little, because the sum of the marginal benefits for those affected exceeds

the marginal cost to society of providing it at that low level. A possible solution to the problem of free riding is to have government or some other agent collect the funds to provide the socially efficient amount of the public good.

Several caveats ought to be noted. First, while government can theoretically help to achieve the efficient amount, governments have their own institutional features likely to hinder achieving that level politically even if it were known. Second, many goods are not purely nonrival: for instance, roads and parks are nonrival when few people are using them, but become more rival when crowded. On the other hand, roads and parks are also excludable, so producers could recover their costs of provision. Third, private means of addressing public goods problems often arise, for example, advertisers paying for television and radio broadcasts, as well as websites. In many cases, private individuals may provide a public good voluntarily: for example, churches that make their playground land available for others, or the millions of websites on the Internet. While unlikely to provide the efficient amount (because users do not pay directly for what they want), some level is still provided. In these more complicated cases, the most appropriate means of providing the socially optimal amount will depend upon the particular circumstances, requiring prudential assessment to choose between market or government provision.

Finally, technological developments may change the excludability and rivalry of the good. For example, the rise of the Internet has made it easier for people to benefit from music (or other intellectual property like books or movies) paid for by others—that is, has made them more nonrival. Similarly, technology can also make goods more excludable: for example, satellite dish companies can arrange their receivers so that people can use the signal only if they have paid the company. The signal remains purely nonrival, but it has now been rendered excludable. In the case of intellectual property (ideas are completely nonrival), governments can also help by providing legal means of shoring up excludability (making copying of files illegal), not necessarily by providing them.

Given the "public" name, it is important to distinguish public goods from other goods or services. Goods are "public" based upon their characteristics of nonrivalry and nonexcludability. It is not a function of government or common *ownership*, such as a good owned by the public like a park or road. Nor is it an issue of government *payment and production*, as for public schools, police, and fire protection.

Moreover, despite similar terms and some conceptual overlap, a public good is not the same as a common good as conceived in Catholic social thought. The intent to obtain the most benefit from scarce resources—by allocating to those cases that provide the most utility per dollar—certainly connects with the Catholic principle of the universal destination of goods: that they are to benefit all. But that doesn't imply that a society should spend tremendously on public goods. Most goods and services—especially the necessities of food, clothing, shelter, and medical care—are rival (private) goods, not public goods. Providing excessive amounts of a public good (e.g., fireworks) at the expense of other important private goods would thus not meet the needs of human dignity and would undermine the efficiency improvement any collective provision might have sought to achieve.

More importantly, within economics, the normative case for public goods rests largely upon utilitarian grounds—how much utility the good or service may provide—with little room for additional considerations. For example, pornographic or crass media on the Internet are nonrival and nonexcludable, and thus public goods by definition. Within Catholic social thought, however, the Church would consider the good/service itself in its capacity to contribute to the common good, broadly defined; in this case, these would not qualify, since they would detract from love of God and growth in virtue. Given this, the common good would meet the definition of a public good for economics—and is in fact the most important and purest public good—but public goods are not necessarily part of the common good of Catholic social thought.—John D. Larrivee and Jeffrey D. Crook Jr.

BIBLIOGRAPHY AND FURTHER READING: Coleman, John A. "The Common Good." In *Modern Catholic Social Teaching*, edited by Kenneth Himes and Lisa Cahill, 538–539. Washington, DC: Georgetown University Press, 2005; Samuelson, Paul. "The Pure Theory of Public Expenditure." *Review of Economics and Statistics* 36, no. 4 (1954): 387–389; Sandmo, Agnar. "Public Goods." In *The New Palgrave: A Dictionary of Economics*, vol. 3, edited by John Eatwell et al., 1064–1065. New York: Stockton, 1987. *See also* COMMON GOOD; UNIVERSAL DESTINATION (OR PURPOSE) OF GOODS

· R ·

RACISM, CATHOLIC SOCIAL TEACHING ON
At its highest levels and in its most solemn and authoritative documents, the Catholic Church is today clear and unequivocal in its condemnation of invidious racial discrimination. In 1965, the Second Vatican Council proclaimed, "Every type of discrimination affecting the fundamental rights of the person, whether social or cultural, on grounds of . . . race, color [etc.] should be overdone and done away with, as contrary to the purpose of God" (*GS* # 29). Nor is this an abstract moral pronouncement removed from practical import and without consequences. *Gaudium et Spes* continues: "The equal dignity of persons demands access to more human and equal conditions of life. And the excessive economic and social inequalities among members or peoples of the same human family are a scandal and at variance with social justice, equity, the dignity of the human person and, not least, social and international peace" (*GS* # 29).

The Church explains its position in this fashion: "Since all men and women possessed of a rational soul and created in the image of God have the same nature and origin, and since they have been redeemed by Christ and enjoy the same divine calling and destiny, the basic equality of which they all share needs to be increasingly recognized" (*GS* # 29). The *Catechism of Catholic Church* affirms this judgment from the 1960s, developing the reasons behind it. "Society ensures social justice when it provides conditions that allow associations or individuals to obtain what is their due, according to their nature and vocation. . . . Social justice can be obtained only in respecting the transcendent dignity of man. The person represents the ultimate end of society, which is ordered to him. . . . Respect for the human person entails respects for the rights that flow from his dignity as a creature. These rights are prior to society and must be recognized by it" (*CCC* # 1928–1930).

Popes of the late 20th and early 21st centuries have extended and applied this consistent condemnation of racism. Because "all men are equal by reason of their natural dignity," John XXIII insisted in 1963's *Pacem in Terris*, "racial discrimination can in no way be justified" (# 44). On the contrary, "he who possesses certain rights has likewise the duty to claim those rights as marks of his dignity, while all others have the obligation to acknowledge those rights and respect them" (*PT* # 44). Within a few years, Paul VI declared that "racism is not the exclusive lot of young nations . . . [but is] still an obstacle to collaboration among disadvantaged nations and a cause of division and hatred whenever individuals and families see the inviolable rights of the human person held in scorn, as they themselves are unjustly subjected to a regime of discrimination because of their race or their color."

Pope John Paul II applied this specifically to treatment of Native Americans in 1999, calling on the Church in the United States to "devote special attention to those ethnic groups which even today experience discrimination. Every attempt to marginalize indigenous peoples must be eliminated. This means, first of all, respecting their territories and the pacts with them; likewise efforts must be made to satisfy their legitimate social, health, and cultural requirements. And how can we overlook the need for reconciliation between the indigenous peoples and the societies to which they belong?" In St. Louis that same year, he called more generally on the United States "to put an end to every form of racism, a plague . . . [and] one of the most persistent evils of the nation."

In 1989, the Pontifical Council for Justice and Peace (PCJP) asserted unequivocally, "Racism and racist acts must be condemned," and had urged "legislative, disciplinary, and administrative measures" and "a whole range of initiatives." This was not a problem merely for officeholders, it said, but "a responsibility of the citizens concerned." A statement from the March 1990 Worldwide Ecumenical Assembly in Seoul goes so far as "to confess and repent of our complicity, voluntary or not, in the racism that pervades the Church [itself]" as well as the wider society.

Two qualifications are needed. First, expressions of hostility to the Jewish people have been frequent in Catholic history. Since Jews are not considered a race in the more recent senses of that disputed term and because anti-Jewish sentiment was based in interpretations of Jewish responses to Jesus, his mission, and his followers, however, that issue is best considered separately. Second, though the emphasis here is properly on the Church's social thinking rather than behavior, the Church's stand on racism cannot be honestly or adequately depicted without some acknowledgment of much behavior by prominent churchmen at variance with these lofty proclamations.

As early as 1435, well before Columbus's expeditions, Pope Eugene IV condemned the recent Iberian enslavement of the Canary Islanders, demanding these black people be "restored to their earlier liberty" and remain "totally and perpetually free." Pope Paul III, decrying racialized chattel enslavement as a stratagem devised by "the enemy of the human race," decreed that "Indians and all other peoples—even though they are outside the faith—who shall hereafter come to the knowledge of Christians . . . should not be deprived of their liberty or possessions . . . and are not to be reduced to slavery. . . . [W]hatever happens to the contrary is

to be considered null and void and having no force of law." Nevertheless, these and later condemnations were undermined by other inconsistencies and seldom enforced.

Two examples may at least give the flavor of the larger phenomenon. Bartolomeo de las Casas (1474–1566), the forceful and eloquent Dominican critic of Iberian mistreatment of the colonized people of the Americas, himself advocated replacing Indian slaves with Africans, though he eventually repudiated and deeply repented this position. In the United States, the Healy family is now widely celebrated as including several of the 19th century's most prominent African American Catholics, comprising a Josephite priest, a bishop, and a Jesuit president of Georgetown University. It is important to note, however, that that university's Jesuits owned slaves in Maryland, that the family hid its descent from a black bondswoman, and that family members held slaves, sought runways' return in court, and, in a particularly odious episode, sold away members of one slave family in apparent retaliation for their escape and court battles to secure their freedom.

So it is appropriate that the 1990 Worldwide Ecumenical Assembly statement quoted above confessed racism in the Church. Recently a pope went further, begging forgiveness for the involvement of churchmen and institutions in the mistreatment of Africans. John Paul II did this on at least three occasions during the first half of his papacy, during visits to Senegal's Gorée Island slave house and to Santo Domingo in 1992 as well as to Cameroon in 1985. At Gorée, recalling Pope Pius II's epistolary characterization of slavery as "*magnum scelus*" ("an enormous crime"), John Paul condemned the slave trade as "a tragedy of the civilization that claimed to be Christian," one perpetrated by "people who were baptized, but did not live their faith." Pointedly calling the slave quarters a "model" for the Nazi concentration camps, he cried out, "In all truth and humility, this sin of man against man, this sin of man against God must be confessed. . . . From this African shrine of Black sorrow, we implore heaven's forgiveness." In Rome, later that year, he specified, "This request for pardon is primarily addressed to the inhabitants of the new land, to the Indios, and then to those who were brought from Africa as slaves" (General Audience, St. Peter's, October 21, 1992). John Paul II insisted, somewhat hyperbolically, that "the Church never ceased to defend the slaves against the[ir] unjust situation," reminding an audience of Brazilian bishops of Pope Benedict XIV's 1741 excommunication of Catholics who kidnapped, traded, or mistreated Native American bondsmen.

These official and explicit solemn Church de-nunciations of racism were proclaimed from Rome in the latter half of the 20th century, but the U.S. bishops were slow to respond, even with racial violence and bigotry all around them. In 1958, four years after the U.S. Supreme Court had deemed state segregation un-constitutional, they belatedly affirmed that racial justice was a neglected but "transcendent moral issue" and that "the heart of the race question is moral and religious," deploring "poisoned attitudes." Seconding federal re-pudiation of the old doctrine of "separate but equal" in *Brown v. Board of Education*, the National Conference of Catholic Bishops (NCCB) held that American racist discrimination "in itself and by its very nature imposes a stigma of inferiority upon the segregated people," lead-ing to "the denial of basic human rights to the Negro." However, it is reported that this joint statement resulted from Vatican pressure, with the U.S. bishops so reluctant that there was strong sentiment for ignoring, on tech-nical grounds, an order from the dying Pope Pius XII.

This statement proclaimed humans equal from the universality of God's creating, redeeming, and calling us and recalled his command to love all with "a firm pur-pose to do good." The bishops forthrightly grounded their repudiation of racist discrimination on God's love and Christ's death for all humanity, on the command to love everyone as neighbor, on the way Christianity transcends all human distinctions and divisions, and on equal rights required by the natural law. The NCCB issued related documents 10 and again 20 years later, giving minimal attention to its theological grounding in a somewhat panicky document published among the riots and assassinations of 1968 and surrounding it with sometimes murky social theory in 1979's pastoral let-ter "Brothers and Sisters to Us." The latter insightfully notes that racism sometimes consists in "indifference," but more problematically claims that the "sin [of rac-ism] is social in nature in that each of us, in varying degrees, is responsible." This patent overstatement is compounded by confusing talk of "absence of personal fault for evil" for which we are nonetheless "respon-sible." Still, a charitable reading could take this as saying what they better formulated in their reminder to "resist and undo injustices we have not caused, lest" we "share in guilt" by "tacitly endors[ing the] evil."

Catholic teaching on racism is chiefly pastoral and moral (i.e., meant to shape conscience and character), not philosophical/conceptual or sociological. Still, we must ask what the Church takes itself to condemn when it speaks out against racism, race discrimination, and racial prejudice. Of what does it understand these

to consist? In 1989, in "The Church and Racism," the PCJP defined *racial prejudice*, "in the strict sense of the term," as "awareness of the biologically determined superiority of one's own race or ethnic group with respect to others," and *racism* as "contempt for a race characterized by its ethnic origin, color, or language." Against these, it demands the "respect for every person and every race [that] is respect for basic rights, dignity, fundamental equality."

The PCJP document speculated that 15th- and 16th-century colonizers "began to develop a racist theory in order to justify their actions." Against this, it noted, Las Casas worked to articulate "universal human rights based on the dignity of the person, regardless of his or her ethnic . . . affiliation." The PCJP insisted that "no human group, however, can boast of having a natural superiority over others or of exercising any dis-crimination that affects the basic rights of the person" and pledged that "the Church wants first and foremost to change racist attitudes," while noting also the exis-tence of "institutionalized," "social," and, triggered by immigration, "spontaneous" racism.

"The Church and Racism" calls for political and legislative change, but sagely observes that "racism will disappear from legal texts only when it dies in people's hearts." The Church "asks God to change hearts" and calls for "formation of a non-racist conscience." So understood, "the evil of racism" is chiefly a moral vice, its sinfulness rooted in the equal dignity derived from the essence and calling of all humanity, our creation in God's image, and Christ's brotherhood and salvific sacrifice. At the personal level, racism extends beyond prejudices and even hostility to include racialized unconcern; nor is it limited to the mind, but extends also to personal actions and even becomes woven into social practices and institutionalized. The personal atti-tudes are original and fundamental, but the institutional manifestations may be more conspicuous and more harmful. Racism is thus seen to exist at different levels, to characterize things of different types, to take different forms, to affect people in a variety of ways, and to be immoral for clear and familiar reasons.

On this insightful foundation, other Catholic thinkers have begun to elaborate fuller accounts. Cardi-nal George, for example, distinguishes spatial (especially residential), internalized, personal, institutional, and cultural forms of racism. This Catholic understanding of racism as centered in personal attitudes contrary to charity and justice—attitudes that can infect and even permeate social institutions and practices—resembles recent sophisticated social theoretic analyses, which variously portray racism as a disjunction of antipathy and prejudice, a combination of discriminatory actions and negative attitudes, or some form of disrespect. It also contrasts with some other currently influential views in ways that expose the latter's faults.

Recent nonessentialist views, which insist there is no such thing as racism as such but only varied "racisms," face difficulty both explaining what makes each type a form of racism and accounting for the fact that racism is always and necessarily immoral. How can it be vicious essentially, by its nature, if it has no essence, no nature? Whereas some, including devotees of radical forms of black (liberation) theology, reduce racism to maldistribution of political and economic power, the Church recognizes that racist social arrangements and institutional actions are immoral because of what emerge from and express them, not what they cause, and that racism ends only with internal conversion. (Still, the Catholic Church recognizes that justice requires continued efforts to rectify racism's effects even after it has vanished.)

On the political left, some theorists advance ideological or overly institutional understandings of racism, but then face problems accommodating racist persons, beliefs, attitudes, and remarks, especially when subjects are socially isolated and disconnected. Meanwhile, on the political right, some characterize efforts to help black people as ill conceived by affording them race preferences or special solicitude with "affirmative," "liberal," "soft," or "reverse" racism. But these supposed forms of racism seem to lack any strong link to racial ill will, neglect, contempt, violations of human dignity, and so forth, which intuitively we think are aspects of racism and which the Catholic understanding captures. Those who theorize racism solely as hostility against the Other overlook the ways in which members of targeted groups can internalize racism into a kind of racial self-hatred or self-contempt, while those for whom racism is just a dominant group oppressing a subordinated one neglect the possibility of the suppressed racializing their resentment of their oppressor into a kind of "antiracist racism."

Certain social understandings of racism, in their advocates' counterproductive zeal to capture widely diverse instances of racism, end up too nebulous, restricting racism only to vague "social structures," "oppression," "culture," and "symbol systems." People who seek a solution to white racism in inflated nonwhite racial pride, loyalty, and identification miss the Christian truth that anyone's real identity lies not in particularities of race but in a universal solidarity rooted in God's creating, calling, and redeeming us. Thus, the Catholic understanding of racism that is sketched in papal and Vatican documents and expanded by some American bishops corrects, marks improvement over, and can be used to instruct numerous influential competitors.

Finally, Catholic opposition to racism, founded in its understandings of human dignity, the dependence of social justice on interpersonal justice, and the calling of the political order, is continuous with the Church's countercultural pro-life stance (in protective solidarity with the unborn, the afflicted, the abandoned, and the despairing) against abortion, embryo-destructive research, infanticide, euthanasia, and physician-assisted suicide as well as its courageous 20th-century stand against statist totalitarianism from both right and left.—J. L. A. Garcia

BIBLIOGRAPHY AND FURTHER READING: Accatolli, Luigi. *When a Pope Asks Forgiveness: Mea Culpas of John Paul II.* New York: St. Paul's, 1998; Panzer, Joel. *The Popes and Slavery.* New York: Alba House, 1996; Pontifical Council for Justice and Peace. "The Church and Racism." 1988; Pontifical Council for Justice and Peace. "The Church and Racism: Introductory Update." Contribution to the World Conference against Racism, Racial Discrimination, Xenophobia, and Related Intolerance, 2001. *See also* AFFIRMATIVE ACTION; ANTI-SEMITISM AND THE CHURCH; LAS CASAS, BARTOLOME DE; SLAVERY

RAHNER, KARL, SJ (1904–1984) A German Jesuit priest, Karl Rahner was one of the best known, most prolific, most widely read, and most influential Catholic theologians of the 20th century. He taught at Innsbruck, Munich, and Münster, and among his doctoral students who themselves became prominent theologians were Johann Baptist Metz and Herbert Vorgrimler. As an advisor to the German-speaking bishops at the Second Vatican Council, Father Rahner was considered at the time, and has been recognized since, as one of the most important *periti*, or theological experts, at the council. His published work on a wide variety of theological, philosophical, and pastoral subjects is vast and, indeed, prodigious, and although his work has been somewhat eclipsed in recent years, he remains one of the most important Catholic figures in what became known as the conciliar and postconciliar eras of the Catholic Church.

Rahner was born in Freiburg im Breisgau, Germany, on March 5, 1904, and died in Innsbruck, Austria, on March 30, 1984. One of seven children, he was born into a family thoroughly grounded in both religious and cultural Catholicism. His father was a gymnasium professor. His older brother, Father Hugo Rahner (1900–1968), entered the Society of Jesus in 1919, three years before Karl himself entered in 1922. Never as well known or prolific as his younger brother, Hugo was nevertheless distinguished as both a theologian and historian, particularly in his seminal Mariological study *Our Lady and the Church* (1951; English translation, 1961). In part because of his strong Catholic family background, Karl Rahner always considered himself to be a "man of the Church," working within and for its traditions, even when he occasionally exhibited something less than strict adherence to its established teachings.

Rahner's extensive traditional Jesuit education took place in Austria and the Netherlands as well as in Germany. He was an outstanding Latinist and came to speak the language fluently. Alfred Delp, a Jesuit priest later martyred by the Nazis, was one of his Latin students. Rahner was eventually sent by his Jesuit superiors to the University of Freiburg for a doctorate in philosophy, but his dissertation on the epistemology of St. Thomas Aquinas was rejected. He subsequently acquired a doctorate in theology at Innsbruck, where he also taught for many years. He was ordained to the sacred priesthood in 1932. During the years of World War II, he served as a parish priest, and throughout his priestly life he maintained a strong interest and presence in the pastoral work of the Church.

By the time the Second Vatican Council was convened by Blessed Pope John XXIII in 1962, Rahner was well established as a professor, writer, and editor, and his prominence at the council was therefore quite an expected thing. One of the other periti with whom he worked closely at the council was the young Father Joseph Ratzinger, with whom he later coauthored a book (*Revelation and Tradition*, 1966), leading some observers to conclude that the future pope was a "disciple" of Rahner's—an idea belied, however, by the later remark, which became famous, of Cardinal Ratzinger's, in his 1977 book *Milestones*, that the two German theologians "lived on two different theological planets." For while Pope Benedict XVI has consistently styled himself an Augustinian, Rahner started out, and to some extent remained, a "transcendental Thomist," influenced by Joseph Maréchal and his school. In some respects, however, Rahner also moved beyond transcendental Thomism; his theological views, in fact, were always characterized by the number, variety, and range of both his subject matter and his approaches. He was greatly influenced, for example, by the views of the towering 19th-century German philosopher G. W. F. Hegel

as well as by the controversial 20th-century German philosopher Martin Heidegger, whose lectures he had attended at the University of Freiburg.

With these philosophical interests in particular, the Jesuit theologian developed his own distinctive theological anthropology, which constituted the background or framework of much of his theological output. One of his constant themes involved continuing explorations into nature and grace, that is, into man's graced experience of the self-disclosure of an otherwise "hidden" God. His approach was characteristically "experiential," in fact, and he usually proceeded on the basis of a Christology or a pneumatology "from below." Two early works of his that influenced his later investigations were *Geist in Welt* (1939; Eng. trans., *Spirit in the World*, 1968) and *Hörer des Wortes* (1941; Eng. trans., *Hearer of the Word*, 1994). Yet another important single work of his was *Grundkurs des Glaubens* (1976; Eng. trans., *Christian Faith: An Introduction to the Idea of Christianity*, 1978).

Significantly, however, most of Karl Rahner's writings came in the form of shorter articles or monographs on selected subjects that were regularly gathered into a series entitled *Schriften zur Theologie* (*Theological Investigations*). Eventually there were more than 20 volumes of these, of which at least 14 volumes were translated into English. The topics investigated included practically every subject in any way related to faith or theology, including scripture, belief, development of doctrine, tradition, the mission of the Church, mystery and symbol, evolution, incarnation, action and contemplation, the priesthood, sacraments, presence of the Spirit, eschatology, women in the Church, the theology of hope, prayer, the laity, ideology, the theology of death, liturgy, freedom in the Church—and this is only a partial list!

Rahner's work as an editor was equally formidable. He edited several volumes of the venerable and traditional *Enchiridion symbolorum* (Heinrich Denzinger and Peter Hünermann, 1952–1957). Among his more significant editorial achievements was the *Lexikon für Theologie und Kirche* (1957–1965). He was one of the founding editors after the Second Vatican Council of the "liberal" theological journal *Concilium*. Rahner is perhaps best known today, however, for his editorship of the massive six-volume *Sacramentum mundi* (1967–1969), the aim of which was to formulate, accurately and concisely, with the help of many authors, the present-day understanding of the Christian faith. Rahner himself wrote many of the articles in this collection.

Among the themes for which Rahner is best known was his theory of the "anonymous Christian"— the idea that divine grace inheres in human beings even before and apart from the Christian revelation and the sacraments of the Church, and that salvation is therefore possible for those in the world who have not formally "believed" and been "baptized." Rahner incurred much opposition and even severe criticism on account of this theory, in particular from the formidable Hans Urs von Balthasar, a one-time colleague. It was argued by more than one critic that the notion that non-Christians could be "anonymous Christians," whether consciously or otherwise, diminished and downgraded the fundamental Christian idea that the first and main point of the faith is that salvation depends on and is realized by belief and life in Jesus Christ. The mission and imperative of Christian evangelization is presumably lessened if people can be saved anyway, apart from belief in and incorporation into Christ in his Church.

Rahner believed, however, that the interior grace that reconciles people with God is present before and apart from baptism—for example, in converts who come to believe and desire baptism—and that his theory of the anonymous Christian was a legitimate development of the teaching contained in the Second Vatican Council's *Dogmatic Constitution on the Church* (*LG* # 16) that those who seek God with a sincere heart and try to do his will according to their lights can be saved.

Father Karl Rahner, SJ, was indisputably one of the preeminent Catholic theologians of the 20th century. His work helped define a whole era. Nevertheless, it must also be recorded—and not to his credit—that like many other theologians in the "permissive" climate of the post–Vatican II era, he unfortunately allowed himself to adopt or support positions that sometimes diverged from those of the Church's magisterium. It is true that he did speak out publicly against some of the extreme positions of Father Hans Küng, a former colleague, in effect agreeing with the judgment of the Congregation for the Doctrine of the Faith (CDF), which had officially declared in 1979 that Küng could no longer be considered a Catholic theologian. Rahner himself, however, similarly espoused views at times that were incompatible with the Church's teaching.

In a number of articles, for example, Rahner sanctioned and essentially approved the dissent from Pope Paul VI's 1968 encyclical *Humanae Vitae* that so many of his theological colleagues had adopted following the issuance of that encyclical (although he was never one of the leaders of the massive theological dissent from *Humanae Vitae*). Again, in volume 20 of his *Theological Investigations*, he expressly declined to accept or endorse the teaching formulated by the CDF and

approved by the pope that the Church had no power to ordain women to the sacred priesthood. This was a teaching that Pope John Paul II would later declare to be "definitive" in *Ordinatio Sacerdotalis*. Similarly—and unhappily—one of Rahner's last acts was to write to the bishops of Peru in 1983 in support of Gustavo Gutierrez and his defective "liberation theology"—a theology and a theologian both expressly rejected by Church authority. Thus, although Karl Rahner's theological legacy is both rich and abundant, in the end it has to be judged a mixed legacy.—Kenneth D. Whitehead

BIBLIOGRAPHY AND FURTHER READING: Kerr, Fergus. *Twentieth-Century Catholic Theologians: From Neo-Scholasticism to Nuptial Mysticism*. Malden, MA: Blackwell, 2002; McCool, Gerald A. *A Rahner Reader*. New York: Crossroad, 1957; Rahner, Karl, SJ. *Belief Today: Theological Meditations*. New York: Sheed & Ward, 1965; Rahner, Karl, SJ. *The Church after the Council*. New York: Herder & Herder, 1966; Rahner, Karl, SJ, ed. *Encyclopedia of Theology: The Concise Sacramentum Mundi*. New York: Seabury Press, 1975; Vorgrimler, Herbert. *Karl Rahner: His Life, Thought, and Works*. Glen Rock, NJ: Paulist Press, 1966. *See also* CHURCH, THE (NATURE, ORIGIN, AND STRUCTURE OF); *DOMINUS IESUS*; HEGEL, GEORG WILHELM FRIEDRICH; HEIDEGGER, MARTIN; KÜNG, HANS; *LUMEN GENTIUM*; THEOLOGY

REASON   The philosophical psychology that has been developed by the scholastic tradition identifies three basic acts of the human intellect: simple apprehension, judgment, and reason. *Simple apprehension* is that act of the intellect by which, through abstraction, a mind comes to know the essential nature of whatever object is presented to it by the senses. Once the mind grasps the essential nature of an object, it then conceives an idea of it. The end product of simple apprehension, then, is the idea, and the idea is the means through which the mind knows the object.

The second act of the intellect is *judgment*. It is by this act that the mind ascertains real, that is, extramental, existence. I can entertain a particular idea, say, the idea of cat, and thus know perfectly well the essential nature of the object I am thinking about—but the idea in itself tells me nothing one way or another about whether there is an actually existing thing, external to my mind, which corresponds to my idea. It is the act of judgment, expressed linguistically by a proposition, which fulfills this task. If I were to predicate something of the idea of cat, for example, by formulating the statement, "The cat is in the kitchen," then I have made a declaration as to what is or is not actually the case in the objective order of things, for that statement is either true or false.

Reason is the third act of the intellect. As is the case with judgment, it is actually a process. With judgment, the process is one by which idea is conjoined to idea to form existentially significant propositions; reason is the process by which proposition is conjoined to proposition to form arguments. We say that human beings are possessed of reason, which simply means that they have the capacity to engage in the reasoning process, the defining characteristic of which is the act of *inference*. This is an act whereby the mind, beginning with a proposition that is known to be true, moves to a second proposition that is seen also to be true, necessarily so, and precisely *because of* the truth of the first proposition. If I know it to be a fact that the cat is in the kitchen, then I can conclude with the fullest confidence that the cat is not in the bedroom. The fact that the cat is actually in the kitchen *entails*, we say, the impossibility of the cat being in the bedroom; or, taking a different point of view, we say that the cat's nonpresence in the bedroom is *inferred* by the known fact that the cat is now definitely in the kitchen.

The success of the reasoning process rests upon the meeting of two critically important conditions. In the first instance, our starting points must be sound: the proposition from which we infer a further proposition must itself be true. Obviously, if I begin with a false proposition, nothing which I infer from it follows necessarily. If I were to claim that the cat is not in the bedroom because the cat is in the kitchen, when in fact it is *not* in the kitchen, then my claim lacks a logical foundation. The second condition that has to be met if reasoning is to be successful, assuming the starting proposition to be true, is that any inference made from the proposition must find its warrant in the proposition itself. If from the fact that the cat is in the kitchen I conclude that the cat under discussion is black and goes by the name of Felix, that conclusion is not warranted because it extends beyond the information provided in the initial proposition. Any proposition, B, is legitimately inferred from another, A, only if proposition B stays within the conceptual bounds established by proposition A. There is nothing in the bare knowledge that there is a cat in the kitchen which allows me to say anything about its color or its name.

It was Aristotle who famously defined man as the rational animal, the animal whose very essence is declared by the presence of reason. St. Thomas Aquinas identified reason as the first principle of all human action. By that he meant that reason—the ability to think discursively, to move from truth to truth—was the source, the elementary explanation, for everything we do as human beings. Man's reasoning power is of course fallible, and we can make mistakes in exercising it, sometimes rather egregious ones. What is worse, we can deliberately employ reason to subvert rather than to serve the truth, thus betraying its very nature and purpose.

Historically, there have been two prominent ways of misconstruing human reason. The first is to make too much of it; the second is to make too little of it. The mistake of making too much of reason is called *rationalism*, a phenomenon which saw its birth in the Renaissance, came to full maturity in the Enlightenment of the 18th century, and continues to be a factor in contemporary culture, though in somewhat muted form. Rationalism, at bottom, represents a naturalistic way of viewing man and his place in the world; if it does not explicitly deny the reality of the supernatural, it systematically ignores it as something not worthy of the attention of "rational" creatures. In its most extreme form, rationalism regards human reason as a power of potentially unbounded capacities, which, by dint of its own prowess, will eventually succeed in overcoming all the problems that now beset the human race. In this respect, it has a certain Promethean quality to it: the idea that man is sufficient unto himself.

One of the more common ways rationalism finds expression today is in the form of *scientism*, that attitude which regards the methods of empirical science as the only proper means by which truth can be attained. According to this way of looking at things, people are acting irrationally if they suppose that something can be taken to be a fact—the existence of angels, for example—if it cannot be verified by the empirical sciences. The heady optimism displayed by the intelligentsia of the 18th century, who regarded themselves as living in the "Age of Reason," was inevitably to see disappointment. Few things are more irrational than the failure to recognize the limitations of human reason.

The mistake of making too *little* of human reason is pronouncedly displayed in the phenomenon called *fideism*. While the advocates of rationalism tend to drift toward atheism, the fideists, by way of contrast and as the name indicates, are very much theists; commonly, they are deeply committed in their religious beliefs. Perhaps overly impressed by the often extreme abuses to which human reason can be put, especially when applied to God and the things of God, some fideists have opted for the unfortunate expedient of throwing the baby out with the bathwater. Human reason is seen by them as a positively dangerous faculty, and the only right and perfectly safe way to God is either through feeling or by blindly clinging to a faith regarded as directly antithetical to reason. The general tendency of fideism is to drive a wedge between reason and faith. If a fideist were a professional philosopher, for example, he would take care to keep his philosophy and his faith in separate and noncommunicating compartments. He would consider it quite improper, if not perhaps bordering on the blasphemous, to apply philosophical reasoning to truths that can be known by faith alone.

The Catholic position unhesitantly rejects both rationalism and fideism, and basically for the same reason: they are both distortions of reality. Rationalism takes a God-given power and invests it with godlike attributes. It is an obviously irreligious stance, for it fails to show the proper kind of gratitude to God for one of his most precious gifts, by exaggerating it. Less obviously, the stance of fideism also smacks of the irreligious, for it, too, fails to show proper gratitude to God for one of his most precious gifts, in this case by denigrating it. In referring to the Scriptural assertion that man was created in the image and likeness of God, St. Augustine explains that we human beings, in however faint and feeble a way, are like God in that we possess intellect and will. God created us as rational creatures, as beings whose very nature it is to reason, and that is precisely how God intended that we should come to him.

There could not be a more conspicuously un-Catholic position than one that would attempt to engineer a divorce between faith and reason. Catholicism has always recognized that the two are not only perfectly compatible but actually depend upon and nurture one another. Augustine's motto, *Credo ut Intelligam* ("I Believe in Order That I Might Understand"), and the motto of St. Anselm, *Fides Quaerens Intellectum* ("Faith Seeking Understanding"), express principles that are like second nature to the Catholic mind. In modern times, the landmark encyclical of Pope Leo XIII, *Aeterni Patris* (1879), gives beautiful and powerful emphasis to the fact that, for the Catholic, faith and reason always go hand in hand.

Aristotle, besides defining man as the rational animal, also describes him as a political animal—a creature, that is to say, whose very nature it is to live in community with other men—and therefore as one who must be capable of achieving the various virtues that living in a community requires. By way of reinforcing that point of view, St. Thomas cites as one of the basic precepts of the natural law man's inborn inclination to live in society, with all which that necessarily implies. The two

ways of identifying man—as a rational animal and as a social animal—are, of course, intimately bound up with one another. Man cannot properly function as a social animal, that is, as someone who actively contributes to the common good of the society of which he is a member, without making proper use of his reason. In fact, the only way the common good can be achieved and maintained is through the proper exercise of reason. There is no denying, therefore, the critical importance of reason for man as a social animal, and, ideally, reason should reign in any political community.

Only a cursory glance at human history would tell us that such an ideal is seldom if ever realized in any given society. Perhaps the societies that have come closest to the ideal have been those monarchies whose rulers have been saints. If we look at most of the political societies we find in the world today, we cannot help but notice the tenuous role that reason plays in their governance. For one thing, as mentioned earlier, rationalism continues to exert significant influence in contemporary societies, and rationalism stands as an excellent example of the abuse of reason.

The specific linguistic form in which the reasoning process expresses itself, as we saw, is argument. What is most evident about contemporary political discourse is the singular absence in it of argument. It is a typical practice of ideological antagonists regularly to fail to address issues, and instead to spend most of their rhetorical energies attacking the persons of those with whom they disagree. Regarding the contemporary scene as a whole, there seems to be a general abandonment of reason in favor of what Alisdair MacIntyre has called *emotivism*, the belief that all moral judgments are really nothing more than the expressions of personal preference. But nothing is more precarious than to abandon reason, for that is effectively to abandon man.—D. Q. McInerny

BIBLIOGRAPHY AND FURTHER READING: Gilson, Etienne. *Methodical Realism*. Front Royal, VA: Christendom Press, 1990; Maritain, Jacques. *An Essay on Christian Philosophy*. New York: Philosophical Library, 1955; McInerny, Ralph. *Rhyme and Reason: St. Thomas and Modes of Discourse*. Milwaukee: Marquette University Press, 1981. *See also* AETERNI PATRIS; AQUINAS, ST. THOMAS; ARISTOTLE; EMOTIVISM; RATIONALISM

REGENSBURG ADDRESS OF POPE BENEDICT XVI   Pope Benedict XVI captured the world's attention on the relationship of faith and reason in his eloquent lecture at Regensburg, Germany, on September 12, 2006. By quoting a dialogue between Byzantine emperor Manuel II Paleologus and an educated Persian on the subject of Christianity and Islam, Pope Benedict dove deeply into the modern crisis of Truth, the conflict between Islam and the Western world, and the distortion of truth and reason by the moral relativism of our modern world. The pope continued a dialogue on reason that dates back to the philosophers of Greece—a dialogue that he insists must take place in every age. Benedict continued the dialogue of his predecessor, Pope John Paul II, who wrote extensively on this topic and more particularly in his encyclicals *Veritatis Splendor* and *Fides et Ratio*.

Joseph Ratzinger began addressing the crisis of Truth and the relationship of faith and reason in his early writings. In 1968, his book on the Creed, *Introduction to Christianity*, spelled out the modern crisis of reason and truth. In commenting on the change in thinking and understanding of reason, Cardinal Ratzinger sees the shift from "*Verum est ens*" ("Being is Truth") to the modern equation "*Verum quia factum*" ("Truth is what one makes"). This formula, he comments, "denotes the real end of the old metaphysics and the beginning of the specifically modern attitude of the mind."

This is clearly a thesis that has been on Ratzinger's mind for a long time. It is significant that on the eve of his election as pope, he addressed this same idea in his homily. George Weigel explains: "Benedict XVI has long been concerned that the West risks the possibility of a new Dark Age. What he described in a sermon on the day before his election as a 'new dictatorship of relativism' is one dimension of the problem. If there is only 'your truth' and 'my truth' and nothing that we understand as 'the truth,' then on what principled basis is the West to defend its greatest accomplishments: equality before the law, tolerance and civility, religious freedom and the rights of conscience, democratic self-governance? If the only measure of us is *us*, isn't the horizon of our aspiration greatly foreshortened?"

A year and a half later, Ratzinger addressed the same point now as Pope Benedict XVI. He received great recognition this time because it touched on a volatile question: Is it reasonable to use violence to do the will of God? He broke into the very issue that plagues our modern culture not only in the understanding of the relationship of faith and reason as it touches Christian–Islamic relations but also in the understanding of faith and reason in the context of the Western world's embrace of relativism and the limitations it has placed on reason and science. In a sense, he hit the "daily double" when he spoke at Regensburg. By addressing the great crisis of the modern alienation of faith from

reason, he confronted two modern issues: the lack of reason within Islamic fundamentalism and Western civilization's abandonment of faith.

It is important to interject at this point that Pope Benedict is not looking to return to the pre-Enlightenment era. His objective is to restore in modern thinking the compatibility of faith with reason, relating them to the modern study of science.

Benedict XVI sets out to convince his listeners that the Judeo-Christian revelation in its union with Greco-Roman culture can speak to all men, in all times, and in all cultures. "I believe we can see the profound harmony between what is Greek in the best sense of the word and the Biblical understanding of faith in God. Modifying the first verse of the Book of Genesis, the first verse of the whole Bible, John began the prologue to his Gospel with the words 'In the beginning was the Logos.' This was the very word used by the Emperor: 'God acts with Logos.' Logos means both reason and word—a reason that is creative and capable of self-communication, precisely as reason."

Rev. James Schall, SJ, who wrote extensively on the Regensburg lecture, comments on the above passage: "The word 'harmony' already indicates that things not the same somehow belong together in a higher whole. The principal issue that concerns the Pope is the status of *reason* within Hebrew and Christian Scriptures, which are themselves admittedly not philosophical tractates. 'What has Athens to do with Jerusalem?' asks Tertullian is a question going back to the beginnings of Christianity. The Pope, at this point, does a remarkable thing. He intimates that both in the Old and New Testament there are intimations of reason." Essentially, what the pope is stating is that *Logos* is intrinsic to both revelation and philosophy.

The Judeo-Christian God acts in accordance with reason: In the beginning was the Word, the Logos. This understanding of God was revealed in the Old Testament and hinted at in the writings of pagan philosophers. In the Septuagint to some degree and certainly in the New Testament, we can trace the unity of the revealed religion of Jerusalem and the wisdom of the philosophers of Athens each supporting the other. The Catholic tradition has embraced this unity throughout its reflection on the questions pertaining to truth, goodness, and God. We know St. Augustine's debt to Plato, and St. Thomas Aquinas's affinity for Aristotle. Our understanding of God comes through the unfolding encounter between faith and reason.

Schall observes that "the heart of the Regensberg Lecture is the expectation that God will not violate reason based on the view that God will not contradict Himself. . . . The principle of non-contradiction is the essence of what it is to be reasonable." This is the point where the pope raises the question of dialogue not only with Islamic culture (or any culture, for that matter) but also with the modern age of relativism. Whether it is an absolutely transcendent Allah who is purely willful and not true to reason, or the voluntarism of a Duns Scotus, or the subjectivity of the age of relativism, the pope is calling to put on the table for discussion that reason in its fullest meaning is necessary to confront the challenges of our day. He argues for a broader understanding of reason. The modern age has placed limits on reason, and Pope Benedict refers to this as the "dehellenization of Western culture."

The Regensberg lecture became a key opportunity for the pope to outline the three stages of dehellenization of Western culture in the modern age: Stage 1, the Reformation and its desire to return to pure faith and *sola scriptura*, which wound up rejecting philosophical insights to better understand the revelation of God; Stage 2, the liberal theology of the 19th and 20th centuries, led by the works of Adolf von Harnack, returning simply to the Jesus of History, indifferent to his divinity; and Stage 3, the false notion that with cultural pluralism, one should restore the New Testament to its simple message without the imprint of the Greek spirit.

The modern age desires to limit the power of reason. Ultimately, by restricting the scope of reason, one is able to ignore the reality of "What Is" or "What is True." When one can ignore the *truth*, then one is quite willing to do as one pleases.

How does the pope resolve this issue? He does not want to step back in time. He is much too progressive to do that. He resolves to settle this issue by reconciling faith and reason with modern science. In a brilliant response to a young person at a meeting in preparation for World Youth Day, he responds spontaneously to a question about "intelligent design."

For Benedict XVI, "The Great Galileo said that God wrote the book of nature in the form of mathematical language. He was convinced that God gave us two books: that of Sacred Scripture, and that of nature. And the language of nature—this was his conviction—is mathematics, which is therefore a language of God, of the Creator." Later in his response the pope comments: "It seems an almost incredible thing to me that an invention of the human intellect and the structure of the universe coincide: The mathematics we invented really gives us access to the nature of the universe and permits us to use it. I think that this intersection between what we have thought up and how nature unfolds and behaves is an enigma and a great challenge, because we see that, in the end, there is one logic that links these two: our reason could not discover the other if there were not an identical logic at the source of both."

At this point, we can see how we have come full circle in Joseph Ratzinger's analysis of the crisis of Truth in the modern age and his proposal for a solution. In 1968, he commented that man's understanding of Truth shifted from *Verum est ens* to *Verum quia factum*, from "Truth is Being" to "Truth is what one makes."

Soon after becoming pope, he commented, "In this sense, it seems to me that mathematics—in which God as such does not appear—shows us the intelligent structure of the universe. Now there are theories of chaos, but these are limited because if chaos had the upper hand, all technology would become impossible. Technology is trustworthy only because our mathematics is trustworthy. Our science, which ultimately makes it possible to work with the energies of nature, presupposes the trustworthy, intelligent structure of matter, . . . the 'design' of creation."

The Regensburg lecture may have gone unnoticed had some Muslims not reacted so violently to Benedict's quote from the 14th-century dialogue between Emperor Manuel II Paleologus and an educated Persian. The emperor commented on the relationship of faith and violence stating: "Show me just what Mohammed brought that was new, and there you will find things only evil and inhuman, such as his command to spread by the sword the faith he preached." The assassination of Sister Leonella Sgorbati in Mogadishu, along with other intimidating actions and threats, brought much attention to the Regensburg lecture—a lecture that actually called for true dialogue of religions and cultures. In response to the violence, the pope neither remained silent nor retracted his comments.

At a general audience on September 20, 2006, Pope Benedict stated: "This quotation, unfortunately, lent itself to possible misunderstanding. For the careful reader, however, it emerges clearly that I did not want to make my own in any way the negative words pronounced by the medieval emperor in this dialogue and their controversy did not express my personal conviction. My intention was rather different: starting out from that Manuel II said later in a positive way, using a very beautiful word, about how reason should guide in the transmission of faith, I wished to explain that not religion and violence, but religion and reason, go together."

In the words of Father Schall: "Sorting out what was spoken in Regensburg is, I think, an intellectual enterprise that awaits the attention of every person who is concerned about intelligence and truth and, indirectly, about their consequences in the realm of action. This lecture is fundamentally important for our time. It is almost the first one that really understands the fuller dimensions of what our time is intellectually about."—Kenneth Hoagland, SM

BIBLIOGRAPHY AND FURTHER READING: Benedict XVI. "The Regensburg Academic Lecture." *Origins* 36 (September 28, 2006): 248; Benedict XVI. "Response to a Question about Intelligent Design at a Meeting with Youth in Preparation for World Youth Day." *First Things*, June/July 2006; Ratzinger, Joseph. *Introduction to Christianity*. San Francisco: Ignatius Press, 1990; Schall, James V. *The Regensburg Lecture*. South Bend, IN: St. Augustine's Press, 2007. *See also FIDES ET RATIO*; POPE BENEDICT XVI; SCIENCE; *VERITATIS SPLENDOR*

RELIGIOUS PLURALISM, THE POLITICAL PROBLEM OF

"Religious pluralism" describes a political community in which citizens hold diverse and sometimes irreconcilable worldviews. It is the situation of most contemporary nation-states in the West since the 17th century. A difficult problem in political philosophy is whether it is possible to articulate a defensible theory that could serve as a stable and acceptable ground for the contemporary Western pluralistic political order, one in which citizens subscribe to rival and irreconcilable comprehensive doctrines. In light of the 21st-century "war on terror," where antagonists are portrayed as holding diametrically opposed belief systems locked in violent conflict with little hope of peaceful resolution, the problem of securing a peaceful and just political order acceptable to men inhabiting radically different intellectual and spiritual worlds has taken on a new level of urgency.

Enlightenment thinkers in the wake of the Wars of Religion and the breakup of Christendom of the late 16th and early 17th centuries called into dispute the prior theoretical and practical imperative of legal favoritism and political establishment of particular Christian confessions for the sake of religious unity, proposing instead a policy of general religious toleration and disestablishment for the sake of civic peace. The political theorists at this time were challenged to articulate a coherent account of a political order that could peacefully accommodate intrareligious divisions in a social order still generally united in Christian conviction. The solution they proposed was a political order based not upon any particular Christian doctrine, but upon principles universally acceptable, based upon a noncontroversial conception of "reason."

However, with the dechristianization, secularization, and balkanization of Western society that has taken place since the time of the Enlightenment, and especially since the massive violence of the wars of the 20th century—wars inspired and exacerbated by secular as well as religious ideologies—the Enlightenment's hope in the power of human reason to articulate and apply universally acceptable moral and political principles to secure peace has greatly diminished. Nevertheless, political theorists have not given up on the attempt to articulate a theoretically justifiable and practically effective foundation for a political order suitable for our ideologically diverse post-Enlightenment and postmodern age. This is an especially difficult task in the present-day Western milieu of *deep* pluralism, with individuals committed to an ever increasing number of not only diverse but also irreconcilable worldviews, both secular and religious.

To understand more precisely why religious pluralism is a *political* problem, it is important to clarify the meaning of the word *political*. Like *rhetoric*, *politics* has a rather negative connotation in contemporary Western culture, suggesting, at best, ruling class/interest group wrangling leading either to halfhearted pragmatic compromises or to partisan ideological triumphs. At worst, politics is mendacious, manipulative rhetoric and backroom deals—essentially, force and fraud benefiting a very select few at the expense of the rest of us. Understood according to Catholic social teaching, however, it connotes principled, communally deliberated decision making in light of and for the genuine common good, including especially the needs of the poor, oppressed, and marginalized. Politics is, ideally, a whole way of life, not a compartmentalized activity alongside of others. It is traditionally that human, communal activity involving, incorporating, and situating all others; it is *architectonic*, subordinate only to the activity of religion, which encompasses, incorporates, and elevates all of human activity, and should certainly not be restricted to an hourly activity on Sunday in a church, but to all times and places. Thus, politics and religion are truly *meta*-activities or practices.

Another term that must be clarified before the political problem of religious pluralism can be both adequately understood and grappled with is *rights*, and its relation to the *good*. The Church supports human rights in both theory and in practice, but only if they are understood as correlative with goods and are embodied in law with this understanding. If rights are to have coercive and legal force, it must be possible for a citizen to see these rights as good for him and for others, and, if he is a Christian, as somehow reconcilable with the rights of God. He must see his rights as positively related to and even constitutive of his quest for the good and the virtues he needs to obtain it.

In Catholic social teaching, there is no question about the origin and character of rights: They come as gifts from God ordered to our good, which is ultimately salvation. Popes have declared this notion of rights forcefully and without change: "Rights stem from our duties to move toward our appropriate end," as one commentator on Leo XIII's *Rerum Novarum* (1892) put it. Pius XI in the 1930s said, "The first right is to do one's duty," and, "The basic fact [is] that man as a person possesses rights he holds from God." The Church has not always explicitly articulated or upheld the idea of political and human rights, but since Leo XIII in the late 19th century, the moral and political necessity of legal rights has been a staple of Catholic social doctrine.

Thus, for the Church, even though it supports the political institution of rights, the good is prior to the right, and rights make no sense and have no authority unless they have their origin and normative character from God. There is a political problem, then, when rights are not seen by the institutions that are charged with determining and enforcing them to have this relation to the good and this divine authority. On the other hand—and this is why the political problem is one related to religious pluralism—since the good is primary but conceptions of the good held by citizens in Western democracies differ substantially and irreconcilably, then human rights risk being perpetually negotiable in terms of whatever conception of the good can be agreed upon, which is bound to be quite thin and even one not in accordance with Truth. This negotiable "good" can endanger those on the margins of society whose beliefs and lifestyles seem politically dangerous to the majority—or even just uncomfortably odd.

It would be impossible to do justice to the variety of competing theories on the topic of the political problem of religious pluralism here. However, we can divide the many theorists into two basic camps, based upon how they answer one fundamental question: Is religious pluralism good or bad? The vast majority of contemporary political theorists consider religious pluralism not only politically but also ethically good. Theorists with a serious religious persuasion tend to consider religious pluralism as unfortunate, yet intractable and inextricable, or at least such if freedom of conscience

is to be preserved, so they are committed to thinking and working within what they deem as the natural and permanent political given of deep pluralism.

There are relatively very few thinkers in academia and in public life who oppose the celebration or normalizing of religious pluralism and reject the conception of a truth-and-good-agnostic-and-neutral state charged with policing this pluralism. The radical orthodoxy movement is a quite influential, though minute in number, example of this opposition. There is an even fewer number of nontheistic thinkers who oppose liberal pluralism, such as Stanley Fish (who advocates a more open and combative public square monitored by neither the politically or religiously correct), the "new atheists" (who seem to want to get rid of Christianity all together), and certain neopagan, neo-Nietzschean thinkers.

One might ask how any Catholic could be against religious pluralism when the Church itself unequivocally endorses religious freedom and political tolerance. But this is to misunderstand what this opposition means and entails. Diversity, variety, freedom, and tolerance are godly values. Yet there must be adequate and authentic freedom for groups who believe the same things about ultimate realities to live out their beliefs together in a way that is not constricted to the private, subpolitical realm or relegated to the merely idiosyncratic. Catholic social teaching proclaims the *public* and *political* importance, even indispensability, of the question of the good. Religious pluralism is a problem because it is not good, strictly speaking, to have deep disagreement about religious truth in Western culture.

As David Gallagher writes: "It would be better, all things considered, to have unanimity among the body politic on the ultimate questions, and if there were such agreement, a number of matters consequent upon the shared comprehensive doctrine could enter political life. Public life would be richer, would produce more good for its citizens, if it included aspects of the transcendent. . . . The point here is that when we accept the unity of reason, then it seems a mistake to take the liberal approach to political life as *in principle* the best or the only adequate one. It may be the best here and now, but only because we are in a defective situation, that of widespread error concerning ultimate questions."

In *Heart of the World*, David Schindler writes: "A nonconfessional state is not logically possible, in the one real order of history. The state cannot finally avoid affirming, in the matter of religion, a priority of either 'freedom from' or 'freedom for'—both of these priorities implying a theology." If there ever can be a solution to the political problem of religious pluralism, the indispensable condition for its emergence will be when Catholic and other religious believers develop new ways of enabling citizens, social institutions, cultural practices, and the state itself—if only on the local and small scale at first—to affirm the kind of freedom and embody the kind of politics that is neither against nor neutral to God.

Religious pluralism is a political problem because politics is fundamentally about how human beings organize their lives together to achieve what they consider their individual good and the common good. If we cannot agree about the good, then we have a serious political problem, and the project of privatizing and depoliticizing our disagreements is not a permanent solution. Disagreement or ignorance about the human good is fundamentally a religious problem, and the good is politically unavoidable; this is why the modern, liberal project of "privatizing the good," to use Alasdair MacIntyre's phrase, is not an answer to the political problem of religious pluralism. It only hides the issue, preventing the question about the human good from being genuinely asked.—Thaddeus J. Kozinski

BIBLIOGRAPHY AND FURTHER READING: Cavanaugh, William T. *The Myth of Religious Violence*. Oxford: Oxford University Press, 2009; Gallagher, David M. "Rawls, Liberalism, and the Unity of Reason." In *Is a Culture of Life Still Possible in the U.S.? Proceedings from the Twentieth Convention of the Fellowship of Catholic Scholars*. South Bend, IN: St. Augustine's Press, 2000; Kozinski, Thaddeus J. *The Political Problem of Religious Pluralism: And Why Philosophers Can't Solve It*. Lanham, MD: Lexington Books, 2010; MacIntyre, Alasdair. "Politics, Philosophy and the Common Good." In *The MacIntyre Reader*, edited by Kelvin Knight. Notre Dame, IN: University of Notre Dame Press, 1998; Olsen, Glenn W. *The Turn to Transcendence: The Role of Religion in the Twenty-First Century*. Washington, DC: Catholic University of America Press, 2010; Schindler, David. *Heart of the World, Center of the Church*. Grand Rapids, MI: Eerdmans, 1996. *See also* CIVIL LIBERTIES; COMMON GOOD; *DIGNITATIS HUMANAE*; FREEDOM OF CONSCIENCE; FREEDOM OF SPEECH; HUMAN RIGHTS; MacINTYRE, ALASDAIR C.; MARITAIN, JACQUES; NATURAL LAW; POLITICS; RELIGIOUS LIBERTY; RELIGIOUS RELATIVISM/INDIFFERENTISM; SEPARATION OF CHURCH AND STATE; TOLERATION

RELIGIOUS RELATIVISM/INDIFFERENTISM

In his 1990 encyclical *Redemptoris Missio*, Blessed Pope John Paul II lamented the fact that "one of the most serious reasons for the lack of interest in the missionary task is a widespread indifferentism, which, sad to say, is found also among Christians. It is based on incorrect theological perspectives and is characterized by a religious relativism which leads to the belief that 'one religion is as good as another'" (*R.Miss.* # 36). This observation by John Paul II helps in understanding the meaning of "indifferentism" and "religious relativism." Fundamentally, these refer to a general attitude that one religion is as good as another because truth is something relative, that it depends on the perspective and needs of the individual or group rather than any correspondence to what is ultimately real or true.

The term *indifferentism* derives from the belief that there is no fundamental difference between the various religions or that it is a matter of "indifference" whether one belongs to one religion as opposed to another. Historically, indifferentism arose in Europe during the Enlightenment of the 18th century (though there were earlier antecedents). To some extent, indifferentism was seen as a way to transcend the religious conflicts of the Wars of Religion that engulfed Europe in the turmoil following the Protestant reform movements. It is important, though, to distinguish "religious indifferentism" from the right to religious freedom in civil society affirmed by the Second Vatican Council's Declaration on Religious Freedom, *Dignitatis Humanae* (1965). Religious indifferentism is based on the belief that one's choice of religion is a matter of personal preference rather than truth. *Dignitatis Humanae*, however, explicitly states that "every man has the duty, and therefore the right, to seek the truth in matters religious in order that he may with prudence form for himself right and true judgments of conscience, under use of all suitable means" (# 3). This truth can be found in the Catholic Church because "the Church is, by the will of Christ, the teacher of the truth. It is her duty to give utterance to, and authoritatively to teach that truth which is Christ Himself" (*DH* # 14).

Indifferentism can take different forms. "Negative indifferentism" shows no interest in religion and therefore sees religious affiliation as a matter of indifference. "Positive religious indifference," on the other hand, believes religion is something good or positive, but, in a spirit of egalitarianism, does not wish to claim that one religion is better or truer than another. Sometimes, there is "irreligious indifferentism," which is often connected to atheism or agnosticism. Judging all religions to be false or unverifiable, this form of indifferentism looks down upon religious communities and therefore sees little difference between one or the other.

In terms of Catholic history, the first magisterial interventions against indifferentism took place in the 19th century. In his encyclical *Ubi Primum* of 1824, Pope Leo XII criticized a certain sect, which, "putting on airs of piety and liberality professes what they call 'tolerantism' or indifferentism, and extols it not only in matters of politics, about which We are not speaking, but also in matters of religion" (Denz–Hün, 2720). What Leo found objectionable is the belief that "man can embrace or adopt any sect or opinion that attracts him according to his own private judgment without any danger to his salvation" (Denz–Hün, 2720).

In 1832, Pope Gregory XVI issued his encyclical *Mirari Vos*, which was directed against the liberal ideas of Felicité de Lammenais. Gregory objected to what he calls "indifferentism," which is described as "that wrong opinion according to which . . . man can attain the eternal salvation of his soul by any profession of faith, provided his moral conduct conforms to the norms of right and good" (Denz–Hün, 2730).

Pope Pius IX, in his 1846 encyclical *Qui Pluribus*, responded to various errors of the day, among which is "the dreadful system or the lack of difference in any religion [indifferentism], which is profoundly contrary even to the natural light of reason, by which these crafty men, after abolishing all distinction between virtue and vice, truth and error, honesty and turpitude, claim that men can gain eternal salvation in the practice of any religion" (Denz–Hün, 2785).

Pius also criticized indifferentism in his 1863 encyclical *Quanto Conficiamur Moerore*. He described as "altogether contrary to the Catholic faith" the opinion that "men who live in errors, estranged from the true faith and Catholic unity, can attain eternal life" (Denz–Hün, 2865). He distinguished, however, between those who suffer from invincible ignorance and, by following the natural law, "are disposed to obey God and to lead a virtuous and correct life" (Denz–Hün, 2866). These can attain eternal life because God, who knows the hearts of men, "will not permit, in his infinite goodness and mercy, anyone who is not guilty of an involuntary fault to suffer eternal punishment" (Denz–Hün, 2865). The same, however, cannot be said about those "who stubbornly remain separated from the unity of the Church and from the Roman Pontiff" (Denz–Hün, 2867).

A year later, Pius IX attached to his encyclical *Quanta Cura* (1864) a collection of 80 erroneous propositions. In this "Syllabus of Errors," proposition 16 states: "Men can find the way of salvation and attain eternal salvation by the practice of any religion whatsoever" (Denz–Hün, 2916). Also pertinent is the error found in proposition 18: "Protestantism is nothing else than a different form of the same true Christian religion, in which it is possible to serve God as well as in the Catholic Church" (Denz–Hün, 2918).

The Second Vatican Council (1962–1965) made an effort to speak in more positive terms with respect to both other Christian groups (the Decree on Ecumenism, *Unitatis Redintegratio*) and non-Christian religions (*Declaration on the Relation of the Church to Non-Christian Religions*, or *Nostra Aetate*). Moreover, the civil right to religious freedom was affirmed in *Dignitatis Humanae*. While the possibility of salvation for non-Christians was acknowledged in *Lumen Gentium* (# 16), there was still the recognition that it is "through Christ's Catholic Church alone, which is the universal help to salvation, that the fullness of the means of salvation can be obtained" (*UR* # 3).

After the Second Vatican Council, the movements of ecumenism (promoting unity among all Christians) and interreligious dialogue (promoting greater understanding and respect among different religions) were encouraged by both the Holy See and conferences of bishops. Unfortunately, some theologians misinterpreted and misapplied the teachings of the council. Ignoring or obscuring its affirmation of the Catholic Church possessing "the fullness of the means of salvation," some ecumenists started to downplay the differences between the Catholic Church and other Christian bodies. Various forms of intra-Christian indifferentism emerged, either consciously or unconsciously. Some Catholic pastors would routinely invite non-Catholic Christians to Holy Communion, ignoring the teaching of *Unitatis Redintegratio* not to use "worship in common" (*communicatio in sacris*) indiscriminately as a means for the restoration of unity among Christians (*UR* # 8). In a similar way, differences between Christianity and other religions were downplayed, and some theologians began to use political terms in assessing doctrinal beliefs. Thus, proclaiming Jesus as the only Savior was judged to be "imperialistic," "intolerant," or "chauvinistic."

By the 1980s, the magisterium began to recognize the seriousness of the problem. John Paul II's 1990 encyclical *Redemptoris Missio* explicitly mentions the dangers of religious relativism and indifferentism (*R.Miss.* # 36). The Congregation for the Doctrine of the Faith (CDF) issued warnings or "notifications" on writings of theologians that were perceived as tending toward religious relativism. These included interventions concerning books by Rev. Leonardo Boff, OFM (1985); Rev. Tissa Balasuriya (1997); Rev. Anthony De Mello, SJ (1998); and Rev. Jacques Dupuis, SJ (2001).

Probably the most comprehensive document of the CDF on religious relativism and indifferentism was the declaration *Dominus Iesus* of 2000. While recognizing positive aspects in non-Christian religions and the possibility of non-Christians being saved, *Dominus Iesus* insisted on the necessity of the Church for salvation (*DI* # 20); the Church must be affirmed as "the universal sacrament of salvation" (*DI* # 20; cf. *LG* # 48). For those who are not formally and visibly members of the Church, "salvation is accessible by virtue of a grace which, while having a mysterious relationship to the Church, does not make them formally part of the Church, but enlightens them in a way which is accommodated to their spiritual and material situation" (*DI* # 20). This, though, does not relativize Christ as the one Savior, since this saving grace comes from Christ and is the result of his sacrifice. Because the Church is "the instrument of salvation for all humanity" (cf. Acts 17: 30–31), it is necessary to rule out "in a radical way, that mentality of indifferentism 'characterized by a religious relativism which leads to the belief that 'one religion is as good as another'" (*DI* # 22; cf. *R.Miss.* # 36).—Robert L. Fastiggi

BIBLIOGRAPHY AND FURTHER READING: Congregation for the Doctrine of the Faith. "Declaration *Dominus Iesus* on the Unicity and Salvific Universality of Jesus Christ and the Church." 2000; Denzinger, Heinrich, and Peter Hünermann. *Enchiridion symbolorum definitionum et declarationum de rebus fidei et morum*, 40th ed. Freiburg: Herder, 2005; Parente, Pietro, et al. *Dictionary of Dogmatic Theology*. Translated by E. Doronzo, OMI. Milwaukee: Bruce, 1951; Pope, Stephen J., and Charles Hefling, eds. *Sic et No: Encountering "Dominus Iesus"*. Maryknoll, NY: Orbis, 2002; Ratzinger, Joseph. *Truth and Tolerance: Christian Belief and World Religions*. San Francisco: Ignatius Press, 2004. *See also* ATHEISM; *DOMINUS IESUS*; ENLIGHTENMENT, AGE OF THE; *LUMEN GENTIUM*; *MIRARI VOS*; MORAL RELATIVISM

REVIEW OF SOCIAL ECONOMY   The *Review of Social Economy* is a journal that addresses the subject of social economics. Mark Lutz notes that social economics is about maximizing human welfare. It acknowledges a common good that is seminal and a social dimension in economic affairs that must be recognized. The fact that these elements have not been paramount concerns in the history of mainstream economics underscores the difficulty that social economics has had in being fully accepted by the larger field. The fulcrum point of the current era is that of economic efficiency as well as an

individualist liberalism. Thus, social economics can be looked at as alternative economics, an economics outside the mainstream.

In 1941, Rev. Thomas F. Divine, SJ, then the dean of the College of Business Administration at Marquette University, proposed the establishment of an association of persons with an interest in "bringing the principles of economic ethics into contact with economic reality." The Catholic Economic Association (CEA), the predecessor of the Association for Social Economics (ASE), was founded (consisting of economics professors from various universities). The famed Msgr. John A. Ryan, the honorary president of the CEA, a social activist and prominent "New Dealer," suggested in 1942 that the association concern itself with the ethical aspects of economic policies and programs, and that it suggest needed reforms in them. Ryan, who helped to develop the ASE and the *Review of Social Economy*, was influenced by the economic thought of British economist John Hobson (sometimes referred to as the "godfather" of the British Labour Party)

Out of all of this emerged the Association for Social Economics, and from that the *Review of Social Economy*, which began publication in 1944 as a double volume consisting of papers that had been delivered at the annual meetings of the ASE in December 1942 and January 1944. The two Jesuit founders of the association, Father Divine and Rev. Bernard W. Dempsey, SJ (an economics professor at St. Louis University) published articles in the first issue. Divine was the first president of the ASE, and Dempsey, its third.

The Second Vatican Council and the many changes in the Catholic Church in the 1960s and afterward were momentous. The ASE had initially restricted membership to members of the Catholic faith, but it removed this restriction in 1970, which resulted in changes in the kinds of articles that were published in the journal. Whereas in the earlier period there were more articles published on the papal social encyclicals and on Catholic social thought, that has been less the case in the last few decades.

The influence of journals is sometimes hard to measure, and the *Review of Social Economy* is no exception. Two studies that examined the overall impact factor of economic journals found that the *Review of Social Economy* ranked in the lower tier of ranked journals. However, it should be remembered that economic journals devoted to social economy will have a difficult time when compared with top journals like the *Quarterly Journal of Economics*, the *Journal of Accounting and Economics*, or the *American Economic Review*. When compared with other journals devoted to social economics, however, it fares better.

Since 1944, the *Review of Social Economy* has published peer-reviewed, scholarly articles on the multifaceted, complex relationships between social values and economics. The journal has attempted to bridge the gap between social and economic policy that the late economist Kenneth Boulding so adroitly addressed. It has examined how social justice can be incorporated into economic policies and programs and has promoted discourse on socioeconomic matters, a discourse that needs greater attention than it has received in the past.—Thomas D. Watts

BIBLIOGRAPHY AND FURTHER READING: Buckley, Louis F. "Early Years of the Association for Social Economics." *Forum for Social Economics* 14, no. 1 (1984): 63–83; Lutz, Mark A. *Economics for the Common Good: Two Centuries of Social Economic Thought in the Humanistic Tradition.* London: Routledge, 1999; O'Boyle, Edward J. "The Best of the *Review of Social Economy*, 1944–1999." *Review of Social Economy* 63, no. 3 (2005): 317–322. *See also* AMERICAN CATHOLIC SOCIOLOGICAL SOCIETY; *CATHOLIC HISTORICAL REVIEW*; *CATHOLIC SOCIAL SCIENCE REVIEW*; ECONOMIC DEVELOPMENT, CHURCH TEACHING ON

RHONHEIMER, MARTIN (1950–)

RHONHEIMER, MARTIN (1950–) Martin Rhonheimer was born in Zurich, Switzerland, in 1950. He grew up in a family of converts, with extended relations including both Jews and Protestants. This familiar and cultural context accustomed Rhonheimer from his youth to intellectual exchange and debate. While attending a Benedictine boarding school from ages 13 to 20, which included a two-year program in Thomistic philosophy, he received a solid foundation for his intellectual vocation. On this basis, he continued to study philosophy along with history and political science, completing a doctorate in philosophy from the University of Zurich. Having completed his theological studies in Rome, Rhonheimer was ordained a Catholic priest in 1983 and is incardinated in the Prelature of Opus Dei.

While at the University of Zurich, Rhonheimer worked from 1972 to 1978 as an assistant to the distinguished German political philosopher Hermann Lübbe. He later served as assistant to Otfried Höffe at the University of Fribourg in Switzerland and worked on a scholarship with Thomistic scholar Wolfgang Kluxen at the University of Bonn. Rhonheimer is a corresponding academician for the Pontifical Academy of St. Thomas Aquinas, serves on the boards of two journals,

and is a professor of ethics and political philosophy at the Pontifical University of the Holy Cross. In addition to dozens of scholarly articles and book chapters, he has written roughly a dozen books, some of which have been translated into multiple languages, including German, Italian, Spanish, and English.

Rhonheimer initially established his reputation in what might be called Thomistic fundamental ethics through his 1987 book *Natur als Grundlage der Moral* (*Nature as Foundation of Morality*), which anticipated several themes treated in Pope John Paul II's 1993 encyclical *Veritatis Splendor*. Rhonheimer became known to English-language readers in the early to mid-1990s through his articles in defense of encyclical, and through the translation of the above monograph as *Natural Law and Practical Reason* (2000), which revealed his knowledge of the primary and secondary literature, both European and American, and his detailed argumentation. Rhonheimer's work in Thomistic "action theory" in support of *Veritatis Splendor* has been a major stimulus for a wide range of publications on the subject, and his closely related writings in Thomistic natural law (*Natural Law and Practical Reason*), along with his systematic articulation of Thomistic virtue ethics (*The Perspective of Morality: Philosophical Foundations of Thomistic Virtue Ethics*), provide a further stimulus for contemporary Thomistic ethics.

As introduced at greater length in the editor's introduction to *The Perspective of the Acting Person*, Rhonheimer's work in fundamental Thomistic ethics includes the following emphases. First, as opposed to advancing some new theory, he sees himself as a faithful interpreter of Aquinas, building upon the work of other interpreters and uncovering the underlying structure of Aquinas's thought in order to respond to subsequent questions and challenges. Second, he reads Aquinas as offering what is fundamentally a rational (i.e., based on right reason) virtue ethics in the Aristotelian tradition (i.e., not primarily as an ethic of law). Third, like *Veritatis Splendor*, he emphasizes the importance of understanding Thomistic ethics as one of the "first person" perspective that considers matters like moral action and natural law from the viewpoint of deliberating toward ends and choosing means, which perspective is distinguished from that of the ethicist who is considering these matters more as an observer. Fourth, Rhonheimer proposes significant advances in the understanding of Aquinas's account of practical reason, including its relation to natural law and to the thought of Aristotle, which together allow him to explain how the truth-attaining capacity of the intellect applies also in the practical realm. Fifth, he offers a reading of the much disputed topic of Aquinas's action theory that is well grounded in the primary texts, is integrated into his systematic presentation of Thomistic ethics, and explains and upholds the contested Catholic teaching that some kinds of human actions are intrinsically evil—meaning they are so in every time and place and without regard for further ends of the agent or the circumstances that are outside the object.

Besides his work in Thomistic fundamental ethics, Rhonheimer's philosophical writings address what might be called applied ethics, political philosophy, and—more recently—debates concerning evolution and intelligent design.

In applied ethics, Rhonheimer tends to focus on the most difficult problems, frequently offering detailed philosophical analyses of disputed questions of relevance to Catholic moral theology. This focus on contested questions is evident in the title of his *Ethics of Procreation and the Defense of Human Life: Contraception, Artificial Fertilization and Abortion*, which was recently published in English, building upon works previously published in German, Italian, and English. His treatment of the ethics of procreation is grounded in the teaching of Aquinas, but includes further developments in response to later challenges. Rhonheimer offers an extensive and rigorously argued defense of the encyclical *Humanae Vitae* that builds upon his retrieval and further articulation of Thomistic action, virtue, and natural law theory.

In his *Ethics of Procreation*, Rhonheimer also explains how the Catholic allowance of the use contraceptives (i.e., anovulant pills) under the threat of rape violates neither the teaching of *Humanae Vitae* regarding conjugal chastity (i.e., the intrinsic evil of contraceptive acts) nor that of *Veritatis Splendor* regarding intrinsically evil acts (i.e., their universal and permanent immorality). This volume also provides a detailed rebuttal of leading contemporary arguments to justify elective abortion, along with a discussion of how—consistent with the foundational principles and political procedures of a constitutional democratic state—one can argue for public policies that uphold the sanctity of human life and the traditional, procreative family unit. Rhonheimer also attempts to resolve disputed questions in medical ethics, such as whether it is permissible to do a salpingotomy (removal of lodged embryo) and not just a salpingectomy (removal of tube) to resolve a tubal pregnancy; this requires the clarification of various key points, including the meaning of the prohibition against killing, to show that physically causing death is morally evil to the extent that it is a violation of justice, which explains, for example, how it can be permissible to kill in self-defense or in war.

Rhonheimer's work in political philosophy addresses various complex questions in this field. In contrast to some contemporary Catholic writers who offer radical critiques of "liberalism" (understood as constitutional democracy and the market economy), he sees the political institutions (legislatures, courts, etc.) and political culture (i.e., an ethos of peace, freedom, justice) of modern states as historical and philosophical achievements. Rhonheimer discusses the necessity of political philosophy understood as "fundamental political ethics," addresses the relation of its Aristotelian and modern forms, makes clear why natural law does not completely address political ethics, and explains its relation to Catholic social teaching. A recurring theme for him is the basic political ethos of the constitutional democratic state, which affirms peace, liberty, and a basic measure of justice. He agrees with the widespread critique that modern "liberals" have an "anthropological problem," according to which freedom is disconnected from authentic goods, and he assesses the anthropological implications of leading contemporary political philosophies.

Whereas some Catholic philosophers consider an Aristotelian/Thomistic understanding of the common good to be incompatible with the modern state, Rhonheimer argues for their compatibility, centered on his distinction between the "integral common good" (the complete fulfillment of persons and groups through their own praxis) and the "political common good," which is achievable through the political process, providing the basis for the integral good. He also explores the relationship between civil law, authority, and truth and argues that the Hobbesian assertion that authority makes law—in its original sense and today—should be understood in light of an understanding that law must be grounded in reason and not mere decisions. Whereas, on the one hand, Rhonheimer defends "secularity" understood as the nonestablishment of religion and implying a properly Christian way of participating in the secular state, he critiques as "soft totalitarianism" those forms of "laicism" or "secularism" that seek to detach modern states from the stable values of the Christian tradition. He also offers an interpretation of John Paul II's 1991 encyclical *Centesimus Annus*, reading it as both accepting the democratic constitutional state and the market economy and criticizing those elements of modern societies that oppose human dignity.

A brief summary of some additional themes treated in Rhonheimer's writings in political philosophy include an assessment of John Rawls's *Political Liberalism*, which appreciates it as providing much philosophical truth while criticizing it for irrationally and inconsistently excluding natural law thinking and for failing to appreciate the family (i.e., based on marriage between persons of different sex) as a natural institution; an appreciation of human rights and a discussion of their universal relevance, the realization of which depends on establishing an overlapping consensus between citizens; an assessment of contemporary writings on "multicultural citizenship," including a judgment that while pluralism is compatible with the constitutional democratic state, multiculturalism is not, because it fails to accept the basic political ethos of such states, which includes a shared conception of citizenship and of the legal order; a historical argument that Christianity introduces into Western history "a clear separation between politics and religion"; and a discussion of the present situation in which the Church carries out its spiritual mission in the secular state.—William F. Murphy Jr.

BIBLIOGRAPHY AND FURTHER READING: Rhonheimer, Martin. *Changing the World: The Timeliness of Opus Dei*. New York: Scepter, 2009; Rhonheimer, Martin. "Christian Secularity, Political Ethics and the Culture of Human Rights." *Josephinum Journal of Theology* 16, no. 2 (2009): 250–272; Rhonheimer, Martin. *Ethics of Procreation and the Defense of Human Life: Contraception, Artificial Fertilization and Abortion*. Edited by William F. Murphy Jr. Washington, DC: Catholic University of America Press, 2010; Rhonheimer, Martin. *Natural Law and Practical Reason: A Thomistic View of Moral Autonomy*. New York: Fordham University Press, 2000; Rhonheimer, Martin. *The Perspective of Morality: Philosophical Foundations of Thomistic Virtue Ethics*. Washington DC: Catholic University of America Press, 2011; Rhonheimer, Martin. *The Perspective of the Acting Person: Essays in the Renewal of Thomistic Moral Philosophy*. Edited with an introduction by William F. Murphy Jr. Washington, DC: Catholic University of America Press, 2008; Rhonheimer, Martin. "The Political Ethos of Constitutional Democracy and the Place of Natural Law in Public Reason: Rawls' Political Liberalism Revisited." *American Journal of Jurisprudence* 50 (2005): 1–70. *See also* ETHICS; PHILOSOPHY, DISCIPLINE OF; POLITICAL PHILOSOPHY; THEOLOGY; THOMISM/NEO-THOMISM; VIRTUE-ETHICS

RIGHT TO LIFE MOVEMENT Also known as the pro-life movement, the right to life movement is a diverse and loosely coordinated group of individuals and organizations that has as its main objective the ending of abortion. It also opposes euthanasia, assisted suicide, and infanticide and has become involved in related issues such as the use of embryonic stem cells for research. It first arose in the mid-1960s in response to nationwide efforts to promote easier access to abortion. Because of the wide range of strategies, tactics, and emphases advocated by various elements in the movement, generalizations about it are difficult.

Local groups opposed to abortion appeared in several states by 1966 and 1967. One of the first permanent organizations was in Troy, New York, founded by Ed Golden. In 1967, the first statewide group, the Virginia Society for Human Life, was founded, followed later that year by a New York State group. In 1968, Minnesota Citizens Concerned for Life was established. Other states that had early groups include Ohio, Florida, California, Michigan, Illinois, and Pennsylvania.

The first national organization appeared in 1967 when the U.S. Catholic Conference (USCC) asked Msgr. James McHugh, director of its Family Life Bureau, to head a new National Right to Life Committee (NRLC). Initially, the NRLC was composed of McHugh and his assistant Michael Taylor. It functioned as a clearinghouse for information and helped stimulate the creation of new groups. It held the first of three national conferences in 1970 at Barat College in Lake Forest, Illinois. A second was held at Macalester College in St. Paul in 1971, and a third in Philadelphia in 1972. In 1973, a new National Right to Life Committee was incorporated as a nondenominational body independent of the USCC. It held the first of its conventions in June of that year in Detroit. From its start, it has been the most significant right to life organization in the country.

Other organizations with a national reach had developed by 1973. These included Americans United for Life (1971), the National Youth Pro-Life Coalition (1971), and Feminists for Life (1972). More groups have been formed since, such as the American Life League in 1979.

Right to life groups fought from the first to reverse a national campaign to liberalize, and later to abolish, the abortion laws. While a number of states did substantially loosen their abortion laws, including California, New York, Hawaii, and Washington, pro-life forces were able to get a repeal of the liberal 1970 New York law through the legislature in 1972, although it was vetoed by Gov. Nelson Rockefeller. In that year, they also defeated, by wide margins, referenda in North Dakota and Michigan that proposed to significantly loosen abortion laws.

The January 22, 1973, Supreme Court decisions in *Roe v. Wade* and *Doe v. Bolton* radically changed the picture for the movement. What had been a series of state contests became a national controversy. The decisions accelerated the transition of the NRLC to its new structure and status and posed an immediate question: How should the movement respond? An obvious answer for many was the passage of a Human Life Amendment (HLA). But what form should it take? Should it simply reverse *Roe v. Wade* and return the issue to the states, or should it seek to protect life beginning at conception? Bitter divisions over the scope and wording of an HLA weakened the movement. By 1983, it was clear that no version would get through Congress.

The attack on abortion took other forms. One was to block federal funding, a goal achieved by the so-called Hyde Amendment, named after Rep. Henry Hyde of Illinois, a series of annual amendments to federal legislation barring the use of federal funds for abortion. First enacted in 1976, it was upheld by the Supreme Court in *Harris v. McRae* in 1980. As well, a series of laws at the state level attempted to limit and regulate abortion, leading to numerous court battles and some limited victories. The most consequential Supreme Court decisions included *Webster v. Reproductive Health Services* in 1989 and *Planned Parenthood v. Casey* in 1992. The latter decision affirmed the right of the states to impose some restrictions, but gave abortion a more secure constitutional basis than it had under *Roe*.

As it became clear that an HLA would not be passed and that legislation could only trim away at abortion, the political focus of the movement turned to securing a reversal of *Roe* through the appointment of pro-life Supreme Court justices. A series of battles over judicial appointments, especially over the attitudes to abortion of nominees, has become a feature of American politics, starting with Ronald Reagan's nomination of Robert Bork in 1987.

The nomination of Bork had as its background the close relationship that had developed between the Republican Party and the right to life movement. It was not obvious at the start of the abortion controversy how the two national parties would align on the issue. As the Democratic Party shifted left as a consequence of opposition to the Vietnam War, however, it became identified by the early 1970s as sympathetic to abortion. In 1976, Ellen McCormack entered the race for the Democratic presidential nomination on an explicitly pro-life platform. She succeeded in drawing attention to the issue, but it was clear that pro-lifers had no future in the Democratic Party. Many pro-lifers who had been

Democrats began to drift into the Republican Party, which in 1976 adopted a moderately pro-life position in its platform. Abortion became a major factor in the growth of the "New Right" in the 1970s and 1980s.

The election of Reagan in 1980 brought a sympathetic presence to the White House, but little of substance was done to advance the movement's cause. The "Mexico City Policy" was implemented, barring funds to groups performing or advocating abortion in other countries, and, as noted above, Bork, a critic of the *Roe* decision, was nominated to the Supreme Court. Reagan's first nomination to the Court—Sandra Day O'Connor—was, however, strongly opposed by right to lifers. As well, after initial efforts, abortion was clearly not a priority for the administration, which saw economic, defense, and foreign policy objectives as primary.

George H. W. Bush was pro-life and maintained his predecessor's policies, but did nothing to advance them. During his presidency, the *Webster* and *Casey* decisions were announced by the Supreme Court. The *Webster* decision, which permitted some restrictions on abortion, led to a resurgence of pro-choice activism.

The administration of Bill Clinton sought to advance access to abortion, but experienced mixed success. The Freedom of Access to Clinic Entrances (FACE) Act was passed in 1994, but the radical Freedom of Choice Act failed. While many observers had predicted that the surge in pro-choice activism after *Webster* spelled the doom of the pro-life movement, its success in blocking the Freedom of Choice Act proved them wrong. As well, in 1993 the movement opened a new line of attack, seeking a ban on "partial birth" abortions of late-term pregnancies. Congress voted for such a ban, but it was vetoed by President Clinton.

The Partial-Birth Abortion Ban Act was passed in 2003 and signed by President George W. Bush, a strong pro-life supporter. By focusing on the partial birth abortion issue, the movement was able to dramatize the whole question of abortion and shift public opinion in a pro-life direction.

The election of Barack Obama in 2008 brought into office a deeply committed abortion supporter. The most serious battle of the first years of his presidency was over the Patient Protection and Affordable Care Act, which sought a national system of medical coverage. The status of abortion in that coverage was one of the most controversial aspects of the Act, which in fact opened the way for the ending of the Hyde Amendment, despite a claim to the contrary by supporters of the Act.

The right to life movement has been of particular importance to Catholics. Many, but by no means all, of the movement's leaders have been Catholics. The Catholic Church has provided support at the parish, diocesan, and national level, with the U.S. Conference of Catholic Bishops' Secretariat of Pro-Life Activities playing an active and effective role in debates over abortion and euthanasia. Nonetheless, many pro-lifers have felt that Church support for the movement has been inconsistent, with some bishops notably more helpful than others. As well, the view advanced by Joseph Cardinal Bernardin in 1983 that abortion should be part of a "consistent life ethic," or "seamless garment," proved intensely controversial. Some pro-lifers saw it as an attempt to provide cover for politicians who supported abortion but opposed capital punishment and war and who supported an expansion of the welfare state. Others hailed it as a welcome step away from the—in their view—too close embrace of the Republican Party and conservative politics by the right to life movement.

Another challenge for Catholics was the question of politicians who, while professing their adherence to Catholicism, supported pro-abortion policies. The most notable rationale for these was provided by Gov. Mario Cuomo of New York in a speech given at the University of Notre Dame in 1984. His theme of "personal opposition" combined with the "refusal to impose morality" was adopted by many Catholic leaders. Controversies over whether such politicians should be able to receive Communion became frequent. It was clear from public opinion data that many Catholics, including frequent church attendees, were not opposed to abortion. This pointed to a major failure of catechesis.

The right to life movement had always had a Protestant presence, but this became more pronounced in the late 1970s with an influx of evangelicals. New organizations such as the Moral Majority, the Christian Action Council, and Focus on the Family became prominent.

One form of activity for pro-lifers was direct action campaigns. These went back to the 1970s with the work of John Cavanaugh-O'Keefe and later Joan Andrews, among others. The most prominent form of direct action was Operation Rescue, founded in 1986 by Randall Terry. Under legal pressure, the movement was in decline by the early 1990s and was effectively killed by the FACE Act of 1994. More long lived was the Pro-Life Action League headed by Joe Scheidler, who endured a 20-year ordeal in the courts, finally winning a Supreme Court victory over the National Organization for Women in 2006. Enormous attention was paid

by the mass media to a very small number of violent activists, who were not connected to the mainstream pro-life movement. The murders of several abortionists were denounced by all major pro-life groups, but the movement was nonetheless smeared with the labels of "violent" and "extremist."

A major focus of pro-life activity was the creation of crisis pregnancy centers. The first of these was Birthright, founded in 1968. Others include Heartbeat International and Care Net. Abortion supporters have made determined efforts to limit the activity of these centers, which have had a remarkable impact. With more than 2,300 of them in operation across the United States in 2008, they have arguably played a major role in the drop in the abortion rate.

The overall impact of the movement is hard to gauge. While it has not achieved its objective of reversing *Roe v. Wade*, it has done several things. It has kept abortion alive as a controversial topic and has prevented its unthinking acceptance as a normal part of society. Public opinion about abortion has become more, not less, pro-life, with large numbers of people accepting it in "difficult" cases, such as incest, rape, and fetal deformity, but not approving of its current scope. In public opinion polls, half of respondents describe it as "morally wrong." As well, the Hyde Amendment and the ban on partial birth abortion, as well as numerous state laws restricting abortion, make it clear that the right to life movement has had real impact.

There are right to life movements in other countries, notably Canada, Great Britain, Australia, and New Zealand. The International Right to Life Federation, Human Life International, and the World Youth Alliance are all active internationally. The relatively greater power of the movement in the United States has been explained in terms of its federal structure and relatively weak political parties, which were more open to citizen activism.

A substantial literature has developed about the movement, but much of what has been written has been highly polemical in character; even work by social scientists often shows clear limitations due to the commitments of the authors. The most widely cited study of the movement, by Kristin Luker, *Abortion and the Politics of Motherhood* (1984), argues that for pro-life women the defense of the fetus is a defense of the value of their own lives; the acceptance of abortion would degrade the value of motherhood, an institution central to their self-definition. Hence, pro-life activism is both a symbolic defense of their own values and a defense of a real material interest. This interpretation has limited power and reduces a complex movement to a single motivation. The movement has some very divergent elements: for some, abortion is linked to contraception; for others, it is connected to the general problem of violence. Pro-lifers have sought alliances on the left and the right and interpret abortion in a number of different frames.

As a powerful and prominent social movement, it has attracted considerable attention from theorists of social movements. At their best, these studies come to see the complexity of the movement and abandon simplistic stereotypes of right to lifers as "zealots," "misogynists," and "fundamentalists." A notable recent work is Ziad Munson's *The Making of Pro-Life Activists: How Social Mobilization Works* (2008).

The movement has shown considerable ability over the years to find new forms of expression. The annual Life Chains in many cities and a lively presence on the Internet demonstrate a continued vitality. In the immediate wake of the *Roe* decision, it was predicted that the furor over abortion would quickly die down and the right to life movement would disappear. That this has not happened demonstrates that it is deeply rooted and widely popular, and one of the most significant social movements in American history.—Keith M. Cassidy

BIBLIOGRAPHY AND FURTHER READING: Cassidy, Keith. "Interpreting the Pro-Life Movement: Recurrent Themes and Recent Trends." *Life and Learning* 9 (1999): 249–266; Cassidy, Keith. "The Right to Life Movement: Sources, Development and Strategies." In *The Politics of Abortion and Birth Control in Historical Perspective*, edited by Donald Critchlow, 128–159. University Park: Pennsylvania State University Press, 1996; Gorney, Cynthia. *Articles of Faith: A Frontline History of the Abortion Wars.* New York: Simon & Schuster, 1998; Karrer, Robert N. "The National Right to Life Committee: Its Founding, Its History and the Emergence of the Pro-Life Movement Prior to *Roe v. Wade.*" *Catholic Historical Review* 97, no. 3 (2011): 527–557; Kelly, James R. "From Counter-Movement to Transforming Movement? Towards the Crystallization and Dual Challenge of the Consistent Ethic of Life." *Life and Learning* 11 (2001): 166–227. *See also* ABORTION; CONSISTENT ETHIC OF LIFE (SEAMLESS GARMENT); PRO-LIFE ORGANIZATIONS; *ROE v. WADE/DOE v. BOLTON*

· S ·

SARTRE, JEAN-PAUL (1905–1980) Jean-Paul Sartre was born in Paris on June 21, 1905, the son of Jean-Baptiste Sartre and Anne Marie Schweitzer Sartre.

When Jean-Baptiste, who was a marine engineer, died of a fever in Indochina shortly after the birth of his son, Anne Marie went with Jean-Paul to live with her parents, and it was in the Schweitzer household, under the doting care of his grandfather, Charles, a Protestant and a professor of languages, that Jean-Paul was raised. The Schweitzer household was not remarkable for its religious observance, and Sartre's mother took a less than fully earnest attitude toward the Catholicism to which she had converted. Her son was baptized a Catholic and presumably made his first Communion, but in the end it was the influence of his grandfather that had the greater effect on him. In his autobiography *The Words*, Sartre writes: "I was led to disbelieve not by a conflict of dogmas but by my grandfather's indifference." Atheism was to become a mainstay of the peculiar brand of existential philosophy that he was subsequently to develop.

Sartre received the *bacalauréat en philosophie* from the *École Normale Supérieure*, and, in 1930, the prestigious *agrégation en philosophie* from the same institution. Over the course of the 1930s, Sartre was busily occupied in a variety of ways: fulfilling the mandatory obligation of military service, teaching first at Le Havre Lycée, followed by taking a post at the Lycée Laon, and then, toward the end of the decade, residing in Germany to devote himself to an intense study of the thought of Edmund Husserl and Martin Heidegger. Both of these philosophers were to have a significant influence on the development of his own thought. At the outbreak of World War II, Sartre was mobilized into the army, where he served in a meteorological unit until he was captured and imprisoned by the Germans. After a year of internment, he was released and repatriated as a civilian, following which he returned to Paris. There he taught at the Lycée Pasteur and, along with Albert Camus, whom he befriended at the time, became active in the French Resistance.

In 1945, Sartre founded the journal *Les Temps Modernes*, which was to become a very influential voice within French intellectual circles during the postwar period. A prolific writer since his boyhood, Sartre was eventually able to give up teaching and support himself by the products of his pen, for many of his writings, especially his fiction and drama, quickly gained wide popular appeal. Though a committed leftist throughout his life, Sartre's relation with the Communist Party was erratic; for a time he was a member of the party, but he resigned in protest over certain of its policies. Simone de Beauvoir, one of the inspiring sources of the modern feminist movement, whom Sartre had met when they were students together in Paris, became his lifelong companion, though their union was never legalized. For them, marriage was a bourgeois institution, and anything smacking of the bourgeois was anathema to these two products of French middle-class society. Sartre turned down the Nobel Prize for literature in 1964 because he felt the award had become an instrument of the Cold War. When Jean-Paul Sartre died, in Paris in 1980, more than 50,000 people spontaneously gathered together to honor his memory.

Sartre's remarkable talents as a writer displayed themselves in a variety of impressive ways. Besides his specifically philosophical works, he wrote and published fiction, drama, journals, and literary criticism. Those of his works that were not specifically philosophical, particularly his novels and plays, nonetheless served as vehicles, and very effective ones, for promoting his philosophic views. It is very likely that more people became enamored of existentialism by being exposed to his literary productions—such as the novel *Nausea* (1938) and the plays *The Flies* (1943) and *No Exit* (1945)—than by any serious encounter with his philosophical works. Toward the end of *No Exit*, one of the characters, Garcin, makes the biting comment, prompted by his experience with the other two characters in the play: "Hell is—other people!" That statement can stand as an accurate enough characterization of the spirit of Sartre's existential psychology, according to which the signal mark of all human relations is permanent, irresoluble conflict. Every individual is burdened with a penchant for employing his freedom in a fruitless attempt to negate the freedom of his fellows.

Being and Nothingness (1943), *Existentialism Is a Humanism* (1945), and *Critique of Dialectical Reason* (1960) are among Sartre's principal philosophical works. *Being and Nothingness*, which is subtitled *An Essay in Phenomenological Ontology*, is his magnum opus and provides an excellent example of the phenomenological method at work, allowing us at once to see the virtues of the method as well as its distinct limitations. Sartre did not write philosophy as he wrote fiction and drama, but gave himself over to a fulsome, belabored form of expression that proves to be remarkably efficient in inhibiting the clear communication of ideas.

All the basic tenets of Sartre's philosophy can be found in *Being and Nothingness*, the chief among which, from the point of view of ontology, is the notion that existence precedes essence. A practical application of this notion results in the conclusion that there is no human nature. We exist as unqualifiedly free creatures, and to the extent that we ever succeed in achieving something by way of essence, it is through the exercise

of our freedom. Not to exercise that freedom, to fail to make the choices that could eventuate in acquiring an essence, is to display what Sartre calls "bad faith"—a willingness to acquiesce to the status of being a mere thing. Through the exercise of his freedom, man defines himself and invents the moral values by which he guides his life. There are no objective moral standards. Sartre rejects the notion of substance, which is logically consistent with the attitude he takes toward essence and existence. The "nothingness" of which Sartre makes much in *Being and Nothingness* is, as he explains, simply what is understood by the classical notion of privation, and he argues that this nothingness/privation takes ontological priority over being.

Sartre's whole philosophical edifice is founded on his ontology, and therein lies a problem of major proportions, for his ontology is, to put it mildly, severely wanting. His pivotal notion—that "for human reality essence comes after existence"—is simply incoherent, a metaphysical misconception of the first order. Essence and existence are absolutely inseparable, for they are not "things" but the foundational and inextricably conjoined principles of every created entity. To say that existence comes before essence is to talk nonsense, for, supposing that to be true, we would have to imagine the impossible: the act of existing without a *subject* of existence. Sartre asserts that there is no human nature, yet he regularly makes reference to what he calls "Human Reality" or "the human condition." If there is no human nature, what is the import of the word *human* in those phrases?

The metaphysical instability of Sartre's philosophy is further demonstrated by the claim that privation—which, as noted, is what he means by "nothingness"—is ontologically prior to being. But here, once again, he is positing an impossibility. Being, understood as any particular existent, can be said to be in privation in a number of respects, serving as it does as the subject of privation. Privation, in other words, presupposes being; it can in no way be prior to being. It is impossible to have simply a lack, a privation; it is necessary to have *something*, an existent being, that is lacking in one way or another.

Sartre's existentialism, it might be supposed, can be applauded for the emphasis it gives to freedom and responsibility, but both of those concepts, as he understands them, are seriously flawed. His philosophy is not the humanism he supposes it to be; indeed, there is something positively antihuman at its very core. Surely it has to be counted as one of the most pessimistic philosophies ever formulated, and Camus was not amiss in seeing it as essentially nihilistic. Sartre, in insisting that atheism was an integral component of existentialism, was being not a little presumptuous, for existentialism was well established by the time he came upon the scene, being the brainchild of such formidable Christian thinkers as Søren Kierkegaard (first and foremost), Nicolai Berdyaev, and Gabriel Marcel. And Sartre was completely out of bounds in claiming that atheism was a prerequisite for any serious philosophy. Just the opposite is the case: Without an openness to the transcendent, the very possibility of philosophy is radically undermined.—D. Q. McInerny

BIBLIOGRAPHY AND FURTHER READING: Aronson, Ronald. *Camus and Sartre.* Chicago: University of Chicago Press, 2004; Barrett, William. "Sartre." Chapter 10 of *Irrational Man: A Study in Existential Philosophy.* Garden City, NY: Doubleday, 1958; Danto, Arthur Coleman. *Sartre.* New York: Viking Press, 1975; Desan, Wilfrid. *The Tragic Finale.* Cambridge, MA: Harvard University Press, 1954; King, Thomas Mulvihill. *Sartre and the Sacred.* Chicago: University of Chicago Press, 1974; Lescoe, Francis J. "Jean Paul Sartre." Chapter 6 of *Existentialism with or without God.* New York: Alba House, 1974; Warnock, Mary. *The Philosophy of Sartre.* New York: Barnes & Noble, 1965. *See also* CAMUS, ALBERT; PHILOSOPHY, DISCIPLINE OF

SCALABRINI, BLESSED GIOVANNI BATTISTA

(1839–1905) Giovanni Battista Scalabrini was born in Fino Mornasco, near Como, Italy. He was ordained a priest in the diocese of Bergamo in 1863 and held positions as teacher, seminary rector, and pastor. Pope Pius IX, acting on recommendations from St. John Bosco, consecrated Scalabrini Bishop of Piacenza in 1876. During his 29 years as bishop, Scalabrini struggled to bolster his people's faith during the difficulties in Italy arising from the Italian Risorgimento. He defended Pius IX's condemnation of the new Italian state, but also encouraged him to pursue a *rapprochement* between church and state.

As bishop, Scalabrini provided a practical social charity as he also pursued more systemic social and economic reform. He sold his belongings and opened his residence to assist ill farmers and workers. He founded an institute for deaf-mutes and organized protection for young women facing both economic and sexual exploitation in the rice fields. He worked to catechize youth and encouraged mutual aid societies, rural banks, cooperatives, Catholic Action Centers, workers' associations, and legitimate trade unionism. Scalabrini's zeal reflected that of a remarkable community of contemporary Italian Catholic activists, including SS. Don Bosco, Louis

Orione, Pope Pius X, Frances Xavier Cabrini, and Luigi Guanella and Blessed Cardinal Andrew Ferrari of Milan, all of whom he knew. He also became an outspoken contributor to a growing body of modern Catholic social teachings addressing the "social question," expressed by figures such as Wilhelm Emmanuel von Ketteler, Giuseppe Toniolo, and Pope Leo XIII.

Scalabrini's eventual reputation as an apostle to immigrants, however, grew from a commitment to social justice that developed out of his own experiences. During episcopal visitations through his diocese, Scalabrini learned that more than 10% of his people had emigrated. Among the reasons for the emigrations were legal problems, political problems, and the lure of wealth, but most were emigrating because poverty forced them to leave.

Scalabrini recognized that emigration and immigration were not inherently bad, since migration was a fundamental natural right. He believed that in the modern world, furthermore, human migration would become commonplace, permit people to develop their talents, and offer them better lives. That position contrasted with prevailing opinions in the Church that viewed the mass migrations of the time as a temporary phenomenon. But Scalabrini also understood that the emigration he witnessed was usually not the carefully reasoned choice his ideas portrayed; it was often a last desperate attempt to survive.

For Scalabrini, all of the conditions causing, and resulting from, mass emigration needed to be addressed. First, mass emigration was a humiliation to Italy. Second, Scalabrini insisted that the Italian government had a moral obligation to ensure that Italy's emigrants not be abused. Third, recruiters encouraging emigration were not to profiteer off of the human exodus, and they were to be held accountable for what they had promised. Fourth, the *padrone* and *bossatura* systems, which exploited hapless emigrants once they arrived abroad, had to be abolished on both sides of the Atlantic.

Most importantly, Scalabrini feared that not only the hardships of emigration but also the breaking of the average Italian emigrants' social bonds with family and community posed serious threats to their Catholicity. The Italians' religion and culture, he insisted, constituted an essential unity, and the disruption of one necessarily endangered the other, which threatened to unravel their entire sense of self and dignity.

Critical to Scalabrini's assessment of the emigration question was the issue of integration versus assimilation. All that was really necessary was integration: one could do business and seek a livelihood in a new land without being forced to surrender one's ethnic and religious identity—and one's dignity—in order to do so. Immigrants, he pointed out, not only took from their adopted homes but also contributed: the world at large needed to respect that reality—it rarely did—and develop immigration policies accordingly. While Scalabrini did see assimilation as inevitable, he viewed it as a slow process that would develop over many generations. Prematurely forcing assimilation, he insisted, did spiritual, cultural, and social violence to immigrants. Meanwhile, Scalabrini saw exciting religious and cultural possibilities for the entire world provided by large, diverse ethnic populations abroad who maintained their unique identities and traditions.

Still, Scalabrini remained more pastor than theoretician in advocating for immigrants. He wrote pamphlets, addressed the Italian government, launched a magazine, *L'Emigrato Italiano*, and made the urgency of his apostolate known both to fellow bishops and to the Holy See, which eventually led the Church to develop systematic policies and teachings on human migration issues.

But suffering emigrants needed more immediate attention. Scalabrini therefore formed a congregation of priests who would themselves become immigrants to minister to migrants and immigrants abroad. This venture coalesced in 1887 into the Missionaries of St. Charles—more commonly known as the Scalabrinian Fathers—which provided Italian immigrants the priests they needed, their desperately needed spiritual care, a link to their homeland, and advocates who would speak out against indignities they faced abroad. In 1892, Scalabrini established the St. Raphael's Society for the Protection of Emigrants, a confraternity of lay volunteers offering assistance to migrants. With Father Giuseppe Marchetti and Mother Assunta Marchetti, Scalabrini founded the Missionary Sisters of St. Charles (Scalabrini Sisters) in 1895.

Scalabrini followed up the work of his congregations and societies with pastoral visits. In 1901, he visited operations in the United States. In 1904, he visited Brazil, which, along with many other Latin American countries, also attracted huge waves of Italian immigration. In addition, Scalabrini helped to arrange pastoral care for German and Polish immigrants, and encouraged Mother Cabrini to direct her efforts to immigrants in the United States instead of developing a missionary apostolate in China.

All of Scalabrini's efforts earned him the title of "Father of the Migrants" by the time of his death in 1905. The Scalabrinians continued, after some initial instability, to develop an international ministry to migrants, emigrants, and immigrants. They are active today in 30 countries on six continents. Pope John Paul II beatified Scalabrini in 1997.—Martin F. Ederer

BIBLIOGRAPHY AND FURTHER READING: Francesconi, Mario. *Blessed John Baptist Scalabrini, Bishop and Founder (1839–1905): Father to the Migrants.* Translated by Angelo Susin, c.s. New York: St. Charles Mission Center, 1999; Francesconi, Mario. *G. B. Scalabrini: A Shepherd to Migrants.* Translated by Angelo J. Susin, c.s. New York: Missionaries of St. Charles, 1988; Tomasi, Archbishop Silvano M., c.s. *For the Love of Immigrants: Migration Writings and Letters of Bishop John Bapt. Scalabrini (1839–1905).* New York: Center for Migration Studies, 2000; Zizzamia, Alba. *A Vision Unfolding: The Scalabrinians in North America, 1888–1988.* Staten Island, NY: Center for Migration Studies, 1989. *See also* IMMIGRATION IN THE UNITED STATES (HISTORICAL OVERVIEW); IMMIGRATION POLICY IN THE UNITED STATES; POPE LEO XIII

SCALIA, ANTONIN (1936–) Antonin Scalia has had a distinguished career as a lawyer, law professor, and jurist. He has served as an associate justice of the U.S. Supreme Court since 1986. He is widely regarded as one of the most important leaders in the conservative legal movement that rose to prominence in the last decades of the 20th century. Scalia has been an influential proponent of judicial restraint based on a textualist or originalist approach to legal interpretation. He has also reflected on the importance of his Catholic faith and on the relationship between his faith and his public responsibilities.

Scalia was born in New Jersey in 1936. When he was six years old, his father Salvatore, who had immigrated to the United States from Sicily, took a faculty position at Brooklyn College, and the Scalia family moved to Queens, New York. Antonin attended schools in New York City and graduated first in his class from St. Francis Xavier, a military preparatory school in Manhattan. He graduated from Georgetown University as the valedictorian. Scalia then attended Harvard Law School, where he earned a position on the *Law Review* and graduated magna cum laude. During this time, he met his wife, Maureen McCarthy; they married in 1960 and are the parents of nine children, one of whom is a priest.

Scalia worked in private practice before beginning his academic career at the University of Virginia School of Law; he also taught at the University of Chicago Law School. Scalia served as an early advisor to the Federalist

Society, an influential group of conservative and libertarian lawyers and law students. He also served with distinction in government positions, including several years as the assistant attorney general for the Office of Legal Counsel in the U.S. Justice Department. Scalia became a federal appeals court judge in 1982, and in 1986, he was nominated by President Ronald Reagan to the Supreme Court and was confirmed unanimously by the Senate.

As a jurist, Justice Scalia is best known for his approach to the interpretation of legal texts. With respect to statutory interpretation, Scalia focuses on the text and has long argued that "legislative history should not be used as an authoritative indication of a statute's meaning." His approach to constitutional interpretation is similar. He focuses on the original *meaning* of the text, not on what the original draftsmen intended and not on what contemporary interpreters think the text ought to mean. This approach to interpretation accords with Scalia's view that social policy ought to be set by the democratic branches of government. According to Scalia, "In a democracy, it is not the function of law to establish any more social policy than what is fairly expressed by legislation, enacted through prescribed democratic procedures." Judges have the responsibility to ascertain the meaning of laws so as to further the policy choices made by the people. Judges are not, Scalia maintains, to use their judicial power to promote their own views of desirable social policy.

In many cases, Scalia's method of interpretation results in a posture of judicial restraint. Scalia largely rejects the idea of judicial recognition and enforcement of nontextual rights such as the right to privacy (which is not explicitly set forth in the U.S. Constitution). Prominent examples of this deferential approach include his votes opposing the use of the Due Process Clause to protect abortion, assisted suicide, and homosexual sodomy.

Scalia is quite willing to uphold the constitutionality of laws that promote morality and is often viewed as the Court's most consistent defender of traditional morality. Some have criticized him for this very reason. These critics cite his votes in the due process cases (abortion, assisted suicide, and homosexual sodomy) as examples of him using his judicial role to support positions that coincide with his religious or political views. Scalia has maintained, however, that his views in abortion cases (to take perhaps the most prominent example) are the result of his recognition that the Constitution doesn't say anything about abortion at all. So, according to Scalia, the Constitution does not prohibit

the legislature from taking any position on abortion. "The States may, if they wish, permit abortion on demand, but the Constitution does not require them to do so. The permissibility of abortion, and the limitations upon it, are to be resolved like most important questions in our democracy: by citizens trying to persuade one another and then voting."

Many Catholics have criticized Justice Scalia's position. According to these critics, his approach neglects the role that the natural law ought to play in judicial decision making. Scalia's view, though, does not reflect an acceptance of legal positivism (which would imply that there is a sharp separation between law and morality). His view is more a consequence of his judicial philosophy: Scalia does not believe that judges have the authority to enforce the natural law in opposition to the text of the relevant constitutional or statutory provisions. A judge's proper role is to enforce the relevant law, whether based on the Constitution or legislation. The judge is not, according to this view, permitted to change or update the meaning of the Constitution or statute to suit his own views; the judge's authority extends only to enforcing the political choices made by the people. The people are, of course, permitted to use the natural law in enacting laws (to, for example, attempt to pass laws restricting abortion), but judges are limited to enforcing the Constitution. (Scalia has noted that a judge who was faced with the prospect of cooperating with an immoral law would be required to resign or to recuse himself; such a judge ought not, though, use his judicial position to invalidate the law unless the Constitution so required.) Under this view, the judge ought not bring his own views (from the natural law or whatever source) into his judicial decisions.

Although Scalia's approach to interpretation frequently requires deferring to the judgment of the legislative branch, this approach does not always result in the constitutionality of governmental actions being upheld. In fact, Scalia has been quite willing to invalidate the actions of the democratic branches when such actions violate individual rights clearly expressed in the Constitution. Scalia, for example, has been an aggressive proponent of freedom of speech (he has voted to protect flag burning, for instance), the right to keep and bear arms, and the right of the accused to confront the witnesses against him. These examples illustrate that this method of interpretation does not necessarily result in the judge's votes being consistent with his political views (be they conservative or liberal). Scalia has also voted to invalidate laws that depart from the structure set forth in the Constitution. So, for example, he has been a strong advocate for enforcing principles of separation of powers and of federalism. He has strongly protected the prerogatives of the executive branch from incursions by the legislative or judicial branches. His dissent from the Court's decision upholding the constitutionality of the independent counsel is one example of this approach. He has also stressed the importance of preserving state sovereignty.

The justice's approach to interpretation and to the proper role of a judge has been influential. Although he hasn't always succeeded in convincing his judicial colleagues of the merits of his views (as the outcome of cases involving abortion and homosexual rights reflect), most acknowledge that he has changed the terms of the debate.

Scalia has spoken frequently about the importance of his Catholic beliefs. Although he does not believe that he should bring his Catholic beliefs to bear on his judicial decisions, he has been a forceful supporter of a strong religious faith. He has encouraged Catholics to live lives of faith and reason. For example, he urged a gathering of the Knights of Columbus to "have the courage to have your wisdom regarded as stupidity. Be fools for Christ. And have the courage to suffer the contempt of the sophisticated world."—Richard S. Myers

Bibliography and Further Reading: Biskupic, Joan. *American Original: The Life and Constitution of Supreme Court Justice Antonin Scalia.* New York: Farrar, Straus & Giroux, 2009; Rossum, Ralph A. *Antonin Scalia's Jurisprudence: Text and Tradition.* Lawrence: University Press of Kansas, 2006; Scalia, Antonin. *A Matter of Interpretation: Federal Courts and the Law.* Princeton, NJ: Princeton University Press, 1997; Scalia, Antonin. "Of Democracy, Morality, and the Majority." Address at the Gregorian University on May 2, 1996. *Origins* 26, no. 6 (1996). *See also* CONSTITUTIONALISM; NATURAL LAW; *ROE v. WADE/DOE v. BOLTON*

SCIENTISM   Scientism is a naturalistic modern ideology in which empirical science is considered to be the only valid way to knowledge. It holds that other disciplines such as philosophy, ethics, sociology, psychology, religion, and so on are subjective and do not provide an avenue to truth that is free from matters of opinion and varied cultural values. Proofs derived from the scientific method are considered to exclude opinion and subjective judgment so as to be universally valid. However, as knowledge is limited to only sense knowledge derived from the observation of phenomena, what is not within the purview of empirical science is not worthy of consideration. The distinguishing feature of scientism is its

exclusion of the transcendent, which manifests itself in society in ways discussed below. Darwinian evolutionism is a scientistic dogma. The attempt to "demythologize" the sacred Scriptures shows the penetration of scientism even into theology.

Scientism has flourished with the notable successes of technology over the past few centuries. Technological achievements have followed one after another at an almost exponential rate since the 17th century. Today we have achieved advancements in fields such as biology, information processing, and physics that have turned yesterday's science fiction into today's scientific reality. The ability to represent physical reality in mathematical expressions and to manipulate these abstracted representations has given mankind a hitherto unimaginable control over nature.

However, scientism is, in fact, a self-negating ideology. It cannot be shown by empirical methods that empirical science is the only valid way to knowledge. Scientism presupposes philosophical assumptions such as the reality of a world governed by causes the human intellect can discover and describe. Yet these basic principles can be justified only by metaphysics, the relevance of which scientism denies.

The philosophical antecedents of scientism can be traced back to positivism, and before that to nominalism. Nominalism arose in ancient Greece with the philosopher Heraclitus, who denied being: All is flux; all is becoming. Plato and Aristotle successfully opposed such a philosophy, which would have destroyed civilization. However, nominalism arose again in the 14th century with William of Ockham. And it was largely due to his influence that the great medieval synthesis of philosophy up to St. Thomas Aquinas was fractured. Nominalism denies that universals have any real existence. Only individual objects exist, to which we subjectively give a name based on common features. Thus, "mankind" does not exist—only Peter, Betty, John, and so on. Nominalism makes natural theology impossible. Hence, knowledge of God is not something that can be achieved by natural reason. Ironically, if nominalism were true, empirical science would be a meaningless pursuit, because the scientific method presumes the reality of universals. For example, one could not refer to the properties of silver, a universal concept, but only to this piece of silver and that piece of silver. Nominalism leads on the one hand to fideism, and on the other hand to agnosticism and atheism. And it is through agnosticism and atheism that nominalism leads to positivism.

Positivism holds that the only authentic knowledge is that which is based on sense perception and positive verification. Auguste Comte is perhaps the most famous proponent of positivism in the 19th century. Positivism is reductionist. For example, it contends that all processes are reducible to physico-chemical processes. Biological organisms are reducible to physical systems. Thought is reduced to brain activity. Positivists hold that the scientific method is to be used in all sciences to explain and predict phenomena, and problems not susceptible to solution by the scientific method are deemed to be illusory problems. Scientific knowledge must be true for all times and places and must be capable of being empirically tested, such as by controlled experimentation. Scientific inquiry must be independent of political, moral, or personal values held by the researchers. But since valid knowledge is reduced to sense knowledge, "the God hypothesis is no longer needed." Accordingly, metaphysics and belief in God are rejected. Positivism sees theistic religion as at best irrelevant and, more commonly, an impediment to true science. It is functionally atheistic.

Eric Voegelin considered progressivism, positivism, and scientism to be variants of gnosticism, which, for Voegelin, is an "immanentization of the Christian eschaton," that is, transformation of society by treating the transcendent as if it were no more than part of the here and now. Sociologist Jacques Ellul provides a penetrating analysis of modern technical civilization in *The Technological Society*. He examines the influence of "technique," a systematic manipulation of technology and social factors such as law and economics with the paramount goal of maximizing efficiency, and sees it as an autonomous force that ultimately drives society to a totalitarian police state. It is a dehumanized pragmatism with no purpose other than its own increase, a mechanization of society that excludes all spiritual and moral values. As such, it is concomitant with a scientistic worldview.

Because of its atheism, scientism results in loss of the supernatural virtue of hope. The two fundamental transgressions against hope—presumption and despair—are both manifested in the present scientistic world: presumption as techno-utopianism and despair as techno-dystopianism.

The progressivist utopianism of scientism can be seen, for example, in *The New Atlantis* written by Sir Francis Bacon and published in 1627. Modern inventions, including ships that travel underwater, were written of with almost glowing approval. Indeed, with the Enlightenment, technology was seen to be the way to a new golden age. In modern times, this techno-utopian hubris has led to transhumanism, which is a movement seeking to overcome biological and physical limitations to create a new man, a "post-human" with enhanced physical and mental qualities. This is to be done through genetic engineering and the use of human–computer interfaces such as computer chip implants in the brain. Ultimately, transhumanists desire to escape the limitations of all physical instrumentalities. It is an attempt by man to divinize himself through technology.

The dark side of scientism is exposed in the arts, especially in modern science fiction films and literature. For example, the 1956 movie *Forbidden Planet* dealt with what can result from such attempts of self-divinization by escaping physical instrumentalities: an entire race of advanced beings destroyed by each other in a single night, each having let loose his subconscious "monsters from the id" backed with all the power of an enormous machine that gave material reality to thoughts.

Modernist techno-utopianism has developed into its obverse: a postmodern techno-dystopianism that focuses on high technology in a dysfunctional society. Currently, it can be seen in cyberpunk, a genre of science fiction beginning in the mid-1980s, characterized by the depiction of advanced technology in a degenerate social order. Cyberpunk is popularized in literary works such as *Neuromancer* by William Gibson and stories by Philip K. Dick and in such futuristic/film noir movies as *Matrix* and *Blade Runner* (a film version of Dick's *Do Androids Dream of Electric Sheep?*). The imagery of modern cyberpunk films derives largely from Fritz Lang's silent movie *Metropolis*. This type of fiction is typically set in a dark, oppressive world and features computers, artificial intelligence, and cyberspace. With androids (machines that act like humans) and humans modified with computer implants and/or machine parts, cyberpunk explores themes concerning the definition of humanity. There is an utter lack of any reference to God or the supernatural. It is a world glittering with artificial illumination but bereft of goodness, charity, innocence, nature, or joy. Behind the fantasy of techno-dystopian science fiction is a grim realism.

Of these two trends, the presumption of techno-utopianism is worse and has far more serious consequences. The despair of the dystopians is grounded in a sense of the nihilistic world that arises from a Godless scientism in a technological society. They see that something is seriously wrong, even though they haven't the light to see the reason or cure. But at least they recognize the spiritual darkness as such and do not mistake it for light.

On the other hand, the idealism of the techno-utopians leads them to desire the transformation of society effected by scientism. They cannot distinguish good from evil, because these concepts depend upon a natural moral order, which in turn depends upon a purpose for which human beings exist. And any such purpose must be directed to some transcendent reality, for a thing cannot be its own purpose any more than it can be its own cause. The only remaining standard of judgment for the techno-utopians is a pragmatic utilitarianism, which vacillates with the perception of one's current material interests. The techno-utopians usurp divine prerogatives to become like gods. This is the primal sin, which is a direct attack on God's majesty.

Scientism culminates in a loss of the sense of what it means to be human; a loss of common sense, of the good, the beautiful, and the true; and the loss of our ultimate fulfillment in eternal happiness. It is a major component of the spiritual disorder and cultural breakdown of Western civilization.—Adrian T. Calderone and Maria F. Calderone

BIBLIOGRAPHY AND FURTHER READING: Ellul, Jacques. *The Technological Society*. New York: Vintage Books, 1964; McCafferty, Larry, ed. *Storming the Reality Studio: A Casebook of Cyberpunk and Postmodern Fiction*. Durham, NC: Duke University Press, 1991; Smith, Wolfgang. *Cosmos and Transcendence: Breaking through the Barrier of Scientistic Belief*. San Rafael, CA: Sophia Perennis, 2008; Voegelin, Eric. *Modernity without Restraint*. Columbia: University of Missouri Press, 2000. *See also* GNOSTICISM; HUMANISM; TRANSHUMANISM; UTOPIANISM; VOEGELIN, ERIC

SCOTTISH ENLIGHTENMENT THOUGHT

The 18th century, the century in which Enlightenment thought saw its full flowering, was dubbed the Age of Reason. The proponents of Enlightenment thought, carried away by a heady optimism in their skewed interpretation of human history, believed that mankind had at last passed beyond its stages of childhood and adolescence and was now on the verge of achieving complete maturity. Freed from superstition and what Enlightenment thinkers regarded as a debilitating subservience to the Christian religion, men would henceforth be under the exclusive guidance of reason, "the only oracle of man." It was reason that would lead mankind out of the darkness into the light, and on to a golden age of universal human fulfillment.

England, France, Germany, and Scotland were the countries in which Enlightenment thought saw its most elaborate development. What was peculiarly characteristic of Scottish Enlightenment thought was that, while it rendered due respect to reason, it did not go overboard in emphasizing its excellence, and, especially in the realm of moral philosophy, gave significant emphasis to the importance of the emotions. It thus represented, in the main, a more balanced philosophical stance and has come to be known as the "commonsense" school of philosophy. There are several important figures associated with the Scottish Enlightenment, but four of them in particular stand out as being especially significant for the important contributions they made in giving the movement its defining characteristics. These four are David Hume (1711–1776), Francis Hutcheson (1694–1746), Adam Smith (1723–1790), and Thomas Reid (1710–1796).

Hume, whose single most significant philosophical work was *A Treatise on Human Nature* (1740), must be counted as one of the most influential thinkers of the modern era, although the influence he exerted has not, unfortunately, been all that beneficial. That is because Hume was a radical skeptic, and skepticism is the bane of philosophy. He did not hesitate to identify himself as a philosopher, and he professed to take great pleasure in philosophizing, yet he was firmly convinced that there was no certitude—about anything whatsoever—that can be arrived at through philosophy. What is so paradoxical about Hume is that he was a man who throughout his life assiduously exercised his reason—in this, he was a typical child of his age—and yet estimated that exercise to be essentially futile. Along with John Locke and George Berkeley, Hume makes up a triad that has come to be known as the British empiricists. They are called empiricists because they took sense experience as the point of departure for their philosophizing, which in itself is commendable enough, but they were not empiricists in a way that philosophical realism would be prepared to recognize. They must, in fact, be regarded at bottom as philosophical idealists, for in their thinking they gave primacy of place to things of the mind, rather than to things in the world.

Hume's skepticism led him to deny the reality of substance, even including that substance which is the human person. Equally notorious was his denial of causality. If B always accompanies or follows upon A, he argued, it is only through habit, not through any intellectual conviction, that we claim A to be the cause of B; we have no way of ever *knowing* if there is an actual causal connection between the two. It would be difficult to deal effectively with the practicalities of daily life if one were to be directed by Hume's theories about our knowledge of the world, and Hume himself knew this. And for that reason, in order to extricate himself from the quagmire of skepticism in which he had become mired, he called in a deus ex machina, Nature, which supplies one with that commonsense assurance of the reality of oneself and of the world, allowing a person to act *as if* he and that world were what they appear to be, and that he had real knowledge of both. Bertrand Russell commented aptly when he wrote that Hume's philosophy "represents the bankruptcy of 18th century reasonableness."

Francis Hutcheson, a Presbyterian minister, was the professor of moral philosophy at the University of Glasgow, and while much of his writings were accordingly devoted to ethical questions, he also made noteworthy contributions to the field of aesthetics. In what may be considered his most important work, *Inquiry into the Original of Our Ideas of Beauty and Virtue* (1725), Hutcheson laid down the basic principles relating to his theory of the "moral sense," the idea that each person is naturally inclined toward altruism and possessed of an innate capacity—having more to do with our emotive selves than our intellectual selves—whereby we are enabled to make correct judgments concerning the distinction between moral right and wrong. This theory, and indeed the basic thrust of his whole philosophy, was intended to counter the naturalism of thinkers like Thomas Hobbes and Bernard de Mandeville, who fostered the notion that the motives for human behavior were essentially egoistical.

One of Hutcheson's students at the University of Glasgow, and the man who succeeded him as professor of moral philosophy there, was Adam Smith, who is best known for his most influential work—a work through which, it is commonly agreed, Smith gave birth to the modern science of economics—*An Inquiry into the Nature and Causes of the Wealth of Nations* (1776). But Smith was principally a moral philosopher, and this is in evidence in all of his writings. His first book, *The Theory of Moral Sentiments* (1759), which drew high praise from Hume, Edmund Burke, and Immanuel Kant, proposed the thesis that all human beings are bound together by a natural sympathy, which explains the general amity that prevails among them.

The Wealth of Nations argued elaborately for what has come to be known as "economic liberalism." Smith believed that government should exert only minimal influence on economic affairs, leaving it to individuals freely to conduct themselves as they see fit in the public arena, guided by self-interest alone. On the face of it, this would seem to be a formula for social chaos, but Smith's confidence in human nature persuaded him that self-interest and natural sympathy would act cooperatively with one another in such a way as to serve the common good, and that in the end everyone in the society would prosper. In this, it would seem that he was assuming an altogether too benign attitude toward human nature and did not take sufficient account of the deleterious effects of original sin. All in all, as in the case of the famous "invisible hand," there are a number of features of Smith's economic theory that, from a scientific point of view, are not entirely convincing.

When Smith resigned his position as professor of moral philosophy at Glasgow in 1764, he was replaced by Thomas Reid, who became the most well known proponent of Scottish commonsense philosophy, as well as a pointed critic of the philosophy of Hume. It was Hume's skepticism that was the focus of Reid's attention, for he rightly saw it as directly undermining not only philosophy, but human reason itself.

In *An Inquiry into the Human Mind, on the Principles of Common Sense* (1764), as well as in later works, Reid developed, as his major philosophical project, a concerted effort to counter the flaws of what he called the "ideal system." What he was basically referring to by that term was modern philosophical idealism, principally represented by thinkers such as René Descartes, Locke, Berkeley, and Hume. Reid confronts Hume's skepticism with telling criticism on every major point, doing so simply by making in each case a direct appeal to common sense, that "faculty" by which we can be assured of having immediate and reliable knowledge of the reality of the external world. As to Hume's skepticism with respect to causality in particular, Reid argues that causal relations are not to be regarded as exotic and elusive secrets of nature that the human mind can never successfully comprehend, but as real events of which we are given clear and trustworthy confirmation by the deliverances of our senses. Causality is a ubiquitous feature of our familiar everyday world, and our knowledge of it is to be taken as the knowledge of a first principle. It is not, in the first instance, a conclusion of a process of reasoning—as Hume supposed it had to be—but rather one of the foundational truths upon which the process of reasoning depends.—D. Q. McInerny

BIBLIOGRAPHY AND FURTHER READING: Bryson, Gladys. *Man and Society: The Scottish Inquiry of the Eighteenth Century.* Princeton, NJ: Princeton University Press, 1945; Davie, G. E. *The Scottish Enlightenment, and Other Essays.* Edinburgh: Polygon, 1991; Kemp, Susan N. *The Philosophy of David Hume.* London: Macmillan, 1941; Russell, Bertrand. "Hume." Chapter 17 of *A History of Western Philosophy*, book 3, part 1. New York: Simon & Schuster, 1945; Small, Albion W. *Adam Smith and Modern Sociology.* Chicago: University of Chicago

Press, 1907; Wood, Paul B. *Thomas Reid and the Scottish Englishtenment.* Toronto, 1985. *See also* ENLIGHTEN-MENT, AGE OF THE; HUME, DAVID; PHILOSO-PHY, DISCIPLINE OF; SMITH, ADAM

SHAKESPEARE, WILLIAM (1564–1616) William Shakespeare was born in 1564, during the reign of Queen Elizabeth I, in Stratford-upon-Avon Warwickshire, England. His parents were Catholic, and his formative years were spent during a period of intense persecution. Several members of his mother's extended family were executed for their alleged role in "papist plots," and his father was fined in 1592 for his Catholic "recusancy," that is, his refusal, in conscience, to attend Anglican services.

The facts of Shakespeare's life suggest that he remained a believing Catholic throughout his life and that his Catholic faith informed his works. Before his arrival in London, there is evidence that he might have spent some time as a schoolmaster in a militantly Catholic home in Lancashire, and there is also evidence that he was forced to leave his hometown of Stratford in a hurry because of persecution by Sir Thomas Lucy, the bane of Stratford's Catholic population.

In London, Shakespeare's patron, the Earl of Southampton, was a well known Catholic, from a staunchly Catholic family, who had the Jesuit St. Robert Southwell as his confessor. There is considerable documentary evidence to suggest that Shakespeare and Southwell were acquainted before the latter's arrest in 1592. Southwell was tortured repeatedly during his imprisonment in the Tower of London and hanged, drawn, and quartered at Tyburn in 1595. He would later be canonized as one of the Forty Martyrs of England and Wales. There is also good circumstantial evidence that the young Shakespeare may have met another Jesuit martyr, St. Edmund Campion, and it seems likely that he knew the martyred priest Robert Dibdale, who would later be beatified by the Church.

If Shakespeare counted priests among his friends, we know that he counted those who persecuted Catholics among his enemies. Court records show that he found himself embroiled in a legal dispute with William Gardiner, a justice of the peace of singularly disreputable character. Gardiner had earned a reputation for persecuting London's Catholic community, of which Shakespeare was now a part.

During the final years of Elizabeth's reign, Shakespeare became involved in a controversial play about St. Thomas More, who had been martyred for his Catholic faith on the orders of the Queen's father, Henry VIII,

more than 60 years earlier. The play was blocked by Sir Edmund Tilney, Master of the Revels, who was Elizabeth's official censor. In spite of Shakespeare's best efforts to make the play acceptable, Tilney refused to lift the ban on its performance.

One of the most convincing pieces of evidence for Shakespeare's Catholicism is his purchase of the Blackfriars Gatehouse in March 1613. This house was a notorious center of Catholic activity and had been raided by the authorities. Having purchased the Gatehouse, Shakespeare chose to lease it to John Robinson, an active Catholic whose brother had entered the English College at Rome to train for the priesthood. Robinson was not merely a tenant but a valued friend. He visited Shakespeare in Stratford during the poet's retirement and was seemingly the only one of the Bard's London friends who was present during his final illness, signing his will as a witness.

Shakespeare died on St. George's Day, 1616, leaving the bulk of his wealth to his daughter Susanna, who had been listed as a recusant Catholic 10 years earlier. Other beneficiaries of his will included several of his recusant Catholic friends. It is evident, therefore, as the Anglican clergyman Richard Davies lamented in the late 1600s, that Shakespeare "dyed a papist."

Throughout the plays, Shakespeare's Catholicism manifests itself in a philosophical dialectic with the emergent atheism (de facto if not always de jure) of the embryonic Enlightenment. Although allusions to the doctrinal disputes of the Reformation and Counter-Reformation are present in the plays, they are eclipsed by the overarching dialectic with secularism. Shakespeare's heroes and heroines are invariably adherents of tradition-oriented philosophy and religion, motivated in their choices and their actions by an implicit understanding of Christian orthodoxy and a desire to conduct themselves with traditional virtue. His villains, in contrast, are machiavels, disciples of the new cynical creed of Machiavelli, who are motivated solely by a self-serving desire to get what they want. Shakespeare's greatest heroines—such as Cordelia, Portia, Desdemona, and Isabella—exhibit a self-sacrificial love emblematic of the Christian saint. His great villains—such as Edmund, Goneril, Regan, and Cornwall in *King Lear*; King Claudius in *Hamlet*; Iago in *Othello*; or the demonically twisted Macbeths—are all philosophical iconoclasts, ripping to shreds Christian philosophy and openly defying orthodox moral theology.

In *Hamlet*, Shakespeare defends the Christian realism of St. Augustine and St. Thomas Aquinas against the nascent relativism of the late Renaissance. In Polonius's famous advice to his son, we see the enunciation of a philosophy of life rooted in self-serving relativism, a philosophy that would lead to his son's unwitting and ultimately fatal manipulation by King Claudius. Prince Hamlet, on the other hand, begins with an egocentric tendency toward skepticism and nihilism, but grows in wisdom through his prevailing adherence to the objectivity of Christian realism. His growth from this solid foundation in philosophy to a revitalized faith, the latter evoked and invoked by his reference to the Gospel as the play approaches its providential climax, is the triumph of traditional virtue over the Machiavellian realpolitik of Polonius and Claudius.

Hamlet can be seen as a companion piece to *Macbeth*, the latter being an inversion of the former. Whereas Hamlet is tempted to despair but grows in the light of realism, Macbeth begins in triumph but descends into the darkness of nihilism, declaring that life "is a tale / Told by an idiot, full of sound and fury, / Signifying nothing." Hamlet overcomes Machiavellianism through the power of Christian realism and virtue; Macbeth loses his power, and his reason, by succumbing to relativism and the Machiavellianism it spawns. Macbeth is, therefore, an anti-Hamlet. Whereas Hamlet ascends purgatorially, through the acceptance of suffering, so that the noble Horatio can say with confidence following Hamlet's death that flights of angels are singing him to his rest, Macbeth descends, through his enslavement to pride and personal ambition, to an inferno of his own devising.

In *King Lear*, the same theme of purgative suffering is pursued in the midst of a political dynamic animated by what the Church would now call subsidiarity. Cordelia's decision to retain a virtuous silence in defiance of her father's wrath and at the cost of her disinheritance and exile is rooted in a principled refusal to bestow unto Caesar that which is not rightfully his. Her courage in the face of draconian secularism is reminiscent of the example of Antigone in Aeschylus's *Oedipus* cycle, but also of St. Thomas More's refusal to kowtow to the secular fundamentalism of Henry VIII or, more generally, of the refusal of England's Catholics to abandon their faith in the face of ruthless state-sponsored persecution.

The Merchant of Venice explores several political themes, but its overarching dynamic is the tension that exists between the worldliness of Venice and the otherworldliness of Belmont, epitomized in the respective philosophies of Shylock and Portia. The venality of Venice demands that the law be employed to crush the malefactor with merciless abandon; the wisdom of

Belmont insists that mercy must prevail or "none of us should see salvation." Once again, secularism (Venice) is seen to be at loggerheads with Christian orthodoxy (Belmont), and once again, Shakespeare comes down solidly on the side of the latter.

Shakespeare's condemnation of usury in *The Merchant of Venice* serves as further evidence of his Catholicism, not only in its conformity with the Catholic Church's traditional teaching on the subject but also in its implicit criticism of Calvinism for sanctioning the practice of usury. Since there was no Jewish presence in England in Shakespeare's time, the Jews having been expelled by Edward I three hundred years earlier, and since usury was practiced almost exclusively by Puritans, it has been suggested by several scholars that Shakespeare's characterization of Shylock is a veiled caricature of a Puritan. Such artistic subterfuge would have been necessary due to the Elizabethan government's ban on the portrayal of contemporary political and religious controversy on the stage.

Further evidence of the Bard's Catholicism is evident in his attitude toward monarchy and kingship. It is noteworthy, for instance, that the plays written during the reign of Elizabeth are preoccupied with questions of legitimacy. Many Catholics questioned the legitimacy of Elizabeth, arguing that her father's relationship with Anne Boleyn was adulterous. It is equally noteworthy that such questions of legitimacy become less prevalent in the plays written after the accession of James I, whose legitimacy was not in question. Instead, the Jacobean plays are far more concerned with the essence of kingship itself.

King James advocated the divine right of kings, whereby a king's subjects were duty-bound to obey the monarch at all times, even if he behaved tyrannically. At the other end of the political spectrum, the radical republicanism of the Puritans sought the abolition of the monarchy. Against these two extremes, Catholic political philosophy represented a via media in which monarchy was seen as a legitimate form of government but the monarch was as subject to the moral law as were his subjects. The political philosophy of Shakespeare's late plays reflects the Catholic position. King Lear's usurpation of powers beyond his rightful jurisdiction leads to disaster and widespread injustice. His radical conversion on the heath, reminiscent of the equally radical conversion of St. Francis, signifies his acceptance and embrace of his own mortality and sinfulness. Yet his acceptance of the mystical equality that he shares with his subjects, under God, does not negate the reality of his kingship nor the rights and responsibilities that accompany it.

He has ceased to be a bad king and has become a good king, but he remains a king.

Shakespeare's most powerful depiction of a good king is his description of St. Edward the Confessor in *Macbeth*. Set against the self-serving Machiavellian machinations of Macbeth, the English king's sanctity and the miraculous healing power that accompanies it serve as an iconic antidote to the poison of tyrannical ambition.

In recent years, from Leo XIII's *Rerum Novarum* (1891) and Pius XI's *Quadragesimo Anno* (1931) to John Paul II's *Centesimus Annus* (1991) and Benedict XVI's *Caritas in Veritate* (2009), the Church has delineated its social teaching in terms of subsidiarity. Such teaching on the role and responsibility of secular power is explored with timely and timeless resonance in the works of the world's greatest playwright.—Joseph Pearce

BIBLIOGRAPHY AND FURTHER READING: Alvis, John E., and Thomas G. West. *Shakespeare as Political Thinker*. Wilmington, DE: ISI Books, 2000; Hadfield, Andrew. *Shakespeare and Renaissance Politics*. London: Arden Shakespeare/Thompson Learning, 2004; Pearce, Joseph. *The Quest for Shakespeare: The Bard of Avon and the Church of Rome*. San Francisco: Ignatius Press, 2008; Pearce, Joseph. *Through Shakespeare's Eyes: Seeing the Catholic Presence in the Plays*. San Francisco: Ignatius Press, 2010. *See also* FISHER, ST. JOHN; LITERATURE; MORE, ST. THOMAS; USURY

SHILS, EDWARD A. (1910–1995)   Edward A. Shils was an internationally renowned sociologist, brilliant scholar, and sophisticated secular humanist with an extraordinary range of intellectual interests. They included the topics of social integration between "center" and "periphery"; the continuing saliency of tradition within modern life; the various forms of moral attachment; the roles played in society by higher education, science, intellectuals, ideology, charisma, literature, religion, and culture; the development of the "new states"; the nature of "mass society," secrecy, and privacy; the institutionalization of sociology as an academic discipline; critiques of the sociology and distribution of knowledge and rational choice/exchange theory, among many others. These seemingly disparate topics of analysis were ultimately united through the length and breadth of a remarkable academic career that witnessed an organic development in his social analysis. As Shils states in his posthumously published autobiography: "I have really been chipping away on the same rock. The rock is a single problem. What is the problem? It is the problem of all of classical sociology and political theory, namely,

the nature and conditions of consensus, or of social solidarity, or loyalty" (2006, pp. 158–159). The reception of the impressive Shilsian intellectual corpus has suffered significantly given the dominant left-wing, politicized, and antinomian perspectives institutionalized in academia from the mid-1960s through to the present.

Long anchored in the Sociology Department and the Committee on Social Thought at the University of Chicago, Shils nonetheless traveled frequently outside the United States and held numerous joint and visiting appointments with prestigious European institutions of higher learning. He came from a humble working-class, Eastern European Jewish background in Philadelphia, where his father was a cigarmaker. He earned a bachelor's degree in French literature at the University of Pennsylvania in 1931. A significantly self-made man, he never sought out earning a doctorate, and his superlative achievements and the state of higher education during his early years never absolutely required it. The precocious Shils first appeared at the University of Chicago in 1932 and flourished in that intellectually stimulating environment for the rest of his life. In the words of one of his many accomplished students, Steven Grosby, "Shils was a man who loved knowledge for its own sake. . . . [It] was, for him, the expression, par excellence, of the freedom of the mind" (2006, p. 10).

A sophisticated representative of Enlightenment thinking, Shils had an exalted understanding of the potential and, in many cases, actual role of intellectuals and professionals in promoting the common good. This understanding, however, was mitigated by his awareness of their ofttimes irrational revulsion for their own societies and, conversely, both the destructive visions they were capable of proposing and realizing and the set of selfish vested interests they were capable of defending. His keen interest in, and advocacy for, serious science, scientists, and scholarship and of enlightened politicians and devoted civil servants in the formation of social policy based on reason and empirically based research was reflected, in part, in his founding and cofounding, respectively, of *Minerva* and the *Bulletin of Atomic Scientists*.

Shils cannot be easily pigeonholed as either a conservative or a progressive. A staunch defender of academic freedom as a necessary requirement in the search for truth, he opposed the excesses of McCarthyism (*The Torment of Secrecy*, 1956). Shils was clear that academic freedom was not a license for academics to pontificate on issues outside of their fields of expertise or to propagate political opinions in the classroom. At the same time, as reported by his close confidant, Joseph

Epstein, Shils—along with then University of Chicago president Edward Levi—was instrumental in insuring that "the University of Chicago did not knuckle under to the student protest in the middle 1960s and was never humiliated and, subsequently, diminished by it the way that Berkeley, Columbia, Michigan, and other universities had been" (1997, p. 23). For Epstein, Shils "performed the function of conscience for a number of people—many students along with some professors—and indeed for entire institutions. It is an invaluable service, but not one that everyone finds congenial or that pays handsome dividends for the person willing to take it up. . . . The price of Edward's courage was loneliness" (1997, pp. 2–3, 23). As Shils put it himself, "I do not think that I marched to any drummer" (2006, p. 155).

Shils was extraordinarily generous to his students in sharing his time, knowledge, and editorial skills, yet he was incredibly demanding of them. Completing a doctorate under Shils was quite an accomplishment, a tribute to the talent, discipline, and sacrifice of the student. At the same time, as Grosby notes, "He demanded an independence of thought; he could not have been less interested in establishing a 'school.' To cultivate 'followers'—so easy a temptation among professors—was abhorrent to him" (2006, p. 155). For Grosby, Shils "was a man of the highest and finest character" (2006, p. 12).

The receipt of many important awards was part and parcel of Shils's acclaimed international status as a scholar. In 1971, the University of Chicago named him a distinguished service professor. The National Council for the Humanities selected him in 1979 to present the Jefferson Lecture, the most prestigious national award in the humanities. In 1983, he was awarded the Balzan Prize, an honor granted to scholars in fields ineligible for consideration for the Nobel Prize.

Part of the Shilsian intellectual project was the integration of elements of the philosophical and theoretical orientation of European sociologists with the more empirical and applied bent of American practitioners of the discipline. Throughout his illustrious career, Shils was a relentless pursuer of social analysis that was objective and nonideological. A member of both the American Academy of Arts and Sciences and the American Philosophical Society, he attempted to incorporate knowledge and insight from history, the other social sciences, the humanities, and the natural sciences into an essentially sociological understanding of reality. A relatively early attempt at a highly deductive, systematic, unified, and comprehensive understanding of society and social life was his *Toward a General Theory of Action* (1952), coauthored with his longtime friend and sometimes collaborator, Harvard University sociologist Talcott Parsons.

As an indication of his attempt at universalism in scholarship and the building up of a general sociology, Shils was not sympathetic to the development of specific sociologies, whether based on national worldviews (e.g., a "French" or "German" sociology) or some other perspective (e.g., a "Marxist" or "feminist" or "Catholic" sociology). In other words, Shils rejected the claim that—in a discipline that was, to the naked eye, pluralistic—all sociological schools of thought are necessarily undergirded by philosophical (and theological) assumptions that are irreconcilable. For Shils, any metaphysical considerations that are an intrinsic aspect of the sociological/scholarly enterprise represent, theoretically, a reflection of some unified, if partially implicit, secular system of thought that mirrored reality.

In terms of the issue of the autonomy of the social sciences, Shils was closer to the positivistic quest for a truth unmediated by historical and biographical contingencies than he was to that branch of the sociology of knowledge that argues that the pursuit of an objective truth never fully capable of being apprehended must navigate itself through the fiery brook of relativity of competing intellectual claims, taking from each whatever partial truth was valid. Shils, however, was no simple follower of Auguste Comte or proponent of any form of scientism. While stating that "it is not entirely out of the question that there will come a time when the human race as a whole shares a common collective self-consciousness formed around the image of a single body of knowledge in which all human beings, except infants, participate," he quickly adds, "I do not foresee any such far ranging changes" (2006, pp. 134–135). Shils's realism, respect for the nonrational aspects of human existence, and acknowledgment of the complexities and mysteries of life precluded him from seriously embracing any form of utopian expectation for the future.

Although operating from a secular humanistic framework with roots in the Enlightenment tradition, Shils—like the intellectual he admired most, Max Weber—manifested a respect for tradition in social life and the importance, for collectivities and individuals, of the "sacred," whether defined from a supernatural or nonsupernatural perspective. Examining both the limits that tradition imposes on innovation and the inevitability of change in tradition, he rejected any clear-cut positing of tradition as over and against innovation. For Shils, the sacred or charismatic is capable of existing in attenuated and diffuse as well as intense and concentrated forms, with modern societies characterized by a "dispersion of charisma." "Mass culture," for Shils and contra the perspective of most intellectuals, was basically a positive phenomenon characterized by the increasing incorporation of once marginal groups and individuals into the cultural and political affairs of the societal center.

It is important to note Shils's eventual "turn against Karl Mannheim," in the words of Jefferson Pooley. Early in his career, Shils had translated and was sympathetic to the line of argumentation put forth by Mannheim in *Ideology and Utopia* and *Man and Society in the Age of Reconstruction*. He ultimately came to reject a Mannheimian version of the sociology of knowledge because he concluded that it did not grant sufficient autonomy to intellectual activity vis-à-vis the realm of culture, posited a situational determinism that did not acknowledge the continuity of tradition, was relativistic, and was incapable of attaining objectivity and truth in social analysis.

Abandoning his earlier "grand theory" and highly deductive system-building attempts with Parsons, Shils eventually and essentially pursued his quest for universal knowledge and a general sociology more empirically, inductively, and pragmatically through the authoring of hundreds of substantive essays. Many were published in a three-volume collection of selected papers: *The Intellectuals and the Powers* (1972), *Center and Periphery* (1975), and *The Calling of Sociology, and Other Essays on the Pursuit of Learning* (1980). His last full-length published manuscript was *Tradition* (1981). In all of his writings, Shils demonstrated a sophisticated understanding of the mutually shaping relationship between theory and sociohistorical realities in social science scholarship. What Shils stated in his introduction to *Intellectuals* stands for all his essays published in his post-Parsons period: "Despite the occasional fragmentary character of these essays, they represent the movement toward . . . more comprehensive and coherent understanding." Shils left two massive monographs, *Love, Belief, and Civility* and *Movements of Knowledge*, to the Joseph Regenstein Library of the University of Chicago; only several fragments of these works have been published as articles.

Recognizing the roles of both consensus and conflict in social life, Shils was centrally concerned with the issue of moral and social integration. Like Emile Durkheim, he held that all functioning societies have a "center" that gives form and articulation to many of the activities of social life. However, his analysis of moral and social integration in modern life—using the categories of "primordial," "personal," "sacred," and "civil" ties, among other considerations—was more complex and subtle than anything offered in a basic Durkheim-

ian analysis. Conversely, his critique of rational choice/exchange theory involves "its excessive inclusiveness and its disregard for what it is unable to include" (2006, p. 195), that is, obligations of a "non-rational" and "non-economic" nature. Furthermore, Shils asserts, "There is a concern for the common good simultaneously experienced in many individuals . . . [although] I do not argue that these persons think only of the common good" (2006, p. 14).

Shils's insistence that primary group attachments maintained their saliency in modern, "gesellschaft" social contexts made permanent contributions to the subdisciplines of military sociology and the sociology of communications and represented a stinging critique of the "theory of mass society" generated by a European sociological tradition depicting modern individuals as overly atomized and prone to totalitarian and authoritarian manipulation. Central here was a study, "Cohesion and Disintegration in the Wehrmacht," coauthored with Morris Janowitz, on the consequences of primary group attachments, or the lack thereof, for the German military during World War II.

Another central Shilsian concern involved the development of the new states in non-Western countries, which tied together his focus on the role of intellectuals and the need for, and nature of, societal integration. He had a special interest in, and fondness for, Indian civilization.

Shils respected the social functionality and ritualistic grandeur of the world's major religions, while intellectually refusing to accept the doctrinal foundations of any one of them. According to Epstein, Shils "once described himself to a devout Catholic acquaintance as a 'pious agnostic.' He just couldn't make the leap into faith. I don't think this was by any means the central drama in his life. Faithfulness to his own exacting standards provided that. But he believed in religion . . . because he thought . . . [it] enhanced society by strengthening its bonds, preserving its traditions, making it deeper and richer" (1997, p. 28).

Shils's never-ceasing fascination with the cultures and religions of the world included a not insignificant amount of time spent in conversation with Pope John Paul II. As Epstein recounts: "In the last seven or eight years of his life, Edward attended conferences at Castel Gandolfo, the summer residence of the Pope. Edward admired the Pope for his intelligence and character and there is reason to believe that his admiration was reciprocated, my guess is on the selfsame grounds" (1997, p. 6). In an amusing aside, Epstein recounts a dream Shils experienced and shared with him: "In the dream he had been made a cardinal. It was quite wonderful, he said. He wore the red hat and robes of a cardinal, and he was permitted to roam the inner recesses of the Vatican, searching the archives in complete freedom. 'And you know, Joseph,' he said, 'no one asked that I believe any of the Church's doctrine.' He paused, then added, 'Jacques Maritain arranged for the whole thing'" (1997, p. 6).

"The Sanctity of Life," republished in *Center and Periphery* (1972), is a particularly useful essay in highlighting the fundamental difference between a Catholic worldview and Shils's own sophisticated secular humanistic perspective—the latter concerned centrally "with the freedom of human beings to guide their actions in light of reason and experience." The difference involves at least two fundamental and related issues. One is Shils's seemingly "natural law"–like analysis of a "proto-religious 'natural metaphysic,'" which, while arguing for "a conception of the 'normal' or the 'natural'" and one "whose chief feature is the affirmation that life is sacred," nonetheless proves itself inadequate, at least from a Catholic frame. The second is Shils's refusal to grant, in theory, that religion is coequal with reason as an authentic source of knowledge. By implication, Shils rejects the Catholic argument, as put forth especially by St. Thomas Aquinas, regarding the compatibility of, and mutually supporting role between, faith and reason. Instead, Shils, at best, compartmentalizes the supernatural and the natural and, at worst, reduces religion to the secular realm.

Regarding the first issue, the natural metaphysic of Shils is deficient from a Catholic perspective in terms of its acceptance of the morality of abortion. For Shils, "a foetus, for some of the period of gestation, does not qualify for the sanctity which is attributed to life. It is still organically part of the mother; it has still not begun to learn, and by virtue of that it has not yet begun its path to individuality." Regarding the second issue, Shils claims that Christianity enjoyed a long run in its plausibility not because of the truthfulness of its specific doctrinal claims derived from revelation, but "because it was able to conform for so many centuries to a deeper proto-religious 'natural metaphysic.'" The Shilsian vision "is not primarily about the reestablishment of a Christianity which is shorn of its historical and mythological accretions. . . . It is the proto religion, the 'natural metaphysic' of the sanctity of life, which must be rehabilitated."

As Shils states in "The Calling of Sociology," "sociological analysis can make peace with rational natural law or with the natural law based on the theory of moral sentiments, but it cannot make a completely comfortable home with natural law based on a religion of revelation. . . . There must be some awareness of the sociological denial of the final claims of religion in general or any of the great world religions of revelation in particular." He thus rejected the opportunity to expand his partially useful philosophical anthropological investigation of a natural metaphysic into an analysis affirming the existence of what Rudolph Otto referred to as the "holy" or "numinous" as a nonreducible religious reality and, derivatively, to oppose the intrinsically morally repulsive and evil act of abortion.

Shils also ignored, was indifferent to, or rejected the less radical option (from his secular stance) of employing his philosophical anthropological ruminations in a search for something akin to the "various signals of transcendence," as proposed by Peter L. Berger. For Berger, the same general kind of empirically based and inductive philosophical anthropological inquiry into the fundamentals of the human condition that Shils engaged in can point to the existence of something outside of secular reality. Berger's investigation uncovered various "signals of transcendence," thus affirming the intellectual plausibility of the supernatural realm.

In the final analysis, Shils's incredibly fertile imagination and intellect was limited to roaming, albeit at the very edges of, what Eric Voegelin termed a "contracted existence." Nonetheless, the case most definitely remains that Catholic scholars and social scientists have much to reflect on, and even more to learn from, Edward A. Shils—as an individual of goodwill, strong moral inclinations, broad ecumenical concerns, and brilliance of mind who devoted his life incessantly to the pursuit of truth, civility, and a humane and consensual society respecting an ordered liberty.—Joseph A. Varacalli

BIBLIOGRAPHY AND FURTHER READING: Ben-David, Joseph, and Terry Nichols Clark, eds. *Culture and Its Creators: Essays in Honor of Edward Shils*. Chicago: University of Chicago Press, 1977; Pooley, Jefferson. "Edward Shils' Turn against Karl Mannheim: The Central European Connection." *American Sociologist* 38 (2007): 364–382; Pooley, Jefferson. "Fifteen Pages That Shook the Field: *Personal Influence*, Edward Shils, and the Remembered History of Mass Communications Research." *Annals of the American Academy of Political and Social Science* 608 (November 2006): 130–156; Shils, Edward. *A Fragment of a Sociological Autobiography: The History of My Pursuit of a Few Ideas*. Edited and with an introduction by Steven Grosby. New Brunswick, NJ: Transaction, 2006; Shils, Edward. *Portraits: A Gallery of Intellectuals*. Edited and with an introduction by Joseph Epstein. Chicago: University of Chicago Press, 1997;

Turner, Stephen. "Edward Shils, 1910–1995." *Tradition and Discovery* 22 (1996): 5–9; Varacalli, Joseph A. "Book Review of Edward Shils' *Tradition.*" *Sociological Analysis* 43, no. 4 (1982): 391–393. *See also* BERGER, PETER L.; DURKHEIM, EMILE; PARSONS, TALCOTT; SOCIOLOGY: A CATHOLIC CRITIQUE; SOCIOLOGY, CHICAGO SCHOOL OF; SOCIOLOGY OF KNOWLEDGE: A CATHOLIC CRITIQUE; WEBER, MAX

SIMMEL, GEORG (1858–1918) Georg Simmel, a philosopher and central figure in the founding of the discipline of sociology, exercised wide influence through his writing and teaching. An original thinker and virtuoso lecturer, Simmel was the primary teacher of Ernst Bloch and Georg Lukács. Karl Mannheim, Walter Benjamin, and Max Scheler also attended his seminars and were influenced by him. He left behind no disciples or school of thought, however, that would carry on his legacy. Simmel also belonged to no school and formulated no strict method, and throughout his writings he failed to identify a basic set of ideas or outlook that would be proper to his thought. This does not mean that there was not a unity to them. In contrast to positivism, Simmel's method is interpretive; his work revolves around his project in grounding social forms in a priori intuitions, moving toward a revelation of the universal significance of a particular context by capturing snapshots of society in order to reveal the interconnections between different spheres and types of human interactions.

Simmel studied at the University of Berlin, completing a doctoral dissertation on Immanuel Kant in 1881. Four years later, he became a lecturer there, teaching many different subjects. Simmel's prolific writings likewise have a wide range, including psychology, art, philosophy, and sociology. He could see analogies and connections between different levels, and each individual work of his contains a multiplicity of topics and perspectives. He wrote over a hundred essays, as well as a number of monographs, including books on the philosophy of history, religion, and Arthur Schopenhauer and Friedrich Nietzsche. Simmel's two major books were *Soziologie* (1908; *Sociology*), and *Philosophie des Geldes* (1900; *The Philosophy of Money*). He was a master of the essay form, writing for the most part footnote-free prose. *Sociology* itself was a collection of essays from the 1890s and the following decade.

Though he was at the center of the intellectual life of his era, Simmel was never fully appreciated in the academy. Baptized Protestant but of Jewish descent, part of the explanation for this may have been anti-Semitism. A year after *The Philosophy of Money* was published, he was raised from lecturer to extraordinary professor at Berlin, but this excluded him from having a voice in university affairs. Only in the last four years of his life did he occupy an academic chair at Strasbourg University, where he was somewhat out of his element away from the bustling city life of his native Berlin.

The first decade of the 20th century was enormously productive for Simmel, beginning with *The Philosophy of Money* in 1900. The book, a philosophical meditation on the new money economy that had developed, considers both the meaning of money and its effect on the inner life of human beings. Beyond narrow economics, Simmel approaches money as a cultural phenomenon that can reveal the nature of social relationships generally. Practical life is inevitably evaluative, and the realm of value is equally primordial with concrete reality. Man ascribes values to things, a phenomenon to which we gain particularly good access by considering money, since it is a pure means, valuable only because it can get something else. Through economic exchange, the realm of values develops an objectivity that appears independent of a personal subjective evaluation. Money is thus a paradigm for culture, as most social relationships can likewise be regarded as an exchange, even when they at first blush appear one-sided, and can also take on the appearance of an impersonal and objective substance, bringing into convergence the two realms of value and neutral objects. An approach to social reality that fastens on its substance while losing a sense of its relational aspects is in danger of becoming absolute, however, as can be seen, for example, in socialism.

Sociology was more influential than *The Philosophy of Money*, at least on German sociology. Simmel tried to orient sociology toward basic interactions, rather than being obsessed with large social structures. Very attentive to the question of the size of a social group, he described the ways an increase in the number of people in an organization fundamentally changes its character. The presence of the stranger in a group is another important basic social element analyzed by Simmel. The alien who does not belong reveals a society's particularity to itself, shattering its naïve confidence that it is universal and orienting it toward a new goal.

In line with a German tradition that kept apart the natural and human sciences, Simmel resisted reducing society to individuals. Sociology cannot be positivistic; it studies the forms of interaction of individuals, which are more than the sum of their parts. The objective truth of social relations is different from that of objects of nature, and the social sciences cannot gain a true and exact representation of reality; its scholarship is comparable, rather, to the painting of an object. Social reality is dynamic, and any description of it has to be selective; therefore, the representation of it can be found not in laws, but rather in relationships that are found with some regularity. Reality as we experience it is socially constructed, arising out of living relationships, including religion, in which the believer lives out a vital relationship with God. Multiple explanations of reality coexist—for example, religious, historical, and scientific—without one exclusively dominating. Truth is not relative but relational, found in the situation with which man finds himself confronted and in which he must make an ethical judgment. Deeply committed to human individuality, Simmel objects to Kant's categorical imperative as excluding specifically individual ethical judgments.—Philip J. Harold

BIBLIOGRAPHY AND FURTHER READING: Frisby, David. *Sociological Impressionism: A Reassessment of Georg Simmel's Social Theory*. London: Heinemann, 1981; Helle, Horst Jürgen. *Georg Simmel: Einführung in seine theorie und methode* [*Georg Simmel: Introduction to His Theory and Method*]. Munich: R. Oldenbourg, 2001. *See also* MEAD, GEORGE HERBERT; SOCIAL SCIENCE METHODOLOGIES; SOCIETY, CONCEPT OF; SOCIOLOGY: A CATHOLIC CRITIQUE; SOCIOLOGY OF KNOWLEDGE: A CATHOLIC CRITIQUE; SOCIOLOGY OF RELIGION

SINGER, PETER ALBERT DAVID (1946–)

Peter Singer is a prominent professor of bioethics at Princeton University and an influential philosopher in the utilitarian ethics tradition. Born on July 6, 1946, in Melbourne, Australia, he was educated at the University of Melbourne and the University of Oxford, receiving a BPhil degree from the latter in 1971. He studied under Richard M. Hare, whose philosophical views influenced Singer's own adoption of preference utilitarianism, the view that morally right actions are those that maximize the fulfillment of the interests or preferences of all beings involved. He is known chiefly for his views on animal liberation and bioethics, particularly regarding the issues of abortion, infanticide, and euthanasia.

Singer gained prominence in the public eye with the publication of *Animal Liberation* (1975), a book that became influential for the modern animal liberation movement and remains his best known popular work. In *Animal Liberation*, Singer argued against "speciesism" (a term popularized by Singer, though originally coined by psychologist Richard Ryder), the view that the in-

terests of one species, merely because its members are members of that species, take precedence over the interests of other species. Human beings, of course, naturally tend to give precedence to the interests of the human species. For Singer, the root of the very possibility of a being's having interests consists in its ability to suffer. Insofar as this ability is common to many animals besides humans, as evidenced both by their behavioral responses to pain and by their physiological similarity to human beings, these other animals may, at least in principle, have interests that merit equal consideration with human interests. The suffering of a horse and the suffering of a human, if equal in extent, are equally evil and ought equally to be prevented when possible. According to this line of reasoning, if we can prevent a great quantity of animal suffering at a lesser cost to ourselves, we are morally obliged to do so.

Singer argued that to take different attitudes toward the suffering of different species on the basis of distinct characteristics, such as the capability for rational thought, is to draw an arbitrary division between their interests, since a being's interest in avoiding suffering is not based on such characteristics as rational thought but rather on the ability to suffer. Consequently, speciesism is no different in principle from racism or sexism; all three are based on arbitrary divisions. In support of this view, Singer observed that some human persons, such as infants and those with severe mental disabilities, exhibit less rational, conscious behavior than some nonhuman animals. Proponents of speciesism, if their preference for human interests were indeed based on humans' possession of rationality and consciousness, would therefore place less value upon the interests of such persons than they would upon the interests of nonhuman animals. That they instead place more value upon the interests of such human persons suggests that speciesism is not a rational ethical principle but merely the prejudice of the dominant species.

In *The Way We Eat: Why Our Food Choices Matter* (2006), coauthored with Jim Mason, Singer brought these ethical principles to bear on the ethics of eating and factory farming, particularly regarding what he saw as the cruel and inhumane treatment of animals raised for food, practices discussed at length in *The Way We Eat*. Singer and Mason argued for vegetarianism and perhaps veganism as the more ethical dietary habit. It should be noted that Singer did not place animals on par with humans in every respect; his focus in these works was on the morality of inflicting physical suffering and death on other beings. Though for Singer, vegetarianism is a moral norm, it is not a moral absolute;

it would not be morally impermissible to eat animals if this were necessary for survival.

Singer is well known for his views on abortion, infanticide, and euthanasia. In his most comprehensive work on ethics, *Practical Ethics* (1979), he defended all three practices as being morally legitimate and even desirable in certain circumstances. Unlike many advocates of abortion, Singer rejected the notion that the moment of birth constitutes a reality-based demarcation between personhood and the lack thereof or in any other way forms a morally significant dividing line. Instead, he based his defense of abortion on the more general ethical claim that the interests of beings, and therefore their rights, derive from features such as self-consciousness, rationality, autonomy, and the ability to wish to continue living. On this view, since a human fetus does not possess any of these traits, except potentially, it cannot be said to have interests or a right to life as an adult human can have. Consequently, Singer maintained, there is no compelling reason to think that abortion is morally justifiable but that infanticide is not. While acknowledging the practical difficulties involved in determining the degree to which an infant possesses the characteristics of rationality and self-consciousness, and agreeing that as a matter of public policy the law should err on the side of life, he suggested that, in at least some cases, a legal right to life should not come into effect for some period of time after birth, mentioning one month as a reasonable possibility.

A similar process of reasoning applies in the case of euthanasia and physician-assisted suicide, according to Singer. If consciousness and self-awareness are prerequisites to any right to life, then human beings in a persistent vegetative state or similarly incapacitated no longer have such a right. Similarly, voluntary euthanasia may be permitted because possessors of rights are able to waive their rights, and standard objections to killing human beings do not apply in such a case.

For the most part, Singer's views on bioethics directly conflict with those of the Catholic Church. According to Catholic teaching, abortion is always forbidden, and states must legally protect every human being's right to life, which begins at conception (*DVi* # III). The Church likewise condemns infanticide (*GS* # 51) and euthanasia (*CCC* # 2277). It is important to note the fundamental reasons for this disagreement. In the Catholic view, human rights are ultimately rooted in a common human dignity arising from the fact that all human beings are persons endowed with a rational soul, possessing the same nature and end (*GS* # 29). Granted this common dignity, it is no surprise that even unborn

infants and wholly incapacitated human persons are deemed to possess a right to life equal to that of any other human person. Because human beings share their nature in common, and dignity and rights are rooted in this common nature, all human persons enjoy the same rights. But the unique status of this common human nature depends on the union of the human body with the rational soul (*DVi* # I.9). Thus, if the idea of the rational soul is rejected and human beings are viewed as purely physical creatures, it becomes difficult to see in what sense human beings can be said to share a common nature and hence a common dignity. Singer himself denied that human embryos have a rational nature in any actual sense, having only a genetic structure that makes them potentially rational, and his bioethics depend ultimately on this claim. Absent a common human nature, human rights must be grounded elsewhere, in features such as actually expressed rationality, self-consciousness, or an ability to show a desire to continue living.

Singer's animal ethics, too, are at odds with Catholic teaching for the same fundamental reason: that he locates the basis for a being's interests and rights in its ability to suffer rather than in the dignity of its nature, leading to a kind of parity between human and animal suffering, which the Church rejects. Animals should not be elevated to the same status as human persons, according to the Church (*CCC* # 2418). Likewise, vegetarianism is not a moral imperative (*CCC* # 2417).

On the other hand, there is a point of agreement between Singer's animal ethics and Catholic teaching. Singer portrays at length what he believes to be the cruel and abusive treatment of animals in factory farming and similar conditions, and—just to the extent that such practices cause unnecessary suffering for the animals involved—the Church sides with Singer in condemning them. To cause animals unnecessary suffering is "contrary to human dignity" (*CCC* # 2418), and though man has indeed been given dominion by God over the rest of creation, including other animals, this dominion is not absolute but "requires a religious respect for the integrity of creation" (*CCC* # 2415). Animals should be treated with kindness (*CCC* # 2416).

Singer's views on bioethics have drawn criticism from various sides, particularly from those in the prolife movement and advocates of the disabled. Upon Singer's appointment to Princeton University in 1999, Steve Forbes, a graduate of Princeton and a member of its board of trustees, wrote a letter to the university in which he announced that he would cease financial support of Princeton as long as Singer continued to teach there. A number of Singer's European lectures have been criticized in advance or interrupted by protesters, in some cases resulting in cancellation. Singer, however, has suggested that his views appear threatening only to those who misunderstand them or interpret them outside of the larger context of his ethical system.—Michael J. Bolin

BIBLIOGRAPHY AND FURTHER READING: Singer, Peter. *Animal Liberation*. New York: HarperCollins, 2009; Singer, Peter. *Practical Ethics*, 3rd ed. New York: Cambridge University Press, 2011; Singer, Peter, and Jim Mason. *The Way We Eat: Why Our Food Choices Matter*. Emmaus, PA: Rodale, 2006. *See also* ABORTION; ANIMAL RIGHTS; ASSISTED SUICIDE; BIOETHICS; *DONUM VITAE*; EUTHANASIA; *GAUDIUM ET SPES*; INFANTICIDE; PERSISTENT VEGETATIVE STATE, FEEDING AND HYDRATING PERSONS IN; UTILITARIANISM

SIRI, CARDINAL GIUSEPPE (1906–1989) It is difficult to think of an archbishop and cardinal who was more influential in the 20th century than Giuseppe Siri. The books and conferences on him continue unabated more than 20 years after his death. His fame was therefore not a transient phenomenon but, as Pope John Paul II said, the acknowledgment of "the zeal with which he has always faced the theological and social problems of our time, asserting with rigor and clarity the primacy of the truth, and making known to everybody that the road to the true social good must pass through Christ."

Born in Genoa in 1906, Giuseppe Siri entered into the minor seminary when he was 10 years old. He was ordained in 1928 and, a year later, obtained his doctorate summa cum laude in theology from the Gregorian University. Named a bishop in 1944, he was the archbishop of Genoa for more than 40 years, from 1946 to 1987. Pope Pius XII made him a cardinal in 1953, while Pope John XXIII named him to be the first president of the Italian Bishops' Conference in 1959 (a post he would occupy until 1965), a member of the central preparatory commission of the Second Vatican Council in 1960, and, in the same year, papal legate to celebrate the wedding between King Baudouin I of Belgium and Doña Fabiola. Cardinal Siri died in 1989 and is buried in the Cathedral of St. Lawrence in Genoa.

An influential participant in four conclaves (1958, 1963, and the two in 1978), Siri made obedience to the supreme authority of St. Peter's successors the hallmark of his spiritual and pastoral life, which allowed him to be a trusted advisor to all the popes he served irrespective of any differences of views. At the Second Vatican Council, his main intervention stressed the primacy of the Roman pontiff as a sign of Catholicity. Accordingly, in 1987, he addressed a moving appeal to Marcel Lefebvre begging him, on his knees, not to separate from Rome. Cardinal Siri's commitment to the deliberations of the Second Vatican Council led him to found the theological journal *Renovatio* and promote an authentic interpretation of the Council against all postconciliar abuses.

A first-class theologian (he taught dogmatics from 1931 to 1946), Siri's writings encompass the whole spectrum of theological reflection, from dogmatic to pastoral themes, from spirituality to the social doctrine of the Church. His clear style and forceful reasoning are in the best Thomistic tradition, which he wholeheartedly embraced throughout his life. His best known writing, *Gethsemane*, challenges the contemporary theological movement in its very premises, starting from the relationship between the natural and supernatural orders.

Before being elevated to the episcopate, Siri had already written and acted on social themes. He introduced the "workers' Easter" (reaching workers in their workplace) and promoted workers' chaplaincies, the Italian "social weeks," and many other social and charitable initiatives, always indicating that justice in society can be done only if truth triumphs and the eyes are turned to the full Truth who is God. In the wake of the tragic acceptance of divorce and abortion in Italy in the 1970s, Siri was firm in vindicating indissolubility as an essential property of marriage and in denouncing as legalized infanticide any law (or, better, mockery of a law) condoning abortion, which can never be accepted for the simple reason that the fifth commandment can never be abrogated.

Unbending in upholding natural morality and Catholic teaching, Siri was a caring pastor, always eager to help his flock at any personal cost. (His favorite prayer was "To you, Lord, amen, amen, whichever is the price.") His commitment to the common good of his city was exemplary, ever since he succeeded against all odds in negotiating with the Nazis their surrender and avoiding the total destruction of the Genoa harbor. In his daily life, sustained by prayer, he followed some basic rules: prioritize what has real value, choose the more difficult path, and adhere to the Gospel, which is the exact opposite of the spirit of the world. He had a deep sense of God's majesty and an equally deep appreciation of the need for man (and especially for an ordained minister) to lead a simple and frugal life, of which his own life set the example.—Maurizio Ragazzi

BIBLIOGRAPHY AND FURTHER READING: Lai, Benny. *Il Papa non eletto: Giuseppe Siri cardinale di Santa Romana Chiesa*. Bari: Laterza, 1993; Siri, Giuseppe. *Gethsemane: Reflections on the Contemporary Theological Movement*. Eng. trans. Chicago: Franciscan Herald Press, 1981; Siri, Giuseppe. *Il primato della verità: Lettere pastorali sull'ortodossia*. Pisa: Giardini, 1984; Siri, Giuseppe. *La ricostruzione della vita sociale*, 2nd ed. Rome: Editrice AVE, 1944; Siri, Giuseppe. *Omelie per l'anno liturgico*. Verona: Fede & Cultura, 2008; Spiazzi, Raimondo. *Il Cardinale Giuseppe Siri, Arcivescovo di Genova dal 1946 al 1987*. Bologna: Edizioni Studio Domenicano, 1990. *See also* ABORTION; DIVORCE; LITURGY AND SOCIAL ORDER; POPE BLESSED JOHN XXIII; POPE PIUS XII; THOMISM/NEO-THOMISM; VATICAN COUNCIL, SECOND

SOCIAL CATHOLICISM, AMERICAN ETHNICS AND

The concept of social justice, as promulgated particularly by Pope Leo XIII, was advanced by various American immigrant groups of the late 19th and early 20th century and continues to have relevance into the 21st century. This period has seen a positive association between Catholic ethnic groups and the utilization of moral principles in a complex industrial and technological society.

For over a century, the doctrines of Catholic social teaching that speak to issues of poverty, wealth, economics, and social organization has influenced American society in general and ethnic groups in particular. Social Catholicism was, accordingly, the beginning of a departure from a Catholic perspective that had in the past limited social action to the realm of corporal works of mercy (e.g., aiding the poor, the hungry, and the homeless) while neglecting other societal concerns such as fair wages, safe and healthful working conditions, and labor's right to organize and engage in collective bargaining. Preoccupation with corporal works of mercy was understandable as basic to the Church's mission, which was then taxed to the utmost to perform these deeds due to the pressing needs of millions of new arrivals in the late 19th century—a time that also coincided with virulent anti-Catholicism that sought to portray that ancient religion as an inauthentic expression of Americanism.

Nativists viewed the accelerated immigration of the period, primarily from southern and eastern European cultures, as confirmation of their worst fears, while for newcomers the concomitant hostility added to the challenge of being uprooted from all that was recognizable and familiar. Catholics played prominent roles in the call for social justice as workers sought to protect their rights in an increasingly industrialized society by creating and organizing labor unions, not only in Europe but also in the United States. By the late 1880s, these conspicuous stirrings for social justice within U.S. Catholic circles were making an impact in Rome and accordingly were said to have influenced Leo XIII to issue his notable groundbreaking "labor encyclical," *Rerum Novarum*, in 1891, which was singular in that it did not view the wage contract as intrinsically evil, but rather as a natural right of the worker.

Irish immigrants and their descendants were primarily responsible for the alliance between the Catholic community and the labor movement. Church leaders like Cardinal James Gibbons, Msgr. John Ryan, and "labor priests" such as Msgr. George Higgins established a firm link with the labor movement, while layman Terrence Powderly, the son of an Irish immigrant, became the founder of the Knights of Labor. With Irish descendants serving as presidents of more than 50 of 110 unions within the American Federation of Labor by the late 19th century, Irish Catholics had become the most prominent leaders in the American labor movement. American Catholic labor participation served to promote the Church's fervent advocacy for social justice and equity for workers and their families.

The U.S. Catholic response to *Rerum Novarum* was gradual—embraced by some churchmen but ignored by others. No American churchman welcomed the encyclical more fervently than did Father John Ryan. He made it his life's work to integrate moral theology and social thought with American progressivism, thereby providing a Catholic critique of U.S. capitalism that affirmed the existence of fundamental natural human rights. Ryan wielded enormous influence via his position as head of the Social Action Department of the National Catholic Welfare Council and as an informal advisor to Franklin D. Roosevelt's New Deal.

Although the first German immigrant organizations predated the publication of the first social encyclicals, German Americans responded positively to the social action call in the early decades of the 20th century. A case in point is that of Frederick P. Kenkel, a "conservative reformer," who for decades served as director of the Catholic Verein and as editor-in-chief of the German-language daily paper, *Amerika*, transforming it into an English-language magazine. Kenkel sought to educate German American Catholics about the shortcomings of U.S. society and the appropriateness of Catholic social action to tackle those ills. He was instrumental in the establishment of a women's branch affiliated with the Central Verein, started a young people's section, and worked with others to promote parish credit unions. German American Catholic women, in turn, spoke on behalf of working women within their ethnic group who were exploited by the capitalistic system, and they likewise became strong advocates for children's day care facilities as well as traveler's aid societies to protect women at railroad stations and ports. The social reform mission of the Catholic Church served to energize the Central Verein as the German ethnic organization coupled its support of labor rights with its opposition to socialist propaganda. Accordingly, it endorsed progressive ideas such as workers' compensation laws and enactment of the Federal Farm Credit Act of 1916.

The Catholic advocacy for justice for the worker victims of the voracious industrialization that prevailed during the early stages of mass immigration clearly resonated with millions of immigrants from southern and eastern Europe then entering the country. One example involving Italians is the creation of immigrant aid organizations, such as the San Raffaele Society established in 1893, after Pope Leo XIII had become aware of the problems faced by these immigrants. Prompted also by the efforts of Bishop John Scalabrini and his religious order, the Congregation of St. Charles Borromeo—popularly known as Scalabrinians—the San Raphael Society opened centers in New York City, Boston, and elsewhere to serve the needs of newly arrived Italian immigrants by providing meals, temporary shelter, and jobs until they made their way into American society. The lifework of a number of Scalabrinian priests, themselves Italian immigrants, further illustrates the development of social activism in this period. Father Antonio Demo, a member of the Scalabrinian order, for example, provided stalwart leadership not only in religious matters for his flock in Lower Manhattan, where he served for years as pastor of Our Lady of Pompei, but also in matters that went beyond the strictly religious, such as his efforts to bring about an elementary parochial school and a day care center for the immigrant community.

The work of Mother Frances Xavier Cabrini is another example of Italians and Italian Americans engaged in social Catholicism. She was already well known in Italy for her charitable works when she met with Pope Leo XIII, who significantly supported her work. Mother Cabrini also conferred with Bishop Scalabrini, who persuaded her to extend her ministry in the United States among poor and exploited Italian immigrants who were genuinely in need of help and direction as they struggled to survive in an unfriendly environment. In response, she marshaled meager resources to found orphanages, hospitals, schools, and day care centers—67 institutions altogether throughout Italian enclaves in the United States, many of which continue to operate in our time, assisting other more recently arrived immigrants. She also established the Missionary Sisters, a congregation of sisters that continues her worldwide ministry. Cabrini became the first U.S. citizen to be canonized a saint of the Catholic Church.

Still another example of Italians involved in Catholic social action is Sylvester Andriano. He was a layman who emigrated from northern Italy early in the 20th century, was educated at St. Mary's College, California, and became a major participant in the promotion of social action based on Catholic principles promulgated by Leo XIII by teaming up with San Francisco archbishop John Mitty. Andriano specifically rejected the left-wing interpretation of the inevitability of class warfare, favoring instead the promotion of cooperation between workers, business owners, and government officials. Unfortunately, he was opposed by a combination of anti-Catholic Italians, Italian Masonic Order members, anticlericals, socialists, and communists, who succeeded in ousting him from his influential position by accusing him of being a fascist tool—a charge subsequently proven to be false.

Social Catholicism was also central to the activities of ethnic groups from eastern and central Europe. One example could be found in their advocacy of an educational policy for their children that led the Chicago public school system to offer English-language basic adult education and literacy classes to Lithuanian and Polish immigrants. Lithuanian and Polish immigrant community leaders—parish priests, newspaper editors, and the professional elite—called on members of their communities in various immigrant publications to attend these classes. In addition to these programs in the Chicago schools, Lithuanian organizations such as the Lithuanian Women's Educational Society and the Aurora Society and such Polish organizations as the Polish National Alliance and the Polish Women's Alliance established classes for their respective immigrant groups. Although participation in the education programs was limited because of the work demands imposed on breadwinners, the programs did provide an opportunity for at least some to improve their status in society. By aiding their children to become educated and by emphasizing their responsibilities to the poor, these U.S. Catholic ethnic organizations were engaging in social Catholicism.

The social Catholicism legacy endures more than a century later among descendants of Eastern Europeans, especially among the Polish ethnic group. When a wave of post-1980 Polish immigrants put new pressure on both the public and parochial school systems of Chicago to meet the needs of these newcomers, a number of Catholic schools instituted bilingual programs for them, brought in Polish-speaking volunteers to help Polish children, and developed Saturday schools that offer specialized language and cultural classes unavailable in the regular school systems. The latter programs were designed to encourage their children to learn and appreciate their heritage.

Another example of the ongoing tradition of social Catholicism among Polish Catholics was evident when Thomas Wenski became the new archbishop of Miami in 2010. On the national stage, Wenski has long been a leader in social justice matters within the U.S. Catholic Church, especially on immigration matters, an interest he attributes in part to the Church's teachings and in part to his personal history as the son of Polish immigrants to America. As a young priest, his fluency with the Haitian Creole language enabled him to be of service to the Haitian community in Miami. When asked about his passion for justice for immigrants, Archbishop Wenski responded: "My father was an immigrant. He was born in Poland and immigrated to the United States when he was about two years old. I think that has given me empathy for the immigrant experience. Then when I was a young seminarian, I learned Spanish in the seminary, because I thought I was going to be working with Cuban refugees in Miami. I did that in my early years of priesthood, but very quickly I also started learning Haitian Creole and I spent 18 years working with Haitians in South Florida." He continued: "Immigration has always been a part of the history of this country, and more importantly it's been a part of the history of the Catholic Church in this country. Some of the anti-immigrant feeling in this country can be understood as a revival of the Know-Nothing movement of the past, which sometimes was a veiled anti-Catholicism."

Immigration continues to be a major and controversial issue in the United States of the 21st century, one that has divided the body politic and that has meaning for Catholics and non-Catholics alike. Notwithstanding the welter of arguments proposed as Americans debate all sides of the immigration question, for Catholics, the principles of social Catholicism that permeated the subject in the 1890s and at the turn of the 20th century still serve as instructive and illuminating guidelines of the moral principles that should shape American society.—Salvatore J. LaGumina

BIBLIOGRAPHY AND FURTHER READING: Dolan, Jay P. *The American Catholic Experience: A History from Colonial Times to the Present.* New York: Doubleday, 1985; Liptak, Dolores, RSM. *Immigrants and Their Church.* New York: Macmillan, 1989. *See also* CABRINI, ST. FRANCES XAVIER; CATHOLIC CENTRAL UNION (VEREIN) OF AMERICA; IMMIGRATION IN THE UNITED STATES (HISTORICAL OVERVIEW); IMMIGRATION POLICY IN THE UNITED STATES; KNIGHTS OF LABOR; RYAN, JOHN AUGUSTINE; SCALABRINI, BLESSED GIOVANNI BATTISTA

SOCIAL CONSTRUCTIONISM Social constructionism refers to how we know and how we become (for the while) certain about what we unproblematically take to be the outside-our-mind realities. The first element of the term suggests that the determinative factors in our grasp of the exterior *really* real, as contrasted with the interior thoughts we have about them, are *societal*; the second, that our apparent apprehensions actually reflect a subterranean and subconscious internalization of our surrounding culture, especially of its language with its undetected category-forming structure. Though the term is employed more by sociologists and social psychologists than by others, *social constructionism* has conceptual affinities with almost all of the powerhouse terms in contemporary philosophy and literary criticism, most of which, in Paul Ricoeur's evocative phrase, embrace a "hermeneutic of suspicion," such as *postmodernism, deconstructionism, genealogy,* and *discursive regime.* Although it shares the limitations of the extreme and a priori *antifoundationalism* associated with postmodernist thought, the social constructionist turn in sociology has many fruitful applications that have an affinity with perennial themes in Catholic social thought, especially the social nature of the human person and the aspiration for human solidarity. But, social constructionism does not share this tradition's permanent concern with the transcultural category of the *intrinsically evil* nor its fear that the radical relativism associated with dominant forms of social constructionism, as opposed to a healthy contextualism, will erode the link between justice and truth.

Although there were several significant intellectual predecessors, such as Emile Durkheim and George Herbert Mead in sociology and Alfred Schutz in philosophy, the explicit phrase lodged itself into the sociological mainstream with the influential and very readable 1966 work by Peter L. Berger and Thomas Luckmann provocatively entitled *The Social Construction of Reality*. Berger and Luckmann persuasively invited the reader to look deeper into her taken-for-granted world and achieve some distance—the current term is *reflexivity*—from all that she would otherwise take as natural or even plausible. The overcoming of ethnocentrism, of course, is typically what anthropology teachers have always encouraged, but the term *social construction of reality* promised a depth and comprehensiveness that was far more challenging that any invitation to a tolerant humanism. In the social constructionist framework, everything was essentially ethnocentric, including our sense of justice. In social constructionist thought, *morals* tend to be reduced to *mores* with weightier and more formal public sanction.

Two much cited research findings vividly, and frighteningly, display the powerful impact that significant others and social roles—besides language, the two core elements in a social constructionist perspective—have on what we come to think we perceive and what we come to think we should do. In the first, Solomon Asch showed that, in an experimental group setting, when asked about the comparative length of a projected stick (bigger than the other? smaller? the same?) people will reverse their original and obviously correct answer and surprisingly often agree with the clearly mistaken answer that all of the surrounding experimenter-hired plants unanimously gave. The second, Stanley Milgram's 1963 Naziesque experiment, found that when their faux research psychiatrist, replete with clinical white gown and professorial glasses, instructed them to increasingly up the pain-causing maximum of a supposedly memory-prompting electrical voltage to a correspondingly increasing-screaming faux patient, about half of his subjects disengaged from their normal reactions and complied with the professional's directive.

A happier example of a social constructionist effect was achieved in a famous experiment by Robert Rosenthal and Lenore Jacobson, who told elementary school teachers that, through a scientific psychometric appraisal, they had identified several students—whom the researchers had actually randomly selected—as late bloomers, that is, kids who, though they presently seemed average and did only average work, would, as the year unfolded, blossom into superior students. And so, with the increased attention and higher expectations paid to these students by their newly scientifically alerted teacher, bloom they did into a higher self-regard and higher grades.

As summarized by a social constructionist perspective, what we see as "obvious" and what we feel as "appropriate" are powerfully shaped and determined not by *naturally given* realities—or, as in the onomatopoetic Kantian phrase, by any *ding-an-sich*—but are made to appear plausible and natural by socially constructed authorizations embedded into familiar social roles experienced as significant or authoritative others.

The Milgram and Asch experiments are extreme (and by today's social science research standards, unprofessional) examples of a social constructionist perspective. Indicative of the more commonplace use of this perspective is that, in just about every introductory sociology textbook's chapters on gender and race, the student learns that what we—that is, the society—presently think about the roles of men and women and their mutual expectations have changed hugely over time. The anatomical facts remain the same, but their cultural meanings in our society now urge us toward an ever deepening equality. Sociologists summarize these historical and ongoing changes with the phrase the "social construction of gender." In familiar social science terms, *nurture* shapes (forms, determines, interprets, encodes) *nature*.

Similarly, the student learns that *race*, and especially any putative causal psychological or cultural dimensions—such as IQ or entrepreneurial motivation—associated with race, has no valid genetically based meaning, but has been historically ascribed by the more powerful to colonized or subordinated others on the socially constructed rationalization that these physical differences are *naturally* associated with innately inferior human potentialities. Indeed, social scientists now refer to the "invention of race."

In a context broader than race and gender (such as how a society defines deviance, beauty, the socially desirable, and so on), the sociological and social psychological perspective called *labeling theory* can be considered a subset of the more generic social constructionism.

So far in this analysis of the core dimensions of a social constructionist perspective, the emphasis has been on changing cultural values as institutionalized in social roles and enacted by significant others as they impact on perceptions and behaviors. But the perspective is most powerfully expressed in the analyses of the relationships between language and thought, especially in what is known as the Whorfian thesis (after Benjamin Lee Whorf, a student of Edward Sapir) that our language does not simply express our thoughts but determines their logic and their scope. For example, because the

Eskimos have many different words for the distinct kinds of snow they experience, while we (at least in Brooklyn) have only a few snow terms (almost all of them beginning with the adjective "damn"), the Eskimos can "see" a great variety of snow while Brooklynites can only see, say, two kinds (shoveled and unshoveled). In Ludwig Wittgenstein's much cited phrase, "The limits of my language mean the limits of my world."

Countering such an extreme linguistic determinism, current research shows that even prelinguistic children manifest aptitudes for differentiation in such key cognitive categories as position, cause and effect, and agency. The less deterministic truth contained in any Whorfian-like hypothesis is that language powerfully affects what a culture values and subtly directs what we pay attention to and how we frame what we are thinking and what we think we should do. Although vocabularies do not *determine* what any given individual thinks, it does, for example, make a great difference to civil discourse, and thus to social policy, whether a society characterizes a military initiative as an "invasion" or a "liberation," or the opposition to abortion as "antichoice" rather than "pro-life."

In an April 2011 address to a plenary assembly of the Pontifical Council for Social Communications, Pope Benedict XVI called attention to the fact that new technologies not only change the way people communicate but embody a vast cultural transformation. Language does not, he said, simply provide a provisional coating of concepts but "the living and palpitating context in which the thoughts, concerns and projects of men are born to the conscience and are molded in gestures, symbols and words." Human beings, he added with what we might call a social constructionist flair, not only *use*, but in a certain way *inhabit*, their language.

The attention that Pope Benedict and others give to the reality-formative dimensions of language strongly urges us to correct any deterministic reading of a social constructionist perspective. We do, after all, experience ourselves as deciding whether, for example, to characterize a war as *just*, and these moral understandings have deepened over time. A pertinent example of a community reflecting on its foundational sources in the context of the lessons of history and contemporary global challenges is Catholicism's Second Vatican Council (1962–1965). In terms of interreligious witness and cooperation against the all too common resort of nations to military violence, the increasing inequality within and among nations, and the omnipresent threat of nuclear annihilation, the council's decrees on ecumenism, on religious freedom, and on relationships

with non-Christian religions challenged church leaders and members to efficaciously recall that their Catholic Christianity transcends national boundaries and national history and that a divided Christianity hinders a convincing global presence.

From a social constructionist perspective, we would anticipate an ongoing postconciliar search for new vocabularies that redirect religious consciousness toward new visions emerging from more comprehensive integrities and for new shared actions, gradually making ecumenism and interfaith cooperation the contemporary taken-for-granted inner consciousness of religion. Though the achievements of ecumenism and of the interfaith movement are as much promissory as actual, they are significant. Distinctive directing vocabularies have emerged, such as *koinonia*, a Greek term that churches in dialogue use to express the solidarity and mutual sharing that they already have and that they are called to deepen; *differentiated consensus*, which expresses the agreements on doctrine that churches have achieved with the recognition that divisions remain; *hierarchy of truths*, the acknowledgment that some church teachings are core, such as the Incarnation, and others are historically conditioned, such as the structurings of authority; and *reception*, the grassroots church sharing in prayers and cooperative works of social justice through which otherwise academic ecumenical agreements are experienced as a lived reality and thus achieve an experiential authority. The present state of ecumenism only faintly approximates the reality these emerging and directive terms intend, which is always the case when the social constructivist perspective is viewed from an activist, transformative perspective.

In pursuit of a less deterministic social constructionist perspective, the "social imaginary" is an apt term that not only can characterize the modern ecumenical and interfaith movements but also more generically signifies the human capacity to go beyond the unquestioned determinative impact of cultural meanings encoded in language and in institutions, roles, and social expectations to achieve a more transforming engagement. Charles Taylor characterizes the social imaginary as applying the moral imagination to the social imagination, whereby our taken-for-granted everyday life includes the expectation that it should have more justice and more human solidarity. The social imaginary, like the social constructionist perspective it enlarges, penetrates consciousness far deeper than disengaged intellectual schemes; it points to the ways ordinary people imagine their social existence and their common expectations about their lives in common and the images, most often religious, in which they are embedded. When given a corrective activist direction, the social constructionist perspective can be considered a vital part of the social science corpus, awaiting its next round of sudden relevance when unarticulated new aspirations prompt an emergent search for new terms or transformations of earlier social constructions.—James R. Kelly

BIBLIOGRAPHY AND FURTHER READING: Fuchs, Lorelei F., SA. *Koinonia and the Quest for an Ecumenical Ecclesiology.* Grand Rapids, MI: Eerdmans, 2008; Gergen, Kenneth J. "The Social Constructionist Movement in Modern Psychology." *American Psychologist* 40, no. 3 (1985): 266–275; Marsh, James L. *Critique, Action, and Liberation.* New York: New York University Press, 1995; Pinker, Stephen. *The Stuff of Thought: Language as a Window into Human Nature.* New York: Penguin Books, 2008; Taylor, Charles. *Modern Social Imaginaries.* Durham, NC: Duke University Press, 2004; Zimbardo, Philip. *The Lucifer Effect: Understanding How Good People Turn Evil.* New York: Random House, 2008. *See also* BERGER, PETER L.; ETHNOCENTRISM; EVIL; MEAD, GEORGE HERBERT; SOCIOLOGY: A CATHOLIC CRITIQUE; TAYLOR, CHARLES M.

SOCIAL DARWINISM The term *social Darwinism* originated in the last decades of the 19th century and was used to describe elements of both progressive and conservative thought common to that era. At the most general level, social Darwinism implies the application of supposedly Darwinian principles to the characteristics of different groups of people, particularly as they relate to intellectual capacity, relative capability, and socioeconomic class. Its roots in Darwin's own work are the subject of considerable debate. Representatives from the natural sciences often reject the application of evolutionary principles to specific social or political programs, in spite of some of Darwin's own words. Though there is no universally agreed-upon list of characteristics of social Darwinism, concepts such as the struggle for survival, natural selection, and restraint prompted by limited resources often figure prominently in social Darwinist reasoning, even if the terms themselves are not always used. Many of the basic ideas in social Darwinism were present in social theory before Darwin's own work was widely known, though it is a mark of his influence that his name became shorthand for the entire framework. The term is often used now to indict any set of principles or policies that may imply or reinforce various forms of social inequality.

Social theorists such as Auguste Comte or Emile Durkheim imported such concepts as functional integration, adaptation, and stasis from biology into the newly emerging social sciences, especially sociology. Social Darwinism went beyond this sort of comparative reasoning to argue that select groups of people were less well suited than others for the demands of the social order. British social philosopher Herbert Spencer, often credited as the originator of the term "survival of the fittest," is widely recognized as one of the first major proponents of social Darwinian thinking. Numerous undergraduates in the United States encountered evolution more from Spencer's work than any other source, and he was always more popular in America than in Europe.

In line with Lamarckian evolutionary principles that allowed for acquired traits, such as learning, to be inherited, Spencer believed that industrial society had progressed to the point that it could and should take control over its own evolution. Individuals and societies could and should act so as to ensure the survival of the fittest rather than simply recognizing this struggle as nature's mechanism for improving the species. Accordingly, Spencer favored social policies that allowed individuals to advance themselves, such as laissez-faire economics and the repeal of compulsory poor relief laws, believing that the strong would then advance over the unfit. In his mind, such a system would advance both the individual and the society. Under this system, society would be relieved of the burden imposed by caring for weaker members. These and similar views were in direct tension with Catholic ideas about social justice, the inherent dignity of every person, and the value of charity, many of which were emerging in new forms to suit modern social conditions. Spencer's approach influenced numerous philosophers, historians, and social theorists, including such notables as Asa Grey, William Sumner, and Henry Ward Beecher, some of whom went further than Spencer himself in terms of advocating policies consistent with the philosophy of social Darwinism.

Probably the most infamous application of social Darwinism is the eugenics movement in Europe and the United States in the early 20th century. Eugenicists believed that our understanding of biology and hereditary had progressed such that we could improve the species overall by tracking genetic lines of undesirable traits and pruning them from the gene pool. Thus, they favored segregation, and in many cases sterilization, for those deemed unfit. The determination of one's fitness was the responsibility of institutions such as the Eugenics Record Office in Cold Spring Harbor, New York, which claimed to be able to identify and track traits such as "feeble-mindedness" and "deafmutism." Though not always expressly tied to social Darwinism, it provided both a philosophical framework and a historical antecedent for the efforts of the eugenicists.

Eugenic science was enormously influential in the opening decades of the 20th century, coinciding as it did with several progressive movements aimed at social reform and the promotion of human well-being. Various states passed measures allowing for the forcible sterilization of private citizens, and the U.S. Supreme Court upheld the constitutionality of such laws in its 1927 decision in *Buck v. Bell.* Writing for the Court, Justice Oliver Wendell Holmes held that the state's interest in promoting the health of its citizens was sufficient to justify the sterilization of Virginian Carrie Buck, whose family had been labeled "feeble-minded" by the state of Virginia.

Support for eugenic programs was widespread, but there were critics as well. Several scientists, especially geneticists, held that the recordkeeping of the various eugenic offices was sloppy and insufficient given the decisions being made, and furthermore that the entire eugenic framework assumed a greater understanding of hereditary and the influence of environment than was possible at the time. Eugenic science, they claimed, was not really science at all.

Religious voices were scattered and inconsistent when it came to the moral and ethical implications of eugenic practices. Many progressive religious voices found in eugenics another tool for the betterment of social conditions and the alleviation of suffering. Dean Walter Sumner of Chicago's Episcopal Cathedral of SS. Peter and Paul promoted his plan to require couples seeking marriage to have a certificate of health from a medical professional before the ceremony could be performed. The American Eugenic Society's Committee on Cooperation with Clergymen sponsored sermon contests stressing the common ground between their aims and those of the churches, namely, promoting a higher quality of life. Harry Emerson Fosdick, one of the most notable progressive religious leaders of the era, served on the Society's Advisory Council, as did Father John Cooper. The influential Father John A. Ryan, onetime head of the Department of Social Action of the National Catholic Welfare Council, served on the Committee on Cooperation with Clergymen, though his reasons for doing so are unclear. He was critical of the eugenic project's tendency to evaluate the worth of individuals, preferring to think in broader terms about social reform. G. K. Chesterton was perhaps the most celebrated critic of eugenics, identifying it as a social evil based on bad science bent on appropriating the power of the state to violate the most basic rights of the individual.

Catholic opposition to eugenic policies was strong and consistent, particularly as the eugenic movement forged both ideological and institutional alliances with advocates of birth control. This was most clearly stated in Pope Pius XI's 1930 encyclical *Casti Connubii*, which held that the state could not gratuitously "tamper with the integrity of the body" and specifically identified eugenics as violating this basic principle (*CC # 70*). On the practical level, Catholic organizations lobbied against sterilization bills in state legislatures, and advocates of eugenic policies recognized the Catholic Church as one of their most effective opponents. Though eugenics is only one example of social Darwinian thinking, it is often identified along with the Holocaust as one of the main factors in the discrediting of social Darwinism. The Catholic Church's campaign against eugenics represents one of its most focused efforts to combat social Darwinism.—Steven L. Jones

BIBLIOGRAPHY AND FURTHER READING: Bruinius, Harry. *Better for All the World: The Secret History of Forced Sterilization and America's Quest for Racial Purity.* New York: Knopf. 2006; Hofstadter, Richard. *Social Darwinism in American Thought.* New York: George Braziller, 1959; Rosen, Christine. *Preaching Eugenics: Religious Leaders and the American Eugenics Movement.* New York: Oxford University Press, 2004; Spencer, Herbert. *The Study of Sociology.* New York: D. Appleton, 1874. *See also* DURKHEIM, EMILE; EUGENICS; RYAN, JOHN AUGUSTINE; SOCIAL DARWINISM AND THE NAZIS

SOCIOLOGY, CHICAGO SCHOOL OF While most students of sociology look to such 19th-century social science thinkers as Alexis de Tocqueville, Auguste Comte, Emile Durkheim, Herbert Spencer, and Max Weber to understand the origins of the discipline of sociology, the reality is that in the United States, the community of social scientists working at the University of Chicago from 1915 to 1935 must be acknowledged as the real force in shaping the future of 20th-century American sociology. And although Catholics were not represented on the faculty of the university during these early days, the Chicago School recognized and appreciated the important role that the U.S. Catholic Church played in creating community for the 20th-century immigrants from the Catholic countries of western and eastern Europe.

The Chicago School pioneered empirical research and a variety of methods, both qualitative and quantitative, shaping not only sociology but also creating such related fields of study as urban ecology, urban planning, community studies, race and ethnic relations, deviance, and criminology. A "school" in sociology can be thought of in the same way the term is used by art historians to designate a group of artists who share a certain style, technique, or set of symbolic expression within a given time frame. For example, the Impressionists can be seen as part of a school because the artists within the school share similar techniques.

As in the art world, the founder or founders of a school within sociology are dominant and visionary. Other sociologists are drawn to the emerging school because they share a set of ideas or beliefs that are articulated by these founders—often in disagreement with the ideas or beliefs that are prevailing in the discipline at the time. Those who join the emerging school then help to recruit others who share their thoughts. Collaboration in scholarly activity is characteristic of a school, and this activity flourishes within academic settings—especially in a metropolitan area that is more likely to draw talented scholars desiring an urban experience in which to study. A journal or academic press like the one started at the University of Chicago is helpful—in fact, almost required, so that the members of the school can work collaboratively and can communicate with a wider scholarly public. But, what is most important in an emerging school is a new vision for the discipline that attracts followers who share that vision.

What drew sociologists to the Chicago School was the school's rejection of what some social scientists have called the "armchair philosophizing" of the 19th century. Abandoning what the Chicago sociologists viewed as the elitist theorizing about how society "ought" to function, the Chicago School began with the idea of looking closely at society as it is. Embracing a more formal, systematic approach to data collection and analysis that had begun in Germany, the earliest sociologists of the Chicago School—including Albion W. Small, the founding department chair; William I. Thomas; Robert E. Park; Ernest W. Burgess; and Louis Wirth—developed a set of standard assumptions and themes that were adapted and implemented by those who followed. The primary assumption for the Chicago School was that qualitative methodologies, especially those used in systematic naturalistic observation, were best suited for the study of urban social phenomena.

As the founding chair of the Sociology Department at the University of Chicago, Small was able to influence future developments of the school through his departmental leadership. But, although Small played an important role in the earliest days of the emerging Chicago School, the role of the university itself cannot be minimized. Its first president, William Rainey Harper, is described by Martin Bulmer in his comprehensive history, *The Chicago School of Sociology* (1986) as "determined to make the university one of the foremost universities in the country." President Harper's conception of the university as a center for research and inquiry was distinctly different from the undergraduate college. Harper appointed senior professors to teach exclusively in the graduate schools "with the goal of training graduate students to push out along new lines of investigation." Determined that research should be fostered, Harper appointed Small as head professor of social science in 1892 at the age of 38.

As Bulmer notes, "Small was an unlikely figure to establish the world's first department of sociology." Born in Maine in 1854, Albion Small was raised in the Puritan family of a Baptist minister. As an undergraduate at Colby College, he studied Greek, Latin, mathematics, and moral philosophy, and he then went to Newton Theological Seminary in Massachusetts, graduating as a Baptist minister in 1879. Rather than accepting a position in the ministry, however, Small joined a number of other liberal Protestants who moved from divinity to sociology and went to Germany to study the social sciences. There, he acquired an ethical view of social science that held out the promise of social reform. When he returned from Germany, Small spent a year of graduate study at Johns Hopkins University, where he furthered his ideas on coupling social reform with empiricism.

It was this interest in social reform informed by a systematic study of social phenomena that characterized the Chicago School from its earliest days. And although, as Bulmer points out, Small's own intellectual contributions to the development of sociology were less striking than those who followed him to Chicago, he created an institutional setting and atmosphere in which other scholars could investigate and teach.

In addition to sociology, President Harper had already provided fertile ground for philosophy, which had produced the first "school" at the university with John Dewey's pragmatism. Like Small, Dewey was influenced by his graduate work in the scientific method and the rigors of experimentalism at Johns Hopkins. Dewey brought these methods to Chicago's Philosophy Department, where the absence of rigid boundaries between disciplines at the University of Chicago helped encourage collaboration beyond the departments. Small facilitated this because he believed that the task of sociology was to synthesize the findings of the social and natural sciences, and he encouraged graduate students to take courses in philosophy, economics, psychology, history, political science, and divinity.

The links between sociology, divinity, and social welfare were also strong in these early days. While the divinity school acquired a sociological orientation, the Sociology Department in the early years had a marked Christian inclination. Bulmer points out that this was reflected in the collaboration between the two departments in the creation of a section within the divinity school to teach "ecclesiastical sociology." Many of the early graduate students in sociology were, like Small, from clerical backgrounds or had studied divinity.

While some Chicago sociologists moved sharply in a secular direction, the influence of liberal Protestantism remained—and with it, the links between sociology and social welfare were strong. Although these relationships eventually became strained as sociology strove to become an independent academic discipline apart from a concern with social improvement and reform, sociology continues to be influenced today by a conflicting desire to both study society and reform it.

For the earliest sociologists of the Chicago School, the city of Chicago became the laboratory for studying social interaction and urban social relations. Social structures were viewed as a complex web of dynamic processes, much like an ecosystem, progressing toward maturity. In an attempt to understand why city development and land use varied throughout the city, Ernest Burgess examined the parallels between natural and social systems and developed a complex ecological model called "concentric zone theory" that, although criticized for being "too localized," is still studied today by students of urban planning.

In addition to urban ecology, Chicago School sociologists noted that areas within the city were always in a state of flux, cycling through different developmental stages. They noted that some areas of the city remained crime- and delinquency-prone even when the people who populated the crime-prone areas moved on and new people moved in—regardless of the ethnicity or the race of the urban dwellers. They identified the complex intergroup patterns of social interaction within regions of the city as the notion of "social worlds." The development of this concept is still important today as sociologists studying the different subcultures that exist within a city look to the Chicago School to understand the diversity in the norms, values, and behaviors of those living within specific areas of the city. In fact, the theory of subcultures begun within the Chicago School

is still used today in the sociological study of the emergence of urban youth gangs whose values, norms, and behaviors are a product of the subcultures that endure long after one youth cohort is replaced by another.

In the early days of the Chicago School, the city's Catholic ethnic enclaves provided the data for studying the diversity of these social worlds. Focusing on the role of the influx of immigrants during the early 1900s, William Thomas proposed the concept of social disorganization theory in his Polish immigration studies. In the first American sociological classic book, *The Polish Peasant* (1918), Thomas postulated that the environment of the city itself acts as a force to render structures, relationships, and norms of the "homeland" irrelevant to the new living situation of the immigrants, and the abandonment of these traditional structures led to social disorganization and instability.

Yet Thomas also noted that it was the local Catholic parish and the maintenance of many tightly bound communal living practices that helped Polish immigrants promote stability and maintenance of community in the midst of disorganization. He found that the effects of disorganization are mitigated only by the degree to which there are stable constants in the transition. For many immigrant groups, including the Irish, the Italians, and the Poles, the Catholic Church and its parish community provided that stability. Providing pastors who shared the ethnicity of the parishioners, and offering the kind of traditional Masses that were celebrated in the native language of the parishioners, Chicago's Catholic churches helped urban dwellers create their own urban villages within the city.

Along these same lines, Louis Wirth concluded that there was a conflict in the culture between old values and new urban experiences that led to social disorganization among Jewish immigrant communities. And although the more pessimistic theory of disorganization that Wirth developed maintained that the emergence of bureaucracies created an impersonal, segmented, and superficial lifestyle that would lead to community breakdown, he celebrated the personal freedom and mobility that the city offered to its inhabitants. Wirth's book *Urbanism as a Way of Life* shaped the direction of urban sociology and is still an important text in the discipline of urban planning.

Robert Park was especially well prepared to study the behavior of those living in these subcultures because of his background as a newspaper reporter. Journalism gave Park the "value-free" opportunity to see all aspects of city life firsthand. Attending court sessions and investigating social problems for the newspaper provided opportunities that most academically oriented sociologists never had. Park's ethnographic research was shaped by his journalism background, as he wrote, "One might fairly say that a sociologist is merely a more accurate, responsible and scientific reporter."

Any attempt to recover the values-based, theologically informed sociology of the past was rejected at the University of Chicago as advances in research methodology began to encourage a move in a more quantitative direction. Some of the qualitative methods of the past began to seem somewhat antiquated to a contemporary observer in the late 1920s. By the 1930s, the influence of other disciplines, notably statistics and economics, began to emerge as the Chicago sociologists moved in a quantitative direction, preferring survey research and analyzing large data sets. This movement toward a scientific, value-free sociology brought with it a rejection of theological ways of thinking—and a complete secularization of the discipline—that continues today.—Anne Hendershott

BIBLIOGRAPHY AND FURTHER READING: Bulner, Martin. *Chicago School of Sociology: Institutionalization, Diversity and the Rise of Sociological Research.* Chicago: University of Chicago Press, 1986; Lutters, Wayne G., and Mark S. Ackerman. *An Introduction to the Chicago School of Sociology.* Palo Alto, CA: Interval Research, 1996; Shils, Edward, ed. *Remembering the University of Chicago: Teachers, Scientists and Scholars.* Chicago: University of Chicago Press, 1991; Thomas, William I., and Florian Znaniecki. *The Polish Peasant in Europe and America.* Boston: Badger Press, 1920. *See also* THOMAS, WILLIAM I.

SOCIOLOGY OF KNOWLEDGE: A CATHOLIC CRITIQUE

The "sociology of knowledge," a term coined by Max Scheler, is a subdiscipline of sociology that focuses on the relationship of knowledge (both cognitive and normative) in civilization to its "social location" or "social-structural base" from which it is either generated or granted plausibility. Like the broader discipline itself, the sociology of knowledge as an academic field of study and as a general intellectual perspective arose as a response to the forces of exaggerated social change and widespread pluralism that tended to undermine what philosopher Alfred Schutz termed the "taken-for-granted" assumptions of social life in European civilization and, more specifically, in academic circles in Germany in the 1920s. Accepted as a premise is the position of Peter L. Berger and Thomas Luckmann in *The Social Construction of Reality: A Treatise in the Sociology of Knowledge* that the sociology of knowledge is centrally concerned with all that passes for everyday knowledge in society (e.g., symbols, values, norms, language) and should not be restricted merely to the realm of grand ideas and articulated philosophies, as was the case for many of the earlier practitioners of the subdiscipline.

One of the central, related, and, in certain cases, debatable foundational issues in the subdiscipline involves the nature and scope of various "social locations" or "social-structural bases" of knowledge. Knowledge can be either generated or granted plausibility from *civilization-wide, subcultural,* or *countercultural* locations. In premodern, traditional contexts, the social location of knowledge usually is civilization-wide, where a religion or philosophy provides what Emile Durkheim in *The Elementary Forms of the Religious Life* terms a "collective consciousness" or what Berger in *The Sacred Canopy* calls an overarching "sacred canopy" of meaning that provides overall form and articulation to social life. The Durkheimian school of sociology, consisting of Durkheim's colleagues and students (e.g., Marcel Mauss, Maurice Halbwach, Marcel Granet, and Lucien Levy-Bruhl), argued in essence that all civilizations are characterized by a collective consciousness with a common set of cognitive and normative definitions of social reality.

It is debatable whether, and in what manner, modern contexts, characterized by their pervasive pluralism, have an effective and functioning collective consciousness that centrally shapes the hearts and minds of its inhabitants. Some argue, for instance, that American civilization in the mid-1960s was held together by a nondenominational theistic American "civil religion," as discussed by Robert Bellah, or by a nontheistic "American way of life," as put forth by Will Herberg. Others suggest that, in the modern context, a civilization's subgroups can be held together merely by the acceptance of common procedural and legal norms. Still others claim that intrinsic to a modern social context characterized by a radical pluralism is the threat and reality of what James D. Hunter has termed "culture wars."

Modern contexts almost always have countercultures, small groups of individuals who band together to live a life based on beliefs that are in fundamental opposition to that of the larger civilization. Some countercultures are "passive," in that they withdraw from but do not actively oppose the societal mainstream (e.g., the Amish in the United States); others are "active," in rebellion or revolt (e.g., the early Black Panther Party). Almost all inhabitants of modern life participate actively in various subcultures that are influenced simultaneously by the broader civilization and by less inclusive groups and social institutions (along racial, ethnic, socioeconomic, career, organizational, scientific, lifestyle, and other lines). Subcultures can be placed on a continuum, with some closer to assimilation to the broader civilization (e.g., contemporary Irish Americans) and others closer to a countercultural stance (e.g., first-generation immigrants from the less developed and industrialized countries living in the United States).

The Catholic evaluation of the nature of participation in, and acceptance of, the lifestyles associated with and generated by these social locations depends on their compatibility with the dictates of the natural law. Furthermore, it is fair to conclude that, as American mainstream civilization becomes progressively more hostile to an authentic expression of the Catholic faith, serious Catholics are increasingly rejecting a passive assimilation into mainstream American culture and are actively migrating to, and attempting to create, vibrant Catholic subcultures veering—as non-Catholic definitions of reality become ever more powerful—toward a countercultural stance.

A second issue revolves around the relationship between, variously put, culture and social structure, ideas and material states of being, or norms and interests. The three ideal-typical options here are those of *cultural determinism*, *structural determinism*, and the positing of a *dialectical relationship* between culture and structure. In the first option, exemplified by the sociological work of both Pitirim Sorokin (*Social and Cultural Dynamics*) and Talcott Parsons (*The Evolution of Societies*), symbolic culture is viewed as ultimately determinative of how society is structured and how individuals think and act. The structural position is exemplified, par excellence, by Karl Marx; in the Marxist formulation, it is the "substructure" of economic class interests that overwhelmingly shapes cultural directives and normative guidelines that represent an epiphenomenal reality of social institutions termed the "superstructure." The dialectical vision, epitomized by the work of Berger and Luckmann, sees cultural and material states of being in an ongoing, mutually shaping relationship, with priority given to neither culture nor social structure.

The Catholic position, as exemplified by the perspective of John Henry Newman's theory of the organic development of doctrine, is not coterminous with any of these three options. It shares with the cultural determinists a fundamental understanding of the human being as primarily a cultural being who is modified by the awareness that cultural attachments are mediated and affected by—but not reduced to—material states of being, historical and personal realities and exigencies, and the reality of a common human nature. Furthermore, a sacramental, integrative, and incarnational Catholic worldview posits that portion of culture that is consistent with (following St. Thomas Aquinas) the natural law and divine law as representing a semi-autonomous reality. This is a reflection of the Catholic belief that some social constructions can lay claim to a status of being both objective and truthful. Werner Stark similarly claims that, through the use of a long and laborious phenomenological analysis of sociohistorical reality, "the absolute is recognizable . . . in, through, and under the relative . . . 'to the absolute through the relative is our device'" (*Sociology of Knowledge*, 196).

A third issue involves the role of the individual as an actor in social context. On the one hand, all practitioners of the sociology of knowledge as a subdiscipline of sociology would reject the radically economics-like position that the human mind can be totally independent either of the cultural-socialization influences that are attendant to any social location/social structural base or of the role of inherited tradition and culture. On the other hand, some sociologists of knowledge—especially those of Marxist bent—view, or come close to viewing, the human mind as passive and inert in the face of culture and socialization, thus promoting a sociological version of determinism. Any Catholic practitioner of the sociology of knowledge must acknowledge that human beings simultaneously are influenced both by their social location and by the power of the human mind to reflect on the nature and causes of socialization, thus creating the grounds for the assignment of responsibility for human thinking and actions, mitigated by such factors as the nature of one's inherited and present social environment, stage of human development, and state of mental health. Put another way and translated into common sociological terminology, Catholic sociologists must incorporate some version of an "actionist" perspective to counterbalance the typical sociological emphasis on "structure" and the environment, as well as other forms of deterministic thought.

A fourth issue entails just *how* knowledge is generated and manipulated—one of the central concerns of what E. Doyle McCarthy refers to as the "new sociology of knowledge." Is it generated by the population at large from the "ground up" through the generic processes of social and symbolic interaction? Or is it generated from the "top down" by societal elites who control the most powerful sectors and organizations of society? If it is the latter, is the knowledge created by elites intended to promote what they see as the common good as portrayed by the "structural-functionalist" perspective in sociology, or is it purposely manipulated via the use of "ideologies" to serve their vested interests, as understood by the various "conflict" theories in sociology?

Empirically, is it the case that knowledge is generated *both* through general social interaction and by societal elites, but with the important proviso that the latter have a disproportionate ability to generate knowledge that dominates the "official" or "public-sphere" social institutions which control the flow of power, prestige, and wealth in the society? Conversely, is it the case that societal elites have the ability to control the distribution of knowledge in society and to stop the flow of any knowledge that is subversive to the societal status quo?

If the latter is correct, is the domination primarily orchestrated by scientific, technological, government, and cultural elites, as both predicted and promoted by advocates of positivism? In contemporary American civilization, have such elites cut off religiously based ideas from entering into dialogue in an American public sphere dominated by secularism of one sort or another, as was argued by Richard John Neuhaus (*The Naked Public Square*) and William Rusher (*The Coming Battle for the Media*)?

Or is the domination exercised by capitalistic, business elites, as understood by Marxists and such thinkers as C. W. Mills (*The Power Elite*)? Noam Chomsky (*Manufacturing Consent: The Political Economy of the Mass Media*, coauthored with Edward Herman) makes the case that the architects of a capitalist/business dominance in the United States, with its veneer of democracy, have effectively blocked any serious opposition to its hegemonic control of society. The argument here is that they have accomplished this not through the outright coercion typically utilized by elites in totalitarian societies, but by various subtle means and the manipulation of those institutions that Marxists view as part of the superstructure (e.g., government and mass media).

Or, indeed, as prophesized by some of the true believers and utopians of the Left, might there someday be a worldwide dominance of power, wealth, and the distribution of knowledge on the part of a successful revolutionary class acting under the guise of promoting a worldwide communist revolution?

Are there any organizations or social locations that consciously see and promote themselves as a neutral arbiter between competing interests and visions and are primarily concerned with the building up of a "good society" and promoting the common good? Catholic scholars might make the case that the only major or-ganization in contemporary world civilization capable, in theory, of producing something approaching Karl Mannheim's ideal of a "socially unattached intelligentsia" approximating objectivity in social analysis as discussed in his *Ideology and Utopia* is the Catholic Church. In the quest for objectivity, however, these Catholic scholars claim that one would necessarily have to go beyond merely employing the methodological device proposed by Mannheim of juxtaposing competing social and historical perspectives which, they argue, is incapable in and by itself of transcending relativity. They would make the case for the necessary incorporation of a metaphysically based natural law analysis or a phenomenological analysis searching for absolutes underlying the relativity of empirical analysis while cultivating simultaneously a Catholic cultural and ethical sensibility as an interpretative framework.

Related here is the question, put forth by Berger and Luckmann (*Social Construction of Reality*, 12), of whether the primary goal of the sociology of knowledge is the "sociology of error" or the "sociology of truth." Is the goal the linking of social thought to socioeconomic background and social location, thus focusing on the distorting consequences of ideological thought as in the tradition initiated by Mannheim? Or is the primary goal to pursue truth through an analysis of cultural life as in the tradition of Stark, for whom one strives for truth by going through the relative? A Catholic sociology would consider both enterprises important, but the emphasis would clearly be on the latter, that is, the attempt to navigate the "fiery brook of relativity" in search of an ultimate truth that is only, in the final analysis, understood in its completeness and complexity by God alone.

A fifth issue focuses on how different theories of social change portray the present and future state of what passes for knowledge in civilization. The three dominant sociological visions are the *classical*, the *Marxist*, and the *cyclical*. The classical—exemplified in different variations by, among others, Auguste Comte, Max Weber, Emile Durkheim, and Ferdinand Tonnies—views the fundamental transition in human history from "traditional" to "modern" social contexts, the latter characterized by, among other things, the ascendancy of science and advanced technology, government and bureaucracy, and pluralism and individuation. The issue of the compatibility of these changes with a Catholic vision depends on whether they develop in a compatible manner with the universal moral law. Many contemporary Catholic observers of these developments have chronicled, as a reflection of secularization, the unfortunate ascendancy in civilization of the dysfunctions associated with scientism, bureaucratization, relativity, and egotism, all fostered by gnostic-like social elites.

Marxist theory, for its part, sees the fulcrum point of history to be the violent overthrow of capitalism and the ushering in of secularist socialist forms of government (and, theoretically at some unspecified end point, of an anarchistic communist world order). Catholic social thought rejects Marxist theory on many grounds. Among these are its positing of the fundamental dichotomy between human beings based on socioeconomic classes; its advocacy of unrestrained violence as a legitimate political strategy; its essentially materialistic vision of the ends of man and, derivatively, its conception of poverty in basically economic terms; and its defense of a ruthless, gnostic-like "dictatorship of the proletariat." Note should be made in passing of the so-called Marxist-Freudian synthesis (see, e.g., Herbert Marcuse, *Eros and Civilization*), combining the two exaggerations of positing the human being as both essentially economic and sexual beings with, to boot, overly passive minds easily manipulated by capitalistic elites through the institutions in society that they allegedly control. Those accepting of a Catholic frame, however, can certainly find compatible the Marxist claims that, cognitively, one's social class position shapes (although does not determine) the way individuals think and act and affects their "life chances" in society and, normatively, a sufficient distribution of material goods and services is a foundational prerequisite for the creation of a good society.

Finally, the cyclical theory of social change views distinctive constellations of ideas and other forms of knowledge appearing, attenuating, and resurging in a periodic, recurring manner. Another way of putting this is that social change is viewed as occurring within limits, which are set by some more or less constant understanding of human nature. The two primary examples of sociological cyclical theories of social change are propounded by Pitirim Sorokin and Vilfredo Pareto.

For Sorokin, in his *Social and Cultural Dynamics*, civilizations swing back and forth between, and are distinguished by, three different ways in which truth is presented: the "sensate" (or empirical), the "ideational" (or spiritual), and the "idealistic" (a "rational" compromise between the empirical and the spiritual). Sorokin proposed a "principle of limits," through which, when a society moves too far in one direction, the multifaceted needs of human nature force as a corrective a social movement in another direction. For him, contemporary modern civilizations have become excessively sensate,

and he therefore predicts that the pendulum will inevitably swing back to the ideational and, eventually, to the idealistic, only to see the cycle continually repeated.

For Pareto (*The Mind and the Society*), and following a tradition in Italian thought that goes back to ancient Roman antiquity, every society is not only ruthlessly ruled by some political elite but, over time, all societies witness a "circulation of elites" between what Niccolò Machiavelli termed the "foxes" and the "lions." The psychic makeup of lions and foxes is rooted in nature, or what Pareto referred to as "residues." Lions rule by force, and foxes, by cunning. For Pareto, the apparent strength of each human category of elites simultaneously represents its own weakness, which leads to the cyclical replacement of lions by foxes and vice versa.

Catholic social thought would insist on the analytical inclusion of a conception of a basically constant human nature in any theoretical framework used to analyze social life. While appreciating the incorporation of this perennially relevant consideration in the framework of both Sorokin and Pareto, Catholic social thought would, however, reject the deterministic bent of both and insist on modifications better incorporating an individual sense of free will and the ability of individuals to attempt to rationally construct a humane civilization enlightened by the truth of the Gospel, the natural law, and ideas consistent with Catholic social doctrine.

A sixth and final issue that some, especially Catholic, social thinkers would consider important in any overview of the sociology of knowledge is the question of whether there is any universal yardstick available that can be used to judge the various manifestations of "knowledge," morality, beauty, and utility empirically found throughout world history and civilization.

An affirmative answer would be put forth, variously, by (1) those religions claiming a monopoly of absolute truth; (2) an Enlightenment positivism that views science not merely as a means to enriching civilization in a material sense but also as providing a universal, "rational" philosophical blueprint for social organization and individual living—that is, scientism; (3) social worldviews that hypothesize some nonscientific social blueprint as coterminous with the future of mankind (e.g., Marx's communist world order or Durkheim's "religion of humanity"); and (4) natural law or universal rights analysis that posits that there are universal standards for conduct that are rooted in human nature.

Conversely, a negative answer would be put forth by various other schools of thought. One would be a cultural relativism that is prominent in many academic disciplines—especially, in the social sciences, within anthropology and sociology; within cultural anthropology, the work of Margaret Mead exemplifies this position. Even more dramatically, the denial of any universal standard for evaluation is also apparent in the perspectives of atheists, nominalists, deconstructionists, and subjectivists, who deny the existence not only of any objective truth but also of any meaning system that transcends either one's historical and social location or the self. The work of Michel Foucault is one prominent example.

Probably the most important, if not the most radical, opposition to any version of the sociology of knowledge that is compatible with a Catholic understanding of reality comes from the mainstream of a sociological profession that restricts—absolutely and religiously, if you will—all academic inquiry to the empirical realm and considers any discussion of "absolutes," in Robert Merton's words, "as wholly foreign to empirical inquiry" ("Sociology of Knowledge," 472). Critiquing the work of Scheler, Merton states that Scheler "seeks to escape a radical relativism by resorting to a metaphysical dualism. He posits the realm of 'timeless essences' which in varying degrees enter into the content of judgments; a realm utterly distinct from that of historical and social reality" (472). A Catholic intellectual response here would be that the metaphysical and empirical realms are simultaneously distinctive *and* related. Put another way, the metaphysical and empirical necessarily overlap in reality and hence in social analysis; all social scientific activity is inevitably tied to some set of metaphysical assumptions, whether recognized or not.

The Catholic religion affirms that there is an absolute understanding of truth that is provided both through reason—the natural law as a reflection of the divine law—and through revelation—Scripture and tradition. The Catholic Church advocates what can be termed a "realistic multiculturalism." This stance acknowledges that eternal truth is inevitably mediated through both sociohistorical context and the individual and that there can be found varying degrees and amounts of truth within different cultures, historical contexts, groups, religions, philosophies, and stated beliefs of individuals throughout time and space. Indeed, this is precisely the goal of the Catholic sociologist of knowledge Werner Stark, who proposed a "synoptic doctrine of man" as the solution to the "problem of relativity" (*Sociology of Knowledge*, 196). For Stark, by abstracting the "common human element" by way of the phenomenological method, the scholar can develop a body of knowledge that could "claim a quasi-scientific status" (197) that would be truly ecumenical and would

enable one to glimpse "verities that are more than the products of a narrow valley or a passing day" (346).

In a compatible and related manner, Scheler argued that all perception and thought presupposed the existence of an absolute realm of eternal values written into the heart that are ranked along a spiritual/moral-to-material/biological continuum. For him, each civilization, group, and individual personality has a specific "ethos." The plurality of worldviews readily apparent in the empirical world reflects, for him, the reality that various people apprehend and prioritize the sphere of eternal values from different angles and with different priorities. Social and individual discord and pathology—a "disorder of the heart"—results when values of lower rank, those closer to the biological/materialistic endpoint, are prioritized and institutionalized over values of higher rank, those closer to the spiritual/moral endpoint. Catholic scholars looking to develop further a sociology of knowledge perspective that shares a compatibility with the Catholic worldview could profitably start their enterprise by reviewing the work of Scheler and Stark.—Joseph A. Varacalli

BIBLIOGRAPHY AND FURTHER READING. Berger, Peter L., and Brigitte Berger. *Sociology: A Biographical Approach*, 2nd ed. New York: Basic Books, 1975; Berger, Peter L., and Thomas Luckmann. *The Social Construction of Reality: A Treatise in the Sociology of Knowledge.* New York: Doubleday, 1966; Coser, Lewis A. *Masters of Sociological Thought*, 2nd ed. New York: Harcourt Brace Jovanovich, 1977; Mannheim, Karl. *Ideology and Utopia: An Introduction to the Sociology of Knowledge.* Translated by Louis Wirth and Edward Shils. New York: Harcourt, Brace & World, 1936; McCarthy, E. Doyle. "Knowledge, Sociology of." In *The Blackwell Encyclopedia of Sociology*, online version, pp. 2482–2485. http://www.sociology-encyclopedia.com, 2006; Merton, Robert A. "The Sociology of Knowledge." Chapter 12 of *Social Theory and Social Structure*, rev. larger ed. Glencoe, IL: Free Press, 1957; Scheler, Max. *Problems of a Sociology of Knowledge.* Translated with an introduction by Manfred S. Frings. London: Routledge & Kegan Paul, 1980; Stark, Werner. *The Sociology of Knowledge: An Essay in Aid of a Deeper Understanding of the History of Ideas.* London: Routledge & Kegan Paul, 1958; Varacalli, Joseph A. "Multiculturalism, Catholicism, and American Civilization." *Homiletic and Pastoral Review* 96, no. 4 (1994): 47–55; Varacalli, Joseph A. "Review of Max Scheler's *Problems of a Sociology of Knowledge.*" *Contemporary Sociology* 11, no. 2 (1982): 198–199; Varacalli, Joseph A. "Sociology, Feminism, and the Magisterium." *Homiletic and Pastoral Review* 89, no. 10 (1989): 60–66. *See also* BERGER, PETER L.;

CULTURAL RELATIVISM; DURKHEIM, EMILE; MARX, KARL; MARXISM; PARSONS, TALCOTT; SHILS, EDWARD A.; SOCIAL CONSTRUCTIONISM; SOROKIN, PITIRIM ALEXANDROVITCH

SOVEREIGNTY According to the concept of sovereignty, there is a supreme power in a state that can make the law and is itself above the law. The idea of sovereignty is a modern idea, and it is tied to the concept of the state, a political entity that claims final authority over a territory. The origins of the modern state go back to the late medieval period, when it began to replace a feudal order wherein rule possessed neither sovereignty nor territoriality. The concept of sovereignty is not to be found in Greek political thought, and neither did the Romans fully develop it. Roman *imperium* did not mean the political territory Rome ruled, but the *power* to rule; empire as a concept did not refer to a territorial entity, but the *ecumene*, the horizon of a whole civilization; and finally, even when Roman law was most developed, custom was still seen as a fundamental source of law, which could not be overridden. The other fundamental source of Roman law was the will of the emperor, and the rediscovery and study of Roman law gave impetus to trends otherwise developing in the late Middle Ages toward the modern understanding of sovereignty.

The idea of sovereignty was, however, irrelevant in the medieval period. There was no room for it to develop in a society in which rule was personal and lacking in territorial fixity and exclusivity. Customary laws, though enough for small, unconnected communities, were not sufficient when these social segments started becoming connected into a larger whole ruled from a central government, as was starting to be the case by the 13th century. But even then sovereignty could not be conceptualized, as it was incompatible with a plurality of overlapping authorities, from regional communities all the way up to the Holy Roman emperor and pope, with each ruler in this great chain of duties limited to his proper sphere.

In-kind payments and personal loyalties were the foundation for the economic and political system of feudalism, but this started to change with the expansion of the European economy in the late 11th century. Trade increased, and the resulting monetarization of the economy had a centralizing effect, just as the currency shortage of the earlier medieval period was a large factor in the decentralized nature of feudalism. In a money economy, a central power is able to control the periphery through cash payments, particularly for military service.

England, which due to its small size and insular status developed more rapidly than the kingdoms on the continent, was the first to develop in practice something like a concept of sovereignty. In the 15th and 16th centuries, the Tudor monarchs used the idea of the "divine right of kings" to buttress the prestige of the ruler; it also meant that God picked the successor to the crown, thus stabilizing the transition from one monarch to the next. Although they did not mean by this that the king could make the law at his pleasure, in practice the king controlled Parliament and, by the middle of the 16th century, had the accepted ability to take the initiative in acting, freed from the limits of custom. An inchoate idea of sovereignty was behind King Henry VIII's break from Rome, which treated the Church as a mere political body to be integrated into the mystical body of the realm, of which the king was the head. Previously, the Church had secularized the idea of the mystical body of Christ to mean the Church itself as a legal person, and the state followed that lead by transferring the concept of the mystical body to it.

The incipient notion of sovereignty became articulate with Jean Bodin (1529/30–1596), whose book *Six Books of the Commonwealth* (*Six livres de la république*, 1576) was widely read in England right after its publication, well before its translation 30 years later. Sovereignty is the very essence of a commonwealth for Bodin, who was writing against the Huguenot revolutionaries in France; therefore, revolt against a legitimate ruler can never be justified. Bodin derives sovereignty not from any historical determination of what the supremacy of the state in fact consists of, but rather from the very concept of the state itself, which he defines as the making of legislation over subjects without their consent. This is a rejection of the then dominant conception of the ruler as a judge who upholds the justice that is present in the social laws and customs he finds already in place. Bodin's defense of private property, however—according to him, taxation always requires consent—is an embarrassment for his theory of absolute sovereignty.

In an early work, Bodin had argued that the Parlement of Paris should be able to veto legislation of the king that was unjust, but he rejected that later in *Six Books*. Bodin was explicitly denying a countertheory to absolutism, which in the 16th to 18th centuries held that the sovereign power must be exercised through prescribed channels, such as assemblies and courts, which see it as their duty to abrogate the portions of decrees that are unreasonable and unjust. Since such faulty decrees are the inevitable product of fallen human nature of the men who happen to be king, failure to execute them in the name of the ideal royal will in fact help the monarchs retain their majesty. The theory of absolute sovereignty, by contrast, deemphasizes the fact that the sovereign ruler is a fallible human being and focuses on abstract sovereignty rather than the actual sovereign ruler. The separation of sovereignty from the monarch was first made by François Hotman (1524–1590).

The concept of sovereignty was formed as a response to disorder and revolution; it was searching for a clearly delineated supreme authority that would bring order to chaos. This was the dominant motivation behind the work of Thomas Hobbes (1588–1679), the greatest English-speaking political theorist, whose ideas in his great work *Leviathan* (1651) pushed the idea of absolute sovereignty the farthest it could go. For Hobbes, sovereignty came from the people considered as individuals, who, in the state of nature—an intolerable violent anarchy—all contract together to create a sovereign to rule them. No contract could then be made with the sovereign, who is a mortal god, can never be in error, rules by fear, and cannot even be criticized by his subjects. Hobbes rigorously expounds the logic of sovereignty as entailing that the sovereign power is independent of all custom and natural law. If there are rights held by the people prior to and apart from the sovereign, then the sovereign isn't really sovereign.

Hobbes's theories were often deplored and were not widely accepted; however, they set the terms of future debate on the concept of sovereignty. A grant of unlimited power to the ruler was too unappetizing a prospect, but granting this power to the community was not. Calvinist political philosopher Johannes Althusius (1557–1638) was the first to place sovereignty in the people. Jean-Jacques Rousseau (1712–1778) built his famous notion of popular sovereignty on a Hobbesian foundation of total submission to the state in his *Social Contract* (1762). Rousseau in fact wanted to uphold a strict distinction between the representatives of the people and the people themselves. For him, the laws must be restricted, rarely changed, and ratified by the people in the cases when they must be changed. Torn from the context of his thought, however, the idea of popular sovereignty was pressed into service of parliamentary sovereignty, which Rousseau explicitly condemns in many places.

The idea of popular sovereignty widespread today is a troubling one. The typical frame in which the foundations of modern freedoms are viewed—that formerly power was in bad hands (monarchs) but now is in good hands (the people)—is mistaken, as Bertrand de Jouvenel has lucidly shown. Boundless sovereignty, the unregulated right to legislate, is a modern idea. All the power of the absolute monarch has been transferred over to the people, but this change is hardly an effective safeguard against tyranny and injustice, since the people are just as prone to abuse power as a king would be. The *Compendium of the Social Doctrine of the Church* states that the people in their entirety are the subject of sovereignty, but also that "the mere consent of the people is not ... sufficient for considering 'just' the ways in which political authority is exercised" (*CSDC* # 395).

The Catholic Church teaches us that sovereignty belongs to God, and political power comes from God. This was emphasized by Pope Leo XIII, who held that "no human being has a natural right to bind another, for this power is divine, and can only be participated," as Russell Hittinger explains it. Man can attempt to enforce his will by violence on others, but fear is a weak foundation for government, as St. Thomas Aquinas teaches. "As authority rests chiefly on moral force," writes Pope John XXIII in *Pacem in Terris*, "it follows that civil authority must appeal primarily to the conscience of individual citizens, that is, to each one's duty to collaborate readily for the common good of all" (*PT* # 48). Moral authority is the only strong adhesive the state requires, and indeed the sine qua non of the institution of the modern state is its citizens identifying with it. Popular sovereignty is insufficient and dangerous, on account of the power exercised by modern states. In *Immortale Dei*, Leo XIII called the sovereignty of the people "without any reference to God" a doctrine "exceedingly well calculated to flatter and to inflame many passions, but which lacks all reasonable proof, and all power of insuring public safety and preserving order" (*ID* # 31).

More fundamentally, the problem is not so much popular sovereignty as absolute sovereignty, the idea that unchecked power of legislation is of the essence of the modern state. Much more in line with Catholic social teaching is a theory of sovereignty that, like the previously mentioned theory of the regulated royal will, sees human authority for what it is: always relative and conditioned. The notion of absolute state sovereignty has been condemned by Pope Pius XII in *Ad Summi Pontificatus*, which noted that it not only harms the internal life of nations but also, by sapping the unity and vigor of international society, harms the relations between peoples.

The term *sovereignty* itself does not have to entail absolute sovereignty, however. The *Compendium of the Social Doctrine of the Church* recognizes the importance of the idea, understood as the proper independence of a nation from outside interference, "an expression of the freedom that must govern relations between States," which represents "the subjectivity of a nation, in the political, economic, social, and even cultural sense." But it continues: "*National sovereignty is not, however, absolute. Nations can freely renounce the exercise of some of their rights in view of a common goal,* in the awareness that they form a 'family of nations' where mutual trust, support and respect must prevail" (*CSDC* # 435).

Rather than seeing sovereignty as absolute power, we should see it as a sphere of responsibility. In Pope Benedict XVI's address to the United Nations in 2008, the pope said that "every State has the primary duty to protect its own population from grave and sustained violations of human rights, as well as from the consequences of humanitarian crises, whether natural or man-made" and spoke of this concept of a "responsibility to protect" as part of the foundation of the modern state. The "responsibility to protect" is the pope's proposal for a new name of sovereignty.—Philip J. Harold

BIBLIOGRAPHY AND FURTHER READING: Hinsley, F. H. *Sovereignty*, 2nd ed. Cambridge: Cambridge University Press, 1986; Jouvenel, Bertrand de. *Sovereignty: An Inquiry into the Political Good.* Translated by J. F. Huntington. Indianapolis: Liberty Fund, 1997; Spruyt, Hendrik. *The Sovereign State and Its Competitors.* Princeton, NJ: Princeton University Press, 1994; Witte, John, Jr. and Frank S. Alexander, eds. *The Teachings of Modern Roman Catholicism: On Law, Politics, and Human Nature.* Introduction by Russell Hittinger. New York: Columbia University Press, 2007. *See also* AUTHORITY; BODIN, JEAN; HOBBES, THOMAS; INTERNATIONAL LAW; INTERNATIONAL RELATIONS: CATHOLIC PERSPECTIVE ON; MYSTICAL BODY OF CHRIST, SOCIAL SIGNIFICANCE OF; STATE, CATHOLIC THOUGHT ON

SPE SALVI Pope Benedict XVI's second encyclical, *Spe Salvi,* bears some similarities with the first encyclical of his pontificate, *Deus Caritas Est,* which explores the theological and social meaning of love. *Spe Salvi,* which was presented on November 30, 2007, explores another theological virtue—hope—and considers both the theological and social dimensions of this virtue. The title is taken from Romans 8: 24 which reads, "In hope we are saved." The encyclical contains 50 sections and about 19,000 words, making it longer than many papal

encyclicals. That Benedict write on the meaning of hope is noteworthy, as his predecessor, Blessed John Paul II, frequently spoke of hope in encyclicals, homilies, and other speeches—although he never wrote an encyclical on the meaning of hope. Moreover, many encyclicals seem to the bear the work of many writers, but this encyclical expresses themes and theological concerns that have long been important to Pope Benedict.

Spe Salvi begins with a discussion of the meaning of hope and its relation to faith (# 2–9). Herein, Benedict discusses several passages from the New Testament and argues that hope is essentially connected to faith. Accordingly, it would be accurate to speak of "hope-faith" as a compound concept. Hope is also presented as not merely *informative,* but *performative,* and here Benedict utilizes the terminology of the British philosopher of language J. L. Austin (although Austin is not identified in the text). Hope as performative means not only that human beings gain knowledge through having hope but also that hope changes the lives of human beings. Benedict gives the example of St. Josephine Bakhita, the one-time slave, who in the midst of her suffering and misfortune became a Christian and experienced hope and liberation from her suffering and in her final years took vows as a member of a religious order. Hope then makes us perform differently in the world, but, Benedict also asserts, our performance is not that of a social revolutionary, like the Roman slave Spartacus, who attacks the existing social order.

Benedict, drawing upon his work as a Scripture scholar, also engages in an analysis of how hope-filled faith is understood in the New Testament. He argues that it is in reality a substance—as in the *substance* (in Greek, *hypostasis*) of things hoped for (Hebrews 5: 1). He states that his interpretation differs from that of Martin Luther, who understood hope-faith not as an objective reality but as an interior attitude of standing firm.

After characterizing hope as an objective reality, Benedict then considers how hope is "life-changing and life-sustaining" in this life, even though the great hope is for eternal life (# 10–12). According to Benedict, Christians do not merely seek life without end, but have hope for eternal life with God, which is a transformation. Eternal life means not only life without end but also an experience of happiness for the person in this world and a transformation in the next world.

Benedict then argues that the experience of hope is not simply an individual experience, where an individual separates himself from others while having private hope (# 13–15). Here he cites 20th-century theologian Henri du Lubac, who presents salvation as a "social reality" (*SS* # 14). Benedict states that "this community-oriented vision of the 'blessed life' is certainly directed beyond the present world . . . it also has to do with the building up of this world" (# 15). The pope says that Christian believers are closely connected with other Christian believers in living out this hope-faith and asserts that even the medieval contemplatives, who might be characterized by some as having abandoned the world, were connected to and concerned for the world through the nobility of their manual labor and their prayer.

The encyclical then engages how the modern world has expressed and sometimes rejected hope (# 16–23). Benedict asserts that the true meaning of hope—both for this world and the next—has been modified by intellectual currents in modernity that are directly at odds with the Christian conception. He says that the modern world has hope for scientific progress that will overcome the great problems facing human beings, such as diminishing bodily health and insufficient material well-being. This section not only refers to ideas but also, unlike some other ecclesiastical documents, specifically names people. Thus, it is Francis Bacon who poured his hope into the capacities of modern natural science.

Another related dimension of modern hope was hope in the power of reason. Benedict cites the French revolutionaries as attempting to have a political rule based entirely upon reason. The discussion of the misuse of reason when it is separated from revelation was also developed in Pope Benedict's Regensberg Address; for Benedict, reason is always to be utilized in the context of revelation.

He also cites the hope expressed by some early in the 19th century that the industrial revolution would give rise to a new social reality. When continual progress was not made toward a better society, this provided an opportunity for Marx's call for revolution. Marxism is then the fruit of an unrealized and unrealistic social hope for this world. Benedict adeptly recognizes that Marxism not only fails as an economic system but also fails to provide a ground of hope.

In an article in *Christian Century* (May 20, 2008) about this encyclical, the eminent Protestant theologian Jurgen Moltmann writes critically of Pope Benedict for devoting attention to social theories that are no longer actively considered, such as Marxism or the Kantian hope for enlightenment by reason. Benedict's purpose, however, is to offer a historical account of the improper development of social hope and to indicate that Chris-

tianity provides an alternative account of hope that is not only otherworldly. Modernity then, he explains, needs "a dialogue with Christianity and its concept of hope" (*SS* # 22). Our world, according to Benedict, needs this account of hope, because the means for secular hopes—reason and technological progress—have even turned against hope. Technological progress, for example, has in some instances undermined hope. With this in mind, Benedict cites German social theorist Theodor Adorno's quip that the world has progressed "from the sling to the atom bomb" (*SS* # 22).

As an alternative to the insufficient secular hopes, Benedict then outlines the "shape of Christian hope" (# 24–31). True Christian hope does allow for a hope for incremental progress in material matters. Moreover, there could be some moral improvement for human societies, but the social world will not be reconstituted to become perfect, and there will not always be improvement. "The right state of human affairs, the moral well-being of the world can never be guaranteed simply through structures alone," writes Benedict (*SS* # 24). Human beings, with the freedom they have, may make good or bad choices, and therefore "the kingdom of good will never be definitively established in this world" (*SS* # 24). The pope says that there is always work to be done in improving this world, both in a material and spiritual sense. Christians can and should seek to engage the world, even while realizing that the world will not be perfected by human action.

Christians, asserts Benedict, need to realize that the ground of all hopes is God. Man can be aided by science, but "man is redeemed by love" (*SS* # 26). The source of that love is God. "Man's great, true hope which holds hope firm in spite of all disappointments can only be God" (*SS* # 27). Christians then depend upon God for the hope for this world, not only for the hope for the next. God gives this hope to us to experience in this world not merely as individuals but in the midst of human communities. Benedict cites several Christian figures who expressed a communal sense of hope, but he gives particular attention to St. Augustine—a figure not often associated with having hope for this world. Augustine preferred the life of contemplation, but realized that he needed to work in the Christian community and to "transmit hope" to that community (*SS* # 29).

Pope Benedict concludes his account of hope by stating that "we need the greater and lesser hopes that keep us going day by day . . . but these are not enough with the great hope" (*SS* # 31). The "great hope" is a gift from God, and this hope is present in this world. It is substance that we can experience and have, not simply an awareness of some present state. Benedict writes that God's "love alone gives us the possibility of soberly preserving day by day, without ceasing to be spurred on by hope, in a world which by its very nature is very imperfect" (*SS* # 31).

The second half of *Spe Salvi* (# 32–47), like the second half of *Deus Caritas Est*, concerns the means by which the virtue is practiced. First, prayer is presented as a school of hope (# 32–35). He cites a book of prayers by the late Cardinal Nguyen Van Thuan called *Prayers of Hope*, which describes the prayer life of an individual who spent many years in prison. Prayer is not merely asking God for needs, but a means of purification and thus a means to "become ministers of hope for others" (*SS* # 34).

After prayer, action is offered as a means of practicing the virtue of hope. We can act to build a better world, but "we cannot 'build' the kingdom of God by our own efforts [because] what we build will always be the kingdom of man with all of its limitations" (*SS* # 35). The this-worldly hope we have can be shown to others and encouraged in others by our actions. This hope can give us "courage to place ourselves on the side of good even in seemingly hopeless situations" (*SS* # 36). If our hopes are purely this-worldly, individuals can often practice fanaticism or have diminished hope when faced by setbacks, large or small. Benedict adds that action can limit suffering in the world, but cannot eliminate it. Here he calls Christians to suffer with those who are suffering; he cautions, however, that Christians should not lose hope because they cannot eliminate all suffering. Moreover, those who blame God for suffering will undermine the source of hope.

That prayer and action in this world is a setting and school for hope is not surprising, but the third "setting" for hope is the judgment of and for human beings (# 41–48). The "last things" are not typically considered as related to this worldly hope, but Pope Benedict demonstrates that not only does this world look forward to the next, but the eternal judgment can provide meaning for this world. The resurrection is presented as a means of "undoing of past suffering," and the future justice corrects the injustice of this world (*SS* # 33). This section of the encyclical includes a brief discussion of purgatory, as a means of purifying and transforming individuals as they transition to "communion with God" (*SS* # 47).

There is one final dimension in this account of hope that has social implications. Benedict concludes by restating that hope itself is not completely individualistic. Our hope is nourished by our membership in a Christian community. "Our hope is always essentially also hope for others," he says (*SS* # 48). In the end, hope, accordingly to Benedict, is both this-worldly and otherworldly at the same time. It is for us and for others simultaneously. It comes from God and goes to others at the very same time. The encyclical then concludes with a reflection on Mary (# 49–50) with a special reference to her title as the "mother of hope."

In both *Spe Salvi* and his other encyclicals, Pope Benedict XVI is expressing themes important in both his academic and ecclesiastical work about the unity and essential integration of faith and life. The theological virtues of faith, hope, and love are both the foundation and essence of the social life and of our personal faith. *Spe Salvi* is not merely a restating of previous social teaching; it is, in addition, a challenge to all Christians to love God and others and have a proper hope for this world and the next.—Michael L. Coulter

BIBLIOGRAPHY AND FURTHER READING: McDonagh, Phillip. "Uncovering the Sources of Creation: Pope Benedict XVI on Hope." *Logos* 13, no. 4 (2010): 96–129; Ratzinger, Joseph. *Church, Ecumenism, and Politics: New Endeavors in Ecclesiology*. San Francisco: Ignatius Press, 2008; Ratzinger, Joseph. *Eschatology, Death, and Eternal Life*, 2nd ed. Translated by Michael Waldstein; translated and edited by Aidan Nichols. Washington DC: Catholic University of America Press, 2007. *See also CARITAS IN VERITATE; DEUS CARITAS EST; MAGISTERIUM; POPE BENEDICT XVI; REGENSBURG ADDRESS OF POPE BENEDICT XVI*

SPINOZA, BENEDICT DE (1632–1677)

Baruch de Spinoza was born in Amsterdam into a community of Jews that had settled in the Netherlands after having been expelled from their native Portugal. Besides receiving a traditional Talmudic education, he was encouraged by his teachers to learn Latin and to acquaint himself with modern philosophy. Spinoza mastered the Latin language and became deeply immersed in modern philosophy; as a result of the latter, he began first to question, and then eventually to abandon, his Jewish faith. In 1656, at the age of 24, he was formally excommunicated from the Amsterdam synagogue, having been accused and found guilty of heresy. It was at this time that he changed his name to Benedict and decided to devote his life to philosophy.

After moving from Amsterdam in 1660, Spinoza lived in various places in the Netherlands until, in 1670, he settled permanently in The Hague. He supported himself by grinding lenses, a skill he had learned in his youth; it was an ideal occupation for him, allowing ample time for study and writing. All in all, Spinoza's life was simple and uneventful. He had a small coterie of friends with whom he shared his ideas, and he carried on a steady correspondence with a number of fellow philosophers. He was himself, in due course, to gain considerable notoriety as a philosopher, and in 1673 he was offered the chair in philosophy at the University of Heidelberg. In the letter he sent to the authorities at that institution declining their offer, he wrote: "I do not look for any higher worldly position than that which I now enjoy." Spinoza died, of consumption, in The Hague on February 20, 1677, at the age of 44.

The two thinkers who contributed most to the shaping of Spinoza's philosophical thought were René Descartes and Thomas Hobbes. It was the influence of Descartes that made him a committed rationalist—that is to say, one who believes that human reason is the final arbiter of reality and truth. And it was chiefly the influence of Hobbes that explains why his philosophy is, as one commentator correctly puts it, "thoroughly naturalistic and deterministic." In the world as seen by Spinoza, there is no room for the supernatural; everything is reduced to the level of the natural.

Only two of Spinoza's principal works were published during his lifetime: *The Principles of Cartesian Philosophy* in 1663, and *Treatise on Theology and Politics* (*Tractatus Theologico-Politicus*) in 1670. The latter work, which was published anonymously, was officially banned for the questionable views it contained on religion and the Bible. Among his other writings, Spinoza's *Improvement of the Understanding*, his first serious philosophical work, shows the clear influence of Descartes and is reminiscent of the French philosopher's *Discourse on Method*. In the first half of the 1660s, he wrote a fragment called the *Improvement of the Understanding* (*De Intellectus Emendatione*) and completed his most important work, *Ethics Geometrically Demonstrated* (*Ethica More Geometrica Demonstrata*), which he had modeled on Euclid. Very likely because of the unfriendly reception given to his *Treatise on Theology and Politics*, Spinoza made no attempt to publish the *Ethics* during his life. It was published the year of his death, along with two other works, the *Treatise on the Rainbow* and the unfinished *Treatise on Politics*.

In *Treatise on Theology and Politics*, Spinoza states his intention "to examine the Bible afresh in a careful, impartial, and unfettered spirit." The work is addressed specifically to "philosophical readers." As for "the rest of mankind," they would be better off not reading the treatise, for, given the prejudices they embrace in the name of religion, he "cannot expect that it contains anything to please them." Spinoza's naturalism is on full display in this work, although an unwary reader, misled by his elusive language, might believe that he is dealing with a man whose philosophy and theology are not as errant as in fact they are. For example, the term *God* is to be found throughout the text, but the referent of the term is certainly not the object of Christian or Jewish belief. A key phrase for understanding Spinoza's thought is *Deus sive natura* ("God or Nature"). "God," in other words, is to be taken as just another term for Nature, referring to the sum total of the physical universe.

Spinoza insists that the Bible is to be interpreted in its own terms, which means that one should not apply to it the rational standards employed by philosophy, a mistake Spinoza thought had been made by the medieval commentator Moses Maimonides. The principal value of the Bible is to be found in its moral content. As a historical document, it is a shambles, and if any modern historian were to model himself on the biblical writers, "the commentators would cover him with contempt." The miracles of the Bible are explained away. The prophets were doubtless good and sincere men, but they lacked philosophical acumen. In many respects, this work anticipates the open atheism of Ludwig Feuerbach's *The Essence of Christianity* two centuries later.

The *Treatise on Politics*, which Spinoza was working on when he died and which clearly reflects the thought of Hobbes, is at bottom an elaborate development of the primitive doctrine that might makes right. In the "state of nature," a lawless environment, it is the individual's might that will decide if he is fit enough to survive. The state of nature is eventually replaced by civil government, to which individuals surrender their personal rights to action in exchange for the peace and security provided by the government. The state, as the sole source of law and its sole interpreter, establishes the criteria for the morality that will guide the lives of the citizens, definitively determining what will count for justice and equity. And the state is the authoritative voice in matters of religion. In this work, Spinoza lays down impressively thorough and detailed constitutions for monarchical and oligarchical forms of government.

Spinoza's *Ethics*, despite its title, is considerably more than a treatise on moral philosophy, although that is its main focus. It is a work that treats matters pertaining to general metaphysics, theology, political philosophy, and psychology. Spinoza argues that there is but a single substance, God or Nature, which is the cause of itself and has both material and spiritual dimensions. All else in existence, including human beings, are accidents or modes of the one substance. There are no absolute moral values, and the ethical system that Spinoza develops amounts to being a combination of utilitarianism and hedonism. He writes that "every man is bound [i.e., necessitated by nature] to seek what is useful for himself," and what is superficially altruistic behavior is essentially self-serving behavior. Elsewhere we read the succinct formula: "Good: every kind of pleasure; evil: every kind of pain."

The *Ethics* contains a considerable amount of interesting and perceptive descriptive psychology, but the ethical system it presents is fatally flawed on account of a glaring and unresolved contradiction between Spinoza's unvarying commitment to determinism, on the one hand, and the appeals he makes to human freedom, on the other. As it turns out, however, Spinoza's "freedom" is like his "God," in that the term does not have the meaning normally attached to it. To be "free," in his terms, is only to do what nature dictates; it is to act out the inevitable. Equally problematic is his notion of rights: to exercise a right, for him, is to act according to whatever power an individual might possess, but that power has been predetermined by nature. To exercise a right, then, is simply to behave as you must necessarily behave.

Spinoza discusses the classic antipathy between reason and the passions and seems to be following the traditional wisdom in advocating the need to opt for the guidance of reason and not to allow ourselves to fall prey to the passions. But this assumes that we have a real choice in the matter, which, according to Spinoza's own fundamental principles, we in fact do not. Because of the unbending demands of an all-encompassing and totally deterministic nature, reason is no more under our control than are our passions. How we reason, how we emote—both have been decided beforehand.

The harsh reality of our ethical situation, as understood by Spinoza, cannot be better described than by Spinoza himself, which he does for us in the *Improvement of the Understanding*: "The soul acts according to fixed laws; and is, as it were, an immaterial automaton." When it comes to ethical matters, one would not want to go to Benedict de Spinoza for guidance.—D. Q. McInerny

BIBLIOGRAPHY AND FURTHER READING: Collins, James Daniel. *The Continental Rationalists: Descartes, Spinoza, Leibniz*. Milwaukee: Bruce, 1966; Donagan, A. *Spinoza*. Chicago: University of Chicago Press, 1989; Wolfson, Harry A. *The Philosophy of Spinoza*. New York: Meridian Books, 1960. *See also* AGNOSTICISM AND ATHEISM; FEUERBACH, LUDWIG ANDREAS; RATIONALISM

SPORTS IN MODERN AMERICA: A CATHOLIC CRITIQUE To keep up with the writings of social scientists about sports (which have mushroomed in quantity since 1976) is to recognize instantly that most social scientists are approaching sports *instrumentally*. Social scientists usually view sports as a means to social betterment, racial or gender parity, or some version of "social justice," usually undefined. All this is well and good. Yet it is precisely at this point that the Catholic intellectual tradition has something far more daring, profound, and indispensable to place squarely in the center of inquiry. The Catholic critique of modern American sports is that their promoters, participants, and commentators miss the crucial point altogether. Sports do not in essence belong to the kingdom of means, and they are not in the first place instruments to some further end. Sports belong to the kingdom of ends. Sports, especially the great liturgical sports (usually trivialized as "spectator sports"), are like culture itself and cult ends in themselves. Play also is an end in itself. To workaday persons, it may seem aimless. To those involved, it seems the one thing worth doing, worth resting in, worth taking joy in.

The Catholic intellectual tradition in this respect has something far more original (and important) to say about sports than most other modern intellectual traditions. Recall briefly the paradigm shift brought to sports by Joseph Pieper's *Leisure, the Basis of Culture*; Johan Huizinga's *Homo Ludens*; Hugo Rahner's *Man at Play*; James Schall's two books, *Far Too Easily Pleased: A Theology of Play, Contemplation, and Festivity* and *Play On: From Games to Celebrations*; and even Paul Weiss's metaphysical study, *Sport: A Philosophical Inquiry*. In a parallel vein, the great wartime immigrant scholar at Harvard University, and later Dartmouth College, Eugen Rosenstock-Huessy wrote that when he kept trying to find concrete examples in the lives of undergraduates to make the points that were readily available in European history, art, and literature, he lit with great success on the experience of American students of the 1930s and 1940s with athletics. Once he started linking the main concepts of the liberal arts to his students' familiarity with rugged sports such as crew, baseball, football, basketball, and track and field, these concepts flashed light for his students in their own fund of human experience.

The modern mind tends to be organized around the two realities of power ("Knowledge is power") and work ("Don't just stand there—do something about it"), both breathlessly pursued in the good name of "progress." Such a focus of mind is the lens through which many journalists and social scientists perceive sports. Compared with their serious colleagues on the news, science, and business pages, many sports journalists seem vaguely ashamed of reporting on "kid stuff." What are *sports* doing to change the world? When such journalists look at sports, they are visibly preoccupied with its financial side, its excesses, and its psychology, social science, and internal social conflicts.

In the eighth edition (2009) of D. Stanley Eitzen's *Sport in Contemporary Society*, parts 2, 3, and 4 focus on "socialization"—among youth, in the mass media, and Native American names and mascots. Parts 5 through 9 address "problems of excess," such as overzealous parents, sexual assault, drugs, and big-time college sports. Parts 10, 11, and 12 examine "structured inequality" in relation to race/ethnicity, gender, and sexuality. And the final part 13 includes three articles on "globalization." The 2011 ninth edition offers more studies of the same general type: problems, shortcomings, excesses.

All of these are worthy subjects, and they are well researched and well argued. They teach us much that is interesting. Still, they are far afield from the central issue—they could as well be found in other sections of a newspaper, such as business, society, or the television pages. They do little to describe or probe into sports *as sports*, just for the joy of it. Most sports reporting tells us little about the actual narrative of the game, its heroic acts, its unforgettable plays.

The truth is that all the sociological faults of sports explain virtually nothing about what it is in sports that excites us in victory and depresses us in defeat; their beauty; their wonderfully high standards (as close to perfection in one activity as humans can get); their power to draw, hold, and uplift our attention; their power to ennoble us and to enlarge our sense of the beauty of the human race. All these things sports do just by *being*. Sports are what they are, and that much is good and beautiful and worth resting in. They represent in a way the contemplative side of life (as distinct from the workaday, merely pragmatic, means-oriented busyness of the largest part of our lifetimes). Sports make workaday life worthwhile, beautiful, more in tune with our heroic possibilities, more noble.

"Cult," runs the proverb, "is the beginning of culture." The greatest works of art and the inner guides to life in the ancient worlds of Greece and Rome were centered around the cults of the gods and the nobility of spirit they were intended to elicit from us. The astonishing architecture of the cathedrals of Paris and Cologne, and the breathtaking paintings, frescoes, sculptures, and tapestries they both sponsored and inspired,

grew out of the cult of the Creator of all humans and the God-Man slain on account of the evil acts of all human beings, Redeemer of good out of evil, and beauty out of ugliness, suffering, and despair. Similarly, the public games of the Olympics and the medieval jousts and heart-stopping horse races like the Palio of Siena are inconceivable apart from festivals honoring the highest visions and meaning-giving acts to which humans are called.

Among American journalists and social scientists, the favorite word for our central sporting events such as games of baseball, basketball, and football (and in some regions, hockey) is "entertainment." But *entertainment* is demonstrably an inadequate term. When a Monday Night Football game of some importance is being shown in a hotel bar, a newcomer does well to stand in respectful silence for a while, until a break in the action, since most of the spectators are absorbed by the drama in the arena and resist being interrupted. They are in a frame of mind more inward and contemplative than extroverted and this-worldly. At a college football game, while the game is in play, intense fans move as little as possible. Game time is a bit like the high holy moments, when respectful silence and concentration are in order. During halftime, when the marching bands and twirlers and singers appear—*that* is the time of entertainment, and nearly everybody gets up for food or to go to the bathroom. The game itself is not entertainment. Its power goes far beyond diversion. Sometimes the game so absorbs us that at the end we feel exhausted, as if we have played it ourselves. Coming out of a really great game is like coming out of another and better world, now suddenly returned to the profane, prosaic, unbeautiful world of finding one's automobile.

It is in such ennobling and absorbing activities that most of us first come closest to the act of contemplation—the act of sitting in wonder before acts good-in-themselves, beautiful, heroic, fraught with contingency, danger, and possibilities of failure. Al Gionfriddo's leaping catch against the left field wall; Willie Mays's blazing speed and then nonchalance in holding out his glove for another impossible catch; the heart the Dallas Mavericks display in coming back again and again from adversity and the seeming certainty of defeat; the intensity of each man's play on the part of the overmatched Boston Bruins, time and again on the verge of elimination by the great Vancouver Canucks; George Blanda's fairy-tale string of last-minute victories by an impossible placekick or an unlikely pass—all these were heroic acts in which flawed individuals seemed in the grip of some superior presence to rise above all probabilities and present to all with eyes to see works of great and unforgettable beauty.

It is in the moments when we are so caught up in playing or in participant-viewing (essentially different from mere spectating) that we come closest to experiencing human existence outside of time. We lose all sense of passing time. We are absorbed into a wordless *now*, which totally captures our concentration and our awe.

Indeed, some sculptures of athletes in motion, and some photographs so brilliantly shot at just the right timeless moment, give humans a sense of the eternal dimension in a particular human action. A living moment. As Shakespeare wrote about a lover whom he presented in a peerless sonnet, as long as men could read she was immortalized.

It has shocked some that in my earlier writings I have called certain sports events "liturgies." But the dictionary definition of *liturgy* is "a rite or body of rites prescribed for public worship," and *rite* is defined as "a set form for conducting a ceremony; a ceremonial act or action." A participant knows exactly what forms to expect as a football, baseball, or basketball "ceremony" is about to get under way. And, in the United States at least, the ceremonies at our great sports liturgies (and also our political liturgies, such as presidential inaugurations or the ceremonies and addresses on Memorial Day or the Fourth of July) are very often consecrated by a prayer to the Divine—or, when not, by acts of piety and reverence toward a nation and a history much "blessed." These last obeisances are done with recognition that it is not the *nation-state* that is being honored, but rather the Providence that has so blessed it (so many, many times, as George Washington well insisted), "under Whom" the nation is one, and "in Whom" its citizens trust. Observing all this with some amazement, G. K. Chesterton described America as "a nation with the soul of a church."

Despite being founded in an intellectual framework of Protestantism, with its emphasis on the individual, America has over the generations developed a public, communal way of celebrating its fundamental "truths" (as the Declaration of Independence puts it), both in its great political events and in its sporting events.

All three of our major liturgical sports were invented by Americans to celebrate an important—but different—radiation of who we are as a distinctive and even exceptional nation, unlike any other. Each of our three most widely beloved public ceremonial forms—baseball, football, and basketball—is structured as a narrative.

Football is a narrative of the will to "run for daylight" through 11 hulking monsters intent on stopping you; it is a narrative of overcoming obstacles by sheer spunk and wit. Baseball is a Lockean narrative of liberty and law (the voice of the law rules on every play), ordered, symmetrical, designed to see if round-the-world clipper ships can "come home." Basketball is the narrative of urban shiftiness, feint, deception, and laser-like passing to penetrate a tall, active, and fired-up defense.

As we live through these narratives again and again, with all their built-in contingencies and probabilities of error and defeat, we live through our national narrative. That narrative is not exactly the Christian narrative, nor the Jewish, nor the Greek, nor the Roman. But it demonstrably derives from them, and in some ways, recapitulates them. It presents ways of entering into and living through analogies of all four of those life-narratives (and maybe others).

It is hard to imagine how much poorer the United States would be—culturally, morally, aesthetically, and contemplatively—if it wholly lacked these three great ceremonial actions, these teachers both of personal courage and communal intensity. These ceremonies are also regular, repeated, dangerous risks of symbolic death and ashes in defeat, and going through once again the resurrection that comes with victory, especially a victory eked out by coming from behind against serious adversity.

As is usual, a Catholic critique begins with an appreciation for *what is*. Such a critique gains its distinctiveness by diving through perceptions that arise from a preoccupation with pleasure or utility, digging deep into those first things that are ends in themselves. In the Catholic way of thinking, we do not play in order to work, we work in order to play. This is a variation of the signature phrase of St. Benedict, the great founder of European civilization (and recognized as such on the Medal of Europe, given each year to persons who enrich that civilization): "*Laborare et orare.*"

Laborare et ludere. The reward, the endgame, is *play*. The boring, instrumental stuff is *work*. Moderns tend to think of the human being as "Man the worker and doer." But there is an older, and more enriching, set of priorities: *Homo ludens.* For human beings, the most important thing is the realm of ends, of being and beauty and truth. This depth we come closest to in play. It is so in the interior life. It is also so in the experience of the great highlights and intuitions of eternity, the heroic, and the more-than-human that even young boys and girls begin first to know in sports.

I know of nothing that has taught my son and two daughters, and their children, so much about the depths of life than their experiences of courage, teamwork, defeat, victory, and pain in the sports they loved in school. To go in a matter of weeks from being the one whose inexcusable misplay lost a key game for your teammates to one whose last-second three-pointer won them the championship is a narrative beyond the capacity of any father to communicate to his children in words. Sports do not teach us every lesson about life. What they do lead us into is invaluable.—Michael Novak

BIBLIOGRAPHY AND FURTHER READING: Huizinga, Johan. *Homo Ludens.* Boston: Beacon Press, 1955; Pieper, Joseph. *Leisure, the Basis of Culture.* New York: Pantheon, 1964; Rahner, Hugo. *Man at Play.* New York: Herder & Herder, 1967; Schall, James. *Far Too Easily Pleased: A Theology of Play, Contemplation, and Festivity.* Beverly Hills: Benzinger, 1976; Schall, James. *Play On: From Games to Celebrations.* Philadelphia: Fortress Press, 1971; Weiss, Paul. *Sport: A Philosophic Inquiry.* Carbondale: Southern Illinois University Press, 1974. *See also LABOREM EXERCENS*; LEISURE; WORK, CATHOLIC UNDERSTANDING OF

STEPINAC, CARDINAL ALOYSIUS (1898–1960) Aloysius Viktor Stepinac was born in 1898 to Josip and Barbara Stepinac in Brezarić, a village that is now a part of Croatia. He was the fifth of eight children. In 1909, he moved to Zagreb to undertake his studies, graduating in 1916. Prior to his 18th birthday, he was drafted into the Austro-Hungarian Army. During World War I, he served on the Italian front and was taken prisoner by the Italians. After the formation of the short-lived State of Slovenes, Croats, and Serbs, Stepinac was no longer treated as an enemy by the Italians and was permitted to volunteer for the Yugoslavian legion. A few months later, he was honorably discharged with the rank of second lieutenant. He returned home in the spring of 1919 and was given an award for his heroism.

After the war, Stepinac enrolled in the University of Zagreb, but he left it after one semester and returned home to help his father. In 1924, he traveled to Rome to study for the priesthood. Stepinac was ordained on October 26, 1930, and said his first Mass at the Basilica di Santa Maria Maggiore on November 1. The next year, he became a parish curate in Zagreb.

Stepinac was made the coadjutor bishop to the Diocese of Zagreb in 1934. When Archbishop Anton Bauer died on December 7, 1937, Stepinac, though still under 40, succeeded him as the archbishop of Zagreb. Pope Pius XII declared 1940 a jubilee year for Croats to celebrate 1,300 years of their Christianity, and that same year, the Franciscan order celebrated 700 years in Croatia. During the combined celebration, Stepinac joined the Franciscan Third Order.

On March 25, 1941, Italy, Germany, and Yugoslavia signed an agreement bringing Yugoslavia into the Axis. Two days later, a group of Serbian nationalists seized control of Belgrade and announced that they were siding with the Allies. As a result, Germany invaded Yugoslavia. Croat Fascists then declared an independent Croatia. The new Croat government was led by Ante Pavelic and his brutal group, the Ustash.

There had been a long history of hatred between the predominantly Catholic Croats and the mainly Orthodox Serbs, and the Ustashi government began to exact revenge against the Serbs for years of perceived discrimination. According to some accounts, as many as 700,000 Serbs were slaughtered. Because the Ustashi leaders claimed to be Catholic, many charges have been leveled against the Catholic Church in Croatia, including that it engaged in forcible conversions, that Church officials hid criminals after the war, that Nazi gold made its way from Croatia to the Vatican, and that Catholic leaders supported the brutality toward the Serbs.

At first, Archbishop Stepinac tried to work with the Ustashi government, but before long he became an outspoken critic. A speech he gave on October 24, 1942, is typical of many he made refuting Nazi theory: "All men and all races are children of God; all without distinction. Those who are Gypsies, Black, European, or Aryan all have the same rights. . . . For this reason, the Catholic Church had always condemned, and continues to condemn, all injustice and all violence committed in the name of theories of class, race, or nationality. It is not permissible to persecute Gypsies or Jews because they are thought to be an inferior race." The Associated Press reported that "by 1942 Stepinac had become a harsh critic of that Nazi puppet regime, condemning its genocidal policies, which killed tens of thousands of Serbs, Jews, Gypsies and Croats." He thereby earned the enmity of the Croatian dictator Pavelic.

The Vatican refused to recognize the Independent State of Croatia or receive a Croatian representative. When Pavelic traveled to the Vatican, Stepinac refused to accompany him, and although the secretary of state granted him an audience, it was not the diplomatic one he had wanted. Notes from both Ustashi and Vatican sources show that Pavelic was deeply offended.

There is simply no credible evidence that Stepinac, the pope, or other Vatican officials behaved inappropriately. The Vatican expressly repudiated forcible conversions in Croatia, and the archbishop regularly spoke against them. In August 1942, the Grand Rabbi of Zagreb, Dr. Miroslav Freiberger, wrote to Pius XII expressing his most profound gratitude "for the limitless goodness that the representatives of the Holy See and the leaders of the Church showed to our poor brothers."

In 1944–1945, Communist partisans under Josip Broz Tito conquered the Balkans, occupied Zagreb, and established the Socialist Federation of Yugoslavia. That government immediately undertook severe persecution of the Catholic Church. Before coming to power, the Communists had used Stepinac's speeches in their propaganda, as he had often spoke out against Nazi ideology and the violation of human rights committed by Pavelic. Now that they had power, however, Stepinac was a threat.

The Communists held a show trial of Stepinac so they could convict him of supporting the Ustashi government. Similar trials were held for religious leaders in many areas where Communists took control, and they were widely recognized for the sham that they were.

Pope Pius publicly protested Stepinac's prosecution, noting that the archbishop had saved thousands of people from the Nazis. The president of the Jewish Community in the United States, Louis Braier, said that Stepinac was a "great man of the Church . . . [who] spoke openly and fearlessly against the racial law. After His Holiness, Pius XII, he was the greatest defender of the Jews in persecuted Europe." During the war, Meir Touval-Weltmann, a member of a commission to help European Jews, wrote a letter of thanks for all that the Holy See had done and enclosed a memorandum of thanks that stated: "Dr. Stepinac has done everything possible to aid and ease the unhappy fate of the Jews in Croatia."

Stepinac was sentenced to 16 years of hard labor, but due to protests throughout the democratic world and Jewish testimony to the good work he had done, he was moved to house arrest in 1951. Almost immediately, Pope Pius made him a cardinal. He died under house arrest in 1960. Later testing on his exhumed body proved that he had been slowly poisoned.

After throwing off the shackles of Communism, one of the first acts of parliament in the newly independent state of Croatia in 1992 was to condemn "the political trial and sentence passed on Cardinal Alojzij Stepinac in 1946." Stepinac was condemned, declared the parliament, "because he had acted against the violence and crimes of the communist authorities, just as he had acted during the whirlwind of atrocities committed in World War II, to protect the persecuted,

regardless of the national origin or religious denomination." He was beatified as a martyr on October 3, 1998, at which time Pope John Paul II described him as a man who had the strength to oppose the three great evils of his century: Fascism, Nazism, and Communism.—Ronald J. Rychlak

BIBLIOGRAPHY AND FURTHER READING: Rychlak, Ronald J. "Cardinal Stepinac, Pope Pius XII, and the Roman Catholic Church during the Second World War." *Catholic Social Science Review* 14 (2009): 367–383. Tanjić, Željko. *Cardinal Stepinac: A Witness to the Truth* (Zagreb: Glas Koncila, 2009) [in English and Croatian]; *See also* COMMUNISM; FASCISM; NAZISM

STEWARDSHIP OF CREATION   The word *stewardship* has common currency in environmental ethics, although how the term is understood varies, as do views as to whether it is a sound approach. One of the more common versions is succinctly articulated by the Roman Catholic bishops of the Columbia Watershed region: "Stewardship is the traditional Christian expression of the role of people in relation to creation. Stewards, as caretakers for the things of God, are called to use wisely and distribute justly the goods of God's earth to meet the needs of God's children. They are to care for the earth as their home and as a beautiful revelation of the creativity, goodness and love of God. Creation is a 'book of nature' in whose living pages people can see signs of the Spirit of God present in the universe, yet separate from it." The keys to this understanding of stewardship are, first, that the Earth has been created by God, who transcends it; second, that it was created by God to serve two purposes: to bear witness to his glory and to serve the needs of every human individual, both physical and spiritual; and third, that God has entrusted us with the task of seeing that these purposes are realized.

Many secular forms of environmentalism adopt divergent views, either directly divinizing nature or expressing awe before nature, while failing to acknowledge its source. The notion of stewardship then, when not simply rejected, either takes the form of extending equal respect and care to all life forms or of justly distributing the Earth's resources among humans on exclusively humanitarian grounds (the Environmental Protection Agency's website on stewardship exemplifies the latter approach).

The other main determinant of one's position regarding stewardship is one's view of human transcendence. For the Christian, the notions that material creation is ordered to human well-being and that God has placed humanity in charge of caring for creation are rooted in the idea that human beings are created in the image of God. Only rational beings are capable of sharing in God's own life, and as such, nonrational beings are ordered to them. Likewise, only rational beings are capable of understanding the purposes of creation, and thus only they are capable of caring for it.

Many secular environmentalists—and strangely enough certain religious ones, as well—condemn the view that nature is ordered to us as anthropocentric and "speciesist." Yet, we could not have a moral responsibility to safeguard the Earth if we did not transcend nature by virtue of our faculties of intellect and free will. Moreover, if there was no God to endow us with these faculties, we would be just one animal species among others, and gone would be any reason to care for other natural beings apart from their contribution to our reproductive fitness. Contrary to what certain environmentalists think, it is the denial of God and of our likeness to him that warrants a utilitarian anthropocentric exploitation of the planet. The Christian view of environmental stewardship avoids the extremes of saying that we can do whatever we please with the things on the planet and that we are just one species among others.

Most secular views of environmental stewardship agree with the Christian view that the Earth is meant to sustain all humans, both those living today and those in future generations, and that it is a matter of justice to see that this is assured. As the Catholic Church notes, environmental issues are in some sense right-to-life issues, since human beings cannot survive without water, food, and other goods derived from the Earth. The Church maintains that ownership of private property is generally a suitable means to see that people peaceably and efficiently derive from the Earth what they need, but also notes that such ownership is only a means and cannot licitly prevent people in need from deriving sustenance from the Earth.

The theological underpinnings of Christian stewardship of creation are hardly new; they go back to Genesis: the Creator God pronounces nonrational creation to be good, creates humans in his image, and charges them with caring for the garden. The reasons for the emphasis on stewardship in recent times are threefold. First, environmental problems have become more acute in our day than in previous ages due to increases in population, technology, and industrialization, along with globalization. Second, false ideologies, such as those that denigrate human dignity, have been widely disseminated of late in response to environmental problems. Third, our technological prowess and the materialism it has facilitated have fostered mentalities and lifestyles that are hostile to stewardship. The Catholic Church, the Orthodox Church, and other Christian faith communities have of late been responding to the need to provide the faithful with guidance in regard to these developments. The Catholic Church's views are to a varying extent shared by other Christian groups.

The issue of human population is certainly one where the Catholic Church's notion of stewardship differs from that of most secular environmentalists and of certain Christian denominations as well. The Church does not deny that there can arise situations that call for limiting family size in order to prevent nature from being overtaxed to the point that human life in a given area is threatened and nature no longer witnesses to God's glory. However, as a general rule, Church teaching enjoins us to "be fruitful and multiply," understanding that each human being is created in the image of God and called to an eternal destiny. The Church notes that the problem of limited resources vis-à-vis the human population is not so much one of the number of people as it is of how those people behave. Habits of greed and immoderate consumption and desperate practices employed by the poor have taken an increasing toll on our planet as our numbers increase. In the cases where limiting family size is called for, Pope Benedict XVI has pointed to the need for "human ecology"—that is, that we respect the natural cycles of our bodies. It is ironic that those who protest the effect of herbicides on frog reproduction often sterilize themselves through various forms of contraception.

When it comes to technology, the Church affirms that "applied research is a significant expression of man's dominion over creation" (*CCC* # 2293), while at the same time insisting that creation is not to be used as if it were a mere instrument to satisfy our wishes. Technology is, of course, what made industrialization possible. The rapid rate at which products were henceforth produced, plus some of the products themselves (e.g., electric devices, plastics) resulted in a far more rapid depletion of the Earth's resources, accompanied by a significant increase in pollution. Regarding these developments, the Church reminds us of our responsibility to reduce consumption, to foster scientific research concerning renewable energy and other sustainable practices, and to educate others how to use the environment in a way that respects the God-given order inherent in it.

Globalization has brought with it the possibility of people on one part of the globe exploiting the environment (as well as the people) on other parts of the globe.

To give one example, First World nations are willing to pay for large amounts of soybeans or corn, thus inducing poorer countries to cut down their forests to make room for these crops, despite the loss of biodiversity this entails. In response to such situations, the Church calls upon the faithful to practice solidarity, which is a virtue that counteracts systematic injustices. But this is generally easier said than done. Often individuals are unaware of corporate and other social practices that result in uncalled-for environmental destruction. Nonetheless, some have the responsibility of heightening others' awareness of these problems, and informed individuals can put pressure on business and government to change environmentally disastrous practices—witness the increased availability of sustainably grown fair-trade products in response to consumer demand. The solidarity the Church calls us to also requires that richer nations share aid and knowledge so that developing nations are able to put in place cleaner technologies.

In addition to speaking to the changes in society that have exacerbated environmental problems in our day, the Church also considers why Christians have allowed these things to go on and identifies changes that need to be made in minds and in hearts: "Serious ecological problems call for an effective change of mentality leading to the adoption of new lifestyles" (*CSDC* # 486).

In many cases, Christians have lost the sense that creation is a gift of God to the entire human family and that it is meant to give glory to God. Many of us have no connection with nature to speak of; we do not know how our food is grown and have little contact with trees, birds, and other living things. Many of us live in a world reduced to the "reality" that is delivered to us via electronic devices. Thus, the Church insists that we need to recover an attitude of gratitude for the Earth and its fruits and to cultivate a spirit of contemplativeness in the face of God's creation.

The Church, as already noted, continually reminds us that proper care of the environment is a question of simple justice. Catholics need to realize that selfish attitudes of greed, laziness, hedonism, and consumerism result in others wrongfully being deprived of the goods of the Earth. The Church further points out that proper treatment of the environment will not be achieved until we address the poverty that both drives people to counterproductive uses of the environment and leaves them the first victims of environmental degradation.

The two central changes in mentality the Church calls for, then, are none other than being mindful of the true purposes of creation. The hallmark of being a good steward is to be prudent. Essential to prudence is to measure means by the end; how we use the Earth is to be measured by its purposes of giving glory to God and sustaining the entire human family. Prudent decisions and actions, however, depend on the practice of the other three cardinal virtues. Accordingly, the Church enjoins upon us changes in our lifestyles. We are to practice trust in providence, justice, and generosity as an antidote to greed, as well as the specific form of justice—solidarity—to reform political and other social structures that are causing needless environmental destruction and poverty. We are to practice simplicity (a form of temperance) as an antidote to consumerism and hedonism, and self-discipline (a form of courage) as an antidote to laziness.

Prudence is especially needed in sorting wants from needs, and legitimate wants from forms of overindulgence. Prudence is of the utmost importance when we make decisions in which we must weigh human benefit against the preservation of ecosystems, especially in those cases where the scientific knowledge needed to make a good decision is of questionable reliability. When the latter obtains, we are to employ the "precautionary principle," weighing risks against benefits the best we can as to what current scientific research indicates is likely to obtain, while remaining attentive to revisions in scientific theories. In this context, we need to keep in mind the lesson of the "Galileo affair": that the Church's authority extends to faith and morals but not to matters scientific.

In conclusion, the Catholic notion of environmental stewardship is far from being new; it is solidly rooted in a scripturally based theology of creation, one in which the transcendent God commands our first parents, created in his image, to care for creation. What is new is the urgency of our call to be responsible stewards in light of the extensive unnecessary destruction of God's creation that has occurred in recent history. Practice of the Christian virtues of prudence, justice, courage, and temperance, animated by love of God and neighbor, has become more important than ever, given our increased ability and hence responsibility to insure that creation fulfills its God-given purposes of witnessing to his goodness and sustaining the entire human family. While many secular environmentalists disagree with the Catholic Church on matters of divine and human transcendence, the Church's views here are philosophically defensible, and accordingly its views on environmental stewardship are compelling and balanced from a purely rational standpoint.—Marie I. George

BIBLIOGRAPHY AND FURTHER READING: Benedict XVI. "If You Want to Cultivate Peace, Protect Creation." Address for World Day of Peace, January 1, 2010; Catholic Bishops of the Watershed Region. "The Columbia River Watershed: Caring for Creation and the Common Good." Pastoral letter, January 2001; John Paul II. "Peace with God the Creator, Peace with All of Creation." Address for World Day of Peace, January 1, 1990.
See also ENVIRONMENTALISM; STEWARDSHIP

SUPPLY-SIDE ECONOMICS Supply-side economics is a school of thought within macroeconomics devoted to expanding the productivity (supply) of the economy by a combination of fiscal policies of low marginal tax rates and limited regulation and of monetary policy aimed at stabilizing price levels. These policies are intended to provide incentives to expand output by increasing the returns to working, saving, and investing. While originally intended as a short-run approach to stimulate the economy in response to the sluggish conditions of the 1970s, these policies also establish long-run conditions for growth by stabilizing people's expectations of the future. The economics profession has adopted many of the elements of supply-side theory, particularly its emphasis on individual response to incentives, expectations, and productivity and the role of individual initiative. This shift is also recognized in more recent papal encyclicals, which have moved from encouraging government policies for controlling the economy to setting the right long-run conditions for entrepreneurs to move into areas of opportunity.

As a discipline, macroeconomics largely arose after World War II as a response to the Great Depression, seeking to explain how the overall economy works and to devise policies to deal with fluctuations in it, particularly to avoid further severe downturns. Keynesianism (named for British economist John Maynard Keynes) became the dominant theoretical framework for most macroeconomic theory from the 1940s to the 1970s. Keynesian theory assumes that the economy is prone to instability and unlikely to correct itself from economic swings and thus needs constant correction by government. Government can do this, the Keynesians explain, by actively managing aggregate demand—that is, how much output is wanted by consumers, businesses, government, and foreign countries. For example, cutting taxes or increasing spending when aggregate demand is low is thought to raise demand and stimulate the economy, while reversing these when aggregate demand is too high slows it down. This is thus known as *demand-side* economics.

Weaknesses of the demand-side theories themselves were slowly identified during the 1950s and 1960s: challenges of timing, crowding out of private investment, income smoothing, expectations, and so forth. Supply-side economics then rose to prominence in response to high U.S. inflation and unemployment of the 1970s and the inability of the Keynesian models of the time to explain their simultaneous occurrence.

The earliest and most influential proponents of supply-side policy were economists Robert Mundell and Arthur Laffer. Mundell had actually begun his case for supply-side policies in the early 1960s while working at the International Monetary Fund. As part of his pioneering work on macroeconomic policy in an open economy, he argued that Keynesian policies would be undermined by offsetting movements in capital across countries. On the other hand, lower marginal tax rates could stimulate an economy, while stable money would attract capital from abroad. Though not due to Mundell's arguments, that combination was ultimately adopted. President John F. Kennedy dropped the top marginal tax rate from 90% to 70%, while the Federal Reserve Bank kept money tight. The policy resulted in growth for much of the rest of the 1960s.

This successful economic policy was ultimately undercut, however, when the nation embarked on the War on Poverty and the Vietnam War, the simultaneous cost of which resulted in increasing deficits. As the Federal Reserve increased the money supply to accommodate the deficits, inflation rose so much that in the early 1970s the United States had to pull out of the Bretton Woods agreement (the fixed exchange rate system adopted in the 1940s), and President Richard Nixon ordered price controls. Growth slowed, while unemployment and inflation rose (peaking at over 10% per year).

In response, Mundell and Laffer began to put some of Mundell's earlier work together more actively in the early 1970s. They argued that the combination of high tax rates, a progressive tax system with many brackets, and high inflation created a disincentive for people to work and save.

High and variable inflation saps economic vitality by raising the risk of economic transactions and by inducing people to spend more effort on protecting themselves from the swings (for example, investing in commodities like gold rather than productive assets) and less on improving productivity. This becomes more problematic as inflation increases, because the higher the inflation rate, the greater the (unpredictable) magnitude of swings in it. In addition, because inflation does not affect all markets evenly, these fluctuations undermine the information role of prices by artificially distorting relative prices across industries. Inflation also creates incentives to spend before the currency value erodes, rather than to save. These problems were compounded by the tax code at the time: since taxes were paid on capital gains not adjusted for inflation, many people paid taxes on what were real losses. These effects undermined the efficiency of the economy at its heart: the incentives to work, save, or invest.

High tax rates in themselves discourage initiative by reducing returns on productive effort. There was also a negative synergistic effect with inflation: with a complicated structure of high graduated marginal tax rates that were not indexed for inflation, ordinary salary raises people received to adjust for rising cost of living (itself rising rapidly due to high inflation) perversely placed more and more people's income into higher tax brackets, even though their real income hadn't risen. This raised taxes in real dollars for the government, while resulting in lower real income for most people.

Mundell, Laffer, and a growing circle of other economists, policy makers, and journalists argued through the late 1970s that bringing down both inflation and the marginal tax rates would stimulate the economy by raising the returns for work and stabilizing expectations regarding taxes and inflation. Mundell also argued that the Federal Reserve Bank should target its emphasis to maintaining stable price levels and nothing more.

The supply-side economists argued rates should be low and constant, and thus predictable. Key to this was cutting the *marginal* tax rates people actually faced, thereby raising the return to individual effort at the margin and expanding effort now and in the future. Marginal tax rates, rather than average tax rates, are critical because they are the tax rate people face on *additional* economic activity. Thus, lowering marginal tax rates increases the incentive to engage in more economic activity. Other forms of tax cuts do not affect the incentives at the margin: tax rebates only return taxes paid for *past* economic activity, rather than encouraging increases in economic activity now or in the future. And Keynesian tax cuts—on again, off again to stimulate economies—are unlikely to provide much stimulus across time since people aren't sure what future tax rates to expect.

This general program was adopted with shocking success: Tax rates were reduced in the early 1980s (and reduced further in 1986), and the Federal Reserve Bank brought inflation under control. The result was the beginning of a long period of high growth, with low inflation and low unemployment.

While initially viewed with suspicion by much of the rest of the profession, over the long run, most economists adopted at least some of the supply-side insights, recognizing the impact of incentives, the importance of lower marginal tax rates, and the need for inflation to be low and predictable. Numerous countries around the world adopted supply-side strategies, and Mundell was awarded a Nobel Prize. Robert Lucas, himself a Nobel laureate for his work in macroeconomics, argues that the supply-side reduction in marginal tax rates of the 1980s and the accompanying inflation stabilization were the two top macroeconomic policy changes of the last fifty years.

While Mundell, Laffer, and others synthesized the supply-side ideas to address the conditions of the 1970s in the short run, supply-side policies have an important long-run role: maintaining low tax rates and inflation to stabilize people's expectations. Contrary to a Keynesian approach of frequent but unpredictable government intervention to guide the economy, supply-side policies emphasize keeping tax, regulation, and inflation rates low and consistent and making policy predictable so individuals can plan their economic activity more effectively, without fear of negative policy-induced changes.

This long-run focus is enormously important. To a major extent, demand-side policies functioned by smoothing out spending flows across time, not by improving efficiency overall. In contrast, supply-side policies improve productivity, and thus growth, over time. While differences in growth rates over time may seem small, moving a country from a 1% to a 2% growth rate will result in far larger gains in well-being over time because gains compound every year. Lucas believes these long-run gains in growth far exceed potential improvements from demand management.

An implication of supply-side economics is that cutting tax *rates* can result in higher tax *revenues* overall, if initial tax rates were very high. All tax-rate increases discourage productive effort, but tax revenue is a function of both the rate and the level of activity. At very low tax rates, tax-rate increases discourage additional activity, but the increases in tax rates more than offset the decreased activity. Inevitably, however, at some tax rate, tax revenues hit a peak, and thereafter further increases in the tax rate discourage so much taxable activity that revenues begin to fall. This tax rate–tax revenue relationship became popularized as the Laffer curve and has often erroneously been misrepresented as the entirety of supply-side thought—mischaracterized as implying that tax rate cuts *always* yield tax revenue increases (a meaning Laffer never intended). Those mischaracterizations miss the more important insight of the school's focus on growth and incentives and misconstrue Laffer's more sophisticated point about the rate–revenue relationship.

Supply-side economics is itself part of a broader trend within economics that recognizes the critical role of individual actions, rather than governmental ones, in economic growth. It is individuals, not the government, who decide to pursue a college education, major in accounting, invest in a project, or develop an idea. Growth is merely the sum total of such decisions across the population, across time.

This emphasis on the role of individuals, especially entrepreneurs, rather than the government, coincides with the principle of subsidiarity—of leaving more scope for human freedom to act at the most appropriate level. It also recognizes that people are the most important resource for an economy. Papal encyclicals considering economic issues have captured this understanding. Recent encyclicals reflect a shift from the classic Keynesian sense that governments ought to manage their economies—implied, for example, in *Mater et Magistra* (# 54)—to a position in *Centesimus Annus* that government's more appropriate economic role is to establish the right conditions for individual initiative and a recognition of the role of entrepreneurs as creative actors.—John D. Larrivee, Richard Creek, and John Streifel

BIBLIOGRAPHY AND FURTHER READING: Domitrovic, Brian. *Econoclasts: The Rebels Who Sparked the Supply-Side Revolution and Restored American Prosperity.* Wilmington, DE: ISI Books, 2009; Lucas, Robert. "Macroeconomic Priorities." *American Economic Review.* 93, no. 1 (2003): 1–14; Lucas, Robert. "Mortgages and Monetary Policy." *Wall Street Journal*, September 19, 2007; Skousen, Mark. *The Making of Modern Economics: The Lives and Ideas of the Great Thinkers*, 2nd ed. Armonk, NY: M. E. Sharpe, 2009. See also CAPITALISM; *CENTESIMUS ANNUS*; ENTREPRENEUR; FREE MARKET ECONOMY; INFLATION; KEYNES, JOHN MAYNARD, AND KEYNESIANISM

SYMBOLIC INTERACTIONISM Symbolic interactionism is one of the major theoretical perspectives in sociology. For the interactionist, society consists of organized and patterned interactions among individuals. Thus, research by interactionists focuses on easily observable, face-to-face interactions rather than the large-scale surveys or "societal-level" studies of relationships involving social institutions performed by functionalists or conflict theorists. Using qualitative data-gathering techniques rather than large-scale survey instruments, interactionists focus on the subjective micro-level aspects of social life, rather than on objective, macro-level aspects of social systems.

The symbolic interactionist researcher seeks to understand how actors jointly define meanings and construct lines of action within those settings. Rather than survey data collection or quantitative data analysis, the preferred method for the symbolic interactionist is ethnography and participant observation research in which those being observed are unaware that one of the group members is actually a sociologist. The symbolic interactionist would argue that close contact and immersion in the everyday lives of the participants is necessary for understanding the meaning of actions, the definition of the situation itself, and the process by which actors construct the situation through their interaction.

While Max Weber, the German sociologist and economist, and American philosopher George Herbert Mead were the first to emphasize the subjective meaning of human behavior, Herbert Blumer, a sociologist from the University of Chicago, is responsible for coining the term *symbolic interactionism*, as well as for formulating the most prominent version of the theory.

Blumer was influenced by John Dewey, who insisted that human beings are best understood in relation to their environment. In fact, Blumer believed that people act toward things based on the meaning those things have for them. For him, and for social interactionists generally, norms, values, and beliefs are not static—they are always changing based on the situation. Meanings are derived from social interaction and are modified through the interpretation of those involved in the interaction itself.

An individualistic theory—yet rejecting a psychological perspective—Blumer's symbolic interactionism maintains that "human beings interpret or define each others' actions instead of merely reacting. . . . Their response is based on the meaning which they attach to such actions." For Blumer, social structures exist "only in the minds of sociologists who spend too much time in their studies [on social structures] and too little doing direct observation." This theory is in opposition to structural functionalism and conflict theories, both of which posit an existing social structure. For the interactionist, social structures are always changing and new ones emerging—nothing is static because it is constantly being redefined and reinterpreted.

Within social interactionism, humans are pragmatic actors who continuously adjust their behavior to the actions of others. The way humans do this is to interpret the actions of others and then "rehearse" alternative lines of action before they act. Blumer suggests that there are three core principles: meaning, language, and thought. The principle of *meaning* claims that humans act toward people and things based on the meanings that they have given to those people or things. *Language* is the second core principle because speech gives humans a means to negotiate meaning through symbols. By engaging in speech acts with others (symbolic interaction), humans come to identify meaning. The third core principle is *thought*, which modifies each individual's interpretation of symbols. Thought requires "role taking" or imagining the possible different points of view of the Other.

Symbolic interactionism is pragmatic, because the emphasis on symbols, negotiated reality, and the social construction of society leads to an interest in the roles people play and the ways in which reality is constructed. Erving Goffman, a prominent symbolic interactionist, maintains that roles are critical to understanding the social construction of society. For Goffman, role taking is the most important mechanism for interaction because it permits us to take other perspectives to see what our actions might mean to the other actors with whom we interact.

The focus is on interaction and on the meaning of events to the participants in those events—and this shifts the attention of interactionists away from stable norms and values toward more changeable, continually readjusting social processes based upon what interactionists call the "definition of the situation." Unlike functionalists, who seek stability in the social system, interactionists focus on negotiation among members of society to create temporary, socially constructed relations that remain in constant flux.

The shift of attention away from stable social structures, norms, and values to the social construction of reality is the key to understanding symbolic interactionism. But, for Catholics, as norms and values become socially constructed and open to negotiation by human beings, this shift in perspective can be viewed as a threat to natural law. Drawing from St. Thomas Aquinas, Catholics believe that there are social (and moral) rules of society that are unchangeable and cannot be violated. Catholics believe that social structures—or society and the rules of nature and of nature's God—exist separate from the actors who create them.

Yet, there are Christian symbolic interactionists, such as Peter Berger, who maintain that although this theory can be viewed as a form of humanism, it is not necessarily hostile to religion. In *Invitation to Sociology*, Berger writes, "The very phenomenon of religion as such can be socially located in terms of specific functions, such as its legitimation of political authority or its assuagement of social rebellion." As such, the universality of religion is explicable in terms of its social functions—for example, the meaning it provides. Moreover, changes in religious patterns in the course of history can also be interpreted in sociological terms. From this perspective, the individual derives his worldview socially—including his view of religion and God—in very much the same way that he derives his roles and his identity. And, for Berger, society, in the same way, "supplies our values, our logic and the store of information (or, for that matter, misinformation) that constitutes our knowledge." This is not hostile to religion, but rather helps support the role that religion plays in helping to shape our beliefs, values, norms, and behaviors.

In *Creation Social Science and Humanities Quarterly*, Donald Ratcliff maintains that, although some Christians would have reservations about symbolic interaction theory because it "overemphasizes human autonomy," he believes we must recognize that God has endowed us with choice. Symbolic interaction theory does not deny an objectively real world, but rather that our construction of the world is what we act upon in daily life. When meanings are shared, interaction is possible. Ratcliff maintains that God's constructing through creation is reflected in the social constructing of humans as stated by symbolic interactionism. "We construct our sometimes faulty views of reality, an imperfect image of God's original construction of the real world and its inhabitants. As the Apostle Paul stated: 'We see as through a glass darkly,' while God sees perfectly."

The sociology of deviance is heavily influenced by symbolic interactionism because this theoretical perspective demonstrates that, in major cultural transitions, words often change their meanings as new norms evolve and old cultural constraints loosen. Those wishing to change a label of deviance on a given behavior may get involved in a political campaign to do this by changing the language related to that behavior. The deviance status of a number of behaviors—including premarital sex, homosexuality, same-sex marriage, divorce, contraception, and abortion—has been dramatically changed through a political and media campaign that has pushed for standards of behavior based on individual desires rather than moral categories. The media campaign involves changing the language so that the sexually promiscuous teenager is redefined as "sexually adventurous." Abortion is redefined as just another "choice," and same-sex marriage is redefined as equivalent to heterosexual marriage. Even suicide has been redefined from an act that was viewed as "deeply disturbed" to one that involves "choice" and "dignity."

From a Catholic perspective, the real problem at the core of symbolic interactionism is that there are no moral absolutes and no permanent moral authority structure. For a hierarchical Church with an elaborate authority structure, this is a problem. Rather than a set of moral precepts and an unchanging natural law, meaning is constantly shifting as language changes. From the rights-based, pro-choice rhetoric of those promoting assisted suicide, same-sex marriage, or abortion to the medical jargon of those promoting a disease model of addiction, advocates for redefinitions of deviance know that the side that wins the linguistic high ground generally wins the debate.—Anne Hendershott

BIBLIOGRAPHY AND FURTHER READING: Blumer, Herbert. *Symbolic Interactionism: Perspective and Method.* Englewood Cliffs, NJ: Prentice Hall, 1969; Goffman, Erving. *The Presentation of Self in Everyday Life.* Edinburgh: University of Edinburgh, Social Sciences Research Centre, 1958; Ratcliff, Donald. "Creation, Redemption and Sociological Theory." *Creation Social Science and Humanities Quarterly* 10, no. 4 (1988): 14–20. *See also* DEWEY, JOHN; NATURAL LAW; SOCIOLOGY: A CATHOLIC CRITIQUE; WEBER, MAX

· T ·

TAYLOR, CHARLES M. (1931–) Charles Taylor is a Canadian Catholic philosopher who has made major intellectual contributions in the fields of political philosophy, the history of philosophy, and the philosophy of the social sciences. Taylor has been both a student and a teacher at McGill University and Oxford University. His most recent teaching appointment was in the philosophy and law departments at Northwestern University. Taylor has received numerous awards, including the Kyoto Prize (sometimes called the Japanese Nobel) in arts and philosophy and the Templeton Prize for research about spiritual realities.

Beyond his academic endeavors, Taylor has also been involved in politics, running several times for Parliament in the 1960s as a member of the New Democratic Party. In 2007, he served as one of the heads of the Bouchard Taylor Commission, a commission of inquiry to seek reasonable accommodation on cultural differences in the province of Quebec.

Taylor is a postanalytic philosopher who seeks the clarity and rigor of analytical thought but is both historical and interdisciplinary in his approach. In pursuing his quest to unpack the sources and dimensions of the "modern malaise," Taylor draws on a diverse range of sources, from Aristotle to Ludwig Wittgenstein and Georg Hegel to Maurice Merleau-Ponty.

Much of Taylor's work has been a communitarian critique of modern and liberal understandings of the self. He has often noted the importance of social institutions in the development of individual meaning and identity. Indeed, he has utilized and explored the term *social imaginary*, which references the interlocking dimensions of the individual and a community through reflexivity, self-constitution, market exchange, public opinion, and many other forms and qualities. In this exploration, Taylor has criticized many Anglo-American political theorists, from John Locke to John Rawls, who have ignored the fact that individuals act within thick contexts supplied by societies. He is in accord with Wittgenstein that political action presupposes a background or a "form of life." In this form of life, we obey rules as a form of practice that draws on our habits and dispositions. These habits and dispositions provide the "sense of things," an unarticulated background for our actions.

If he is critical of liberal political thinkers, Taylor does not abandon politics as a vehicle for social development. Indeed in the *Ethics of Authenticity* (1991), Taylor warns against abandoning political life and seeking a private quest for authenticity—this narrows the possibilities for human life. Full authenticity requires openness to "horizons of significance," and this quest offers possible connection to larger political, social, or religious forms of connection.

In *Sources of the Self* (1992), Taylor offers a more systematic antidote to the "modern malaise," beginning with an exploration of the archeology of the self in Western thought from the time of Plato. He begins by recognizing three major sources of our moral frameworks. The first is the respect we accord human life, and it is from this respect for life that we have moral obligations. The second refers to beliefs about values we bring to our daily actions and choices. The third source focuses on the human dignity afforded to both ourselves and others based on our roles in society.

Taylor is a critic of modern ethical theories, such as utilitarianism and Kantian ethics. Having detached themselves from their historical frameworks, such modern approaches deny the historical and cultural backgrounds that produce their proposed goods such as justice, beneficence, and equality. The effort to get outside our cultural and historical frameworks in modern thought has contributed to incoherence in the development and expression of modern ethics. The modern approach fails to address the issue of substantive qualitative distinctions among moral goods. The naturalism of modernity accepts goods, but reduces these goods to a single level and cannot express allegiance to any notion of ultimate goods. Taylor rejects this approach and assesses the general level of goods through "hypergoods," which provide criteria for judging other goods and thus provide a coherent moral framework.

Constantly wrestling with the meaning of modernity, Taylor more explicitly explores its meaning for religious traditions in *A Catholic Modernity* (1990). For Taylor, the project of Christendom was problematic, if well intentioned. As a historical project, the effort to create Christendom inevitably involved coercion and the co-opting of noble ideals by narrow interests. Substituting other secular philosophies in the place of Christendom does not, however, necessarily offer a better prospect for human flourishing. Nonetheless, Taylor concedes that the modern world allows for certain positive developments, such as developing certain ethical concepts further than would have been possible in Christendom. For example, modernity has allowed the affirmation of universal human rights of life, freedom, citizenship, and self-realization that depend on the "radical unconditionality" of modernity.

In *A Secular Age* (2007), Taylor once again systematically explores the predicament of the modern self operating in a different context than earlier Christians did. He notes how theology in the premodern world sought the divine form that would provide a template for the Church, politics, and culture. With the advent of the modern world, the seeking of form came to be replaced by the imposing of form in religion and politics. This "intellectual deviation," a desire within theology to impose form, was then co-opted by secular forces in the past few centuries. The secular world has sought to impose on the inert matter of the universe a code of form that is not intrinsic to the universe but is a man-made creation.

The modern person is thus guided by a code that provides moral order, but a moral order that is imposed and is disengaged from our social and natural environments. The resulting "buffered selves" seek mutual benefit in a political order that is based on the securing of individual rights. This vision of mutually assured individual rights seeks to create a "new sociality."

In contrast to the atomism of the buffered self in the modern world, Taylor proposes an alternative in the ideal of communion. In a life of communion, we live as porous selves implicated in each others' lives, the cosmos, and God. Instead of the mutual benefit of the buffered selves, humanity in communion relies on *agape*, a form of unconditional, self-giving, thoughtful love.

According to Taylor, we are in a "new predicament." The buffered self's ethic of mutual benefit has been challenged by a variety of positions such as moralism and romanticism. These alternatives and the realities of modern life produce "cross pressures" that result in "dilemmas" for the materialist and individualist trajectories of modern life. The result is an opening—a space where a variety of options are available. In addition to the buffered self and religion, there is room for wandering and seeking without choosing a specific path. Thus, we have a landscape that includes atheism, agnosticism, materialism, and an array of "intermediate positions." An example of an intermediate position is a person who professes a creed but does not practice his faith.

Religions may not have easy or complete answers to the dilemmas posed by the modern world, but their answers are more sufficient than those of the modern perspective. Religions survive because they draw on deep resources and fundamental insights. A religion today can recognize that we are pulled toward the good and away from evil at the "unquiet frontiers of modernity." Hence, a conversion to belief from an immanent framework remains possible. The positive gains of modernity are retained in such a conversion, but in a more comprehensive and fecund framework.

In addition to his impressive body of work on the many facets of modernity, Taylor has explored the challenges and opportunities of multiculturalism, most notably in his lecture "The Politics of Recognition." The modern world has emphasized the ahistorical sameness of all citizens, and this modern perspective has the inherent danger of promoting a homogenizing tyranny through ideas like Jean-Jacques Rousseau's general will. For Taylor, a focus on dignity in a postmodern politics of identity or multiculturalism is an antidote to this tyranny and promotes a politics of difference, allowing for the distinctiveness of an individual or group within a political structure of equal recognition. One of his most recent multicultural concerns is "Islamaphobia," the trend toward universal fear of Islam, which Taylor cites as a form of "block thinking" where a diverse reality is reduced to an indissoluble unity.

Taylor's work has been subject to numerous criticisms. Some contend that his work is poorly organized and lacking in clarity of expression. Taylor has also been accused of being too apologetic toward modern thinking even as he raises his complex criticisms of its thought. He is sometimes criticized for being a problem solver rather than a careful systematic thinker or is painted as trying to encompass too much in his narrative of modernity. As for multiculturalism, it is suggested that he seems to offer a goal of equality without providing a viable process to arrive at such an outcome.—Phillip M. Thompson

BIBLIOGRAPHY AND FURTHER READING: Taylor, Charles. *A Secular Age*. Cambridge, MA: Harvard University Press, 2007; Taylor, Charles. *Sources of the Self*. Cambridge, MA: Harvard University Press, 1989; Tully, James, and Daniel M. Weinstock, eds. *Philosophy in an Age of Pluralism: The Philosophy of Charles Taylor in Question*. Cambridge: Cambridge University Press, 1995. *See also* COMMUNITARIANISM; MacINTYRE, ALASDAIR C.; MULTICULTURALISM

TECHNOLOGY The English word *technology* traces its roots to the Greek *techne*, which means "skill" or "craft." The Greek verb *technazo* means "to employ a skill or craft," and what we call a *technique* refers to the particular manner in which one does so. Originally, technology referred to the science or study of the practical arts (*techne* + *logos*), and thus a school calling itself an "institute of technology" would typically be one that built its curriculum around fields such as engineering. A distinction is commonly made between science and technology, the basic import of which is that science concerns itself principally with theoretical knowledge, whereas technology devotes itself to developing practical applications of theoretical knowledge. In this sense, technology is often called "applied science." A nuclear physicist focuses his attention on the atomic structure of uranium; with the knowledge gained by the physicist, a *technician* then constructs a very powerful explosive device (although, in a case such as this, the physicist and the technician may be one and the same person).

While there is a certain usefulness to the distinction between science and technology, it should not be overplayed. Though the two are distinct, they are rarely completely separate. It would be wrong, therefore, looking at things from a historical perspective, to suppose that science was chronologically anterior to technology. As a matter of fact, science and technology invariably accompany one another, by reason of the fact that they are closely interdependent. Advances in what we might call "pure" science were often made possible only because of technology, in the form of instrumentation of one kind or another. For example, our greatly increased knowledge of astronomy accompanied the technology represented by the telescope. Almost all successful experimental science is explained by its heavy dependence on technology, and often the peculiar demands of a particular experiment will engender improvements in the very technology of which it makes use.

Considered in the broadest possible terms, technology can be understood to refer to any material object at all that is not part of the human body, but extends or enhances the power of or renders more efficient the practical exertions of the human body. This object could be man-made, an artifact, such as a flint arrowhead that forms part of a weapon used for hunting, or it could be a natural object, such as a sturdy stick used as a cane. As in the case of those two examples, technology can be of the most primitive kind, but, of course, when it comes to the matter of artifacts, technology can take on wondrous complexity in the form of, say, a computer, the premier artifact of modern technology.

It goes without saying that technology has a direct and very important bearing on the social scene. The history of the human race in general and the history of technology are inextricably bound up with one another. One might reasonably argue that the progress of any society, as a society, is closely allied to its technological progress; the more technological sophistication a particular society can show, the more humane the environment it can provide for its members. Nevertheless, technology always has significant consequences for society, whatever the nature of those consequences. As is true of everything that is wrought by man, technology has an inescapably moral dimension to it. There is no such thing as a morally neutral technology, its moral quality being determined in each case by the uses to which it is put.

There have been certain benchmark periods in the history of technology, such as the scientific revolution of the 17th century and the industrial revolution that began in the late 18th century and flourished in the 19th. The industrial revolution altered the entire face of Western civilization, transforming it from a dominantly agrarian society to a dominantly urban one. The two world wars, especially the second, are noteworthy for the wide range of new and exotic technologies they gave birth to. One of the most interesting things about the history of technology is its steady acceleration over the past two hundred years, an acceleration that has now reached a fairly dizzying pace.

While great benefits have accrued to mankind as a result of technology, specifically in such fields as medicine, agriculture, communication, and transportation, it cannot be denied that technology has a dark side to it. And as it continues to accelerate and becomes a yet more pervasive and insinuating factor in contemporary life, technology's two-sided nature becomes increasingly evident. While some technologies are put to impressively constructive uses—and their benefits cannot be sufficiently lauded—others are intended by their nature only for destruction. Moreover, a good portion of the energy and ingenious thinking that has gone into the development of technology over the centuries has been devoted to the production of artifacts whose purpose is to kill rather than to cure.

The whole purpose of technology is to make man a more efficient operative. Technology enables man to do things that, without it, would be quite beyond his capacity. And therein lies the great and abiding temptation of technology. Technology can instill within man such a heady sense of power that he deludes himself into believing that the mere capacity to do something entails a warrant for doing it. A fatal transference is made from "This can be done" to "This *should* be done."

Technology has a way of taking on a life of its own, and in certain circumstances there are signs of a disconcerting Frankensteinian reversal taking place, whereby an artifact that was masterfully made by man ends up being man's master. A constantly accelerating technology tends to feed on itself, in the sense that often, and for purely economic reasons, there is a propensity to go in for novelty just for the sake of novelty. We are urged to believe, by intensive, pervasive, and incessant advertising, that the technologically new is necessarily the technologically improved. But, as experience has shown, the latest product is not always a better product, and in fact the replacement is sometimes decidedly inferior to what has been replaced.

The more thoroughly and irreversibly a society becomes immersed in technology—which represents the realm of the artificial—the greater is the possibility that the members of that society will grow gradually more distanced from the realm of the natural, specifically in the form of their own human nature. In other words, the more man becomes comprehensively dependent on his machines, to the point perhaps where that dependence begins to curtail his freedom, the more alienated he becomes from himself. Given the pervasiveness and sophistication of modern technology, many of our artifacts, which began as luxury items in our lives, have eventually assumed the imperative character of needs, and what was once liberating turns out, paradoxically, to be positively confining. The sheer proliferation of the products of technology, especially with those exclusively dedicated to entertainment—which

itself has become a massive industry—can so surround and encumber our lives that, besides being a scandal to Christian simplicity, keep us in a state of almost constant and debilitating distraction. The one thing necessary pales into the peripheral.

There have been some philosophers and artists who have envisioned an apocalyptic future in which technology so gains the ascendency that it effectively swamps the human. Should it ever transpire that man loses control over the products of his own making, it will only be because he had antecedently lost control over himself.

Plato, in the *Republic*, draws a number of instructive parallels between the individual and society, particularly in terms of justice. The individual is just, he argues, insofar as he maintains rational control over his passions, which results in psychological order. Comparably, a society is just insofar as it is ordered, and that order is maintained, as on the individual level, by the reign of the rational.

So long as a society maintains rational control over technology, technology will play its proper role as servant, not master. A society succeeds in doing this by keeping clearly and practically in mind the elementary distinction between ends and means. Technology is a means, not an end in itself; it is only when it becomes the latter that disorder is introduced, within the individual or within a society as a whole. Rightly regarded, rightly employed, technology should serve, however remotely, those transcendent ends that have to do with the ultimate destiny of man.—D. Q. McInerny

BIBLIOGRAPHY AND FURTHER READING: Barrett, William. *Death of the Soul: From Descartes to the Computer.* New York: Anchor Books, 1987; Marcel, Gabriel. *Men against Humanity.* Chicago: Regnery, 1952; Queffélec, Henri. *Technology and Religion.* New York: Hawthorne Books, 1964. *See also* SCIENCE; SCIENTISM

TEILHARD DE CHARDIN, PIERRE, SJ (1881–1955)

Pierre Teilhard de Chardin was born in an 18th-century manor in the Auvergne district of France on May 1, 1881, the fourth of 11 children. He was raised in a devout Catholic household, where every evening his father, Emmanuel, led the family in prayer. From his earliest boyhood, he showed a vibrant interest in the natural world—an interest that was to eventuate in the total dedication he would give to scientific studies as an adult. At age 10, Teilhard was sent to be educated at a Jesuit boarding school, and eight years later, having passed his baccalaureate, he joined the Society of Jesus.

When the French government expelled all religious orders from the country in 1902, Teilhard, now having completed his novitiate, emigrated with his community to Jersey. It was there that he pursued studies in philosophy. A fellow Jesuit, and one of his closest friends, Father Pierre Leroy, wrote of him in this period: "He studied scholastic philosophy, becoming familiar with its methods and terminology, without, however, adopting its spirit." In 1905, Teilhard was sent to teach physics and chemistry at Holy Family College in Cairo, where he remained for three years. He returned to England in 1908 and completed his theological studies; he was ordained a priest in 1912.

During World War I, Teilhard served at the front as a stretcher bearer, for which he was awarded the Médaille Militaire and the Légion d'Honneur. The war over, he then embarked upon his specifically scientific education, studying under Marcellin Boule at the Natural History Museum in Paris and in 1922 being awarded a doctorate in geology from the Sorbonne. For the next two years, he taught geology at the Institut Catholique in Paris, but he was summarily relieved of his teaching duties by his Jesuit superiors because of concerns they had over the orthodoxy of some of the views he was espousing. In the period between 1924 and the end of World War II, Teilhard lived and worked in France and in China, where he was engaged in paleontological research; he also traveled throughout the world in pursuit of various scientific interests. In 1946, Teilhard returned to France, where he lived until 1951, when, because of new restrictions put upon his activities by his Jesuit superiors, he moved to New York. There, he was a member of the Wenner Gren Foundation, an institute sponsoring research in anthropology. Teilhard died in New York City on Easter Sunday, 1955.

Though Teilhard wrote a good deal over the course of his life, he was not permitted to publish. Immediately after his death, however, his works quickly found their way into print, and within a very short time they created quite a sensation, especially within Catholic circles. There was a time, in the late 1950s and 1960s, when he assumed a larger-than-life status in the minds of some, who regarded him as a seer, an inspired prophet announcing an entirely new way of thinking about the Christian faith and how it fit into the larger scheme of things. He was the subject of extravagant praise: Queen Marie-José called him "a figure-head in the unfolding of a new cycle in the life of mankind"; Bernard Wall, the general editor of the works of Teilhard, saw him as "a unique figure who cut his way through what in some sense were virgin forests of the mind"; and Jean

Priveteau described him as "one of the greatest minds the world has known." Teilhard has been the subject of a great many books and scholarly articles.

Teilhard regarded himself first and foremost as a priest and a religious. But after that, he very much wanted to be recognized as a scientist, or—a term he seemed to prefer—a naturalist. A good many of his published works can be broadly identified as scientific treatises, though none of his books limits itself to a single, tightly circumscribed subject area. Works like *The Divine Milieu* (1957) and *Hymn of the Universe* (1961) are best categorized as poetic meditations that range into issues having significant theological import. As a self-identified mystic, he presumably would not have been against people regarding him as a seer, someone whose insights disclosed the foundational aspects of reality. Even in his scientific treatises, he gives much emphasis to the importance of "vision," the ability to see beneath the surface of things and there to discover the dynamic essence of the cosmos.

There is common agreement that Teilhard's single most important work is *The Phenomenon of Man*, which was written between 1946 and 1948 and published in 1955, the year of his death. In it, we find all the key elements of his sweeping evolutionary cosmology. Teilhard was totally committed to evolutionary theory, but it was an evolutionary theory very much of his own making. He was clearly influenced by the thought of Charles Darwin, although neither *The Origin of Species* nor *The Descent of Man* had as much influence on shaping the peculiar cast of his thought as did Henri Bergson's *Creative Evolution*.

Teilhard showed due deference to Darwin and extolled evolutionary theory as being in effect a "theory of everything," the crowning glory of human thought. But it would be quite wrong to consider him an orthodox Darwinian, for he took marked exception to the English naturalist on several points. For example, whereas Darwin asserted that man differed from the animals in degree but not in kind, Teilhard maintained that not only was man radically superior to all other creatures, he was the climactic end point—the very purpose—of evolution. And whereas contemporary Darwinists like Richard Dawkins insist that there is no design or direction in evolution, Teilhard saw the whole evolutionary process as a divinely instigated and controlled upward and onward progression from matter to mind, a process that involved the spiritualization, even the divinization, of matter. He was not altogether unlike the ancient Greek philosopher Thales, who saw "soul" in all matter; matter, for Teilhard, was "pre-life," and life itself an epiphenomenon of matter.

The whole thrust of the grand, cosmic drama of evolution, as Teilhard envisioned it, begins in the sphere of the geological and is directed ineluctably toward life and, eventually, life in its highest form: intellectual life, which blossoms forth in what he called the "noosphere." From there, the ascent continues until it culminates in the Omega Point, or the Hyper-Personal, or God-Omega—the ultimate term of a steadily converging universe.

Teilhard's evolutionary theory is certainly fascinating, but judged by strict scientific standards—by which he supposedly would want it to be judged—it is considerably less than compelling. Perhaps the thorniest element in the theory is his notion of complexification of matter, the "law of complication," whereby matter is gradually transformed, over eons of time and supposedly by an entirely natural process, into conscious life. Here we have a head-on clash with the principle *omne vivum de vivo*, all life comes from life. *The Phenomenon of Man* is fraught with serious philosophical and logical problems, as is demonstrated by any number of occasions where we witness athletic leaps to conclusions from grounds that are manifestly weak or not even fully apparent.

As for Teilhard's thought taken as a whole, especially when it is exercised within the realm of theology, it is not difficult to see why his Jesuit superiors saw fit to remove him from a teaching position and prohibited the publication of his writings. For one thing—and by no means an unimportant one when it comes to theology—his style is beset by a debilitating ambiguity. He makes free use of arresting but not necessarily clarifying neologisms, and he has the habit of employing ordinary terms without honoring their ordinary meanings. Among specific problems with his theological thought, one can cite the advocacy of a qualified pantheism; a noncommittal attitude toward the doctrine of original sin; leaving open the possibility of polygenesis, which was explicitly condemned by Pope Pius XII in his encyclical *Humani Generis*; and, in general, a failure to draw a clear distinction between the natural and the supernatural.

In *The Peasant of Garonne*, Jacques Maritain wrote a pointed critique of the thought of Teilhard de Chardin, which he ended with the bland comment: "He was without a doubt a man of great imagination." It is no small gift to be possessed of a great imagination, but it carries with it special responsibilities; the greater the imagination, the greater the need for logic and metaphysics.—D. Q. McInerny

BIBLIOGRAPHY AND FURTHER READING: Blondel, Maurice. *Pierre Teilhard de Chardin*. New York: Herder & Herder, 1967; Duggan, G. H. *Teilhardism and the Faith*. Cork, Ireland: Mercer Press, 1968; Lubac, Henri de. *Teilhard Explained*. New York: Paulist Press, 1968; Lukas, Mary. *Teilhard*. Garden City, NY: Doubleday, 1977; Mooney, Christopher F. *Teilhard de Chardin and the Mystery of Christ*. New York: Harper & Row, 1966; Rabat, Oliver. *Teilhard de Chardin*. New York: Sheed & Ward, 1961; Smith, Wolfgang. *Teilhardism and the New Religion*. Rockford, IL: Tan Books, 1988. *See also* EVOLUTION; JAKI, STANLEY L., OSB; KING, THOMAS M., SJ; MODERNISM AND NEO-MODERNISM; SCIENCE; THEOLOGY

THEOLOGICAL STUDIES   *Theological Studies* is a quarterly journal of theology, published under the auspices of the Jesuit order in the United States. Supported by Marquette University and Georgetown University, it has been under the general editorship of David G. Schultenover, SJ, since 2006. Its first issues appeared in 1940 under the leadership of William J. McGarry, SJ. After his untimely death in 1941, he was succeeded by John Courtney Murray, SJ (1941–1967); Walter J. Burghardt, SJ (1967–1990); Robert Daly, SJ (1991–1995); and Michael A. Fahey, SJ (1996–2005).

The context for the decision to found *Theological Studies* was the need for a first-rate American journal of Catholic theology other than the *American Ecclesiastical Review*. (The *New York Review* was short lived, 1905–1908. It had been published at St. Joseph's Seminary in Dunwoodie, New York, but under pressure from Rome was suppressed by the archbishop of New York during the modernist crisis.) The *American Ecclesiastical Review* had been suspended briefly by local authorities after pressure from the Vatican, but it resumed publication. It was sometimes perceived not to have the degree of freedom appropriate to scholarly research.

Finding that there was no American equivalent to such European Jesuit journals as the *Nouvelle Revue Théologique* (1869), *Zeitschrift für Katholische Theologie* (1876), *Recherches de Sciences Religieuses* (1913), *Gregorianum* (1920), or *Bijdragen* (1938), the six theological faculties then staffed by the Society of Jesus in the United States—Alma College (California), St. Mary's College (Kansas), West Baden College (Indiana), Weston College (Massachusetts), and Woodstock College (Maryland), and the diocesan seminary in suburban Chicago, St. Mary of the Lake (Mundelein, Illinois)—undertook the project.

In the course of its history, *Theological Studies* has played a critical role in the development of theological trends, not only in the sphere of English-language studies in theology but globally. There is a vast range of topics covered in this journal, but of special importance here is the regular appearance over the years of a column entitled "Notes on Moral Theology." The changing tone and content of this series of articles provides a telling record of certain important trends and shifts in the views prevalent among prominent Catholic moralists during this period.

In the course of his 25 years of editorial service, Father Murray used the pages of *Theological Studies* to exemplify the level of scholarship to which figures like Msgr. John Tracy Ellis, the dean of Catholic historians, challenged Catholics to rise in his 1955 essay "American Catholics and the Intellectual Life." Father Bernard Lonergan, SJ, for instance, published the series of five articles on the concept of *Verbum* in St. Thomas Aquinas that was seminal for the distinctive theological stance that he came to articulate. Murray himself published more than 20 of his own essays in *Theological Studies*, including a series of pieces that reflected upon the teachings of Pope Leo XIII in the area of Catholic social doctrine. He regularly published essays on the natural moral law and ordered liberty, on the role that Catholicism could and should play in the American form of democratic government, and (until silenced by Rome in 1955 for having criticized Cardinal Alfredo Ottaviani) on religious freedom and the relations of church and state. Many of his views would, however, eventually influence the Second Vatican Council's *Declaration on Religious Freedom*.

During Father Burghardt's term as editor, the journal formally expanded its editorial board and its stable of authors. Moving from the original idea of using the faculties of the Jesuit theologates, the journal gradually saw widespread participation by university professors from around the globe. As a result, the nature of the articles published gradually changed, and one can easily trace the growing polarization of theological viewpoints. There are articles, for instance, by Francis Schüssler Fiorenza and Gustavo Gutiérrez on liberation theology; by Karl Rahner, SJ, on the implications of the Second Vatican Council for change in the Church; by Raymond Brown and Joseph Fitzmyer, SJ, on the Scriptures; by Rosemary Radford Ruether and Sandra Schneider on feminist theology; and by Avery Dulles, SJ, on revelation, faith, ecclesiology, and ecumenism. Under subsequent editors, the pages of *Theological Studies* have continued to provide a venue for the most prominent names in theology, not only in these areas but also in such fields as ecumenical theology, historical theology, spirituality, canon law, and patristics.

The annual "Notes on Moral Theology" columns deserve special attention here. These began quite modestly in 1940 with several pages of reflections by McGarry on topics ranging from fundamentalism in biblical interpretation to questions about the morality of testicular transplants. But gradually the notes came to focus exclusively on moral issues, presumably out of the long-term Jesuit concern with casuistry. From 1947 to 1956, Rev. John C. Ford, occasionally joined by Rev. Gerald A. Kelly, wrote articles discussing questions of ethics and reviewing publications in the area from other U.S. and European periodicals.

Rev. Richard A. McCormick, SJ, composed the notes from 1965 to 1987, and since then there has been a team of authors who have divided the labors in accord with their own specialties within moral theology. In the articles subsequent to the promulgation of *Humanae Vitae* in 1968, one can rather clearly see Father McCormick's growing embrace of proportionalist and consequentialist strategies of moral argument in the course of what he himself called a "theological revolution" in the area of morality. To its credit, *Theological Studies* also published the work of McCormick's critics, for example, "The Disvalue of Ontic Evil" by Rev. Paul M. Quay, SJ, in 1985, which argued that an equivocation in the use of the term *ontic evil* and its cognates renders it impossible for moralists of the proportionalist school ever to formulate a "self-consistent position."

Among the most significant articles that have ever appeared in this journal is one published during World War II by John C. Ford, SJ. In "The Morality of Obliteration Bombing," an essay published in 1944, a year before the dropping of atomic bombs on Hiroshima and Nagasaki, Ford argued that bombings of this type constituted "an immoral attack on the rights of the innocent." On a related theme, *Theological Studies* in recent years has offered ongoing discussion of questions like the morality of nuclear deterrence and of preemptive strikes. It has also provided a venue for a variety of medico-moral topics, human rights issues, and problems in the area of Catholic social teaching.—Joseph W. Koterski, SJ

BIBLIOGRAPHY AND FURTHER READING: Burghardt, Walter J., SJ. "A Half Century of *Theological Studies*: Retrospect and Prospect." *Theological Studies* 50 (1989): 761–785. *Theological Studies* website, http://www.ts.mu .edu. *See also* COMMUNIO; CONSEQUENTIALISM;

McCORMICK, RICHARD A.; MORAL THEOLOGY: A SURVEY; MURRAY, JOHN COURTNEY, SJ; PROPORTIONALISM; RAHNER, KARL, SJ; SOCIETY OF JESUS

THOMAS, WILLIAM I. (1863–1947) William Isaac Thomas was an American sociologist and pioneer of social psychology who cowrote, with Florian Znaniecki, *The Polish Peasant in Europe and America*, the seminal early study of Polish immigrants in the United States. Thomas was born, reportedly of Pennsylvania Dutch extraction, in the Appalachian region of Virginia, the son of a farmer who was also a Methodist minister. Later, he would recall the social world he was brought up in as being still essentially that of the 18th century, and his youth as more concerned with hunting than books. Any religiosity derived from his upbringing seems to have been gradually abandoned in adulthood, and in his intellectual maturity, he would take relatively little interest in religion as a sociological problem, in comparison to, for instance, his collaborator Znaniecki.

As a young man, Thomas attended the University of Tennessee, where he excelled academically and socially, studying modern and classical languages and showing for the first time a powerful and restless intellect. It was here that he decided to pursue scholarship as his career, and as a young faculty member at Tennessee, he was sent to Germany for a year to pursue the new German model of specialist scholarship, which he greatly admired, although his own interests were always broader than those defined by emerging disciplinary boundaries. In Germany, he became interested in ethnography, and this seems to have colored his decision to return to school (after a brief stint teaching English at Oberlin College) to study sociology in the new doctoral program at the University of Chicago, in 1894.

In the years that followed his doctorate (1896), Thomas developed the main themes and ideas that would characterize his scholarly work thereafter. From Herbert Spencer and American evolutionary anthropologists like L. H. Morgan, he took an interest in social development, but Thomas rejected their unilinear models of social evolution. He accepted with Sigmund Freud that human beings have certain basic desires that exist beyond the immediate control of consciousness, but rejected Freud's sexual basis of the personality as too simplistic. John Dewey's pragmatism and early behaviorism also had some influence on his thought, whereas from Oswald Spengler he acquired an interest in social disorganization and decline.

There is little doubt Thomas regarded himself as an empiricist open to a variety of theoretical approaches insofar as they could explain human action in society, but without being wedded to any one of them. He had an early interest in physical anthropology and published a book on sexual differences with regard to society (*Sex and Society*, 1907), which interpreted them in part on the basis of supposed metabolic differences between men and women. In the longer run, however, he tended to stress the fundamental biological unity of humanity with regard to both sex and race, in particular interpreting differences in intellectual attainment through different degrees of connection to wider social spheres rather than inherent factors.

Although he professed the requirement that science and politics be kept separate, it is worth noting his open association with the more leftist progressive circles, with which he had contact through his pacifist wife (among others), and it would be the politically progressive wealthy widow Helen Culver who would underwrite his research into the Polish peasant immigrants, who were then regarded as the cause of many social problems, especially in Chicago.

The Polish Peasant in Europe and America, eventually to reach five volumes, was conceived initially by Thomas, and the basic plan for it existed before Znaniecki joined the project. Although the Polish philosopher helped considerably in shaping its theoretical framework, the focus on the individual as framed in letters, autobiography, and similar documents reflects Thomas's emerging interests, as well as his method of collecting and commenting on materials and sources, which in turn closely follows his unusual teaching practices. The interest in the social disorganization of Polish peasant society and attempts to reorganize it on a new basis in the United States also reflects his long-term interests. Several major pieces of the interpretive apparatus come from Thomas's social psychology: the four inherent wishes of human beings (desire for novel stimulations, desire for recognition by others, desire for mastery and control, and the desire for security), the focus on the formation of attitudes of individuals in relation to society and social norms, and the importance (and often great variability) of the way individuals, societies, and cultures define the meaning of human situations. The focus on values, the national question, and the distinction between the nuclear and extended peasant family, on the other hand, came rather from the interests of Znaniecki. It has been argued that the concern for the human situation of peasants from an underdeveloped rural area trying to adapt to a modern

American urban area likely reflects Thomas's own life experience, and the social distance he traveled from Appalachian country boy to cosmopolitan professor at the University of Chicago.

In 1918, before full publication of *The Polish Peasant*, Thomas was caught on a private trip with the wife of an Army officer and was charged with violating the Mann Act, which forbade the transport of girls and women across state lines for immoral purposes. The ensuing scandal led to his dismissal from the University of Chicago, and he never held long-term regular academic employment again, instead teaching at a variety of institutions and devoting himself to his research projects. The most significant of his later works include *The Unadjusted Girl* (1923) and *Primitive Behavior* (1937).—Paul J. Radzilowski

BIBLIOGRAPHY AND FURTHER READING: Bogardus, Emory C. "The Sociology of William I. Thomas." *Sociology and Social Research* 34 (1949): 34–48; Burgess, Ernest W. "William I. Thomas as a Teacher." *Sociology and Social Research* 32 (1948): 760–764; Coser, Lewis A. "William I. Thomas." In *Masters of Sociological Thought: Ideas in Historical and Social Context*, 2nd ed., 530–536. New York: Harcourt, 1977; Thomas, Evan A. "The Collaboration of William I. Thomas and Florian Znaniecki: A Significant Event in the History of Polish and American Cultural Connections." *Polish American Studies* 49, no. 1 (Spring 1992): 67–75; Thomas, William I. *Primitive Behavior: An Introduction to the Social Sciences*. New York: McGraw-Hill, 1937; Thomas, William I., and Florian Znaniecki. *The Polish Peasant in Europe and America*. 5 vols. Chicago: University of Chicago Press; Boston: Badger Press, 1918–1920; Znaniecki, Florian. "William I. Thomas as a Collaborator." *Sociology and Social Research* 32 (1948): 765–767. *See also* IMMIGRATION IN THE UNITED STATES (HISTORICAL OVERVIEW); SOCIOLOGY: A CATHOLIC CRITIQUE; SOCIOLOGY, CHICAGO SCHOOL OF; ZNANIECKI, FLORIAN

TOLKIEN, J. R. R. (1892–1973) Born in South Africa of English parents, the future fantasy writer and Oxford linguist J. R. R. Tolkien was already living in England by age three. His outlook and self-image would exemplify a rural, pastoral England that was already disappearing in the early 20th century, but that would significantly influence the rich setting of his imaginary literary creations. Tolkien suffered the loss of his father at the age of four, followed by the death of his mother eight years later.

Tolkien's mother had a major influence on her famous son in spite of her early death. She made the bold decision in the England of that time to leave the Anglican Church and be received into the Catholic Church. The hostility of most of her relatives to this dramatic move is said to have, in Tolkien's eyes at least, contributed to her death at the young age of 34. She zealously raised her two sons in her newfound Catholic faith. This momentous decision by his mother is likely the most influential formative event of Tolkien's youth. Until his death, Tolkien would be a devout practicing Roman Catholic, stubbornly loyal to the faith for which his widowed mother was willing to suffer the loss of financial support from her relatives. In 1953, Tolkien described *The Lord of the Rings* (1954–1955), his most famous and massive work, written as a sequel to *The Hobbit* (1937), as "a fundamentally religious and Catholic work; unconsciously so at first, but consciously in the revision." Mabel Tolkien was also an educated woman who first introduced Tolkien to the study of other languages, a lifelong interest that would be central to his academic and writing career.

The Shire of Tolkien's works reflects the pastoral England of Tolkien's early childhood memory. The reluctant adventurers Bilbo and Frodo Baggins come from a content and introspective setting, not from our now common, frenzied cosmopolitan cities. The origin of the hobbit adventurers is similar to that of Cervantes's Don Quixote, the Spanish adventurer who emerges from the stark plains of La Mancha in rural Castile—not from Madrid—to reaffirm old-fashioned chivalrous values. The parallel to Don Quixote is biographically well founded. Before her death, Tolkien's mother appointed Father Francis Morgan as guardian for her two boys. The Spanish-speaking Father Morgan was apparently of Anglo-Spanish descent due to his family's connections to the sherry trade, and his library of Spanish books provided the young Tolkien with early exposure to Spanish literature and language. T. A. Shippy, a prominent Tolkien scholar, justly compares the duo of Frodo and Sam Gamgee to that of Don Quixote and Sancho. What is apparent is that Tolkien clearly seems to prefer the simple folk beyond the urban megalopolis. This preference is consistent with Tolkien's known dislike for industry's invasion of the countryside. Tolkien would likely sympathize with the "small is better" view popularized by humanistic economist E. F. Schumacher.

The clear contrast to the sane, human scale of the Shire is the crazed military-industrial complex created by the evil wizard Saruman in Isengard in his quest to conquer Middle-earth, a quest manipulated by the ultimate evil power of Sauron. The clanging noise, gluttonous felling of trees, and smoky hyperactivity, all directed by one megalomaniac figure, depicts the social opposite of the bucolic, peaceful, and content Shire in which each individual lives within sane limits. The parallel to the Catholic principle of subsidiarity is fruitful: both this principle of Catholic social doctrine and *The Lord of the Rings* share an aversion to and suspicion of excessive scale in social organization and activity. Tolkien's distaste for large, impersonal organizations and forces may account for part of the trilogy's continuing popularity, which blossomed in the United States in the confused, antiestablishment turmoil of the 1960s.

To the probable surprise of many today, the old-fashioned, strictly Catholic Tolkien presents a powerful literary "green" view of the world. As a prime example of this view, we have the delightful and pivotal role of the Ents, giant walking and talking trees, in defeating the forces of evil in *The Lord of the Rings*, a role that testifies to Tolkien's confirmed love of trees and of the natural life and beauty that trees powerfully incarnate and represent. Yet, any surprise today toward Tolkien as a very contemporary exponent of the green perspective is misplaced once people recall the lavish biblical celebration of creation, St. Francis of Assisi, and the Catholic Church's continuing suspicion of the harmful effects of unrestrained market or state capitalism in its social teachings.

Yet, this green view is never isolated from the wider moral battle between good and evil and remains just one dimension of that wider conflict. Since ancient times—as exemplified, for example, in the *Aeneid*—the virtue of piety is seen as the restraint and humility of the successful epic hero who refuses the temptation to megalomania, in contrast to the wizard Saruman who surrendered to it. Tolkien emphasizes in his masterwork how the refusal to use highly convenient evil means, such as the ring, even for good ends, is the key to moral survival and the triumph of good over evil. This theme of the relation of means and ends is quite relevant to the modern rejection of unpopular Catholic teachings on sexual morality, especially regarding contraception, abortion, and reproductive technologies. Thus, the theme of the corruption of power represented by the ring is even more central to *Lord of the Rings* than the green dimension. Wanton destruction of the Earth or of goodness itself emerges from unrestrained lust for power, incited by the alluringly seductive and very "technologically" effective ring. An obvious suspicion of concentration of power is evident, again consistent with the principle of subsidiarity, which favors the least intrusive and least bureaucratic response to social problems. The social vision of Tolkien is thus wise, not

simplistically ideological, in its sophisticated and shrewd recognition of the dangers of the human lust for power even when the goals are ostensibly presented as good, as done by Saruman in his attempt to win over to his schemes the good wizard Gandalf.

Another detectable social theme in *The Lord of the Rings* is that of hierarchy and egalitarianism. Again, the picture is not simplistically ideological but nuanced, as one would expect in a great work of literature. The relation of Frodo and Sam, as noted before, parallels that of the knight Don Quixote and the humble squire Sancho. The knight and the peasant are inseparable, yet the social class distinction is obvious in both pairs of adventurers. Tolkien's fantasy world is one in which hierarchy (kings, queens, stewards, commoners) is accepted as normal. Yet, in the Shire at least, the hierarchy is quite softened and indirect. Sam certainly acts as the social inferior of Frodo; yet, there is no trace of humiliating or debasing subservience by Sam or of the brutal exercise of raw superior power by Frodo. Their differing social status is overwhelmed by the reality of a deep and deepening affectionate friendship as their tribulations proliferate. The same trend is seen in the Don Quixote–Sancho pairing. Easygoing friendship in the face of hardship makes differing social status nonproblematic both in the Shire world and in La Mancha. In contrast, the world of Saruman, Sauron, and their Orcs is marked by the exercise of the raw power of command. There is no bond of friendship, as the savage infighting and arguments among the orcs and Saruman's break with Gandalf demonstrate.

The depictions of Shire society are also marked by a strong "middle-class" aura: Hobbits occupy different social stations, but on the whole, no impression is created of a wide social chasm or of any master–slave mentality. Just as Cervantes's work can be viewed as a critique of the social distance of that time, so today the generally egalitarian nature of the Shire can likewise be viewed as a critique of modern society's obsession with credentials and relative prestige. Deep friendship freely and easily crosses social boundaries.

Finally, Tolkien portrayed the origins of the world presented in *The Lord of the Rings* in a work long dear to his heart, *The Silmarillion* (1977). This posthumously published work, in a way, provides a "sociological" catalogue of the diverse characters determining the fate of Middle-earth and recites the origins of the struggle between good and evil in Middle-earth. Ilúvatar, the chief and omnipotent creator, creates the most powerful beings, the Valar, who sing the world into being and govern creation in an almost godlike capacity. The Elves, while not as powerful as the Valar, are endowed with extraordinary beauty and wisdom, as well as immortality. In contrast to the Elves, Men are mortal. Otherwise, Men share with the Elves many traits, but to a lesser qualitative degree.

In *The Silmarillion*, the refusal to accept one's place in the world (i.e., a "*non serviam*") by magnifying one's allotted role has enormous consequences. Out of a desire to increase his own importance and power, Melkor, the mightiest Valar, introduces discord into the harmonious song of Ilúvatar. Eventually, Melkor's desire for domination makes him a Satanic figure and the chief antagonist to Ilúvatar. Fëanor, one of the mightiest of the Elves, creates extraordinarily beautiful jewels called "silmarils," the name from which the title *Silmarillion* derives. The silmarils in turn exert a corrupting influence on Fëanor, who becomes jealously possessive of them. When the silmarils are stolen by Melkor, Fëanor and his sons swear an oath to destroy anyone, good or evil, who takes or holds a silmaril. Through this oath, the pride and greed of Fëanor, even after death, result in the misfortune of many throughout the course of *The Silmarillion*. The disordered desires of Melkor and Fëanor ultimately lead to their destruction. The narratives of *The Silmarillion* show that when characters act in a way that contradicts their uniquely assigned identities, they harm not only themselves or only one class of beings, but the entire created order.—Oswald Sobrino and Elena J. Sobrino

BIBLIOGRAPHY AND FURTHER READING: Becker, Alida, ed. *A Tolkien Treasury*. Philadelphia: Running Press, 1989 (with essays by W. H. Auden, Colin Wilson, and Edmund Wilson); Carpenter, Humphrey. *J. R. R. Tolkien: A Biography*. New York: Houghton Mifflin, 2000; Carpenter, Humphrey, ed., with Christopher Tolkien. *The Letters of J. R. R. Tolkien*. New York: Houghton Mifflin, 2000; Pearce, Joseph. *Tolkien: Man and Myth*. San Francisco: Ignatius Press, 1998; Shippey, T. A. *J. R. R. Tolkien: Author of the Century*. New York: Houghton Mifflin, 2002; Shippey, T. A. *The Road to Middle-earth: How J. R. R. Tolkien Created a New Mythology*. New York: Houghton Mifflin, 2003; Tolkien, J. R. R. *The Tolkien Reader*. New York: Ballantine Books, 1966. *See also* BELLOC, HILAIRE; CAPITALISM; CHESTERTON, GILBERT KEITH; INDUSTRIALIZATION; LITERATURE; SUBSIDIARITY

TOLSTOY, LEV (LEO) NIKOLAEVICH (1828–1910)

Possibly the most well known Russian writer of the 19th century, Leo Tolstoy presents a unique challenge to his readers due to the diversity of his accomplishments and the dynamism of his thought: in his long and multifaceted career, Tolstoy succeeded as a brave soldier, a brilliant fiction writer, an innovative pedagogue, a controversial political philosopher, a scathing social critic, a wealthy landowner, and a prophetic head of a new religious movement (the Tolstoyans).

Born September 9, 1828, at the idyllic family estate of Yasnaya Polyana, south of Moscow, Tolstoy inherited this beautiful land in 1847 and maintained it as his home until his final "escape," which ended tragically with his sudden illness and death at the unknown railway station of Astapovo. Tolstoy lost his mother at two and his father at nine, so after his happy early childhood spent in Yasnaya, he was passed through the hands of several relatives that lived in various places. Perhaps due to this displacement and despite enjoying all the typical comforts of his social station, Tolstoy eventually developed a profoundly antagonistic attitude to his class and all its privileges.

In 1844, Tolstoy began his studies at Kazan University with unsystematic readings in Rousseau, Dickens, and Schiller, displaying an early and serious interest in moral philosophy. By 1847, he decided to leave the university without any degree and to settle down at his family estate. From 1851 to 1854, Tolstoy served in the army, taking active part in the wretched Crimean War. In 1862, he married Sophia Bers, who brought him decades of genuine family bliss, bearing 13 children and sharing her husband's every endeavor.

Although his literary debut with the autobiographical trilogy *Childhood* (1852), *Boyhood* (1854), and *Youth* (1856) gained immediate and enthusiastic acclaim, Tolstoy never relished his popularity, and in 1859 he resolved to abandon artistic pursuits for more serious endeavors of managing his estate and educating his serfs' children. His pedagogical activity and the many duties of a busy country squire and paterfamilias did not, however, preclude Tolstoy from finishing his monumental novel *War and Peace* (1869). His literature for children also gained recognition and was adopted by many nations' schools. In the mid-1870s, during his work on the second large novel *Anna Karenina* (1877), Tolstoy was assailed by intense doubts about the meaningfulness of human existence and suffered from severe depression and suicidal thoughts. The climax of this crisis is known as Tolstoy's "conversion" into the worldview of human significance grounded in service to the moral ideals of Christianity. Hence, 1878 is held by many as a divide between the Tolstoy of the brilliant literary output and the Tolstoy of the extremist anarchist polemic.

The publication of Tolstoy's *Confession* (1882) was stopped by the censor, as were other writings that followed this watershed text, which, as Tolstoy himself noted, broke completely from his previous literary aspirations. In spite of the factual validity of Tolstoy's break from the style and content of his earlier fiction writing, a certain continuity of themes, philosophical concerns, and even expressive techniques exists between the novelist Tolstoy and the publicist Tolstoy. Such leitmotifs as (1) deromanticizing patriotic heroism, military valor, class distinction, personal glory, and other traditional ideals; (2) insistent pursuit of Truth through meticulous and often malicious-sounding examination of human consciousness and activity; and (3) courageous probing of the conflicted relationship between the individual and the collective, all continue to occupy Tolstoy's attention in his nonfiction writings. Moreover, Tolstoy never stopped using estrangement to represent familiar and routinely accepted social and political phenomena in unrecognizably different and disturbing light. Tolstoy's ethical argument often depends on showing the sheer absurdity of contemporary culture, which justifies and glorifies the most base and egotistical impulses while still promoting elevated Christian ethics.

From 1880 to 1883, Tolstoy wrote three books on religion: *A Study of Dogmatic Theology, A Harmony and Translation of the Four Gospels*, and *What I Believe*, and from this time on, devoted all of his energy to a methodical explication and impassioned defense of his religious views. As a teacher of a radically new way of life, Tolstoy engaged an astonishing variety of political and cultural topics: socialism, anarchism, pacifism, colonialism, capital punishment, vegetarianism, human mortality and sexuality, public health and education, famine, and countless others. In his essay *On Life* (1886–1887), Tolstoy expressed his dualistic view of human existence comprised of the inauthentic and evil life of the body and life's true and good spiritual essence. *What Then Should We Do?* (1886) articulated most clearly Tolstoy's socialist thought by proposing a complete abolition of money and private property as a genuine and realistic solution to the problem of poverty. Here, Tolstoy condemned philanthropy as hypocritical, for it assisted the poor without eliminating poverty.

The Kingdom of God Is within You (1893) developed at length two major themes of Tolstoy's religious thought: anarchism and nonresistance to evil, both of which Tolstoy presented as key Christian concepts rejected by organized Christianity but propagated by sectarians both in Russia and abroad. In this large polemic, Tolstoy first demonstrated how the Christian message of forgiveness, meekness, and peace contradicted aggressive Christian practices of division and strife. According to Tolstoy, the antiauthoritarian and anticlerical content of the Gospels annuls all forms of organized religion as well as all governmental institutions.

After enumerating all the known examples of Christian resistance to violence and hierarchy, and regretfully admitting that these instances of Christian anarchism have been so few, the bulk of the text then treats the history of what Tolstoy sees as a "perversion" of the Gospel message and establishment of Christian governments supported by churches. Tolstoy claims that the transformative moral teachings of Christ were deliberately obfuscated by religious doctrines and too hastily dismissed by the modern scientific, or secular, worldview. Such shocking absence of clear spiritual orientation in life naturally produced intense contradiction, tension, and suffering within Christian civilization.

Because Tolstoy defined Christ's message as a rational instruction of the human will to become progressively more harmonized and eventually merged with the transcendent source of all life—that is, God—he finds its clearest expression in the Sermon on the Mount. Thus, to live for God, as a true child of God, every Christian should labor toward the establishment of human brotherhood based on the law of equality and love. Tolstoy understood human brotherhood not simply as a collective but as an equal relation of every member to his or her divine existential foundation in God. Thus, Tolstoy denied any mystical content of Christ's message and took it as a reasonable call to a total reformation of human life on egalitarian and peaceful principles.

Consequentially, Tolstoy rejected both capitalism, which promoted violent exploitation of the labor force, and Marxism, which promised to be no less violent. Hence, Lenin's definition of Tolstoy as a "mirror of the Russian Revolution" is deliberately false, since Tolstoy offered his contemporaries a genuinely revolutionary solution to the present cultural contradiction (between egalitarian ideals of the West and its oppressive practices): total abstinence from human addiction to power. If the violence continued, Tolstoy prophesied a real and immediate endangerment not only to human rationality but to human survival itself.

Despite the conventional view of Tolstoy as a skeptic and a pessimist, he remained hopeful about the final triumph of the Kingdom of God within each soul. Meanwhile, he encouraged believers to refuse participation in such government-enforced activities as taxes, oaths, jury duty, and military service.

Both Tolstoy's polemical writings and his late fiction works, particularly stories like "The Death of Ivan Ilyich" (1887), "The Kreutzer Sonata" (1889), and his last novel *Resurrection* (1899), forged his reputation as the "conscience of humanity." In the 1900s, Tolstoyan communities began to appear both in Russia and abroad. Countless pilgrims visited the writer daily, and via his correspondence, he influenced even more people in various parts of the world. For example, *The Kingdom of God* produced a life-changing effect on Mohandas Gandhi, who adopted many of Tolstoy's principles for his own pedagogical and political undertakings.

Simultaneously, Tolstoy became a divisive figure in Russia, especially after the Orthodox Church excommunicated him as a heretic in 1901. His followers suffered governmental reprisals, and most of his post-1880 writings were banned. This reaction to Tolstoy's theological writings stems not exclusively from their radical ideas but also from their irritating and irreverent tone of moral certitude, rationalistic reductionism, vitriolic parody, peremptory didacticism, and cultural nihilism. Overall, Tolstoy's late thought displayed a genuine pathos of urgency and sincerity combined with a highly intolerant spirit of what Mikhail Bakhtin calls "monologism," or linguistic practice that finalizes all discussion rather than stimulates dialogue. Having denounced all existing forms of cultural creativity, Tolstoy promoted highly simplistic ways of being in the world: agrarian ("bread") labor, nonacquisitive communal economy, anarchy, asceticism, vegetarianism, extreme self-sufficiency, and independence.—Svetlana Corwin

BIBLIOGRAPHY AND FURTHER READING: Boot, Alexander. *God and Man According to Tolstoy.* New York: Palgrave Macmillan, 2009; Gustafson, Richard. *Leo Tolstoy: Resident and Stranger.* Princeton, NJ: Princeton University Press, 1986; Kaufmann, Walter, ed. *Religion from Tolstoy to Camus.* New Brunswick, NJ: Transaction, 1994; Matual, David. *Tolstoy's Translation of the Gospels: A Critical Study.* Lewiston, NY: Edwin Mellen, 1992; Medzhibovskaya, Inessa. *Tolstoy and the Religious Culture of His Time: A Biography of a Long Conversion, 1845–1885.* Lanham, MD: Lexington Books, 2008; Nickell, William. *The Death of Tolstoy: Russia on the Eve, Astapovo Station, 1910.* Ithaca, NY: Cornell University Press, 2010; Orwin, Donna Tussing, ed. *The Cambridge Companion to Tolstoy.* New York: Cambridge University Press, 2002; *See also* DOSTOEVSKY, FYODOR MIKHAILOVICH; LITERATURE; NIHILISM; ORTHODOX CHURCHES, SOCIAL TEACHINGS OF; SOROKIN, PITIRIM ALEXANDROVITCH

TRADITION: ITS MEANING AND PURPOSE In an era when the notion of change is almost an obsession and the members of the leadership class call themselves progressives, history is a subject constantly being rewritten and tradition is regarded as the "heavy hand of the past," to be discarded. It is the new that is admired, the forward-looking that is encouraged, and independence from the past that is respected. Traditions, customs, and ceremonies are regarded as quaint observances best left to those suffering from nostalgia or to those who enjoy looking to the past rather than to the future.

However, there is a price to be paid by those who ignore their history. Wisdom can be hidden in the ways of the past. There are good reasons why certain traditions have persisted through time. Lessons from the past can provide guidance for the future. All this we know, and tension exists between the desire to move rapidly and confidently toward the future and the awareness that to abandon completely the past is to court disaster.

Edward Shils, in his book *Tradition*, gives the term *tradition* a broad definition. For him, it is anything that is transmitted or handed down from the past to the present. The definitive criterion is that it is passed down over a span of at least three generations. A "generation," of course, is of indeterminate duration, depending on circumstances. Within a school or college, for example, a generation may be four years; within a tribe or nation, it may be the average life span of the members. There are some traditions that have survived over countless generations, for example, monotheism.

In *The Meaning of Tradition*, French theologian Yves Congar, OP, refers to tradition as "the continual presence of a spirit and of a moral attitude, the continuity of an *ethos*." He cites the definition of tradition provided by French sociologist Mikel Dufrenne: "Tradition . . . implies a spontaneous assimilation of the past in understanding the present without a break in the continuity of a society's life and without considering the past as outmoded." With regard to the notion of continuity, Congar adds that tradition goes beyond mere continuity because it also contains movement and progress in positive values. Thus, tradition continues the past but also goes beyond it, adding to it, improving it, and discarding what is nonessential.

There are three crucial institutions in the work of transmitting tradition, according to Shils: schools, churches, and the family. The first two have a function that Shils says has an "irreducible intellectuality." The schools pass on skills and knowledge, whereas the churches pass on doctrine that centers on man's nature and purpose. The family, on the other hand, inculcates moral beliefs as well as patterns, images, and customs that are family centered. Together, these three institutions pass on the moral and intellectual beliefs that contribute to the basic structure of society. In Shils's words: "These institutions provide the internal spine and the outer frame of the culture which maintains a society. When they fail to do so, the society is in danger of losing its character as a society."

Thus, there is a correlation between the functions of the schools, churches, and families and the well-being of society. The weakening of these institutions is followed by a decline in both the intellectual and moral virtues of the citizenry. As citizens become less understanding of and less cooperative with the legal function of society, that is, less law-abiding, there is a need for even more laws and law enforcement. Freedom under law is maximized with a virtuous people and minimized with a decline in virtue.

Despite living in an era of great flux, Shils points out that the social life of many nations is lived under the influence of enduring institutions and under rules from a long-standing past. Most people seem to realize instinctively that there are inherent values worth preserving and forces for social stability worth maintaining in the inheritance that has been passed down. It is the preservation of these old beliefs and customs that constitute conservatism in its proper meaning.

Aligned against the common people and their appreciation of what has been handed down over many generations are the forces of the educated and political elites who are enamored with the idea of progress. As Shils observes: "The novelty of the modern belief [in progress] is its assertion that it lies within human power to bring human existence closer to perfection on earth."

It is the antithetical view of the influential forces resident in the academy and the political order that has dampened the enthusiasm among ordinary citizens for practices of the past. Since no one wants to be considered "stuck in the past" and therefore backward, the authentic meaning and value of tradition have grown dim in the minds of the people. This is especially true of the young, who are told that they are the hope of the future and that they must throw off the influences of hearth and church and become "independent" and "authentic individuals." What is lost as a result of the influence of progress is what Shils calls "substantive traditionality," which he defines as "the appreciation of the accomplishment and wisdom of the past and of the institutions especially impregnated with tradition, as well as the desirability of regarding patterns inherited from the past as valid guides."

The outlook of the Enlightenment, with its worship of analytical reason and scientific knowledge, has been substituted for substantive traditionality. As a result, Christian religious beliefs, respect for authority, and what Richard Weaver in *Ideas Have Consequences* calls the need for a "threefold piety"—respect for nature, our neighbor, and the past—have been weakened.

James Kurth, in an article entitled "Western Civilization: Our Tradition," elaborates further on the three traditions to which Western civilization is heir: the Classical culture of Greece and Rome; the Christian religion, particularly Western Christianity, and the Enlightenment of the modern era. With regard to the first, Kurth tells us, Greece passed on the ideas of a republic and of liberty, and Rome passed on the ideas of empire and law. When combined, the Classical tradition passed on the important concept of liberty under law.

Christian tradition further strengthened this concept of liberty under law when it established the sanctity of the individual person and called for obedience to an otherworldly authority that ruled over both peasant and king. American theologian John Courtney Murray, SJ, in *We Hold These Truths: Catholic Reflections on the American Proposition*, confirms Kurth's view with his observation that "the new Christian view was based on a radical distinction between the order of the sacred and the order of the secular." Murray quotes Pope Gelasius I, who in 494 wrote to the Byzantine emperor Anastasius I: "Two there are, august Emperor, by which the world is ruled on original and sovereign right—the consecrated authority of the priesthood and the royal power." Says Murray: "The emphasis on the word 'two' bespoke the revolutionary character of the Christian dispensation."

The third tradition, that of the Enlightenment, provided the ideas of analytical reason and empirical science as the main sources of knowledge of the physical universe. It was also the source of the free market in economics and liberal democracy in government.

The Classical tradition survived in the United States, Kurth tells us, through the 1950s, but was overcome by the two forces of the democratic and commercial spirit that were the products of the Enlightenment. The waning of the Classical tradition led to the loss of such ideas as aristocracy, hierarchy, honor, and duty as integral to a sound education. These were supplanted by the doctrine of equalitarianism.

The death of Classical tradition was followed by an attack on Christian tradition. The faith in the power of reason and science as the only avenues to truth led to the denigration of religion and the natural-law moral position supported by the Catholic Church. The secular spirit took over the universities and the media and, with technological developments, led to a moral relativism that, in turn, led to the sexual revolution, the weakening of the family, and the legalization of abortion.

There is a more specialized meaning of the idea of tradition when it is used in its theological sense, especially by the Catholic Church. The Church distinguishes within revelation between Scripture and tradition, the first referring to that portion of revelation that has been written down by the inspired authors, both of the Old and the New Testament, and the second to the oral tradition that preceded the inspired word and was later collected in written form.

In the early Church, the oral tradition was the only normative tradition until about 150. By that time, the preaching of Jesus and his Disciples had been committed to writing in the New Testament and also became normative. A third source of tradition in addition to the Divine and the Apostolic is the ecclesiastical, which has its origin in the post-Apostolic Church. The authenticity of Sacred Scripture and Sacred Tradition is guaranteed through the work of the Holy Spirit acting through the Church. The Church maintains the deposit of faith, which includes the oral tradition, the sacraments, and the liturgy under the guidance of the Holy Spirit.

In the development of tradition, a special place must be given to the Greek and Latin Fathers of the early Church. These were men of learning who wrote commentaries on Scripture and defended the faith in the early centuries in the midst of controversies and schisms. Their writings are still studied today in the continuing search for further clarification of the orthodox position of the Church in matters of faith. Also important in understanding the notion of tradition is the role of the magisterium, the teaching authority of the Church, which is composed of the bishops under the leadership of the pope. It is the role of the magisterium to protect, authenticate, and declare the deposit of faith.

The teaching function of the church is divided into two categories. The first is the sacred magisterium, which deals with infallible teachings. These include the pope's ex cathedra pronouncements, decrees from ecumenical councils, and the teachings of what is called "the ordinary and universal magisterium." The second category is the ordinary magisterium, and this includes teachings that may be fallible. These include non–ex cathedra teachings of the pope, ecumenical councils,

and pronouncements of individual bishops. An example of fallible teachings would be the social teachings of the Church and papal or presbyterial theological teachings that fall under the heading of opinions.

The Catholic Church gives preeminence to the role of Sacred Scripture, but not an exclusive one. This is made clear in the Dogmatic Constitution on Revelation, *Dei Verbum*, which, following in the footsteps of the Council of Trent and the First Vatican Council, declared that a close connection existed between Scripture and tradition: "For both of them, flowing from the same Divine wellspring, in a certain way merge into a unity and tend toward the same end" (*DVb* # 9). Thus it is clear that the Church, under the guidance of the Holy Spirit, relies on two sources for the truths of Faith: Sacred Scripture and Sacred Tradition.—Robert A. Preston

BIBLIOGRAPHY AND FURTHER READING: Congar, Yves, OP. *The Meaning of Tradition.* Translated by A. N. Woodrow. San Francisco: Ignatius Press, 2004; Kurth, James. "Western Civilization, Our Tradition." *Intercollegiate Review*, Fall 2002/Spring 2004, 5–13; Murray, John Courtney, SJ. *We Hold These Truths: Catholic Reflections on the American Proposition.* Kansas City, MO: Sheed & Ward, 1960; Shils, Edward. *Tradition.* Chicago: University of Chicago Press, 1981. *See also* MAGISTERIUM; SHILS, EDWARD A.; TRADITIONALIST CATHOLIC MOVEMENT; WEAVER, RICHARD MALCOLM

TRANSHUMANISM *Transhumanism* refers to the attempt to free humanity from its biological limitations. Transhumanists advocate the use of various types of rapidly developing technology, especially bioengineering, to accomplish this purpose. Some transhumanists imagine the creation of a new type of human being with genetically engineered biological features so far removed from natural human biology as to warrant classification as "posthuman."

Sir Julian Huxley is credited with coining the term *transhumanism* in 1957. He wrote: "The human species can, if it wishes, transcend itself—not just sporadically, an individual here in one way, an individual in another way, but in its entirety, as humanity. We need a name for this new belief. Perhaps *transhumanism* will serve: man remaining man, but transcending himself by realizing new possibilities of and for his human nature." In a similar vein, the World Transhumanist Association defines transhumanism as "the intellectual and cultural movement that affirms the possibility and desirability of fundamentally improving the human condition through applied reason, especially developing and making widely available technologies to eliminate aging and to greatly enhance human intellectual, physical and psychological capacities." Political philosopher Francis Fukuyama, on the other hand, described transhumanism as the world's most dangerous idea.

There are four technological areas in which society has witnessed particularly rapid advancement in the past 20 to 30 years: biotechnology, information technology, wireless technology, and nanotechnology. These technologies enable us to do things inconceivable even a few decades ago. But these new potentials present new dimensions of ethical dilemmas.

Genetic engineering enables the genetic material of one type of being to be incorporated into the genetic material of another to produce a type of being never before seen in nature. For example, the genes of fireflies have been inserted into a tobacco plant to create a plant that glows in the dark. Cloning of animals, transgenic plants, and a host of other developments are historical events, not futuristic speculations. A U.S. patent application is on file detailing the creation of an artificial life form.

Such technology can be used for therapeutic and pharmaceutical purposes. Genetic engineering enables us to use living organisms—bacteria, for example—as miniature drug factories to manufacture pharmaceuticals that otherwise could not be produced. It has been proposed to use genetically modified viruses to introduce modified DNA into target organisms, for example, to overcome naturally occurring genetic abnormalities.

But portions of human genetic material can be merged with the genetic material of an animal to produce hybrid beings. It has been proposed to use genetic engineering to modify the DNA of animals to produce human-compatible organs for the purposes of organ harvesting and implantation into humans. But such technology can also enable the creation of human-animal hybrids. The ethical status of such beings remains a question.

Transhumanism also contemplates the modification of human DNA to produce "superior humans" with enhanced physical potentials. But any technology that can be used to create humans with enhanced potentials can also be used to create humans with inferior potentials. This topic was treated in *Brave New World* by Aldous Huxley.

Some transhumanists desire to escape mortality by integration of human beings with machines. There is already the possibility of implanting computer chips in the human brain. Neural implants, human–computer interfaces—these are concepts which just a few years

ago were the subjects of science fiction but are now the subjects of U.S. patents. One should also consider the possibility of wireless communication between a neural computer implant and some remote control center.

Transhumanization is, in some sense, an old concept. Dante Alighieri expressed the idea of transhumanization in canto 1 of *Paradiso*, written sometime in the early 1300s. Dante wrote: "To represent transhumanize in words / Is not possible, the example, then, suffice / Him for whom grace the experience reserves."

Transhumanization is not a concept alien to Christianity—rather, it is our Christian hope. But in Christianity, transhumanization is a matter of God's grace. Although we can begin the process of transhumanization in this life by living in the state of God's grace, completion of the process is meant for a future life, an eternal life, of intimacy with God. In our present life in this world, grace does not destroy or change human nature; it works *through* human nature and perfects it. Through grace we are transformed into an image of Christ. But we must await our resurrection for final transformation with new bodies in the world to come. In the journey of our life, we must take as our companions the Christian virtues of patience and perseverance.

In modern, technology-based transhumanism, one can see the philosophical influences of materialism, Enlightenment thinking, gnosticism, scientism, evolutionism, and secular humanism, which have plagued Western thought over the past few centuries. Ultimately, transhumanism arises from a repudiation of Divine Providence.

Proponents of transhumanism extol its potentials to improve human biology. However, it presents profound dangers to individuals and society. It is likely to become the new face of eugenics. We might have a society stratified into the genetically enhanced and the genetically deprived. As some transhumanists suggest, it would be considered unethical *not* to enhance the biological potentials of children. The state might even require parents to agree to the genetic enhancement of their children or face accusations of child abuse. Within a thoroughly secularized society where natural law and divine law are banished from public discourse, such a nightmare world is a likely outcome of transhumanism taken to its logical conclusion.

The Church has begun to examine transhumanism. The 2002 International Theological Commission document entitled *Communion and Stewardship: Human Persons Created in the Image of God* addresses some of the ethical issues raised by transhumanism. It warns against mankind usurping the role of God: "Neither science nor technology are ends in themselves; what is technically possible is not necessarily also reasonable or ethical." The document also considers cloning, germ-line genetic engineering, enhancement genetic engineering, and therapeutic interventions.—Adrian T. Calderone

BIBLIOGRAPHY AND FURTHER READING: Huxley, Julian. *Transhumanism: New Bottles for New Wine.* London: Chatto & Windus, 1957; International Theological Commission. *Communion and Stewardship: Human Persons Created in the Image of God.* Rome: International Theological Commission, 2002. *See also* DANTE ALIGHIERI; ENLIGHTENMENT, AGE OF THE; EVOLUTION; HUMANISM; SCIENTISM; UTOPIANISM

TYN, TOMAS, OP (1950–1990) Father Tomas Tyn is the perfect example of a saintly theologian writing and operating after the Second Vatican Council. He was endowed with a solid Thomistic formation centered on non-negotiable values of a dogmatic and moral character and animated by an intense priestly and consecrated life and a typically Dominican zeal to preach the truth.

Born in Brno, Czechoslovakia, on May 3, 1950, Tyn absorbed from his family Christian principles that the country's Communist regime hindered the profession of publicly. When only 12 years old, Tyn started expressing a vivid desire for priestly and religious life. Having completed his primary education in Brno, Tyn obtained a scholarship that allowed him to study for a bachelor's degree at the Lycée Carnot in Dijon, France, where he met the Dominican Father Henri-Marie Féret. He took advantage of his time in Dijon to study languages, both contemporary (German and Russian in addition to French) and ancient (Latin, Greek, and Hebrew). In the meantime, as a consequence of the Soviet invasion of Czechoslovakia in 1968, his parents and their two other children, Helena and Paul, were able to escape the country and found refuge in West Germany.

After obtaining his bachelor's degree in 1969, Tyn left France for Germany, where on September 28, 1969, he became a Dominican novice in Warburg, Westphalia. At the Dominican *studium* of nearby Walberberg, he studied philosophy and theology, getting a lectorate in theology with a dissertation on rest and motion in Plato. In 1972, he was attracted to the community of St. Dominic in Bologna, Italy, by the postconciliar *aggiornamento*, truthful to Church tradition, promoted by Father Enrico Rossetti. At St. Dominic's Church, Tyn pronounced his solemn vows on July 19, 1973.

Tyn's priestly ordination in Rome, by Pope Paul VI on June 29, 1975, was accompanied by the offering of his life for the freedom of the Church in Czechoslovakia. Shortly thereafter, he got his licentiate in theology with a bulky dissertation in Latin on divine grace and justification, written under the supervision of a well-known Dominican theologian, Father Alberto Galli. In his dissertation, Tyn compared the profound and faithful teaching of St. Thomas Aquinas with Martin Luther's mistakes, which still influence neo-modernist views. He then further explored this subject in his doctoral dissertation, completed in 1978 at the Angelicum under the direction of the French Dominican Felice Lagutaine.

Having returned to Bologna, Father Tyn taught moral theology at the Dominican studium, of which he became deputy principal in 1980. His teaching, always engaging and faithful to Church doctrine, also touched upon social ethics, and he did not shy away from confronting such evils as abortion or from exploring themes of family ethics, political systems, democracy, freedom and justice, economics, and education. Tyn's activities were not isolated to teaching, as he was actively engaged in preaching and apostolate within different settings, often to the benefit of unbelievers who were thus attracted to the Church. He was untiring, as well, in his sacramental ministry of the confessional and his direction of souls, some of whom he directed toward the consecrated life.

On Sundays, Tyn would walk for miles to celebrate Mass at St. James outside the Walls in Bologna, where he also showed his concern for the spiritual needs of engaged and newly married couples. In the convent life, he was a sociable and humble friar, always attentive to his religious brothers' ideas and always avoiding superfluous talk. He was fully committed to the Dominican rule of life and enjoyed friendship, the beauty of nature and art, and classical music.

A great lover of the liturgy, prayer, and contemplation, Tyn was piously devoted to Mass and the Holy Eucharist. While welcoming the liturgical reforms of the Second Vatican Council in continuity with Church tradition, he had special love for the Tridentine Mass, which he regularly celebrated. As a good Dominican, he was devoted to the Virgin Mary and to the Rosary, admiring the Marian spirituality of St. Louis-Marie de Montfort.

A regular participant in learned discussions among scientists, philosophers, and theologians, Tyn authored numerous writings, mainly on philosophical and theological subjects, some of which have not yet been published. His philosophical investigations led him to explore issues of metaphysics, rational theology, natural and social ethics, logic, and the theory of knowledge.

His favorite themes in theology were the theological virtues, the relationship between grace and free will, Mariology, and the Eucharist. Tyn's most significant scholarly contribution remains his volume on metaphysics and the concept of participation, *Metafisica della sostanza*. In this book, published posthumously in 1991, he discusses extensively the notion of "person," rejecting the idea that reduces it to pure relation and therefore recognizing the full dignity, as human persons, of embryos, the mentally disabled, and the dying, even when they have only a partial or diminished capacity to relate to others.

When only 39 years old, as his intellectual life was flourishing, Father Tyn was attacked by lung cancer, which led to his death in a couple of months amid great suffering, which he heroically accepted and did not prevent him from celebrating Mass until the end. He died at his family's house in Neckargemünd near Heidelberg, Germany, on January 1, 1990, while his motherland was being freed from the yoke of a Communist regime— and the vows of his ordination were accomplished. His remains are in the local cemetery of Neckargemünd. Shortly after his death, many in Italy (where he had lived his adult life) and the Czech Republic (where he is considered as a national hero) promoted the cause of his beatification, which was solemnly opened by the archbishop of Bologna, Cardinal Caffarra, on February 25, 2006.—Giovanni Cavalcoli, OP

BIBLIOGRAPHY AND FURTHER READING: Cavalcoli, Giovanni. *La liberazione della libertà: Il messaggio di P. Tomas Tyn ai giovani*. Verona: Fede & Cultura, 2008; Cavalcoli, Giovanni. *Padre Tomas Tyn, un tradizionalista postconciliare*. Verona: Fede & Cultura, 2007. Tyn, Tomas. *La beata sempre Vergine Maria Madre di Dio: Omelie mariane del servo di Dio Padre Tomáš Tyn*. Edited by Rosanna Schinco. Bologna: Carta Bianca Editore, 2009; Tyn, Tomas. *Metafisica della sostanza: Partecipazione e analogia entis*. Edited by Giovanni Cavalcoli. Verona: Fede & Cultura, 2009; *See also* AQUINAS, ST. THOMAS; COMMUNISM; DOMINIC, ST., AND THE DOMINICAN TRADITION; HUMAN LIFE (DIGNITY AND SANCTITY OF); MODERNISM AND NEO-MODERNISM; PLATO; POPE PAUL VI; TYRANNY AND TYRANNICIDE; VATICAN COUNCIL, SECOND

· V ·

VIANNEY, ST. JEAN-MARIE-BAPTISTE (1786–1859)

Jean-Marie Vianney was born on May 8, 1786, in the country village of Dardilly in France to Matthew and Marie, who were simple farmers, devout Catholics, and the parents of six children. Shortly after his birth, France was ravaged by the French Revolution and infamous Reign of Terror. Religion was banned, churches were closed, and church land was confiscated. Celebration of and attendance at Mass became a crime. As a result, some people turned against religion, and others became lax in keeping their faith. However, staunch Catholics continued to attend forbidden Masses in private homes, barns, and elsewhere, conducted by hunted priests. Such was the faith of the Vianney family.

One incident that speaks of the fervor of faith in the Vianney household took place prior to Jean-Marie's birth. In July 1770, his grandfather, Pierre Vianney, welcomed a mendicant monk into his home to share a meal. As it turned out, the wayfaring monk later became St. Benedict Joseph Labré. Jean-Marie's father, Matthew, never tired of telling this story as an illustration of Christian charity.

There are multiple determinants that shape the course of a person's life. We can understand the character and love of God of Jean-Marie Vianney by knowing his environment and influences from early on. His devotion to God and his fellow man was fostered by an exceptional Catholic upbringing by his parents. Vianney was not physically imposing. He had brown hair and blue eyes and was rather short and frail. Never did he manifest vanity or self-indulgence, and he contented himself with matters spiritual, not material. Vianney discerned as a teenager that his vocation was to be a priest. He received his First Holy Communion surreptitiously when he was 13 years old. Since public worship was forbidden, the joyous event took place in a private home, where an outlaw priest offered the Mass and administered the sacrament of Holy Communion to 15 children.

The Reign of Terror and persecution of the Catholic Church came to an abrupt halt when the first consul signed a concordat with the pope reestablishing the Church in France in 1802. At age 19, Vianney was able to enter a newly opened seminary in the nearby town of Écully. He was deficient in French grammar and Latin. Although he was promoted the next year to the major seminary of St. Irene in Lyons, he was dismissed after failing the term examination. The head of the minor seminary at Écully, Father Charles Balley, perceived a great holiness in Vianney, however, and resolved to tutor him. After a year of theology taught by Balley, Vianney passed his examination and was ordained on August 13, 1815, at age 29.

Father Vianney was appointed as assistant to his beloved mentor, Father Balley, who was also pastor of the church at Écully. Vianney was then appointed pastor of the church at Ars, whose young pastor, Father Antoine Deplace, succumbed to tuberculosis a month after his arrival. Ars was considered a backwater for the clergy. It was a very small town with four taverns and negligible religious zeal.

As the new curé of Ars, Vianney was determined to improve the faith and morals of his parish. Forthwith, he visited all the families of the village, from the mayor and uppermost citizens to the lowliest peasant. He helped the poor and needy, selling his personal possessions. The priest did not ignore the youth of Ars and its environs, either. In November 1824, Vianney purchased a small house near the church to be used as a school. Though Vianney had had little schooling when he was a child, he was a proponent of education and labored tirelessly for the cause. In so doing, he prepared disadvantaged youngsters for law-abiding, productive lives. Students who were orphans and destitute waifs were given free room and board. The house, named La Providence, became the school and domicile for girls, who were taught skills to make a living. For the boys in the parish, Vianney raised money with his begging cup to fund the construction of a Catholic school in 1849 and paid the tuition of needy boys.

Over 35 years at Ars, Father Vianney endeared himself to all the people of the parish and beyond. The transformation of Ars has been documented by pilgrims who flocked to see this holy priest of God. In a gift of grace for his singular piety and self-renunciation, God granted Vianney the ability to heal a nun's tuberculosis, a woman's paralyzed left arm, a man's paralyzed legs, a child who was blind, and another child who was blind and deaf. At least 30 miracles were accredited to Vianney, including 17 after his death. During the last year of his life in 1859, more than a hundred thousand pilgrims journeyed to Ars to receive his blessings and confession. On May 31, 1925, this dedicated priest was canonized a saint by Pope Pius XI, who 10 years later declared St. Jean-Marie Vianney to be the patron of all parish priests. The shrine holding the incorrupt body of the saint is at the church of Ars, where 500,000 people come each year.—Alexander LaPerchia

BIBLIOGRAPHY AND FURTHER READING: Cristiani, Leon. *Saint John Vianney: The Village Priest Who Fought God's Battles.* Boston: Pauline Books & Media, 1994; Rutler, George William. *Saint John Vianney: The Curé d'Ars Today.* San Francisco: Ignatius Press, 1988; Trochu, Francis. *The Curé d'Ars: St. Jean-Marie-Baptiste Vianney.* Rockland, IL: Tan Books, 1977. *See also* PARISH AS AN AGENT OF EVANGELIZATION

VOLTAIRE (1694–1778)   Voltaire was the pen name of François-Marie d'Arouet, a French writer, intellectual, and social reformer who played a primary role in promoting the philosophical movement known as the Enlightenment. He remains the best known of the 18th-century philosophers and is widely credited with setting the Western agenda for the following centuries.

Voltaire was born into a wealthy family of the lower French aristocracy. He received an excellent education from the Jesuits at the prestigious Collège Louis-le-Grand in Paris. Early in his youth, he became a playwright specializing in works of both mischievous satire (leading to his first confinement in the Bastille in 1717) and serious classicism (with his first theatrical success, *Oedipus*, in 1718). His talent for witty conversation made him a popular figure in literary circles.

Faced with charges of libel in 1726, Voltaire chose exile in England, ultimately spending three years there, during which time his philosophy began to mature. When he was allowed to return to France, Voltaire skillfully invested his family inheritance, achieving financial independence and freedom from the prevailing system of patronage.

His reestablishment in French society was so complete that by 1732 he was residing at the Court of Versailles. The 1734 publication of a work that promoted English natural philosophy provoked such controversy, however, that he was forced to flee Paris and find refuge at the estate of Emilie du Châtelet, who became his intellectual collaborator and lover until her death in 1749. The ultimate acceptance of Voltaire's defense of Newtonian science created a public view of Voltaire as a guardian of philosophical truth against error and prejudice.

Voltaire continued to write prodigiously, pouring forth works of drama, poetry, fiction, and narrative history. In 1745, he became royal historiographer of France, which led him to write a universal history that became his most influential work in his own lifetime, *Essais sur les moeurs et l'esprit des nations*. In the meantime, he joined the court of Frederick the Great in Prussia, a sojourn that ended badly when Voltaire was dismissed for causing intellectual dissension. Rather than returning to France, Voltaire purchased a chateau in Switzerland as his permanent residence.

From this point on, Voltaire devoted himself to fighting for what he termed the "party of humanity" against what he saw as fanaticism and superstition, a stance encapsulated in his famous motto, "*Écrasez l'infâme!*" ("Crush the infamy!"). To that end, Voltaire was an enthusiastic supporter of and contributor to the *Encyclopédie*, an attempt by French philosophers to encapsulate all wisdom that could be gained through human reason.

Voltaire often married philosophical reflection with social advocacy, as with his public defense of Jean Calas, a French Protestant erroneously executed for the murder of his son. In 1778, Voltaire made a triumphant return to Paris, welcomed by enormous crowds shouting, "Calas man!" Voltaire died only weeks later, probably the most famous man in Europe. He was denied a Christian burial but was ultimately interned in the Pantheon, in 1791, before a crowd of 200,000.

Voltaire's philosophy was not systematic. He was not an especially profound or original thinker (except perhaps in historiography—to which he contributed the concept of history as a form of social science), and he had no formal university training. His legacy remains strongest in its linkage of philosophical reflection with satirical polemicism on behalf of social reform, the strength of that linkage resting on intellectual assumptions in four areas: liberty, skepticism, science, and morality.

Those with the ability to use reason, Voltaire believed, were capable of choosing their own free actions through the prompting of the individual conscience. However, he never thought that most human beings, even if rigorously educated, would be capable of exercising the discipline and self-control necessary for wisdom. For the many who were not able to harness the potential of reason (those Voltaire referred to as "*la canaille*," "the rabble"), religion, backed by established political authority, would remain indispensable as the guarantor of public order. Thus, Voltaire supported a state religion that would confine itself to the public teaching of morality and to the maintenance of buildings, rites, and registers of births, weddings, and burials.

Voltaire's skepticism derived from his belief that no authority—especially the religious—should be free from the challenge of critical reason. Thus, although Voltaire was opposed to atheism and believed in a purposeful design to the universe, he was entirely hostile to clerical power, which he saw as responsible for oppression through the promotion of superstition. Therefore, almost everything he wrote was steeped in anticlericalism.

On the other hand, he was a strong proponent of the value of empirical science. In Voltaire's view, empirical and experimental reasoning was sufficient basis for gaining knowledge of universal and certain truth. To him, this contrasted with religious thinking, which promoted fallacy and caused sectarian disputation be-

cause it was based upon faith in irrational revelation that corrupt authorities used to promote obedience and docility.

Voltaire believed that morality should be determined by the positive valuation of material pleasure. This led him to attack what he saw as the repressive tradition of Catholic asceticism. In his view, the ultimate moral conclusion of the free rational conscience devoted to pleasure would be sociability and mutual benefit. This would, in turn, create a profound admiration and respect for the interests and opinions of others.

In sum, the philosophy Voltaire professed asserted that privileged men must have the freedom to apply rational criticism to institutions of power. To accomplish this, organized religions must diminish in authority. Scientific reasoning could then be used to determine morality for an enlightened society. Natural religion and the state were necessary to encourage socially beneficial behavior from the ordinary masses.

To fully comprehend the impact of Voltaire upon the Catholic Church, three factors must be considered: his historical context, the debt his thought owes to Catholic tradition, and the manner in which Catholics continue to address issues he raised using language he pioneered.

First, Voltaire lived during the autumn of Gallicanism. The Gallican church was semiautonomous from Rome, pseudo-conciliar in governance, and scornful of Tridentine reform. It was also closely allied to the French state. It was a church of aesthetic grandeur and high culture. It was also a church that gave its powerful positions to corrupt nobles and assiduously protected its property rights, while enforcing obedience and ruthlessly extracting wealth from poor parishioners whose faith was inarticulate and whose main role was to pay for the whole complex edifice. Though many French clerics criticized their ecclesiastical structures, the French church was incapable of reforming itself. It was this church that Voltaire criticized and sought to diminish. Indeed, it was the immorality of the French clerics and clerical structures of his time that principally offended Voltaire and convinced him that religious institutions failed at what he saw as their primary duty—instilling morality. He maintained a belief in the social need for a revealed religion that would be maintained as the dominant, though not exclusive, confession within a state.

Second, historians have noted many points of consensus between Enlightenment philosophy and Christian theology. Voltaire inherited many traits of Catholic thought, though he reconstituted their structure. He postulated truth as universal, though accessible to reason, not faith. He shared a conviction that beliefs should be reasonably demonstrated, but believed that such demonstration must be inductive, not deductive. And he shared a pessimism about human nature, though he did not identify it as sin; rather, he acknowledged a sort of natural weakness (though even here, he was probably reflecting his Jesuit education). Voltaire understood the limitations of reason, but differed from Catholicism on what constituted these limits; where Catholicism proposes that what is inaccessible to human reason is illuminated by faith, Voltaire believed that what is inaccessible to reason is nonsensical. He retained a belief in natural law—though independent from divine wisdom. His pursuit of human reform was a secular formulation of the idea of conversion—with education, not baptism, as its means of initiation. He had an intimate knowledge of the Bible and celebrated the person of Jesus, not as savior but as a great teacher of natural religion.

Finally, Voltaire, in secularizing certain Catholic understandings of the natural order and in virtually inventing the concept of public opinion, expanded the audience for these ideas. The debates Voltaire provoked concerning the possibilities and limitations of human reason, the origin and maintenance of morality, and the role and function of authority, along with the rhetoric he used to promote these debates and the audience to which he communicated them, resulted in a Catholicism that ultimately accommodated itself to, and used the language of, concepts such as respect for the human person, freedom of conscience, and contractual government to appeal to a more global public. While he sought to reduce the influence of the Catholic Church, he encouraged movement toward a faith and practice at once more personal and more profound. In this way, he was partially responsible for influencing the Catholic Church to adapt to, and become complicit in, the making of modernity.—Troy Feay

BIBLIOGRAPHY AND FURTHER READING: Gay, Peter. *The Enlightenment: An Interpretation*. Vol. 1, *The Rise of Modern Paganism*, rev. ed. New York: W. W. Norton, 1995; Israel, Jonathan. *Enlightenment Contests: Philosophy, Modernity, and the Emancipation of Man, 1670–1752*. Oxford: Oxford University Press, 2006; McMahon, Darrin M. *Enemies of the Enlightenment: The French Counter-Enlightenment and the Making of Modernity*. Oxford: Oxford University Press, 2001; Melton, James Van Horn. *The Rise of the Public in Enlightenment Europe*. Cambridge: Cambridge University Press, 2001; Pearson, Roger. *Voltaire Almighty: A Life in Pursuit of Freedom*. London: Bloomsbury, 2005; Saul, John Ralston. *Voltaire's Bastards: The Dictatorship of Reason in the West*. New York: Free Press, 1992; Van Kley, Dale K. "Christianity as Casualty and Chrysalis of Modernity: The Problem of Dechristianization in the French Revolution," *American Historical Review* 108, no. 4 (2003): 1081–1104; Zinsser, Judith. *La Dame d'Esprit: A Biography of the Marquise du Châtelet*. New York: Viking, 2006. *See also* ATHEISM; AUTHORITY; ENLIGHTENMENT, AGE OF THE; RATIONALISM; REASON

· W ·

WEAVER, RICHARD MALCOLM (1910–1963)

Although he wrote other books, including *Visions of Order* (1964), *The Ethics of Rhetoric* (1953), and *The Southern Tradition at Bay* (1968), Richard Weaver will always be known as the author of *Ideas Have Consequences* (1948), the book that brought him recognition as one of the leading intellectual conservatives of the mid-20th century.

Weaver was born in Weaverville, North Carolina, grew up in Lexington, Kentucky, and received his bachelor's degree in English (1932) from the University of Kentucky. He went on to receive a master's degree in English (1934) from Vanderbilt University and his doctorate in English (1943) from Louisiana State University. A very private person, this lifelong bachelor joined the faculty at the University of Chicago in September 1944 and taught there in the English Department until his untimely death on April 3, 1963.

Weaver was a critic of modern culture. The point of view from which he criticized the decline of Western civilization was that of *metaphysical realism*, a position that recognizes two realities: the reality of the universal (e.g., human nature), which is eternal and unchanging, and the reality of the particular (e.g., the individual person), which is temporal, spatial, and subject to change. Thus, each existing thing is an individual manifestation of a universal nature.

The opposing point of view, that of *nominalism*, recognizes only the reality of the individual. In the nominalistic view, the universal is a mental fiction that is useful for categorizing reality. It is only a name (*nomina* in Latin, from which comes nominalism). William of Ockham, a 14th-century Franciscan theologian, is the founder of nominalism, and Weaver argues that it is from this historical point that the decline of the West begins. He traces the downward trajectory from the High Middle Ages, with its metaphysical and theological concerns, to the rise of science, with its concern for the study of individual entities. No longer, Weaver points out, was there interest in what the world was for; rather, the dominant issue was how the world works.

If only the individual is real, then it follows that the knowable is coextensive with the sensible. But because the individual is subject to change, it further follows that it cannot be the basis for truth. Thus, truth—which must be based upon the reality of the unchanging, eternal, and universal—is denied and in its place is substituted the fact; thus the statements "It is true that . . ." and "It is a fact that . . ." become synonymous.

Weaver saw clearly the myriad implications that resulted from what he called the "fateful doctrine" of nominalism. He traces the cultural changes from a decline of the importance of religion in public life to the rise of a rampant secularism, from the movement in education away from the study of the Western intellectual tradition to an emphasis on careerism, and from a concern within society for the common good to a pursuit of the private good of each individual. These fundamental changes are reflected in a decline in moral life, family life, and cultural life, but are most manifest, Weaver claims, in the breakdown of community life. He sees as the fundamental problem a loss of common agreement on core issues. How, he asks in his lively rhetorical style, can men live together in harmony when they no longer agree on the basic questions of life?

This loss of basic agreement has led to the rise of what Weaver calls the "Great Stereopticon," which comprises the newspaper, the radio, and the motion picture. These conspire to provide to an unreflective public "a systematic indoctrination [in a materialistic worldview] from day to day of the whole citizenry through channels of information and entertainment."

What can be done to counteract this cultural decline? Weaver's answer is that we must find a way to get people to recognize the reality of the transcendent. One way to do this is through the study of language, because "all metaphysical community depends on the ability of men to understand one another." Also, "words in common human practice express something transcending the moment."

Thus, Weaver falls back upon that panacea of all reformers: proper education. For him, that would include teaching that man lives in a created order, in a moral universe, and that he is intelligent and free. Thus, the human person is able to grasp the meaning and purpose of life and to pursue justice under law. "Rational society is a mirror of the logos," Weaver writes, "and this means that it has a formal structure that enables apprehension."

One can only wonder how optimistic Weaver was that his analysis and recommendations would be heeded. His writings, however, are still worth reading because his prescience has been recognized.—Robert A. Preston

BIBLIOGRAPHY AND FURTHER READING: Smith, Ted, III, ed. *In Defense of Tradition: Collected Shorter Writings of Richard M. Weaver, 1929–1963*. Wilmington, DE: ISI Press, 2000; Weaver, Richard M. *The Ethics of Rhetoric*. Chicago: Regnery, 1953; Weaver, Richard M. *Ideas Have Consequences*. Chicago: University of Chicago Press, 1948; Weaver, Richard M. *Visions of Order*. Baton Rouge: Louisiana State University Press, 1964; Weaver, Richard M. *The Southern Tradition at Bay*. New Rochelle, NY: Arlington House, 1968. *See also* CONSERVATISM IN THE UNITED STATES; KIRK, RUSSELL AMOS; TRADITION: ITS MEANING AND PURPOSE

WILHELMSEN, FREDERICK D. (1923–1996)

Frederick D. Wilhelmsen, known as "Fritz" by his family and friends, was one of the 20th century's preeminent Thomistic philosophers. He was born on May 18, 1923, to Ed and Clare Wilhelmsen in Detroit. His father was a Danish Lutheran and his mother a Swiss Catholic. Young Fritz grew up in the Catholic ghetto of Detroit. His parents encouraged his studies, being especially careful to introduce him to the writings of such profound intellectual and spiritual Catholic scholars as John Henry Cardinal Newman, Christopher Dawson, and Hilaire Belloc. Later, Wilhelmsen would mature as a serious student of the thinking of the French Thomistic philosopher Jacques Maritain.

In Detroit, his parish church was the transcendent center of a higher calling in life, elevating him and his family above the mundane circumference of the secular world that was becoming ever more dominant in American society. James Lehrberger wrote of him: "From his youth on, Dr. Wilhelmsen put his talents and unflagging energy at the service of his Catholic faith. The very taproot of his life and the animating center of his thought was dedication to what he often called 'the Catholic thing.'"

Wilhelmsen entered the University of Detroit following high school, but left that institution to serve three years in the Army as a medic during World War II. While stationed in San Francisco, Wilhelmsen married Virginia Bretz, an Anglican who later converted to Catholicism. From that marriage came three daughters: Alexandra, Elizabeth, and Francesca Juliana. Following his honorable discharge from the Army, Wilhelmsen enrolled at the University of San Francisco and in 1947 earned his bachelor's degree in philosophy. Soon thereafter, he earned a master's degree in philosophy at the University of Notre Dame, studying under two noted students of Maritain, Msgr. Gerald Phelan and Yves Simon.

Wilhelmsen then accepted a teaching position at Santa Clara University. There, in 1956, he attracted international attention when he led a major public protest against President Dwight Eisenhower's refusal to aid the Hungarian freedom fighters in their fight against the Hungarian Communists.

After his brief term on the faculty at Santa Clara, Wilhelmsen moved to Spain, where he earned his doctorate in philosophy from the University of Madrid in 1958. He wrote his doctoral dissertation on Maritain's Thomism. Wilhelmsen then served on the faculty of University of Navarre in Pamplona.

In 1953, Wilhelmsen published the first of 16 scholarly books, *Hilaire Belloc, No Alienated Man: A Study in Christian Integration*, which was an expansion of his 1952 review "No Alienated Man" published in *America*. That review article was the first published of almost three hundred such efforts that spanned more than 40 years.

Following his stay at the University of Navarre, Wilhelmsen returned to the United States in 1965 and joined the faculty of the University of Dallas, where he would remain as a professor of philosophy and politics for the rest of his life. Wilhelmsen was part of a faculty team that established its graduate Institute of Philosophic Studies. Along with those developments, Wilhelmsen, with his Catholic intellectual reputation maturing, became increasingly in demand as a lecturer and visiting professor, accepting offers to serve in Argentina, Mexico, Peru, Nicaragua, and Iraq.

Meanwhile, in addition to his deepening understanding of the natural law and his dedication to the teachings of St. Thomas Aquinas, Wilhelmsen and his family were drawn to the Carlist cause in Spain. His publications were increasingly focused on Thomistic thought, and he interpreted the political struggles in Spain in part from this perspective. In common with such other Catholic scholars as Cardinal Newman and Dawson, Wilhelmsen saw political developments as having theological foundations. Lehrberger stressed this perception of Wilhelmsen's understanding of human history: "Since God took to himself human nature, human nature was validated in its own right. This was true above all for man's capacity to know the truth, i.e., for his reason or mind. Dr. Wilhelmsen's supreme faith in the Incarnation undergirded his unwavering confidence in the mind's capacity to know the real."

In addition to his scholarship, Wilhelmsen worked with L. Brent Bozell in publishing *Triumph*, a magazine that both Wilhelmsen and Bozell hoped would mature as an authentic Catholic voice of opinion while being the "journalistic organ of the Christian Commonwealth Institute" that Wilhelmsen and Bozell had founded. His work with *Triumph* began in 1966, shortly after he arrived at the University of Dallas, and continued for a decade.

At the heart of Wilhelmsen's view of a human society as a sacral (as opposed to a secular) world was his faith in the Catholic Church and its teachings. From his days as a youth in the Catholic part of Detroit, he saw what he clearly perceived as beauty of the highest kind in his parish church and all that it represented. This splendor of the divine he pursued all of his life, living his Catholic life to the fullest and defending the Church and its teaching.

On May 21, 1996, Wilhelmsen collapsed from a heart attack at his home and died en route to the hospital. No one spoke more clearly of Wilhelmsen than his former student and colleague R. A. Herrera, who wrote: "Fritz Wilhelmsen accomplished much and had the unusual merit of being more than what he accomplished. He was a profound and acute interpreter of St. Thomas, a political thinker of substance, and one of the first, together with his friend Marshall McLuhan, to explore the new and threatening horizon of electronic technology. Wilhelmsen was a writer of elan, an essayist of rare perception, something of a contemporary Belloc, a writer he admired and in many ways resembled."— Patrick Foley and Donald J. D'Elia

BIBLIOGRAPHY AND FURTHER READING: Herrera, R. A. "Frederick D. Wilhelmsen." *Catholic Social Science Review* 1 (1996): 283; Lehrberger, James, O. Cist. "Christian Troubadour: Frederick D. Wilhelmsen." *Intercollegiate Review* 32, no. 2 (1997); Wilhelmsen, Frederick D. *Citizen of Rome: Reflections from the Life of a Roman Catholic.* LaSalle, IL: Sherwood Sugden, 1980. *See also* AQUINAS, ST. THOMAS; MARITAIN, JACQUES; SIMON, YVES R.

WOMEN'S RELIGIOUS ORDERS AND THE SOCIAL APOSTOLATE

Women religious have made valuable contributions to the social apostolate of the Catholic Church throughout its history. Impelled by the love of God, they have undertaken many courageous works in the service of God and neighbor. They were especially important in the expansion and development of the Catholic Church in the United States and continue to meet important social needs today.

Women's religious communities can be generally divided into two groups: contemplative and active. Contemplative women support the apostolate of the Church through their lives of prayer, sacrifice, and union with God. The French Carmelite St. Thérèse of Lisieux (1873–1897) exemplifies this gift of fruitfulness in the enclosure. The lives of women contemplatives are a source of hidden vitality for the Church.

Active women religious also consider their vowed lives of union with God to be their greatest contribution to the Church. Traditionally, these women see themselves first of all as "brides of Christ" through their vows of poverty, chastity, and obedience. Their close union with Christ enables them to engage in apostolic works as spiritual mothers and sisters to all the children of God. The apostolate is seen as a sharing in the work of Christ, their spouse. Although the apostolate is secondary, there have been many cases in which women experienced Christ's call to religious life as a vocation to minister to him present in the needy.

The history of the social works of women religious in the Church is rich and varied, often with an emphasis on education and care of the sick. In the early Church, women dedicated to God through the practice of virginity served in their families and communities. Early monasteries for women were founded by saints such as North African bishop St. Augustine of Hippo (354–430) and Italian monk St. Benedict of Nursia (480–546). Augustinian religious sometimes nursed the sick, while the Benedictines contributed to the apostolate of the Church through the same works often associated with male Benedictines: hospitality, copying of manuscripts, preservation of culture, and serving as a spiritual center for the surrounding population.

During the Middle Ages, mendicant orders such as the Dominicans, Franciscans, and Carmelites arose. In these groups, the priests and brothers formed the First Order. Second Order contemplative sisters sometimes operated schools from their convents, while Third Order groups developed with more freedom of movement to serve apostolic needs in the Church. During these years, women religious worked in hospices, hospitals, and orphanages, taking care of pilgrims, teaching girls, and performing a variety of other works. After the Council of Trent (convened 1545), strict cloistering was enforced on contemplative sisters, as well as some Third Order religious who were temporarily forced to become cloistered contemplatives. To fill the resulting need, congregations devoted to particular active apostolates in the Church emerged.

In the United States, more than 400 communities of women religious have contributed to the social apostolate of the Church. They have been outstanding examples of holiness while providing much-needed labor and inspiration to the developing Church in America. It is impossible to catalogue the contributions of so many dedicated women; a description of a few of the most prominent communities must suffice. The works most commonly performed by religious sisters in the United States can be grouped into the three ministries of teaching, caring for orphans, and nursing.

One of the earliest communities in the United States that undertook the work of teaching was the Sisters of Charity. American founder St. Elizabeth Bayley Seton began this community in Emmitsburg, Maryland, in 1809. As their work expanded to include nursing and the care of orphans, the sisters of the initial foundation branched out to form six different congregations of religious sisters. The first of many communities of Dominican Sisters in the United States was established in 1822 at Bardstown, Kentucky; these teaching sisters founded a daughter house in Somerset, Ohio, in 1830. In 1847, the School Sisters of Notre Dame from Germany settled in Baltimore, Maryland; they expanded, doing substantial work through their service in many parochial schools. The Sisters of Charity of Providence came from Canada to open their first American house in 1856 in what would become the state of Washington, and from there, they rapidly spread through the west. The Missionary Sisters of the Sacred Heart of Jesus, founded by naturalized U.S. citizen St. Frances Xavier Cabrini, established its first American foundation in 1889; these sisters aided Italian immigrants by running orphanages and hospitals as well as schools.

In early years, religious communities often began their work of teaching by opening paying academies for refined girls in conjunction with free schools for the poor. In 1861, there were almost 1,500 Catholic schools in the United States. After the Civil War, there was an even greater expansion of parochial schools made possible principally by the availability of religious sisters. The Third Plenary Council of Baltimore (1884) identified parish schools as necessary to the development of the Church in the United States. The Council Fathers mandated that schools should be erected alongside parish churches whenever possible. In the east, parochial schools were seen as bastions of Catholic culture in the face of Protestantism. These schools were the key to preserving the Catholic faith of immigrant children as they became acculturated to their new country. In the west, Catholic schools were often the only ones available for the education of the population.

After 1920, Catholic high schools were founded in some locations. These were more likely to be established on the initiative of the local bishop than of women religious, although religious sisters served in many of them. In 1945, there were 2,000 Catholic high schools with sisters as teachers. The need to train sisters to teach also led to the establishment of Catholic colleges by women religious.

Some of the same communities that were involved in teaching were also important in the care of orphans. The first American Catholic orphanage was founded in Philadelphia in 1816 by Sr. Rose White of the Sisters of Charity, a branch of Mother Seton's foundation. French sisters of the Society of the Sacred Heart established their U.S. foundation in St. Charles, Missouri, in 1818 under the leadership of St. Rose Philippine Duchesne; these sisters ran orphanages, academies, and schools and were distinguished by their apostolate among the Native American peoples. The Congregation of the Sisters of the Holy Family was founded in the United States in 1842 by Sr. Henriette Delille; her congregation of black sisters operated orphanages, shelters for homeless women, and schools. By 1900, there were 322 Catholic orphanages in the United States, fulfilling a genuine need in the country. The number of orphanages gradually decreased during the next century, as life expectancy increased and government and work-funded social services grew.

In comparison to the other two apostolates, American Catholic nursing had a slow beginning. Most Catholic hospitals were founded after the Civil War, during which at least 580 sisters served as nurses on both sides. In the east, hospitals staffed by sisters helped Catholics, the poor, and ethnic immigrants who could not communicate with English-speaking doctors. Paralleling the situation of Catholic schools, Catholic hospitals often offered the only available medical services in the west.

Among the communities that were important in nursing were the Sisters of Mercy from Ireland, established in America in 1843. Also prominent were the Sisters of St. Joseph, who arrived from France in 1836 and established their first motherhouse in Carondelet, Missouri. American Rose Hawthorne Lathrop founded the Dominican Congregation of St. Rose of Lima in New York in 1896 to meet the needs of dying cancer patients; her sisters are also known as the Servants of Relief for Incurable Cancer. Various Franciscan congregations also distinguished themselves in the field of nursing. One notable offshoot of Franciscan hospital work is the renowned Mayo Clinic, which branched off from St. Mary's Hospital, opened in 1889 through the efforts of Mother Alfred Moes of the Sisters of St. Francis and Dr. W. W. Mayo.

Since the 1960s, many women religious have abandoned the traditional apostolates of their communities to pursue individual ministry working in such roles as prison chaplains, political lobbyists, and advocates for various causes of social justice. These changes in community life and apostolate have become sources of controversy since the Second Vatican Council.

At the same time, new foundations of women religious have arisen in order to meet current social needs. The Daughters of St. Paul, founded in 1915 in Italy, made its first American foundation in 1932. Its motherhouse is in Boston. The work of these women is to evangelize through promoting the Catholic press and media, and the scope of their work has expanded alongside the rapid growth of modern technology. Mother Mary Angelica, a Poor Clare nun from Alabama, made another important contribution to Catholic media in 1981 by launching the Eternal Word Television Network (EWTN), the world's first Catholic satellite television network.

New communities have also been founded to continue traditional apostolates. For example, the Dominican Sisters of Mary, Mother of the Eucharist was founded in 1997 in response to Pope John Paul II's call for a new evangelization. The sisters of this community are primarily teachers. They join previously existing communities in filling the continuing need for religious sisters in Catholic schools.

Other groups have come into existence to challenge the expansion of the modern "culture of death." Blessed Teresa of Calcutta opened her first American house of the Missionaries of Charity in 1971 to care for the "poorest of the poor"—those considered valueless or unreachable by mainstream society. The Sisters of Life, a group active in pro-life ministry, was founded in New York in 1991 by John Cardinal O'Connor to promote the sacredness of human life in his diocese.—Albert Marie Surmanski, OP

BIBLIOGRAPHY AND FURTHER READING: Dolan, Jay P. *The American Catholic Experience: A History from Colonial Times to the Present*. New York: Image Books, 1985; Fialka, John J. *Sisters: Catholic Nuns and the Making of America*. New York: St. Martin's Press, 2003; McCarthy, Thomas P., CSV. *Guide to the Catholic Sisterhoods in the United States*. Washington, DC: Catholic University of America Press, 2002; Stewart, George C., Jr. *Marvels of*

Charity: History of American Sisters and Nuns. Huntington, IN: Our Sunday Visitor, 1994. *See also* ANGELICA, MOTHER (RITA RIZZO); CABRINI, ST. FRANCES XAVIER; DREXEL, MOTHER KATHARINE; SETON, ST. ELIZABETH ANN BAYLEY; SISTERS OF LIFE

· X ·

XAVIER, ST. FRANCIS (1506–1552)   St. Francis Xavier was born on April 7, 1506, in his family's castle in the Kingdom of Navarre. When he was six years old, Navarre was overtaken by King Ferdinand of Aragon, resulting in financial harm to Francis's family. Thus, in 1525, Francis left his family and traveled to Paris to study at the College of St. Barbara where he formed friendships with Blessed Pierre Lefavre (Peter Favre) and St. Ignatius of Loyola. The charity and piety of Lefavre and Ignatius had a profound effect on Francis and brought about in him a conversion. Under the leadership of Ignatius, they and other confreres founded the Society of Jesus (Jesuits). On the Solemnity of Our Lady's Assumption in 1534, they took their first vows of poverty, chastity, and obedience at Montmartre. On June 24, 1537, Francis was ordained a priest.

After receiving his licentiate in philosophy, Francis Xavier traveled with Ignatius and his fellow Jesuits into Italy. Wherever he went, Francis displayed a great zeal for the corporal works of mercy. In Venice, he overcame his fear of physical infirmities by ministering to the incurables in hospitals. Later, after receiving a vision from St. Jerome, he traveled to Bologna, where he catechized children, visited those confined to prisons and hospitals, heard confessions, and preached in the piazzas. When he himself became sick, he was summoned to Rome, where he eventually recovered. There, he was also reunited with Ignatius, who was in the process of trying to convince Pope Paul III officially to declare the Jesuits a religious order in the Church. Temporarily, Francis became secretary to Ignatius before setting out in March 1540 for India to convert the Eastern lands conquered by the Portuguese.

Francis left Europe with the blessing of Paul III and the title of apostolic legate. He arrived at the port city of Goa, where he preached against the debauchery among the Portuguese colonialists, and then traveled to the Indian coast and preached there. Earnestly wishing to convert Indians, he successfully translated the Catechism, the Ten Commandments, the Ave Maria, and the Pater Noster into Malabar. Francis was so successful that he was reported to have converted whole villages in one day. In one month alone, he converted about 10,000 people. Children were especially attracted to him. Francis would instruct the children to teach their parents and other family members the fundamentals of the Catholic faith. Among adults, Francis's main pastoral concern was the elimination of idolatry. Not all of Francis's projects were fruitful, however. He tried but failed to convert the relatively peaceful Brahmins of the region. In some cases, the spread of Catholicism was inhibited by the cruelty and prejudice of the Portuguese and their savage raids against pagan Indians. Newly converted Christians suffered, too, being martyred for the faith that had been planted by Francis. Some of the native Indians, due to a lack of priests in the region, abandoned Christianity altogether and reverted to their old ways after Francis's departure.

After visiting the Shrine of St. Thomas the Apostle, Francis decided to travel to Malacca and the Moluccan Islands. On these islands, Francis converted both Muslims and pagans. He even converted Queen Neachile, a daughter of the king of Tidor. The presence of Christianity, however, was the occasion for persecution here, too. As in India, when Francis left Malacca and the Moluccas, some of the converted returned to their former way of living.

While in Malacca, Francis was introduced to a Japanese man, Anger (Han-Siro), who wished to be instructed in the ways of Christianity. Eventually, Anger was baptized with the Christian name Paul. With this, Francis began thinking of the conversion of Japan. In due course, he went to Japan and preached in Kagoshima, where he also studied Japanese and translated Catholic texts into a new language. He traveled throughout Japan, ministering in many different places and establishing small Christian communities. Francis entered into dialogue with the *bonzes* (Buddhist monks or clergy), even though this often led to heated arguments. Still, during trying moments, Francis exhibited a calm deportment and was unfailingly humble.

After spending more than two years in Japan, Francis returned to India. He immediately began envisioning the conversion of China, but died on the way to China on December 3, 1552, his eventual feast day. He is recognized as one of the greatest Jesuit saints and was canonized with Ignatius of Loyola in 1622. St. Francis Xavier's body was interred in Goa, the place of his mission—while his right arm, the arm with which he baptized, is enshrined in the Church of the Gesù in Rome.

The Protestant Reformation left great religious and political turmoil in Europe. The life of St. Francis

Xavier was an example of strength and vitality for the Church. He taught the Catechism and the Creed and took pains to have them translated into the native languages of the Far East. While Catholic theology was acrimoniously debated on the European continent, Francis placed emphasis on precisely those things that had come under attack in the Reformation: the sacraments and their institution by Christ, devotion to the Blessed Virgin Mary, and a meditational and sacrificial priesthood.

St. Francis Xavier was also a forerunner in the field of ecumenism. While preaching throughout the Far East, he encountered the adherents of all the great religious traditions, including Muslims, Buddhists, and Hindus. Without exception, he treated the leaders of these religions with complete respect. In return, he was held in high esteem, known throughout the East as the "holy Father."—Robert J. Batule and Thomas F.X. Varacalli

BIBLIOGRAPHY AND FURTHER READING: Biodrick, James. *Saint Francis Xavier.* New York: Wicklow Press, 1952; Coleridge, Henry J. *The Life and Letters of Saint Francis Xavier.* 2 vols. London: Burns & Oates, 1872; Montguerre, Jean-Marc. *Saint Francis Xavier.* Garden City, NY: Doubleday, 1963. *See also* IGNATIUS OF LOYOLA, ST.; SAINTS AND SOCIAL ACTION; SOCIETY OF JESUS; WORKS OF MERCY, CORPORAL AND SPIRITUAL

· Z ·

ZNANIECKI, FLORIAN (1882–1958) Florian Znaniecki was a Polish American sociologist and philosopher. He was born in Prussian Poland into a gentry family, which moved to the Russian partition when Znaniecki was very young. His early life was marked by discontinuities. As a youth, he had broad interests, but was most drawn to literature in the vein of the Polish romantic tradition, which still held strong sway among the Polish intellegentsia and which was strongly associated with the Polish national cause. Znaniecki as a youth gained modest acclaim as a lyric poet, but his attempts to produce larger-scale poetic works were judged failures by critics.

At the same time, under the influence of romantic nationalist messianism and the works of Friedrich Nietzsche, he dreamed of founding a new, optimistic "religion of humanity." Since he had discovered his poetic talents insufficient for such a grand purpose, Znaniecki turned his interests away from literature. Meanwhile, he was expelled from the University of Warsaw in 1902, after only one semester of study, for agitating against the authorities' policy of Russian-language-only education. He grew tired of courting the aristocracy, and since it remained the main patron of Polish-language culture in Warsaw in the face of official hostility, he decided to go abroad.

Attempting to re-create himself and become a man of the people, Znaniecki faked his own drowning in Switzerland and went off to join the French Foreign Legion. One month after arriving in French Algeria, however, he was injured on sentry duty and was discharged. The highly varied jobs he took in France proved unsatisfying, so he returned to school, studying philosophy, psychology, and sociology at the universities of Geneva, Zurich, and Paris (where he attended lectures by Emile Durkheim) and graduating eventually in 1910 with a doctorate in philosophy from the Jagiellonian University in Krakow, Austrian Poland.

Between 1910 and 1914, Znaniecki resided again in Warsaw, where he offered instruction in philosophy. He also became head of the Society for the Welfare of Emigrants, an organization that attempted to keep up the Polish diaspora's ties to the home country, as well as to inform Poles about the true prospects and dangers of emigration. Despite his other duties, he found time to publish several books in philosophy, along with many articles and reviews. These were intended to sketch out his own philosophical system, which stressed the primacy of the category of "values," regardless of whether such values were theoretical, aesthetic, moral, social, or religious. According to Znaniecki, *all* these kinds of values are in some degree cognitive and productive of knowledge about reality outside the mind, not just those linked with science or formal thought.

Agreeing with the pragmatists, Znaniecki stressed the primacy of human *action* in establishing and maintaining values, including those that are intellectual, religious, or spiritual in nature. Even perennial values to him were human creations, and at root all values were profoundly relative. Znaniecki took over from Henri Bergson the idea of creative evolution, although he rejected his biologism. He saw the role of intellectual and artist as furthering the evolution of culture by inventing new values, which are then passed to the rest of society.

In the primacy he gave to values, Znaniecki almost hypostatizes them: According to him, values are fundamental to philosophy and alone can bridge the gap in modern thought between the objective and subjective spheres, since they have both an individual, subjective manifestation and an exterior, objective, and social manifestation, while in themselves being neither objective or subjective. They also implicate the larger, nonhuman world, as well as the world of the human spirit.

In 1914, Znaniecki took up an offer from William I. Thomas, an American sociologist at the University of Chicago he had met in Warsaw, to come and help him in the United States in compiling a work on Polish immigrants. The result of their collaboration would be the five-volume *The Polish Peasant in Europe and America*, one of the monumental achievements of American sociology in the period. Although the work had already been conceived in large measure by Thomas, Znaniecki significantly shaped the theoretical aspect of the work, writing the methodological reflection in the first volume.

The work was devoted, in significant measure, to the question of social and cultural disorganization of peasant societies in emigration, as well as their attempts to reorganize themselves in the context of modern American society. Thomas and Znaniecki were rather more impressed with the disorganization of peasant society in the United States than its reorganization, and their work's attention to such social and moral problems as crime and out-of-wedlock births proved controversial among Polish American audiences. Znaniecki, for his part, was disappointed by what he saw as the limited cultural horizons of Polish Americans and their lack of interest in such intellectual leadership as he could provide. Nonetheless, the cooperation with Thomas proved formative of his later theoretical views. Thomas's interest in social psychology and especially social attitudes increased Znaniecki's interest in lived experience, as well as the way social realities mediate between values and the external human world.

Znaniecki returned to newly independent Poland in 1920 and took up a position in sociology at the University of Poznań, from which he exercised a strong influence on interwar Polish sociology. When World War II broke out, he was finishing a visiting professorship in the United States and elected to stay, settling by 1940 at the University of Illinois at Urbana-Champaign, where he remained for the rest of his life in the Sociology Department.

Znaniecki continued to research and write prolifically. His later work built off his work with Thomas, but tended to abandon his social psychological approaches. He regarded them as too rigid to account for the complexity of human society—focused as they were on the needs and drives of individuals. Instead, Znaniecki proposed a focus on social *roles*, defined as the total set of social functions, norms, and perceived realities invested in some definite activity in society. The role of the teacher, thus, would include all the teacher does and expects of himself professionally, as well as all the actions and expectations attached to his activity on the part of students and any others involved in his functioning. From interrelated social roles, larger social systems and societies derive.

His later work stresses culture and norms in shaping social realities, but to him the primary engine of *social change* remained changes in *values*, which end up over time being translated into new social norms. Although Znaniecki regarded himself as an empiricist and encouraged broad-based research of all kinds, he was not entirely happy with the postwar trend toward quantitative methods in sociology, regarding them as a retreat from real social theory—which to him was essentially humanistic—into a mere "saving of appearances."

Znaniecki was not in any strict sense a Catholic thinker, however much he endeavored to maintain proper personal relations with Polish and Polish American clergy. All religious practices, perceptions, and ideas seem to remain for him essentially human phenomena, created by man, however real (or beneficial) they may be in a social sense. His analysis of Polish peasant Catholicism is instructive in this regard. He differentiated within it three distinct religious systems typically under common Catholic names and symbols: besides conventional Catholic belief, there was a system of religious solidarity with all creation, as well as a system of pagan spirits and gods. All these were sequentially created by men in human history and were welded together on the surface of culture, although they remain *functionally* distinct. Znaniecki also identified certain aspects of Catholic sacramental belief as "magical." Yet his great interest in religion, culture, common values, and norms, as well as his suspicion of any crude reductionism applied to human realities, arguably show a lingering Catholic influence on his work.—Paul J. Radzilowski

BIBLIOGRAPHY AND FURTHER READING: Dulczewski, Zygmunt. *Florian Znaniecki: Życie i Dzieło (Florian Znaniecki: Life and Work)*. Poznań: Wydawnictwo, 1984; Thomas, Evan A. "The Collaboration of William I. Thomas and Florian Znaniecki." *Polish Review* 49, no. 1 (1992): 67–75; Thomas, William I., and Florian Znaniecki. *The Polish Peasant in Europe and America*. 5 vols. Chicago: University of Chicago Press, 1918–1920; Znaniecki, Florian. *Cultural Reality*. Chicago: University of Chicago Press, 1919; Znaniecki, Florian, et al. *What Are Sociological Problems?* Poznań: Wydawnictwo, 1994; Znaniecki-Lopata, Helena. "A Life Record of the Immigrant." *Society* 13, no. 1 (November–December 1975): 64–74. *See also* IMMIGRATION IN THE UNITED STATES (HISTORICAL OVERVIEW); SOCIOLOGY: A CATHOLIC CRITIQUE OF; THOMAS, WILLIAM I.

Index to Volume 3

List of Entries and Authors, Volumes 1–3

Contributors

Marynita Anderson, Nassau Community College–SUNY

Mike Aquilina, St. Paul Center for Biblical Theology

Rev. Robert John Araujo, SJ, Loyola University of Chicago Law School

Michael Barber, John Paul the Great Catholic University

Mary Ellen Barrett, *Long Island Catholic*

Most Rev. Msgr. Robert J. Batule, Seminary of the Immaculate Conception, Huntington, NY

Rev. John Berry, Anscombe Bioethics Centre

Michael J. Bolin, Wyoming Catholic College

David G. Bonagura Jr., Seminary of the Immaculate Conception, Huntington, NY, and Kellenberg Memorial High School, Long Island, NY

Patrick H. Breen, Providence College

Howard Bromberg, University of Michigan Law School

Grattan T. Brown, Belmont Abbey College

E. Christian Brugger, St. John Vianney Theological Seminary

Steven Brust

Adrian T. Calderone, Society of Catholic Social Scientists

Maria F. Calderone, Fashion Institute of Technology–SUNY

Keith M. Cassidy, University of Guelph and Our Lady Seat of Wisdom Academy

Frank J. Cavaioli, Farmingdale State College–SUNY (retired)

Rev. Giovanni Cavalcoli, OP, Theological Faculty of Emilia-Romagna, Bologna

Clarke E. Cochran, Texas Tech University

James Como, York College–CUNY

Rev. John J. Conley, SJ, Loyola University of Maryland

Derry Connolly, John Paul the Great Catholic University

Travis Cook, Belmont Abbey College

Svetlana Corwin, Belmont Abbey College

Rev. John J. Coughlin, OFM, Notre Dame Law School

Michael L. Coulter, Grove City College

Richard Creek, Mount St. Mary's University

Jeffrey D. Crook Jr., Mount St. Mary's University

Alfred R. D'Anca, College of Mount St. Vincent

Donald J. D'Elia, SUNY New Paltz

William C. Duncan, Marriage Law Foundation

Martin F. Ederer, Buffalo State College–SUNY

Andrew M. Essig, De Sales University

Robert L. Fastiggi, Sacred Heart Major Seminary

Troy Feay, Belmont Abbey College

Rev. Kevin L. Flannery, SJ, Gregorian University

Patrick Foley, *Catholic Southwest: A Journal of History and Culture* (editor emeritus)

Paul T. Foster, John Paul II Catholic High School

Philip A. Franco, Diocese of Brooklyn

Maggie Gallagher, Institute for Marriage and Public Policy

J. L. A. Garcia, Boston College

Anne Barbeau Gardiner, John Jay College–CUNY (emeritus)

Marie I. George, St. John's University

Robert P. George, Princeton University

Jane H. Gilroy, Molloy College

Gary D. Glenn, Northern Illinois University

Luke Gormally, Anscombe Bioethics Centre

Robert F. Gorman, Texas State University–San Marcos

Rev. Msgr. George P. Graham, St. Bernard's Parish, Diocese of Rockville Center

David L. Gregory, St. John's School of Law

Steven D. Greydanus, *National Catholic Register*

Patrick Guinan, University of Illinois at Chicago

Philip J. Harold, Robert Morris University

Anne Hendershott, King's College (New York)

Richard Hinshaw, *Long Island Catholic*

Bro. Kenneth Hoagland, SM, Kellenberg Memorial High School, Long Island, NY

Dominic Iocco, John Paul the Great Catholic University

Steven L. Jones, Grove City College

Christopher Kaczor, Loyola Marymount University

Daniella E. Keller, St. John's School of Law

James R. Kelly, Fordham University

M. Brett Kendall, Fordham University

Thomas C. Kohler, Boston College Law School

Rev. Joseph W. Koterski, SJ, Fordham University

Thaddeus J. Kozinski, Wyoming Catholic College

Michael P. Krom, St. Vincent College

James Krug, Kellenberg Memorial High School, Long Island, NY

Salvatore J. LaGumina, Nassau Community College–SUNY

Alexander LaPerchia, Mercy College (retired)

John D. Larrivee, Mount St. Mary's University

Mark S. Latkovic, Sacred Heart Major Seminary

Kevin P. Lee, Campbell University School of Law

Gerald Malsbary, Belmont Abbey College

Thomas Masters, New City Press

William E. May, John Paul II Institute for Studies on Marriage and Family at the Catholic University of America (emeritus) and Culture of Life Foundation

David McGinley, Mount St. Mary's University

D. Q. McInerny, Our Lady of Guadalupe Seminary

Rev. David Vincent Meconi, SJ, St. Louis University

Robert Moynihan, *Inside the Vatican*

William F. Murphy Jr., Pontifical College Josephinum

Clare E. Myers, University of Dallas

Richard S. Myers, Ave Maria School of Law

William Newton, International Theological Institute

Michael Novak, Ave Maria University

Michael Pakaluk, Ave Maria University

William J. Parente, University of Scranton

Joseph Pearce, Ave Maria University

Joseph J. Piccione, OSF Healthcare System

Robert A. Preston, Belmont Abbey College

Enrico Maria Radaelli, Associazione Internazionale *Sensus Communis*

Paul J. Radzilowski, Madonna University

Maurizio Ragazzi

Ronald J. Rychlak, University of Mississippi School of Law

Clara Sarrocco, New York C. S. Lewis Society

Florence Maffoni Scarinci, Nassau Community College–SUNY

D. Brian Scarnecchia, Ave Maria School of Law and Franciscan University of Steubenville

Elizabeth R. Schiltz, St. Thomas University School of Law

Kevin E. Schmiesing, Acton Institute

Stephen R. Sharkey, Alverno College

Russell Shaw, Pontifical University of the Holy Cross

Elena J. Sobrino, University of Michigan–Flint

Oswald Sobrino, editor, Logos blog, and Sacred Heart Major Seminary

Tara Stone, John Paul the Great Catholic University

Lee J. Strang, University of Toledo Law School

Rev. Peter M. J. Stravinskas, Catholic Education Foundation

John Streifel, Mount St. Mary's University

Rev. D. Paul Sullins, Catholic University of America

Sr. Albert Marie Surmanski, OP, Dominican Sisters of Mary, Mother of the Eucharist

Phillip M. Sutton, psychologist and therapist

Ronald B. Thomas Jr., Belmont Abbey College

Phillip M. Thompson, Aquinas Center for Theology at Emory University

Piero A. Tozzi, Alliance Defense Fund

Amy Uelmen, Georgetown University Law Center

Joseph A. Varacalli, Nassau Community College–SUNY

Thomas F. X. Varacalli, Louisiana State University

Leticia C. Velasquez, KIDS (Keep Infants with Down Syndrome)

Thomas D. Watts, University of Texas–Arlington

Kenneth D. Whitehead, Fellowship of Catholic Scholars

About the Editors

Michael L. Coulter, PhD, is professor of political science and humanities at Grove City College in Grove City, Pennsylvania. He is a coeditor of the two original volumes of the *Encyclopedia of Catholic Social Thought, Social Science, and Social Policy* (Scarecrow Press, 2007) and has contributed to, among other works, *Perspectives on Political Science, The Journal of Markets and Morality, Encyclopedia of the Supreme Court, Family in America*, and *Encyclopedia of American Religion and Politics*.

Richard S. Myers is professor of law at Ave Maria School of Law in Naples, Florida. He is a coeditor of the two original volumes of the *Encyclopedia of Catholic Social Thought, Social Science, and Social Policy* and of *St. Thomas Aquinas and the Natural Law Tradition: Contemporary Perspectives* (2004). He has published extensively on constitutional law, including articles in the law reviews of Ave Maria School of Law, Catholic University, Notre Dame, and Washington and Lee. He is the vice president of University Faculty for Life and the executive secretary of the Society of Catholic Social Scientists.

Joseph A. Varacalli, PhD, is State University of New York Distinguished Service Professor and the director of the Center for Catholic Studies at Nassau Community College–SUNY. A cofounder of the Society of Catholic Social Scientists, he is also a coeditor of the two original volumes of the *Encyclopedia of Catholic Social Thought, Social Science, and Social Policy*. His other recent book publications are *The Catholic Experience in America* (2006) and *Bright Promise, Failed Community: Catholics and the American Public Order* (Lexington Books, 2001).

CPSIA information can be obtained at www.ICGtesting.com
Printed in the USA
BVOW040957300312

286135BV00002B/1/P